T0180694

Lecture Notes in Artificial Intelligence 12997

Subseries of Lecture Notes in Computer Science

More information about this subseries at http://www.springer.com/series/1244

Alexey Karpov · Rodmonga Potapova (Eds.)

Speech and Computer

23rd International Conference, SPECOM 2021
St. Petersburg, Russia, September 27–30, 2021
Proceedings

Editors
Alexey Karpov [ID]
St. Petersburg Federal Research Center
of the Russian Academy of Sciences
St. Petersburg, Russia

Rodmonga Potapova [ID]
Moscow State Linguistic University
Moscow, Russia

ISSN 0302-9743 ISSN 1611-3349 (electronic)
Lecture Notes in Artificial Intelligence
ISBN 978-3-030-87801-6 ISBN 978-3-030-87802-3 (eBook)
https://doi.org/10.1007/978-3-030-87802-3

LNCS Sublibrary: SL7 – Artificial Intelligence

This Springer imprint is published by the registered company Springer Nature Switzerland AG
The registered company address is: Gewerbestrasse 11, 6330 Cham, Switzerland

SPECOM 2021 Preface

The International Conference on Speech and Computer (SPECOM) has become a regular event since the first SPECOM held in St. Petersburg, Russia, in October 1996. SPECOM was established 25 years ago (a of a quarter century!), by the St. Petersburg Institute for Informatics and Automation of the Russian Academy of Sciences (SPIIRAS) and the Herzen State Pedagogical University of Russia, thanks to the efforts of Yuri Kosarev and Rajmund Piotrowski.

SPECOM is a conference with a long tradition that attracts researchers in the area of speech technology, including automatic speech recognition and understanding, text-to-speech synthesis, and speaker and language recognition, as well as related domains like digital speech processing, natural language processing, text analysis, computational paralinguistics, multi–modal speech, and data processing or human–computer interaction. The SPECOM conference is an ideal platform for know-how exchange – especially for experts working on Slavic or other highly inflectional languages – including both under-resourced and regular well–resourced languages.

In its long history, the SPECOM conference was organized alternately by the St. Petersburg Institute for Informatics and Automation of the Russian Academy of Sciences and by the Moscow State Linguistic University (MSLU) in their home towns. Furthermore, in 1997 it was organized by the Cluj–Napoca Subsidiary of the Research Institute for Computer Technique (Romania), in 2005 by the University of Patras (in Patras, Greece), in 2011 by the Kazan Federal University (in Kazan, Russia), in 2013 by the University of West Bohemia (in Pilsen, Czech Republic), in 2014 by the University of Novi Sad (in Novi Sad, Serbia), in 2015 by the University of Patras (in Athens, Greece), in 2016 by the Budapest University of Technology and Economics (in Budapest, Hungary), in 2017 by the University of Hertfordshire (in Hatfield, UK), in 2018 by the Leipzig University of Telecommunications (in Leipzig, Germany), in 2019 by the Boğaziçi University (in Istanbul, Turkey), and in 2020 by SPIIRAS/SPC RAS (fully online).

SPECOM 2021 was the 23rd event in the series, and this time it was organized by the St. Petersburg Federal Research Center of the Russian Academy of Sciences (SPC RAS, which now includes SPIIRAS) in cooperation with MSLU, and held during September 27–30, 2021 in an online format. The conference was sponsored by HUAWEI (Russian Research Center) as a general sponsor, as well as ASM Solutions Ltd. and Alpha Cephei Inc. (Moscow, Russia). SPECOM 2021 was also supported by the International Speech Communication Association (ISCA) and the Saint Petersburg Convention Bureau. Monomax PCO was the official conference service agency.

SPECOM 2021 was held jointly with the 6th International Conference on Interactive Collaborative Robotics (ICR 2021), where problems and modern solutions of human–robot interaction were discussed.

During the SPECOM 2021 and ICR 2021 conferences, keynote lectures were given by Junichi Yamagishi (National Institute of Informatics, Tokyo, Japan) on "Automatic Detection of Generated Voices and Faces: ASVspoof and Deepfake Detection", by

Mac Schwager (Stanford University, Stanford, USA) on "Enabling Robots to Cooperate and Compete: Distributed Optimization and Game Theoretic Methods for Multiple Interacting Robots", as well as by researchers of HUAWEI (Russian Research Center).

Due to the ongoing COVID–19 pandemic, for the second time, SPECOM 2021 was organized as a fully virtual conference. The virtual conference, in an online format via Zoom, had a number of advantages including an increased number of participants because listeners could take part without any fees, essentially reduced registration fees for authors of the presented papers, no costs for travel and accommodation, a paperless green conference with only electronic proceedings, free access to video presentations in YouTube after the conference, comfortable home conditions for presenters, etc.

This volume contains a collection of submitted papers presented at SPECOM 2021 which were thoroughly reviewed by members of the Program Committee and additional reviewers consisting of more than 100 famous specialists in the conference topic areas. In total, 74 accepted papers out of 163 papers submitted for SPECOM/ICR were selected by the Program Committee for presentation at the conference and for the inclusion in this book. Theoretical and more general contributions were presented in common plenary sessions. Problem–oriented sessions as well as panel discussions brought together specialists in niche problem areas with the aim of exchanging knowledge and skills resulting from research projects of all kinds.

We would like to express our gratitude to all authors for providing their papers on time, to the members of the Program Committee for their careful reviews and paper selection, and to the editors and correctors for their hard work in preparing this volume. Special thanks are due to the members of the Organizing Committee and Monomax PCO for their tireless effort and enthusiasm during the conference organization.

September 2021

Alexey Karpov
Rodmonga Potapova

Organization

The 23rd International Conference on Speech and Computer (SPECOM 2021) was organized by the St. Petersburg Federal Research Center of the Russian Academy of Sciences (SPC RAS, St. Petersburg, Russia) in cooperation with the Moscow State Linguistic University (MSLU, Moscow, Russia). The conference website is: http://www.specom.nw.ru/2021.

General Chairs

Alexey Karpov   SPC RAS, Russia
Rodmonga Potapova   MSLU, Russia

Program Committee

Shyam Agrawal, India
Tanel Alumäe, Estonia
Elias Azarov, Belarus
Peter Birkholz, Germany
Milana Bojanić, Serbia
Nick Campbell, Ireland
Eric Castelli, France
Josef Chaloupka, Czech Republic
Khalid Choukri, France
Vladimir Chuchupal, Russia
Vlado Delić, Serbia
Olivier Deroo, France
Febe De Wet, South Africa
Anna Esposito, Italy
Yannick Estève, France
Vera Evdokimova, Russia
Mauro Falcone, Italy
Vasiliki Foufi, Switzerland
Todor Ganchev, Bulgaria
Philip Garner, Switzerland
Gábor Gosztolya, Hungary
Tunga Gungör, Turkey
Abualseoud Hanani, Palestine
Ruediger Hoffmann, Germany
Marek Hrúz, Czech Republic
Kristiina Jokinen, Japan

Oliver Jokisch, Germany
Denis Jouvet, France
Tatiana Kachkovskaia, Russia
Alexey Karpov, Russia
Heysem Kaya, The Netherlands
Tomi Kinnunen, Finland
Irina Kipyatkova, Russia
Daniil Kocharov, Russia
Liliya Komalova, Russia
Evgeny Kostyuchenko, Russia
Mikko Kurimo, Finland
Benjamin Lecouteux, France
Natalia Loukachevitch, Russia
Elena Lyakso, Russia
Joseph Mariani, France
Konstantin Markov, Japan
Jindřich Matoušek, Czech Republic
Yuri Matveev, Russia
Ivan Medennikov, Russia
Peter Mihajlik, Hungary
Nobuaki Minematsu, Japan
Wolfgang Minker, Germany
Iosif Mporas, UK
Ludek Muller, Czech Republic
Bernd Möbius, Germany
Sebastian Möller, Germany

Additional Reviewers

Organizing Committee

Alexey Karpov (Chair)
Andrey Ronzhin
Rodmonda Potapova
Daniil Kocharov
Irina Kipyatkova
Dmitry Ryumin

Dmitriy Levonevskiy
Natalia Kashina
Anastasiya Molotilova
Irina Novikova
Natalia Dormidontova
Denis Ivanko

Contents

Text-Independent Speaker Verification Employing CNN-LSTM-TDNN Hybrid Networks

Jahangir Alam$^{(\boxtimes)}$, Abderrahim Fathan, and Woo Hyun Kang

Computer Research Institute of Montreal, Montreal, Quebec H3N 1M3, Canada
{Jahangir.Alam,Abderrahim.Fathan,Woohyun.Kang}@crim.ca
https://www.crim.ca/en/

Abstract. Time Delay Neural Network (TDNN)-based speaker embeddings extraction have become the dominant approach for text-independent speaker verification. Several single and hybrid deep learning architectures have been proposed for improving the performance. In this paper, we propose yet another hybrid configuration that employs Convolution Neural Network (CNN), TDNN and Long Short-Term Memory (LSTM) for training and extraction of speaker discriminant utterance level representations. In the proposed framework, we also use SpecAugment for on the fly data augmentation and multi-level statistics pooling from across CNN, LSTM and TDNN layers for aggregating the frame level information into utterance level speaker embeddings via fully connected layers. For performance evaluation of the proposed framework, speaker verification experiments are carried out across NIST SRE 2016, Voxceleb and Short duration Speaker Verification (SdSV) challenge 2021 corpora. Evaluation metrics chosen for performance evaluation are equal error rate (EER), minimum decision cost function (minDCF), and actual decision cost function (actDCF). Experimental results depict the proposed hybrid approach yielding improvements over the original TDNN, TDNN-LSTM hybrid architecture, as well as some other previously-proposed approaches.

Keywords: Speaker verification · SpecAugment ·
CNN-TDNN-LSTM · Multi-level statistics pooling · PLDA.

1 Introduction

Various technological solutions are gradually being implemented to deal with identity theft, spoofing attacks, document fraud, and new threats such as terrorism or cybercrime. One such technology is the speaker verification or voice biometrics. Due to its invasive nature and ease of accessibility, voice biometric technology has quickly established itself as the most pertinent means to identify and authenticate a person based on a set of recognizable and verifiable voice characteristics which are unique and specific to that person. In the past, applications using biometrics have been primarily instigated by authorities for military

© Springer Nature Switzerland AG 2021
A. Karpov and R. Potapova (Eds.): SPECOM 2021, LNAI 12997, pp. 1–13, 2021.
https://doi.org/10.1007/978-3-030-87802-3_1

access control, criminal or civil identification under a strictly regulated legal and technical framework. Nowadays, banking, retail, call centers, and mobile commerce sectors are demonstrating a real urge for the benefits of biometrics. As millions of smart device (such as smartphone, Google Home, Amazon Alexa etc.) users are unlocking their devices with a voice, awareness and acceptance of voice biometrics (or speaker verification) have been boosted in the recent past years [11,24].

1.1 Related Work

State-of-the-art speaker verification systems represent the acoustic properties of an utterance by a compact and fixed-dimensional vector using a Time Delay Neural Network (TDNN), known as speaker embedding or x-vector [23]. On the top of this speaker embedding, a suitable backend, such as Probabilistic Linear Discriminant Analysis (PLDA) or cosine similarity, is normally used for scoring and then making verification decisions. On text-independent speaker recognition, this approach promises to achieve the best performance compared to earlier i-vector [4] - based speaker verification paradigm.

The TDNN model of x-vector/PLDA framework consists of a stack of dilated 1-dimensional convolution layers which operate across the time dimension. The convolutional stack is followed by a temporal pooling layer, which simply aggregates component-wise mean and standard deviation over the time axis. The output of the pooling layers are finally projected into a compact and fixed dimensional speaker embeddings using two fully-connected layers. This output is finally fed to the output layer to yield outputs corresponding to conditional log-probabilities over a set of speakers in the training data [23].

Despite being successful in matched settings, the x-vector approach still provides poor verification performance when there exists domain-mismatch between train and test settings. To improve the performance and to make deep learning-based speaker verification robust, various single and hybrid approaches have been proposed. Especially the hybrid approaches, which employ non-TDNN neural network modules such as Long-Short Term Memory (LSTM) and Convolutional Neural Network (CNN) to the x-vector framework, were able to achieve noticeable enhancement in the speaker verification performance. It has been shown in [9,19,30] that the robustness of x-vectors can be improved by adding residual connections between the frame-level layers or replacing the TDNNs with ResNets [12,15] or DenseNet [17]. It was found in [5] that enhancing the multi-scale temporal features at a granular level by the Res2Net blocks [6] and re-calibrating the channel-wise feature responses by the squeeze-and-excitation units [13] could improve the robustness of speaker embeddings. Performance of TDNN and TDNN-LSTM architectures with/without multi-head attention have been explored in [2]. SpecAugment based on the fly spectral data augmentation was shown to provide promising results in speech recognition task [20]. Later, this augmentation technique has been investigated for the speaker verification task [26].

Moreover, various temporal pooling techniques were proposed, such as Self-Attentive Pooling (SAP) and Statistics Pooling (SP), which have a notable impact on learning discriminative and robust utterance-level representations. In [25], a TDNN-LSTM hybrid architecture with multi-level pooling was proposed, which successfully exploits the complimentary information encoded by the TDNN and LSTM layers.

1.2 Our Contributions

In various speech processing applications, such as speech and speaker recognition, TDNN, CNN, and LSTM networks have demonstrated improved performance over the Deep Neural Network (DNN). These models are known to be complementary in their modeling competencies. For example, TDNN and CNN are adept at reducing changes in frequency, while the LSTMs are good for sequential & temporal modeling. On the other hand, DNN is suitable for mapping input features to more separable regions. In order to exploit the complementary information modeled by different network modules, several single and hybrid architectures [1,8,14,16,25] were proposed for boosting the performance of the TDNN-based x-vector/PLDA [23] speaker verification paradigm. In this paper, we propose yet another hybrid architecture that employs multi-level statistics [25] for capturing the complementarity by combining statistics from different network modules. Moreover, our proposed model incorporates on the fly data augmentation using SpecAugment [20] to further enhance the robustness of the performance. To be concrete, in this work, our contributions can be outlined as follows:

- In order to capture complementarity of CNN, LSTM and DNN/TDNN networks and to improve speaker verification performance, we propose a hybrid deep learning architecture that employs CNN, LSTM and TDNN networks for learning more discriminative local (i.e., frame level) descriptors. Proposed model, in addition to offline data augmentation, also incorporates on the fly data augmentation based on SpecAugment and multi-level statistics pooling for fusing statistics from all three network modules.
- Unlike the conventional multi-level statistics pooling, the proposed system extracts not only the global statistics, but also the local statistics to exploit the short-durational characteristics encoded by different networks.
- We perform an investigative study on the influence of multi-level statistics pooling with different single (e.g., TDNN) and hybrid network (e.g., TDNN-LSTM, proposed approach, etc.) for speaker verification.
- We perform evaluation of our proposed approach across three diverse datasets and compare performances with the original TDNN [23], TDNN-LSTM hybrid architecture [14,25], as well as some other previously-proposed approaches.
- To the best of our knowledge, proposed approach is new and till now, nobody has tried this approach for text-independent speaker verification task.

2   Proposed Architecture

The main motivation behind using hybrid deep learning architectures in various speech processing applications is to bag the complementarity that exists among CNN, LSTM, TDNN, and DNN modules. In order to effectively bag this complementarity, we propose a hybrid configuration, as depicted in Fig. 1, that employs CNN, TDNN, LSTM with local statistics pooling layers.

2.1   SpecAugment and CNN-based Feature Extraction

Mel-frequency cepstral coefficients (MFCC) are used as input features to this hybrid model, which are passed through the IDCT-layer (inverse discrete cosine transform) to obtain d-dimensional Mel-Filterbank (MFB) features. The MFCCs, being decorrelated, are more easily compressible without any information loss and therefore, take less storage space than MFB coefficients.

Over the MFB features, SpecAugment is applied on the fly, where both time and frequency masking are performed. For a MFB feature sequence with n frames, the policy for time and frequency masking are as follows:

- Frequency masking: for a randomly sampled $f \sim unif(0, F)$ and $f_0 \sim unif(0, d - f)$, the Mel-frequency channels $[f_0, f_0 + f)$ are masked, where F is the frequency mask parameter.
- Time masking: for a randomly sampled $t \sim unif(0, T)$ and $t_0 \sim unif(0, n - t)$, the time steps $[t_0, t_0 + t)$ are masked, where T is the time mask parameter.

The augmented spectral features are then passed through 5 2-dimensional CNN (2D-CNN) layers to capture the local spectral characteristics.

2.2   TDNN-LSTM-based Frame-Level Network

The 2D-CNN module is then followed by a frame-level network which is composed of TDNN and LSTM layers, to extract local descriptors with sufficient temporal information for speaker discrimination. The frame-level network used in our proposed approach is similar to the TDNN-LSTM approach presented in [14], where the second TDNN layer of the standard x-vector [23] is replaced with a LSTM layer.

2.3   Multi-level Statistics Pooling

In the proposed architecture, we use Multi-Level Statistics Pooling (MLSP) [25] for aggregating statistics from the last layers of CNN, LSTM and TDNN blocks in order to capture speaker specific information from different spaces and learn more discriminative utterance level representations by bagging complementarity available in CNN, LSTM and TDNN networks. Similar to the standard x-vector, the proposed system extracts the first- and second- order statistics. However, unlike the conventional x-vector, the proposed architecture extracts the statistics not only globally (across the entire utterance), but also locally (across adjacent frames) to exploit the short-durational correlation. As depicted in Fig. 1, each module (i.e., TDNN, LSTM) takes both the frame-level outputs from the previous model, and the local statistics extracted from them as input.

After propagating the input features to the frame-level network, a global statistics pooling is performed to aggregate the local descriptors obtained from the TDNN and LSTM blocks. The global first- and second- order statistics are concatenated to a fixed-dimensional utterance-level representation.

The pooled statistics are then projected into a 512-dimensional embedding vector via two fully-connected layers. Once the training is completed, the embeddings are extracted from the fully-connected layer close to the global statistics pooling layer.

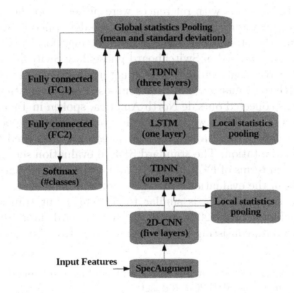

Fig. 1. Schematic diagram of our proposed hybrid architecture for automatic speaker verification task.

3 Experiments

3.1 Experimental Setups

Following the KALDI [21] SRE16 recipe [23], we performed data augmentation on top of original training data by corrupting them using additive noises, babble and music from MUSAN data and reverberation from the simulated RIRs (room impulse response) database. Note that, MUSAN and RIRs datasets are publicly available from http://www.openslr.org. In addition to the noise and RIR augmentation, we also performed on the fly augmentation, more specifically the

SpecAugment technique which provided promising results in the speech recognition task [20].

MFCCs are extracted using an analysis window size of 25 ms over a frame shift of 10 ms and features are normalized using short-time cepstral mean normalization over a window of 300 frames. Energy-based voice activity detector is used for removing non-speech frames from the signal.

For experiments on NIST SRE 2016, 23-dimensional features were extracted and for other cases, the dimension of MFCCs is 40.

3.2   Experiments on NIST SRE 2016

In the NIST SRE 2016 [22] experiments, we compared the performance of systems with different frame-level network architectures and pooling schemes, which are described in Table 1.

Results for the systems with references were picked from the corresponding publication. All the systems without references are developed by us, which were trained following the standard Kaldi x-vector settings for NIST SRE16. The training data was comprised of Switchboard phase 2, 3; Switchboard Cellular 1, 2; and the NIST SREs 2004–2010. The training utterances are mostly spoken in English. The SRE16 evaluation data was composed of conversational telephone speech recordings collected outside North America, spoken in Tagalog and Cantonese languages. The PLDA was trained only on the SRE augmented portion and the unlabeled SRE16 data (from major languages) was used for the unsupervised PLDA adaptation. The standard SRE16 evaluation set [22] is used for reporting results in terms of EER, minDCF and actDCF. Information about the number of trials in the evaluation test set is reported in Table 2.

Note that system MP [25] is similar to System 4 but trained on a large dataset that includes: SREs 2004–2010, all Switchboard data; all Fisher data and all Voxceleb data consisting of speech recordings from 20,803 speakers.

Table 1. Frame-level network architectures and pooling strategies for the systems experimented on the NIST SRE 2016 dataset.

System #	Augmentation	Neural feature extractor	Frame-level network			Pooling
			Layer #1	Layer #2	Layer #3∼5	
System 1	RIR + Noise	-	TDNN	TDNN	TDNN	SP
System 2		-				MLSP
System 3		-		LSTM		SP
System 4		-				MLSP
System 5		5 layers 2D-CNN				SP
System 6						MLSP
System 7 (proposed)	RIR + Noise + SpecAugment					

Results and Discussion. Table 3 presents results on the SRE16 evaluation set for the pooled, Cantonese and Tagalog language conditions in terms of official evaluation metrics EER (%), minDCF and actDCF. We can see that our proposed approach outperformed all the systems considered in this table by a significant margin on all conditions in terms of all considered metrics. We can also observe that whether MLSP used with single (i.e., System 1 and System 2) or hybrid architectures (System 3 to System 7), it always helped to improve performance compared to its counterpart (i.e., system without MLSP). These findings prove the effectiveness of using multi-level pooling in terms of verifying the speaker. Also, from the results from System 5 to System 7, it could be seen that CNN and SpecAugment + CNN can help boosting the speaker verification performance.

Table 2. Some statistics of SRE16 evaluation test set in terms of numbers of speakers, total number of trials and target trials.

Partition	# Speakers	# Trials	# Target trials
Cantonese	100	965396	19298
Tagalog	101	1021332	17764
Pooled	201	1986728	37062

3.3 Experiments on Voxceleb

In the VoxCeleb experiments, only the Voxceleb2 development set that contains only 5,994 speakers with 1,092,009 utterances was used for training. For training the system, similar data augmentation was performed as done in the experiments for NIST SRE 2016. PLDA was trained on portion of training data i.e., without data augmentation. Results are reported on all three Voxceleb 1 test sets, namely, VoxCeleb1_O: original Voxceleb 1 test set, VoxCeleb1_E: Extended Voxceleb 1 test set, and VoxCeleb1_H: Voxceleb 1 hard test set. Results are reported in terms of EER(%) only. For all experiments speaker discriminant neural networks are trained on the augmented VoxCeleb2 development data and speaker verification performances are evaluated on the three test sets presented in Table 4.

Results and Discussion. In Table 5, we present results on all the three test partitions of Voxceleb 1 dataset in terms of EER(%) metrics for the systems including our proposed hybrid approach. It can be observed from the reported results that our proposed approach provided better performances compared to all systems with a substantial margin. On Voxceleb1 hard test set, our system yielded almost similar performance to that of SpecAugment+ResNet34 system [26]. We can say that our proposed approach yields consistent and generalized performance across different datasets.

3.4 Experiments on Task 2 of SdSV Challenge 2021

In the SdSV Challenge 2021 [29] experiments, we did not use any in-domain data (i.e., SdSV challenge 2021 Task 2 training data) for training our proposed speaker discriminant neural network. Instead, we used our pre-trained network from Sect. 3.3 and then did extract embeddings from all SdSV challenge 2021 Task 2 data i.e., train, development and evaluation. Number of trials in the evaluation set is $4,619,310$. Since the labels for in-domain data are available, the SdSV challenge 2021 Task2 development and evaluation sets are scored using a supervised PLDA adaptation technique [7]. In supervised PLDA adaptation, two PLDA models were trained, one on out-of-domain (i.e., Voxceleb 2 development) data and the second on in-domain (SdSV2021 Task 2 training data) training data. After that, the PLDA parameters (i.e. across-class and within-class covariances) were adapted by doing interpolation [7]. Optimal interpolation parameter was selected based on development set results and was set to $\alpha = 0.95$. Official evaluation metrics EER (%) and minDCF are used for reporting results.

Results and Discussion. Table 6 shows the results on the Task 2 evaluation set of SdSV2021 challenge attained with our proposed method. For comparison, we use x-vector- baseline provided by the organizer. We can see from the presented results that proposed approach outperformed the challenge baseline with a large margin. In Fig. 2, DET (detection error trade-off) plot of our proposed system's performance on the evaluation set is depicted. DET plot shows the overall performance as well as performances by splitting the trials based on language and gender. Table 7 depicts the detailed results obtained by our proposed approach on different sub-conditions of evaluation set trials. We can observe that the performance on male trials is better than that on female trials. Again, better performance is achieved on English trials than Farsi trials.

Table 3. Speaker verification performance on the evaluation set of the NIST SRE16. Results are reported in terms of EER (%), minDCF, and actDCF. "-" indicates results are not reported in [25].

System	Pooled			Cantonese			Tagalog		
	EER	minDCF	actDCF	EER	minDCF	actDCF	EER	minDCF	actDCF
TDNN [23]	8.66	0.610	0.620	4.69	0.420	0.430	12.63	0.760	0.810
System #1	8.32	0.585	0.591	4.28	0.3826	0.394	12.33	0.755	0.787
System #2	8.07	0.568	0.573	3.84	0.356	0.374	12.22	0.746	0.771
System #3	7.84	0.562	0.567	4.06	0.359	0.386	11.63	0.740	0.748
System #4	7.84	0.559	0.565	3.93	0.356	0.384	11.66	0.736	0.745
System #5	7.53	0.552	0.559	3.58	0.348	0.383	11.54	0.727	0.736
System #6	7.10	0.534	0.540	3.43	0.309	0.349	10.76	0.719	0.731
MP ($\lambda = 0$) [25]	6.68	-	-	3.51	-	-	9.74	-	-
System #7 (proposed)	6.49	0.521	0.533	3.09	0.287	0.345	9.89	0.713	0.721

Table 4. Some statistics of voxceleb 1 test sets in terms of numbers of speakers, recordings, total number of trials and target trials.

Test sets	# Speakers	# Recordings	# Trials	# Target trials
VoxCeleb1_O	40	4874	37720	18860
VoxCeleb1_E	1251	145375	581480	290743
VoxCeleb1_H	1190	138137	552536	276270

Table 5. Speaker verification performance on the three test partitions of Voxceleb 1 corpus reported in terms of equal error rate (EER). Here, VoxCeleb1_O: original Voxceleb 1 test set, VoxCeleb1_E: Extended Voxceleb 1 test set, and VoxCeleb1_H: Voxceleb 1 hard test set. AMS stands for additive margin softmax.

	Scoring	EER (%)
		Voxceleb1_O
Chung et al. [3]	Cosine	3.95
Xie et al. [28]	Cosine	3.22
Hajavi et al. [10]	Cosine	4.26
Xiang et al. [27]	Cosine	2.69
Monteiro et al. [18]	Learned sim.	2.51
SpecAugment+TDNN [26]	PLDA	2.59
SpecAugment+TDNN+AMS [26]	Cosine	1.96
SpecAugment+ResNet34 [26]	PLDA	1.68
Proposed	PLDA	**1.55**
		Voxceleb1_E
Chung et al. [3]	Cosine	4.42
Xie et al. [28]	Cosine	3.13
Xiang et al. [27]	Cosine	2.76
Monteiro et al. [18]	Learned sim.	2.57
SpecAugment+TDNN [26]	PLDA	2.77
SpecAugment+TDNN+AMS [26]	Cosine	2.31
SpecAugment+ResNet34 [26]	PLDA	1.80
Proposed	PLDA	**1.75**
		Voxceleb1_H
Chung et al. [3]	Cosine	7.33
Xie et al. [28]	Cosine	5.06
Xiang et al. [27]	Cosine	4.73
Monteiro et al. [18]	Learned sim.	4.73
SpecAugment+TDNN [26]	PLDA	4.83
SpecAugment+TDNN+AMS [26]	Cosine	4.02
SpecAugment+ResNet34 [26]	PLDA	**3.08**
Proposed	PLDA	**3.00**

Table 6. Speaker verification results on the evaluation set of Task 2 for the SdSV challenge 2021. Results are reported in terms of official evaluation metrics EER and minDCF. Baseline refers to SdSV challenge 2021 baseline.

System	EER (%)	minDCF
Baseline	10.65	0.4318
Proposed	3.86	0.1780

Table 7. The detailed results of our proposed system on the Task 2 of SdSV challenge 2021 evaluation subset with trials partitioned into different sub-conditions.

Condition	EER(%)	minDCF
Overall Results	3.86	0.1780
Male	2.38	0.1191
Female	4.70	0.2083
English	2.00	0.0948
Farsi	3.28	0.1402
English-Male	1.35	0.0722
English-Female	2.28	0.1062
Farsi-Male	2.02	0.0985
Farsi-Female	3.91	0.1607

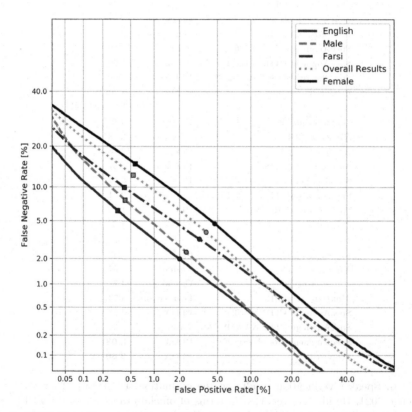

Fig. 2. DET (detection error trade-offs) plot of our proposed system's performance on the evaluation set of Task 2 for SdSV challenge 2021. Network is trained on only Voxceleb 2 dev data and scoring is done using supervised PLDA adaptation.

4 Conclusion

In this work, we introduced a hybrid deep learning architecture for text-independent speaker verification task. The core module of our proposed approach is comprised of CNN, TDNN, and LSTM networks for mapping input hand-crafted features into more discriminative local descriptors. The local descriptors are then converted into global utterance level representations using multi-level pooling layer that pools the statistics from the last layers of CNN, LSTM and TDNN blocks, and thereby, assists in learning more discriminative speaker embeddings by capturing speaker specific information from different regions across the hybrid network. Moreover, the proposed system extracts not only the global statistics, but also the local statistics from each of the CNN, LSTM and TDNN blocks to exploit the information latent in short durational local regions. Performances of our proposed approach were evaluated by conducting speaker verification experiments on three diverse datasets NIST SRE 2016, Voxceleb, and SdSV challenge 2021. On NIST SRE 2016, proposed system yielded 6.49%, 3.09%, and 9.89% EERs on pooled, Cantonese and Tagalog, respectively. On Voxceleb evaluation sets Voxceleb1_O, Voxceleb1_E, and Voxceleb1_H, we achieved an EER of 1.55%, 1.75% and 3.00%, respectively. Overall, proposed hybrid approach demonstrated consistently better performance across diverse corpora.

References

1. Bhattacharya, G., Alam, J., Kenny, P.: Deep speaker recognition: modular or monolithic?. In: Proceedings Interspeech 2019, pp. 1143–1147 (2019)
2. Chen, C., Zhang, S., Yeh, C., Wang, J., Wang, T., Huang, C.: Speaker characterization using TDNN-LSTM based speaker embedding. In: ICASSP 2019–2019 IEEE International Conference on Acoustics, Speech and Signal Processing (ICASSP), pp. 6211–6215 (2019)
3. Chung, J.S., Nagrani, A., Zisserman, A.: Voxceleb2: deep speaker recognition. arXiv preprint arXiv:1806.05622 (2018)
4. Dehak, N., Kenny, P.J., Dehak, R., Dumouchel, P., Ouellet, P.: Front-end factor analysis for speaker verification. IEEE Trans. Audio Speech Lang. Process. **19**(4), 788–798 (2011)
5. Desplanques, B., Thienpondt, J., Demuynck, K.: Ecapa-tdnn: emphasized channel attention, propagation and aggregation in tdnn based speaker verification. Interspeech 2020, October 2020. http://dx.doi.org/10.21437/Interspeech.2020-2650
6. Gao, S., Cheng, M., Zhao, K., Zhang, X., Yang, M., Torr, P.H.S.: Res2net: a new multi-scale backbone architecture. CoRR abs/1904.01169 (2019). http://arxiv.org/abs/1904.01169
7. Garcia-Romero, D., McCree, A.: Supervised domain adaptation for i-vector based speaker recognition. In: 2014 IEEE International Conference on Acoustics, Speech and Signal Processing (ICASSP), pp. 4047–4051 (2014)
8. Garcia-Romero, D., Sell, G., Mccree, A.: MagNetO: x-vector magnitude estimation network plus offset for improved speaker recognition. In: Proceedings Odyssey 2020 The Speaker and Language Recognition Workshop, pp. 1–8 (2020)
9. Gusev, A., et al.: Deep speaker embeddings for far-field speaker recognition on short utterances (2020)

10. Hajavi, A., Etemad, A.: A deep neural network for short-segment speaker recognition. In: Proceedings Interspeech (2019), pp. 2878–2882 (2019)
11. Hansen, J.H.L., Hasan, T.: Speaker recognition by machines and humans: a tutorial review. IEEE Sig. Process. Mag. **32**(6), 74–99 (2015)
12. He, K., Zhang, X., Ren, S., Sun, J.: Deep residual learning for image recognition. CoRR abs/1512.03385 (2015). http://arxiv.org/abs/1512.03385
13. Hu, J., Shen, L., Sun, G.: Squeeze-and-excitation networks. CoRR abs/1709.01507 (2017). http://arxiv.org/abs/1709.01507
14. Huang, C.L.: Speaker characterization using TDNN, TDNN-LSTM, TDNN-LSTM-attention based speaker embeddings for NIST SRE 2019. In: Proceedings Odyssey 2020 The Speaker and Language Recognition Workshop, pp. 423–427 (2020)
15. Li, N., Tuo, D., Su, D., Li, Z., Yu, D.: Deep discriminative embeddings for duration robust speaker verification. In: Proceedings Interspeech (2018), pp. 2262–2266 (2018)
16. Liang, T., Liu, Y., Xu, C., Zhang, X., He, L.: Combined vector based on factorized time-delay neural network for text-independent speaker recognition. In: Proceedings Odyssey 2020 The Speaker and Language Recognition Workshop, pp. 428–432 (2020)
17. Lin, W., Mak, M.W., Yi, L.: Learning mixture representation for deep speaker embedding using attention. In: Proceedings Odyssey 2020 The Speaker and Language Recognition Workshop, pp. 210–214 (2020)
18. Monteiro, J., Albuquerque, I., Alam, J., Hjelm, R.D., Falk, T.: An end-to-end approach for the verification problem: learning the right distance. In: International Conference on Machine Learning (2020)
19. Novoselov, S., Shulipa, A., Kremnev, I., Kozlov, A., Shchemelinin, V.: On deep speaker embeddings for text-independent speaker recognition. CoRR abs/1804.10080 (2018). http://arxiv.org/abs/1804.10080
20. Park, D.S., et al.: SpecAugment: a simple data augmentation method for automatic speech recognition. In: Proceedings Interspeech (2019), pp. 2613–2617 (2019)
21. Povey, D., et al.: The kaldi speech recognition toolkit (2011)
22. Sadjadi, S.O., et al.: The 2016 NIST speaker recognition evaluation. In: Proceedings Interspeech (2017), pp. 1353–1357 (2017)
23. Snyder, D., Garcia-Romero, D., Sell, G., Povey, D., Khudanpur, S.: X-vectors: robust dnn embeddings for speaker recognition. In: 2018 IEEE International Conference on Acoustics, Speech and Signal Processing (ICASSP), pp. 5329–5333 (2018)
24. Sztahó, D., Szaszák, G., Beke, A.: Deep learning methods in speaker recognition: a review (2019)
25. Tang, Y., Ding, G., Huang, J., He, X., Zhou, B.: Deep speaker embedding learning with multi-level pooling for text-independent speaker verification. In: ICASSP 2019–2019 IEEE International Conference on Acoustics, Speech and Signal Processing (ICASSP), pp. 6116–6120 (2019)
26. Wang, S., Rohdin, J., Plchot, O., Burget, L., Yu, K., Černocký, J.: Investigation of specaugment for deep speaker embedding learning. In: ICASSP 2020–2020 IEEE International Conference on Acoustics, Speech and Signal Processing (ICASSP), pp. 7139–7143 (2020)
27. Xiang, X., Wang, S., Huang, H., Qian, Y., Yu, K.: Margin matters: Towards more discriminative deep neural network embeddings for speaker recognition. arXiv preprint arXiv:1906.07317 (2019)

28. Xie, W., Nagrani, A., Chung, J.S., Zisserman, A.: Utterance-level aggregation for speaker recognition in the wild. In: ICASSP 2019–2019 IEEE International Conference on Acoustics, Speech and Signal Processing (ICASSP), pp. 5791–5795. IEEE (2019)
29. Zeinali, H., Lee, K.A., Alam, J., Burget, L.: Short-duration speaker verification (SdSV) challenge 2021: the challenge evaluation plan (2021)
30. Zhang, R., et al.: ARET: aggregated residual extended time-delay neural networks for speaker verification. In: Proceedings Interspeech (2020), pp. 946–950 (2020)

End-to-End Voice Spoofing Detection Employing Time Delay Neural Networks and Higher Order Statistics

Jahangir Alam$^{(\boxtimes)}$, Abderrahim Fathan, and Woo Hyun Kang

Computer Research Institute of Montreal (CRIM),
Montreal, Qubec H3N 1M3, Canada
{jahangir.alam,abderrahim.fathan,woohyun.kang}@crim.ca
https://www.crim.ca/en/

Abstract. Technological progress and proliferation of sophisticated software has made it easier than ever to spoof a person's voice and audio in general. Like other biometrics, speaker verification is vulnerable to spoofing attacks. Detecting these attacks using the artifacts present in the recordings is a major challenge. Current trend in spoofing detection is to employ deep learning architectures to perform end-to-end detection by employing a pooling layer which aggregates the frame-level information into utterance-level embeddings. To do so, only the first or first and second order statistics are normally pooled across temporal dimension. In this paper, we investigate the influence of higher order statistics, such as third and fourth order moments, on spoofing detection performance. A Time Delay Neural Network (TDNN) architecture is used on the top of linear frequency cepstral coefficients for carrying out spoofing detection experiments on the ASVspoof2019 challenge logical access and physical access corpora. Experiments results, in terms of equal error rate (EER) and minimum tandem detection cost function (min-tDCF), show that inclusion of higher order statistics is accommodating for improving the performance of spoofing detection systems.

Keywords: Voice spoofing detection · Higher order statistics · TDNN · GMM · LFCC · ASVspoof2019.

1 Introduction

Spoofing refers to a phenomenon in which a person or computer program imitates a target speaker for malicious purposes, such as political gains, fake news, unauthorized access, and fraudulent scams, etc. Spoofing attacks with regards to automatic speaker verification (ASV) can be broadly classified into two categories: replay or physical access (PA) attacks at the sensor-level, and synthetic or logical access (LA) attacks, which are also known as audio deepfakes, generated using speech synthesis and voice conversion algorithms. Replay attacks consist of playing back the pre-recorded voice of a target speaker to spoof the system [7,22,34]. Recent advancements in deep learning algorithms for speech synthesis

© Springer Nature Switzerland AG 2021
A. Karpov and R. Potapova (Eds.): SPECOM 2021, LNAI 12997, pp. 14–25, 2021.
https://doi.org/10.1007/978-3-030-87802-3_2

and voice conversion/cloning algorithms have demonstrated a potential to generate synthetic speech based on text or utterances of the target speaker that are nearly indistinguishable from target speaker's genuine speech. Some examples include WaveNet [16], Tacotron [30], DeepVoice3 [20]. Current consumer smart devices and recent techniques in speech synthesis, voice conversion (VC) [9], and generative models such as GANs [12,17,26,31] make it easier for an imposter to impersonate and forge data of a legitimate user which in turn poses increasingly more threats to voice biometrics.

With the acceptance and competences of voice spoofing on the rise, creating defenses against those voice spoofing attacks or audio deepfakes used for malicious intent is becoming more essential than ever.

1.1 Related Work

In order to make voice biometrics secure against spoofing attacks many standalone spoofing detection systems have been proposed in the literature and evaluated on the datasets of ASVpoof challenges [10,29,35]. The most effective countermeasures against spoofing attacks are found to be the low-level acoustic features typically extracted at 10 ms intervals and designed to detect artifacts in synthetic/replayed speech [1,18,19,23,27,28,37]. Previously, most of the research works in this direction focused on the development/investigation of more discriminative hand-crafted countermeasures, namely, Linear Frequency Cepstral Coefficients (LFCC) [2,3,23], Constant-Q Cepstral Coefficients (CQCC) [28] and its variant [1], Cochlear Filter Cepstral Coefficients Instantaneous Frequency (CFC-CIF) [18] and so on.

A standard Gaussian Mixture Model (GMM) as classifier is found to perform excellently on the logical access task [13,23,24,28]. Recent trends in voice antispoofing is to employ deep learning architectures in an end-to-end or modular (i.e., two-step) fashion on the top of raw signal/hand-crafted features to discriminate between bonafide and spoof speech signals [4,11,13–15,21,25,33,39]. Frequency masking based on the fly data augmentation with the ResNet network using large margin cosine loss (LMCL) was introduced in [4]. In [39], one class softmax loss with ResNet18 architecture was proposed. Feature genuinization based light CNN system was presented in [33]. In order to improve generalization of anti-spoofing systems to unseen test data, several variants of softmax loss were also adopted [4,39]. Transfer learning approach with a ResNet has also been explored for spoofing detection task [21].

The key idea in deep learning based spoofing detection is to use some kind of deep learning architecture, such as ResNet, on top of hand-crafted/learned features for capturing more discriminative local descriptors which are then aggregated to generate final fixed dimensional utterance level embeddings. The embeddings are then fed into a classifier which discriminates whether the input audio is a spoof attack or genuine. Conventionally, a two-stage approach was popularly adopted, where the classifier (e.g., support vector machine, SVM) and the embedding extraction network is trained separately. However, in order to mutually optimize the decision hyperplane and the embedding feature space, various end-to-end approaches [4,11,13–15,21,25,33,39] were proposed in the past few years, where the neural classifier is trained jointly with the embedding extraction network.

In both the two-stage and end-to-end approaches, usually a pooling layer is incorporated where only the first (i.e., mean) or first and second order (i.e., standard deviation) statistics are normally pooled together across the temporal dimension [4,13–15,39] to obtain utterance-level representations. However, no previous researches have been done in the field of deep learning-based anti-spoofing that include higher order statistics (HOS), i.e., 3rd order and 4th order moments denoted as skewness and kurtosis, respectively, for learning global representations of utterances. In [38], a multi-task learning based text-independent speaker verification was proposed where the auxiliary task was to reconstruct the first, second, and higher-order statistics of the original input utterance.

1.2   Our Contributions

We believe that not only the first and second order statistics, but also the skewness and kurtosis of the frame-level features may carry essential information for obtaining a discriminative embedding adequate for anti-spoofing. Therefore in this paper, we propose an end-to-end anti-spoofing countermeasure system which uses HOS for obtaining the utterance-level embeddings. To be more precise, our contributions can be summarized as:

- Develop a Time Delay Neural Network (TDNN)-based end-to-end voice spoofing detection system by incorporating Higher Order Statistics (HOS) on their own and in addition to the first and second order statistics.
- Perform an investigative study on the influence of HOS and different combinations of 1st, 2nd, 3rd and 4th order statistics for logical and physical access spoofing attacks detection.
- Perform comparison with various existing and recently proposed deep learning-based spoofing detection systems.

2   Spoofing Detection Using TDNN and HOS

In various speech-based applications time delay neural network (TDNN) is found to be very successful. In this section, we provide a description of our end-to-end spoofing detection approach that employs a TDNN architecture with angular additive margin (AAM) softmax loss and includes HOS (higher order statistics) both alone and in combination with mean and standard deviation in statistics pooling.

In Table 1, we present a summary of the employed TDNN architecture which is made up of a sequence of dilated 1-dimensional convolutions across the temporal dimension, followed by a statistics pooling layer. In the statistics pooling layer, the statistics of the last TDNN layer outputs are computed over time and concatenated element-wise. For example, if we use all four statistics (i.e., with

$n = 4$), the first-, second-, third-, and fourth-order statistics are concatenated, thus resulting in a 2,048-dimensional supervector. The pooled statistics are then projected into 256-dimensional vector representations, known as embeddings, through two fully-connected layers. The output is a softmax layer employing AAM softmax loss variant, where each of its output nodes corresponds to one class in the training data.

2.1   Higher Order Statistics (HOS)

In this work, by HOS we mainly refer to 3rd- and 4th-order moments which are also known as skewness and kurtosis, respectively. The HOS have been applied to many tasks for the estimation of the shape of unimodal distributions. Given frame-level features of the final convolutional layer h_d as depicted in Table 1, the mean μ, standard deviation σ, skewness s, and kurtosis k can be computed as:

$$\mu = \frac{1}{D} \sum_{d=1}^{D} h_d, \tag{1}$$

$$\sigma = \frac{1}{D} \sum_{d=1}^{D} (h_d - \mu)^2, \tag{2}$$

$$s = \frac{1}{D} \sum_{d=1}^{D} (h_d - \mu)^3, \tag{3}$$

$$k = \frac{1}{D} \sum_{d=1}^{D} (h_d - \mu)^4, \tag{4}$$

where D represents the number of frames in the input features. The skewness measures the lack of symmetry in the data distribution while the kurtosis is actually the measure of outliers present in the distribution. When all four different statistics described above are pooled together the output of pooling layer can be formulated as:

$$v = [\mu, \sigma, s, k]. \tag{5}$$

Exploiting the knowledge of the data distribution can help the classification system to successfully learn the optimal decision boundary between different classes. While the first- and second- order moments are sufficient to be considered when dealing with a dataset with Gaussian distribution, real-life signals like speech are known to have non-Gaussian distribution [32]. Therefore the anti-spoofing countermeasure system may benefit from taking the HOS into account, which can help train the network to understand the precise distribution of the frame-level representation of the genuine and spoofed speech.

2.2 Additive Angular Margin (AAM) Softmax

The most popular approach for learning neural embedding models is optimizing the Softmax loss which is tailored for seen data set, but typically does not learn deep representations or embeddings that are discriminative enough for unseen test set. Some recent works on voice anti-spoofing improved generalization capability to unseen test data by employing one class softmax (OCS) [39] and large margin cosine loss (LMCL) [4] variants of classification loss functions. In this work, we use AAM variant of softmax which can be formulated as [36]:

$$L_{AAM} = -\frac{1}{N} \sum_{i=1}^{N} log(\frac{e^{s(cos(\theta_{y_i},i+m))}}{Z_1}), \tag{6}$$

where $Z_1 = e^{s(cos(\theta_{y_i},i+m))} + \sum_{j=1,j\neq i}^{c} e^{scos\theta_{j,i}}$, N is the batch size, c is the number of classes, y_i corresponds to label index, $\theta_{j,i}$ represents the angle between the column vector of weight matrix W_j and the i-th input sample to the projection layer x_i, where both W_j and x_i are normalized. The scale factor s is used to make sure the gradient is not too small during the training and m is a hyperparameter that encourages the similarity of correct classes to be greater than that of incorrect classes by a margin m.

In this work, for all models, we empirically choose $s = 20$ and $m = 0.75$ based on validation set performance.

Table 1. TDNN architecture used in this work. D indicates the duration of features in number of frames and F the feature vector dimensionality. n indicates the number of statistics combined in statistics pooling layer. If all four (i.e., mean, standard deviation, skewness, and kurtosis) statistics are used then $n = 4$.

Layer	Input dimension	Output dimension	Dilation
Conv1d+ReLU	F × D	512 × D	1
Conv1d+ReLU	512 × D	512 × D	2
Conv1d+ReLU	512 × D	512 × D	3
Conv1d+ReLU	512 × D	512 × D	1
Conv1d+ReLU	512 × D	512 × D	1
Statistics Pooling	512 × D	2048 (with n = 4)	–
Linear+ReLU	2048	256	–
Linear+ReLU	256	256	–
AAM Softmax	256	# classes	–

3 Experiments

3.1 ASVspoof2019 Challenge Corpora

The ASVspoof 2019 challenge provides a common framework with a standard corpora for conducting spoofing detection research both on LA and PA attacks.

The LA dataset includes bonafide and spoof speech signals generated using various state-of-the-art voice conversion and speech synthesis algorithms. The PA data is generated according to different replay configurations by simulating channel characteristics across three room sizes, three distances to the microphone, and three levels of reverberation. A summary of the LA and PA corpora in terms of training (Train), development (Dev) and evaluation (Eval) partitions and number of recordings is presented in Table 2. In both LA and PA tasks, development and evaluation subsets constitute the seen and unseen test sets in terms of spoofing attacks. For more details about the corpora, the interested readers are referred to [6].

3.2 Evaluation Metrics

The official evaluation metrics of ASVspoof2019 challenge, equal error rate (EER) and minimum tandem detection cost function (min-tDCF) [8], are used for performance evaluation. The lower the values of EER and min-tDCF the better performance is attained. The ASV scores provided by the challenge organizer are used for computing min-tDCF.

Table 2. Summary of ASVspoof2019 logical Access (LA) and physical access (PA) corpora in terms of training (Train), development (Dev) and evaluation (Eval) partitions and number of recordings.

Set	# Speakers	# Recordings			
		Logical Access		Physical Access	
		Bonafide	Spoof	Bonafide	Spoof
Train	20	2,580	22,800	5,400	48,600
Dev.	20	2,548	22,296	5,400	24,300
Eval.	67	7,355	63,882	18,090	116,640

3.3 Experimental Setup

As local frame-level hand-crafted features we use 60-dimensional Linear Frequency Cepstral Coefficients (LFCC) extracted using 25 ms analysis window over a frame shift of 10 ms. The neural network architecture is based on TDNN with statistics pooling layer. No data augmentation is performed. Training is carried out using Stochastic Gradient Descent (SGD) optimizer for the parameters in the loss functions [15, 39] in a standard classification setting. Balanced mini-batches of size 64 samples are used for both LA and PA tasks. The learning rates were set at 0.0003 and performance is monitored on the validation set. Polyak's momentum is also employed with its coefficient set to 0.9.

3.4 Results

Results Using Combination of Different Order Statistics. Table 3 presents spoofing detection performance on evaluation set of ASVspoof2019 PA task. Presented results were obtained using TDNN architectures and eleven combinations of different order (1st, 2nd, 3rd and 4th) statistics used while performing statistics pooling. It is observed that pooling HOS alone (e.g., system TDNN_s34) or in combination with 1st or 2nd or 1st & 2nd order statistics (e.g., systems TDNN_s13, TDNN_s14, TDNN_s23, TDNN_s24, TDNN_s123, TDNN_s124, TDNN_s134, TDNN_s234 and TDNN_s1234) helped us to achieve better performance i.e., reduction of EER and min-tDCF values, compared to when only 1st and 2nd order statistics were pooled. These findings suggest that HOS assists in detecting acoustic cues/artifacts that are more discriminative for the detection of spoofing attacks. In short, inclusion of HOS is found to be effective for PA attacks detection task.

We further verify the effectiveness of using HOS for LA attacks or audio deepfakes detection task by conducting similar experiments on ASVspoof2019 LA corpus as done for PA task. These results are reported in Table 4 in terms of EER and min-tDCF evaluation metrics. We can see from the presented results, almost similar trends in performance were achieved as attained in Table 3 which has led to the conclusion that pooling of HOS on their own or in conjunction with lower order statistics (i.e., mean and standard deviation) is supportive for both replay and synthetic speech detection tasks. Best performances were achieved on both LA and PA tasks with system TDNN_s23 in which standard deviation and skewness are simply concatenated over time during statistics pooling to learn global embeddings from local descriptors. Therefore, based on this evidence, we choose system TDNN_s23 for comparison with other most recent or previously proposed single best voice anti-spoofing systems in Sect. 3.4.

Table 3. Spoofing detection performance with TDNN architecture using different combination of statistics on the evaluation set of the *Physical Access (PA)* task of the ASVspoof 2019 challenge. TDNN_s12 denotes a TDNN-based spoofing detection system that only uses first and second order statistics during statistics pooling, where concatenated numbers in the subscript indicate the order (1st, 2nd, 3rd, and 4th orders) statistics included in the system.

System_statistics	EER (%)	min-tDCF
TDNN_s12	1.802	0.0539
TDNN_s13	1.354	0.0378
TDNN_s14	1.438	0.0412
TDNN_s23	1.343	0.0385
TDNN_s24	1.537	0.0445
TDNN_s34	1.470	0.0428
TDNN_s123	1.422	0.0403
TDNN_s124	1.502	0.0453
TDNN_s134	1.433	0.0423
TDNN_s234	1.493	0.0437
TDNN_s1234	1.437	0.0436

Table 4. Voice spoofing detection performance with TDNN architecture using different combination of statistics on the evaluation set of the *Logical Access (LA)* task of the ASVspoof 2019 challenge.

System statistics	EER (%)	min-tDCF
TDNN_s12	4.280	0.1079
TDNN_s13	3.481	0.0836
TDNN_s14	3.154	0.0780
TDNN_s23	3.050	0.0729
TDNN_s24	3.452	0.0893
TDNN_s34	3.086	0.0710
TDNN_s123	3.563	0.0964
TDNN_s124	4.253	0.0917
TDNN_s134	3.831	0.0943
TDNN_s234	3.519	0.0863
TDNN_s1234	3.424	0.0857

Comparison with Some Existing Single Best Approaches. In this section, we compare the performances of the best performing systems (LA:TDNN_s23, PA:TDNN_s23), selected from previous section, with other existing single best systems as well as the ASVspoof2019 challenge baselines. Tables 5 and 6 provide a comparison of performances of our best systems with other published single best systems in terms of EER and min-tDCF, on LA and PA tasks, respectively. From Table 5 it can be observed that, except the ResNet18+OCS system [39], our TDNN_s23 system outperformed all other systems, considered here for comparison purpose, with a substantial margin. Though TDNN_s23 system could not provide better performance than the ResNet18+OCS system, we believe that by including self-attentive pooling of either standard deviation and skewness (as done in system TDNN_s23) or skewness and kurtosis (similar to system TDNN_s34) in ResNet18+OCS system can lead us to achieve better results than the one reported in [39]. Unfortunately, some of the systems considered in Table 5 did not report detection results on PA task, thus we could not compare those systems' performances to our system in Table 6. By observing the results from Table 6 we can say that our HOS-based TDNN system achieved the best performance on simulated replay attacks detection.

On a final note, statistics pooling, be it Self-Attentive Pooling (SAP) or simple Statistics Pooling (SP), has a notable impact on learning discriminative and robust utterance-level representations and inclusion of HOS alone or jointly with lower order statistics during pooling operation supports to capture some acoustic cues which are evidently more discriminative for voice anti-spoofing.

We achieved our best and consistent performance across LA and PA tasks when 3rd order statistics were combined with 2nd order statistics during pooling operation. For this reason we did not try to incorporate 5-th and/or 6-th order statistics, i.e., hyperskewness and/or hypertailedness, in this work.

Table 5. Spoofing detection performance on the evaluation set of the *logical access* (LA) task of the ASVspoof 2019.

System	EER (%)	min-tDCF
CQCC-GMM [6]	9.57	0.2366
LFCC-GMM [6]	8.09	0.2116
CQCC-GMM [13]	8.91	0.2157
ResNet [13]	6.38	0.1423
TDNN [14]	7.00	0.1653
System A [5]	7.66	0.179
ResNet + LMCL [4]	3.49	0.092
ResNet18+OCS [39]	2.19	0.059
OLFCC + GMM [24]	3.50	0.090
RawNet2 [25]	4.66	0.1294
FG-LCNN [33]	4.07	0.102
FFT-LCNN [11]	4.53	0.103
MelSpec + ResNet34 [21]	5.32	0.151
ResNet + OC-SVM [39]	4.44	0.115
TDNN_s23 (*Ours*)	**3.05**	**0.0729**

Table 6. Spoofing detection performance on the evaluation set of the *physical access* task of the ASVspoof 2019.

System	EER (%)	min-tDCF
CQCC-GMM [6]	11.04	0.2454
LFCC-GMM [6]	13.54	0.3017
CQCC-GMM [13]	11.16	0.2478
ivector/PLDA [13]	10.18	0.2687
MelSpec + ResNet34 [21]	5.74	0.1514
ResNet [13]	1.98	0.0579
TDNN [14]	1.77	0.0597
TDNN_s23 (*Ours*)	**1.34**	**0.0385**

4   Conclusion

In this work, we carried out an investigative study on the influence of higher order statistics, such as third and fourth order moments, in addition to the first and second order statistics on the performance of a stand-alone spoofing detection system. A standard TDNN architecture with statistics pooling and additive angular margin softmax was used to perform end-to-end spoofing detection. The hand-crafted linear frequency cepstral coefficients (LFCC) were used as local frame-level countermeasure to the input of TDNN. Simulation experiments were conducted on the ASVspoof2019 LA and PA corpora and results were reported on the unseen evaluation test sets. Experimental results, in terms of EER and min-tDCF, show that inclusion of 3rd and/or 4th order statistics with the 1st and/or 2nd order statistics yielded improvement in spoofing detection performances on both LA and PA tasks. On both tasks, best performances were achieved when 2nd and 3rd order statistics were pooled to obtain a fixed dimensional and compact utterance-level countermeasure vector, i.e., embedding. Compared to the GMM-based baseline systems and most of the other existing deep learning based single systems, our approach (TDNN_s23) depicted better performance.

In future work, we plan to incorporate higher order statistics (specifically 3rd order stats in combination with standard deviation) with ResNet architecture and one class softmax classification loss [39] paradigm for voice antispoofing. Our results can be reproduced with the toolkits released with articles [15] and [39].

References

1. Alam, J., Kenny, P.: Spoofing detection employing infinite impulse response-constant q transform-based feature representations. In: 2017 25th European Signal Processing Conference (EUSIPCO), pp. 101–105. IEEE (2017)
2. Alam, M.J., Kenny, P., Bhattacharya, G., Stafylakis, T.: Development of CRIM system for the automatic speaker verification spoofing and countermeasures challenge 2015. In: Sixteenth Annual Conference of the International Speech Communication Association (2015)
3. Alam, M.J., Kenny, P., Gupta, V., Stafylakis, T.: Spoofing detection on the asvspoof2015 challenge corpus employing deep neural networks. In: Proceedings Odyssey, pp. 270–276 (2016)
4. Chen, T., Kumar, A., Nagarsheth, P., Sivaraman, G., Khoury, E.: Generalization of audio deepfake detection. In: Proceedings Odyssey 2020 The Speaker and Language Recognition Workshop, pp. 132–137 (2020)
5. Chettri, B., Stoller, D., Morfi, V., Ramírez, M.A.M., Benetos, E., Sturm, B.L.: Ensemble models for spoofing detection in automatic speaker verification. In: Proceedings Interspeech (2019), pp. 1018–1022 (2019)
6. consortium, A.: ASVspoof 2019: automatic speaker verification spoofing and countermeasures challenge evaluation plan (2019). https://www.asvspoof.org/asvspoof2019/asvspoof2019_evaluation_plan.pdf. Accessed 13 May 2020
7. Evans, N.W., Kinnunen, T., Yamagishi, J.: Spoofing and countermeasures for automatic speaker verification. In: Interspeech, pp. 925–929 (2013)
8. Kinnunen, T., et al.: T-DCF: a detection cost function for the tandem assessment of spoofing countermeasures and automatic speaker verification. arXiv preprint arXiv:1804.09618 (2018)
9. Kinnunen, T., et al.: A spoofing benchmark for the 2018 voice conversion challenge: Leveraging from spoofing countermeasures for speech artifact assessment. arXiv preprint arXiv:1804.08438 (2018)
10. Kinnunen, T., et al.: The asvspoof 2017 challenge: assessing the limits of replay spoofing attack detection. In: Proceedings Interspeech, (2017), pp. 2–6 (2017)

11. Lavrentyeva, G., Novoselov, S., Tseren, A., Volkova, M., Gorlanov, A., Kozlov, A.: STC antispoofing systems for the asvspoof2019 challenge. In: Proceedings Interspeech (2019), pp. 1033–1037 (2019)
12. Lorenzo-Trueba, J., Fang, F., Wang, X., Echizen, I., Yamagishi, J., Kinnunen, T.: Can we steal your vocal identity from the internet?: Initial investigation of cloning obama's voice using gan, wavenet and low-quality found data. arXiv preprint arXiv:1803.00860 (2018)
13. Monteiro, J., Alam, J.: Development of voice spoofing detection systems for 2019 edition of automatic speaker verification and countermeasures challenge. In: 2019 IEEE Automatic Speech Recognition and Understanding Workshop (ASRU), pp. 1003–1010 (2019)
14. Monteiro, J., Alam, J., Falk, T.: A multi-condition training strategy for countermeasures against spoofing attacks to speaker recognizers. In: Proceedings Odyssey 2020 The Speaker and Language Recognition Workshop, pp. 296–303 (2020)
15. Monteiro, J., Alam, J., Falk, T.H.: Generalized end-to-end detection of spoofing attacks to automatic speaker recognizers. Comput. Speech Lang. **63**, 101096 (2020)
16. van den Oord, A., et al.: Wavenet: a generative model for raw audio. CoRR arXiv:1609.03499 (2016).
17. Oord, A.V.D., et al.: Wavenet: a generative model for raw audio. arXiv preprint arXiv:1609.03499 (2016)
18. Patel, T.B., Patil, H.A.: Combining evidences from mel cepstral, cochlear filter cepstral and instantaneous frequency features for detection of natural vs. spoofed speech. In: Sixteenth Annual Conference of the International Speech Communication Association (2015)
19. Patel, T.B., Patil, H.A.: Effectiveness of fundamental frequency (f 0) and strength of excitation (SOE) for spoofed speech detection. In: 2016 IEEE International Conference on Acoustics, Speech and Signal Processing (ICASSP), pp. 5105–5109. IEEE (2016)
20. Ping, W., et al.: Deep voice 3: 2000-speaker neural text-to-speech. CoRR arXiv:1710.07654 (2017)
21. RahulT, P., Aravind, P.R., Ranjith, C., Nechiyil, U., Paramparambath, N.: Audio spoofing verification using deep convolutional neural networks by transfer learning. ArXiv:abs/2008.03464 (2020)
22. Sahidullah, M., et al.: Introduction to voice presentation attack detection and recent advances. In: Marcel, S., Nixon, M.S., Fierrez, J., Evans, N. (eds.) Handbook of Biometric Anti-Spoofing. ACVPR, pp. 321–361. Springer, Cham (2019). https:// doi.org/10.1007/978-3-319-92627-8_15
23. Sahidullah, M., Kinnunen, T., Hanilçi, C.: A comparison of features for synthetic speech detection (2015)
24. Tak, H., Patino, J., Nautsch, A., Evans, N., Todisco, M.: Spoofing attack detection using the non-linear fusion of sub-band classifiers. In: Proceedings Interspeech 2020, pp. 1106–1110 (2020)
25. Tak, H., Patino, J., Todisco, M., Nautsch, A., Evans, N., Larcher, A.: End-to-end anti-spoofing with rawnet2. In: IEEE (ed.) ICASSP 2021, IEEE International Conference on Acoustics, Speech and Signal Processing, Toronto, Canada (Virtual Conference), June 2021, pp. 6–11. Ontario (2021)
26. Tamamori, A., Hayashi, T., Kobayashi, K., Takeda, K., Toda, T.: Speaker-dependent wavenet vocoder. In: Interspeech 2017, pp. 1118–1122 (2017)
27. Tian, X., Wu, Z., Xiao, X., Chng, E.S., Li, H.: Spoofing detection from a feature representation perspective. In: 2016 IEEE International Conference on Acoustics, Speech and Signal Processing (ICASSP), pp. 2119–2123. IEEE (2016)

28. Todisco, M., Delgado, H., Evans, N.: Constant q cepstral coefficients: a spoofing countermeasure for automatic speaker verification. Comput. Speech Lang. **45**, 516–535 (2017)
29. Todisco, M., et al.: Asvspoof 2019: future horizons in spoofed and fake audio detection. arXiv preprint arXiv:1904.05441 (2019)
30. Wang, Y., et al.: Tacotron: a fully end-to-end text-to-speech synthesis model. CoRR arXiv:1703.10135 (2017)
31. Wang, Y., et al.: Tacotron: towards end-to-end speech synthesis. arXiv preprint arXiv:1703.10135 (2017)
32. Wielgus, A., Magiera, W., Smagowski, P.: Efficiency of the nonlinear schur-type estimation algorithms for higher-order stochastic processes. In: International Conference on Signals and Electronic Systems (2018)
33. Wu, Z., Das, R.K., Yang, J., Li, H.: Light convolutional neural network with feature genuinization for detection of synthetic speech attacks. In: Proceedings Interspeech 2020, pp. 1101–1105 (2020)
34. Wu, Z., Evans, N., Kinnunen, T., Yamagishi, J., Alegre, F., Li, H.: Spoofing and countermeasures for speaker verification. Surv. Speech Commun. **66**, 130–153 (2015)
35. Wu, Z., et al.: Asvspoof 2015: the first automatic speaker verification spoofing and countermeasures challenge. In: Sixteenth Annual Conference of the International Speech Communication Association (2015)
36. Xiang, X., Wang, S., Huang, H., Qian, Y., Yu, K.: Margin matters: towards more discriminative deep neural network embeddings for speaker recognition. arXiv preprint arXiv:1906.07317 (2019)
37. Xiao, X., Tian, X., Du, S., Xu, H., Chng, E.S., Li, H.: Spoofing speech detection using high dimensional magnitude and phase features: the NTU approach for asvspoof 2015 challenge. In: Sixteenth Annual Conference of the International Speech Communication Association (2015)
38. You, L., Guo, W., Dai, L., Du, J.: Multi-task learning with high-order statistics for x-vector based text-independent speaker verification (2019)
39. Zhang, Y., Jiang, F., Duan, Z.: One-class learning towards synthetic voice spoofing detection. IEEE Sig. Process. Lett. **28**, 937–941 (2021)

Assessing Velar Gestures Timing in European Portuguese Nasal Vowels with RT-MRI Data

Nuno Almeida[1(✉)], Conceição Cunha[2], Samuel Silva[1], and António Teixeira[1]

[1] IEETA / DETI - University of Aveiro, Aveiro, Portugal
{nunoalmeida,sss,ajst}@ua.pt
[2] Institute of Phonetics and Speech Processing, LMU Munich, Germany
cunha@phonetik.uni-muenchen.de

Abstract. European Portuguese (EP) nasal vowels are characterised by their dynamic nature entailing a gradual variation from an oral into a nasal configuration. The analysis of velar dynamics assumes a particular relevance for improving our understanding of nasal vowel production with an impact, e.g., on articulatory synthesis. Following on previous work, considering EMA and real-time magnetic resonance imaging (RT-MRI), at 14 fps, this study revisits the work regarding the characterisation of EP nasal vowels by analysing gesture timings considering articulatory data obtained from RT-MRI of the vocal tract at a higher frame rate (50 fps) and a larger number of speakers. The analysis, considering eleven EP speakers, characterises the duration of opening and closing velar gestures and explores synchronisation with the previous oral gesture (start-to-release lag) and the potential influence of vowel height in this regard.

Keywords: Nasal vowels · European Portuguese · Gestural timing · Real-time magnetic resonance.

1 Introduction

Portuguese is characterised by having five nasal vowels ([6~], [e~], [i~], [o~], [u~], SAMPA notation adopted throughout) and several nasal diphthongs and thriphthongs. Nasal sounds are roughly defined by the lowering of the soft palate (velum), resulting in the opening of the velo-pharyngeal port and the coupling of the nasal and oral passages. But their production is much more complex. A relevant finding regarding Portuguese nasality entails its unfolding in the temporal dimension, as first observed by Lacerda and Head [6]: the course of nasality in the vowels is typically defined by an incremental movement from oral to nasal. In this regard, adopting the Articulatory Phonology framework, and working with acoustic data, Albano [1] provides a gestural explanation for Brazilian Portuguese nasal vowels encompassing a velum gesture which is delayed with respect to the tongue body gesture – and this is the reason for an oral onset –, and depending on the amount of overlap of the velum gesture with the following oral gesture (e.g., as in "canto" [k6~tu]), a consonantal segment can appear.

Understanding nasality, and having a more precise description of its underlying mechanisms and timings is important to foster an understanding of speech production,

© Springer Nature Switzerland AG 2021
A. Karpov and R. Potapova (Eds.): SPECOM 2021, LNAI 12997, pp. 26–35, 2021.
https://doi.org/10.1007/978-3-030-87802-3_3

in general, with applications, for instance, in speech therapy, but it is also crucial to realistically represent the movement of the involved articulatory gestures in articulatory-based speech synthesis [17, 18].

Our team has devoted particular attention to the study of the dynamic pattern of European Portuguese nasal vowels considering several technologies such as EMA [11–13, 15] and RT-MRI [3, 4, 7–9]. These previous works observed that: (1) the opening movement of the velum is longer than the closing gesture, regardless of speech rate; (2) the onset of velum opening seems to follow the release of the preceding oral constriction (start-to-release lag around 20 − 30 ms); and (3) a consonantic segment is observed, at the end of the vowel, resulting from an overlap between the velum closing gesture and the oral gesture. Nevertheless, although these previous works provide insights into the temporal organisation of nasal vowels, the typically low number of speakers involved is still a limitation to what can definitely be concluded, particularly regarding speaker idiosyncrasies and related strategies in the implementation.

Advances on the technologies considered to study these matters open up novel opportunities to revisit the study of nasal vowels in its multiple dimensions. RT-MRI images exhibiting good image quality and with frame rates reaching 50 fps is the precious source of information to study nasal vowels with a view over the whole vocal tract dynamics that goes beyond the more granular data provided by the pellets in EMA. However, dealing with the amount and complexity of the RT-MRI data for these matters is a challenge in itself: While in EMA the movement of the velum is directly provided by the data of a particular pellet, in RT-MRI, the image data needs to be processed to locate and extract the anatomical structures of interest and derive the relevant profiles. Given the amount of data, these studies need to be performed as automatically as possible. However, due to the sometimes noisy nature of the data, this may require the adoption of increasingly complex pre-processing and analysis methods to ensure the quality of the data and a proper depiction of the studied phenomena.

In this study, we add to previous articulatory analysis by considering a 50 fps RT-MRI data of the vocal tract to analyse the temporal course of velar movement and its synchronisation with the preceding oral gesture. Given the dynamic nature of how nasality unfolds, the higher time resolution of the RT-MRI data (compared with 14 fps in previous works) is paramount for a more precise determination of synchronisation and timings. Furthermore, a larger number of speakers is considered (11) providing a wider view over inter-speaker variability. Our overall aim is, therefore, to present a first exploration of the articulatory data provided by this new data set and contribute to further complement previous work regarding the study of nasal vowel dynamics with a focus on the velum. Additionally, we seek to inform the requirements for future studies - both regarding the inner-workings of nasal vowels that deserve a more in-depth analysis and how to deal with the RT-MRI data to serve that purpose.

The remainder of this article is organised as follows: Sect. 2 presents an overview of the considered data and the methods adopted for their processing and analysis; The results thus obtained are reported in Sect. 3 followed by an overall discussion of the main findings in Sect. 4; finally, Sect. 5 presents some conclusions and ideas for further work.

2 Methods

2.1 Articulatory Data

Sagittal real-time image sequences of the vocal tract, acquired at 50 fps, and collected for 11 European Portuguese native speakers were considered. The images were acquired at the Max-Planck-Institute in Göttingen, Germany, using a 3T Siemens Prisma Fit MRI System equipped with a 64-channel head coil. The acquisition method provided real-time image sequences of the vocal tract in a midsagittal plane of the speaker at 50 fps [19]. Speech sound was synchronously recorded using an optical microphone (Dual Channel-FOMRI, Optoacoustics) and annotated using Praat [2].

The recorded speech material considered for the work presented here consists of words containing the five EP nasal vowels [6~, e~, i~, o~, u~] preceded by the oral consonant /p/, as in [p6~tu, pi~tu]. All words were randomised and repeated in two prosodic conditions embedded in one of three carrier sentences alternating the verb as follows: (diga ('Say'); ouvi ('I heard'); leio ('I read')) as in 'Diga pato, diga pato baixinho' ('Say duck, Say duck gently'). Here we analyse only the first repetition of the token in each sentence. Figure 1 shows some examples of images extracted from the recorded RT-MRI sequences.

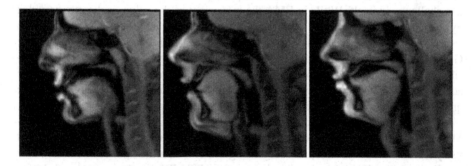

Fig. 1. Illustrative samples of RT-MRI images included in the collected data. From left to right, images selected during the production of /6~/, /i~/, and /u~/ for speakers S05, S06, and S07 respectively. Note the different tongue configurations and the lowered velum visible in all images.

For this work, we considered the same processed data obtained in our previous work [3] consisting of the estimated aperture of the vocal tract and data for an estimate of lip aperture and velar movement based on regions of interest placed at the lips and velum region [3]. The velum movement data is obtained from the Principal Component Analysis (PCA) performed after the alignment of all the samples of the corpus.

In order to identify the data of interest to study velar movement and inter-gestural timings, the annotations performed on the audio were considered to select the segment containing the nasal vowel and the flanking consonants.

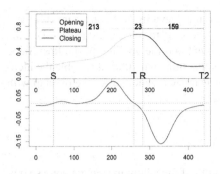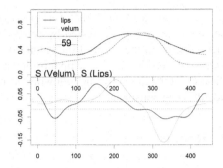

Fig. 2. Illustrative examples for the computation of relevant articulatory events and durations. On the left, based on the first derivative of velar aperture (bottom curve), the onset (S) of the opening gesture, target (T), release (R) and release offset (T2) are computed, enabling the computation of the opening, plateau, and closing times. On the right, based on the first derivatives of the velar and lip aperture curves (presented at the bottom of the graph), the release for the oral constriction (S lips) and the onset (S) of the velar opening gesture are determined and the start-to-release lag (SRL) is computed.

2.2 Post-processing and Determination of Articulatory Events

Despite the high frame rate of the RT-MRI data, 50 Hz, a greater number of samples per second can enable a finer determination of the different vocal track events in the lips and velum movement. Using R, we have interpolated the values obtained from the processed RT-MRI data, fitting a cubic smoothing spline to the original data to create more resolution. In order to eliminate some noise in the data the FFT (fast Fourier transform) is computed and all frequencies 12 Hz are removed.

The filtered data, showing lip aperture and velum height, over time, was then processed following a procedure similar to the one adopted to analyse EMA data: the first derivative of these curves was computed (yielding articulator velocity) and supported the determination of articulatory events adopting a decision threshold of 10% of the maximum value of the derivative. An illustrative sample of these computations can be seen in Fig. 2. For instance, the onset of velum aperture movement is set to the instant when the derivative is increasing and crosses the 10% threshold and the plateau stage is the region where velocity is inverted, noticeable by the derivative crossing zero and delimited from 10% to −10% of the maximum value of the derivative.

For each of the articulators of interest, i.e., lip and velar aperture, a set of events of interest were labelled. For each velum gesture we have the: movement start (S); achievement of the target (T); target release (R); and release offset (T2).

2.3 Timings

Based on the the differences between the times for the labelled events the time of opening, plateau and closing were computed. Figure 2 illustrates the events determined for a velar cycle. Inter-gestural timing was quantified as the time between gestural events derived, as described above, from the first derivative of velar and lip aperture curves.

As in previous work [13], the overlap between the previous oral consonant (C1) and the velum gesture was assessed by computing the start-to-release lag (SRL), i.e., the interval between the onset of the velum movement and the aperture of the lips. Since we are not considering tongue tip movement, at this time, which would enable the identification of the target for the following /t/, no analysis is reported for the overlap with the following consonant.

3   Results

In a first instance, we performed a characterisation of the velum movement across vowels and speakers. All durations of interest, i.e., velar opening, plateau, and closing, were computed automatically from the events labelled in the velum curves.

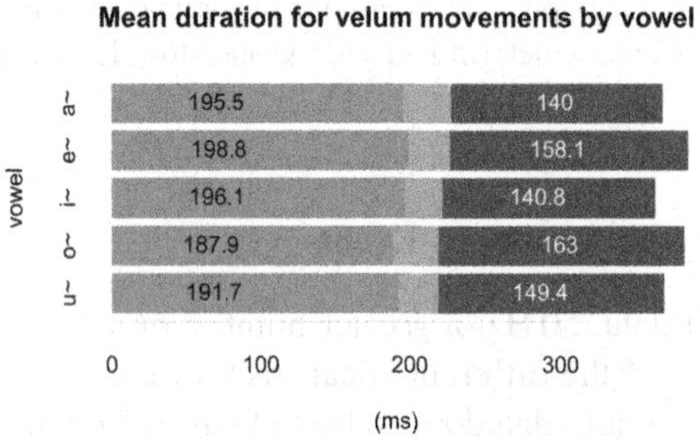

Mean duration for velum movements by vowel

Vowel	Total	Opening	Plateau	Closure
a~	368 ± 54	195 ± 52	33 ± 14	140 ± 31
e~	385 ± 62	199 ± 70	28 ± 13	158 ± 47
i~	363 ± 62	196 ± 53	26 ± 14	141 ± 33
o~	383 ± 57	188 ± 53	32 ± 17	163 ± 39
u~	369 ± 58	192 ± 50	28 ± 12	149 ± 46

Fig. 3. Mean duration and standard deviation (ms) for velar movements (opening, plateau, and closure) for each EP nasal vowel.

Figure 3 presents the mean opening, plateau and closing durations for EP nasal vowels obtained by averaging the data from all speakers. Overall, the velar cycle duration, considering all vowels, 374 ms. It can be observed that, with some small differences in total duration, mostly due to a variable duration of the closing phase, among vowels, all vowels seem to follow a similar trend: (1) similar opening phase; (2) short plateau; and (3) the closing phase always having a shorter duration than the opening phase.

To assess the vowel effect, separate repeated measures ANOVAs for all four durations were made considering vowel as a within factor. The analysis showed no significant vowel effect for all measures (results in Table 1).

Table 1. Results for the assessment of the effect of vowel and speaker in different parameters characterising velar movement using a repeated measures ANOVA.

	Total	Opening	Plateau	Closing
Vowel	$F = 0.88, p = 0.478$	$F = 0.181, p = 0.948$	$F = 1.053, p = 0.382$	$F = 1.342, p = 0.257$

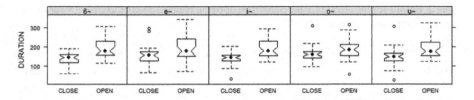

Fig. 4. Closing and opening gesture duration for all vowels. A repeated measues ANOVA shows a significantly higher opening time and this is observed consistently for all vowels.

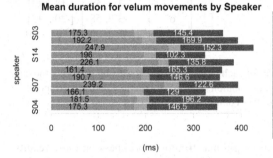

SPK	Total	Opening	Plateau	Closure
S04	350 ± 58	175 ± 57	28 ± 10	146 ± 18
S05	404 ± 47	182 ± 76	26 ± 12	196 ± 62
S06	325 ± 24	166 ± 19	30 ± 14	129 ± 24
S07	393 ± 68	239 ± 61	31 ± 12	123 ± 22
S08	355 ± 57	191 ± 50	18 ± 5	147 ± 19
S10	360 ± 37	161 ± 23	33 ± 10	165 ± 25
S13	384 ± 72	226 ± 54	22 ± 11	136 ± 52
S14	324 ± 56	196 ± 83	26 ± 15	102 ± 50
S01	426 ± 63	248 ± 58	25 ± 14	152 ± 33
S02	393 ± 46	192 ± 42	31 ± 11	170 ± 24
S03	362 ± 45	175 ± 22	41 ± 22	145 ± 39

Fig. 5. Mean duration and standard deviation (ms) of velar movements (total, opening, plateau, and closure) for each speaker, gathering data from all nasal vowels.

Regarding the obverved tendency of a longer opening than closing duration, a repeated measures ANOVA showed that the opening time significantly higher than closing time $[F = 68.57, p < 0.001]$, with CI 95 % of $[185.2, 202.6]$ and $[144.1, 156.7]$ for opening and closing time, respectively. This effect is clear for all vowels as shown in Fig. 4.

Figure 5 shows velum movement characterisation per speaker, obtained by averaging the data for all vowels produced by that speaker. In here, the total duration of the velar cycle is noticeably variable, across speakers, but the tendency of a shorter closing phase than the opening is still observable. ANOVAs revealed significant speaker effect in all measured durations ($p < 0.001$).

Finally, considering our initial hypothesis that low vowels may be more strongly nasalised than high vowels, the results for velum opening duration were also analysed for differences based on vowel height. Repeated measures ANOVAs for the 4 times, performed separately, considering 2 groups of vowels (high=[i~, u~], non-high=[6~, e~, o~]) showed no significant differences for all measured parameters. ANOVAs results are summarised in Table 2.

Regarding the inter-gestural timing concerning the preceding consonant (/p/), Fig. 6 shows boxplots for the SRL per vowel along with the mean and standard deviations. These results show a wide variability among vowels ranging form clearly positive values for /6~/ to clearly negative mean values for /u~/. Notably, a strong dispersion (with a large standard deviation between 60 ms and 90 ms) of the values is also observed with the lower end of the 95% confidence interval for /u~/ near −70 ms.

Table 2. Results for the effect of vowel height on different parameters characterising velar movement using repeated measures ANOVA.

	Total	Opening	Plateau	Closing
V height	$F = 2.733, p = 0.1$	$F = 0.157, p = 0.692$	$F = 2.48, p = 0.118$	$F = 1.779, p = 0.184$

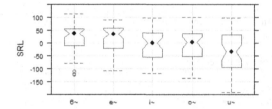

vowel	SRL (ms)	CI (95%)
6~	20 ± 60	[2 .. 39]
e~	10 ± 59	[-8 .. 28]
i~	-2 ± 55	[-18 .. 14]
o~	-3 ± 58	[-20 .. 15]
u~	-43 ± 90	[-70 .. -15]

Fig. 6. Start-to-release lag (SRL) obtained for each of the EP nasal vowels by gathering the data from all speakers. On the left, boxplot representation; on the right, table with the corresponding mean SRL values, standard deviation and 95% confidence interval (CI).

To assert the effect of vowel, their height and frontness/backness on these results, repeated-measure ANOVAS were performed for each. For these analyses, vowels were divided in different groups: high ([i~, u~]), not-high ([6~, e~, o~]), front ([e~, i~]), and back (o~, u~). The results of the analyses are presented in Table 3 and show a significant effect of all factors.

Table 3. Results for the effects of vowel, vowel height, and vowel frontness/backness in the start-to-release lag (SRL) using repeated measures ANOVA.

	Vowel	v. height	v. front/back
SRL	$F = 7.347, \ p < 0.001***$	$F = 14.73, \ p < 0.001***$	$F = 8.852, \ p < 0.005**$

4 Discussion

Regarding the total duration of the velum cycle, its mean values are in line with those reported in previous works for EP nasal vowels (see Table 4) strengthened by the number of consider speakers, in this study. Although the amount of data in previous studies does not allow any definitive conclusion, it seems that larger vowel durations (slower speech rate) have been measured for the studies using RT-MRI. In this context, one important difference is the speaker's position during acquisition (supine for RT-MRI and sited for EMA). However, some studies have shown that the acquisitions of speech data for speakers in supine position are not much influenced by gravity if the corpus does not include sustained productions. In those cases, sounds are artificially sustained so that the vocal tract is in a stable position for image capturing, a practise most common in static MRI studies. Nevertheless, studies on velar dynamics – aimed primarily to study deglutition [14] – , seem to show a different velar behaviour when in supine

Table 4. Overall results for total duration of velar cycle in EP nasal vowels along with the start-to-release lag (SRL) found in previous studies considering different technologies and number of speakers.

Ref.	Technology	# Speakers	Total duration	Close vs Open	SRL (CI %95)
Oliveira et al. [13]	EMMA	1	307 ms	smaller	—
Oliveira et al. [12]	EMMA	1	300 ms	smaller	[23 .. 43] ms
Martins et al. [9]	14 fps RTMRI	2	333 to 437 ms	smaller	—
Present study	50 fps RTMRI	11	324 to 426 ms	smaller	[−70 .. 39] ms

position. This may be an indication that speakers tend to adopt a slower speech rate – as a more comfortable rate –, in this position, but further studies are required to be able to assert it. Another distinguishing aspect between RT-MRI and EMA acquisitions, potentially influencing the differences in observed duration, is the ambient noise present in the first, related with the acquisition equipment, since the presence of ambient noise has also been shown to yield an increased duration of vowels [5, 10].

As observed in previous work [9, 12], the closing gesture duration is shorter than the opening gesture and this is observed for all vowels. Additionally, there is a notable variation of total duration among speakers, which may be the result of different speech rates, but the closing gesture is always shorter that the opening gesture.

Regarding the duration of the opening stage of the velum, if lower vowels were more strongly nasalised than higher vowels, we would expect a shorter duration of the opening gesture, for instance for [6~], than for [i~] or [u~]. However, our analysis did not show any significant difference among vowels.

The observed mean SRL is different among vowels, with a large negative value (−43 ms) for [u~], although the 95% confidence interval goes above 20 ms for all vowels. In previous work [12], although just for one speaker, a mean SRL as low as −1.6 ms (and as high as 32.9 ms) was observed, but only when the speaker was instructed to speak at a higher rate. In this light, the values of SRL obtained for the vowels [6~, e~, i~, o~] are inline with those results. The positive values of SRL (for [a~] and [e~]) entail that the onset of velum opening follows constriction release (lips) and seems to corroborate the results in [12] possibly explained by the motor constraints imposed by the need for the velum to be closed to produce the preceding stop (/p/). Such lag entails that the initial part of the nasal vowel, after the release of the oral constriction and until the onset of velar opening, has a configuration that is similar to its oral congener. This is consistent with the nasal vowel having a first oral stage.

However, vowels [i~] and [o~] present a marginally negative mean SRL that appeared, in previous studies, only for fast speech rates [12]. In fact, SRL seems to be affected by heightness and backness. One possibility, given the supine position, is that some adjustments to the oral and velar gestures needs to happen due to gravity. Nevertheless, vowel [u~] shows a very low mean value of SRL (−43 ms) which raises some questions. Since the method used to infer velum movement is dependent on a region of interest approach, and since the backness of the tongue, for this vowel, puts it in close proximity with the velum, two aspects can potentially contribute to this value: (1) a need for the velum to anticipate opening onset to account for adjustments given the tongue's proximity; (2) the proximity of the two structures results in image artefacts which influence the region-based method to infer velar aperture. To more precisely assert the impact of each of these factors, the extraction of the velar data needs to move into a model-based segmentation framework, as proposed in [16], allowing the measurement of distances between the velum and the pharyngeal wall instead of estimating it based on pixel intensities.

A stronger nasalisation might be achieved by a shorter duration of the opening gesture, which our data did not show, or by a smaller SRL. Our results show a significant effect of vowel height, but also of backness, with the SRL value found for [u~] advising caution on taking major conclusions without a closer inspection of the data, as discussed above, and also paying attention to the strategies adopted by each speaker.

5   Conclusion

This paper presents a characterisation of nasal vowel timings for European Portuguese from articulatory data extracted from RT-MRI images of 11 speakers. The number of considered speakers enables a broader perspective over the nasality of EP nasal vowels and the results confirm a previously observed tendency of a closing velum gesture shorter than the opening movement. Additionally, the new results for SRL partially confirm previous findings using EMA [12], but raise some questions that need to be further explored, namely regarding a shortening of the mean SRL value for some of the vowels, and a large negative value appearing for [u~].

In this regard, the analysis presented here is based on velum and lip aperture data that is extracted from the RT-MRI sequences considering regions-of-interest. Therefore, although a good surrogate for the actual movement of the articulators, it is more prone to image noise and artefacts than having distances computed from landmarks in the anatomy. This explains the number of outliers found in our data and should be address, in the future, with a more robust approach to the data extraction, e.g., resorting to segmentations of the vocal tract, e.g., evolving the method proposed in [16] to cope with this novel data.

One important aspect that needs to be addressed for a more complete characterisation of gestures timing for EP nasal vowels concerns the coordination with the subsequent oral targets (concerning the following consonant). This assessment should enable a greater insight over aspects such as the existence and nature of a nasal tail (N) as reported in [12]. Adding to this objective, the consideration of additional contexts should also be addressed.

Acknowledgements. This work is partially funded by the German Federal Ministry of Education and Research (BMBF, KZ:01UL1712X), IEETA Research Unit funding (UIDB/00127/2020), by Portugal 2020 under the Competitiveness and Internationalization Operational Program, and the European Regional Development Fund through project SOCA–Smart Open Campus (CENTRO-01–0145-FEDER-000010), project MEMNON (POCI-01–0145-FEDER-028976). A word of thanks is due to Dr Christopher Carignan for sharing the scripts serving as basis for extracting the lip and velar aperture data from the RT-MRI sequences.

References

1. Albano, E.C.: O português brasileiro e as controvérsias da fonética atual: pelo aperfeiçoamento da fonologia articulatória. DELTA: Documentação de Estudos em Lingüística Teórica e Aplicada **15**, 23–50 (1999)
2. Boersma, P.: Praat: doing phonetics by computer [computer program] (2020). http://www.praat.org/
3. Cunha, C., Almeida, N., Frahm, J., Silva, S., Teixeira, A.: Data-driven analysis of nasal vowels dynamics and coordination: Results for bilabial contexts. In: Proceedings IberSPEECH 2021, pp. 215–219 (2021). http://dx.doi.org/10.21437/IberSPEECH.2021-46
4. Cunha, C., et al.: On the role of oral configurations in european portuguese nasal vowels. In: Proceedings Interspeech 2019, pp. 3332–3336 (2019). http://dx.doi.org/10.21437/Interspeech.2019-2232
5. Junqua, J.C.: The lombard reflex and its role on human listeners and automatic speech recognizers. J. Acoust. Soc. Am. **93**(1), 510–524 (1993)
6. Lacerda, A., Head, B.: Análise de sons nasais e sons nasalizados do português. Revista do Laboratório de Fonética Experimental de Coimbra **6**, 5–70 (1966)
7. Martins, P., Carbone, I., Silva, A., Teixeira, A.: An MRI study of European Portuguese nasals. In: Interspeech. Antuérpia (2007)
8. Martins, P., Carbone, I., Pinto, A., Silva, A., Teixeira, A.: European Portuguese MRI based speech production studies. Speech Commun. **50**(11–12), 925–952 (2008)
9. Martins, P., Oliveira, C., Silva, S., Teixeira, A.: Velar movement in European Portuguese nasal vowels. In: Proceedings of IberSpeech-VII Jornadas en Tecnología del Habla and II Iberian SLTech Workshop, Madrid, Spain, pp. 231–240 (2012)
10. Ngo, T., Akagi, M., Birkholz, P.: Effect of articulatory and acoustic features on the intelligibility of speech in noise: an articulatory synthesis study. Speech Commun. **117**, 13–20 (2020)
11. Oliveira, C.: Do grafema ao gesto: Contributos Linguísticos para um Sistema de Síntese de base articulatória. Universidade de Aveiro, Aveiro, Dissertação de doutoramento (2009)
12. Oliveira, C., Martins, P., Teixeira, A.: Speech rate effects on European Portuguese nasal vowels. In: InterSpeech. Brighton (2009)
13. Oliveira, C., Teixeira, A.: On gestures timing in European Portuguese nasals. In: ICPhS. Saarbrücken (2007)
14. Perry, J.L., Bae, Y., Kuehn, D.P.: Effect of posture on deglutitive biomechanics in healthy individuals. Dysphagia **27**(1), 70–80 (2012)
15. Rossato, S., Teixeira, A., Ferreira, L.: Les nasales du portugais et du français: une étude comparative sur les données emma. Journées d' Etude sur la Parole (2006)
16. Silva, S., Teixeira, A.: Unsupervised segmentation of the vocal tract from real-time MRI sequences. Comput. Speech Lang. **33**(1), 25–46 (2015)
17. Teixeira, A., Oliveira, C., Barbosa, P.: European Portuguese articulatory based text-to-speech: first results. In: Teixeira, A., de Lima, V.L.S., de Oliveira, L.C., Quaresma, P. (eds.) PROPOR 2008. LNCS (LNAI), vol. 5190, pp. 101–111. Springer, Heidelberg (2008). https://doi.org/10.1007/978-3-540-85980-2_11
18. Teixeira, A., Martinez, R., Silva, L.N., Jesus, L., Príncipe, J., Vaz, F.: Simulation of human speech production applied to the study and synthesis of European Portuguese. EURASIP J. Appl. Sig. Process. **9**, 1435–1448 (2005)
19. Uecker, M., Zhang, S., Voit, D., Karaus, A., Merboldt, K.D., Frahm, J.: Real-time MRI at a resolution of 20 ms. NMR in Biomed. **23**(8), 986–994 (2010)

Designing and Deploying an Interaction Modality for Articulatory-Based Audiovisual Speech Synthesis

Nuno Almeida[(⊠)], Diogo Cunha, Samuel Silva, and António Teixeira

IEETA/DETI, University of Aveiro, Aveiro, Portugal
nunoalmeida@ua.pt
https://www.ieeta.pt

Abstract. Humans communicate with each other in a multimodal way. Even with several technologies mediating remote communication, face-to-face contact is still our main and most natural way to exchange information. Despite continuous advances in interaction modalities, such as speech interaction, much can be done to improve its naturalness and efficiency, particularly by considering the visual cues transmitted by facial expressions through audiovisual speech synthesis (AVS). To this effect, several approaches have been proposed, in the literature, mostly based in data-driven methods. These, while presenting very good results, rely on models that work as black boxes without a direct relation with the actual process of producing speech and, hence, do not contribute much to our understanding of the underpinnings of the synergies between the audio and visual outputs. In this context, the authors proposed a first proof of concept for an articulatory-based approach to AVS, supported on the articulatory phonology framework, and argued that this research needs to be challenged and informed by fast methods to translate it to interactive applications. In this article, we describe further evolutions of the pronunciation module of the AVS core system along with the proposal of a set of interaction modalities to enable its integration in applications to enable a faster translation into real scenarios. The proposed modalities are designed in line with the W3C recommendations for multimodal interaction architectures making it easy to integrate with any applications that consider it.

Keywords: Audiovisual speech synthesis · Articulatory · Interaction modality · Multimodal interaction

1 Introduction

Speech is our most natural way to communicate with other humans. In recent years, we have witnessed a strong evolution of speech technologies boosting advances in speech interaction with applications and digital personal assistants. Most current speech interaction solutions are limited to the auditory signal. However, the visual features of speech production, such as the movement of the lips,

© Springer Nature Switzerland AG 2021
A. Karpov and R. Potapova (Eds.): SPECOM 2021, LNAI 12997, pp. 36–49, 2021.
https://doi.org/10.1007/978-3-030-87802-3_4

provide additional cues that can result in a greater resilience of speech communication, even in less adequate contexts, such as noisy environments. Additionally, the consideration of an avatar can foster the sense of a more humanized system and enables exploring facial cues, e.g., to emphasize affective speech content.

Most of the approaches to AVS, nowadays, rely on the acquisition of a large set of data to create models for synthesis (e.g., [4]) and provide very good results for many application scenarios. Nevertheless, the resulting models work as 'black boxes' controlled by parameters that do not relate, for instance, with the anatomy involved in speech production. This, mostly entails that we are evolving the technology for AVS, but not particularly evolving our knowledge on audiovisual speech production. In this context, approaching audiovisual speech synthesis from an anthropomorphic perspective, i.e., trying to understand the human process of speech articulation and how it relates with the visual cues, may still be far from providing as much quality as data-driven approaches but, importantly, can serve the research on audiovisual speech production and enables controlling and analyzing the system using parameters that are more understandable and have a close relation with the different anatomical parts. This may enable a greater flexibility in understanding how the audio and visual components of speech relate, can be an important tool in speech therapy contexts, and can even support the study regarding how different limitations to the speech production apparatus (e.g., partial lip/face paralysis resulting from a stroke) can impact audiovisual speech production.

Advancing an articulatory-based AVS system poses several challenges at different levels: (a) requires the integration and deployment of a set of complex technologies to support the articulatory approach, such as the articulatory model and all the subsystems (e.g., pronunciation) enabling to go from a written sentence to a format that these models can process to compute articulator trajectories; (b) requires 3D modeling technology for building an avatar that supports rigging, i.e., the manipulation of the facial expression by moving a set of anchor points; (c) the speech audio needs to be synthesized with acceptable quality and keeping the required levels of synchronization with the visual stream; and (d) it is important to be able to easily deploy the whole system, even at early stages, since this will foster easier evaluation of its performance and opens the routes to challenge it in environments outside the lab informing improvements and prioritizing requirements.

In this context, following on the work presented in [14] and adopting the conceptual framework proposed by the authors in [15], this work contributes with: (a) improvements to the audiovisual speech synthesis core, namely through evolutions on a pronunciation module for European Portuguese, used to feed an articulatory model aligned with the Task Dynamics framework, making it more versatile than our previous work which relied on dictionaries; and (b) a set of interaction modalities abiding to the requirements of the W3C multimodal interaction recommendations, allowing an easy integration with other applications already adopting the multimodal interaction framework, for instance the one in Almeida et al. [1].

The remainder of this document is structured as follows. Section 2 provides a brief overview regarding previous work on articulatory-based audiovisual speech synthesis and a summary of aspects about developing multimodal interactive systems deemed relevant to contextualize the present work. Then, Sect. 3 describes the evolution of the pronunciation module for EP and Sect. 4 explains the overall architecture and features of an audiovisual speech synthesis interaction modality. Finally, Sect. 5 presents conclusions and overall perspectives for future advances.

2   Background and Related Work

To contextualize the contributions provided in this document, the following sections briefly describe current approaches to AVS along with previous work, by the authors, regarding articulatory-based AVS for European Portuguese.

Additionally, a brief background and related work is also provided regarding multimodal interaction and its development, relevant to support the overall design decisions for the proposed AVS interaction modalities.

2.1   AudioVisual Speech Synthesis

Several research areas can profit from the evolution of the AudioVisual Speech Synthesis with application scenarios ranging from talking avatars as means to provide a more humanized, expressive and resilient way (e.g., no ambient noise) of providing speech output, to a form of providing a more controlled creation of stimuli supporting research in human perception while hearing and seeing speech [21].

Audiovisual speech can be defined, as proposed in an extensive review on the subject by Mattheyses and Verhelst [5], by four aspects: (a) the properties of the input (e.g., text or audio); (b) the properties of the output; (c) the definition of visual articulators; and (d) how the different visual configurations are predicted.

One possible approach to perform the visual part of the audiovisual speech synthesis is the use of visemes. A viseme defines the representation of the relevant visual articulators associated with a phoneme. Defining visemes for each phoneme requires a lot of effort and it is time consuming, and this is why some approaches using this method opt to use the same viseme for several phonemes when the visible part is similar (e.g., lips for /m/ and /p/) [13]. Then, having a set of visemes, for each phoneme in a word or sentence, the corresponding viseme is shown. However, one important aspect in speech is that the sounds are not produced in isolated form. Instead, the configuration of our vocal tract (and, by extension, of the visual facial features) changes, over time, in a fluid movement from one phoneme to another in a process know as coarticulation. In simple terms, this entails that the configuration of the vocal tract to produce a particular sound is often influenced by the sounds that come before and after.

With visemes, the coarticulation is usually approached by interpolation between the existing visemes, used as key frames, but improved approaches have been proposed using trisemes entailing that for a phoneme (P) multiple visemes may exist that were modeled for various combinations of $(P_p \; \mathbf{P} \; P_n)$, where P_p and P_n are phones that precede or succeed the phone of interest.

The advances in data-driven approaches have also provided notable improvement in the quality of the proposed audiovisual synthesis systems for instance by advancing the viseme approach [20] and by boosting the proposal of photo-realistic audiovisual synthesis (e.g., [4,16].

Concerning audiovisual speech synthesis for European Portuguese only a few works have been proposed. One notable example [13] considered a viseme-based approach allowing the visual animation synthesis from text or audio speech and noting that a small set of visemes impaired the quality of the output.

2.2 Articulatory-Based Audiovisual Synthesis

In Silva and Teixeira [15] the authors proposed a conceptual framework for creating the conditions to foster a more structured evolution of the research in articulatory-based AVS. The main rationale supporting the proposal was that the actual use of the AVS module, from early on, in scenarios where it can be seen and tested by users, would challenge and inform the research providing feedback, refining the requirements, and identifying issues.

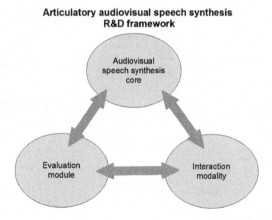

Fig. 1. Conceptual framework for development of audiovisual speech systems (from [15]).

Furthermore, being able to deploy the proposed system easily, to different platforms can also improve how it can be formally evaluated (e.g., through perceptual tests with users or automated assessment using ground truth speaker data). To this end, the conceptual framework (see Fig. 1) proposed three main modules: (a) the audiovisual synthesis core, responsible for creating the synthesis from text; (b) the interaction modalities, providing a fast track for translating the audiovisual features into applications; and (c) the evaluation module that would provide automated and supervised features for formal assessment of performance.

Aligned with this conceptual framework, the authors proposed a first proof-of-concept [14] for the AVS core module adopting an articulatory-based approach relying on the TADA [6,12] – TAsk Dynamic Application. In this approach, the rationale was to take an articulatory model that, given an input text, can compute how the different articulators (e.g., lips, tongue) need to move, over time, to utter it. One notable difference of this approach towards the use of visemes is that coarticulation is implicitly computed based on the sequence of phones that needs to be uttered. At the end of the computation, the result is a set of trajectories for the different articulators (e.g., lips, tongue tip) defining the configuration of the vocal tract over time which can also be considered for synthesizing speech using it as input to an articulatory synthesizer (e.g., SAPWindows [17]). The fact that the movements of the articulators and the speech signal are produced from the same tract data is an advantage since they are inherently synchronized.

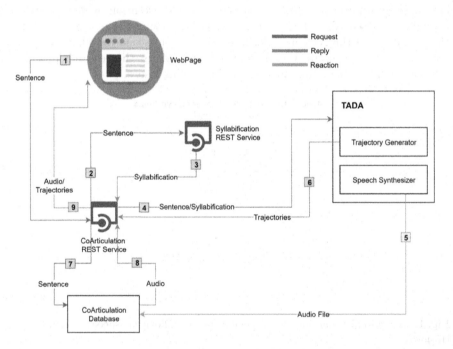

Fig. 2. Overall architecture for the articulatory-based audiovisual speech synthesizer module. At its core is the Task Dynamics Application (TADA) responsible for computing the trajectories of the different vocal tract articulators. The lips trajectories are then used to modify a photo-realistic avatar that is rendered along with the speech audio.

In short, in the first proposal, and following the numbered lines in Fig. 2, (1) a sentence is sent to the coarticulation service – managing the whole process – and is (2) syllabified based on a dictionary containing different European Portuguese words and their syllabification. Next, (3) the syllabified sentence is sent (4) to

TADA, responsible for computing the trajectories of the different articulators (6) to produce the sentence, and a speech audio signal is generated from these trajectories using CASY (5). Since the computations of the trajectories take some time, they are stored, along with the audio to speed the response to future requests of the same sentence (7, 8). Finally, the trajectories and audio are sent to the frontend to get ready for rendering (9). To this end, a photorealistic avatar is modified according to the received trajectories for the lips and rendered in WebGL while the speech audio is played.

This first system showed the viability of the approach and three key points were identified as requiring evolutions towards increasing the performance and adaptability in terms of processing speed and quality of the audiovisual synthesis: (a) generalize the pronunciation to accept words beyond the current approach using a dictionary; (b) increase the speed of articulators' trajectories computation to enable a behavior closer to real-time; (c) improve speech synthesis quality, currently being performed using a simple synthesizer (CASY [11]) as a proof-of-concept.

The work presented in this article mainly contributes with the evolution of the AVS core module beyond the proof-of-concept presented in [14] and in the proposal of a first set of interaction modalities to support its integration in applications, in line with the proposed conceptual framework.

2.3   Multimodal Interaction

The design and development of multimodal interactive systems entails a range of challenges particularly regarding how to deal with the desirable high and transient number of modalities. The complexity associated with some of the modalities can also be an obstacle to their wide use in many applications, since developers need to master all the technology and often cannot reuse previous work since modalities are developed in tight relation with the application core. Furthermore, when multiple modalities are present and can be used in synergy (e.g., speech and gestures), managing the interaction requires additional complexity to fuse the events, which increases the burden to the developer and the complexity of the application.

In this context, several solutions have been presented that try to tackle these challenges putting a particular emphasis in decoupling the interaction modalities and interaction management from the application. In this way, the developer only has to integrate the desired modalities using a very well defined method that is similar across modalities. This enables, for instance, that complex interaction modalities, such as speech input, can be made available of-the-shelf to be used in any application that abides to the specifications.

The W3C have put an effort to propose a set of recommendations for multimodal interactive systems [3] including the definition of the multimodal architecture, a standard markup language for communication and specification of each internal component. Despite some open points, which are being address by the community, such as discovery and registration of new modalities addressed, e.g., by Rodríguez et al. [10], multimodal frameworks based on this architecture have already been proposed supporting the development of multimodal interactive applications, and notable examples are OpenStream Cue-me[1] and the authors previous work, the AM4I framework [1], and its use in the context of Ambient Assisted Living (AAL) [19] and smarthomes [18].

Considering these frameworks, application can profit from adopting them since its decoupled nature allows an easy integration with existent and new modalities. A developer creating an application does not need to handle the variety of technologies used for each modality. Also, when a modality is created there is no need to worry about the application where it will be used. Also, existent, of-the-shelf, modalities can be used as a starting point to interact with new applications based on the multimodal framework, it is easy to interact across multiple devices and new modalities can be created and seamlessly used with already existing applications.

All things considered, given the complexity of the proposed audiovisual speech synthesis and the need to provide an integration solution that can potentially make it available in a wide variety of scenarios, the consideration of a solution aligned with a multimodal framework seems an important route to follow.

3   Evolutions of the Articulatory-Based Audiovisual Synthesis Core

Our first version of the pronunciation module inherited from the team's previous research on an articulatory synthesizer for European Portuguese [17] and was focused on supporting only a small set of words (and some nonsense words) to test the performance of the articulatory synthesizer for particular sounds. In this iteration we tackled this limitation aiming to support the synthesis for any word or sentence.

The new pronunciation module consists of two stages: (1) G2P (Grapheme-to-Phoneme), which converts the sentences' graphemes into their phonetic representation, also including the information regarding stress; and (2) syllabification of the phonetic representation using the notation accepted by TADA.

To make the G2P conversion a Deep Bidirectional Short-Term Memory (DBLSTM) neural network was trained [9]. Figure 3 depicts the overall neural network architecture. This network includes Long Short-Term Memory (LSTM) layers that allow the preservation of a context of past values flowing through it. Additionally, it also uses bidirectional long short-term memory (BLSTM) layers, a particular case of LSTMs, but enabling a context also including future values. In the G2P context, this is particularly suited since, for each grapheme, the network has a context of previous and next graphemes in the current word. As an alternative to the LSTM layers, gated recurrent units (GRUs) were also tested, but performance assessment showed that, even though they speed up training, the provided results were worst.

---

[1] http://www.openstream.com/cueme.html.

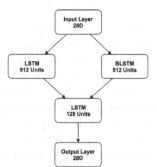

Graphemes	Phonemes	Syllabification
aftas	"aft6S	(-a1_)(f-V0_)(t-60_S)
aplanavas	6pl6n"av6S	(-60_)(pl-60_)(n-a1_)(v-60_S)
caprichamos	k6priS"6muS	(k-60_)(pr-i0_)(S-61_)(m-u0_S)
donativos	dun6t"ivuS	(d-u0_)(n-60_)(t-i1_)(v-u0_S)
vira-o	v"ir6u	(v-i1_)(r-60u_)
infamarão	i~f6m6r"6~w~	(-i~0_)(f-60_)(m-60_)(r-6~1w~_)

Fig. 3. Architecture of the neural network considered to support the G2P and syllabification along with a sample of the dataset. SAMPA is adopted for the phonetic transcription and the syllabification is formatted as required by TADA.

The dataset used for training and testing was created by resorting to a dictionary provided by PROJECTO NATURA[2] containing almost 1 million European Portuguese words and by using a phonetic transcription tool made available by Coimbra's Institute of Telecommunications[3]. Finally, 60% of the resulting set of word + phonetic transcription pairs was randomly selected for training and 20% for validation. The test with 20% of the set had 1.44% of words with wrong prediction.

For syllabification, the same network as the one adopted for G2P was used. For building the dataset to train and test the network, a previous heuristic approach to syllabification was used [7] that only performed syllabification from graphemes. This approach was applied to the PROJECTO NATURA European Portuguese dictionary and the outcomes paired with the corresponding phonetic transcriptions obtained earlier. The syllabifications were inspected to detect any systematic issues or other problems and manually corrected. A 60% training, 20% validation, 20% testing division of the dataset was adopted. The 20% of the set revealed 755 words with a wrong prediction for syllabification (0.38%).

Although the G2P presented by Rao [9] does the conversion on the character level, this models were created at word level. Also, using a larger data set the percentage of prediction error was inferior.

4 Interaction Modality for Audiovisual Speech Synthesis

As argued in Sect. 2, the ability to easily deploy the AVS system is relevant for facilitating its formal evaluation (e.g., perceptual tests) and challenge its performance in scenarios closer to reality. These later conditions of use can inform the development and refinement by providing clear requirements from the end-user perspective, similarly to the approach our team adopted for advancing a speech interaction modality [2].

---

[2] https://natura.di.uminho.pt/wiki/doku.php.
[3] https://www.aclweb.org/anthology/W11-4516/.

Just to provide a potential context for deploying our work, one illustrative scenario for the AVS modality is the smarthome environment where users are surrounded by devices placed in the environment or that they carry with them, and may interact, for instance, with a 'digital butler' to control and obtain information about the house using multiple interaction modalities. In this case, the AVS modality should be available in a wide variety of devices and take advantage of their features, maybe sometimes rendering the talking avatar in the person's tablet, or showing the visual stream in a display, available, e.g., in the living room or the fridge, and sending the audio stream to the user's earphones, connected to the smartphone. Additionally, and considering this scenario as a testbed for the technology, it would be important that updates to the core features of the AVS system (e.g. to improve performance) happened transparently to the user, without requiring changes to the local resources.

From this overall vision and from the characteristics of the proposed AVS system, it follows that its deployment should: (a) be provided in the form of a decoupled interaction modality; (b) be designed according to the multimodal interaction W3C recommendations to enable easy integration in any environments that embrace them; (c) be accessible from multiple devices and operative platforms; (d) enable the rendering of the audio and visual components in separate devices; and (e) keep the heavy computation work on the server side and a decoupling between the modality and these features to allow continuous update of the AVS core system without modifications needed on the application side.

Considering these initial requirements, Fig. 4 depicts the overall architecture to support the demonstration of a AVS output modality integrated in a minimal multidevice multimodal interactive system. To demonstrate the flexibility of a multimodal approach, we depict each component on its own device. A user can interact with an application that integrates any number of input and output modalities. Each of the modalities considered by the application can be executed on any device, e.g., the AVS modality on a computer and a text input modality on a smartphone, while having the application on a tablet. Each modality is independent of one another and independent of the application. The communication between these components is mediated by the interaction manager (IM) and the communication between the different modalities and the IM occurs through MMI Life Cycle events.

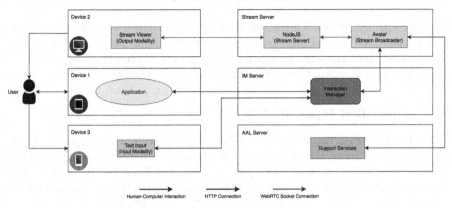

Fig. 4. Overall system architecture integrating the multimodal framework with the AVS modality.

4.1   Audiovisual Speech Synthesis Output Modality

Our AVS modality presents the user with an animated avatar uttering a sentence as requested by the application or user (explained ahead). From a conceptual point-of-view, it is important to understand that the AVS modality is to be considered as one possible form of output of the interactive system to pass a message to the user along with other possibilities. For instance, given a text message, some examples of possible ways of transmitting it to the user might be: (a) written text on a screen; (b) synthesized audio of the message; (c) talking avatar; or (d) a set of pictograms. All these, if present on a system, would be potential candidates for the task. Therefore, the AVS modality is connected to the interaction manager (IM) and it is up to this module to manage which message and when is sent to the AVS modality to be rendered.

To enable the visualization in most devices the modality is composed of three components: (a) **server** - using NodeJS and Socket.io, establishes the initial connection between the broadcaster and clients and allows for the relaying of messages; (b) **broadcaster** - consists of an implementation of the avatar itself that communicates with the support services of the AVS core trough their API, using REST, and manages the communication of the modality with the interaction manager through MMI Life Cycle events; and (c) **client** - consisting mainly of a video and an audio elements to reproduce the tracks of the stream sent by the broadcaster. While the support services are an external component, they are essential to the execution of the modality as they do all the necessary processing on the sentences sent to the Avatar, particularly calculating the vocal tract parameters over time and creating the audio file corresponding to the sentence. During the initial setup, the broadcaster and the clients connect to the server using WebSockets. Then, a new WebRTC connection is created to directly connect the broadcaster and the clients, without the need to send the stream trough the server. The broadcaster creates a stream using as video track, the canvas of the Avatar and, as audio track, the audio file generated by the system. The client receives the stream and reproduces each track in a video or audio element, corresponding to the type of media of the track.

4.2 Sample Text Input Modality

To further illustrate the modularity of our system we created a simple input modality consisting of a text input and a button. Similarly to the AVS modality, the input modality is also completely decoupled from the application and connects to the IM by exchanging MMI Lifecycle events. This serves to show, in a simple manner, that, in the future, new input modalities can be added, such as speech recognition (speech-to-text), to provide the input to be rendered, and no changes need to be made to the Avatar to be able to receive the text and process it.

This input modality allows the user to send sentences to be audio-visually synthesized. These go through the interaction manager that in a more complex system would decide which of the available modalities would be more suitable to do it. In this particular case, only one output modality is present, the AVS modality, and the interaction manager will forward the request to it. The sentences are sent to the Avatar and are processed trough the AVS core system support services, sent back to the modality and directed to the client.

4.3 Test Application

In order to demonstrate the usage of our two modalities, we created a web application. Upon opening the application, the user can see a set of buttons for input and output modalities. In this case, as can be see in Fig. 5, there are only two modalities available.

Clicking on the "Text Input Modality" button will load the corresponding modality using an HTML iframe. Similarly, clicking on the "Avatar Modality" button will load an instance of the Avatar Modality client also using an HTML iframe. This serves to illustrate the inclusion of the modalities in an interface in a dynamic manner, i.e., the modalities exist as independent modules and can be inserted in the application's interface on-demand. So, a developer only needs to integrate the modality, in this manner, and does not have to worry about, for instance, rendering the avatar.

Users can, then, insert a sentence in the text input box and send it to the IM using the "Send" button. The IM will receive the sentence and verify that the destination is the Avatar modality, being the one that was selected, thereby forwarding the message. Once the Avatar receives the sentence, it is processed trough the system (on the support services) and it is displayed in the client. Because an instance of the client was loaded in the application too, users will see and hear the sentence they introduced.

Fig. 5. Screenshot of the modality tester. On the left, two interface elements that enable invoking the input modality (text) and output modality (audiovisual synthesis). These, when selected are dynamically loaded in the interface (on the right).

5   Conclusion

The main contributions of this work are the improvements to the authors' previous work on audiovisual speech and an output modality based on a photorealistic Avatar for audiovisual speech synthesis. The improvements were in the modules to convert words to phonemes and the syllabification, using the G2P to train new models for European Portuguese.

By adopting an approach aligned with the W3C recommendations for multimodal interactive systems, the proposed modality can, for instance, be more easily integrated with ongoing research regarding the proposal of assistive communication technologies for aphasia in project APH-ALARM[4].

While our approach allows other systems to integrate and test the modality, there is still room for improvement. Particularly in two main points: synthesis speed and sound quality. Regarding synthesis speed improvements, these do not need to be as prioritized, since a possible workaround for this is storing the trajectories for each sentence the first time it is synthesized, thereby greatly decreasing the time it takes to output the results on subsequent requests. When it comes to sound quality, it plays a crucial role in the systems' ability to perceptually perform better, and the team is already putting an effort to improve it by exploring state of the art approaches such as WaveGlow [8].

Acknowledgements. This work is partially funded by IEETA Research Unit funding (UIDB/00127/2020), by Portugal 2020 under the Competitiveness and Internationalization Operational Program, and the European Regional Development Fund through project MEMNON (POCI-01-0145-FEDER-028976).

References

1. Almeida, N., Teixeira, A., Silva, S., Ketsmur, M.: The AM4I architecture and framework for multimodal interaction and its application to smart environments. Sensors **19**, 11 (2019). https://doi.org/10.3390/s19112587. Switzerland

---

[4] https://aph-alarm-project.com/index.php/en/.

2. Almeida, N., Silva, S., Teixeira, A.: Design and development of speech interaction: a methodology. In: Kurosu, M. (ed.) HCI 2014, Part II. LNCS, vol. 8511, pp. 370–381. Springer, Cham (2014). https://doi.org/10.1007/978-3-319-07230-2_36

3. Dahl, D.A.: The W3C multimodal architecture and interfaces standard. J. Multimodal User Interfaces 7(3), 171–182 (2013). https://doi.org/10.1007/s12193-013-0120-5

4. Filntisis, P.P., Katsamanis, A., Tsiakoulis, P., Maragos, P.: Video-realistic expressive audio-visual speech synthesis for the Greek language. Speech Commun. 95, 137–152 (2017)

5. Mattheyses, W., Verhelst, W.: Audiovisual speech synthesis: an overview of the state-of-the-art. Speech Commun. 66, 182–217 (2015). https://doi.org/10.1016/j.specom.2014.11.001

6. Nam, H., Goldstein, L., Browman, C., Rubin, P., Proctor, M., Saltzman, E.: Tada (task dynamics application) manual (2006)

7. Oliveira, C.A.M.D.: Do grafema ao gesto: contributos linguísticos para um sistema de síntese de base articulatória. Ph.D. thesis, Universidade de Aveiro (2009). https://ria.ua.pt/handle/10773/4847

8. Prenger, R., Valle, R., Catanzaro, B.: WaveGlow: a flow-based generative network for speech synthesis. In: 2019 IEEE International Conference on Acoustics, Speech and Signal Processing (ICASSP), ICASSP 2019, pp. 3617–3621. IEEE (2019)

9. Rao, K., Peng, F., Sak, H., Beaufays, F.: Grapheme-to-phoneme conversion using Long Short-Term Memory recurrent neural networks. In: 2015 IEEE International Conference on Acoustics, Speech and Signal Processing (ICASSP), pp. 4225–4229 (2015). https://doi.org/10.1109/ICASSP.2015.7178767

10. Rodríguez, B.H., Moissinac, J.C.: Discovery and registration: finding and integrating components into dynamic systems. In: Dahl, D. (ed.) Multimodal Interaction with W3C Standards. Springer, Cham (2017). https://doi.org/10.1007/978-3-319-42816-1_15

11. Rubin, P., Baer, T., Mermelstein, P.: An articulatory synthesizer for perceptual research. J. Acoust. Soc. Am. 70(2), 321–328 (1981)

12. Saltzman, E.L., Munhall, K.G.: A dynamical approach to gestural patterning in speech production. Ecol. Psychol. 1(4), 333–382 (1989)

13. Serra, J., Ribeiro, M., Freitas, J., Orvalho, V., Dias, M.S.: A proposal for a visual speech animation system for European Portuguese. In: Torre Toledano, D., et al. (eds.) IberSPEECH 2012. CCIS, vol. 328, pp. 267–276. Springer, Heidelberg (2012). https://doi.org/10.1007/978-3-642-35292-8_28

14. Silva, S., Teixeira, A., Orvalho, V.: Articulatory-based audiovisual speech synthesis: proof of concept for European Portuguese. In: Proceedings of the Iberspeech, Lisbon, Portugal, pp. 119–126 (2016)

15. Silva, S., Teixeira, A.J.S.: An anthropomorphic perspective for audiovisual speech synthesis. In: BIOSIGNALS, pp. 163–172 (2017)

16. Suwajanakorn, S., Seitz, S.M., Kemelmacher-Shlizerman, I.: Synthesizing Obama: learning lip sync from audio. ACM Trans. Graph. (ToG) 36(4), 1–13 (2017)

17. Teixeira, A., Silva, L., Martinez, R., Vaz, F.: Sapwindows - towards a versatile modular articulatory synthesizer. In: Proceedings of 2002 IEEE Workshop on Speech Synthesis, pp. 31–34 (2002). https://doi.org/10.1109/WSS.2002.1224366

18. Teixeira, A., Almeida, N., Pereira, C., Oliveira e Silva, M., Vieira, D., Silva, S.: Applications of the multimodal interaction architecture in ambient assisted living. In: Dahl, D. (ed.) Multimodal Interaction with W3C Standards. Springer, Cham (2017). https://doi.org/10.1007/978-3-319-42816-1_12

19. Teixeira, A., Almeida, N., Ketsmur, M., Silva, S.: Chapter 6 - effective natural interaction with our sensorized smart homes. In: Neustein, A. (ed.) Advances in Ubiquitous Computing. Advances in Ubiquitous Sensing Applications for Healthcare, pp. 185–222. Academic Press (2020). https://doi.org/10.1016/B978-0-12-816801-1.00006-2
20. Thangthai, A., Milner, B., Taylor, S.: Synthesising visual speech using dynamic visemes and deep learning architectures. Comput. Speech Lang. **55**, 101–119 (2019)
21. Thézé, R., Gadiri, M.A., Albert, L., Provost, A., Giraud, A.L., Mégevand, P.: Animated virtual characters to explore audio-visual speech in controlled and naturalistic environments. Sci. Rep. **10**(1), 1–12 (2020)

Kurdish Spoken Dialect Recognition
Using X-Vector Speaker Embedding

Arash Amani[1]([✉]), Mohammad Mohammadamini[2], and Hadi Veisi[3]

[1] Asosoft Research Group, Tehran, Iran
[2] Avignon University LIA (Laboratoire Informatique d'Avignon), Avignon, France
mohammad.mohammadamini@univ-avignon.fr
[3] Faculty of New Sciences and Technologies, University of Tehran, Tehran, Iran
h.veisi@ut.ac.ir

Abstract. This paper presents a dialect recognition system for the Kurdish language using speaker embedding. Two main goals are followed in this research: first, we investigate the availability of dialect information in speaker embedding, then this information is used for spoken dialect recognition in the Kurdish language. Second, we introduce a public dataset for Kurdish spoken dialect recognition named Zar. The Zar dataset comprises 16,385 utterances in 49 h-36 min for five dialects of the Kurdish language (Northern Kurdish, Central Kurdish, Southern Kurdish, Hawrami, and Zazaki). The dialect recognition is done with x-vector speaker embedding which is trained for speaker recognition using Voxceleb1 and Voxceleb2 datasets. After that, the extracted x-vectors are used to train support vector machine (SVM) and decision tree classifiers for dialect recognition. The results are compared with an i-vector system that is trained specifically for Kurdish spoken dialect recognition. In both systems (i-vector and x-vector), the SVM classifier with 87% of precision results in better performance. Our results show that the information preserved in the speaker embedding can be used for automatic dialect recognition.

Keywords: Speaker embedding · X-vector · Kurdish language · Dialect recognition · Zar dataset

1 Introduction

Spoken dialect/language recognition is the automatic identification of a dialect/language from speech utterances. Spoken dialect/language recognition can be used as a preprocessing step for other speech technologies such as speech dictation, speech to speech translation, speech assistants, etc. [1]. In general, dialect recognition is more difficult than language recognition because the dialects of specific language are almost similar [2].

Earlier generations of language recognition are based on speaker modeling frameworks such as Gaussian Mixture Model (GMM), [4], Factor Analysis (FA) [5]

© Springer Nature Switzerland AG 2021
A. Karpov and R. Potapova (Eds.): SPECOM 2021, LNAI 12997, pp. 50–57, 2021.
https://doi.org/10.1007/978-3-030-87802-3_5

and i-vector [3] systems. Recently, the x-vector speaker modeling is adopted for language recognition [6,7]. The x-vector is a deep learning speaker embedding system that is already proposed for speaker recognition. In the speaker recognition pipeline the Deep Neural Network is trained to classify the speakers and a compact fixed-sized representation for each utterance extracted from a hidden layer [8]. The language recognition recipe of the system is trained with language labels [7]. The original version of x-vectors (i.e. trained for speaker recognition) has shown that besides the speaker's information, it also encodes different characteristics (e.g. gender [9],) and environment variability (room, microphone [9], type of noise [10]).

This paper follows two goals: Firstly, we investigate the possibility of doing dialect recognition with an embedding system that is already trained for speaker recognition. In doing so, we use the x-vector system that classifies speakers. The trained system is used to extract x-vector representation for our dataset that the dialect recognition is done on it. In [6,7] the language/dialect recognition is done with an embedding network that is specifically trained for language recognition but in our work the x-vector network trained for speaker recognition is used. Using speaker embedding for dialect recognition had importance for several reasons. Firstly, the speaker recognition data and recipes are more accessible. Secondly, the dialect feature could be interesting in forensic speaker recognition or privacy preserving voice applications.

The second goal of this research is to present the first dataset for dialect recognition in the Kurdish language. Kurdish is an Indo-European language which is spoken by more than 30 million people in Kurdistan (a region between Turkey, Iran, Iraq, Syria) and by Kurdish diaspora [11]. In a broader accepted taxonomy, the Kurdish dialects are categorized in five main branches: Northern Kurdish (Kurmanji), Central Kurdish (Sorani), Southern Kurdish (Laki and Kalhori), Hawrami (Gorani) and Zazaki [12]. For each dialect there are several sub-dialects. For example, the Central Kurdish branch has Ardalani, Mukriyani, Sorani and Jafi sub-dialects [13]. In this work, we have focused on the main branches and we didn't consider the sub-dialects of each dialect. Spoken dialect recognition is an important task for Kurdish because it can be used as a preprocessing system that can be integrated with automatic speech recognition systems to have specific acoustic models for each dialect.

Kurdish language is not studied broadly in the domain of speech processing. There are just few researches focused on speech processing for this language. Preparing speech resources for this language is crucial to foster research on this language. Asosoft speech corpus is the only speech corpus for the Kurdish language [13]. This corpus is usable for automatic speech recognition and text to speech tasks. The Asosoft speech corpus is in Central Kurdish and it can not be used for dialect recognition. Already in [14], a small data set with 100 utterances is used for speaker recognition in Kurdish language. It deserved to be mentioned that there are some attempts on Kurdish text dialect recognition [15, 16] but to the best of our knowledge the current paper is the first attempt of spoken dialect recognition in the Kurdish. In our work we present a dataset with 16,385 utterances in 49h36min for five main dialects of the Kurdish language.

The covered dialects are Northern Kurdish, Central Kurdish, Southern Kurdish, Hwarami and Zazaki.

The next parts of this paper are organized as: in Sect. 2. the data collection and data prepossessing steps are presented. In Sect. 3 the methodology is described. The experimental setup and results are presented in Sect. 4 and finally, in Sect. 5 the obtained results are discussed.

2 Data Collection

In this section a speech corpus for Kurdish dialect recognition is introduced. The corpus named *Zar* which means dialect in Kurdish. In collecting and designing the speech corpus we considered several points. First of all, we tried to cover all Kurdish dialects. The available Kurdish corpora normally include Northern and Central Kurdish that covers the most population of Kurdish speakers and are used more in both written and spoken form. We covered all Kurdish dialects, even those such as Hawrami that is a zero-resourced dialect and an endangered dialect.

The data is collected mainly from Kurdish public TV and radio websites. The major part of the data is scrapped from the web, even though a smaller part downloaded from the Telegram Channels manually. Table 1 shows the source and original type of scrapped data. The files are a combination of news, dialogue and music in different languages dialects of Kurdish language that we have to review to remove other sounds that include non-proper Kurdish dialects and non Kurdish parts. Each segment may consist of more than one speaker and corrupted by noise. The speakers are male and female. The speaker can be anywhere in studio, in nature, on the street and speak through smart phone or telephone. The data collection and processing is done in the following steps:

1. The collected files were in different audio and video formats. The data is converted into mono channel wav format.
2. The files shorter than 8 s were merged into bigger ones to have enough information in dialect recognition.
3. These files were reviewed manually. Music, other languages or other dialects have been removed from each file if it exists.

The final version of the Zar dataset included 16,385 files results in 49h36m in five dialects of the Kurdish language. We tried to have a balanced data for each dialect. The minimum length of speech files is 8 s and the maximum size is 39 s, The average length of the files is 10.9 s. The general specification of the dataset is shown in Table 2. In Fig. 1 the distribution of file duration for all dialects is shown. The Zar dataset is publicly available in the Github repository[1].

---

[1] https://github.com/ArashAmani/Kurdish-Dialect-Recognition.

Table 1. Source of Data.

Dialect	Source	Type
Hawrami Kurdish	www.sterktv.net	Video
	https://t.me/hawramanhaneberchem	Voice
Zazaki Kurdish	http://sterktv.net/	Video
	https://globalrecordings.net/en/language/12048	Video
Northern Kurdish	https://www.dengeamerika.com/	Audio
	http://www.denge-welat.org/	Video
Central Kurdish	https://www.dengiamerika.com/	Audio
Southern Kurdish	https://prim.dideo.ir/	Video
	https://t.me/radioro_kurdestan	Audio
	https://t.me/shervaadab_razi	Audio

Table 2. General specifications of the Zar dialect recognition dataset.

Dialect	Number	Min Len (Sec)	Max Len (Sec)	Avg Len (Sec)	Total (duration)
Hawrami Kurdish	1876	8	36	11.2	5:49:42
Zazaki Kurdish	3839	8	39	10.4	11:08:23
Northern Kurdish	3603	8	37	11.0	11:00:57
Central Kurdish	3386	8	37	11.1	10:24:08
Southern Kurdish	3681	8	38	11.0	11:13:22
Total	16,385	8	39	10.9	49:36:32

3   Proposed Method

In this section the proposed method is described. The previous research shows that x-vector embedding preserve different characteristics of a speech file. Until now, the researchers have shown that besides the speaker specific information, the x-vectors holds both types of speaker and environment information. Among the speaker characteristics it was shown that x-vectors holds gender [9], accent, emotion [17]. In regard to environment information it is shown that x-vectors can be classified in terms of the recording environment, recording device, type of noise etc. [18]. This behaviour of x-vectors gives us the power of applying this representation to other speech processing applications. In this paper we tried to explore the availability of dialect information in the x-vectors. The experiments are done in this steps:

Step 1. Feature Extraction: The x-vector systems was trained on MFCC features with 25 frame length.

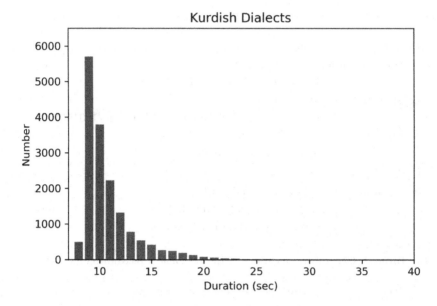

Fig. 1. The distribution of file duration in Zar corpus.

Step 2. x-Vector: In this work the Time Delay Neural Network (TDNN) is used for x-vector extraction [8]. The x-vector network was trained with the clean and augmented version of Voxceleb2. The Musan corpus was used for data augmentation [19]. The x-vector has 512 dimension.

Step 3. Dialect Recognition: To do dialect recognition, we trained Support Vector Machine and Decision Tree models on x-vector speaker embedding. 5-fold cross validation method is used to train and test models. The criterion used on DT is *entropy.* The code is available in the Github repository. Results are discussed Sect. 4.

The configuration of the x-vector dialect recognition is presented in Fig. 2.

4   Results and Discussion

In this section the obtained results are discussed. As it was mentioned in Sect. 3, the experiments are done in three steps. Firstly, the MFCC features are extracted. Then, two systems (i.e. x-vector, and i-vector) are used to achieve a fixed length representation for each utterance. Finally, two classifiers are trained for dialect recognition. In our experiments we used decision tree and support vector machine to classify the dialects. The results are presented in Table 3.

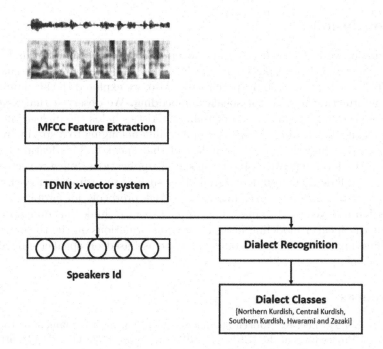

Fig. 2. The configuration of the dialect recognition system using x-vector speaker embedding.

Table 3. Kurdish dialect recognition with x-vector speaker embedding.

System	x-vector			i-vector		
Metric	Precision	Recall	F-measure	Precision	Recall	F-measure
DT	0.65	0.64	0.64	0.67	0.66	0.66
SVM	0.87	0.86	0.86	0.87	0.83	0.83

From the results in Table 3 we can see that x-vector speaker embedding, beside capturing the speaker features, preserve language/dialect information. The results show that however the x-vector is trained basically for speaker recognition system but its performance is better or same as an i-vector system that is trained specifically for dialect recognition. This property of x-vector speaker embedding show that it is important to do more exploration in the characteristics preserved in x-vector speaker embedding.

Another potential reason behind this ability of the x-vector system comes from the channel and environment of the recorded data. Because in our dataset the recording environment for a specific dialect almost are same and it is shown already that x-vectors are sensitive to the recording environment and it is possible to classify the vectors coming from different acoustic environments.

5 Conclusion

In this paper we introduced the first spoken dialect recognition corpus for the Kurdish language. The corpus comprises five dialects of the Kurdish language in 16,385 files resulting 49 h 36 m speech data. Also, we explored the availability of dialect information in x-vector speaker embedding. We observed that x-vector speaker embedding beside the speaker characteristics holds the dialect information. It means that having the speaker embedding belonging to a specific person it is possible to find the language/dialect of that speaker. This feature can be interesting to develop privacy preserving speech applications. Since, x-vectors are sensitive to diffident environment variabilities such as recording device, channel, noise, reverberation etc., developing more strict protocols for probing dialect information in x-vector systems is important. Also we think that domain adaptation at the speaker modeling network or transformations on the the extracted embedding make the dialect recognition systems based on speaker embedding more efficient.

References

1. Li, H., Ma, B., Lee, K.: Spoken language recognition: from fundamentals to practice. In: Proceedings of the IEEE, vol. 101, issue 5, pp. 1136–1159 (2013). https://doi.org/10.1109/JPROC.2012.2237151
2. Biadsy, F., Soltauy, H., Manguy, L., Navratily, J., Hirschberg, J.: Discriminative phonotactics for dialect recognition using context-dependent phone classifiers. In: Proceedings of the IEEE Odyssey: Speaker and Language Recognition Workshop, pp. 263–270, Brno, Czech Republic (2010)
3. Wang, W., Song, W., Chen, Ch., Zhang, Z., Xin, Y.: I-vector features and deep neural network modeling for language recognition. Procedia Comput. Sci. **147**, 36–43 (2019)
4. Torres-Carrasquillo, P., Gleason, T., Reynolds, D.: Dialect identification using Gaussian Mixture Models (2004)
5. Lei, Y., Hansen, J.: Factor analysis-based information integration for Arabic dialect identification. In: 2009 IEEE International Conference on Acoustics, Speech and Signal Processing, pp. 4337–4340 (2009). https://doi.org/10.1109/ICASSP.2009.4960589
6. Hanani, A., Naser, R.: Spoken Arabic dialect recognition using X-vectors. Natural Language Engineering. Cambridge University Press (2020)
7. Snyder, D., Garcia-Romero, D., McCree, A., Sell, G., Povey, D., Khudanpur, S.: Spoken language recognition using X-vectors. In: Proceedings of the Odyssey 2018 The Speaker and Language Recognition Workshop, pp. 105–111 (2018). https://doi.org/10.21437/Odyssey.2018-15
8. Snyder, D., Garcia-Romero, D., Sell, G., Povey, D., Khudanpur, S.: X-vectors: robust DNN embedding for speaker recognition. In: 2018 IEEE International Conference on Acoustics, Speech and Signal Processing (ICASSP), pp. 5329–5333 (2018). https://doi.org/10.1109/ICASSP.2018.8461375
9. Raj, D., Snyder, D., Povey, D., Khudanpur, S.: Probing the information encoded in X-vectors. In: 2019 IEEE Automatic Speech Recognition and Understanding Workshop (ASRU), pp. 726–733 (2019). https://doi.org/10.1109/ASRU46091.2019.9003979

10. Mohammadamini, M., Matrouf, D., Bonastre, J-F., Serizel, R., Dowerah, S., Jouvet, D.: Compensate multiple distortions for speaker recognition systems. In: EUSIPCO (2021)
11. Veisi, H., MohammadAmini, M., Hosseini, H.: Toward Kurdish language processing: experiments in collecting and processing the AsoSoft text corpus. Digit. Scholarsh. Humanit. **35**(1), 176–193 (2020). https://doi.org/10.1093/llc/fqy074
12. Malmasi, S.: Subdialectal differences in Sorani Kurdish. In: Proceedings of the Third Workshop on NLP for Similar Languages, Varieties and Dialects, Osaka, Japan (2016)
13. Veisi, H., Hosseini, H., Mohammadamini, M., Fathy, W., Mahmudi, A.: A Kurdish Speech Recognition System Designing and Building Speech Corpus and Pronunciation Lexicon (2021), https://arxiv.org/abs/2102.07412v1
14. Abdul, Z.: Kurdish speaker identification based on one dimensional convolutional neural network. Comput. Methods Diff. Equat. **7**(4), 566–572 (2019). (Special Issue)
15. Hassani, H., Hamid, O.: Using Artificial Neural Networks in Dialect Identification in Less-resourced Languages - The Case of Kurdish Dialects Identification
16. Hassani, H., Medjedovic, D.: Automatic Kurdish dialects identification. In: Conference: Fifth International Conference on Natural language Processing, Sydney, Australia (2016)
17. Pappagari, R., Wang, T., Villalba, J., Chen, N., Dehak, N.: X-vectors meet emotions: a study on dependencies between emotion and speaker recognition. In: ICASSP (2020)
18. Nandwana, M.K., et al.: The VOiCES from a distance challenge 2019: analysis of speaker verification results and remaining challenges. In: Proceedings of the Speaker and Language Recognition Workshop, pp. 165–170. https://doi.org/10.21437/Odyssey.2020-24
19. Snyder, D., Chen, G., Povey, D.: MUSAN A Music, Speech, and Noise Corpus (2015) arXiv:1510.08484v1

An ASR-Based Tutor for Learning to Read: How to Optimize Feedback to First Graders

Yu Bai[1(✉)], Cristian Tejedor-García[1], Ferdy Hubers[1,2], Catia Cucchiarini[1], and Helmer Strik[1,2,3,4]

[1] Centre for Language and Speech Technology (CLST),
Radboud University Nijmegen, Nijmegen, The Netherlands
y.bai@let.ru.nl
[2] Centre for Language Studies (CLS), Radboud University Nijmegen,
Nijmegen, The Netherlands
[3] Donders Institute for Brain, Cognition and Behaviour,
Radboud University Nijmegen, Nijmegen, The Netherlands
[4] NovoLearning B.V., Nijmegen, The Netherlands

Abstract. The interest in employing automatic speech recognition (ASR) in applications for reading practice has been growing in recent years. In a previous study, we presented an ASR-based Dutch reading tutor application that was developed to provide instantaneous feedback to first-graders learning to read. We saw that ASR has potential at this stage of the reading process, as the results suggested that pupils made progress in reading accuracy and fluency by using the software. In the current study, we used children's speech from an existing corpus (JAS-MIN) to develop two new ASR systems, and compared the results to those of the previous study. We analyze correct/incorrect classification of the ASR systems using human transcripts at word level, by means of evaluation measures such as Cohen's Kappa, Matthews Correlation Coefficient (MCC), precision, recall and F-measures. We observe improvements for the newly developed ASR systems regarding the agreement with human-based judgment and correct rejection (CR). The accuracy of the ASR systems varies for different reading tasks and word types. Our results suggest that, in the current configuration, it is difficult to classify isolated words. We discuss these results, possible ways to improve our systems and avenues for future research.

Keywords: Automatic speech recognition · ASR · Reading tutor · Child speech

1 Introduction

The idea that automatic speech recognition (ASR) technology can be employed to support children learning to read has been around for quite a while [26,32,36]. Various research systems and commercial products have been proposed [11,20,27]

© Springer Nature Switzerland AG 2021
A. Karpov and R. Potapova (Eds.): SPECOM 2021, LNAI 12997, pp. 58–69, 2021.
https://doi.org/10.1007/978-3-030-87802-3_6

that can monitor children while reading and indicate when they encounter difficulties. Fewer ASR-based systems are really capable of providing a kind of guidance and feedback that is comparable to what teachers usually offer in their classrooms. Besides, there is still scarce empirical evidence about the effectiveness of ASR-based systems for Dutch child speech. In the project Dutch Automatic Reading Tutor (DART[1]) we investigate whether such a system can be developed for the initial stages of learning to read (grade 1) when children need to develop accurate and rapid word decoding skills [17, 28]. In this paper we report on experiments that were conducted to investigate the performance of different ASR systems in identifying reading errors and to provide feedback on those errors.

To improve the ASR system in reading tutors, evaluating ASR miscue detection is important. A good reading tutor for children should avoid too many false rejections (FRs), which will lower the credibility of the reading tutor and cause frustration, and detect miscues that pupils can correct [25]. In the previous study, we evaluated the agreement between DART reading tutor with Novo-ASR backend and human transcripts [3]. The highest agreement obtained measured by Cohen's Kappa is .41, which is classified as moderate agreement [18]. In this study, we first developed two ASR systems based on Dutch child speech and investigated the performance of three ASR systems in respect of how accurate the ASR judgments are compared to human judgments. For this purpose we employed various metrics, including Cohen's Kappa, Matthews Correlation Coefficient (MCC), precision, recall and F-measures. The material used in the reading tutor contains four reading tasks designed with different goals and difficulty levels for first graders [2]. We also investigated the ASR accuracy in each reading task and different word types from two reading tasks which contain both words that are familiar to the first graders and new words.

The rest of the paper is organized as follows. Section 2 describes the research background of educational applications aiming at helping children improve reading skills and Kaldi as a framework for ASR technology. Section 3 formulates the aim of the study and describes the reading tutor. Section 4 explains the data used in the experiments, how the new ASR systems were built with kaldi and the procedure of how the three ASR systems were evaluated. The results of performance evaluation of the ASR systems are reported in Sect. 5. Finally, in Sect. 6 we discuss the results, possible ways of improving our systems and new lines of future work.

2   Research Background

Most of the research that has been conducted so far on applying ASR in the context of reading skills acquisition [12, 31, 36] addressed reading skills in English [25, 26, 32]. Many of the studies addressed reading assessment at a global level [5, 35] or were aimed at monitoring children while they read aloud whole passages and at providing some form of support when they encounter difficulties [9]. For

---

[1] http://hstrik.ruhosting.nl/DART/.

English even several commercial products have been made available for this latter purpose, such as the Reading Assistant[2], IBM Reading Companion[3], and the ReadingBuddy[4]. A possible application of ASR could be at earlier stages of the process of learning to read, when children need to acquire grapheme-phoneme connections in order to develop word decoding skills [7]. This process requires intensive practice in reading aloud that cannot always be provided in teacher-fronted education. So far, relatively few studies have investigated to what extent ASR can be employed in this type of application. This is not surprising, as such applications are extremely challenging in terms of ASR performance and accuracy.

Feedback provided by such reading tutor applications is not always correct. Various methods of evaluating ASR-based reading tutoring systems have been discussed. Taking human classification as the criterion, agreement (Cohen's Kappa value) of automatic classifiers turns out to vary for reading tasks with different numbers of syllables [9]. The agreement rate of feedback messages between system judgment and human judgment was used as a measure [1]. Miscue detection rate and false alarm rate can also be used as evaluation metrics [4]. Since most reading tutor applications are task-oriented, their performance can differ from one type of task to another.

Regarding existing ASR technology, Kaldi is one of the most current and state-of-the-art open-source toolkits [29], becoming a highly matured development tool for almost any language in the speech recognition area thanks to its recipe scripts. Kaldi uses a finite-state transducer (FST)-based framework; therefore, any language model can be applied which supports FST. One can easily implement N-gram language model using the SRILM toolkit [19]. Recent research studies integrated Kaldi for assessing the pronunciation of non-native speakers producing non-spontaneous speech [33,34] and spontaneous speech [14,30]. In the case of reading assessment one of the main problems is dealing with child speech [5,9]. In the specific case of first graders this is even more problematic because these children are in the early stages of the reading process and therefore produce many hesitations, disfluencies and broken words. Addressing these difficulties and providing the appropriate feedback online, makes this task extremely challenging

3   Present Study

3.1   Aim of the Study

Developing reading skills is crucial for first-grade pupils. Reading software systems that incorporate ASR are able to provide more opportunities for pupils to practice reading aloud and receiving immediate feedback. In the DART project, we aim to investigate how such reading tutor software with ASR can be best developed and implemented. We especially focus on feasible and suitable forms of feedback on reading accuracy and fluency.

---

[2] http://www.readingassistant.com/.

[3] https://www.ibm.com/ibm/responsibility/downloads/initiatives/ ReadingCompanion.pdf.

[4] http://readingbuddysoftware.com/.

Reading accuracy is an important reading skill and providing appropriate feedback on reading accuracy is crucial in a reading tutor. The forms of feedback depend on the correct/incorrect judgment by the system based on the output of the ASR. The aim of the present study is to gain insight into the accuracy of binary classification based on the outputs of different ASR systems and how to improve them. We investigate to what extent a) using ASR trained on child speech helps improve the agreement with human judgment, b) to what extent the improvement differs in different reading tasks and word types and c) to what extent ASR performance varies in terms of miscue detection and false rejection.

3.2 The Reading Tutor

The reading tutor is based on a reading method for first graders developed by Zwijsen Publishers, 'Veilig Leren Lezen'. It distinguishes two types of exercises: accuracy exercises and fluency exercises and four reading tasks: reading a) isolated words b) sentences c) word lists and d) stories. The accuracy exercises are meant to enhance pupils' reading accuracy of individual words and sentences. Sentences and isolated words are read one by one and each word is analysed by an ASR backend. Based on this analysis, pupils receive feedback on whether the target word or sentence is read correctly. If incorrect, the pupil has to try again (up to three attempts). The fluency exercises aim to improve the pupils' reading fluency and accuracy. In these exercises, pupils read word lists or stories in one go. Subsequently, they receive feedback and have to try the incorrect words or sentences again. Next, pupils have to read the same word list or story again. For more information about the system and the reading materials see [2].

4 Method

4.1 Transcribed Speech Data

In 2020, the first experiment of the DART project was conducted with school children practicing from home because of the pandemic. In spite of the complexities in organising this experiment, we managed to collect 1547 audio recordings which were subsequently transcribed by an annotator using Praat [3]. After filtering recordings that, according to the annotator, were either empty or damaged, or contained excessive background noise, 1132 audio files with 8263 words were left. These data were used to test the accuracy of three ASR systems we compared.

4.2 Kaldi ASR Systems Pipeline

The machine configuration on which the experiment was conducted has Ubuntu 18.04.1 LTS (64-bit operating system), AMD EPYC 7502P 32-Core (64 threads) processor with 2.5–3.35 GHz. We installed Kaldi on the machine. We adopted a classic hybrid training and decoding framework using a simple deep neural network (DNN) with hyperbolic tangent (tanh) nonlinearities [14] after training a context-dependent triphone system with a simple GMM–HMM model [23]. The features are Mel frequency cepstral coefficients (MFCCs) with per-speaker cepstral mean and variance statistics. Since Kaldi underlies on an FST-based framework to build language models from the raw text, we used the SRILM toolkit for building a 4-gram language model [24].

First, we trained monophone models. The first triphone pass used MFCCs, delta and delta–delta features. The second triphone pass included linear discriminant analysis (LDA) and Maximum Likelihood Linear Transform (MLLT). The third triphone pass combined LDA, MLLT and speaker adaptive training (SAT). The next steps included standard Gaussian mixture models (SGMM2), maximum mutual information (MMI) and boosted MMI on top of LDA and MLLT. Finally, we trained the hybrid DNN. For every step mentioned above we applied the appropriate transforms, alignments and decoding techniques for Kaldi[5].

4.3 ASR Systems

The reading tutor used by pupils during the experiments made use of the NovoLearning ASR engine, in which the ASR model (ASR.1) was trained with Dutch adult speech. It calculates probability scores and gives right/wrong feedback according to the adjustable threshold [3]. Two other systems (system ASR.2 and system ASR.3) were built with Kaldi after the experimental tests with children. Both systems employed the same acoustic models trained on 7.5 effective hours of child speech material from the JASMIN corpus [8]. The speakers are from JASMIN's group 1: native children between 7 and 11 years old. Different language models were used in these two models. A 4-gram language model generated from a lexicon of prompts was used in model ASR.2, obtaining a word error rate (WER) value of 38.78% (95% confidence interval [35.18, 42.37]); while a 4-gram language model created from a lexicon of orthographic transcriptions was used in model ASR.3, obtaining a WER of 35.71% (95% confidence interval [32.84, 38.58]).

4.4 Procedure for Performance Evaluation of ASR Systems

The annotator's transcription was compared to the prompt using the dynamic programming (alignment) algorithm ADAPT [15]. This yielded the reference binary classification word scores (0 for incorrect, 1 for correct). See [3] for more information on this procedure. Using the same procedure, the outputs for the ASR systems 2 and 3 (i.e., the recognized words) are aligned with the prompt, yielding the binary classification scores for these ASR systems. Finally, the later ASR binary scores are compared to the reference binary scores (which are based on the annotator's transcription).

For ASR.1 the evaluation procedure is different. The output of ASR.1 contains the words in the prompt with probability measures at word level. These

---

[5] http://kaldi-asr.org/doc/.

probability measures are compared to a threshold to obtain classification scores. In a previous paper [3], we focused on optimizing this threshold.

Two agreement measures were used to evaluate the classification performance. Unbalanced distributions of binary scores were observed in the human annotation, outputs of ASR.1, ASR.2 and ASR.3, which is understandable as pupils generally read more correct words than incorrect words. This is especially the case in Dutch education, in which reading methods are based on incrementally difficult reading levels and children are encouraged to practice words that they are supposed to be capable of reading [21]. A more suitable measure for binary classification in the case of unbalanced data is the MCC [6]. Therefore, we calculated both Cohen's Kappa and MCC as agreement measures for our data. To capture an essence of ASR performance where CA, CR, FA, FR are important, precision, recall and F-measures were also calculated.

Function words, in general have little lexical meaning and mainly express grammatical relation. They are, on average, shorter, are articulated less clearly [10], occur more frequently, and are more familiar to first-grade pupils. Content words possess more semantic content, are less frequent, on average, and often require more reading practice. It is thus interesting to compare the performance of the ASR systems on function vs. content words. To gain insights, agreement measures (Cohen's Kappa and MCC) were calculated for the function words and content words respectively in two reading tasks containing both function words and content words: reading sentences in accuracy exercises and reading stories in fluency exercises.

5   Results

In this section we present an evaluation of three different ASR systems using different performance measures, including Cohen's Kappa, MCC, precision, recall and F-measure. Performance on different types of exercises and comparison between agreement on function words and content words are also presented.

5.1   Performance Evaluation of Different Systems

In the previous study [3] we found that 48 was the threshold that produced the highest agreement between the ASR scores for correct/incorrect and the human judgment [3]. After removing invalid audio recordings, the best threshold shifted to 46. Table 1 illustrates that the highest Cohen's kappa value of ASR.1 is .42 at a threshold of 46. The models trained on JASMIN native children's speech show better agreement with the human-based judgments with Cohen's kappa of .44 for ASR.2 and .53 for ASR.3.

Table 1 also indicates that model ASR.1 has the lowest MCC value of .42. ASR.2 shows slightly better agreement with human-based judgment than ASR.1 with an MCC of .46. Among three models, ASR.3 shows the highest agreement. This is consistent with Cohen's Kappa values.

Table 1. Cohen's Kappa and MCC values of three ASR systems.

Systems	Cohen's Kappa	MCC
ASR.1	.422	.423
ASR.2	.442	.455
ASR.3	.533	.568

Table 2. Correct acceptance rate (CAR), correct rejection rate (CRR), false acceptance rate (FAR), false rejection rate (FRR), precision, recall and F-measure of correct acceptance (CA) and correct rejection (CR).

	Percentage (%)				Precision (%)		Recall (%)		F-measure (%)	
	CA	CR	FA	FR	CA	CR	CA	CR	CA	CR
ASR.1	72.4	9.9	7.6	10.0	90.5	49.8	87.8	56.6	89.1	53.0
ASR.2	68.9	12.1	5.5	13.6	92.6	47.0	83.5	68.7	87.8	55.8
ASR.3	67.3	15.3	2.3	15.1	96.7	50.2	81.6	87.1	88.6	63.7

Table 2 demonstrates correct acceptance (CA), correct rejection (CR), false acceptance (FA), false rejection (FR) rates, precision, recall and F-measure of CA and CR. It shows that there are more CRs and FRs given by the judgment of ASR.2 and ASR.3 while fewer CAs and false acceptances FAs, compared to ASR.1. We see relatively balanced FA and FR in the judgement of ASR.1. Model ASR.3 shows a significant improvement in recall of CR, from 56.6% to 87.10%, but a decrease in recall of CA from 87.85% to 81.64%. In general, all three models show better results for CA, while the precision of CR and F-measure of CR are relatively low. A significant difference in Recall of CR is observed between the three systems.

5.2   Performance on Different Reading Tasks

Cohen's Kappa and MCC are calculated for four different reading tasks. Table 3 suggests that all three models perform worse for isolated words than for sentences, word lists and stories. Cohen's Kappa and MCC values of sentences, word lists and stories are similar. However, the values for isolated words are between .20 and .41. The primary cause of the low agreement for isolated words is due to a consequence of less effective language models for isolated words. After removing isolated words from the data, both Cohen's Kappa and MCC are improved (see Table 4).

Table 3. Cohen's Kappa and MCC values of three ASR systems for different reading tasks.

	Cohen's Kappa				MCC			
	Isolated word	Sentence	Word list	Story	Isolated word	Sentence	Word list	Story
ASR.1	.268	.464	.458	.365	.285	.464	.458	.368
ASR.2	.200	.452	.442	.502	.238	.474	.444	.514
ASR.3	.325	.559	.549	.537	.407	.588	.578	.571

Table 4. Cohen's Kappa and MCC values of three ASR systems after removing isolated words.

Systems	Cohen's Kappa	MCC
ASR.1	.437	.438
ASR.2	.468	.478
ASR.3	.555	.585

5.3 Performance on Function and Content Words

Function words were separated from content words using NLTK [22]. We calculated agreement for function words and content words respectively with different measures (see Table 5). ASR.1 shows similar performance on function words and content words with slightly higher agreement for function words. Contrary to expectations, model ASR.2 and model ASR.3 present higher agreement for function words than content words.

Table 5. Cohen's Kappa and MCC values of three systems for function and content words.

	Cohen's Kappa		MCC	
	Function	Content	Function	Content
ASR.1	.397	.417	.402	.428
ASR.2	.510	.453	.533	.465
ASR.3	.565	.534	.595	.567

6   Discussion and Conclusion

In the current paper we investigated the performance of three ASR systems: the original ASR system (ASR.1) implemented in the reading tutor software used by first-graders, and the two newly developed ASR systems (ASR.2 and ASR.3) trained with JASMIN child speech data. We first obtained binary scores from the outputs of ASR systems and human transcripts as the reference. Then we applied different measures to evaluate the ASR performance.

The results show that with respect to Cohen's Kappa and MCC values, ASR.2 and ASR.3 present better performance than ASR.1. ASR.3 outperformed the other two systems. However, this is not always the case for all measures.

The F-measures of CA are similar for the three ASR systems. The precision of CA is higher for ASR.2 and ASR.3 while the recall of CA is lower for ASR.2 and ASR.3 compared to ASR.1. By using new ASR systems, the F-measure of CR was improved. Although there is a small difference in precision of CR among the three ASR systems, recall of CR significantly improved for ASR.2 and ASR.3. This suggests that lowering the false rejection rate (FRR) is important for further experiments because it influences precision of CR and recall of CA. It is notable that all three systems demonstrate relatively poor performance for Precision of CR, an important point that definitely deserves attention in future experiments.

We also saw different agreement performance on the four reading tasks implemented in the reading tutor. The two newly developed ASR systems achieved better results on sentences, word lists and stories than on isolated words. This is also a point that deserves attention. An important difference between the evaluation of isolated words by the annotator and the ASR system is that the annotator knows which words the pupils should be reading and can therefore compare the incoming signal to what she expected to hear. As a matter of fact, in a preliminary analysis in which we asked five elementary school teachers to give correct/incorrect judgements on 300 isolated words, we observed a very high agreement of 81.67% among the teachers, where all five teachers gave the same correct/incorrect judgement. At the moment, our ASR system does not know which word to expect and therefore cannot make such a specific form of comparison. Adopting a customized language model for isolated words would be a way of dealing with this discrepancy that is expected to enhance the performance of the system on isolated words.

The results demonstrated that ASR.2 and ASR.3 have better performance on function words than on content words while for ASR.1, better results were observed for content words. The expectation was that the ASR systems would provide more accurate feedback on content words than on function words. This was based on the assumption that the pupils would read content words more slowly and carefully. A possible explanation could be that function words occur more frequently and are more familiar to pupils. While content words, particularly new words, are often problematic for first-graders.

Although the present study was limited due to the small amount of transcribed speech data, the results are promising. More data collected from the pupils who used the reading tutor are being transcribed. Future directions for improving the acoustic models and the general performance of the ASR systems includes training with data not only from the JASMIN corpus, but also with a significant amount of new child speech data that are being collected and transcribed. We are also considering to apply transfer learning [13] to other sources of speech data, such as Dutch adult speech and Flemish (a variety of Dutch spoken in Belgium) child speech. Finally, we are examining other techniques for binary classification as a complement to ASR output feedback for children while reading, such as forced alignment [16].

Acknowledgements. The current research is carried out within the 'Dutch ASR-based Reading Tutor' (DART) project (http://hstrik.ruhosting.nl/DART). This work is part of the Netherlands Initiative for Education Research (NRO) with project number 40.5.18540.121, which is financed by the Dutch Research Council (NWO). We would like to thank children who used the reading tutor at home during the pandemic, their parents and teachers who gave us informative feedback and advice in questionnaires and interviews and schools that participated in the experiments.

References

1. Abdou, S.M., et al.: Computer aided pronunciation learning system using speech recognition techniques. In: Proceedings of the Interspeech, pp. 849–852, Pittsburgh, PA, USA, 17–21 September 2006

2. Bai, Y., Hubers, F., Cucchiarini, C., Strik, H.: ASR-based evaluation and feedback for individualized reading practice. In: Proceedings of the Interspeech, pp. 3870–3874, 2020–2842 (2020). https://doi.org/10.21437/Interspeech

3. Bai, Y., Hubers, F., Cucchiarini, C., Strik, H.: An ASR-based reading tutor for practicing reading skills in the first grade: improving performance through threshold adjustment. In: Proceedings of the IberSPEECH 2021, pp. 11–15 (2021). https://doi.org/10.21437/IberSPEECH.2021-3

4. Banerjee, S., Beck, J., Mostow, J.: Evaluating the effect of predicting oral reading miscues. In: Proceedings of the Interspeech, pp. 3165–3168, Geneva, Switzerland, 1–4 September (2003)

5. Black, M.P., Tepperman, J., Narayanan, S.S.: Automatic prediction of children's reading ability for high-level literacy assessment. IEEE Trans. Audio Speech Lang. Process. **19**(4), 1015–1028 (2011). https://doi.org/10.1109/TASL.2010.2076389

6. Boughorbel, S., Jarray, F., El-Anbari, M.: Optimal classifier for imbalanced data using Matthews correlation coefficient metric. Plos One **12**(6), e0177678 (2017). https://doi.org/10.1371/journal.pone.0177678

7. Castles, A., Rastle, K., Nation, K.: Ending the reading wars: reading acquisition from novice to expert. Psychol. Sci. Public Interest **19**(1), 5–51 (2018). https://doi.org/10.1177/1529100618772271

8. Cucchiarini, C., Van hamme, H.: The JASMIN speech corpus: recordings of children, non-natives and elderly people. In: Spyns, P., Odijk, J. (eds.) Essential Speech and Language Technology for Dutch. TANLP, pp. 43–59. Springer, Heidelberg (2013). https://doi.org/10.1007/978-3-642-30910-6_3

9. Duchateau, J., et al.: Developing a reading tutor: design and evaluation of dedicated speech recognition and synthesis modules. Speech Commun. **51**(10), 985–994 (2009). https://doi.org/10.1016/j.specom.2009.04.010

10. Goldwater, S., Jurafsky, D., Manning, C.D.: Which words are hard to recognize? Prosodic, lexical, and disfluency factors that increase speech recognition error rates. Speech Commun. **52**(3), 181 (2010). https://doi.org/10.1016/j.specom.2009.10.001

11. Hagen, A., Pellom, B., Cole, R.: Children's speech recognition with application to interactive books and tutors. In: 2003 IEEE Workshop on Automatic Speech Recognition and Understanding (IEEE Cat. No. 03EX721), pp. 186–191 (2003). https://doi.org/10.1109/ASRU.2003.1318426

12. Hsu, L.: An empirical examination of EFL learners' perceptual learning styles and acceptance of ASR-based computer-assisted pronunciation training. Comput. Assist. Lang. Learn. **29**(5), 881–900 (2016)

13. Joshi, V., Zhao, R., Mehta, R.R., Kumar, K., Li, J.: Transfer learning approaches for streaming end-to-end speech recognition system (2020)
14. Kipyatkova, I., Karpov, A.: DNN-based acoustic modeling for Russian speech recognition using Kaldi. In: Ronzhin, A., Potapova, R., Németh, G. (eds.) SPECOM 2016. LNCS (LNAI), vol. 9811, pp. 246–253. Springer, Cham (2016). https://doi.org/10.1007/978-3-319-43958-7_29
15. Kocharov, D.: Automatic alignment of phonetic transcriptions for Russian. In: Ronzhin, A., Potapova, R., Delic, V. (eds.) SPECOM 2014. LNCS (LNAI), vol. 8773, pp. 123–128. Springer, Cham (2014). https://doi.org/10.1007/978-3-319-11581-8_15
16. Kraljevski, I., Tan, Z.H., Bissiri, M.P.: Comparison of forced-alignment speech recognition and humans for generating reference VAD. In: Proceedings of the Interspeech, pp. 2937–2941. Dresden, Germany, 6–10 September (2015)
17. Kuhn, M.R., Schwanenflugel, P.J., Meisinger, E.B., Levy, B.A., Rasinski, T.V.: Aligning theory and assessment of reading fluency: Automaticity, prosody, and definitions of fluency. Read. Res. Q. **45**(2), 230–251 (2010). https://doi.org/10.1598/rrq.45.2.4
18. Landis, J.R., Koch, G.G.: The measurement of observer agreement for categorical data. Biometrics **33**(1), 159 (1977). https://doi.org/10.2307/2529310
19. Lee, A., Kawahara, T., Shikano, K.: Julius–an open source real-time large vocabulary recognition engine. In: EUROSPEECH 2001, pp. 1691–1694 (2001)
20. Li, X.L., Deng, L., Ju, Y.C., Acero, A.: Automatic children's reading tutor on hand-held devices. In: Proceedings of the InterSpeech, pp. 1733–1736. International Speech Communication Association, Brisbane, Australia, 22–26 September 2008. https://www.microsoft.com/en-us/research/publication/automatic-childrens-reading-tutor-on-hand-held-devices/
21. Limonard, S., Cucchiarini, C., van Hout, R., Strik, H.: Analyzing read aloud speech by primary school pupils: insights for research and development. In: Proceedings of the Interspeech, pp. 3710–3714, Shanghai, China, 25–29 October 2020. https://doi.org/10.21437/Interspeech.2020-2804
22. Loper, E., Bird, S.: NLTK: the natural language toolkit. In: Proceedings of the ACL Workshop on Effective Tools and Methodologies for Teaching Natural Language Processing and Computational Linguistics. Association for Computational Linguistics, Philadelphia (2002)
23. McAuliffe, M., Socolof, M., Mihuc, S., Wagner, M., Sonderegger, M.: Montreal forced aligner: trainable text-speech alignment using Kaldi. In: Proceedings of the Interspeech, pp. 498–502, Stockholm, Sweden, 20–24 August (2017). https://doi.org/10.21437/Interspeech.2017-1386
24. Mohri, M., Riley, M.: Weighted finite-state transducers in speech recognition (tutorial). In: Proceedings of the ICSLP, Denver, Colorado, USA, 16–20 September (2002)
25. Mostow, J.: Is ASR accurate enough for automated reading tutors, and how can we tell? In: Proceedings of the Interspeech, pp. 837–840, Pittsburgh, PA, USA, 17–21 September (2006)
26. Mostow, J., Nelson-Taylor, J., Beck, J.E.: Computer-guided oral reading versus independent practice: comparison of sustained silent reading to an automated reading tutor that listens. J. Educ. Comput. Res. **49**(2), 249–276 (2013). https://doi.org/10.2190/EC.49.2.g
27. Mostow, J., Roth, S.F., Hauptmann, A.G., Kane, M.: A prototype reading coach that listens. In: Proceedings of the AAAI, pp. 785–792, Seattle, Washington, WA, 31 August – September 4 (1994)

28. Pikulski, J.J., Chard, D.J.: Fluency: bridge between decoding and reading comprehension. Read. Teach. **58**(6), 510–519 (2005). http://www.jstor.org/stable/20205516

29. Povey et al. D.: The Kaldi speech recognition toolkit. In: Proceedings of the ASRU, pp. 1–4, Waikoloa, Hawaii, HI, USA, 11–15 December 2011

30. Qian, Y., Evanini, K., Wang, X., Lee, C.M., Mulholland, M.D.: Bidirectional LSTM-RNN for improving automated assessment of non-native children's speech. In: Proceedings of the Interspeech, Stockholm, Sweden, 20–24 August 2017. 1https://doi.org/10.21437/Interspeech.2017-1386

31. Rao, P., Swarup, P., Pasad, A., Tulsiani, H., Das, G.G.: Automatic assessment of reading with speech recognition technology. In: Copyright 2016 Asia-Pacific Society for Computers in Education All rights Reserved. No part of this Book May Be Reproduced, Stored in a Retrieval System, Transmitted, in Any Forms or Any Means, Without the Prior permission of the Asia-Pacific Society for Computers in Education, p. 1. ISBN 9789868473591 (2016)

32. Reeder, K., Shapiro, J., Wakefield, J., D'Silva, R.: Speech recognition software contributes to reading development for young learners of English. Int. J. Comput. Assist. Lang. Learn. Teach. **5**(3), 60–74 (2015). https://doi.org/10.4018/ijcallt.2015070104

33. Sudhakara, S., Ramanathi, M.K., Yarra, C., Ghosh, P.K.: An improved goodness of pronunciation (GoP) measure for pronunciation evaluation with DNN-HMM system considering HMM Transition probabilities. In: Proceedings of the Interspeech, pp. 954–958 (2019)

34. Tejedor-García, C., Cardeñoso-Payo, V., Escudero-Mancebo, D.: Performance comparison of specific and general-purpose ASR systems for pronunciation assessment of japanese learners of Spanish. In: Proceedings of the IberSPEECH 2021, pp. 6–10 (2021). https://doi.org/10.21437/IberSPEECH.2021-2

35. Tepperman, J., et al.: A Bayesian network classifier for word-level reading assessment. In: Proceedings of the Interspeech, pp. 2185–2188, ISCA, Antwerp, Belgium, 27–31 August (2007). http://www.isca-speech.org/archive/interspeech_2007/i07_2185.html

36. Wise, B., et al.: Learning to read with a virtual tutor: foundations to literacy. In: Kinzer, C., Verhoeven, L. (eds.) Interactive Literacy Education: Facilitating Literacy Learning Environments Through Technology. Lawrence Erlbaum, Mahwah (2005) http://citeseerx.ist.psu.edu/viewdoc/summary?doi=10.1.1.120.7734

Velocity Differences Between Velum Raising and Lowering Movements

Peter Birkholz[✉] [iD] and Christian Kleiner

Institute of Acoustics and Speech Communication, Technische Universität Dresden,
Dresden, Germany
{peter.birkholz,christian.kleiner}@tu-dresden.de

Abstract. This study investigated the intrinsic velocities of raising and
lowering movements of the velum that are related to its biomechanical
structure and aerodynamic conditions. To this end, five subjects produced cyclic transitions between nasals and fricatives as in /s-n-s-n-s-.../
with flat intonation and at two specific speaking rates to minimize contextual and prosodic effects. The velar movements were inferred from the
movements of the lateral pharyngeal wall in ultrasound image sequences,
which are strongly correlated. The results indicate that velum raising
was significantly faster than velum lowering for the two male subjects
(24%–49% faster, depending on the subject and speaking rate), but not
for the three female subjects. Possible biomechanical and aerodynamic
reasons for the observed velocity differences are discussed. The results
can inform the interpretation of kinematic data of velar movements with
regard to underlying neural control, and improve movement models for
articulatory speech synthesis.

Keywords: Speech production · Velar movement · Articulator
velocities

1   Introduction

The velocity of an articulator when it approaches the target for a certain speech
sound depends on its biomechanical properties, on the active control by the nervous system, and on aerodynamic conditions [11]. The individual contributions
of these factors to an observed articulatory movement are of great interest in
speech production research, but they are usually hard to disentangle. When one
articulator moves *on average* slower or faster than another one across different phonetic contexts and aerodynamic conditions, this difference is likely due
to their biomechanical differences. For example, the movement of the tongue
towards and away from a velar closure is generally slower than that of the lips
during the formation or release of a bilabial closure [24], which is likely related
to the different masses of the tongue and the lips.

Furthermore, there is evidence that the velocities of articulators also depend
on the *direction* of movement. For example, it was observed that lip retraction is
on average faster than lip protrusion [7], that tongue backing is on average slower

© Springer Nature Switzerland AG 2021
A. Karpov and R. Potapova (Eds.): SPECOM 2021, LNAI 12997, pp. 70–80, 2021.
https://doi.org/10.1007/978-3-030-87802-3_7

than tongue fronting [1, 8, 27], that vocal fold adduction is slower than vocal fold abduction [15], and that the maximum speed of pitch change is significantly higher for pitch lowering movements than for pitch raising movements [28].

For velar movements, it is not completely clear yet whether there is an intrinsic (i.e. biomechanical) difference between raising and lowering velocities. While studies on velar movements during the articulation of European Portuguese nasal vowels indicated that velum lowering takes on average longer than velum raising [18, 21, 25], studies with French nasals and nasalized vowels reported different observations: One study found that the durations of velum raising and lowering are essentially equal, independently from the nasal vowel, its phonetic context and the speaking style [2], while another study found indications that velum raising is faster than lowering [5]. Since the recording of velar movements is rather difficult, all of these studies were based on only 1–3 subjects. Furthermore, they were not specifically designed to explore velocity differences.

The goal of the present study was to gain more insight into the intrinsic direction-dependent velocity differences of the velum using a tailored experimental design and more subjects. The subjects produced alternating raising and lowering movements of the velum in phoneme sequences like /s-n-s-n-s-.../ with flat intonation and specific speaking rates. In this way the phonetic context and prosodic factors were precisely controlled, so that differences between the observed raising and lowering movements can be attributed solely to biomechanical and aerodynamic factors.

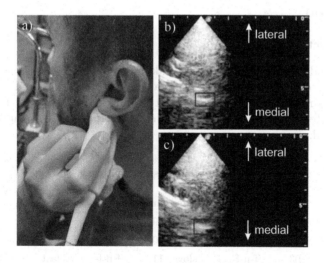

Fig. 1. a) Positioning of the ultrasound transducer for measuring lateral pharyngeal wall movements. b) Ultrasound image for a pharyngeal wall position that corresponds to a lowered velum. c) Ultrasound image for a pharyngeal wall position that corresponds to a raised velum. The blue boxes in b) and c) indicate the tracked region of interest.

As mentioned above, the measurement of velar movements is difficult because of the individual drawbacks of the existing techniques [16]. Real-time MRI of the vocal tract is rather expensive, and the subjects are in supine position [18]. X-ray cinematography [19] is normally not used in speech studies anymore because of its ionizing radiation. Other methods like fiberoptic endoscopy [3–5], electromagnetic articulography [25], or velum-specific measurement devices like the Velotrace [13] or the Nasograph [9] are invasive and unpleasant for the subjects. In the present study, we therefore used an indirect method to track velum movements based on ultrasound. It is based on the observation that the lateral pharyngeal walls (LPW) move medially when the velum raises, and laterally when the velum lowers [22]. LPW movements and velar movements are highly correlated, i.e. parallel in both time course and extent [3,4], and can be detected on ultrasound images when the transducer is placed below one ear of the subject as illustrated in Fig. 1a.

Learning about intrinsic direction-dependent velocities of articulators cannot only benefit the interpretation of kinematic speech data, but can also help to improve the realism and quality of articulatory speech synthesis [6,10,26]. For example, it was found that different intrinsic velocity components for different directions of tongue movement can explain and reproduce the observed loop patterns in tongue trajectories [8,27]. Modeling such more realistic tongue trajectories (as opposed to straight-line paths between the articulatory targets) was found to lead to more natural synthetic speech generated by articulatory synthesis [14,20]. A better model for the movement of other articulators like the velum might further improve the realism and quality of articulatory synthesis.

2   Method

2.1   Subjects and Corpus

Two male and three female German speaking subjects (29–43 years old) participated in the experiment. All subjects gave informed consent and reported no speech or hearing disorders. Each subject produced two times the 16 phoneme sequences listed in Table 1 while the speech audio signal and the velar movements were recorded.

Table 1. Phoneme sequences uttered by the subjects.

Index	Sequence	Rate	Index	Sequence	Rate
01	/s-n-s-.../	slow	09	/s-n-s-.../	fast
02	/s-m-s-.../	slow	10	/s-m-s-.../	fast
03	/f-n-f-.../	slow	11	/f-n-f-.../	fast
04	/f-m-f-.../	slow	12	/f-m-f-.../	fast
05	/n-s-n-.../	slow	13	/n-s-n-.../	fast
06	/m-s-m-.../	slow	14	/m-s-m-.../	fast
07	/n-f-n-.../	slow	15	/n-f-n-.../	fast
08	/m-f-m-.../	slow	16	/m-f-m-.../	fast

Each phoneme sequence consisted of at least five repetitions of a fricative-nasal or nasal-fricative pair. The fricatives and nasals with the alveolar, labiodental, and bilabial places of articulation were selected in such a way that the velum had no or minimal contact with the tongue back at any time for as unrestricted velar movement as possible. Furthermore, the movements of other articulators were small, leading to a low interference with the velar movement. For each pair of a fricative and a nasal there was one sequence that started with the nasal, and one sequence that started with the fricative. The phonemes in a sequence were produced with a flat intonation and at a specific rate as dictated by a metronome (without glottal stops between the phonemes). The slow and fast sequences were produced with 500 ms and 375 ms per phoneme, respectively. With this experimental design, contextual and prosodic factors were precisely controlled so that any potential differences between velar raising and lowering movements can be attributed to biomechanical or aerodynamic factors.

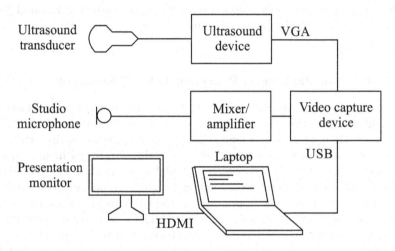

Fig. 2. The measurement setup used in the experiment.

2.2   Experimental Setup and Recording Procedure

Velar movements were measured in terms of lateral pharyngeal wall (LPW) movements as mentioned in the Introduction. This is possible because lateral-medial movements of the LPW are highly correlated with lowering-raising movements of the velum [3,4,23]. The experimental setup is shown in Fig. 2. B-mode scans of the LPW were captured with a medical ultrasound device (SonoScape S2 using a SonoScape 2P1 transducer) at 1.8 MHz with a rate of 50 frames per second. The speech audio signal was recorded with a studio microphone (M930 by Microtech Gefell) fed by a mixer (Behringer MX1602). A video capture device (USB3HDCAP by StarTech) digitized the audio signal and the ultrasound video frames, which were resampled at a rate of 60 frames per second (by doubling every 6th frame). The digital signals were sent via a USB connection to a laptop computer (MSI

GT72 with MS Windows 8.1) where they were recorded and saved with the video grabber software StreamCatcher.

The experiment was performed in a recording studio in individual sessions for each subject. The subjects were seated in a comfortable position with the head stabilized by a headrest. Before the actual recordings the subjects practiced the timed phoneme changes of the utterances. For the recordings, the ultrasound transducer was held by an assistant at a position below the left ear as illustrated in Fig. 2a. The orientation of the probe was carefully adjusted to obtain as clear a picture as possible of the LPW movement. Whether an orientation was suitable was tested with the utterances /n-s-n-s-.../ and /f-s-f-s-.../, where clearly visible movements were expected for the first utterance, and no movements for the second utterance (due to a constantly high velum position). After a suitable probe orientation was found, the utterances in Table 1 were displayed one by one on a presentation monitor and spoken by the subject in two rounds. The phoneme changes after 500 ms (slow) or 375 ms (fast) per phoneme were indicated by click sounds played over the laptop loudspeaker. In the case of ultrasound image artifacts or an incorrectly produced sequence, the utterance was immediately repeated.

2.3   Tracking of the Lateral Pharyngeal Wall Movement

Using the audio data as time reference, the captured ultrasound video files were segmented into the individual utterances using the software VirtualDub2 (http://www.virtualdub.org). Using a custom-made Python script, the LPW movement in each utterance was tracked across the ultrasound image sequence based on the region tracker [17], which is available as the class TrackerCSRT in the Open Source Computer Vision toolbox 4.5 (https://opencv.org). Since not only the position but also the appearance of the LPW in the ultrasound images often changed between the raised velum state and the lowered velum state, the initial frame and region of interest for the tracker had to be carefully selected for each sequence. In 23% of the recorded utterances the tracker failed to follow the LPW movements over at least three velar raising-lowering periods and the corresponding utterances were discarded[1].

Figures 1b and c show example video frames for the two velum states. The tracked region of interest is marked by the blue rectangles. The lower rectangle position in Fig. 1c indicates a more medial LPW position and hence corresponds to a raised velum. An example of the tracked horizontal and vertical positions of the LPW (center of the tracked region) in the ultrasound images over an entire utterance is shown in Figs. 3a and b. Because there was usually not only movement along the vertical axis but also along the horizontal axis, the main movement direction in the image plane was determined by means of a principal component analysis, and the 2D-trajectory was then projected on the first principal component to obtain a one-dimensional position signal (Fig. 3c).

---

[1] The difficulty of finding a good ultrasonic LPW reflection was also reported in [22].

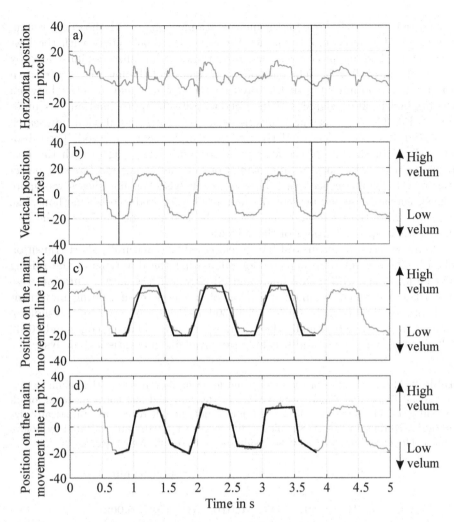

Fig. 3. a, b) Time functions of the horizontal and vertical positions of the lateral pharyngeal wall on the ultrasound images for the utterance /m-s-m-s-.../ (slow speaking rate) by speaker M2. c) Lateral pharyngeal wall position projected on the main movement line (first principal component of the x-y-trajectory; gray curve), and initial approximation by straight-line pieces (black curve). The main movement line was calculated for the trajectory between the vertical black lines in a) and b). d) Approximation of the gray curve in c) by line pieces (black curve) after optimization. Increasing position values in c) and d) correspond to a medial movement of the nasopharyngeal wall and hence to an increasing height of the velum.

2.4 Determination of Movement Velocities

In each LPW position signal three consecutive periods were approximated by a sequence of straight-line pieces. Each period was represented by four line pieces:

one for the raising edge, one for the quasi-stationary phase with the raised velum, one for the falling edge, and one for the quasi-stationary phase with the lowered velum. The line pieces were first prototypically initialized as illustrated by the black lines in Fig. 3c. The endpoint coordinates of the line pieces were then automatically optimized in such a way that the root-mean-square error between the original position signal and its piece-wise linear approximation was minimized (Fig. 3d). The optimization was performed with the function fminsearch in Matlab R2019b, which is a derivative-free simplex search method. The (absolute) slopes of the line pieces for the raising and falling edges (with the unit pixels/second) were taken as approximations of the raising and lowering velocities of the velum, respectively. This approach based on line pieces was more robust against noise and prevented ambiguities compared to other methods, like e.g. smoothing the curve and then taking the maxima and minima of the first derivative as approximations of the velocities.

In a few cases, problems of LPW tracking led to unnaturally short transition phases. These cases were detected by comparing the durations of the raising and falling edges with a threshold, and all edges with a shorter duration were discarded. Since the minimum duration of a complete alternating movement cycle of the velum is in the range of 200–300 ms [24], a conservative threshold of 60 ms was chosen here. Finally there were between 19–40 rising edges and 16–42 falling edges per subject and speaking rate available for statistical analysis.

Table 2. Mean velocities of the raising and lowering movements of the velum in pixels/second ($\overline{v}_{\text{raise}}$ and $\overline{v}_{\text{lower}}$, respectively) at the slow and fast speaking rates for all five subjects. The p values indicate whether or not the differences are statistically significant according to t-tests. Significant differences ($\alpha = 0.01$) are indicated by bold p values. The lowest row presents the results pooled over all five subjects.

Subject	Slow speaking rate			Fast speaking rate		
	$\overline{v}_{\text{raise}}$	$\overline{v}_{\text{lower}}$	p	$\overline{v}_{\text{raise}}$	$\overline{v}_{\text{lower}}$	p
M1	191	145	**0.010**	253	170	**0.002**
M2	278	210	**0.004**	287	232	**0.006**
F1	206	216	0.769	238	227	0.590
F2	260	269	0.747	318	277	0.302
F3	265	234	0.102	234	229	0.801
all	248	217	**0.007**	267	226	**0.000**

3   Results

Figure 4 shows the distributions of the raising and lowering velocities of the velum individually for all five subjects and both speaking rates, and pooled across all subjects for each speaking rate. Table 2 summarizes the mean values $\overline{v}_{\text{raise}}$ and $\overline{v}_{\text{lower}}$ of these distributions. Except for two cases (subjects F1 and F2 at the slow speaking rate) the mean raising velocity of the velum was higher

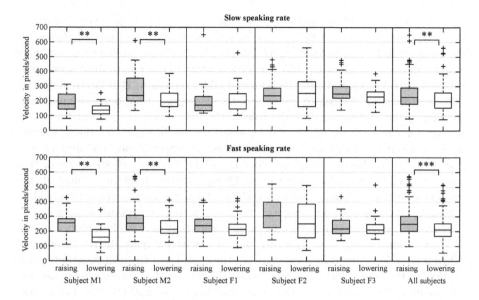

Fig. 4. Distributions of the raising and lowering velocities of the velum (inferred from LPW movement) at the slow and fast speaking rates for all five subjects individually, and pooled across all subjects. Significant differences between the raising and lowering velocities are indicated with ** ($p < 0.01$) or *** ($p < 0.001$).

than the lowering velocity. Based on two-sample two-sided t-tests, the differences were significant for the two male subjects M1 and M2 ($p < 0.01$), and when the data were pooled across all subjects ($p < 0.001$). For the two male subjects, raising movements were 24%–49% faster than lowering movements, depending on the subject and the speaking rate. Across all subjects, velum raising was on average 14% faster than velum lowering for the slow speaking rate, and 18% faster for the fast speaking rate. From the slow to the fast speaking rate, the velocities increased on average by 7.7% and 4.1% for velum raising and lowering, respectively.

4 Discussion and Conclusion

This study found that velum raising was faster than velum lowering for two out of five subjects, which confirms the findings of the studies [5,18,21,25], and that there was no significant difference for three subjects, which confirms the observations of [2]. In contrast to the previous studies, the present study included more subjects and was specifically designed to uncover potential direction-dependent velocity differences. Confounding factors like prosodic and contextual variations, or physical contact between the velum and the tongue were minimized. This leaves essentially biomechanical/muscular or aerodynamic reasons for the observed velocity differences.

With regard to biomechanics, it is generally accepted that velum raising (and retraction) is caused by the activity of the levator palatini [4]. However, the mechanism for velum lowering is not as clear. Some researchers suggest that velum lowering is implemented by the joint activity of the palatopharyngeus and palatoglossus [12]. In contrast, the reviewed EMG studies by Bell-Berti [4] do not provide support for the role of the palatopharyngeus as a velar depressor and had inhomogeneous conclusions for the role of the palatoglossus, i.e., palatoglossus activity for nasal sounds was found for some people, but not for others. Hence, the *basic* mechanism for lowering the velum might simply involve the *suppression* of activity of the levator palatini and rely on the restoring elastic force of the tissue to open the velopharyngeal port. This passive opening mechanism of the velopharyngeal port might simply be slower than the active muscle-controlled closing mechanism for some subjects, which could partly explain our results.

Stevens [24] suggested an *aerodynamic* reason that may explain higher velocities for velum raising than lowering (however without quantitative evidence): When a nasal is followed by an obstruent, the creation of the oral constriction or closure for the obstruent raises the intraoral pressure that exerts a force on the soft palate and so accelerates the raising movement. To find out whether or not this intraoral pressure increase really plays a role for faster raising movements, one could repeat the presented experiment with ingressive speech, where no intraoral pressure would build up. However, our preliminary attempts showed that it is very hard for most subjects to produce the timed phoneme changes with ingressive speech.

In summary, velocity differences between velum raising and lowering occur both in natural (fluent) speech, as indicated in previous studies, and in artificially timed speech, as in the present study. However, the effect size seems to be quite subject-dependent. While confounding contextual and prosodic factors could be minimized with the present experimental design, a discrimination of biomechanical and aerodynamic causes for the observed effect was not possible. In future work, it would be interesting to study potential differences between men and women with regard to velar movements, as our data suggest that the direction-dependent velocity differences were greater for the male speakers. Future work will also explore the potential benefit of including these velocity differences in articulatory speech synthesis. Finally, the correlation between LPW and velar movements should be further substantiated for a higher number of people to ensure that LPW velocity is a reliable surrogate of velar velocity.

Acknowledgments. This study was funded by the German Research Foundation (DFG), grant no. BI 1639/4-1.

References

1. Alfonso, P.J., Baer, T.: Dynamics of vowel articulation. Lang. Speech **25**(2), 151–173 (1982)
2. Amelot, A.: Etude aérodynamique, fibroscopique, acoustique et perceptive des voyelles nasales du français. Ph.D. thesis, Université de la Sorbonne nouvelle-Paris III (2004)

3. Amelot, A., Crevier-Buchman, L., Maeda, S.: Observations of the velopharyngeal closure mechanism in horizontal and lateral direction from fiberscopic data. In: 15th International Congress of Phonetic Sciences, Barcelona, Spain, pp. 3021–3024 (2003)
4. Bell-Berti, F.: Velopharyngeal function: a spatio-temporal model. In: Lass, N. (ed.) Speech and Language: Advances in Basic Research and Practice, pp. 291–316. Academic Press, New York (1980)
5. Benguerel, A.P., Hirose, H., Sawashima, M., Ushijima, T.: Velar coarticulation in French: a fiberscopic study. J. Phon. 5(2), 149–158 (1977)
6. Birkholz, P.: Modeling consonant-vowel coarticulation for articulatory speech synthesis. PLoS ONE 8(4), e60603 (2013)
7. Birkholz, P., Hoole, P.: Intrinsic velocity differences of lip and jaw movements: preliminary results. In: Proceedings of the Interspeech 2012, Portland, Oregon, USA, pp. 2017–2020 (2012)
8. Birkholz, P., Hoole, P., Kröger, B.J., Neuschaefer-Rube, C.: Tongue body loops in vowel sequences. In: 9th International Seminar on Speech Production (ISSP 2011), Montreal, Canada, pp. 203–210 (2011)
9. Dalston, R.M.: Photodetector assessment of velopharyngeal activity. Cleft Palate J. 19(1), 1–8 (1982)
10. Fels, S., Lloyd, J.E., Van Den Doel, K., Vogt, F., Stavness, I., Vatikiotis-Bateson, E.: Developing physically-based, dynamic vocal tract models using ArtiSynth. In: Proceedings of the 7th International Seminar on Speech Production (ISSP 2006), Ubatuba, Brazil, pp. 419–426 (2006)
11. Fuchs, S., Perrier, P.: On the complex nature of speech kinematics. ZAS Pap. Linguist. 42, 137–165 (2005)
12. Halle, M.: On distinctive features and their articulatory implementation. Nat. Lang. Linguist. Theory 91–105 (1983)
13. Horiguchi, S., Bell-Berti, F.: The velotrace: a device for monitoring velar position. Cleft Palate J. 24(2), 104–111 (1987)
14. Iskarous, K., Nam, H., Whalen, D.H.: Perception of articulatory dynamics from acoustic signatures. J. Acoust. Soc. Am. 127(6), 3717–3728 (2010)
15. Kleiner, C., Kainz, M.A., Echternach, M., Birkholz, P.: Speed differences in laryngeal adduction and abduction gestures. J. Acoust. Soc. Am. (submitted)
16. Krakow, R.A., Huffman, M.K.: Instruments and techniques for investigating nasalization and velopharyngeal function in the laboratory: an introduction. In: Nasals, Nasalization, and the Velum, pp. 3–59. Academic Press (1993)
17. Lukežič, A., Vojíř, T., Čehovin, L., Matas, J., Kristan, M.: Discriminative correlation filter tracker with channel and spatial reliability. Int. J. Comput. Vision 126(7), 671–688 (2018)
18. Martins, P., Oliveira, C., Silva, S., Teixeira, A.: Velar movement in European Portuguese nasal vowels. In: Procedings of IberSPEECH 2012, Madrid, Spain, pp. 231–240 (2012)
19. Moll, K.L., Daniloff, R.G.: Investigation of the timing of velar movements during speech. J. Acoust. Soc. Am. 50(2), 678–684 (1971)
20. Nam, H., Mooshammer, C., Iskarous, K., Whalen, D.: Hearing tongue loops: perceptual sensitivity to acoustic signatures of articulatory dynamics. J. Acoust. Soc. Am. 134(5), 3808–3817 (2013)
21. Oliveira, C., Martins, P., Teixeira, A.: Speech rate effects on European Portuguese nasal vowels. In: Proceedings of the Interspeech 2009, Brighton, UK (2009)
22. Ryan, W.J., Hawkins, C.F.: Ultrasonic measurement of lateral pharyngeal wall movement at the velopharyngeal port. Cleft Palate J. 13(2), 156–164 (1976)

23. Serrurier, A., Badin, P.: A three-dimensional articulatory model of the velum and nasopharyngeal wall based on MRI and CT data. J. Acoust. Soc. Am. **123**(4), 2335–2355 (2008)
24. Stevens, K.N.: Acoustic Phonetics. The MIT Press, Cambridge (1998)
25. Teixeira, A., Vaz, F.: European Portuguese nasal vowels: an EMMA study. In: Proceedings of the Eurospeech 2001, Aalborg, Denmark (2001)
26. Teixeira, A.J.S., Martinez, R., Silva, L.N., Jesus, L.M.T., Principe, J.C., Vaz, F.A.C.: Simulation of human speech production applied to the study and synthesis of European Portuguese. EURASIP J. Appl. Signal Process. **9**, 1435–1448 (2005)
27. Thiele, C., Mooshammer, C., Belz, M., Rasskazova, O., Birkholz, P.: An experimental study of tongue body loops in V1-V2-V1 sequences. J. Phon. **80**, 100965 (2020)
28. Xu, Y., Sun, X.: Maximum speed of pitch change and how it may relate to speech. J. Acoust. Soc. Am. **111**(3), 1399–1413 (2002)

Pragmatic Markers of Russian Everyday Speech: Invariants in Dialogue and Monologue

Natalia Bogdanova-Beglarian[1], Olga Blinova[1,2], Tatiana Sherstinova[1,2(✉)], and Tatiana Sulimova[1]

[1] Saint Petersburg State University, Saint Petersburg, Russia
{n.bogdanova,o.blinova,t.sherstinova}@spbu.ru
[2] HSE University, Saint Petersburg, Russia

Abstract. The paper presents the distribution of pragmatic markers (PM) of Russian everyday speech in two types of discourse: dialogical and monologic. PMs are an essential part of any oral discourse, therefore, quantitative data on their distribution are necessary for solving both theoretical and practical tasks related to studies of speech communication, as well as for translation and teaching Russian as a foreign language. The article describes samples from two speech corpora: "One Speaker's Day" (ORD corpus, consisting of mostly dialogue speech, the annotated subcorpus containing 321 504 tokens) and "Balanced Annotated Text Library" (SAT corpus, which consists only of monologues, the annotated subcorpus containing 50 128 tokens). Besides, it presents statistical data of PM distributions obtained for 60 basic (invariant) markers, PMs common in both dialogue and monologue (for example, hesitative marker such as *vot, tam, tak*) are identified, as well as those that are more typical for monologues (boundary markers like *znachit, nu vot, vs'o*) or dialogues ('xeno'-markers like *takoj, grit*; and meta-communicative markers *vidish', (ja) ne znaju*). Special attention is paid to PMs usage both in different communication situations and in speech of different sociolects.

Keywords: Russian everyday speech · Speech corpus · Pragmatic marker · Monologue · Dialogue · Invariants

1 Introduction

Pragmatic markers (PM) are the units of spoken language that have gone through the process of pragmaticalization (see in: [7, 8]). As a result, they lost or significantly reduced the original lexical and/or grammatical meaning and took on a pragmatic meaning instead. As a result, they perform in discourse a limited number of functions. For example, PMs mark the boundaries of replicas (*tak, znachit, nu vot, vs'o*) or introduce someone else's speech (*takoj/aja/ie, tipa (togo chto), grit/gr'u/gr'at, tak i tak mol*, etc.), verbalize speaker's hesitation (*eto samoye, kak ego (jejo, ikh), ili tam*) or his/her reflection about what was already said or was going to be said (*Ili kak tam? Ili kak skazat'? Ili chto? Skazhem tak*) or self-correction (*eto, eto samoe*), express metacommunication (*znaesh', ponimaesh', da, (ja) ne znaju, chto jeshch'o?*), etc.

© Springer Nature Switzerland AG 2021
A. Karpov and R. Potapova (Eds.): SPECOM 2021, LNAI 12997, pp. 81–90, 2021.
https://doi.org/10.1007/978-3-030-87802-3_8

The differences between PMs and discourse words, or discourse markers (DMs), which are understood in linguistics as a very wide class of functional units (see, for example, [1, 2, 9, 10, 13]), are described in paper [3]. A thorough manual annotation of the corpus material with the distinction between PMs and the homonymous significant units preceded the analysis of PMs in the present study (see, for example, [4, 15]). Because of the structural variability of the majority of PMs, the terms of *the basic variant* and *structural variants* (real uses) of the PM were introduced to describe them. The object of quantitative analysis in this paper is the basic variants (or invariants) of PM. What concerns their qualitative description, it is presented in a special dictionary of pragmatic markers [12]. As for PM structural variants, quantitative characteristics of their real uses are presented in [5].

We are fully aware of the fact that quite a long time has passed since the recording of our corpora (ORD recordings were made in 2007–2015, whereas SAT was recorded in 1990s) and the data obtained cannot be considered a reflection of *today's* spoken language. However, regarding to large corpus data, it is always very timeconsuming to collect, systematize, transcribe, annotate and process data, therefore, apparently, it cannot be otherwise. This is close to the situation of creating any dictionary, which, by the time of its release, partly already loses its adequacy to the real state of our language, and even more so to our everyday speech. Cf.: "the codified norm reflects a specific synchronous section of the system and for some time (until the next reference edition is published) remains static, and therefore turns into an increasingly traditional one. The antinomy of constant movement of the objective norm and the periodic stability of the codified one underlies the fundamental impossibility of their full correspondence" [6].

2   Typology of Pragmatic Markers

The annotation of both corpora is based on the developed functional typology of PMs [12], which includes 10 types of markers:

1. **Hesitation markers (X)** – fill in hesitation pauses, most often when searching for the right word to continue the speech or in the course of overcoming a communication difficulty that has arisen:

   - *a / vs'o … a u men'a na da… d… dacha na **etom** / **kak jego**/ na Dunae$ // # a nu / na Dunae$ khorosho* (ORD) (about the peculiarities of the spelling presentation of the ORD material, see: [11: 242–243]).

2. **Reflective markers (F)** – express the speaker's reaction to his/her own speech behavior, in particular, to the results of hesitation search of a word just performed, as well as the degree of satisfaction of the speaker with the found unit as compared with his/her original intention:

   - *nu vot eto vot / odnoobrazie / kotoroe tam bylo / vot eta neustroennost' byta / e-e nu / dejstvovala na men'a ne ochen' / **tak skazhem** / plodotvorno* (SAT).

3. **Boundary/limit-setting markers (G)** – help the speaker to structure his spoken text. They may by starting, navigational or final:

- *v obshchem / v rezul'tate / nu tam nikakoj okhrany dazhe rechi net / v rezul'tate* (ORD) (starting);
- *nu serye tona / i takoe grustnoe nastrojenie // kholodno // nu () to jest' (e-e)* **nu vot v principe** */ nichego ne mogu skazat' / nu nebo mrachnoe / nu eto ja uzhe govorila / nu vot i vs'o *C* (SAT) (navigational);
- *i ona prosto / u neye tam na na urovne podsoznaniya srabatyvayet / net / ne khochu / potomu chto // ya ne znayu pochemu /* **dumayu chto** (ORD) (finalizing).

4. **Deictic marker (D)** – contain three deictic elements in a line, according to the model *vot (…) vot*:

- *bol'she vsego na men'a proizv'ol vpechatlenie eto Kair // to jest' gorod kak eto nazyvaets'a nu vot sejchas by skazala gorod kontrastov // kha-kha vot to jest' tam tam nishcheta roskosh' / e-e* **vot etot vot***/ m-m tak skazat' / gr'az' i v to zhe vrem'a shikarnye / parki* (SAT).

5. **Meta-communicative markers (M)** – help the speaker to comprehend what was said, as well as to establish and then maintain his/her contact with the interlocutor:

- *vs'o eto *N chto kogda vot @* **ty ponimaesh'** *@ kogda vot eto planirovanie bylo / vs'o znaesh' chto vs'o-vs'o eto budet zarplata te-te-te / i vs'o eto* **znaesh'** *vot kak by / chelovek zhdal / zhdal / a potom e… a potom raz / op-op-op / i ty ponimaesh' / chto nichego takoe () / okazyvaets'a ne proiskhodit* (ORD).

6. **Self-correction markers (C)** – help the speaker correct an unintentional speech mistake:

- *vidite / eta prozrachnaya shtuka ona tut* <u>setka</u> *//* **v smysle** <u>karkas</u> *takaya* (ORD).

7. **'Xeno'-marker (K)** – introduce someone else's speech, someone else's thoughts or the speech behavior of another person into the narrative:

- *ja podosh'ol k treneru i govor'u jemu* **tak i tak vot** <u>ja zanimals'a vodnym polo / ennoe kolichestvo let / ja khochu popast' v komandu</u> (SAT).

8. **Rhythm-forming markers (P)** – allow to harmonize rhythmic groups in the speech stream:

- *dev'at' tys'ach* **tam** | *s kopejkami (ORD)*;
- *daby ne dostalos'* | **vot** *jejo sopernice* (SAT).

9. **Markers of approximation (A)** – show the speaker's uncertainty about what he or she is talking about:

- *nu vot nu on znachit byl e gr'aznyj ryzhij kak oni jego v obshchem eto samoe nashli / podobrali / tak **vrode by*** (SAT).

10. **Replacing markers (Z)** – are used instead of someone else's speech, long enumerations or parts of it:

- *snajperka prich'om prilichno strel'aet // *P s etim / s optikoj / **so vsemi delami*** (ORD).

3   The Dialogues Sample (ORD Corpus)

The annotated subcorpus of the ORD includes 195 episodes taken from "speech days" obtained from 104 informants. The total number of tokens is over 300 000. In three episodes no pragmatic markers were found during the annotation process, so the research is carried out on the data of 192 files.

The subcorpus presents everyday dialogues between women and men of three *age groups*: (1) *young people* – from 16 to 34 years old. During this age period people get an education and start their labor activity, in general, the period is characterized by an active attitude to work, often – by career growth and family creation; (2) *the middle age* is 35 to 49 years old. This is a period of active work and, as a rule, the peak of social maturity; (3) *the senior generation* – over 50 years old, the generation that is less actively involved in social life.

According to *the education level*, there are categories of informants who received (1) secondary education (including the secondary specialized one), (2) incomplete higher and (3) higher education (including PhD).

The subcorpus contains speech samples of informants from different *professional groups*:

1. workers employed in production, construction, representatives of blue-collar occupations usually associated with manual labor (RAB);
2. employees of service sector (SO);
3. educational personnel (OBR);
4. military personnel, police and other representatives of power structures (SIL);
5. representatives of creative professions (TVOR);
6. "office workers", specialists in economic activities, specialists in public relations and advertising (OF);
7. information technology specialists (IT),
8. representatives of engineering specialties (INZH);
9. representatives of the humanities (GUM);
10. representatives of natural sciences (EST).

According to *social status* (official position) the following categories of speakers were identified: (1) leaders/heads/executives/employers (RUK), (2) employees or specialists (the majority of participants belongs to this category) (SP), (3) students and cadets (UCH), and (4) non-working people including pensioners (HP).

According to the education data and the kind of professional activities that may be either related or not related with speech activities, we distinguish different *levels of speech competency* (URK): low, medium (for the majority of people) and high.

Social role in which the speaker acts in a particular communicative episode was also took into account. Thus, the following roles have been identified:

- symmetrical: male friends, female friends, colleagues, husband or wife, classmates,
- asymmetric: parent (father or mother), child (son or daughter) and "customer-service" roles.

In *psycholinguistic aspect*, speech of speakers belonging to two main *psychotypes* (extroverts and introverts), five *temperament* groups (melancholic, sanguine, phlegmatic, choleric, as well as a mixed group of choleric-phlegmatic) and three groups that vary by the level of *neuroticism* (high, medium, low) was analyzed.

All these data were taken into account in the further analysis of the distribution of basic (standard) PMs.

4 The Monologues Sample (SAT Corpus)

To obtain a representative sound recordings data of informal speech communication, reflecting different monologue scenarios for different socio-demographic and psychological groups of speakers, monologues of different types recorded from 34 informants were selected from the SAT corpus. The sample includes 50 128 words.

The main principle underlying texts selection for a balanced subcorpus, was justified by the need to analyze speech of different social and professional groups of speakers. It was decided to select texts reflecting various scenarios of generating monologue speech and to provide inclusion speech by representatives of different gender, age and professional groups. The sample included texts of monologues based on 3 types of communicative scenarios typical of speakers' everyday life: (1) retelling (both texts based on a storyline and descriptive texts), (2) description (storyline pictures and landscape images) and (3) free narration for a given topic. The sample contains 34 texts of each type, thus, the subcorpus is balanced, first of all, according to the types of monologue included.

The subcorpus combines the monologue speech of informants belonging to two *professional groups* – lawyers and medical personal (JUR and MED): 5 monologues of different types by 17 informants from each professional group are included; in total the subcorpus contains 170 monologic texts.

Among the informants, women predominate, since the MED subcorpus was recorded only from women. Along with that, the sample of informants in the JUR is gender-balanced (8 women and 9 men).

The age of speakers ranges from 23 to 49 years, 13 speakers belong to age group I (23–34 years old), and 21 speakers belong to the middle-age group II (35–49 years old). 22 informants have a high *speech competency level*, 6 informants have a medium URK and 6 more – a low one.

Before the recording, informants-lawyers took *psychological testing* to determine their level of extraversion/introversion and the type of temperament. It turned out that among 17 informants, the sample included 2 sanguine-extroverts, 7 ambiverts (among them 2 are choleric, 2 phlegmatic, 2 melancholic and 1 sanguine-phlegmatic) and 8 introverts (4 phlegmatic, 1 melancholic, 1 choleric and 2 phlegmatic-melancholic).

All these data were also taken into account in further analysis of the distribution of base (standard) PMs.

5 Research Data

Based on two annotated samples (ORD, 321 504 tokens; and SAT, 50 128 tokens), quantitative characteristics of basic (invariant) PMs were obtained and correlations were established between their appearance in everyday speech and various factors: speech type (dialogue – monologue), place and type of communication, the speaker's social role in a specific communicative macro episode [14], as well as his/her social and psychological characteristics.

Table 1 presents total number of tokens in each analyzed subsamples of different sociolects [5].

Table 1. The number of tokens in the subsamples with various social characteristics.

Gender				
men			women	
171 497			158 390	
Age groups				
young		middle		senior
143 805		67 089		118 993
Education				
incomplete higher / secondary		secondary specialized		higher
47 634		36 313		215 540
URK speech competency level				
low		medium		high
19 983		245 586		54 825
Professional groups				
GUM	EST	INZH	IT	OB
30 493	11 988	30 897	29 105	29 738
OF	RAB	SIL	SO	TVOR
8 989	13 290	1 587	27 041	17 581

6 Statistics of Basic PM (Invariants)

The general vocabulary of basic (standard) PMs includes 60 units [12]. The absolute "leader" for all sociolects is the marker VOT – its frequency is slightly less than a third of the total number of PMs in speech of all speakers. The marker TAM, which has rank 2 both in the general vocabulary and for the most of sociolects, is also quite frequent. The speech of older speakers, a group of speakers with incomplete higher education and executives is an exception, in which the 'XENO'-marker GOVORIT has rank 2. Besides, speech of non-working pensioners also differs: here, meta-communicative marker ZNAESH' is in the second place. The upper zone (top-5) of PMs frequency lists for the main groups of speakers of different gender and age is as follows:

General: VOT, TAM, ETO, GOVORIT, DA.

Men: VOT, TAM, ETO, DA, GOVORIT.

Women: VOT, TAM, GOVORIT, ETO, DA.

Youth: VOT, TAM, KAK BY, DA, ETO.

Middle age: VOT, TAM, GOVORIT, ETO, DA.

Older age: VOT, GOVORIT, ETO, TAM, ZNACHIT.

The almost complete similarity of the sets of markers in these zones is clearly visible, as well as the high rank 3 of marker KAK BY in the speech of young people and the marker ZNACHIT (rank 5) in the speech of older speakers. We can also note the absence in the top 10 of male speech of the contact-establishing marker ZNAESH', which in the general frequency list has a rank of 9 and is present in the upper zones of all other main frequency lists. In speech of young people, meta-communicative marker SLUSHAJ is added to the verb ZNAESH' in this upper zone (rank 10), and in the speech of older speakers – the same contact verb PONIMAESH' (also rank 10).

Among other specific features of the basic PM functioning, it is worth to mention the high 6th rank of the marker ETO SAMOE in male speech, which in the general vocabulary takes only the 10th place, as well as the presence of the marker KOROCHE (GOVOR'A) in the upper part of the frequency vocabulary only in the speech of younger speakers (rank 9). Students' speech is distinguished by the markers KAK BY (rank 3) and KOROCHE (GOVOR'A) (rank 5). This PM also marks the speech of speakers with secondary (rank 6) and incomplete higher (these are mainly students) (rank 9) education, as well as, in general, the speech of speakers with low URK (rank 3). Among the professional groups, this marker is preferred by workers and representatives of "power" structures (rank 3 in both cases).

With a few exceptions, the VOT marker is also "in the lead" in conversations systematized by *the type of communication*. Its share is undoubtedly high in informal, business and educational conversations. In *informal and professional communication*, VOT is 2–2.5 times more frequent than the marker TAM which has the 3rd rank (21.96 and 29.59% vs 11.00 and 11.13%, respectively). In *educational conversation*, rank 2 has a hesitative marker ETO SAMOE, slightly less in frequency than the marker VOT (17.56 vs. 13.36%), followed by DA and TAM in the frequency list (12.21% each). In *public communication*, the VOT marker concedes rank 1 to the deictic marker VOT (…) VOT (29.73%) and shares the second position with KAK BY marker-approximator (16.22% each). In addition, there is a high frequency of TAK SKAZAT' marker (rank 5) in public communication. Being reflexive in its essence, TAK SKAZAT' marker is often used without a reason (especially in public speech), for just a manner of speaking, it usually marks not very high speech competency level of the speaker who wants speak literary and beautiful, but does not know how to do it properly (the phenomenon of hypercorrection).

What regards *the place of communication*, it also reveals the predominance of the VOT marker in everyday speech – mainly in conversations *at home, in the office and on the street*, where it is again 2–2.5 times ahead of the next marker TAM by the frequency of occurrence. In the three other places of communication identified during the analysis of corpus material, the picture is slightly different. Thus, in *hospital* conversations the first three positions in the frequency vocabulary are occupied by markers VOT (21.09%), TAM (18.37%) and GOVORIT (18.37%), which are close in usage. In conversations taking place in *cafes and restaurants*, VOT moves to the 5th place in the frequency list, yielding the leading positions to the markers TAM (18.10%) and DA (17.14%). And in conversations between young cadets in the military barracks, the KOROCHE (GOVOR'A) marker (as a rule, in the reduced form KOROCHE) (23.75 and 19.38%, respectively) is close to the VOT, TAM marker following them (15.63%). The TIPA marker also has a high 4th rank in conversation in military "barracks" (6.88%), being followed by KAK BY marker which has the 5th rank (5.63%).

Additional information on the distribution of PMs basic variants in Russian everyday speech was obtained in the process of social role analysis which takes into account special role of a speaker in a particular communicative episode. The analysis showed that the "leading" position of the VOT marker (rank 1) is preserved for all social roles. The share of this PM is especially high in speech of parents (42.73%). Different markers have the 2nd rank for different social roles: TAM – in speech of friends, client or service workers, parents and children; govorit in speech of colleagues, ZNAESH' – in speech of girlfriends, DA – in speech of classmates. It is worth to mention the high frequency of KOROCHE (GOVOR'A) marker in communication between friends (rank 4) or classmates (rank 3).

The distribution of basic PMs which takes into account the speaker's *psychotype* (extroverts – introverts), did not significantly change the overall picture. As before, the first two positions in the PMs frequency lists in speech of both psychotypes are occupied by VOT and TAM, and the first one is 2.5–3 times more frequent than the second: 24.31 vs 10.64% for extroverts, 29.03 vs 9.08% for introverts. The speech of extroverts is also distinguished by the presence in the top-5 of the 'Xeno'-marker GOVORIT (rank 3), and the speech of introverts – by the presence of meta-communicatives DA and ZNAESH' in the same zone (ranks 3 and 4, respectively).

What concerns speaker's temperament and level of neuroticism, in this aspect the situation is much the same: VOT marker still has the first rank for all cases, although its share turned out to be rather low (as compared to other groups) — 14.0% in speech of speakers with a low level of neuroticism and 14.16% for the mixed phlegmatic-choleric group. In addition, these two groups of speakers prefer the marker KOROCHE (GOVOR'A): its rank, respectively, is 4 for speakers with a low level of neuroticism and 5 for a mixed group of phlegmatic-choleric people. The high rank 2 of the TAM marker is retained in the speech of speakers with low and medium levels of neuroticism, as well as in the speech of sanguine and phlegmatic people. In other groups of speakers, markers DA (speakers with a high level of neuroticism, melancholic and choleric) and GOVORIT (a mixed group of phlegmatic choleric) climbed to the second rank.

It can be seen that the most striking specificity indicator of everyday Russian speech is precisely the pragmatic marker KOROCHE (GOVOR'A), marking the speech of young speakers (primarily students, including cadets), as well as, in general, native speakers with low URK, including workers and law enforcement officers. This marker is typical for "barracks" speech (here, TIPA and KAK BY markers are also very typical), for the social roles of a friend and classmate, as well as for speakers with a low level of neuroticism and a mixed group of phlegmatic choleric people. It should be mentioned that in this case, this marker appears almost exclusively in its reduced form KOROCHE.

7   Conclusion

The paper presents quantitative data on PMs frequency in speech based on two annotated speech corpora (ORD and SAT). The analysis was carried out on the ranked frequency lists of PMs with information on the relative frequency of their usage in dialogues (ORD corpus) and monologues (from SAT corpus). In addition, PMs frequency lists for different communication conditions were obtained (i.e., type of conversation, social role of the speaker, etc.), as well as for different groups of speakers (sociolects). All these data are summarized in the PM dictionary, which, in addition to the paper version, has an electronic one, which makes it possible to listen to audio examples for each type of PMs [12]. The obtained quantitative data should be considered preliminary, since the sample cannot be considered sufficiently representative for all social groups of speakers.

A qualitative analysis of specific uses of PMs was forced to be left outside the scope of this article, as well as quantitative data on the distribution of real uses of PMs and their specific functional types. This may become the subject for another article. In general, the analysis of corpus material showed that PMs indeed regularly appear in everyday speech of speakers of all social groups and in all communicative situations without exception. However, the frequency of certain basic PMs usage varies depending on characteristics of both the speakers themselves and the conditions of communication. These data expand theoretical understanding of PM usage in real everyday communication and can be used in a variety of practical applications, such as speech technologies development, linguistic expertise, translation practice, and teaching Russian as a foreign language.

Acknowledgments. The presented research was supported by Saint Petersburg State University, project # 75254082 "Modeling of Russian megalopolis citizens' communicative behavior in social, speech and pragmatic aspects using artificial intelligence methods".

References

1. Baranov, A.N., Plungyan, V.A., Rakhilina, E.V.: Putevoditel' po diskursivnym slovam russkogo jazyka [Russian Discourse Words Guide]. Moscow (1993)
2. Beliao, J., Lacheret, A.: Disfluency and discursive markers: when prosody and syntax plan discourse. In: 6th Workshop on Disfluency in Spontaneous Speech. Stockholm, Sweden. **54**(1), pp. 5–9 (2013)

3. Bogdanova-Beglarian, N.V., Filyasova, Y.A.: Discourse vs pragmatic markers: a contrastive terminological study. In: 5th International Multidisciplinary Scientific Conference on Social Sciences and Arts, SGEM 2018. Vienna ART Conference Proceedings. **5**(3.1), 123–130 (2018)

4. Bogdanova-Beglarian, N.V., Blinova, O.V., Martynenko, G.Y., Sherstinova, T.Y., Zaides, K.D., Popova, T.I.: Annotirovanie pragmaticheskikh markerov v russkom rechevom korpuse: problemy, poiski, reshenia, rezul'taty [Annotation of pragmatic markers in the Russian speech corpus: problems, searches, solutions, results]. Kompjuternaya lingvistika i intellektual'nye tekhnologii computational linguistics and intellectual technologies. In: Proceedings of the International Conference "Dialogue 2019". **18**(25), 72–85. Moscow (2019)

5. Bogdanova-Beglarian, N.V., Blinova, O.V., Troshchenkova, E.V., Sherstinova, T.Y., Gorbunova, D.A., Zajdes, K.D., Popova, T.I., Sulimova, T.S.: Pragmaticheskie markery russkoj povsednevnoj rechi: kolichestvennye dannye [Pragmatic markers of Russian everyday speech: quantitative data]. Kompjuternaya lingvistika i intellektual'nye tekhnologii computational linguistics and intellectual technologies. In: Proceedings of the International Conference "Dialogue 2021". **20**(27). Moscow. In Print (2021)

6. Bolycheva, E.M.: Foneticheskaya variativnost' v aspekte kodifitsirovannoj normy [Phonetic Variability in the Aspect of the Codified Norm]. Vestnik Moskovskogo universiteta, MSU Vestnik **1**, 69–81 (1996)

7. Degand, L., Evers-Vermeul, J.: Grammaticalization or pragmaticalization of discourse markers? More than a terminological issue. J. Hist. Pragmat. **16**(1), 59–85 (2015)

8. Diewald, G.: Pragmaticalization (Defined) as grammaticalization of discourse functions. Linguistics **49**(2), 365–390 (2011)

9. Diskursivnye slova russkogo jazyka: Opyt kontekstno-semanticheskogo opisaniya [Discursive Words of the Russian language: an experience of context-semantic description] Moscow (1998)

10. Diskursivnye slova russkogo jazyka: varjirovanie i semanticheskoe jedinstvo [Discursive words of the Russian language: variation and semantic unity]. Collection of articles. Moscow (2003)

11. Russkij jazyk povsednevnogo obshchenia: osobennosti funkcionirovania v raznykh social'nykh gruppakh [Everyday Russian language: functioning features in different social groups. collective monograph] St. Petersburg (2016)

12. Pragmaticheskie Markery russkoj povsednevnoj rechi: slovar'-monografia [Pragmatic markers of Russian everyday speech: dictionary-monograph] St. Petersburg. In print (2021)

13. Schiffrin, D.: Discourse markers. Cambridge University Press, Cambridge (1987)

14. Sherstinova, T.: Macro episodes of Russian everyday oral communication: towards pragmatic annotation of the ORD speech corpus. In: Ronzhin, A., Potapova, R., Fakotakis, N. (eds.) SPECOM 2015. LNCS (LNAI), vol. 9319, pp. 268–276. Springer, Cham (2015). https://doi.org/10.1007/978-3-319-23132-7_33

15. Zaides, K., Popova, T., Bogdanova-Beglarian, N.: Pragmatic markers in the corpus "One Day of Speech": approaches to the annotation. In: Proceedings of Computational Models in Language and Speech Workshop (CMLS 2018) Co-Located with the 15th TEL International Conference on Computational and Cognitive Linguistics (TEL 2018). vol. 2303, pp. 128–143 (2018)

Language Adaptation for Speaker Recognition Systems Using Contrastive Learning

Vincent Brignatz, Jarod Duret, Driss Matrouf, and Mickael Rouvier[✉]

LIA, Avignon University, Avignon, France
{vincent.brignatz,jarod.duret,driss.matrouf,
mickael.rouvier}@univ-avignon.fr

Abstract. In this article we propose to study several approaches to adapt a system between two languages. To train the state of the art x-vector Speaker Verification system, we need a huge amount of labeled speech data. If this constraint is satisfied in English (due to Voxceleb), it is not in our target domain: French. We use a supervised Contrastive Learning to transfer knowledge between source and target domain. Among the two other proposed adaptation approaches (Multilingual Learning and Transfert Learning) we show that the one based on Contrastive Learning gives the best performance: about 30% relative gain in term of Equal Error Rate with respect to the baseline system. We also show the robustness of the Contrastive Learning with respect to the duration (from very short to short) as well as to distortion presence (noise, reverberation).

Keywords: Speaker recognition · Domain adaptation · Contrastive learning

1 Introduction

These last years, speaker verification accuracy has drastically improved due to recent advances in machine learning and particularly in deep learning methods. One reason of this success is the generalization capability of Deep Neural Network (DNN) when using very large corpus.

However, a DNN trained on a speaker identification task in [19] still rely heavily on huge amount of labeled data for its results to be accurate. Such large datasets like Voxceleb2 [7] may be available in English. Yet, many variability specific datasets lack labels or are just too small to learn an accurate speaker representation from scratch. Any shift between training and test data, in terms of device, language, duration, noise or other, tends to degrade accuracy of the speaker recognition system. In this study, we investigate domain adaptation approaches for the speaker verification task (SV) in order to reduce the amount of degradation.

Recently, many effective solutions of domain adaptation were proposed [2, 4,13,24]. Some of these approaches work in the embedding space, proposing transformation methods (often linear) attempting to map the embedding from the

© Springer Nature Switzerland AG 2021
A. Karpov and R. Potapova (Eds.): SPECOM 2021, LNAI 12997, pp. 91–99, 2021.
https://doi.org/10.1007/978-3-030-87802-3_9

source space to the target space. However, these approaches become less effective in the context of the latest state-of-the-art systems such as ResNet [26]. Other approaches attempt to adapt the DNN generating the embedding, so that it is optimized to generate efficient embeddings in the target space. In this class of approaches we can find Transfer Learning shows better results by adding a small adaptation specific neural network to the end of the speaker verification system [8]. However, these methods only prove beneficial if enough different speakers are present in the target data. Also, these methods still need a large of amount of labeled data in order to show significant results.

In [25], the authors focus on self-supervised Contrastive Learning approaches, where the goal is to discriminate positive and negative pairs by using a Contrastive Learning framework, such as SimCLR [6]. The main goal of this technique is to achieve accurate speaker representation without using labeled data in target space (or at least in a very small amount).

Unlike [25], we assume in this paper that huge labeled database (like Voxceleb) is available in the source domain to train the DNN (ResNet 34 in our case) by using a cross-entropy criterion. Voxceleb is an English corpus but our domain application is French (the FABIOLE database). We do not have a sufficiently large database in French to learn a new speaker representation system as accurate as the one trained on English data. Our strategy here is to pre-train on the English database and then optimize with the French database. We will propose and compare three adaptation techniques to achieve better performances in the target space (French): Multilingual Learning, the Transfer Learning and the Contrastive Learning.

The article will be organized as follows: In Sect. 2 we will describe our baseline system based on ResNet-34. In Sect. 3 we will describe the three proposed training approaches. In Sect. 4 we present the obtained results and compare the three proposed approach. Finally, in Sect. 5 we will expose our conclusions and perspectives.

2   ResNet-Based Speaker Embedding

An embedding is a high-level speaker feature extracted from a DNN model. The DNN model is trained through a speaker identification task, *i.e.* by classifying speech segments into one of N speaker identities. In that context, the different layers of the DNN are trained to extract information for discriminating between different speakers. The idea is to use one of the hidden layer as the speaker representation (the embedding). One of the main advantage is that embeddings produced by the DNN can generalize well to speakers beyond those present in the training set. The benefits of embeddings in terms of speaker detection accuracy have been demonstrated during the recent evaluation campaigns: NIST SRE [14,17,22], VoxCeleb 2020 [5,20,21] and SdSVC [10,15,23].

The embedding extractor used in this paper is a variant based on ResNet [26]. The ResNet model for extracting embeddings consists of three modules: a *frame-level* feature extractor, a *statistics-level* layer, and *segment-level* representation layers.

- The *frame-level* component is based on the well-known ResNet topology. ResNet (Residual Network) uses stack of many Residual Blocks. A Residual Block is made up of two 2-dimensional Convolutional Neural Networks (CNN) layers separated by a non-linearity (ReLU). The input of Residual Block is added to its output in order to constitute the input of the next Residual Block. Residual blocks allowed to solve the problem of exploding and vanishing gradients. And ResNet have emerged as a family with an extremely deep architectures showing compelling accuracy and nice convergence behaviors.
- The *statistics-level* component is an essential component that converts from a variable length speech signal into a single fixed-dimensional vector. The statistics-level is composed of one layer: the statistics-pooling, which aggregates over frame-level output vectors of the DNN and computes their mean and standard deviation.
- The *segment-level* component maps the segment-level vector to speaker identities. The mean and standard deviation are concatenated together and forward to additional hidden layers and finally to softmax output layer.

The detailed topology of the used ResNet is shown in Table 1. The ResNet is trained using ArcFace softmax to classify speakers contained in the training set. In order to increase the diversity of the acoustic conditions in the training set, a data augmentation strategy is applied using the Kaldi toolkit [16]. This strategy adds four corrupted copies of the original recordings to the training list. The recordings are corrupted by adding noise, music and mixed speech (babble) drawn from the MUSAN database [18] and adding reverberation by using simulated Room Impulse Responses (RIR) [12].

3   Domain Adaptation Approaches

In this section we present three domains adaptations techniques: Multilingual, Transfer and Contrastive Learning. All theses techniques aim to adapt the embedding extractor (ResNet) to the target domain.

3.1   Multilingual Learning

With this technique, we try to include the target data directly in the global optimization process. First, we merge the source and target data in a unique corpus. Then, using this data, we train the generator and classifier on the classification task. The newly obtained dataset contains 1.379.676 utterances for 9.324 speakers. This number of speakers means the dimension of the classifier's fully connected layer is 256×9324. The new corpus contains 64% of English speakers and 79% of English utterances. The training, like the baseline's one, is realized on the speaker classification task. With this approach, we aim to use the large quantity of data available from the source domain while giving the target domain variability to the system.

Table 1. The proposed ResNet-34 architecture. Last row, N is the number of speakers. Batch-norm and ReLU layers are not shown. The dimensions are (Frequency × Channels × Time). The input is comprised of 60 filter banks from speech segments. During training we use a fixed segment length of 400.

Layer name	Structure	Output
Input	–	$60 \times 400 \times 1$
Conv2D-1	3×3, Stride 1	$60 \times 400 \times 32$
ResNetBlock-1	$\begin{bmatrix} 3 \times 3, 32 \\ 3 \times 3, 32 \end{bmatrix} \times 3$, Stride 1	$60 \times 400 \times 32$
ResNetBlock-2	$\begin{bmatrix} 3 \times 3, 64 \\ 3 \times 3, 64 \end{bmatrix} \times 4$, Stride 2	$30 \times 200 \times 64$
ResNetBlock-3	$\begin{bmatrix} 3 \times 3, 128 \\ 3 \times 3, 128 \end{bmatrix} \times 6$, Stride 2	$15 \times 100 \times 128$
ResNetBlock-4	$\begin{bmatrix} 3 \times 3, 256 \\ 3 \times 3, 256 \end{bmatrix} \times 3$, Stride 2	$8 \times 50 \times 256$
Pooling	–	8×256
Flatten	–	2048
Dense1	–	256
Dense2 (Softmax)	–	N
Total	–	–

3.2 Transfer Learning

This technique makes it possible to transfer the knowledge acquired to a source dataset in order to better process a target dataset.

Most machine learning algorithms are based on the assumption that the dataset used for training and the test dataset belong to the same descriptor space and follow the same probability distribution. However, in a number of applications, this is not the case. The retraining of models is also greedy in data and costly in computing time, in particular in deep learning. Fortunately, this process can be optimized thanks to Transfer Learning. The knowledge acquired from the training dataset, henceforth called the source data set, are *transferred* in order to be able to properly process the new data set, called target.

In practice there are several Transfer Learning approaches. Certain techniques modify the source and/or target descriptor spaces in order to make them similar: this is called a feature based transfer. Other approaches carry out the transfer by weighting and/or by choosing certain data from the source set to introduce them into the target set: we speak of a based transfer instance. This methods modify the models themselves in order to transfer knowledge. The approach we propose in this work belongs to this later class.

In our case the ResNet-34 is trained on the development part of the labeled corpus Voxceleb2 [7], the source dataset. The output of the ResNet is a probabilities vector with 5.994 components. The number of speakers in the adaptation corpus is only 3.330 and are different from those of the source corpus.

To adapt the ResNet to the target, we replace the classifier (fully connected layer after the embedding) of size 256×5994 (256 is the embedding size and 5.994 is the number of speakers in training database) by new one of size 256×3330 corresponding to the number of speakers in the adaptation dataset. In the first training step, we let the Embedding generator unchanged while optimizing the new classifier on the target dataset. Then we optimize globally the system using a lower learning rate to fine-tune the extractor and new classifier.

3.3 Contrastive Learning

Contrastive Learning can be used for different purposes. In [25] the authors use this approach to process unlabeled data. In this work, the goal is different: to increase the performance on the target dataset. Here, the Contrastive Learning plays the role of knowledge transfer.

After training the extractor and the classifier on the source data, the classifier is replaced by a projection head. The cost function (cross-entropy) is also replaced by a new cost function called "contrastive loss". This function aims to minimize the distances between examples belonging to the same speakers while maximizing the distances between examples belonging to different speakers.

The authors of [6] found that using a projection head (fully connected layer) and optimizing the contrastive loss at the projection level instead of the embedding level was beneficial. Therefore, the generator is optimized due to back-propagation, and by using a lower learning rate, we can fine tune its weights. When the training is complete, we throw away the projection head and use the newly optimized ResNet generator in our speaker verification systems.

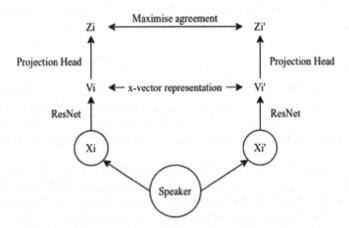

Fig. 1. A schema of the Contrastive Learning pipeline. Two augmented utterances (X_i and X_i') are selected from one speaker. The generator (ResNet) extract the embedding (V_i and V_i') from the utterances' features. The projection head then maps the embeddings to a new space. The generator and projection head are trained to maximize the agreement between the projections (Z_i and Z_i') using the contrastive loss.

In order to maximize inter-class separation and intra-class compactness while adapting the system, we used the Contrastive Learning protocol presented in Fig. 1 from the SimCLR framework [6]. With each mini-batch, we randomly select 2 augmented utterances from N different speakers, getting us $2N$ augmented utterances. Each example is compared to one positive example (from the same speaker) and $2(N-1)$ negative examples (from another speaker). The contrastive loss is then applied and the back propagation occurs.

The contrastive loss function is defined as:

$$l = \frac{1}{N} \sum_{i=1}^{N} -\log \frac{\exp(\cos(z_i, z_i'))}{\sum_{j=1}^{2N} \mathbb{1}_{[j \neq i]} \exp(\cos(z_i, z_j))}, \tag{1}$$

where z_i, z_i' are two augmented utterances from the same speaker, z_j is from the rest of the $2(N-1)$ samples, $\mathbb{1}_{[k \neq i]} \in \{0, 1\}$ is an indicator function evaluating to 1 if $k \neq i$.

Note that, if the SimCLR framework propose a self-supervised learning technique, we used a supervised one. Indeed, in speakers datasets, we often find a number of utterances belonging to the same speaker. This is due to the practicality of recording with volunteers. This inequality between the number of classes and amount of data can lead to scenarios where a lot of utterances are supposed to be from different speaker while they are not. This can have very negative effect on the Contrastive Learning performances.

4   Experiments and Results

We describe in this section the experimental setup in terms of datasets and evaluation protocol.

4.1   Experimental Protocol

The embedding extractor is trained on the development partition of the VoxCeleb2 dataset [7]. This corpus contains speech from celebrities extracted from the *YouTube* platform with a 16 Khz sampling rate. The audio can contain background noise, chatter or laughs overlapping speech and varying room acoustics.

For the target domain (French), two datasets are used. The first dataset was introduced with the French evaluation campaign REPERE [11]. The data was collected from 8 different types of show broadcasted by two French TV channels [9]. The second dataset comes from the *Common Voice* speech corpus [3]. This corpus is community driven and regroup over 2500h of speech in 29 languages. For our purpose, we only use the French part of this dataset. The combination of these two datasets allow us to work with a bigger corpus.

Our test protocol used trials from the FABIOLE [1] corpus. This corpus consists in excerpts from 10 French radios and television shows with good speech quality. It divided the speakers into two categories: 30 target speakers with 100 excerpts each and 100 "impostors" with only one excerpt.

In summary, our application domain is the FABIOLE dataset. The training set consists primarily English speech, whereas the enrollment and test segments are in French. To adapt our system, we use a combination of two French datasets: REPERE and Common Voice. We described the quantity of data in each dataset in the Table 2.

Table 2. Quantity of data in the four corpora.

Corpus	# utt	# speakers
Voxceleb2	1092009	5994
REPERE	163275	2836
Common Voice	124392	494
Fabiole	7000	130

We used The Equal Error Rate (EER) as the performance criterion of speaker verification. EER is the threshold value such that false acceptance rate and miss rate are equals.

4.2   Results

We choose to present the results for 4 set of trails: FABIOLE-A, FABIOLE-B, FABIOLE-A-aug and FABIOLE-B-aug. FABIOLE-A contains trails with duration segment is between 3 and 5s while FABIOLE-B contains very short segments (about 2s). FABIOLE-A-aug and FABIOLE-B-aug are the noisy versions of FABIOLE-A and FABIOLE-B (noise with SNR from 0 to 15 and reverberation). The baseline system is the ResNet trained with the English corpus Voxceleb2 only. We can see in Table 3 that the three proposed methods generally bring gains compared to the baseline system. Except for the Multilingual method which degrades performance in the FABIOLE-A and FABIOLE-A-aug protocols. The Transfer Learning method always brings improvements but is still limited. Among the methods studied in this article, the Contrastive Learning method is by far the best which give a relative gain of about 30% compared to the baseline system.

Table 3. Obtained EER for each protocol.

Protocol	EER (%)			
	Baseline	Multilingual	Transfer Learn.	Contrastive Learn.
FABIOLE - A	2.92	3.83	2.55	**2.01**
FABIOLE - B	7.24	5.94	7.10	**5.00**
FABIOLE - A aug.	3.65	4.74	3.10	**2.74**
FABIOLE - B aug.	10.43	8.83	10.14	**7.60**

5   Conclusion

In this article we studied the possibility of adapting a speaker verification system between two languages. We trained the baseline system on English data but it must be used in French. From the three approaches we compared the Contrastive Learning showed the best performances. With a 30% relative gain regarding the baseline system, the Contrastive Learning techniques show great potential. Even if it can be used in a self-supervised way, we decided, in this work, to use the available labels in our corpora to prevent wrong assumptions. We also show the robustness of the Contrastive Learning with respect to the duration (from very short to short) and the presence of noise and reverberation. We believe in the potential of this approach to adapt a system from a language to another. We must continue to improve this technique by proposing novel approaches regarding the choice of examples on which it is necessary to optimize the cost function. We plan also study the combination of the presented approaches.

References

1. Ajili, M., Bonastre, J.F., Kahn, J., Rossato, S., Bernard, G.: FABIOLE, a speech database for forensic speaker comparison. In: Proceedings of the Tenth International Conference on Language Resources and Evaluation (LREC 2016), pp. 726–733. European Language Resources Association (ELRA), Portorož, May 2016. https://www.aclweb.org/anthology/L16-1115
2. Alam, M.J., Bhattacharya, G., Kenny, P.: Speaker verification in mismatched conditions with frustratingly easy domain adaptation. In: Proceedings of Speaker Odyssey: The Speaker and Language Recognition Workshop, pp. 176–180 (2018). https://doi.org/10.21437/Odyssey.2018-25
3. Ardila, R., et al.: Common voice: a massively-multilingual speech corpus. In: Proceedings of the 12th Language Resources and Evaluation Conference (LREC 2020) (2020)
4. Bousquet, P., Rouvier, M.: On robustness of unsupervised domain adaptation for speaker recognition. In: Kubin, G., Kacic, Z. (eds.) Interspeech 2019, 20th Annual Conference of the International Speech Communication Association, Graz, Austria, 15–19 September 2019, pp. 2958–2962. ISCA (2019). https://doi.org/10.21437/Interspeech.2019-1524
5. Brummer, N., et al.: But+ omilia system description voxceleb speaker recognition challenge 2020 (2020)
6. Chen, T., Kornblith, S., Norouzi, M., Hinton, G.E.: A simple framework for contrastive learning of visual representations. CoRR abs/2002.05709 (2020). https://arxiv.org/abs/2002.05709
7. Chung, J.S., Nagrani, A., Zisserman, A.: Voxceleb2: deep speaker recognition. CoRR abs/1806.05622 (2018). http://arxiv.org/abs/1806.05622
8. Ganvir, S., Lal, N.: Automatic speaker recognition using transfer learning approach of deep learning models. In: 2021 6th International Conference on Inventive Computation Technologies (ICICT), pp. 595–601 (2021). https://doi.org/10.1109/ICICT50816.2021.9358539
9. Giraudel, A., Carré, M., Mapelli, V., Kahn, J., Galibert, O., Quintard, L.: The REPERE corpus: a multimodal corpus for person recognition, pp. 1102–1107 (2012). http://www.lrec-conf.org/proceedings/lrec2012/summaries/707.html

10. Guillermo Barbadillo, S.P.: Veridas solution for SdSV challenge technical report (2019)
11. Kahn, J., Galibert, O., Quintard, L., Carré, M., Giraudel, A., Joly, P.: A presentation of the repere challenge. In: 2012 10th International Workshop on Content-Based Multimedia Indexing (CBMI), pp. 1–6 (2012). https://doi.org/10.1109/CBMI.2012.6269851
12. Ko, T., Peddinti, V., Povey, D., Seltzer, M.L., Khudanpur, S.: A study on data augmentation of reverberant speech for robust speech recognition. In: 2017 IEEE International Conference on Acoustics, Speech and Signal Processing (ICASSP), pp. 5220–5224 (2017). https://doi.org/10.1109/ICASSP.2017.7953152
13. Lee, K.A., Wang, Q., Koshinaka, T.: The coral+ algorithm for unsupervised domain adaptation of PLDA. In: ICASSP 2019-2019 IEEE International Conference on Acoustics, Speech and Signal Processing (ICASSP), pp. 5821–5825. IEEE (2019)
14. Lee, K.A., et al.: The NEC-TT 2018 speaker verification system. In: Interspeech, pp. 4355–4359 (2019)
15. Pierre-Michel Bousquet, M.R.: The LIA system description for SdSV challenge task 2 (2019). https://sdsvc.github.io/2020/descriptions/Team42_Task2.pdf
16. Povey, D., et al.: The kaldi speech recognition toolkit. In: IEEE 2011 Workshop on Automatic Speech Recognition and Understanding. IEEE Signal Processing Society, December 2011. iEEE Catalog No.: CFP11SRW-USB
17. Rouvier, M., Bousquet, P., Ajili, M., Kheder, W.B., Matrouf, D., Bonastre, J.: LIA system description for NIST SRE 2016 (2016). http://arxiv.org/abs/1612.05168
18. Snyder, D., Chen, G., Povey, D.: MUSAN: a music, speech, and noise corpus. CoRR abs/1510.08484 (2015). http://arxiv.org/abs/1510.08484
19. Snyder, D., Garcia-Romero, D., Sell, G., Povey, D., Khudanpur, S.: X-vectors: robust DNN embeddings for speaker recognition. In: 2018 IEEE International Conference on Acoustics, Speech and Signal Processing (ICASSP), pp. 5329–5333 (2018). https://doi.org/10.1109/ICASSP.2018.8461375
20. Thienpondt, J., Desplanques, B., Demuynck, K.: The IDLAB voxceleb speaker recognition challenge 2020 system description. CoRR abs/2010.12468 (2020). https://arxiv.org/abs/2010.12468
21. Torgashov, N.: ID R&D system description to voxceleb speaker recognition challenge 2020 (2020)
22. Villalba, J., et al.: The JHU-MIT system description for NIST SRE18 (2018). https://sdsvc.github.io/2020/descriptions/Team10_Both.pdf
23. Villalba, J., Dehak, N.: The JHU system description for SDSV2020 challenge (2019)
24. Wang, Q., Okabe, K., Lee, K.A., Koshinaka, T.: A generalized framework for domain adaptation of PLDA in speaker recognition. In: ICASSP 2020-2020 IEEE International Conference on Acoustics, Speech and Signal Processing (ICASSP), pp. 6619–6623. IEEE (2020)
25. Xia, W., Zhang, C., Weng, C., Yu, M., Yu, D.: Self-supervised text-independent speaker verification using prototypical momentum contrastive learning (2020). https://arxiv.org/abs/2012.07178
26. Zeinali, H., Wang, S., Silnova, A., Matejka, P., Plchot, O.: BUT system description to voxceleb speaker recognition challenge 2019. CoRR abs/1910.12592 (2019). http://arxiv.org/abs/1910.12592

Evaluating X-Vector-Based Speaker Anonymization Under White-Box Assessment

Pierre Champion[1,2]([✉]), Denis Jouvet[1]([✉]), and Anthony Larcher[2]([✉])

[1] Université de Lorraine, CNRS, Inria, LORIA, 54000 Nancy, France
{pierre.champion,denis.jouvet}@inria.fr
[2] Le Mans Université, LIUM, Le Mans, France
anthony.larcher@univ-lemans.fr

Abstract. In the scenario of the Voice Privacy challenge, anonymization is achieved by converting all utterances from a source speaker to match the same target identity; this identity being randomly selected. In this context, an attacker with maximum knowledge about the anonymization system can not infer the target identity. This article proposed to constrain the target selection to a specific identity, i.e., removing the random selection of identity, to evaluate the extreme threat under a white-box assessment (the attacker has complete knowledge about the system). Targeting a unique identity also allows us to investigate whether some target's identities are better than others to anonymize a given speaker.

Keywords: Speaker anonymization · VoicePrivacy · Anonymization evaluation

1 Introduction

In many applications, such as virtual assistants, speech signal is sent from the user device to the service provider's servers in which data is collected, processed, and stored. Recent regulations, e.g., the General Data Protection Regulation (GDPR) [10] in the EU, emphasize on privacy preservation and protection of personal data. As speech data can reflect both biological and behavioral characteristics of the speaker, it is qualified as personal data [8]. The research reported in this article has been done using the Voice privacy Challenge framework [17], which is one of the first attempts of the speech community to evaluate research on this topic, by producing dedicated protocols, metrics, datasets and baselines.

Speaker anonymization is performed to suppress the personally identifiable paralinguistic information from a speech utterance while maintaining the linguistic content. This is also referred to as *speaker anonymization* [3] or *de-identification* [5]. Recently, Fang et al. [3] proposed an x-vector-based speaker anonymization system based on voice conversion where one of the hyper-parameters used to transform the voice is a target pseudo-speaker identity. In order to choose the

© Springer Nature Switzerland AG 2021
A. Karpov and R. Potapova (Eds.): SPECOM 2021, LNAI 12997, pp. 100–111, 2021.
https://doi.org/10.1007/978-3-030-87802-3_10

anonymization system and hyper-parameters, for a given use case, we must evaluate and rank the performances of each anonymization method. In this first edition of the Voice privacy Challenge, the quality of anonymization is assessed by using state-of-the-art speaker verification system together with an automatic speech recognition system that is used to evaluate the preservation of the linguistic content. In the context of privacy, a game-theoretic reasoning with two agents is defined as follows: one who wishes to anonymize a user's speech (the service provider) and the other (the attacker) who will do everything possible to "break" this anonymity. Introduced in [15], the notion of attacker's knowledge of the anonymization method was introduced, it defines three possible attack scenarios: black-box, white-box, and grey-box. In all approaches, privacy is evaluated by comparing original speech (accessible to the attacker) and anonymous speech published by a service provider. The goal of an effective anonymization system is to allow the publication of speech whose identity is difficult to link to a user's identity, even if the attacker has some knowledge of the anonymization mechanism. In the black-box attacker scenario, privacy is measured by comparing clean, non-anonymized enrollment speech, and anonymized trial speech. In this scenario, the attacker is not aware that speech has been anonymized. In contrast, a white-box attacker is fully aware of the anonymization system and hyper-parameters. Grey-box attackers cover the whole range of possible scenario in-between black and white boxes, when the attacker has a partial knowledge of the anonymization system.

The target pseudo-speaker identity used to anonymize the voices can be generated following multiple strategies [15]. In the *permanent* strategy, used in the VoicePrivacy challenge, all utterances from a speaker are converted using the same target pseudo-speaker. The challenge defines a grey-box attacker that has access to the anonymization toolkit, and thus is able to transform any utterance from her enrollment dataset using the same system and target strategy. However, for a given source speaker, the target pseudo-speaker used by the attacker differs from the one used by the service provider due to the random pseudo-speaker selection process included in the *permanent* strategy. In case the attacker knows the pseudo-speaker, this grey-box scenario turns into a white-box scenario.

We modify the Voice Privacy Challenge scenario into a white-box assessment by targeting a same speaker identity for all utterances from all speakers. This target selection strategy allows us to evaluate the performance of the x-vector-based anonymization system on its own, and generate a report that does not assume that the attacker has knowledge deficiencies. Experiments are performed with a large group of target speaker identity in order to investigate the effect of this identity on the quality of the anonymization.

In the remaining of this article, we first describe the baseline system and voice conversion method in Sect. 2. We then introduce our experimental protocol in Sect. 3 and present our experimental results in Sect. 4. Eventually, we draw our conclusions and propose future avenues in Sect. 5.

2   Anonymization Technique

The anonymization of speaker's identity can be performed with various methods [1,3,7,12,15]. In this article, our contributions are based on the *Baseline-1* (referred to as the *baseline* in this article) of the VoicePrivacy challenge that anonymizes speech using x-vectors and neural waveform models [3].

2.1   The Voice Conversion System

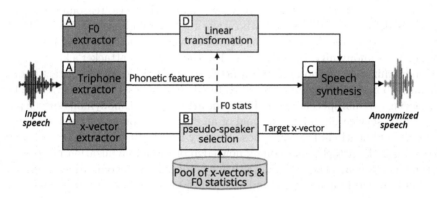

Fig. 1. The speaker anonymization pipeline. Modules A, B, and C are parts of the baseline model. Module D is an enhancement used to coherently alter the F0 values with respect to the selected pseudo-speaker identity.

The baseline system introduced in [3] aims at separating speaker identity and linguistic content from an input speech utterance. Assuming that those features are disentangled, an anonymized speech waveform can be generated after altering only the features that encode the speaker's identity. The anonymization system illustrated in Fig. 1 can be decomposed into three groups of modules. Modules from the *group A* extract different features from the source signal: the fundamental frequency, the phonetic features encoding articulation of speech sounds (Phoneme Posterior-Grams (PPGs) [16]) and the speaker's x-vector. *The module B* derives a new pseudo-speaker identity. The x-vector from each source input speaker is compared to a pool of external x-vectors to select the 200 furthest vectors; 100 of them are randomly selected and averaged to create an anonymized pseudo-speaker x-vector identity. Finally, *the module C* synthesizes a speech waveform from the pseudo-speaker x-vector together with the original PPGs features and F0.

As an enhancement to this baseline, [2] proposed to modify the F0 values (cf. module D in Fig. 1) using the F0 mean and variance statistics associated with each of the x-vector of the pool.

2.2   Design Choices for Anonymization

In the evaluation plan of the VoicePrivacy Challenge, all utterances of a given speaker should be converted to match a single target pseudo-speaker. This strategy, described as *permanent* in [15], ensures that a one-to-one mapping exists between the source speaker identity and the anonymized speaker identity. This requirement allows anonymized voices to be distinguishable from each other. This one-to-one mapping does not apply in-between speech anonymized by the service provider and speech anonymized by the attacker. Speech data anonymized by the service provider corresponds to the trial dataset, and speech available to the attacker corresponds to the enrollment dataset, see Sect. 3.1 for more detail. Figure 2a shows how the *permanent* strategy converts enrollment and trial speech to different anonymized pseudo-speakers.

To select the target pseudo-speaker identity, module B (from Fig. 1) has many hyper-parameters that affect the selection mechanism. According to [2,13,14], the best anonymization results are achieved by picking the pseudo-speaker in a dense region of the x-vector space, randomly targeting male or female gender pseudo-speaker, and modifying the F0 values of the input speech so that it matches the F0 statistics of the real speakers used to generate the pseudo-identity.

The VoicePrivacy challenge's protocol assumes that attackers have access to anonymized trial utterances and original enrollment utterances. During the challenge, two sets of tests are performed following black-box and grey-box attacker scenarios corresponding to situations where the enrollment utterances are original or have been anonymized. In the latter scenario, the attacker has partial knowledge of the system and is able to anonymize the enrollment utterances using the same anonymization system and *permanent* target selection strategy. The pseudo-speaker chosen for each of the enrollment speakers differs from the pseudo-speaker chosen for the trial speakers as the attacker does not have knowledge of the randomly selected speakers used to generate the pseudo-speaker identity. As the voices of the same speakers once anonymized by the service provider (trial) and the attacker (enrollment) are different from each other, this leads to a rather good anonymization performance [17].

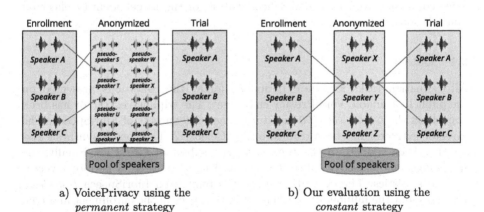

a) VoicePrivacy using the
permanent strategy

b) Our evaluation using the
constant strategy

Fig. 2. Overview of target selection strategies. In the *permanent* strategy pseudo-speakers are randomly selected, first for the trial dataset and then for the enrollment dataset. While our *constant* strategy, always targets the same pseudo-speaker.

With the *permanent* target selection strategy used in the challenge, anonymized voices remain distinguishable and all utterances from the same original speaker are anonymized with the same pseudo-speaker. This process is referred to as pseudonymization. Providing attackers the target's identity of each speaker in the *permanent* strategy evaluates the quality of the voice conversion system and the preservation of the voice distinctiveness [9]. In this paper, we evaluate the privacy of the anonymization technique with the best attacker, that is using the *constant* selection strategy.

3   Experimental Setup

In this evaluation, we want to provide a comprehensive assessment of the voice conversion toolkit under a white-box scenario where the attacker has full knowledge about the system. We change the game between the attacker and the service provider to use the *constant* identity selection strategy defined in [15]. In contrast to the anonymization performed in the VoicePrivacy challenge, the *constant* strategy defines a single pseudo-speaker identity for all speakers in a given dataset. We extend this property to all speakers of the trial and the enrollment datasets so that all of them should have the same anonymized voice identity. We expect good anonymization performance as the voices of all speakers should appear to be spoken by a single identity. This breaks the one-to-one requirement of the challenge, speakers will not be distinguishable from each other. Still, we believe this assessment is complementary to the realistic attacker-based evaluation of the challenge. Figure 2 shows the differences in the target selection strategies between the VoicePrivacy strategy (*permanent* strategy), and the strategy chosen for this study (our *constant* strategy). Experiments are performed with different target speaker identities to provide averaged global results about the voice conversion toolkit, and detailed analysis of the target identity effect on multiple source speakers.

3.1   Dataset

All evaluation tasks for the experiments follow the conditions presented on the publicly available VoicePrivacy challenge[1]. The triphone extractor has been trained on the *train-clean-100* and *train-other-500* subsets of LibriSpeech. The x-vector extractor has been trained on VoxCeleb-1,2. The speech synthesis system has been trained on the *train-clean-100* subset of LibriTTS. Finally, the *train-other-500* subset of LibriTTS has been used to create a pool of x-vector and F0 statistics. The evaluation dataset is built from LibriSpeech *test-clean*. Details about the number of speakers and utterances in the enrollment and trial dataset are reported in Table 1.

---

[1] https://github.com/Voice-Privacy-Challenge.

Table 1. Statistics of the evaluation dataset [17].

Subset		Female	Male	Total
Librispeech test-clean	Speakers in enrollment	16	13	29
	Speakers in trials	20	20	40
	Enrollment utterances	254	184	438
	Trial utterances	734	762	1496

3.2 Utility and Privacy Metrics

To evaluate the performance of the system in both privacy (*speaker's conceal-ing* capability) and utility (*content intelligibility*) two systems and metrics are used. To quantitatively evaluate the privacy, an x-vector-PLDA based Automatic Speaker Verification (ASV) architecture provided by the challenge organizers is used. The privacy protection is measured with the linkability metric: [4] intro-duced two different measures that are calculated based on mated and non-mated likelihood score distributions. In this case, mated scores are computed comparing anonymized speech of the same user. Whereas non-mated scores are computed comparing anonymized speech of different users. The local measure $D_{\leftrightarrow}$ is the local score-wise measure depending upon the likelihood ratio between the mated and non-mated sample's score. The global linkability measure $D_{\leftrightarrow}^{sys}$ is the average value of $D_{\leftrightarrow}$ over all mated scores. To obtain the linkability score for a given speaker, the average is taken from all mated scores of this specific speaker. Work in [6] advocate the use of $D_{\leftrightarrow}^{sys}$ as a robust privacy metric. The lower the $D_{\leftrightarrow}^{sys}$, the better the speakers are anonymized. As the Equal Error Rate (EER%) measure is more often used in speaker verification, we present our result in terms of both EER% and $D_{\leftrightarrow}^{sys}$. The higher the EER%, the better the speakers are anonymized.

For the utility, the pre-trained Automatic Speech Recognition (ASR) system provided by the challenge organizers is used to decode the anonymized speech and compute the Word Error Rate (WER%). In this evaluation, the WER% measure is used to evaluate how the content is kept intelligible. The lower the WER% is, the more intelligible the anonymized speech is. Both ASR and ASV systems are trained on LibriSpeech *train-clean-360* using Kaldi [11].

3.3 Evaluation Methodology

In this experiment, we run the anonymization and evaluation on 40 real target speaker's identities that cover as best as possible the speaker space. Thus, to select the target speakers, we identify 20 female and 20 male clusters of x-vectors in the anonymization pool (*LibriTTS train-other-500*) using K-Means. We then pick the speaker x-vector that is the closest to the centroid of each cluster. The assessment of the anonymization performances will be done for each of those 40 target speaker identities. Real speaker identities are used instead of pseudo-speaker identities derived from multiples speakers.

To evaluate the performances of the anonymization system, we perform the following procedure for the 40 selected target speaker identities. First, we convert all utterances of *Librispeech test-clean* (data corresponding to enrollment and trial) and *Librispeech train-360* to the selected target speaker. Then, we train the ASV model on the anonymized *Librispeech train-360* dataset. Lastly, we evaluate the privacy performances for each of the speakers of *Librispeech test-clean* using the specially trained ASV model. As a result, we obtain one score for each trial speaker of *Librispeech test-clean* and target identities (that is a total of 29 × 40 scores). To evaluate the quality of the conversion process in terms of utility (linked to speech recognition performance), we use a pre-trained ASR model released for the VoicePrivacy Challenge. To study the effectiveness of the F0 anonymization (module D of Fig. 1), we perform the anonymization process, and the associated evaluation, with and without the F0 transformation enabled.

4   Experimental Results

4.1   Global Results

Table 2 compares the anonymization performance on a global scale. The first line presents the linkability when no anonymization is performed (i.e., on original speech data), clean speech encapsulates the speaker's information to a high degree ($D_{\leftrightarrow}^{\mathrm{sys}}$ scores > 0.90). The second and third lines display the linkability when using the voice anonymization system without and with the F0 transformation.

Table 2. Linkability ($D_{\leftrightarrow}^{\mathrm{sys}}$) and EER% scores for original and anonymized speech. For the anonymized data, the mean and standard deviation values are calculated over the 40 experiments (i.e., one for each target speaker). Results on anonymized data are given without and with F0 transformation.

	Female speakers		Male speakers	
	$D_{\leftrightarrow}^{\mathrm{sys}}$	EER%	$D_{\leftrightarrow}^{\mathrm{sys}}$	EER%
Original	0.90	7.66	0.96	1.11
Anon. without F0	0.72 ± 0.01	12.1 ± 0.6	0.77 ± 0.01	9.5 ± 0.6
Anon. with F0	0.74 ± 0.01	11.6 ± 0.6	0.75 ± 0.01	10.6 ± 0.8

In contrast with the original speech results, the anonymized results come from 40 ASV tests, each using a different speaker identity. The mean and standard deviation values are calculated from the 40 evaluations. From the linkability score difference between original and Anon. lines of Table 2 we can conclude that speakers are less linkable to their true identity after applying the x-vector base anonymization system. From the original data to the anonymized speech, linkability scores drop by at least 17%, meaning the anonymization system has some effectiveness. The comparison between the last two lines shows that modifying the F0 values does not help to remove speaker information from the speech signal, as shown by the standard deviation values. This means that the transformation applied was not strong enough to actually remove extra speaker information or that the ASV system is quite robust against such modification. The rather low standard deviation values across all scores show that there is no large variation when changing target speaker identity, this indicates that a given target speaker isn't more suited than another to anonymize the whole dataset. As there are not large scores differences between voice conversion without or with F0 values transformation, the following sections will only analyze the results of the anonymization system that includes the F0 linear transformation.

4.2 Detailed Analysis

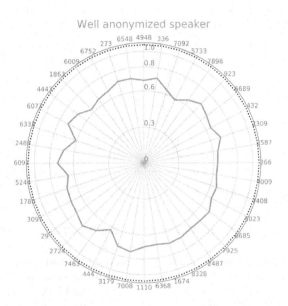

Results on a single test speaker (speaker 5105)

Fig. 3. Linkability scores ($D_{\leftrightarrow}^{\mathrm{sys}}$) obtained using the ASV retrained on anonymized data for each of the 40 target speakers (colored solid line) and on original speech (dotted black circle). Each axis corresponds to a target speaker. The anonymization system lowered the linkability scores, meaning better privacy is achieved. (Color figure online)

We conducted a detailed analysis to check whether a specific target identity is more suited to anonymize one or more speakers of our test dataset. Figure 3 illustrate the visualization used for this study in the case of a single source speaker. The linkability $D_{\leftrightarrow}^{\mathrm{sys}}$ scores are computed for speech anonymized with 40 different x-vectors and F0 statistics.

The black-dot circle indicates the linkability of the speaker on clean original speech signal (note that the original speech does not depend on the target speakers, hence the circle). And, for each of the 40 target speakers, the linkability is presented by the colored solid line. After transforming the speech with 40 target speakers, we can observe that none of the 40 targets are significantly better to anonymize this speaker's voice. The variation between the anonymized linkability scores is more likely due to the difference between the ASV model training rather than a better target choice. This observation also applies to the 29 other speakers of our test dataset. It is also noteworthy that, out of the 40 target identities, 20 of them induce cross-gender voice conversion. Results for same-gender and cross-gender voice anonymization were found similar.

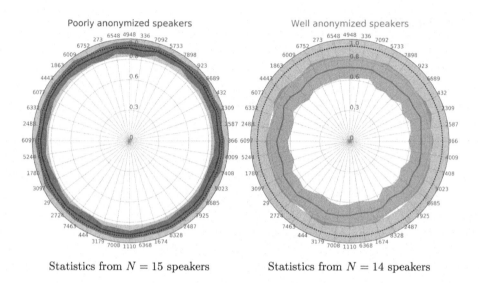

Fig. 4. Mean and standard deviation $D_{\leftrightarrow}^{sys}$ scores obtained for N speakers using retrained ASVs on anonymized data for each of the 40 target speakers (mean and standard deviation corresponding to the colored solid line and light area) and on original speech (dotted black circle and grey area). Each axis corresponds to a target speaker.

Figure 4 shows the linkability $D_{\leftrightarrow}^{sys}$ scores of two groups to illustrate the common anonymization behavior: one for which the anonymization system did not remove speaker information, and the other for which the anonymization did remove some speaker information. For the poorly anonymized speakers, we observe that the distributions of linkability scores on anonymized speech (colored area) completely overlaps the distribution of linkability scores on original speech (grey area). The anonymization system did not remove any speaker information for half of our test speakers. On the other hand, for the well anonymized speakers, the anonymized speech and original speech scores distributions diverge. The difference is distinct, speaker information was removed by the anonymization system for the other half of our test speakers.

4.3 Utility Results

Across all experiments, we evaluated the utility for each 40 target identities. We performed the intelligibility test with the pre-trained ASR system of the VoiecPrivacy challenge. Figure 5 shows the utility scores after anonymization considering each of the 40 target identities. On original clean speech signal, the ASR systems score 4.15 WER$_\%$. When using the same model (trained on clean data) the overall WER$_\%$ on the anonymized data reaches 7.30 WER$_\%$ (average value over the 40 experiments). Retraining the ASR system on anonymized speech improves the WER$_\%$ significantly [17]. The very high utility loss yielded when using speaker 2487 is due to a generalization issue of the anonymization system (with happens with and without the F0 modification), in this case, non-intelligible speech was generated at the beginning of some segments. We conducted an additional test using 100 randomly selected target speaker identities, and were able to find 3 target speaker x-vectors that have the same behavior, with the worse case having a score of 59.37 WER$_\%$. Informal listening test reported that the original speech that produced the faulty x-vector contained singing segments. Further analysis needs to be conducted.

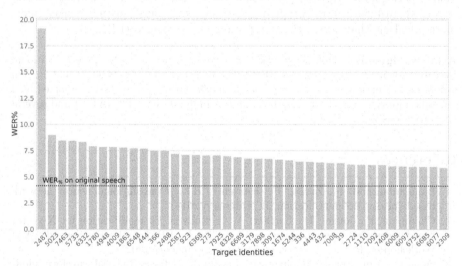

Fig. 5. WER$_\%$ scores obtained by the VoicePrivacy ASR evaluation systems for each of the 40 speakers and on original speech (dotted black line).

5 Conclusion

In this work, we evaluated and analyzed the x-vector-based speaker anonymization system proposed in [3] and F0 extension proposed in [2] under a white-box attack scenario approach and a *constant* target selection strategy. To assess the long-term performance of the voice conversion system and the impact of each of the hyper-parameters (i.e. the x-vector target identity, the F0 linear transformation, and the random gender selection), the use of a *constant* target selection strategy is beneficial. This target selection strategy allows the attacker to have complete knowledge about the system, under those circumstances models and hyper-parameters design choices can be compared as the best attacker will be used to evaluate the anonymization performance.

The experiments done in [2,14] showed that black and grey-box attackers can easily be fooled when enrollment speech and trial speech are anonymized in a different manner, i.e. by selecting the x-vector in different regions, applying the F0 linear transformation and random gender selection. On the contrary, we observed that neither the x-vector target, F0 transformation, or cross-gender conversion actually help to remove the speaker information from the speech signal. We showed that regardless of the hyper-parameters used, privacy protection stays the same. The detailed analysis showed that a given set of hyper-parameters does not help the anonymization system to better anonymize a given source speaker. Furthermore, we concluded that the anonymization system performance depends on the speaker to anonymize, half of our test speakers did not have their privacy improved.

We raise caution on the privacy evaluation procedure, as we've shown that system performance varies depending on the attacker's knowledge and ASV system used. In future work, we plan to evaluate the source of the speaker information leakage that occurs through the phonetic features (PPGs).

Acknowledgments. This work was supported in part by the French National Research Agency under project DEEP-PRIVACY (ANR-18-CE23-0018) and Région Grand Est. Experiments were carried out using the Grid'5000 testbed, supported by a scientific interest group hosted by Inria and including CNRS, RENATER and several Universities as well as other organizations.

References

1. Bahmaninezhad, F., Zhang, C., Hansen, J.H.L.: Convolutional neural network based speaker de-identification. In: Odyssey (2018)
2. Champion, P., Jouvet, D., Larcher, A.: A study of F0 modification for X-vector based speech pseudonymization across gender. In: PPAI 2021 - The Second AAAI Workshop on Privacy-Preserving Artificial Intelligence (2021)
3. Fang, F., et al.: Speaker anonymization using X-vector and neural waveform models. In: 10th ISCA Speech Synthesis Workshop (2019)
4. Gomez-Barrero, M., Galbally, J., Rathgeb, C., Busch, C.: General framework to evaluate unlinkability in biometric template protection systems. IEEE Trans. Inf. Forensics Secur. **13**(6), 1406–1420 (2018)
5. Magariños, C., Lopez-Otero, P., Docio-Fernandez, L., Rodriguez-Banga, E., Erro, D., Garcia-Mateo, C.: Reversible speaker de-identification using pre-trained transformation functions. Comput. Speech Lang. **46**, 36–52 (2017)
6. Maouche, M., Srivastava, B.M.L., Vauquier, N., Bellet, A., Tommasi, M., Vincent, E.: A comparative study of speech anonymization metrics. In: Interspeech (2020)
7. McAdams, S.: Spectral fusion, spectral parsing and the formation of the auditory image. Ph.D. thesis, Stanford (1984)

8. Nautsch, A., Jasserand, C., Kindt, E., Todisco, M., Trancoso, I., Evans, N.: The GDPR & speech data: reflections of legal and technology communities, first steps towards a common understanding. In: Interspeech (2019)

9. Noé, P.G., Bonastre, J.F., Matrouf, D., Tomashenko, N., Nautsch, A., Evans, N.: Speech pseudonymisation assessment using voice similarity matrices. In: Interspeech (2020)

10. European Parliament and of the Council: Regulation (EU) 2016/679 of the European Parliament and of the Council of 27 April 2016. Regulation on the protection of natural persons with regard to the processing of personal data and on the free movement of such data, and repealing Directive 95/46/EC. General Data Protection Regulation (2016)

11. Povey, D., et al.: The kaldi speech recognition toolkit. In: IEEE Workshop on Automatic Speech Recognition and Understanding (2011)

12. Srivastava, B.M.L., Bellet, A., Tommasi, M., Vincent, E.: Privacy-preserving adversarial representation learning in ASR: reality or illusion? In: Interspeech (2019)

13. Srivastava, B.M.L., et al.: Privacy and utility of x-vector based speaker anonymization. Trans. Audio Speech Lang. Process. (2021)

14. Srivastava, B.M.L., et al.: Design choices for x-vector based speaker anonymization. In: Interspeech (2020)

15. Srivastava, B.M.L., Vauquier, N., Sahidullah, M., Bellet, A., Tommasi, M., Vincent, E.: Evaluating voice conversion-based privacy protection against informed attackers. In: IEEE International Conference on Acoustics, Speech, and Signal Processing (2020)

16. Sun, L., Li, K., Wang, H., Kang, S., Meng, H.: Phonetic posteriorgrams for many-to-one voice conversion without parallel data training. In: IEEE International Conference on Multimedia and Expo (2016)

17. Tomashenko, N., et al.: Introducing the VoicePrivacy initiative. In: Interspeech (2020)

Improved Prosodic Clustering for Multispeaker and Speaker-Independent Phoneme-Level Prosody Control

Myrsini Christidou[1]([✉]), Alexandra Vioni[1], Nikolaos Ellinas[1],
Georgios Vamvoukakis[1], Konstantinos Markopoulos[1], Panos Kakoulidis[1],
June Sig Sung[2], Hyoungmin Park[2], Aimilios Chalamandaris[1],
and Pirros Tsiakoulis[1]

[1] Innoetics, Samsung Electronics, Marousi, Greece
{m.christidou,a.vioni}@partner.samsung.com,
{n.ellinas,g.vamvouk}@samsung.com
[2] Mobile Communications Business, Samsung Electronics, Suwon, Republic of Korea

Abstract. This paper presents a method for phoneme-level prosody control of F0 and duration on a multispeaker text-to-speech setup, which is based on prosodic clustering. An autoregressive attention-based model is used, incorporating multispeaker architecture modules in parallel to a prosody encoder. Several improvements over the basic single-speaker method are proposed that increase the prosodic control range and coverage. More specifically we employ data augmentation, F0 normalization, balanced clustering for duration, and speaker-independent prosodic clustering. These modifications enable fine-grained phoneme-level prosody control for all speakers contained in the training set, while maintaining the speaker identity. The model is also fine-tuned to unseen speakers with limited amounts of data and it is shown to maintain its prosody control capabilities, verifying that the speaker-independent prosodic clustering is effective. Experimental results verify that the model maintains high output speech quality and that the proposed method allows efficient prosody control within each speaker's range despite the variability that a multispeaker setting introduces.

Keywords: Controllable text-to-speech synthesis · Fine-grained control · Prosody control · Speaker adaptation

1 Introduction

Neural text-to-speech (TTS) systems, such as Tacotron [24,33], that produce synthetic voice of high quality and naturalness, have paved the way for exploration and control over more elaborate aspects of speech, including prosody and style. In the recent surge of multispeaker and multilingual architectures [21,38], it is valuable to integrate prosodic control mechanisms in such systems by taking advantage of the speaker and prosodic diversity, while also embracing and overcoming the challenges that arise from this heterogeneity.

M. Christidou and A. Vioni—Equal contribution.

© Springer Nature Switzerland AG 2021
A. Karpov and R. Potapova (Eds.): SPECOM 2021, LNAI 12997, pp. 112–123, 2021.
https://doi.org/10.1007/978-3-030-87802-3_11

1.1 Related Work

Since basic neural TTS systems model the average speaking style of the training data, style control is traditionally exerted by using extended models conditioned on a style embedding space [25] that is learned in an unsupervised way. These approaches introduce a Global Style Tokens (GSTs) module [34], or a Variational Autoencoder (VAE) [2,12,37] to learn latent representations of prosody in utterance-level prosody control or transfer. In addition, fine-grained control at frame-level, phoneme-level or word-level resolutions can be achieved using temporal constraints [18], hierarchical modeling [5,26,27], or adversarial learning [8]. In [9], phoneme-level prosody embeddings are modeled using a Gaussian mixture model (GMM) based mixture density network (MDN).

Explicit control over prosodic features such as F0 and duration by extracting these features and using them as input to a prosody encoder has been implemented for utterance-level [11,22,23] and more fine-grained [15,20,31,35] control. In [1], data augmentation is applied to extend the voice range in terms of F0 and duration, and note embeddings are used in parallel to the phoneme sequence, to pursue singing synthesis. [17] inserts prosodic symbols to the phoneme sequence to model accents, pauses, and sentence endings.

Regarding multispeaker systems, several approaches for prosody control and transfer have been carried through. Mellotron [28] constitutes a multispeaker voice synthesis model conditioned on rhythm and continuous pitch contours, that can generate expressive and singing voice. In [19], a controllable voice cloning model based on Tacotron 2, conditioned on a speaker embedding, pitch contour and latent style tokens, enables fine-grained style transfer for an unseen speaker. [16] proposes a method for few-shot speaker adaptation and generation of an unseen speaker's style by incorporating a non-autoregressive feed-forward Transformer along with adaptive normalization. Adversarial learning was employed in [14] to avoid source speaker leakage in prosody transfer tasks, and in [32] to ensure prosodic disentanglement in voice conversion. Also, in [36], a multispeaker Transformer-based model with an ASR module and an utterance-level prosody encoder is fine-tuned to the target speaker for prosody transfer.

However, all the aforementioned approaches for multispeaker prosody control refer to utterance level control; or to a generic prosodic style in the case of a more detailed scale. Alternatively, we propose speaker independent phoneme-level prosody control over F0 and duration in a multispeaker system. Furthermore, we show that the proposed method is feasible even for new speakers with very limited data, as the system maintains the prosody control capability after fine-tuning the model.

1.2 Proposed Method

In this paper we apply prosodic clustering for multispeaker phoneme-level prosody control of F0 and duration in TTS. The discretization and grouping of these features into clusters provides great controllability over prosody in synthesized speech [29], however limited inside the speaker's range since the outermost clusters contain more extreme values which are not frequent in the training data. Using the model for unseen speaker adaptation, would also cause the single speaker clustering method to fail due to the different speaker characteristics.

To address these problems, we have incorporated several preprocessing steps and we have adapted the prosodic clustering method for multispeaker TTS. We apply augmentation transformations to the training data [1], in order to increase the number of samples in the outermost clusters. To minimize stability issues in duration control, we have adopted a balanced duration clustering strategy, assigning an equal number of samples in each cluster instead of using K-Means, as it was done in the single speaker model for both f0 and duration. In addition, we introduce per speaker normalization of F0 with the purpose of neutralizing speaker and gender variations, essentially offering speaker-independent control over the same prosodic space.

The aforementioned modifications allow us to create universal, speaker-independent clusters for F0 and duration. Thus, prosody control capabilities can be extended to previously unseen speakers, after fine-tuning the model with only a few samples. Overall, the contributions of this work are the following: (i) data augmentation for increased control range, (ii) speaker independent clustering via F0 normalization, (iii) balanced duration clustering for better stability, and (iv) speaker adaptation with limited data while maintaining controllability.

2   Method

2.1   Multispeaker Model

The model presented in [29] is adapted to a multispeaker architecture. It is an autoregressive attention-based text-to-speech model, that receives an input sequence of phonemes $p = [p_1, ..., p_N]$ and sequences of F0 and duration tokens $f = [f_1, ..., f_M]$, $d = [d_1, ..., d_M]$ which are jointly referred to as prosodic features.

Each phoneme has a corresponding token for F0 and duration, while word boundaries and punctuation marks do not receive any such tokens, therefore $M < N$. The phoneme sequence is passed into a text encoder which produces a text encoder representation $e = [e_1, ..., e_N]$ and the prosodic feature sequences are concatenated and then passed into a prosody encoder which produces the prosody encoder representation $e' = [e'_1, ..., e'_M]$. On the decoder side, apart from the MoL (Mixture of Logistic distributions) attention module responsible for producing a robust phoneme alignment [10], we use an extra module for the alignment of the prosodic representations. As mentioned in [29], we do not wish the prosodic attention context vector to contain any phoneme information, so we choose to process the prosodic sequence with a separate attention module to enforce this condition.

Each speaker is mapped to a 64-dimensional learnable embedding, which is used to condition the decoder. A variational residual encoder [12] is implemented to model any additional information included in the audio samples other than speaker identity, text and prosodic features, like acoustic conditions and noise.

An adversarial speaker classifier similar to [38] is also added, to induce disentanglement of the phoneme representations and the speakers' identity. The architecture is presented in Fig. 1.

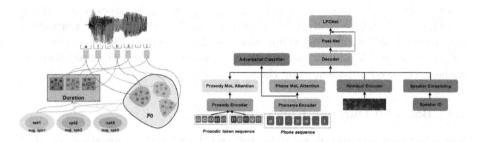

Fig. 1. Multispeaker Prosody Control Model. The prosodic features are firstly clustered. The normalization applied to each cluster is common for every speaker. The single speaker architecture was modified with an Adversarial Classifier, Speaker Embedding and Residual Encoder in order to enable the model to train on multiple speakers.

2.2 Dataset Augmentation

In order to make our system more robust, we have employed voice data augmentation to widen the speaker range regarding F0 and duration, and to increase the number of samples in each cluster, as seen in previous multispeaker [6] and singing synthesis [1,3] papers. The data transformations applied are: pitch shifting by [−6, −4, −2, 2, 4, 6] semitones, and tempo changes by altering speaking rate to [0.70, 0.80, 0.90, 1.10, 1.20, 1.30] of the original one, using the Praat Vocal Toolkit [7]. The selection of alterations to be applied on the utterances was made similarly to [1] so that adequate augmentation was added to enhance the training data, whilst no distortion was introduced to the produced audio. Specifically, we have applied one of these twelve transformations to each spoken utterance in our dataset, with the resulting dataset being double in size compared to the initial one.

We perform clustering on our augmented dataset together with the original one to get new cluster centroids that correspond to the widened F0 and duration ranges. The proposed augmentation method extends the prosodic range, while also enhancing model robustness and voice quality.

2.3 F0 Normalization

Since different speakers have different pitch ranges it is not practical to cluster the F0 values of each speaker separately. We first apply z-score normalization to each speaker's extracted F0 values, and then cluster the normalized values of all speakers together to obtain universal F0 centroids. Thus for each phoneme's corresponding pitch in the dataset we apply:

$$F_0 = \frac{f - \mu_i}{\sigma_i}, i \in speakers \tag{1}$$

where f is the unnormalized F0 and μ, σ are the mean and variance of the respective speaker's F0 values. This way, we deal with gender and speaker variation in pitch and create a mapping from each speaker's F0 values to a common prosodic space, where clustering can be performed universally. The normalization method also facilitates adding new speakers, because the normalized F0 values of the new speakers can be directly mapped to the universal centroids without the need of recomputing them.

2.4 Balanced Duration Clustering

Regarding phoneme durations, it is observed that, for the same phone, typical duration ranges are similar across all speakers, thus duration normalization is not necessary before clustering. However, results from our previous work [29] show that voice quality deterioration is mostly noted in duration control when using the outermost clusters, and not so much in F0 control. Thus, we have adopted a different scheme for extracting duration clusters. Following the single speaker method, clustering is still performed per phoneme, but the K-means algorithm is replaced with a simple balanced clustering method; the average phoneme duration values are sorted in ascending order and grouped into the desired number of intervals, so that each interval contains an equal number of samples. We observe that using this grouping strategy slightly decreases the duration control range, as extreme values are averaged out by being pushed towards the bulk of more frequent phoneme durations, but more importantly increases the duration control stability.

2.5 Speaker Adaptation

The same method as described in the sections above was used to investigate the feasibility of fine-grained prosody control on a previously unseen speaker with a very small number of samples. Extra attention was given so that the selected sentences, that were to be used in the new training, would provide enough phonetic coverage. This means that the utterances would contain each phoneme at least once.

After applying augmentation and z-score normalization to the new speaker's data, we fine-tuned our pretrained model by replacing one of the speakers in the training set with the new speaker. We experimented with various recording time lengths in order to test the model's limits and investigate how many minutes of recorded speech is needed to achieve similar quality results with the speakers in the training set. We found that even with as few as 5.7 min of recordings our model was able not only to reproduce that speaker's voice, but also to manipulate phoneme-level F0 and duration in a similar manner to the voices in our training set.

3   Experiments and Results

An initial multispeaker model is trained on an internal dataset containing three female and two male speakers for a total of 159.7 h of speech. The preprocessing methods described in Sect. 2 are applied to all voice data. A randomly selected augmentation is applied to each utterance in order to create new augmented speakers, doubling the size of the original multispeaker dataset. Considering each speaker together with their augmented version as a new set, z-score normalization of the extracted F0 values is applied for each speaker separately. The duration labels are computed with balanced clustering, while the K-Means algorithm was used to find the optimal centroids for F0 values, with the selected number of clusters both for F0 and duration being fixed to 15. Since the duration values do not vary much from speaker to speaker and the F0 values are normalized, the values of each feature lie in the same space, so the two methods are applied on the full augmented dataset with all of the speakers mixed together.

In order to evaluate the effectiveness of adapting the multispeaker model to unseen speakers, we use the voice of Catherine Byers (Cathy) from the 2013 Blizzard Challenge in two training setups. The first one, referred to as *Cathy-multi*, is a model trained on the multispeaker dataset mentioned above, with the addition of Cathy, resulting in a total duration of 223.9 h. This model is used to generate samples from the target speaker when they are included in the initial training, utilizing their full set of data. For the second model, *Cathy-adapt*, we select 100 recordings from the Cathy dataset containing 7.72 min of speech and fine-tune the initial 5-voice multispeaker model. The selection of recordings is done with a method introduced in [4] which sorts utterances of a speech corpus in descending order of phonological diversity, in order to maximize the phonetic coverage in a small collection of recordings.

The initial multispeaker model is also adapted to another 2 female and 2 male unseen voices by applying the speaker adaptation process independently for each one, in order to obtain results from different target speakers and genders. For this task, we use the LJ Speech dataset [13], an audiobook male voice and two additional internal voices, one female and one male. The corpus selection process to ensure phonetic coverage with 100 sentences for each voice resulted in 10.24, 5.7, 10.83, and 13.17 min of speech respectively. By using these limited data we obtain the respective speaker adapted models, namely *LJ-adapt*, *Audiobook-male-adapt*, *Female-adapt* and *Male-adapt*.

The same preprocessing steps for augmentation, duration and F0 clustering as described above are applied to the adaptation speakers. An important change is that, since the goal is to integrate the new speaker into the already trained model, the duration intervals and F0 centroids are not recomputed, but rather used as pretrained values from the full length multispeaker dataset in order to find the corresponding target speaker values. This process does not introduce any inconsistencies as the normalized F0 values of the new speakers lie in the same universal space with the initial training dataset. The model is fine-tuned for

5K iterations as a single speaker model, after replacing one of the initial speaker identities with the target speaker to obtain the desired voice characteristics.

The voices used in our experiments were of native US English speakers. All audio data was resampled at 24 kHz and the extracted acoustic features consist of 20 Bark-scale cepstral coefficients, the pitch period and pitch correlation, in order to match the modified LPCNet vocoder [30]. The proposed model follows the same architecture as in [29] for the phoneme encoder, prosody encoder, attention mechanism and decoder with the additions described in Sect. 2.1.

For the objective and subjective tests we selected 100 utterances from Catherine Byers' dataset, which were excluded from the training data. Those were used to extract the ground truth prosodic labels. In general, the model is able to synthesize arbitrary text provided that the corresponding prosodic labels are specified; predicted by a separate model, or extracted from a reference utterance.

3.1   Objective Evaluation

In order to evaluate the control capability of the proposed model, a test set is generated for each speaker by assigning the prosody tokens of each sentence to a single cluster in an ascending order. Specifically, this process is applied at one prosodic category at a time, keeping the other category's tokens at their ground truth values.

In Fig. 2 the mean values of F0 and phoneme duration are depicted, calculated over the extracted features of every synthesized test utterance modified according to the specific cluster ID shown in the horizontal axis. The depicted models belong to the configurations Cathy-multi, Cathy-adapt, Female-adapt and Male-adapt. We can observe that all models follow the ascending order of the cluster IDs both in F0 and duration variations, proving that controllability is retained in the multispeaker setup. Cathy-multi and Cathy-adapt perform alike and obtain similar values for the same cluster IDs, proving that prosody control in the same range is possible even with a few data, compared to a large speaker dataset. The rest of the adaptation models present a same ascending behavior, with the male voices assuming lower F0 values from the female ones, despite being trained with a common set of prosodic labels, indicating that our method is indeed speaker and gender independent.

Audio samples of utterance-level and word-level prosodic control are available on our website. Phoneme-level manipulation of F0 and duration is also demonstrated, for which no established protocol exists for objective evaluation. We encourage readers to listen to the audio samples: https://innoetics.github.io/publications/multispeaker-prosody-control/index.html.

3.2   Subjective Evaluation

We performed listening tests in order to assess the quality of the proposed method, with respect to naturalness and speaker similarity. Regarding naturalness, the set of the chosen 100 sentences which were excluded from the training data and modified in terms of F0 and duration were used to synthesize voice

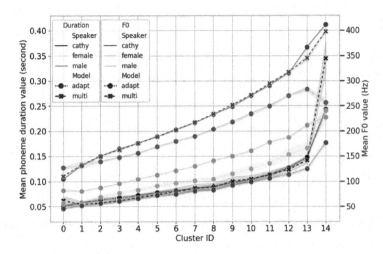

Fig. 2. Sentence level mean F0 and average phoneme duration for ascending cluster IDs with 95% confidence intervals. The left y-axis corresponds to the duration graphs while the right y-axis corresponds to the F0 graphs.

samples from Cathy-multi, Cathy-adapt and Male-adapt models. Listeners were asked to score the samples' naturalness on a 5-point Likert scale.

F0 and duration modification was done by adding or subtracting an offset from the ground truth prosodic labels of each test sentence, with the offsets varying in range $[-11, +11]$. This was straightforward, since the proposed labels for both prosodic features range from 0–14 and are represented as so. Regarding F0, adding or subtracting an offset from the ground truth value leads to synthesized voice with higher or lower pitch, whilst regarding duration, these offsets lead to slower or faster uttered phones, respectively. This method, which verifies the controllability of the model, is now used to evaluate naturalness.

In order to facilitate the Mean Opinion Score (MOS) results' visualization, each prosodic feature was modified independently, while the labels of the other feature retained their ground truth values. In total, 2400 test utterances were rated for naturalness, with each one receiving 20 scores by native speakers via the Amazon Mechanical Turk.

The MOS is depicted as a function of the modification offset in Fig. 3 for the Cathy-multi and the Cathy-adapt models, and in Fig. 4 for the Male-adapt model. Based on the plots, it can be said that the voice samples with modified prosodic tokens retain reasonable naturalness levels in general, with the exception of very low duration offsets. These offsets correspond to extremely fast speech which is generally considered unnatural. Moreover, MOS scores of the voice samples produced by Cathy-adapt are directly comparable in naturalness with the scores of Cathy-multi, over the full modification range, as it can be seen in Fig. 3. Hence, it is shown that, despite been trained with very limited data, the speaker-adapted models' capability of prosodic modification also preserves high voice naturalness, in levels similar to the multispeaker model, which was trained with the full dataset.

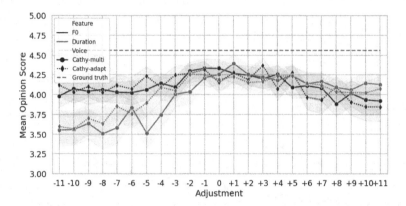

Fig. 3. Mean opinion scores for Cathy-multi and Cathy-adapt with 95% confidence intervals.

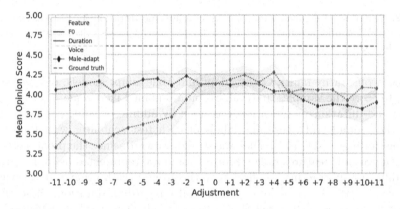

Fig. 4. Mean opinion scores for Male-adapt with 95% confidence intervals.

Regarding speaker similarity, listening tests were performed to evaluate speaker adaptation with limited data. For each speaker adapted model, 20 samples synthesized with ground truth prosodic labels were compared to a reference audio of the respective speaker. Listeners were asked to rate speaker similarity on a 5-point Likert scale. Each utterance received 40 scores by native speakers via the Amazon Mechanical Turk.

Table 1. Speaker similarity MOS for speaker adaptation with 95% confidence intervals.

Voice	Speaker similarity
Cathy-adapt	3.506 ± 0.140
LJ-adapt	3.000 ± 0.142
Female-adapt	3.858 ± 0.124
Male-adapt	3.942 ± 0.117
Audiobook-male-adapt	3.633 ± 0.121

By observing the results in Table 1, it is evident that speaker similarity is adequate for all voices, taking into consideration that speaker adaptation was performed with only few minutes of speech from each speaker, and very satisfactory for the internal voices. Our speaker similarity MOS scores range between values in the same area as the MOS of previous works on multispeaker and speaker adaptation TTS [36, 38]. It can be said that the speaker similarity MOS scores correlate well with the voice recordings quality, since they are higher for internal voices with clear recordings, but deteriorate for voice datasets where noise and artifacts are present.

4   Conclusion

In this paper, we expand upon our previous work on fine-grained prosody control from a single speaker to any number of speakers without compromising the quality of generated speech. We apply augmentation, feature normalization and a universal clustering method for all speakers' recordings so that we can produce universal F0 and duration clusters for training. The same principles are applied to new, previously unseen speakers with very few recordings, in order to test if this method can be used to create synthetic speech similar to the target voice with the same quality and level of control.

Our experiments verify that the multispeaker and speaker adapted models retain the control capability over F0 and duration and generate high quality speech, independently of gender or different voice characteristics. Moreover, the speaker adapted models' scores indicate reasonable similarity to the original speakers' audio, given the short duration and variable quality of the recordings across speakers.

References

1. Angelini, O., Moinet, A., Yanagisawa, K., Drugman, T.: Singing synthesis: with a little help from my attention. In: Proceedings of Interspeech (2020)
2. Battenberg, E., et al.: Effective use of variational embedding capacity in expressive end-to-end speech synthesis. arXiv:1906.03402 (2019)
3. Blaauw, M., Bonada, J.: A neural parametric singing synthesizer modeling timbre and expression from natural songs. Appl. Sci. **7**(12), 1313 (2017)

4. Chalamandaris, A., Tsiakoulis, P., Raptis, S., Karabetsos, S.: Corpus design for a unit selection TTS system with application to Bulgarian. In: Proceedings of 4th Conference on Human Language Technology: Challenges for Computer Science and Linguistics, pp. 35–46 (2009)
5. Chien, C.M., Lee, H.: Hierarchical prosody modeling for non-autoregressive speech synthesis. In: Proceedings of SLT (2021)
6. Cooper, E., Lai, C.I., Yasuda, Y., Yamagishi, J.: Can speaker augmentation improve multi-speaker end-to-end TTS? In: Proceedings of Interspeech (2020)
7. Corretge, R.: Praat Vocal Toolkit (2012–2020). http://www.praatvocaltoolkit.com
8. Daxin, T., Tan, L.: Fine-grained style modelling and transfer in text-to-speech synthesis via content-style disentanglement. arXiv:2011.03943 (2020)
9. Du, C., Yu, K.: Mixture Density Network for Phone-Level Prosody Modelling in Speech Synthesis. arXiv:2102.00851 (2021)
10. Ellinas, N., et al.: High quality streaming speech synthesis with low, sentence-length-independent latency. In: Proceedings of Interspeech (2020)
11. Gururani, S., Gupta, K., Shah, D., Shakeri, Z., Pinto, J.: Prosody Transfer in Neural Text to Speech Using Global Pitch and Loudness Features. arXiv:1911.09645 (2019)
12. Hsu, W.N., et al.: Hierarchical generative modeling for controllable speech synthesis. In: Proceedings of ICLR (2018)
13. Ito, K., Johnson, L.: The LJ Speech Dataset (2017). https://keithito.com/LJ-Speech-Dataset
14. Karlapati, S., Moinet, A., Joly, A., Klimkov, V., Sáez-Trigueros, D., Drugman, T.: CopyCat: many-to-many fine-grained prosody transfer for neural text-to-speech. In: Proceedings of Interspeech (2020)
15. Klimkov, V., Ronanki, S., Rohnke, J., Drugman, T.: Fine-grained robust prosody transfer for single-speaker neural text-to-speech. In: Proceedings of Interspeech (2019)
16. Kumar, N., Goel, S., Narang, A., Lall, B.: Few Shot Adaptive Normalization Driven Multi-Speaker Speech Synthesis. arXiv:2012.07252 (2020)
17. Kurihara, K., Seiyama, N., Kumano, T.: Prosodic features control by symbols as input of sequence-to-sequence acoustic modeling for neural TTS. IEICE Trans. Inf. Syst. **E104.D**(2), 302–311 (2021)
18. Lee, Y., Kim, T.: Robust and fine-grained prosody control of end-to-end speech synthesis. In: Proceedings of ICASSP (2019)
19. Neekhara, P., Hussain, S., Dubnov, S., Koushanfar, F., McAuley, J.: Expressive Neural Voice Cloning. arXiv:2102.00151 (2021)
20. Park, J., Han, K., Jeong, Y., Lee, S.W.: Phonemic-level duration control using attention alignment for natural speech synthesis. In: Proceedings of ICASSP (2019)
21. Ping, W., et al.: Deep voice 3: scaling text-to-speech with convolutional sequence learning. In: Proceedings of ICLR (2018)
22. Raitio, T., Rasipuram, R., Castellani, D.: Controllable neural text-to-speech synthesis using intuitive prosodic features. In: Proceedings of Interspeech (2020)
23. Shechtman, S., Sorin, A.: Sequence to sequence neural speech synthesis with prosody modification capabilities. In: Proceedings of SSW (2019)
24. Shen, J., et al.: Natural TTS synthesis by conditioning WaveNet on mel spectrogram predictions. In: Proceedings of ICASSP (2018)
25. Skerry-Ryan, R., et al.: Towards end-to-end prosody transfer for expressive speech synthesis with Tacotron. In: Proceedings of ICML (2018)

26. Sun, G., et al.: Generating diverse and natural text-to-speech samples using a quantized fine-grained VAE and autoregressive prosody prior. In: Proceedings of ICASSP (2020)
27. Sun, G., Zhang, Y., Weiss, R.J., Cao, Y., Zen, H., Wu, Y.: Fully-hierarchical fine-grained prosody modeling for interpretable speech synthesis. In: Proceedings of ICASSP (2020)
28. Valle, R., Li, J., Prenger, R., Catanzaro, B.: Mellotron: multispeaker expressive voice synthesis by conditioning on rhythm, pitch and global style tokens. In: Proceedings of ICASSP (2020)
29. Vioni, A., et al.: Prosodic clustering for phoneme-level prosody control in end-to-end speech synthesis. In: Proceedings of ICASSP (2021)
30. Vipperla, R., et al.: Bunched LPCNet: vocoder for low-cost neural text-to-speech systems. In: Proceedings of Interspeech (2020)
31. Wan, V., an Chan, C., Kenter, T., Vit, J., Clark, R.: CHiVE: varying prosody in speech synthesis with a linguistically driven dynamic hierarchical conditional variational network. In: Proceedings of ICML (2019)
32. Wang, J., Li, J., Zhao, X., Wu, Z., Meng, H.: Adversarially learning disentangled speech representations for robust multi-factor voice conversion. arXiv:2102.00184 (2021)
33. Wang, Y., et al.: Tacotron: towards end-to-end speech synthesis. In: Proceedings of Interspeech (2017)
34. Wang, Y., et al.: Style tokens: unsupervised style modeling, control and transfer in end-to-end speech synthesis. In: Proceedings of ICML (2018)
35. Zhang, G., Qin, Y., Lee, T.: Learning syllable-level discrete prosodic representation for expressive speech generation. In: Proceedings of Interspeech (2020)
36. Zhang, J.X., et al.: Voice Conversion by Cascading Automatic Speech Recognition and Text-to-Speech Synthesis with Prosody Transfer. arXiv:2009.01475 (2020)
37. Zhang, Y.J., Pan, S., He, L., Ling, Z.H.: Learning latent representations for style control and transfer in end-to-end speech synthesis. In: Proceedings of ICASSP (2019)
38. Zhang, Y., et al.: Learning to speak fluently in a foreign language: multilingual speech synthesis and cross-language voice cloning. In: Proceedings of Interspeech (2019)

Initial Experiments on Question Answering from the Intrinsic Structure of Oral History Archives

Adam Chýlek[(✉)] [ID], Jan Švec [ID], and Luboš Šmídl [ID]

NTIS, University of West Bohemia, Pilsen, Czech Republic
{chylek,honzas}@ntis.zcu.cz, smidl@kky.zcu.cz

Abstract. Large audio archives with spoken content are natural candidates for question answering systems. Oral history archives generally contain many facts and stories that would be otherwise hard to obtain without listening to hours of recordings. We strive for making the archive more accessible by allowing natural language question answering. In this paper, we present challenges our dataset poses. We propose our initial approach that uses questions and answers mined from the archive itself and evaluate the performance in experiments with pretrained language representation and question answering models.

Keywords: Question answering · Datasets · Transformers · The MALACH archive

1 Introduction

Oral history is a method of preserving historical records [1]. It is also a process of conducting an interview during which the interviewer guides the narrator of historically significant events to gain insight into their memories and history. This gives us spoken accounts and subjective opinions that are kept as audio and video recordings to later act as research sources that help us interpret and understand past events. Oral history archives should therefore be transcribed, indexed, or summarized to enable their interpretation.

The Visual History Archive of Holocaust testimonies contains a large amount of information about the Holocaust, general history, and personal stories of Holocaust witnesses in spoken form. The archive is maintained by the USC Shoah Foundation[1], its collection was initiated by the Shoah Visual History Foundation founded by Steven Spielberg. The English part of the dataset [13] contains hundreds of hours of video footage. This makes exploring this valuable resource challenging for historians and the general public.

The research started as part of the Multilingual Access to Large Spoken Archives (MALACH) project[2], hence we reference the USC Shoah Foundation

---

[1] https://sfi.usc.edu/.
[2] https://malach.umiacs.umd.edu/.

© Springer Nature Switzerland AG 2021
A. Karpov and R. Potapova (Eds.): SPECOM 2021, LNAI 12997, pp. 124–133, 2021.
https://doi.org/10.1007/978-3-030-87802-3_12

Visual History Archive as the MALACH Archive. As part of this and subsequent projects, the authors of [14] developed a search engine that allowed searching for any arbitrary text in these audio-visual (AV) archives. Their approach uses automatic speech recognition (ASR) to transcribe speech from the audio recordings [11,15] and then create a searchable index. The use of that engine is similar to the use of full-text search engines - the user provides several words as a query and the system retrieves the AV footage in which the words are uttered. Although it is certainly useful in cases when users know the exact words they want to look for, it is unable to find paraphrases of the user's input and it can not cope with input in natural language.

The motivation for our current research is to build on top of that system and allow the user to ask natural language questions and still receive pointers to the exact time in the AV footage where there are answers to those questions. The user should be able to ask for information mentioned in current footage or, in combination with document retrieval, ask general questions with the entire archive as its knowledge base. As the entire interview's footage can be returned, the user will then be free to explore the answer's context, making the exploration of the archive easier.

For the MALACH archive, we have created a QA system based mainly on expert-defined rules [3]. The knowledge base of this system is limited to a handful of entities (e.g. names, cities, dates). The user's query is transformed into a database search query using several rules. If entities are found in the database the system returns a list of possible answers together with a pointer to the exact time in the AV footage when each answer was uttered. Although this approach allows for a quick transfer to different domains and easy expansion of the knowledge base, its range will always be limited to the expert-defined entities. In our current research, we want to allow users to ask general questions without prior knowledge of what the experts defined as searchable.

It is common that QA systems use a combination of self-supervised learning for language representation and supervised learning for the question answering based on those learned representations. Usually, the datasets used to train the models are created by humans, making it expensive to create new datasets for new domains. We present our experiments that evaluate the possible use of pretrained models in combination with information already present in the MALACH archive. This evaluation should also provide enough insight for future research, e.g. whether this approach is at all viable, which additional data would be needed to improve the performance, or which elements of the proposed approach can be omitted.

We describe in Sect. 3 how we leverage the underlying structure of our dataset to obtain our in-domain QA data. These are used to fine-tune the pretrained models to fit our dataset and the experimental pipelines are evaluated in Sect. 4. The results and our long-term plan on using this QA pipeline as part of a dialogue system are discussed in Sect. 5.

2   Related Work

The question answering tasks have several large publicly available datasets that are commonly used as a starting point for QA systems that are intended to be used in novel domains or with novel machine learning structures. We were inspired by the use of pretrained models in the EfficientQA [8] challenge, although the main goal of that challenge was to create open-domain QA systems and we want to create a system more specific to our domain. Similarly to these systems, we will be using text documents, but the form of those documents differs. Common QA systems are using written encyclopedic text, whereas we will be using transcripts of natural spoken conversations. Also contrary to the approaches used in the challenge, we use only an extractive question-answering [16] approach that retrieves the answer and its span in the context that supports the answer. Although generative question-answering approaches or the combination of both approaches show promising results [6], our ultimate goal is to return a pointer to a spoken segment with the answer and its context. That would be impossible with the generative approach.

There are also annotations for the evaluation of topic detection or information retrieval systems [9] for the MALACH archive. These annotations are limited to hand-picked keywords or topics assigned to segments of output from an automatic speech recognition system (ASR). They can not be used for our task as they do not contain any questions or answers by themselves and since they even lack any time alignment information, they cannot be easily used with human transcriptions or better-performing ASR. We also note that similar oral history archives exist and could benefit from our research, like [18] or the Czech version of the MALACH archive [10].

3   Approach

Based on the related work we use pretrained neural network models for language representation and fine-tune them for our QA task using supervised learning. The data for fine-tuning are mined from the dataset itself (and optionally from an open-domain QA dataset). This approach should allow us to bootstrap further research and make the collection of human-made annotation simpler. To understand why mining is possible, we first describe the MALACH archive.

3.1   Creating the Mined MALACH QA Corpus

The English part of the MALACH archive has several hours of speech in interviews that are even transcribed by human annotators. These transcriptions also contain information about the current speaker (i.e. interviewer or interviewee). We will be using this reference transcription as the source of question-answer pairs and to train the language model networks.

Approximately 17% of the reference transcriptions contain punctuation and that allowed us to identify a question simply by looking for a question mark. We

```
"id": "20040-002-1", "start": 1478, "end": 1541,
"question": "how did they kill the people?",
"answer": "they would shoot 'em, they would drag 'em,
           they would hang 'em.",
"context": [...] was like, you know, it was like part
           of your daily routine. they would shoot 'em,
           they would drag 'em, they would hang 'em.
           They would show you, he- here's [...]
```

Fig. 1. Sample from the mMQA dataset with its context shortened for brevity.

manually sampled some of the questions from an interviewer. We then added the interviewee's answers that immediately followed the interviewer's question. From these samples, we concluded that the answers are truly related to the question and that we can obtain the immediate context for that answer. We have decided to pursue this idea of questions and answers coming from the intrinsic structure of the interviews and use this approach to obtain all the data necessary to train neural network models for the question answering task.

Since most of the reference transcriptions were lacking punctuation, we used a punctuation restoration method based on the work of [2] to add punctuation to all the reference transcripts. This approach uses the RoBERTa-large pretrained language model as the transformer encoder model, followed by a bidirectional LSTM layer and a linear layer that predicts target punctuation token at each sequence position. We then used the question marks to detect the questions and full stops to detect the end of the answer.

This technique yielded 10197 questions and answers. We also require the context and indices of the answer's span in that context. We process the data in the following way:

- Filter the pairs based on simple criteria of the minimal number 3 of words in the question and the maximal number of 20 words in the answer.
- Add the original context of the answer. The interviewee's utterances both preceding and following the answer are kept in this step. We ignore any interruptions from the interviewer and add the utterances to the answer's context as if no interruptions happened.
- Assign a random position to the answer and slice the context accordingly.

This resulted in what we reference as the mined MALACH question answering dataset (mMQA) of 7132, 891, and 891 samples for training, validation, and testing, respectively. An example of this dataset is in Fig. 1. The average sentence length was 10.5 words for questions and 6.5 words for answers.

The MALACH transcriptions enriched with punctuation are also used for the language model fine-tuning, giving us a corpus of 143946 sentences. Each sentence consists of 12.4 words on average.

Table 1. Statistics of the mMQA and SQuAD datasets.

Dataset	Training samples	Validation samples	Avg. question length (words)	Avg. answer length (words)
mMQA	7132	891	10.5	6.5
SQuAD	130319	11873	9.9	3.2

3.2   Transformer Neural Networks

Based on the overview of related research we have chosen the transformer neural networks for the question answering task. These networks have unprecedented performance on a large range of natural language processing tasks.

The transformer networks with pretrained parameters from their original papers and repositories will be used as a starting point for further training, or fine-tuning. We designed several fine-tuning steps as part of a training pipeline and we conduct experiments with different pipelines that we use to obtain the best performing pipeline for our use case.

3.3   Experimental Setup

We want to compare the performance of the unchanged pretrained models and the effect the fine-tuning steps have on the performance of the system. We will be using the exact match (EM) and F1 score as our evaluation metrics since these are the standard metrics reported for the SQuAD [12] benchmark as well.

For the EM score, we compare whether the best answer prediction matches fully the ground truth answer. For the F1 score, we measure the overlap of the tokenized best prediction and the tokenized ground truth answer.

Our experiments will be in the form of a pipeline that starts with pre-trained language representation models. We use the Huggingface Transformers framework [17] to obtain the structure and weights for the transformer models and to fine-tune on the question-answering task. This framework also handles the tokenization of the datasets using the correct tokenizer for each pretrained model.

We have selected the models and their pretrained parameters based on the prevalence in related QA papers and their reported performance on QA tasks such as the SQuAD. The amount of the GPU memory on NVIDIA A100 cards we used for these experiments was also a factor. We will be conducting the experiments with BERT (the base, uncased variant, [5]), ALBERT (large, [7]), and ELECTRA (large, [4]) pretrained models. Since the research in this field is very active and new models or ensembles of models compete for the state-of-the-art status on QA tasks, we consider the selected models as a good starting point for our evaluation with possible improvements left for future research.

Several combinations of fine-tuning steps were designed. As an optional first step, the base language representation model (e.g. BERT) can be further pretrained using the sentences from the MALACH transcribed recordings (the TRS step). Our motivation is to see whether pretraining the language representation

Table 2. The values of the hyperparameters: learning rate (LR), batch size (BS), and number of epochs for the fine-tuning steps.

Model name	Step	Batch size	Learning rate	# of epochs
BERT	TRS	32	$2 \cdot 10^{-5}$	20
	SQ	32	$2 \cdot 10^{-5}$	2
	mMQA	32	$1 \cdot 10^{-6}$	20
ALBERT	TRS	8	$2 \cdot 10^{-5}$	10
	SQ	8	$2 \cdot 10^{-5}$	2
	mMQA	8	$1 \cdot 10^{-6}$	5
ELECTRA	TRS	8	$2 \cdot 10^{-5}$	20
	SQ	8	$2 \cdot 10^{-5}$	2
	mMQA	8	$1 \cdot 10^{-6}$	5

to our domain is at all useful or whether the QA steps that follow can handle that all by themselves.

We are evaluating the impact of using open domain question answering dataset SQuAD during the fine-tuning steps (referred to as SQ step). This dataset provides 130319 training samples. The 7132 training samples from the mMQA dataset are used in the QA fine-tuning step either alone or in combination with the SQ step. See Table 1 for additional dataset statistics. The hyperparameter values were set per base model (BERT, ALBERT, ELECTRA) and they are in Table 2.

We call the combinations of the pretraining and fine-tuning steps a pipeline. The pipelines are named by the order in which the steps are executed during training. For example, "TRS-SQ" is a pipeline that has the base language representation model pretrained first on the TRS data and the resulting model is then fine-tuned for QA on the SQ dataset. On the other hand, an "SQ-mMQA" pipeline does keep the base language representation model intact and directly proceeds to first fine-tune the QA task on the SQ dataset and then on the mMQA dataset.

Another part of the mMQA dataset (891 testing samples) is used for the evaluation of all the pipelines. We consider the SQ pipeline as our baseline since the performance of that pipeline is not tuned to our domain.

4   Results and Discussion

The exact match and F1 metrics for the combinations of fine-tuning steps are in Table 3.

Looking at the baseline pipeline SQ, we can conclude that using the large (albeit marginally related) SQuAD dataset alone is not enough to perform well on our data regardless of the base model used. Since the SQ pipeline performance on its intended domain is good (Table 4) we can say that the baseline models cannot generalize to our domain.

Table 3. Evaluation of each pipeline's performance on the mMQA dataset with 891 samples. We report the exact match (EM) and F1 metrics.

Pipeline	Model	EM	F1
SQ	BERT	1.12	7.29
	ALBERT	1.23	4.66
	ELECTRA	2.69	10.35
TRS-SQ	BERT	1.80	12.43
	ALBERT	2.02	7.00
	ELECTRA	5.39	18.87
SQ-mMQA	BERT	20.09	25.89
	ALBERT	19.98	24.79
	ELECTRA	32.21	38.16
TRS-SQ-mMQA	BERT	22.33	29.81
	ALBERT	18.86	22.49
	ELECTRA	36.00	45.46
TRS-mMQA	BERT	15.49	20.68
	ALBERT	18.86	23.05
	ELECTRA	38.38	51.28
mMQA	BERT	14.48	19.58
	ALBERT	24.47	31.84
	ELECTRA	**40.40**	**51.72**

Table 4. Performance of the SQ pipeline on the SQuAD dataset (11873 samples). We report the exact match (EM) and F1 metrics.

Model	EM	F1
BERT	70.29	73.73
ALBERT	80.83	83.91
ELECTRA	86.51	89.30

The best-performing pipeline with regards to the mMQA dataset is simply running only the mMQA step with the ELECTRA as a base model. This achieves an exact match of 40.4% and an F1 score of 51.72%. The ALBERT model also performs best when used in the single-step setup. The progress of the EM metric is in Fig. 2. Contrary to our intuition, introducing the TRS pretraining step (in the pipeline TRS-mMQA pipeline) did not yield better results. The BERT model on the other hand benefited from the TRS-SQ-mMQA pipeline with the most variety, yet it achieved barely 55% of ELECTRA's performance. This is to be expected, as ELECTRA has the best performance of the 3 base models even on other QA tasks, as reported in its original research paper and as can be seen in Table 4.

The base models play a significant role even on our dataset. It is useful to note the relative performance difference of each language representation model evaluated on the SQuAD dataset in Table 4. Since the performance is commonly reported in QA research papers it can be used as an indicator of a relative performance difference on the mMQA dataset as well.

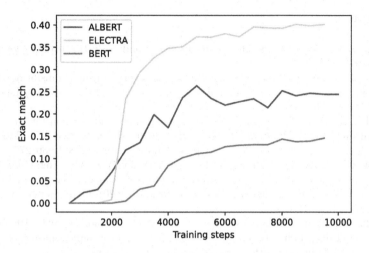

Fig. 2. Progress of the value of the exact match metric for the best-performing mMQA pipeline with regards to the training steps.

5   Conclusion and Future Work

In the search of a general question answering solution for the MALACH archive of the Holocaust testimonies, we can conclude, that the archive is challenging for pretrained models. We have explored and evaluated an approach that uses the underlying structure of the archive to create a pipeline that can bootstrap the research in this particular domain. The conversational nature of the content is a strong starting point for a question answering system. This can allow us to easily obtain human-validated annotations in the future by simply having people assess whether the system gave a valid answer to a valid question instead of creating question-answer pairs from scratch. It can also improve the development of what we consider our main research goal in this topic - a question-answering spoken dialogue system on top of the MALACH archive and other Holocaust-related sources. A user of the dialog system may want to simply explore the vast dataset. We think that the provided answers, their context, and their source will be enough for the user's exploration of the archive. Even though the question answering component does not yet achieve stellar performance. The next step towards creating the dialogue system is finding a suitable approach for document retrieval. The extensiveness of the dataset prohibits us from finding an answer in all possible contexts in a reasonable time. Also challenging will be the transition from the transcribed text to the output of speech-to-text recognizer [15].

Acknowledgements. This work was supported by the European Regional Development Fund under the project Robotics for Industry 4.0 (reg. no. CZ.02.1.01/0.0/0.0/15_003/0000470). Computational resources were supplied by the project "e-Infrastruktura CZ" (e-INFRA LM2018140) provided within the program Projects of Large Research, Development and Innovations Infrastructures.

References

1. Abrams, L.: Oral History Theory. Routledge, London (2016). https://doi.org/10.4324/9781315640761
2. Alam, T., Khan, A., Alam, F.: Punctuation Restoration using Transformer Models for High-and Low-Resource Languages, pp. 132–142 (2020). https://doi.org/10.18653/v1/2020.wnut-1.18
3. Chýlek, A., Šmídl, L., Švec, J.: Question-answering dialog system for large audio-visual archives. In: Ekštein, K. (ed.) TSD 2019. LNCS (LNAI), vol. 11697, pp. 385–397. Springer, Cham (2019). https://doi.org/10.1007/978-3-030-27947-9_33
4. Clark, K., Luong, M.T., Brain, G., Le Google Brain, Q.V., Manning, C.D.: ELECTRA: pre-training text encoders as discriminators rather than generators. In: International Conference on Learning Representations (2020). https://openreview.net/forum?id=r1xMH1BtvB
5. Devlin, J., Chang, M.W., Lee, K., Google, K.T., Language, A.I.: BERT: pre-training of deep bidirectional transformers for language understanding. Technical report (2018). https://github.com/tensorflow/tensor2tensor
6. Fajcik, M., Docekal, M., Ondrej, K., Smrz, P.: Pruning the Index Contents for Memory Efficient Open-Domain QA (2021). http://arxiv.org/abs/2102.10697
7. Lan, Z., Chen, M., Goodman, S., Gimpel, K., Sharma, P., Soricut, R.: ALBERT: a lite BERT for self-supervised learning of language representations. In: International Conference on Learning Representations (2020). https://openreview.net/forum?id=H1eA7AEtvS
8. Min, S., Boyd-Graber, J., Alberti, C., Chen, D., Choi, E., et al.: NeurIPS 2020 EfficientQA Competition: Systems, Analyses and Lessons Learned, pp. 1–27 (2020). http://arxiv.org/abs/2101.00133
9. Pecina, P., Hoffmannová, P., Jones, G.J.F., Zhang, Y., Oard, D.W.: Overview of the CLEF-2007 cross-language speech retrieval track. In: Peters, C., et al. (eds.) CLEF 2007. LNCS, vol. 5152, pp. 674–686. Springer, Heidelberg (2008). https://doi.org/10.1007/978-3-540-85760-0_86
10. Psutka, J., Radová, V., Ircing, P., Matoušek, J., Müller, L.: USC-SFI MALACH Interviews and Transcripts Czech LDC2014S04 (2014). https://catalog.ldc.upenn.edu/LDC2014S04
11. Psutka, J., et al.: System for fast lexical and phonetic spoken term detection in a Czech cultural heritage archive. EURASIP J. Audio Speech Music Process. **2011**(1), 10 (2011). https://doi.org/10.1186/1687-4722-2011-10. http://asmp.eurasipjournals.com/content/2011/1/10
12. Rajpurkar, P., Jia, R., Liang, P.: Know What You Don't Know: Unanswerable Questions for SQuAD (2018). http://arxiv.org/abs/1806.03822
13. Ramabhadran, B., et al.: USC-SFI MALACH Interviews and Transcripts English LDC2012S05 (2012). https://catalog.ldc.upenn.edu/LDC2012S05

14. Stanislav, P., Švec, J., Ircing, P.: An engine for online video search in large archives of the holocaust testimonies. In: Proceedings of the Annual Conference of the International Speech Communication Association, INTERSPEECH, pp. 2352–2353 (2016)
15. Švec, J., Psutka, J.V., Trmal, J., Šmídl, L., Ircing, P., Sedmidubsky, J.: On the use of grapheme models for searching in large spoken archives. In: ICASSP, IEEE International Conference on Acoustics, Speech and Signal Processing - Proceedings, vol. 2018-April, pp. 6259–6263 (2018). https://doi.org/10.1109/ICASSP.2018.8461774
16. Tan, C., Wei, F., Yang, N., Du, B., Lv, W., Zhou, M.: S-Net: from answer extraction to answer synthesis for machine reading comprehension. In: AAAI, pp. 5940–5947 (2018). https://www.aaai.org/ocs/index.php/AAAI/AAAI18/paper/view/16239
17. Wolf, T., et al.: Transformers: State-of-the-Art Natural Language Processing, pp. 38–45 (2020). https://doi.org/10.18653/v1/2020.emnlp-demos.6
18. Zajíc, Z., et al.: Towards processing of the oral history interviews and related printed documents. In: Proceedings of the Eleventh International Conference on Language Resources and Evaluation (LREC 2018) (2018)

Imagined, Intended, and Spoken Speech Envelope Synthesis from Neuromagnetic Signals

Debadatta Dash[1]([✉])[iD], Paul Ferrari[1,2][iD], Karinne Berstis[1], and Jun Wang[1][iD]

[1] University of Texas at Austin, Austin, TX 78712, USA
debadatta.dash@utexas.edu, {karinne,jun.wang}@austin.utexas.edu
[2] Helen DeVos Children's Hospital, Spectrum Health, Grand Rapids, MI 49503, USA
paul.ferrari@spectrunhealth.org

Abstract. Neural speech decoding retrieves speech information directly from the brain, providing promise towards better communication assistance to patients with locked-in syndrome (e.g. due to amyotrophic lateral sclerosis, ALS). Currently, speech decoding research using non-invasive neural signals is limited to discrete classifications of only a few speech units (e.g., words/syllables/phrases). Considerable work remains to achieve the ultimate goal of decoding continuous speech sounds. One stepping stone towards this goal would be to reconstruct the inner speech envelope in real-time from neural activity. Numerous studies have shown the possibility of tracking the speech envelope during speech perception but this has not been demonstrated for speech production, imagination or intention. Here, we attempted to reconstruct the intended, imagined, and spoken speech envelope by decoding the temporal information of speech directly from neural signals. Using magnetoencephalography (MEG), we collected the neuromagnetic activity from 7 subjects imagining and speaking various cued phrases and from 7 different subjects speaking yes or no randomly without any cue. We used a bidirectional long short-term memory recurrent neural network (BLSTM-RNN) for single-trial regression of the speech envelope using all brainwaves (0.3–250 Hz). For the phrase stimuli, we obtained an average correlation score of 0.41 and 0.72 for reconstructing imagined and spoken speech envelope respectively, both significantly higher than the chance level (<0.1). For the word stimuli, the correlation score of the reconstructed speech envelope was 0.77 and 0.82, respectively for intended and spoken speech. Furthermore, to evaluate the efficacy of low frequency neural oscillations in reconstructing spoken speech envelope, we used delta (0.3–4 Hz) and delta + theta (0.3–8 Hz) brainwaves and found that the performance for word stimuli was significantly lower compared to when brainwaves with all frequencies were used but no such significant difference was observed for phrase stimuli. These findings provide a foundation for direct speech synthesis from non-invasive neural signals.

Keywords: Speech envelope · MEG · LSTM

© Springer Nature Switzerland AG 2021
A. Karpov and R. Potapova (Eds.): SPECOM 2021, LNAI 12997, pp. 134–145, 2021.
https://doi.org/10.1007/978-3-030-87802-3_13

1   Introduction

Neurodegenerative disorders such as amyotrophic lateral sclerosis (ALS) may lead the patients towards a state of complete paralysis otherwise being cognitively intact, i.e., locked-in syndrome. The brain might be the only source of communication for these patients. Current commercially available brain-computer interface (BCI) spellers or thought-to-writing can help these patients communicate to a level but at a very slow communication rate (about 10 words or 90 characters per min) [37]. Neural speech decoding paradigm attempts to decode speech information directly from the brain providing promise towards real-time communication assistance, thereby, improving the quality of life for these neurologically impaired patients. Recently, promising results in neural speech decoding have been obtained using either invasive neural signals using electrocorticography (ECoG) [1,2] or non-invasively using electroencephalography (EEG) [22,30] and magnetoencephalography (MEG) [10,11]. However, current research using non-invasive signals is limited to discrete classification of a few speech units (phonemes/words/phrases) rather decoding the continuous speech information which is essential towards the goal of developing speech-BCIs. One stepping stone towards this goal would be to synthesize the inner speech envelope in real-time from neural activity.

Speech envelope tracking has been studied for perception, which has revealed information about listeners' perception and cognitive speech processing. Numerous studies have focused on tracking the amplitude of the perceived speech using the low frequency information within high temporal resolution neurophysiological signals such as electrocorticography (ECoG) [27,33], electroencephalography (EEG) [4,17,32,38], and magnetoencephalography (MEG) [14,20]. This neural speech tracking paradigm or speech entrainment, has provided keen insight into various topics including audiology [36] and neural disorders [23]. In contrast to speech perception, to our knowledge, tracking of the speech envelope during speech production or imagination or intention has not been done, even though it has potential applications including speech decoding based brain-computer interfaces to assist communication in locked-in patients, pre-surgical localization of cortical language areas, and forming a better understanding of neural speech processing for speech production. Thus, in this study, we focused on tracking the slow modulations of spoken, imagined, and intended speech as a foundation towards direct speech synthesis from non-invasive neural signals.

MEG is a non-invasive neuroimaging modality with excellent temporal resolution and good spatial resolution, suitable for exploring the underlying mechanism of cognitive speech processing. With highly sensitive magnetometers and gradiometers, MEG accurately measures the magnetic fields induced due to the post-synaptic cortical neuronal currents. Recent MEG-based speech research such as investigations of MEG oscillations during speech production [6,18] and understanding temporal patterns of neural activations of speech [7,24], etc. provides strong support for using MEG to retrieve cortical speech information. Moreover, MEG signals have been shown to accurately track the speech envelope [13,19,35], although for speech perception rather than production. Furthermore,

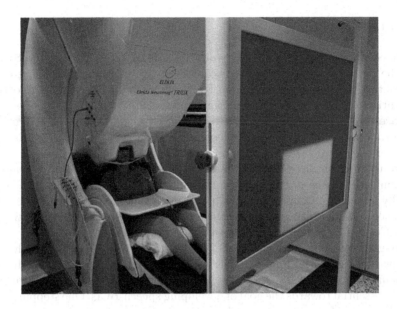

Fig. 1. The Elekta Neuromag MEG unit.

recent developments of wearable, movable, and low-cost MEGs, known as, optically pumped magnetometers (OPM) [3,29], have huge potential in real-world applications, and also have been proven effective for perceived speech envelope tracking [12]. In this study, we used MEG to investigate the potential of neuromagnetic signals to decode the spoken speech envelope.

Traditionally, low frequency cortical oscillations such as delta (0.3–4 Hz) or theta band (4–8 Hz) have been used to track the slow modulations of speech perception [25]. Studies have shown that during continuous speech listening, cortical activity tracks the speech rhythmicity at frequencies matching with the repetition rate of speech units (e.g. delta band for phrases or theta band for words) [12]. In this study, our goal was single-trial speech envelope prediction of short phrases or words, where one trial consists of a single word ($\sim$0.3 s) or a single phrase ($\sim$2 s). Hence, we used a wider band of neural oscillations (0.3–250 Hz) to reconstruct the speech envelope. The benefit of single-trial analysis is in real-time applications of brain-computer interfaces. Also, to verify the role of low-frequency brainwaves on the stimuli period, we performed separate regression analyses for the two types of speech stimuli using the delta and the theta band. Recurrent neural networks have been a widely used approach for modeling EEG [22,26] or MEG [7,10,15,16,21] based sequential neural signals. Since both MEG and the corresponding speech envelope are sequential time varying signals in nature, we used a bidirectional long short-term memory recurrent neural network (BLSTM-RNN) to perform the regression in real-time. In this study, we focused only on subject dependent analysis to perform speech envelope regression.

2 Data Collection

We used two identical Elekta Neuromag TRIUX MEG machines (MEGIN, LCC) for data collection: one at the Dell Children's Medical Center in Austin, TX and the other at the Cook Children's Medical Center in Fort Worth, TX (Fig. 1). Informed consent was obtained from each subject in accordance with the corresponding institutions' research ethics board. The machines are housed within a magnetically shielded room to discard external magnetic interference. The MEG machine consists of 306 channels with 204 planar gradiometers and 102 magnetometer sensors. A DLP projector is situated at about 90 cm from the machine to display the stimuli. For this study, we selected two types of speech production tasks, one cued and the other non-cued. In the non-cued task, subjects spontaneously spoke the words yes or no repeatedly until at least 80 repetitions of each item were produced. Subjects spoke continuously and randomly at their self-paced rate without any specific cue. For the cued task, subjects first imagined and then overtly articulated 5 different short phrases presented psueduo-randomly at least 100 times each. We used 5 commonly used sentences, selected from an alternative and augmentative communication (AAC) list: 1. *Do you understand me*, 2. *That's perfect*, 3. *How are you*, 4. *Good-bye, and* 5. *I need help*. We designed a time-locked protocol that consisted of four segments in a trial: 1. Pre-stimuli (0.5 s) where the subjects were at rest, 2. Perception (1 s): where a stimulus is shown on a screen for the subjects to silently read, 3. Preparation/Imagination (1 s): where the subjects imagined and prepared to speak the previously shown phrase, and 4. Articulation/Production (1.5–2.5 s): subjects were cued to overtly speak the shown phrase. Seven healthy subjects (3 females, mean age: 41 years) performed the cued task and 7 different subjects (4 females, mean age: 25 years) performed the non-cued task. More details about the data collection can be found in our previous study [5]. All MEG data were collected at a 4 kHz sampling frequency and an online filter of 0.3 to 1330 Hz. We also used ECG and EOG electrodes to detect artifacts from cardiac and eye-movements, respectively. Acoustic output was recorded through a standard built-in microphone connected to a transducer placed outside the MSR and digitized by feeding into the MEG ADC in real-time as a separate channel.

3 Methods

3.1 Data Preparation

The MEG data were low passed filtered at 250 Hz and the 60 Hz power line frequency and its harmonics were removed with notch filters. For analysis with low frequency cortical oscillations, the signals were further low-passed with a 4th order Butterworth filter with cutoff frequency 4 Hz for delta band and 8 Hz for delta+theta band. The phrase data were epoched into trials centered on stimulus onset. Via thorough visual inspection, trials containing extremely and unexpected high amplitude artifacts or untimely articulated trials were removed. Since the word stimuli data were collected in a single run, without any cue, we epoched this data with respect to the acoustic onset and offset of each spoken word for speech production trial. First, the speech signals were denoised with a Wiener filter [28]. Second, voice activity detection (VAD) [31] was performed to identify the acoustic onset and offset of the words. Third, after epoching based on VAD labels, each trial was manually visualized and if required, corrected for accurate labels. Last, each trial was segregated to either 'yes' or 'no' class after listening to the acoustic signals. The median length of each trial (yes/no) was about 0.3 s. We segregated the speech intention trial by taking the same length of speech production segment (~0.3 s) prior to acoustic onset for each trial. Considering the effectiveness of gradiometers over magnetometers in noise suppression, only gradiometers were used in this study. Flat and noisy gradiometer channels were removed from the data analysis. After preprocessing, on average, about ~350 trials (~70 trials × 5 phrases) of phrase data and ~170 trials (~85 trials × 2 words) of word stimuli data per subject were retained. The number of retained trials and sensors per subject can be found in Table 1.

Table 1. Details of preprocessed data.

Phrases			Words			
Sub.	Trials/Phrase	Sensors	Sub.	Trials Yes—No		Sensors
S1	74	200	P1	82	84	203
S2	77	201	P2	82	82	203
S3	73	199	P3	67	79	203
S4	78	203	P4	80	105	203
S5	55	196	P5	103	103	203
S6	65	201	P6	100	94	203
S7	63	199	P7	86	101	203

3.2 Regression Model

We performed BLSTM-RNN regression to reconstruct the speech envelope (extracted from the speech signals) from the gradiometer signals. Considering the cognitive variance across subjects [9], we trained and tuned a separate model for each subject and each type of stimulus (phrase or word). Further, separate models were tuned for analysis with low-frequency MEG signals. Table 2 enlists the model architecture details and most common hyperparameter choices across subjects. The model consisted of 5 layers, with initial 3 layers of recurrent bidirectional LSTM units feeding to a fully connected (FC) layer on the top followed by an output regression layer. The input to the model was the z-score normalized ~200-dimensional gradiometer signals trained to regress to a 1-dimensional speech envelope at each sample. A hard-sigmoid activation function was used to update the gate state and tanh for the cell and hidden states. The total number

Table 2. Model architecture and hyperparameters.

Components	Details	
	Phrases	Words
Input	MEG Signals	
Input layer dimension	196–203	203
Sampling rate	1 kHz	4 kHz
Input time points	1500–2500	~1200
Training samples	~200	~140
Output	Speech Envelope	
Output layer dimension	1	1
Output time points	1500–2500	~1200
Number of test samples	~70	~30
Regression Model	BLSTM-RNN	
Depth	5	
LSTM Units in Layer 1	512–640	
Dropout	0.2	
LSTM Units in Layer 2	256	
Dropout	0.2	
LSTM Units in Layer 3	64	
Dropout	0.1–0.2	
Number of FC nodes	50	
Dropout	0.5	
Batch size	10	
Maximum epochs	80–100	
Optimizer	ADAM	
Training method	BPTT	
Initial learning rate	0.004–0.007	
Learning rate drop factor	0.5	
Learning rate drop period	10 epochs	
Gradient threshold method	L_2 Norm	
Gradient threshold value	0.1	
beta1	0.9	
beta2	0.999	
epsilon	1.00E-08	
Loss function	RMSE	

of samples for training and testing were about 280 and 70 for phrases, 140 and 30 for words, respectively. For regularization, 20% dropouts after the BLSTM layers, 50% dropout after the FC layer, and L_2 Norm with gradient threshold value of 0.1 were used. The loss function was root mean square error (RMSE), trained with an ADAM optimizer via backpropagation through time (BPTT) with fixed $\beta 1$, $\beta 2$, and ϵ values of 0.9, 0.999, and 1E-8 respectively.

A 20% holdout cross-validation on training data was used for hyperparameter tuning. The tuned hyperparameters are: number of units in BLSTM layers, number of FC nodes, initial learning rate, batch size, and number of epochs. The number of recurrent units in 3 layers was tuned with a grid search within ranges: 64–640 with increments of 64. The first recurrent layer was the most significant in providing the best performance which ranged between 512–640 across subjects. The number of FC nodes was tuned for values from 10 to 100 with increments of 10. Initial learning rate was tuned with a coarse to fine setting within the range of values of 0.1, 0.01, 0.001, 0.0001. Batch size value was tuned for 10, 16, 32, and 64. Number of epochs was tuned from 50 to 100 with an increment of 10 until convergence in RMSE loss. The final hyperparameter values were chosen based on the least RMSE score on validation data. Pearson correlation score was used as the standard metric to evaluate the regression performance. Correlation scores were calculated between the test trial envelopes and the envelopes predicted with the BLSTM model.

3.3 Comparison of Brainwaves for Regression

Although low frequency brainwaves (delta and theta) have typically been used in traditional speech envelope reconstruction literature, they were implemented in the context of continuous speech listening tasks with longer periods of auditory stimuli. In our study of single-trial analysis, the trial durations were in the range of ~2 s for phrase stimuli and ~0.3 s for the word stimuli. Thus, we used a wide-band with brainwaves of all frequencies (0.3–250 Hz) for regression analysis. The role of high frequency neural oscillations in speech productions has been shown consistently in literature [6,8,34], which motivated us to include the high frequency brainwaves in our analysis. However since the speech envelope is a low frequency signal and matches with the low frequency cortical rhythmic activity, we also performed the regression analysis with only low frequency brainwaves (delta: 0.3–4 Hz and delta+theta: 0.3–8 Hz). We restricted this analysis to spoken speech envelope reconstruction only.

4   Results and Discussion

4.1   Regression Performance

The median value of the correlation scores across trials was calculated for each subject. For spoken speech envelope regression of yes/no data, the average

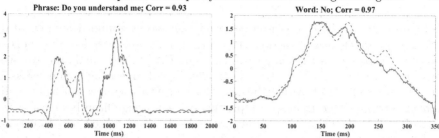

Fig. 2. Exemplary single-trial prediction of a phrase stimulus (do you understand me) (left) and a word stimulus (No) (right) in orange and original speech envelope in blue. (Color figure online)

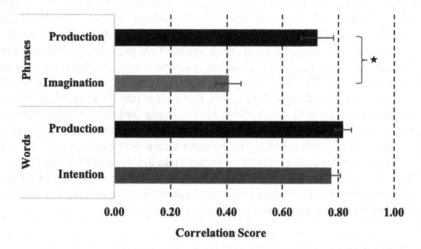

Fig. 3. Regression performance for spoken, imagined, and intended speech envelope. Error bars represent standard error and * denotes statistical significance: $p < 0.05$.

median correlation across subjects was 0.82 ± 0.08. Amongst 7 subjects, the highest performance was a median correlation score of 0.88 and the lowest was 0.67. Similarly, for phrases the average median correlation across subjects was 0.72 ± 0.15, the highest was 0.89 and the lowest was 0.51. Exemplary predictions for a phrase and a word stimulus can be seen in Fig. 2. It's evident that the model was able to learn the slow temporal amplitudes of the speech effectively. Although the average score for the phrases was lower compared to words, interestingly, for phrases, the silence parts of the articulation segment (before acoustic onset and after offset) were predicted accurately. This indicates that the temporal characteristics of the speech and non-speech intervals are well represented in the cortical signals. Since the phrase data were collected in time-locked manner, we trained the entire segment of articulation (2–2.5 s) for speech envelope regression, but for the word stimuli, the period was only from acoustic onset to offset.

Figure 3 shows the comparison of correlation scores obtained for imagined and spoken speech reconstruction of phrase stimuli and intended and spoken speech envelope reconstruction for word stimuli. For phrase stimuli, the average correlation score for reconstructing speech envelope during imagination across 7 subjects was 0.41 ± 0.12. Although the performance was significantly less (1-tail paired t-test; $p < 0.05$) than speech production, it was significantly higher than chance level (0.1). The chance level performance was obtained based on random shuffling of ground truth labels and bootstrapping. This indicates that the speech envelope can be successfully reconstructed during speech imagination. The higher performance for speech production could be due to the contribution of auditory feedback. For the word stimuli, however, the average correlation score for the reconstruction of intended speech envelope was about 0.77 ± 0.09, close to performance for speech production, without any statistically significant difference (1-tail paired t-test; $p = 0.17$). For speech intention, we have used about 0.3 s of data prior to acoustic onset. This period, just before speech production, includes the speech planning stage to articulate the corresponding intended speech. The fact that the speech envelope can be reconstructed by taking neural signals during speech planning has a huge impact towards developing speech-BCIs for ALS patients. Although, this study included only healthy participants, and similar analysis has to be conducted to confirm this hypothesis. It can also be hypothesized that the reconstruction performance for synthesizing intended speech envelope could be higher than synthesizing imagined speech envelope. However, in this study, the performance for reconstructing imagined speech and intended speech aren't directly comparable, considering the tasks are for different stimuli (phrases and words respectively).

4.2 Comparison with Low Frequency Brainwaves

Figure 4 compares the average correlation scores across the subjects for each type of stimuli. It can be seen that, for shorter speech stimuli, all frequencies provided the best performance compared to delta or delta+theta band only (1-tail paired t-test, $p < 0.05$). This further emphasizes the role of high frequency brainwaves in speech production. However, it might also be possible that the temporal characteristics of low frequency neural oscillations (delta or delta+theta) might have been diminished because of the shorter trial duration. This is further illustrated in the performances obtained for the trials with longer periods (phrase stimuli), where no significant difference was observed between the low frequency and wide-band MEG signals. These results indicate that using neural signals with all frequencies might be more efficient for single-trial analysis of speech production envelope regression.

5   Conclusion

In this study, we reconstructed intended, imagined, and spoken speech envelopes from MEG signals. We used a Bidirectional LSTM model for single-trial speech

Regression Performance

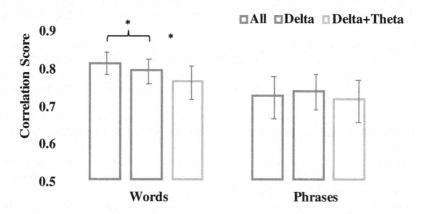

Fig. 4. Average correlation score for words and phrases across subjects with all frequency, delta only, and delta+theta. Error bars represent standard error and * denotes statistical significance: $p < 0.05$.

envelope regression with two types of stimuli (words and phrases). We found that the slow temporal modulations of spoken speech can be efficiently reconstructed with an average correlation of 0.82 for words and 0.72 for phrases. Using only the low frequency brainwaves, we found a similar performance for reconstructing the spoken phrase envelope, however, for shorter speech units (words), the performance was significantly better with neural signals containing all frequencies up to 250 Hz. We also found that it is possible to synthesize the speech envelope during speech imagination and speech intention providing a foundation for direct speech synthesis from non-invasive neural signals.

Acknowledgments. This work was supported by the University of Texas System Brain Initiative under award 362221 and partly by the National Institutes of Health (NIH) under awards R01DC016621 and R03DC013990. We would like to thank Dr. Saleem Malik, Dr. Mark McManis, Kristin Teplansky, Dr. Alan Wisler, Saara Raja, and the volunteering participants.

References

1. Angrick, M., et al.: Speech synthesis from ECoG using densely connected 3D convolutional neural networks. J. Neural Eng. **16**(3), 036019 (2019)
2. Anumanchipalli, G.K., Chartier, J., Chang, E.F.: Speech synthesis from neural decoding of spoken sentences. Nature **568**(7753), 493–498 (2019)
3. Boto, E., et al.: Moving magnetoencephalography towards real-world applications with a wearable system. Nature **555**(7698), 657–661 (2018)
4. Bröhl, F., Kayser, C.: Delta/theta band EEG differentially tracks low and high frequency speech-derived envelopes. Neuroimage **233**, 117958 (2021)

5. Dash, D., Ferrari, P., Wang, J.: Decoding imagined and spoken phrases from non-invasive neural (MEG) signals. Front. Neurosci. **14**, 290 (2020)
6. Dash, D., Ferrari, P., Wang, J.: Role of brainwaves in neural speech decoding. In: 2020 28th European Signal Processing Conference (EUSIPCO), pp. 1357–1361 (2021)
7. Dash, D., Ferrari, P., Dutta, S., Wang, J.: NeuroVAD: real-time voice activity detection from non-invasive neuromagnetic signals. Sensors **20**(8), 2248 (2020)
8. Dash, D., Ferrari, P., Hernandez, A., Heitzman, D., Austin, S.G., Wang, J.: Neural speech decoding for amyotrophic lateral sclerosis. In: Proceedings of Interspeech 2020, pp. 2782–2786 (2020)
9. Dash, D., Ferrari, P., Wang, J.: Spatial and spectral fingerprint in the brain: speaker identification from single trial MEG signals. In: INTERSPEECH, pp. 1203–1207 (2019)
10. Dash, D., Ferrari, P., Wang, J.: Decoding speech evoked jaw motion from non-invasive neuromagnetic oscillations. In: 2020 International Joint Conference on Neural Networks (IJCNN), pp. 1–8. IEEE (2020)
11. Dash, D., Wisler, A., Ferrari, P., Davenport, E.M., Maldjian, J., Wang, J.: MEG sensor selection for neural speech decoding. IEEE Access **8**, 182320–182337 (2020)
12. de Lange, P., et al.: Measuring the cortical tracking of speech with optically-pumped magnetometers. Neuroimage **233**, 117969 (2021)
13. Destoky, F., et al.: Comparing the potential of MEG and EEG to uncover brain tracking of speech temporal envelope. Neuroimage **184**, 201–213 (2019)
14. Ding, N., Simon, J.Z.: Neural coding of continuous speech in auditory cortex during monaural and dichotic listening. J. Neurophysiol. **107**(1), 78–89 (2012). PMID: 21975452
15. Dinh, C., Samuelsson, J.G., Hunold, A., Hämäläinen, M.S., Khan, S.: Contextual MEG and EEG source estimates using spatiotemporal LSTM networks. Front. Neurosci. **15**, 119 (2021)
16. Donhauser, P.W., Baillet, S.: Two distinct neural timescales for predictive speech processing. Neuron **105**(2), 385–393 (2020)
17. Fu, Z., Chen, J.: Congruent audiovisual speech enhances cortical envelope tracking during auditory selective attention. In: Proceedings of Interspeech 2020, pp. 116–120 (2020)
18. Gehrig, J., Wibral, M., Arnold, C., Kell, C.: Setting up the speech production network: How oscillations contribute to lateralized information routing. Front. Psychol. **3**, 169 (2012)
19. Hertrich, I., Dietrich, S., Ackermann, H.: Tracking the speech signal – time-locked MEG signals during perception of ultra-fast and moderately fast speech in blind and in sighted listeners. Brain Lang. **124**(1), 9–21 (2013)
20. Kojima, K., Oganian, Y., Cai, C., Findlay, A., Chang, E., Nagarajan, S.: Low-frequency neural tracking of natural speech envelope reflects the convolution of evoked responses to acoustic edges, not oscillatory entrainment. Not Oscillatory Entrainment (2021)
21. Kostas, D., Pang, E.W., Rudzicz, F.: Machine learning for MEG during speech tasks. Sci. Rep. **9**(1), 1–13 (2019)
22. Krishna, G., Tran, C., Han, Y., Carnahan, M., Tewfik, A.H.: Speech synthesis using EEG. In: ICASSP 2020–2020 IEEE International Conference on Acoustics, Speech and Signal Processing (ICASSP), pp. 1235–1238. IEEE (2020)
23. Lizarazu, M., Lallier, M., Bourguignon, M., Carreiras, M., Molinaro, N.: Impaired neural response to speech edges in dyslexia. Cortex **135**, 207–218 (2021)

24. Memarian, N., Ferrari, P., Macdonald, M.J., Cheyne, D., Luc, F., Pang, E.W.: Cortical activity during speech and non-speech oromotor tasks: a magnetoencephalography (MEG) study. Neurosci. Lett. **527**(1), 34–39 (2012)

25. Meyer, L.: The neural oscillations of speech processing and language comprehension: state of the art and emerging mechanisms. Eur. J. Neurosci. **48**(7), 2609–2621 (2018)

26. Monesi, M.J., Accou, B., Montoya-Martinez, J., Francart, T., Hamme, H.V.: An LSTM based architecture to relate speech stimulus to EEG. In: ICASSP 2020-2020 IEEE International Conference on Acoustics, Speech and Signal Processing (ICASSP), pp. 941–945 (2020)

27. Oganian, Y., Chang, E.F.: A speech envelope landmark for syllable encoding in human superior temporal gyrus. Sci. Adv. **5**(11), eaay6279 (2019)

28. Plapous, C., Marro, C., Scalart, P.: Improved signal-to-noise ratio estimation for speech enhancement. IEEE Trans. Audio Speech Lang. Process. **14**(6), 2098–2108 (2006)

29. Pratt, E.J., et al.: Kernel flux: a whole-head 432-magnetometer optically-pumped magnetoencephalography (OP-MEG) system for brain activity imaging during natural human experiences. In: Optical and Quantum Sensing and Precision Metrology, vol. 11700, p. 1170032. International Society for Optics and Photonics (2021)

30. Sharon, R.A., Narayanan, S.S., Sur, M., Murthy, A.H.: Neural speech decoding during audition, imagination and production. IEEE Access **8**, 149714–149729 (2020)

31. Sohn, J., Kim, N.S., Sung, W.: A statistical model-based voice activity detection. IEEE Signal Process. Lett. **6**(1), 1–3 (1999)

32. de Taillez, T., Kollmeier, B., Meyer, B.T.: Machine learning for decoding listeners' attention from electroencephalography evoked by continuous speech. Eur. J. Neurosci. **51**(5), 1234–1241 (2020)

33. Tang, C., Hamilton, L., Chang, E.: Intonational speech prosody encoding in the human auditory cortex. Science **357**(6353), 797–801 (2017)

34. Towle, V.L., et al.: ECoG gamma activity during a language task: differentiating expressive and receptive speech areas. Brain **131**(8), 2013–2027 (2008)

35. Vander Ghinst, M., et al.: Cortical tracking of speech-in-noise develops from childhood to adulthood. J. Neurosci. **39**(15), 2938–2950 (2019)

36. Vanthornhout, J., Decruy, L., Wouters, J., Simon, J.Z., Francart, T.: Speech intelligibility predicted from neural entrainment of the speech envelope. J. Assoc. Res. Otolaryngol. **19**(2), 181–191 (2018)

37. Willett, F.R., Avansino, D.T., Hochberg, L.R., Henderson, J.M., Shenoy, K.V.: High-performance brain-to-text communication via handwriting. Nature **593**(7858), 249–254 (2021)

38. Zhou, D., Zhang, G., Dang, J., Wu, S., Zhang, Z.: Neural entrainment to natural speech envelope based on subject aligned EEG signals. In: Proceedings of Interspeech 2020, pp. 106–110 (2020)

What Causes Phonetic Reduction in Russian Speech: New Evidence from Machine Learning Algorithms

Maria Dayter⑩ and Elena Riekhakaynen$^{(\boxtimes)}$ ⑩

Saint-Petersburg State University, Universitetskaya Emb. 7/9, 199034 St. Petersburg, Russia
e.riehakajnen@spbu.ru

Abstract. In this paper, we describe the second stage of the study aimed at describing the factors that influence the phonetic reduction of words in Russian speech using machine learning algorithms. We discuss the limitations of the first stage of our study and try to overcome some of them by increasing the dataset and using new algorithms such as random forest, gradient boosting, and perceptron. We used the texts from the Corpus of Russian Speech as the data. The dataset was divided into two separate datasets: one consisted of single words and the other contained multiword units from our corpus. According to the results, for single words the most important features turned out to be the number of syllables and whether the word is an adjective as they were chosen by all algorithms. For the multiword units, the main features were the number of syllables, frequency in Russian spoken texts (in ipm), and token frequency in a given text. In our further research, we are going to expand the dataset and look closer on such features as text type and token frequency in a given text.

Keywords: Phonetic reduction · Speech · Machine learning · Russian

1 Introduction

Over the past 20 years, many studies have shown that we need to study natural speech both for understanding speech production and spoken word recognition, and for solving practical issues associated with automatic speech recognition and synthesis [1–3]. In this paper, we develop a study that was described in [4] where we tried to identify the factors that affect the occurrence of phonetic reduction of words in Russian speech. We understand phonetic reduction of words as the loss of one or more sounds in a word. This phenomenon is widespread in speech [1, 5–7] and is one of the reasons for the obstacles in automatic speech recognition. We assume that finding out the causes of the reduction will allow to cope at least partially with these obstacles. In addition, the factors that influence the occurrence of reduction can be used for the development of automatic text-to-speech systems (as it was proposed, for example, in [8]).

Different methodological solutions to the problem of identifying the crucial factors for phonetic reduction are possible. Traditionally, in this case, linguists conduct

© Springer Nature Switzerland AG 2021
A. Karpov and R. Potapova (Eds.): SPECOM 2021, LNAI 12997, pp. 146–156, 2021.
https://doi.org/10.1007/978-3-030-87802-3_14

descriptive corpus-based studies. They describe how certain combinations of sounds are realized in certain words or phonetic positions, in certain types of speech, etc., in order to subsequently, basing on this information, identify factors that determine whether the word will undergo reduction or not (see, for example, [5, 9, 10]). In [4], we decided to use a different methodology, namely, to apply machine learning algorithms, and provided a brief overview of how such methods are used in phonetic research on the material of various languages. Among the studies of phonetic reduction, the following can be considered to be the closest to us methodologically: the papers in which logistic regression is used to test the assumptions about the influence of various factors on the occurrence of reduction (e.g., [1] based on the data of the American English language, or [11], where reduction in Danish spontaneous speech was studied). In our study, we used the Corpus of Russian Speech as a material (http://russpeech.spbu.ru/; see [12] for more details). All the records in the corpus are provided with orthographic and phonetic transcription (for the principles of transcription, see: http://russpeech.spbu.ru/transkrip.htm). For testing the algorithm, we used the recordings of one radio program and two TV programs from the corpus, with a total duration of 93 min. With the help of a program written in Python, a list of all the words contained in this material was compiled. It included not only single words, but also so-called multiword units (*mozhet_byt'* 'may be', *potomu_chto* 'because', etc. [13]). The preliminary results showed that the higher the frequency of a word form is, the more likely it is to be reduced; the more syllables a word form has, the higher probability of its reduction is; adjectives and parenthetical words tend to be reduced more often than other parts-of-speech. At the same time, some limitations of the study were observed, associated with both the methods used and the selection of the material. In this paper, we are going to discuss and solve some of them.

2   The Previous Study: What Went Wrong?

In our previous study [4], we used such machine learning algorithms as a random forest [14], an extremely randomized tree [15], and logistic regression [16] for predicting phonetic reduction and identifying the factors that determine its occurrence. Balanced accuracy was chosen as the metric to optimize, since the classes in our dataset were unbalanced (32% of words were reduced). As a result, we obtained two lists of features. The first one contained four features (the number of syllables, frequency in Russian spoken texts (hereinafter called "frequency in ipm" and opposed to token frequency in a given text), whether the word is an adjective, whether the word is a parenthetical word), and the second one consisted of five features (the number of syllables, frequency in ipm, whether the word is an adjective, whether the word is a parenthetical word, whether the word is a preposition). We built a logistic regression algorithm for each of the lists. All the features, except for the last one, received positive coefficients, which indicates a positive correlation between the feature and the fact of reduction. The results were good enough (the balanced accuracy was 75%), although not perfect. Therefore, we decided to analyze our data in order to identify the reasons due to which the selected metric did not exceed the value obtained.

   The first step was to calculate bias and variance. Bias is the difference between the true value and the expected value, predicted by the model [17]. Variance is the mean square of the difference between the predicted value and its mean [18]. High bias values indicate that the model failed to find the optimal solution, that is, underfitting occurred. High variance values indicate overfitting [19]. To calculate bias and variance for our dataset, we used the mlextend library (for more details see: http://rasbt.github.io/mlx tend/). For the first algorithm that contained five features we got the following values: bias was 0.19, variance was 0.005. For the second algorithm we obtained the following values: bias was 0.19, variance was 0.004. The bias value turned out to be quite high, which points to the fact that the algorithm was underfitted.

It is worth noticing that when trying to build a neural network, based either on the features mentioned above or on a dataset that contained three features (frequency in ipm, number of syllables, token frequency in a given text) we also failed to overcome the 80 percent threshold, regardless of the fact whether regularization was used. Such amends as increasing the number of layers or neurons were also unsuccessful.

Finally, we performed visualization. The scatterplot matrices (see Fig. 1) show that there are no dependencies in our data, therefore it is impossible for an algorithm to find a dividing surface. Normalization [19] is of little use here (see Fig. 2).

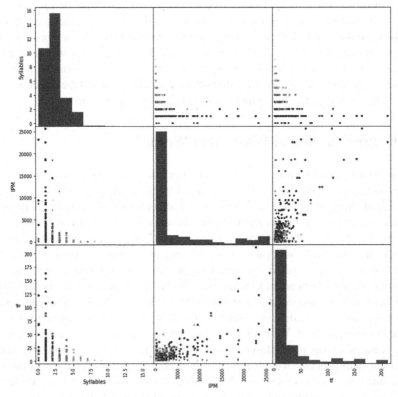

Fig. 1. A scatterplot matrix for syllables, frequency in ipm, and token frequency in a given text before normalization.

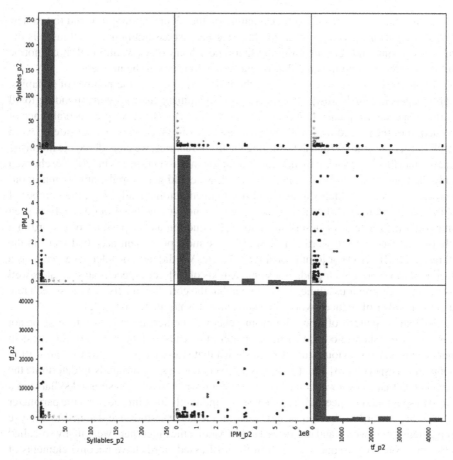

Fig. 2. A scatterplot matrix for syllables, frequency in ipm, and token frequency in a given text after normalization.

There are several possible solutions for the problems mentioned above:

- since decision tree algorithms were used for feature selection, it might be worth trying to use support vector machines instead, due to the fact that this algorithm is better for sparse datasets [17];
- in order to reduce the bias, it may be worth trying to increase the dataset. However, it might have an undesired effect for random forest, therefore it might be better to use a different type of algorithm [17];
- dimensionality may be another important factor in reducing bias. For instance, linear algorithms show less bias when working with larger datasets [17];
- finally, it is possible that our set of features is not big enough for a complete description of such a complex process as phonetic reduction. Adding new features will presumably help to identify patterns and get better results.

In this paper, we decided to focus mainly on the second assumption and to test new types of algorithms. But we tried to elaborate the last assumption as well, as it is the most promising and relevant from the theoretical point of view, although it cannot be fully considered using the data that we have in our corpus at the moment.

In our previous study, we analyzed the following features: the number of syllables, part-of-speech, which was later converted into 18 binary features corresponding to all parts-of-speech, frequency in ipm, token frequency in a given text, presence/absence of reduction of the preceding word, presence/absence of reduction of the considered word itself (target variable). When determining the list of features, we considered the linguistic parameters that were shown to influence reduction in Russian speech in [20]. We checked only the features the information about which we could get from the annotation in our corpus or those for which values could be obtained automatically (e.g., the number of syllables or frequency). For this reason, we have not yet included in our analysis such important parameters for describing phonetic reduction as the position of a word in a phrase and whether the word is followed by the most prominent accented word in the phrase (see [21: 184]) or joint probability [1], etc. We did not consider speech rate as a factor, because our data include not so many texts of different speech rates so far as well as because our previous studies have shown that the correlation between the speech rate and the number of reduced words in a spoken text is not that strong [22].

The stress pattern of a word and, in general, whether the word is stressed or not cannot yet be taken into account in our material, because we do not mark the stress in our corpus, since previous studies have shown that stress patterns of words can shift in spontaneous speech [23] and it is necessary to conduct a separate study to determine the parameters that a corpus annotator should rely on when marking a stressed syllable in a word in spontaneous speech. Nevertheless, we indirectly took into account the parameter of whether a word is stressed or not, since in the current study we decided to analyze separately single words and multiword units. Among the latter there were many so-called phonetic words. Consequently, most of the unstressed words have become elements of multiword units. In addition, compared to the first stage of our study described in [4], we included a text type feature in the list of features, since our corpus contains information about this parameter. This feature is binary as our corpus includes spontaneous monologues and fragments of reading.

3   Random Forest, Gradient Boosting, Perceptron and Feature Selection

As we stated above, in the previous study, we used a random forest and an extremely randomized tree to select the most important features for the occurrence of phonetic reduction. These algorithms were used in combination with the recursive feature elimination with cross-validation (RFECV) method, which recursively selects features and chooses the best feature set using cross-validation [24]. In this study, we decided to use a different method for feature selection, that works as follows: we use those features for which the feature_importance value exceeds the threshold value, which varies from 0.01 to 0.1 when using tree-based algorithms, or those features whose coefficients are not equal to 0 when using linear algorithms. For perceptron, the values of the alpha parameter varied from 0.0001 to 10. These values were chosen randomly.

Since the decision tree algorithm is prone to overfitting (lack of generalization ability), a choice was made in favor of tree-based ensemble methods, namely, random forest and extremely randomized tree.

During the preliminary stage of constructing the algorithm, we imported the dataset, made the feature "PoS" ("part-of-speech") categorical, divided this feature into separate parts-of-speech corresponding to all categories we used for part-of-speech tagging. For this purpose, a dictionary was created, the keys of which were numbers, and the values were the names of parts-of-speech. In order to scale the data, we converted the feature "frequency in ipm" to binary. To do this, we used the value of the third quartile of ipm values for unique word forms as a threshold. The word forms with ipm above 94.68 were classified as the word forms of high frequency.

In this study, we used such algorithms for feature selection as random forest, gradient boosting [16], and perceptron [25]. We built[1] perceptron, logistic regression and neural networks using datasets, in which the values for frequency in ipm and token frequency in a given text were normalized by taking the logarithm [26].

In our previous study, we used a dataset that consisted of 9181 one-word units and 287 multiword ones. In this study, the dataset has been expanded – we added new texts from the Corpus of Russian Speech (http://russpeech.spbu.ru/). Now it contains 14 933 words and 428 compound units.

The algorithms were built separately for single words and for multiword units, since, in our opinion, this makes the data more homogeneous and simplifies the search for patterns. Both resulting datasets were divided into training and test samples (80% and 20% of each dataset respectively).

To write the code, we used the Jupyter Notebook (for more details see: https://jupyter.org/).

The following libraries were used:

- Scikit-learn - for building algorithms;
- Pandas - for data processing;
- NumPy - for working with mathematical functions.
- Keras - for building neural networks [27].

3.1 Working with Single Words

The first algorithm we built was a random forest. As a result, we obtained a list consisting of four features: the number of syllables, frequency in ipm, token frequency in a given text and whether the word is an adjective. Having used perceptron, we got a list that included the following features: the number of syllables, whether the word is a pronoun, whether the word is an adjective, whether the word is a pronominal adjective, whether the word is a noun, whether the word is a preposition. Having used gradient boosting we received the following list of features: the number of syllables, frequency in ipm, whether the word is an adjective, whether the word is a noun, token frequency in a given

---

[1] The source code can be found here: https://github.com/dayterr/sp_article_2021.

text, whether the word is a pronominal adjective and whether the word is an adverb. The accuracy and balanced accuracy for all three algorithms are provided in Table 1.

Table 1. The results of the application of the random forest, perceptron, gradient boosting and logistic regression to the dataset consisting of single words.

Algorithm	Accuracy	Balanced accuracy	Number of features in the list	Logistic regression for the list	
				Accuracy	Balanced accuracy
Random forest	79.85%	76.07%	4	75.39%	66.67%
Perceptron	77.13%	74.77%	6	78.30%	72.13%
Gradient boosting	80.42%	76.20%	7	78.27%	72.13%

To verify our results, we used logistic regression for the three lists of features obtained and received the highest accuracy and balanced accuracy for the list of six features proposed by the perceptron algorithm (see Table 1). The following features received positive coefficients: the number of syllables, whether the word is a pronoun, whether the word is an adjective, whether the word is a pronominal adjective. The features "whether the word is a noun" and "whether the word is a preposition" got negative coefficients. The accuracy for the list with seven features was very close to the one for the list of six features. In the former the following features received positive coefficients: whether the word is an adjective, the number of syllables, whether the word is a pronominal adjective, whether the word is an adverb, frequency in ipm. The features "token frequency in a given text" and "whether the word is a noun" obtained negative coefficients. In the list that we got having used the random forest algorithm the features "number of syllables", "frequency in ipm" and "whether the word is an adjective" received positive coefficients, which may indicate a direct correlation between these features and the fact of reduction; token frequency in a given text received a negative coefficient.

We also implemented neural networks based on the datasets obtained. The binary accuracy for the set of four features turned out to be 78.74%, for the set of six features – 77.2%, for the set of seven features – 78.47%.

3.2 Working with Multiword Units

In order to select the most relevant features for the occurrence of phonetic reduction in multiword units, we used the same algorithms as when working with single words (see Table 2 for the quantitative results).

The list obtained using a random forest algorithm included four features: frequency in ipm, number of words, token frequency in a given text, whether a word is a parenthetical word. Perceptron resulted in the following list of features: whether the word is an adjective, whether the previous word form is reduced, whether the word is a parenthetical word, token frequency in a given text, whether the word is a preposition, whether the word is a numeral, whether the word is an interjection, whether the word is a pronominal noun, type of text, number of syllables, whether a word is pronominal adjective, whether a word is a noun, frequency in ipm, whether a word is a conjunction, whether a word is a verb, whether a word is an adverb, whether a word is a pronoun, whether a word is a pronominal adverb, whether the word is a particle. Having used gradient boosting algorithm, the following list was obtained: frequency in ipm, the number of syllables, token frequency in a given text.

Table 2. The results of the application of the random forest, perceptron, gradient boosting and logistic regression to the dataset consisting of multiword units.

Algorithm	Accuracy	Balanced accuracy	Number of features in the list	Logistic regression for the list	
				Accuracy	Balanced accuracy
Random forest	83.72%	83.64%	4	67.44%	67.78%
Perceptron	77.90%	78.70%	19	69.77%	70.27%
Gradient boosting	81.40%	81.30%	3	62.80%	63.10%

For all the three lists, a logistic regression algorithm was also built. All features in the first list (obtained using the random forest algorithm) and in the third one (obtained using the gradient boosting algorithm) received positive coefficients. In the second list of 19 features, the following features got positive coefficients: whether the word is an adjective, whether the previous word form is reduced, whether the word is a parenthetical word, token frequency in a given text, whether the word is a preposition, whether the word is a numeral, whether the word is an interjection, whether the word is a pronominal noun, type of text, the number of syllables, whether the word is a pronominal adjective, whether the word is a noun, frequency in ipm. The following six features obtained negative coefficients: whether the word is an interjection, whether the word is a verb, whether the word is a pronominal adverb, whether the word is a pronoun, whether the word is an adverb, whether the word is a particle.

4   Discussion and Conclusion

In this study, six different sets of features were obtained using three different algorithms on two different datasets, i.e., single words and multiword units. When working with single words at the stage of feature selection, the gradient boosting algorithm showed the best result: the balanced accuracy for it was 76.20%. For the multiword units, the random forest algorithm showed the best result: its balanced accuracy was 83.64%. Both lists contained the following three features: frequency in ipm, number of syllables, token frequency in a given text.

All three lists for the dataset consisting of single words included such features as the number of syllables and whether the word is an adjective. This is quite understandable, given that the longer a word is the more chances there are that at least one of its phonetic elements will be reduced. As for the adjectives, 99.7% of all adjectives in the dataset are one-word adjectives and 75.3% of them were reduced, i.e., were pronounced with at least one omitted sound.

Two of the three lists for single words included such features as frequency ipm, token frequency in a given text, whether a word is a pronominal adjective, and whether a word is a noun. It can be assumed that nouns are reduced somewhat less frequently: 65.32% of nouns in our dataset did not undergo reduction. Similarly, Schachtenhaufen in [10] shows that nouns in spontaneous Danish also tend not to be reduced unless they are used in grammaticalized constructions. Checking this tendency in other languages seems to be promising from a typological perspective.

For some reason, token frequency in a given text received negative coefficient for the dataset consisting of single words. This result requires further consideration possibly including the analysis of pragmatic aspects of word usage (cf. [28]) as it seems to be strange that the words that are less frequent in a given text tend to undergo reduction more often than more frequent ones.

When working with multiword units, all the three lists included the following features: the number of syllables, frequency in ipm, token frequency in a given text. All these features received positive coefficients when building a logistic regression. As for the parenthetical words that appeared in two lists of features for multiword units, but were not observed in any list of features for single words, we can provide the following explanation. There are slightly more multiword units than single words among parenthetical words in our data: 51.7% (e.g., *mozhet_byt'* 'may be') and 48.3% respectively. However, 76% of all multiword parenthetical units were reduced, whereas only 48.5% parenthetical single words underwent reduction.

Interestingly enough, for multiword units, the logistic regression performed best on the largest list of features. Perhaps this is due to the small size of the dataset itself. It is impossible to draw any far-reaching conclusions on a dataset of this size. The only thing that can be said with a certain degree of confidence is that in addition to frequency in ipm, the number of syllables and token frequency in a given text, there should be some other features that determine whether a word form undergoes phonetic reduction in spontaneous speech. Thus, we are going to consider in our analysis the features discussed at the end of Sect. 2. This will require a further annotation of our corpus data (e.g., adding the information about the position in a phrase and the stress, etc.), but will allow us inter alia to compare our findings to the results of the similar studies on other languages [1, 11].

We are also going to expand the dataset, i.e., to use all texts from our corpus (which includes more than 25000 words now) and look more precisely on such features as text type (as our corpus includes monologues, reading and dialogues) and token frequency in a given text.

Acknowledgments. The research is supported by the grant #19-012-00629 from the Russian Foundation for Basic Research. We are very grateful to the anonymous peer-reviewers for constructive comments on an earlier version of the article.

References

1. Jurafski, D., Bell, A., Gregory, M., Raymond, W.D.: Probabilistic relations between words: evidence from reduction in lexical production. In: Bybee, J., Hopper, P. (eds.) Frequency and the Emergence of Linguistic Structure, pp. 229–254. John Benjamins, Philadelphia (2001). https://doi.org/10.1075/tsl.45.13jur

2. Kipyatkova, I.: Improving Russian LVCSR using deep neural networks for acoustic and language modeling. In: Karpov, A., Jokisch, O., Potapova, R. (eds.) SPECOM 2018. LNCS (LNAI), vol. 11096, pp. 291–300. Springer, Cham (2018). https://doi.org/10.1007/978-3-319-99579-3_31

3. Ernestus, M., Tucker, B.V.: Why we need to investigate casual speech to truly understand language production, processing and mental lexicon. Ment. Lex. **11**(3), 375–400 (2016). https://doi.org/10.1075/ml.11.3.03tuc

4. Dayter, M., Riekhakaynen, E.: Automatic prediction of word form reduction in Russian spontaneous speech. In: Karpov, A., Potapova, R. (eds.) SPECOM 2020. LNCS (LNAI), vol. 12335, pp. 119–127. Springer, Cham (2020). https://doi.org/10.1007/978-3-030-60276-5_12

5. Ernestus, M.: Voice Assimilation and Segment Reduction in Casual Dutch. A Corpus-Based Study of the Phonology-Phonetics Interface. Landelijke Onderzoekschool Taalwetenschap, Utrecht (2000)

6. Spilková, H.: Phonetic Reduction in Spontaneous Speech: An Investigation of Native and Non-Native Production. Norwegian University of Science and Technology, Trondheim (2014)

7. Stoyka, D.A.: Reduced Forms of Russian Speech: Linguistic and Extralinguistic Aspects. PhD thesis, Saint Petersburg (2016). (in Russian)

8. Lobanov, B.M., Tsyrulnik, L.I.: Modeling of intra-word and inter-word phonetic-acoustic phenomena in the synthesizer of Russian speech by text. In: Ideas and Methods of Experimental Study of Speech: Collection of Articles. Art. in Memory of prof. L.A. Chistovich and prof. V. A. Kozhevnikov, pp. 47–63. St. Petersburg (2008). (in Russian)

9. Riekhakaynen, E.: Realization of intervocalic consonant clusters in frequency words of the Russian language. Vestnik Sankt-Peterburgskogo Universiteta, Yazyk i Literatura **17**(4), 672–690 (2020). https://doi.org/10.21638/spbu09.2020.411. (in Russian)

10. Schachtenhaufen, R.: Phonetic reductions and linguistic factors. In: New Perspectives on Speech in Action. Proceedings of the 2nd SJUSK Conference on Contemporary Speech Habits, pp. 167–179. Samfundslitteratur, Frederiksberg (2013)

11. Pharao, N.: Consonant Reduction in Copenhagen Danish: A Study of Linguistic and Extra-linguistic Factors in Phonetic Variation and Change. Det Humanistiske Fakultet, Københavns Universitet, København (2010)

12. Riekhakaynen, E.: Corpora of Russian spontaneous speech as a tool for modelling natural speech production and recognition. In: 10th Annual Computing and Communication Workshop and Conference, CCWC 2020, January 2020, pp. 406–411. IEEE, Las Vegas (2020). https://doi.org/10.1109/CCWC47524.2020.9031251

13. Ventsov, A.V., Grudeva, E.V.: A Frequency Dictionary of Russian. CHSU Publishing House, Cherepovets (2008). (in Russian)

14. Breiman, L.: Random forests. Mach. Learn. **45**, 5–32 (2001). https://doi.org/10.1023/A:1010933404324

15. Geurts, P., Ernst, D., Wehenkel, L.: Extremely randomized trees. Mach. Learn. **63**, 3–42 (2006). https://doi.org/10.1007/s10994-006-6226-1

16. Hastie, T., Tibshirani, R., Friedman, J.: The Elements of Statistical Learning: Data Mining, Inference, and Prediction. Springer, New York (2012). https://doi.org/10.1007/978-0-387-84858-7

17. Aggarwal, C.C.: Machine Learning for Text. Springer, Cham (2018). https://doi.org/10.1007/978-3-319-73531-3
18. Manning, C.D., Raghavan, P., Schütze, H.: An Introduction to Information Retrieval. Cambridge University Press, Cambridge (2009)
19. Alpaydin, E.: Introduction to Machine Learning. MIT Press, Cambridge (2014)
20. Riekhakaynen, E.: Reduction in spontaneous speech: How to survive. In: Heegart, J., Henrichsen, P.J. (eds.) Copenhagen Studies in Language. 43: New Perspectives on Speech in Action: Proceedings of the 2nd SJUSK Conference on Contemporary Speech Habits, pp. 153–167. Samfundslitteratur, Frederiksberg (2013)
21. Knyazev, S.A., Pozharitskaya, S.K.: Modern Russian Language: Phonetics, Correct Pronunciation, Writing System, Spelling. Academic Project, Gaudeamus, Moscow (2011). (in Russian)
22. Riekhakaynen, E.I.: Recognition of Russian Speech: Context + Frequency. St. Petersburg State University, St. Petersburg (2016). (in Russian)
23. Apushkina, I.E.: Stressed and unstressed words in a spontaneous spoken text. In: Cherepovets Scientific Readings–2009: Proceedings of the All-Russian Conference Dedicated to the Day of the City of Cherepovets (November 2–3, 2009). Part 1. Literature Studies and Linguistics at the Beginning of the 21st Century, pp. 57–60. GOU VPO ChGU, Cherepovets (2010). (in Russian)
24. Guyon, I., Weston, J., Barnhill, S., Vapnik, V.: Gene selection for cancer classification using support vector machines. Mach. Learn. **46**, 389–422 (2002). https://doi.org/10.1023/A:1012487302797
25. Freund, Y., Schapire, R.E.: Large margin classification using the perceptron algorithm. Mach. Learn. **37**, 277–296 (1999). https://doi.org/10.1023/A:1007662407062
26. Zumel, N., Mount, J.: Practical Data Science with R. Manning Publications, New York (2020)
27. Sholle, F.: Deep Learning in Python. Piter, St. Petersburg (2018). (in Russian)
28. Pavlova, A.V., Svetozarova, N.D.: Phrasal Stress in Phonetic, Functional and Semantic Aspects. Flinta, Moscow (2017). (in Russian)

Toxic Comment Classification Service in Social Network

Mikhail Dolgushin, Dayana Ismakova, Yuliya Bidulya$^{(\boxtimes)}$, Igor Krupkin,
Galina Barskaya, and Anastasiya Lesiv

University of Tyumen, Tyumen, Russia

Abstract. The article discusses the development of an online tool for moderating
the content of social network groups. The use of classification using machine
learning methods is proposed as the main element of the system. The creation of
the feature set of messages is assumed by extracting the content features of the text,
as well as the use of word embeddings vectors. The authors conducted a series of
experiments to find the best combination of vector representation, content features
and classification method. Tests on a dataset of 11 thousand messages in Russian
showed the result of 87% accuracy. The architecture of the group moderator's web
application with the ability to automatically apply classification results to control
users and display posts is proposed.

Keywords: Social media · Moderation · Toxic detection · Feature extraction ·
Text classification

1 Introduction

The object of study in this work is the moderation of messages and comments in a social
network group to maintain a comfortable climate in this group, encouraging people to
correctly express their opinions on the topic. Inappropriateness is most often expressed as
the presence of toxicity, which is a rude, disrespectful comment that can cause someone
to leave the discussion [1].

This paper presents the initial stage of developing a message moderation system
intended for administrators of social network groups. For the most part, the automation of
moderating messages on social networks comes down to filtering them based on the list of
forbidden words compiled by the moderator. These filters allow you to remove messages
that contain offensive language or some forbidden words. This approach often leads to
the deletion of harmless messages, or, on the contrary, to the omission of comments with
more subtle insults, built on the context and outwardly looking quite neutral. It is for this
reason that social media comments are often moderated manually by moderators either
before or after the [2] publication.

Automatic determination of toxicity in a text using machine learning methods has
been discussed for a long time in publications, however, in the Russian-speaking segment
of social networks, this problem has not yet been sufficiently developed. Research into

© Springer Nature Switzerland AG 2021
A. Karpov and R. Potapova (Eds.): SPECOM 2021, LNAI 12997, pp. 157–165, 2021.
https://doi.org/10.1007/978-3-030-87802-3_15

toxic detection is mainly focused on English, but some work in other languages also exists [3].

The aim of our work is to develop a software that could detect toxicity in the Russian segment of social media VKontakte (https://vk.com/). We study the possibility of using machine-learning algorithms to create a pre-trained model that is stored on the server side and connected as a web-service. One of the main development problems was the lack of Russian-language tagged datasets for training. Another problem is the need to use limited computing resources when developing a web service for moderating messages online.

We consider the problem of toxic detection as a text classification task with a binary choice: a system must predict whether a message should be blocked or non-blocked. Previously, experiments were carried out to select the best set of message properties to determine the toxicity, the presence of which determines the blocking of the message or verification of its author. Our research was carried out using two datasets. The first dataset is provided on the site of the well-known platform Kaggle [4]. With its help, we have selected the most effective algorithms for classifying messages by the presence or absence of toxic statements. A second dataset of 5000 messages we collected and annotated manually [5]. It was used to extract additional features for pre-filtering messages, as well as to train classifiers at the developed web application.

2 Related Work

2.1 Content Moderation of User Generated Content

A huge number of works are devoted to the problem of user generated content moderation. The relevance of the topic is due to the rapid growth in the number of resources with the necessary feedback from users. Content moderation is used in advertising, politics, business and other areas of activity, and the goals may vary. For example, in the electronic media, comments from news readers are screened, and moderation is used to decide which comments should be blocked in accordance with the policy of a particular newspaper [6]. Authors considered eight different categories of comments: disallowed content, threats, hate speech, obscenity, deception & trolling, vulgarity, language, and abuse. Each category provided its own scenarios of actions: from blocking an account to a temporary ban.

One more article [7] was also devoted to media moderation, which used a dataset of a newspaper of more than million comments with labels received from the newspaper's moderators and journalists. More specific categories were used as labels: calumniation, discrimination, disrespect, hooliganism, insult, irony, swearing, threat. Labels were used as attributes of objects, not target classes.

Many works are also devoted to the analysis of messages on social networks. The review article [8] shows the main features of the content and related problems of analysis: general terms, jargon, memes, vocabulary and cultural preferences of social groups can vary significantly; attackers can use special methods to "deceive" moderation algorithms on social networks; the presence of messages with spelling errors and typos complicates the technical processing of texts. In addition, messages represent short texts, which make it difficult to consider the context and build models that reflect fixed expressions and word order.

2.2 Text Classification

Two approaches are used to classify texts during the moderation process. First, for each comment, semantic characteristics associated with toxicity markers are determined, such as the use of harsh words, negative or positive sentiment, the presence of emojis, the mention of proper names or pointers to locations, the type of utterance, characteristics of the message distribution, and so on. The values of these features make up the vector of each message, which is then used to train the system or determine the class using rules [9–11].

The second approach involves constructing a vector of each message using bag of word n-grams or word embeddings for further training of classifiers and neural networks [12]. The following text preprocessing scheme is used: tokenization, removal of stop words, POS markup, extraction of text tags, which results in the display of a bag of words or n-grams [13]. In addition, the representation of texts in embedding models is also widely used in classification problems. The most popular model is Word2vec, representing words from a dictionary mapped to vectors of real numbers [14].

A hybrid of these two approaches is also widely used, when the vector representation of texts is supplemented with content attributes [15].

About classification methods, the most popular and effective are convolutional neural networks, on which such systems for analyzing user content as Perspective (http://www.perspectiveapi.com/) are based. However, traditional methods such as SVM, naive Bayesian method, random forest, etc. [10] also show good results and provide more opportunities for implementation in the form of web applications, since they require less extensive computational resources.

3 Data and Preprocessing

We used two different datasets in this work. First dataset Kaggle Russian Language Toxic Comments Dataset (Dataset 1) [4] is a collection of annotated comments which was published on Kaggle in 2019 and consists of 14,412 unique comments, where 4,826 texts were labeled as toxic, and 9,586 as non-toxic. The length of comment ranges from 21 to 7400 characters, the average length is 175 characters.

For our own dataset (Dataset 2), 5,000 comments were collected and marked up from the social network Vkontakte [5]. It includes 1,150 texts labeled as toxic, and 3,850 texts labeled as non-toxic. The length of comment ranges from 11 to 4100 characters.

Message preprocessing includes tokenization, stop-word and punctuation removal, lemmatization provided by NLTK [16] and Pymorphy2 [17] libraries.

4   Features

4.1   Vector Models

We implemented the set of features that used as the input data for the machine learning classification. At the output, we get labels for messages, depending on presence of toxic in the message text. The features are described below.

In our experiments, we use the following vector models for feature extraction:

1. Term Frequency (TF) vector model is a matrix of unigrams usage frequencies in documents [18]. In this work, we didn't use the TFIDF model, since it shows itself better on long text messages, the use of the TF-matrix is more reasonable. For the same reason higher-level n-grams are not considered. For the TF implementation matrix, the Count Vectorizer acquired in the Scikit-learn library [19] is used with parameter: size 300.
2. Word2Vec [20] is a tool for calculating vector representations of words that implements two main architectures: Continuous Bag Of Words and Skip-gram. The input is a text corpus, and the output is a set of word vec-tors. We applied Word2vec model of Gensim with the following model parameters: size 150, window 10. The final value for each word is obtained by averaging all the numbers in its vector.
3. Doc2Vec [21] is a tool like Word2Vec, but the input is a whole text document. We applied Doc2vec model of Gensim with the following model parame-ters: size 10. The final value for each word is obtained by averaging all the numbers in its vector.
4. FastText [22] is a library containing pre-trained ready-made word representations and a classifier, that is, a machine learning algorithm that breaks words into classes. We used FastText model of Gensim with the following model parame-ters: size 150, window 5.

We applied scaling from 0 to 100 results using the MaxMinScaler class from the Scikit-learn library [19] for all described models except Count Vectorizer.

4.2   Content Features

We have expanded the word vector features with additional features determined from the message content:

- the presence in the text of persona's names,
- the presence in the text of names of locations,
- the presence in the text of names of organizations,
- positive, negative, neutral sentiment,
- the presence of rude words.

These features were extracted using the Dostoevsky [23], SpaCy [24] libraries, as well as the vocabulary of rude words.

5 Experiments and Results

5.1 Classification of Toxic Comments

The goal of the first experiment was to find the best combination of a vector model as feature set and a classification algorithm from the following:

1. Support vector classification (SVC) [25] is a set of similar supervised learning algorithms used for classification and regression analysis problems.
2. The Multinomial Naive Bayesian Classifier (MNB) [25] is a modification of the Naive Bayesian Classifier where function vectors represent the frequencies with which certain events were generated by a polynomial distribution.
3. A support vector machine modification using a naive Bayesian algorithm (NBSVM) is a support vector machine implementation in which vectors are constructed based on the coefficients of the logarithm of the naive Bayesian algorithm as characteristic values. The NBSVM implementation is taken from the Kaggle [26].
4. The Random Forest Classification (RFC) [25] is a classification model using a machine learning algorithm that uses an ensemble of decision trees (decision trees).

For the classifiers Multinomial Naive Bayesian, Support vector classification and Random Forest the classes presented in the SciKitLearn library were used [19]. The experiments were carried out on the Dataset 1. We used cross-validation with stratification to prevent overfitting and to decrease the influence of class imbalance in all classification methods. In addition, a grid search was used in the implementation of the Scikit-learn library for selection of classification parameters [19].

Table 1 demonstrates a F1-measure and accuracy values calculated for features described above in Sect. 4.1.

As follows from the results of Table 1 (in bold), the best values of the F-measure and accuracy in this experiment were obtained using the FastText vectorization and the SVC classifier.

5.2 Content Features Selection

After feature extraction (see Sect. 4.2) we calculated the Pearson correlation for each feature with the target sign of the presence or absence of toxicity in the tagged dataset. The calculated values are shown in Table 2.

The largest coefficient is shown by features: negative, neutral sentiment and the presence of rude words. We expanded word vectors by features with the highest correlation and trained again on the same dataset. The best result was shown by the Word2Vec representation and the SVC classifier. It turned out that the expansion of the feature set led to a low increase in accuracy from 0.864 to 0.872. This model was later used in the development of a web application for moderating social network comments.

Table 1. The results of message classification.

Vector model	Classifier	Class "Toxic", F1	Class "Un-toxic", F1	Accuracy
Term frequency	SVC	.571	.858	.787
	MNB	.385	.839	.745
	NBSVM	.568	.859	.787
	RFC	.410	.844	.753
Doc2Vec	SVC	.745	.892	.851
	MNB	.744	.889	.845
	NBSVM	.715	.864	.816
	RFC	.763	.891	.851
Word2Vec	SVC	.769	.902	.862
	MNB	.742	.894	.849
	NBSVM	.778	.894	.857
	RFC	.771	.903	.864
FashText	SVC	**.786**	**.906**	**.870**
	MNB	.776	.889	.852
	NBSVM	.779	.904	.867
	RFC	.748	.899	.856

Table 2. Pearson's correlation coefficients.

Feature	Coefficient
Person	−0.013
Location	−0.063
Organization	−0.017
Positive	−0.047
Negative	0.361
Neutral	−0.267
Rude words	0.413

6 System Architecture

After analyzing the results of the experiments, we chose an approach to implement a Web application for the automatic determination of toxicity in VKontakte messages.

The application implements functions executed within the following modules (see Fig. 1):

- "ToxicAuth" is a Laravel (https://laravel.com) framework-based backend service that is present an application programming interface (API) for moderator authentication.
- "MainAPI" is a backend service for moderating a social network group. It works with data about comments, users, messages and groups and allows you to assign restrictions to messages or users who have received toxicity labels as a result of classification. Essentially, it links the classification module to the moderator interface.
- "ClassifierAPI" is an application implemented in the Python programming language and the Flask (https://flask.palletsprojects.com) framework. It trains the classifier and displays the class label for an individual message or comment text. The trained model is saved in.csv format and stored on the server. The module interacts with *vk-api* (https://pypi.org/project/vk-api/) to receive messages and comments from the social network, as well as with the "MainAPI" module, transmitting data about toxic messages and users who will be penalized in any way for toxic messages.
- "ClassifierGUI" is a separate graphical interface developed for working with the training sample and the output of training metrics. A graphical interface was developed using the PyQT5 library and developed using the PyQT5 Designer (https://pythonscripts.com/pyqt5).

"ToxicFront" is a frontend application developed using the React.js framework (https://reactjs.org). This is an interface for a group moderator that receives information about users submitting toxic messages or comments and can warn or block such users.

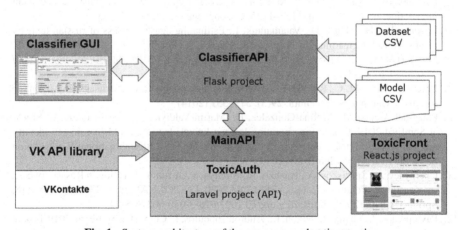

Fig. 1. System architecture of the message moderation service.

7   Conclusion

We investigated the possibility of using machine learning methods to develop the web-application for moderation of Russian-language messages and comments on a social network. Experiments on a sample of eleven thousand messages have shown that the most suitable result is achieved using vectorization of the Word2vec model and classification by the SVM method with the expansion of content features: the presence of rude words, negative and neutral sentiment. The maximum accuracy has reached 87%.

As a result of this work, the first version of software for moderation of social network messages in the Russian-speaking group of VK has been developed. It trained on a hand-made dataset and currently being tested on five groups of social network users.

References

1. Georgakopoulos, S.V., Tasoulis, S.K., Vrahatis, A.G., Plagianakos, V.P.: Convolutional neural networks for toxic comment classification. arXiv preprint arXiv:1802.09957 (2018)
2. Medialogiya–monitoring and analysis of media and social networks (rus.). https://www.mlg.ru
3. Corazza, M., Menini, S., Cabrio, E., Tonelli, S., Villata, S.: A multilingual evaluation for online hate speech detection. ACM Trans. Internet Technol. Assoc. Comput. Mach. 20(2), 1–22 (2020). https://doi.org/10.1145/3377323.hal-02972184
4. Russian Language Toxic Comments. https://www.kaggle.com/blackmoon/russian-language-toxic-comments
5. "Toxicology" project: vk_comments_DS. https://github.com/mihatronych/files/blob/main/ds_of_toxic_messages_from_vk/our_toxic_vk_comments_data.csv
6. Shekhar, R., Pranjić, M., Pollak, S., Pelicon, A., Purver, M.: Automating news comment moderation with limited resources: benchmarking in croatian and estonian. J. Lang. Technol. Comput. Linguist. 34, 49–79 (2020)
7. Pavlopoulos, J., Malakasiotis, P., Androutsopoulos, I.: Deeper attention to abusive user content moderation. In: EMNLP, pp. 1125–1135. Copenghagen, Denmark (2017)
8. Levonevskiy, D., Malov, D., Vatamaniuk, I.: Estimating aggressiveness of russian texts by means of machine learning. In: Salah, A.A., Karpov, A., Potapova, R. (eds.) SPECOM 2019. LNCS (LNAI), vol. 11658, pp. 270–279. Springer, Cham (2019). https://doi.org/10.1007/978-3-030-26061-3_28
9. Lee, J.-T., Yang, M.-C., Rim, H.-C.: Discovering high-quality threaded discussions in online forums. J. Comput. Sci. Technol. 29(3), 519–531 (2014)
10. Plaza-del Arco, F.M., Molina-Gonzalez, D., Martın-Valdivia, T., Urena-Lopez, A.: SINAI at SemEval-2019 Task 6: incorporating lexicon knowledge into SVM learning to identify and categorize offensive language in social media. In: The 13th International Workshop on Semantic Evaluation (SemEval) (2019)
11. Chernyaev, A., Spryiskov, A., Ivashko, A., Bidulya, Y.: A rumor detection in Russian tweets. In: Karpov, A., Potapova, R. (eds.) SPECOM 2020. LNCS (LNAI), vol. 12335, pp. 108–118. Springer, Cham (2020). https://doi.org/10.1007/978-3-030-60276-5_11
12. Pavlopoulos, J., Thain, N., Dixon, L., Androutsopoulos, I.: ConvAI at SemEval-2019 Task 6: offensive language identification and categorization with perspective and BERT. In: SemEval, Minneapolis, USA (2019)
13. Pietro, M.D.: Text Classification with NLP: tf-idf vs Word2Vec vs BERT. https://towardsdatascience.com/text-classification-with-nlp-tf-idf-vs-word2vec-vs-bert-41ff868d1794
14. Camacho-Collados, J., Pilehvar, M.T.: From word to sense embeddings: a survey on vector representations of meaning. arXiv:1805.04032. Bibcode:2018arXiv180504032C (2018)
15. Waseem, Z., Hovy, D.: Hateful symbols or hateful people? predictive features for hate speech detection on Twitter. In: Proceedings of the 2016 Conference of the North American Chapter of the Association for Computational Linguistics: Human Language Technologies. Association for Computational Linguistics, pp. 88–93 (2016)

16. NLTK documentation. https://www.nltk.org
17. Morphological analyzer pymorphy2. https://pymorphy2.readthedocs.io
18. Document-term matrix. https://en.wikipedia.org/wiki/Document-term_matrix
19. Pedregosa, F., et al.: Scikit-learn: machine learning in python. J. Mach. Learn. Res. **12**, 2825–2830. JMLR (2011)
20. Rehurek, R., Sojka, P.: Software framework for topic modelling with large corpora. In: LREC 2010 Workshop on New Challenges for NLP Frameworks, pp. 45–50. Valletta, Malta, May. ELRA (2010). http://is.muni.cz/publication/884893/en
21. Gensim: Doc2vec. https://radimrehurek.com/gensim/models/doc2vec.html
22. Mestre, M.: FastText: stepping through the code. https://medium.com/@mariamestre/fasttext-stepping-through-the-code-259996d6ebc4
23. Dostoevsky: Sentiment Analysis Library for Russian Language. https://pypi.org/project/dostoevsky
24. SpaCy: Industrial-Strength Natural Language Processing. https://spacy.io
25. Wang, S., Manning, C.D.: Baselines and bigrams: simple, good sentiment and topic classification, Department of Computer Science, Stanford University, Stanford 94305. https://nlp.stanford.edu/pubs/sidaw12_simple_sentiment.pdf
26. Wang, Z.: NBSVM. https://www.kaggle.com/ziliwang/nbsvm

Deep Learning Based Engagement Recognition in Highly Imbalanced Data

Denis Dresvyanskiy[1,2(✉)], Wolfgang Minker[1], and Alexey Karpov[3]

[1] Ulm University, Helmholtzstraße 16, 89081 Ulm, Germany
{denis.dresvyanskiy,wolfgang.minker}@uni-ulm.de
[2] ITMO University, Kronverksky Pr. 49, bldg. A, 197101 St. Petersburg, Russia
[3] St. Petersburg Institute for Informatics and Automation of the Russian Academy
Sciences, St. Petersburg Federal Research Center of the Russian Academy of Sciences
(SPC RAS), 14th Line V.O. 39, 199178 St. Petersburg, Russia
karpov@iias.spb.su

Abstract. Engagement recognition is a growing domain in paralinguistics evaluation due to its importance in many human-computer and human-robot applications. Current requirements for such systems are not only to interact, but also to engage the user into interaction as long as possible. To do so, the machine should differ among different levels of engagement to adjust its behavior properly. However, actual models are still far from it, partially due to data quality – usually, engagement recognition datasets are highly biased towards the high-engagement levels, because they are more often and naturally expressed by humans during interaction context. Thus, currently, the development of a reliable engagement recognition system able to detect all engagement levels is necessary. To facilitate it, we introduce a deep learning engagement recognition framework in the context of the DAiSEE corpus, which is a highly imbalanced dataset. We showed that the metric used formerly for evaluating the performance of the models on the DAiSEE dataset is inadequate due to its imbalance and conducted extensive experiments on DAiSEE, suggesting a new baseline performance based on the Unweighted Average Recall metric.

Keywords: Paralinguistics · Engagement recognition · Class imbalance · Face processing · Deep learning

1 Introduction

Nowadays the human-computer interaction (HCI), as well as human-robot interaction (HRI), is becoming a day-to-day routine for more and more people. However, current HCI and HRI systems such as intelligent dialogue assistants and domestic robots endure a lack of paralinguistic characteristics evaluation, although current requirements for such systems are not only to maintain the dialogue, but also to recognize user's state and act appropriately [8,11]. Therefore, one of the actively developing areas in HCI and HRI has become engagement recognition (ER) because of its usefulness, yet complexity in evaluation.

© Springer Nature Switzerland AG 2021
A. Karpov and R. Potapova (Eds.): SPECOM 2021, LNAI 12997, pp. 166–178, 2021.
https://doi.org/10.1007/978-3-030-87802-3_16

Engagement is a complex phenomena, which still has several commonly used scientific definitions, depending on the domain it is used. For example, in terms of interaction between humans (robots) it is defined as the "process by which two (or more) participants establish, maintain and end their perceived connection" [33] or "the value that a participant in an interaction attributes to the goal of being together with the other participant(s) and of continuing the interaction" [30]. Dobrian et al. [10] defined it as "reflection of user involvement and interaction", using engagement as an intermediate position between aforementioned states. Depending on the usage, different engagement definitions were stated in terms of interface quality [31], quality of user experience [29], and social media [18].

This work, according to Kaur et al. [22], relies on the definition of student engagement provided by [13], where it is described as a complex structure consisting of 3 components: behavioral (persistence and participation in learning process), emotional (feelings and interest to the target object or topic), and cognitive engagement (motivation, strategy and efforts to the task under consideration).

The recognition of student engagement has large attention from the industry, especially from Massive Open Online Courses (MOOCs), since more than 90% of students leave chosen course before reaching its end [20,36]. The intelligent learning system, which would be able to recognize the point of starting disengagement and act properly, could make a revolution in MOOCs, dramatically decreasing the student's dropout rate.

Although there are several available databases devoted to ER such as Engagement-in-the-wild [22], DAiSEE [15,21], and NoXi [6], all of them suffer from class imbalance. It is a natural problem for ER due to the difficulty of gathering the low-engagement classes. At the same time, the most important instances are low-engagement classes, since the task for the HCI system is taking into account such cases to prevent the user disengagement and return him/her to the higher points of engagement evaluation scale. Therefore, one of the key requirements for an ER system should be reliability in terms of low-engagement evaluation, which can be reached by training a balanced model using special techniques.

Thus, in this work, we propose the ER framework based on deep learning and focused on the balancing of the classification performance. We analyzed and conducted extensive experiments on the DAiSEE [15], known as a highly imbalanced dataset for recognition of affective states in the e-environment. Moreover, we suggest using another metric (Unweighted Average Recall) to measure the performance of the ER system, since the former one (Accuracy) is not appropriate for highly imbalanced datasets, and provide a new baseline performance, evaluated on the DAiSEE dataset.

The rest of the paper is organized as follows: we describe the background and related work in Sect. 2. Section 3 presents an exploiting dataset analysis. In Sect. 4, we propose our deep learning framework for ER task. Section 5 provides the experimental results and setup of the proposed framework. In Sect. 6 we discuss the results obtained on chosen dataset. Lastly, Sect. 7 summarizes performed work and discuss future research directions in ER with high imbalance.

2   Related Work

In this Section, we firstly observe methods commonly used for ER during HCI and HRI and then shift to the methods exploited within the DAiSEE database.

2.1   Engagement Recognition in HCI and HRI

Overall, the feasibility of determining the user engagement state has already been researched for almost 20 years. Today, as robotization and dialogue systems had become more widespread, ER has started to actively permeate in various HCI and HRI scenarios.

In the context of HCI and e-learning, Yun et al. [38] proposed a deep learning framework based on convolutional neural network (CNN) and temporal dynamics module for preventing overfitting and processing deep embeddings across the temporal dimension. As a result, they reached decent results in comparison with human-level predictions. Kim et al. [23] studied engagement detection in groups of children utilizing special ranking Support Vector Machine (SVM) instead of default one. Authors showed that the fusing of multimodal features benefits more than using them separately. The automatic recognition of engagement in the student environment was examined in [35], where preprocessed data from RGB camera was fed into SVM and Multinomial Logistic Regression classifiers. The implemented system performed with compatible to humans results on the binary classification task. To consider context information while evaluating user engagement state, Heimerl et al. [16] suggested a hybrid system, combining deep learning with Bayesian Networks to increase interpretability of the model. They showed that utilizing multimodal data in combination with their approach can outperform state-of-the-art black-box methods on the same database.

In the context of the HRI, the most common information channels also remain audio and video signals. As for the HCI, researchers tend to use multimodal classical and/or end-to-end machine learning approaches, but the trajectory of the ER investigation is slightly biased towards identifying low-engagement user states to prevent it. For instance, Ben-Youssef et al. [4] introduced a new dataset UE-HRI, which imposed to develop approaches to detect early disengagement time points in the conversation and act properly. Several works have done studies on it, utilizing Echo-state networks [26], classical classificators such as logistic regression [37] and deep neural networks [5], and examining the feasibility of early automatic detection of engagement breakdown in the HRI environment.

Another popular direction in HRI is evaluation of the Visual Focus of Attention (VFOA) itself and related features, since it is important for the robot to identify what or whom a person is looking at. The VFOA is similar to the engagement characteristic in HRI, since humans tend to look on the object they are interested in. For example, Jayagopi et al. [19] introduced the Vernissage corpus for training models capable to evaluate VFOA and corresponding features [27,32].

When analyzing the databases used in the aforementioned studies, it is important to note that all of them are highly imbalanced and shifted towards high-engagement classes. We have summarized the class distributions of observed corpora in Table 1. The column "minor class" represents the least presented category in the corresponding dataset, while the column "Major class" – the most presented category. We should note that in all datasets minor class refers to the lowest-engagement user state and the major class alters between high- and very-high-engagement classes. We also should underline that for our experiments, we have chosen DAiSEE [15], as it is the most imbalanced corpus among presented ones, yet, is popular among datasets devoted to MOOCs.

Table 1. Class distributions in various engagement recognition datasets. The Minor classes are always a low-engagement classes.

ID	Dataset	Minor class	Major class	Ratio
1	NoXi [6]	1.80%	64.80%	1:36
2	Engagement-in-the-wild [22]	4.60%	42.26%	1:9.2
3	UE-HRI [4]	10.00%	90.00%	1:9
4	Children engagement [38]	2.94%	50.00%	1:17
5	Faces of engagement (HBCU) [35]	6.03 %	46.29%	1:7.7
6	Faces of engagement (UC) [35]	5.37%	43.85%	1:8.2
7	**DAiSEE** [15]	**0.71%**	**50.31%**	**1:70.86**

2.2 Engagement Recognition Using DAiSEE

Since collecting and publishing the DAiSEE dataset in 2016, numerous researchers have tried to build and train reliable systems able to differentiate between different levels of engagement. Firstly, we should note that authors of the DAiSEE corpus [15] have provided baseline performance on the collected dataset. They exploited different deep learning models, reaching the highest *Accuracy* equaled to 56.1% with pretrained and fine-tuned 3D-CNN on the DAiSEE corpus. After publishing, different research groups have applied other models to beat the baseline model.

Zhang et al. [39] have employed Inflated 3D Convolutional Network (I3D) to solve binary and four-class tasks. Binarization of the classes was simply done by unifying two low-engagement and two high-engagement classes into 2 different classes. They achieved 98.72% *Accuracy* on binary task, however, the model was not able to perform well on the 4-class task, giving only 52.35% *Accuracy*. In [14], authors constructed 3D-CNN, using focal loss to train it. Nevertheless, the performance of the model was 56.2%, which is greater only on 0.1% in comparison with the baseline. Liao et al. [24] developed Deep Facial SpatioTemporal Network, combining pretrained SE-ResNet-50 (SENet) with Long-Short Term Memory (LSTM) network with Global Attention applied to it. Exploiting implemented model, they have reached 58.84% *Accuracy* on the DAiSEE corpus, outperforming baseline on 2.74%. Next, Huang at all [17] reported on reaching 60.00% *Accuracy* on the 4-class task, using special temporal convolution with bidirectional LSTM (BLSTM) and attention mechanism. The last and very recent paper [1] has implemented ResNet and Temporal Convolutional Network (TCN) hybrid network, leading to 63.90% *Accuracy*, which is the best result on DAiSEE corpus today.

To sum up considered approaches and their effectiveness, we presented them in Table 2. The best result is highlighted in bold. As we can see from the table, deep learning is used in all papers, since the number of data is high and it can satisfy the hunger of neural network approaches.

Table 2. The accuracy performance of observed frameworks on the DAiSEE corpus.

ID	Paper	Approach	Test performance (Acc.)
1	[15]	3D-CNN (baseline)	56.10%
2	[39]	I3D	52.35%
3	[14]	3D-CNN + Focal Loss	56.20%
4	[24]	SENet + LSTM + Global Attention	58.84%
5	[17]	Temporal Convolution + BLSTM + RNN-Attention	60.00%
6	[1]	**Resnet-TCN hybrid**	**63.90%**

3   Dataset Analysis

The DAiSEE corpus is recorded in an e-learning environment and implied the scenario such as a student taking MOOC in the classroom or at home. The target labels were chosen according to 4 affective states, which student can feel during the learning process: engagement, frustration, boredom, and confusion. The video data was collected using a full HD web camera with 1980×1080 resolution and 30 fps, which is enough for detecting changes in participants' faces. The data has varying illumination settings, frequently occurring obstacles, and complete freedom for participants' actions, making DAiSEE truly in-the-wild dataset.

Overall, 112 subjects took part in experiments, resulting in approximately 25 h of video material. For the simplicity of the annotation, all video files were separated into 10-second segments. The crowdsourcing platform CroudFlower was chosen to perform the annotation process, relying on the "wisdom-of-the-crowd". Then, after several post-processing steps (to get more information, please, see [15]), 9068 10-second annotated video segments were obtained. It should be noted that authors provide audio modality along with the video segments. However, due to the e-learning context, participants are mostly silent, resulting in the inefficiency of exploiting the audio modality.

As we mentioned above, the DAiSEE is a highly imbalanced dataset. To demonstrate it, we depicted the class distribution for train, development, and

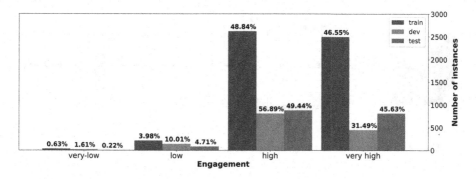

Fig. 1. Class distribution for train, development and test sets of DAiSEE. Please, note: Values located above the bars indicate the proportion of the class within one dataset (different colors refer to different datasets). (Color figure online)

test sets in Fig. 1. It is wide-known that one of the key points in solving imbalance problems is defining the right metric for measuring the model performance. Observing from Table 2, we can note that all papers described above as well as baseline paper considered *Accuracy* as the main metric for model evaluation. However, *Accuracy* is not an adequate performance metric in highly imbalanced datasets such as DAiSEE. We can demonstrate it by predicting always high-engagement class: it already gives **49.37%** *Accuracy*, while generating predictions randomly as high- and very-high-engagement classes gives near **47%** *Accuracy*. As a confirmation, Abedi and Khan in [1] have demonstrated the inability of several models, observed earlier, to predict low- and very-low-engagement classes, although they had a decent *Accuracy* score.

Therefore, working with highly imbalanced data, the good choice is *Unweighted Average Recall* (UAR), because it represents the unbiased evaluation of the model capability to distinguish among various engagement levels, eliminating the drawback of *Accuracy* metric. UAR allows paying attention even to the class with an extremely low number of instances (as very-low-engagement), while does not forget about other widely represented classes, providing the possibility to balance the model during the training process, which is not possible to get with simple weighted metric such as *Accuracy*.

4   Methodology

The proposed framework for ER in highly imbalanced datasets is presented in the Fig. 2. Generally, it consists of 4 different blocks: OpenFace block, EmoVG-GFace2, VGGFace2-SA and Recurrent block. Each block has its own advantages, adding complementary benefit to the overall evaluation. On the one hand, Facial Action Units (FAUs), extracted by OpenFace, have proven themselves as reliable facial features in affective computing. On the other hand, deep embeddings from deep neural networks have been successfully used for the last decade, showing outperforming effectiveness in various paralinguistics tasks. Moreover, we believe

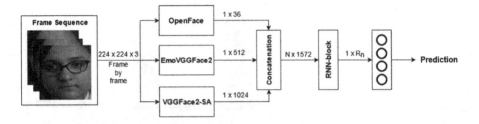

Fig. 2. The pipeline of the proposed framework for engagement recognition.

that deep emotional embeddings, extracted from pretrained on emotion recognition task CNN, can dramatically increase the efficacy of the ER system, since the part of the engagement itself is an emotional engagement [11]. The Recurrent block is responsible for temporal modelling, because the engagement is a long-term process, difficult to detect from only one frame without context. The Recurrent block consists of LSTM and Self-Attention layers.

The OpenFace block is simply the wide-known Facial Behaviour Analysis Toolkit [3], namely the part of the framework responsible for FAU evaluation [2]. We extract FAU features in frame-by-frame way and use them for further evaluations. The description of all other blocks are provided further.

4.1 EmoVGGFace2

The EmoVGGFace2 is based on ResNet50 network architecture pretrained on VGGFace2 dataset [7]. The VGGFace2 is created for face recognition task, providing a rich and diverse facial data for training face identification systems. We fine-tuned provided by authors VGGFace2 model on AffectNet [28] dataset to obtain model able to extract deep emotional embeddings from faces (resulting in EmoVGGFAce2 model). The embeddings were extracted from the first dense layer, which is located right after the last convolutional layer of ResNet50 network architecture. To learn more about the fine-tuning process, the reader is kindly referred to the [12].

4.2 VGGFace2-SA

To get model specialized only on ER, we have constructed VGGFace2-SA model. Structurally, it is composed of ResNet50 network and modified Self-Attention Non-Local Block (SA-NLB) [34]. On top of it we stack two dense layers with 1024 and 4 (softmax) neurons accordingly. SA mechanism was applied for capturing dependencies between high-level features at the end of the ResNet50.

Since we trained created model on the DAiSEE in frame-by-frame way, we slightly modified SA-NLB by omitting temporal dimension of the SA mechanism.

Thus, the input and output of the SA-NLB block were $H \times W \times 1024$, instead of $T \times H \times W \times 1024$, where T - temporal dimension (number of frames), H - height of the feature map, W - width of the feature map and 1024 - the number of channels. We utilized the *embedded Gaussian* version of the SA with softmax function after dot-product inside Non-Local Block.

4.3 Recurrent Block

The main purpose of the recurrent block is to capture temporal dependencies along several frames (namely, corresponding to them extracted embeddings). Structurally, the Recurrent block consists of repeated LSTM layers followed by SA-NLB described earlier. Overall, we added two LSTM-SA-NLB blocks with 512 and 256 units on top of the model. Next, one more LSTM layer with 128 units followed by a dense layer with 4 softmax units was added.

4.4 Methods for Imbalance Elimination

To deal with the class imbalance in DAiSEE, we have applied several balancing techniques. First of all, we augmented low-presented classes leveraging affine transformations (horizontal and vertical flips, shifting, brightness change, shearing, and rotation), cropping out of a random area of the frame, applying Gaussian noise to randomly chosen color channel, worsening the quality of the image and blurring. Note that we applied every augmentation procedure with the probability of 0.1, so every image could have several augmentative changes.

To force both VGGFace2-SA and Recurrent models to pay attention to hardly classified objects, we applied a focal loss [25], which modifies the categorical cross-entropy loss function with the following formula:

$$L = -(1 - p_y)^{\gamma} log(p_y) \tag{1}$$

where $y \in \{0, ..., N - 1\}$, N - the number of classes, $p = (p_0, ..., p_{N-1})$ is the vector of estimated class probabilities over N classes, and γ is a configurable parameter named as focusing parameter. Focal loss has recommended itself as a useful loss function in dealing with imbalanced datasets, since it prevents the model from overwhelming by the vast number of easy-recognizable examples during the training. The authors recommend to take the value of $\gamma \in [0.5, 5]$.

To enhance the model's attention to the low-engagement classes even more, we applied a neat class weighting procedure, named Effective Number of Samples [9], which is proposed for long-tailed datasets, yet can be effectively utilized in highly imbalanced corpora with properly chosen parameters. The main formula for class weights generation is presented below:

$$W_i = \frac{1 - \beta}{1 - \beta^{n_i}} \tag{2}$$

where W_i is the calculated weight for the class i, n_i is a number of instances in the class i, and the β is a configurable parameter. Authors recommend to take the value of $\beta \in \{0.9, 0.99, 0.999, 0.9999\}$. They showed that exploiting such a sophisticated weighting technique in combination with focal loss can significantly improve the performance of the system in comparison with commonly used loss functions on the long-tailed datasets, which could help in high-imbalanced datasets as well.

5   Experimental Results

To be consistent with the authors of the DAiSEE, we followed the same dataset splitting. Firstly, we trained the VGGFace2-SA model on the train set with the following parameters: 50 epochs, SGD optimizer with momentum 0.9, weight decay 0.00001, and learning rate (LR) equaled to 0.0005. Additionally, the LR was monotony decreased to 0.00001 throughout the training. The focal loss with Effective Number of Samples weighting was applied with γ equaled to 2 and β equaled to 0.99999. We have chosen such parameters empirically, running the algorithm several dozen times. During training, the mixup [40] and mentioned augmentation techniques were utilized additionally as well.

Next, deep embeddings and FAUs from all facial frames were extracted. However, to train the Recurrent block, we should have defined the "temporal" parameters: length of the window (how many frames should contain one window) and the size of step (how many windows should shift in relation to the former position). To take more temporal information into account within one window, we also downsampled the frame rate of the videos to 5 fps. We conducted extensive experiments varying the length (10, 15, 20, 25, 30 frames) and step of the slicing window (0.25, 0.4, 0.5, 0.6 - the proportions of the window size), ended up with parameters equaled to 30 frames per window (corresponds to the 6 s) and 0.25 intersection proportion. It should be noted that the best parameters were chosen according to model performance on the development dataset.

Additionally, during training of Recurrent block, the focal loss with Effective Number of Samples weighting was applied. We have conducted an extensive search for β parameter as well, resulting in β equaled to 0.99995.

We have chosen the best system according to the UAR on the development set. The results of the conducted experiments on the test set of DAiSEE corpus are presented in the Table 3. Note that for comparison we included results of other papers, where it was possible to evaluate UAR metric from confusion matrices provided by authors. In addition, we provide the confusion matrix of our system, depicted in Fig. 3, for further discussions. Note that the number of examples in confusion matrix are approximately doubled due to the window cutting procedure.

6   Discussion

The results from Table 3 clearly show the difference in performance measuring by utilizing different metrics. For example, system 5 (ResNet + TCN) has the highest *Accuracy* among other systems, while at the same time it is one of the

Table 3. Results of the ER systems on DAiSEE test set.*

ID	System	Accuracy	UAR
1	Fine-tuned C3D	57.79%	30.66%
2	C3D + TCN	59.92%	31.46%
3	ResNet + TCN + weighted sampling and loss	53.70%	37.11%
4	DFSTN	58.84%	35.50%
5	Resnet + TCN	**63.90%**	33.55%
6	This work	39.02 %	**44.27%**

* The performance metrics of other systems are calculated based on confusion matrices provided by [1] and [24].

most ineffective systems in terms of UAR (the difference with the highest one is 10.72%). However, we believe that UAR is a more representative performance measure, especially in such imbalanced datasets, since it shows the ability of the model to identify all classes **equally well**. The confusion matrix depicted in Fig. 3 demonstrates the capability of the proposed framework to differ among various engagement classes with decent efficacy, taking into account the complexity of the DAiSEE dataset. Moreover, we can see that the most number of predictions are concentrated in the second and fourth quadrant in relation to the center of the picture, which means that model confuses rather between similar engagement levels (high vs very-high or low vs very-low) than between dissimilar ones.

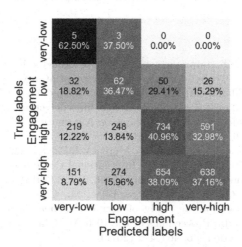

Fig. 3. Confusion matrix of proposed ER system on DAiSEE test set. Please, note: Deeper blue corresponds to the higher percentage of recognition within the concrete engagement level (The sum of every row equals to 100 %). (Color figure online)

In addition, we would like to propose a new baseline performance evaluation measure on the DAiSEE corpus, which is equalled to **44.27%** and based on UAR, instead of leveraged earlier *Accuracy*. Suggested baseline is more reliable for evaluating ER systems on such imbalanced datasets as DAiSEE and will allow researchers to develop more balanced models able to differ among all presented classes, instead of part of them.

7   Conclusion

ER has received a powerful boost over the last decade due to the rapid development of HCI- and HRI-related domains. However, existing corpora obstruct developing efficient ER systems due to the presence of natural, but the high imbalance in relation to the low-engagement classes. In this work, we observed and analyzed such problem on the example of the DAiSEE dataset, which is collected in an e-learning environment and implied for developing student state recognition systems including engagement. Moreover, we have applied various augmentation and class balancing techniques, feature fusion of emotional-based and attention-based deep embeddings, and subsequent temporal modeling of fused features to get a reliable balanced ER system based on facial images. Although, the overall performance of the model reached 44.27%, yet is the highest efficiency measure showed on the DAiSEE dataset in terms of the UAR metric. We discussed and demonstrated why *Accuracy* used earlier is not an adequate performance measure on imbalanced corpora such as DAiSEE and proposed a new baseline metric, which can help future researchers to compare their models in a more balanced and, therefore, reliable way.

References

1. Abedi, A., Khan, S.S.: Improving state-of-the-art in detecting student engagement with ResNet and TCN hybrid network. arXiv preprint arXiv:2104.10122 (2021)
2. Baltrušaitis, T., Mahmoud, M., Robinson, P.: Cross-dataset learning and person-specific normalisation for automatic action unit detection. In: 2015 11th IEEE International Conference and Workshops on Automatic Face and Gesture Recognition (FG), vol. 6, pp. 1–6. IEEE (2015)
3. Baltrusaitis, T., Zadeh, A., Lim, Y.C., Morency, L.P.: Openface 2.0: facial behavior analysis toolkit. In: 2018 13th IEEE International Conference on Automatic Face & Gesture Recognition (FG 2018), pp. 59–66. IEEE (2018)
4. Ben-Youssef, A., Clavel, C., Essid, S., Bilac, M., Chamoux, M., Lim, A.: UE-HRI: a new dataset for the study of user engagement in spontaneous human-robot interactions. In: Proceedings of the 19th ACM International Conference on Multimodal Interaction, pp. 464–472 (2017)
5. Ben-Youssef, A., Varni, G., Essid, S., Clavel, C.: On-the-fly detection of user engagement decrease in spontaneous human-robot interaction using recurrent and deep neural networks. Int. J. Soc. Robot. 11(5), 815–828 (2019)
6. Cafaro, A., et al.: The NoXi database: multimodal recordings of mediated novice-expert interactions. In: Proceedings of the 19th ACM International Conference on Multimodal Interaction, pp. 350–359 (2017)

7. Cao, Q., Shen, L., Xie, W., Parkhi, O.M., Zisserman, A.: VGGFace2: a dataset for recognising faces across pose and age. In: 2018 13th IEEE International Conference on Automatic Face & Gesture Recognition (FG 2018), pp. 67–74. IEEE (2018)
8. Cerrato, L., Campbell, N.: Engagement in dialogue with social robots. In: Jokinen, K., Wilcock, G. (eds.) Dialogues with Social Robots. LNEE, vol. 999, pp. 313–319. Springer, Singapore (2017). https://doi.org/10.1007/978-981-10-2585-3_25
9. Cui, Y., Jia, M., Lin, T.Y., Song, Y., Belongie, S.: Class-balanced loss based on effective number of samples. In: Proceedings of the IEEE/CVF Conference on Computer Vision and Pattern Recognition, pp. 9268–9277 (2019)
10. Dobrian, F., et al.: Understanding the impact of video quality on user engagement. Commun. ACM **56**(3), 91–99 (2013)
11. Doherty, K., Doherty, G.: Engagement in HCI: conception, theory and measurement. ACM Comput. Surv. (CSUR) **51**(5), 1–39 (2018)
12. Dresvyanskiy, D., Ryumina, E., Kaya, H., Markitantov, M., Karpov, A., Minker, W.: An audio-video deep and transfer learning framework for multimodal emotion recognition in the wild. arXiv preprint arXiv:2010.03692 (2020)
13. Fredricks, J.A., Blumenfeld, P.C., Paris, A.H.: School engagement: potential of the concept, state of the evidence. Rev. Educ. Res. **74**(1), 59–109 (2004)
14. Geng, L., Xu, M., Wei, Z., Zhou, X.: Learning deep spatiotemporal feature for engagement recognition of online courses. In: 2019 IEEE Symposium Series on Computational Intelligence (SSCI), pp. 442–447. IEEE (2019)
15. Gupta, A., D'Cunha, A., Awasthi, K., Balasubramanian, V.: DAiSEE: towards user engagement recognition in the wild. arXiv preprint arXiv:1609.01885 (2016)
16. Heimerl, A., Baur, T., André, E.: A transparent framework towards the context-sensitive recognition of conversational engagement, pp. 7–16 (2020)
17. Huang, T., Mei, Y., Zhang, H., Liu, S., Yang, H.: Fine-grained engagement recognition in online learning environment. In: 2019 IEEE 9th International Conference on Electronics Information and Emergency Communication (ICEIEC), pp. 338–341. IEEE (2019)
18. Jaimes, A., Lalmas, M., Volkovich, Y.: First international workshop on social media engagement (SoME 2011). In: ACM SIGIR Forum, vol. 45, pp. 56–62. ACM, New York (2011)
19. Jayagopi, D.B., et al.: The vernissage corpus: a conversational human-robot-interaction dataset. In: 2013 8th ACM/IEEE International Conference on Human-Robot Interaction (HRI), pp. 149–150. IEEE (2013)
20. Jordan, K.: Initial trends in enrolment and completion of massive open online courses. Int. Rev. Res. Open Distrib. Learn. **15**(1), 133–160 (2014)
21. Kamath, A., Biswas, A., Balasubramanian, V.: A crowdsourced approach to student engagement recognition in e-learning environments. In: 2016 IEEE Winter Conference on Applications of Computer Vision (WACV), pp. 1–9. IEEE (2016)
22. Kaur, A., Mustafa, A., Mehta, L., Dhall, A.: Prediction and localization of student engagement in the wild. In: 2018 Digital Image Computing: Techniques and Applications (DICTA), pp. 1–8. IEEE (2018)
23. Kim, J., Truong, K.P., Charisi, V., Zaga, C., Evers, V., Chetouani, M.: Multimodal detection of engagement in groups of children using rank learning. In: Chetouani, M., Cohn, J., Salah, A.A. (eds.) HBU 2016. LNCS, vol. 9997, pp. 35–48. Springer, Cham (2016). https://doi.org/10.1007/978-3-319-46843-3_3
24. Liao, J., Liang, Y., Pan, J.: Deep facial spatiotemporal network for engagement prediction in online learning. Appl. Intell. 1–13 (2021)

25. Lin, T.Y., Goyal, P., Girshick, R., He, K., Dollár, P.: Focal loss for dense object detection. In: Proceedings of the IEEE International Conference on Computer Vision, pp. 2980–2988 (2017)
26. Liu, T., Kappas, A.: Predicting engagement breakdown in HRI using thin-slices of facial expressions. In: Workshops at the Thirty-Second AAAI Conference on Artificial Intelligence (2018)
27. Massé, B., Ba, S., Horaud, R.: Tracking gaze and visual focus of attention of people involved in social interaction. IEEE Trans. Pattern Anal. Mach. Intell. 40(11), 2711–2724 (2017)
28. Mollahosseini, A., Hasani, B., Mahoor, M.H.: AffectNet: a database for facial expression, valence, and arousal computing in the wild. IEEE Trans. Affect. Comput. 10(1), 18–31 (2017)
29. O'Brien, H.L., Toms, E.G.: What is user engagement? A conceptual framework for defining user engagement with technology. J. Am. Soc. Inform. Sci. Technol. 59(6), 938–955 (2008)
30. Poggi, I.: Mind, hands, face and body: a goal and belief view of multimodal communication. Weidler (2007)
31. Quesenbery, W.: Dimensions of usability. Content and complexity: information design in technical communication (2003)
32. Sheikhi, S., Odobez, J.M.: Combining dynamic head pose-gaze mapping with the robot conversational state for attention recognition in human-robot interactions. Pattern Recogn. Lett. 66, 81–90 (2015)
33. Sidner, C.L., Lee, C., Kidd, C.D., Lesh, N., Rich, C.: Explorations in engagement for humans and robots. Artif. Intell. 166(1–2), 140–164 (2005)
34. Wang, X., Girshick, R., Gupta, A., He, K.: Non-local neural networks. In: Proceedings of the IEEE Conference on Computer Vision and Pattern Recognition, pp. 7794–7803 (2018)
35. Whitehill, J., Serpell, Z., Lin, Y.C., Foster, A., Movellan, J.R.: The faces of engagement: automatic recognition of student engagement from facial expressions. IEEE Trans. Affect. Comput. 5(1), 86–98 (2014)
36. Yang, D., Sinha, T., Adamson, D., Rosé, C.P.: Turn on, tune in, drop out: anticipating student dropouts in massive open online courses. In: Proceedings of the 2013 NIPS Data-Driven Education Workshop, vol. 11, p. 14 (2013)
37. Youssef, A.B., Clavel, C., Essid, S.: Early detection of user engagement breakdown in spontaneous human-humanoid interaction. IEEE Trans. Affect. Comput. (2019)
38. Yun, W.H., Lee, D., Park, C., Kim, J., Kim, J.: Automatic recognition of children engagement from facial video using convolutional neural networks. IEEE Trans. Affect. Comput. 11(4), 696–707 (2018)
39. Zhang, H., Xiao, X., Huang, T., Liu, S., Xia, Y., Li, J.: An novel end-to-end network for automatic student engagement recognition. In: 2019 IEEE 9th International Conference on Electronics Information and Emergency Communication (ICEIEC), pp. 342–345. IEEE (2019)
40. Zhang, H., Cisse, M., Dauphin, Y.N., Lopez-Paz, D.: mixup: beyond empirical risk minimization. arXiv preprint arXiv:1710.09412 (2017)

Intraspeaker Variability of a Professional Lecturer: Ageing, Genre, Pragmatics vs. Voice Acting (Case Study)

Anna Dunashova[1,2(✉)]

[1] Moscow State Institute of International Relations (MGIMO University), 76, Prospekt Vernadskogo, Moscow 119454, Russian Federation
[2] Moscow State Linguistic University, 38 Ostozhenka Street, Moscow 119034, Russian Federation

Abstract. This paper reports the results of a case study analyzing the intraspeaker variability of the prosodic level a professional lecturer under several factors at play, namely voice ageing, genre, pragmatics, and voice acting. The goal of the study is to establish the range of prosodic variability of David Crystal, a prominent lecturer. The prosodic features analyzed are frequency, intensity, duration, and voice quality; the method used is acoustic analysis. The results not only expand the existing theory on intraspeaker variability due to the newly received voice quality data, but will also serve as a measuring stick for analyzing other lecturers or public speakers. The key study findings comprise the ability of the speaker in question to resist age-related changes and to preserve the control over temporal parameters, pitch range, and harmonic-to-noise-ratio (HNR). The decline in shimmer and jitter values was documented to decrease harshness in voice and express agreeableness in an interview while high NHR values were noticed to accompany lectures. No voice quality parameter changed under the influence of pragmatic intention. Constructing several individual prosodic portraits of a speaker in different age, genre, pragmatics environments allowed for the recreation of the speaker's prosodic level, but it is the examination of voice acting that proved to be vital as it allows to analyze the wider scope of the speaker's variability.

Keywords: English · Intraspeaker variability · Voice quality · Ageing · Genre · Pragmatics · Voice acting

1 Introduction

Intraspeaker variability has long been subject to serious scientific scrutiny as both anthropocentric paradigm and interest in speaker identification prove it to be one of modern linguistics' top priorities. It is argued that "a linguistics of a community without a linguistics of an individual cannot adequately explain language use" [13]. Social and forensic phonetics are, thus, increasingly focusing on personal speech characteristics which convey a speaker's biological, social and psychological information.

© Springer Nature Switzerland AG 2021
A. Karpov and R. Potapova (Eds.): SPECOM 2021, LNAI 12997, pp. 179–189, 2021.
https://doi.org/10.1007/978-3-030-87802-3_17

As of now research has been carried out on various aspects of prosodic variability: age [20], sex [19], social background [19], style [7, 9, 10], pragmatics [4], emotions [2, 17] etc. However, these studies have been based on large corpora consisting of speech samples taken from different individuals, not the same individual displaying variability in speech production. Furthermore, the speech of a lecturer has been explored from the perspective of a lecture as a genre, not a lecturer as an individual. Moreover, those "individual portraits" [16] of one speaker that have been drawn focus mostly on longitudinal study of a life-long change in mono-genre speech of individual public figures.

For example, Queen Elizabeth II has been found to exhibit changes in the direction of the community change. J. Harrington et al. have analyzed Queen's Christmas messages broadcast every year since 1952 and examined the changes in her vowel quality. The results indicate small shifts towards SSB (Standard Southern British) in the formant frequency of vowel realization which made the researchers conclude that the social changes in the 60s may have driven the Queen via her speech to narrow the distance between herself and her subjects [11]. Another study examined long-time changes in vowel realization of television presenters Sir David Attenborough and David Dimbleby. Both experiments showed "relatively little change and a good deal of resistance to alterations" with the only distinguished change being a drift in David Attenborough's GOAT vowel [12]. Yet another study examined the way social status may influence sound realization and looked into the speech of Associate Justice Ruth Bader Ginsburg. The data included her speeches first as a lawyer arguing cases before the Supreme Court in the 1970's and then as a Justice on the Court from 1993 onward and highlighted r-vocalization and THOUGHT-raising [18]. To our knowledge no longitudinal study has been conducted on prosodic variability of one individual across various genres.

It stands to reason that human voice undergoes notable acoustic changes throughout lifetime. These changes are documented to be resulted from various anatomical alterations affecting the respiratory system, vocal tract and larynx [15]. Such age-related changes may even adversely affect one's communication skills. Having said that, it is essential to acknowledge the individual character of a rate at which these changes happen to a particular speaker since voice habits are known to be responsible for the rate of voice ageing. For example, earlier research has shown that singing as well as reading aloud provides certain protection against age-related effects [1, 14]. Acoustic analysis shows that elderly individuals with regular singing training generally enjoy greater voice stability [1], greater amplitude, and a wider phonation range than those without [14]. The studies prompt further questions about what voice habits are beneficial to voice preservation, whether or not lecturing slows down voice ageing, and to what extent the ageing factor is to be taken under consideration when analyzing the variability of a speech of a particular speaker in question.

The ageing factor might well be the key factor influencing language change within a person across lifespan. However, when exploring the prosodic level of an individual from a synchronic approach, it is mostly situational conditioning that determines prosodic behaviour of a speaker. The effect of genre (after D. Biber we opt for the term genre when distinguishing between the following situations: lecture, reading, interview [4]) and pragmatics, including language play and voice acting, has been exhaustively described

[3, 7] but to our knowledge no research has been done on the extent of style- and intention-conditioned prosodic variability of one speaker. Thus, sociolinguists in general and sociophoneticians in particular have explored both auditor-related and environmental factors that may lead to variation in speech production but there exists a lack of studies devoted to prosodic variability of one individual under the influence of various factors at play.

This paper aspires to analyze the extent of intraspeaker variability of a professional lecturer under the influence of various factors (ageing, genre, pragmatics) and his variability when doing voice acting. The following research questions are addressed:

– What is the range of prosodic variability of a professional lecturer under the influence of ageing, genre and pragmatic intentions?
– How does the intraspeaker variability in voice acting differ from real life situationally conditioned intraspeaker variability?
– Is there any change in the voice quality parameters accompanying the genre choice and pragmatic intentions?

2 Methodology

2.1 Data

The data for the case study in question were collected from the available recordings of David Crystal's speeches. Being a role-model for aspiring lectures-to-be, with an impressible accomplishment record and a great variety of publicly available materials, David Crystal was a clear choice for our analysis of intraspeaker variability of a professional lecturer due to his showcase professionalism. Furthermore, his interest in voice acting allowed us to explore the wider array of prosodic variability.

First, in order to analyze the effect ageing has on the prosody level of the speaker in question we collected data from reading samples of two time periods spanning 15 years. The recordings comprise emotionally neutral narrative episodes from two audiobooks voiced by D. Crystal: "St. John's Gospel" (2000) and "Just a Phrase I'm Going Through" (2015).

Second, in order to explore the effect genre has on the intraspeaker variability same-time period data comprising reading ("Just a Phrase I'm Going Through" (2015)), interview with David Crystal's son ("Ben Crystal & David Crystal. Sunday Brunch" (2014)) and lecture ("Is Control of English Shifting Away from British and American Native Speakers" (2014)), were collected.

Third, for the purpose of analyzing the effect pragmatic intentions have on the prosodic variability of one speaker we eliminated the potential ageing and genre impact and examined the prosodic make-up of intentions varying within an hour-long lecture ("The Future of Englishes" 2008). The pragmatic intentions used are described in D. Crystal's book "The Gift of the Gab. How Eloquence Works" (2016); they are based on the results of psychological studies on attention spans, and include the following: presenting information peak, information lull (giving the audience an opportunity to relax), telling a personal story (establishing rapport with the audience), recapitulation of the main points, and conclusion [8].

Finally, voice acting, together with imitating and mimicking, constitutes part of D. Crystal's personality as he regularly resorts to these types of speech production in his professional activities. Thus, this aspect of D. Crystal's prosody level could not be omitted. To analyze artistic prosodic variability of a professional lecturer we collected sections of the audiobook "Just a Phrase I'm Going Through" where D. Crystal voices nine different characters resorting to prosodic variation. The selected material was then categorized into three age-gender groups of characters' voices: children's, adult male or adult female.

The duration of the overall corpus is 3 h 15 min. The duration of the narrow corpus is 38 min. The following Table 1 gives summary of the experimental corpus.

Table 1. Experimental corpus.

Title	Genre	Year
Just a Phrase I'm Going Through	Reading	2000
St. John's Gospel	Reading	2015
Ben Crystal and David Crystal. Sunday Brunch	Interview	2014
Is Control of English Shifting Away from British and American Native Speakers	Lecture	2014
The Future of Englishes	Lecture	2008

2.2 Measurements

The speech from the recordings was segmented into syntagms and analyzed with Praat software (version 6.0.46) [5]. Using a custom Praat script, we extracted the following parameters:

- fundamental frequency (f0) parameters (Hz): f0 minimum, f0 maximum, f0 medium, f0 range, and f0 SD;
- amplitude parameters (dB): intensity minimum, intensity maximum, and intensity medium;
- voice quality parameters: shimmer (dB), jitter (%), and harmony/noise ratio (HNR) (dB).

Temporal parameters were collected manually and included:

- average syllable duration (ASD) is the mean duration of a syllable in a morpheme;
- phonation/pausation ratio (PPR) is the ration of phonation time to pausation time.

Based on the obtained data we have constructed individual prosodic portraits of the speaker in the aforementioned situations. Then, all data were analyzed using Jamovi software (version 1.2.27.0) [21]. Statistical analyses included one-way analysis of variance (ANOVA), used for three or more groups of data to gain information about the dependent and independent variables. Moreover, post hoc tests and Mann-Whitney U Test were run to compare differences between two groups of data. All the acoustic and temporal measures were used as the dependent measures, a criterium of $p = 0.05$ being used to establish significance.

3 Results

3.1 The Ageing Impact on Prosodic Variability

ANOVA analysis found a significant age effect on the following acoustic measures: f0 ($F = 24.1$, $p < 0.01$, $\eta^2 = 0.131$), ASD ($F = 11.9$, $p = 0.01$, $\eta^2 = 0.158$), shimmer ($F = 52.1$, $p < 0.01$, $\eta^2 = 0.453$), and jitter ($F = 24.3$, $p < 0.01$, $\eta^2 = 0.279$). Table 2 gives summary of the obtained data.

Table 2. Values of acoustic measures across the two ages.

Age	F0	F0 min	F0 max	F0 SD	Int[a]	Int max	ASD	PPR	Shimmer	Jitter	HNR
59	100	70	483	21	59	81	220	2.67:1	1.17	3.44	8.12
74	110	74	471	27	69	81	181	3.79:1	1.80	4.39	7.76

[a] int = intensity

F0 was found to be increasing with age; the findings are consistent with the previously published findings on the decrease of f0 in men until 50 and its gradual rise in the years after; therefore, the results are not surprising [15]. Perturbation measures (shimmer and jitter) and their increase (see Fig. 1) revealing the age-induced instability of vocal cords were also expected. Thus, on the whole, f0, shimmer, and jitter are once again proven to be age dependent.

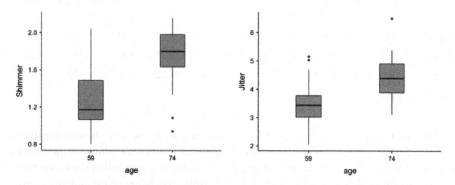

Fig. 1. The boxplots of shimmer and jitter values for the two ages (59 and 74).

However, the value change of ASD parameter is opposite to what was expected. Articulation rate and speech tempo are documented to slow down with older age. Yet, acoustic analysis shows the decrease of ASD parameter and thus, increase of articulation rate. Admittedly, temporal measurements are known to be most varying as they are controlled by the speaker himself who adjusts speech tempo to the communicative situation. Having said that, the finding shows that, when having a choice, D. Crystal opts for accelerated tempo therefore proving that age has not affected his control over temporal characteristics of his speech.

Interestingly, no age effect was found on HNR despite the fact that HNR has been documented to decline with age due to a widening gap between the vocal folds. Even though medium values do show a decline with age, the correlation is not significant ($p = 0.194$). This demonstrates the speaker's preserved ability to display voice resonance. Furthermore, proceeding to the amplitude parameters we observe the wider intensity range value in the recording of an older age which points at the acquired expressiveness (53 dB and 61 dB at the age of 59 and 74 respectively). Admittedly, sound equipment may have had certain effect on the intensity level of the sound. However, we analyze the available recordings as they are due to the fact that they were processed and made available online in this form. Vocal range value was found to stay stable (33 st) despite the documented tendency towards its narrowing in men with age.

3.2 The Genre Impact on Prosodic Variability

ANOVA analysis found genre to have a significant effect on the following acoustic measures: f0 ($F = 7.42$, $p < 0.01$, $\eta^2 = 0.086$), f0 SD ($F = 40.9$, $p < 0.01$, $\eta^2 = 0.341$), ASD ($F = 9.80$, $p < 0.01$, $\eta^2 = 0.123$), shimmer ($F = 59.5$, $p < 0.01$, $\eta^2 = 0.429$), jitter ($F = 74.1$, $p < 0.01$, $\eta^2 = 0.484$), and HNR ($F = 39.0$, $p < 0.01$, $\eta^2 = 0.331$). Post hoc tests were run to clarify the comparisons between the genres. Table 3 gives summary on the genre effect on intraspeaker prosodic variability.

Table 3. Values of acoustic measures across the three genres (interview, reading, and lecture).

Genre	F0	F0 min	F0 max	F0 SD	Int[a]	Int max	ASD	PPR	Shimmer	Jitter	HNR
Interview	115	74	496	29	67	76	166	8:1	1.19	2.52	5.65
Reading	110	74	471	27	69	81	181	3.79:1	1.80	4.39	7.76
Lecture	105	73	499	72	69	89	197	5.22:1	1.22	3.58	7.60

[a] int = intensity

F0 was found to be genre dependent. This said, post hoc test showed similarity between lecture and reading values with only interview values standing out; the finding may be explained by a more casual atmosphere of a conversation with a family member revealing the modal voice of the speaker. F0 SD, while also being genre-dependent, was found to stand out during a lecture which is explained by a high linguistic expressiveness and frequent shifts between low and high pitch. As expected, ASD values indeed undergo genre impact as they are situationally conditioned and consciously controlled by the speaker.

Surprisingly, voice quality measures displayed variability dependent on genre. All the three measures (shimmer, jitter, and HNR) demonstrate the lowest values during interview (see Table 3) which increase during a lecture and reading. Seeing as no age-related impact could have taken place, the rise in the values may be accounted for by the emotional activation of the speaker. It has been described that the increase of shimmer and jitter values correlate with strong emotions which are part of public speaking and artistic reading; at the same time agreeableness tends to be accompanied by a decline in voice harshness, hence, by a decline in shimmer and jitter values that we can observe in an interview [17].

No genre effect was found on f0 min, f0 max, f0 range, intensity values, and phonation/pausation ratio. Vocal range remained stable at 33 st.

3.3 The Pragmatics Impact on Prosodic Variability

A significant effect of pragmatic intention on prosodic variability was found on only the following fundamental frequency measures: f0 ($F = 6.01$, $p < 0.01$, $\eta^2 = 0.143$), f0 SD ($F = 4.82$, $p = 0.01$, $\eta^2 = 0.118$), f0 max ($F = 4.37$, $p = 0.02$, $\eta^2 = 0.108$). No significant effect was found on other acoustic measures which show their predominant dependency on age or genre factor. Table 4 gives summary on the pragmatics effect on intraspeaker prosodic variability.

Table 4. Values of acoustic measures across the five intentions (story, recapitulation, peak, lull, conclusion).

Intention	F0	F0 min	F0 max	F0 SD	Int[a]	Int max	ASD	PPR	Shimmer	Jitter	HNR
Story	105	72	497	26	66	82	214	5:1	1.21	2.61	7.92
Recap[b]	114	73	495	35	66	80	222	4.8:1	1.20	2.60	7.85
Peak	113	74	478	33	66	81	208	6.7:1	1.13	2.56	7.85
Lull	139	73	495	57	65	82	238	3.3:1	1.19	2.74	8.25
Conclusion	114	74	385	23	64	81	200	4.6:1	1.15	1.28	7.92

[a] int = intensity
[b] recap = recapitulation

Concerning f0 values, post hoc tests showed recapitulation, peak and conclusion to have similar f0 values (see Fig. 2) which implies their shared intention of intonational accentuation of the key information.

Interestingly, lull is characterized by a higher pitch, which distinguishes it from other intentions and lets the audience know when it is allowed to defocus. It also demonstrates the highest f0 SD values, which also lays emphasis on this part of the lecture.

Personal story, told by the speaker in order to establish rapport with the audience, is notable for the lowest f0 value (105 Hz) and highest f0 max value (497 Hz), which shows a wider pitch range that allows for a greater expressiveness.

Vocal range remained stable at 33 st across all the intentions.

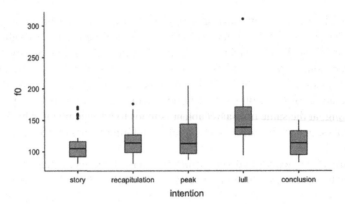

Fig. 2. The boxplots of f0 values for the *story,* recapitulation, peak, lull, and conclusion intentions.

3.4 The Prosodic Variability of Voice Acting

We hypothesize that David Crystal resorted to gender- and are-related language stereotypes for the purpose of creating characters. For that reason, the nine characters voiced by D. Crystal were split into three gender-age groups: adult male, adult female, children. Statistical tests were run to compare the prosodic make-up of the three groups. ANOVA analysis found a significant effect on the following acoustic measures: f0 ($F = 17.9$, p < 0.01, $\eta^2 = 0.449$), f0 min ($F = 7.22$, p $= 0.02$, $\eta^2 = 0.247$), shimmer ($F = 3.62$, p < 0.035, $\eta^2 = 0.141$), and HNR ($F = 8.46$, p < 0.01, $\eta^2 = 0.278$). Table 5 gives summary on the effect of voice acting on intraspeaker prosodic variability.

Table 5. Values of acoustic measures across the three characters' age-gender groups (adult male, adult female, children's).

Gender-age	F0	F0 min	F0 max	F0 SD	Int*	Int max	ASD	Shimmer	Jitter	HNR
Adult male	103	64	497	54	70	80	288	1.64	3.36	8.50
Adult female	169	74	416	69	73	79	212	1.00	3.00	10.00
Children's	154	75	306	48	71	80	279	1.56	3.13	12.20

Interestingly, when voice acting David Crystal resorts to narrowing down his pitch range. When doing children's voices, he narrows the range to 24 st, which is much narrower than when doing adult male (35 st), and adult female (30 st) voices (see Fig. 3). Pitch range is documented to expand up until middle age [19]. Moreover, wide pitch range being a distinctive feature of high social status we may presume that by giving adult male characters a wider vocal range, David Crystal highlighted their importance and social status.

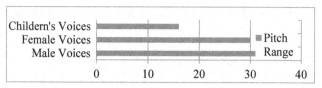

Fig. 3. Pitch range of the three age-gender character groups (adult male, adult female, children's).

F0 values were found to skyrocket dramatically with adult female characters (169 Hz) which correlates with a robust language stereotype of female voices sounding higher than men's [6]. HNR values demonstrate resonance in voice and carry age-related changes. D. Crystal displays great control over the parameter; children's voices sound most resonant, adult female voices demonstrate a smaller level of resonance, giving away the older age. Adult male characters show the smallest values of HNR which come closer to D. Crystal's mode voice (see Fig. 4).

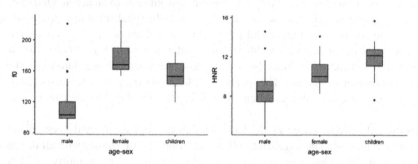

Fig. 4. The boxplots of f0 and HNR values for the three age-gender groups.

4 Conclusion and Discussion

The case study showed a high degree of intraspeaker variability and voice control in David Crystal which may be due to his vast public speaking experience. Table 6 summarizes the difference between David Crystal's intraspeaker variability under the influence of the ageing, genre and pragmatics factors and his intraspeaker variability when voice acting.

The case study revealed the following characteristics of David Crystal's prosodic level:

– Generally, f0 values of the speaker vary from 100 to 115 Hz but when in voice acting the value increases to 179 Hz getting closer to, but not reaching the female average value of 200 Hz;
– Despite the ageing impact, David Crystal demonstrates a wide pitch range, only narrowing it down for the artistic purposes;

Table 6. The range of variability of acoustic values under the influence of age, genre, pragmatics vs voice acting.

Acoustic parameter	Ageing/genre/pragmatics	Voice acting
Pitch range	28–33 st	14–32 st
F0	100–115 Hz	102–179 Hz
ASD	166–222	178–417
Shimmer	1.13–1.80 dB	1.00–1.78 dB
Jitter	2.21–4.39%	1.89–4.28%
HNR	5.56–8.25 dB	7.53–15.7 dB

- Despite the ageing impact, David Crystal enjoys a firm control over the temporal parameters of his speech, varying speech tempo from slow to an accelerated one;
- Voice quality parameters reflect not only the age of the speaker but also his emotional state. The decline in shimmer and jitter values was documented to decrease harshness in voice and express agreeableness in an interview while high NHR values were noticed to accompany lectures. No voice quality parameter changed under the influence of pragmatic intention. The speaker is able to vary the parameters, especially the HNR one, to a greater degree when voice acting (mimicking, language playing etc.).

Admittedly, corpus-based studies show a lot about language use and a general development direction of a language. But only a collection of case studies with all the peculiarities of an individual may tell us more about intraspeaker variability. "Although "voiceprints" are not as individual as fingerprints, people do have fairly consistent and fairly distinct acoustic voices" [13]. As is illustrated by David Crystal's example, ageing has an inevitable effect on the prosodic level of speech production, but the degree of this effect differs depending on an individual's experience. The results illustrate that due to a long and consistent lecturing experience, pitch range and the control over temporal parameters can be preserved despite the general population age-related tendency. Moreover, voice quality parameters (shimmer, jitter, HNR), despite them being considered to be fairly constant and consistent within a person, can display a great variability.

Thus, constructing several individual prosodic portraits of a speaker in different age, genre, pragmatics environments allow for the recreation of the speaker's prosodic level which contributes to better speaker recognition and identification. The analysis of voice acting/mimicking/language play shows the wider scope of intraspeaker variability and, thus, should be taken into account. Voice quality parameters should always be factored in as they carry age-group belonging and emotional state of the speaker. The further research will expand on the material used by introducing more genres and pragmatic intentions; it will also implement the spectral features analysis to present a more extensive portrait of a speaker.

References

1. Awan, S.N.: Phonetographic profiles and F0-SPL characteristics of untrained versus trained vocal groups. J. Voice **5**(1), 41–50 (1991)
2. Bachorowski, J.A., Owren, M.J.: Vocal expression of emotion: acoustic properties of speech are associated with emotional intensity and context. Psychol. Sci. **6**, 219–224 (1995)
3. Berry, M., Brown, S.: Acting in action: prosodic analysis of character portrayal during acting. J. Exp. Psychol. Gen. **148**(8), 1407–1425 (2019)
4. Biber, D.: Variation across speech and writing. In: Biber, D., Finegan, E. (eds.) Sociolinguistic Perspectives on Register, pp. 31–56. Oxford University Press, Oxford (1994)
5. Boersma, P., Weenink, D.: Praat: doing phonetics by computer [Computer program]. Ver. 6.0.46 (2017). www.praat.org/
6. Cartei, V., Cowles, H.W., Reby, D.: Spontaneous voice gender imitation abilities in adult speakers. PLoS ONE **7**(2), e31353 (2012)
7. Crystal, D., Davy, D.: Investigating English Style. Indiana University Press, Bloomington (1969)
8. Crystal, D.: The Gift of the Gab. How Eloquence Works, 1st edn. Yale University Press, New Haven (2016)
9. Dunashova, A.V.: Stilisticheskaya variativnost' prosodicheskih harakteristik yazykovoj lichnosti (Stylistic Variability of an Individual). Teoreticheskaya i prikladnaya lingvistika **27**(1), 22–30 (2021). (in Russian)
10. Goldman, J.-P., Prsir, T., Christodoulides, G., Auchlin, A.: Speaking style prosodic variation: an 8-hour 9-style corpus study. In: 7th International Conference on Speech Prosody, Proceedings, Dublin, Ireland, pp. 105–109 (2014)
11. Harrington, J.: Monophthongal vowel changes in received pronunciation: an acoustic analysis of the Queen's Christmas broadcasts. J. Int. Phon. Assoc. **30**, 63–78 (2000)
12. Hinton, M.: Changes in received pronunciation: diachronic case studies. Res. Lang. **13**(1), 21–35 (2015)
13. Johnstone, B.: The Linguistic Individual: Self-expression in Language and Linguistics. Oxford University Press, Oxford (1996)
14. Lortie, C.L., Rivard, J., Thibeault, M., Tremblay, P.: The moderating effect of frequent singing on voice aging. J. Voice **31**(1), 112.e1–112.e12 (2017)
15. Linville, S.E.: Vocal Ageing. Singular Publishing Group, San Diego (2001)
16. Potapova, R.K., Potapov, V.V.: Yazyk, Rech, Lichnost' (Language, Speech, Personality). YazykiSlavyanskoyKultury, Moscow (2006). (in Russian)
17. Scherer, K.R.: Vocal communication of emotion: a review of research paradigms. Speech Commun. **40**, 227–256 (2003)
18. Shapp, A., LaFave, N., Singler, J.V.: Ginsburg v. Ginsburg: A Longitudinal Study of Regional Features in a Supreme Court Justice's Speech. University of Pennsylvania Working Papers in Linguistics, vol. 20, no. 2, pp. 148–158 (2014)
19. Shevchenko, T.I.: Sociofonetika: nacionalnayaisocialnayaidentichnost' v anglijskomproiznoshenii (Sociophonetics: national and social identity in English pronunciation), 2nd edn. URSS, Moscow (2016).(in Russian)
20. Shevchenko, T., Sokoreva, T.: Corpus data on adult life-long trajectory of prosody development in American English, with special reference to middle age. In: Karpov, A., Jokisch, O., Potapova, R. (eds.) SPECOM 2018. LNCS (LNAI), vol. 11096, pp. 606–614. Springer, Cham (2018). https://doi.org/10.1007/978-3-319-99579-3_62
21. The jamovi project: jamovi (ver. 1.2.27.0) (2020). https://www.jamovi.org

An Ensemble Approach for the Diagnosis of COVID-19 from Speech and Cough Sounds

Abderrahim Fathan, Jahangir Alam$^{(\boxtimes)}$, and Woo Hyun Kang

Computer Research Institute of Montreal, Montreal, QC H3N 1M3, Canada
{abderrahim.fathan,jahangir.alam,woohyun.kang}@crim.ca
https://www.crim.ca/en/

Abstract. Mass COVID-19 infections detection has shown to be a very hard problem. In this work, we describe our systems developed to diagnose COVID-19 cases based on coughing sounds and speech. We propose a hybrid configuration that employs Convolution Neural Network (CNN), Time Delay Neural Network (TDNN) and Long Short-Term Memory (LSTM) for the extraction of coughing sound and speech embeddings. Moreover, the proposed framework utilizes SpecAugment-based on-the-fly data augmentation and multi-level statistics pooling for mapping frame level information into utterance level embedding. We employ classical support vector machines, random forests, AdaBoost, decision trees, and logistic regression classifiers for the final decision making, to determine whether the given feature is from a COVID-19 negative or positive patient. We also adopt an end-to-end approach employing ResNet model with a one-class softmax loss function for making positive versus negative decision over the high resolution hand-crafted features. Experiments are carried out on the two subsets, denoted as COVID-19 Speech Sounds (CSS) and COVID-19 Cough Sounds (CCS), from the Cambridge COVID-19 Sound database and experimental results are reported on the development and test sets of these subsets. Our approach outperforms the baselines provided by the challenge organizers on the development set, and shows that using speech to help remotely detect early COVID-19 infections and eventually other respiratory diseases is likely possible, which opens a new opportunity for a promising cheap and scalable pre-diagnosis way to better handle pandemics.

Keywords: COVID-19 · Computational paralinguistics · Deep representations · Data augmentation · CNN-TDNN-LSTM · Multi-level statistics pooling

1 Introduction

Since the start of the current COVID-19 pandemic situation, finding an efficient and scalable solution to diagnose COVID-19 infections has been an urgent task. A low-cost real-time pre-diagnosis of COVID-19 infection that is accessible anywhere and anytime holds a great potential to help control the spread of new infections.

© Springer Nature Switzerland AG 2021
A. Karpov and R. Potapova (Eds.): SPECOM 2021, LNAI 12997, pp. 190–201, 2021.
https://doi.org/10.1007/978-3-030-87802-3_18

Various challenges have been organized, such as the COVID-19 Speech Sounds (CSS) and COVID-19 Cough Sounds (CCS) sub-challenges (using the Cambridge COVID-19 Sound database) from the Computational Paralinguistics ChallengE (ComParE) 2021 [25], diagnosing COVID-19 using acoustics (DiCOVA) challenge 2021 [16], to help promote this idea, where binary classification on COVID-19 (or not) infection has to be made based on coughing sounds and speech.

Clinical observations of symptomatic patients of COVID-19 have shown that the virus moderately or often seriously impairs the functions of the lower and mid respiratory tract. Since the vibration of the vocal folds is the primary source of our human phonation (voice), this paper investigates this possibility to use speech deep learning models to diagnose COVID-19 cases based solely on coughing sounds and speech. Our features show a high discriminative capability using 5 types of classifiers, achieving 77.0% and 72.7% Unweighted Average Recall (UAR) on the CSS and CCS sub-challenges respectively with a single system, and reach as high as 82.6% and 80.3% UAR on the development sets using majority vote ensemble systems, which outperform the baseline features and classifiers proposed by the organizers.

The remainder of this work is organized as follows: Sect. 2 discusses the related work to our paper. Components of our proposed systems and training procedure are detailed in Sect. 3. Experimental setup, results and discussion appear in Sect. 4 and conclusions in Sect. 5.

2   Related Work

The literature on diagnosing COVID-19 from voice, coughs and other respiratory sounds anomalies is very recent and sparse [6]. [21] provides a recent review of computer audition for diagnosing COVID-19, which concludes that data is still sparse and results often lack sufficient validation. On the other hand, [12] found concrete evidence of the association of abnormal breath sounds in the oscillation patterns during phonation, crackles and asymmetries in vocal resonances and indistinguishable murmurs with COVID-19 infection. Moreover, [14] classifies cough recordings based on convolutional neural networks made up of one Poisson biomarker layer and 3 pre-trained ResNet50's in parallel, outputting a binary pre-screening diagnostic. Their approach achieves a high COVID-19 sensitivity on their collected data.

Another work [22] attempts to detect COVID-19 by analyzing the speech envelope, pitch, cepstral peak prominence and the formant center-frequencies. This study observes high rank eigenvalues tending toward relatively lower energy in post-COVID-19 cases. Additionally, [5] proposes a method that analyzes the differential dynamics of the glottal flow waveform (GFW) during voice production to identify features in them that are most significant for the detection of COVID-19 from voice. Finally, researchers have also used crowd-sourced data [4,11] with data-driven end-to-end deep learning methods for this purpose. However, the data remain scarce, and their deep learning models were prone to overfitting.

In the same spirit, and as a contribution to the aforementioned line of work, this paper studies the application of several state-of-the-art deep learning systems and curated augmentations to diagnose COVID-19 infections. We demonstrate that our features have a high discriminative capability using 5 types of classifiers and lead to much better classification performance than the baseline systems considered in this work for the purpose of comparison of performances.

3   Description of Our Adopted Approaches

With the advent of deep learning, current trend in speech processing applications is to employ single or hybrid deep learning architectures for automatically learning the intermediate feature representation relevant to the downstream task. As these deep feature extraction approaches are less dependent on human knowledge and are more optimized toward the target task (e.g., classification), the resulting representations may lead to improved performance over the classical techniques [15]. In this section, we describe our proposed approach for supervised representations learning as well as the residual neural network [10]-based end-to-end approach for the diagnosis of COVID-19 cases based on coughing sounds and speech.

3.1   Data Augmentation

Training data provided for the CCS and CSS sub-Challenges [25] is very small. Such small dataset may not be sufficient for the system to learn the full manifold of the input feature distribution, and therefore is likely to deteriorate the classification performance. In order to increase the size and variability of the training set, we perform a 4-fold data augmentation on top of the original training data by corrupting them using additive noise from the MUSAN data and the reverberation from the simulated RIRs (room impulse responses) database. Note that, MUSAN and RIRs datasets are publicly available from http://www.openslr.org. This can increase the training size up to 5 times the original training samples.

In addition to this offline data augmentation, we also performed on the fly data augmentation using the spectral augmentation technique proposed in [18]. This augmentation is known as SpecAugment and was found to provide promising results in speech recognition tasks. In this work, over the 40-dimensional Mel filterbank (MelFB) input features, SpecAugment is applied on the fly, where both time and frequency masking are performed.

3.2   Deep Supervised Feature Representations

In order to learn more discriminative feature representations, we propose a hybrid configuration, as shown in Fig. 1, that employs Convolution Neural Network (CNN), Time Delay Neural Network (TDNN) and Long Short-Term Memory (LSTM) networks. 40-dimensional Mel filterbank (MelFB) coefficients are used as input features to this hybrid model and on the fly SpecAugment is performed on top of MelFB features. Augmented MelFB is then passed through CNN (stack of five 2-D convolution layers), TDNN1 (one dilated 1-D convolution layer), LSTM (one layer), TDNN (comprised of three dilated 1-D convolutional layers) for frame-level processing and thereby, end up mapping input features into more discriminative local descriptors. The local descriptors are then converted into global utterance level representations with the application of a pooling layer which simply concatenates element-wise first-, and second-order statistics (i.e., mean and standard deviation) over time. In this work, we use multi-level statistics pooling [27] for aggregating statistics from the last layers of CNN, LSTM and TDNN blocks in order to capture class specific information from different spaces and learn more discriminative utterance-level representations. Pooled statistics are then projected into 512- or 256-dimensional feature representations, through two fully-connected layers and a softmax layer. The hybrid network is then trained to classify the input speech, determining if it is from a COVID-19 negative or a positive patient.

Once the network is trained, the extracted features from the last fully connected layer are then used as input of different classifiers to diagnose COVID-19 cases (positive versus negative). We denote these features here as *Deep Features (DF)*. Kaldi toolkit [20] is used for training and extracting our proposed DF.

3.3   End-to-End Diagnosis with ResNet

Inspired by [13,29], in this work, we built a system for diagnosing COVID-19 cases (positive versus negative) based on coughing sounds and speech signals in an end-to-end fashion. To do so, we employ an 18-layer deep residual neural network (ResNet18) with attentive statistics pooling and one class softmax (OCS) loss on top of the 64-dimensional MelFB features. One class softmax (OCS) is formulated to boost the generalization capability to unseen test data by introducing two different margins for each class to better identify the normal speech and cough sounds (negative class) while still isolating the anomalies in the positive patients without overfitting to only the most common anomalies. One-class softmax can be formulated as [29]:

$$L_{OCS} = -\frac{1}{N} \sum_{i=1}^{N} log(1 + e^{\alpha(m_{y_i} - \hat{w}_0 \hat{x}_i)(-1)^{y_i}}), \tag{1}$$

where $x_i \in R^D$ and $y_i \in \{0, 1\}$ are the D-dimensional embedding vector and label of the ith sample respectively. N is the mini-batch size and m_{y_i} defines the compactness margin for class label y_i. The larger is the margin, the more compact the embeddings will be. w_0 is the weight vector of our target class embeddings. Both $\hat{w}_0$ and $\hat{x}_i$ are normalizations of w_0 and x_i respectively.

Training is carried out, in a standard classification setting, using Stochastic Gradient Descent (SGD) optimizer for the parameters in the loss functions. Balanced mini-batches of size 64 samples are used for both CSS and CCS tasks. The learning rates were set at 0.0003 and performance is monitored on the validation set. Similar to [29], we set $\alpha = 20$, $m_0 = 0.9$ and $m_1 = 0.2$ for the hyperparameters in the one class softmax loss function.

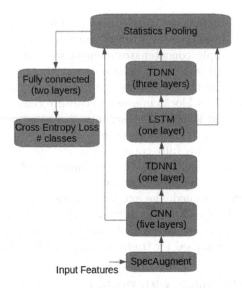

Fig. 1. Block diagram of our adopted hybrid architecture which is used for the extraction of utterance level embeddings from the speech and cough recordings. Input hand-crafted features are mapped into local descriptors which are then aggregated to yield final fixed dimensional utterance level feature representations. As input features, we use 40-dimensional Mel filterbank (MelFB) input features.

4   Experiments

4.1   Database

Table 1 presents the summary of both CCS and CSS subsets from the Cambridge COVID-19 Sound corpus [4,9]. For both CCS and CSS, only cough sounds and voice recordings, respectively, were included. Only participants with available COVID-19 positive/negative test results were included separately, and only the audio data and the corresponding COVID-19 test labels were provided in the train and development sets of the CCS and CSS databases. For CCS, each participant provided one to three forced coughs in each cough recording. On the other hand, for CSS, each speech sample contains a patient uttering the phrase "I hope my data can help to manage the virus pandemic." in one language (from English, Italian, or German, etc.), one to three times. All the audio data was resampled and converted to single channel 16 kHz, 16 bits PCM format, and further recording-wise normalization was performed. Figures 2 and 3 show random samples of audio spectrograms of negative and positive patients for the CCS and the CSS sub-challenges. From the spectrograms, it could be easily observed that there is a distinctive spectral difference between the audio from the positive and negative patients.

Table 1. Number of recordings per class in the Train/Dev/Test splits of the CCS and CSS databases. Here, CCS and CSS stand for COVID-19 Cough Sounds and COVID-19 Speech Sounds, respectively.

	# Recordings				
	CCS		CSS		Total (CCS/CSS)
	Negative	Positive	Negative	Positive	
Train	215	71	243	72	286/315
Dev.	183	48	153	142	231/295
Test	Blinded	Blinded	Blinded	Blinded	208/283

Fig. 2. Sample STFT (Short-time Fourier Transform) spectrograms of a positive (left) and a negative (right) audio files from the COVID-19 CCS train set.

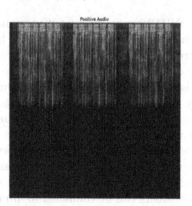 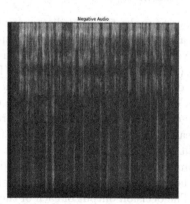

Fig. 3. Sample STFT (Short-time Fourier Transform) spectrograms of a positive (left) and a negative (right) audio files from the COVID-19 CSS train set.

4.2   Baseline COVID-19 Diagnosis Systems

Baseline COVID-19 diagnosis systems [25] considered here for comparison purposes are based on various utterance level feature representations, namely, COMPARE functionals which are 6373-dimensional static feature vectors resulting from the computation of statistics over low-level descriptor contours [7,24,28], Bag-of-Audio-Words (BoAW) [23] which are histograms of acoustic low-level descriptors, following quantisation based on a codebook, auDEEP feature set obtained through unsupervised representation learning with recurrent sequence-to-sequence autoencoders [1,8], DiFE (Dutch Linguistic Feature Extractor)-based linguistic features [26], and DEEP SPECTRUM toolkit-based 2048-dimensional vector level features extracted using pre-trained Convolutional Neural Networks (CNNs) [2,3]. They all employ linear SVM classifier for the prediction of COVID-19 infections from speech and coughing sounds. Best baselines over the development set are included in Table 2 and Table 3.

4.3   Evaluation Measure

Since the evaluation data is highly unbalanced, and as required in the challenge [25], we employ Unweighted Average Recall (UAR) as an evaluation measure (metric) instead of accuracy. UAR is simply defined as the unweighted average of both classes recalls achieved by our system. Since the UAR aims to ensure that all classes are recognized with equally good recall, it can boost the relative importance of the positive minority class.

4.4   Classifiers

In order to make the final diagnosis of COVID-19 cases into positive or negative patients based on coughing and speech embeddings, we used classical Support Vector Machines (SVM), Random Forests (RF), AdaBoost (AB), Decision Trees (DT), and Logistic Regression (LR) classification algorithms. Due to the small dataset available for training the classifier and the relatively high dimensional embeddings, a single classifier may fail to learn the accurate manifold of the embedding distribution, thus produce a hyperplane with low discrimination capability. Therefore, we believe that the classification system can greatly benefit from using number of different classifiers, which will each learn different discriminative features from the embeddings to distinguish between the positive and the negative patients, and would benefit from employing randomized subsets. The decision output of each of these classifiers can be combined to improve the robustness and generalizability of the system. To combine the classification decisions, fusion is performed with Majority Voting (MV) and a minimum of three systems are required to perform MV-based fusion.

Following the work and provided baselines in [25], we use Scikit-Learn library [19] to evaluate the different performances of generated feature representations. Parameters of each classifier function are optimized by cross-validated grid-search over a parameter grid in Scikit-Learn (data scaler, parameters, estimators, solvers, etc.). The classifier is then fit on the generated train features to learn file classification into negative or positive. Finally, each system is evaluated on the development set, and further predictions for the test set are generated, for which true labels are blinded by the organizers. All feature representations were scaled to zero mean and unit standard deviation.

4.5 Results and Discussion

In addition to our proposed feature extraction-based systems, Our ensembles' study also includes the baseline feature extractors and classifiers [25] based on the COMPARE [28] and BoAWs [23] features, as well as deep unsupervised representation learning using the auDEEP toolkit[1] and deep feature extraction from pre-trained CNNs using the DEEP SPECTRUM toolkit[2]. We extend the evaluation of these features to all of our 5 classifiers.

Table 2. Performance evaluation of the different proposed architectures on the development set of the CCS task in terms of the UAR (%) metric. Higher values are better. Here, CCS stands for COVID-19 Cough Sounds. As classifier, Support Vector Machines (SVM), Random Forests (RF), AdaBoost (AB), Decision Trees (DT), and Logistic Regression (LR) classification algorithms are used.

Features (classifier)	UAR (%)
DF256 (AB)	72.7
DF512VAD (LR)	71.8
DF512VAD (RF)	71.7
DF256VAD_11Augmentations (LR)	71.6
DF256VAD (SVM)	71.4
DF256 (SVM)	71.3
DF512_fused (AB)	71.1
DF256VAD (LR)	71.0
DF256 (LR)	71.0
DF256 (RF)	70.6
DF256VAD_11Augmentations (SVM)	70.6
DF256_noDataAugmentation (SVM)	70.5
DF256VAD (DT)	70.2
DF512VAD (SVM)	70.1
openXBoW (RF)	69.7
auDeep (RF)	65.7
ResNet18 (end-to-end)	66.0
Best development set performance [25]	67.6
Best ensemble (majority vote)	80.3

---

[1] https://github.com/auDeep/auDeep.
[2] https://github.com/DeepSpectrum/DeepSpectrum.

Table 2 and Table 3 summarize the results of our best performing systems for the CCS (COVID-19 Cough Sounds) and the CSS (COVID-19 Speech Sounds) tasks respectively, compared to the baselines. VAD denotes the use of voice activity detector to remove non speech frames, and unless specified otherwise, all systems use on the fly data augmentation using SpecAugment [18]. DF512_fused is the case where 256-embeddings from the last two fully connected layers are extracted and then concatenated (i.e., feature-level fusion) to provide the final 512-dimensional deep features as output.

Table 3. Performance evaluation of the different proposed architectures on the Development set of the CSS task in terms of the UAR (%) metric. Higher values are better. Here, CSS stands for COVID-19 Speech Sounds. In this case, Support Vector Machines (SVM), Random Forests (RF), Decision Trees(DT), and Logistic Regression (LR) classification algorithms are used as classifiers.

Features (classifier)	UAR (%)
DF512 (RF)	77.0
DF512 (LR)	76.6
DF256_comb (LR)	75.9
DF512_comb (LR)	75.8
DF512 (SVM)	75.6
DF256 (RF)	75.6
DF512VAD (RF)	75.2
DF256VAD (SVM)	75.0
DF256VAD (RF)	74.7
DF256 (SVM)	74.7
DF256_finetune_from_ASV (RF)	74.5
openXBoW (RF)	73.7
DF512_noDataAugmentation (RF)	73.5
auDeep (RF)	68.1
opensmile (RF)	65.9
deepspectrum (RF)	63.6
ResNet18 (end-to-end)	70.0
Best development set performance [25]	70.5
Best ensemble (majority vote)	82.6

We can easily observe that several variants of our proposed system achieve very high performance, and outperform original baselines of the challenge. In particular, our DF256 and DF512 systems with 256- and 512-dimensional deep features respectively, and using on-the-fly SpecAugment data augmentation, are able to achieve 72.7% UAR on the CCS sub-challenge and 77.0% UAR on the

CSS sub-challenge. Tables also show the discriminative power and robustness of our representations across several classifiers. Moreover, using our end-to-end ResNet18-based approach also yields a relatively high performance of 70.0% UAR compared to the CSS baseline features.

We further explore 3 additional ideas: (1) combine CCS and CSS data during training in DF256_comb and DF512_comb, (2) use a total of 11 offline augmentations (white and pink noise, pitch shift, time stretch, speed tuning, audio mix, reverberance, time and frequency masking, sparse warping, SpecAugment) for a total of 10 times original data in DF256VAD_11Augmentations, and (3) finetune a pre-trained speaker discriminant neural network model trained on the Voxceleb dataset [17] on COVID-19 speech/COVID-19 cough sounds in DF512_comb.

Additionally, We also experimented with 2 ensemble systems based on majority voting (MV) that achieve very high performance on the development set. Our best CCS ensemble system (MV of 6 systems) achieves a high performance of 80.34% UAR, while the best CSS ensemble system (MV of 3 systems) achieves a performance of 82.59% on the dev set. From this result, we can safely assume that these classifiers (i.e., RF, LR, SVM) are learning complementary information about the spectrum for distinguishing the positive patients from the negative patients.

Table 4 shows the very decent performance of our only 3 submitted systems for evaluation on the test set. ResNet18-based end-to-end proposed system was not included in our majority voting (MV) ensemble systems as it was not ready at time of submission. Finally, we find it worth mentioning that we were able to achieve equally very good performance (above 80% UAR) on the development set with MV-based ensemble systems comprising more systems from Table 2 and Table 3 respectively (e.g. all systems) but we were unable to evaluate them on the test set due to the time limit of the challenge. These latter systems hold the potential to perform much better on the test set as they comprise more systems and thus could be more robust and generalize better.

Table 4. Results of our 3 submissions (or trials) on the Dev/Test splits of the CCS (COVID-19 Cough Sounds) and CSS (COVID-19 Speech Sounds) corpora. The last row shows the best possible performances of the organizer's baselines (not same systems across Dev and Test sets).

System	UAR (%)			
	Dev		Test	
	CSS	CCS	CSS	CCS
Submission 1	78.6	77.4	64.9	73.3
Submission 2	78.3	80.3	65.7	70.0
Submission 3	82.5	80.2	65.5	68.3
Best Baselines [25]	70.5	67.6	72.1	73.9

5   Conclusion

To detect COVID-19 infections from voice and cough sounds, we introduce our deep supervised feature representations based on Convolution Neural Network (CNN), Time Delay Neural Network (TDNN), and Long Short-Term Memory (LSTM) and an end-to-end ResNet-based architecture. Our approach outperforms the considered baseline systems on the development set in terms of UAR metric, achieves very decent results on the test set, and allows us to infer the high potential of the generated representations to be used as discriminative features for classification of positive vs negative subjects.

References

1. Amiriparian, S., Freitag, M., Cummins, N., Schuller, B.: Sequence to sequence autoencoders for unsupervised representation learning from audio. Universität Augsburg (2017)
2. Amiriparian, S., et al.: Snore sound classification using image-based deep spectrum features (2017)
3. Amiriparian, S., Gerczuk, M., Ottl, S., Cummins, N., Pugachevskiy, S., Schuller, B.: Bag-of-Deep-Features: noise-robust deep feature representations for audio analysis. In: Proceeding of IJCNN, pp. 1–7. IEEE (2018)
4. Brown, C., et al.: Exploring automatic diagnosis of COVID-19 from crowdsourced respiratory sound data. In: Proceedings of the 26th ACM SIGKDD International Conference on Knowledge Discovery & Data Mining, pp. 3474–3484 (2020)
5. Deshmukh, S., Ismail, M.A., Singh, R.: Interpreting glottal flow dynamics for detecting COVID-19 from voice. arXiv preprint arXiv:2010.16318 (2020)
6. Deshpande, G., Schuller, B.: An overview on audio, signal, speech, & language processing for COVID-19. arXiv preprint arXiv:2005.08579 (2020)
7. Eyben, F., Weninger, F., Gross, F., Schuller, B.: Recent developments in openS-MILE, the Munich open-source multimedia feature extractor. In: Proceedings of ACM ICM, pp. 835–838 (2013)
8. Freitag, M., Amiriparian, S., Pugachevskiy, S., Cummins, N., Schuller, B.: auDeep: unsupervised learning of representations from audio with deep recurrent neural networks. J. Mach. Learn. Res. **18**(1), 6340–6344 (2017)
9. Han, J., et al.: Exploring automatic COVID-19 diagnosis via voice and symptoms from crowdsourced data, pp. 8328–8332 (2021)
10. He, K., Zhang, X., Ren, S., Sun, J.: Deep residual learning for image recognition. CoRR abs/1512.03385 (2015). http://arxiv.org/abs/1512.03385
11. Imran, A., et al.: AI4COVID-19: AI enabled preliminary diagnosis for COVID-19 from cough samples via an app. Inf. Med. Unlocked **20**, 100378 (2020)
12. Ismail, M.A., Deshmukh, S., Singh, R.: Detection of COVID-19 through the analysis of vocal fold oscillations. arXiv preprint arXiv:2010.10707 (2020)
13. Khalid, H., Woo, S.S.: OC-FakeDect: classifying deepfakes using one-class variational autoencoder. In: Proceedings of IEEE/CVF CVPR Workshops, pp. 2794–2803 (2020)
14. Laguarta, J., Hueto, F., Subirana, B.: COVID-19 artificial intelligence diagnosis using only cough recordings. IEEE Open J. Eng. Med. Biol. **1**, 275–281 (2020)

15. Latif, S., Rana, R., Khalifa, S., Jurdak, R., Qadir, J., Schuller, B.W.: Deep representation learning in speech processing: Challenges, recent advances, and future trends. CoRR abs/2001.00378 (2020). http://arxiv.org/abs/2001.00378

16. Muguli, A., et al.: Dicova challenge: dataset, task, and baseline system for COVID-19 diagnosis using acoustics (2021)

17. Nagrani, A., Chung, J.S., Zisserman, A.: VoxCeleb: a large-scale speaker identification dataset. CoRR abs/1706.08612 (2017). http://arxiv.org/abs/1706.08612

18. Park, D.S., et al.: SpecAugment: a simple data augmentation method for automatic speech recognition. Proc. Interspeech **2019**, 2613–2617 (2019)

19. Pedregosa, F., et al.: Scikit-learn: machine learning in Python. J. Mach. Learn. Res. **12**, 2825–2830 (2011)

20. Povey, D., et al.: The Kaldi speech recognition toolkit (2011)

21. Qian, K., Schuller, B.W., Yamamoto, Y.: Recent advances in computer audition for diagnosing covid-19: An overview. arXiv preprint arXiv:2012.04650 (2020)

22. Quatieri, T.F., Talkar, T., Palmer, J.S.: A framework for biomarkers of COVID-19 based on coordination of speech-production subsystems. IEEE Open J. Eng. Med. Biol. **1**, 203–206 (2020)

23. Schmitt, M., Schuller, B.: OpenXBOW: introducing the Passau open-source cross-modal bag-of-words toolkit (2017)

24. Schuller, B., et al.: The interspeech 2013 computational paralinguistics challenge: social signals, conflict, emotion, autism. In: Proceedings of INTERSPEECH (2013)

25. Schuller, B.W., et al.: The interspeech 2021 computational paralinguistics challenge: COVID-19 cough, COVID-19 speech, escalation & primates. arXiv preprint arXiv:2102.13468 (2021)

26. Stappen, L., Rizos, G., Hasan, M., Hain, T., Schuller, B.W.: Uncertainty-aware machine support for paper reviewing on the interspeech 2019 submission corpus. In: Proc. Interspeech, pp. 1808–1812 (2020)

27. Tang, Y., Ding, G., Huang, J., He, X., Zhou, B.: Deep speaker embedding learning with multi-level pooling for text-independent speaker verification. In: Proceedings of IEEE ICASSP, pp. 6116–6120 (2019)

28. Weninger, F., Eyben, F., Schuller, B.W., Mortillaro, M., Scherer, K.R.: On the acoustics of emotion in audio: what speech, music, and sound have in common. Front. Psychol. **4**, 292 (2013)

29. Zhang, Y., Jiang, F., Duan, Z.: One-class learning towards synthetic voice spoofing detection. IEEE Sig. Process. Lett. **28**, 937–941 (2021)

Where Are We in Semantic Concept Extraction for Spoken Language Understanding?

Sahar Ghannay[1], Antoine Caubrière[2(✉)], Salima Mdhaffar[2],
Gaëlle Laperrière[2], Bassam Jabaian[2], and Yannick Estève[2]

[1] Université Paris-Saclay, CNRS, LISN, 91400 Orsay, France
sahar.ghannay@limsi.fr
[2] LIA - Avignon Université, Avignon, France
{antoine.caubrière,salima.mdhaffar,gaelle.laperriere,bassam.jabaian,
yannick.esteve}@univ-avignon.fr

Abstract. Spoken language understanding (SLU) topic has seen a lot of progress these last three years, with the emergence of end-to-end neural approaches. Spoken language understanding refers to natural language processing tasks related to semantic extraction from speech signal, like named entity recognition from speech or slot filling task in a context of human-machine dialogue. Classically, SLU tasks were processed through a cascade approach that consists in applying, firstly, an automatic speech recognition process, followed by a natural language processing module applied to the automatic transcriptions. These three last years, end-to-end neural approaches, based on deep neural networks, have been proposed in order to directly extract the semantics from speech signal, by using a single neural model. More recent works on self-supervised training with unlabeled data open new perspectives in term of performance for automatic speech recognition and natural language processing. In this paper, we present a brief overview of the recent advances on the French MEDIA benchmark dataset for SLU, with or without the use of additional data. We also present our last results that significantly outperform the current state-of-the-art with a Concept Error Rate (CER) of 11.2%, instead of 13.6% for the last state-of-the-art system presented this year.

Keywords: Spoken language understanding · End-to-end approach · Cascade approach · Self supervised training

1 Introduction

Spoken language understanding (SLU) refers to natural language processing tasks related to semantic extraction from the speech signal [34], like named entity recognition from speech, call routing, slot filling task in a context of human-machine dialogue...

Usually, SLU tasks were processed through a cascade approach that consists in applying first an automatic speech recognition (ASR) process, followed by a

A. Karpov and R. Potapova (Eds.): SPECOM 2021, LNAI 12997, pp. 202–213, 2021.
https://doi.org/10.1007/978-3-030-87802-3_19

natural language processing module applied to the automatic transcription [14]. For both automatic speech recognition and natural language processing, deep neural networks (DNN) have made great advances possible, leading to impressive improvements of qualitative performance for final SLU tasks [1,11,35].

These three last years, end-to-end neural approaches, based on deep neural networks, have been proposed in order to directly extract the semantics from speech signal, by using a single neural model [18,29]. A first advantage of such approaches consists in a joint optimization of the ASR and NLP part, since the unique neural model is optimized only for the final SLU task. Another advantage is the limitation of the error propagation: when using a cascade approach, an error in the first treatment implies errors in the following ones. In a neural end-to-end approach, the model decision is delayed to the output layer: all the information uncertainty is handled until the final decision.

Very recently, works on self-supervised training with unlabeled data open new perspectives in term of performance for automatic speech recognition and natural language processing [2,16]. They can be applied to SLU task.

This study presents experimental results on the French MEDIA benchmark dataset. This benchmark dataset is one of the most challenging benchmarks for SLU task. In this paper, we present a brief overview of the performance evolution of state-of-the-art systems on this benchmark dataset. We also present an approach that takes benefit from acoustic-based and linguistic-based models pre-trained on unlabelled data: this approach represents the next milestone to be surpassed.

2   MEDIA Dataset

The French MEDIA corpus [5], is dedicated to semantic extraction from speech in a context of human-machine dialogues for a hotel booking task. This dataset was created as a part of the Technolangue project of the French government in 2002. Its main objective is to set up an infrastructure for the production and dissemination of language resources, the evaluation of written and oral language technologies, the participation in national and international standardisation bodies and an information monitoring in the field.

The MEDIA dataset is made of telephone dialogue recordings with their manual transcriptions and semantic annotations. It is composed of 1257 dialogues from 250 different speakers, collected with a Wizard-of-Oz setting between two humans: one plays a computer, the other plays the user. The dataset is split into three parts (train, dev, test) as described in Table 1. In this work, we used the user part of MEDIA, since it has both speech and semantic annotations.

The semantic domain of this corpus is represented by 76 semantic concept tags such as *room number, hotel name, location, etc..* Some more complex linguistic tags, like co-references, are also used in this corpus.

The following sentence (translated from French) is an example of the MEDIA content: "I would like to book one double room in Paris up to one hundred and thirty euros". It will be annotated as (I would like to book, *reservation*), (one, *number-room*), (double room, *room-type*), (up to, *comparative-payment*), (one hundred and thirty, *amount-payment*), (euros, *currency-payment*).

Table 1. The official MEDIA dataset distribution.

Data	Nb Words	Nb Utterances	Nb Concepts	Nb Hours
train	94.2k	13.7k	31.7k	10 h46 m
dev	10.7k	1.3k	3.3k	01 h13 m
test	26.6k	3.7k	8.8 k	02 h59 m

In [4], Béchet and Raymond showed why the MEDIA task can be considered as the most challenging SLU benchmark available, in comparison to other well-known benchmarks such as ATIS [13], SNIPS [12], and M2M [31].

3 Overview of Approaches Proposed for the MEDIA Benchmark

3.1 Cascade Approach

Conventional SLU systems are designed as a cascade of components. Each of them solves separately a specific problem. First, an ASR module, trained on a large amount of data, maps speech signals to automatic transcriptions. This is then passed on to a natural language understanding (NLU) module that predicts semantic information from the automatic transcriptions. In this approach, error propagation is unavoidable, despite the performance of current ASR and NLU systems. In addition, those modules are optimized separately under different criteria. The ASR system is trained to minimize the word error rate (WER), while the NLU module is trained to minimize the concept error rate (CER) in case of slot filling task. This separate optimization suggests that a cascade SLU system is suboptimal.

Working on automatic transcriptions, for an SLU task on MEDIA corpus, is highly challenging. Many approaches have been proposed. Early NLU approaches were based on generative models such as Stochastic finite state transducers (FST), on discriminative or conditional models such as conditional random fields (CRFs) and support vector machines(SVMs)[21]. In the light of the success of neural approaches in different fields, some studies developed neural architectures for SLU task. In [27], the author presents the first recurrent neural architecture dedicated to SLU for the ATIS benchmark corpus. This neural model was applied to transcriptions despite speech signals directly. In [32,33], for the first time, an encoder-decoder neural network structure with attention mechanism [3] was proposed for this task. This time, it was on manual and automatic transcriptions from the MEDIA corpus. In order to reduce the unavoidable SLU performance decline due to ASR errors, the authors in [33] have proposed ASR confidence measures to localize ASR errors. These confidence measures have been used as additional SLU features to be combined with lexical and syntactic features, useful for characterizing concept mentions. In [32], the authors proposed an approach to simulate ASR errors from manual transcriptions, to improve the performance of SLU systems. The use of the resulting corpus prepares the SLU system to ASR errors during their training and makes it more robust to ASR errors.

3.2   End-to-End Approach

As seen in the previous section, one problem with cascaded approaches is the propagation of errors through the components. The intermediate transcription is noisy due to speech recognition errors, and the NLU component has to deal with these errors. The other problem comes from the separate optimizations of the different modules.

To tackle these issues, end-to-end approaches were proposed in order not to use an intermediate speech transcriptions. This kind of approach aims to develop a single system directly optimized to extract semantic concepts from speech.

SLU end-to-end systems are usually trained to generate both recognized words and semantic tags [15,18].

Until now, mainly two kinds of neural architectures have been proposed on the MEDIA benchmark. The first one is based on the use of the Connectionist Temporal Classification (CTC) loss function [20], while the other one is based on the use of an encoder-decoder architecture with attention mechanism [3].

CTC Approach
In this work, we call CTC approach the neural architecture trained by using the CTC loss function. This loss function allows the system to learn an alignment between the input speech and the word and concept sequences to produce.

To our knowledge, the best-published results with a CTC approach on MEDIA were obtained by [6]. In this study, the authors proposed a neural architecture largely inspired by the DeepSpeech 2 speech recognition system. The neural architecture is a stack of two 2D-invariant convolutional layers (CNN), followed by five bidirectional long short term memory (bLSTM) layers with sequence-wise batch normalization, a classical fully connected layer, and the softmax output layer. As input features, we used spectrograms of power to normalize audio clips, calculated on 20ms windows. This system was trained following the curriculum-based transfer learning approach, which consists in training the same model through successive stages, with different tasks ranked from the most generic one to the most specific one. The authors used speech recognition tasks, then named entity extraction and finally semantic concept extraction tasks.

Encoder-Decoder Approach with Attention Mechanism
The encoder-decoder architecture was initially implemented in the machine translation context. This approach quickly showed its benefits for the speech recognition task [7–9], and more recently for SLU tasks [28,29].

The encoder-decoder architecture is divided into two main parts. First, an encoder receives the speech features as input, and provides its hidden states to build a high-level representation of the features. This high-level representation is then passed on to an attention module. It identifies the parts of these representations that are relevant for each step of the decoding process. Next, the attention module computes a context vector from these representations to feed the decoder. Finally, the decoder processes the input context vectors to predict the transcription of speech, enriched with semantic concepts. At each decoding time step, a new context vector is computed from the encoded speech representations. Unlike CTC approaches, the output sequence size of an encoder-decoder approach does not depend on the input sequence size.

A recent study [28] used a similar architecture and obtained the state-of-the-art performance for the MEDIA task. The encoder part is composed of four 2-dimensional convolution layers followed by four bLSTM layers. Each convolution layer is followed by a batch normalization. The decoder part is a stack of four bLSTM layers, two fully connected layers, and a softmax layer. The input features of the network are 40-dimensional MelFBanks with a Hamming window of 25 ms and 10 ms strides.

This encoder-decoder system is trained following the curriculum-based transfer learning, with the same data used for the CTC approach presented in Sect. 3.2, except for the named entity extraction task which was not used.

3.3 System Performance

SLU systems can be evaluated with different metrics. Historically, on the MEDIA corpus, two metrics are jointly used: the Concept Error Rate (CER) and the Concept/Value Error Rate (CVER). The CER is computed similarly to the Word Error Rate, by only taking into account the concepts occurrences in both the reference and the hypothesis files. The CVER metrics is an extension of the CER. It considers the correctness of the complete concept/value pair. In the example in Sect. 2, both "one hundred and thirty" and *amount-payment* have to be correct to consider the concept/value pair (one hundred and thirty,*amount-payment*) as correct. Errors on the value component can come from a bad segmentation (missing or additional words in the value) or from ASR errors.

Table 2 presents the best results obtained on the official MEDIA benchmark dataset, by the main families of approaches presented in the two previous sections. By computing the 95% confidence interval, we observe a 0.7 confidence margin for CER and 0.8 for CVER, when the CER is 13.6% and the CVER 18.5%. Until now, the best result was reached by an end-to-end encoder-decoder architecture with attention mechanism, trained by following a curriculum transfer-learning approach [28].

4   Improving the State of the Art

In the previous section we present state-of-the-art performances. Recently, unsupervised learning on huge amount of data have been successfully proposed to pre-train Transformers-based models [2,16]. Thanks to these models, ASR state-of-the-art performance [2] and NLP state-of-the-art performance [16] have been

Table 2. Best results obtained on the official MEDIA benchmark dataset, by the main families of approaches presented in this paper. Results are given in both Concept Error Rate and Concept/Value Error Rate.

Architecture	Model	CER	CVER
Cascade (2018)	HMM/DNN ASR + neural NLU [32]	20.2	26.0
Cascade (2018)	HMM/DNN ASR + CRF [32]	20.2	25.3
Cascade (2019)	HMM/TDNN ASR + CRF [6]	16.1	20.4
End-to-end (2019)	E2E CTC [6]	16.4	20.9
End-to-end (2021)	E2E encoder-decoder with attention [28]	**13.6**	**18.5**

outperformed, with respectively wav2vec and BERT models. In this section, we present a cascade system using both BERT and wav2vec optimized on the MEDIA task.

4.1 BERT and CamemBERT Models

For the NLU module, we propose to use the one that achieved the state-of-the-art result on manual transcriptions of MEDIA corpus [19]. This system is based on a fine-tuning of BERT [16] on MEDIA SLU task using the French CamemBERT [26] model.

BERT [16] is a deeply bidirectional, unsupervised language representation model, which stands for Bidirectional Encoder Representations from Transformers. It is designed to pre-train deep bidirectional representations from unlabeled text, taking into account both left and right context in all layers. The resulting pre-trained BERT model can be fine-tuned with just one additional output layer, to create state-of-the-art models for a wide range of NLP tasks. BERT is pre-trained using a combination of masked language modeling objective and next sentence prediction on a large corpus which include the Toronto Book Corpus and Wikipedia.

The French CamemBERT model is based on RoBERTa (Robustly Optimized BERT Pre-training Approach) [25] which is based on BERT. CamemBERT is similar to RoBERTa, which dynamically change the masking pattern applied to the training data, and remove the next sentence prediction task. In addition, it uses the whole word masking and the SentencePiece tokenization [24]. The CamemBERT model is trained on the French CCNet corpus composed of 135 GB of raw text.

4.2 Wav2vec Models

Wav2vec 2.0 [2] is a model pre-trained through self-supervision. It takes raw audio as input and computes contextual representations that can be used as input for speech recognition systems. It contains three main components: a convolutional feature encoder, a context network and a quantization block. The convolutional feature encoder converts the audio signal into a latent representation. This representation is given to the context network which takes care of the context. The context network architecture consists of a succession of several transformer encoder blocks. The quantization network is used to map the latent representation to quantized representation.

In [17], the authors released French pre-trained wav2vec 2.0 models. Two models have been released for public use[1], a large one and a base one. In this study, we use the large configuration which encodes raw audio into frames of 1024-dimensional vectors. The models are pre-trained in a unsupervised way with 3K hours of unlabeled speech. Details about data used to train the wav2vec models can be found in [17]. The trained model is composed of about 300M parameters.

To get better ASR results than the ones we could reach by fine-tuning the French wav2vec 2.0 model, on the MEDIA training data only, we suggest to, first, fine-tune on external audio data, as proposed in [6] or [28]. To make the experiments reproducible, instead of using the Broadcast News data used in these works, we used the CommonVoice French dataset[2] (version 6.1), collected by the Mozilla Foundation, and much easily accessible. The train set consists of 425.5 h of speech, while the validation and test sets contain around 24 h of speech.

4.3   Cascade Approach with Pre-trained Models

As written before, we propose in this work to use a cascade approach, with pre-trained models for each component. The ASR system is composed of the large pre-trained French wav2vec model, a linear layer of 1024 units, and the softmax output layer. First, we optimize the ASR system on the French CommonVoice dataset. Then, we fine-tune it for speech recognition on the French MEDIA corpus, the wav2vec weights being updated at each training stage. The loss function used at each fine-tuning step is the CTC loss function. We call the final ASR model W2V • Common Voice • M_{ASR}.

The NLU system is applied on the automatic transcriptions provided from the ASR system, to obtain semantic annotations. This system is based on the fine-tuning of the French CamemBERT [26] model, on the manual transcriptions of MEDIA corpus. It achieved state-of-the-art result on manual transcriptions of MEDIA corpus [19], yielding to 7.56 of CER when there is no error in the transcription.

4.4   Results and Discussion

The experimental result obtained with the proposed cascade approach is presented in Table 3. We compare the performance of this cascade system, named *W2V • Common Voice • M_{ASR} + CamemBERT*, to the E2E encoder-decoder

---

[1] https://huggingface.co/LeBenchmark.

[2] https://commonvoice.mozilla.org/fr/datasets.

model proposed in [28], that reached the best result on this task until now, and other wav2vec-based models. All the wav2vec-based models presented in Table 3 were implemented thanks to the SpeechBrain toolkit[3], including the fine-tuning of the wav2vec models.

Like in Sect. 3.3, the results are evaluated in terms of CER and CVER. Our new system yields to 17.64% of relative CER improvement and 7.02% of relative CVER improvement, by reaching respectively 11.2% of CER and 17.2% of WER. The result shows the effectiveness of unsupervised pre-trained models like wav2vec and BERT in such a scenario. Notice that the $W2V \bullet Common Voice \bullet M_{ASR}$ model allows us to have an effective ASR system that achieved 8.5% of WER.

In system (1), the wav2vec model is fine-tuned directly on MEDIA SLU (M_{SLU}) task. In system (2), the wav2vec model is first fine-tuned on the Common Voice data then on M_{SLU} task, and a beam search decoding is applied. In systems (3) and (4) the wav2vec model is first fine-tuned on the Common Voice data, then on MEDIA ASR (M_{ASR}), and last on M_{SLU} task, using the greedy or the beam search decoding using a 5-gram language model to rescore. This language model is trained on the manual transcriptions of M_{SLU} training data only.

It is worth to mention that even before the generalisation of the use of neural networks for sequential tagging tasks, such as the slot filling task investigated in this paper, several efforts have been made to better take into account the ASR system errors during the semantic labeling. Many approaches have been proposed for a joint decoding between speech recognition and understanding, considering the n-best recognition hypotheses during the semantic annotation [22,23,30]. When neural networks have become state-of-the-art systems for SLU, end-to-end approaches have gradually replaced cascade approaches and have shown very good performance, allowing the semantic labeling of a speech signal and minimising the impact of transcription errors on the SLU performance. However, these architectures need a large amount of data and often use pre-trained external module that have been trained separately in out-of-context data. The results presented in Table 3 show that if such pre-trained models are used in a cascade architecture, the resulting system reaches or even exceeds the performance of the end-to-end based one. In addition, the result of the cascade system reinforces the idea of the use of pre-trained models at the encoder (wav2vec) and decoder (BERT) levels within end-to-end architecture, as proposed in [10]. This leads us to conclude that the two architectures remain valid and competitive and that the choice should be made according to the availability of additional data and the pre-training models.

---

[3] https://speechbrain.github.io.

Table 3. Performance on Test MEDIA in terms of CER and CVER scores of the proposed cascade and end-to-end systems using pre-trained models. "•" formalizes a transfer learning step during the training of the E2E system.

Architecture	Model	CER	CVER
End-to-end	Encoder-decoder [28]	13.6	18.5
	(1) W2V • M_{SLU} (Beam 5g)	18.8	23.6
	(2) W2V • Common Voice • M_{SLU} (Beam 5g)	15.8	20.4
	(3) W2V • Common Voice • M_{ASR} • M_{SLU} (greedy)	15.4	20.5
	(4) W2V • Common Voice • M_{ASR} • M_{SLU} (Beam 5g)	14.5	18.8
Cascade	W2V • Common Voice • M_{ASR} + CamemBERT	**11.2**	**17.2**

5   Conclusion

In this paper, we present a brief overview of the recent advances on the French MEDIA benchmark dataset for SLU. We propose a system based on a cascade approach, that takes benefit from acoustic-based and linguistic-based models pre-trained on unlabelled data: wav2vec models for the ASR system, and BERT-like model for the NLU system. Experimental results show that our system outperforms significantly the current state of the art with a Concept Error Rate (CER) of 11.2% instead of 13.6% for the last state-of-the-art system presented this year.

This new advance reinforces the idea of the use of pre-trained models at the encoder (wav2vec) and decoder (BERT) levels within an end-to-end architecture. This will be explored in our future work.

This study leads us to conclude that the two architectures (cascade *vs.* end-to-end) remain valid and competitive and that the choice should be made according to the availability of additional data and relevant pre-trained models.

Acknowledgments. This work was granted access to the HPC resources of IDRIS under the allocation 2020-AD011011838 made by GENCI.

References

1. Amodei, D., et al.: Deep speech 2: end-to-end speech recognition in English and mandarin. In: International Conference on Machine Learning, pp. 173–182. PMLR (2016)
2. Baevski, A., Zhou, H., Mohamed, A., Auli, M.: wav2vec 2.0: a framework for self-supervised learning of speech representations. arXiv preprint arXiv:2006.11477 (2020)
3. Bahdanau, D., Cho, K., Bengio, Y.: Neural machine translation by jointly learning to align and translate. arXiv preprint arXiv:1409.0473 (2014)
4. Béchet, F., Raymond, C.: Benchmarking benchmarks: introducing new automatic indicators for benchmarking spoken language understanding corpora. In: Interspeech, Graz, Austria (2019)

5. Bonneau-Maynard, H., Rosset, S., Ayache, C., Kuhn, A., Mostefa, D.: Semantic annotation of the French media dialog corpus. In: INTERSPEECH (2005)
6. Caubrière, A., Tomashenko, N., Laurent, A., Morin, E., Camelin, N., Estève, Y.: Curriculum-based transfer learning for an effective end-to-end spoken language understanding and domain portability. In: Proceedings Interspeech 2019, pp. 1198–1202 (2019). https://doi.org/10.21437/Interspeech.2019-1832
7. Chan, W., Jaitly, N., Le, Q., Vinyals, O.: Listen, attend and spell: a neural network for large vocabulary conversational speech recognition. In: 2016 IEEE International Conference on Acoustics, Speech and Signal Processing (ICASSP), pp. 4960–4964. IEEE (2016)
8. Chiu, C.C., et al.: State-of-the-art speech recognition with sequence-to-sequence models. In: 2018 IEEE International Conference on Acoustics, Speech and Signal Processing (ICASSP), pp. 4774–4778. IEEE (2018)
9. Chorowski, J., Bahdanau, D., Cho, K., Bengio, Y.: End-to-end continuous speech recognition using attention-based recurrent NN: first results. arXiv preprint arXiv:1412.1602 (2014)
10. Chung, Y.A., Zhu, C., Zeng, M.: SPLAT: speech-language joint pre-training for spoken language understanding. In: Proceedings of the 2021 Conference of the North American Chapter of the Association for Computational Linguistics: Human Language Technologies, pp. 1897–1907 (2021)
11. Collobert, R., Weston, J., Bottou, L., Karlen, M., Kavukcuoglu, K., Kuksa, P.: Natural language processing (almost) from scratch. J. Mach. Learn. Res. **12**, 2493–2537 (2011)
12. Coucke, A., et al.: Snips voice platform: an embedded spoken language understanding system for private-by-design voice interfaces. arXiv preprint arXiv:1805.10190 (2018)
13. Dahl, D.A., et al.: Expanding the scope of the ATIS task: The ATIS-3 corpus. In: Human Language Technology: Proceedings of a Workshop held at Plainsboro, New Jersey, 8–11 March 1994 (1994)
14. De Mori, R.: Spoken language understanding: a survey. In: 2007 IEEE Workshop on Automatic Speech Recognition & Understanding (ASRU), pp. 365–376. IEEE (2007)
15. Desot, T., Portet, F., Vacher, M.: Towards end-to-end spoken intent recognition in smart home. In: 2019 International Conference on Speech Technology and Human-Computer Dialogue (SpeD), pp. 1–8. IEEE (2019)
16. Devlin, J., Chang, M.W., Lee, K., Toutanova, K.: BERT: pre-training of deep bidirectional transformers for language understanding. In: NAACL-HLT. Association for Computational Linguistics, Minneapolis, Minnesota, June 2019. https://doi.org/10.18653/v1/N19-1423. https://www.aclweb.org/anthology/N19-1423
17. Evain, S., et al.: Lebenchmark: a reproducible framework for assessing self-supervised representation learning from speech. In: Interspeech, Brno, Czechia (2021)
18. Ghannay, S., et al.: End-to-end named entity and semantic concept extraction from speech. In: 2018 IEEE Spoken Language Technology Workshop (SLT), pp. 692–699. IEEE (2018)
19. Ghannay, S., Servan, C., Rosset, S.: Neural networks approaches focused on French spoken language understanding: application to the MEDIA evaluation task. In: Proceedings of the 28th International Conference on Computational Linguistics, pp. 2722–2727. International Committee on Computational Linguistics, Barcelona, Spain (Online), December 2020. https://doi.org/10.18653/v1/2020.coling-main.245. https://www.aclweb.org/anthology/2020.coling-main.245

20. Graves, A., Fernández, S., Gomez, F., Schmidhuber, J.: Connectionist temporal classification: labelling unsegmented sequence data with recurrent neural networks. In: Proceedings of the 23rd International Conference on Machine Learning, pp. 369–376 (2006)

21. Hahn, S., et al.: Comparing stochastic approaches to spoken language understanding in multiple languages. IEEE Trans. Audio Speech Lang. Process. **19**(6), 1569–1583 (2010)

22. Hakkani-Tü, D., Béchet, F., Riccardi, G., Tur, G.: Beyond ASR 1-best: using word confusion networks in spoken language understanding. Comput. Speech Lang. (2005). https://doi.org/10.1016/j.csl.2005.07.005. https://hal.archives-ouvertes. fr/hal-01314993

23. Jabaian, B., Lefèvre, F.: Error-corrective discriminative joint decoding of automatic spoken language transcription and understanding. In: Bimbot, F., et al. (eds.) INTERSPEECH 2013, 14th Annual Conference of the International Speech Communication Association, Lyon, France, 25–29 August 2013, pp. 2718–2722. ISCA (2013). http://www.isca-speech.org/archive/interspeech_2013/i13_2718.html

24. Kudo, T., Richardson, J.: SentencePiece: a simple and language independent subword tokenizer and Detokenizer for neural text processing. In: Proceedings of the 2018 Conference on Empirical Methods in Natural Language Processing: System Demonstrations, pp. 66–71. Association for Computational Linguistics, Brussels, Belgium, November 2018. https://doi.org/10.18653/v1/D18-2012. https://www. aclweb.org/anthology/D18-2012

25. Liu, Y., et al.: Roberta: a robustly optimized BERT pretraining approach. arXiv preprint arXiv:1907.11692 (2019)

26. Martin, L., et al.: CamemBERT: a tasty French language model. In: Proceedings of the 58th Annual Meeting of the Association for Computational Linguistics (2020)

27. Mesnil, G., He, X., Deng, L., Bengio, Y.: Investigation of recurrent-neural-network architectures and learning methods for spoken language understanding. In: Interspeech, pp. 3771–3775 (2013)

28. Pelloin, V., et al.: End2end acoustic to semantic transduction. In: ICASSP 2021–2021 IEEE International Conference on Acoustics, Speech and Signal Processing (ICASSP), pp. 7448–7452 (2021). https://doi.org/10.1109/ICASSP39728.2021. 9413581

29. Serdyuk, D., Wang, Y., Fuegen, C., Kumar, A., Liu, B., Bengio, Y.: Towards end-to-end spoken language understanding. In: 2018 IEEE International Conference on Acoustics, Speech and Signal Processing (ICASSP), pp. 5754–5758. IEEE (2018)

30. Servan, C., Raymond, C., Béchet, F., Nocera, P.: Conceptual decoding from word lattices: application to the spoken dialogue corpus MEDIA. In: The Ninth International Conference on Spoken Language Processing (Interspeech 2006 - ICSLP), Pittsburgh, United States, September 2006. https://hal.archives-ouvertes.fr/hal-01160181

31. Shah, P., et al.: Building a conversational agent overnight with dialogue self-play. arXiv preprint arXiv:1801.04871 (2018)

32. Simonnet, E., Ghannay, S., Camelin, N., Estève, Y.: Simulating ASR errors for training SLU systems. In: Proceedings of the Eleventh International Conference on Language Resources and Evaluation (LREC 2018). European Language Resources Association (ELRA), Miyazaki, Japan, May 2018. https://www.aclweb. org/anthology/L18-1499

33. Simonnet, E., Ghannay, S., Camelin, N., Estève, Y., De Mori, R.: ASR error management for improving spoken language understanding. In: Interspeech 2017, Stockholm, Sweden, August 2017

34. Tur, G., De Mori, R.: Spoken Language Understanding: Systems for Extracting Semantic Information From Speech. Wiley (2011)
35. Vaswani, A., et al.: Attention is all you need. arXiv preprint arXiv:1706.03762 (2017)

Learning Mizo Tones from F0 Contours Using 1D-CNN

Parismita Gogoi[1(✉)], Sishir Kalita[1], Wendy Lalhminghlui[1],
Priyankoo Sarmah[1], and S. R. M. Prasanna[2]

[1] Indian Institute of Technology Guwahati, Guwahati 781039, India
{parismitagogoi,sishir,wendy,priyankoo}@iitg.ac.in
[2] Indian Institute of Technology Dharwad, Dharwad 580011, India
prasanna@iitdh.ac.in

Abstract. This work attempts to build an automatic 1D-CNN based tone recognizer of Mizo, an under-studied Tibeto-Burman language of North-East India. Preliminary research findings have confirmed that along with four canonical tones of Mizo (High, Low, Rising and Falling), a phenomenon of Rising tone sandhi (RTS) with distinct phonetic characteristics are also observed. As per the authors' knowledge, no work has been reported to identify the RTS along with four distinct tones. Moreover, previous tone recognition works have explored hand-crafted features derived from F0 contour which may not provide the explicit representation of a specific tone category. To address these issues, current work attempts to incorporate the RTS along with four lexical tones and learn tone specific features directly from F0 contours using a 1D-CNN model. Experimental results conducted for speaker independent case show that the proposed 1D-CNN model achieves an accuracy of 68.18%.

Keywords: Tone sandhi · Mizo · F0 contour · 1D-CNN

1 Introduction

Mizo is a tone language belonging to the Tibeto-Burman language family, spoken in Mizoram province in the Northeast of India, Western Burma (Myanmar), and Eastern Bangladesh. Tone languages show variation in tone patterns of every syllable (i.e., fundamental frequency (F0) and its harmonics). Mizo has four distinct lexical tones or patterns: High (H), Low (L), Rising (R), and Falling (F) [5,8,9,28]. Figure 1 shows the F0 contours of the four phonological tones present in Mizo. The figure is plotted using the data referred in the present work. Table 1 presents a set of minimal tonal pairs in Mizo [15]. Previous acoustic studies on Mizo tones have shown that the four Mizo tones are distinct from each other in terms of F0 slope and average F0 [27,28]. In terms of average F0, Rising vs. Low and Falling vs. High tones do not show any significant difference. However, in terms of F0 slope, all four tones are significantly distinct from each other [9,28]. Apart from the four distinct tones of Mizo, previous works on Mizo tones have reported the existence of a Rising Tone Sandhi (RTS) in the

© Springer Nature Switzerland AG 2021
A. Karpov and R. Potapova (Eds.): SPECOM 2021, LNAI 12997, pp. 214–225, 2021.
https://doi.org/10.1007/978-3-030-87802-3_20

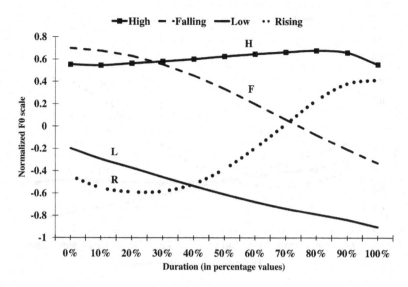

Fig. 1. The averaged normalized F0 contours of four Mizo tones [15].

language [5,9,27,31]. Tone sandhi is a phonological process which changes the canonical tone of a syllable, due to contextual effects of the preceding or the following tone [14,15]. For instance, in Mandarin Chinese, a tone 3 (Falling-Rising tone) preceding another tone 3 changes to tone 2 (Rising) [29]. In Mizo, it is noticed that a Rising tone preceding a Falling or a High tone loses its rising contour and becomes a lower register tone, as shown in the examples in Table 2 and in Fig. 2. Figure 2 is also plotted using the data referred in the present work. However, as reported in the previous study, at least phonetically, it is not identical to any of the other four phonological tones in Mizo (see Fig. 2) [9,14]. The resulting sandhi tone retains the duration of the canonical Rising tone but is significantly shorter than the canonical Low tone. In terms of pitch height, the sandhi tone is between the High tone and the Low tone in Mizo. Additionally, it is reported that the low tone derived from RTS can be categorically perceived by the native speakers of Mizo [14].

The presence of RTS in Mizo is observed by analyzing the behaviour of the four tones in trisyllabic phrases [27]. The two trisyllabic phrases in (Table 2)

Table 1. Mizo lexical words with the four contrasting tones [15].

Tone	Word	Meaning
High	/vai/	'chaff'
Low	/vai/	'dazzle'
Rising	/vai/	'search'
Falling	/vai/	'wave'

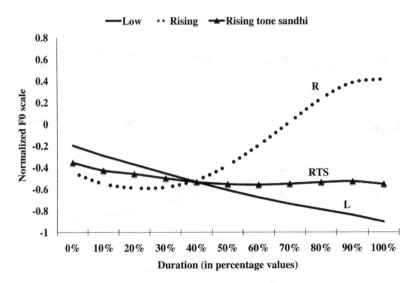

Fig. 2. The averaged normalized F0 contours of rising, low, and the derived low tone from RTS in Mizo [15].

Table 2. RTS phenomenon in initial and medial position of Mizo trisyllabic phrases.

Phrases	Meaning	Underlying tone	Surface tone
kor sen moi	A beautiful white shirt	R-H-H	RTS-H-H
a hal ta	He has burnt it	L-R-F	L-RTS-F

show the RTS phenomenon in the initial and medial position of the phrases whenever Rising tone is followed by High or Falling tone (Fig. 2).

2   Previous Works and Motivation

Tone recognition has been a crucial task in developing speech technology for tonal languages, such as Mandarin, Cantonese, and Mizo. Tone recognition plays a key role in performance improvement in learning system as well as in speech recognition [12]. In our previous works on speech recognition, it was found that incorporation of tonal information improves the Mizo ASR performance [7] and Mizo digit recognition performance [13,25]. Most of the works related to tone recognition reported in the literature are on the Mandarin. Classical machine learning methods, such as Gaussian Mixture Model, Support Vector Machine (SVM), Hidden Markov Model (HMM) are successfully applied for tone recognition on segmented syllable for Mandarin [4,19,32]. In recent years, Neural Networks (NNs) have proven to be successful in tone modeling tasks. Tones in Mandarin monosyllables were recognized using multilayer perceptron by extracting ten features of fundamental frequency and energy contours [2,18]. Ryant et al. trained segment-level models to classify syllables in Mandarin with a DNN for frame-level 5-tone classification and a single-layer NN at syllable level [23]. An error rate of 16.86% was obtained when inputs are raw MFCCs. One of six tone classes was classified with DNN model when input to the DNN is 40-dimensional MFCCs [24]. Authors proposed a fully automated method of tone classification of syllables in Mandarin [3] using convolutional Neural Network (CNN) with MFCCs as input to classify four tones in Mandarin, whereas, spectrogram as the input for CNN was explored in [21]. A method was developed using tone nucleus modeling and neural network classifier where a syllable F0 contour was explored [30].

In case of Cantonese, tone recognition was done for isolated Cantonese syllables using suprasegmental features extracted from the voiced portion of a monosyllabic utterance [9]. Three layers feed forward neural network was used to classify these features achieving an accuracy of 89.0% for single-speaker and 87.6% for multi-speaker, respectively [16]. HMM was used for tone recognition in Cantonese for continuous spoken speech [17]. The work in [17] was further explored using SVM to achieve better performance in speaker-independent condition [20].

A few preliminary works have also been reported in the direction of Mizo tone recognition. In a perceptual study conducted on Mizo speakers, it has been found that average F0, slope, and duration are very important acoustic cues to correctly identifying the Mizo tones [11]. Based on this observation, authors develop a threshold-based Mizo tone recognition system for four phonological categories using pitch height and F0 slope features [26]. However, this method possesses two main shortcomings - (1) the approach for identifying tones was threshold-based and no statistical method was incorporated, and (2) the Mizo database used for the work was considerably small. Later, to address these issues, a DNN-based tone recognition system with six F0 derived acoustic features as front-end was proposed [9]. However, this work did not include the sandhi tone, only four class classification of Mizo tones was performed.

From the above discussion, it is clear that existing works have mostly focused on features extracted from the speech signal (MFCCs) or from the F0 contour (e.g., height and slope). Then, those features are used as input to train a machine learning model. It is mentioned earlier that the average F0 does not show any significant difference for Rising vs. Low and Falling vs. High tones. It can be seen from Fig. 1 that the High tone in Mizo is fairly static, while the other tones have dynamic F0 contours. The Falling tone begins from the same point of initiation of High tone and the Low tone has a falling contour [9]. The Rising tone has an initial downward dip and then rises up from about 40% of the total duration [9]. However, the hand-crafted features computed from F0 contour may not explicitly capture the above-mentioned salient cues for each tone class. Moreover, to the best of our knowledge, no previous works incorporated the sandhi tone in the recognition system. Although, its recognition is important to analyze the tonal co-articulation effects and improve performance of speech technology based systems. It is shown in Fig. 2 that RTS and Low tones are quite similar though a Mizo speaker can easily perceive the difference. However, representing this kind of minute variation using the hand-crafted features may be difficult, and leads to poor recognition performance. Considering these issues, current work proposes an approach based on CNN for tone recognition, which will learn the tone class directly from the F0 contour. CNN is a machine learning technique that learns patterns present in the data and provides robust representations that are robust to local variations in the data. We have explored one-dimensional (1D) CNN, and F0 contour computed from each syllable will be fed to the network and let the network to learn relevant features. It is expected that the proposed 1D-CNN-based method will outperform our previous DNN-based method trained using F0 derived features. Hence, the key contributions of this work can be highlighted as follows:

- Proposal of a 1D-CNN for learning tone class directly from F0 contour.
- Incorporation of RTS in Mizo tone recognition system and analyze how it interacts with other four tone classes.

The remainder of this paper is organized as follows. Section 3 describes the speech corpus used in this work. Section 4 discusses the tone classification model used for the recognition of Mizo Tones. In Sect. 5, we present the experimental results. Finally, the paper is concluded in Sect. 6.

3   Mizo Speech Corpus

The Mizo speech corpus used in this work is prepared from 19 (10 male and 9 female) native Mizo speakers. The speech corpus has its size in 1.8 h of token duration. The speech data was collected in a soundproof recording booth using a Tascam DR100 MKII linear PCM recorder connected to a Shure SM10A unidirectional head-worn, close-talk microphone [9,14]. All the speakers were born and brought up in Mizoram, and their average age was 22. Printed sets of meaningful trisyllabic Mizo phrases were provided, comprising of three monosyllabic words with all the possible combinations of the four Mizo lexical tones resulting in 64 distinct tone combinations [9]. Each tone combination consists of five unique phrases which were recorded three times by each speaker. The Tone Bearing Unit (TBU) in Mizo is the syllable rime, made up of vowel nucleus or vowel with a sonorant coda. Accordingly, tone boundary was segmented and annotated by native Mizo speakers by listening and visually examining the pitch track of the TBU using Praat [1]. Figure 3 provides the annotation of one trisyllabic phrase /lei lai aŋ/ *Let's dig the ground*. This is obtained from one female speaker's first iteration. In this phrase, /lei/ is Rising tone, /lai/ is Low tone and /aŋ/ is Rising tone resulting in a Rising-Low-Rising tone combination.

4   Methodology

In this section, a detailed discussion about the proposed tone recognition system on isolated syllables in Mizo is presented. Initially, the estimation of F0 contour

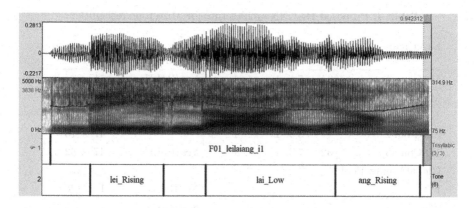

Fig. 3. The Praat picture of tone annotated trisyllabic phrase obtained from one female speaker in Rising-Low-Rising combination.

and its speaker-wise normalization are discussed. Following that, 1D-CNN-based tone detection system using the estimated F0 contour is described. The development of the baseline system based on DNN model with six F0 features as input to compare the performance of the proposed system is also discussed in this section.

4.1 Estimation of F0 and Normalization

Due to the non-uniform number of tone samples in different classes of the Mizo speech corpus (Sect. 3), we develop one dataset from the corpus for the classification purpose. Among the five tone classes, only $3,611$ samples are from the RTS category. Hence, we partition the dataset into 14983 syllables as training examples and 6437 syllables as testing examples. Thus, the total tone examples in our present dataset are $21,420$. The detailed structure of dataset can be seen in Table 3. The training dataset is balanced to have similar number of files in each tone categories. Speakers present in train set are not included in test set to make the study speaker-independent. The average duration of the five tones across all the 19 speakers are around 140 ms. The F0 values were automatically extracted at every 2% interval of the total duration using PRAAT software [1,9], and the

Table 3. Mizo dataset.

Tone	Training examples	Testing examples
High (H)	3000	1765
Low (L)	3000	1362
Rising (R)	3000	1129
Falling (F)	3000	1553
Rising Tone Sandhi (RTS)	2983	628
Total	14983	6437

Table 4. Proposed 1D-CNN architecture for Mizo tone recognition.

Layer name	Size	Kernel size	Stride	Batch norm/ Activation	Output size
1D-Conv-1	8	7 × 1	1	Yes/ReLU	51 × 8
MaxPool-1	–	3 × 1	1	–	49 × 8
1D-Conv-2	16	7 × 1	1	Yes/ReLU	49 × 16
MaxPool-2	–	3 × 1	1	–	47 × 16
1D-Conv-3	32	7 × 1	1	Yes/ReLU	47 × 32
GlobalAveragePool	–	–	–	–	1 × 32
FC	128	–	–	No/ReLU	1 × 128
FC	5	–	–	Softmax	1 × 5

values are collected in a spreadsheet. For speaker-independent tone recognition, the speaker effect needs to be removed from the F0 contour [9]. The z-score normalization is considered to be the best method for gender normalization [22]. Z-score normalization is achieved with the equation: $x^* = \frac{x-\mu}{\sigma}$, where μ is the mean F0, and σ is the standard deviation of the F0 values considered for mean F0. After F0 normalization is done, speaker-dependent F0 values are non-existent while the shape of the original F0 contour and its relative height is maintained [9]. Here, the F0 contour profile is time-aligned by a technique described in [9,16], and make each F0 contour of size 51 samples. This is performed to equal each tone recorded with different duration for input to the 1D-CNN.

4.2   Proposed 1D-CNN-based Tone Detection System

Our proposed system fully automates the five tone classification of isolated syllables in Mizo. The CNN takes F0 contour as the only input data and classify the syllables into one of the five tones in Mizo. The proposed 1D-CNN architecture can be seen in Table 4. The hyper-parameters of the network are tuned such that the difference of train set and test accuracies is reduced and does not overfit the model. Here, batch normalization is used after each of the 3 convolutional layers. After the batch normalization, ReLU activation is used, and following that, max pooling is applied. We have used a kernel size of 3 × 1 in the pooling layer. This is true for first two of the convolutional blocks (convolutional layer + batch normalization + ReLU activation + max pooling). However, after the ReLU activation of the third convolutional layer, we have used a global average pooling layer to map the output of activation function into one vector and to reduce the dimensionality. The number of filters are 8, 16, and 32 for first, second and third convolutional layers, respectively. The filter size is 7 for all the CNN layers. The output of the global average pooling layer is fed into a dense layer of size 128, where ReLU is used as an activation function. Finally, in the last layer, softmax activation function is applied and it has 5 nodes corresponding to five tone classes.

The CNN network is trained with random initialization of weights & biases and optimized using stochastic gradient descent (SGD) optimizer to minimize the

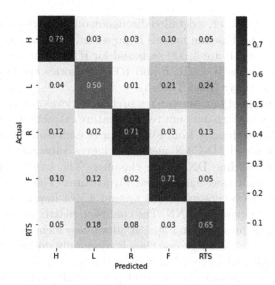

Fig. 4. Confusion matrix of 1D-CNN based system.

categorical cross-entropy loss between the target label and network output. The feature kernels are fine trained by back-propagation of the gradient across the convolutional layers [10]. Early stopping regularization technique is adopted here to determine the stopping of the fine-tuning procedure. Our method is implemented in the Keras toolkit [6]. We have used an initial learning rate of 0.001 for SGD optimizer. The network is trained for 300 epochs with a batch size of 32.

4.3 Baseline Tone Detection System Using DNN

A baseline tone detection system using a set of six acoustic features derived from F0 contour is developed as mentioned in our previous work [9]. The six features computed from Fundamental Frequency (F0) contours are (i) F0_slope, (ii) F0_height, (iii) F0_variance, (iv) Initial_F0, (v) Final_F0, and (vi) F0_difference [9]. A detailed description of feature extraction process can be found in [9]. A DNN model is implemented using these features in the Keras toolkit [6]. The hyper-parameters of the networks are tuned to achieve the optimum performance on the test samples to derive that 2 hidden layers with 64 neurons is optimum. The output layer is a softmax layer of 5 dimension, one output for each of the five Mizo tones. The SGD optimizer is considered to train the model with a learning rate of 0.001. The network is trained for 300 epochs with a batch size of 64. ReLU is used as the activation function in each hidden layer.

5   Results and Discussion

This section describes the results of the proposed tone recognition system. Initially, a brief discussion on the database preparation for training and evaluating the model is provided. Later, a detailed discussion on the performance evaluation for both proposed and baseline models is presented. The training examples for four tones H, L, R and F are 3,000 each and for RTS, there are 2983 syllables. Testing examples for the H, L, R, F and RTS categories are 1765, 1362, 1129, 1553 and 628 respectively (refer Table 3).

The primary focus of our present research is to develop a robust automatic tone recognition tool, which does not require feature extraction, rather the model learns the tone classes directly from F0 contour of each isolated syllables. When evaluated, our proposed 1D-CNN method achieves substantially higher accuracy compared to baseline DNN tone classifier. The baseline DNN classifier has shortcomings as it uses handcrafted F0 features. This result is presented in Table 5, and, it can be observed that around 4.59% improvement is achieved using 1D-CNN as compared to DNN. The confusion matrix for the best performing 1D-CNN model is presented in Fig. 4. It allows easy identification of confusion between the five tone classes e.g., one class is commonly mislabeled as the other. The evaluated results are in conformity with the acoustic and perception study carried on four Mizo canonical tones and perceptually categorical rising tone sandhi [15]. The percentage of correct and incorrect prediction accuracies are summarized and broken down by each class.

The confusion matrix also shows that High and Falling tones are correctly labeled with 79% and 71% accuracy, respectively. While the Rising tones are identified with an accuracy of 71%, Low tones are identified with an accuracy of 50%. The Rising sandhi tone is predicted correctly with 65% accuracy. From the confusion matrix, it is clear that 18% of the tone sandhi stimuli are confused as a Low tone. While, 8% of tone sandhi is categorized as Rising tone. It is also found that 24% of Low tones are wrongly classified as sandhi tones. These behaviour of the classification results may be due to the inherent nature of sandhi tone, which is already discussed in the introduction section. However, it is desirable to get better accuracy in detecting the Low tone. Incorporation of other cues apart from the F0 contour may be helpful. Hence, a detailed analysis will be required, which will be done in our future research.

Error analysis reveals that in the case of sandhi tone, our 1D-CNN classifier labels 18% of the sandhi tone stimuli as Low tones. This is not a significantly high amount of mislabeling; rather it confirms that canonical Low tone and the emerging 'Low tone' due to sandhi rules are phonetically different. It is posited that the 1D- CNN based automatic tone recognizer is able to fairly distinguish the neutralized Rising sandhi tone from the phonological Low tone using statistical modelling.

Table 5. Accuracy of tone recognition for DNN and 1D-CNN models.

Model	Input	Accuracy (%)
DNN	F0_slope, F0_height, F0_variance, Initial_F0, Final_F0, F0_difference	63.59
1D-CNN	F0 contour	68.18

It can be summarized that the notable difference between our CNN model and DNN models [9] is in the type of features used in the network input layer. The features in our CNN model are learned automatically from F0 contours, whereas features are manually handcrafted in the baseline DNN model. Experimental results show that the proposed 1D-CNN model performs better with an accuracy of about 68% than the DNN baseline system which gives about 63% accurate results.

6   Conclusion

Tone concatenation, defined as tone sandhi rules, leads to changes in F0 contours. In Mizo, Rising tone sandhi changes into a Low tone when it is followed by either High tone or Falling tone. Recent works have shown that the F0 contour of Rising tone sandhi and the canonical Low tone in Mizo are different [15]. The speakers of Mizo can distinguish the Low tone derived out of rising tone sandhi from the canonical Low tone as analyzed in perception test in [15]. This acoustic investigation motivates us to consider this Low tone derived out of Rising tone sandhi as a perceptually categorical fifth tone along with four other canonical tones in Mizo and build the five-class tone recognizer. This is an attempt to automatically identify the neutralized Rising tone in Mizo from a Low tone using 1D-CNN system using F0 contour as the only input data. Also, an attempt is being made to detect the five Mizo tones using DNN as the baseline model with six F0 features as input data [9]. From the confusion matrix, it is clear that only 18% of the tone sandhi stimuli are mislabelled as a Low tone. Experimental results show that the proposed 1D-CNN model performs better with an accuracy of 68% than the DNN baseline system, which gives 63% accurate results.

In the work, 1D-CNN provides better performance than the DNN-based method. The performance of the system can be improved by adding more number of examples in the database for CNN training. As it is found that around 24% Low tone is detected as RTS; therefore, a detailed future exploration to derive discriminable cues will be required.

Another issue of this system is the requirement of F0 estimation, which may be difficult in a noisy situation. This issue can be overcome by learning tone-specific features from the raw speech signal, but this requires very large database. Future work is planned in this direction. Also, another future work is planned to learn the tone characteristics using the 2D-CNN with narrow-band spectrogram as the input to the network.

Acknowledgements. The speech corpus used in this work was developed for the project titled "Acoustic and Tonal Features based Analysis of Mizo", funded by the Ministry of Electronics & Information Technology (MeitY), Ministry of Communication & Information Technology (MC&IT), Government of India.

References

1. Boersma, P.: PRAAT, a system for doing phonetics by computer. Glot Int. **5**(9/10), 341–345 (2001)
2. Chang, P.C., Sun, S.W., Chen, S.H.: Mandarin tone recognition by multi-layer perceptron. In: International Conference on Acoustics, Speech, and Signal Processing, pp. 517–520. IEEE (1990)
3. Chen, C., Bunescu, R., Xu, L., Liu, C.: Tone classification in mandarin Chinese using convolutional neural networks. In: Interspeech 2016, pp. 2150–2154 (2016). https:// doi.org/10.21437/Interspeech.2016-528.   http://dx.doi.org/10.21437/Interspeech. 2016-528
4. Chen, X.X., Cai, C.N., Guo, P., Sun, Y.: A Hidden Markov Model applied to Chinese four-tone recognition. In: ICASSP 1987. IEEE International Conference on Acoustics, Speech, and Signal Processing, vol. 12, pp. 797–800. IEEE (1987)
5. Chhangte, L.: Mizo Syntax. Ph.D. thesis, University of Oregon (1993)
6. Chollet, F., et al.: Keras link url. https://keras.io/
7. Dey, A., et al.: Robust mizo continuous speech recognition. In: INTERSPEECH, pp. 1036–1040 (2018)
8. Fanai, L.: Some aspects of the lexical phonology of mizo and english: an autosegmental approach. Ph.D. thesis, CIEFL, Hyderabad, India (1992)
9. Gogoi, P., Dey, A., Lalhminghlui, W., Sarmah, P., Prasanna, S.R.M.: Lexical tone recognition in mizo using acoustic-prosodic features. In: Proceedings of The 12th Language Resources and Evaluation Conference, pp. 6460–6463. European Language Resources Association, Marseille, France, May 2020
10. Goodfellow, I., Bengio, Y., Courville, A.: Deep Learning. MIT Press, Cambridge (2016)
11. Govind, D., Sarmah, P., Prasanna, S.R.M.: Role of pitch slope and duration in synthesized Mizo tones. In: Speech Prosody (2012)
12. Kaur, J., Singh, A., Kadyan, V.: Automatic speech recognition system for tonal languages: state-of-the-art survey. Arch. Comput. Methods Eng. **28**(3), 1039–1068 (2020). https://doi.org/10.1007/s11831-020-09414-4
13. Kothapalli, V., et al.: Robust recognition of tone specified mizo digits using CNN-LSTM and nonlinear spectral resolution. In: 2018 15th IEEE India Council International Conference (INDICON), pp. 1–5. IEEE (2018)
14. Lalhminghlui, W., Mazumdar, P., Sarmah, P.: Behaviour of tone sandhi in different morphological structures in Mizo. In: Paper presented at The 23rd Himalayan Languages Symposium, Tezpur University, Tezpur (2017)
15. Lalhminghlui, W., Sarmah, P.: Production and perception of rising tone sandhi in Mizo. In: Proceedings TAL, pp. 114–118 (2018)
16. Lee, T., Ching, P.C., Chan, Y.H., Mak, B.: Tone recognition of isolated Cantonese syllables. IEEE Trans. Speech Audio Process. **3**(3), 204–209 (1995)
17. Lee, T., Lau, W., Wong, Y.W., Ching, P.: Using tone information in Cantonese continuous speech recognition. ACM Trans. Asian Lang. Inf. Process. (TALIP) **1**(1), 83–102 (2002)
18. Li, X., et al.: Mandarin Chinese tone recognition with an artificial neural network. J. Otol. **1**(1), 30–34 (2006)
19. Liu, L.C., Yang, W.J., Wang, H.C., Chang, Y.C.: Tone recognition of polysyllabic words in Mandarin speech. Comput. Speech Lang. **3**(3), 253–264 (1989)
20. Peng, G., Wang, W.S.Y.: Tone recognition of continuous Cantonese speech based on support vector machines. Speech Commun. **45**(1), 49–62 (2005)

21. Gao, Q., Sun, S., Yang, Y.: ToneNet: a CNN model of tone classification of mandarin Chinese. In: Interspeech 2019 (2019)
22. Rose, P.J.: Considerations on the normalization of the fundamental frequency of linguistic tone. Speech Commun. **10**(3), 229–247 (1991)
23. Ryant, N., Slaney, M., Liberman, M., Shriberg, E., Yuan, J.: Highly accurate mandarin tone classification in the absence of pitch information. In: Proceedings of Speech Prosody (2014)
24. Ryant, N., Yuan, J., Liberman, M.: Mandarin tone classification without pitch tracking. In: 2014 IEEE International Conference on Acoustics, Speech and Signal Processing (ICASSP) (2014)
25. Sarma, B.D., Dey, A., Lalhminghlui, W., Gogoi, P., Sarmah, P., Prasanna, S.: Robust Mizo digit recognition using data augmentation and tonal information. In: Proceedings 9th International Conference on Speech Prosody, vol. 2018, pp. 621–625 (2018)
26. Sarma, B.D., Sarmah, P., Lalhminghlui, W., Prasanna, S.R.M.: Detection of Mizo tones. In: Interspeech, pp. 934–937 (2015)
27. Sarmah, P., Dihingia, L., Lalhminghlui, W.: Contextual variation of tones in Mizo. In: Interspeech, pp. 983–986 (2015)
28. Sarmah, P., Wiltshire, C.R.: A preliminary acoustic study of Mizo vowels and tones. J. Acoust. Soc. India **37**(3), 121–129 (2010)
29. Wang, W.S., Li, K.P.: Tone 3 in Pekinese. J. Speech Lang. Hear. Res. **10**(3), 629–636 (1967)
30. Wang, X.D., Hirose, K., Zhang, J.S., Minematsu, N.: Tone recognition of continuous mandarin speech based on tone nucleus model and neural network. IEICE Trans. Inf. Syst. **E91.D**(6), 1748–1755 (2008)
31. Weidert, A.: Componential Analysis of Lushai Phonology, vol. 2. John Benjamins Publishing (1975)
32. Yang, W.J., Lee, J.C., Chang, Y.C., Wang, H.C.: Hidden Markov model for Mandarin lexical tone recognition. IEEE Trans. Acoust. Speech Signal Process. **36**(7), 988–992 (1988)

OCR Improvements for Images
of Multi-page Historical Documents

Ivan Gruber[1,2(✉)] , Marek Hrúz[1,2] , Pavel Ircing[1,2] , Petr Neduchal[1,2] ,
Tomáš Zítka[2] , Miroslav Hlaváč[1,2] , Zbyněk Zajíc[1,2] , Jan Švec[1,2] ,
and Martin Bulín[1,2]

[1] Faculty of Applied Sciences, New Technologies for the Information Society,
University of West Bohemia, Univerzitní 8, 301 00 Plzeň, Czech Republic
{grubiv,mhruz,ircing,neduchal,mhlavac,zzajic,honzas,bulinm}@ntis.zcu.cz
[2] Faculty of Applied Sciences, Department of Cybernetics, University of West
Bohemia, Univerzitní 8, 301 00 Plzeň, Czech Republic
zitkat@ntis.zcu.cz

Abstract. This work presents a pipeline for processing digitally scanned
documents, reading their textual content, and storing it in a dataset for
the purpose of information retrieval. The pipeline is able to handle images
of various quality, whether they were obtained by a digital scanner or
camera. The image can contain multiple pages in any layout, but an
approximate upright orientation is assumed. The pipeline uses Faster R-
CNN to detect individual pages. These are then processed by a deskew
algorithm to correct the orientation, and finally read by the Tesseract
OCR system that has been retrained on a large set of synthetic images
and a small set of annotated real-world documents. By applying the
pipeline, we were able to increase the word recall to 60.56% which is
an absolute gain of 19.19% from the baseline solution that uses only
Tesseract OCR. A demo of the proposed pipeline can be found at https://
archivkgb.zcu.cz/.

Keywords: Document digitization · Document layout analysis ·
Optical character recognition · Image preprocessing

1 Introduction

This paper describes new results achieved within the project that was introduced
in the last year's SPECOM paper [3]. Let us summarize here that the main goal
of the project is to design and test a robust pipeline that would take (often
imperfectly) scanned historical documents, apply several image pre-processing
techniques that have the potential to improve the consequent Optical Character
Recognition (OCR), and finally store the resulting electronic text in a specially
designed database with index. The database is then accessed through a carefully
designed GUI that enables a multifaceted search in the stored documents.

The processed documents are historical materials found in the archives of
NKVD (People's Commissariat for Internal Affairs) in the post-soviet states and

© Springer Nature Switzerland AG 2021
A. Karpov and R. Potapova (Eds.): SPECOM 2021, LNAI 12997, pp. 226–237, 2021.
https://doi.org/10.1007/978-3-030-87802-3_21

are related to the history of (former) Czechoslovakia. As such, the scanned materials are not only of a technical quality which poses a serious challenge for OCR techniques (mix of typewritten and handwritten materials, poor image quality) but also regularly contain texts in multiple languages, often with completely different alphabets (Czech vs. Russian). The physical quality of the scanned documents is also deteriorated and often there are more documents in one scan, frequently overlapping each other.

The techniques and algorithms presented in this paper are applicable to a large variety of use cases and are of course not limited to the data mentioned above. The described task however serves as a useful benchmark. We describe the processing pipeline and report the achieved results as an ablation study.

2   Related Work

The automatic processing of scanned historical documents is a trending topic nowadays. Even if we restrict our focus to the Czech Republic only, we can find for example the project PERO [8,9] or the HDPA framework described in [12]. The number of projects worldwide is of course even substantially larger but they often focus only on just one aspect of historical document processing—such as extracting tables from handwritten tabular documents [11], generating synthetic data for OCR training [18] or even post-editing the OCR output [13]. Our work, however, aims for a more complex approach targeting all the modules of the processing pipeline.

Moreover, each of the projects is focused on rather different types of the processed documents and the overall experience shows that the approach tailored to each individual project brings a substantial improvement in effectiveness. Our method differs from the others mainly by the possibility of processing a larger variety of input documents. Our main contributions include a robust visual detection of individual (possibly overlapping) pages, an efficient deskewing algorithm, and improving the OCR results by training models on synthetic data.

3   Processing Pipeline

The proposed pipeline is depicted in Fig. 1. The input of the system is a digital image depicting one or more individual pages. The image might be scanned or photographed, the layout of the individual pages in the image is not restricted to any special form. This makes the task of OCR more difficult and some pre-processing techniques need to be applied before the document can be read. The first algorithm denoted "Page segmentation" segments the image into regions containing individual pages. The algorithm outputs only the pages that are mostly fully visible and thus suitable for reading. The next step in the pipeline is the "Page deskew" algorithm that rotates the segmented pages so that they are upright. After this step, we perform the OCR using Tesseract [16] to obtain a set of words and their locations on the page. These are then also transformed into the coordinate system of the original image. It should be noted that handwritten texts are ignored by Tesseract and we would like to address this problem by using OCR for handwritten texts in our future research. Finally, we insert the detected texts into a database and create an index allowing the user to search for words and/or phrases.

Fig. 1. Processing pipeline.

As was already mentioned in the Introduction, the GUI built on top of the database (archive) processed by the proposed pipeline allows users to search in the database based on several criteria (e.g. the name of the file, language, source of the document, or other available metadata). However, the main focus is on the "fulltext" search when the user can input an arbitrary word or short phrase and the database is searched for the occurrence of such a query. Since the list of retrieved "hits" is usually rather short – as the users tend to search for very specific words and phrases – we choose to present even the results with smaller confidence scores obtained from the OCR and let the user decide whether the returned result is of interest.

In such a setup, it makes more sense to maximize the word recall (as opposed to precision) since a missed occurrence is much more serious error than a false alarm. Thus we use the mentioned word recall as the ultimate measure of the effectiveness of the methods proposed in this paper.

4   Page Segmentation

The first step in our processing pipeline is the page segmentation, in which the main goal is to segment an input image into regions containing individual document pages. Nevertheless, during this step, we are interested only in pages suitable for further processing, i.e. fully visible pages.

Because of the very complicated and unique nature of the processed scanned documents, available pre-trained algorithms for document layout analysis [15] do not provide satisfactory results. Therefore, we decided to train our model.

We manually annotated 3000 randomly chosen images, which resulted in 3189 annotated pages in total (some of the documents contained, for example, non-occluded photos, which resulted in more than one annotated page per document). Each page is annotated using a polygon shape with any number of vertexes. For training purposes, these polygons are converted into bounding boxes. The dataset is randomly split into training and validation sets, containing 2700 and 300 images respectively.

To detect the pages, we trained a detection neural network Faster R-CNN [14] using ResNet50 [4] as its backbone. Even though Faster R-CNN is not the state-of-the-art approach anymore, it provides very robust results and is frequently used for document layout analysis. This means that many pre-trained models for layout analysis are publicly available, therefore we can utilize the transfer learning technique. We utilized the implementation in Detectron2 framework [19] and pre-trained weights from newspaper navigator dataset [10]. The model was trained during 10 epochs with the images in the original resolution with batch size $bs = 1$ using SGD optimizer with learning rate $lr = 0.001$ without any data augmentations. The model reached mean average precision $mAP_{50} = 0.993$ on the validation set. For exemplary results see Fig. 2.

5 Deskew Algorithm

The second method in the processing pipeline is the deskew algorithm developed for correcting small skew angle of the scanned document. It is an enhanced version of the algorithm used in our previous research [20] and evaluated in [2]. The method is based on the detection of the skew angle in the frequency domain computed using the Fast Fourier Transform algorithm. The main difference of the new method proposed in this paper is in the searching procedure. Instead of rotating the whole center part of the 2D frequency spectrum, only pixels on a particular line are sampled to compute their sum. The deskew algorithm can be summarized as follows.

1. Load the image and apply 2D Fourier transform.
2. For all angles (with precision on a defined decimal order) in the specified range:
   (a) Sample the 2D spectrum in locations lying on a line with a particular angle that passes through the center of the spectrum image
   (b) Compute the sum of the sample values.
3. Get argmax of the computed sums where the argument is the angle of the line.
4. Rotate the image by the value opposite to the calculated angle.

The properties of the method are similar to the older version, but there are a few improvements. The new version is faster because it uses fewer locations to compute the sum of the values on the line, and it avoids rotations of the whole spectrum center.

To verify the algorithm and its accuracy, several tests were performed. A dataset composed of 500 synthetic text documents containing salt and pepper noise was used in the first verification test. In contrast to the real documents, this dataset contains ground-truth information that can be used to verify the proper function of the deskew algorithm. The results of the algorithm were compared with ground truth data for three settings of the angle step – i.e. the rotation

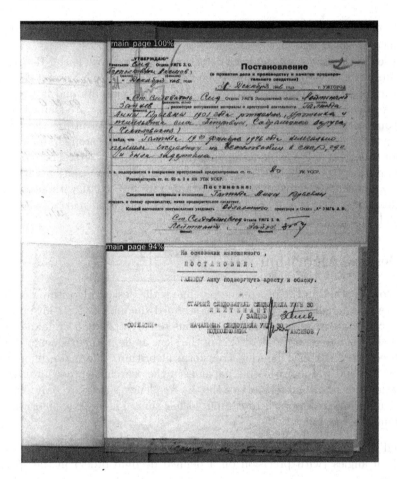

Fig. 2. Page segmentation - exemplary results of page detection algorithm in one image containing two main pages. Document source: Sectoral State Archive of the Security Services of Ukraine (HDA SBU).

step of the algorithm for searching maximal response in frequency spectrum. In particular, the step was set to 0.5, 0.25, and 0.1°. Results are summarized in Table 1.

In all cases, the average error of the method is under 0.3°. The average error of the angle step of 0.1° is smaller than in the case of the step of 0.5. On the other hand, the maximal error is larger. It shows that the method becomes more sensitive when the angle step is too small–the method obtained good results in all three cases.

In two additional tests, a set of 50 unannotated real historical documents were used. The goal of this algorithm was to verify consistency in the case of

Table 1. Results of the deskew algorithm on the synthethic dataset. Errors are computed as a mean and a maximum of absolute differences between estimated angle and ground-truth data.

Angle step [°]	Average error [°]	Maximal error [°]
0.5	0.284	1.433
0.25	0.265	1.270
0.1	0.255	1.629

downsampling and cropping of the input image. Therefore results of downsampled and cropped documents are compared with results of original documents. In other words, the original documents were processed by the deskew algorithm. These results were used as ground-truth. During the evaluation, estimated angles of cropped and downsampled images were compared with these ground-truth data. Results of downsampling are listed in Table 2 and results of cropping are listed in Table 3. The angle step was set to 0.25° in the case of both of these experiments because this setting had the best combination of average and maximal error in the first experiment.

Table 2. Results of the deskew algorithm on downsampled documents. The error is computed as an angle deviation w.r.t. result of the original image (column 100%).

Size of image [%]	100	80	66	50	25
Average error [°]	0.00	0.06	0.06	0.13	0.25
Maximal error [°]	0.00	0.25	0.25	0.75	0.75
Processing time [s]	2.89	2.08	1.56	1.04	0.43

The downsampling was tested on five sizes of the input documents. Each size is represented as the relative reduction of the size w.r.t. the original image. The error is also computed as an angle deviation w.r.t. the result of the original size of the input image (first column of the table). It can be seen that the error grows with a reduction of the input image size, but the maximum deviation is still smaller than 1° in the case of 25% image size. The benefit of downsampling is a significant reduction in the processing time. The computing time of the smallest images is only 14.88% of the original image processing time.

Table 3. Results of the deskew algorithm on cropped documents. Each side of an input image is cropped by the crop value.

Crop value [%]	0	1	2	4	10	20	25
Average error [°]	0	0.05	0.05	0.12	0.13	0.13	0.20
Maximal error [°]	0	0.5	0.5	0.75	1.0	1.0	1.0
Processing time [s]	3.17	2.91	2.89	2.76	2.18	1.48	1.12

The results of the cropping experiment are similar. Both average error and maximal error grow with the increase of the cropped area. On the other hand, even in the case of 25% crop from each side (reduces 50% of the image in both image dimension axis), the maximal angle error is equal to one degree. The processing time is decreasing in a similar way as in the downsampling experiment. The processing time of the largest crop is only 35.33% of the computing time of the original image with no crop.

Overall, based on the presented results, the proposed deskew algorithm is stable and robust against both the downsampling and cropping of the input image. Moreover, the algorithm is sufficiently accurate for use with scanned documents.

6   Optical Character Recognition

OCR is a method of recognizing characters of a given alphabet from digital images. Nowadays, methods based on deep neural networks provide the best results. In our solution, we use the Tesseract framework, which is based on an LSTM recurrent neural network [5]. Although the system performs very well on standard digitally scanned documents, the accuracy deteriorates quickly when the text has a different appearance from the network's training data. One option is to manually annotate large quantities of new training data from the target domain. This process is usually very time-consuming. Another option is to automatically generate the training data that resemble the target domain as closely as possible. In this work, we explore the second option. The description of the synthesis of the training data is described in the next section. It should be noted that in this work we retrain only the model for the Russian language because the majority of the documents are in Russian. Furthermore, we observed better performance of the models for the Latin alphabet.

6.1   Synthetic Document Generation

We have used our previously developed document generator presented in [1]. The generator uses Variational Auto-Encoder (VAE) [7] to generate background images simulating the look of old paper. The synthetic text was generated using publicly available typewriter fonts of Cyrillic characters (GTW, LITERPLA, TTWPGOTT). The document generator was improved over the previous version by adding the capability to generate a differently structured block of text with different fonts. We have prepared a pipeline that takes random sentences from Russian and Ukrainian texts and renders them on a randomly generated background from the previously mentioned VAE. The output of the pipeline is a digital image depicting the input text together with annotations in the form of individual letters' pixel coordinates and bounding boxes. The data is then used for training Tesseract to improve the recognition rate for our target data. Figure 3 shows real data and their synthetic equivalent generated by our pipeline.

На допросе 11/X-1949 года с участием	На допросе 11/X-1949 года с участием
На допросе 11/X-1949 года с участием	На допросе 11/X-1949 года с участием
На допросе 11/X-1949 года с участием	На допросе 11/X-1949 года с участием
На допросе 11/X-1949 года с участием	На допросе 11/X-1949 года с участием

Fig. 3. Real data compared to synthetic data generated from our pipeline. The real world data are in the first row. The second, third, and fourth lines depict three random samples produced by our generator before (left) and after (right) histogram matching. Real document source: Sectoral State Archive of the Security Services of Ukraine (HDA SBU).

6.2 Tesseract Retraining

To extract text from pre-processed documents we used Tesseract OCR engine version 4.1.1[1]. This is the latest version that uses LSTM neural network for OCR. However, publicly available models[2] do not provide sufficient accuracy on wildly scanned typewritten text. To alleviate this, we fine-tune the pre-trained model on synthetic data and a sample of annotated real-world data. In our experiments, we use two training sets and one testing set. The first training set is composed of synthetic data, the second one contains only real-world data. The testing set is composed of real-world data only.

For training, we generated 1546 full text pages, each containing 4000 to 6000 characters in approximately 50 lines with resolution of 2480×3504 pixels. This amounts to an average resolution of 20×30 per character, roughly corresponding to the resolution in the real-world data. However, these generated pages featured a very different color spectrum from the real-world data. To alleviate this we used histogram matching algorithm[3] with real-world samples as targets, see Fig. 3. Additionally, we augmented the data with random contrast and random gamma transformations.

Native speakers annotated 100 documents of real-world data. From these, we cropped 473 single-line inscriptions for the purpose of Tesseract fine-tuning. The rest of the data in the form of 161 cropped multi-line inscriptions were used as the test set. Cropping the test set to paragraphs eliminates errors introduced by unreliable Tesseract segmentation, thus allowing us to evaluate the OCR part of Tesseract only.

In all cases, we trained Tesseract for 3000 iterations using Adam optimizer [6] with per layer adaptive learning rate starting at 10^{-4} and batch size equal to one.

The results of the experiments are reported in Table 4. For synthetic data, we report train errors on the synthetic training set, whereas for real and combined data we report errors on the real-world data training set. The original model of Tesseract OCR achieves, on real test data, character error rate (CER) of 28.5%

---

[1] https://github.com/tesseract-ocr/tesseract/releases/tag/4.1.1.

[2] https://github.com/tesseract-ocr/tessdata_best.

[3] http://paulbourke.net/miscellaneous/equalisation/.

and word error rate (WER) of 64.2%. These results fall short of the expected performance of OCR, which achieves CER under 5% in standard cases (e.g. [17]). When training on the synthetic data only, Tesseract is able to achieve very low training CER and WER. This unfortunately does not meaningfully impact the performance on the real-world test data. When training on the real-world data only, Tesseract training errors are relatively high, however, performance on the testing set does improve both in CER and WER. When training on synthetic and then real world data, training CER and WER improves significantly along with moderate improvement on testing set. This finally improves performance on full-text search task as measured by word recall.

Table 4. Tesseract performance for different training data.

Data	Train set		Test set	
	CER	WER	CER	WER
Pre-trained	–	–	28.5%	64.2%
Synthetic	3.8%	8.5%	27.3%	64%
Real world	39%	59%	27.4%	60.3%
Combined	28%	48%	**25.9%**	**58.7%**

7 Results and Ablation Study

As was already mentioned, the main goal of our processing pipeline is to improve word recall to maximize the probability of document retrieval. In this section, we analyze the effect of the specific parts of the pipeline. We also list precision for each of them to show the precision-recall trade-off. For the testing, we used 80 annotated documents (different documents than 100 documents used for the Tesseract retraining experiment). Word recall is calculated only for words with more than 2 letters, this results in 6255 unique words in total. Furthermore, the text is converted to lowercase only, and all non-alphanumeric characters are deleted. The results are reported in Table 5.

Baseline word recall using the original scans and Tesseract only is 41.37%. Such poor result is caused primarily by the difficult nature of the original documents.

When the important page is detected and only its crop is processed, the word recall improves by 3.81%. We believe it is caused by the fact that Tesseract's layout analyzer has a much easier job to parse the input image into meaningful regions, when only one page is presented. The usage of the deskew algorithm (with an angle step of 0.25° and a crop value of 0%) improves the final word recall by 5.83% using alone, and by 7.07% using in conjunction with the page segmentation. We believe that this is caused by two main factors. Firstly, it is a well-known fact that Tesseract has major problems with rotated text (i.e. it is not good for texts in the wild). Secondly, the deskew algorithm performs generally much better in conjunction with the page segmentation, because it is not confused by the fact that many different pages with different rotations can be presented on the scan.

The usage of retrained Tesseract in conjunction with the previous steps results in an additional improvement of 1.10%, i.e. in the total improvement of 8.17% comparing to the baseline approach.

Lastly, we observe huge word recall improvement (additional 11.02%), while using both the unprocessed and the processed image scans as inputs into the retrained Tesseract and concatenating the results. We argue this is caused by the following phenomena.

The first phenomenon is a major fail of certain processing pipeline parts. For example, wrongly detected pages result in fatal failure of the whole pipeline or wrongly rotated image can cause huge problems for OCR. Moreover, chaining small mistakes can also cause major problems at the end of the pipeline. All these possibilities play a role in the decrease of the total word recall improvement. However, due to the great results of the single processing parts, we believe, this is only a part of the problem.

The second, much more common phenomenon, is Tesseract's inability to detect (and then read) certain text paragraphs after the processing, despite the fact that they are equally difficult or even easier to read for a human. We observe this phenomenon across a huge variety of input images and we believe the problem lies in Tesseract's segmentation algorithm. In our future research, we would like to address this problem by parsing the individual pages into logical text blocks (titles, headings, paragraphs, etc.) using a layout parser. These blocks will be used as inputs into Tesseract separately.

Table 5. Word recall and precision while using certain parts of our processing pipeline.

Approach	Word recall	WR gain	Precision
Baseline	41.37%	+0.00%	76.74%
+Crop	45.18%	+3.81%	86.25%
+Deskew	47.20%	+5.83%	79.21%
+Crop+Deskew	48.44%	+7.07%	87.41%
+Crop+Deskew+Retraining	49.54%	+8.17%	**88.19%**
Unprocessed+Processed	**60.56%**	**+19.19%**	78.26%

8 Conclusion and Future Work

This paper presents a novel processing pipeline for the digitization of historical documents. The pipeline is composed of three major parts - page segmentation, page deskew, and optical character recognition. Firstly, we extensively tested each of the parts separately. Secondly, we provide an ablation study regarding the performance of the whole pipeline. The total improvement of word recall while using the pipeline is more than 19%.

In our future work, we would like to address the problem with Tesseract's text segmentation via a novel segmentation algorithm, which will segment the whole image into logical blocks. From our observations, this step greatly improves Tesseract's performance overall. Moreover, to improve the document archive structure, we would like to add a document classification algorithm into the pipeline.

Acknowledgements. This research was supported by the Ministry of Culture Czech Republic, project No. DG20P02OVV018. Access to computing and storage facilities owned by parties and projects contributing to the National Grid Infrastructure Meta-Centrum provided under the programme "Projects of Large Research, Development, and Innovations Infrastructures" (CESNET LM2015042), is greatly appreciated.

References

1. Bureš, L., Gruber, I., Neduchal, P., Hlaváč, M., Hrúz, M.: Semantic text segmentation from synthetic images of full-text documents (2019)
2. Bureš, L., Neduchal, P., Müller, L.: Automatic information extraction from scanned documents. In: Karpov, A., Potapova, R. (eds.) SPECOM 2020. LNCS (LNAI), vol. 12335, pp. 87–96. Springer, Cham (2020). https://doi.org/10.1007/978-3-030-60276-5_9
3. Gruber, I., et al.: An automated pipeline for robust image processing and optical character recognition of historical documents. In: Karpov, A., Potapova, R. (eds.) SPECOM 2020. LNCS (LNAI), vol. 12335, pp. 166–175. Springer, Cham (2020). https://doi.org/10.1007/978-3-030-60276-5_17
4. He, K., Zhang, X., Ren, S., Sun, J.: Deep residual learning for image recognition. In: Proceedings of the IEEE Conference on Computer Vision and Pattern Recognition, pp. 770–778 (2016)
5. Hochreiter, S., Schmidhuber, J.: Long short-term memory. Neural Comput. **9**(8), 1735–1780 (1997)
6. Kingma, D.P., Ba, J.: Adam: a method for stochastic optimization. In: Bengio, Y., LeCun, Y. (eds.) 3rd International Conference on Learning Representations, ICLR 2015, San Diego, CA, USA, 7–9 May 2015, Conference Track Proceedings (2015)
7. Kingma, D.P., Welling, M.: Auto-encoding variational Bayes. In: 2nd International Conference on Learning Representations, ICLR 2014, Banff, AB, Canada, 14–16 April 2014, Conference Track Proceedings (2014)
8. Kodym, O., Hradiš, M.: Page layout analysis system for unconstrained historic documents. arXiv preprint arXiv:2102.11838 (2021)
9. Kohút, J., Hradiš, M.: TS-Net: OCR trained to switch between text transcription styles. arXiv preprint arXiv:2103.05489 (2021)
10. Lee, B.C.G., et al.: The newspaper navigator dataset: extracting and analyzing visual content from 16 million historic newspaper pages in chronicling America. arXiv preprint arXiv:2005.01583 (2020)
11. Lehenmeier, C., Burghardt, M., Mischka, B.: Layout detection and table recognition – recent challenges in digitizing historical documents and handwritten tabular data. In: Hall, M., Merčun, T., Risse, T., Duchateau, F. (eds.) TPDL 2020. LNCS, vol. 12246, pp. 229–242. Springer, Cham (2020). https://doi.org/10.1007/978-3-030-54956-5_17

12. Lenc, L., Martínek, J., Král, P., Nicolao, A., Christlein, V.: HDPA: historical document processing and analysis framework. Evol. Syst. **12**(1), 177–190 (2020). https://doi.org/10.1007/s12530-020-09343-4

13. Poncelas, A., Aboomar, M., Buts, J., Hadley, J., Way, A.: A tool for facilitating OCR postediting in historical documents. arXiv preprint arXiv:2004.11471 (2020)

14. Ren, S., He, K., Girshick, R., Sun, J.: Faster R-CNN: towards real-time object detection with region proposal networks. IEEE Trans. Pattern Anal. Mach. Intell. **39**(6), 1137–1149 (2016)

15. Shen, Z., Zhang, R., Dell, M., Lee, B.C.G., Carlson, J., Li, W.: Layout-parser: a unified toolkit for deep learning based document image analysis. arXiv preprint arXiv:2103.15348 (2021)

16. Smith, R.: An overview of the tesseract OCR engine. In: Ninth International Conference on Document Analysis and Recognition (ICDAR 2007), vol 2, pp. 629–633. IEEE, Curitiba, September 2007. iSSN: 1520–5363

17. Smith, R., Antonova, D., Lee, D.S.: Adapting the tesseract open source OCR engine for multilingual OCR. In: Proceedings of the International Workshop on Multilingual OCR, pp. 1–8 (2009)

18. Vögtlin, L., Drazyk, M., Pondenkandath, V., Alberti, M., Ingold, R.: Generating synthetic handwritten historical documents with OCR constrained GANs. arXiv preprint arXiv:2103.08236 (2021)

19. Wu, Y., Kirillov, A., Massa, F., Lo, W.Y., Girshick, R.: Detectron2. https://github.com/facebookresearch/detectron2 (2019)

20. Zajíc, Z., et al.: Towards processing of the oral history interviews and related printed documents. In: Proceedings of the Eleventh International Conference on Language Resources and Evaluation (LREC 2018) (2018)

X-Bridge: Image-to-Image Translation with Reconstruction Capabilities

Ivan Gruber[1,2]([✉]) [iD], Marek Hrúz[1,2] [iD], Miloš Železný[1] [iD], and Alexey Karpov[3] [iD]

[1] Faculty of Applied Sciences, New Technologies for the Information Society,
University of West Bohemia, Univerzitní 8, 301 00 Plzeň, Czech Republic
{grubiv,mhruz,zelezny}@ntis.zcu.cz
[2] Department of Cybernetics, University of West Bohemia,
Univerzitní 8, 301 00 Plzeň, Czech Republic
[3] SPIIRAS, St. Petersburg Federal Research Center of the Russian Academy
of Sciences (SPC RAS), St. Petersburg, Russia
karpov@iias.spb.su

Abstract. This work presents a novel method for image-to-image translation named X-Bridge. The method is based on a conditional adversarial network. X-Bridge is a supervised method build upon the Pix2pix approach, however, it extends the original system with an additional reconstruction path and a shared-latent space assumption between the original and the reconstruction path. With these modifications, we argue that the qualitative results provided by X-Bridge overcome other state-of-the-art methods in terms of similarity between translated and corresponding images, robustness, generalization capacity, and translated features preservation. This assumption is confirmed with provided quantitative results. We demonstrate the power of this approach on the challenging facial image-to-sketch translation task. Code is available at: https://github.com/YvanG/Cross-modal-Bridge.

Keywords: Image-to-image translation · Generative adversarial networks · Heterogeneous face recognition

1 Introduction

Many computer vision problems require translation of images from one domain to another. For example attribute transfer, inpainting, style transfer, or super-resolution. Image-to-image cross-domain translation can also overcome the differences between two different modalities in the heterogeneous face recognition task. Thanks to the ability to generate sharp realistically-looking images, approaches based on Generative Adversarial Networks (GANs) [2] are the most popular and promising for all the above-mentioned tasks.

In this paper, a novel supervised approach called X-Bridge, proposed within dissertation work [3], is presented. X-Bridge is a supervised method designed specifically for precise and robust image-to-image translation with high feature preservation. The structure of X-Bridge stems from the Pix2pix approach [8],

© Springer Nature Switzerland AG 2021
A. Karpov and R. Potapova (Eds.): SPECOM 2021, LNAI 12997, pp. 238–249, 2021.
https://doi.org/10.1007/978-3-030-87802-3_22

however, inspired by UNIT [10], it assumes shared-latent space across two different domains. The main attribute of shared-latent space is that a pair of corresponding images $(x, \hat{x})$ from two different domains $\mathcal{X}, \hat{\mathcal{X}}$ can be mapped to the same latent code z in a shared-latent space $\mathcal{Z}$. The performance of X-Bridge is tested on various image-to-sketch translation tasks. Qualitative and qualitative results and its comparison with state-of-the-art methods are presented.

2   Related Work

In recent years, several deep generative models were proposed for image-to-image translation. Most of existing approaches are based on supervised learning [8,9,17], however, models based on unsupervised learning became very popular lately [6,10,19]. We decide to use the two most significant methods, one from each group, as a baseline in our experiments. These two methods are described in more detailed manner in the following subsections.

2.1   Pix2pix

Pix2pix [8] is a method designed for image-to-image translation. To the best of our knowledge, it provides state-of-the-art results among different translation tasks. Originally, it was trained on the Cityscapes dataset and CMP Facades dataset. Both datasets have a very similar concept - they contain pairs of RGB image and their semantic (per-pixel) segmentation. The method was later also tested on a day-night photo translation task and a pose transfer task. The method generally provides very good results for all of the above-mentioned tasks.

In our experiments, we are using the original Pix2pix architecture. The only change is the usage of Instance normalization [14] instead of the batch normalization [7] - we observe better training stability and faster convergence while using instance normalization.

2.2   UNIT/MUNIT

UNIT [10] and MUNIT [6] are other methods designed for image-to-image translation tasks, whereas MUNIT is one of the best unsupervised methods available. Its main advantage is the ability to use the same model for both image-to-sketch and sketch-to-image translation. It stems from shared-latent space assumption, i.e., it is assumed that two corresponding images from two different domains can be mapped to the same latent code in a shared-latent space. Such an assumption also implies cycle consistency, i.e., the result of a translation of already translated image should be the original image. The method was tested on the Cityscapes dataset and also on a day-night photo translation task. MUNIT provides very realistic results in both of these experiments. Apart from the unsupervised manner of the training of MUNIT, its biggest advantage is the fact that one network can be used for all translation directions. In our experiments, we are using the original MUNIT implementation without any changes.

3   X-Bridge Method

X-Bridge is composed of five main parts: encoder, two generators, and two discriminators. Each part is a different convolutional neural network. These parts create two main paths of the method: translation path, and reconstruction path. Each path can be imagined as a separated GAN and has its own generator and discriminator, whereas both of them share one encoder.

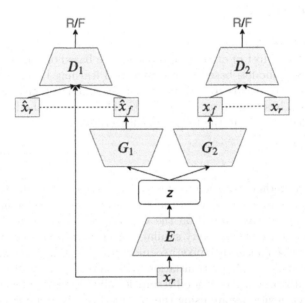

Fig. 1. X-Bridge pipeline. E = encoder, G_1, G_2 = generators, D_1, D_2 = discriminators, z = latent space. Dotted line indicates L_1 loss. x_r is real input from the first domain, x_f is reconstructed fake image from the first domain, $\hat{x}_f$ is translated fake image from the second domain, $\hat{x}_r$ is corresponding real image from the second domain. The translation path is on the left, whereas, the reconstruction path on the right.

The task of the translation path is to translate an input image x from domain $\mathcal{X}$ to the other domain $\hat{\mathcal{X}}$ generating image $\hat{x}$. The whole process can be divided into a few steps. First, the encoder E encodes important information from an input real image x_r into the shared-latent space $\mathcal{Z}$. Second, the generator G_1 decodes this information and generates a translated fake image $\hat{x}_f$ from the second domain $\hat{\mathcal{X}}$. In the following equations the encoder E and the generator G_1 are denoted together as EG_1. Third, during the training, same as in the traditional GAN, the fake images $\hat{x}_f$ with real images $\hat{x}_r$ from the second domain are introduced to the discriminator D_1, which distinguishes between the real and the fake ones. The translation path in X-Bridge approach utilizes a conditional discriminator, which means there is additionally the original image x_r on the input of the discriminator. This prevents mode collapse and forces the generator to generate the corresponding image pair. The translation path is, in principle, the same as the Pix2pix method. The loss function of the translation path can be expressed as:

$$L_{TR}(EG_1, D_1) = \mathbb{E}_{x_r, \hat{x}_r}[\log D_1(x_r, \hat{x}_r)]$$
$$+\mathbb{E}_{x_r, z}[\log(1 - D_1(x_r, EG_1(x_r, z)))]. \tag{1}$$

The task of the reconstruction path is to encode original image x_r into the shared-latent space $\mathcal{Z}$ and then to reconstruct it in the original domain as x_f. During the training, the discriminator is utilized again, however, the standard one this time. Conditional discriminator would be too difficult for the generator G_2 to overcome because, for the real image, the conditional input and the real input are identical. In other words, it would be very easy for the discriminator to learn, that the difference between real images and reference images is always exactly zero. This would lead to a very unbalance performance of the generator and discriminator and thus problematic training. In the following equations the encoder E and generator G_2 are denoted together as EG_2. The addition of the reconstruction path motivates the shared encoder to preserve information about important features, to generalize better, and to learn important regularities across both domains. The loss function of the reconstruction path can be expressed as:

$$L_R(EG_2, D_2) = \mathbb{E}_{x_r}[\log D_2(x_r)] + \mathbb{E}_{x_r, z}[\log(1 - D_2(EG_2(x_r, z)))]. \tag{2}$$

Testing proves [8] the benefit of mixing the traditional GAN objective function with some metric loss to further motivate the generators to produce an image corresponding with the original input. X-Bridge employs L_1 distance in both paths. Additional losses are defined as follows:

$$L_{11}(EG_1) = \mathbb{E}_{x_r, \hat{x}_r, z}\left[\|\hat{x}_r - EG_1(x_r, z)\|_1\right], \tag{3}$$

$$L_{12}(EG_2) = \mathbb{E}_{x_r, z}\left[\|x_r - EG_2(x_r, z)\|_1\right]. \tag{4}$$

The final loss is then defined as follows:

$$L_F = \min_{EG_1, EG_2} \max_{D_1, D_2} L_{TR}(EG_1, D_1) + \lambda_1 L_{11}(EG_1)$$
$$+\lambda_R[L_R(EG_2, D_2) + \lambda_2 L_{12}(EG_2)], \tag{5}$$

where λ_1 and λ_2 are proportional constants affecting the amount of influence of additional metric loss. λ_R is proportional constant affecting the learning speed of the reconstruction path. Generally, λ_R should be much lower than 1, because the reconstruction is generally easier, and also a good translation is the primary goal of the X-Bridge method. For the X-Bridge pipeline, see Fig. 1.

Inspired by Pix2pix, X-Bridge also employs Markovian discriminators [9] in both of its paths. This discriminator tries to classify if each $N \times N$ patch in an image is real or fake. The discriminator is run across all the patches, averaging all responses to provide the final output.

In X-Bridge, the shared-latent space is primarily enforced by the shared encoder. However, to further enforce it, the first few layers (high-level layers) of the generators are sharing their weights. Different weights in low-level layers allow generators to specialize in the specific domain. Sharing the first four layers provides the best results during our experiments.

To improve the propagation of important features, skip connections between the last four layers of the encoder, and the first four layers of the generators are added. Specifically, the skip connections are implemented as channel concatenation of all channels between each ith layer and $(n-i)^{th}$ layer, where n is a total number of layers [12]. Element-wise addition (residual skip connection [4]) was also tested, however, the current implementation provides better results.

For the X-Bridge detail architecture, see Table 1.

Table 1. Structure of the X-Bridge architecture. Both generators have the same structure, while sharing parameters between Deconv2D-R and all Deconv2D-U layers. Both discriminators have the same structure, except the translation discriminator is conditional, whereas, reconstruction discriminator is not. If not said otherwise, all the convolutions and the deconvolutions have stride 2. Conv2D-L denotes 2D convolution, followed by Leaky ReLU. Conv2D-IL is followed by instance normalization and Leaky ReLU. Conv2D-U denotes encoder's Conv2D-IL with an additional skip-connection between Conv2D-U and corresponding Deconv2D-U layers in the generators. Conv2D-R denotes convolution, followed by ReLU. Deconv2D-IR denotes 2D deconvolution, followed by instance normalization and ReLU, Deconv2D-R is followed be ReLU. Deconv2D-U denotes Deconv2D-IR with additional skip-connection input from the corresponding encoder's layer. Deconv2D-T denotes deconvolution, followed by the Tanh activation function. Conv2D-IR1 denotes 2D convolution with stride 1, followed by instance normalization and Leaky ReLU. Conv2D-1 denotes 2D convolution with stride 1.

Encoder	Generator	Discriminator
Conv2D-L($64, 4 \times 4$)	Deconv2D-R($512, 4 \times 4$)	Conv2D-L($64, 4 \times 4$)
Conv2D-IL($128, 4 \times 4$)	Deconv2D-U($512, 4 \times 4$)	Conv2D-IR($128, 4 \times 4$)
Conv2D-IL($256, 4 \times 4$)	Deconv2D-U($512, 4 \times 4$)	Conv2D-IR($256, 4 \times 4$)
Conv2D-IL($512, 4 \times 4$)	Deconv2D-U($512, 4 \times 4$)	Conv2D-IR1($512, 4 \times 4$)
Conv2D-U($512, 4 \times 4$)	Deconv2D-IR($256, 4 \times 4$)	Conv2D-1($1, 4 \times 4$)
Conv2D-U($512, 4 \times 4$)	Deconv2D-IR($128, 4 \times 4$)	
Conv2D-U($512, 4 \times 4$)	Deconv2D-IR($64, 4 \times 4$)	
Conv2D-C($512, 4 \times 4$)	Deconv2D-T($3, 4 \times 4$)	

4   Experiments

To demonstrate the power of the X-Bridge approach, we decided to test it primary on the facial image-to-sketch task. We argue this task is very challenging for the same reasons as face recognition or face synthesis generally. Human faces as objects are very similar to each other and the main differences between the faces of two different persons are in relatively small details. A change of these details can be very influential on the person's identification. Therefore, it is very desirable to preserve as many details as possible during the image-to-image translation.

4.1   Dataset

To the best of our knowledge, there exist two suitable datasets for the training of facial image-to-sketch translation systems. First, the CUFS dataset [16], which is divided into three main sub-parts and should contain 606 photo-sketch pairs in total. However, the photos from the second and the third part are no longer available online. This means there remains only a CUHK dataset containing 188 images of students from Honk Kong university. Despite its small size, it is a very popular dataset. All the photos are in the frontal pose, normal lighting conditions, and with a neutral expression. All the sketches are drawn by the same artist. Apart from the small size, the main limitation is the fact there are only Asians of one ethnic group in the dataset. This is a very limiting factor for the training of the system because of the total omission of the other races, there is a high probability that the fully-trained system would have problems with generalization and, therefore, with the translation of different data.

The second possible dataset is CUFSF [18]. CUFSF includes 1194 sketches drawn by an artist, which corresponds to images from the color-FERET dataset. Unfortunately, there are some inaccuracies in pair filenames, therefore, only 895 pairs can be easily constructed. Sketches are provided in two versions - original version, and a cropped version. All the corresponding RGB images can also be cropped according to coordinates of the center of the eyes and the tip of the nose, which are provided by the authors of the dataset. All the photos are in the frontal pose, normal lighting conditions, and with a neutral expression. The pre-processed images have a resolution of 256×256 pixels.

Apart from the bigger size of this dataset, the main advantage is the presence of different ethnic groups among the drawn subjects, therefore, for the training, we decide to use the CUFSF dataset instead of the CUHK. In all the following experiments the cropped versions of the sketches are used. To enrich the training data, we use a horizontal flip and random noise addition. All the data values are normalized from 0 to 1. The data are split into three subsets (training, validation, testing) in proportion of 80-10-10.

Moreover, for the testing of the image-to-sketch translation robustness to the rotation, we utilize color-FERET dataset [11], which provides, for each identity, at least six different facial images in a control environment (lighting conditions, neural expression), with large pose variations. For the purposes of the testing, each image is cropped according to provided coordinated and all images are converted to gray-scale and resized to a resolution of 256×256 pixels.

4.2   Qualitative Results

During the experiments, the tested models are trained for 150 epochs with mini-batch size of 1 using Adam optimizer. It should be noted we train only one model for the MUNIT method, whereas two models for both the Pix2pix method and the X-Bridge method (one model for each translation direction). The patch size N for Markovian discriminators is heuristically set to the value = 70. Furthermore, λ_1 and λ_2 (Eq. 5) are heuristically set to the value = 100. λ_R is set to the value = 0.1. That means the shared encoder is affected ten times less by the reconstruction path than by the translation path.

In the first experiment, we test the image-to-sketch translation. A comparison of the results can be seen in Fig. 2. All methods provide very realistic and precise results, however, we argue that the both supervised models outperform the MUNIT approach, which has problems generating sharp images and therefore also small details. Pix2pix and X-Bridge reach comparable results.

Fig. 2. Image-to-sketch translation comparison.

In the second experiment, we test the sketch-to-image translation task. The results can be seen in Fig. 3. The obtained results are, qualitatively speaking, worse, which is caused by the fact that sketch-to-image translation is arguably harder translation direction than image-to-sketch. MUNIT outputs are more blurry than the results of both supervised methods. We claim that X-Bridge preserves more features, for example different shapes of eyes. On the one hand, thanks to it, the results look a little bit odd, and the translated image is more prone to the artist's faults. On the other hand, in the heterogeneous face recognition real-world applications, we would like to preserve as many details as possible to ensure the correct identification of the person.

Moreover, comparing to Pix2pix, we observe better performance of X-Bridge in terms of generalization, i.e. it has smaller problems with the translation of earrings, glasses, etc., see Fig. 4.

In the third experiment, we test robustness to non-planar rotation. As testing data, we use the color-FERET dataset utilizing non-frontal images, for exemplary results, see Fig. 5. For all tested methods, a decrease in quality occurs in terms of detail preservation. Moreover, Pix2pix is unable to overcome the fact

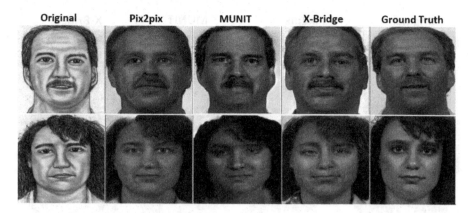

Fig. 3. Sketch-to-Image translation comparison.

Fig. 4. Comparison of translating subject with glasses. All methods correctly drew glasses into the sketch, however, Pix2pix was unable to correctly draw the right eye behind the glasses, and the sketch generated by MUNIT is of lower quality overall, which suggest the glasses cause problems. On the other hand, X-Bridge was able to preserve sketch details quite well and it generates both eyes under the glasses.

that the right ear of the subjects is occluded and tries to model it in both cases. In the top row, Pix2pix believes the glasses are "a weird ear", whereas, in the bottom row, it models at least small remnants of the right ear. On the other hand, MUNIT and X-Bridge "understand" the fact that the ear is occluded and are not forced to model it.

To test the ability to handle sketches drawn in a different style than the training sketches, we utilize data from the CUHK dataset. The sketches are cropped and resized to a resolution of 256 × 256 pixels. The comparison of exemplary results can be found in Fig. 6. We believe the obvious decrease (for all methods) in the quality of the translated images is caused by the change of the drawing style. Especially the fact that the faces on the sketches from the original dataset are much darker and shaded than in the CUHK sketches seems problematic for the translation. In this experiment, MUNIT proves the best ability to handle the change of the drawing style. In comparison to Pix2pix, the decrease in quality

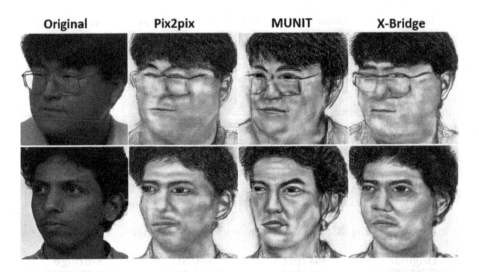

Fig. 5. Comparison of translation of a facial photo in a non-frontal pose.

is lower for the X-Bridge approach. The results of both supervised approaches implicate their over-fitting to the drawing style.

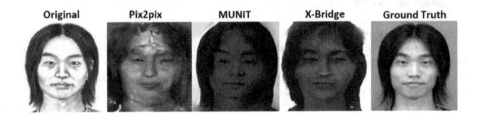

Fig. 6. Sketch-to-Image translation - CUHK dataset.

In Fig. 7 the X-Bridge's ability to handle real images taken in a semi-controlled environment can be seen. The photo is taken using a mobile camera, and the face is detected automatically using the Viola-Jones Cascade face detector [15]. The generated sketch preserves the pose of the subject almost flawlessly, the translation of hair is also very realistic and detailed. The facial features preservation is worse than for the images from the testing database, however, we argue the mutual resemblance is still quite satisfactory.

At last, we provide results from the X-Bridge's reconstruction path, see Fig. 8. It can be seen that X-Bridge reaches almost flawless results in reconstructing the original images in both tested tasks. It should be noted that reconstruction results are usually a little bit brighter than the original image.

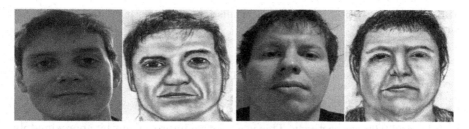

Fig. 7. Image-to-sketch translation using X-Bridge. There are original real images in the odd columns and generated sketches in the even columns.

Fig. 8. X-Bridge reconstruction path output. Input images in the odd columns and the outputs in the even columns.

In conclusion, we argue that qualitative results provided by X-Bridge overcome other tested methods in terms of facial features preservation, details generation, and generalization capacity.

4.3 Quantitative Results

There are two different performance metrics used for GAN evaluation - Inception Score (IS) [13], and Fréchet Inception Distance (FID) [5]. However, despite the existence of these metrics, we argue, that none of them is suitable to evaluate the performance of GAN in the image-to-image translation task. To further elaborate, higher IS or FID does not directly ensure the preservation of fine-grained information essential for precise and detailed translation. Due to the above-mentioned reasons, we decided to utilize our own metric.

In the first step, using the tested method, we translate the whole testing set from the sketch modality into the image modality. In the second step, we extract features from the translated set and also from the corresponding original real images. In the last step, we calculate the similarity of these corresponding images. As a feature extractor, we utilize pretrained ArcFace architecture [1] without any further fine-tuning. The ArcFace utilizes cosine similarity during its training, therefore, we do the same in our experiment. The results for all the tested methods can be found in Table 2.

X-Bridge overcomes both tested state-of-the-art methods by a large margin. In comparison with MUNIT, and Pix2pix, X-Bridge improve cosine similarity

Table 2. Comparison of average cosine similarity for the testing data. The higher is better.

Tested method	Pix2pix	MUNIT	X-Bridge
Cosine similarity	0.38 ± 0.11	0.27 ± 0.10	0.44 ± 0.10

by 0.17, and 0.06, respectively. This is a relative improvement by approximately 62%, and 16%, respectively.

5   Conclusion

Despite the huge progress of generative adversarial networks, image-to-image translation is still a challenging problem. In this paper, we present a novel method for image-to-image translation called X-Bridge, while addressing some issues of the existing ones. By providing qualitative and quantitative results from image-to-sketch translation task, we show superior ability of X-Bridge to preserve important features, its improved robustness and also generalization capacity.

In our future research, we would like to focus on the unsupervised image-to-image translation tasks. We see big potential in such approaches and we believe that they can help with the translation of modalities, where obtaining a large amount of data is problematic or too expensive.

Acknowledgments. This research was supported by the Technology Agency of the Czech Republic, project No. TN01000024. Access to computing and storage facilities owned by parties and projects contributing to the National Grid Infrastructure Meta-Centrum provided under the programme "Projects of Large Research, Development, and Innovations Infrastructures" (CESNET LM2015042), is greatly appreciated. This research was also partially supported by the RFBR, project No. 20-04-60529.

References

1. Deng, J., Guo, J., Xue, N., Zafeiriou, S.: Arcface: additive angular margin loss for deep face recognition. In: Proceedings of the IEEE Conference on Computer Vision and Pattern Recognition, pp. 4690–4699 (2019)
2. Goodfellow, I.J., et al.: Generative adversarial nets. In: Proceedings of the 27th International Conference on Neural Information Processing Systems, NIPS 2014, vol. 2, pp. 2672–2680. MIT Press, Cambridge (2014)
3. Gruber, I.: Heterogenní rozpoznávání lidské tváře ze skic obličeje (2019)
4. He, K., Zhang, X., Ren, S., Sun, J.: Deep residual learning for image recognition. In: Proceedings of the IEEE Conference on Computer Vision and Pattern Recognition, pp. 770–778 (2016)
5. Heusel, M., Ramsauer, H., Unterthiner, T., Nessler, B., Hochreiter, S.: GANs trained by a two time-scale update rule converge to a local nash equilibrium. In: Advances in Neural Information Processing Systems, pp. 6626–6637 (2017)

6. Huang, X., Liu, M.Y., Belongie, S., Kautz, J.: Multimodal unsupervised image-to-image translation. In: Proceedings of the European Conference on Computer Vision (ECCV), pp. 172–189 (2018)

7. Ioffe, S., Szegedy, C.: Batch normalization: accelerating deep network training by reducing internal covariate shift. In: International Conference on Machine Learning, pp. 448–456. PMLR (2015)

8. Isola, P., Zhu, J.Y., Zhou, T., Efros, A.A.: Image-to-image translation with conditional adversarial networks. In: Proceedings of the IEEE Conference on Computer Vision and Pattern Recognition, pp. 1125–1134 (2017)

9. Li, C., Wand, M.: Precomputed real-time texture synthesis with Markovian generative adversarial networks. In: Leibe, B., Matas, J., Sebe, N., Welling, M. (eds.) ECCV 2016. LNCS, vol. 9907, pp. 702–716. Springer, Cham (2016). https://doi.org/10.1007/978-3-319-46487-9_43

10. Liu, M.Y., Breuel, T., Kautz, J.: Unsupervised image-to-image translation networks. In: Proceedings of the 31st International Conference on Neural Information Processing Systems, pp. 700–708 (2017)

11. Phillips, P.J., Moon, H., Rizvi, S.A., Rauss, P.J.: The feret evaluation methodology for face-recognition algorithms. IEEE Trans. Pattern Anal. Mach. Intell. $22(10)$, 1090–1104 (2000)

12. Ronneberger, O., Fischer, P., Brox, T.: U-Net: convolutional networks for biomedical image segmentation. In: Navab, N., Hornegger, J., Wells, W.M., Frangi, A.F. (eds.) MICCAI 2015. LNCS, vol. 9351, pp. 234–241. Springer, Cham (2015). https://doi.org/10.1007/978-3-319-24574-4_28

13. Salimans, T., Goodfellow, I., Zaremba, W., Cheung, V., Radford, A., Chen, X.: Improved techniques for training GANs. In: Advances in Neural Information Processing Systems, pp. 2234–2242 (2016)

14. Ulyanov, D., Vedaldi, A., Lempitsky, V.S.: Instance normalization: the missing ingredient for fast stylization. CoRR abs/1607.08022 (2016)

15. Viola, P., Jones, M.: Rapid object detection using a boosted cascade of simple features. In: Proceedings of the 2001 IEEE Computer Society Conference on Computer Vision and Pattern Recognition, CVPR 2001, vol. 1, pp. I-511–I-518 (2001). https://doi.org/10.1109/CVPR.2001.990517

16. Wang, X., Tang, X.: Face photo-sketch synthesis and recognition. IEEE Trans. Pattern Anal. Mach. Intell. $31(11)$, 1955–1967 (2009)

17. Wang, X., Gupta, A.: Generative image modeling using style and structure adversarial networks. In: Leibe, B., Matas, J., Sebe, N., Welling, M. (eds.) ECCV 2016. LNCS, vol. 9908, pp. 318–335. Springer, Cham (2016). https://doi.org/10.1007/978-3-319-46493-0_20

18. Zhang, W., Wang, X., Tang, X.: Coupled information-theoretic encoding for face photo-sketch recognition. In: Proceedings of IEEE Conference on Computer Vision and Pattern Recognition (CVPR) (2011)

19. Zhu, J.Y., Park, T., Isola, P., Efros, A.A.: Unpaired image-to-image translation using cycle-consistent adversarial networks. In: Proceedings of the IEEE International Conference on Computer Vision, pp. 2223–2232 (2017)

Who is Selling to Whom – Feature Evaluation for Multi-block Classification in Invoice Information Extraction

Hien Thi Ha[✉] and Aleš Horák

Natural Language Processing Centre, Faculty of Informatics, Masaryk University,
Botanická 68a, 602 00 Brno, Czech Republic
{xha1,hales}@fi.muni.cz

Abstract. The invoice information extraction task aims at unifying the automatized processing of invoices in structured forms and in the form of a scanned image. Recognizing the pieces of information where a specific value is identified with a keyword (such as the invoice date) is a relatively well-managed task. On the other hand, identification of multi-block information on the invoice, such as distinguishing the seller, buyer, and the delivery address, is much more challenging due to versatile invoice layouts.

In this work, we present a new technique of feature extraction and classification to recognize the seller, buyer, and delivery address text blocks in scanned invoices based on a combination of complex layout and annotated text features. The method does not only consider the block positional features but also the relation between blocks and block contents at a higher level. The technique is implemented as a module of the OCRMiner system. We offer its detailed evaluation and error analysis with a dataset of more than five hundred Czech invoices reaching the overall macro average F1-score of 94%.

Keywords: OCR · Invoice · Block type classification · Seller · Buyer · Delivery address

1 Introduction

An invoice is a time-stamped commercial document that itemizes and records a transaction between a buyer and a seller [13]. Thus, in an invoice, seller and buyer are two parties having totally different rights and obligations. Classification of the invoice as a sales invoice (on the seller's side) or a purchase invoice (on the buyer's side) on one hand helps companies to keep track of relevant actions, e.g. the buyer will check received products or make the payment by the due date. On the other hand, the process helps Taxation offices to monitor goods and services tax duties of the provider.

Recognizing and extracting the key text items from scanned invoices have a huge commercial potential which attracts significant interest of big companies.

© Springer Nature Switzerland AG 2021
A. Karpov and R. Potapova (Eds.): SPECOM 2021, LNAI 12997, pp. 250–261, 2021.
https://doi.org/10.1007/978-3-030-87802-3_23

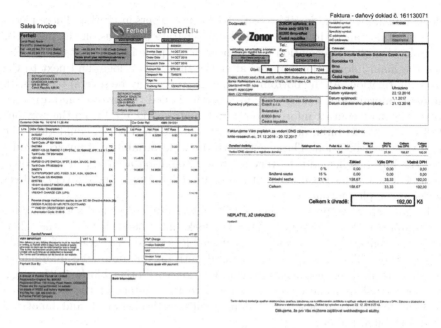

Fig. 1. Examples of parties blocks: sellers in purple boxes, buyers in blue, and delivery addresses in orange. The actual information is modified to ensure privacy. (Color figure online)

Several challenges to tackle this problem have been organized recently, for example, the Robust Reading Challenge on Scanned Receipt OCR and Information extraction (SROIE) at ICDAR 2019 [15] or Mobile-Captured Image Document Recognition for Vietnamese Receipts at RIVF2021.[1] Recent works on this field also focus on analysing both text and layout features [9,24,25]. However, the exploited layout features are limited to the positions (bounding boxes) of text items only. Positional relations between blocks and the semantic information of the surrounding blocks are not taken into account. To the best of our knowledge, there is no work fully differentiating parties (i.e. buyer, seller, and receiver) in invoices. The reason may lie in the difference between invoices and receipts. While invoices always require full name and contact details of both the provider and the customer, receipts usually contain only the supplier identification.

The previously introduced OCRMiner system [10] exploits layout and text analysis in the invoice image information extraction. The system is based on a logical analysis assigning informative labels to each text block using manual rules based on rich annotations. The block types include title, general information (e.g. invoice number, invoice date, order number, order date), payment information, bank information, buyer/seller/delivery address, and page number. Among these blocks, the buyer, seller, and delivery address are the most complex. They involve organization name (ORG), address, company identity (ID),

---

[1] https://www.rivf2021-mc-ocr.vietnlp.com/.

telephone number, fax, email, website, and contact person (PER). These pieces of information can be in different blocks at separate positions on the page. For example, the seller information may appear in the page header containing ORG then the main information appears after the title with a logo, and next to the buyer information. At the bottom of the page, there may be several blocks with the bank information, website, the person who issued the invoice, and a repetition of the main contact information (ORG, address, ID, etc.) from the previous blocks. The blocks often do not have keywords attached which could guide the block type identification. These facts with the wide variability of invoice layouts keep the buyer, seller and delivery address recognition accuracy at low scores. Figure 1 shows invoice examples with separate seller, buyer, and delivery address blocks in complex layouts.

In this paper, we present a new OCRMiner module designed specifically for this complex task of classifying the text blocks into four categories: the seller, buyer, the delivery address, and empty if the block does not contain information of those three. The new approach is based both on the annotated information and the semantics of the block layout in relation with other blocks in the page. The contextual information is not limited to the content of the surrounding blocks since it concerns also the alignment with parties keywords and annotated entities through the page.

The next section summarises related works in this area. The details of pre-processing, feature extraction and classification model are given in Sect. 3. In Sect. 4, we offer a detailed evaluation of the method with a Czech invoice dataset.

2   Related Work

One of the main challenges of the invoice processing task is the huge variety of layout formats. Although the predefined set of fields is mandatory, i.e. the invoice number, date, price, seller, and buyer, their positions are not fixed. Therefore, many invoice analysis systems consider a particular layout as a class, usually connected to a particular vendor. Smartfix [16,20] or CBR-DIA [12] are examples of such methods which classify invoices into the known and unknown classes based on their layout graphs using case-base reasoning. These systems must manage a large number of classes which may grow over time due to new providers or layout updates.

A template-based method is proposed in [2,7]. The key idea is to group documents generated by the same template and then to design extraction rules for each group. This method is not scalable to large bulks of document groups.

Liu et al. [17] proposed graph convolution to train graph embeddings which are then combined with word embeddings before feeding them into a standard BiLSTM-CRF neural network used in the named entity recognition approaches. The graph embeddings include relation position between text segments but they are limited to the direct neighbours only. Moreover, the graph embeddings training needs a large amount of manually labeled invoice graphs.

With the success of Transformers [22] and deep languages models trained on large volumes of text (BERT [5] and its variants [23]) in NLP tasks, several models trained to join text and visual features have been introduced recently. LayoutLM [24], LAMBERT [9], or PICK [25] gained the state of the art results of the information extraction task in ICDAR 2019 challenges with the receipt dataset [14]. The layout-awareness features employed in these models include positional embeddings [9], image embedding [19,25] or an ensemble of both [24]. Nevertheless, only visual features of word or sequence are used, the relation between block contents are not yet taken into account. This relation is an essential feature in classifying the invoice party blocks, especially for the complex layouts with separate blocks without keywords attached to them. Moreover, training the deep models needs a huge amount of data which is difficult to adapt to other languages.

In ICDAR 2019 [15], or RIVF 2021[2], the information extraction task consisted in extracting the company name and address from scanned receipts, however, of the supplier only. While an invoice is a document, sent by seller to buyer, that requests payment for products or services, a receipt is the proof of payment. An invoice includes name and contact information of both the supplier and the customer whereas a receipt contains the information of the supplier only. Therefore, the tasks did not require the seller/buyer distinction.

In [4], the party information is extracted by searching the OCRed text for previously saved client records. These records are stored in a database containing all information about the clients, e.g. the company name, VAT number, or the address. This method needs to update every time they have a new client or when a client changes their information. Moreover, one company can be a supplier in one transaction, and a customer in another transaction. This method does not differentiate the role of the party in the invoice.

In a previous work [11], we extracted information, including party information, from scanned contracts using an adapted annotation pipeline. Different from invoices, the party information in contracts is often not dispersed but concentrated in one area. While the role of each party in an invoice is sometimes ambiguous, their roles in a contract are stated clearly in the text.

3 The Method

3.1 Pre-processing and Annotations

The annotation process in Fig. 2 is similar to [10] with several important enhancements. The invoice image is first processed by an optical character recognition (OCR) engine.[3] OCRMiner then builds the hierarchical layout model of the pages and applies a series of annotation tasks to enrich the analysis by adding

---

[2] https://rivf2021-mc-ocr.vietnlp.com/challenge.
[3] The system uses the open source Tesseract-OCR [21] version 4.1.0 with the page segmentation mode set to "11".

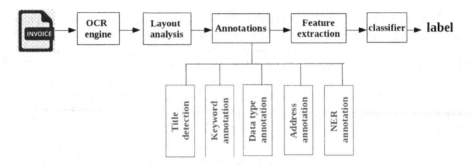

Fig. 2. The processing pipeline.

valuable information about named entities, keywords, structured data types, and parts of addresses based on the output of natural language processing tasks.

In the hierarchical layout model, the blocks are built from the line chunks identified by Tesseract using the "sparse text" page segmentation mode. The process of building blocks from lines is based on the style, alignment, and distance between the lines.

The named entity recognition (NER) module is currently based on the Slavic BERT model [1] in which the deep bidirectional unsupervised language model BERT (Bidirectional Encoder Representations from Transformers) [6] was pre-trained on stratified Wikipedia data for Bulgarian, Czech, and Polish and News data for Russian. The Slavic BERT NER model was evaluated with the Balto-Slavic Natural Language Processing Shared Task dataset where it acquired the F1 score of 93.9% for the Czech language.

The global layout annotation enriches the block annotation with the information about its perceived position on the page. The absolute position separates blocks horizontally (absolute x) into "left" and "right" columns and vertically into five parts involving "header", "top", "middle", "bottom", "footer". A block is in the header or footer regions if the distance from it to the top or bottom of the page is less than 10% of the page height. The remaining area is equally divided into 3 parts marked as "top", "middle", and "bottom".

3.2 Feature Extraction

Besides the textual features, recent invoice analysis works pay attention to the visual features. The current text features are mainly pre-trained word embeddings by either word2vec [18], or BERT models. In case of visual features, the information besides plain bounding box coordinates includes image features extracted by Convolutional Neural Networks (CNN) [19,25] or graph embeddings by Graph Convolution [17,25]. Some works learn the visual embeddings by using the transformer architecture on the bounding box coordinates [9,24].

OCRMiner also makes use of both textual and layout features, but the semantics of this information is organized in the way used by humans when reading an

```
AdiAdiA, s.r.o.
Brolzova  2087/10b          IČ: 60771771      mobil:                    tel.: +420-205120555
60800  Brno-Líšeň           DIČ: CZ60771771    www: www.adiadia.cz       fax: +420-205120526
Česká republika                                e-mail: adiadia@adiadia.cz
                            C 16877 vedená u rejstříkového soudu v Brně
```

FAKTURA - DAŇOVÝ DOKLAD   170110189

Fig. 3. Multi-blocks information example. "IČ" denotes a company ID, "DIČ" is a VAT number.

invoice. The invoice parties blocks are different from the other blocks in including special entities, such as ORG, LOC, PER[4] and specific regulatory information, such as the company VAT number. These features rely on the block's text, whereas differentiating between the invoice parties mainly rely on the positional relations between blocks. Moreover, in many cases a party's information is spread into several blocks in vertical or horizontal direction. In such cases, not only the position but also the content of surrounding blocks are important.

OCRMiner extracts these features from the layout and semantic annotations in the pre-processing steps. Firstly, the semantic features search the block's annotations for either BUYER, SELLER, or DELIVERY ADDRESS keywords, or pieces of a company information, i.e. ORG, PER, LOC, CITY, POSTCODE, ID, or VAT NUMBER. The partial information helps to distinguish party labels from a non-party one ("empty" in the module classification) while the buyer/seller/delivery address keywords contribute to differentiating those 3 labels. Then, the layout features identify the area of the page that the block belongs to, i.e. on the left or the right part (absolute x), in the header, top, middle, bottom, or footer part (absolute y). Thirdly, the module checks if the neighbour blocks also contain invoice party information. Figure 3 presents an example of an invoice party information in four separate blocks at the top of the page. However, in many cases a company information is not only broken down into two or more blocks but these blocks appear in a vicinity of the other party block (as can be seen in Fig. 1). In such cases, the regional alignment[5] with the party keywords is an important distinguishing feature.

In addition, a numeric information about entities in the block which are repeated through the invoice is computed. This is based on the observation that the seller information or its contact is often repeated at the bottom of the page. Features indicating whether the text contains numbers, alphabetic characters, or capitalized words are also included. The total number of extracted feature types is 159.

3.3 The Classifier

The module output needs a declarative approach capable of justifying the results of the block type classification. That is why recent neural network approaches

---

[4] An organization name, a location or a personal name.

[5] i.e. alignment on the same left or right part of the page (same column), or at the same header, top, middle, bottom, or footer of the page (same row).

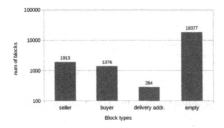
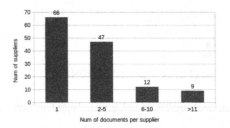

Fig. 4. The blocks statistics.   **Fig. 5.** Suppliers statistics.

were exempt from the process. The current implementation exploits the Random forest (RF) [3] technique. RF is an ensemble classifier consisting of a large number of decision trees voting for the most popular output. The generalization error of random forests depends on the strength of the individual classifiers in the forest and the correlation between them. The less correlation and the more strong the trees are, the lower the generalization error is, i.e. the better results are obtained. Two main techniques to minimize the correlation between individual trees are the bootstrap aggregation (bagging) and the random input selection. Experiments shows that the random forest technique is among the best classifiers for small and medium datasets [8].

4   Experiments and Evaluation

The evaluation dataset includes 532 real invoices from 134 different suppliers in the Czech Republic. Each supplier has a different layout, i.e. the information and position of the buyer and the seller are different between different suppliers. Approximately a half of them ($66/134 \approx 49\%$) have only one invoice, and more than a third ($47/134 \approx 35\%$) have less than 5 invoices. Three suppliers take a quarter of total invoices, which are 44, 42, and 52 respectively. The numbers of invoices per supplier are presented in Fig. 5.

The total number of extracted blocks is 21,932. The number of blocks in each category is illustrated in Fig. 4. Twenty two blocks have more than one label (2 blocks having all three types: seller, buyer, delivery address, and 20 blocks having two out of these three). This is caused by the small positional distance between the blocks, which hinders them from splitting. The dataset is shuffled and divided into the training, validation and testing subsets in the 64:16:20 ratio.

The random forest hyperparameters were tuned on the validation set using the randomized search cross validation leading to the values of bootstrap: *False*, max_depth: 30, max_features: *sqrt*, min_samples_leaf: 1, min_samples_split: 2, and n_estimators: 190.

Using the rich set of the extracted features, the overall results reach 94–95% precision for all the classes and above 90% recall for the seller and buyer classes. The precision, recall, and F1-score of each type as well as average measurements are listed in Table 1. The highest F1-score of 99% was expectedly achieved with

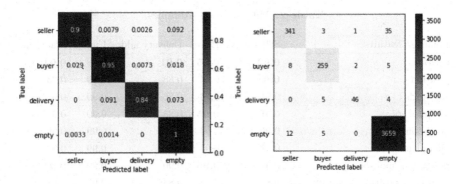

Fig. 6. Confusion matrix with and without normalization.

the empty class and the lowest F1-score of 88% with the delivery address class. The overall macro average F1-score reached **94%** with the weighted average of 98%. Figure 6 details the confusion measures in distinguishing each pair of classes. Only 3 seller blocks (0.79% of all seller blocks) are misrecognized as buyer blocks and 8 buyer blocks (2.9%) are misclassified into seller blocks. The unrecognized seller, buyer, delivery address blocks correspond to 9.2%, 1.8%, and 7.3% of the subset. A detailed error analysis reveals that 30% of missing party blocks are due to the situation where the seller information is stamped at the lower part of invoices. Such blocks are often erroneous, and split by the signatures when processed by the OCR engine. The second most frequent error cause corresponds to the situation where the party blocks are fragmented into small blocks containing one piece of information, e.g. telephone number, city, or street name. In both cases, the annotations are not strong enough to classify the blocks into party classes. The analysis also reveals that 76% of "false positives" in empty class are actually pieces of parties' information that are not labeled.

In order to evaluate the contribution of each group of features, a series of ablation tests was performed with dropping one or more feature groups and re-running the classification with the same hyper-parameters. The features are

Table 1. Evaluation of multi-class classifier.

Label	Precision	Recall	F1-score	Support
seller	0.94	0.90	0.92	380
buyer	0.95	0.95	0.95	274
delivery addr.	0.94	0.84	0.88	55
empty	**0.99**	**1.00**	**0.99**	3676
accuracy			0.98	4385
macro avg	**0.96**	**0.92**	**0.94**	4385
weighted avg	0.98	0.98	0.98	4385

Table 2. Ablation tests examples.

Removed features	Seller class	Buyer	Delivery addr.	Empty	Macro avg
entities	**0.92**	**0.95**	**0.91**	0.99	**0.94**
position	**0.92**	0.94	0.88	0.99	0.93
keywords	0.91	0.94	0.86	0.99	0.93
morphology	0.91	**0.95**	0.88	0.99	0.93
neighbours	0.90	0.94	0.88	0.99	0.93
alignments	0.91	0.94	0.87	0.99	0.93
position + morphology	0.91	**0.95**	0.90	0.99	**0.94**
entities + position + morphology	0.88	0.93	0.84	0.99	0.91
all except neighbours	0.76	0.87	0.78	0.97	0.85

grouped into block entities (entities), block keywords (keywords), block position (position), block text morphology (morphology), block neighbours annotations (neighbours), party alignments (alignments), and others. The ablation tests results are presented in Table 2. The set of features is well balanced as removing any one of the feature groups deteriorates the macro average F1-score by 1% at most. For example, when the block entities features are removed, the remaining most important features are "have keyword VAT number", "have keyword company ID", "vertical position", and "number of capitalized words". The important information about the block neighbours' features alone reaches the F1-score of 0.85 setting a baseline for the other improvements.

To identify the most important features, the task was additionally split into two sub-tasks. First, the party and non-party blocks are classified with 94% F1-score. Using the same set of features, the party class is then categorized into the

Table 3. Feature importance of classifying party and non-party (left) and classifying parties (right).

Ind	Feature	Importance	Ind	Feature	Importance
3	Has VAT#	0.0768	19	Horizontal position	0.0961
2	Has LOC	0.0645	31	Same col. with buyer keyw	0.0802
0	Has PER	0.0564	35	Same col. with seller keyw	0.0798
14	Has keyw VAT#	0.0499	20	Vertical position	0.0594
15	Has keyw ID	0.0462	29	Alignment with buyer keyw	0.0441
18	Vertical pos	0.0441	32	Same row with buyer keyw	0.0440
1	Has company name	0.0376	88	Has right block	0.0285
9	Has POSTCODE	0.0355	110	Has bottom block	0.0274
6	Num of capitals	0.0282	44	Top bl has ORG	0.0240
5	Has numbers	0.0250	33	Alignment with seller keyw	0.0216

Table 4. Classification among parties and classification of party and non-party blocks.

Class	Precision	Recall	F1-score	Class	Precision	Recall	F1-score
seller	0.97	0.99	0.98	non-party	0.99	0.99	0.99
buyer	0.99	0.96	0.98	party	0.97	0.94	0.96
accuracy			0.98	accuracy			0.98
macro avg	0.98	0.98	0.98	macro avg	0.97	0.96	0.96
weighted avg	0.98	0.98	0.98	weighted avg	0.98	0.98	0.98

seller and buyer classes.[6] This second subtask reaches a F1-score of 98% on both the seller and buyer classes. Detailed results of these sub-tasks are illustrated in Table 4. Based on the feature importance analyses in Table 3, it may be further deduced that the content of the block (e.g. whether it contains location, VAT number, person, company id, etc.) and its vertical position in the page are the most important features to distinguish the party and non-party blocks. The layout features such as the relative position in the page, and the alignments with the seller and buyer keywords are the most important features to identify the specific invoice party.

5   Conclusion and Future Directions

In this paper, we have presented the results of a new method for multi-block classification in the invoice information extraction task. The most important part lies in the feature extraction process that in combination with a declarative learning process reaches **94%** of macro average F1-score for the seller, buyer and delivery address recognition. This method can be easily adapted to other languages.

The detailed analysis showed that most of the errors happen in (erroneously) fragmented party blocks. Therefore, we will experiment with grouping the party block fragments by integrating region boundary detection with the output of the OCR engine. In addition, the features used in the method rely on annotations, therefore, the more accurate annotations, the better the classification can be. We plan to re-train the NER module on a large invoice dataset obtained from publicly available web registries.

Acknowledgments. This work has been partly supported by the Ministry of Education of the Czech Republic within the LINDAT/CLARIAH-CZ research infrastructure LM2018101 and by Konica Minolta Business Solution Czech within the OCRMiner project.

---

[6] Whereas the buyer usually identifies the headquarters of the company, the actual delivery address may be the same or at a different branch. So, to simplify this part of the evaluation, the delivery address is merged into the buyer class.

References

1. Arkhipov, M., Trofimova, M., Kuratov, Y., Sorokin, A.: Tuning multilingual transformers for named entity recognition on Slavic languages. In: BSNLP 2019, p. 89 (2019)
2. Bart, E., Sarkar, P.: Information extraction by finding repeated structure. In: Proceedings of the 9th International Workshop on Document Analysis Systems, pp. 175–182. ACM (2010)
3. Breiman, L.: Random forests. Mach. Learn. **45**(1), 5–32 (2001)
4. Bureš, L., Neduchal, P., Müller, L.: Automatic information extraction from scanned documents. In: Karpov, A., Potapova, R. (eds.) SPECOM 2020. LNCS (LNAI), vol. 12335, pp. 87–96. Springer, Cham (2020). https://doi.org/10.1007/978-3-030-60276-5_9
5. Devlin, J., Chang, M.W., Lee, K., Toutanova, K.: BERT: pre-training of deep bidirectional transformers for language understanding. arXiv preprint arXiv:1810.04805 (2018)
6. Devlin, J., Chang, M.W., Lee, K., Toutanova, K.: BERT: pre-training of deep bidirectional transformers for language understanding. In: Proceedings of the 2019 Conference of the North American Chapter of the Association for Computational Linguistics: Human Language Technologies, (Long and Short Papers), Minneapolis, Minnesota, vol. 1, pp. 4171–4186. Association for Computational Linguistics, June 2019. https://doi.org/10.18653/v1/N19-1423. https://www.aclweb.org/anthology/N19-1423
7. Esser, D., Schuster, D., Muthmann, K., Schill, A.: Few-exemplar information extraction for business documents. In: ICEIS (1), pp. 293–298 (2014)
8. Fernández-Delgado, M., Cernadas, E., Barro, S., Amorim, D.: Do we need hundreds of classifiers to solve real world classification problems? J. Mach. Learn. Res. **15**(1), 3133–3181 (2014)
9. Garncarek, Ł., Powalski, R., Stanisławek, T., Topolski, B., Halama, P., Graliński, F.: LAMBERT: layout-aware (language) modeling using BERT for information extraction (2020)
10. Ha, H.T., Medved', M., Nevěřilová, Z., Horák, A.: Recognition of OCR invoice metadata block types. In: Sojka, P., Horák, A., Kopeček, I., Pala, K. (eds.) TSD 2018. LNCS (LNAI), vol. 11107, pp. 304–312. Springer, Cham (2018). https://doi.org/10.1007/978-3-030-00794-2_33
11. Ha, H.T., Horák, A., Bui, M.T.: Contract metadata identification in Czech scanned documents. In: ICAART 2021, pp. 795–802. SCITEPRESS (2021)
12. Hamza, H., Belaid, Y., Belaïd, A.: A case-based reasoning approach for invoice structure extraction. In: Ninth International Conference on Document Analysis and Recognition, vol. 1, pp. 327–331. IEEE (2007)
13. Hayes, A.: Invoice (2020). https://www.investopedia.com/terms/i/invoice.asp
14. Huang, Z., et al.: ICDAR 2019 competition on scanned receipt OCR and information extraction. In: 2019 International Conference on Document Analysis and Recognition (ICDAR), pp. 1516–1520. IEEE (2019)
15. Jaume, G., Ekenel, H.K., Thiran, J.P.: FUNSD: a dataset for form understanding in noisy scanned documents. In: 2019 International Conference on Document Analysis and Recognition Workshops (ICDARW), vol. 2, pp. 1–6. IEEE (2019)
16. Klein, B., Dengel, A.R., Fordan, A.: *smartFIX*: an adaptive system for document analysis and understanding. In: Dengel, A., Junker, M., Weisbecker, A. (eds.) Reading and Learning. LNCS, vol. 2956, pp. 166–186. Springer, Heidelberg (2004). https://doi.org/10.1007/978-3-540-24642-8_11

17. Liu, X., Gao, F., Zhang, Q., Zhao, H.: Graph convolution for multimodal information extraction from visually rich documents. arXiv preprint arXiv:1903.11279 (2019)
18. Mikolov, T., Sutskever, I., Chen, K., Corrado, G., Dean, J.: Distributed representations of words and phrases and their compositionality. arXiv preprint arXiv:1310.4546 (2013)
19. Patel, S., Bhatt, D.: Abstractive information extraction from scanned invoices (AIESI) using end-to-end sequential approach. arXiv preprint arXiv:2009.05728 (2020)
20. Schulz, F., Ebbecke, M., Gillmann, M., Adrian, B., Agne, S., Dengel, A.: Seizing the treasure: transferring knowledge in invoice analysis. In: 10th International Conference on Document Analysis and Recognition, pp. 848–852. IEEE (2009). https://doi.org/10.1109/ICDAR.2009.47
21. Smith, R.W.: Hybrid page layout analysis via tab-stop detection. In: 10th International Conference on Document Analysis and Recognition, pp. 241–245. IEEE (2009)
22. Vaswani, A., et al.: Attention is all you need. arXiv preprint arXiv:1706.03762 (2017)
23. Wolf, T., et al.: Transformers: state-of-the-art natural language processing. In: Proceedings of the 2020 Conference on Empirical Methods in Natural Language Processing: System Demonstrations, pp. 38–45. Association for Computational Linguistics, Online, October 2020. https://www.aclweb.org/anthology/2020.emnlp-demos.6
24. Xu, Y., Li, M., Cui, L., Huang, S., Wei, F., Zhou, M.: LayoutLM: pre-training of text and layout for document image understanding. In: Proceedings of the 26th ACM SIGKDD International Conference on Knowledge Discovery & Data Mining, pp. 1192–1200 (2020)
25. Yu, W., Lu, N., Qi, X., Gong, P., Xiao, R.: PICK: processing key information extraction from documents using improved graph learning-convolutional networks. In: 25th International Conference on Pattern Recognition (ICPR 2020), pp. 4363–4370. IEEE (2021)

Multimodal Corpus Analysis of Autoblog 2020: Lecture Videos in Machine Learning

Abner Hernandez[1] and Seung Hee Yang[2(✉)]

[1] Pattern Recognition Lab, Friedrich Alexander University Erlangen-Nürnberg,
Erlangen, Germany
`abner.hernandez@fau.de`
[2] Department of Artificial Intelligence in Biomedical Engineering,
Friedrich Alexander University Erlangen-Nürnberg, Erlangen, Germany
`seung.hee.yang@fau.de`

Abstract. This paper introduces a lecture video corpus, Autoblog 2020. With the increase of online learning in universities, there is a demand for a systematic toolchain development for lecture video processing. However, the existing lecture video corpus does not satisfy the requirement for such tasks, and lecture transcription and analyses are relatively unexplored areas in speech and natural language research. Autoblog 2020 Corpus is developed towards the end goal of free video-to-blog post conversion software that supports making video presentations more accessible. It will include automatic editing of disfluencies, automatic speech recognition (ASR), and spoken term extraction so that researchers can process and share their contents more efficiently. In this paper, we present a description of the corpus, linguistic analyses and preliminary experiment results regarding ASR, keyword extraction, and segmentation. The results will be used in future work to develop a video-to-blog post conversion.

Keywords: Video lecture corpus · Speech recognition · Keyword extraction · Automatic segmentation · Audio-visual processing

1 Introduction

Recently, we have seen a dramatic increase in online lectures and conference presentations due to the COVID-19 outbreak [16]. A growing number of these resources are publicly available on video-sharing websites such as YouTube. Open source videos enable students to learn anywhere and anytime, increase learning opportunities for students with disabilities, and help professionals to share recent advancements in their fields.

However, automatic lecture video processing still has a large room to benefit from the development of speech and language technology using deep learning. For example, more effective learning would be possible if students and researchers can search for a particular slide using keywords that are uttered during a lecture, along with blog posts of the corresponding video resources. Concise blog-like

A. Karpov and R. Potapova (Eds.): SPECOM 2021, LNAI 12997, pp. 262–270, 2021.
https://doi.org/10.1007/978-3-030-87802-3_24

versions of videos would allow students to skim through lecture material and take notes of important key details. Moreover, researchers can make presentations more accessible and increase the impact of their research and visibility.

In order to address such needs, it is necessary to develop a lecture corpus that is designed particularly for these problems. Existing lecture speech corpora include the Corpus of Japanese classroom Lecture speech Contents [21], LECTRA [20], and the classroom lecture speech developed by MIT research group [11]. However, these datasets are insufficient to benefit from the state-of-the-art speech and language processing technologies because they are recorded in classroom environments. The TED-LIUM 3 dataset [6] is another speech corpus consisting of 452 h of audio from TED conference videos. While the TED-LIUM dataset is useful for speech recognition research, it does not make the associated videos available. Massive Open Online Course (MOOC) lecture videos, such as from Coursera, are a recent trend, but the videos, audio, or transcripts are often not open-source and in some cases not free.

For the purpose of developing a comprehensive toolchain, videos that are pre-recorded in a clean environment with a lower degree of spontaneity are necessary.

This paper introduces Autoblog 2020, our lecture video corpus in the deep learning domain. The corpus is built to enable an interactive and systematic tool for lecture videos. Currently, the corpus consists of 43 video lectures for a Pattern Recognition course amounting to 11.4 h. Moreover, we are in the process of organizing and generating transcripts for 4 other courses with an extra 168 videos and 55 h of audio. We will provide transcriptions for all videos, their raw unedited counterparts, and all slides of each lecture available in .pdf documents. Autoblog 2020 will continue to expand as we accumulate the number of lectures with transcriptions, with the goal of enabling fast, accurate, and easy processing of lecture materials.

We organize the rest of the paper as follows. Related studies are presented in Sect. 2. A description of the corpus is introduced in Sect. 3. Preliminary experiment results from the corpus are presented in Sect. 4. In, Sect. 5 we discuss future work and conclude the paper.

2   Related Work

Corpus design, ASR, video summarization, and keyword-spotting are the main tasks involved in video lecture processing. This section presents the related works in the fields. Automatic transcription performance in the lecture video domain has been a topic of interest for several years. Previously, a corpus of MIT courses amounting to 168 h of transcribed videos was collected for the purpose of automatically transcribing and indexing audio-visual academic lectures [11]. This corpus was mainly built for investigating language models with different vocabulary for ASR and keyword spotting performance. Results indicate that keywords can be obtained even with highly erroneous transcriptions. Furthermore, including additional speech data leads to more accurate transcriptions, but has a marginal effect on keyword retrieval. Similarly, a corpus of Japanese class-room lectures (CJLC) was collected in [21] for building robust speech recognition of lecture speech. The performance of speech recognition using CJLC data was compared when training different language models [7]. The study showed that including lecture syllabus information to language models resulted in an increased word accuracy of 2.4%. Although the lecture videos from MIT and CJLC are recorded in classroom settings, the videos in Autoblog 2020 Corpus are pre-recorded, which are more similar to what one encounters in online classes in today's COVID-19 environment.

Besides ASR, video lecture processing has been researched in keyword spotting and automatic summarisation tasks. Text content on PDF slides via Optical Character Recognition was used in [8], and results indicated that the method performs better than words selected at random. Linguistic features were used in [4] for keyword extraction, such as prosodic features from the speech signal, and lexical features from lecture slides and transcripts. All features showed promising keyword extraction results.

For automatic lecture video summarisation, handwriting features were used in [9], while histogram-based video features for generating a concise preview video were explored in [18]. For the same task, image and text processing techniques are used in [17]. Results indicate that students studying with summarised materials obtained better scores on pre-lecture quizzes.

Much research has been done in audio-visual speech processing in order to improve ASR and keyword spotting tasks. Studies have found that audio features along with visual features such as lip movement can significantly improve the performance of ASR in the presence of noise [1,13,19]. Another growing field of research in audio-visual processing is keyword spotting. Traditionally, only the speech signal has been used for detecting keywords, but studies suggest that visual information can also be useful. A 128-dimensional feature vector representing a given speech signal and its corresponding lip movements was shown to produce excellent results for multiple data sets [5]. Similarly, visual feature extraction using an 18-layer spatio-temporal ResNet along with audio features improves the performance of keyword spotting with clean and noisy audio data [10].

The survey of the previous research highlight that there has been significant research directed toward speech and language processing, and that lecture video processing can enjoy many benefits from these existing methods. Given that the Autoblog Corpus videos consist of both PDF slides and the lecturer's facial expressions, the keyword spotting and summarisation tasks can benefit from a multi-modal approach. Our effort towards Autoblog 2020 Corpus aims to enable multi-modal audio-visual processing methods for a systematic tool chain development. Currently, we developed a preliminary website[1] for several tasks such as extracting text from SBV files containing the recognized text and the timestamps, automatic segmentation of sentences boundaries, PDF to JPEG conversion, JPEG to GIF conversion, and movie to GIF conversion.

---

[1] https://autoblog.tf.fau.de.

3   Corpus Description

Autoblog 2020 Corpus includes one full semester course recording of Pattern Recognition lectures. Every semester, more lectures are being recorded and accumulated. Table 1 shows the number of hours, lectures, editing progress, and lecture slide availability. The full course contains 43 videos and is 11.4 h. Manually corrected transcriptions of the ASR results, raw unedited videos in additions to the edited versions, and pdf files of lecture slides are available. Future courses will also consist of the same data collection scheme. Example screenshots of a lecture slide (a), along with the lecturer's face (b), are displayed in Fig. 1. All videos have the same format, with lecture slides on the left and the lecturer on the right.

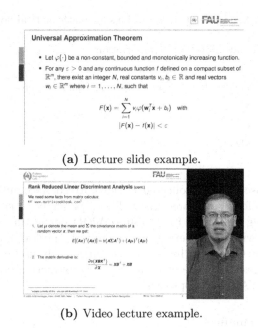

(a) Lecture slide example.

(b) Video lecture example.

Fig. 1. Screenshot examples of lecture format.

4   Corpus Analysis

In order to quantify the characteristics of Autoblog 2020 Corpus, we have examined the performances of ASR, sentence segmentation, and analyzed keyword extraction results.

As many lectures in Autoblog 2020 are becoming available on video sharing websites such as YouTube, we utilized its automatic captioning system in order to obtain transcription results [2]. All outputs are hand-corrected by an annotator. Since the lecture materials heavily rely on mathematic equations and

Table 1. Description of the Pattern Recognition course for the Autoblog 2020 corpus.

Material	Pattern recognition course
# of videos	43
Duration (hours)	11.4
Availability of unedited versions	Yes
Manually corrected ASR transcripts	Yes
Lecture slides in PDF	yes

formulas, attention is made to annotate as spoken by the lecturer, instead of using mathematical notation. See Table 2 for some examples.

Table 2. Examples of transcriptions for mathematical notation.

Math notation	Transcription
$f(x)$	f of x
$p(x\|y = 0)$	p of x given y equals to zero
$\hat{x}$	x hat
x'	x prime
Δx	delta x

Reference transcripts are collected for all Pattern Recognition lectures and then used for the following three tasks. First, we analyse the performance of ASR by calculating the Word Error Rate (WER) per lecture video. Since the output of ASR is without punctuations, we test the performance of a sentence boundary detector. Obtaining full stops are particularly useful when uploading transcripts to blogs. Lastly, we examine keyword extraction performance using the unsupervised YAKE [3] approach.

4.1   ASR Performance

After uploading the video on YouTube, we calculate WER's of each lecture using our human annotations and the automatic captioning output. The average WER is 6.25% for 38 Pattern Recognition lectures. Depending on the courses, the overall performance varies with a WER range between 2.65% to 15.73%. Example errors are shown in Table 3, which shows that proper nouns and mathematical terms are often misrecognised. Future work will implement an in-house ASR system for the task, fine-tuned towards lecture videos in the deep learning domain.

4.2   Sentence Segmentation

Once the automatic transcription results are obtained, the next step in the video processing would be sentence segmentation. Sentence boundary detection was

Table 3. Example errors in Pattern Recognition lecture.

Reference	Hypothesis
a creative commons for *zero* license	a creative commons for *xero* license
friedrich alexander university *erlangen* nuremberg	friedrich alexander university *along* nuremberg
so r1 r2 up to *rm* where m is the number of observations	so r-hand side1 r2 up to *our m* is the number of observations
now the minimization using the *l2norm* is something that we've already seen	now the minimization using the *two norm* is something that we've already seen

conducted using a bi-directional long short-term memory with conditional random fields(BiLSTM-CRF). The segmentation model consists of an input layer with Glove [12] embeddings, followed by a hidden layer where the BiLSTM maps those embeddings to hidden sequences. Lastly, a CRF output layer which takes in hidden sequences and computes probabilities of tokenization labels. In this case, the labels denote whether a word is at a sentence boundary.

Results are compared when using a model pretrained with close to one million English sentences from the tatoeba dataset [14]. We also fine-tuned the model with 7,112 sentences from the Deep Learning lecture transcripts, which is another course that will be added to the Autoblog corpus. The deep learning lecture transcripts were used during fine-tuning in order to prevent overfitting and improve generalizeability of the model. The task is treated as a classification problem where the model predicts for each given word whether there is a sentence boundary. A correct prediction of a sentence boundary is a true positive, while a correct prediction of no boundary is a true negative. Similarly, a false positive occurs if the model incorrectly predicts a sentence boundary and a false negative when failing to predict a boundary.

To measure the performance we calculate precision, recall and F1. From Table 4 we see that a base model can achieve an F1 score of 53%, while a fine-tuned model can reach 80.87%. Figure 2 contains example sentence boundary predictions for the manually parsed sentences in (a). The base model (b) incorrectly ends sentences two, three and five, but correctly predicts the start of sentence one, two and five. As expected, the fine-tuned model (c) outperforms the base model and correctly segments sentence one, two and five.

Table 4. Segmentation task results for Pattern Recognition lectures.

Dataset	Measure (%)	Base-model	Finetuned-model
Pattern recognition	Precision	56.84	80.66
	Recall	49.99	81.52
	F1	53.00	80.87

1. we'll give a brief sketch of the ideas of neural networks.
2. lets have a look at multilayer perceptrons.
3. you see that we talked about this here only about very basic concepts.
4. if you're interested in neural networks we have an entire class on deep learning where we talk about all the details.
5. here we will stay rather on the surface.

(a) Manual segmentation.

1. we'll give a brief sketch of the ideas of neural networks.
2. lets have a look at multilayer.
3. perceptrons you see that we talked about this here only about very basic concepts if you're interested in neural networks.
4. we have an entire class on deep learning where we talk about all the details.
5. here we will stay rather on the surface you may know that neural networks are extremely popular ....

(b) Base-model segmentation.

1. we'll give a brief sketch of the ideas of neural networks.
2. lets have a look at multilayer perceptrons.
3. you see that we talked about this here only about very basic concepts if you're interested in neural networks.
4. we have an entire class on deep learning where we talk about all the details.
5. here we will stay rather on the surface.

(c) Finetuned segmentation.

Fig. 2. Example predictions for sentence boundaries.

4.3   Keyword Extraction

After using ASR, keywords can be extracted from the spoken text. Keywords are extracted from transcripts using the unsupervised YAKE approach [3]. This approach was shown to be more effective than other unsupervised statistical methods such as term frequency-inverse document frequency (TF-IDF) [15]. The YAKE algorithm involves five steps: text pre-processing and candidate term identification, feature extraction, computing term score, n-gram generation and computing candidate keyword score and data deduplication and ranking. Before feeding our transcripts to the YAKE algorithm, we clean the texts by removing stop words, removing punctuation and lemmatising the remaining words. The top 5 keywords are extracted for each individual lecture. Examples of the extracted keyword results for four different lectures can be seen in Table 5.

Table 5. Top 5 keywords for 4 lectures in Autoblog 2020.

Kernel PCA	Laplacian SVM	Gradient Descent	LDA
kernel	vector	step	matrix
feature	decision	direction	covariance
vector	boundary	size	transform
time	laplacian	gradient	lambda
eigenvector	datum	function	compute

Looking at the keywords, we can see the YAKE algorithm accurately extracts what is expected from specific lecture topics. The kernel-PCA lecture contains keywords such as kernel, eigenvector, features. While the laplacian SVM and

Gradient Descent lectures contain relevant keywords such as decision boundary, laplacian, gradient, step. Similarly, keywords such as matrix, transform, lambda and covariance were extracted from the Linear Discriminant Analysis (LDA) lecture.

5   Discussion and Conclusion

The current paper introduces the video lecture corpus Autoblog 2020, which contains useful data for video lecture processing. The future goal with Autoblog is to produce blog-like versions of lecture content, and we have conduct several experiments to show how the data can be utilized.

First, we examine the WER for Pattern Recognition lectures using the features available in YouTube and our manual annotations, which obtained an average WER of 6.25%. Second, as ASR outputs do not contain full stops, we investigate the ability to train a neural network to predict sentence boundaries even with no punctuation. A base model trained on close to a million English sentences could segment sentences with an F1 score of 53%. Fine-tuning the model can achieve an F1 score up to 80.87%. Lastly, we extracted keywords from lecture transcripts using the unsupervised YAKE algorithm. The resulting output was consistent with what is expected given the lecture material.

In conclusion, we introduce a new lecture video corpus called Autoblog, designed to make the research contents more accessible and visible for students and researchers. In the future, more videos of full courses will be added, along with transcripts, PDF's of slides, raw unedited videos, and other data useful for processing lecture videos.

Acknowledgments. This work was supported by the Deutscher Akademischer Austauschdienst (DAAD) in the International Programmes Digital (IP Digital).

References

1. Afouras, T., Chung, J.S., Senior, A., Vinyals, O., Zisserman, A.: Deep audio-visual speech recognition. IEEE Trans. Pattern Anal. Mach. Intell. (2018)
2. Alberti, C., Bacchiani, M.: Automatic captioning in youtube (2009). https://ai.googleblog.com/2009/12/automatic-captioning-in-youtube.html. Accessed 09 June 2021
3. Campos, R., Mangaravite, V., Pasquali, A., Jorge, A., Nunes, C., Jatowt, A.: Yake! keyword extraction from single documents using multiple local features. Inf. Sci. **509**, 257–289 (2020)
4. Chen, Y.N., Huang, Y., Kong, S.Y., Lee, L.S.: Automatic key term extraction from spoken course lectures using branching entropy and prosodic/semantic features. In: 2010 IEEE Spoken Language Technology Workshop, pp. 265–270. IEEE (2010)
5. Handa, A., Agarwal, R., Kohli, N.: A multimodel keyword spotting system based on lip movement and speech features. Multimedia Tools Appl. **79**(27), 20461–20481 (2020)

6. Hernandez, F., Nguyen, V., Ghannay, S., Tomashenko, N., Estève, Y.: TED-LIUM 3: twice as much data and corpus repartition for experiments on speaker adaptation. In: Karpov, A., Jokisch, O., Potapova, R. (eds.) SPECOM 2018. LNCS (LNAI), vol. 11096, pp. 198–208. Springer, Cham (2018). https://doi.org/10.1007/978-3-319-99579-3_21

7. Kogure, S., Nishizaki, H., Tsuchiya, M., Yamamoto, K., Togashi, S., Nakagawa, S.: Speech recognition performance of CJLC: corpus of Japanese lecture contents. In: Ninth Annual Conference of the International Speech Communication Association (2008)

8. Koka, R.S., Chowdhury, F.N., Rahman, M.R., Solorio, T., Subhlok, J.: Automatic identification of keywords in lecture video segments. In: 2020 IEEE International Symposium on Multimedia (ISM), pp. 162–165. IEEE (2020)

9. Lee, G.C., Yeh, F.-H., Chen, Y.-J., Chang, T.-K.: Robust handwriting extraction and lecture video summarization. Multimedia Tools Appl. **76**(5), 7067–7085 (2016). https://doi.org/10.1007/s11042-016-3353-y

10. Momeni, L., Afouras, T., Stafylakis, T., Albanie, S., Zisserman, A.: Seeing wake words: audio-visual keyword spotting. In: The 31st British Machine Vision Conference (2020)

11. Park, A., Hazen, T.J., Glass, J.R.: Automatic processing of audio lectures for information retrieval: vocabulary selection and language modeling. In: Proceedings (ICASSP 2005) IEEE International Conference on Acoustics, Speech, and Signal Processing, vol. 1, pp. I-497. IEEE (2005)

12. Pennington, J., Socher, R., Manning, C.D.: Glove: global vectors for word representation. In: Proceedings of the 2014 Conference on Empirical Methods in Natural Language Processing (EMNLP), pp. 1532–1543 (2014)

13. Petridis, S., Stafylakis, T., Ma, P., Cai, F., Tzimiropoulos, G., Pantic, M.: End-to-end audiovisual speech recognition. In: 2018 IEEE International Conference on Acoustics, Speech and Signal Processing (ICASSP), pp. 6548–6552. IEEE (2018)

14. Raine, P.: Building sentences with web 2.0 and the tatoeba database. Accents Asia **10**(2), 2–7 (2018)

15. Salton, G., McGill, M.J.: Introduction to modern information retrieval (1986)

16. Schwarz, M., Scherrer, A., Hohmann, C., Heiberg, J., Brugger, A., Nuñez-Jimenez, A.: COVID-19 and the academy: it is time for going digital. Energy Res. Soc. Sci. **68**, 101684 (2020)

17. Shimada, A., Okubo, F., Yin, C., Ogata, H.: Automatic summarization of lecture slides for enhanced student preview technical report and user study. IEEE Trans. Learn. Technol. **11**(2), 165–178 (2017)

18. Subudhi, B.N., Veerakumar, T., Yadav, D., Suryavanshi, A.P., Disha, S.: Video skimming for lecture video sequences using histogram based low level features. In: 2017 IEEE 7th International Advance Computing Conference (IACC), pp. 684–689. IEEE (2017)

19. Tao, F., Busso, C.: End-to-end audiovisual speech recognition system with multi-task learning. IEEE Trans. Multimedia **23**, 1–11 (2020)

20. Trancoso, I., Martins, R., Moniz, H., Mata, A.I., Viana, M.C.: The lectra corpus-classroom lecture transcriptions in European portuguese. Econ. Theor. **1**(17), 15-1 (2008)

21. Tsuchiya, M., Kogure, S., Nishizaki, H., Ohta, K., Nakagawa, S.: Developing corpus of Japanese classroom lecture speech contents. In: LREC (2008)

Text and Synthetic Data for Domain Adaptation in End-to-End Speech Recognition

Juan Hussain[1]([✉]), Christian Huber[1], Sebastian Stüker[1],
and Alexander Waibel[1,2]

[1] Interactive Systems Lab, Karlsruhe Institute of Technology, Karlsruhe, Germany
{juan.hussain,sebastian.stueker}@partner.kit.edu,
{christian.huber,alexander.waibel}@kit.edu
[2] Carnegie Mellon University, Pittsburgh, PA, USA
alexander.waibel@cmu.edu

Abstract. Neural sequence-to-sequence systems deliver state-of-the-art performance for automatic speech recognition (ASR). When training such systems, one often faces the situation where sufficient amounts of training data for the language in question are available, however, with only small amounts of data for the domain in question. This problem is even bigger for end-to-end speech recognition systems that only accept transcribed speech as training data, which is harder and more expensive to obtain than text data. To alleviate this problem we supplement an end-to-end ASR system with a Text-Encoder which injects text-only input directly into the decoder. In addition, we compare the performance of using text-only input with synthetic speech. Furthermore, we prove for a specific domain that using a very small amount of transcribed speech and a sufficient amount of text-only data from the target domain outperforms adapting with a large amount of domain transcribed speech. Finally, we improve with the Text-Encoder learning new words, e.g., named entities, with no need for any context.

Keywords: Speech recognition · Domain adaptation · Text-encoder

1 Introduction

Lately, end-to-end approaches to automatic speech recognition (ASR) have started to outperform traditional Bayes Classifier based approaches that used neural networks to estimate the emission probabilities of Hidden Markov Models for acoustic modeling and n-gram models for language modeling. The end-to-end approaches can be roughly divided into CTC [8], RNN-T [7] and Sequence-to-Sequence (S2S) [2] models. In this work we will focus on Sequence-to-Sequence models.

S2S models can be adapted to a new domain, given large amounts of transcribed speech data. If such data is not available in sufficient amounts, the question arises how adaptation can be done anyway. One common case is the availability of a small

© Springer Nature Switzerland AG 2021
A. Karpov and R. Potapova (Eds.): SPECOM 2021, LNAI 12997, pp. 271–278, 2021.
https://doi.org/10.1007/978-3-030-87802-3_25

amount of transcribed speech and sufficient amounts of text-only data for the target domain.

In this paper we present experiments with a chosen domain where small amounts of transcribed audio is insufficient for achieving a well-performing adaptation, as we will see in Sect. 4.1. We use additional textual data from the target domain either in conjunction with a multi speaker text-to-speech (TTS) systems (Sect. 3.3) or with a Text-Encoder (Sect. 3.4). Furthermore, we combine the textual domain data with the transcribed speech data from the target domain (Sect. 4.3). Finally, we also experiment with the Text-Encoder for learning new words, e.g., named entities where no context is provided. We introduce the method in Sect. 4.3.

2   Related Work

In our previous work [10] we adapted an S2S ASR system with a small amount of domain transcribed speech using a batch weighting scheme, in order to avoid the problem of catastrophic forgetting during adaptation. The amount of data was sufficient to achieve satisfying results, however, applying the method for other domains with wider language variability yielded insufficient performance. Our work in this paper focuses on enhancing the adaption with text-only data using a Text-Encoder. Several previous works used text input for speech recognition, however, the scenarios considered where different from ours. [11] used text data for semi-supervised learning. The speech and Text-Encoder is shared and supplied with a sub-sampling layer for speech to achieve a similar dimensionality as text. In [4], a separate encoder for text is employed for low resource speech recognition. Adversarial training is used to increase the similarity between speech and text features. Other work employed synthetic audio, as in [21]. They show that the method improves the recognition for utterances with out-of-vocabulary (OOV) words. Other related works enhances the model by re-scoring the output with a language model via two pass decoding. [16] incorporated a multi corpora language model for second pass re-scoring, while [5] and [18] re-score with a second model by attending to the audio or as in [9], in which the second model attends to both the audio and the output using a deliberation model.

3   Method and Training

3.1   Baseline

As our baseline system we use a long short-term memory (LSTM) based sequence-to-sequence model [14]. The encoder consists of six layers, the decoder of two. Before the encoder, two convolutional neural network (CNN) layers with 32 filters and a stride of two are used to down-sample the audio features. The LSTM-layers of the encoder and the decoder have a model dimension of 1024. As output vocabulary, we use a byte-pair encoding (BPE) [20] with 4000 tokens trained on the training data.

3.2   Training and Domain Data

The baseline model is trained on the HOW2 [19] and TED [17] data sets (see Table 1). For the adaptation of the model we use the Wall Street Journal (WSJ) data set [6,13]. As text-only data from the Wall Street Journal domain we use [12] and refer to this data set as TXT-WSJ. It contains two million lines of text data. The validation and test set for the baseline (HOW2+TED) and for the target domain (WSJ) can be seen in Table 1.

3.3   Synthesized Speech

For the TTS system we use Flite [1]. We synthesized audio from the TXT-WSJ data and refer to this as Synthetic TXT-WSJ. Thereby we select for each sentence one of 16 different speakers to obtain speaker variability.

Table 1. Summary of the English speech data-sets.

Corpus	Speech data	Utterances
How2+Ted training set	789 h	473K
How2+Ted validation set	18.3 h	11K
WSJ training set	80 h	36k
WSJ validation set	3.2 h	1421
Synthetic TXT-WSJ training set	4500 h	2M
Ted test set	2.6 h	1155
WSJ test set	1.1 h	503

3.4   Text-Encoder

In the following sections we describe the Text-Encoder model as well as the training process for the domain adaptation or learning new words with no context.

Model Architecture. While in [11] one encoder is used for both text and speech, we use a separate encoder for each input as Fig. 1 shows. We take the speech encoder and the decoder from our pre-trained baseline ASR model. The Text-Encoder has a simple architecture consisting of an LSTM-layer followed by a deconvolution layer [15] followed again by an LSTM-layer. Since the length of the text token sequence is much shorter than the speech feature sequence length, we use a deconvolution layer to up-sample the input features. The up-sampling maps the text token sequence to a higher dimensionality similar in length to the speech feature sequence. Thereby, we aim to produce a similar features presentation to the one generated by the speech encoder.

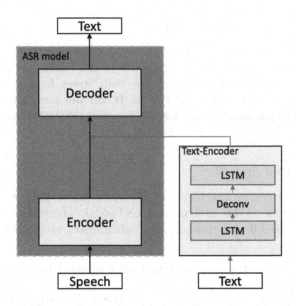

Fig. 1. Model architecture. Left: Baseline ASR model. Right: Text-Encoder architecture in detail.

Training of the Text-Encoder for Domain Adaptation. We alternate the training between two cases:

- In the first case, the Text-Encoder is trained with frozen decoder until saturation. We input noised text sequences from a large text corpus to the Text-Encoder and reconstruct the clean sequences by the frozen decoder. The noise we use is applied by masking tokens (substitute them with the masking token) with a probability of 0.2 (similar to [3]).
- In the second case, we train the Text-Encoder and the decoder on both text and speech inputs. In this case we freeze the speech encoder. We apply one pass from the Text-Encoder and one pass from the speech encoder, accumulate the gradient and update the parameters after reaching about 12000 input text tokens.

The reason for freezing the speech encoder in the second case is that we noticed degradation in the performance as the decoder was trying to adapt the speech encoder to generate similar features as the Text-Encoder. Our baseline speech encoder was already trained thoroughly and reached a satisfying level of abstraction for speech features. Therefore, compromises with the Text-Encoder do not benefit the model, instead harm the general performance of it. Besides, using a discriminator for adversarial training as in [4] for motivating the speech encoder to generate a similar output to Text-Encoder was not of advantage in our case. Our suggestion is that we have a different case than in [4]. They train a system for low-resourced-language i.e. very few transcribed speech data are available to reach a well trained speech encoder. In our case we have enough speech data and could reach a very good performing baseline as mentioned above. Our speech encoder is able to reach a sufficient abstraction on general domain.

Training of the Text-Encoder for New-Word Learning. We try to use the Text-Encoder to approach the problem of the new words or words not seen during the training (also known as Out-of-Vocabulary Problem OOV). We assume that those words.

We take the parallel training set which we used for training the baseline. From this set we take only the text. In each text utterance, we insert a word from the new-word list in a random place. We avoid to place the tokens of new words between tokens of a single word in the training utterance. Thereafter, we train the model using this text data with the Text-Encoder. Each time we insert the words in a new random location in order to avoid harming the language model learned by the decoder with fixed not real contexts.

Similar to the training for domain adaption above, we noise the text input of the Text-Encoder. The difference here is that the text is supplied with randomly inserted new words we want to recognize. We noticed here that adding more noise yields better results. Therefore, We mask with the probability 0.3 instead of 0.2 and insert random tokens to the input with the probability of 0.3 within tokens of the training text.

It is worth to mention that we employ here only the transcription of the training set and not big text corpora, to study the effect of our method without adding additional information.

4   Results

4.1   Basic Adaptation Methods

To examine our methods of domain adaptation using text data or synthetic data, we first employ the conventional adapting methods, such as, fine-tuning and batch-weighting [10]. Fine-tuning yields good performance on the new domain but the model suffers from catastrophic forgetting (Table 2). For the rest of the experiments we use batch-weighting with ratio 0.9 for the original training data and 0.1 for the new domain data. From Table 2 we notice that adapting with 80 hours of data (experiment Batch-Weighting-80) obviously outperforms adapting with only two hours (experiment Batch-Weighting-02).

4.2   Comparison Synthetic Speech and Text-Encoder

Using the Synthetic TXT-WSJ dataset to adapt the model (experiment Batch-Weighting (Synthesis)) improves over the baseline as well as over the approach using only texts from new domain (experiment Batch-Weighting (Text-Encoder)). Another Experiment (Batch-Weighting (Synthesis + Text-Encoder)) shows comparable results. Despite the slight improvement of the above mentioned methods, we are still far from the results of using additional transcribed audio (Sect. 4.1 and 4.3).

We also tried to use a separate encoder for the synthetic audio initialized with the encoder of the baseline. However, these experiments did not show improvements over using one encoder for both the synthetic and the real audio.

4.3 Results with Text-Encoder

Result for Domain Adaption. Remarkably, the results of using two hours (experiment Batch-Weighting-02 (Text-Encoder)) and 80 hours (experiment Batch-Weighting-80 (Text-Encoder)) WSJ are comparable in the case of injecting the decoder with the additional large new domain texts from TXT-WSJ using Text-Encoder (Sect. 3.3). Our interpretation is that only little amount of data is needed for the speech encoder to capture and adapt towards speech features of the new domain. Such features might be the recording channel characteristics or the speaking style. Moreover, the decoder adaptation needs language characteristics of the new domain, which is achievable only with a large text data set, such as, the two million lines TXT-WSJ.

Table 2. Summary of the results.

Method	Additional data	WER Ted	WER WSJ
Baseline	–	7.40	12.60
Fine-tuning	WSJ-80 h	10.27	5.55
Batch-Weighting-80	WSJ-80 h	7.33	5.51
Batch-Weighting-02	WSJ-2 h	7.80	8.54
Batch-Weighting (Synthesis)	Synthetic TXT-WSJ	**7.35**	9.51
Batch-Weighting (Text-Encoder)	TXT-WSJ	7.48	11.34
Batch-Weighting (Synthesis + Text-Encoder)	Synthetic TXT-WSJ + TXT-WSJ	7.54	**9.22**
Batch-Weighting-80 (Synthesis)	WSJ-80 h + Synthetic TXT-WSJ	7.21	**4.74**
Batch-Weighting-80 (Text-Encoder)	WSJ-80 h + TXT-WSJ	6.98	4.89
Batch-Weighting-02 (Text-Encoder)	WSJ-2 h + TXT-WSJ	**6.83**	4.85

Result for New Words. We experimented the Text-Encoder for learning new words problems as described in Sect. 4.3. A set of 69 words containing mainly named entities. For the test we put the names in a context and recorded them. The baseline model recognizes only 15.9% percent of the new words. After training with the Text-Encoder we obtain 43.5% accuracy of the new word. The WER of the baseline 32.1% is also reduced by the Text-Encoder to 27.1%. Furthermore, the model does not loose the generality as the WER on the TED test-set remains the same.

5 Conclusion

In this work we extend our previous work on domain adaptation with batch-weighting to domains with language variability that need larger amounts of transcribed speech from the target domain. We examined using textual data directly either with a supplemented Text-Encoder or after synthesizing it with a multi-speakers TTS system. We obtain better results with synthesizing text if we do not employ transcribed data from the target domain. However, the results are comparable when using only a small amount of transcribed speech from the target domain. Furthermore, we notice that the performance equalizes when using small or large amount of transcribed speech data as long as we use enough amounts of textual data. The reason might be that the system is able to capture sufficient information from a small amount of transcribed data related to the audio and speaking characteristics. However, the system looks for language modeling information in the large amount textual data. In addition, we were able to improve the recognition of OOV without using additional context. In future works, we will focus on the training mechanism and the model structure of the Text-Encoder to achieve at least the performance of multi-speaker synthesis in scenarios in which no transcribed speech data is available. Furthermore, we will experiment to extract the audio and speaking characteristics with even smaller amounts of transcribed speech from the target domain. For the OOV problem, we will experiment to insert the words in large text corpus or generate contexts for the new-words.

References

1. Black, A.W., Lenzo, K.A.: Flite: a small fast run-time synthesis engine. In: 4th ISCA Tutorial and Research Workshop (ITRW) on Speech Synthesis (2001)
2. Chorowski, J., Bahdanau, D., Serdyuk, D., Cho, K., Bengio, Y.: Attention-based models for speech recognition. arXiv preprint arXiv:1506.07503 (2015)
3. Devlin, J., Chang, M.W., Lee, K., Toutanova, K.: BERT: pre-training of deep bidirectional transformers for language understanding. arXiv preprint arXiv:1810.04805 (2018)
4. Drexler, J., Glass, J.: Combining end-to-end and adversarial training for low-resource speech recognition. In: 2018 IEEE Spoken Language Technology Workshop (SLT), pp. 361–368. IEEE (2018)
5. Gandhe, A., Rastrow, A.: Audio-attention discriminative language model for ASR rescoring. In: ICASSP 2020–2020 IEEE International Conference on Acoustics, Speech and Signal Processing (ICASSP), pp. 7944–7948. IEEE (2020)
6. Garofolo, J.S., Graff, D., Paul, D., David, P.: CSR-I (WSJ0) Sennheiser LDC93S6B. https://doi.org/10.35111/ap42-7n83
7. Graves, A.: Sequence transduction with recurrent neural networks. arXiv preprint arXiv:1211.3711 (2012)
8. Graves, A., Fernández, S., Gomez, F., Schmidhuber, J.: Connectionist temporal classification: labelling unsegmented sequence data with recurrent neural networks. In: Proceedings of the 23rd International Conference on Machine Learning, pp. 369–376 (2006)
9. Hu, K., Sainath, T.N., Pang, R., Prabhavalkar, R.: Deliberation model based two-pass end-to-end speech recognition. In: ICASSP 2020–2020 IEEE International Conference on Acoustics, Speech and Signal Processing (ICASSP), pp. 7799–7803. IEEE (2020)

10. Huber, C., Hussain, J., Nguyen, T.N., Song, K., Stüker, S., Waibel, A.: Supervised adaptation of sequence-to-sequence speech recognition systems using batch-weighting. In: Proceedings of the 2nd Workshop on Life-long Learning for Spoken Language Systems, pp. 9–17 (2020)
11. Karita, S., Watanabe, S., Iwata, T., Ogawa, A., Delcroix, M.: Semi-supervised end-to-end speech recognition. In: Interspeech, pp. 2–6 (2018)
12. Linguistic Data Consortium: ACL/DCI LDC93T1. https://doi.org/10.35111/vdfv-av77
13. Linguistic Data Consortium, NIST Multimodal Information Group: CSR-II (WSJ1) Sennheiser LDC94S13B. https://doi.org/10.35111/5jkw-xt28
14. Nguyen, T.S., Stueker, S., Niehues, J., Waibel, A.: Improving sequence-to-sequence speech recognition training with on-the-fly data augmentation. In: ICASSP 2020–2020 IEEE International Conference on Acoustics, Speech and Signal Processing (ICASSP), pp. 7689–7693. IEEE (2020)
15. Noh, H., Hong, S., Han, B.: Learning deconvolution network for semantic segmentation. In: Proceedings of the IEEE International Conference on Computer Vision, pp. 1520–1528 (2015)
16. Raju, A., Filimonov, D., Tiwari, G., Lan, G., Rastrow, A.: Scalable multi corpora neural language models for ASR. arXiv preprint arXiv:1907.01677 (2019)
17. Rousseau, A., Deléglise, P., Esteve, Y.: TED-LIUM: an automatic speech recognition dedicated corpus. In: LREC, pp. 125–129 (2012)
18. Sainath, T.N., et al.: Two-pass end-to-end speech recognition. arXiv preprint arXiv:1908.10992 (2019)
19. Sanabria, R., et al.: How2: a large-scale dataset for multimodal language understanding. arXiv preprint arXiv:1811.00347 (2018)
20. Sennrich, R., Haddow, B., Birch, A.: Neural machine translation of rare words with subword units. arXiv preprint arXiv:1508.07909 (2015)
21. Zheng, X., Liu, Y., Gunceler, D., Willett, D.: Using synthetic audio to improve the recognition of out-of-vocabulary words in end-to-end ASR systems. In: ICASSP 2021–2021 IEEE International Conference on Acoustics, Speech and Signal Processing (ICASSP), pp. 5674–5678. IEEE (2021)

Speaker-Invariant Speech-to-Intent Classification for Low-Resource Languages

Anosha Ignatius[✉] and Uthayasanker Thayasivam

University of Moratuwa, Moratuwa, Sri Lanka
anoshai@uom.lk

Abstract. Deep Neural Networks based speech embedding techniques have delivered significant results in speech processing applications such as automatic speech recognition and spoken intent detection systems. Still, the presence of para-linguistic information such as speaker characteristics, accent, pronunciation, and emotional expression cause performance degradation in speech tasks where only the linguistic content is required. Over time many techniques have been proposed to address this problem by disentangling the underlying para-linguistic content from the speech signal. The most common approach is to incorporate speaker representations in speech recognition systems. However, it has been less studied for speech intent identification and these speech recognition models require large amounts of labeled training data. In the case of low resource languages, when only a limited amount of data is available, transfer learning approach is adopted. In this paper, we present a speech-to-intent classification model with i-vector based speaker normalization evaluated on Sinhala, and Tamil speech intent datasets. We explore the use of pretrained acoustic models to address the problem of data scarcity. Experimental results show that the proposed approach is effective in improving the performance of the speech intent classification system.

Keywords: Speech recognition · Para-linguistic information · Speaker characteristics · Low-resource languages

1 Introduction

Spoken intent detection has gained a high research interest in the field of speech processing. A number of recent studies [4,17,28] have yielded promising results with the development of Deep Neural Network (DNN) based models and the availability of large amounts of training data. However, their performance can be greatly compromised due to a mismatch between testing and training conditions. It is because they are subjected to variations in the speaking manner caused by speaker characteristics, emotional expressions, and environmental differences. This type of information present in speech signals beyond the verbal content is referred to as para-linguistic information. Therefore, carrying out extensive research on this area is of great importance for developing techniques

© Springer Nature Switzerland AG 2021
A. Karpov and R. Potapova (Eds.): SPECOM 2021, LNAI 12997, pp. 279–290, 2021.
https://doi.org/10.1007/978-3-030-87802-3_26

that compensate for the speaker variability and improve the robustness of the speech-to-intent systems. The challenge in building a speech-to-intent system that is robust against speaker variability is that it requires a large amount of labeled training data. Further, the training data should cover speakers from a wide range of ages and accents but the available datasets failed to do so. Under low resource conditions where a significant amount of labeled training data is not available, it is difficult to separate linguistically irrelevant speaker information encoded in the speech features and it could lead to poor generalization of the model. This is because, supervised acoustic modeling relies on large amounts of transcribed speech data to ensure robustness against speaker variability.

DNN based speech embedding models are generally trained using acoustic feature vectors representing both the time domain and frequency domain information in the speech signal. Acoustic feature vectors are extracted using various feature extraction techniques such as Mel Frequency Cepstral Coefficients (MFCC) [37], Linear Predictive Codes (LPC) [1] and Perceptual Linear Prediction (PLP) [19]. Existing solutions for normalizing the speaker variations incorporate speaker information by augmenting the acoustic features with speaker representing vectors. This helps in disentangling the underlying speaker information in the speech signal by learning better representations. Vectors representing the speaker-specific information are obtained by mapping the variable-length speech utterance to a fixed dimensional vector. Prior studies have explored mainly two types of such techniques: i-vector approach [32] and DNN based speaker embedding [31,33]. By providing speaker representations to the DNN as additional input features, DNNs are trained to be aware of the presence of speaker information. This approach is referred to as speaker aware training and it enables the acoustic model to normalize speaker effects, thus leading to a better generalization of the model to unseen conditions.

Several studies have investigated speaker aware training methods to remove speaker related information from the speech signal while retaining the linguistic content in DNN based ASR models [10,13,25,30,35]. Though speaker normalization techniques for ASR systems have been investigated for many years, it has been less studied in speech-to-intent models even for high resource languages. To our knowledge, only Tomashenko et al. [34] have conducted research on speaker adaptation for end-to-end Spoken Language Understanding (SLU) models. In the case of a low resource scenario, unsupervised speech representations that separate speaker traits from linguistic content have been experimented to address the problem of data scarcity [7–9]. Such representations learnt with an available large data set of unlabeled speech recordings can be used in downstream applications like speech intent classification with only a small amount of labeled training data through transfer learning approach.

In this paper, we explore speech intent classification with speaker normalization for low resource settings using Sinhala and Tamil Languages dataset. We present an i-vector based speaker normalization with transfer learning for speech intent classification of Sinhala and Tamil speech data. Experimental results show that incorporating the i-vectors to compensate for the speaker variability is effective in improving the recognition accuracy. The rest of the paper is organized as follows: Sect. 2 reviews the related work on speaker normalisation and unsupervised speech representation learning. Section 3 describes the methodology used in our approach. We detail the experimental setup and the datasets used in Sect. 4. Section 5 presents a detailed analysis of the obtained results. Finally, the paper is concluded in Sect. 6.

2 Related Work

Acoustic DNN models can be made invariant to speaker variability by providing speaker information. Speaker information can be modelled using speaker representing vectors. Speaker vectors encode long-term speaker traits and states that are difficult to learn with acoustic models using short-term features. Long-term speaker traits include biological trait primitives such as height, weight, age, gender, ethnicity, culture, and personality. i-vector is an effective method to map a variable-length speech segment to a low dimensional representation that captures speaker characteristics. i-vectors have been extensively used in speaker identification and verification tasks. i-vectors are also used for speaker normalization in ASR systems where augmenting the acoustic features with i-vectors transforms the input features to a speaker normalized space. Speaker representating vectors can also be extracted using DNN based embedding techniques where a DNN is trained to discriminate between speaker classes and the speaker representing vectors are extracted at the bottleneck layer. Recent DNN embeddings such as x-vectors [33] and h-vectors [31] achieved better performance in speaker identification and verification tasks. These vectors are not generally used for speaker normalisation since experiments have not shown consistent improvements in performance when compared with i-vectors.

Feature augmentation techniques include directly appending the speaker vectors to acoustic features and providing transformed features to the DNN during training. It helps the DNN learn to normalize the speaker effects, thereby improving the performance. The conventional i-vector based augmentation method uses i-vectors as additional input features that are concatenated with the acoustic features. Providing speaker information at the input enables the DNN to normalize the signal and make it invariant to speaker effects [30,35]. Sri Garimella et al. proposed passing the i-vectors through a nonlinear hidden layer before combining them with the acoustic features [13]. Using a nonlinear hidden layer to transform the i-vectors showed improvement over directly appending them to the acoustic features.

Two types of feature mapping neural networks ivecNN and adaptNN are presented in the paper by Miao et al. where i-vectors are used as additional inputs to project acoustic features into a speaker normalized space [25]. In ivecNN, a bias vector is estimated and added to the original features making the resulting feature space speaker-independent. In adaptNN, multiple adaptation layers are used under the initial DNN acoustic model where each adaptation layer except the last one appends the i-vector to its output. Experimental results showed that these two networks achieve better performance over the original DNN. Xiaodong

Cui et al. proposed an embedding-based speaker adaptive training approach [10] where speaker vectors are mapped to layer dependent element-wise affine transformations through a control network. The resulting affine transformations are applied to the internal feature representations at the outputs of the selected hidden layers in the acoustic model to facilitate speaker normalization.

Speaker Aware Speech Transformer, a standard speech transformer [36] with a speaker attention module (SAM) is presented in the paper by Zhiyun Fan et al. [11]. SAM includes a speaker knowledge block that consists of a group of i-vectors extracted from the training data. Given a speech utterance, the similarity of the acoustic feature vector and each i-vector from the group of basic speakers in the speaker knowledge block is computed with the attention mechanism to obtain the weight for each basic i-vector. The soft speaker embedding is extracted as the weighted sum of the basic i-vectors and a weighted combined speaker embedding vector is fed to the decoder. This helps the model to normalize the speaker variations and leads to better generalization to unseen test speakers. A similar approach where the attention mechanism is used to select the relevant speaker i-vectors for each frame from the memory is proposed by Jia Pan et al. [27]. Speaker-aware speech transformers proved to be more effective than other feature augmentation techniques using i-vectors.

Under low resource settings, unsupervised learning method uses large amounts of unlabeled data to learn useful speech representations that can be incorporated into several downstream applications. Autoencoder is one such network that involves the reconstruction of its inputs. It consists of an encoding network that extracts a latent representation and a decoding network that tries to reconstruct the original data using the latent representation. By applying constraints, the network is made to learn a latent representation that discards irrelevant para-linguistic information while preserving the information necessary for perfect reconstruction. Factorized Hierarchical Variational Autoencoder (FHVAE) [16] is proposed by Wei-Ning Hsu et al. to learn disentangled representations from sequential data. It can be used to separate linguistic content and speaker information in speech signals in an unsupervised way. The FHVAE learns to factorize sequence-level (speaker information) and segment-level (phonetic content) attributes of speech into different latent variables [12,15]. Jan Chorowski et al. presented a Vector Quantized Variational Autoencoder (VQ-VAE) that learns a representation to capture high-level semantic content while being invariant to the underlying speaker information by conditioning the decoder on speaker identity [6]. VQ-VAE yielded a significant performance in the phonetic unit discovery task indicating a better separation between phonetic content and speaker information.

Another unsupervised objective, Auto-regressive Predictive Coding (APC) [7–9] proposed by Yu-An Chung et al. can be used as a pre-training approach for learning meaningful speech representations. It is trained to predict the spectrum of future frames n steps ahead of the current one using the past values to infer more global structures in speech. Experiments conducted using intermediate representations obtained from the APC model indicate that different levels of speech information are captured by the APC model at different layers. Lower layers contain more speaker information while the upper layers provide more phonetic content. A combination of the internal representations extracted across different layers could be beneficial in learning disentangled representations for speech recognition tasks. In speech processing, APC and other unsupervised acoustic features such as wav2vec [29], Mockingjay [23], Tera [22], audio Albert [5], and NPC [21] have been applied for tasks such as phoneme recognition, automatic speech recognition, speaker recognition, speech to text translation and Spoken Language Understanding (SLU). Edmilson et al. conducted SLU experiments for predicting intent and entity labels and the results showed that wav2vec outperforms filterbank features [26]. The aforementioned research studies show that unsupervised learning methods can be effectively applied to large amounts of unlabeled data to extract speaker invariant features that help in improving the robustness of low resource speech recognition systems.

3   Methodology

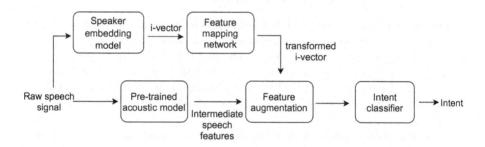

Fig. 1. Architecture of the proposed model.

In Sect. 2, we showed that using i-vectors to augment the acoustic features is beneficial in building speaker invariant acoustic models. Additionally, unsupervised speech representations have been found to be effective in many speech processing applications. Therefore, our basic idea is to use transfer learning approach, where we make use of an acoustic model pre-trained on a high resource language data to extract feature representations for low resource language speech data. In order to compensate for the speaker effects, we augment these features with i-vectors extracted at the utterance level. Speaker i-vectors are passed through a feature mapping network which consists of multiple fully connected layers with sigmoid activation function and an output layer with rectified linear activation function. The transformed i-vectors are then appended to the features extracted using pre-trained models. The output is then fed to the intent classifier to predict the intent of the given speech utterance. Figure 1 shows the architecture of the proposed model.

4 Experiment

In this work, we experimented with four separate feature representations listed below, each of them pre-trained on English speech data to generate feature representations for speech intent data. We selected two ASR models used in the work by Yohan et al. [17,18] and two self-supervised features since their efficacy has been proved in SLU tasks.

1. Character probability representation
2. Phoneme probability representation
3. Autoregressive Predictive Coding (APC)
4. Non-autoregressive predictive Coding (NPC)

We built intent classifier models with these features and compared their performance with the combined feature augmentation with i-vectors. We used SIDEKIT toolkit [20] for i-vector extraction. The i-vector extractor generates a 100 dimensional i-vector using MFCCs as input features.

4.1 ASR Intermediate Representations

As presented in [17,18] we used the DeepSpeech model [2,14] which has been trained on the Common Voice American English corpus to extract the character probability representation. Deepspeech model is trained to predict the text transcription for a given sequence of acoustic features. MFCCs are used as input features and the model converts them into a sequence of character probabilities. The optimal transcript is obtained using the probabilities through beam search algorithm.

To get phoneme probability representation, we used the end-to-end SLU model of Lugosch et al. [24] which has been pre-trained on the LibriSpeech English corpus. The model is first pre-trained to predict words and phonemes, and then trained on the end-to-end SLU task discarding the word and phoneme classifiers. We selected phoneme probabilities which are used as intermediate pre-training targets in this model to generate input features for our intent classification task.

4.2 Self-supervised Features

APC and NPC representations are extracted using self-supervised learning methods as mentioned in Sect. 2. To derive high-level feature representations, APC incorporates an autoregressive model that predicts future frame that is n steps ahead of input frame while NPC tries to predict the input depending on the neighbors within the receptive field without using the autoregressive property. We extracted these self-supervised features using APC and NPC models pre-trained on the LibriSpeech English corpus.

4.3 Dataset

Table 1. Details of the Dataset (I - Number of inflections, S - Number of samples).

Intent	Sinhala		Tamil	
	I	S	I	S
Request Acc. balance	8	1712	7	101
Money deposit	7	1306	7	75
Money withdraw	8	1548	5	62
Bill payments	5	1004	4	46
Money transfer	7	1271	4	49
Credit card payments	4	795	4	67
Total	39	7624	31	400
Size in hours	7.5		0.5	

To evaluate the performance of the proposed approach, we used Sinhala and Tamil speech intent dataset [3] which contains Sinhala and Tamil speech recordings of six intents related to the banking domain. All the audio recordings have been collected through mobile phones via crowdsourcing. The Sinhala dataset consists of 7624 samples, that is 7.5 h of speech data from 215 speakers including both male and female speakers while the Tamil dataset consists of 400 samples, that is 0.5 h of speech data from 40 speakers. The length of each audio recording is less than 7 s. Table 1 shows the details of the dataset.

5 Results

We split the initial dataset into training and testing sets with a train-test split ratio of 80:20 and employed 5-fold cross-validation to measure the overall classification accuracy. The results obtained on the test sets for each language are presented in Table 2. It shows a comparison of average accuracy values between approaches without using and with using i-vectors.

Table 2. Average accuracy values obtained for 4 different intent classification models trained with Sinhala and Tamil speech dataset.

Dataset	Character Prob		Phoneme Prob		APC		NPC	
	Without i-vectors	With i-vectors	Without i-vectors	With i-vectors	Without i-vectors	With i-vectors	Without i-vectors	With i-vectors
Sinhala speech intent dataset	0.81	0.83	0.92	0.93	0.97	**0.98**	0.93	0.94
Tamil speech intent dataset	0.32	0.44	0.49	**0.51**	0.25	0.43	0.25	0.46

Incorporating the speaker information using i-vectors has resulted in slightly improved performance in all the four models compared. Even though the improvement is minor, we can clearly observe it in all four models. It indicates that the proposed method of augmenting acoustic features is more effective in predicting intents than the previous approaches. The highest accuracy of 98 % is achieved for Sinhala dataset when NPC features are combined with the i-vectors and it has outperformed the results obtained in the previous work [17]. We can see that the unsupervised pre-trained acoustic features further improve the performance. However, phoneme probability features achieved the highest accuracy of 51 % for Tamil dataset.

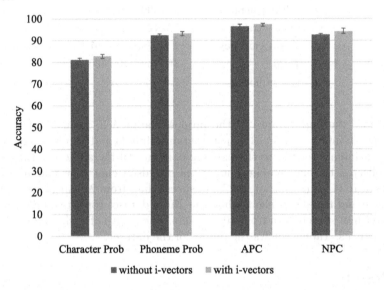

Fig. 2. Plot of average accuracy with standard deviation for 5-fold cross validation (Sinhala dataset).

Figure 2 plots the average test accuracy for the four models evaluated on the Sinhala speech dataset and the error bar shows the standard deviation for 5-fold cross validation. It shows that there is an improvement in accuracy with minimal variance when using features augmented with i-vectors.

Table 3. Comparison of F1 scores obtained for each intent in Sinhala speech dataset.

Intent	Character Prob		Phoneme Prob		APC		NPC	
	Without i-vectors	With i-vectors	Without i-vectors	With i-vectors	Without i-vectors	With i-vectors	Without i-vectors	With i-vectors
Request Acc. balance	0.91	0.95	0.98	0.98	0.99	0.99	0.95	0.97
Money deposit	0.77	0.77	0.89	0.92	0.96	0.97	0.94	0.93
Money withdraw	0.76	0.79	0.87	0.90	0.96	0.97	0.91	0.90
Bill payments	0.74	0.78	0.90	0.91	0.94	0.96	0.90	0.89
Money transfer	0.86	0.88	0.95	0.97	0.99	0.98	0.96	0.98
Credit card payments	0.81	0.77	0.91	0.89	0.96	0.97	0.92	0.93
Average	**0.810**	**0.824**	**0.917**	**0.930**	**0.966**	**0.974**	**0.930**	**0.934**

Table 3 shows the detailed results of the Sinhala dataset with F1-score values for each intent for the four models and their relative comparison with the speaker normalized ones. In the best performing model with APC features, all classes achieve more than 0.96 F1-score. Type 1 intent shows the highest F1-score among all. Type 6 intent also reports 0.97 f1-score even with a lower number of data samples. These results clearly demonstrate the effectiveness of our proposed approach of i-vector based feature augmentation and using self-supervised features for speech intent classification.

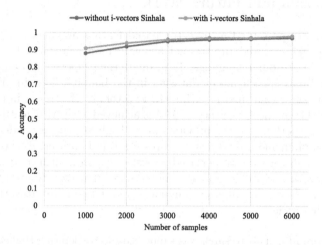

Fig. 3. Plot of accuracy variation with training data size for intent classification with APC features (Sinhala dataset).

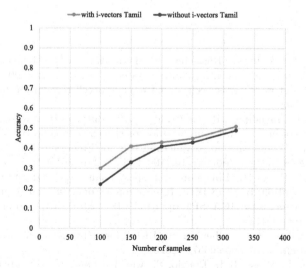

Fig. 4. Plot of accuracy variation with training data size for intent classification with phoneme probability features (Tamil dataset).

Accuracy values for the best performing model for varying sizes of training data are plotted in Fig. 3 and Fig. 4 for Sinhala and Tamil datasets respectively. We can observe that the accuracy achieved for the model with i-vectors is always higher than that for the model without i-vectors regardless of the training data size. Further, the large difference observed at low number of samples indicate that the i-vector based speaker normalisation is more beneficial when the training data size is small.

6   Conclusion and Future Work

In this paper, we presented an i-vector based feature augmentation for intent classification and we used pre-trained acoustic models to transfer the learnt knowledge to low resource language. To evaluate the proposed approach, we used Sinhala and Tamil speech intent datasets in the banking domain. The experimental results show that incorporating the i-vectors is effective in improving the performance. The highest accuracy of 98% is achieved with APC features for Sinhala dataset outperforming the previous work. Highest accuracy value of 51% is achieved with phoneme probability features for Tamil dataset. In the future, we intend to evaluate other unsupervised acoustic features, such as, wav2vec 2.0, Mockingjay, Tera and audio Albert. Further, we plan to extend this work by including more data from different languages and domains to prove the generalizability of the model.

Acknowledgments. This research was supported by Accelerating Higher Education Expansion and Development (AHEAD) Operation of the Ministry of Education, Sri Lanka funded by the World Bank.

References

1. Aida-zade, K., Ardil, C., Rustamov, S.: Investigation of combined use of MFCC and LPC features in speech recognition systems. Sig. Process. (2007)
2. Amodei, D., et al.: Deep speech 2: end-to-end speech recognition in English and mandarin (2015)
3. Buddhika, D., Liyadipita, R., Nadeeshan, S., Witharana, H., Jayasena, S., Thayasivam, U.: Voicer: a crowd sourcing tool for speech data collection. In: 2018 18th International Conference on Advances in ICT for Emerging Regions (ICTer), pp. 174–181 (2018). https://doi.org/10.1109/ICTER.2018.8615521
4. Chen, Y.P., Price, R., Bangalore, S.: Spoken language understanding without speech recognition. In: 2018 IEEE International Conference on Acoustics, Speech and Signal Processing (ICASSP), pp. 6189–6193 (2018). https://doi.org/10.1109/ICASSP.2018.8461718
5. Chi, P.H., et al.: Audio albert: a lite BERT for self-supervised learning of audio representation. arXiv:2005.08575 (2020)
6. Chorowski, J., Weiss, R.J., Bengio, S., van den Oord, A.: Unsupervised speech representation learning using WaveNet autoencoders. IEEE/ACM Trans. Audio Speech Lang. Process. **27**, 2041–2053 (2019)

7. Chung, Y.A., Glass, J.R.: Generative pre-training for speech with autoregressive predictive coding. In: ICASSP 2020–2020 IEEE International Conference on Acoustics, Speech and Signal Processing (ICASSP), pp. 3497–3501 (2020)

8. Chung, Y.A., Hsu, W.N., Tang, H., Glass, J.R.: An unsupervised autoregressive model for speech representation learning. arXiv:1904.03240 (2019)

9. Chung, Y.A., Tang, H., Glass, J.: Vector-quantized autoregressive predictive coding. In: INTERSPEECH (2020)

10. Cui, X., Goel, V., Saon, G.: Embedding-based speaker adaptive training of deep neural networks, pp. 122–126 (2017). https://doi.org/10.21437/Interspeech.2017-460

11. Fan, Z., Li, J., Zhou, S., Xu, B.: Speaker-aware speech-transformer. In: 2019 IEEE Automatic Speech Recognition and Understanding Workshop (ASRU), pp. 222–229 (2019)

12. Feng, S., Lee, T.: Improving unsupervised subword modeling via disentangled speech representation learning and transformation. In: INTERSPEECH (2019)

13. Garimella, S., Mandal, A., Strom, N., Hoffmeister, B., Matsoukas, S., Parthasarathi, S.H.K.: Robust i-vector based adaptation of DNN acoustic model for speech recognition. In: INTERSPEECH (2015)

14. Hannun, A., et al.: DeepSpeech: scaling up end-to-end speech recognition. arXiv:1412.5567 (2014)

15. Hsu, W.N., Glass, J.R.: Extracting domain invariant features by unsupervised learning for robust automatic speech recognition. In: 2018 IEEE International Conference on Acoustics, Speech and Signal Processing (ICASSP), pp. 5614–5618 (2018)

16. Hsu, W.N., Zhang, Y., Glass, J.R.: Unsupervised learning of disentangled and interpretable representations from sequential data. In: NIPS (2017)

17. Karunanayake, Y., Thayasivam, U., Ranathunga, S.: Sinhala and Tamil speech intent identification from English phoneme based ASR. In: 2019 International Conference on Asian Language Processing (IALP), pp. 234–239 (2019)

18. Karunanayake, Y., Thayasivam, U., Ranathunga, S.: Transfer learning based free-form speech command classification for low-resource languages. In: ACL (2019)

19. Këpuska, V., Elharati, H.: Robust speech recognition system using conventional and hybrid features of MFCC, LPCC, PLP, RASTA-PLP and hidden Markov model classifier in noisy conditions. J. Comput. Commun. **3**, 1–9 (2015). https://doi.org/10.4236/jcc.2015.36001

20. Larcher, A., Lee, K.A., Meignier, S.: An extensible speaker identification sidekit in Python. In: 2016 IEEE International Conference on Acoustics, Speech and Signal Processing (ICASSP), pp. 5095–5099 (2016)

21. Liu, A.H., Chung, Y.A., Glass, J.: Non-autoregressive predictive coding for learning speech representations from local dependencies. arXiv:2011.00406 (2020)

22. Liu, A.T., Li, S.W., Lee, H.Y.: TERA: self-supervised learning of transformer encoder representation for speech. arXiv:2007.06028 (2020)

23. Liu, A.T., Yang, S., Chi, P.H., Hsu, P.C., Lee, H.Y.: Mockingjay: unsupervised speech representation learning with deep bidirectional transformer encoders. In: ICASSP 2020–2020 IEEE International Conference on Acoustics, Speech and Signal Processing (ICASSP), pp. 6419–6423 (2020)

24. Lugosch, L., Ravanelli, M., Ignoto, P., Tomar, V., Bengio, Y.: Speech model pre-training for end-to-end spoken language understanding. arXiv:1904.03670 (2019)

25. Miao, Y., Zhang, H., Metze, F.: Towards speaker adaptive training of deep neural network acoustic models. In: INTERSPEECH (2014)

26. Morais, E., Kuo, H., Thomas, S., Tuske, Z., Kingsbury, B.: End-to-end spoken language understanding using transformer networks and self-supervised pre-trained features. arXiv:2011.08238 (2020)
27. Pan, J., Liu, D., Wan, G., Du, J., Liu, Q., Ye, Z.: Online speaker adaptation for LVCSR based on attention mechanism. In: 2018 Asia-Pacific Signal and Information Processing Association Annual Summit and Conference (APSIPA ASC), pp. 183–186 (2018)
28. Poncelet, J., Van hamme, H.: Multitask learning with capsule networks for speech-to-intent applications. In: ICASSP 2020–2020 IEEE International Conference on Acoustics, Speech and Signal Processing (ICASSP), pp. 8494–8498 (2020). https://doi.org/10.1109/ICASSP40776.2020.9053832
29. Schneider, S., Baevski, A., Collobert, R., Auli, M.: Wav2vec: unsupervised pre-training for speech recognition. In: INTERSPEECH (2019)
30. Senior, A., Lopez-Moreno, I.: Improving DNN speaker independence with i-vector inputs. In: 2014 IEEE International Conference on Acoustics, Speech and Signal Processing (ICASSP), pp. 225–229 (2014). https://doi.org/10.1109/ICASSP.2014.6853591
31. Shi, Y., Huang, Q., Hain, T.: H-VECTORS: utterance-level speaker embedding using a hierarchical attention model. In: ICASSP 2020–2020 IEEE International Conference on Acoustics, Speech and Signal Processing (ICASSP), pp. 7579–7583 (2020). https://doi.org/10.1109/ICASSP40776.2020.9054448
32. Shum, S., Dehak, N., Dehak, R., Glass, J.: Unsupervised speaker adaptation based on the cosine similarity for text-independent speaker verification. In: Odyssey (2010)
33. Snyder, D., Garcia-Romero, D., Sell, G., Povey, D., Khudanpur, S.: X-vectors: Robust DNN embeddings for speaker recognition. In: 2018 IEEE International Conference on Acoustics, Speech and Signal Processing (ICASSP), pp. 5329–5333 (2018). https://doi.org/10.1109/ICASSP.2018.8461375
34. Tomashenko, N., Caubrière, A., Estève, Y.: Investigating adaptation and transfer learning for end-to-end spoken language understanding from speech. In: Proceedings of the Interspeech 2019, pp. 824–828 (2019). https://doi.org/10.21437/Interspeech.2019-2158
35. Yu, C., Ogawa, A., Delcroix, M., Yoshioka, T., Nakatani, T., Hansen, J.: Robust i-vector extraction for neural network adaptation in noisy environment. In: INTERSPEECH (2015)
36. Zhao, Y., Li, J., Wang, X., Li, Y.: The SpeechTransformer for large-scale mandarin chinese speech recognition. In: ICASSP 2019–2019 IEEE International Conference on Acoustics, Speech and Signal Processing (ICASSP), pp. 7095–7099 (2019). https://doi.org/10.1109/ICASSP.2019.8682586
37. Zhen, B., Wu, X., Liu, Z., Chi, H.: On the importance of components of the MFCC in speech and speaker recognition. In: INTERSPEECH, vol. 37, pp. 487–490 (2000)

Speaker-Dependent Visual Command Recognition in Vehicle Cabin: Methodology and Evaluation

Denis Ivanko$^{(\boxtimes)}$ ⓘ, Dmitry Ryumin ⓘ, Alexandr Axyonov ⓘ, and Alexey Kashevnik ⓘ

St. Petersburg Federal Research Center of the Russian Academy of Sciences, St. Petersburg 199178, Russia

{ivanko.d,ryumin.d,axyonov.a,alexey.kashevnik}@iias.spb.su

Abstract. This work presents a scalable solution to speaker-dependent visual command recognition in vehicle cabin. The goal of this work is to recognize a limited number of most frequent driver's requests based on his/her lip movements. Unlike previous works that have focused on automated lip-reading in controlled laboratory environment, we tackle this problem in real driving conditions based on the recorded RUSAVIC dataset. Due to limiting the scope of the task to speaker-dependency and vocabulary of 50 phrases, the models that we train surpass the performance of previous work and can be used in real-life speech recognition applications. To achieve this, we constructed end-to-end methodology that require only 10 repetition of each phrase in order to achieve reasonable recognition accuracy up to 54% based purely on video information. Our key contributions are: (1) we introduce a novel approach to visual speech data preprocessing and labeling, designed to tackle real-life drivers data from vehicle cabin; (2) we investigate to what extent lip-reading is complimentary to improve visual command recognition, depending on the set of recognizable commands; (3) we train, adapted for our task and compare three state-of-the-art CNN architectures, namely MobileNetV2, DenseNet121, NASNetMobile to evaluate the performance of developed system. The proposed system achieved word recognition rate (WRR) of 55% for a vehicle parked at the crossroad task and 54% for driving scenarios.

Keywords: Automated lip-reading · Visual speech recognition · Vehicle cabin · Machine learning · End-to-End · CNN · LSTM

1 Introduction

According to the US National Safety Council reports that cell phone use while driving leads to 1.6 million crashes each year. Nearly 390,000 injuries occur each year from accidents caused by texting while driving. 1 out of every 4 car accidents is caused by texting and driving [1].

A potential solution to the problem could be the use of automatic speech recognition system, that enable to process driver's acoustic and visual data and perform the certain

© Springer Nature Switzerland AG 2021
A. Karpov and R. Potapova (Eds.): SPECOM 2021, LNAI 12997, pp. 291–302, 2021.
https://doi.org/10.1007/978-3-030-87802-3_27

activities (like writing messages, process incoming/outcoming calls and control some other desired functions) without distracting driver's hands from steering wheel and eye contact from the road.

Despite the significant success achieved in the recent years in the field of automatic speech recognition this real-life scenario remains particularly challenging. Modern acoustic speech recognition systems perform really well in a quiet controlled office conditions, however when heavy noise occur the speech recognition accuracy of such systems degrades rapidly. Unfortunately, uncontrolled noisy situations happen regularly in busy traffic conditions.

There is a consensus among researchers that acoustic speech signal is the primary cue for automatic speech recognition, but at the same time the visual observation of the lips, teeth, tongue and jaw contribute to better recognition, especially when the acoustic signal degraded or even inaccessible.

Visual speech recognition (or lip-reading) is a difficult skill for human to learn, however in a severe noisy environment we all start to pay attention to the lip's movements of interlocutor during conversation in order to better understand the meaning [2]. Obviously, human speech perception is a multimodal process and based on this knowledge, there has been significant progress in the performance of automatic speech recognition systems in the recent years due to the availability of large-scale datasets and the development of modern neural network architectures [3, 4].

It is impossible to underestimate the potential of a machine that can lip read and it opens up a variety of applications, starting from dictation messages to a phone in a noisy environment, improving general performance of automated speech recognition, transcribing silent films, resolving multi-talker simultaneous speech scenarios, etc. [5].

In current research, we focused on visual command recognition in vehicle cabin scenario. Based on our previous research [6] we determined a set of 50 requests, most frequently asked by driver's. We record the data in two real-life scenarios: driving conditions and vehicle parked near busy intersection, we introduce a novel approach to visual speech data preprocessing and labeling, we train end-to-end automated lip-reading system based on three modern state-of-the-art convolutional neural network architectures, namely MobileNetV2, DenseNet121, NASNetMobile. In this work, we mainly research speaker-dependent scenarios, keeping in mind that usually vehicle has one driver and it is important to more accurately recognize his/her voice commands. The results of this research are planning to be used for building noise-robust audio-visual speech recognition system in car environments.

2   Related Work

To date, a lot of scientific research has been devoted to the topic of automated lip-reading. The initial attempts relied mainly on substantial prior knowledge and were focused mainly on isolated words or digits recognition tasks [7–10]. Traditional HMM-based speech recognition concept was forged back then following the steps of rapidly developing acoustic speech recognition. In [11] multi-stream HHMs were introduced that improved upon earlier models by using additional visual features to the lip contours. Later in [12] the coupled version of HMM were used to jointly model audio and video streams to predict sequences of words. We refer the reader to the survey of [13] for additional details. However, it should be noted, that the performance of earlier lip-reading systems remained rather low.

More recent attempts include combination of advanced machine learning pipelines, computer vision techniques and traditional speech processing approaches [14–18]. As mentioned in [14], the processing of lips motion features and generalization upon speakers have been considered open challenge. Recent advances in deep learning have made it possible to overcome these limitations in a certain way. Nevertheless, a lot of studies still devoted to isolated word classification, either by learning visual represenations [19, 20], multimodal representations [21, 22] or combining DNNs with traditional speech processing approaches [23, 24].

According to modern approaches to automated visual speech recognition, the task can be divided into three sequential stages: region-of-interest (ROI) detection, visual features extraction and visual speech recognition. The visualization of this pipeline is presented in the Fig. 1.

Identifying a region-of-interest area that contains the mouth motion is the very important step in the construction of a reliable lip-reading system. The main reason behind it that the quality of ROI significantly affects the resulting speech recognition accuracy. To extract ROIs, many researchers relied on the active appearance models (AAM) [25], Haar-like feature based boosted classification framework [26], skin color thresholding [27], etc. To correctly crop the mouth region in images we need to localize certain facial landmarks such as chin, nostrils, corners of the lips, etc. For the following informative features extraction detected ROI must be cropped and normalized. In recent decades, facial landmarks tracking has been an active research topic due to its widespread use in computer vision tasks.

To date, there are several basic types of visual features existing in scientific literature. The most widespread of them are: pixel-based features [28] – raw pixel data used directly or after some image processing; geometry-based features [29] – geometric information of the talking mouth is extracted as features; model-based features [30] - a model of the mouth motion is built and model parameters are used as visual features, or a combination of mentioned above features [31].

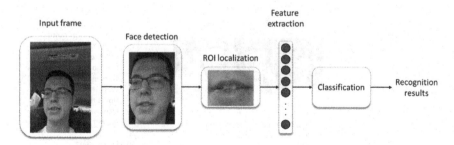

Fig. 1. Automated lip-reading pipeline example.

LipNet model [14] was the first end-to-end model that handles sentence-level lip-reading by predicting sequences of characters. The model used spatiotemporal convolutions followed by gated recurrent units (GRUs) and was trained with the CTC loss function. It was evaluated on a GRID corpus with very limited vocabulary and achieved WER of 11.4% in controlled office conditions. Several end-to-end architectures were subsequently introduced in the works [32–35].

The most of the abovementioned research were evaluated on the data recorded in a quiet office environment. However, it is obvious that driving a vehicle is accompanied by a rather active head turns from side to side. The driver often is turned to the camera at different angles, which greatly complicates automatic lip-reading by using video information. At the same time, the presence of strong acoustic noise during driving significantly degrades the results of speech recognition by voice. To date, there were only five attempts to collect such data: AVICAR [36], AV@CAR [37], Czech AVSC [38], CENSREC-2-AV [39] and RUSAVIC [6]. And only the most recent RUSAVIC dataset devoid of the shortcomings of previous ones, such as low quality of video data, asynchrony, low fps, etc. Thus, we can state with confidence the lack of research in the area and state the need to develop a reliable visual command recognition system in vehicle cabin.

3 Data

In current research we use the RUSAVIC dataset video data. The main characteristics of the recorded corpus are shown in (Fig. 2). In general, it consists of mp4 files for each recording session of every speaker. Each speaker performed 10 recording sessions and was captured by three Samsung Galaxy S20+ smartphones from three different angles (20°, 0°, −20°) with FullHD video resolution and 60 fps recording rate. We proposed our developed mobile application for data recording in the paper [6].

During each recording session speaker uttered 50 phrases. These phrases have been determined in our previous work [6] as the most frequent driver requests for smartphones, based on the open-source data of speech recognition engines, such as Alexa Auto, Yandex Drive, Google Drive, etc.

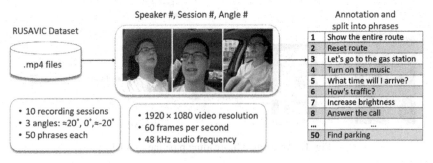

Fig. 2. RUSAVIC dataset structure.

Fig. 3. A snapshot of video stream and recording environment.

Some examples of the recorded phrases are depicted on the (Fig. 2, right) and some snapshots of the speakers and recording conditions are shown on (Fig. 3). In current research we use the data of two different scenarios: (1) uncontrolled driving environment including different lighting conditions, active head turns, traffic noise, etc. (Fig. 3, upper row) and (2) vehicle parked near busy intersection, also including different lighting conditions, normal head turns, traffic noise, etc. (Fig. 3, bottom row).

4   Proposed Methodology

In this section, we describe the strategy used to effectively build speaker-dependent lip-reading system and train the models, making best use of the limited amount of data available. We split this process into sequential execution of the three following stages: (1) visual data preprocessing and labelling; (2) mouth region detection and extraction; (3) DNN model training and evaluation.

4.1   Visual Data Preprocessing and Labelling

Since there is no out of the box solution to process and label visual speech data, we come up with our own method. The functional scheme of it is depicted on (Fig. 4).

Implementation of the proposed methodology allows to process raw audio-visual data of the recording sessions of RUSAVIC dataset and results in obtaining properly splitted and labelled video files in accordance with the uttered phrases. In turn, it involves sequential execution of several indispensable processing steps:

(1) extract separate audio (.wav files) and video (frames) information from raw recording session of original dataset;
(2) determine the number of threads per CPU in order to obtain optimal processing speed;

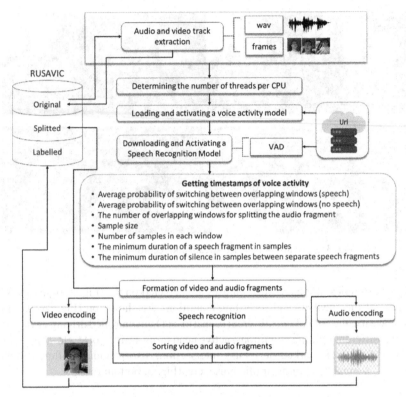

Fig. 4. Functional scheme of visual data processing and labelling method.

(3) download from the cloud voice activity model that allow the detection of the presence or absence of human speech based on the processing of audio information. In current research we used voice activity model provided by Vosk API [40] for that purposes;

(4) download from the cloud speech recognition model. We used an open-source and free Python toolkit Vosk [40] for acoustic speech recognition in order to obtain timestamps of uttered phrases. It also allows to perform fine-tuning by set up some additional parameters, such as average probability of switching between overlapping windows (speech/no speech), the minimum duration of speech samples/silence samples, the size of the samples and its number in each window, etc. (Fig. 4);

(5) the next step is to form splitted video and audio fragments based on the data provided by activity detection model and save them into the dataset;

(6) perform speech recognition using uploaded and attuned speech recognition model;

(7) sort and label video and audio fragments in accordance with recognizable vocabulary. In our case 50 most frequent driver's requests;

(8) encode video (based on desired type and quality of encoding) and audio (based on the number of channels) and save the labelled data into the dataset.

4.2 Mouth Region Detection and Extraction

In accordance with the defined strategy the next step after labelling visual data is to crop the region-of-interest (mouth region) from each frame of the video. To this end we use the state-of-the-art solution of MediaPipe Face Mesh [41] that is able to estimate 468 3D face landmarks in real-time even on mobile devices. Landmark map and face detection results depicted on the (Fig. 5). In addition, this solution was bundled with the Face Geometry module that bridges the gap between the face landmark estimation and useful real-time augmented reality applications. The face geometry data consists of common 3D geometry primitives, including a face pose transformation matrix and a triangular face mesh.

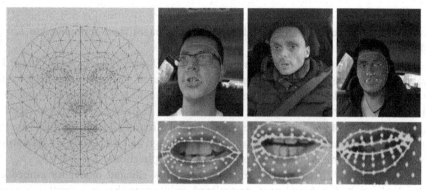

Fig. 5. Face Mesh face landmark map (left), face detection results (upper right), extracted mouth regions (lower right).

The face detection machine learning pipeline consist of two real-time deep neural network models that work together [41]: a detector that operates on the full image and computes face locations and a 3D face landmark model that operates on those locations and predicts the approximate surface geometry via regression.

4.3 Model Training

Traditional approaches separated the problem of automated lip-reading into two stages: designing or learning visual features and speech recognition. More recent deep lip-reading approaches are end-to-end trainable. Motivated by novel advances in visual speech decoding we decided to implement and train state-of-the-art end-to-end architecture with deep convolutional neural network (CNN) for on-the-fly features extraction, followed by long-short-term-memory (LSTM) layers for classification. The general structure of the model is shown in (Fig. 6).

One of the prerequisites for training a NN-based model is the fixed-dimensional input layer. However, it is obvious, that mouth regions extracted from different speakers, various recording conditions and distance to camera are subject to change. Thus, the first step is to reduce cropped mouth images to single dimension. In current research it

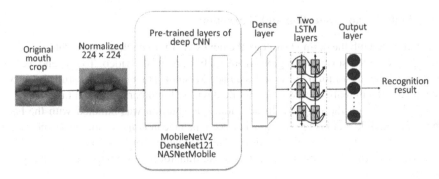

Fig. 6. General architecture of the model.

was determined experimentally and all input mouth images were normalized to 224 × 224 pixels.

Due to limited amount of data available (only 10 repetitions of each phrase by speaker) it is impossible to train deep CNN from scratch. Therefore, we tried to get the best use of modern transfer learning approaches and applied three different pre-trained deep CNN architectures, namely MobileNetV2, DenseNet121 and NASNetMobile. Those NN topologies were chosen by a particular reason. First of all, these are the state-of-the-art models that appeared only 2–3 years ago and trained on a vast amount of visual data for various computer vision tasks and applications.

MobileNetV2 [42] is a second generation of class efficient model for embedded vision application. It is based on a streamlined architecture that uses depth-wise separable convolutions except for the first layer which is a full convolution. In total, the network consists of 154 layers. All CNN layers are followed by a batchnorm and ReLU nonlinearity. Down sampling is handled with strided convolution. A final average pooling reduces the spatial resolution to 1 before the fully connected layer. It was trained using RMSprop with asynchronous gradient descent.

DenseNet121 [43] architecture was inspired that CNNs can be substantialy deeper, more accurate and efficient is they contain shorter connections between layers close to the input and those close to the output. In DenseNet each layer connects to every other layer in a feed-forward fashion. We used the network of 427 layers in total. The DenseNet used in our experiments has three dence blocks that each has equal number of layers. Before entering the first dense block a convolution is performed on the input images. For convolutional layers with kernel size 3 × 3, each side of the inputs is zero-padded by one pixel to keep the feature-map size fixed. We use 1 × 1 convolution followed by 2 × 2 average pooling as transition layers between two dense blocks. At the end of the last dense block, a global average pooling is performed.

NASNetMobile [44] is a scalable architecture for image classification and consist of two repeated building blocks termed Normal Cell and Reduction Cell. In current research we applied the latest 769 layers architecture. For full NN structure refer to original work [44].

Thus, we take deep pre-trained CNN models of three different architectures, remove the last classification layer and use them for features extraction from our mouth images.

Video sequences are split into batches of 30 frames with 50% overlap (15 frames). Total number of batches equals 9 (270 frames). Pre-trained CNN block followed by a fully connected layer with L2 regularization. Its margin was fine-tuned for each speaker in order to better generalize on the speaker-specific data. Extracted features are then processed by two standard LSTM layers, using similar L2 regularization, Adam optimizer and fine-tuned dropout followed by a fully connected output layer.

5 Evaluation Experiments

In this section we evaluate and compare the proposed architecture on different speakers and training strategies. We train three separate speaker-dependent visual command recognition systems on the data of RUSAVIC dataset. Table 1 shows the recognition accuracy of different systems.

Maximum number of epochs was 100 and training was interrupted if the accuracy does not increase for 5 epochs. For each speaker the train and test data were split 80:20 ratio. Thus, for each phrase we have 8 samples used for training and 2 samples used for testing, multiplied on the total number of phrases (50) results in total of 100 test samples for each speaker.

We trained as described in 4.3 section. We tested different pre-trained state-of-the-art CNN topologies, such as MobileNetV2, DenseNet121 and NASNetMobile. As we can see from the table 1, MobileNetV2 features extraction architecture clearly outperforms the other two by a small margin from 2 to 6% of accuracy. It is clear that all architectures demonstrated comparable results, nevertheless MobileNetV2 generalized on the provided data a slightly more accurate.

Table 1. Accuracy comparison of different architectures of speaker-dependent visual command recognition systems.

Speaker #	CNN topology	Number of CNN layers	Acc, % (epoch)
	MobileNetV2	154	55 (12)
1	DenseNet121	427	49 (24)
	NASNetMobile	769	47 (19)
	MobileNetV2	154	53 (17)
2	DenseNet121	427	51 (9)
	NASNetMobile	769	46 (23)
	MobileNetV2	154	54 (32)
3	DenseNet121	427	52 (27)
	NASNetMobile	769	51 (29)

Along with this, the first two speaker-dependent system were trained on the data, when a vehicle was parked near busy intersection and a system #3 was trained on the actual driving data. Despite our concern that real driving scenario would have lower speech recognition accuracy due to more active head turns the actual results are almost equal for all three systems.

As we can see from the Table 1, visual speech recognition accuracy differs from 46% on system #2 using NASNetMobile architecture to 55% on system #1 using MobileNetV2 architecture. Thus, we can conclude that only with 10 repetition of voice command we can obtain about 50% speech recognition accuracy based purely on visual information of speaker's lips movements at 50 different classes.

6 Conclusion and Future Work

In this paper, we introduced a scalable solution to speaker-dependent visual command recognition in vehicle cabin. We have described the strategy used to effectively build speaker-dependent lip-reading system and train the models, making best use of the limited amount of data available. We have covered this process from the prospect of three sequential stages, namely: visual data preprocessing and labelling; mouth region detection and extraction; DNN model training and evaluation.

We constructed end-to-end methodology, that require only 10 repetition of each phrase in order to achieve reasonable recognition accuracy up to 54% on 50 different classes based purely on video information. Our key contributions are: (1) we introduced a novel approach to visual speech data preprocessing and labeling, designed to tackle real-life drivers data from vehicle cabin; (2) we investigated to what extent lip-reading is complimentary to improve visual command recognition, depending on the set of recognizable commands (3) we have trained and compared three state-of-the-art CNN architectures, namely MobileNetV2, DenseNet121, NASNetMobile to evaluate the performance of developed system. The proposed system achieved word recognition rate (WRR) of 55% for a vehicle parked at the crossroads task and 54% for different driving scenarios with 50 recognizable classes.

In further research, it is planned to shift from the speaker-dependency of current visual speech recognition system, by (1) expanding RUSAVIC corpus with more data (number of speakers and real-driving recordings) and (2) researching the NN-based architectures to better tackle end-to-end lip-reading task.

Acknowledgments. This research is financially supported by the Russian Foundation for Basic Research (project No. 19-29-09081 мк).

References

1. Schroeder, P., Meyers, M., Kostuniuk, L.: National survey on distracted driving attitudes and behaviors, Report No. DOT HS 811 729. National Highway Traffic Safety Administration, Washington, DC (2019)
2. McGurk, H., MacDonald, J.: Hearing lips and seeing voices. Nature **264**, 746–748 (1976)
3. Shillingford, B., Assael, Y., Hoffman, M., et al.: Large-Scale Visual Speech Recognition. In: arXiv eprint 1807.05162, pp. 1–21 (2018)
4. Chen, X., Du, J., Zhang, H.: Lipreading with DenseNet and resBi-LSTM. Signal Image Video Process **14**, 981–989 (2020)

5. Afouras, T., Chung, J.C., Senior, A., et al.: Deep Audio-visual Speech Recognition. In: IEEE Transactions on Pattern Analysis and Machine Intelligence, pp. 1–13 (2018)
6. Kashevnik, A., et al.: Multimodal corpus design for audio-visual speech recognition in vehicle cabin. IEEE Access **9**, 34986–35003 (2021)
7. Papandreou, G., Katsamanis, A., Pitsikalis, V., Maragos, P.: Adaptive multimodal fusion by uncertainty compensation with application to audiovisual speech recognition. IEEE Trans. Audio Speech Lang. Process. **17**(3), 423–435 (2009)
8. Gurban, M., Thiran, J.P.: Information theoretic feature extraction for audio-visual speech recognition. IEEE Trans. Signal Process. **57**, 4765–4776 (2009)
9. Ivanko, D., et al.: Using a high-speed video camera for robust audio-visual speech recognition in acoustically noisy conditions. In: Karpov, A., Potapova, R., Mporas, I. (eds.) SPECOM 2017. LNCS (LNAI), vol. 10458, pp. 757–766. Springer, Cham (2017). https://doi.org/10.1007/978-3-319-66429-3_76
10. Zhao, G., Barnard, M., Pietikainen, M.: Lipreading with local spatiotemporal descriptors. IEEE Trans. Multimedia **11**(7), 1254–1265 (2009)
11. Potamianos, G., Graf, H.P., Cosatto, E.: An image transform approach for hmm based automatic lipreading. In: IEEE Conference on Image Processing, pp. 173–177 (1998)
12. Ivanko, D., et al.: Multimodal speech recognition: increasing accuracy using high speed video data. J. Multimodal User Interfaces **12**(4), 319–328 (2018). https://doi.org/10.1007/s12193-018-0267-1
13. Zhou, Z., Zhao, G., Hong, X., Pietikainen, M.: A review of recent advances in visual speech decoding. Image Vis. Comput. **32**, 590–605 (2014)
14. Assael, Y., Shillingford, B., Whiteson, S., Freitas, N.: LipNet: end-to-end sentence-level lipreading. In: GPU Technology Conference, pp. 1–14 (2017)
15. Hinton, G., et al.: Deep neural networks for acoustic modeling in speech recognition: the shared views of four research groups. IEEE Signal Process. Mag. **29**(6), 82–97 (2012)
16. Chung, J.S., Zisserman, A.: Lip reading in the wild. In: Asian Conference on Computer Vision, pp. 87–103 (2016)
17. Wand, M., Schmidhuber, J.: Improving speaker-independent lipreading with domain adversarial training. Interspeech **2017**, 3982–3987 (2017)
18. Kagirov, I., Ryumin, D., Axyonov, A.: Method for multimodal recognition of one-handed sign language gestures through 3D convolution and LSTM neural networks. In: International Conference on Speech and Computer, pp. 191–200 (2019)
19. Stafylakis, T., Tzimiropoulos, G.: Combining residual networks with LSTMs for lipreading. In: Interspeech, pp. 3652–3656, ISCA (2017)
20. Wand, M., Koutnik, K., Schmidhuber, J.: Lipreading with long short-term memory. International Conference on Acoustics, Speech, and Signal Processing, pp. 6115–6119 (2016)
21. Petridis, S., Wang, Y., Li, Z., Pantic, M.: End-to-end multi-view lipreading. In: British Machine Vision Conference, pp. 1–14 (2017)
22. Sui, S., Bennamoun, M., Togneri, R.: Listening with your eyes: towards a practical visual speech recognition system using deep Boltzmann machines. In: ICCV, pp. 154–162 (2015)
23. Noda, K., Yamaguchi, Y., Nakadai, K., et al.: Lipreading using convolutional neural network. In: Interspeech, pp. 1149–1153 (2014)
24. Almajai, I., Cox, S., Harvey, R., Lan, Y.: Improved speaker independent lip reading using speaker adaptive training and deep neural networks. In: IEEE International Conference on Acoustics, Speech, and Signal Processing, pp. 2722–2726 (2016)
25. Newman, J., Cox, S.: Language identification using visual features. In: Proc. IEEE Audio Speech and Language Processing, vol. 20, no. 7, pp. 1936–1947 (2012)
26. Lan, Y., Theobald, B., Harvey, R.: View independent computer lip-reading. In: Proc. International Conference Multimedia Expo (ICME), pp. 432–437 (2012)

27. Estellers, V., Thiran, J.: Multi-pose lipreading and audio-visual speech recognition. In: EURALISP Journal Advanced Signal Processing, vol. 51 (2012)

28. Huang, Z., Zeng, Z., Liu, B., et al.: Pixel-BERT: Aligning Image Pixels with Text by Deep Multi-Modal Transformers. In: arXiv: 2004.00849, pp. 1–17 (2020)

29. Ivanko, D., Ryumin, D., Axyonov, A., Železný, M.: Designing advanced geometric features for automatic Russian visual speech recognition. In: Karpov, A., Jokisch, O., Potapova, R. (eds.) SPECOM 2018. LNCS (LNAI), vol. 11096, pp. 245–254. Springer, Cham (2018). https://doi.org/10.1007/978-3-319-99579-3_26

30. Rajagopal, A., et al.: A deep learning model based on multi-objective particle swarm optimization for scene classification in unmanned aerial vehicles. IEEE Access **8**, 135383–135393 (2020)

31. Ivanko, D., Ryumin, D., Kipyatkova, I., et al.: Lip-Reading Using Pixel-Based and Geometry-Based Features for Multimodal Human-Robot Interfaces. Smart Innovation, Systems and Technologies, vol. 154, pp. 477–486. Springer, Singapore (2020)

32. Xu, K., Li, D., Cassimatis, N., Wang, X. LCANet: End-to-end lipreading with cascaded attention-ctc. arXiv preprint arXiv:1803.04988, pp. 1–10 (2018)

33. Ryumina, E., Karpov, A.: Facial expression recognition using distance importance scores between facial landmarks. CEUR Workshop Proceedings **2744**, 1–10 (2020)

34. Thanda, A., Venkatesan, S.M.: Audio visual speech recognition using deep recurrent neural networks. In: Multimodal Pattern Recognition of Social Signals in Human-Computer-Interaction, pp. 98–109 (2017)

35. Ryumina, E., Ryumin, D., Ivanko, D., Karpov, A.: A Novel Method for Protective Face Mask Detection Using Convolutional Neural Networks and Image Histograms. ISPRS-International Archives of the Photogrammetry, Remote Sensing and Spatial Information Sciences **XLIV-2/W1-2021**, 177–182 (2021)

36. Lee, B., et al.: AVICAR: Audio-Visual Speech Corpus in a Car Environment. In: 8th International Conference on Spoken Language Processing, ICSLP 2004, pp. 1–5 (2004)

37. Ortega, A. et al.: AV@CAR: A Spanish multichannel multimodal corpus for in-vehicle automatic audio-visual speech recognition. In: LREC, pp. 1354–1359 (2004)

38. Miloš, M., Milo[š]železny, M., Císař, P.: Czech Audio-Visual Speech Corpus of a Car Driver for In-Vehicle Audio-Visual Speech Recognition. In: International Conference on Audio-Visual Speech Processing, AVSP, pp. 1–5 (2003)

39. Kawasaki, T., et al.: An audio-visual in-car corpus "CENSREC-2-AV" for robust bimodal speech recognition. In: Vehicle Systems and Driver Modelling, pp. 181–190 (2017)

40. Vosk offline speech recognition API Kaldi based, [online] Available: https://alphacephei.com/vosk/

41. Kartynnik, Y., Ablavatski, A., Grishchenko, I., Grundmann, M.: Real-time Facial Surface Geometry from Monocular Video on Mobile GPUs. In: CVPR Workshop on Computer Vision for Augmented and Virtual Reality 2019, IEEE, pp. 1–4 (2019)

42. Howard, A., Zhu, M., Chen, B., et al.: MobileNets: Efficient Convolutional Neural Networks for Mobile Vision Applications. In arXiv:1704.04861, pp. 1–9 (2017)

43. Huang, G., Liu, Z., et al.: Densely Connected Convolutional Networks. In: IEEE Conference on Computer Vision and Pattern Recognition (CVPR), pp. 2261–2269 (2018)

44. Barret, Z., Vijay, V., Jonathon, S., Quoc, L.: Learning Transferable Architectures for Scalable Image Recognition. In: Conference on Computer Vision and Pattern Recognition (CVPR), pp. 8697–8710 (2018)

Optimised Code-Switched Language Model Data Augmentation in Four Under-Resourced South African Languages

Joshua Jansen van Vueren$^{(\boxtimes)}$ and Thomas Niesler

Department of Electrical and Electronic Engineering, Stellenbosch University,
Stellenbosch, South Africa
{jjvanvueren,trn}@sun.ac.za

Abstract. Code-switching in South African languages is common but data for language modelling remains extremely scarce. We present techniques that allow recurrent neural networks (LSTMs) to be better applied as generative models to the task of producing artificial code-switched text that can be used to augment the small training sets. We propose the application of prompting to favour the generation of sentences with intra-sentential language switches, and introduce an extensive LSTM hyperparameter search that specifically optimises the utility of the artificially generated code-switched text. We use these strategies to generate artificial code-switched text for four under-resourced South African languages and evaluate the utility of this additional data for language modelling. We find that the optimised models are able to generate text that leads to consistent perplexity and word error rate improvements for all four language pairs, especially at language switches. This is an improvement on previous work using the same speech data in which text generated without such optimisation did not provide improved performance. We conclude that prompting and targeted hyperparameter optimisation are an effective means of improving language model data augmentation for code-switched speech recognition.

Keywords: Code-switching · Language model data augmentation · LSTM · Speech recognition · Under-resourced languages · African languages · Bantu languages

1 Introduction

Code-switching is the use of more than one language within and between sentences, a phenomenon that is pervasive in multilingual countries such as South Africa. Language switches are known to occur on the intra-word (prefix/suffix), word (insertional), and phrase (alternational) level [22]. One can further distinguish between intra-sentential, and inter-sentential switching [7]. Accurate modelling of code-switching is challenging due to its spontaneous nature and the severe lack of data.

© Springer Nature Switzerland AG 2021
A. Karpov and R. Potapova (Eds.): SPECOM 2021, LNAI 12997, pp. 303–316, 2021.
https://doi.org/10.1007/978-3-030-87802-3_28

Various strategies for the augmentation of code-switched data have been explored and can be categorised as neurally generative and syntactically constrained. Generative adversarial networks (GANs), part-of-speech (POS) tags [5], and hybrid BERT-GAN architectures [9] have been used to generate code-switched sentences from a monolingual Mandarin corpus either by learning which words or phrases should be translated into English or by masking tokens one-by-one in the input sequence. The synthesized datasets were pooled with the code-switched training sets and used to train RNN and n-gram language models. Although it was found that the n-gram perplexity worsened, when used in ASR experiments the performance was slightly improved. The RNN language model was evaluated solely using perplexity and improved over a baseline result.

In [16], a code-switched corpus is synthesized by aligning and embedding words and phrases from parallel monolingual English and Mandarin text according to the matrix language frame (MLF) theory [17]. A code-switch probability is assigned to each pair of aligned phrases and used to generate code-switched sequences for LSTM pre-training. This pre-training improved perplexity, lead to faster convergence, and improved ASR performance in lattice rescoring. Aligned parallel English-Mandarin text was also used in [13] to generate code-switched sentences that were subsequently fused with data generated by a pointer-generator neural network. A RNN composed of two LSTMs that separately model monolingual segments was shown to reduce perplexity in [10], where the current language is used as a signal to select the LSTM which models the next word. In [20] speech synthesized using novel algorithms and code-switched text generated using equivalence constraint theory (ECT) were incorporated into the training data, thereby improving English-Hindi ASR performance. With a similar aim, [24] improved perplexities and word error rates for Dutch-Frisian code-switching through the augmentation of acoustic and text data. Large artificial code-switched corpora were generated using an LSTM trained on a small amount of in-domain code-switched text. Text was also manually translated from Dutch to Frisian utilising an open-source web-service. Finally, ASR transcriptions were incorporated into the training data. In [23] code-switched bigrams synthesised using word embeddings were shown to improve both perplexity and speech recognition performance at language switches. In further work, an LSTM was used to augment English-isiZulu data, thereby decreasing perplexity [3].

Here, we build on the work described in [2,3,24]. We also train LSTMs on severely under-resourced code-switched data and then use these to generate artificial text with which to augment the training set. However, we extend these approaches by introducing the targeted optimisation of the text generation to produce sequences with useful code switches. To do this, we apply an extensive hyperparameter search that optimises text generation quality. Such targeted hyperparameter optimisation for code-switches has not been reported on before.

The remainder of this paper is organised as follows. Section 2 describes the datasets utilised for experimentation. Section 3 details the experimental setup and Sect. 4 presents the results. Finally, Sect. 5 concludes.

2   Dataset

This work uses a manually transcribed corpus of code-switched speech compiled from South Africa soap opera episodes [21]. The speech in this corpus includes four South African Bantu languages (isiZulu, isiXhosa, Sesotho and Setswana) as well as English. Table 1 shows the subdivision of the corpus into four bilingual sub-corpora: English-isiZulu (EZ), English-isiXhosa (EX), English-Sesotho (ES), and English-Setswana (ET).

Table 1. The soap opera corpus, showing the total number of word tokens, word types, and code switches in the four bilingual sub-corpora. CS_{EB} indicates the number of switches from English to a Bantu language, while CS_{BE} indicates switches from Bantu to English. The final column indicates the duration of the audio data.

Pair	Partition	English		Bantu		Total				
		Tok	Typ	Tok	Typ	Tok	Typ	CS_{EB}	CS_{BE}	Dur
EZ	Train	28033	3608	24350	6788	52383	10396	2236	2743	4.81 h
	Dev	832	414	734	452	1566	866	175	198	8.00 min
	Test	2457	870	3199	1435	5656	2305	688	776	30.4 min
EX	Train	20324	2630	12215	5086	32539	7716	776	1003	2.68 h
	Dev	1153	484	1147	762	2300	1246	91	113	13.7 min
	Test	1149	498	1502	889	2651	1387	328	363	14.3 min
ES	Train	15395	2255	19825	2086	35197	4339	1565	1719	2.36 h
	Dev	843	437	2227	614	3067	1050	156	166	12.8 min
	Test	1794	659	2265	535	4054	1193	403	396	15.5 min
ET	Train	16180	2361	19570	1448	35725	3808	1885	1951	2.33 h
	Dev	1170	514	2539	539	3707	1052	224	251	13.8 min
	Test	1970	729	2979	526	4939	1254	505	526	17.8 min

All four Bantu languages are agglutinative. Furthermore, isiZulu and isiXhosa have a conjunctive orthography, leading to larger vocabularies (Table 1) than Sesotho and Setswana, which have a more disjunctive orthography.

Table 2. Out-of-domain monolingual corpora.

Language	English	isiZulu	isiXhosa	Sesotho	Setswana
Tokens	471M	3.25M	0.99M	0.23M	2.84M

We also use the five out-of-domain monolingual corpora outlined in Table 2. This data was gathered from transcriptions of conversations, newspaper reports and web text [2]. The table shows that, while substantial out-of-domain text resources are available for English, much less is available than the four under-resourced Bantu languages.

3   Experimental Strategy

Our generative LSTM [11,12] consists of 3 layers: an embedding layer, an LSTM layer and a dense layer. Gated recurrent units (GRUs) [6] and dropout [14] were found to be ineffective in preliminary experiments. Adam [15] was used for gradient descent and cross entropy as the optimisation criterion. All LSTMs were implemented using Tensorflow [1], all n-gram language models are trigrams with Witten-Bell discounting trained using the SRILM toolkit [19].

Speech recognition experiments were performed using KALDI [18] according to the procedure in [4]. The training procedure is broken into two sections: multilingual pre-training, and language adaptation. The multilingual pre-training trains a CNN-TDNN-F acoustic model on the pooled data from all four sub-corpora as detailed in Table 1. The adaptation phase fine-tunes the pre-trained CNN-TDNN-F by training for two epochs on the relevant bilingual sub-corpus.

3.1   Metrics

In addition to perplexity (PP), to pinpoint the difficulties encountered at language switches, we also consider the code-switched perplexity (CPP) as first defined in [23]. CPP is the perplexity when calculated only across the language switches, while monolingual perplexity (MPP) is the perplexity calculated within monolingual stretches of text.

Similarly, in speech recognition experiments we make use of the code-switched bigram (CSBG) error, which is the speech recognition error computed only for words immediately following a language switch [3]. By observing this figure, the impact of our interventions specifically on code-switching can be assessed.

3.2   Text Synthesis and N-Gram Augmentation

To generate text, the start sequence token <s> is presented to the generative model as input. The model then returns a categorical probability distribution over the possible next words as well as the hidden and cell state vectors. Using random sampling, a next word is chosen from the categorical distribution. This word token and the hidden and cell state vectors are then presented to the model as a new input. This continues until the end sequence token </s> is synthesized, or the sequence length reaches a predetermined maximum limit.

$$p_i = \frac{\exp(z_i/\tau)}{\sum_j \exp(z_j/\tau)} \tag{1}$$

Random sampling allows more diverse samples to be obtained from the inner-representation of the LSTM. The unnormalized likelihoods (z_i) output by the dense layer can be focused or spread by multiplication with a heuristic temperature value τ, as shown in Eq. 1, where p_i is the resultant probability.

Prompting. Neural networks trained to accomplish downstream natural language processing (NLP) tasks are typically either pre-trained and adapted to a task-domain or 'prompted' by syntactic characters [8]. We apply prompting to our LSTM model in an attempt to generate code-switched sequences more effectively and reliably. During training, we mark all sequences containing code-switches with the special start sequence token $<s_{cs}>$, while monolingual sequences begin with token $<s_{mono}>$. In combination with this technique, the discarding of monolingual sequences (ablation) is also considered. This results in four text generation strategies, listed in Table 3.

Table 3. The four considered text generation strategies.

Strategy	Discard monolingual sequences (ablation)	Use special start token (prompting)
All$_{Text}$		
CS$_{Text}$	×	
All$_{Prompt}$		×
CS$_{Prompt}$	×	×

Evaluating the Quality of Artificially-Generated Text. To determine whether the synthesized data is useful, it is used to train an n-gram language model, which is linearly interpolated with a baseline n-gram language model (LM$_B$) trained only on the training set (Table 1). The interpolation weight λ is optimised to minimise the development set perplexity. During preliminary experiments it became apparent that the optimal perplexity of this interpolated model was generally not observed for text generated by LSTMs that had been trained until convergence on the development set, which was observed to be reached after only a few training epochs ($N_E \lesssim 10$). Instead, text generated using LSTMs for which training was allowed to continue after convergence provided greater perplexity improvements. Therefore, the number of training epochs was also considered to be a hyperparameter that was explicitly optimised.

3.3 Hyperparameter Tuning

Fig. 1 shows how optimization is split into three phases.

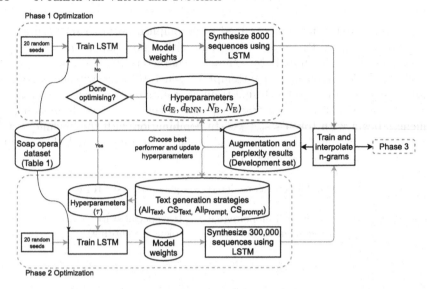

Fig. 1. Block diagram of the hyperparameter and text generation tuning strategy used to optimise the generative LSTMs.

Table 4. Hyperparameters considered for optimisation.

Symbol	Description	Considered range
N_B	Batch size	$\{8, 16, 32, 64, 128, 256\}$
d_{RNN}	NN dimension	$\{16, 32, 64, 128, 256, 512, 768\}$
d_E	Embedding dimension	$\{2, 4, 8, 16, 32, 64, 128, 256\}$
N_E	Training epochs	$\{5, 10, 15, ..., 60\}$
τ	Temperature	$\{0.75, 1.0, 1.25, 1.5\}$

Phase One: N_B, d_{RNN}, d_E and N_E. In Phase One, 20 separate LSTMs are initialised, each with a different random seed. These models are trained on the training sets in Table 1 and then used to generate 20 respective sets of artificial text, each 8000 sequences in length and without ablation (All$_{Text}$, Table 3). Each of these sets of text is used to train an n-gram language model that is subsequently interpolated with the baseline n-gram (LM$_B$) after which the perplexities described in Sect. 3.2 are calculated and stored. The hyperparameters in Table 4 are tuned one at a time, repeating the above procedure for each considered value while holding the other parameters constant. Optimal hyperparameter values were chosen based on the mean over the 20 experiments. Since the hyperparameters N_B, d_{RNN} and d_E influence the rate of convergence, the models are first evaluated for $N_E = \{20, 40, 60\}$ epochs. Subsequently, N_E is optimized over the range in Table 4. Due to the computational complexity of this process, only one pass for each hyperparameter was performed.

Phase Two: τ. Phase Two of the optimization process utilised the best performing hyperparameters from Phase One to train 20 new LSTM models for each of the four text generation strategies in Table 3. For each strategy, 300,000 sequences are synthesized and this synthesis is repeated for the temperatures τ listed in Table 4. The set of 20 models associated with the text generation strategy with the best average performance was then used to generate 20 final datasets consisting of 1 million sequences each. The 20 sets of 1 million sequences are used to train 20 n-gram language models, which are each interpolated with the baseline n-gram (LM_B). The interpolated n-gram with the lowest code-switched perplexity (CPP) on the development set is then selected to be used in the third and final phase of augmentation experiments.

Table 5. Phase Three language models. LM_B: Baseline, LM_{B+S}: Baseline interpolated with language model trained on synthesized text, LM_{B+M}: Baseline interpolated with language models trained on monolingual text, LM_{B+S+M}: Baseline interpolated with both synthesized and monolingual language models.

Label	Train	Synth	English	Bantu
LM_B	×			
LM_{B+S}	×	×		
LM_{B+M}	×		×	×
LM_{B+S+M}	×	×	×	×

Phase Three: Interpolation. In Phase Three, we consider the four augmented n-gram language model configurations listed in Table 5. The baseline (LM_B) is trained only on the training set (Table 1). LM_{B+S} indicates an interpolation between the n-gram trained on the training set (LM_B) and the best performing n-gram trained on the synthesized dataset of 1 million sequences from Phase Two. LM_{B+M} indicates an interpolation between LM_B and two n-gram language models each trained on the respective out-of-domain monolingual corporus shown in Table 2. LM_{B+S+M} indicates an interpolation between LM_B, an n-gram language model trained on the synthesized dataset, as well as the two n-gram language models trained on the out-of-domain monolingual corpora. The resulting four interpolated n-gram language models in Table 5 are used in ASR experiments.

4   Experimental Results

We note at the outset that, in our previous work on the same speech datasets, synthesizing text using an LSTM without the hyperparameter optimisation we proposed here afforded only insubstantial ($<1\%$) improvements in perplexity over the baseline, and no improvements in speech recognition accuracy [2].

4.1 Hyperparameter Tuning

Table 6 shows the hyperparameter optimization process in Phase One (Sect. 3.3) for the English-isiZulu sub-corpus. Similar behaviour was observed for the other three language pairs. Each row reports the successive optimisation of the first four hyperparameters in Table 4. We see that interpolation with a language model trained on the synthesized dataset after optimising the first four hyperparameters leads to a 1.4% relative reduction in perplexity over the baseline LM_B. We expect only small perplexity improvements in Phase One due to the small amount of text generated. More substantial improvements are achieved in Phase 2 of the optimisation procedure. We also note from the table that code-switched perplexities (CPP) are much higher than overall perplexities (PP). This indicates the high degree of uncertainty the n-gram has as language switches. Reducing this uncertainty is the primary objective of our data augmentation.

Table 6. Development set perplexity (PP) and optimal average interpolation weight (λ) between the baseline LM_B and an n-gram trained on the synthesized text for the English-isiZulu sub-corpus. Each row indicates the optimization a successive hyperparameter (Par) and its best performing value (Value).

Par	Value	λ	$Loss_{Train}$	$Loss_{Dev}$	PP	CPP
LM_B	–	–	–	–	626	3226
N_B	32	0.94	2.46	4.32	622 ± 2.2	3257 ± 28.9
d_{RNN}	512	0.94	1.5	6.16	622 ± 1.6	3270 ± 27.8
d_E	64	0.9	1.25	5.87	616 ± 3.7	3235 ± 48.1
N_E	35	0.9	1.42	5.51	617 ± 2.5	3244 ± 36.4

We illustrate the effectiveness of the hyperparameter tuning strategy and the need to choose effective parameters in Fig. 2. The figure shows the average relative improvement over the four language pairs afforded by the language model incorporating the synthesized data relative to the baseline language model (LM_B) when optimising each hyperparameter. It is clear from the figure that each hyperparameter has an associated optimum.

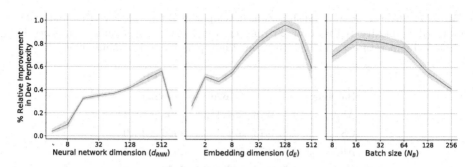

Fig. 2. Relative improvement in development set perplexity achieved during the successive optimisation of the three hyperparameters: neural network dimension d_{RNN}, embedding dimension d_{E}, and batch size N_{B}. Average improvements are calculated over the four language pairs and the three epochs ($N_{\text{E}} = \{20, 40, 60\}$) at which the 8000 sequences in Phase One of hyperparameter tuning are synthesised.

In Phase Two of our optimization process (Sect. 3.3) the temperature (τ) is optimised for each of the text generation strategies in Table 3. Table 7 presents these optimal temperatures for the English-isiZulu sub-corpus. We see that, of the values considered, $\tau = 1.5$ was optimal for all text generation strategies. We also observe that including all generated text (All_{Text}) reduces perplexity and code-switched perplexity by 6.71% and 9.92% respectively relative to the baseline. When only sequences with language switches are retained (CS_{Text}), both perplexity and code-switched perplexity show greater relative improvements of 8.79% and 17.4%. Prompting increased the proportion of synthesised sequences that contain code-switches from 32.0% (All_{Text}) to 87.6% (All_{Prompt}) and affords further perplexity improvements. Finally, combining both ablation and prompting (CS_{Prompt}) produced the best result of the four strategies and reduces perplexity and code-switched perplexity by 9.58% and 20.1% relative to the baseline. When this optimised LSTM is used to generate a larger dataset (1,000,000 sequences), further gains are achieved.

Table 8 presents the perplexity and code-switched perplexity of the interpolated language model for four temperatures when using the CS_{Prompt} strategy (Row 5 in Table 7). When artificial text is generated without modifying the LSTM distribution, the perplexity of the resulting interpolated language model is 6.23% better than the baseline. For the optimized temperature, this improvement increases to 9.58% for the overall perplexity and a more substantial 18.3% for the code-switched perplexity.

We note that higher temperatures produce lower perplexities and therefore more surprising predictions are more helpful for language modelling. Furthermore, the mixture weight λ shifts towards the synthesized language model the more the synthesized data is optimized. Finally, the standard deviation of the perplexities is two orders of magnitude smaller than the corresponding means for both PP and CPP, indicating a high degree of consistency.

Table 7. Mean ± stdev English-isiZulu development set perplexity (PP) and code-switched perplexity (CPP) over 20 runs for the four text generation strategies in Table 3. Temperature τ and average optimal interpolation weight λ are indicated.

Strategy	τ	λ	PP	CPP
Baseline	–	–	626	3226
All$_{Text}$	1.5	0.76	584 ± 2.5	2906 ± 56.3
CS$_{Text}$	1.5	0.73	571 ± 3.1	2666 ± 67.0
All$_{Prompt}$	1.5	0.73	568 ± 4.1	2628 ± 77.1
CS$_{Prompt}$	1.5	0.73	566 ± 2.5	2579 ± 61.8
1 Mil	1.5	0.73	559 ± 3.6	2513 ± 57.5

Table 8. Mean ± stdev English-isiZulu development set perplexity (PP) and code-switched perplexity (CPP) over 20 runs when interpolating LM$_B$ with an n-gram language model trained on the data generated using CS$_{Prompt}$ text synthesis for different temperatures τ. The associated average optimal interpolation weight is indicated by λ.

τ	λ	PP	CPP
–	–	626	3226
0.75	0.82	587 ± 3.5	3045 ± 61.9
1.0	0.75	570 ± 2.3	2798 ± 48.7
1.25	0.72	565 ± 3.8	2636 ± 60.9
1.5	0.73	566 ± 2.5	2579 ± 61.8

4.2   Speech Recognition

Table 9 shows the perplexities and word error rates achieved by each of the four augmented language model configurations outlined in Table 5 for all four language pairs.

We see again that the code-switched perplexity (CPP) is much larger than the overall perplexity (PP) for all language pairs. Furthermore, the larger vocabularies (Table 1) of isiZulu and isiXhosa are reflected in the higher perplexities, when compared with Sesotho and Setswana. Finally, we see that the speech recognition error rate at language switches (CSBG) is much higher than the overall word error rate.

Table 9 shows that the language models incorporating the synthesized data (LM$_{B+S}$) reduce code-switched perplexities by between 6.8% and 19.9% relative to the baseline (LM$_B$). Furthermore, Table 9 shows that, for all four language pairs, the language models that incorporate synthesized data (either LM$_{B+S}$ or LM$_{B+S+M}$) achieved improvements over the baseline in terms of overall word error rate (1.76% to 2.83% absolute) and also code-switched bigram error (0.86% to 1.37% absolute). From this we conclude that the synthesized text is able to reliably reduce the confusion around code-switched points. Additionally, we note

Table 9. Test set perplexity (PP), code-switched perplexity (CPP), monolingual perplexity (MPP), word error rate (WER), monolingual English and Bantu word error rates (WER_{ENG}, WER_{BAN}) and code-switched bigram (CSBG) error for the four language model configurations in Table 5.

Pair	Model	PP	CPP	MPP	WER	WER_{ENG}	WER_{BAN}	CSBG
EZ	LM_B	842.4	3637	534.8	41.40	36.56	45.12	62.66
	LM_{B+S}	758.5	**2912**	500.8	42.15	36.67	46.36	**61.52**
	LM_{B+M}	624.9	3550	367.4	**38.39**	31:35	**43.81**	62.67
	LM_{B+S+M}	**597.3**	2954	**365.8**	38.57	31.29	44.18	61.69
EX	LM_B	1018.0	5171	624.9	42.53	36.71	46.98	68.29
	LM_{B+S}	979.8	**4818**	611.3	41.83	36.08	**46.23**	**66.92**
	LM_{B+M}	**790.0**	5055	**456.2**	**40.56**	30.87	47.98	67.64
	LM_{B+S+M}	793.6	4883	463.5	40.77	31.0	48.24	68.06
ES	LM_B	285.9	1166	209.0	49.56	40.2	**56.95**	66.88
	LM_{B+S}	269.7	1016	202.5	49.49	39.44	57.44	66.53
	LM_{B+M}	**223.1**	1080	**158.9**	**47.14**	33.98	57.53	66.69
	LM_{B+S+M}	223.9	**979.4**	163.0	47.23	34.71	57.12	**65.91**
ET	LM_B	224.5	1025	154.3	40.80	31.01	47.23	54.90
	LM_{B+S}	202.3	864.8	142.8	40.24	29.96	47.0	**54.04**
	LM_{B+M}	179.8	963.3	120.6	**38.36**	26.23	46.34	54.47
	LM_{B+S+M}	**171.7**	**815.5**	**118.4**	38.56	26.84	**46.28**	54.91

that the reduction in code-switched error rate achieved by our language models incorporating the synthesized data (LM_{B+S}) is not achieved by incorporating only the monolingual data (LM_{B+M}). This emphasises the importance of obtaining more code-switched data, which we achieved here through synthesis.

Language models incorporating only the out-of-domain monolingual data (LM_{B+M}) substantially lower the overall and the monolingual perplexities (by between 19.9% and 31.3%) relative to the baseline. These language models also improve the speech recognition performance, outperforming the baseline by between 1.97% and 3.01% absolute in terms of word error rate. The strong correspondence between decreases in monolingual and overall perplexities and word error rate is due to the fact that, despite code switches, most speech remains monolingual. As expected, however, the additional monolingual data has little effect on the code-switched perplexity.

We also note that, for all four language pairs, the language models that incorporate only monolingual data (LM_{B+M}) result in the best overall word error rate, marginally outperforming the language models that also incorporate synthesized data (LM_{B+S+M}) by between 0.09% and 0.21% absolute. However, the columns WER_{ENG} and WER_{BAN} of Table 9 show that this is due mostly to an improvement in the English word error rate (absolute improvements of between 4.78% and 6.22%). Importantly, this is often at the expense of the

Bantu word error rate. Additionally the inclusion of only the monolingual data only marginally affects the recognition error at code-switches (between 0.01% worse and 0.65% better). In terms of code-switched bigram error, the language models which incorporated only the synthesized data outperformed the baseline language models and also the language models which incorporated only the monolingual data for all four language pairs.

5 Conclusion

We have presented a strategy that optimises an LSTM specifically for the purpose of generating code-switched utterances that can be used for language model augmentation. We find that, while our previous LSTMs that are not optimised in this way did not afford improvements, the optimised models are able to generate text the leads to consistent and substantial perplexity and word error rate improvements in all four considered language pairs, especially at language switches. We also see that, although out-of-domain but monolingual data does produce slightly better average speech recognition performance, this improvement is primarily seen for English and is at the expense of the performance in the four under-resourced languages as well as at language switches. We conclude that the hyperparameter tuning, ablation and prompting are effective techniques for improving the speech recognition accuracy at language switches severely under-resourced code-switched datasets.

Acknowledgments. We would like to thank the Council for Scientific and Industrial Research (CSIR), Department of Science and Technology, South Africa for providing access to their CHPC cluster. We gratefully acknowledge the support of Telkom South Africa.

References

1. Abadi, M., et al.: TensorFlow: large-scale machine learning on heterogeneous systems. White Paper (2015)
2. Biswas, A., van der Westhuizen, E., Niesler, T., de Wet, F.: Improving ASR for code-switched speech in under-resourced languages using out-of-domain data. In: Proceedings of the 6th International Workshop on Spoken Language Technologies for Under-Resourced Languages (SLTU), Gurugram, India (2018)
3. Biswas, A., Yilmaz, E., de Wet, F., van der Westhuizen, E., Niesler, T.: Semi-supervised development of ASR systems for multilingual code-switched speech in under-resourced languages. In: Proceedings of the 12th Language Resources and Evaluation Conference (LREC), Marseille, France (2020)
4. Biswas, A., Yılmaz, E., de Wet, F., van der Westhuizen, E., Niesler, T.: Semi-supervised acoustic model training for five-lingual code-switched ASR. In: Proceedings of Interspeech, Graz, Austria (2019)

5. Chang, C.T., Chuang, S.P., Lee, H.Y.: Code-switching sentence generation by generative adversarial networks and its application to data augmentation. In: Proceedings of Interspeech, Graz, Austria (2019)
6. Cho, K., et al.: Learning phrase representations using RNN encoder-decoder for statistical machine translation. In: Proceedings of the Conference on Empirical Methods in Natural Language Processing (EMNLP), Doha, Qatar (2014)
7. Deuchar, M.: Welsh-English code-switching and the matrix language frame model. Lingua **116**(11), 1986–2011 (2006)
8. Devlin, J., Chang, M.W., Lee, K., Toutanova, K.: BERT: pre-training of deep bidirectional transformers for language understanding. arXiv preprint arXiv:1810.04805 (2018)
9. Gao, Y., Feng, J., Liu, Y., Hou, L., Pan, X., Ma, Y.: Code-switching sentence generation by BERT and generative adversarial networks. In: Proceedings of Interspeech, Graz, Austria (2019)
10. Garg, S., Parekh, T., Jyothi, P.: Code-switched language models using dual RNNs and same-source pretraining. In: Proceedings of the Conference on Empirical Methods in Natural Language Processing (EMNLP), Brussels, Belgium (2018)
11. Graves, A.: Generating sequences with recurrent neural networks. arXiv preprint arXiv:1308.0850 (2013)
12. Hochreiter, S., Schmidhuber, J.: Long short-term memory. Neural Comput. **9**(8), 1735–1780 (1997)
13. Hu, X., Zhang, Q., Yang, L., Gu, B., Xu, X.: Data augmentation for code-switch language modeling by fusing multiple text generation methods. In: Proceedings of Interspeech, Shanghai, China (2020)
14. Jozefowicz, R., Zaremba, W., Sutskever, I.: An empirical exploration of recurrent network architectures. In: Proceedings of the International Conference on Machine Learning (2015)
15. Kingma, D.P., Ba, J.: Adam: a method for stochastic optimization. arXiv preprint arXiv:1412.6980 (2014)
16. Lee, G., Yue, X., Li, H.: Linguistically motivated parallel data augmentation for code-switch language modeling. In: Proceedings of Interspeech, Graz, Austria (2019)
17. Myers-Scotton, C.: Duelling Languages: Grammatical Structure in Codeswitching. Oxford University Press, Oxford (1997)
18. Povey, D., et al.: The Kaldi speech recognition toolkit. In: Proceedings of the IEEE Workshop on Automatic Speech Recognition and Understanding (ASRU), Hawaii, USA (2011)
19. Stolcke, A.: SRILM-an extensible language modeling toolkit. In: Proceedings of the Seventh International Conference on Spoken Language Processing (ICSLP), Colorado, USA (2002)
20. Taneja, K., Guha, S., Jyothi, P., Abraham, B.: Exploiting monolingual speech corpora for code-mixed speech recognition. In: Proceedings of Interspeech, Graz, Austria (2019)
21. van der Westhuizen, E., Niesler, T.: A first South African corpus of multilingual code-switched soap opera speech. In: Proceedings of the Eleventh International Conference on Language Resources and Evaluation (LREC). European Language Resources Association (ELRA), Miyazaki (2018)
22. van der Westhuizen, E., Niesler, T.: Automatic speech recognition of English-isiZulu code-switched speech from South African soap operas. Procedia Comput. Sci. **81**, 121–127 (2016). 5th Workshop on Spoken Language Technologies for Under-resourced languages (SLTU), Yogyakarta, Indonesia

23. van der Westhuizen, E., Niesler, T.R.: Synthesised bigrams using word embeddings for code-switched ASR of four South African language pairs. Comput. Speech Lang. **54**, 151–175 (2019)

24. Yılmaz, E., van den Heuvel, H., van Leeuwen, D.: Acoustic and textual data augmentation for improved ASR of code-switching speech. In: Proceedings of Interspeech, Hyderabad, India (2018)

Synthesis Speech Based Data Augmentation for Low Resource Children ASR

Virender Kadyan[1,3], Hemant Kathania[2,3(✉)], Prajjval Govil[3], and Mikko Kurimo[3]

[1] Speech and Language Research Centre, School of Computer Science, University of Petroleum and Energy Studies, Dehradun, Uttarakhand, India
vkadyan@ddn.upes.ac.in
[2] Department of Electronics and Communication Engineering, National Institute of Sikkim, Ravangla, India
hemant.kathania@aalto.fi, hemant.ece@nitsikkim.ac.in
[3] Department of Signal Processing and Acoustics, Aalto University, Espoo, Finland
{prajjval.govil,mikko.kurimo}@aalto.fi

Abstract. Successful speech recognition for children requires large training data with sufficient speaker variability. The collection of such a training database of children's voices is challenging and very expensive for zero/low resource language like Punjabi. In this paper, the data scarcity issue of the low resourced language Punjabi is addressed through two levels of augmentation. The original training corpus is first augmented by modifying the prosody parameters for pitch and speaking rate. Our results show that the augmentation improves the system performance over the baseline system. Then the augmented data combined with original data and used to train the TTS system to generate synthesis data and extended dataset is further used for augmented by generating children's utterances using text-to-speech synthesis and sampling the language model with methods that increase the acoustic and lexical diversity. The final speech recognition performance indicates a relative improvement of 50.10% with acoustic and 57.40% with language diversity based augmentation in comparison to that of the baseline system respectively.

Keywords: Low resource · Children speech recognition · Prosody modification · Speech synthesis · Tacotron

1 Introduction

In recent years, Automatic speech recognition (ASR) system for children speech is an active area of research. It also showed a significant progress on inclusive ASR technologies. At the same time, spoken interfaces are utilized increasingly in smart devices through applications like Amazon Alexa, Google Home and Apple Siri [27]. The wide and successful real world use of such a general purpose spoken interface requires a vast amount of training data for the ASR system [4].

© Springer Nature Switzerland AG 2021
A. Karpov and R. Potapova (Eds.): SPECOM 2021, LNAI 12997, pp. 317–326, 2021.
https://doi.org/10.1007/978-3-030-87802-3_29

Still, only a few languages like English, Chinese and Arabic have sufficient speech and language data resources and, in fact, most other languages spoken in the world have low or even zero resources. Research programs like IARPA Babel have facilitated ASR development in many low resourced languages [19], but there are still languages like Punjabi spoken in Indian part of Punjab where speech resources for children are zero and for adults very small[1] even though it is spoken by as many as 105 million native speakers.

For building large vocabulary ASR system large amount of training data is required. This challenge occurs because of the high necessity of acoustic, speaker and linguistic variability and the cost of the large-scale human transcription work. In the past, efforts have been made to explore training data of other languages to be employed via multilingual deep neural networks. Additional corpora have been generated through in or out domain strategies using transfer learning [32], model-agnostic meta learning algorithm [5], and triangular architecture [21] etc. They contributed towards higher recognition rate in various other languages [14]. A few studies on low resource languages have investigated whether limited training speakers could be extended using single or multiple data augmentation [8,9,19]. Recently various data augmentation approaches have been explored using language adaptive DNN [15], mapping of acoustic feature through conversion of adult voice into child voice, processing of corrupted clean data [6,12], and speech dereverberation [29] are simulated using Generative adversarial network (GAN) [27], speed, volume and spectogram perturbation. These approaches works through masking of time or frequency parameters [11].

So far, few general purpose ASR has focused upon data augmentation using the training speakers only. This can be performed, for example, by prosody modification of the training data [10,25]. This augmentation approach is not much beneficial for ASR system. It occurred due to lack of robustness in parameter estimation. Consequently, prosody transfer based ASR-TTS methods are also found to be effective in generation of audios through voice conversion [30].

Till date very limited work on text-to-speech synthesis (TTS) have been employed for low resource languages [2]. A few other voice mapping techniques between train or test utterances have been performed by Tacotron 2 [26], Transformer TTS [13] and Fast Speech [22]. Unfortunately, on small training sets this generates unnatural voices which are not beneficial for training the ASR system. A range of approaches have been examined to overcome such issues. These involve either tuning the original voice or generation of utterances from the text data. This has recently created a lot of attention by cascading ASR-TTS for generation of synthetic copies. This behaves like a recognition-conversion system which carries language specific information [7,16]. The task of generation of audios from text is leveraged using TTS synthesis [3]. For most languages it is easier to find or prepare text than speech corpora. A TTS helped in replication of its training data. It contain the characteristics which is similar to the training of an ASR model. However, this approach is well suited for low resource languages where there is no training data. Previous studies on data augmentation

---

[1] LDC-IL, Punjabi Raw Speech Corpus, https://data.ldcil.org/punjabi-raw-speech-corpus last accessed 2021/05/10.

mostly focused on individual approaches only. Not much work has been reported on examining the effect of TTS under low resource circumstances. Though this study includes cascading of TTS-ASR for generation of synthetic data not only on original speech but also indulge the characteristics of prosody data which provide speech which is equivalent to that of human original audios quality.

In this paper, we first collected new speech data for Punjabi children, and created a baseline ASR system using TDNN acoustic model in Kaldi. However, the baseline result was poor because of the limited amount of training data. To capture more acoustic and speaker variability to alleviate the data scarcity we tried two types of data augmentation methods. Initial augmentation was performed by modifying prosody parameters (pitch and speaking rate) to introduce more acoustic variability. Further we used the prosody based augmented data to generate synthetic speech data using a Tacotron-based TTS system. In the TTS system we investigated acoustic and lexical diversity methods in data generation. We also explored sampling new sentences from our language model in addition to both the diversity models.

2   Data

In this study, a Punjabi language children speech corpus has been collected from native speakers of India part of Punjab. Despite being spoken or written by large number of speakers it is still declared as under-resource language. Our self created corpus was built through read speech. The Punjab School Education Board books were read aloud by pupils from 7 to 14 years. A few pupils also contributed spontaneous speech by explaining on a certain topic like about themselves, their community etc. The corpus was collected from 79 speakers (35 male and 44 female) which were further divided into train and test speakers in 80:20 ratio. No speakers nor sentences occur both in the train and test data. Corpus statistics like age group, duration etc. are presented in Table 1. The collected speech were varying with different prosody parameters like speaking rate (SR), and pitch. It resulted into huge variations among speech which were collected from different speakers. Pupils up to 10 years old spoke long sentences by concatenating or by taking a short pause between two continuous sentences but above 10 years old pupils spoke sentences fluently. The corpus was recorded through mobile devices in a controlled noise-free environment. The speech data was sampled at 16 kHz. Each speaker spoke long sentences of up to 8–9 words.

3   Baseline System

We used a Kaldi toolkit-based recipe to train the baseline ASR system [18]. It utilizes conventional MFCC features using 40 channel Mel-filterbank with a frame size of 25 ms and frame shift of 10 ms to train DNN and TDNN-based acoustic models [1,17]. For normalization, cepstral feature-space maximum likelihood linear regression (fMLLR) was used. The fMLLR transformations for the training and test data were generated using the speaker adaptive training [20]. LDA-MLLT+SAT based GMM alignment labels were used to train the DNN and

Table 1. Indian Punjabi speech corpus details.

Purpose	Training	Testing
No. of speakers	63 (28 m and 35 f)	16 (7 m and 9 f)
Speaker age	7–14 years	7–14 years
No. of sentences	8420	2250
Duration (h)	12.20	2.50
Vocabulary size	8587	2588

TDNN acoustic models. The initial as well as final learning rates were kept as 0.005 and 0.0005, respectively. Further Tanh nonlinearity was used in the DNN architecture. The number of hidden nodes was kept at 512 whereas a total of 3 hidden layers are employed in it. On the other hand, i-vector [24] based speaker adaptation was used for the TDNN based acoustic model. The decoding is then performed using a bigram language model for the DNN system and a 4-g maximum entropy language model built using SRILM toolkit [28] for the TDNN system. Baseline WER's for the DNN and TDNN-based systems are given in Table 2. From Table 2 it can be noted that the TDNN system outperforms the DNN so for further study we used the TDNN system.

Table 2. WER obtained on the baseline DNN and TDNN acoustic models.

Acoustic model	WER (%)
DNN	12.73
TDNN	9.18

4   Data Augmentation

In this paper, we tried to implement three type of augmentation approaches like prosody based data augmentation (Sect. 4.1), TTS based data augmentation (Sect. 4.2) and language model sampling based data augmentation (Sect. 4.3).

4.1   Prosody Based Data Augmentation

We change two types of prosody parameters, the pitch scale (PS) and the speaking rate (SR), systematically to add more prosody variation in the children's speech (Sect. 2). We then augment the modified data to the original corpora for further system development. To modify the pitch and speaking rate, we have explored Time Scale Modification (TSM) based on Real-Time Iterative Spectrogram Inversion with Look-Ahead (RTISI-LA) algorithm [10,31]. Both these prosody parameters are tunable and we varied the pitch modification factor s from 0.65 to 1.45 to modify pitch and the speaking rate modification factor α

from 0.65 to 1.85 with a step size of 0.10. The best values of pitch 0.85 and speaking rate 1.15 were selected on the lower WER of test set and later these values are utilized for further experimentation. RTISI-LA algorithm constructs a high-quality time-domain signal from its short-time magnitude spectrum. The effect of the prosody based data augmentation made to the original data is reported in Table 3. We found that combining the pitch scale and speaking rate based data augmentation improves most over the baseline.

Table 3. WER obtained on prosody modification based data augmented system.

System type	WER (%)
Original (O)	9.18
O+SR	9.06
O+PS	8.98
O+PS+SR	7.84

4.2 Speech Synthesis Based Data Augmentation

In the previous section, we proposed prosody based data augmentation to capture more acoustic variability. The prosody modified data was then combined with the original data to train a TTS model based on Tacotron2 [26]. This not only provides the effect of synthesized copies of the original audios, but it also induces characteristics of the prosody modified audios. To produce diverse speaker representation on train utterances we employed an acoustic diversity method which improved the ASR performance over the baseline ASR. Consequently, the impact of lexical diversity for TTS utterances was evaluated using Tacotron 2. Only few synthetic utterances were not found to be useful and others were resemble to natural speakers' audios. Finally we can artificially increase the acoustic and lexical diversity of the training data.

Acoustic Diversity. In this section, a Tacotron2 based text-to-speech synthesis model architecture was used to process an input text sequence. It is a combination of encoder-decoder network with an attention mechanism, and a Wavenet based Vocoder. It takes input as a sequence of text in Punjabi language, which is encoded by encoder. In the first part of the encoder, the character sequence is converted into a word embedding vector. The input text sequence embedding is encoded by 3 convolution layers each containing 512 filters of shape 5 × 1, followed by a bidirectional LSTM layer of 250 units for each direction. Tacotron 2 also uses 'Local sensitive attention' which takes the encoder output as input and tries to summarize the full encoded sequence as a fixed length context vector for each decoder output step. Later, a decoder is employed which is an autoregressive recurrent neural network. It predicts a mel spectrogram from the encoded input sequence one frame at a time. The output of the attention layer is passed through a small pre-net containing 256 hidden ReLU (Rectified Linear Unit) units. The pre-net output and attention context vector are concatenated and passed through a stack of LSTM layers. The output of the LSTM layer is projected through a linear transform to predict the target spectrogram frame. This helps in prediction of a normalized weight vector which can be further employed for aggregation on the basis of attention history. The predicted mel spectrogram is passed through convolution postnet layers. The postnet layer predicts a residual to add to the prediction to improve the overall reconstruction. Finally, the mel spectrogram is transformed into time domain waveforms by modified Wavenet vocoder. The mel spectrograms are mapped to a fixed dimensional embedding vector, known as deep speaker vectors (d-vectors). These d-vectors are frame-level speaker discriminative features that represent the speaker characteristics. The proposed system uses three different approaches to generate d-vectors for inference to handle speaker diversity in the synthesized data. Training of the TTS is done with a GMM based attention model followed by LSTM layers. All the local encoder input is processed and fed to its decoder. This provides data duplicates by synthesized data which was later used for training utterances augmentation. In these, training data was extended by combining one more type of augmented data i.e. synthesized copies which were generated with the help of training utterances. It has been performed by using three different types of speaker conditioning information [23]:

– Original (O'): A set of d-vector is employed as speaker condition information on train data. In this, the output is synthetic copies that resemble to the source data.
– Sampled (S): In this case d-vectors were obtained on random selection of speakers which were different in characteristics to that of source utterances and synthesized utterances. Apart, these speaker information were seen earlier by the synthesizer.
– Random (R): A random set of 256 dimensional vector information were generated after projected them on unit hypersphere through L2 normalization. It was employed further for d-vector and employed in synthesized utterances.

In these types of synthesized dataset, the acoustic diversity (AD) helped in controlling of speaker diversity among the training dataset. It was performed by extracting speaker information as d-vectors. On the basis of O', S, and R synthetic speech, different augmented data has been generated which were further added to original data to train an ASR system. It was generated on basis of data in train, train+test and train+new speaker based TTS model. The resulting augmented data introduced more speaker variability. As shown in Table 4 the Sampled (S) type gives a lower WER than others and the best performance was achieved by further augmentation of baseline + tacotron (O'+S+R) data.

Lexical Diversity. The purpose of using Lexical Diversity (LD) based TTS synthesis was to generate audio from text transcripts while using the model speaker's characteristics. It helped in production of speech which resulted into

Table 4. WER obtained on acoustic diversity based augmented ASR system.

AD	WER (%)
None	–
Original (O')	6.69
Random (R)	7.14
Sampled (S)	6.27
O+O'+R+S	5.62

Table 5. WER obtained on lexical diversity based augmented ASR system.

LD	WER (%)
Sampled (S')	4.84
Original (O")	4.79
S'+O"	4.18

addition of lexical as well as acoustic variations in our train data. One approach to add lexical diversity is to use the transcripts in the test data by ignoring the audios corresponding to them. Two types of augmented data were generated as Original (O") and Sampled (S'). In case of S' there was no involvement of test audio whereas in O" the speakers were synthesized from the test speakers' audios. In such case it significantly enhanced the performance of ASR system which would not be generally true in real world situations. However, such LD approach could be beneficial in speaker and domain specific ASR applications. However, the LD results presented in Table 5 show that O" where augmenting was based on knowledge of the test audios is only slightly better than S' which was augmented with only test transcripts and copies of train utterances. To obtain more gain on ASR performance, the output audios generated from combination of O" + S" systems were further pooled with the baseline.

4.3 Language Model Sampling

To further boost the performance of AD and LD based augmented systems, Language model sampling has been performed with most common lexicon based utterances of Punjabi language that had a maximum length of 15 words. The collected utterances were synthesized and pooled with training set audios to lower the WER of the AD and LD systems. The utterance augmentation was found to be beneficial to some extent as depicted in Tables 6. These systems achieved the lowest WER of 4.58% and 3.91% on AD or LD augmented system. However, the system performance degraded when too much variation of training utterances was augmented as synthetic utterances. The best results were found at augmenting 10K utterances as presented in Table 6.

Table 6. WER obtained on language model sampling augmentation for the baseline ASR system using acoustic diversity (AD) and lexical diversity (LD).

LMS	WER (%)	
	AD	LD
0	5.62	4.18
5K	4.71	4.02
10K	4.58	3.91
25K	4.97	4.17

5 Conclusion

We have collected new speech data for Punjabi children to build ASR system in this language specifically for children's speech. The baseline system built on this data was not good. So to capture more acoustic and speaker variability for this kind of limited training data scenario we have investigated data augmentation methods. Firstly, we explored prosody based data augmentation and found improvement in system performance. Secondly, characteristics of Tacotron 2 was demonstrated in two ways: first training synthesis by introducing multi-speaker variability as acoustic diversity, and later by adding new utterances using language model as lexical diversity. Each method was experimented alone or through a combination which shows more performance improvement. System performance has been obtained on general and domain-specific systems through Tacotron 2 model. The best system provided a relative improvement of 50.10% with AD and 57.40% with LD method on LMS over the baseline system.

References

1. Dahl, G., Yu, D., Deng, L., Acero, A.: Context-dependent pre-trained deep neural networks for large vocabulary speech recognition. IEEE Trans. Speech Audio Process. **20**(1), 30–42 (2012)
2. Dalmia, S., Sanabria, R., Metze, F., Black, A.W.: Sequence-based multi-lingual low resource speech recognition. In: Proceedings of the ICASSP, pp. 4909–4913. IEEE (2018)
3. Du, C., Yu, K.: Speaker augmentation for low resource speech recognition. In: Proceedings of the ICASSP, pp. 7719–7723. IEEE (2020)
4. Evermann, G., et al.: Development of the 2003 CU-HTK conversational telephone speech transcription system. In: Proceedings of the ICASSP, vol. 1, pp. I-249. IEEE (2004)
5. Gu, J., Wang, Y., Chen, Y., Cho, K., Li, V.O.: Meta-learning for low-resource neural machine translation. arXiv preprint arXiv:1808.08437 (2018)
6. Hannun, A., et al.: Deep speech: scaling up end-to-end speech recognition. arXiv preprint arXiv:1412.5567 (2014)
7. Hartmann, W., Ng, T., Hsiao, R., Tsakalidis, S., Schwartz, R.M.: Two-stage data augmentation for low-resourced speech recognition. In: Proceedings of the INTERSPEECH, pp. 2378–2382 (2016)

8. Kadyan, V., Shanawazuddin, S., Singh, A.: Developing children's speech recognition system for low resource Punjabi language. Appl. Acoust. **178**, 108002 (2021)
9. Kanda, N., Takeda, R., Obuchi, Y.: Elastic spectral distortion for low resource speech recognition with deep neural networks. In: 2013 IEEE Workshop on Automatic Speech Recognition and Understanding, pp. 309–314. IEEE (2013)
10. Kathania, H., Singh, M., Grósz, T., Kurimo, M.: Data augmentation using prosody and false starts to recognize non-native children's speech. In: Proceedings of the INTERSPEECH 2020 (2020). To appear
11. Ko, T., Peddinti, V., Povey, D., Khudanpur, S.: Audio augmentation for speech recognition. In: Sixteenth Annual Conference of the International Speech Communication Association (2015)
12. Kathania, H.K., Kadiri, S.R., Alku, P., Kurimo, M.: Study of formant modification for children ASR. In: Proceedings of the ICASSP, pp. 7429–7433 (2020)
13. Li, N., Liu, S., Liu, Y., Zhao, S., Liu, M.: Neural speech synthesis with transformer network. In: Proceedings of the AAAI Conference on Artificial Intelligence, vol. 33, pp. 6706–6713 (2019)
14. Müller, M., Stüker, S., Waibel, A.: Language adaptive DNNs for improved low resource speech recognition. In: Proceedings of the INTERSPEECH, pp. 3878–3882 (2016)
15. Müller, M., Waibel, A.: Using language adaptive deep neural networks for improved multilingual speech recognition. In: Proceedings of the 12th International Workshop on Spoken Language Translation (IWSLT) (2015)
16. Park, D.S., et al.: SpecAugment: a simple data augmentation method for automatic speech recognition. arXiv preprint arXiv:1904.08779 (2019)
17. Povey, D., et al.: Semi-orthogonal low-rank matrix factorization for deep neural networks. In: Yegnanarayana, B. (ed.) Proceedings of the INTERSPEECH 2018, pp. 3743–3747. ISCA (2018)
18. Povey, D., et al.: The Kaldi Speech recognition toolkit. In: Proceedings of the ASRU, December 2011
19. Ragni, A., Knill, K., Rath, S.P., Gales, M.: Data augmentation for low resource languages (2014)
20. Rath, S.P., Povey, D., Veselý, K., Černocký, J.: Improved feature processing for deep neural networks. In: Proceedings of the INTERSPEECH (2013)
21. Ren, S., Chen, W., Liu, S., Li, M., Zhou, M., Ma, S.: Triangular architecture for rare language translation. arXiv preprint arXiv:1805.04813 (2018)
22. Ren, Y., et al.: FastSpeech: fast, robust and controllable text to speech. In: Advances in Neural Information Processing Systems, pp. 3171–3180 (2019)
23. Rosenberg, A., et al.: Speech recognition with augmented synthesized speech. In: 2019 IEEE Automatic Speech Recognition and Understanding Workshop (ASRU), pp. 996–1002. IEEE (2019)
24. Saon, G., Soltau, H., Nahamoo, D., Picheny, M.: Speaker adaptation of neural network acoustic models using i-vectors. In: 2013 IEEE Workshop on Automatic Speech Recognition and Understanding, Olomouc, Czech Republic, 8–12 December 2013, pp. 55–59. IEEE (2013)
25. Shahnawazuddin, S., Ahmad, W., Adiga, N., Kumar, A.: In-domain and out-of-domain data augmentation to improve children's speaker verification system in limited data scenario. In: Proceedings of the ICASSP, pp. 7554–7558. IEEE (2020)
26. Shen, J., et al.: Natural TTS synthesis by conditioning WaveNet on Mel spectrogram predictions. In: Proceedings of the ICASSP, pp. 4779–4783. IEEE (2018)

27. Sriram, A., Jun, H., Gaur, Y., Satheesh, S.: Robust speech recognition using generative adversarial networks. In: Proceedings of the ICASSP, pp. 5639–5643. IEEE (2018)
28. Stolcke, A.: SRILM - an extensible language modeling toolkit. In: Hansen, J.H.L., Pellom, B.L. (eds.) INTERSPEECH 2002. ISCA (2002)
29. Wang, K., Zhang, J., Sun, S., Wang, Y., Xiang, F., Xie, L.: Investigating generative adversarial networks based speech dereverberation for robust speech recognition. arXiv preprint arXiv:1803.10132 (2018)
30. Zhang, J.X., et al.: Voice conversion by cascading automatic speech recognition and text-to-speech synthesis with prosody transfer. arXiv preprint arXiv:2009.01475 (2020)
31. Zhu, X., Beauregard, G.T., Wyse, L.L.: Real-time signal estimation from modified short-time Fourier transform magnitude spectra. IEEE Trans. Audio Speech Lang. Process. **15**(5), 1645–1653 (2007)
32. Zoph, B., Yuret, D., May, J., Knight, K.: Transfer learning for low-resource neural machine translation. arXiv preprint arXiv:1604.02201 (2016)

End-to-End Russian Speech Recognition Models with Multi-head Attention

Irina Kipyatkova[✉]

St. Petersburg Federal Research Center of the Russian Academy of Sciences (SPC RAS),
SPIIRAS, St. Petersburg, Russia
kipyatkova@iias.spb.su

Abstract. The aim of the current research was to improve the Russian end-to-end speech recognition system developed in SPC RAS by application of multi-head attention. The system was created by joining Connectional Temporal Classification model and attention-based encoder-decoder. The models with following attention types were created and researched: dot-product attention, additive attention, location-based attention, and multi-resolution location-based attention. The experiments of using different number of attention vectors were performed. The models were trained on a small Russian speech corpus of 60 h by application of transfer learning with English as non-target language. The usage of multi-head attention reduced word error rate for dot-product and additive attention comparing to the results obtained with one attention vector.

Keywords: End-to-end speech recognition · Attention mechanism · Multi-head attention · Encoder-decoder · Russian speech

1 Introduction

In recent years, attention-based encoder-decoder has become a widespread model for sequence-to-sequence task which includes automatic speech recognition (ASR) [1]. In encoder-decoder the encoder transforms an input sequence $\mathbf{X} = (x_1, \ldots, x_T)$ into an intermediate sequence $\mathbf{H} = (h_1, \ldots, h_T)$. Based on this intermediate sequence, the decoder generates an output sequence $\mathbf{Y} = (y_1, \ldots, y_I)$, with generated symbols being used as additional inputs when predicting the next symbol. Attention mechanism selects a portion of the input sequence, which is used for prediction of the next output symbol. One type of attention mechanism is multi-head attention [2], in which multiple attention vectors are used to track different areas of input data.

Attention-based encoder-decoder architecture is used in end-to-end ASR systems which incorporate all models of the standard ASR system, namely acoustic model, language model and vocabulary (lexical model) [3]. Moreover, in end-to-end models this architecture can be used jointly with model based on Connectionist Temporal Classification (CTC) [4]. In this case two loss functions are used by combining them using weighted sum as follows [5]:

$$L = \lambda L_{CTC} + (1 - \lambda)L_{att}, \tag{1}$$

© Springer Nature Switzerland AG 2021
A. Karpov and R. Potapova (Eds.): SPECOM 2021, LNAI 12997, pp. 327–335, 2021.
https://doi.org/10.1007/978-3-030-87802-3_30

where L_{CTC} is an objective for CTC and L_{att} is an objective for attention-based model, λ is a weight of CTC model, $\lambda \in [0, 1]$.

In many recent papers different types of attention mechanisms are investigated. For example, an application of self-attention in CTC model was researched in [6]. The proposed model allowed the authors to outperform other end-to-end models (CTC, encoder-decoder, joint CTC/encoder-decoder and other) in terms of word error rate (WER).

In [7] character-aware attention was used to take into account morphological relationships for prediction of both subword units as well as whole words. In the paper it was proposed to use separate recurrent neural network in parallel to encoder in order to generate subword unit representations. A trigger attention was suggested in [8]. In the proposed model, at each time step of decoder, the trigger attention controls encoder states at which attention mechanism looks upon. For online speech recognition monotonic attention [9] can be used.

Multi-head decoder for end-to-end speech recognition was presented in [10]. In the proposed model, multiple decoders were used for each attention and their outputs were combined to generate final output. Moreover, different attention functions were used for each head.

Application of multi-head attention in joint CTC/encoder-decoder model was described in [11], where it was proposed to perform multiplication of outputs from two consecutive layers of the encoder for computation the attention score. Thus long-term dependencies were included in the calculation of the attention score.

The aim of this research was to explore multi-head attention in end-to-end Russian speech recognition system, combining encoder-decoder and CTC models. The rest of the paper is organized as follows. In Sect. 2 we present our CTC/encoder-decoder end-to-end speech recognition model, in Sect. 3 we describe multi-head attention mechanism, the experimental results are given in Sect. 4, in Sect. 5 we make a conclusion to our work.

2   Architecture of End-to-End Speech Recognition Model

In the research, we used joint CTC-attention based encoder-decoder model. The similar architecture was proposed in [5]. The architecture of the used model is presented on Fig. 1, where $\mathbf{X}$ is an input vector, $\mathbf{H}$ is a vector of hidden states obtained from encoder, y_i is the output on i-th iteration, λ is CTC weight, and ψ is language model (LM) weight. Model's topology is described in [12]. Filter banks features were used as input. The first block of the model was feature extraction block that was VGG model [13] with residual connection (ResNet) [14]. Bidirectional Long Short-Term Memory (BLSTM) network with highway connections [15] was used as encoder. Highway connection solves the vanishing gradient problem. Highway network contains special gates controlling the information flow. In our previous research we found out that the usage of highway connections in encoder network improves speech recognition results [16]. Long Short-Term Memory (LSTM) network was used as decoder. In decoder, the multi-head attention was applied. The applied types of attention are described in the next section.

The main model's parameters are presented in Table 1.

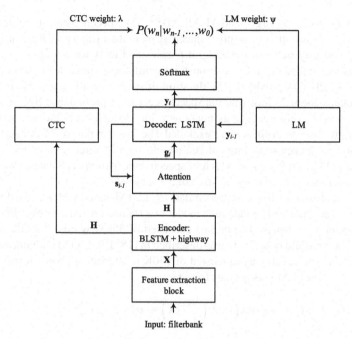

Fig. 1. Architecture of End-to-End Speech Recognition Model.

Table 1. Parameters of the used end-to-end model.

Parameter	Value
The dimension of feature extraction block's output	128
The number of layers in encoder	5
The number of units in each layer in encoder	512
Dropout rate in encoder	0.4
The number of layers in decoder	2
The number of units in each layer in decoder	512
CTC weight at training stage	0.3
CTC weight at decoding stage	0.5

The model was trained with the help of transfer learning method with English speech data used as non-target data (360 h of English data from LibriSpeech [17] corpus were used for pretraining). Transfer learning was used for initialization of weights of networks of the encoder and the feature extraction block. Then models were trained on Russian speech data composed from the Russian speech corpus collected at SPC RAS as well as free speech corpora Voxforge[1] and M-AILABS[2]. The speech corpus recorded in SPC RAS [12, 18] contains utterances pronounced by more than 100 native Russian speakers. Mostly phonetically rich and meaningful phrases and texts were used for recordings. The corpus was collected in clean acoustic conditions, a signal-to-noise ratio (SNR) at least 35–40 dB was provided. The duration of speech data is about 30 h. Voxforge corpus contains about 25 h of Russian speech recordings pronounced by 200 speakers, but unfortunately, some recordings contains a lot of noises, hesitations, self-repairs, etc., therefore some recordings were excluded.The Russian part of M-AILABS corpus contains 46 h of speech recordings of audiobooks read by three speaker (two men and one woman). As a result we had 60.6 h of speech data. This speech dataset was splitted into validation and trains parts with sizes of 5% and 95%.

Due to small size of Russian speech dataset, LSTM-based LM was used at speech recognition experiments. The language model was trained on text corpus collected from online Russian newspapers. The corpus consisted of 350M words (2.4 GB data). The text data collection and processing was described in [18, 19]. LSTM contained one layer with 512 cells. The vocabulary consisted of 150K most frequent word-forms from the training text corpus. LM was used as follows:

$$y_i = \underset{y_i}{\mathrm{argmax}} \left(log P\left(y_i^{hyb} | \mathbf{X} \right) + \psi \, log P_{LM} \left(y_i^{hyb} \right) \right), \tag{2}$$

where y_i^{hyb} is output of joint CTC and encoder-decoder model.

The end-to-end Russian speech recognition model was trained and tested using ESPnet toolkit [20] with a PyTorch as a back-end part.

3   Encoder-Decoder with Multi-head Attention

The attention based encoder-decoder model works as follows. Encoder transforms the input sequence $\mathbf{X} = (x_1, \dots x_T)$ into hidden state h_t:

$$\mathbf{h}_t = Encoder(\mathbf{X}) \tag{3}$$

Decoder predicts the next symbol $\mathbf{y}_i$ depending on the previous symbol $\mathbf{y}_{i-1}$, vector of decoder's hidden state on previous step $\mathbf{s}_{i-1}$, and a vector $\mathbf{r}_i$ defined as follows:

$$\mathbf{r}_i = \sum_{t=1}^{T} \alpha_{i,t} \mathbf{h}_t, \tag{4}$$

where α_i is vector of attention weights.

Thus, the sequence of symbols at output of decoder is defined as follows:

$$P(\mathbf{y}_i | \mathbf{y}_{1:i-1}, \mathbf{X}) = Decoder(\mathbf{r}_i, \mathbf{s}_{i-1}, \mathbf{y}_{i-1}) \tag{5}$$

---

[1] http://www.voxforge.org/.
[2] https://www.caito.de/2019/01/the-m-ailabs-speech-dataset/.

The attention mechanism helps the decoder to decide on which time frames and how much attention the decoder should pay to predict the output sequence at the appropriate time step [21]. In [2] attention is defined as mapping a query and a set of key-value pairs to an output, where the query ($\mathbf{q}_t$), keys ($\mathbf{k}_t$), values ($\mathbf{v}_t$), and output are all vectors. The query, key, and value vectors are computed as follows:

$$\mathbf{k}_t = \mathbf{W}_k \mathbf{h}_t, \tag{6}$$

$$\mathbf{v}_t = \mathbf{W}_v \mathbf{h}_t, \tag{7}$$

$$\mathbf{q}_t = \mathbf{W}_q \mathbf{s}_{t-1}. \tag{8}$$

Keys, values, and quires are packed together into matrices $\mathbf{K}$, $\mathbf{V}$, and $\mathbf{Q}$ respectively. The dimension of keys and quires is d_k, and dimension of values is d_v.

There are several types of attention mechanism. In this paper the following four types of attention [10] are researched:

- dot-product attention;
- additive attention;
- location-based attention;
- multi-resolution location-based attention (in case of multi-head attention).

Dot-product scaled attention is computed as follows [2]:

$$\alpha_i = softmax\left(\frac{\mathbf{Q}\mathbf{K}^\mathrm{T}}{\sqrt{d_k}}\right)\mathbf{V}. \tag{9}$$

Additive attention computes the compatibility function using a feed-forward network with a single hidden layer [2]:

$$\alpha_i = softmax\left(\frac{\mathbf{g}^\mathrm{T} tanh(\mathbf{Q} + \mathbf{K})}{\sqrt{d_k}}\right)\mathbf{V}, \tag{10}$$

where $\mathbf{g}$ is a vector of weights.

Location-based attention proposed in [22] takes into account alignment obtained at previous step. At first, vectors $\mathbf{f}_i$ are extracted for every position of previous alignment α_{i-1} by convolution with matrix $\mathbf{F}$:

$$\mathbf{f}_i = \mathbf{F}\alpha_{i-1}. \tag{11}$$

The obtained vectors $\mathbf{f}_i$ are used for computation of the attention:

$$\alpha_i = softmax\left(\frac{\mathbf{g}^\mathrm{T} tanh(\mathbf{Q} + \mathbf{f}_i + \mathbf{K})}{\sqrt{d_k}}\right)\mathbf{V}. \tag{12}$$

In multi-head attention several attention vectors are computed in parallel, this allows the model to jointly attend to information from different representation at different positions [2]. The resulting attention vector (α_i^{MH}) is computing by concatenation of all attention vectors:

$$\alpha_i^{MH} = Concat(head_1, \dots head_j, \dots head_M)\mathbf{W_o}, \tag{13}$$

where $head_j = Attention(\mathbf{K}, \mathbf{V}, \mathbf{Q})$, $\mathbf{W_o}$ – is a matrix of parameters, M – the number of attention vectors. All described above types of attention can be realized as multi-head attention. Moreover, in case of multi-head attention, multi-resolution location-based attention can be performed which is computed by using convolution filters of different size for every attention vector.

4   Results of Experiments on Russian Speech Recognition

Experiments on continuous Russian speech recognition were performed on our test speech corpus consisting of 500 phrases pronounced by 5 speakers. The phrases were taken from online newspaper which was not used for LM training. During experiments we used beam search pruning method similar to the approach described in [23]. Our method is described in detail in [24]. At the decoding stage we used gumbel-softmax function instead of softmax [25]. During our previous experiments we have obtained CER = 14.9 and WER = 37.1 without usage of transfer learning method. Transfer learning method allowed us to decrease CER to 10.5% and WER to 28.0%. These results were obtained with the usage of described above model architecture and location-aware attention in decoder network.

First, experiments on speech recognition using models with one attention vector in decoder were performed. All mentioned above types of attention were tried. Then speech recognition with end-to-end models with multi-head attention in decoder were carried out. Obtained results in terms of character error rate (CER) and word error rate (WER) are presented in Tables 2 and 3.

Table 2. Experimental results on speech recognition using models with multi-head attention in terms of CER (%).

Type of attention	Number of attention vectors				
	1	2	3	4	5
Dot-product	10.9	10.8	10.9	10.6	10.8
Additive	11.9	12.0	12.0	11.2	11.6
Location-based	10.9	11.0	**10.1**	10.7	11.8
Multi-resolution location based	11.9	11.4	12.5	12.3	12.3

Table 3. Experimental results on speech recognition using models with multi-head attention in terms of WER (%).

Type of attention	Number of attention vectors				
	1	2	3	4	5
Dot-product	30.3	29.3	29.2	30.0	**28.6**
Additive	31.9	30.7	31.2	**28.8**	29.2
Location-based	**27.5**	28.3	28.4	27.9	30.7
Multi-resolution location based	**27.9**	30.1	29.9	31.6	30.3

As we can see from the tables, application of multi-head attention allows to decrease WER when dot-product and additive attentions were used. As well we increased the number of attention vectors in dot-product attention up to 6 and obtained further CER and WER reduction, in this case CER was equal to 11.0 and WER was equal to 28.1. Application of several attention weights for location based attention did not lead to WER decreasing that can be connected with overtraining.

5 Conclusion and Future Work

In the paper, a joint CTC/encoder-decoder with the multi-head attention was investigated for application in Russian end-to-end speech recognition system. The usage of several attention weights allowed to slightly decrease WER for dot-product and additive attention. For dot-product attention the relative reduction of WER was 6% comparing to the usage of one attention vector. For additive attention WER relative reduction of 10% was achieved. Application of several attention vectors in location-based attention did not lead to improvement of speech recognition results that can be connected with overtraining, because training corpus of Russian speech was small. Therefore, the further researches will be connected with enlarging the training data and experimenting with the usage of other language as non-target language for transfer learning.

Acknowledgements. This research was supported by the Russian Foundation for Basic Research (project No. 19-29-09081) and by the state research № 0073-2019-0005.

References

1. Sutskever, I., Vinyals, O., Le, Q.V.: Sequence to sequence learning with neural networks. In: Advances in Neural Information Processing Systems. pp. 3104–3112 (2014)
2. Vaswani, A. et al.: Attention is all you need. arXiv preprint arXiv:1706.03762 (2017). https://arxiv.org/abs/1706.03762
3. Markovnikov, M., Kipyatkova, I.: An analytic survey of end-to-end speech recognition systems. SPIIRAS Proc. **58**, 77–110 (2018)

4. Graves, A., Fernández, S., Gomez, F., Schmidhuber, J.: Connectionist temporal classification: labelling unsegmented sequence data with recurrent neural networks. In: Proceedings of the 23rd International Conference on Machine Learning. pp. 369–376 (2006)

5. Kim, S., Hori, T., Watanabe, S: Joint ctc-attention based end-to-end speech recognition using multi-task learning. In: Proceedings of IEEE International Conference on Acoustics, Speech and Signal Processing (ICASSP-2017), pp. 4835–4839 (2017)

6. Salazar, J., Kirchhoff, K., Huang, Z.: Self-attention networks for connectionist temporal classification in speech recognition. In: Proceedings of IEEE International Conference on Acoustics, Speech and Signal Processing (ICASSP-2019), pp. 7115–7119 (2019)

7. Meng, Z., Gaur, Y., Li, J., Gong, Y.: Character-aware attention-based end-to-end speech recognition. In: Proceedings of IEEE Automatic Speech Recognition and Understanding Workshop (ASRU), pp. 949–955 (2019)

8. Moritz, N., Hori, T., Le Roux, J.: Triggered attention for end-to-end speech recognition. In: Proceedings of International Conference on Acoustics, Speech and Signal Processing (ICASSP-2019), pp. 5666–5670 (2019)

9. Raffel, C., Luong, M.-T., Liu, P.J., Weiss, R.J., Eck, D.: Online and linear-time attention by enforcing monotonic alignments. In: Proceedings of International Conference on Machine Learning, pp. 2837–2846 (2017)

10. Hayashi, T., et al.: Multi-head decoder for end-to-end speech recognition. arXiv preprint arXiv:1804.08050 (2018). https://arxiv.org/abs/1804.08050

11. Qin, C.-X., Zhang, W.-L., Qu, D.: A new joint CTC-attention-based speech recognition model with multi-level multi-head attention. EURASIP J. Audio, Speech, Music Proc. 2019(1), 1–12 (2019)

12. Kipyatkova, I., Markovnikov, N.: Experimenting with attention mechanisms in joint CTC-attention models for Russian speech recognition. In: Karpov, A., Potapova, R. (eds.) SPECOM 2020. LNCS (LNAI), vol. 12335, pp. 214–222. Springer, Cham (2020). https://doi.org/10.1007/978-3-030-60276-5_22

13. Simonyan, K., Zisserman, A.: Very deep convolutional networks for large-scale image recognition. ArXiv preprint arXiv:1409.1556 (2014). https://arxiv.org/abs/1409.1556

14. He, K., Zhang, X., Ren, S., Sun, J.: Deep residual learning for image recognition. In: Proceedings of the IEEE Conference on Computer Vision and Pattern Recognition, pp. 770–778 (2016)

15. Srivastava, R.K., Greff, K., Schmidhuber, J.: Highway networks. arXiv preprint arXiv:1505.00387 (2015). https://arxiv.org/abs/1505.00387

16. Kipyatkova, I.S., Karpov, A.A.: A comparative study of neural network architectures for integrated speech recognition system. J. Instrum. Eng. 63(11), 1027–1033 (2020). (In Russian)

17. Panayotov, V. et al.: Librispeech: an ASR corpus based on public domain audio books. In: IEEE International Conference on Acoustics, Speech, and Signal Processing (ICASSP-2015), pp. 5206–5210 (2015)

18. Kipyatkova, I., Karpov, A.: Class-based LSTM Russian language model with linguistic information. In: Proceedings 12th International Conference on Language Resources and Evaluation LREC-2020, ELRA, Marseille, France, pp. 2470–2474 (2020)

19. Kipyatkova, I., Karpov, A.: Lexicon size and language model order optimization for Russian LVCSR. In: Železný, M., Habernal, I., Ronzhin, A. (eds.) SPECOM 2013. LNCS (LNAI), vol. 8113, pp. 219–226. Springer, Cham (2013). https://doi.org/10.1007/978-3-319-01931-4_29

20. Watanabe, S. et al.: Espnet: end-to-end speech processing toolkit. In: INTERSPEECH-2018, pp. 2207–2211 (2018)

21. Karmakar, P., Teng, S.W., Lu, G.: Thank you for attention: a survey on attention-based artificial neural networks for automatic speech recognition. arXiv preprint arXiv:2102.07259 (2021). https://arxiv.org/abs/2102.07259

22. Chorowski, J.K., Bahdanau, D., Serdyuk, D., Cho, K., Bengio, Y.: Attention-based models for speech recognition. In: Advances in Neural Information Processing Systems, pp. 577–585 (2015)

23. Freitag, M., Al-Onaizan, Y.: Beam search strategies for neural machine translation. ArXiv preprint arXiv:1702.01806 (2017). https://arxiv.org/abs/1702.01806

24. Markovnikov, N., Kipyatkova, I.: Investigating joint CTC-attention models for end-to-end Russian speech recognition. In: Salah, A.A., Karpov, A., Potapova, R. (eds.) SPECOM 2019. LNCS (LNAI), vol. 11658, pp. 337–347. Springer, Cham (2019). https://doi.org/10.1007/978-3-030-26061-3_35

25. Jang, E., Gu, S., Poole, B.: Categorical reparameterization with gumbel softMax. ArXiv preprint arXiv:1611.01144 (2016). https://arxiv.org/abs/1611.01144

Word-Level Style Control for Expressive, Non-attentive Speech Synthesis

Konstantinos Klapsas[1][(✉)], Nikolaos Ellinas[1], June Sig Sung[2], Hyoungmin Park[2], and Spyros Raptis[1]

[1] Innoetics, Samsung Electronics, Athens, Greece
k.klapsas@partner.samsung.com, {n.ellinas,s.raptis}@samsung.com
[2] Mobile Communications Business, Samsung Electronics, Seoul, Republic of Korea
{js6.sung,hm94.park}@samsung.com

Abstract. This paper presents an expressive speech synthesis architecture for modeling and controlling the speaking style at a word level. It attempts to learn word-level stylistic and prosodic representations of the speech data, with the aid of two encoders. The first one models style by finding a combination of style tokens for each word given the acoustic features, and the second outputs a word-level sequence conditioned only on the phonetic information in order to disentangle it from the style information. The two encoder outputs are aligned and concatenated with the phoneme encoder outputs and then decoded with a Non-Attentive Tacotron model. An extra prior encoder is used to predict the style tokens autoregressively, in order for the model to be able to run without a reference utterance. We find that the resulting model gives both word-level and global control over the style, as well as prosody transfer capabilities.

Keywords: Text-to-speech · Prosody control · Expressive speech synthesis

1 Introduction

Since neural text-to-speech models such as Tacotron [16,22] significantly improved the quality and naturalness of speech synthesis systems, there has been an increased interest in approaches that expand on the basic architecture by explicitly modeling the prosody of the synthesized speech. This can be done either by using a reference from which prosody is copied [17], or by manually controlling the prosody on an utterance [24], or fine-grained level [12].

Of particular interest to our work is the Global Style Tokens mechanism (GST) [24] which assigns for each utterance a style embedding that is learned in an unsupervised way as a combination of a given number of Style Tokens. A precursor to GST [23], has a similar architecture, where the tokens are extracted at a phoneme level. Our approach is an extension of this architecture, where the tokens are extracted at the word level, something that provides more refined control than the GST architecture yet it operates at a more intuitive level than the phoneme level.

© Springer Nature Switzerland AG 2021
A. Karpov and R. Potapova (Eds.): SPECOM 2021, LNAI 12997, pp. 336–347, 2021.
https://doi.org/10.1007/978-3-030-87802-3_31

A new family of models that has recently gained traction is the Non-Attentive family [15,27] which, instead of using attention to align the phoneme encoder outputs with the target spectrogram, employs extra modules to directly predict the duration of each phoneme. The ground-truth durations are used during training both as a target for the prediction, and as the input for the decoder. This removes a number of artifacts that are typically observed in attention models, allowing for a more immediate and robust control of duration related properties, such as speaking rate. We leverage this by conditioning the duration prediction module to the style embeddings, thereby gaining the ability to control the speaking rate via the tokens that comprise the embeddings.

1.1 Related Work

A number of approaches based on VAEs have been successful in learning latent representations in an unsupervised manner [5,28]. While this is usually done at the utterance level, fine-grained approaches that align the target mel-spectrogram with the phonetic features via an attention mechanism have also been explored. In [19], after this alignment is obtained, a hierarchical VAE structure is used where phonetic information is conditioned on word-level aggregated acoustic features, while in [20] a quantization module is used in order to discretize the latent information.

While VAE methods have the advantage that it is possible to synthesize audio without a reference by manipulating the latent variables directly, systems which require a given reference audio have also been investigated, aiming to copy the prosody from a different speaker [6,10]. The features extracted from the reference audio are aligned at the phoneme level in order to achieve fine-grained prosody transfer.

There have also been several approaches that, similarly to ours, aggregate the information at a word level [4,7]. Most of these works condition the style embeddings purely on the textual information instead of the acoustic features, as is done in the original formulation of GSTs. Additionally, a number of these models condition on linguistic embeddings that are derived from pre-trained text models such as BERT [3,25].

1.2 Our Contributions

Our main contributions in this paper are:

- we modify the GST architecture to achieve word-level prosody control conditioned on acoustic features.
- we propose a word sequence encoder that helps disentangle the text content from style information.
- we incorporate a prior autoregressive encoder [20] that allows synthesis without the need for a reference, without compromising the control capabilities of the model.
- we investigate and demonstrate the control abilities of such configuration in a non-attentive architecture.

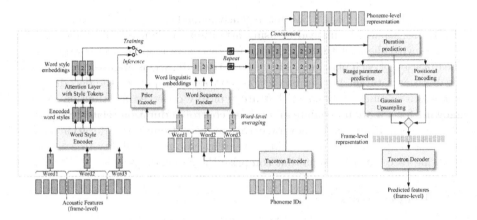

Fig. 1. Architecture of full model.

2   Method

2.1   Word Style Encoder

The frame-level acoustic features are first aligned with the phonemes of the training utterances using a forced-alignment system [14]. We employed an HMM monophone acoustic model trained using flat start initialization and implemented with the HTK toolkit [26], similarly to ASR forced alignment models. After the alignments are obtained for each utterance in the training set, the duration of each phoneme is extracted and then used to train the prediction module of the Non-Attentive Tacotron. The phonemes are then aligned with the words, using the known phone-word alignment.

For each word, an encoder summarizes the corresponding acoustic sequence into a fixed length vector that contains the prosodic information for the word. This vector is then used as a query to an attention module and a weighted average of a fixed number of style tokens is obtained via softmax. Similar to [24], the tokens are initialized randomly and their values are updated by back propagation.

The output of the softmax is the word style embedding that is then replicated for each phoneme of the word, concatenated with the Non-Attentive Tacotron encoder outputs and sent to the decoder for reconstruction. By concatenating the style tokens with the phoneme encoder outputs, we essentially condition the duration prediction module on the style. We therefore expect the style information to contain information about the speaking rate, and indeed we find that some tokens correspond directly to the speaking rate. We elaborate more on the interpretability of the tokens in Sect. 3.5.

This model requires a reference utterance, since it learned during training to expect a valid combination of different tokens for each word, and generates unintelligible speech if a single token is used. However, it is possible to increase the weight the model assigns to any token manually, thus biasing the style of any particular word towards the given token. This can be done by adding the embedding vector of the given token to the full embedding matrix, as is done in [23]. This process can be done to all the words of the sentence, thereby gaining global style control, or it can be done to any individual word, using the default embeddings from the ground truth for the rest of the words.

To increase the robustness of the process of directly controlling the token weights, we estimate the distribution of each token's weights in the training corpus and then apply changes to the token weights that are multiples of their standard deviation. We find that this offers a unified way to control weights across tokens, inducing style changes that are perceptually similar in intensity for all tokens.

2.2   Word Sequence Encoder

For the model architecture as described, it was observed that the word style embeddings contain a lot of phonetic information. In order to disentangle the style and phonetic representation of each word, a second word-level encoder was used, conditioned only on phonetic information.

This encoder takes as input the Tacotron encoder outputs and, after they are passed through a linear layer, their average is extracted for every word. The obtained sequence, is passed through a bidirectional word-level LSTM and concatenated with the encoder outputs and the word style embeddings. Like the style tokens and style encoder, it is only trained through the reconstruction loss. A stop gradient operation is used so that the Tacotron encoder does not get updated by the gradient that passes through the word sequence encoder.

The output of the module contains information that is already present on the text but aggregates it at the same level as the word style encoder. Therefore, the decoder learns to rely on the style embeddings only for style information since the remaining phonetic information is already modeled.

2.3   Prior Autoregressive Encoder

In order to synthesize without a reference utterance, a prior autoregressive encoder similar to the one proposed in [20] is used to generate a sequence of word style embeddings, given only the textual information. This model is trained to predict each word style embedding given the text and all the previous embeddings.

The prior encoder takes as inputs the outputs of both the phoneme encoder and the word sequence encoder. The phoneme encoder output is first averaged across each word and concatenated with the output of the word sequence encoder. A stop gradient operator is used for both other encoders, so that only the parameters of the prior model are updated. An extra rnn cell is used which, given this word-level sequence, predicts the word embeddings autoregressively by maximizing the likelihood of the embedding sequence.

The embeddings are predicted in the same space as the output of the token attention module, i.e. this model tries to predict the weighted combination of the tokens at once. This is similar to the TPSE-GST architecture from [18] where they predict the global style tokens from textual information. During inference the encoder requires only the phoneme encodings and a vector of zeros that is fed as the initial state of the rnn cell.

The parameters of the Tacotron model and the extra word-level encoders are not updated with the loss of this prior encoder. Therefore, it can be trained after the rest of the model is done training or simultaneously, without affecting the rest of the training procedure. It was observed, however, that training the models simultaneously leads to better performance.

During inference, the prior encoder predicts plausible style embeddings which are fairly rich in expressiveness. Moreover, it is possible to directly manipulate the prior embeddings by adding weighted style token vectors at any word's embedding, thus biasing those words towards a specific desired style.

We find that using the prior encoder in place of the reference does not significantly deteriorate nor the quality nor the expressiveness of the produced speech. Furthermore, no additional fine-tuning of the token weights is required, since the weights that correspond to meaningful changes in style are the same ones as those with a given reference.

The architecture of the full model, including all three encoders can be seen in Fig. 1.

3   Experiments

3.1   Experimental Setup

The models were evaluated on a subset of the Blizzard Challenge 2013 single-speaker audiobook dataset [8] which contains 85 h of speech with highly varying prosody. All audio data was first resampled to 24 kHz before the extraction of acoustic features.

Similar to [2], the acoustic features that were used for these experiments are 22 LPC features, i.e. 20 Bark-scale cepstral coefficients, the pitch period and the pitch correlation, that are then vocoded using the LPCNet Vocoder [21]. We use a custom implementation of the Non-Attentive Tacotron decoder model [15] in which the durations of each phoneme are predicted given the encoder outputs and then a Gaussian upsampling is applied in order to get the correct length of the acoustic features. A content-based attention [13] with a softmax is used to predict the weights of 15 style tokens. The number 15 was chosen empirically as the maximum number of tokens that can be used without the decoder learning to ignore a large number of them. The size of the token embeddings is 128, also found via experimentation.

We use the Adam optimizer [9] with parameters (0.9, 0.999) for training the networks with batch size 32. We use the same learning rate schedule as the Non-attentive Tacotron, with a linear ramp-up for 4K steps and then decay at half every 50K steps. We also apply L2 regularization with factor 10^{-6}.

All of the following evaluations were done on a subset of 1000 utterances from the dataset that were not seen by the model during training.

Audio samples and illustrations from the experiments are available at https://innoetics.github.io/publications/word-style-tokens/index.html.

3.2 Reconstruction Performance

We use F_0 frame error (FFE), Voice Decision Error (VDE) and Gross Pitch Error (GPE) [1] as well as mel-cepstral distortion (MCD) [11] as objective evaluation metrics for the reconstruction performance. We compare our model with the baseline Non-Attentive Tacotron both when we reconstruct from a given sentence and when we synthesize using the embeddings predicted by the prior encoder. DTW was used to align the ground-truth sequences with the outputs of each model. The results are shown in Table 1.

Table 1. Objective evaluation scores for reconstruction. Lower is better.

Model	FFE	VDE	GPE	MCD
Non Attentive Tacotron	30.3	6.1	34.1	5.8
Proposed model with prior	34.5	6.5	39.0	5.9
Proposed model with reference	11.5	4.9	9.3	4.9

As expected the reconstruction is significantly better for the model when using the reference embeddings. The performance using the prior embeddings is only slightly worse than that of the baseline Non Attentive Tacotron, indicating that the prior does indeed learn how to capture an average style of a sentence.

3.3 Subjective Evaluation

We evaluate the naturalness of our samples with a Mean Opinion Score (MOS), ranging from 1 to 5. We compare samples from the baseline Non-Attentive Tacotron with the samples synthesized with the prior embeddings, and with the reference embeddings. We also include scores for samples biased towards four tokens from the prior embeddings, for three different biasing weights, that correspond to 1, 2 and 4 standard deviations from the mean of the respective tokens, in either direction. The tokens were chosen for their clear semantic interpretation (further explored in Sect. 3.5) and the weights were chosen to range from minor but perceptible changes to very clear changes while keeping the speech intelligible. The samples were crowdsourced and raters who assigned unusually low ratings to ground truth samples were excluded from the analysis, leaving 38 raters.

The results are shown in Table 2. The quality of the speech synthesized from the prior model is only slightly worse than the baseline Non-Attentive Tacotron, which could be partly attributed to the fact that the latter seems to model prosody more conservatively. Furthermore, while the quality degrades as larger biases are imposed towards specific tokens, as is expected, the generated speech is still perceived as mostly natural, even when the changes are substantial.

Table 2. MOS evaluation scores

Model	MOS
Natural speech (ground truth)	4.41
Non Attentive Tacotron	4.33
Proposed with prior	4.27
Proposed with reference	4.28
Proposed with token weight −4 stds	3.82
Proposed with token weight −2 stds	4.26
Proposed with token weight −1 stds	4.27
Proposed with token weight +1 stds	4.30
Proposed with token weight +2 stds	4.16
Proposed with token weight +4 stds	4.03

3.4 Objective Assessment of Model's Generative Behavior

The generative behavior of the model has also been examined in terms of the acoustic properties of its generated audio files. Three models have been examined:

1. A plain Non-Attentive Tacotron model without any extra component for modeling styles,
2. A variation of our proposed model where the input of the Prior Encoder is simply the word-level aggregated phoneme encoder outputs,
3. Our proposed model as seen in Fig. 1 where the Prior Encoder gets as additional input the outputs of the Word Sequence Encoder, as described in Sect. 2.3.

The properties examined were the pitch and phoneme durations. Inference was performed using each of the three models and the synthesized audio was segmented using an acoustic model trained on the full dataset. From there, phoneme durations were obtained which were then z-normalized per phone-class using statistics from the full dataset.

The distribution of these normalized duration values for all phonemes in each of the three generated datasets is shown in Fig. 2a. The pitch contours of all generated files were calculated on a frame basis (excluding unvoiced frames). These were used to calculate the distributions of: (i) these raw values (Fig. 2b); as well as (ii) the standard deviation of pitch per audio file (Fig. 2c). Kernel-density estimation was used to estimate each of the distributions above, using Gaussian kernels and empirically selected bandwidths in each case.

As evident from these figures, the phoneme durations (Fig. 2a) in the audio generated by Models 2 and 3 which include style-related components are similar to those of the plain Model 1. The style-aware Models 2 and 3 tend to generate speech with pitch spanning a higher range (Fig. 2b), Model 3 even more so compared to Model 2. They also tend to generate higher pitch variation within each generated utterance (Fig. 2c).

These indicate that the style-aware models tend to generate richer pitch patterns than the plain model. This behavior may be partly attributed to the larger size of these models and their, thus, increased modeling capacity.

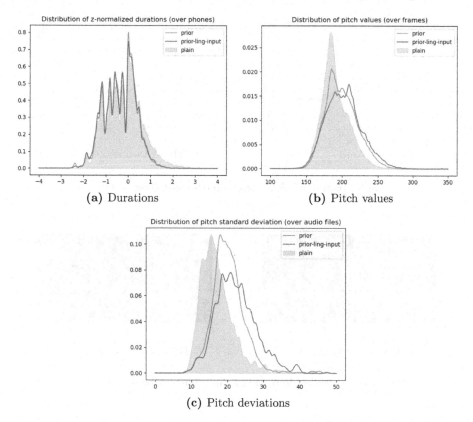

(a) Durations   (b) Pitch values

(c) Pitch deviations

Fig. 2. Distributions of relevant characteristics.

3.5 Interpretability of Tokens

A general weakness of unsupervised methods such as GSTs and VAEs is that the representations of style that the models learn depends heavily on training factors such as initialization, hyperparameters etc. However, we find that across all our experiments, a number of the tokens had simple intuitive interpretations. In particular, we find that some tokens were directly related to the pitch and some to the speaking rate and that this fact was generally consistent and independent of the details of each particular training. Additionally, we often find that by adding the embedding of a particular token with a negative weight corresponds to the conceptually opposite change than by adding the embedding with a positive weight. For example, the token that corresponds to higher speaking rate, has a slow-down effect when subtracted rather than added to the style embedding. This is consistent with the findings in [24].

In Fig. 3, we see the difference of a token that controls the pitch when added with a positive or a negative sign to the embedding matrix. In Fig. 4 we see the same for a duration controlling token.

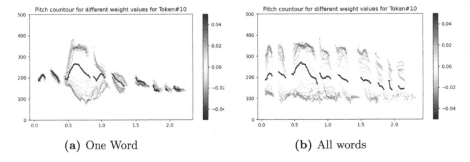

(a) One Word   (b) All words

Fig. 3. Increasing/decreasing a pitch-controlling token.

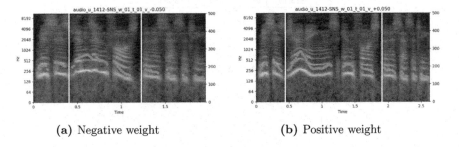

(a) Negative weight   (b) Positive weight

Fig. 4. Increasing/decreasing a duration-controlling token.

3.6   Style Transfer

We also find that it is possible to do style transfer from a different given sentence (or word) by using the embeddings from that target sentence. The transfer is more successful when the number of phonemes in the source and target words are similar.

We observe that despite the fact that the two encoders are disentangling to some extend the phonetic information from the style information, the naive implementation of style transfer still sometimes results to unintelligible words. We address this by synthesizing using a mixture of the weights of the prior encoder and the style of the target sentence. Since the prior encoder predicts the style embeddings given the phonemes of the target sentence, it results to more intelligible speech, by reducing somewhat the transfer ability.

Figure 5 shows the F_0 plots of the target sentence compared with the sentence synthesized from prior embeddings, and with the embeddings of the given sentence. We find that indeed the style transfer does manage to match the desired F_0.

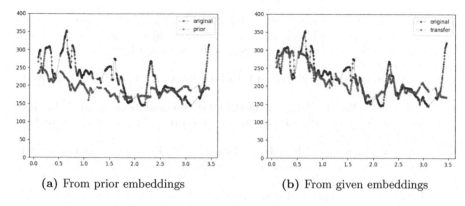

(a) From prior embeddings   (b) From given embeddings

Fig. 5. Style transfer.

4   Conclusion

As demonstrated in the experiments, the proposed model offers word-level style modeling with fairly robust control capabilities. Many of the emergent style tokens seem well correlated to perceptually relevant and interpretable aspects of the speaking style, also making it possible to transfer styles across words and utterances in a meaningful way. This is further enhanced by the proposed model's non-attentive nature which virtually removes any repeat/omit failures that are typical in Tacotron-like architectures. Some keys directions for further research will focus on integrating pre-trained linguistic word embeddings and investigating alternative ways to meaningfully control the style.

References

1. Chu, W., Alwan, A.: Reducing F0 frame error of F0 tracking algorithms under noisy conditions with an unvoiced/voiced classification frontend. In: Proceedings of the International Conference on Acoustics, Speech and Signal Processing (ICASSP), pp. 3969–3972. IEEE (2009)
2. Ellinas, N., et al.: High quality streaming speech synthesis with low, sentence-length-independent latency. In: Proceedings of the Interspeech (2020). https://doi.org/10.21437/Interspeech.2020-2464
3. Hayashi, T., Watanabe, S., Toda, T., Takeda, K., Toshniwal, S., Livescu, K.: Pre-trained text embeddings for enhanced text-to-speech synthesis. In: Proceedings of the Interspeech (2019)
4. Hono, Y., et al.: Hierarchical multi-grained generative model for expressive speech synthesis. In: Proceedings of the Interspeech (2020)
5. Hsu, W.N., et al.: Hierarchical generative modeling for controllable speech synthesis. In: Proceedings of the International Conference on Learning Representations (ICLR) (2019)
6. Karlapati, S., Moinet, A., Joly, A., Klimkov, V., Saez-Trigueros, D., Drugman, T.: CopyCat: many-to-many fine-grained prosody transfer for neural text-to-speech. In: Proceedings of the Interspeech (2020)

7. Kenter, T., Wan, V., Chan, C.A., Clark, R., Vit, J.: CHiVE: varying prosody in speech synthesis with a linguistically driven dynamic hierarchical conditional variational network. In: Proceedings of the 36th International Conference on Machine Learning (2019)

8. King, S., Karaiskos, V.: The Blizzard challenge 2013. In: Blizzard Challenge Workshop (2013)

9. Kingma, D.P., Ba, J.: Adam: a method for stochastic optimization. In: Proceedings of the International Conference on Learning Representations (ICLR). arXiv:1412.6980 (2015)

10. Klimkov, V., Ronanki, S., Rohnke, J., Drugman, T.: Fine-grained robust prosody transfer for single-speaker neural text-to-speech. In: Proceedings of the Interspeech (2019)

11. Kubichek, R.: Mel-cepstral distance measure for objective speech quality assessment. In: Proceedings of IEEE Pacific Rim Conference on Communications Computers and Signal Processing, vol. 1, pp. 125–128 (1993)

12. Lee, Y., Kim, T.: Robust and fine-grained prosody control of end-to-end speech synthesis. In: Proceedings of the International Conference on Acoustics, Speech and Signal Processing (ICASSP), pp. 5911–5915. IEEE (2019)

13. Luong, T., Pham, H., Manning, C.D.: Effective approaches to attention-based neural machine translation. In: Proceedings of the 2015 Conference on Empirical Methods in Natural Language Processing, pp. 1412–1421. Association for Computational Linguistics, September 2015

14. Raptis, S., Tsiakoulis, P., Chalamandaris, A., Karabetsos, S.: Expressive speech synthesis for story telling: the INNOETICS' entry to the blizzard challenge 2016. In: Proceedings of the Blizzard Challenge (2016)

15. Shen, J., et al.: Non-attentive Tacotron: robust and controllable neural TTS synthesis including unsupervised duration modeling. arXiv:2010.04301 (2020)

16. Shen, J., et al.: Natural TTS synthesis by conditioning WaveNet on Mel spectrogram predictions. In: Proceedings of the International Conference on Acoustics, Speech and Signal Processing (ICASSP), pp. 4779–4783. IEEE (2018)

17. Skerry-Ryan, R., et al.: Towards end-to-end prosody transfer for expressive speech synthesis with Tacotron. In: Proceedings of the 35th International Conference on Machine Learning, pp. 4693–4702 (2018)

18. Stanton, D., Wang, Y., Skerry-Ryan, R.: Predicting expressive speaking style from text in end-to-end speech synthesis. In: 2018 IEEE Spoken Language Technology Workshop (SLT), pp. 595–5602 (2018)

19. Sun, G., Zen, H., Weiss, R.J., Wu, Y., Zhang, Y., Cao, Y.: Fully-hierarchical fine-grained prosody modeling for interpretable speech synthesis. In: Proceedings of the International Conference on Acoustics, Speech and Signal Processing (ICASSP). IEEE (2020)

20. Sun, G., et al.: Generating diverse and natural text-to-speech samples using a quantized fine-grained VAE and autoregressive prosody prior. In: 2020 IEEE International Conference on Acoustics, Speech and Signal Processing (ICASSP), pp. 6699–6703 (2020)

21. Valin, J., Skoglund, J.: LPCNet: improving neural speech synthesis through linear prediction. In: Proceedings of the International Conference on Acoustics, Speech and Signal Processing (ICASSP), pp. 5891–5895. IEEE (2019). https://doi.org/10.1109/ICASSP.2019.8682804

22. Wang, Y., et al.: Tacotron: towards end-to-end speech synthesis. In: Proceedings of the Interspeech, pp. 4006–4010 (2017)

23. Wang, Y., et al.: Uncovering latent style factors for expressive speech synthesis. In: ML4Audio Workshop, NIPS (2017)
24. Wang, Y., et al.: Style tokens: unsupervised style modeling, control and transfer in end-to-end speech synthesis. In: ICML (2018)
25. Xiao, Y., He, L., Ming, H., Soong, F.K.: Improving prosody with linguistic and BERT derived features in multi-speaker based mandarin Chinese neural TTS. In: Proceedings of the International Conference on Acoustics, Speech and Signal Processing (ICASSP), pp. 6704–6708. IEEE (2020). https://doi.org/10.1109/ICASSP40776.2020.9054337
26. Young, S., et al.: The HTK Book (version 3.5a) (2015)
27. Yu, C., et al.: DurIAN: duration informed attention network for multimodal synthesis. arXiv:1909.01700 (2019)
28. Zhang, Y.J., Pan, S., He, L., Ling, Z.: Learning latent representations for style control and transfer in end-to-end speech synthesis. In: Proceedings of the International Conference on Acoustics, Speech and Signal Processing (ICASSP), pp. 6945–6949. IEEE (2019)

Perceiving Speech Aggression with and without Textual Context on Twitter Social Network Site

Liliya Komalova[1,2]([⊠]) [iD] and Diana Kulagina[2]

[1] Institute of Scientific Information for Social Sciences of the Russian Academy of Sciences, Nakhimovsky prospect, 51/21, Moscow 117418, Russia
komalova@inion.ru
[2] Moscow State Linguistic University, Ostozhenka str., 38, Moscow 119034, Russia

Abstract. The Internet has become the leading place for the emergence and spread of aggressive behavior. All major social network sites today work in one way or another to maintain a respectful atmosphere within their communities. Besides all this work to harmonize communication, today speech aggression is still a common fact within internet-communication on social network sites. The paper explores speech aggression perception in internet-communication of Russian speaking Twitter users. We suppose that taking into account such factors as communicative situation and communicative context, when analyzing the fact of speech aggression implementation, will increase the accuracy of determining the nature (direction) of speech aggression in the process of speech communication on social network sites. Based on ten tweet stimuli selected we perform an empirical research recruiting 45 Russian speaking recipients and asking them to detect speech aggression in tweets without and within textual context. The results of the research argue that indeed, the presence of textual context influences the interpretation of the tweet as an offensive or a defensive aggressive speech act.

Keywords: Perception · Text analysis · Internet mediated communication · Speech aggression · Levels of language

1 Introduction

1.1 Literature Review

In 2015, the Internet media The Village launched a media project "Evil Moscow" with the aim to draw attention to aggression and its presence in the daily life of Moscow residents. The authors of the project pointed to the existence of a number of contradictions, acting as a source and catalyst for (offensive, defensive, etc.) aggressive actions. The project noted that the presence of aggression in the interaction between relatives within the family circle increased three times from 1981 to 2011 [6]. Moreover, approximately 80% of murders occur on domestic grounds. The death rate among women who died violently includes 33–50% of women who are victims of a husband or lover [1]. Television and radio

© Springer Nature Switzerland AG 2021
A. Karpov and R. Potapova (Eds.): SPECOM 2021, LNAI 12997, pp. 348–359, 2021.
https://doi.org/10.1007/978-3-030-87802-3_32

broadcasts daily messages containing descriptions and scenes of violence: according to statistics, 65% of news items on the NTV channel include scenes of violence, and on the First Channel this indicator stands at 44% [18].

The Internet has become the leading place for the emergence and spread of aggressive behavior. VKontakte social network site records 17 obscene words per 1000 words of neutral vocabulary; My World (Moy Mir) detects 16 obscene words, Twitter – 15 words, Odnoklassniki – 15.4 words; the lowest indicator is found by Facebook – 13 words. The Children Online (Deti online) state service line, notes that 40% of requests are caused by a confrontation with aggression on the Internet; 25% of those who applied say that they face bullying on a daily basis [5].

In 2019, experts from Brand Analytics searched for Russian speaking internet-sites where verbalized aggression is concentrated and reproduced. Researchers were interested in revealing virtual places where interlocutors verbalize aggression more often. The leading positions were taken by sites of an entertainment nature, whose average age of users varies between the range of 12–30 years (2ch.hk, yaplakal.com, pickabu.ru, etc.); they are followed by sites dedicated to cybersport (prodota.ru, dota2.ru, etc.); and forums where users hold discussions on hot political topics (echo.msk.ru, politforums.net, bolshoyforum.com, etc.) [3].

A countless number of texts on various topics and styles are published on the Internet every day. Studies of the media environment show that negative news arouses the greatest interest among the audience, regardless of age and social status [8]. Manifesting negative content on television and radio, as well as on the Internet, the authors often deliberately "malignantly affect the communicative space and make it hostile" [11, p. 31]. So, offensive speech aggression appeals an increased attention of the audience to such content, while simultaneously polarizing the media space, making it hostile.

Today modern technologies make it possible to take control over user behavior on the Internet with the help of artificial intelligence based on speech processers. In 2017, the world's largest social network site Facebook launched a program to combat hate speech and terrorist propaganda [17]. Company officials claim they were using technologies such as artificial intelligence to find and eliminate unwanted language on their platform. In 2021, Facebook decided to increase the effectiveness of its technologies by engaging users themselves in the fight against hate speech [7]. Although 95% of hate speech is removed from the platform by the site itself, some messages and posts containing hate speech or incitement to aggression, nevertheless, are tested by algorithms and end up in the users' feed. To counter unwanted messages, Facebook encourages users to actively participate in content filtering, which results in efficiency increase of the algorithms up to 99% [ibid.].

The Russian social network site VKontakte also fights hate speech and tests a neural network to automatically recognize text data with aggressive statements [19]. The new VKontakte recognition system covers a wider range of manifestations of aggression and, accordingly, includes more tasks. The neural network is taught to define such types of insults as a manifestation of xenophobia, racism, sexism, homophobia, etc. [ibid.]. A new complaint function "Hate speech" has also been added.

The owners and developers of YouTube video hosting are also making changes to the process of posting comments on videos [13]. In December 2020, the function of analyzing comments for the content of offenses (bullying, hate speech and other kinds of nasty comments) was launched: the system checks future comments and, if it detects offensive statements, displays a reminder "keep comments respectful" [2].

The examples cited indicate that all major social network sites today work in one way or another to maintain a respectful atmosphere within their communities. Besides all this work to harmonize communication, today speech aggression is still a common fact within internet-communication on social network sites.

1.2 Research Question and the Hypothesis

Communication, in which speech aggression is manifested, has the character of an inter-action of high emotional and psychological tension, in which the boundaries between interlocutors are erased and it becomes almost impossible to make a judgment about who the aggressor is, what caused harm, whether those actions were intentional.

The working hypothesis of the research lies in the assumption that the distinction between offensive (initial) and defensive (response) types of speech aggression will make it possible to localize the focus (starting point) of aggression, which, firstly, becomes a trigger for the subsequent reaction in the form of speech aggression (assuming that aggression is a possible way of reacting in a specific communicative situation), secondly, it marks the norms of communication in a particular situation (whether the very way of such a response is discussed as possible and acceptable), thirdly, it divides interlocutors into at least three groups: (a) those who agree with the aggressor, (b) those who disagree with the aggressor, and (c) those who remain neutral.

From the standpoint of an external observer, the distinction between the offensive or defensive nature of speech aggression is subjective and depends on the competence of the perceiving subject, her/his involvement in the communication situation, as well as the attitude towards the communication partner.

We suppose that taking into account such factors as communicative situation[1] and communicative context[2], when analyzing the fact of speech aggression implementation, will increase the accuracy of determining the nature (direction) of speech aggression in the process of speech communication on social network sites.

2 Methodology

Stimuli Construction.

---

[1] Communicative context within this work is understood as macro-context – the linguistic environ-ment of a particular speech unit (a word, a phrase, an utterance, etc.). This context is wider then a phrase and goes beyond one utterance [4]. Within this work context means tweets following the stimuli tweet.

[2] Communicative situation means a structural speech entity realized in space and time. The com-municative situation characterizes the circumstances of communication in general, its incentives, its participants, etc. It includes interlocutors (a sender of the messages and recipient(s)), topic of communication (about what interlocutors communicate), motive to communicate (why they communicate), aims of interlocutors (what results they want to reach), code used by them (how they communicate), communicative style used by them (common talks, official speech etc.), place and time of communication (where and when interlocutors communicate), communicative environments (social prescriptions, taboos etc.), and ethnic peculiarities [16].

The research material was collected out of the social network site Twitter. The size of a message (post or tweet) on Twitter is 230 characters, which implies a clear, succinct wording of the statement. According to A. Perez [14], the average publication on Twitter contains 33 characters. Also, due to these limitations and the specifics of the language style, users often use abbreviations and emoji, the latter help to express a thought more expressively and more accurately [12].

When selecting the textual data on Twitter, the following criteria were taken into account:

- the relative novelty of the publication (tweets must be posted no longer than a year ago);
- the content of discussion should touch upon socially significant topics;
- the interlocutors participating in discussion threads should manifest clearly opposed positions or speak "for" and "against" someone's position;
- at least 20 interlocutors must actively participate in the discussion thread (each of them must publish at least three informative posts);
- the language of the studied text data must be authentic, the interlocutors must express their thoughts freely.

The selection of the text data was carried out by the method of continuous sampling by the date of April 21, 2020.

We analyzed only the tweets containing the so-called markers of speech aggression [9, 10]:

- morphological features: words' forms changing with diminutives expressing derogatory, indulgent attitude, suffixes with the meaning of humiliation, insulting, the use of already established word-forming models and their derivatives with negative semantic coloring, language creativity for elaboration words-hybrids containing neutral component that changes its semantic coloring depending on the context (such words formally do not violate the rules of etiquette, which creates complexity in their detection using automated instruments);
- lexical/lexico-semantical features: lexemes with a negative connotation from the semantic field "aggression", dysphemisms, xenophobia, amplifying vocabulary (all, in general, the most, etc.), invectives, direct appeals and questions containing a negative assessment of the object of discussion;
- grammatical features: verbs in the imperative mood, verbs of affective influence, verbal adjectives, the imperative in the infinitive form, etc.;
- syntactic-stylistic features: textual organization based on a contrast between notions, using colloquial words, abusive vocabulary, incomplete impersonal sentences;
- pragmatic features: the transition to personalities, belittling the importance ("everyone", "any", etc.), speech genres of accusation, reproach, insulting and ridicule speech acts, pursuit of strategies for lowering the status of the object of aggression, distancing from the addressee, etc.;
- graphic features and punctuation: often used exclamation or question marks punctuation, ellipses at the end or middle (a kind of breaking) of a sentence, quotation marks or dashes when transmitting other people's words or to give a different intonation to

the utterance, swear words with a modified spelling using punctuation marks such as ".", "!", "*" etc. Figure 1–2 shows examples of stimuli tweets without and within textual context (translation from Russian into English is given in Table 2).

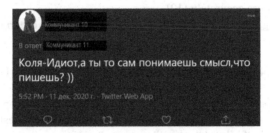

Fig. 1. Example of tweet #10 without textual context.

Fig. 2. Example of tweet #10 within textual context.

2.1 Recruitment of Participants

The Google Forms platform was used to create and conduct the research. The study was conducted on native Russian speaking adult subjects. All of them are Internet users. Invitation to the survey was published on online communities' sites dedicated to linguistics. A total number of 45 unique respondents took part in the research (Table 1).

2.2 Experiment Procedure

The methodology of the study assumes the following procedure. We explained to the subjects, what speech aggression was, and gave examples of offensive (initial) and defensive (response) types of speech aggression. Then we selected ten tweets (Table 2) out of the collected textual data[3] and used them as stimuli. Table 2 shows stimuli tweets used

---

[3] Tips for hate speech data annotation see in [20].

Table 1. Demographic data on the subjects participated in the research.

Recipients' age groups	Males	Females	Total number
18–24	9	18	27
25–30	3	6	9
31–40	2	4	7
41–50	1	0	1
51+	0	2	2
Total number	15	30	45

Table 2. Stimuli tweets (translation from Russian into English).

Tweet No	Textual content of the tweet
1	Communicant #1: How to explain to idiots that we got the difficulties of the 90s not because the USSR collapsed, but because it was? And the "Time of Troubles", was not because Ivan the Terrible died, but because he lived. And you rush there again. At 27 Mach, on an unpredictable fucking trajectory
2	Communicant #2: Yeah, I broke my arm not because I fell, but because I was walking. A man died not because he got sick, but because he lived. The house burned down not because it was set on fire, but because it was made of wood. (it itself is to blame and it deserves it). Homegrown fucking philosophers
3	Communicant #3: No way! I propose to observe and mock. I have long understood that, firstly, they are unteachable, and secondly, they cannot see beyond the tip of their nose
4	Communicant #4: Let's say this way: you, sir, fluidly crapped yours pants with your conclusions
5	Communicant #5: Useless. As I was recently haughtily told: "Now it has become fashionable to scold the USSR." We are such mods that we are fucking
6	Communicant #6: Well, explain – why in the 1930s during the deep crisis and the "Great Depression" America did not disintegrate as a country? Any thoughts in your head about this?
7	Communicant #7: so how many likes this nonsense collected… I suspect what the level of intelligence have those who left them…
8	Communicant #8: Are the idiot's explanations interesting to anyone?
9	Communicant #9: No, well, this is logical: you will also die because you lived. But here it became interesting to me: do you believe in your invulnerability and immortality? Just, if not, then your delirium cannot be taken seriously
10	Communicant #10: Kolya is an Idiot, but you yourself understand the meaning of what you write?))

for the first step of the experiment: each tweet is a message from different people. The recipients analyzed the stimuli based on the questionnaire posted on Google Forms. At the first step of the research the stimuli tweets were presented separately, at the second step – with textual context (comments – following tweets) consisting of one, two or three comments to the tweet (the added comments were taken from real communication threads and followed after the stimuli tweets from the first experimental step). The task was (1) to detect what type of speech aggression the stimuli represented (offensive or defensive), if there were any, (2) to describe speech features recipients thought were marking speech aggression. Then we analyzed the data obtained at two research stages.

3   Results

3.1   Results of the First Research Step

Results of the first research step are presented on Fig. 3. The speech style used by interlocutors twitting should be called colloquial, mainly vernacular vocabulary is used.

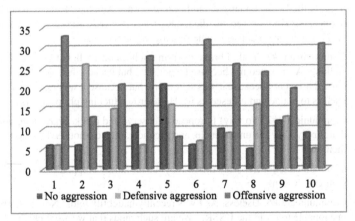

Fig. 3. Detection of speech aggression at the first research step (tweets without textual context): X-axis shows numbers of stimuli tweets (from 1 to 10), Y-axis shows number of participants' answers (from 0 to 45).

There is no total consensus between the recipients towards whether the analyzed tweets represent aggression or not, but most of them suppose that most the stimuli tweets (except tweet #5) are speech aggression acts: tweets #1, 3, 4, 6, 7, 8, 9, 10 are of offensive type, tweet #2 is of defensive type.

In addition, we asked the participants whether they would respond to such tweets if they had participated in the thread. Their answers are presented on Table 3.

Table 3. Supposed potential reactions (responds in %) of participants to stimuli tweets.

Tweet No	In %			
	Disagree with the author at all	Agree with the author	Agree with the statement but not with the wording	Would refrain from any response
1	2.6	7.7	17.9	71.8
2	2.8	5.6	0	91.7
3	14.7	0	0	85.3
4	0	12.5	0	87.5
5	5.1	2.6	7.7	84.6
6	14.3	2.9	2.4	82.9
7	12.2	0	2.4	85.4
8	6.1	3	6.1	84.8
9	2.8	0	2.8	94.4
10	1.6	7.7	17.9	72.8

Most of the participants answered that they prefer to ignore such tweets and not being involve in such communication at all. We see that participants totally disagree with the statement presented in tweets #3, 6, 7. Some participants would agree with the statement presented in tweet #4, and some participants would agree with the statement but not with wording of tweets #1, 10. At the same time, when we asked the participants what kind of reaction they would use, they answered that they would probably use speech aggression in response in case such speech aggression is addressed directly to them.

The results of analysis of speech features the recipients think to be indicative in speech aggressive detection are presented on Table 4. The following categories were presented as a list of checkboxes for participants, and examples were given to make sure the participants could identify speech markers correctly (we used results of our previous work [9, 10, 15] to train the recipients).

We can resume that the most indicative features are lexical. Punctuation, syntactic-stylistic and grammatical features are also in the list of most significant markers of aggressive speech.

3.2   Results of the Second Research Step

Results of the second research step are presented on Fig. 4. We see that in total assessment, within differentiation between males and females answers, only #5 tweet's evaluation has a drastic shift from "no aggression" to "defensive aggression" marking (Fig. 5). We see mild shifts in all other tweets evaluations. The most significant are seen in tweets #3, 9, 10. In tweet #3 presence of textual context smoothed the differences between "no aggression", "defensive aggression" and "offensive aggression" evaluations. Tweet #9 evaluations became more inclined towards offensive aggression, and tweet #10 evaluations – towards defensive aggression.

Table 4. Speech markers indicating aggression.

Tweet No	In %				
	Punctuation	Syntactic-stylistic features	Morphological features	Grammatical features	Lexical features
1	15	9	2	9	39
2	7	12	2	3	39
3	18	20	1	14	33
4	1	8	3	5	32
5	1	3	3	3	24
6	8	2	4	26	37
7	19	18	0	3	35
8	11	1	0	2	40
9	6	5	1	5	33
10	25	2	3	1	26

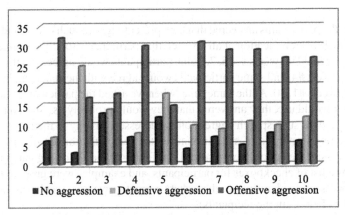

Fig. 4. Detection of speech aggression at the second research step (tweets within textual context): X-axis shows numbers of stimuli tweets (from 1 to 10), Y-axis shows number of participants (from 0 to 45).

After incorporation of textual context to the same ten tweets the results of speech classification changed (Table 5): adding textual context in form of comments after the tweet changes recipients' decision to classify the tweet as aggressive; we see less marks "no aggression" and more marks "defensive/offensive aggression" in "within context" tweets.

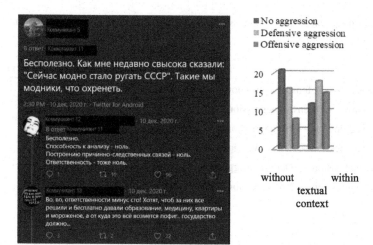

Fig. 5. Tweet #5 and its evaluation without and within textual context.

Table 5. Comparison of speech aggression detection in tweets without and within textual context.

Tweets' No	No aggression		Defensive aggression		Offensive aggression	
	Without context	Within context	Without context	Within context	Without context	Within context
1	6	6	6	7	33	32
2	6	3	26	25	13	17
3	9	13	15	14	21	18
4	11	7	6	8	28	30
5	21	12	16	18	8	15
6	6	4	7	10	32	31
7	10	7	9	9	26	29
8	5	5	16	11	24	29
9	12	8	13	10	20	27
10	9	6	5	12	31	27
Total	95 →	71	119 →	124	236 →	255

In female group recipients changed their minds in 53.6% of cases when analyzing tweets within textual context; male recipients – in 47.7%. We noticed that for males' group the most frequent shift was from "no aggression" to "offensive aggression" and from "defensive aggression" to "offensive aggression"; for females' group – from "defensive aggression" to "offensive aggression" and from "offensive aggression" to "defensive aggression" (Table 6).

Table 6. Comparison of speech aggression detection in tweets without and within textual context (number of cases in %).

Shift	In males' group	In females' group
No aggression → Defensive aggression	7.69	6.79
No aggression → Offensive aggression	12.3	8.57
Defensive aggression → No aggression	1.54	4.64
Defensive aggression → Offensive aggression	11.5	13.9
Offensive aggression → Defensive aggression	8.46	12.9
Offensive aggression → No aggression	6.15	6.79
Total	47.7	53.6

4   Conclusion

Indeed, the presence of textual context following a tweet influences the interpretation of the tweet itself. Even if it was described as offensive (initial) speech aggression manifestation when analyzed separately, textual context could shift this interpretation of the notion from offensive to defensive type of aggressive speech act or vice versa, or even to neutralize it.

It is also fair to note that most participants would ignore the tweet containing aggressive speech if it was not addressed to them but would respond it if they were the addressee. Moreover, their response would also contain speech aggression of defensive type.

References

1. Aggression in figures: Who, where and why hurts others. https://www.the-village.ru/village/city/situation/164541-agressiya-v-tsifrah
2. Bell, K.: YouTube will remind users to 'keep comments respectful' before posting (2020). https://www.engadget.com/youtube-pop-up-keep-comments-respectful-185717715.html
3. Data mining of society: aggressiveness on social media and the newest technologies to detect them (2019). https://br-analytics.ru/blog/agressivnost/
4. Dominikan, A.: Types of contexts according to different scientific approaches. Vestnik TvGU. Series: Philology **4**, 125–131 (2017)
5. Every second schoolchild in Russia faced aggression on the Internet (2014). https://ict-online.ru/news/n105989/
6. Evil Moscow. https://www.the-village.ru/tags/%D0%97%D0%BB%D0%B0%D1%8F%20%D0%BC%D0%BE%D1%81%D0%BA%D0%B2%D0%B0
7. Facebook launches campaign to drive out hate speech. https://en.ejo.ch/media-politics/hatespeech
8. Kolezev, D.E.: Negativity bias: why do news websites keep focusing in negative events. In: Mass media Priorities and Values of the Journalism as a Profession, pp. 33–36. Ural University Press, Ekaterinburg (2018)
9. Komalova, L.R.: Aggressogen Discourse: The Multilingual Aggression Verbalization Typology. Sputnik+, Moscow (2020)

10. Komalova, L.R.: Language and Speech Aggression. INION RAN, Moscow (2015)
11. Koshkarova, N.N.: The space of conflict discourse in the genre of political interviews. Vestnik of Chelyabinsk State University **17**, 54–59 (2010)
12. Krylov, Y.V.: Emodji's semantics in the virtual dialogue. Vestnik of Omsk State Pedagogical University. Humanitarian Studies 2, pp. 50–52 (2017)
13. No trolls are welcome here: YouTube will fight insulting speech in video comments (2020). https://rg.ru/2020/12/07/youtube-budet-borotsia-s-oskorbleniiami-v-kommentariiah-k-video.html
14. Perez, S.: Twitter's doubling of character count for 140 to 280 had little impact on length of tweets (2018). https://techcrunch.com/2018/10/30/twitters-doubling-of-character-count-from-140-to-280-had-little-impact-on-length-of-tweets
15. Potapova, R., Komalova, L.: Lexico-semantical indices of "deprivation – aggression" modality correlation in social network discourse. In: Karpov, A., Potapova, R., Mporas, I. (eds.) SPECOM 2017. LNCS (LNAI), vol. 10458, pp. 493–502. Springer, Cham (2017). https://doi.org/10.1007/978-3-319-66429-3_49
16. Serebrykova, A.Yu.: About components of communicative situation. Bulletin of the South Ural State University. Series: Linguistics **15**(158), 30–32 (2009)
17. Tur, A.: Facebook launches program to combat hate speech and terrorist propaganda in the UK (2017). https://www.theverge.com/2017/6/23/15860868/facebook-hate-speech-terrorism-uk-online-civil-courage-initiative
18. Violence on TV screen as a market factor and basis for modeling the world for the domestic audience (2014). https://ctyzyrka.ru/studproekt/103-nasilie-na-televizionnom-ekrane-kak-faktor-rynka-i-osnova-miromodelirovaniya-dlya-otechestvennogo-zritelya
19. VKontakte tests new neural network to combat hate speech (2020). https://vk.com/press/no-hate-speech
20. Wassem, Z.: Are you a racist or am I seeing things? Annotator influence on hate speech detection on Twitter. In: Proceedings of 2016 EMNLP Workshop on Natural Language Processing and Computational Social Science, pp. 138–142. Austin, TX (2016)

Assessing Speaker Interpolation in Neural Text-to-Speech

Roman Korostik[1(✉)], Javier Latorre[2], Sivanand Achanta[3],
and Yannis Stylianou[2]

[1] ITMO University, Saint Petersburg, Russia
roman.korostik@pm.me
[2] Apple, Cambridge, UK
[3] Apple, Cupertino, USA

Abstract. This paper presents a study on voice interpolation in the framework of neural text-to-speech. Two main approaches are considered. The first one consists of adding three independent speaker embeddings at 3 different positions within the model. The second one substitutes the embedding vectors by convolutional layers, kernels of which are computed on the fly from reference spectrograms. The interpolation between speakers is done by linear interpolation between the speaker embeddings in the first case, and between convolution kernels in the second. Finally, we propose a new method for evaluating interpolation smoothness using agreements between interpolation weights, objective and subjective speaker similarities. The results indicate that both methods are able to produce smooth interpolation to some extent, with the one based on learned speaker embeddings yielding better results.

Keywords: Speech synthesis · Text-to-speech · Suprasegmentals representation

1 Introduction

Since the introduction of neural text-to-speech, the quality of speech synthesis has improved dramatically. Moreover, techniques such as multi-speaker training and fine-tuning have allowed to create voices for new speakers or new styles with less data. However, in order to create a new voice, some speech data is still required. One way to alleviate this limitation is to try to factorise the different supra-segmental characteristics of speech such as speaker identity, style, emotion, etc., so they can be transferred from one voice to another [4,12,13,15,30,32]. Usually, this is achieved by using a global speaker/style representation vector. The vector comes from either an embedding table (if labels are available), or from a reference spectrogram passed through an encoder module. This vector is used as bias within one or more of the layer of the neural-TTS architecture. Most of these approaches work well for mimicking a given style, especially

---

R. Korostik—Work done during internship at Apple.

© Springer Nature Switzerland AG 2021
A. Karpov and R. Potapova (Eds.): SPECOM 2021, LNAI 12997, pp. 360–371, 2021.
https://doi.org/10.1007/978-3-030-87802-3_33

when some fine-tuning is allowed. However, creating new speakers/styles out of the existing ones by interpolating between their representation vectors is much harder. In that case, the interpolated speaker/style is often closer to the reference speaker/style with the largest interpolation weight, or it jumps randomly between the references speakers/styles.

In contrast, in HMM-based TTS, interpolation was achieved simply by interpolating between the means of the corresponding models [21,27,34]. In this paper, we explore ways to achieve this interpolatability property of HMM-based TTS with neural-TTS and how to evaluate it for creating new voices. To do this we trained two models, one based on three bias vectors for each speaker added at 3 different points of the model architecture, and another in which these vectors are replaced by 3 dynamic convolutional layers (CNN). The latter may be viewed as similar to the maximum-likelihood linear regression (MLLR) matrices in HMM-based TTS.

Our main contributions:

- we introduce dynamic convolutions for modelling speaker in neural-TTS,
- we propose applying multiple independent speaker vectors at different points on the model architecture,
- we describe a new method of evaluating speaker interpolatability.

The rest of the paper is organised as follows. Section 2 discusses the most relevant work on speech synthesis and other machine learning tasks. Section 3 describes our approach to style and speaker modelling. Section 4 describes our method of evaluating speaker interpolatability. Section 5 describes the model architecture, training procedure and data used. Section 6 provides the results of the evaluation. Section 7 discusses the results and finally in Sect. 8 conclusions are drawn.

2   Related Work

The most common approach in neural text-to-speech, popularised by Tacotron 2 [26], is to use two networks: text-to-spectrogram and spectrogram-to-waveform (vocoder). We base our model on EATS [6] and use WaveRNN [16] as vocoder.

Learning latent style space is an actively researched topic [12,30,37]. However, properties of the latent style space beyond typical F_0 range, pace [22,25] and class separability (e.g. emotion [28], recording quality [11,12]) are not often explored.

Works on speaker modelling in neural text-to-speech are usually concerned with transfer learning [15] and adaptation to external (possibly low-quality) data [3,4,13,20].

Predicting weights of a neural network from input was first introduced in [24], adding "fast" weights to horizontal connections in recurrent modules. More recent works include [5] and [19]. For a comprehensive overview we refer reader to a recent survey of dynamic networks [10].

Use of dynamic convolutions in this work was inspired by [31], where this approach was used for machine translation. Conceptually, the most relevant work is [1] where authors present a deep latent model of images in which every image is parameterized by its own convolution kernel. Dynamic convolutions have also been used in neural TTS [2] as a part of effort on stabilizing attention in Tacotron. It serves as an example of successful usage of dynamic layers in TTS, although in a completely different context.

3   Prosody/Style Modelling

Text-to-speech is a one-to-many task: a text can be pronounced in many ways. Borrowing from recent work on generative models for images, we define style as everything a neural TTS model can learn from speech data beyond text content. It includes features such as speaker identity, emotion, transmission channel, etc. In this paper, we consider style and speaker identity to be global utterance-level features.

3.1   Vectors

When labels are available (speaker, domain, etc.), the simplest way of representing a global feature is to learn an embedding table with a vector for every possible class. In our experience, a set of learned embeddings usually does not allow for interpolating between different classes, resulting in unstable behaviour. For example, when averaging vectors for two speakers, perceived speaker identity switches back and forth between those two speakers across a single utterance, not giving an in-between speaker.

The dominating unsupervised approach for modelling style is to extract a fixed-length vector from a variable-length spectrogram using a neural network. This vector is concatenated or added to an intermediate representation in the main model. The spectrogram encoder subnetwork can be trained jointly with the main model or obtained externally.

The aim of popular architectures, such as GST [30] and VAE[1] [12,17,37], is to learn a meaningful continuous latent space to allow combination and manipulation of style. For example, averaging vectors for fast and slow speech is expected to give speech of moderate pace.

3.2   Dynamic Layers

A bias vector interacts with the input sequence by shifting every token in the same direction (and concatenating is very similar [7]), but we don't expect to modify every segment of the output in the same way. For example, when adding

---

[1] Analogous to GST, VAE in context of text-to-speech is usually seen as an auxiliary module to the main network; the whole model can be interpreted as a variational autoencoder of spectrograms with decoder conditioned on input text.

an 'expressive prosody' vector, we expect F_0 to go up and down in different parts of the utterance, compared to a 'flat prosody' vector. Thus, a single vector might be too simple for representing style and its components.

We propose to make interactions between representations of style and text content more complex by using a 'dynamic' layer, meaning its weights depend on data and are computed on-the-fly. After compressing the reference spectrogram into a vector of fixed length, we interpret this vector as weights of a layer, and put it inside the main network. It this way, operation 'shift by a vector' is replaced by a more complex one, such as matrix multiplication or generalized convolution, introducing a number of multiplicative interactions.

Similar to previous models [12,37], we augment a neural TTS model with a spectrogram reference encoder. It transforms each spectrogram into a fixed-width vector, which is being fed into VAE projections. The sample from the VAE posterior is projected to a higher-dimensional space, and result is reinterpreted as weights tensor of a convolution. In other words, for every training utterance we infer weights of a convolutional layer from the target spectrogram. Encoder then uses that layer to predict the spectrogram from the text.

3.3 Several Places of Conditioning

The most common approach to conditioning on a global variable is to add its representation at a single place in the main network. Motivated by existence of hierarchy in speech, we propose to use several places of conditioning, for example at the beginning of the text encoder, in the middle and in the end. For learned embeddings this means having different look-up tables. In unsupervised case this means having a separate spectrogram encoder for each place of conditioning.

4   Evaluation Methodology

A good style representation should allow smooth transition between different styles. Recent work shows that it is possible to learn smooth manipulation of pitch and tempo as global variables [12,22,25]. Still, smooth manipulation of more complex global features in text-to-speech remains largely unexplored. While it is easy to check smoothness of transitions between e.g. lower and higher pitch by calculating F_0 and durations, objectively assessing manipulation of more abstract features is more complicated.

Although perceived speaker identity is a high-level feature, quantifying objective similarity to a speaker is easier than assessing other high-level features such as 'style' and 'emotion'. Thus, we restrict our attention to a model's ability to interpolate between speakers: given reference utterances from speakers A and B, we hope to produce a series of utterances in which perceivable speaker characteristics gradually change from A to B.

We construct test sets by randomly choosing n speaker pairs from the training set and t texts from an internal text-to-speech test set. Unit of analysis is speakerA-speakerB-text triple.

4.1 Objective Evaluation

To perform objective evaluation, we use a pre-trained deep speaker verification (SV) model. That model is used to calculate SV vectors for reference utterances and synthesized speaker-interpolated utterances. Then, cosine similarity is used to measure similarity of interpolated samples to the two references. The hypothesis is that as we go from speaker A to speaker B, similarity to speaker A should drop and similarity to speaker B should rise. We quantify these drops and rises in similarities using Spearman correlation between interpolation coefficients and similarities to speaker A and speaker B. These two correlations for speaker A and speaker B are used as objective metrics of a model's ability to interpolate between speakers.

4.2 Subjective Evaluation

To quantify speaker similarity subjectively, we conduct an ABX test. Stimuli A and B are reference utterances from two different speakers from the corpus. Stimulus X is a synthesized sample with latent style variable l set to

$$l = (1 - \alpha)\, l_A + \alpha\, l_B, \ \alpha \in [0, 1],$$

where l_A and l_B are latent vectors for references A and B. Participants are asked to choose which reference is more similar to X in terms of speaker identity. Possible answers are 'A', 'B' and 'neither', with an optional text field for commentary. Answers from several participants are then converted to scores ranging from 0 to 1.

We then calculate Spearman correlation between objective scores and subjective scores. It is used as a measure of agreement between objective and subjective judgements for a given speaker-speaker-text combination.

5 Setup

5.1 Architecture

We use a modification of EATS [6] denoted as MEATS (modified EATS, Fig. 1a). Compared to the original architecture, it drops the adversarial waveform decoder in favor of a more a traditional setup with a separate neural vocoder. The spectrogram decoder consists of 3 blocks of dilated convolutions with residual connections, with each block refining the output spectrogram in three steps. The text encoder consists of 10 blocks of dilated convolutions with residual connections. Batch normalization in the encoder [14] is replaced with weight normalization [23]. Following the original paper, we train the model using SoftDTW and total duration losses.

All encoder and decoder layers in synthesizer have dimensions and number of channels set to 256.

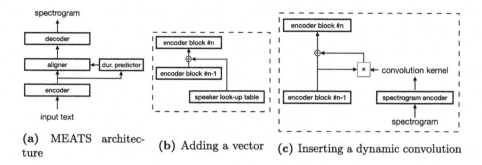

(a) MEATS architecture   **(b)** Adding a vector   **(c)** Inserting a dynamic convolution

Fig. 1. Architecture charts of used models.

In our experiments, we compare two different representations for speaker identity: learned embedding tables (Fig. 1b), and dynamic convolutions (Fig. 1c). In both, there are three independent representations used after encoder blocks #0, #5 and #9: learned embeddings are broadcasted and added, dynamic convolutions are applied.

For dynamic layers, architecture and parameters of the reference encoder follow [30]. Dimensions of VAE latent spaces are set to 32. Dynamic layers have form of grouped [18] 1D convolutional layers with 256 channels, 64 groups and kernel width of 3. The mapping from the latent space to the space of convolution weights is a single fully-connected layer with weight matrix of size 32 × 3072.

The model is optimized using Adam with $\beta_1 = 0.9$, $\beta_2 = 0.999$, learning rate starts from 0.0003 with cosine annealing. The model is trained until 3M steps on 8 GPUs with batch size 64.

For vocoder, we use WaveRNN [16]. We train a universal WaveRNN on LibriTTS [36] instead of VCTK to prevent overfitting to its speakers. Because of the dataset mismatch audio quality is not excellent, but still good enough for our investigation.

5.2 Data

We perform all experiments on VCTK [33]. It is a multispeaker English corpus with total duration of 24 h. There are 108 speakers, out of which 45 are recognized as male and 63 as female. Average duration of recordings per speaker is 13.4 min.

6 Results

6.1 Speakers

We divide speakers in VCTK into clusters by fitting a GMM to mean F_0 of their utterances. Two clusters is a reasonable model; the groups roughly correspond to speakers perceived as male and female. The space between those clusters is not well covered (Fig. 3).

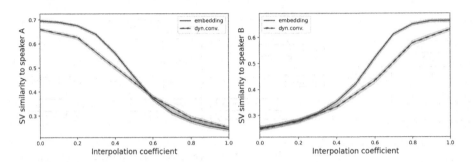

Fig. 2. Interpolation point vs. SV similarity.

6.2   Objective

For initial objective evaluation, we randomly choose 20 speaker pairs from the training set and 50 texts from an internal text-to-speech test set, giving us 1000 speaker-speaker-text combinations. For each combination, we generate 11 samples with latent space vector moving from reference A to reference B linearly in steps of 0.1. Reference utterances for speakers are taken from the corpus. We then calculate speaker vectors for both generated samples and references using a pre-trained deep speaker verification model. Cosine similarity of samples to references are calculated then. Figure 2 displays average SV similarity for every interpolation point. It shows that moving from speaker A to speaker B in the latent space results in drop of similarity to speaker A and rise of similarity to speaker B.

6.3   Subjective

For subsequent subjective evaluation, we randomly choose 70 speaker pairs from different clusters, and 100 speaker pairs from same clusters. For each speaker pair we randomly choose 5 texts from an internal text-to-speech test set. Reference utterances for speakers are taken from the corpus. For each speaker-speaker-text combination we generate 6 samples where latent space vector is moving from reference A to reference B linearly in steps of 0.2. Objective similarities are calculated as above.

Figure 5 shows box plot of listeners' judgements on similarity to speaker B for every interpolation point for model with 3 speaker embeddings. Plot shows that interpolation between speakers from same clusters is smooth, but for pair of speakers from different clusters similarity graph resembles step function rather than a line, suggesting that the model does not generalize to speakers with typical F_0 between clusters. It also shows that when forced to choose, subjects agree about the change-point.

Figure 4 shows box plots of agreements between objective and subjective similarities for every speaker-speaker-text for models with 3 lookup tables and

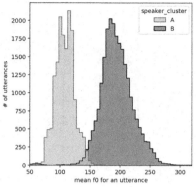
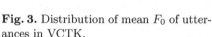
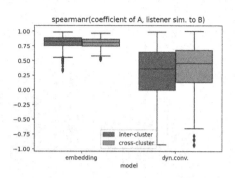

Fig. 3. Distribution of mean F_0 of utterances in VCTK.

Fig. 4. How SV similarity to speaker A correlates with listeners' judgments on similarity to speaker A.

3 dynamic convolutions. Plot suggests that model with 3 independent learned speaker embeddings performs better than the model with dynamic convolutions.

We note that the option 'neither' was never selected by any of the participants.

Overall, objective and subjective evaluation shows that simpler model using learned speaker embeddings performed better than the novel approach based on dynamic convolutions.

7   Discussion

7.1   On Architecture and Hyperparameter Exploration

Preliminary research showed that using a single speaker embedding table did not allow for speaker interpolation. Models using various existing approaches to conditioning on a global variable (such as adding output of the spectrogram encoder, or both adding a vector and multiplying by a vector [8]) produced unintelligible speech. Models with dynamic convolutions were the only ones that produced intelligible speech and allowed for speaker interpolation. Later we decided to try three learned speaker embeddings added at different encoder levels. To our surprise, this model also allowed to interpolate between speakers, giving a simpler working baseline.

As for hyperparameters of models with dynamic convolutions, using higher dimension of the latent space ($d = 256$) resulted in unintelligible speech samples. Using deeper mappings from the VAE latent space to the space of convolution kernels further increased variance of agreement between interpolation coefficients and objective metrics, as did spherical interpolation. Overall, our hyperparameter exploration showed that the initial guess hit a spot where the model works. We lowered dimension of the weights space by using grouped convolutions, but

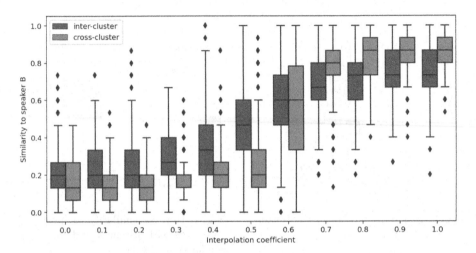

Fig. 5. Distribution of listeners' judgements on similarity to speaker B for every interpolation point; model with 3 embedding tables.

it might be beneficial to restrict it even more by switching to depthwise or lightweight convolutions.

7.2 On Several Places of Conditioning

It has been shown that in convolutional networks later representations correspond to higher-level features [35]. Conditioning on a global variable in three different places was supposed to test if varying global variables at different levels would correspond to changes at different levels of speech hierarchy. Experiments showed that independently modifying global variables either has no effect or leads to generation of unintelligible speech; thus, we resorted to modifying all three global variables simultaneously. Perhaps global variables should be conditioned on one another in order to better reflect this goal in the network architecture.

7.3 On Speaker Identity and Other Features in Text-to-Speech

Speaker identity consists not only of vocal tract characteristics (timbre), but also of a speaker's own habits of imposing melody and rhythm onto the phoneme sequence. These habits are hard to accurately describe using just durations, intensity, and F_0 values, but humans are good at perceiving them nevertheless. While F_0 and durations are useful proxies for subjective impressions of pitch and rhythm, we should be more aware of the distinction between acoustic and auditory phenomena.

This line of reasoning extends to other features such as emotions [9,28], expressiveness [29], etc. Indeed, it is hard to describe those features without resorting to human judgements, as they are not easily and robustly connected to acoustic features. They are auditory and should be treated as such. When building a model, the end metric can only be expressed by questions we can ask in listening experiments.

On the other hand, there is a more general question related to generative modelling: what do we *expect* to be the result of changing representations related to style? For example, what do we expect to hear if we mix a statement and a question? If we mix speakers of different English dialects? If we mix representations of speech from different sociolinguistic groups, e.g. those who have masculine and feminine patterns of speech?

We have made a step towards addressing these concerns, choosing speaker identity as the feature of study. We expressed our expectations for the model and assessed it using two lenses: a speaker verification model and a subjective listening test.

8 Conclusion

This paper explores different approaches to create new voices by interpolating between existing speakers, and proposed a new approach to evaluate the interpolability of a model. Two new approaches were analysed. The first approach consists of adding 3 independent learned speaker embeddings at 3 different points of the model. The second one replaces these 3 speaker vectors by 3 CNN layers which weights are obtained on-the-fly from acoustic references of the target speaker. The interpolation between speakers is achieved by linearly interpolating between the speaker representation, i.e., the learned embeddings or the CNN weights. A new evaluation method using agreement between objective and subjective speaker similarities is also proposed. The results of such evaluation showed that for both approaches the interpolation weights correlate positively with agreement between objective and subjective metrics of speaker similarity. It also shows that the bias vector approach works in general better than the dynamic CNN one, probably because due to its relative simplicity allowed for its parameters to be computed more robustly. Despite these results, we believe this direction in the design space of neural TTS models should be explored further. While evaluated on a non-autoregressive model, replacing bias vectors with dynamic layers can be easily done in more conventional architectures such as Tacotron. Robustness of such changes is yet to be explored.

References

1. Athar, S., Burnaev, E., Lempitsky, V.: Latent convolutional models. In: 7th International Conference on Learning Representations, ICLR 2019 (2019)
2. Battenberg, E., et al.: Location-relative attention mechanisms for robust long-form speech synthesis. In: ICASSP 2020–2020 IEEE International Conference on Acoustics, Speech and Signal Processing (ICASSP), pp. 6194–6198. IEEE (2020)
3. Chen, Y., et al.: Sample efficient adaptive text-to-speech. arXiv preprint arXiv:1809.10460 (2018)

4. Cooper, E., et al.: Zero-shot multi-speaker text-to-speech with state-of-the-art neural speaker embeddings. In: ICASSP 2020–2020 IEEE International Conference on Acoustics, Speech and Signal Processing (ICASSP), pp. 6184–6188. IEEE (2020)
5. Denil, M., Shakibi, B., Dinh, L., Ranzato, M., De Freitas, N.: Predicting parameters in deep learning. arXiv preprint arXiv:1306.0543 (2013)
6. Donahue, J., Dieleman, S., Bińkowski, M., Elsen, E., Simonyan, K.: End-to-end adversarial text-to-speech. arXiv preprint arXiv:2006.03575 (2020)
7. Dumoulin, V., et al.: Feature-wise transformations. Distill 3(7), e11 (2018)
8. Dumoulin, V., Shlens, J., Kudlur, M.: A learned representation for artistic style. arXiv preprint arXiv:1610.07629 (2016)
9. Habib, R., et al.: Semi-supervised generative modeling for controllable speech synthesis. arXiv preprint arXiv:1910.01709 (2019)
10. Han, Y., Huang, G., Song, S., Yang, L., Wang, H., Wang, Y.: Dynamic neural networks: a survey. arXiv preprint arXiv:2102.04906 (2021)
11. Hsu, W.N., et al.: Disentangling correlated speaker and noise for speech synthesis via data augmentation and adversarial factorization. In: ICASSP 2019–2019 IEEE International Conference on Acoustics, Speech and Signal Processing (ICASSP), pp. 5901–5905. IEEE (2019)
12. Hsu, W.N., et al.: Hierarchical generative modeling for controllable speech synthesis. arXiv preprint arXiv:1810.07217 (2018)
13. Hu, Q., Marchi, E., Winarsky, D., Stylianou, Y., Naik, D., Kajarekar, S.: Neural text-to-speech adaptation from low quality public recordings. In: Speech Synthesis Workshop, vol. 10 (2019)
14. Ioffe, S., Szegedy, C.: Batch normalization: accelerating deep network training by reducing internal covariate shift. In: International Conference on Machine Learning, pp. 448–456. PMLR (2015)
15. Jia, Y., et al.: Transfer learning from speaker verification to multispeaker text-to-speech synthesis. arXiv preprint arXiv:1806.04558 (2018)
16. Kalchbrenner, N., et al.: Efficient neural audio synthesis. In: International Conference on Machine Learning, pp. 2410–2419. PMLR (2018)
17. Kingma, D.P., Welling, M.: Auto-encoding variational Bayes. arXiv preprint arXiv:1312.6114 (2013)
18. Krizhevsky, A., Sutskever, I., Hinton, G.E.: ImageNet classification with deep convolutional neural networks. In: Pereira, F., Burges, C.J.C., Bottou, L., Weinberger, K.Q. (eds.) Advances in Neural Information Processing Systems, vol. 25. Curran Associates, Inc. (2012). https://proceedings.neurips.cc/paper/2012/file/c399862d3b9d6b76c8436e924a68c45b-Paper.pdf
19. Ma, N., Zhang, X., Huang, J., Sun, J.: WeightNet: revisiting the design space of weight networks. arXiv preprint arXiv:2007.11823 (2020)
20. Moss, H.B., Aggarwal, V., Prateek, N., González, J., Barra-Chicote, R.: BOFFIN TTS: few-shot speaker adaptation by Bayesian optimization. In: ICASSP 2020–2020 IEEE International Conference on Acoustics, Speech and Signal Processing (ICASSP), pp. 7639–7643. IEEE (2020)
21. Pucher, M., Schabus, D., Yamagishi, J., Neubarth, F., Strom, V.: Modeling and interpolation of Austrian German and Viennese dialect in hmm-based speech synthesis. Speech Commun. 52(2), 164–179 (2010)
22. Raitio, T., Rasipuram, R., Castellani, D.: Controllable neural text-to-speech synthesis using intuitive prosodic features. arXiv preprint arXiv:2009.06775 (2020)
23. Salimans, T., Kingma, D.P.: Weight normalization: a simple reparameterization to accelerate training of deep neural networks. In: Proceedings of the 30th International Conference on Neural Information Processing Systems, pp. 901–909 (2016)

24. Schmidhuber, J.: Learning to control fast-weight memories: an alternative to dynamic recurrent networks. Neural Comput. **4**(1), 131–139 (1992)
25. Shechtman, S., Sorin, A.: Sequence to sequence neural speech synthesis with prosody modification capabilities. In: Proceedings of the 10th ISCA Speech Synthesis Workshop, pp. 275–280 (2019)
26. Shen, J., et al.: Natural TTS synthesis by conditioning WaveNet on Mel spectrogram predictions. In: 2018 IEEE International Conference on Acoustics, Speech and Signal Processing (ICASSP), pp. 4779–4783. IEEE (2018)
27. Tachibana, M., Yamagishi, J., Onishi, K., Masuko, T., Kobayashi, T.: HMM-based speech synthesis with various speaking styles using model interpolation. In: Speech Prosody 2004, International Conference (2004)
28. Um, S.Y., Oh, S., Byun, K., Jang, I., Ahn, C., Kang, H.G.: Emotional speech synthesis with rich and granularized control. In: ICASSP 2020–2020 IEEE International Conference on Acoustics, Speech and Signal Processing (ICASSP), pp. 7254–7258. IEEE (2020)
29. Wang, Y., et al.: Uncovering latent style factors for expressive speech synthesis. arXiv preprint arXiv:1711.00520 (2017)
30. Wang, Y., et al.: Style tokens: unsupervised style modeling, control and transfer in end-to-end speech synthesis. In: International Conference on Machine Learning, pp. 5180–5189. PMLR (2018)
31. Wu, F., Fan, A., Baevski, A., Dauphin, Y.N., Auli, M.: Pay less attention with lightweight and dynamic convolutions. arXiv preprint arXiv:1901.10430 (2019)
32. Xiao, Y., He, L., Ming, H., Soong, F.K.: Improving prosody with linguistic and BERT derived features in multi-speaker based mandarin Chinese neural TTS. In: ICASSP 2020–2020 IEEE International Conference on Acoustics, Speech and Signal Processing (ICASSP), pp. 6704–6708 (2020). https://doi.org/10.1109/ICASSP40776.2020.9054337
33. Yamagishi, J., Veaux, C., MacDonald, K., et al.: CSTR VCTK corpus: English multi-speaker corpus for CSTR voice cloning toolkit (version 0.92) (2019)
34. Yoshimura, T., Masuko, T., Tokuda, K., Kobayashi, T., Kitamura, T.: Speaker interpolation in HMM-based speech synthesis system. In: Fifth European Conference on Speech Communication and Technology (1997)
35. Zeiler, M.D., Fergus, R.: Visualizing and understanding convolutional networks. In: Fleet, D., Pajdla, T., Schiele, B., Tuytelaars, T. (eds.) ECCV 2014. LNCS, vol. 8689, pp. 818–833. Springer, Cham (2014). https://doi.org/10.1007/978-3-319-10590-1_53
36. Zen, H., et al.: LibriTTS: a corpus derived from LibriSpeech for text-to-speech. arXiv preprint arXiv:1904.02882 (2019)
37. Zhang, Y.J., Pan, S., He, L., Ling, Z.H.: Learning latent representations for style control and transfer in end-to-end speech synthesis. In: ICASSP 2019–2019 IEEE International Conference on Acoustics, Speech and Signal Processing (ICASSP), pp. 6945–6949. IEEE (2019)

A Mobile Application for Detection of Amyotrophic Lateral Sclerosis via Voice Analysis

Denis Likhachov[1](✉), Maxim Vashkevich[1] ⓘ, Elias Azarov[1], Katsiaryna Malhina[2], and Yuliya Rushkevich[2] ⓘ

[1] Belarusian State University of Informatics and Radioelectronics, 6 P. Brovky Street, 220013 Minsk, Belarus
likhachov@bsuir.by

[2] Republican Research and Clinical Center of Neurology and Neurosurgery, 24 F. Skoriny Street, 220114 Minsk, Belarus

Abstract. Analysis of the state of the art in the field of treatment and diagnosis of a rapidly progressing neurological disease of the amyotrophic lateral sclerosis (ALS) revealed a lack of tools for early diagnosis and monitoring the course of the disease. This paper proposes a method for evaluating the state of the voice function of patients with ALS, intended for use in a mobile application. As a speech probe a long pronunciation of the vowel sound / a / is used from which acoustic features (jitter, shimmer, degree of vibrato pathology, etc.) are extracted. Applying a classifier based on the method of linear discriminant analysis to the obtained vector of parameters, it is possible to obtain an estimate whether the presented voice is pathological and possible progress of the disease. For training and verification of the proposed method, a database of 64 voices (33 healthy, 31 patients with ALS), recorded at the Republican Research and Clinical Center of Neurology and Neurosurgery (Minsk, Belarus), was used. To test the proposed method, a prototype of the mobile application «ALS Expert» was developed with the ability to record, process voice and display the results of voice analysis. The results indicate that the acoustic analysis of the voice and the resulting objective parameters are a promising direction for solving this problem.

Keywords: Speech processing · Detection of pathology in the voice · Amyotrophic lateral sclerosis

1 The Relevance of Solving the Problem of Developing Affordable Non-invasive Methods for Early Diagnosis of ALS

The most common type of motor neuron disease (MND) is amyotrophic lateral sclerosis (ALS). This disease is characterized by damage to the motor neurons of the brain and spinal cord, conducting corticospinal pathways with the development of muscle atrophy, bulbar and respiratory disorders. The rapid progression of the disease leads to a violation of the functions of breathing and swallowing, the ability to move independently. The

A. Karpov and R. Potapova (Eds.): SPECOM 2021, LNAI 12997, pp. 372–383, 2021.
https://doi.org/10.1007/978-3-030-87802-3_34

life expectancy of patients with ALS is 3–5 years. According to the conducted studies, the one-year survival rate of patients with ALS is 80.3% [95% CI 76.6–84.1], the 2-year survival rate decreases to 51% [95% CI 46.3–55.8], the 3-year survival rate decreases to 30.9% [95% CI 26.2–35.5]. Currently, there is an increase in mortality rates from ALS and its prevalence, which is probably due to improved diagnostic capabilities and an increase in the number of patients seeking medical care [1]. Early diagnosis of ALS allows you to actively influence the course of the disease, preserving the quality of life of the patient.

Speech and swallowing disorders develop either at the onset of the disease or are associated with the progression of the disease, occurring in more than 80% of all cases of ALS. In the early stages of the disease, speech disorders are skipped by doctors due to the rarity of the pathology. The consequence of this is the wrong diagnosis and the appointment of treatment with the use of unnecessary, and sometimes dangerous for ALS types of therapy or even surgical treatment.

Thus, the main tasks of the doctor are a quick and objective diagnosis, monitoring the patient's status in dynamics for its timely correction, especially speech and swallowing [2]. The development and testing of tools for the diagnosis, monitoring and evaluation of patients' status is a necessary criterion for the implementation of effective actions on the part of the doctor. The process of speech production involves cortical and subcortical structures, and therefore is particularly sensitive to the death of motor neurons. This means that speech analysis for early diagnosis of ALS can be useful for identifying both people with the bulbar form of the disease and people with other forms of ALS who have concomitant bulbar disorders.

Currently, active research is underway aimed at developing a system for detecting speech disorders caused by ALS [3–7].

The aim of this paper is to develop a method for diagnosing and tracking speech disorders in people with ALS, adapted for use in a mobile application. The main advantages of creating a system for early diagnosis of the disease and monitoring its course in the form of a mobile application are its ease of use and high availability. It should also be noted that the mobile application does not impose strict restrictions on the place of testing and does not require it to be carried out in a specially equipped room. This allows testing both directly by the doctor and by the patient independently.

2 Specificity of ALS Diagnostics by Voice Analysis

2.1 Speech Tasks Used in ASL Detection Systems

Currently available research systems for detecting speech disorders associated with ALS differ in the speech tasks used in them. Thus, in [8, 9], a count from one to ten was used as a speech task. In [10–12], it is proposed to use several speech tests consisting in the utterance of monosyllabic words, notes, and a long sound [and]. In [13], the test signal contained the short phrase "one, two, three". Phrases of general content (such as "I need help", etc.) were used as a speech task in the works [14, 15].

In [5], the participants were asked to read a specially designed short text passage ("Bamboo passage") [16]. This passage is designed to make it easier to automatically search for pauses between words. To do this, the voiced consonants in it are placed on the borders of words, since they better emphasize the border between the word and the pause than the deaf consonants.

Some researchers use shorter, but specially selected sentences. Thus, in [6] only the first sentence from the "bamboo passage" was used, and in [17] the speech task consisted of repeating the sentence "Buy Bobby a puppy" ten times. It can be noted that the sentence uses explosive consonants [p] and [b], the pronunciation of which requires a coordinated work of articulatory organs. Other examples of specially developed proposals can be found in [18].

In some studies dedicated to the detection of speech disorders in ALS, a special type of speech task is used – the diadochokinetic (DDC) test [15, 19]. The DDC test consists of quickly pronouncing syllables (for example, "pa - / ta/ - ka" or "bu - / ter/ - kap") with maximum speed and accuracy in one breath. This test is widely used in differential diagnosis and for detecting disorders in the muscular apparatus of speech [20].

Sometimes a long-drawn-out vowel sound is used as a speech task. It can be included in the test of several speech tasks [19, 20] or can act as a single source of information [21, 22].

In [14], the repetition of listened phrases and spontaneous speech were used as speech tasks.

Summarizing the above data, we can say that the speech tasks used in the systems for detecting speech disorders caused by ALS are divided into the following groups:

1) simple short phrases of general meaning [13–15];
2) short specially designed sentences [6, 17];
3) specially designed passages of the text [5];
4) diadochokinetic (DDC) test [4, 15, 19];
5) prolonged pronouncing of a vowel sound [23, 24];
6) a complex test consisting of several types of speech tasks [10–12, 21, 22].

2.2 Acoustic Voice and Speech Features Used in ALS Detection Systems

The choice of acoustic features for detecting speech disorders in ALS is an open question, and researchers solve it in different ways.

In [6], for the purpose of early diagnosis of ALS, a set of a very large number of acoustic features (6861 features) was used, which were extracted from the analyzed signal using a special OpenSMILE toolkit. For classification, all features were grouped into seven categories: cepstral coefficients, formants, energy parameters, pitch frequency, spectral parameters, time parameters, and parameters that evaluate the quality of the speech signal. The OpenSMILE library was also used in [15, 25].

In [5], the researchers used the speed of speech (number of words per minute), the speed of articulation (number of syllables per second), and the ratio of the duration of pauses to the duration of the speech task to differentiate people with and without symptoms of the disease. It has been experimentally shown that the use of indicators of speech speed and articulation is a fairly promising approach for the diagnosis of ALS.

To identify changes in speech motor skills that can be associated with ALS, it was proposed in [4] to use four speech features: 1) coordination; 2) consistency; 3) speed; 4) precision. The coordination and consistency of speech with multiple repetition of certain syllables were evaluated using the voice onset time – the length of time that passes between the release of a stop consonant and the onset of voicing. The speed and accuracy were evaluated by analyzing the frequency response of the second formant (F2). The experimental verification of the approach proposed in [4] was performed by analyzing speech recordings from two groups: a control group (18 people) and those with ALS symptoms (14 people). The data obtained were analyzed using a linear mixed model (LMM). With a sufficient degree of confidence, it was shown that coordination, speed and accuracy of speech can be associated with the deterioration of speech function in patients with ALS.

2.3 Classification Methods Used in Systems for Detecting Speech Disorders in ALS

The efficiency of the currently existing classifier models depends on the features, structure, and patterns [26] that are present in the analyzed data. For the task of detecting speech disorders in ALS, classification based on the support vector machine (SVM – support vector machine) is most often used [6, 7, 15, 17, 25]. Sometimes researchers use deep neural networks (DNN-deep neural network) and convolutional neural networks (CNN-convolutional neural network) [7, 14, 15]. In [19], the XGBoost (Extreme Gradient Boosting) method was used for classification. In [9, 13, 23, 24], the classification was based on the linear discriminant analysis (LDA) method.

Despite the growing popularity of convolutional neural networks and deep learning methods, the application of these approaches to the task of detecting speech disorders associated with ALS has not yet shown a significant advantage over other classification methods. For example, the researchers in [14] obtained a detection accuracy of 75–77% when using convolutional neural networks. The popularity of classification based on the support vector machine can be explained by its relatively low computational complexity (compared to a neural network) and its freely distributed software implementation in the form of the libSVM library. The advantages of the method are its resistance to retraining and high efficiency. For example, in [6], a classifier based on the support vector machine with a linear kernel function was used. The classifier was trained using speech recordings from 123 people divided into three groups: control group, with pronounced symptoms and with initial symptoms of the disease. To identify patients with severe ALS symptoms, a high classification accuracy index (AUC = 0.91 − 0.99) was obtained. However, in the context of the problem considered in this paper, the support vector method has a serious drawback. The result of his work is very difficult to interpret [26]. For a doctor, it is not enough just to know what result the detection system gave after analyzing the voice, but it is important to understand on the basis of what the decision was made. In this respect, the LDA-based classification approach is in a better position. This method is close to the linear regression model and its result can be easily interpreted.

3 The Proposed Method for Evaluating the State of the Voice Function in Patients with ALS

3.1 The Used Acoustic Features

This paper is based on the results obtained earlier in [23, 24]. These papers describe systems for detecting speech disorders in patients with ALS based on linear discriminant analysis (LDA). The simplest test for long-term phonation of sound (a) was used as a speech task. The following acoustic features were extracted from the phonation record: 1) jitter; 2) shimmer; 3) pitch periods entropy (PPE); 4) the pathology vibrato index (PVI); 5) noise parameters (HNR and GNE); 6).

Jitter – a measure of the change in the pitch frequency. It is an indicator of the pronator system stability of the speech formation subsystem (when the neuromotor function is impaired, this indicator increases). In a simplest case jitter is defined as

$$J_{loc} = \frac{1}{N-1} \sum_{i=2}^{N} |T_i - T_{i-1}| / \frac{1}{N} \sum_{i=1}^{N} |T_i|, \tag{1}$$

where T_i – is length of the i-th pitch period, N is total number of pitch periods in the voice signal.

According to (1) jitter estimates short-term variations in pitch period duration. This small variation cannot be accounted to voluntary changes of pitch and therefore attributed to violation of neuromotor control of the phonatory system.

In general case, jitter estimated as a period perturbation quotient (PPQ) on L consecutive pitch periods:

$$J_{ppqL} = \frac{\frac{1}{N-L+1} \sum_{i=1+(L-1)/2}^{N-(L-1)/2} \left| T_i - \frac{1}{L} \sum_{n=i-(L-1)/2}^{i+(L-1)/2} T_n \right|}{\frac{1}{N} \sum_{i=1}^{N} |T_i|}, \tag{2}$$

As a rule, parameter L is takes the values $3, 5$ and 55 [29, 30]. As a measure of pitch frequency instability directional perturbation factor (DPF) is used.

Shimmer – a measure of the variation in the acoustic wave amplitude during phonation. An increase in this parameter, considering the natural decline in the intensity of the voice, indicates the presence of speech disorders. In a simplest case shimmer is defined as:

$$S_{loc} = \frac{1}{N-1} \sum_{i=2}^{N} |A_i - A_{i-1}| / \frac{1}{N} \sum_{i=1}^{N} A_i, \tag{3}$$

where A_i – is amplitude of the i-th pitch period.

In general case, shimmer estimated as amplitude perturbation quotient (APQ) on L consecutive pitch periods:

$$S_{apqL} = \frac{\frac{1}{N-L+1} \sum_{i=1+(L-1)/2}^{N-(L-1)/2} \left| A_i - \frac{1}{L} \sum_{n=i-(L-1)/2}^{i+(L-1)/2} A_n \right|}{\frac{1}{N} \sum_{i=1}^{N} |A_i|}, \tag{4}$$

As a rule, parameter L is takes the values 3, 5, 11 and 55 [29, 30].

PPE [24] is used to evaluate the violation of the ability to control the stability of the pitch frequency during the prolonged utterance of sounds. An increase in this parameter indicates that the natural level of pitch variation is exceeded.

Vibrato is the rapid and regular oscillation of the pitch frequency during prolonged phonation. In patients with ALS, this parameter is characterized by high-frequency components (about 9–14 Hz). The algorithm for calculating PVI is given in [23, 24].

We also used parameters HNR (*harmonic noise ratio*) and GNE (*glottal noise excitation ratio*) that characterized noise component of the voice signal [Michaelis-97]. HNR and GNE calculated on a frame-by-frame basis, therefore, as a result of such an analysis, a set of values of each parameter are obtained, which can be considered as a random variable. For the HNR and GNE values, the median (HNR_{me} and GNE_{me} and the interquartile range (HNR_{IRQ} and GNE_{IRQ} were calculated. Table 1 summarized features used for train LDA classifier model.

Table 1. Features extracted from vowel /a/.

Parameter group	Number of features	List of features
Frequency perturbation	6	$J_{loc}, J_{ppq3}, J_{ppq5}, J_{ppq55} J_{ppq63}$, DPF
Amplitude perturbation	5	$S_{loc}, S_{apq3}, S_{ppq5}, S_{ppq11}, S_{ppq55}$
Based on F0-contour	2	PPE, PVI
Noise	4	GNE_{me}, GNE_{IQR}, HNR_{me}, HNR_{IQR}
Total	17	

3.2 Jitter and Shimmer Parameters Optimization

In the literature described the cases of use J_{ppqL} and S_{apqL} parameters with fixed values of L (as mentioned above). In this work we carried out optimization of this parameters in order to find the optimal value of L. The following criterion was used:

The J_{ppqL} and S_{apqL} parameters can be applied at fixed values of L (as mentioned above). In this paper, these parameters were optimized in order to find the optimal value of L. The following criterion was used:

$$C(L) = \frac{\left(\text{mean}\left(J_{ppqL}^{(H)}\right) - \text{mean}\left(J_{ppqL}^{(P)}\right)\right)^2}{\text{var}\left(J_{ppqL}^{(H)}\right) + \text{var}\left(J_{ppqL}^{(P)}\right)}, \tag{5}$$

where $J_{ppqL}^{(H)}$ is the values of jitter calculated for the control group with parameter L, $J_{ppqL}^{(P)}$ is the values of jitter calculated for the ALS group with parameter L, mean($\cdot$) is the operator of calculating the average value, $var(\cdot)$ is the operator variance.

The problem of finding the optimal value of L is formulated as

$$L_{opt} = \underset{L \in [3,155]}{\text{argmax}} \ C(L), \tag{6}$$

According to criterion (16), in (17) the value of L is searched for which the difference of the average value of J_{ppqL} between the control group and the group of patients with ALS is maximal, and the variation of J_{ppqL} within each group is minimal. For the S_{apqL} parameter, a similar procedure was used to find the optimal value of L.

Figure 1 shows the results of optimization jitter and shimmer parameters. It turned out that optimal window size for jitter is equal to 63 pitch periods. In turn, for the shimmer, the optimal window size is equal to 11 pitch periods.

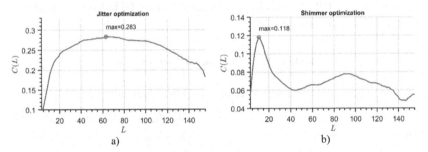

Fig. 1. The result of voice perturbation parameters optimization: a) Jitter, $L_{opt} = 63$; b) Shimmer, $L_{opt} = 11$.

3.3   Classifier Models

In this work we used two popular machine learning techniques to build classifier model: linear discriminant analysis and k nearest-neighbor. In this section we briefly describe those approaches.

Using LDA analysis, the vector of input parameters is transformed into a single value z, on the basis of which a decision on the presence of a disease is made.

Let there be a training data set $\{(\mathbf{x}^{(i)}, y_i)\}$, $i = 1, 2, \ldots m..$ In this case, $\mathbf{x}^{(i)}$ is a. d-dimensional vector of acoustic features derived from analysis of the recording of the i-th voice from the database, y_i is the corresponding class label (for a healthy voice use the label "-1", for the voice of the patient with als – "1").

In the method of LDA data are interpreted as points in d-dimensional space, that which is sought in the one-dimensional projection:

$$z = \mathbf{w}^T \mathbf{x}, \tag{7}$$

where $\mathbf{w}$ is the vector defining the normal to the hyperplane to be projected onto. The idea of the LDA method is to find a hyperplane for which, as a result of projecting a training set on it, the intra-class variance would be minimal, and the inter-class difference would be maximum (so-called Fisher criterion [27]).

The classification function in the LDA method has the following form:

$$f(\mathbf{x}) = \text{sign}\left(\mathbf{w}^T \mathbf{x} - b\right),$$

(8)

where $\mathbf{x}$ is the vector of acoustic features, b is the offset, and sign(a) is the function that returns the sign of the number a. If $f(\mathbf{x}) = 1$, then vector $\mathbf{x}$ belongs to the class of patients with ALS, and if $f(\mathbf{x}) = -1$, it belongs to the class of healthy patients. The offset b is a threshold value, so for the input $\mathbf{x}$ vector, if $\mathbf{w}^T\mathbf{x} > b$, then it is classified as belonging to the class of ALS patients, otherwise to the class of healthy ones.

The selection of the offset b can be done as follows. The first stage is the projection of all vectors from the training data set into a one-dimensional space using the expression (7). At the second stage, a value of b is produced that would allow optimal separation of the marked data in a one-dimensional space according to a pre-specified criterion (the criterion can be obtaining maximum sensitivity, specificity, etc.).

The idea of k nearest-neighbor (kNN) classification is to assigning label to data sample based on the k closest points $\mathbf{x}^{(i)}$ in the training set. Classification function of the kNN method is defined as follows:

$$f(\mathbf{x}) = \text{sign}\left(\frac{1}{k} \sum_{\mathbf{x}^{(i)} \in N_k(\mathbf{x})} y_i\right),$$

(9)

where $N_k(\mathbf{x})$ – k nearest neighbor from training set closest to $\mathbf{x}$. We used Mahalanobis distance to measure the distance between data samples.

3.4 The Database of Voices

To train the LDA model proposed in this paper, a database of voices was collected at the Republican Research and Clinical Center of Neurology and Neurosurgery (Minsk, Belarus). The voices of 64 people were recorded, of which 33 were healthy (13 men, 20 women) and 31 patients with ALS with signs of bulbar disorders (17 men, 14 women). The average age in he healthy group was 50.2 years (SD 13.8) for men and 56.1 (SD 9.7) for women. The average age in the ALS group was 61.1 years (SD 7.7) for men and 57.3 (SD 7.8) for women. Each participant was asked to pronounce the long vowel sound /a/ in one breath for as long as possible with a comfortable pitch and volume. The voice was recorded using a smartphone with a headset (sampling rate 44.1 kHz) and stored as uncompressed 16-bit wav files. The average duration of the recordings was 4.1 s. The Matlab functions used for voice analysis are hosted in a public repository[1]. The voice database is also available in public GitHub repository[2].

3.5 Train and Validation of Classifier Models

Our goal was to obtain a classifier with a small number of features. It was assumed that no more than one feature from each group can be selected into the feature vector.

[1] https://github.com/Mak-Sim/Troparion.

[2] https://github.com/Mak-Sim/Minsk2020_ALS_database.

An exception was made only for features based on F0-contour: the feature vector must include at least one of these features or both. According to this formulation of the problem, there are $7 \times 6 \times 3 \times 5 = 630$ variants of feature vector that satisfy the requirements. This number of options is small, so all of them can be verified by direct search.

For each possible variant of the feature vector, the quality of the classifier model was assessed using the *k-fold cross-validation method* [28] (for k = 9). Classifiers were found with the highest accuracy, sensitivity, specificity and AUC. The results for the LDA-based classifiers are shown in **Table 2**.

Table 2. Results of LDA-based classification.

Feature vector	Accuracy, %	Sensitivity, %	Specificity, %	AUC, \%
J_{loc}, PPE, PVI,GNE$_{me}$	**77.7 ± 2.5**	84.7 ± 2.8	70.4 ± 4.3	0.81 ± 0.02
J_{ppq63}, PPE	66.7 ± 2.0	**95.0 ± 2.2**	37.6 ± 3.5	0.77 ± 0.02
PVI	60.7 ± 1.4	32.9 ± 1.9	**89.4 ± 1.8**	**0.83 ± 0.01**

The classifier that uses the parameters jitter, PPE, PVI and the noise parameter GNE has the highest accuracy. The greatest specificity is obtained by using the optimized jitter and PPE parameter. The PVI-based classifier showed the highest specificity and AUC.

For kNN-based classifier were tested different values of parameter $k = \{1, 3, 5, 7, 9\}$. It was found that the best performance characteristics obtained for value $k = 1$. For 3-component feature vector J_{ppq63}, PPE, PVI the kNN-classifier give the following results: accuracy 83,9 ± 2,5, sensitivity 82,7 ± 4,9, specificity 85,2 ± 3,4, AUC 0.84 ± 0.03.

For the kNN-based classifier, the accuracy results were slightly better than for the LDA-based classifier. However, the preference was given to the LDA-based classifier, because its output can be converted into the probability of belonging of data sample to a given class [28]. This option is valuable for the doctor, since classification system provides not only the final decision, but also an estimation of its reliability.

3.6 ALS Expert Mobile Application

To test the proposed method for assessing the state of the voice function, a prototype of the ALS Expert mobile application was created (see Fig. 2), which is focused on performing two main functions: early diagnosis of ALS and monitoring the state of speech apparatus for ALS patients in dynamics.

ALS Expert[3] is an application for the Android operating system. The computational core of the application analyzes the digitized speech signal in accordance with the mathematical model described above. It was implemented in the C++ programming language. The UI and application logic are implemented with Flutter, a custom UI toolkit for building mobile apps from Google.

---

[3] https://drive.google.com/file/d/14U-t2ajWX5ILfNWx9hBZG1UfpHlhW197/view?usp=sharing.

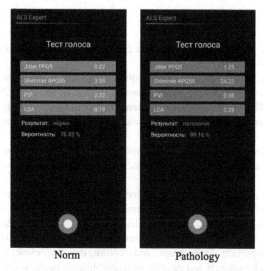

Norm   Pathology

Fig. 2. Examples of output results in the ALS Expert application.

The procedure for evaluating the status of the patient's voice function is conducted by a doctor and consists of the following. The patient performs a speech task (drawls the sound /a/). The result of uttering the sound /a/ is recorded using the built-in microphone or headset microphone and processed by the application's computing core. The result of the application is the values of the acoustic parameters, which are further analyzed by the doctor.

4 Conclusion

In this paper, a method was proposed for evaluating the state of the voice function in patients with ALS. The method is based on LDA classifier that used to determine if a voice belongs to a group of healthy people or a group of ALS patients. Our goal was to obtain the classifier with a small number of features. To study the efficiency of the classification, four groups of acoustic parameters were used: frequency perturbation, amplitude perturbation, features based on F0-contour and noise parameters. It was found that the classifier that uses the parameters jitter, PPE, PVI and GNE has the highest accuracy. The greatest specificity is obtained by using the optimized jitter and PPE parameter. The PVI-based classifier showed the highest specificity and AUC.

The obtained results indicate that the developed method can be used for evaluating of the voice function state in patients with ALS. The proposed method was developed considering the specifics of use in a mobile application (limited computing power, the impossibility of performing complex combined voice tests, etc.). The strengths of this approach: 1) ease of organization and execution of the test – a simple test for the long pronunciation of the vowel / a / is used; 2) the result is available immediately after the test; 3) possibility of automatic data accumulation; 4) relative low cost of the technical solution. However, the proposed method and its software implementation are experimental and require further clinical testing and verification.

References

1. Rushkevich, Y.N., Likhachev, S.A.: Modern concepts of motor neuron disease. Meditsinskie novosti, pp. 23–31 (2019)
2. Rushkevich, Y.N., Likhachev, S.A.: Epidemiology of motor neurone disease in the Republic of Belarus. Neurology and Neurosurgery Eastern Europe. 4, 551–561 (2018)
3. Eshghi, M.: Reduced task adaptation in alternating motion rate tasks as an early marker of bulbar involvement in amyotrophic lateral sclerosis. In: Procedings of Interspeech, pp. 4524–4528 (2019)
4. Rowe, H.P., Green, J.R.: Profiling speech motor impairments in persons with amyotrophic lateral sclerosis: an acoustic-based approach. In: Proceedings of Interspeech, pp. 4509–4513 (2019)
5. Connaghan, K.P.: Use of beiwe smartphone app to identify and track speech decline in amyotrophic lateral sclerosis. In: Proceedings of Interspeech, pp. 4504–4508 (2019)
6. Gutz, S. E.: Early identification of speech changes due to amyotrophic lateral sclerosis using machine classification. In: Proceedings of Interspeech, pp. 604–608 (2019)
7. Suhas, B.N.: Comparison of speech tasks and recording devices for voice based automatic classification of healthy subjects and patients with amyotrophic lateral sclerosis. In: Proceedings of Interspeech, pp. 4564–4568 (2019)
8. Rushkevich, Y.N.: Clinical experience of speech signal time-frequency analysis in the diagnostics and monitoring of bulbar dysfunction. Eastern Europe. 3, 429–439 (2017)
9. Gvozdovich, A.D., Rushkevich, Y.N., Vashkevich, M.I.: Detection of bulbar amyotrophic lateral sclerosis based on speech analysis. Doklady BGUIR. 6, 52–58 (2018). (in Russian)
10. Osipov, A.N.: Mobile app to collect diagnostic information through the registration of speech signals. BIG DATA Advanced Analytics: collection of materials of the fourth international scientific and practical conference, Minsk, Belarus, 2018 editorial board: Batura, M. etc. Minsk, BSUIR, pp. 343–347 (2018)
11. Kul, T.P., Rushkevich, Y.N., Lihachev, S.A.: Adaptation of digital signal processing methods to the analysis of speech in neurological pathologies. Doklady BGUIR. 7, 128–132 (2018)
12. Kul, T.P., Mezhennaya, M.M., Rushkevich, Y., Osipov, A.N., Likhachev, S.A., Rushkevich, I.V.: Methodical and hardware-software for recording and processing speech signals for diagnosis of neurological diseases. Informatics. 16(2), 27–39 (2019). (in Russian)
13. Vashkevich, M., Gvozdovich, A., Rushkevich, Y.: Detection of bulbar dysfunction in ALS patients based on running speech test. In: Ablameyko, S.V., Krasnoproshin, V.V., Lukashevich, M.M. (eds.) PRIP 2019. CCIS, vol. 1055, pp. 192–204. Springer, Cham (2019). https://doi.org/10.1007/978-3-030-35430-5_16
14. An, K., Kim, M., Teplansky, K., Green, J., Campbell, T., Yunusova, Y., Heitzman D., Wang, J.: Automatic early detection of amyotrophic lateral sclerosis from intelligible speech using convolutional neural networks. In: Proceedings of Interspeech, pp. 1913–1917 (2018)
15. Wang, J., Kothalkar, P.V., Cao, B., Heitzman, D.: Towards automatic detection of amyotrophic lateral sclerosis from speech acoustic and articulatory samples. In: Proceedings of Interspeech, pp. 1195–1199 (2016)
16. Yunusova, Y.: Profiling speech and pausing in amyotrophic lateral sclerosis (ALS) and frontotemporal dementia (FTD). PLoS ONE 11(1), 1–18 (2016)
17. Bandini, A., Green, J.R., Zinman, L., Yunusova, Y.: Classification of bulbar ALS from kinematic features of the jaw and lips: towards computer-mediated assessment. In: Proceedings of Interspeech, pp. 1819–1823 (2019)
18. Liss, J.M., LeGendre, S., Lotto, A.J.: Discriminating dysarthria type from envelope modulation spectra. J. Speech Language Hearing Res. 5(53), 1246–1255 (2011)

19. Spangler, T.: Fractal features for automatic detection of dysarthria. Spangler, T., Vinodchandran, N.V., Samal, A., Green, J.R. In: IEEE EMBS International Conference on Biomedical Health Informatics (BHI), pp. 437–440. Orlando, USA, Orlando (2017)

20. Wang, Y.-T., Kent, R.D., Duffy, J.R., Thomas, J.E.: Analysis of diadochokinesis in ataxic dysarthria using the motor speech profile programTM. Folia phoniatrica et logopaedica: official organ of the International Association of Logopedics and Phoniatrics (IALP). **61**(1), 1–11 (2009)

21. Green, J.R., et al.: Bulbar and speech motor assessment in ALS: challenges and future directions. Amyotrophic Lateral Sclerosis and Frontotemporal Degeneration. **14**, 494–500 (2013)

22. Yunusova, Y., Rosenthal, J.S., Green, J.R., Shellikeri, S., Rong, P., Wang, J., Zinman, L.H.: Detection of bulbar ALS using a comprehensive speech assessment battery. In: Proceedings of the International Workshop on Models and Analysis of Vocal Emissions for Biomedical Applications, pp. 217–220 (2013)

23. Vashkevich, M., Petrovsky, A., Rushkevich, Y.: Bulbar ALS detection based on analysis of voice perturbation and vibrato. Signal Processing: Algorithms, Architectures, Arrangements, and Applications (SPA), 267–272 (2019)

24. Vashkevich, M., Rushkevich, Y.: Detection of impairment of speech function in patients with ALS based on analysis of voice signal. Digital Signal Proc. **4**, 33–41 (2019)

25. Norel, R., Pietrowicz, M., Agurto, C., Rishoni, S., Cecchi, G.: Detection of amyotrophic lateral sclerosis (ALS) via acoustic analysis. In: Proceedings of Interspeech, pp. 377–381 (2018)

26. Kelleher, J.D., Mac Namee, B., D'arcy, A.: Fundamentals of machine learning for predictive data analytics: algorithms, worked examples, and case studies. MIT Press (2020)

27. Bishop, C.M.: Pattern recognition. Machine Learning. Springer Verlag. New York (2006)

28. Flach, P.: Machine learning: the art and science of algorithms that make sense of data. Cambridge University Press (2012)

29. Baken, R.J., Orlikoff, R.F.: Clinical measurement of speech and voice, p. 864, 2nd edn. Thomson Learning (2000)

30. Moran, R.J.: Telephony-based voice pathology assessment using automated speech analysis. IEEE Trans. Biomed. Eng. **53**(3), 468–477 (2006)

31. Michaelis, D., Gramss, T., Strube, H.W.: Glottal-to-noise excitation ratio–a new measure for describing pathological voices. Acta Acust. Acust. **83**(4), 700–706 (1997)

Child's Emotional Speech Classification by Human Across Two Languages: Russian & Tamil

Elena Lyakso[1]([⊠]) [ID], Olga Frolova[1] [ID], Nersisson Ruban[2] [ID], and A. Mary Mekala[3] [ID]

[1] The Child Speech Research Group, St. Petersburg State University, St. Petersburg, Russia
[2] School of Electrical Engineering, Vellore Institute of Technology, Vellore, India
[3] School of Information Technology & Engineering,
Vellore Institute of Technology, Vellore, India

Abstract. We examined the features of cross-cultural recognition of four basic emotions "joy – neutral (calm state) - sadness - anger" in the spontaneous and acting speech of Indian and Russian children across Russian and Tamil languages. Cross-cultural studies point that although basic emotion recognition is universal; emotion recognition is more accurate when speakers and receivers come from the same culture than the other cultures. The results showed that Russian and Indian experts recognized correctly the emotional states of children by their speech, but with different accuracy. Both groups of experts agreed on the state of sadness via spontaneous and acting speech of Russian children and the neutral state in spontaneous speech and anger state in the acting speech of Indian children. The importance of cultural recognition are that Indian experts classify more speech samples of spontaneous and acting speech from Russian children as reflecting a state of anger, Russian experts - a state of joy and a neutral state in the acting speech of Tamil children. Differences were revealed in the acoustic characteristics of the speech of Russian and Indian children, reflecting the basic emotions. Experts, when recognizing emotions in spontaneous speech, rely on the pitch values, in acting speech - on the intensity. The novelty of our finding lies in the cross-cultural recognition of emotions from the speech of children and the comparison of two distant languages - Russian and Tamil.

Keywords: Perceptual experiment · Child spontaneous speech · Child acting speech · Tamil language · Russian language · Acoustic features of speech

1 Introduction

The study of recognition of human emotions by voice has a long history [1]. Human speech expresses emotional meaning not only through semantics but also through certain attributes of the voice, for example, pitch or loudness.

In investigations of the emotions manifestations in voice, facial expressions, and behavior, the questions about the existence of basic (innate) and acquired (social) emotions [2–6], about the influence of the culture and language specificity on the expressions

© Springer Nature Switzerland AG 2021
A. Karpov and R. Potapova (Eds.): SPECOM 2021, LNAI 12997, pp. 384–396, 2021.
https://doi.org/10.1007/978-3-030-87802-3_35

and recognition of the emotions [6], e. g., on the role of prior cognitive experience in judgment when listening to vocal material [7] are discussed. Socio-cultural rules [8], the age and gender of the speaker and the listener [9, 10], and types of emotions [7] play an important role in emotional states recognition. Cross-cultural researches discussed in [5, 6, 8, 11] are devoted to solving these issues. Cross-cultural studies often indicate that while basic emotion recognition is universal, emotion recognition is more accurate when speakers and receivers come from the same culture compared to other cultural groups [5, 6, 12]. The results of the study (in which Dutch and Japanese listeners categorized and rated Dutch and Japanese vocalizations expressing nine emotions including anger and triumph, two socially disengaging emotions) demonstrate that Japanese vocalizations of socially disengaging emotions, especially anger, are challenging to interpret for Western listeners [13]. Consistent with previous studies both Dutch and Japanese listeners were generally able to recognize emotions expressed by both in-group and out-group members at the above chance level [14].

A meta-analysis of 37 cross-cultural studies of emotion recognition from speech prosody and nonlinguistic vocalizations, including expressers from 26 cultural groups and perceivers from 44 different cultures showed that a wide range of positive and negative emotions can be recognized with incredible accuracy in intercultural conditions and the impact on the recognition based on the diversity of the culture of the expresser and the perceiver [11].

The frame of Dialect theory argues that although emotional communication is culturally universal, it is characterized by accents that reflect the distinct cultural style for expressing nonverbal cues [15]. Cross-cultural studies on the recognition of emotions by voice and speech of Indian and European participants are unitary [8]. Cross-cultural studies of emotional prosody recognition by Hindi and Canadian English listeners were conducted [8]. Pseudoutterances conveying four basic emotions, expressed in English and Hindi, were presented to English and Hindi-speaking listeners. Results showed that in each language condition, native listeners were faster and more accurate than non-native listeners to recognize emotions. In this particular study, participants from India were born and raised in different parts of India and all spoke Hindi in the home to both parents while growing up; each had moved as a young adult to Montreal, Canada, to study or work [8]. The Eighth Schedule to the Indian Constitution contains a list of 22 scheduled languages, one of which is Tamil. As far as is known, there are no cross-cultural data on the recognition of the basic emotions via speech by native Russian and native Tamil listeners. Russian is one of the East Slavic languages which belong to the Indo-European family. Tamil is one of the classical languages in the world [16]. Tamil is a language of the Tamil-Kannada group of Eurasian languages which belongs to the Dravidian family. Both languages have an ancient origin, and the countries where these languages are used have a centuries-old original culture. Cross-cultural recognition of emotions from the voice and speech of children speaking Russian and Tamil is an even more difficult challenge in comparison with the cross-cultural recognition of emotions via speech of adults. The results of recognition of basic emotions in the voice of children by native speakers of two different language groups will be able to supplement existing knowledge about cross-cultural perception of emotions. These findings can be used to amplify dialect theory and hypothesis about the influence of previous cognitive experiences on the recognition of vocal emotions. The children of younger school age are the most interesting group for this research, because such children have not yet fully mastered the cultural traditions of emotional manifestations, and their development in the appropriate cultural environment has already influenced their emotional sphere.

The hypothesis of the study is to test the assumption that basic emotions in the speech of Russian and Indian children will be recognized by native speakers of Russian and Tamil languages, but dialect-specific recognition features will be revealed. The goal of the study is to compare the cross-cultural recognition of four emotions "joy – neutral (calm state) – sadness – anger" in the spontaneous and acting speech of children aged 8–12 years across Russian and Tamil languages. The research tasks are to examine the ability of Russian and Indian experts to recognize the state of Russian and Indian children by their speech, determine the acoustic features of emotional speech and correctly recognized speech samples.

2   Methods

2.1   Speech Data Collection

To study the cross-linguistic recognition of the emotional state of Indian and Russian children of 8–12 years of age via their speech by humans and machine, two language-specific corpora of emotional speech are created. Each corpus contains records of spontaneous speech and acting speech of 8–12 years old children. Russian corpus includes emotional speech of 95 children, Indian corpus contains speech data of 40 children. Speech recording was carried out according to a standardized protocol. Each recording session for every child included a dialogue with the experimenter (with a standard set of questions [17]) and the acting speech – words and phrases reflecting the emotional state, and meaningless texts.

The experimenter began the dialogue with the request to say child's name and age. Then the experimenter consistently asked questions:

For example:

– Do you like to go to school? What do you like in school (classes or play with friends)? What are your favorite tasks? Why? Do you have any hobbies? What are your favorite movies, cartoons, books, games (computer/desktop/mobile)?
– What do you dislike at the school? What lesson do you dislike the most? Why? Are you angry with anyone? How often do you get angry? If there is a conflict, do you fight right away or do you first find out the cause of the conflict?
– Do you know what sadness is? How do you feel if you are sad? When (in what situations) do you think a person experiences sadness?

The set of words and phrases both for Russian and Indian children: the words and phrases reflecting different emotional states "joy – neutral – sadness – anger" were selected according to the lexical meaning of words /- I love when it is beautiful, I am scared, dark and scared /, etc. The children should pronounce the speech material, manifesting the emotional state. This task was designed to show how children could demonstrate different states in vocal expressions.

The recording time varied from 30 min to 60 min and included a training session for pronouncing meaningless texts. The place of recording of child's speech and behavior was the laboratory. The annotation of the child's emotional speech was made on four categories (based on video recordings and the recording situation protocol) "joy – neutral – sadness – anger" by two Russian speaking speech specialists for Russian children and by two Tamil speaking speech specialists for Tamil speaking children. The speech samples were assigned to the corresponding emotional category when there was an agreement between the two annotators (they did not participate in subsequent perceptual experiments). The recordings of speech of children were made by the "Marantz PMD660" recorder with external microphone "SENNHEIZER e835S" with the following settings: the sampling rate was set to 16,000 Hz and the mono audio channel was used in all the recording sessions. Parallel with the recording of the speech, the child's behavior and facial expression were recorded using a video camera "SONY HDR-CX560E". The recording was carried out in rooms without special soundproofing. The distance from the child's face to the microphone did not exceed 50 cm (30–50 cm). All speech files were stored in .wav format, 44.100 Hz, 16 bits per sample.

Emotional speech recordings from 30 children aged 8–12 years were selected for human recognition from speech corpora: 12 Russian-speaking children (born and living in St. Petersburg, Russia), 18 Tamil speaking children (born and living in Vellore, India). Two types of speech were used: spontaneous speech and acting speech. Spontaneous speech – the phrases were selected from the child's replies in dialogs with the experimenter. The utterance of meaningless was used as an acting speech, reflecting various emotional states [18, 19]. A compromise between spontaneous and natural acting speech is the standardization of speech material [20], for example, reciting nonsense. Acting speech - Russian children pronouncing a meaningless text – the first quatrain of "Jabberwocky", the poem by Lewis Carroll [21], and the meaningless (sentence) by L.V. Shcherba "glokaya kuzdra" (1930) [22]; Indian children spoke the meaningless text about Grandpa [23] and Tamil meaningless phrases.

2.2 Listeners

To investigate whether the listener's native language affects the recognition of the emotional state of children which is reflected in their speech, we conducted a study with two groups of participants. Participants were listeners speaking the Russian and Tamil languages, who were invited to listen to speech samples of Russian and Indian children, pronounced in different emotional states. Their results were subjected to cross-comparisons in subsequent analyzes. In total, 26 listeners participated in the experiment. Both native Russian and native Tamil (Indian) listeners have special education in speech sciences and professional experience in the field of speech science - experts. Demographics of the experts' groups are summarized in Table 1.

Table 1. Summary of listeners group demographics. Age is given in years.

	Russian	Indian
Number	13	13
Mean age	35.8	37.6
SD age	12.6	10.7
Professional experience, mean age	12.8	13.7
Professional experience, SD age	8.8	9.2

2.3 Data Analysis

The study includes two methods: perceptual study and spectrographic analysis of child speech. The study was carried out according to the common protocol.

Perceptual study: The 6 test sequences included the spontaneous and acting speech of Russian and Tamil children (4 tests of spontaneous speech for 45 speech samples; 2 tests of acting speech for 16 speech samples). Each test was listened to by 10 experts. For all the studies, the experts indicated their information in the questionnaire: gender, age, and experience in interacting with children. The task for experts was to identify four classes: "joy - neutral - sadness - anger". There was no preliminary training for the experts. The experts listened to each test once. Experts listened to the test sequences through headphones "SENNHEIZER". The speech intensity level in the tests during playback was 60–70 dB. The experiment was carried out in a laboratory condition. The noise level did not exceed 20 dB. Confusion matrixes for perceptual experiments were prepared. We compared how native speakers recognize emotions from the speech of children of their own nationality with other nationality; and between the spontaneous speech and acting speech.

Spectrographic analysis of the speech material was carried out in the Cool Edit Pro sound editor and Praat v.6.1.42 [24]. The temporal and spectral characteristics of speech were automatically calculated, based on the algorithms implemented in the Cool Edit Pro sound editor, the intensity was automatically calculated in Praat. For all speech samples which are included in the test sequences, the duration (ms) of a word, phrase or utterance was determined; by word, phrase, utterance: pitch values (F0, Hz) - average, F0 max, F0 min, and intensity values E (dB). F0 is the main characteristic of the voice, resulting from the swaying of vocal folds. F0 statistics are one of the most important features that correlate with emotional vocal expressions. A higher and wider range of F0 [9, 25–27] and energy (intensity) [25] are usually associated with high-arousal emotions compared to neutral speech.

For each utterance, the range of F0 was calculated by subtracting the minimum F0 from the maximum F0 values: F0 range = F0max-F0min; the ratio of intensities cor-responding to F0max - E0max and F0min - E0min normalized concerning E0 - E0max/E0, E0min/E0, the ratio E0max/E0min were calculated. The rate of meaningless speech was determined as the number of syllables per second.

Statistical data analysis was carried out using non-parametric tests: Mann-Whitney test, Regression analysis.

All procedures were approved by the Health and Human Research Ethics Committee of Saint Petersburg State University and written informed consent was obtained from parents of the child participant. Signed consent forms are filled by the parent of each Indian child.

3   Results

3.1   Characteristics of Stimulus Material

Spontaneous speech of Indian children is characterized by higher values of pitch than the speech of Russian children (Z-score $= 9.119$; $p < 0.00001$ - Mann-Whitney test), and pitch range for sad, joy, and anger states ($p < 0.005$). Pitch values of acting speech of Russian children are higher vs speech of Indian children (Z-score $= 2.164$ $p < 0.03$), pitch range significantly less for sadness state ($p < 0.05$) (Fig. 1 A, B). Intensity ratio (E0max/E0min) for stressed vowels of words is higher for joy state for acting Russian speech vs joy state for Russian spontaneous speech and anger state for acting Tamil speech (Fig. 1 C). The range of intensity values of acting speech samples is higher for Tamil speech vs Russian speech ($p < 0.001$) (Fig. 1 E). The rate of meaningless speech is higher for Indian children's emotional speech to Russian children's speech. The minimum speech rate for Russian children was in sadness speech; for Indian children, the speech rate doesn't differ significantly in different emotional states, at the highest speed in neutral speech (Fig. 1 F).

3.2   Perceptual Data: Spontaneous Speech vs Acting Speech

Russian Speaking Children's Spontaneous Speech. Russian experts recognized the state of joy (60% of correct answers) and neutral (84%) in the speech of Russian speaking children better vs the state of sadness (44%) and anger state (25% accuracy). They attributed the largest number of speech samples to a neutral state (Table 2). Indian experts recognized the emotional state of anger (46%) better than Russian experts did. Indian experts classified the state of joy (39%), the state of sadness (36%), and the neutral state (46%) in the speech of Russian children worse than Russian experts did. Russian and Indian experts agreed on the state of sadness via a child's spontaneous speech (recall 0.44 & 0.36). Russian experts recognized the emotional state of Russian children better than Indian experts ($p < 0.0001$ – Mann-Whitney test) – particularly for the neutral state ($p < 0.0001$) and joy ($p < 0.01$) but not for sadness and anger.

Tamil Speaking Children's Spontaneous Speech. Indian experts recognized the neutral state (86% of correct answers), sadness state (86%), and anger state (81%) in the speech of Tamil speaking children better vs the state of joy (80%) (Table 2).

Russian experts recognized the neutral state (72%) and the state of sadness (58%) in the speech of Tamil-speaking children better vs the states of joy and anger.

The average recognition recall (UAR) of the emotional state from the spontaneous speech of Russian children for Russian experts was 0.53; for Indian experts – 0.42; UAR for spontaneous Tamil speech for Russian experts - 0.54, for Indian experts – 0.83.

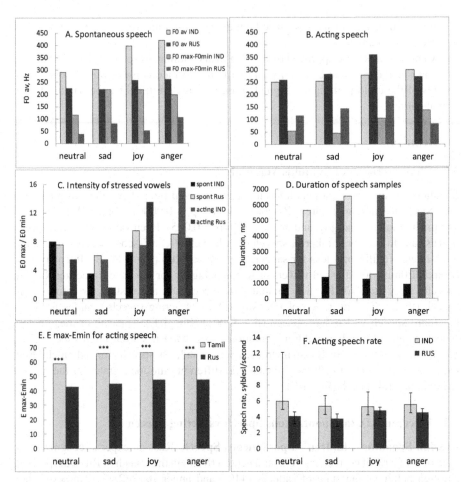

Fig. 1. Characteristics of stimulus material: A, B – pitch values and pitch values range – A - spontaneous speech, B - acting speech; C – the intensity of pitch of stressed vowels from words (the ratio of the E maximum value to the E minimum); D – duration of speech samples; E - Intensity range for acting speech; F – Acting speech rate. Vertical axis: A, B – Pitch values, Hz; C - intensity ratio [E0 max/E0min], dB; D – speech samples duration, ms; E – Intensity range [Emax-Emin], dB; F- speech rate, syllables/second. Horizontal axis – emotional state "neutral (calm) – sadness – joy – anger". *** - p < 0.001 - Mann-Whitney test.

The agreement between Indian and Russian experts for neutral state classification for speech of Tamil children was revealed (recall 0.72 & 0.86). Indian experts recognized all the emotional states of Tamil children better than Russian experts.

Russian Speaking Children's Meaningless Speech. Russian experts better recognized a state of joy (98% of correct answers), worse - a neutral state (65%) via Russian children's acting speech. Indian experts better recognized the state of sadness (88%), worse recognized the neutral state (48%) (Table 3). Both groups of experts determined

Table 2. Confusion matrixes for emotion classification by Russian and Indian experts in the spontaneous speech of Russian and Indian children, %.

Russian speech								
	Joy		Neutral		Sadness		Anger	
	R	I	R	I	R	I	R	I
Joy	**60**	**39**	36	25	3	18	1	18
Neutral	9	7	**84**	**46**	6	31	1	16
Sadness	5	13	45	31	**44**	**36**	6	20
Anger	9	11	47	22	19	21	**25**	**46**
Total	83	70	212	124	72	106	33	100
Recall	0.6	0.39	0.84	0.46	0.44	0.36	0.25	0.46
Precision	0.72	0.56	0.40	0.37	0.61	0.34	0.76	0.46
F1-score	0.66	0.46	0.54	0.41	0.51	0.35	0.38	0.46

Unweighted Average Recall (UAR) – Russian (R) - **0.53**; Indian (I) - **0.42**

Tamil speech								
	Joy		Neutral		Sadness		Anger	
	R	I	R	I	R	I	R	I
Joy	**42**	**80**	35	17	8	2	15	1
Neutral	11	6	**72**	**86**	10	6	7	2
Sadness	7	1	31	9	**58**	**86**	4	4
Anger	24	5	29	11	5	3	**42**	**81**
Total	84	92	167	123	81	97	68	88
Recall	0.42	0.80	0.72	0.86	0.58	0.86	0.42	0.81
Precision	0.50	0.87	0.43	0.70	0.72	0.89	0.62	0.92
F1-score	0.46	0.88	0.54	0.77	0.64	0.87	0.5	0.86

Unweighted Average Recall (UAR) – R - **0.54**; I - **0.83**

Note: R – Russian experts, I – Indian experts

the state of sadness equally well (85% and 88% of the answers of Russian and Indian experts; recall - 0.85 & 0.88).

Tamil Speaking Children's Meaningless Speech. Russian experts better recognized a state of anger (84% of correct answers), worse - a state of sadness (62%) via Tamil children's acting speech. Indian experts better recognized the state of anger (85%), worse recognized the state of sadness (48%) (Table 3). Both groups of experts determined the state of anger equally well (84% and 85% of the answers of Russian and Indian experts; recall - 0.84 & 0.85).

UAR of the emotional state from the acting speech of Russian children for Russian experts was 0.80; for Indian experts – 0.73; UAR for acting Tamil speech for Russian experts - 0.71, for Indian experts – 0.61.

Table 3. Confusion matrixes for emotion classification by Russian and Indian experts in the acting speech of Russian and Indian children, %.

Russian speech

	Joy		Neutral		Sadness		Anger	
	R	I	R	I	R	I	R	I
Joy	**98**	**70**	2	25	0	0	0	5
Neutral	5	10	**65**	**48**	30	42	0	0
Sadness	0	0	15	12	**85**	**88**	0	0
Anger	17	10	10	5	3	0	**70**	**85**
Total	120	90	92	90	118	130	70	90
Recall	0.98	0.70	0.65	0.48	0.85	0.88	0.7	0.85
Precision	0.82	0.78	0.71	0.53	0.72	0.68	1.0	0.94
F1-score	0.89	0.74	0.68	0.51	0.78	0.77	0.82	0.89

Unweighted Average Recall (UAR): R – **0.80**; I – **0.73**

Tamil speech

	Joy		Neutral		Sadness		Anger	
	R	I	R	I	R	I	R	I
Joy	**67**	**56**	17	29	11	14	5	1
Neutral	19	40	**70**	**54**	11	4	0	2
Sadness	14	14	23	36	**62**	**48**	1	2
Anger	10	7.5	6	7.5	0	0	**84**	**85**
Total	110	117.5	116	126.5	84	66	90	90
Recall	0.67	0.56	0.70	0.54	0.62	0.48	0.84	0.85
Precision	0.61	0.48	0.60	0.43	0.74	0.73	0.93	0.94
F1-score	0.64	0.51	0.65	0.48	0.67	0.58	0.88	0.89

Unweighted Average Recall (UAR): R - **0.71**; I - **0.61**

3.3 Acoustic Features of Emotional Speech

Acoustic features of speech correctly classified by both Indian and Russian listeners (probability 0.75–1.0).

A. For spontaneous speech the correlation was revealed between emotional state of children: and

F0 max - $F(1,35) = 4.264$ p < 0.05 ($R^2 = 0.109$ $\beta = 0.33$) - Regression analysis,
F0max-F0min - $F(1,35) = 4.212$ p < 0.05 ($R^2 = 0.107$ $\beta = 0.328$),

B. For acting speech:
intensity of pitch of stressed vowels from words (E0min/E0) - $F(1,18) = 6.972$.
p < 0.02 ($R^2 = 0.279$ $\beta = -0.528$), E max/Emin - $F(1,18) = 12.379$ p < 0.003.
($R^2 = 0.408$ $\beta = 0.638$),
speech samples Emax-Emin - $F(1,11) = 7.807$ p < 0.02 ($R^2 = 0.415$ $\beta = 0.644$).

Acoustic features of the speech of children correctly recognized by experts belonging to the same language environments.

A. Indian children: For spontaneous speech, the correlation was revealed between the emotional state of children and:
F0 average - $F(1,60) = 30.317$ p < 0.000 ($R^2 = 0.336$ $\beta = 0.579$);
F0 max - $F(1,60) = 31.068$ p < 0.000 ($R^2 = 0.341$ $\beta = 0.584$);
F0 min - $F(1,60) = 6.585$ p < 0.02 ($R^2 = 0.099$ $\beta = 0.315$).
For acting speech between emotional state of children and:
F0 average - $F(1,12) = 4.943$ p < 0.05 ($R^2 = 0.292$ $\beta = 0.54$).
F0 max - $F(1,12) = 9.55$ p < 0.01 ($R^2 = 0.443$ $\beta = 0.666$);
F0max-F0min - $F(1,12) = 17.662$ p < 0.002 ($R^2 = 0.595$ $\beta = 0.772$);
E0max/E0min - $F(1,12) = 12.560$ p < 0.005 ($R^2 = 0.511$ $\beta = 0.715$).

B. Russian children: For spontaneous speech the correlation was revealed between emotional state of children and F0 average –
$F(1,46) = 10.231$ p < 0.003 ($R^2 = 0.182$ $\beta = 0.427$).
For acting speech: between emotional state of children and E0 min/E0 of stressed vowels from words - $F(1,8) = 8.788$ p < 0.02 ($R^2 = 0.524$ $\beta = -0.724$);
speech samples Emax-Emin - $F(1,8) = 11.730$ p < 0.01 ($R^2 = 0.595$ $\beta = 0.771$).

4 Discussion

The results of the study on the material of the Russian and Tamil languages showed the ability of cross-cultural (Russia-India) recognition of the emotional state through the speech of children belonging to different linguistic environments. They complement the data obtained on the material of other languages - a cross-cultural study of English and Hindi listeners [8], recognition of vocal emotions in Spanish, Chinese, Arabic, and English speech by English listeners [28], a cross-cultural study of the emotional tone of voice recognition by native Chinese and British speakers [29]. Russian and Indian experts agreed on the state of sadness via spontaneous and acting speech of Russian children and the neutral state in spontaneous speech and anger state in the acting speech of Indian children. The manifestation of emotions in the spontaneous speech of Indian children is more expressive in comparison with Russian peers that are correlated with higher values of voice pitch - the basic feature of emotional speech. The accuracy of recognizing children's emotions by spontaneous speech was higher among experts with a similar culture with children.

One interesting culture-specific phenomenon observed in our data was that Indian experts chose more speech samples from Russian children as anger in spontaneous speech vs Russian experts. Furthermore, anger is well recognized by both groups of experts in the acting speech of children of two nationalities. Our findings converge with previous work on vocal emotion recognition, e.g. [28–31] that negative information is very important for the formation of impressions, e.g. [32]. Anger is considered a very arousing emotional condition. Anger is critical to motivating action and approaching and is considered a survival response inherent in all living things [33]. Acoustic features of the speech of Russian and Indian children correctly assigned by Russian and Indian experts to the corresponding emotions were identified. The listeners rely on similar acoustic features while determining corresponding emotions via speech – pitch values for spontaneous speech, and intensity – for acting speech. These data fit into the general framework of research on the acoustic characteristics of emotional speech, e.g. [26, 34, 35]. At the same time, the novelty of our research lies in the cross-cultural recognition of emotions from the speech of children and the comparison of two distant languages - Russian and Tamil.

5 Conclusion

The result of the study confirmed the hypothesis about the ability of experts of two nationalities to recognize four basic emotions from the speech of children of the same nationality and another, but with varying accuracy. The native Russian experts were more accurate in recognizing the emotional states of children in the acting speech vs spontaneous speech. The native Tamil-speaking experts were more accurate in recognizing the emotional states of Russian children in the acting speech while the emotional states of Indian children in the spontaneous speech. Russian and Indian experts agreed on the state of sadness via spontaneous and acting speech of Russian children and the neutral state in spontaneous speech and anger state in the acting speech of Indian children. The specifies of recognition are that Indian experts classify a more number of speech samples of spontaneous and acting speech of Russian children as reflecting a state of anger, Russian experts - a state of joy and a neutral state in the acting speech of Tamil children. Differences were revealed in the acoustic characteristics of the speech of Russian and Indian children, reflecting basic emotions. Experts, when recognizing emotions in spontaneous speech, rely on the pitch values, in acting speech - on the intensity of speech.

The limitation: we examine the reflection of emotional states of children in one (Tamil) of more than 22 Indian state languages and a small number of participants of the study.

Future work: to carry out the automatic recognition of emotions from the speech of children to use this data in the development of interfaces and systems for teaching children with atypical development and developmental disorders accompanied by emotional disorders.

Acknowledgments. The research was financially supported by the Russian Foundation for Basic Research (project 19-57-45008–IND) – for Russian researchers, and Department of Science and Technology (DST) (INTRUSRFBR382) - for Indian researchers.

References

1. Darwin, C.: The Expression of the Emotions in Man and Animals. John Murray, London (1872)
2. Ekman, P.: Universals and cultural differences in facial expressions of emotions. In: Cole, J. (ed.) Nebraska Symposium on Motivation, 1971, vol. 19, pp. 207–282. University of Nebraska Press, Lincoln (1972)
3. Ekman, P.: Basic emotions. In: Dalgleish, T., Power, M.J. (eds.) Handbook of Cognition and Emotion, pp. 45–60. John Wiley & Sons, Ltd, Hoboken (1999)
4. Izard, K.: Human Emotions. Plenum Press, New York (1977)
5. Elfenbein, H.A., Ambady, N.: On the universality and cultural specificity of emotion recognition: a meta-analysis. Psychol. Bull. **128**(2), 203–235 (2002)
6. Sauter, D.A., Eisner, F., Ekman, P., Scott, S.K.: Cross-cultural recognition of basic emotions through nonverbal emotional vocalizations. Proceedings of the National Academy of Science of the United States of America **107**(6), 2408–2412 (2010)
7. Nordström, H., Laukka, P., Thingujam, N.S., Schubert, E., Elfenbein, H.A.: Emotion appraisal dimensions inferred from vocal expressions are consistent across cultures: a comparison between Australia and India. R. Soc. Open Sci. **4**(11), 170912 (2017)
8. Jiang, X., Paulmann, S., Robin, J., Pell, M.D.: More than accuracy: Nonverbal dialects modulate the time course of vocal emotion recognition across cultures. J. Exp. Psychol. Hum. Percept. Perform. **41**, 597–612 (2015)
9. Goy, H., Pichora-Fuller, M.K., van Lieshout, P.: Effects of age on speech and voice quality ratings. J. Acoust. Soc. Am. **139**(4), 1648–1659 (2016)
10. Lausen, A., Schacht, A.: Gender differences in the recognition of vocal emotions. Front. Psychol. **9**, 882 (2018)
11. Laukka, P., Elfenbein, H.A.: Cross-cultural emotion recognition and in-group advantage in vocal expression: a meta-analysis. Emot. Rev. **13**(1), 3–11 (2020)
12. Thompson, W.F., Balkwill, L.L.: Decoding speech prosody in five languages. Semiotica **158**, 407–424 (2006)
13. Yoshie, M., Sauter, D.A.: Cultural norms influence nonverbal emotion communication: Japanese vocalizations of socially disengaging emotions. Emotion **20**(3), 513–517 (2020)
14. Cordaro, D.T., Keltner, D., Tshering, S., Wangchuk, D., Flynn, L.M.: The voice conveys emotion in ten globalized cultures and one remote village in Bhutan. Emotion **16**(1), 117–128 (2016)
15. Elfenbein, H.A.: Nonverbal dialects and accents in facial expressions of emotion. Emot. Rev. **5**, 90–96 (2013)
16. Stein, B.: Circulation and the historical geography of Tamil country. J. Asian Stud. **37**(1), 7–26 (1977)
17. Lyakso, E.E., Ruban, N., Frolova, O.V., Gorodnyi, V.A., Matveev, Y.N.: Approbation of a method for studying the reflection of emotional state in children's speech and pilot psychophysiological experimental data. Int. J. Adv. Trends Comput. Sci. Eng. **9**(1), 649–656 (2020)
18. Liu, P., Pell, M.D.: Recognizing vocal emotions in Mandarin Chinese: a validated database of Chinese vocal emotional stimuli. Behav. Res. Methods **44**(4), 1042–1051 (2012). https://doi.org/10.3758/s13428-012-0203-3
19. Castro, S.L., Lima, C.: Recognizing emotions in spoken language: a validated set of Portuguese sentences and pseudo sentences for research on emotional prosody. Behav. Res. Methods **42**(1), 74–81 (2010)
20. Schuller, B., et al.: Cross-corpus acoustic emotion recognition: variances and strategies. IEEE Trans. Affect. Comput. **1**(2), 119–131 (2010)

21. Carrol, L.: Through the Looking-Glass and What Alice Found There. Macmillan and Co, London (1872)
22. http://languagehat.com/glokaya-kuzdr
23. Heyman, M., Satpathy, S., Ravishankar, A.: The Tenth Rasa: An Anthology of Indian Nonsense. Penguin Books India, New Delhi (2007)
24. https://www.fon.hum.uva.nl/praat
25. Johnstone, T., Scherer, K.R.: Vocal communication of emotion. In: Lewis, M., Haviland, J. (eds.) Handbook of Emotions, 2nd edn., pp. 220–235. Guilford Press, New York (2000)
26. Breitenstein, C., Lancker, D.V., Daum, I.: The contribution of speech rate and pitch variation to the perception of vocal emotions in a German and an American sample. Cogn. Emot. **15**(1), 57–79 (2001)
27. Lyakso, E., Frolova, O.: Emotion state manifestation in voice features: chimpanzees, human infants, children, adults. In: Ronzhin, A., Potapova, R., Fakotakis, N. (eds.) SPECOM 2015. LNCS (LNAI), vol. 9319, pp. 201–208. Springer, Cham (2015). https://doi.org/10.1007/978-3-319-23132-7_25
28. Chronaki, G., Wigelsworth, M., Pell, M.D., Kotz, S.A.: The development of cross-cultural recognition of vocal emotion during childhood and adolescence. Sci. Rep. **8**, 8659 (2018)
29. Paulmann, S., Uskul, A.K.: Cross-cultural emotional prosody recognition: evidence from Chinese and British listeners. Cogn. Emot. **28**, 230–244 (2014)
30. Lausen, A., Hammerschmidt, K.: Emotion recognition and confidence ratings predicted by vocal stimulus type and prosodic parameters. Humanit. Soc. Sci. Commun. **7**(2), 1–17 (2020)
31. Cowen, A.S., Elfenbein, H.A., Laukka, P., Keltner, D.: Mapping 24 emotions conveyed by brief human vocalization. Am. Psychol. **74**(6), 698–712 (2019)
32. Baumeister, R.F., Bratslavsky, E., Finkenauer, C., Vohr, K.D.: Bad is stronger than good. Rev. Gen. Psychol. **5**(4), 323–370 (2001)
33. Gilam, G., Hendler, T.: Deconstructing anger in the human brain. Curr. Top. Behav. Neurosci. **30**, 257–273 (2017)
34. Kamiloğlu, R.G., Fischer, A.H., Sauter, D.A.: Good vibrations: a review of vocal expressions of positive emotions. Psychon. Bull. Rev. **27**(2), 237–265 (2020). https://doi.org/10.3758/s13423-019-01701-x
35. Guo, D., Yu, H., Hu, A., Ding, Y.: Statistical analysis of acoustic characteristics of Tibetan Lhasa dialect speech emotion. In: SHS Web of Conferences. 25: 01017 (2016)

Analysis of Dialogues of Typically Developing Children, Children with Down Syndrome and ASD Using Machine Learning Methods

Olesia Makhnytkina[1]($\boxtimes$) (iD), Aleksey Grigorev[2]($\boxtimes$) (iD), and Aleksander Nikolaev[2] (iD)

[1] ITMO University, Saint Petersburg 197101, Russian Federation
makhnytkina@itmo.ru
[2] Saint Petersburg State University, Saint Petersburg 191124, Russian Federation

Abstract. In this paper, we propose an approach for determining significant differences in speech of typically developing children, children with Autism Spectrum Disorder (ASD) and Down syndrome. To start solving this problem, we performed an automatic graphemic and morphological analysis of transcribed children's dialogues. Sixty-two children (20 children with typical development, 14 with Down syndrome, 28 with autism spectrum disorder) discussed standard set of questions with experimenters; for further analysis, only the children's replicas were used. A total of 25 linguistic features were extracted from each dialogue: the number of replicas, the number of sentences, the number of tokens, the number of pauses, the number of unfinished words and the part of speech composition. To reduce the dimensionality, we performed Kruskal-Wallis tests to assess differences in these features among the studied groups of children, which allows to select 12 significant features. These features were incorporated into tree models such as Gradient Boosting, Random Forest, Ada Boost. All machine learning methods showed high performance, which allows to conclude about a good differentiating ability of features. Our best method showed a classification accuracy of 83%.

Keywords: Linguistic features · Autism spectrum disorder · Down syndrome · Machine learning

1 Introduction

A speech of each person has distinctive features, but at the same time researchers highlight specific signs, which are characteristic for groups of texts, for example, works of different genres or texts by people belonging to different groups.

Graphematic, lexico-morphological features are considered among such signs. Linguistic characteristics, for which differences have been identified for the target groups of texts, are used for classification of texts. So, in the work [1] the morphological features of single words, «adjective + noun» constructions, text dynamism, the average length of words and sentences are considered for solving the problem of classification of texts by style. Morphological and lexical features are also significant for solving the problem of texts classification by gender of authors [2], age [3].

© Springer Nature Switzerland AG 2021
A. Karpov and R. Potapova (Eds.): SPECOM 2021, LNAI 12997, pp. 397–406, 2021.
https://doi.org/10.1007/978-3-030-87802-3_36

A large number of studies focus on a speech of typically developing (TD) children (materials of the annual international conference «Problems of ontolinguistics»). For children with atypical development such studies are few.

For children with autism spectrum disorders (ASD), it has been shown that their speech is represented mainly by vocalizations, single words and short simple phrases [4–6]. Children with ASD have a poorer vocabulary than their typically developing peers and have difficulty building sentences. Children with ASD may have difficulty understanding other people's speech [7]. Nouns predominate in the vocabulary of children with ASD [5, 8]. There is a specific use of words by children with ASD, in particular, the use of words in the wrong meaning. There is the lag of children with ASD in comparison with TD children in the acquisition of grammatical constructions: prepositions of direction, plural, auxiliary and modal verbs, personal and demonstrative pronouns [9]. Children with ASD differ from TD children in the use of personal [10] and subject [11] pronouns.

It was shown, that children with Down syndrome (DS) have a shorter length of utterances comparing to TD children, their speech has poor intelligibility, but intelligibility improves with increasing age in adolescence. Children with DS are more likely to skip verbs than TD children; children with DS use fewer words in speech than they understand, have less expressive vocabulary [12]; they use prepositional phrases more often and use more verbs than nouns [13]. It was shown on the material of German language, that children with DS have difficulties with verbal inflection: building of past tense forms [14], subject – predicate agreement [15].

Analysis of parts of speech of Russian-speaking children aged 6–7 years showed that TD children use mainly nouns and verbs in speech, children with ASD and DS - particles and vocalizations. It was revealed that children with ASD use significantly less verbs, adjectives, adverbs, numbers, prepositions and conjunctions in speech in comparison with TD peers. For children with DS, a significantly lower frequency of the use of verbs, pronouns, adjectives, adverbs, numbers, prepositions and conjunctions was found than for TD children [16]. Statistical analysis of the text of speech of children with DS showed the most frequent use of words /дать 'give' – 0.37; мама 'mom' – 0.36; mom 'that' – 0.12; да 'yes' – 0.07/, /спасибо 'thanks' – 0.07/ [17]. In children with ASD aged 5–11 the proportion of answers adequate to the question asked by the experimenter is less than in TD children. Proportion of verbal and gesture answers is also less than in TD children. The feature of children with ASD was missing answers. The predominant type of cue in children with ASD is a single word, in TD children - a simple phrase. Children with ASD are less likely than TD children to use yes/no answers and cues consisting of a few simple phrases. Complex sentences are found only in the speech of TD children. In children with ASD and TD children, words with one or two syllables are most common. Words of four and five syllables children are less common in children with ASD than in TD children. Nouns prevail in the responses of children with ASD and TD children. Children with ASD use adverbs, pronouns and function words less often than TD children. Phonetic analysis showed the presence in the speech of children with ASD of phonemes atypical for the Russian language, the lack of formation of some groups of consonants and consonant substitutions [18]. However, in all the studies presented linguistic analysis of children's speech was performed manually. This is primarily due to the lack of formation of various aspects of speech in children with atypical development. However, the first work of linguistic analysis of the text of children with highly functional children with ASD using automatic analysis showed the possibility of using the method to analyze the speech of children with atypical development. Thus, the use of linguistic features together with acoustic ones for the detection of ASD was considered in [19]. It was shown that the value of the F1-score in detecting children with typical development was 0.78, and for children with ASD - 0.73.

One of the limitations in the use of morphological features in the problems of classification of texts of children with typical development, ASD is that most researchers carry out the markup manually. However, the high quality of modern morphological analyzers for the Russian language makes it possible to make markup automatically, which help to mark up a large amount of data in a short period of time without involving of linguists [20]. It was shown in [21] that the accuracy of automatic morphological labeling of children's texts is only 1–2% lower than that of adults' texts, which allows to use tools for automatic detection of part of speech markup for dialogues of children with typical development, ASD and DS.

The aim of the our study was to identify the linguistic features of speech of typically developing children, children with ASD and Down syndrome for the classification of dialogue texts of children using machine learning methods at a high performance.

2 Datasets

In our study, we used the original dataset containing hand-transcribed dialogues of children with typical development, Down syndrome, and autism spectrum disorder. This observational child study was approved by the Ethics Committee of the St. Petersburg State University. The sample included speech material of boys aged 8 to 11 years. The choice of male children is due to the standardization of the sample by gender, associated with a higher frequency of occurrence of informants with ASD [22]. The choice of the age of the informants is due to the beginning of the education of children with atypical development in school. TD children attended comprehensive school, children with ASD and DS - special school. The speech material of children was recorded in a school, laboratory and child center using the Marantz PMD660 digital tape recorder with a SENNHEIZER e835S extension microphone. The recording situation was a dialogue between the experimenter and the child with a standard set of questions. The replies of children were selected for analysis. The transcription of the dialogues was carried out by 4 experts - specialists in the field of the study of children's speech. In total, the dataset contains 69 files with dialogues, 62 children were interviewed, including 20 children with typical development, 14 with Down syndrome, 28 with autism spectrum disorder. The descriptive characteristics of the dataset are presented in the table (Table 1):

Table 1. Description of the dataset.

Features	TD	DS	ASD
Number of replicas	834	1173	2550
Number of sentences	1105	1206	2930
Number of tokens	5319	1737	5348

3   Methods

Graphematic analysis is the primary step in the automatic natural language processing. The main task of graphematic analysis is to isolate structural units from the input text, namely, paragraph sentences, words (tokens), punctuation marks, etc. As a result of graphematic analysis, sentences and words were identified, punctuation marks were analyzed - the sequence "…" was highlighted, which in the text denoted a pause.

After carrying out graphematic analysis, descriptive characteristics were calculated for the following features:

1. The number of replicas of the respondent in the dialogue.
2. The number of sentences in the replicas of the respondent in the dialogue.
3. The number of pauses in the replicas of the respondent in the dialogue.
4. The number of unfinished words in the respondent's replicas in the dialogue.
5. The average number of tokens in the respondent's sentences in the dialogue.
6. The average number of tokens in the replicas of the respondent in the dialogue.

Morphological text analysis is the process of determining the grammatical meaning of word forms and highlighting their stems. The task of morphological analysis is to determine the normal form from which a given word form was formed, as well as to obtain a set of its morphological characteristics. Morphological characteristics are a set of key-value pairs. The role of the key is, for example, part of speech, gender, number, case, mood, tense and other features of words used in Russian. A value is any specific value that a given attribute (key) can take. For example, the key "number" can take on the values "singular", "plural".

After morphological analysis, the values of the following signs were calculated for each child:

1. Relative frequency of adjectives (full) ADJF.
2. Relative frequency of adjectives (short) ADJS.
3. Relative frequency of adverbs ADVB.
4. Relative frequency of comparatives COMP.
5. Relative frequency of conjunction CONJ.
6. Relative frequency of verbs (infinitive) INFN.
7. Relative frequency of interjections INTJ.
8. Relative frequency of non-existent words None.
9. Relative frequency of nouns NOUN.
10. Relative frequency of pronouns-nouns NPRO.
11. Relative frequency of numerals NUMR.
12. Relative frequency of particles PRCL.
13. Relative frequency of predicatives PRED.
14. Relative frequency of prepositions PREP.
15. Relative frequency of participles (short) PRTS.
16. Relative frequency of verbs (personal form) VERB.

For each feature, the mean, standard deviation and coefficient of variation were determined. The coefficient of variation (CV) is calculated as the ratio of the standard deviation of a random variable to the mean. It is used to compare the variability of the same attribute in several populations with different mean. If the value of the coefficient of variation does not exceed 0.33 (33%), then the population is considered homogeneous, and if it is more than 0.33 (33%), then it is heterogeneous.

The use of a large number of features in classification models with a small number of samples leads to overfitting, in connection with this, a reduction in dimension is carried out. At the first stage, the significance of the features is evaluated. To test the hypotheses about the difference between three independent samples in terms of the severity of the studied trait, the Kruskal-Wallis H Test was used. At the second stage, data sets were formed with features having differences at the significance levels of 0.05, 0.01, 0.001.

To solve the problem of classifying dialogues in accordance with the presence or absence of a diagnosis in children, classical machine learning methods were used. The basic method was Gradient Boosted Decision Trees, which showed good results in solving the problem of text classification of children with typical development and children with ASD [19]. Gradient Boosted Decision Trees is an ensemble of decision trees that are trained sequentially. In order to improve the quality of classification, other ensembles of models based on decision trees are used in the work: random forest classifier, AdaBoost classifier. To assess the generalizing ability of the considered classification algorithms, the LeaveOneOut cross-validation method was used. All considered methods were implemented using scikit-learn library in Python.

4   Results & Discussion

Descriptive statistics of linguistic features obtained from the results of graphematic analysis are presented in Table 2.

Linguistic features according to the results of graphematic analysis are generally not homogeneous, only the number of sentences in one replica turned out to be uniform for all groups of children.

Significant differences are observed for the signs "the number of sentences in 1 replica", "the number of tokens" - significantly more in TD children compared to the corresponding data for children with ASD and DS; "The number of tokens in the replica" and "the number of tokens in the sentence" are the smallest in children with DS, "the number of pauses" is characterized by great variety, is the smallest in children with DS.

The data obtained using automatic processing generally coincide with the data obtained on the material of the Russian language, where the linguistic analysis of the speech of children was carried out manually [16, 18]. Descriptive statistics of linguistic features obtained from the results of morphological analysis are presented in Table 3.

Among the features, according to the results of morphological analysis, only the relative frequencies of the main parts of speech in the dialogues of children with typical development turned out to be homogeneous: adjective, adverb, noun, particle, verb. Significant differences between the three classes (groups of children - TD, DS, ASD) at the level of 0.001 are observed for the signs: "relative frequency of adjectives (full)", "relative frequency of adverbs", "relative frequency of comparatives", "relative frequency of conjunctions", "relative frequency of verbs (infinitive)", " relative frequency

Table 2. Descriptive statistics of linguistic features.

Features	Descriptive statistics	TD	DS	ASD	The Kruskal-Wallis H Test value	Significance level
Number of replicas	Mean	41.70	83.79	72.86	0.93	>0.05
	CV	*0.29*	0.99	0.94		
Number of sentences	Mean	55.25	86.14	83.71	0.08	>0.05
	CV	0.35	1.00	0.96		
Number of sentences in 1 replica	Mean	1.33	1.03	1.12	23.72	<0.001
	CV	*0.19*	*0.03*	*0.14*		
Number of tokens	Mean	265.95	124.07	152.80	14.34	<0.001
	CV	0.51	1.20	1.11		
Number of tokens in 1 replica	Mean	6.91	1.33	1.81	44.61	<0.001
	CV	0.73	*0.18*	0.37		
Number of tokens in 1 sentence	Mean	4.91	1.29	2.01	45.84	<0.001
	CV	0.49	*0.17*	0.38		
Number of pauses	Mean	8.90	0.86	4.77	16.49	<0.001
	CV	1.01	2.32	1.84		
Number of unfinished words	Mean	1.00	0.57	0.40	7.86	<0.05
	CV	1.41	2.24	3.38		

of non-existent words", "relative frequency of pronouns-nouns", "relative frequency of prepositions" (Table 4).

All the considered methods define the dialogues of children with typical development with the same quality. However, the dialogues of children with atypical development, with the same classification accuracy for all classes equal to 0.81, were classified with different performance: GradientBoostingClassifier showed better metrics for dialogues of children with Down syndrome than RandomForestClassifier and AdaBoostClassifier, and AdaBoostClassifier better defined dialogues of children with ASD. Combining the three classifiers and using the majority rule (VotingClassifier) to predict class labels achieved an accuracy of 83%. As a result, 95% of dialogues of children with typical development were correctly classified (19 out of 20, one dialogue was mistakenly attributed to ASD), 57% of dialogues in children with Down syndrome (8 out of 14, 6 dialogues were erroneously attributed to ASD), 86% of dialogues of children with ASD (30 out of 35, two were mistakenly attributed to the dialogue of children with typical development and 3 to the dialogues of children with Down syndrome).

Table 3. Descriptive statistics of linguistic features.

Features	Descriptive statistics	TD	DS	ASD	The Kruskal-Wallis H Test value	Significance level
None	Mean	2.35	46.76	29.22	34.98	<0.001
	CV	0.82	0.52	0.79		
ADJF	Mean	9.69	2.11	4.57	26.51	<0.001
	CV	*0.31*	1.39	1.01		
ADJS	Mean	0.28	0.16	0.36	2.41	>0.05
	CV	1.50	2.58	2.55		
ADVB	Mean	8.52	2.66	3.40	25.78	<0.001
	CV	*0.32*	1.32	1.32		
COMP	Mean	0.75	0.03	0.01	50.85	<0.001
	CV	0.84	3.74	5.91		
CONJ	Mean	10.09	2.46	4.79	27.45	<0.001
	CV	0.34	1.15	0.81		
GRND	Mean	0.00	0.00	0.05	5.28	>0.05
	CV	0.00	0.00	3.08		
INFN	Mean	2.48	0.09	1.13	28.75	<0.001
	CV	0.78	2.35	2.14		
INTJ	Mean	2.20	17.11	6.19	13.54	<0.01
	CV	0.72	1.34	1.05		
NOUN	Mean	19.91	22.47	25.40	3.10	>0.05
	CV	*0.25*	0.57	0.53		
NPRO	Mean	7.20	1.59	2.96	25.57	<0.001
	CV	0.40	1.45	1.03		
NUMR	Mean	2.00	0.29	1.93	13.66	<0.01
	CV	0.74	2.35	1.69		
PRCL	Mean	15.36	8.49	10.55	9.76	<0.01
	CV	*0.26*	0.83	0.92		
PRED	Mean	1.26	2.45	1.24	1.80	>0.05
	CV	0.65	2.36	1.26		
PREP	Mean	8.30	2.46	5.12	19.40	<0.001
	CV	0.36	1.21	0.84		

(continued)

Table 3. (*continued*)

Features	Descriptive statistics	TD	DS	ASD	The Kruskal-Wallis H Test value	Significance level
PRTS	Mean	0.02	0.34	0.01	1.40	>0.05
	CV	3.08	3.74	5.91		
VERB	Mean	9.85	4.29	8.09	10.79	<0.01
	CV	*0.27*	1.10	1.02		

Table 4. Classification results.

Method	Class	Precision	Recall	F1- score	Accuracy
GradientBoostingClassifier	TD	0.90	0.95	0.93	0.81
	DS	0.64	0.64	0.64	
	ASD	0.82	0.80	0.81	
RandomForestClassifier	TD	0.90	0.95	0.93	0.81
	DS	0.70	0.50	0.58	
	ASD	0.79	0.86	0.82	
AdaBoostClassifier	TD	0.90	0.95	0.93	0.81
	DS	0.75	0.43	0.55	
	ASD	0.78	0.89	0.83	
VotingClassifier	TD	0.90	0.95	*0.93*	*0.83*
	DS	0.73	0.57	*0.64*	
	ASD	0.81	0.86	*0.83*	
Baseline	TD	0.71	0.86	0.78	0.76
	ASD	0.82	0.66	0.73	

Experimental results significantly exceed the baseline. At the same age of children, the severity of autistic disorders in children was different, which was reflected in their speech material. Children with ASD in the study [19] are highly functional autistic with well-formed speech, in our study - with moderate and severe autistic symptoms. The difference may be due to the simultaneous analysis of texts and acoustic characteristics of the speech of TD children and children with ASD in [19], and classifications of children's dialogues into three groups - TD, ASD, DS in our study.

5   Conclusion

The research presents the results of the analysis of linguistic features obtained from the dialogues of children of 3 groups: with typical development, Down syndrome and ASD.

In total, 25 features were considered, and for 12 of them there are differences for the groups at the significance levels of 0.001. The highlighted features make it possible to differentiate quite well the dialogues of children with typical and atypical development, which is confirmed by the fact that, with a relatively small number of features, all classifiers considered in the article showed high performance. Our best approach yielded a correct classification of 83% of the dialogues, with the best performance achieved for the dialogues of children with typical development. Confusion was observed in the automatic classification of dialogues between children with TD and ASD, children with ASD and DS. On average, the values of significant linguistic features of dialogues in children with ASD are between the values of features for the dialogues of TD and DS children.

Future: To reduce the amount of confusion between the dialogues of children with TD and ASD, dialogues of children with ASD and DS, we plan to consider additional linguistic features characterizing the peculiarities of the use of verbs (category of number, type, mood, tense, face), nouns (category of number, category of animation), pronouns (category of person). In addition, we plan to combine the two modalities (audio and text), which can also improve the quality of the classification models.

Acknowledgments. The study is financially supported by the Russian Science Foundation (project № 18-18-00063) and the Russian Foundation for Basic Research (project 19-57-45008–IND_a).

References

1. Dubovik, A.R.: Automatic determination of the stylistic affiliation of texts by their statistical parameters. Computational Linguistics and Computational Ontologies **1**, 29–45 (2017). (in Russian: Dubovik, A.R.: Avtomaticheskoye opredeleniye stilisticheskoy prinadlezhnosti tekstov po ikh statisticheskim parametram. Komp'yuternaya lingvistika i vychislitel'nyye ontologii 1, 29–45 (2017))
2. Sboev, A., Litvinova, T., Gudovskikh, D., Rybka, R., Moloshnikov, I.: Machine learning models of text categorization by author gender using topic-independent features. Procedia Comput. Sci. **101**, 135–142 (2016)
3. Cheng, J.K., Fernandez, A., Quindoza, R.G.M., Tan, S., Cheng, C.: A model for age and gender profiling of social media accounts based on post contents. In: Cheng, L., Leung, A., Ozawa, S. (eds.) ICONIP 2018. LNCS, vol. 11302, pp. 113–123. Springer, Cham (2018). https://doi.org/10.1007/978-3-030-04179-3_10
4. Rapin, I., Dunn, M.A., Allen, D.A., Stevens, M.C., Fein, D.: Subtypes of language disorders in school-age children with autism. Dev. Neuropsychol. **34**(1), 66–84 (2009)
5. Tek, S., Mesite, L., Fein, D., Naigles, L.: Longitudinal analyses of expressive language development reveal two distinct language profiles among young children with autism spectrum disorders. J. Autism Dev. Disord. **44**(1), 75–89 (2014)
6. Lyakso, E., Frolova, O.: Speech features of typically developing children and children with autism spectrum disorders. Abstract book. In: BIT 's 7th Annual Word Congress of Neurotalk – 2016. Innovation of Neuroscience. p. 35 (2016)
7. McGregor, K.K., et al.: Associations between syntax and the lexicon among children with or without ASD and language impairment. J. Autism Dev. Disord. **42**(1), 35–47 (2012)

8. Boorse, J., Cola, M., Plate, S., et al.: Linguistic markers of autism in girls: evidence of a "blended phenotype" during storytelling. Mol. Autism **10**, 14 (2019)

9. Boucher, J.: Research review: structural language in autistic spectrum disorder – characteristics and causes. J. Child Psychol. Psychiatry **53**(3), 219–233 (2012)

10. Mazzaggio, G., Shield, A.: The production of pronouns and verb inflections by Italian children with asd: a new dataset in a null subject language. J. Autism Dev. Disord. **50**(4), 1425–1433 (2020). https://doi.org/10.1007/s10803-019-04349-7

11. Terzi, A., Marinis, T., Zafeiri, A., Francis, K.: Subject and object pronouns in high-functioning children with ASD of a null-subject language. Front. Psychol. **10**(1301), 1–8 (2019)

12. Chapman, R., Hesketh, L.: Language, cognition, and short-term memory in individuals with Down syndrome. Down Syndrome Research and Practice **7**(1), 1–7 (2001)

13. Hesslinga, A., Brimo, D.M.: Spoken fictional narrative and literacy skills of children with Down syndrome. J. Commun. Disord. **79**, 76–89 (2019)

14. Penke, M.: Regular and irregular inflection in Down syndrome – new evidence from German. Cortex **116**, 192–208 (2019)

15. Penke, M.: Verbal agreement inflection in German children with Down syndrome. J. Speech Lang. Hear. Res. **61**(1), 2217–2234 (2018)

16. Gorodnyi, V.A., Lyakso, E.E.: Speech characteristic of children 6–7 years old with autism spectrum disorders and Down syndrome. Theor. Appl. Linguist. **4**(2), 22–37 (2018). (In Russian: Gorodnyi, V.A., Lyakso, E.E.: Kharakteristika rechi detey 6–7 let s rasstroystvami autisticheskogo spektra i sindromom Dauna. Teoreticheskaya i prikladnaya lingvistika **4**(2), 22–37 (2018))

17. Lyakso, E.E., Frolova, O.V.: Verbal behavior of mothers when interacting with children with Down syndrome. Theor. Appl. Linguist. **6**(1), 103–124 (2020). (in Russian: Lyakso, E.E., Frolova, O.V.: Rechevoye povedeniye materey pri vzaimodeystvii s det'mi s sindromom Dauna. Teoreticheskaya i prikladnaya lingvistika **6**(1), 103–124 (2020))

18. Nikolaev, A.S., Frolova, O.V., Gorodnyi, V.A., Lyakso, E.E.: Characteristics of the responses of children 5–11 years old with autism spectrum disorders in dialogues with adults. Questions of psycholinguistics **4**(42), 92–105 (2019). (in Russian: Nikolayev, A.S., Frolova, O.V., Gorodnyi, V.A., Lyakso, E.E.: Kharakteristika otvetnykh replik detey 5–11 let s rasstroystvami autisticheskogo spektra v dialogakh so vzroslymi. Voprosy psikholingvistiki **4**(42), 92–105 (2019))

19. Cho, S., Liberman, M., Ryant, N., Cola, M., Schultz, R., Parish-Morris, J.: Automatic detection of Autism Spectrum Disorder in children using acoustic and text features from brief natural conversations. In: Interspeech 2019: 20th Annual Conference of the International Speech Communication Association, pp. 2513–2517 (2019)

20. Kuzmenko, E.: Morphological analysis for russian: integration and comparison of taggers. In: Ignatov, D.I., et al. (eds.) AIST 2016. CCIS, vol. 661, pp. 162–171. Springer, Cham (2017). https://doi.org/10.1007/978-3-319-52920-2_16

21. Huang, R.: An Evaluation of POS Taggers for the CHILDES Corpus. CUNY Academic Works, New York (2016)

22. Nicholas, J.S., Charles, J.M., Carpenter, L.A., King, L.B., Jenner, W., Spratt, E.G.: Prevalence and characteristics of children with Autism-spectrum disorders. Ann. Epidemiol. **18**(2), 130–136 (2008)

Speaker Adaptation with Continuous Vocoder-Based DNN-TTS

Ali Raheem Mandeel[1(✉)], Mohammed Salah Al-Radhi[1],
and Tamás Gábor Csapó[1,2]

[1] Department of Telecommunication and Media Informatics, Budapest University
of Technology and Economics, Budapest, Hungary
aliraheem.mandeel@edu.bme.hu, {malradhi,csapot}@tmit.bme.hu
[2] MTA-ELTE Lendület Lingual Articulation Research Group, Budapest, Hungary

Abstract. Traditional vocoder-based statistical parametric speech synthesis can be advantageous in applications that require low computational complexity. Recent neural vocoders, which can produce high naturalness, still cannot fulfill the requirement of being real-time during synthesis. In this paper, we experiment with our earlier continuous vocoder, in which the excitation is modeled with two one-dimensional parameters: continuous F0 and Maximum Voiced Frequency. We show on the data of 9 speakers that an average voice can be trained for DNN-TTS, and speaker adaptation is feasible 400 utterances (about 14 min). Objective experiments support that the quality of speaker adaptation with Continuous Vocoder-based DNN-TTS is similar to the quality of the speaker adaptation with a WORLD Vocoder-based baseline.

Keywords: Speech synthesis · DNN · TTS · Continuous vocoder

1 Introduction

Speech processing has brought the attention of researchers and industry as well during the last decades. The rapid advancement in digital technology has led to a wider variety of speech processing functions (such as speech recognition, speech synthesis, dialogue control, and so on) is becoming a central mechanism for creating a human-computer communication interaction. Speech could be used in a variety of industries, including machine control using natural speech rather than written commands, surveillance, healthcare, and the Internet of Things. The technique of converting text into artificial speech is known as speech synthesis which is opposite to Automatic speech recognition (ASR) [11]. Nowadays, all efforts are devoted to producing a sound similar to the natural sound.

Text-to-speech (TTS) synthesis in the state-of-the-art is based on computational parametric methods. Its benefit is the availability of speaker adaptation techniques, which allow for the creation of a unique voice based on any target speaker. The speech signal is broken down into parameters expressing excitation fundamental frequency (F0) and speech spectrum in the parametric model, which are then loaded into a machine learning system. In the synthesis, the parameter

© Springer Nature Switzerland AG 2021
A. Karpov and R. Potapova (Eds.): SPECOM 2021, LNAI 12997, pp. 407–416, 2021.
https://doi.org/10.1007/978-3-030-87802-3_37

chains are reconverted to voice signal using rebuild approaches (excitation models, vocoders) after the mathematical model has been learned on the training data. When it comes to speech synthesis solutions, if the system is configured for real-time low latency use, it is possible to produce audible speech output with a live person. An example is the use at government websites (e.g. the Hungarian Chatbot using TTS techniques at https://ugyfelkapu.gov.hu/), which should be prepared for extremely high loads, and therefore, real-time synthesis of speech is extremely important. Figure 1 shows the statistical parametric speech synthesis system's basic components.

While TTS systems are now intelligible, existing parametric techniques do not allow for absolute naturalness in real-time systems, and there is still potential for advancement in terms of being as similar to human speech as possible. While there are vocoding approaches that produce natural-sounding synthesized speech (e.g. STRAIGHT and WORLD), they are usually computationally costly and hence unsuitable for real-time execution. With minimal training and adaptation data, a speech synthesis system should have the ability to produce the voice of any speaker. A substantial advantage of SPSS (statistical parametric speech synthesis) above unit-selection speech synthesis is its versatility in altering speaker traits, emotions, and speaking styles, which is due to the potential performance of speaker adaptation [22]. Additionally, the efficiency of DNN-based adaptation is superior to HMM-based adaptation [18]. Meanwhile, Deep neural networks (DNN) have significantly improved SPSS according to [16,19], and [12].

The capability to generate new voices utilizing just a limited quantity of adaptation data from an objective speaker can be achieved using adaptation techniques [15]. Because of its function in linking linguistic and acoustic features, the acoustic model's constraint reduces the level of speech naturalness. The continuous vocoder outperforms other traditional vocoders with discontinuous F0 because the vocoder parameters are simple [5]. Our novel contribution in this work to use the continuous vocoder with speaker adaptation in Merlin (a speech synthesis toolkit that uses neural networks to create speech) [20]. We show on the data of 9 speakers that an average voice can be trained, and speaker adaptation is feasible with limited data of 400 utterances (about 14 min). Objective experiments support that the quality is similar to the WORLD-based baseline.

This paper is organized in the following sections: An overview of the related scientific papers, including the novel methods in speech adaptation based text-to-speech synthesis. In the second section, the methodology was described and the design, tools, and dataset were clarified. After that, in section three, the results were explained. Finally, the conclusion was mentioned in section four.

2   Related Work

Until 2013, voice synthesis was dominated by unit-selection synthesis and Hidden Markov model (HMM)-based voice synthesis. There are many fusion approaches between unit selection and statistical parametric synthesis. A review presents the main technique of statistical parametric speech synthesis [8]. According to

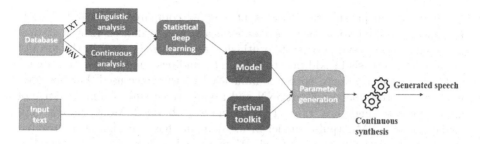

Fig. 1. Schematic diagram of statistical parametric speech synthesis.

the authors, the combination of the two approaches will carry the advantages of both and eliminate some drawbacks. The adaptability and controllability of statistical parametric speech synthesis (SPSS) over unit-selection speech synthesis is a significant benefit. Speech synthesis employing a hidden Markov model (HMM) has many benefits, including the ability to alter the speaker's identity, emotion, and speech style [17]. This technique, however, is a long way from natural speech. [21] used a mixture density output layer to solve the inability of DNNs to estimate variances in SPSS (MDNs). It will calculate maximum probability density functions above actual-valued production features based on the equivalent input characteristics. The findings indicate that better predicting acoustic features improved the naturalism of synthesized voice.

[7] used a fusion method to modeling the speech signal to obtain more normal synthesized speech than the purely statistical version. Via spectrogram kernel filtering, the speech was decomposed into a harmonic and a noise burst component. A vocoder and statistical parameter generation are used to model the harmonic component, while concatenation is used to model the burst part. The final synthesized waveform is created by combining the dual channels.

A new method for using sinusoidal vocoders in DNN-based statistical parametric speech synthesis (SPSS) was introduced by [14]. At the statistical modeling and synthesis stages, the system uses sinusoids as a simple parameterization (DIR) or an intermediate spectral parameterization (INT). Both approaches lead to improving modeling accuracy, according to the findings. Other objective functions can be chosen and tailored for the fusion process to increase the perceptual outcome in the potential work of this research.

A comprehensive and experimental study of speaker adaptation with deep neural network (DNN) based speech synthesis was conducted by [18]. Adapting to a neural network can be done in three ways. The first method involves performing feature space transformations, the second entails augmenting speaker-particular features as feedback to neural networks, and the third method includes model adaptation. The future work of this study to consternate on more precise modeling of the source-filter interaction using the DNN-based approach, as this model has been shown to be insufficient for significantly improving segmental speech efficiency.

In statistical parametric speech synthesis, [2] compared STRAIGHT, glottal, and sinusoidal vocoding. Vocoder accuracy was evaluated in a statistical parametric speech synthesis system utilizing four distinct voices in the form of assessment-synthesis in addition to TTS. The findings suggest that the superiority of vocoder-produced speech is influenced by the voice used. Furthermore, using the glottal vocoder GlottDNN and a male voice with a limited range of expression, the single best-rated TTS system was obtained. Moreover, the sinusoidal vocoder PML (pulse model in log-domain) has the highest aggregated result in all of the tests conducted. [1] presented a new vocoder synthesizer (Vocaine) with an Amplitude Modulated-Frequency Modulated speech model. Vocaine Outperform STRAIGHT unit-selection speech synthesis in computation and match them in performance. Maximum Voiced Frequency is employed for combing voiced and unvoiced excitation by a residual-based vocoder to remove artifacts created by creaky speech in the SPSS [9]. The vocoder's parameters are all continuous, so Multi-Space Distribution isn't needed when training the HMMs.

[13] used the same speech data and controlled laboratory conditions to compare various vocoders in a large-scale listening exercise. The responses were then studied and visualized using K-means clustering and multidimensional scaling, as well as the interaction between the various vocoders. The Vocoders are used to convert acoustic parameters into human voices and vice versa. In text-to-speech synthesis, the vocoders are the most critical part. A Vocoder acts as both an analyzer and a synthesizer. It analyzes speech by transforming the waveform into a series of parameters that reflect the vocal-folds excitation signal and filtering the excitation signal with a vocal-tract filter transfer tool. Otherwise, it reconstructs the initial speech signal from the used parameters. There are several types of vocoders such as STRAIGHT, WORLD, Mel - generalised cepstral vocoder, adaptive harmonic model, Glottal vocoder, and Harmonic model, etc. [13]. The continuous vocoder, despite being an alternative solution, hasn't been tested in speaker adaptation yet.

3   Methodology

3.1   Speech Corpora

The studies were carried out using the VCTK-Corpus [6]. This CSTR VCTK Corpus contains speech data from 109 (with 47 of them being male) English speakers who speak with a variety of accents. Approximately 400 sentences are read by each speaker. Over 9 speakers, we ran the average speech model (AVM) (six females and three males). The waveforms in this database are re-sampled to 16 kHz.

3.2   Continuous Vocoder

In the Continuous vocoder [10], the fundamental frequency (F0) is determined on the input waveforms during the analysis stage. Following this, the MVF parameter is determined from the speech signal. The speech signal is then subjected to gamma = −1/3 with 24-order Mel-Generalized Cepstral analysis (MGC) and alpha = 0.42 as the next move. The frameshift is 5 ms in both measures. Furthermore, in the voiced portions of the opposite filtered residual signal, the Glottal Closure Instant (GCI) algorithm is utilized to discover the glottal period limitations of particular periods. A PCA residual is constructed from these F0 cycles, which will be used in the synthesis process. White noise is used during the synthesis process because the frequencies are greater than the MVF value. To eliminate any residual buzziness and reduce the noise portion, applying a time-domain envelope to the unvoiced segments is proposed as a method of modeling unvoiced sounds [3] and [4]. The vocoders use different parameters as can see in the Table 1.

Table 1. The vocoders types and their parameters.

Vocoder name	Parameters per frame
Continuous	F0: F0: 1 + MVF: 1 + MGC: 24
STRAIGHT	F0: 1 + Aperiodicity: 1024 + Spectrum: 1024
WORLD	F0: 1 + Band aperiodicity: 5 + MGC: 60
Mel - generalised cepstral vocoder	MGC: 24 + F0: 1, Pulse plus noise excitation
Glottal vocoder	F0:1, Energy:1, HNR: 5, Source LSF: 10, Vocal tract LSF: 30, natural pulse
Harmonic model	2 * k harmonics + F0:1, Harmonic excitation
Adaptive harmonic model	2 * k + F0:1, Harmonic excitation

3.3   Build an Average Voice Model (AVM)

Over the range of 9 speakers, we created the average voice model (AVM) (six females and three males). We set up the data and directories, prepared the labels, prepared acoustic features (MGC, MVF, and lf0) using the continuous vocoder. Then we trained duration and acoustic models. Finally, we synthesized speech. We used a Feedforward neural network of 6 hidden layers with tangent hyperbilic units (1024 neurons, 265 batch size, sgd optimizer, and 25 epochs). This neural network is the most basic kind of networks. This architecture is known as a Deep Neural Network (DNN) when there are enough layers. Several layers of hidden units, each performing a nonlinear operation, are used to estimate the output from the signal. It uses linguistic features as input data to estimate vocoder parameters.

3.4   Adapt the AVM for the Adapt Speaker

We did the adaptation with multiple speakers (2 females, and 2 males). We adapted the four speakers (p234, p236, p237, and p247) using a Feedforward neural network with the continuous vocoder. MGC, MVf, and F0 are the parameters used in this vocoder. The adaptation data for each speaker is 400 utterances (about 14 min).

4   Results

Objective and subjective analyses were performed in order to meet our purposes and to validate the feasibility of the proposed process. We independently checked our continuous vocoder parameters with speaker adaptation in deep neural networks using MCD, and F0-CORR, and spectrogram analysis in the objective evaluation. Moreover, a subjective listening experiment was used to test them.

4.1   Objective Evaluation

1. MCD (dB): Distortion of Mel Cepstral measurement 60-dimensional coefficients for each training model were measured. The efficiency of the continuous vocoder systems against the WORLD baseline scheme could be concluded based on these findings.

$$MCD = \frac{1}{N} \sum_{j=1}^{N} \sqrt{\sum_{i=1}^{K} (x_{i,j} - y_{i,j})^2} \qquad (1)$$

x and y are the actual and synthesized voice signals of ith cepstral coefficients. The MCD errors on the validation (dev) and test sets results are described in the Table 2. It seems that the WORLD vocoder has a bit better (i.e., lower MCD) than continuous vocoder.

Table 2. MCD errors on the dev/test sets.

Spkr	WORLD vocoder	Continuous vocoder
P234	5.309/5.251	5.440/5.434
P236	5.540/5.400	5.795/5.547
P237	5.152/5.072	5.370/5.240
P247	5.347/5.335	5.502/5.483

2. F0-CORR: the correlation is a reflection of how closely reference and produced data are related (linearly related). Overall, Frame by frame, a measurement is made. F0-CORR shows good results for continuous vocoder as the values reaching 1 and higher than the baseline vocoder (Table 3).

$$F0 - CORR = \frac{\sum_{i=1}^{n} (x_i - \overline{x})(y_i - \overline{y})}{\sqrt{\sum_{i=1}^{n} (x_i - \overline{x})^2} \sqrt{\sum_{i=1}^{n} (y_i - \overline{y})^2}} \qquad (2)$$

Table 3. F0-CORR on the dev/test sets.

Spkr	WORLD vocoder	Continuous vocoder
P234	0.456/0.511	0.730/0.755
P236	0.607/0.596	0.480/0.588
P237	0.582/0.553	0.760/0.721
P247	0.608/0.655	0.766/0.682

3. Spectrogram Analysis: the visual representation of synthesized sounds by both vocoders has been shown in Fig. 2. We show four spectrogram plots of two speakers (a female and a male) with two vocoders (continuous and WORLD) who read the sentence "I had faith in them.". As can be seen in the spectrograms, the continuous vocoder separates the voiced and unvoiced frequencies of speech, according to the MVF parameter (i.e., the spectral content below MVF is voiced, and above MVF is unvoiced). The WORLD vocoder handles the voicing via band aperiodicities, therefore, such a strong separating curve is not visible in the spectrogram.

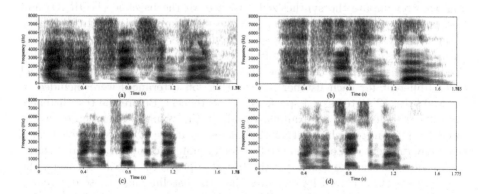

Fig. 2. The spectrogram plot of four synthesised sounds (a) a female voice using continuous vocoder (b) a male voice using continuous vocoder (c) a female voice using WORLD vocoder (d) a male voice using WORLD vocoder.

4.2 Subjective Listening Test

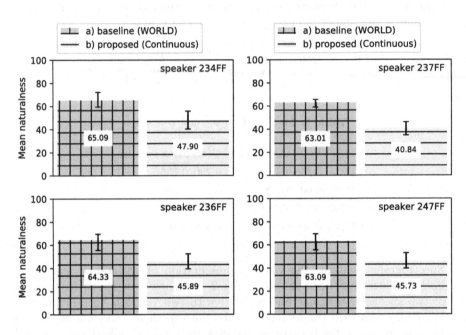

Fig. 3. MOS scores for the naturalness question. Higher value means better overall quality. Errorbars show the bootstrapped 95% confidence intervals.

In order to compare TTS versions, we conducted an online MOS-like test. Our aim was to compare the synthesized sentences of the baseline (WORLD) and the proposed (Continuous) vocoders. In the test, the listeners had to rate the naturalness of each stimulus on a scale, from 0 (very unnatural) to 100 (very natural). We chose seven sentences from the CMU-ARCTIC corpus and synthesized them with the four target speakers. The samples appeared in randomized order (different for each listener). Altogether, 56 utterances were included in the MOS test (2 systems × 4 speakers × 7 sentences). Before the test, listeners were asked to listen to an example to adjust the volume. Each sentence was rated by 11 non-English speakers (2 females, 9 males; 23–39 years old), in a silent environment. On average, the test took 8 min to complete. Figure 3 shows the average naturalness scores for the tested approaches. For all speakers, the proposed system achieved lower scores than the baseline; and these differences are statistically significant (Mann-Whitney-Wilcoxon ranksum test, with a 95% confidence level). Although the naturalness scores of the Continuous vocoder did not reach that of the WORLD vocoder, but we can conclude that the speaker adaptation experiment with the proposed vocoder was successful.

5   Conclusion

Recent neural vocoders, while capable of high naturalness, also fall short of the criteria for real-time synthesis. In applications requiring low computational complexity, traditional vocoder-based statistical parametric speech synthesis can be beneficial (e.g. a chatbot in a high-load environment like a government website). We use our earlier continuous vocoder in this article, in which the excitation is modeled with two one-dimensional parameters: continuous F0 and Maximum Voiced Frequency. We demonstrate that an average voice can be trained using data from nine speakers, and that speaker adaptation using just 400 utterances is possible (about 14 min).

Acknowledgments. The research was partly supported by the European Union's Horizon 2020 research and innovation programme under grant agreement No. 825619 (AI4EU), and by the National Research Development and Innovation Office of Hungary (FK 124584 and PD 127915). The Titan X GPU used was donated by NVIDIA Corporation. We would like to thank the subjects for participating in the listening test.

References

1. Agiomyrgiannakis, Y.: Vocaine the vocoder and applications in speech synthesis. In: ICASSP, pp. 4230–4234. IEEE (2015)
2. Airaksinen, M., Juvela, L., Bollepalli, B., Yamagishi, J., Alku, P.: A comparison between straight, glottal, and sinusoidal vocoding in statistical parametric speech synthesis. IEEE/ACM Trans. Audio Speech Lang. Process. **26**(9), 1658–1670 (2018)
3. Al-Radhi, M.S., Abdo, O., Csapó, T.G., Abdou, S., Németh, G., Fashal, M.: A continuous vocoder for statistical parametric speech synthesis and its evaluation using an audio-visual phonetically annotated Arabic corpus. Comput. Speech Lang. **60**, 101025 (2020)
4. Al-Radhi, M.S., Csapó, T.G., Németh, G.: Time-domain envelope modulating the noise component of excitation in a continuous residual-based vocoder for statistical parametric speech synthesis. In: INTERSPEECH, pp. 434–438 (2017)
5. Al-Radhi, M.S., Csapó, T.G., Németh, G.: A continuous vocoder using sinusoidal model for statistical parametric speech synthesis. In: Karpov, A., Jokisch, O., Potapova, R. (eds.) SPECOM 2018. LNCS (LNAI), vol. 11096, pp. 11–20. Springer, Cham (2018). https://doi.org/10.1007/978-3-319-99579-3_2
6. Bakhturina, E., Lavrukhin, V., Ginsburg, B., Zhang, Y.: Hi-Fi multi-speaker English TTS dataset. arXiv preprint arXiv:2104.01497 (2021)
7. Beskow, J., Berthelsen, H.: A hybrid harmonics-and-bursts modelling approach to speech synthesis. In: SSW, pp. 208–213 (2016)
8. Black, A.W., Zen, H., Tokuda, K.: Statistical parametric speech synthesis. In: ICASSP, vol. 4, pp. IV-1229. IEEE (2007)
9. Csapó, T.G., Németh, G., Cernak, M.: Residual-based excitation with continuous F0 modeling in HMM-based speech synthesis. In: Dediu, A.-H., Martín-Vide, C., Vicsi, K. (eds.) SLSP 2015. LNCS (LNAI), vol. 9449, pp. 27–38. Springer, Cham (2015). https://doi.org/10.1007/978-3-319-25789-1_4

10. Csapó, T.G., Németh, G., Cernak, M., Garner, P.N.: Modeling unvoiced sounds in statistical parametric speech synthesis with a continuous vocoder. In: EUSIPCO, pp. 1338–1342. IEEE (2016)

11. Habeeb, I.Q., Fadhil, T.Z., Jurn, Y.N., Habeeb, Z.Q., Abdulkhudhur, H.N.: An ensemble technique for speech recognition in noisy environments. Indones. J. Electr. Eng. Comput. Sci. **18**(2), 835–842 (2020)

12. Hashimoto, K., Oura, K., Nankaku, Y., Tokuda, K.: The effect of neural networks in statistical parametric speech synthesis. In: ICASSP, pp. 4455–4459. IEEE (2015)

13. Hu, Q., Richmond, K., Yamagishi, J., Latorre, J.: An experimental comparison of multiple vocoder types. In: SSW8, pp. 135–140 (2013)

14. Hu, Q., Wu, Z., Richmond, K., Yamagishi, J., Stylianou, Y., Maia, R.: Fusion of multiple parameterisations for DNN-based sinusoidal speech synthesis with multi-task learning. In: INTERSPEECH, pp. 854–858 (2015)

15. Lanchantin, P., Gales, M.J., King, S., Yamagishi, J.: Multiple-average-voice-based speech synthesis. In: ICASSP, pp. 285–289. IEEE (2014)

16. Ling, Z.H., Deng, L., Yu, D.: Modeling spectral envelopes using restricted Boltzmann machines and deep belief networks for statistical parametric speech synthesis. IEEE Trans. Audio Speech Lang. Process. **21**(10), 2129–2139 (2013)

17. Tokuda, K., Nankaku, Y., Toda, T., Zen, H., Yamagishi, J., Oura, K.: Speech synthesis based on hidden Markov models. Proc. IEEE **101**(5), 1234–1252 (2013)

18. Wu, Z., Swietojanski, P., Veaux, C., Renals, S., King, S.: A study of speaker adaptation for DNN-based speech synthesis. In: Interspeech, pp. 879–883 (2015)

19. Wu, Z., Valentini-Botinhao, C., Watts, O., King, S.: Deep neural networks employing multi-task learning and stacked bottleneck features for speech synthesis. In: ICASSP, pp. 4460–4464. IEEE (2015)

20. Wu, Z., Watts, O., King, S.: Merlin: an open source neural network speech synthesis system. In: SSW, pp. 202–207 (2016)

21. Zen, H., Senior, A.: Deep mixture density networks for acoustic modeling in statistical parametric speech synthesis. In: ICASSP, pp. 3844–3848. IEEE (2014)

22. Zen, H., Tokuda, K., Black, A.W.: Statistical parametric speech synthesis. Speech Commun. **51**(11), 1039–1064 (2009)

Automatic Recognition of the Psychoneurological State of Children: Autism Spectrum Disorders, Down Syndrome, Typical Development

Yuri Matveev[1]([⊠]) [ID], Anton Matveev[1] [ID], Olga Frolova[2] [ID], and Elena Lyakso[2] [ID]

[1] ITMO University, St. Petersburg, Russia
[2] Saint Petersburg State University, St. Petersburg, Russia

Abstract. In this paper, we explore the problem of automatic recognition of psychoneurological states: Autism Spectrum Disorders, Down Syndrome, Typical Development of 7–10 years old children from their speech in the Russian language. We described the results of fully automatic recognition based on our proprietary speech dataset. Along with SVM, we used the ComParE features from Computational Paralinguistic Challenges. The results on our dataset showed high performance of automated recognition of psychoneurological states of 7–10 years old children from their speech. The results are theoretically and practically valuable, they will expand the knowledge about human voice uniqueness, possibilities of diagnostics of human psychoneurological states by voice and speech features, and creation of alternative communicative systems.

Keywords: Automatic recognition · Psychoneurological state · Down syndrome · Autism spectrum disorders

1 Introduction

Speech disorders are accompanied by many diseases and atypical development of children. Autism is a developmental disorder and is defined as a triad of impairments: atypical development of reciprocal social interaction, atypical communication and speech, and restricted, stereotyped, and repetitive behaviors [1]. Autism spectrum disorders (ASD) is characterized by impairments in language and social-emotional cognition. A wide range of speech disorders is described for children with ASD: from the rough delay of formation to the outstripping development rate [2]. The severity of autistic disorders affects the level of speech development in children with ASD [3].

Children with Down syndrome (DS) have specifics in the vocal tract structure - a smaller volume of the oral and nasal cavities, lowering of the lower jaw, a narrow palate, and shorter length of the vocal tract vs typically development (TD) children. The specificity of children and adults with DS is a large folded tongue and muscular hypotonia [4]. These anatomical peculiarities cause less speech intelligibility and articulation clarity [5], the less difference between values of formant frequencies of the cardinal vowels /i/

© Springer Nature Switzerland AG 2021
A. Karpov and R. Potapova (Eds.): SPECOM 2021, LNAI 12997, pp. 417–425, 2021.
https://doi.org/10.1007/978-3-030-87802-3_38

and /u/ [6] than in TD peers. People with DS have traditionally been characterized as friendly and very sociable, charming personalities with positive mood [7, 8]; children with ASD have communication problems. ASD and DS were selected as developmental disorders, accompanied by speech impairment.

Recognition of psychoneurological states by voice and speech features is a necessary component of the diagnosis of developmental disorders and can be used as an additional method. At present, systematized data on the reflection of the psychoneurological states (identified based on an objective evaluation) in the features of voice and speech of an informant considering their basic diagnosis are absent in the Russian language. The data of perceptual studies in which different groups of listeners correctly classified a child by the category of "developmental disorders or typical development" when listening to the child's speech samples [9–11] are known.

Automatic speech recognition of children's speech has its difficulties associated with large acoustic variability of speech, including incorrect pronunciation due to ongoing biological changes in growth, the development of vocabulary and language skills [12].

In the last 10–15 years, affective computing has been the subject of intense research. Series of ComParE challenges have shown the main approaches to affective computing (including recognition of ASD) [13]. In overviews [14, 15] on techniques to recognize ASD and DS based on voice and speech is found that most used in automatic recognition are GeMAPS/eGeMAPS features and SVM classifiers.

The goal of our study is automatic classification of psychoneurological states of Russian primary school children: Autism Spectrum Disorder, Down Syndrome, and Typical Development as control.

The rest of the article is structured as follows: Sect. 2 introduces a description of the dataset of speech recordings of Russian speaking 7–10 years old children. Section 3 gives description of the proposed schema for automated recognition. Section 4 describes results of experiments on the recognition of the psychoneurological states. Section 5 provides conclusions.

2   Dataset

There are few databases that contain speech of children with atypical development. We know, for example, speech databases of children with Specific Language Impairment (SLI) [16], 5–12-year-old Chinese children with cleft palate [17], and two databases created in 2016 on Czech language material and containing the speech of typically developing children (TD) and children with SLI [18].

We use the database "AD_Child.Ru" (Atypical Development Child.Ru) [19], which contains the speech of 392 children aged 4–16 years with atypical development and TD children (control), totally 1.5 Tb:

- 265 children with atypical development: with autism spectrum disorders (ASD), Down syndrome (DS), mixed specific developmental disorders (MSDD), intellectual disabilities – mental retardation (ID), cerebral palsy (CP), mild neurological disorders;
- 127 typically developing (TD) children (control).

The children were diagnosed by a medical doctor.

The speech material is represented by recordings in model situations (dialog with parents, dialog with an experimenter, retelling a fairy tale or a cartoon, story based on a picture), emotional speech in the Russian language. The recording for every child with ASD and DS was made from three to ten times, due to the difficulty of interacting with children and obtaining speech material.

The recordings of informants' speech material were made in kindergarten, at school, in the laboratory, and Child center. The recording was carried out in the rooms without special soundproofing. The records were made by the digital recorder "Marantz PMD660" with external highly directional microphone "SENNHEIZER e835S" and video camera "SONY HDR-CX560E". The distance from the child's face to the microphone did not exceed 50 cm (30–50 cm).

Speech files were stored in Windows PCM format WAV, 44.100 Hz, 16 bits per sample; video files were in AVI format. The speech material is accompanied by information about the child's psychophysiological and psychoneurological state, includes the results of tests and questionnaires [20] and also recording of child's behavior in parallel.

For this research, from the "AD-Child.Ru" database we selected audio files for 78 male children 7 to 10 years old with ASD, DS, and typical development (TD).

There are several studies suggesting a prevalence of males in the referred populations of DS [21] and ASD [22]. Among children who meet the ASD criteria, the true male to female ratio is closer to 3:1 [22]; sex ratio of children with DS 1,3:1 [21]. A prevalence of boys was observed in all forms of trisomy 21, except from the mosaic variant [23]. Thus, the speech material of boys was chosen for standardization.

The age range corresponds to early school age and does not cover the pubertal period, during which hormonal changes have a significant effect on the structure of the vocal folds and, accordingly, the characteristics of the voice [24]. The lower age (7 years) coincides with the beginning of the systematic education of children at school that requires them to concentrate their attention and, if possible, to produce a verbal response; that allows to record the speech material of children.

Traditionally, speech of highly functional autists is used for analysis (e.g. [14]). In our study speech material of children with moderate and severe ASD (CARS score 38–50 [25]) was taken for analysis. Diagnosis of ASD is difficult due to a variety of symptoms. Two groups of children with atypical development – DS, and moderate and severe ASD - were selected for the study, since there are similarities between these diagnoses in terms of speech level and intellectual impairments.

Distribution of children by psychoneurological states and age in the dataset is given in Table 1. As we can see from Table 1, the distribution of children by age is approximately balanced, but distribution of children by psychoneurological states is imbalanced due to the DS state.

After filtering for noise, we have a total of 3095 recordings available for analysis. As we can see from Table 2, the distribution of recordings by psychoneurological states is also imbalanced.

Table 1. Distribution of children 7–10 years old by psychoneurological states in the dataset: number of children (males).

Age, years	ASD	DS	TD	Total
7	10	3	10	23
8	9	6	5	20
9	7	2	7	16
10	6	3	10	19
Totally	32	14	32	78

Table 2. Distribution of recordings by psychoneurological states.

State	Number of recordings
ASD	1750
DS	834
TD	511
Totally	3095

3   Description of the Schema for Automated Recognition

Traditional approaches use handcrafted features derived based on expert experience. Research in recent decades has led to the emergence of a large number of different acoustic parameters extracted from speech signals for recognition of a speaker identity and its paralinguistic characteristics.

The most popular is the ComParE feature set [13, 26], which consists of 6,373 features from the openSMILE library (https://github.com/audeering/opensmile-python). The success of ComParE features can be attributed to several factors: they are easy to calculate, widely known in the community, and well designed for specific applications of voice-based affect recognition.

In [26] it was suggested to use the Geneva Minimalistic Acoustic Parameter Set (GeMAPS) for various areas of automatic voice analysis such as paralinguistic voice analysis. These features were selected due to their ability to reflect affective physiological changes in the process of speech production. In our experiments we have investigated the automatic recognition of psychoneurological states based on eGeMAPS features sets, which is the extension of GeMAPS [27]. We used version 2 of the extended Geneva Minimalistic Acoustic Parameter Set (eGeMAPS) with 88 parameters.

As it noted in [26], most of the participants in the Autism Sub-Challenge applied different algorithms on the ComParE acoustic feature set, and as a classifier applied SVM. Authors of [14, 15] also noted that in automatic disorder recognition (ASD, DS) combination of GeMAPS/eGeMAPS - SVM is the most popular.

All our experiments are done using scikit-learn machine learning library for the Python programming language.

The openSmile library v. 2.0 was used to extract acoustic features from each recording.

As a classifier we used SVM with a linear kernel from scikit-learn machine learning library: C-Support Vector Classification (https://scikit-learn.org/stable/modules/genera ted/sklearn.svm.SVC.html). For all other parameters we used the default values.

As a tool for classification model evaluation we used a multi-class confusion matrix library PyCM written in Python [28]. Different evaluation metrics have been used in different competitions depending on the type of task. In our experiments, we used Accuracy, Precision, Recall, F1-score and their average values for multiclass classifiers.

Our datasets for training and testing models of psychoneurological states are relatively small in size. To overcome this problem, especially when it is difficult or impossible to augment a dataset, the cross-validation method is used, which provides protection against hypotheses "imposed by data", the so-called "Type III error". In our experiments, we use Stratified K-Folds cross-validator (https://scikit-learn.org/stable/modules/genera ted/sklearn.model_selection.StratifiedKFold.html) with the value of K = 6. This validator provides a better balance of classes, which is especially important for us since we have a small number of speakers.

4   Experimental Results

This section describes the experimental details and results.

During the experiments, we obtained the following results for recognition of psychoneurological states using GeMAPS-SVM Schema, see Table 3 and Table 4.

Due to the imbalance of the classes, we use a raw normalized confusion matrix.

Table 3. Row normalized confusion matrix for psychoneurological states' predictions (%).

True state	Predicted state		
	ASD	DS	TD
ASD	74.78	13.35	11.87
DS	33.53	62.28	4.19
TD	31.30	3.48	65.22

Table 4. Accuracy of psychoneurological states' predictions.

State	Accuracy	Precision	Recall	F1
ASD	0.70	0.54	0.75	0.62
DS	0.82	0.79	0.62	0.70
TD	0.83	0.80	0.65	0.72
Average	0.78	0.71	0.67	0.68

Our results for Russian-speaking children 7–10 years old correlate with the known results.

It is found in [14] that human raters have accuracy of 67%, and machine-learning methods have accuracy ranging from 70% to 96% for separating individuals with ASD (children and adults). In [26] it was reported that along with SVM, the ComParE features yielded competitive performance in the participants' field of the Autism Sub-Challenge with the best UAR at 69.4%. Our results with the accuracy at 70% and recall at 75% for Russian-speaking children 7–10 years old are comparable to the state-of-the-art results.

Authors of [15] reported results of automatic identification of people with DS (GeMAPS-SVM schema) with a very high accuracy, above 95%. But this was achieved for adults; and in [15] it was pointed out that there is a significant difference in speech features between adults and children with DS. Our results for Russian-speaking 7–10 years old children with accuracy from 82,00% to 85,57% are consistent with data of the perceptual study for Russian-speaking 11–12 years old children [10].

The results showed that the ASD is often classified as TD and DS, while DS as ASD only, which is consistent with the results of perceptual experiments [9, 10].

TD children are classified worse than ASD and less than in the study on the material of the French language [26] that may be explained by different conditions of recording. The conversation between the child and experimenter was conducted in a free form. The child did not articulate sounds clearly, as when answering in the lesson, but demonstrated true spontaneous speech. Spontaneous Russian speech is characterized by flaccid articulation in comparison with the tense articulation of the French language [29].

The novelty of the results of our study is caused by the use of the spontaneous speech material of children with atypical development low level of speech formation. The results showed high performance of automated recognition of psychoneurological states of children aged 7 to 10 years. The work was performed on the material of the Russian language, which is characterized by the specific features of articulation patterns and intonation [30]. This finding allows to use these methods in the future for the purpose of additional rapid diagnosis of the characteristics of developmental disorders in children and to use it to create systems of alternative communication for children with a low level of speech formation.

5   Conclusion

This paper reports the results of automatic recognition of ASD, DS and TD psychoneurological states of Russian-speaking 7–10 years old children.

Experiments demonstrated promising results with relatively high accuracies on discriminating between psychoneurological states of children from their speech based on ComParE features from the openSMILE library v. 2.0. The used classifiers (SVM) performed above chance and has accuracy higher than human raters and comparable to the state-of-the-art results.

It is obvious that the main limitation of our approach is the lack of data.

First of all, we plan to continue collecting data to be able to use more sophisticated machine learning methods to improve the performance of children's state recognition by their speech.

Second, we plan to use deep neural networks (DNN). In the last decade, DNNs have been increasingly used for pattern recognition tasks, including recognition of emotional states from speech signals. Recent results show that in direct comparisons, handcrafted features usually lose to DNN-extracted features.

However, the main obstacle is that the size of existing emotional speech datasets is not yet large enough to extract deep features that reflect true emotional states. Another obstacle is that many databases are provided with annotations from multiple annotators, and these annotations often differ and are not true. In addition, these datasets are often imbalanced.

As the size of the training datasets increases, there will be a chance to create more effective deep models that specialize in recognition of emotional states. For example, pre-trained deep models may become readily available in the form of feature extractors similar to handcrafted features. Unfortunately, techniques such as knowledge transfer or data augmentation have ultimately failed yet to fully compensate for the lack of data in recognition of emotional states.

We have already started to explore the problem of data augmentation [31] using generative adversarial networks (GAN). Our experiments have shown improvements in the naturalness of synthesized speech. But for such a special kind of speech as the speech of children with different types of development, we need to explore peculiarities of this speech that have to be considered in synthesis.

Due to a very small size of the corpus evaluable for experiments it was not possible to investigate the use of DNN for the current task.

We described the results of fully automatic recognition based on our proprietary speech dataset for Russian-speaking 7–10 years old children. The results showed high performance of automated recognition of psychoneurological states of children 7 to 10 years old from their speech.

This schema may be further used for creating human-computer interfaces for informants with atypical development.

The long-term goal of our research is to develop systems that will assist informants with ASD and DS for communication and speech training. The results will be theoretically and practically valuable, they will expand the knowledge about human voice uniqueness, possibilities of diagnostics of a human state by their voice and speech features, and creation of alternative communicative systems.

Acknowledgments. The study is financially supported by the Russian Science Foundation (project № 18-18-00063) and the Russian Foundation for Basic Research (project 19-57-45008–IND_a).

References

1. Kanner, L.: Autistic disturbances of affective contact. Nervous Child **2**, 217–250 (1943)
2. Bonneh, Y.S., Levanov, Y., Dean-Pardo, O., Lossos, L., Adini, Y.: Abnormal speech spectrum and increased pitch variability in young autistic children. Front. Hum. Neurosci. **4**, 1–7 (2011)
3. Lyakso, E., Frolova, O.: Early development indicators predict speech features of autistic children. In: Proc. 2020 International Conference on Multimodal Interaction (ICMI'20 Companion) – WoCBU'20 Workshop, pp. 514–521 (2020)

4. Kanamori, M.W., Brown, J., Williams-Smith, L.: Otolaryngologic manifestations of Down syndrome. Otolaryngol. Clin. North Am. **33**(6), 1285–1292 (2000)
5. Kent, R.D., Vorperian, H.K.: Speech impairment in Down syndrome: a review. J. Speech Lang. Hear. Res. **56**(1), 178–210 (2013)
6. Moura, C.P., Cunha, L.M., et al.: Voice parameters in children with Down syndrome. J. Voice. **22**(1), 34–42 (2008)
7. Dykens, E., Hodapp, R.M., Evans, D.W.: Profiles and development of adaptive behavior in children with Down syndrome. Am. J. Ment. Retard. **98**(5), 580–587 (1994)
8. Fidler, D.J.: The emerging Down syndrome behavioral phenotype in early childhood implications for practice. Infants Young Child. **18**(2), 86–103 (2005)
9. Lyakso, E., Frolova, O., Gorodniy, V., Grigovev, A., Nikolaev, A., Matveev, Yu.: Reflection of the emotional state in the characteristics of voice and speech of children with Down syndrome. In: Proceedings SpeD 2019, 10th IEEE International Conference on Speech Technology and Human-Computer Dialogue, pp. 1–6. Timisoara, Romania (2019)
10. Frolova, O., Gorodnyi, V., Nikolaev, A., Grigorev, A., Grechanyi, S., Lyakso, E.: Developmental disorders manifestation in the characteristics of the child's voice and speech: perceptual and acoustic study. In: Salah, A.A., Karpov, A., Potapova, R. (eds.) SPECOM 2019. LNCS (LNAI), vol. 11658, pp. 103–112. Springer, Cham (2019). https://doi.org/10.1007/978-3-030-26061-3_11
11. Lyakso, E., Frolova, O.: Adult recognition of the emotional state and intonation in speech of children with Autism Spectrum Disorders: a pilot study. Int. J. Autism Relat. Disabil. **18**(3), 1–5 (2018)
12. Kumar, M., Kim, S.H., Lord, C., Lyon, T.D., Narayanan, S.: Leveraging linguistic context in dyadic interactions to improve automatic speech recognition for children. Comput. Speech Lang. **63**(101101) (2020)
13. Schuller, B.W., Zhang, Y., Weninger, F.: Three recent trends in Paralinguistics on the way to omniscient machine intelligence. J. Multimodal User Interfaces **12**(4), 273–283 (2018). https://doi.org/10.1007/s12193-018-0270-6
14. Fusaroli, R., Lambrechts, A., Bang, D., Bowler, D.M., Gaigg, S.B.: Is voice a marker for Autism Spectrum Disorder? A systematic review and meta-analysis. Autism Res. **10**, 384–407 (2017)
15. Corrales-Astorgano, M., Escudero-Mancebo, D., González-Ferreras, C.: Acoustic characterization and perceptual analysis of the relative importance of prosody in speech of people with Down syndrome. Speech Commun. **99**, 90–100 (2018)
16. Tomblin, J.B.: The EpiSLI database: a publicly available database on speech and language. Lang. Speech Hear. Serv. Sch. **41**(1), 108–117 (2010)
17. He, L., Zhang, J., Liu, Q., et al.: Automatic evaluation of hyper-nasality based on a cleft palate speech database. J. Med. Syst. **39**(5) (2015)
18. Grill, P., Tučková, J.: Speech databases of typical children and children with SLI. PLOS ONE **11**(3), #e0150365 (2016)
19. Lyakso, E., Frolova, O., Kaliyev, A., Gorodnyi, V., Grigorev, A., Matveev, Y.: AD-Child.Ru: speech corpus for Russian children with atypical development. In: Salah, A.A., Karpov, A., Potapova, R. (eds.) SPECOM 2019. LNCS (LNAI), vol. 11658, pp. 299–308. Springer, Cham (2019). https://doi.org/10.1007/978-3-030-26061-3_31
20. Lyakso, E., Frolova, O., Karpov, A.: A new method for collection and annotation of speech data of atypically developing children. In: Proc. of 2018 International Conference on Sensor Networks and Signal Processing, pp. 175–180 (2018)
21. Verma, R.S., Huq, A.: Sex ratio of children with trisomy 21 or Down syndrome. Cytobios. **51**, 206–207 (1987)

22. Loomes, R., Hull, L., Mandy, W.: What is the male-to-female ratio in Autism spectrum disorder? A systematic review and meta-analysis. J. Am. Acad. Child Adolesc. Psychiatry **56**(6), 466–474 (2017)
23. Kovaleva, N.V., Btomo, V., Körblein, A.: Sex ratio in Down syndrome. Studies in patients with confirmed trisomy. Tsitologiia i genetika **35**(6), 43–49 (2001)
24. Kadakia, S., Carlson, D., Sataloff, R.T.: The effect of hormones on the voice. Care of the professional voice. J. Sing. **69**(5), 571–574 (2013)
25. Schopler, E., Reichler, R.J., DeVellis, R.F., Daly, K.: Toward objective classification of childhood autism: Childhood Autism Rating Scale (CARS). J. Autism Dev. Disord. **10**(1), 91–103 (1980)
26. Schuller, B., Weninger, F., Zhang, Y., et al.: Affective and behavioural computing: lessons learnt from the first computational paralinguistics challenge. Comput. Speech Lang. **53**, 156–180 (2019)
27. Eyben, F., Scherer, K.R., Schuller, B.W., et al.: The Geneva minimalistic acoustic parameter set (GeMAPS) for voice research and affective computing. IEEE Trans. Affect. Comput. **7**, 190–202 (2016)
28. PyCM: Multiclass confusion matrix library in Python. https://joss.theoj.org/papers/10.21105/joss.00729
29. Bubnova, G.I.: The articulation base of the Russian and French languages: a dynamic aspect. Bulletin of the Moscow State Linguistic University. Humanit. Sci. **9**(825), 47–56 (2019)
30. Svyatozarova, N.D.: The Intonation System of the Russian Language. Leningrad University Publishing House, Leningrad (1982)
31. Kaliyev, A., Zeno, B., Rybin, S.V., Matveev, Y.N., Lyakso, E.E.: GAN acoustic model for Kazakh speech synthesis. Int. J. Speech Technol. **24**(3), 729–735 (2021). https://doi.org/10.1007/s10772-021-09840-0

Study on Acoustic Model Personalization in a Context of Collaborative Learning Constrained by Privacy Preservation

Salima Mdhaffar[1]([✉]) [iD], Marc Tommasi[2] [iD], and Yannick Estève[1] [iD]

[1] LIA - Avignon Université, Avignon, France
{Salima.Mdhaffar,Yannick.Esteve}@univ-avignon.fr
[2] Université de Lille, CNRS, Inria, Centrale Lille, UMR 9189 - CRIStAL, Lille, France
marc.tommasi@inria.fr

Abstract. This paper investigates different approaches in order to improve the performance of a speech recognition system for a given speaker by using no more than 5 min of speech from this speaker, and without exchanging data from other users/speakers. Inspired by the federated learning paradigm, we consider speakers that have access to a personalized database of their own speech, learn an acoustic model and collaborate with other speakers in a network to improve their model. Several local personalizations are explored depending on how aggregation mechanisms are performed. We study the impact of selecting, in an adaptive way, a subset of speakers's models based on a notion of similarity. We also investigate the effect of weighted averaging of fine-tuned and global models. In our approach, only neural acoustic model parameters are exchanged and no audio data is exchanged. By avoiding communicating their personal data, the proposed approach tends to preserve the privacy of speakers.

Experiments conducted on the TEDLIUM 3 dataset show that the best improvement is given by averaging a subset of different acoustic models fine-tuned on several user datasets. Our approach applied to HMM/TDNN acoustic models improves quickly and significantly the ASR performance in terms of WER (for instance in one of our two evaluation datasets, from 14.84% to 13.45% with less than 5 min of speech per speaker).

Keywords: Automatic speech recognition · Privacy-protection · Collaborative learning · Acoustic models · Personalization

1 Introduction

User interface of modern electronic and personal devices are more and more based on voice interaction and this tendency would probably continue increasing during the next years. Automatic speech recognition (ASR) is the technology at the core of voice interaction systems. To attain a satisfactory level of usability, ASR models need to be trained with a huge amount of training data costly to be collected and

A. Karpov and R. Potapova (Eds.): SPECOM 2021, LNAI 12997, pp. 426–436, 2021.
https://doi.org/10.1007/978-3-030-87802-3_39

annotated. But an important issue with the data collection is privacy preservation. Indeed, some users are now very reluctant to use software solutions that do not preserve their privacy. Efforts towards privacy have been made by European states and the General Data Protection Regulation (GDPR) for instance constraints the way to realize data collection. Speech signals can be considered as sensitive information because in addition to the linguistic content, speech also brings information about the speaker: identity, gender, age, health, emotion...[8].

Different levels of privacy preservation can be defined according to the private information to preserve. Two main approaches have been proposed depending on the information to hide. In the Interspeech VoicePrivacy Challenge [13], the aim of privacy preservation consisted in modifying the speech representation features, trying to remove the speaker identity without removing the linguistic content. In this scenario, the data is first anonymized, and then collected. Even if very promising results have been reached with these contributions, data anonymization is still imperfect and negatively impacts the performance of ASR systems. Another approach consists in avoiding to share data: data is only used locally, on the user device, to personalize the model to this user. Then the models are exchanged, assuming that adapted models contain less sensitive information than the data itself. Such approaches have been used in different works for speech recognition [7], mainly through the use of distributed learning to speech the acoustic model train process [16].

Instead of targeting the improvement of a single general model by sharing anonymized data or applying a distributed learning approach, we propose in this paper to focus on the personalization of an initial model to each user. Inspired by widespread of powerful personal devices, we consider speakers that have access to a personalized database of their own speech. In this scenario, closely related to personalized federated learning [5,14], it is possible to both locally fine-tune an acoustic model and collaborate with other speakers in a network to improve their own model.

The paper is organised along the following lines. Section 2 presents related works. Section 3 details the model adaptation. The experimental setup are described in Sect. 4. The experimental results are presented in Sect. 5 before concluding and giving some perspectives in Sect. 6.

2   Related Work

In this study the term 'personalization' can be interpreted as 'speaker adaptation', more used in the speech community. A nice overview of speaker adaptation techniques for neural acoustic models has been presented in [1], that classifies adaptation techniques into three categories: embedding-based approaches that relies to the use of auxiliary speaker-dependent features like i-vectors [3], model-based approaches that relies to speaker data to update the neural weights, and data augmentation approaches 'which attempt to synthetically generate additional training data with a close match to the target speaker, by transforming *the existing training data'*. No approach based on the use of collaborative training was mentioned in this paper for speaker adaptation, but collaborative training has already been investigated for acoustic model training. In [2,7], federated learning was applied to improve a general shared acoustic model with the goal of privacy preservation, but no speaker adaptation was targeted. Federated learning was also experimented in [4] to speed up the training process and improve the shared general acoustic model performance.

3   Model Adaptation

Our objective is to locally improve the acoustic model for a target speaker by taking advantage from both local pre-existing data and from pre-existing models specific to other users. In our scenario, a global acoustic model is available, trained on the initial corpus. This global model is distributed to all the devices, on which it is possible to fine-tune a local instance of the global model by exploiting locally the user data. These local models can be shared in order to indirectly take benefit from the local data used to their adaptation, through a model averaging.

Since the number of speakers (*i.e.* devices) can be very high, and so the number of adapted models, it seems relevant to propose a strategy to better select these local models that could be use to adapt the model of a target speaker. In a classical hybrid HMM/DNN speech recognition acoustic features like MFCC (Mel-Frequency Cepstral Coefficients) are generally augmented with additional speaker-specific features like i-vectors [6] or x-vectors [12] that can capture information about the speaker. In this work, we assume that this kind of information cannot be exchanged between the different devices since we want to avoid to share explicit knowledge about the speaker and the linguistic content present in the data. To select the best candidate models from the other speakers, we suggest to consider the euclidean distance between candidate models and the model fine-tuned on the target user data.

Our study explores different ways to adapt a HMM/DNN acoustic model through the use of model averaging, local fine-tuning, or a combination of these approaches. The aim of this adaptation is to modify the parameters of the (generic) neural network involved in the HMM/DNN architecture. Fine-tuning consists in continuing the training process of the generic acoustic model on a small dataset of the target speaker, by taking care on avoiding overfitting. Model averaging consists on computing a model whose each weight is the average of the weights extracted from a set of models that share the same neural topology.

Figure 1 illustrates the adaptation approach explored in this work. In this framework, no user data is shared: the fine-tuning is made locally, only adapted models can be exchanged.

4   Experimental Setup

This section describes the ASR system, the experimental methodology and the datasets used for the experiments on speaker adaptation through fine-tuning and

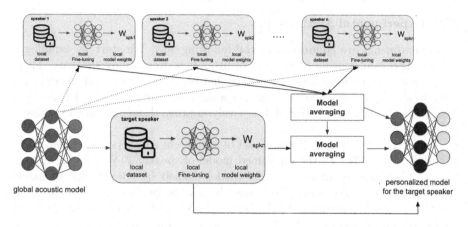

Fig. 1. Model personalization for a target speaker.

model averaging, applied in addition to the classical use of i-vectors as auxiliary input features for neural network speaker adaptation.

4.1   ASR System

The ASR system is based on the Kaldi toolkit [9]. Acoustic models are based on a chain-TDNN approach [10]. The chain-TDNN setup is based on 13 layers with dimension 512 and is trained on cepstral mean and variance normalized 40-dimensional MFCC features concatenated with 9 left and 9 right neighbor frames. We also incorporates i-vectors as an additional input features. The acoustic model has about 14 million parameters. The initial and final learning rates were equal to 0.00025 and 0.000025 respectively. Training audio samples were randomly perturbed in speed and volume during the training process. This approach is commonly called audio augmentation.

When fine-tuning the generic model on target speaker data, we modify only the value of learning rate (the initial and final learning rates were equal to 0.000025 and 0.000015 respectively) and all hyperparameters (i.e. learning rate and local epochs number) are assumed to be homogeneous among all workers.

We make available complete recipes for building the generic acoustic model and the fine-tuned models[1].

As described below, the TEDLIUM 3 dataset was used to train the acoustic models. Data used to train the model is not a part of the TEDLIUM 3 data and is described in [11]. The language model used in our experiment is a 4-gram model, which was pruned to 10 million n-grams.

---

[1] https://github.com/mdhaffar/Acoustic_model_personalisation.

4.2 Experimental Methodology

The experiments are conducted in the following way. We start by building a generic ASR model using a large set of utterances from many speakers. Then, every speaker is associated with a worker that fine-tunes the generic model with a fresh set of utterances of the given speaker. We obtain a set of fine-tuned ASR models. Then we try to collaboratively improve these fine-tuned models in different ways.

Let us consider in the following a set of n different speakers. Let us denote by G the generic model, P_s the fine-tuned model of speaker s. We call an average model of a given set of models, the model defined by the average of model parameters component wise. We denote by $\bar{P}_s$ the per-speaker average of all fine-tuned models $P_{s'}$ except P_s: i.e. $\bar{P}_s = \frac{1}{n-1}\sum_{s'\neq s} P_{s'}$. For a given speaker s and an integer k, we denote by $\bar{B}_s^{\leq k}$ the average of the k best models, measured by the WER on the set of utterances of s used to fine-tune P_s.

We also performed a hierarchical clustering on personal models represented by the vector of their weights of the first layer only. This choice of the first layer as a representative layer comes from a preliminary study we made. This study showed us that the word error rate obtained by using an acoustic model fine tuned on a non-target speaker and the Euclidean distance between the first layer of this model and the first layer of the model fine-tuned on the target speaker data is the most correlated, in comparison to the use of other layers. This is illustrated by Fig. 2.

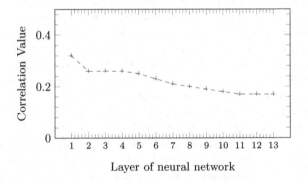

Fig. 2. Pearson correlation between WER and Euclidian distance in function of the layer order on the *perso*1 dataset, described in Sect. 4.3.

For the hierarchical clustering, we use the Numpy library[2] with the *ward* linkage function. Let us recall that the principle of the hierarchical clustering is to build a hierarchy of clusters in bottom-up fashion. The Euclidean distance

---

[2] https://docs.scipy.org/doc/scipy/reference/generated/scipy.cluster.hierarchy.linkage.html.

between weight vectors is used to compute the distance between neural network models. In an iterative process, the two closest clusters are successively merged until only one remains. The output can be represented by a dendrogram. The Ward linkage function [15] is used to evaluate the distance between clusters. It is based on minimum variance method and allows to minimize the total within-cluster variance.

Using this dendrogram, for a given speaker s and an integer k, we compute $\bar{D}_s^{\leq k}$ the average of k closest models to P_s (in terms of distance within the dendrogram).[3]

We perform different kinds of aggregation of the fine-tuned models using a weighted average combined to:

1. the generic model G,
2. or the per-speaker average of all fine-tuned models $\bar{P}_s$
3. or the k-best fine-tuned models $\bar{B}_s^{\leq k}$ (models that have the lowest WER on data from speaker s)
4. or the k-nearest neighbours models $\bar{D}_s^{\leq k}$ where the similarity is given by a dendrogram of Euclidean distance between model weights
5. or the average of k models taken at random among all fine-tuned models $\bar{R}_s^k$.

The weighted average of P_s with one these models $M \in \{G, \bar{P}_s, \bar{B}_s^{\leq k}, \bar{D}_s^{\leq k}, \bar{R}_s^k\}$ is computed by $\alpha P_s + (1-\alpha)M$, i.e. in a component-wise convex combination of the weights.

4.3 Datasets

All experiments to train acoustic models were conducted with the TEDLIUM 3 dataset, a large corpus of 452 h of TED talks given by 2,295 speakers. The dataset is ready for training ASR systems but also dedicated to speaker adaptation tasks. We processed the dataset in an original way for this set of experiments. We split it into three parts so that the sets of speakers in each part are pairwise disjoints. Characteristics of the three parts are reported in Table 1. The first part is called *generic* and has been used to train an initial acoustic model for ASR. The two other parts called *perso1* and *perso2* are used for 2 distinct trials of model personalization and evaluation. In each part $p \in \{perso1, perso2\}$, for each speaker s, we consider a small subset of 5 min of speech data called $train_p^s$ to fine-tune a per-speaker model and the remaining is called $test_p^s$ and used for evaluation. These datasets are never shared (or merged) with other data. We consider them as personal and private datasets belonging to speakers. The average duration of $test_p^s$ data is presented in the third line in Table 1. For the reproductibility of experimental results by research community, we give the list of the new division of the dataset[4].

---

[3] Note that this set may not be unique and we build it iteratively, starting from the closest cluster and choosing models uniformly at random in the last iteration.

[4] https://github.com/mdhaffar/Acoustic_model_personalisation.

Table 1. TEDLIUM3 dataset.

	Generic	perso1	perso2
Duration (hours)	200	150	170
Duration of speech (hours)	170	125	150
Average duration per speaker (minutes)	-	8.5	8.1
Number of speakers	880	650	765

5   Experimental Results

In our experiments, we take k equals to 50, except for $\bar{B}_s^{\leq k}$, where $k = 10$. We measure the average of WER of different models on the $test_p^s$ data. In a more formal way, if we denote by $WER(M, S)$ the word error rate of model M on the dataset S, then we compute averages in the following way. For each part $p \in \{perso1, perso2\}$, and for a base model M_s in $\{G, \bar{P}_s, \bar{B}_s^{\leq k}, \bar{D}_s^{\leq k}, R_s^k\}$, we compute the average WER on part p as $\frac{1}{n}\sum_{s=1}^{n} WER(\alpha P_s + (1 - \alpha)\bar{M}_s, test_p^s)$. The word error rate of the generic model G and the fine-tuned model P_s are given in Table 2.

Table 2. Word Error Rate of the generic and the fine-tuned models.

	perso1	perso2
Generic model G	15.43	14.84
Speaker model P_s	15.04	14.63

The values of average WER for the different base models computed as explained above are reported in Table 3 for the values of $\alpha = 0$, when the private data of the given speaker has not been used and $\alpha = 1/2$ when the fine-tuned model and the other model equally contribute to the averaged model. A graphical representation of the results is given in Fig. 3 for α varying between 0 and 1.

Table 3. Results of collaborative learning with ($\alpha = 0.5$) and without ($\alpha = 0$) fine-tuned model of the target speaker.

	$\alpha = 0$		$\alpha = 0.5$	
Base model	perso1	perso2	perso1	perso2
G	15.43	14.84	14.43	13.92
$\bar{P}_s$	15.21	14.62	14.38	13.82
$\bar{D}_s^{\leq 50}$	15.49	14.81	14.59	14.01
$\bar{R}_s^{50}$	15.25	14.66	14.35	13.84
$\bar{B}_s^{\leq 10}$	14.72	13.8	14.13	13.45

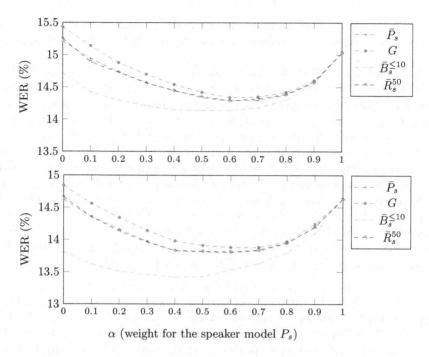

Fig. 3. WER according to different weighted average of P_s with four different aggregated models: all fine-tuned models $\bar{P}_s$, generic model G, 10-best (WER) fine-tuned models $\bar{B}_s^{\leq 10}$, 50 random models $\bar{R}_s^{\leq 50}$ on *perso1* (top) and *perso2* (bottom).

The significance of our results is measured using WER and using the 95% confidence interval. Confidence interval for the *perso1* is 0.08 and 0.07 for *perso2*. Confidence interval means that if the improvement in WER exceed this value, we can consider it as significant improvement. The generic model G is considered as a good model as it is trained by mixing all the training data such that training is carried out on public dataset. WER of G evaluated on the test part of the two datasets *perso1* and *perso2* are presented in line 1 in Table 2. We observe that the values are significantly different. The second line in Table 2 presents results for the speaker model (the local model trained by fine-tuning using only 5 min of speech from the target speaker). Compared to the generic model in Table 2, speaker model improves the WERs for the two sets *perso1* and *perso2*. It is also treated as a good model since it is trained using data from the target speaker.

Table 3 shows results obtained under various aggregation of acoustic model. Results are given for two configurations: with and without the local fine-tuned model of the target speaker.

Collaborative Learning Without the Local Fine-Tuned Model of the Target Speaker ($\alpha = 0$): The second line presents results of aggregation of all fine-tuned models except the target speaker. An improvement is shown compared to the generic model (from 15.43% to 15.21% for *perso1* and from 14.84% to

14.62% for *perso*2). This improvement is significant since it exceeds the confidence interval value (the absolute gain for *perso*1 is 0.22 (0.22 > 0.08) and the same for *perso*2).

The third line in Table 3 presents results of aggregation of k-nearest neighbours models. The selection of k-nearest neighbours models does not improve results compared to the generic model and the model of all speakers (15.49% WER for *perso*1 and 14.81% WER for *perso*2). This selection is compared to a random selection. Results are presented in the line 4 in Table 3. Results of random selection are better than the results of dendrogram-based selection. Surprisingly, the benefit of using close models is not empirically demonstrated. This may be due to several factors. Either the distance is not reflecting a notion of usefulness or some amount of diversity is necessary to obtain models that behave well on new data. It should be noted that the first layer has maybe a too large number of parameters to compute a meaningful distance. We also tried to reduce the dimension of this vector, but the impact on the correlations with the WER (computed in a similar way than in Fig. 2) was not observable.

Collaborative Learning with the Local Fine-Tuned Model of the Target Speaker $(\alpha = 0.5)$: As shown in Table 2, the fine-tuned model using a small local dataset improves WER compared to the generic model. So, we decide to take benefit from this improvement by aggregating models obtained with $\alpha = 0$ with the fine-tuned model of the target speaker (note that this model is trained with a very small dataset). Results in Table 3 shows a significant improvement in WER for all kinds of aggregation.

Acoustic models are prone to overfitting when the training dataset is limited. This could explain why the speaker model P_s cannot get very high performance, since speakers' models are trained using only 5 min. Averaging speakers' models with the target speaker model allows us to produce a more accurate model than the target speaker model. The weight value used to combine the target speaker model P_s and an aggregated model has an influence on the resulting model combination. This is illustrated in Fig. 3. Results in Fig. 3 show also that with a good aggregated model, there is less need of the fine-tuned model P_s to get better results. This is particularly visible when combining P_s to the $\bar{B}_s^{\leq 10}$ aggregated model, made by averaging the ten models fine-tuned on other speakers that got the lowest WERs when applied to the target speaker data. This final combined model outperforms all the other ones, but its usage seems unrealistic since a local decoding process on the target user data is necessary for all the available non-target speaker models P_s'. However, these results provide good indications to continue this work on acoustic model collaborative personalization with privacy preservation constraints.

6   Conclusion

In this paper, we investigate a collaborative learning algorithm to locally improve the performance of an automatic speech recognition system, without sharing data (but models). In this purpose, we suggest to take benefit from acoustic models that have been separately fine-tuned for each user, in addition to the local fine-tuning on the target speaker data. Two kinds of local personalizations are explored, based on a fine-tuning processed on local data, and model averaging. Significant improvements are observed when these two local personalizations are combined through a weighted average. We also observed that a random selection of non-target speaker models gives better results than a non-naive approach. In a scenario where computations are not limited, a selection of non-target speaker models based on their performances – in terms of WER – on the target speaker data gives the best results.

Acknowledgements. This work was supported by the French National Research Agency under project DEEP-PRIVACY (ANR-18-CE23-0018).

References

1. Bell, P., Fainberg, J., Klejch, O., Li, J., Renals, S., Swietojanski, P.: Adaptation algorithms for neural network-based speech recognition: an overview. arXiv preprint arXiv:2008.06580 (2020)
2. Cui, X., Lu, S., Kingsbury, B.: Federated acoustic modeling for automatic speech recognition. In: ICASSP 2021–2021 IEEE International Conference on Acoustics, Speech and Signal Processing (ICASSP), pp. 6748–6752. IEEE (2021)
3. Dehak, N., Kenny, P.J., Dehak, R., Dumouchel, P., Ouellet, P.: Front-end factor analysis for speaker verification. IEEE Trans. Audio Speech Lang. Process. **19**(4), 788–798 (2010)
4. Dimitriadis, D., Kumatani, K., Gmyr, R., Gaur, Y., Eskimez, S.E.: A federated approach in training acoustic models. In: Proceedings of Interspeech (2020)
5. Fallah, A., Mokhtari, A., Ozdaglar, A.: Personalized federated learning with theoretical guarantees: a model-agnostic meta-learning approach. In: Larochelle, H., Ranzato, M., Hadsell, R., Balcan, M.F., Lin, H. (eds.) Advances in Neural Information Processing Systems, vol. 33, pp. 3557–3568. Curran Associates, Inc. (2020). https:// proceedings.neurips.cc/paper/2020/file/24389bfe4fe2eba8bf9aa9203a44cdad-Paper.pdf
6. Gupta, V., Kenny, P., Ouellet, P., Stafylakis, T.: I-vector-based speaker adaptation of deep neural networks for French broadcast audio transcription. In: 2014 IEEE International Conference on Acoustics, Speech and Signal Processing (ICASSP), pp. 6334–6338. IEEE (2014)
7. Leroy, D., Coucke, A., Lavril, T., Gisselbrecht, T., Dureau, J.: Federated learning for keyword spotting. In: ICASSP 2019–2019 IEEE International Conference on Acoustics, Speech and Signal Processing (ICASSP), pp. 6341–6345. IEEE (2019)
8. Nautsch, A., Jiménez, A., Treiber, A., Kolberg, J., Jasserand, C., Kindt, E., Delgado, H., Todisco, M., Hmani, M.A., Mtibaa, A., et al.: Preserving privacy in speaker and speech characterisation. Comput. Speech Lang. **58**, 441–480 (2019)
9. Povey, D., et al.: The kaldi speech recognition toolkit. In: IEEE 2011 Workshop on Automatic Speech Recognition and Understanding. No. CONF, IEEE Signal Processing Society (2011)
10. Povey, D., et al.: Purely sequence-trained neural networks for ASR based on lattice-free MMI. In: Interspeech, pp. 2751–2755 (2016)

11. Rousseau, A., Deléglise, P., Esteve, Y.: Enhancing the TED-LIUM corpus with selected data for language modeling and more ted talks. In: LREC, pp. 3935–3939 (2014)
12. Snyder, D., Garcia-Romero, D., Sell, G., Povey, D., Khudanpur, S.: X-vectors: Robust DNN embeddings for speaker recognition. In: 2018 IEEE International Conference on Acoustics, Speech and Signal Processing (ICASSP), pp. 5329–5333. IEEE (2018)
13. Tomashenko, N., et al.: Introducing the voice privacy initiative. arXiv preprint arXiv:2005.01387 (2020)
14. Wang, K., Mathews, R., Kiddon, C., Eichner, H., Beaufays, F., Ramage, D.: Federated evaluation of on-device personalization (2019)
15. Ward, J.H., Jr.: Hierarchical grouping to optimize an objective function. J. Am. Stat. Assoc. **58**(301), 236–244 (1963)
16. Zhang, W., et al.: Distributed deep learning strategies for automatic speech recognition. In: ICASSP 2019–2019 IEEE International Conference on Acoustics, Speech and Signal Processing (ICASSP), pp. 5706–5710. IEEE (2019)

USC: An Open-Source Uzbek Speech Corpus and Initial Speech Recognition Experiments

Muhammadjon Musaev[1], Saida Mussakhojayeva[2], Ilyos Khujayorov[1],
Yerbolat Khassanov[2], Mannon Ochilov[1], and Huseyin Atakan Varol[2(✉)]

[1] Computer Systems, Tashkent University of Information Technology named after
Muhammad Al-Khwarizmi, Tashkent, Uzbekistan
[2] Institute of Smart Systems and Artificial Intelligence (ISSAI),
Nazarbayev University, Nur-Sultan, Kazakhstan
{saida.mussakhojayeva,yerbolat.khassanov,ahvarol}@nu.edu.kz

Abstract. We present a freely available speech corpus for the Uzbek
language and report preliminary automatic speech recognition (ASR)
results using both the deep neural network hidden Markov model (DNN-
HMM) and end-to-end (E2E) architectures. The Uzbek speech corpus
(USC) comprises 958 different speakers with a total of 105 h of transcribed audio recordings. To the best of our knowledge, this is the first
open-source Uzbek speech corpus dedicated to the ASR task. To ensure
high quality, the USC has been manually checked by native speakers. We
first describe the design and development procedures of the USC, and
then explain the conducted ASR experiments in detail. The experimental
results demonstrate promising results for the applicability of the USC for
ASR. Specifically, 18.1% and 17.4% word error rates were achieved on the
validation and test sets, respectively. To enable experiment reproducibility, we share the USC dataset, pre-trained models, and training recipes
in our GitHub repository (https://github.com/IS2AI/Uzbek_ASR).

Keywords: Dataset · Speech recognition · End-to-end · Transformer ·
Conformer · LSTM · DNN-HMM · Uzbek · Low-resource

1 Introduction

In this paper, we present an open-source Uzbek speech corpus (USC) dedicated
to advancing automatic speech recognition (ASR) research for the Uzbek language. Uzbek is the official language of Uzbekistan also spoken in other neighboring countries, such as Afghanistan, Kazakhstan, Kyrgyzstan, Tajikistan, and
Turkmenistan. It is an agglutinative language spoken by over 35 million people
worldwide [2], which makes it the second-most widely spoken language in the
Turkic languages family. With the USC, we aim to promote the development
and usage of the Uzbek language in speech-enabled applications, such as message dictation, voice search, voice command, and other voice-controlled smart
devices. We also believe that the USC will help to facilitate the development of

© Springer Nature Switzerland AG 2021
A. Karpov and R. Potapova (Eds.): SPECOM 2021, LNAI 12997, pp. 437–447, 2021.
https://doi.org/10.1007/978-3-030-87802-3_40

assistive technologies in the Uzbek language for people with special needs (e.g., the hearing impaired).

Previously, several works have addressed Uzbek speech recognition [21, 23]. However, to the best of our knowledge, there has been no work presenting an open-source Uzbek speech corpus of high quality and sufficient size for training robust speech recognition systems. As a result, there is no generally accepted common Uzbek dataset, and thus, each research group conducts experiments and reports results on their internal data. This hinders experiment reproducibility and performance benchmarking, which retards the further development of Uzbek ASR technologies.

To address this problem, we created the USC dataset containing around 105 h of transcribed audio recordings spoken by 958 speakers from different regions and age groups. The USC is primarily designed for the ASR task, however, it can also be used to aid other speech-related tasks, such as speech synthesis and speech translation. To the best of our knowledge, the USC is the first open-source Uzbek speech corpus available for both academic and commercial use under the Creative Commons Attribution 4.0 International License[1]. We expect that the USC will be a valuable resource for the general speech research community and become the baseline dataset for Uzbek ASR research. Therefore, we invite other researchers to use our dataset and help to further explore it with us.

To demonstrate the reliability of the USC, we conducted initial ASR experiments using both the hybrid deep neural network hidden Markov model (DNN-HMM) and end-to-end (E2E) architectures. Additionally, we investigated the impact of neural language models (LMs) and data augmentation techniques on the Uzbek speech recognition performance. In our experiments, the best DNN-HMM ASR system achieved 18.8% and 23.5% word error rates (WER) on the validation and test sets, respectively. The best E2E ASR system achieved 18.1% and 17.4% WERs on the validation and test sets, respectively. These results showcase the high quality of audios and transcripts in the USC.

The main contribution of this work is two-fold:

- We developed the first open-source speech corpus for the Uzbek language.
- We conducted initial Uzbek speech recognition experiments using both the conventional DNN-HMM and recently proposed E2E architectures.

The rest of the paper is organized as follows: Sect. 2 reviews past works on Uzbek speech recognition and datasets. Section 3 extensively describes the USC dataset construction procedures. The speech recognition experiments and obtained results are presented in Sect. 4. Lastly, Sect. 5 concludes the paper and points out directions of future work.

---

[1] https://creativecommons.org/licenses/by/4.0/.

2   Related Work

Speech is the most natural means of communication between humans, and researchers have long dreamed of employing it for interacting with machines. As a result, ASR research has attracted a great deal of attention over the past few decades [36]. In particular, various ASR architectures [4,5,12,13] and annotated datasets [8,25,31] for training have been introduced. Unfortunately, most of the datasets are developed for popular languages such as English, Spanish, and Mandarin whereas less popular languages do not get much attention. Consequently, the less popular languages face an acute shortage of research and development of ASR technologies [7].

To address the aforementioned problem, many datasets have been developed in less popular languages. For example, to advance speech processing research in Kazakhstan, researchers developed open-source Kazakh speech corpora for building speech recognition [17] and speech synthesis [24] applications. To enable speech research and increase accessibility of speech-enabled applications for illiterate users, Doumbouya et al. [9] released 150 h of transcribed audio data for West African languages. Similarly, several large-scale multilingual speech corpora construction projects were initiated, e.g., VoxForge [3], Babel [10], M-AILABS [32], and Common Voice [6]. However, these projects do not include the Uzbek language yet.

In the context of the Uzbek language, some works have previously attempted Uzbek speech recognition. For example, Musaev et al. [23] developed an ASR system for geographical entities using a dataset consisting of 3,500 utterances. Similarly, the authors of [21] developed a read speech recognition system using 10 h of transcribed audio. The works of [20] and [22] addressed spoken digit and voice command recognition systems under the limited vocabulary scenarios, respectively. It should be mentioned that the datasets used in these works were very limited and specialized for narrow application domains. Other existing Uzbek datasets are prohibitively expensive or publicly unavailable [1]. Therefore, the development of an open-source Uzbek speech corpus of sufficient size is of paramount importance.

3   The USC Dataset Construction

The Uzbek data collection project was conducted with the ethical approval of the Expert Committee consisting of members from the Tashkent University of Information Technology named after Muhammad Al-Khwarizmi. Each reader participated voluntarily and was informed of the data collection and use protocols. The dataset was collected by two means: crowdsourcing and audiobooks.

3.1   Crowdsourcing

The crowdsourcing process consisted of three main stages–namely, text collection, text narration, and audio checking, which will be thoroughly described in the following sections.

Text Collection. We first collected Uzbek textual data from various sources including news portals, electronic books from modern Uzbek literature and national legislation database. The texts were collected automatically using web crawlers and they cover a wide range of topics such as politics, finance, entertainment, and law. In addition, we manually filtered the collected texts to eliminate defects peculiar to web crawlers and exclude non-Uzbek sentences and inappropriate content (e.g., user privacy and violence). We kept sentences containing borrowed words from other languages such as English. Lastly, we removed sentences containing numerals and sentences with more than 30 words. In total, over 100 thousand sentences were prepared for narration.

Text Narration. To narrate the collected sentences, we employed the Telegram [33] messaging platform, which is widely used in Uzbekistan. Specifically, we developed a Telegram bot that first presents a welcome message with instructions and then starts the narration process (see Fig. 1a). During the narration process, the bot sends a sentence to a reader and receives the corresponding audio recording. The bot allowed readers to listen to recorded audio and decide whether to submit or re-record it. In addition, the bot stored the reader IDs and other information including the age, gender, and geographical location. We attracted readers aged 18 or above by advertising the data collection project in social media, news, and open messaging communities on WhatsApp and Telegram.

(a) Data collection bot

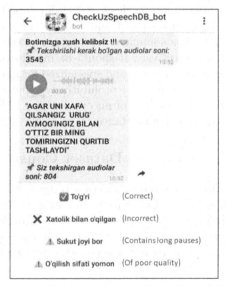

(b) Data checking bot

Fig. 1. Examples of interaction with the Telegram bots during the (a) data collection and (b) data checking stages.

Audio Checking. To ensure the high quality of collected data, we developed an additional Telegram bot for checking the audio recordings. Different from the audio collection bot, the checker bot sends an audio recording and the corresponding sentence to an examiner (see Fig. 1b). As examiners, we recruited several volunteers among native Uzbek speakers. The examiners were instructed to inspect received audios with the sentences and mark them as "correct", "incorrect", "contains long pauses", or "of poor quality". Audio and sentence pairs marked as "correct" were added to the final speech corpus. For pairs marked as "incorrect", the audio recording was removed, and the sentence was transferred to the audio collection bot for re-reading. For pairs marked as "contains long pauses" or "of poor quality", we manually applied additional quality improvement procedures (e.g., trimming long pauses, splitting audio into several segments, and normalizing audio) and then added the pairs to the final speech corpus. To make our dataset close to the real-world scenarios, we kept utterances containing background noises.

3.2 Audiobooks

To collect data from audiobooks, we extracted freely available audiobooks narrated by 20 Uzbek audiobook narrators. From each book, we took only a 30-minute audio excerpt to balance the data contributed by each speaker. These excerpts were automatically segmented and aligned with the corresponding text by using the Aeneas Python library [30]. The generated segments were manually inspected and then added to the final speech corpus.

3.3 Dataset Statistics and Structure

The dataset statistics are reported in Table 1. In total, over 108,000 utterances were collected resulting in around 105 h of transcribed speech data. The utterance duration and length distributions are shown in Fig. 2. We split the dataset into training, validation, and test sets. The speakers in these sets are non-overlapping. For experiment reproducibility, we ask researchers planning to use our dataset to follow the provided splitting.

The USC dataset is structured as follows. We split the dataset into three folders corresponding to the training, validation, and test sets. Each folder contains

Table 1. The USC dataset specifications.

Category	Train	Valid	Test	Total
Duration (hours)	96.4	4.0	4.5	104.9
# Utterances	100,767	3,783	3,837	108,387
# Words	569.0k	22.5k	27.1k	618.6k
# Unique Words	59.5k	8.4k	10.5k	63.1k
# Speakers	879	41	38	958

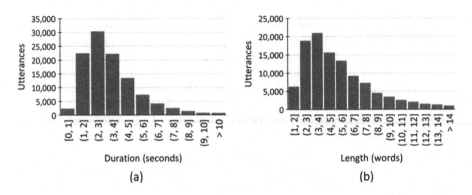

Fig. 2. Utterance (a) duration and (b) length distributions in the USC.

audio recordings and transcripts. The audio and corresponding transcription file-names are the same, except that the audio recordings are stored as WAV files, whereas the transcriptions are stored as TXT files using the UTF-8 encoding. All the transcriptions are represented using the Uzbek Latin alphabet consisting of 29 letters and the apostrophe symbol.

4   Speech Recognition Experiments

We conducted speech recognition experiments to demonstrate the reliability of the USC dataset. We built both DNN-HMM and E2E speech recognition models using our dataset (see Sect. 3) and evaluated them using the character error rate (CER) and word error rate (WER) metrics. We did not use any external data and other available linguistic resources such as lexicon, pronunciation models, and vocabulary. Note that we left the detailed performance comparison of various ASR architectures for the Uzbek language as future work. Hence, in our experiments, we used the standard ASR architectures with the recommended specifications (i.e., number of encoder and decoder blocks, number of layers, layer dimensions, optimizer, initial learning rate, number of training epochs, and so on).

4.1   Experimental Setup

We trained all ASR models using the training set on a single V100 GPU running on the NVIDIA DGX-2 server. The hyper-parameters were tuned using the validation set, and the best-performing models were evaluated using the test set. The characteristics of the built DNN-HMM and E2E ASR systems are described in the following sections. For more information on the implementation details and hyper-parameter values, we refer the interested readers to our GitHub repository[2].

---

[2] https://github.com/IS2AI/Uzbek_ASR.

The DNN-HMM ASR. To build DNN-HMM ASR systems, we used the Kaldi framework [28] and followed the Wall Street Journal (WSJ) recipe. The acoustic model was constructed using the factorized time-delay neural networks (TDNN-F) [27] trained with the lattice-free maximum mutual information (LF-MMI) [29] training criterion. The inputs were Mel-frequency cepstral coefficients (MFCC) features with cepstral mean and variance normalization extracted every 10 ms over a 25 ms window. In addition, we applied data augmentation techniques based on the three-way speed perturbation [19] and spectral augmentation [26].

Due to the strong grapheme-to-phoneme relation in Uzbek, we employed a graphemic lexicon. The graphemic lexicon is comprised of 59.5k unique words extracted only from the training set. As a language model (LM), we used the Kneser-Ney smoothed 3-gram LM[3] trained on the transcripts of the training set and with the vocabulary covering all words in the graphemic lexicon.

The E2E ASR. To build E2E ASR systems, we used the ESPnet framework [35] and followed the WSJ recipe. In particular, we built three types of E2E ASR architectures based on the 1) long short-term memory (LSTM) [16], 2) Transformer [34], and 3) Conformer [14] networks. All E2E ASR architectures were jointly trained with the connectionist temporal classification (CTC) [11] objective function under the multi-task learning framework [18]. The input speech features were represented as an 80-dimensional filterbank features with pitch computed every 10 ms over a 25 ms window. The output units were represented using 29 characters consisting of 26 letters[4], the apostrophe symbol, and special tokens <*unk*> and <*space*>. The batch size in all E2E ASR models was set to 64. To prevent overfitting, we applied data augmentation techniques based on speed perturbation and spectral augmentation. The results for the Transformer and Conformer based E2E ASR models are reported on the average model constructed using the last 10 checkpoints.

In addition, we built a character-level LSTM LM using the transcripts of the training set. The LSTM LM was constructed as a stack of two layers each with a memory cell size of 650. It was employed during the decoding stage using shallow fusion [15] for all the E2E architectures. For decoding, we set the beam size to 20 and the LSTM LM interpolation weight to 1 in all the E2E ASR models.

1) E2E-LSTM ASR. The LSTM-based E2E ASR was constructed using 3 encoder and 1 decoder blocks. Each encoder block consists of a bidirectional LSTM layer with 1,024 units per direction. The decoder block consists of a unidirectional LSTM layer with 1,024 units. The interpolation weight of the CTC objective was set to 0.5 and 0.3 for the training and decoding stages, respectively. The model was trained for 100 epochs using the Adadelta optimizer [37].

---

[3] We trained several N-gram LMs with different orders and smoothing techniques and picked the one that obtained the best perplexity score on the validation set.

[4] Note that the Uzbek Latin alphabet contains 29 letters, however, some of the letters are represented using digraphs (e.g., ng, sh, ch, o' and g'), which we broke down into smaller units and obtained 25 letters. The 26th letter is 'w' obtained from international words.

2) E2E-Transformer ASR. The Transformer-based E2E ASR was constructed using 12 encoder and 6 decoder blocks. We set the number of heads in the self-attention layer to 4 each with 256-dimension hidden states and the feed-forward network dimensions to 2,048. The interpolation weight for the CTC objective was set to 0.3 for both the training and decoding stages. The model was trained for 160 epochs using the Noam optimizer [34] with an initial learning rate of 10 and 25k warm-up steps. The dropout rate and label smoothing were set to 0.1.

3) E2E-Conformer ASR. The specifications of the Conformer-based E2E ASR are similar to the Transformer-based model. It was also constructed using 12 encoder and 6 decoder blocks with a similar number of attention heads and feed-forward network dimensions. However, the interpolation weight for the CTC objective was set to 0.2 and 0.3 for the training and decoding stages, respectively. The model was trained for 100 epochs using the Noam optimizer [34] with an initial learning rate of 5 and 25k warm-up steps. The dropout rate and label smoothing were set to 0.1.

4.2   Experiment Results

Table 2 presents the experiment results in terms of the CER and WER on the validation and test sets. All ASR models achieve competitive results. Specifically, the best result is achieved by the E2E-Conformer, followed by the E2E-Transformer, the DNN-HMM, and then the E2E-LSTM model. We observed

Table 2. The CER (%) and WER (%) results of different ASR models built using USC. The impact of language model (LM), speed perturbation (SP), and spectral augmentation (SA) are also reported.

Model	LM	SP	SA	Valid		Test	
				CER	WER	CER	WER
DNN-HMM	Yes	Yes	No	6.9	18.8	7.5	23.5
	Yes	Yes	Yes	6.9	19.9	8.1	24.9
E2E-LSTM	No	No	No	13.8	43.1	14.0	44.0
	Yes	No	No	14.9	30.0	14.3	31.4
	Yes	Yes	No	13.7	27.6	14.4	30.6
	Yes	Yes	Yes	12.6	24.9	12.0	27.0
E2E-Transformer	No	No	No	12.3	35.2	9.4	31.6
	Yes	No	No	11.7	25.7	8.7	23.9
	Yes	Yes	No	10.7	23.9	8.4	23.0
	Yes	Yes	Yes	9.9	21.4	7.6	21.0
E2E-Conformer	No	No	No	12.7	37.6	10.7	35.1
	Yes	No	No	11.5	27.5	9.7	26.3
	Yes	Yes	No	9.2	21.7	7.5	21.2
	Yes	Yes	Yes	**7.8**	**18.1**	**5.8**	**17.4**

that integrating LMs into E2E ASR is effective for the Uzbek language, where absolute WER improvements of 7.7%–12.6% are achieved on the test set. The application of speed perturbation to the E2E ASR models gains additional absolute WER improvements of 0.8%–5.1% on the test set. Spectral augmentation further improves the E2E ASR models by absolute WERs of 2.0%–3.8% on the test set, however, it does not improve the performance of the DNN-HMM model. Overall, the lowest WER results are 18.1% and 17.4% on the validation and test sets respectively, which were achieved by the E2E-Conformer. These results successfully demonstrate the utility of the USC dataset for training ASR models.

5   Conclusion

We developed an open-source Uzbek speech corpus containing around 105 h of transcribed audio recordings spoken by 958 speakers. The corpus was carefully checked by native speakers to ensure high quality. We believe that our corpus will further advance Uzbek speech processing research and become the primary dataset for comparing different ASR technologies among different research groups. In addition, we conducted preliminary ASR experiments using both the hybrid DNN-HMM and state-of-the-art E2E architectures. The best ASR model trained on our dataset achieved 18.1% and 17.4% WERs on the validation and test sets respectively, which demonstrates the reliability of the USC. In future work, we plan to further increase our dataset size and conduct additional ASR experiments.

References

1. Speechocean's Uzbek speech corpus. http://en.speechocean.com/datacenter/details/1847.html. Accessed 21 May 2021
2. Uzbek language. https://en.wikipedia.org/wiki/Uzbek_language. Accessed 20 May 2021
3. Voxforge. http://www.voxforge.org/. Accessed 11 May 2021
4. Hinton, G., et al.: Deep neural networks for acoustic modeling in speech recognition: the shared views of four research groups. IEEE Signal Process. Mag. **29**(6), 82–97 (2012)
5. Abdel-Hamid, O., Mohamed, A., Jiang, H., Deng, L., Penn, G., Yu, D.: Convolutional neural networks for speech recognition. IEEE ACM Trans. Audio Speech Lang. Process. **22**(10), 1533–1545 (2014)
6. Ardila, R., et al.: Common voice: a massively-multilingual speech corpus. In: LREC, pp. 4218–4222. ELRA (2020)
7. Besacier, L., Barnard, E., Karpov, A., Schultz, T.: Automatic speech recognition for under-resourced languages: a survey. Speech Commun. **56**, 85–100 (2014)
8. Bu, H., Du, J., Na, X., Wu, B., Zheng, H.: AISHELL-1: an open-source Mandarin speech corpus and a speech recognition baseline. In: Proceedings of the O-COCOSDA, pp. 1–5. IEEE (2017)
9. Doumbouya, M., Einstein, L., Piech, C.: Using radio archives for low-resource speech recognition: towards an intelligent virtual assistant for illiterate users. In: Proceedings of the AAAI Conference on Artificial Intelligence, pp. 14757–14765. AAAI Press (2021)

10. Gales, M.J.F., Knill, K.M., Ragni, A., Rath, S.P.: Speech recognition and keyword spotting for low-resource languages: Babel project research at CUED. In: Proceedings of the Workshop on Spoken Language Technologies for Under-Resourced Languages (SLTU), pp. 16–23. ISCA (2014)

11. Graves, A., Fernández, S., Gomez, F.J., Schmidhuber, J.: Connectionist temporal classification: labelling unsegmented sequence data with recurrent neural networks. In: Proceedings of the International Conference on Machine Learning (ICML), Pittsburgh, Pennsylvania, USA, 25–29 June 2006, pp. 369–376 (2006)

12. Graves, A., Jaitly, N.: Towards end-to-end speech recognition with recurrent neural networks. In: Proceedings of the International Conference on Machine Learning (ICML), Beijing, China, 21–26 June 2014, vol. 32, pp. 1764–1772 (2014)

13. Graves, A., Mohamed, A., Hinton, G.E.: Speech recognition with deep recurrent neural networks. In: Proceedings of the IEEE International Conference on Acoustics, Speech and Signal Processing (ICASSP), pp. 6645–6649. IEEE (2013)

14. Gulati, A., et al.: Conformer: convolution-augmented transformer for speech recognition. In: Proceedings of INTERSPEECH, pp. 5036–5040. ISCA (2020)

15. Gülçehre, Ç., et al.: On using monolingual corpora in neural machine translation. CoRR abs/1503.03535 (2015). http://arxiv.org/abs/1503.03535

16. Hochreiter, S., Schmidhuber, J.: Long short-term memory. Neural Comput. 9(8), 1735–1780 (1997)

17. Khassanov, Y., Mussakhojayeva, S., Mirzakhmetov, A., Adiyev, A., Nurpeiissov, M., Varol, H.A.: A crowdsourced open-source Kazakh speech corpus and initial speech recognition baseline. In: Proceedings of the Conference of the European Chapter of the Association for Computational Linguistics, pp. 697–706. Association for Computational Linguistics, April 2021

18. Kim, S., Hori, T., Watanabe, S.: Joint CTC-attention based end-to-end speech recognition using multi-task learning. In: Proceedings of the IEEE International Conference on Acoustics, Speech and Signal Processing (ICASSP), pp. 4835–4839 (2017)

19. Ko, T., Peddinti, V., Povey, D., Khudanpur, S.: Audio augmentation for speech recognition. In: Proceedings of INTERSPEECH, pp. 3586–3589 (2015)

20. Musaev, M., Khujayorov, I., Ochilov, M.: Image approach to speech recognition on CNN. In: Proceedings of the International Symposium on Computer Science and Intelligent Control (ISCSIC), pp. 57:1–57:6. ACM (2019)

21. Musaev, M., Khujayorov, I., Ochilov, M.: Development of integral model of speech recognition system for Uzbek language. In: Proceedings of the IEEE International Conference on Application of Information and Communication Technologies (AICT), pp. 1–6. IEEE (2020)

22. Musaev, M., Khujayorov, I., Ochilov, M.: The use of neural networks to improve the recognition accuracy of explosive and unvoiced phonemes in Uzbek language. In: Proceedings of the Information Communication Technologies Conference (ICTC), pp. 231–234. IEEE (2020)

23. Musaev, M., Khujayorov, I., Ochilov, M.: Automatic recognition of Uzbek speech based on integrated neural networks. In: Aliev, R.A., Yusupbekov, N.R., Kacprzyk, J., Pedrycz, W., Sadikoglu, F.M. (eds.) WCIS 2020. AISC, vol. 1323, pp. 215–223. Springer, Cham (2021). https://doi.org/10.1007/978-3-030-68004-6_28

24. Mussakhojayeva, S., Janaliyeva, A., Mirzakhmetov, A., Khassanov, Y., Varol, H.A.: KazakhTTS: an open-source Kazakh text-to-speech synthesis dataset. CoRR abs/2104.08459 (2021). https://arxiv.org/abs/2104.08459

25. Panayotov, V., Chen, G., Povey, D., Khudanpur, S.: Librispeech: an ASR corpus based on public domain audio books. In: Proceedings of the IEEE International Conference on Acoustics, Speech and Signal Processing (ICASSP), pp. 5206–5210. IEEE (2015)
26. Park, D.S., et al.: SpecAugment: a simple data augmentation method for automatic speech recognition. In: Proceedings of INTERSPEECH, pp. 2613–2617 (2019)
27. Povey, D., et al.: Semi-orthogonal low-rank matrix factorization for deep neural networks. In: Proceedings of INTERSPEECH, pp. 3743–3747 (2018)
28. Povey, D., et al.: The Kaldi speech recognition toolkit. In: Proceedings of the IEEE Workshop on Automatic Speech Recognition and Understanding (2011)
29. Povey, D., et al.: Purely sequence-trained neural networks for ASR based on lattice-free MMI. In: Proceedings of INTERSPEECH, pp. 2751–2755 (2016)
30. ReadBeyond: Aeneas. https://www.readbeyond.it/aeneas/
31. Hernandez, F., Nguyen, V., Ghannay, S., Tomashenko, N., Estève, Y.: TED-LIUM 3: twice as much data and corpus repartition for experiments on speaker adaptation. In: Karpov, A., Jokisch, O., Potapova, R. (eds.) SPECOM 2018. LNCS (LNAI), vol. 11096, pp. 198–208. Springer, Cham (2018). https://doi.org/10.1007/978-3-319-99579-3_21
32. Solak, I.: The M-AILABS speech dataset. https://www.caito.de/2019/01/the-m-ailabs-speech-dataset/. Accessed 11 May 2021
33. Telegram FZ LLC and Telegram Messenger Inc.: Telegram. https://telegram.org
34. Vaswani, A., et al.: Attention is all you need. In: Proceedings of the Annual Conference on Neural Information Processing Systems, 4–9 December 2017, Long Beach, CA, USA, pp. 5998–6008 (2017)
35. Watanabe, S., et al.: ESPnet: end-to-end speech processing toolkit. In: Proceedings of INTERSPEECH, Hyderabad, India, 2–6 September 2018, pp. 2207–2211 (2018)
36. Yu, D., Deng, L.: Automatic Speech Recognition. SCT, Springer, London (2015). https://doi.org/10.1007/978-1-4471-5779-3
37. Zeiler, M.D.: ADADELTA: an adaptive learning rate method. CoRR abs/1212.5701 (2012). http://arxiv.org/abs/1212.5701

A Study of Multilingual End-to-End Speech Recognition for Kazakh, Russian, and English

Saida Mussakhojayeva, Yerbolat Khassanov, and Huseyin Atakan Varol[✉]

Institute of Smart Systems and Artificial Intelligence (ISSAI),
Nazarbayev University, Nur-Sultan, Kazakhstan
{saida.mussakhojayeva,yerbolat.khassanov,ahvarol}@nu.edu.kz

Abstract. We study training a single end-to-end (E2E) automatic speech recognition (ASR) model for three languages used in Kazakhstan: Kazakh, Russian, and English. We first describe the development of multilingual E2E ASR based on Transformer networks and then perform an extensive assessment on the aforementioned languages. We also compare two variants of output grapheme set construction: combined and independent. Furthermore, we evaluate the impact of LMs and data augmentation techniques on the recognition performance of the multilingual E2E ASR. In addition, we present several datasets for training and evaluation purposes. Experiment results show that the multilingual models achieve comparable performances to the monolingual baselines with a similar number of parameters. Our best monolingual and multilingual models achieved 20.9% and 20.5% average word error rates on the combined test set, respectively. To ensure the reproducibility of our experiments and results, we share our training recipes, datasets, and pre-trained models (https://github.com/IS2AI/MultilingualASR).

Keywords: Speech recognition · Multilingual · End-to-end · Dataset · Transformer · Kazakh · Russian · English

1 Introduction

This work aims to study the effectiveness of a multilingual end-to-end (E2E) automatic speech recognition (ASR) system applied to three languages used in Kazakhstan: Kazakh, Russian, and English. Kazakhstan is a multinational country where Kazakh is the official state language, whereas Russian and English are the languages of interethnic and international communication commonly used in business, science, and education. These three languages are part of a large-scale cultural project initiated by the government named "The Trinity of Languages" [1]. The goal of the project is the mastery of the aforementioned languages by the Kazakhstani people. This will presumably enable citizens' successful integration into the international economic and scientific environments. In this regard, we initiate the first study of a single joint E2E ASR model applied to simultaneously recognize the Kazakh, Russian, and English languages.

© Springer Nature Switzerland AG 2021
A. Karpov and R. Potapova (Eds.): SPECOM 2021, LNAI 12997, pp. 448–459, 2021.
https://doi.org/10.1007/978-3-030-87802-3_41

Having a single ASR model for multiple languages considerably simplifies training, deployment, and maintenance [28]. In particular, this is advantageous for multilingual communities where several languages are used for communication. A multilingual ASR system can automatically detect an input language and produce corresponding transcripts without prompting for language or requiring visual and tactile interfaces. This becomes especially useful when ASR is employed in a pipeline of a larger system, such as message dictation, voice command recognition, virtual assistants, a transcription engine on online audio/video sharing platforms (e.g., YouTube), and so on.

Recently presented E2E ASR architectures have been shown to be effective for the multilingual speech recognition task [8,24,32]. It has also been demonstrated that the E2E approaches achieve comparable results to the conventional deep neural network-hidden Markov model (DNN-HMM) ASR [12,14]. Moreover, they significantly reduce the burden of developing ASR systems thanks to the encapsulation of the acoustic, pronunciation, and language models under a single network. Importantly, the E2E ASR models obviate the need for a pronunciation model, which requires significant human effort to be constructed and often proves critical to overall performance [12]. All these features make the E2E architectures attractive for the multilingual speech recognition task.

This work leverages the above-mentioned advantages and studies the multilingual E2E ASR systems applied to simultaneously recognize the Kazakh, Russian, and English languages. Specifically, we thoroughly explore the performance of the Transformer-based E2E architecture [34]. To the best of our knowledge, this is the first study of multilingual E2E ASR dedicated to these languages. We also compared the use of two different grapheme set construction methods (i.e., combined and independent). We also analyzed the impact of language models and data augmentation techniques, such as speed perturbation [23] and spectral augmentation [27]. We found that the multilingual models can achieve comparable results to strong monolingual baselines, despite having a similar number of parameters. To enable experiment reproducibility and facilitate future research, we share our training recipes, datasets, and pre-trained models[1].

Besides conducting the first detailed study of multilingual E2E ASR for Kazakh, Russian, and English, other contributions of this paper are:

- We introduce a 7-h evaluation set of transcribed Kazakh-accented English audio recordings (i.e., native Kazakh speakers reading English sentences extracted from the SpeakingFaces dataset [3]).
- We introduce a 334-h manually-cleaned subset of the OpenSTT dataset [30] for the Russian language, which can also be used to train robust standalone Russian ASR systems.

The rest of the paper is organized as follows: Sect. 2 briefly reviews related works on multilingual ASR. Sections 3 and 4 describe the multilingual models and datasets used in our experiments, respectively. Section 5 presents the experimental setup and obtained results. Section 6 discusses the important findings and highlights potential future work. Finally, Sect. 7 concludes this paper.

---

[1] https://github.com/IS2AI/MultilingualASR.

2   Related Work

A single model capable of recognizing multiple languages has been a long-term goal of the speech recognition community and remains an active area of research for decades [8,28,32]. The use of a single model for several languages simplifies the ASR production pipeline significantly, since maintaining one model per language becomes cumbersome as the number of languages increases. Furthermore, multilingual ASR systems leverage cross-lingual knowledge transfer, which has been shown to improve recognition performance, especially for low-resource languages [7].

Prior works on multilingual ASR have explored both hybrid DNN-HMM [10] and E2E [32] architectures. Both small- and large-capacity multilingual models with up to ten billion parameters have been studied [24]. Offline and streaming speech recognition modes of multilingual ASR have also been investigated [17]. The authors of [4] developed multilingual models capable of recognizing over 100 languages simultaneously. The prior works have also studied different approaches to further improve the multilingual speech recognition performance, such as multi-task [16] and transfer [8] learning. In multi-task learning, a model is jointly trained with other tasks, such as language identification (LID), whereas, in transfer learning, a model pre-trained on other languages (usually high-resource ones) is fully or partially fine-tuned using the target languages. However, to the best of our knowledge, there is no prior work dedicated to simultaneous recognition of the Kazakh, Russian, and English languages.

Among the aforementioned three languages, Russian and English are considered resource-rich, i.e., a large number of annotated datasets exist [2,6,31] and extensive studies have been conducted, both in monolingual and multilingual settings [4,25,28]. On the other hand, Kazakh is considered a low-resource language, where annotated datasets and speech processing research have emerged only in recent years [19,26]. The authors of [19] presented the first crowdsourced open-source Kazakh speech corpus and conducted initial Kazakh speech recognition experiments on both DNN-HMM and E2E architectures. Similarly, the authors of [26] presented the first publicly available speech synthesis dataset for Kazakh. Previously, the Kazakh language was part of several multilingual studies under the IARPA's Babel project [9,16,18], and it was also explored in the context of Kazakh-Russian [21,33] and Kazakh-English [5] code-switching.

This work is the first to study the multilingual E2E ASR systems dedicated to Kazakh, Russian, and English, which we believe will further progress the speech processing research and advance the speech-enabled technology in Kazakhstan and its neighboring countries. These languages belong to different language families (i.e., Kazakh belongs to Turkic, Russian to Slavic, and English to Germanic), which poses an additional challenge to our work. Therefore, we posit that our work will be of interest to the general speech research community, especially for researchers from the post-Soviet states, where Russian and English are also commonly spoken as lingua francas.

3   Speech Recognition Models

In our experiments, we consider three languages $(\mathcal{L}_{kz}, \mathcal{L}_{ru}, \mathcal{L}_{en})$, each with a corresponding grapheme set $(\mathcal{G}_{kz}, \mathcal{G}_{ru}, \mathcal{G}_{en})^2$. In addition, each language has its own independent training set $(\{\mathcal{X}_{kz}, \mathcal{Y}_{kz}\}, \{\mathcal{X}_{ru}, \mathcal{Y}_{ru}\}, \{\mathcal{X}_{en}, \mathcal{Y}_{en})\})$, where $\mathcal{X}$ is an input sequence of acoustic features and $\mathcal{Y}$ is a corresponding target sequence.

The training dataset for the multilingual models is constructed by combining all the three datasets without any form of re-weighting or re-balancing:

$$\{\mathcal{X}_{all}, \mathcal{Y}_{all}\} = \{\mathcal{X}_{kz}, \mathcal{Y}_{kz}\} \cup \{\mathcal{X}_{ru}, \mathcal{Y}_{ru}) \cup \{\mathcal{X}_{en}, \mathcal{Y}_{en}\} \tag{1}$$

and the grapheme set for the combined dataset is similarly obtained as follows:

$$\mathcal{G}_{all} = \mathcal{G}_{kz} \cup \mathcal{G}_{ru} \cup \mathcal{G}_{en} \tag{2}$$

3.1   Monolingual Model

We begin by training randomly-initialized monolingual ASR models for each language using the corresponding training data $\{\mathcal{X}_i, \mathcal{Y}_i\}$ and grapheme set $\mathcal{G}_i$, where $i \in (kz, ru, en)$. These models are encoder-decoder networks based on the Transformer architecture [34] and they will be used as a baseline.

3.2   Multilingual Model

Next, we train a joint model using the multilingual dataset $\{\mathcal{X}_{all}, \mathcal{Y}_{all}\}$ and combined grapheme set $\mathcal{G}_{all}$. The joint model is also based on the Transformer architecture; however, it is a single model whose parameters are shared across all three languages. This model is not given any explicit indication that the training dataset is composed of multiple languages. For the sake of fair comparison, we set the number of parameters and the structure of multilingual and monolingual models to be similar.

Independent Grapheme Set. To alleviate the impact of language confusion in multilingual models, we explored the joint model trained using the independent grapheme sets. To achieve this, we appended each character with the corresponding language code as follows:

Kazakh: 'с ә л е м' → 'с_kz ә_kz л_kz е_kz м_kz'
Russian: 'п р и в е т' → 'п_ru р_ru и_ru в_ru е_ru т_ru'
English: 'h e l l o' → 'h_en e_en l_en l_en o_en'

The training procedure and structure of the independent grapheme set joint model is similar to the standard joint model, except the output layer size is increased from $|\mathcal{G}_{all}|$ to $|\mathcal{G}_{kz}| + |\mathcal{G}_{ru}| + |\mathcal{G}_{en}|$.

---

2 Note that the Kazakh and Russian grapheme sets overlap since they both use Cyrillic script.

Table 1. The dataset statistics for the Kazakh, Russian, and English languages. Utterance and word counts are in thousands (k) or millions (M), and durations are in hours (h). The overall statistics 'Total' are obtained by combining the training, validation, and test sets across all the languages.

Languages		Corpora	Duration	Utterances	Words
Kazakh	train	KSC [19]	318.4 h	147.2k	1.6M
	valid		7.1 h	3.3k	35.3k
	test		7.1 h	3.3k	35.9k
Russian	train	OpenSTT-CS334	327.1 h	223.0k	2.3M
	valid		7.1 h	4.8k	48.3k
	test-B (books)	OpenSTT [30]	3.6 h	3.7k	28.1k
	test-Y (YouTube)		3.4 h	3.9k	31.2k
English	train	CV-330	330.0 h	208.9k	2.2M
	valid	CV [6]	7.4 h	4.3k	43.9k
	test		7.4 h	4.6k	44.3k
	test-SF	SpeakingFaces [3]	7.7 h	6.8k	37.7k
Total	train	–	975.6 h	579.3k	6.0M
	valid		21.6 h	12.4k	127.5k
	test		29.1 h	22.5k	177.3k

4   Datasets

To conduct multilingual speech recognition experiments, we used three datasets corresponding to the Kazakh, Russian, and English languages. The dataset specifications are provided in Table 1. To diminish the performance degradation caused by the challenges peculiar to unbalanced data [24], we made the training set sizes of languages similar (in terms of duration). Additionally, all audio recordings were resampled to 16 kHz and 16-bit format prior to training and evaluation. All datasets used in our experiments are available in our GitHub repository (See footnote 1).

4.1   The Kazakh Language

For Kazakh, we used the recently presented open-source Kazakh Speech Corpus (KSC) [19]. The KSC contains around 332 h of transcribed audio crowdsourced through the Internet, where volunteers from different regions and age groups were asked to read sentences presented through a web browser. In total, around 153,000 recordings were accepted from over 1,600 unique devices. All accepted recordings were manually checked by native Kazakh speakers. In the KSC, all texts are represented using the Cyrillic alphabet, and audio recordings are stored in the WAV format. For the training, validation, and test sets, we used the standard split of non-overlapping speakers provided in [19].

4.2   The Russian Language

For Russian, we used a manually-cleaned subset extracted from the Russian Open Speech To Text (OpenSTT) dataset [30]. The OpenSTT is a multidomain (e.g., radio, lectures, phone calls, and so on) dataset consisting of over 20,000 h of transcribed audio data. However, the provided transcriptions are unreliable since they were obtained automatically by using ASR systems, YouTube subtitles (user-provided and auto-generated), and so on. Clean transcriptions are provided only for the three validation sets from the books, YouTube, and phone calls domains.

To obtain more reliable training data, we hired fluent Russian speakers and manually re-transcribed a randomly selected 334-h subset of the OpenSTT. We selected recordings only from the books and YouTube domains. We named our clean subset OpenSTT-CS334 and its corresponding 334-h original version OpenSTT-ORG334. For the validation set, we randomly selected a 7-h subset of the OpenSTT-CS334, and left the remaining 327 h for training. For the test set, we used the official validation sets of OpenSTT from the books (test-B) and YouTube (test-Y) domains to match the selected training data.

4.3   The English Language

For English, we used a 330-h subset of Mozilla's Common Voice (CV) project [6] that we will further address as the CV-330. The CV is a multilingual dataset intended for speech technology research and development. Its construction procedure is similar to the KSC, where volunteers are recruited to read and verify sentences. The CV-330 consists of validated recordings that received the highest number of up-votes. For evaluation purposes, we randomly extracted 7-h subsets from the standard validation and test sets provided in the CV. Note that the speakers and texts in the training, validation, and test sets are non-overlapping.

We used an additional evaluation set (test-SF) consisting of Kazakh-accented English recordings extracted from the SpeakingFaces dataset [3]. SpeakingFaces is a publicly available multimodal dataset comprised of thermal, visual, and audio data streams. The audios were recorded using a built-in microphone (44.1 kHz) of a web-camera (Logitech C920 Pro HD) at a distance of approximately one meter. The dataset consists of over 13,000 audio recordings of imperative sentences[3] spoken by 142 speakers of different races. We selected recordings spoken by Kazakhs, which resulted in the total of 75 speakers, each uttering around 90 commands. Since the total size of the selected recordings is insufficient to build robust ASR systems, we use them only for evaluation purposes. The produced evaluation set is gender balanced (38 females and 37 males), with the average speaker age of 26 years (ranging from 20 to 47). To the best of our knowledge, this dataset will be the first open-source Kazakh-accented English data, and it will be more suited for assessing the English speech recognition capability of our E2E ASR models.

---

[3] Verbal commands given to virtual assistants and other smart devices such as 'turn off the lights', 'play the next song', and so on.

5   Speech Recognition Experiments

In this section, we describe the experimental setup for both the monolingual and multilingual E2E ASR models, as well as the obtained results. The multilingual and monolingual models were configured and trained similarly for fair comparison. The results are reported using the word error rate (WER) metric.

5.1   Experimental Setup

All E2E ASR systems were trained on the training sets, using the V100 GPUs running on an Nvidia DGX-2 server; hyper-parameters were tuned on the validation sets, and the final systems were evaluated on the test sets (see Table 1). For all systems, the input acoustic features were represented as 80-dimensional log Mel filter bank features with pitch computed every 10 ms over a 25 ms window, and the output units were represented using the character-level graphemes.

To train the E2E ASR systems, we used the ESPnet toolkit [35] and followed the Wall Street Journal (WSJ) recipe. The E2E architecture was based on the Transformer network [34] consisting of 12 encoder and 6 decoder blocks. It was jointly trained with the Connectionist Temporal Classification (CTC) [11] objective function under the multi-task learning framework [22]. The interpolation weight for the CTC objective was set to 0.3 and 0.4 during the training and decoding stages, respectively. For the Transformer module, we set the number of heads in the self-attention layer to 8 each with 512-dimension hidden states, and the feed-forward network dimensions to 2,048. In addition, a VGG-like convolution module [29] was used to pre-process the input audio features before the encoder blocks. All models were trained for 120 epochs using the Noam optimizer [34] with the initial learning rate of 10 and 25k warm-up steps. We set the dropout rate and label smoothing to 0.1. For data augmentation, we used a standard 3-way speed perturbation [23] with factors of 0.9, 1.0, and 1.1, and the spectral augmentation [27]. We report results on an average model constructed using the last ten checkpoints.

To evaluate the impact of language models (LM) on recognition performance, we built character-level LMs using the transcripts of the training sets. The LMs were built as a 2-layer long short-term memory (LSTM) [15] network with a memory cell size of 650 each. We built both monolingual and multilingual LSTM LMs for monolingual and multilingual E2E ASRs, respectively. The multilingual LSTM LM was trained on the combined training set. The LSTM LMs were employed during the decoding stage using shallow fusion [13]. For decoding, we set the beam size to 60 and the LSTM LM interpolation weight to 0.6. The other hyper-parameter values can be found in our GitHub repository (See footnote 1).

5.2   Experiment Results

The experiment results for the three languages are given in Table 2. To obtain an average WER over all the languages, we weighted the WERs by the amount of data in the validation and test sets.

Table 2. The WER (%) results of monolingual (mono), multilingual (multi), and independent grapheme set (multi-igs) models. The results showing the impact of language model (LM), speed perturbation (SP), and spectral augmentation (SA) are also reported. The average WER is computed by weighting the WERs using the amount of data in the validation and test sets.

Model	Kazakh		Russian			English			Average	
	valid	test	valid	test-B	test-Y	valid	test	test-SF	valid	test
mono	21.5	18.8	15.2	17.2	33.7	29.8	34.6	62.0	22.0	34.3
+LM	15.9	13.9	11.5	14.5	28.8	24.7	29.1	57.7	17.3	29.7
+LM+SP	15.3	12.7	9.8	13.4	25.5	23.1	26.7	53.9	15.9	27.3
+LM+SP+SA	**9.4**	8.0	**7.5**	**11.8**	**21.9**	**16.3**	**18.9**	41.6	**11.1**	20.9
multi	20.4	16.3	13.7	16.5	31.5	28.0	32.2	56.0	20.5	31.4
+LM	15.4	12.6	11.2	14.7	28.0	23.7	27.5	51.4	16.7	27.6
+LM+SP	14.4	11.8	10.2	13.8	25.8	22.5	26.4	48.3	15.6	26.0
+LM+SP+SA	9.7	**7.9**	8.2	12.5	23.3	17.1	19.9	39.5	11.7	21.1
multi-igs	20.7	16.6	13.8	16.5	31.3	27.7	32.4	56.4	20.5	31.6
+LM	15.9	12.8	11.3	14.6	27.7	23.4	27.4	51.6	16.7	27.6
+LM+SP	14.9	12.1	10.4	13.6	25.8	22.4	26.1	49.9	15.8	26.3
+LM+SP+SA	9.7	**7.9**	8.3	12.5	23.2	**16.3**	**18.9**	**38.3**	11.5	**20.5**

Monolingual Model. The results of monolingual models show that applying LMs and data augmentation consistently improves the WER performance for all languages, where an average WER improvement of 13.4% was achieved on the test sets (from 34.3% to 20.9%). The best WER result for Kazakh is 8.0% on the test set. The best WER results for Russian are 11.8% and 21.9% on the test-B and test-Y sets, respectively. Notice that recognizing YouTube recordings (i.e., test-Y) is more challenging than audiobooks (i.e., test-B) since the former contains recordings with the spontaneous speech. The best WER results for English are 18.9% and 41.6% on the test and test-SF sets, respectively. Presumably, the poor WER performance on the latter is mostly due to the domain mismatch between the training and test-SF sets because the English training set recordings are read by native English speakers, whereas the test-SF recordings are read by native Kazakh speakers. Moreover, these sets have been collected differently. The best average WER result on the test sets for the monolingual models is 20.9%.

We conducted additional experiments to evaluate the quality of our manually-cleaned subset OpenSTT-CS334. Specifically, we compared the obtained WER results of the monolingual Russian E2E ASR from the previous experiment against a model trained on the original subset OpenSTT-ORG334. Both models were configured and trained similarly. The experiment results given in Table 3 show that the model trained on our clean subset achieves absolute WER improvement of 6.6% for the test-B and 3.1% for the test-Y compared to the model trained on the original subset. These results demonstrate the utility of our OpenSTT-CS334 subset.

Table 3. The comparison of WER (%) results obtained by monolingual Russian ASR models trained on our clean subset OpenSTT-CS334 and corresponding original subset OpenSTT-ORG334.

Model	Training set	Russian		
		valid	test-B	test-Y
mono +LM+SP+SA	OpenSTT-CS334	7.5	11.8	21.9
	OpenSTT-ORG334	12.5	18.4	25.0

Multilingual Model. The use of LMs and data augmentation is also effective for the multilingual models, where an average WER improvement of 10.3% was achieved on the test sets (from 31.4% to 21.1%). The general trend in the WER performances is similar to the monolingual models. For example, the best WER for Kazakh is 7.9%, which is very close to the monolingual baseline. Slightly worse WERs compared to the monolingual baselines are achieved for Russian, with the test-Y set being more challenging than the test-B set. Likewise, small WER degradations are observed for English, and the performance on the test-SF set is poorer than on the test set. However, it is important to mention that the multilingual models achieve noticeable WER improvement of 2.1% on the test-SF set compared to the monolingual baseline (39.5% versus 41.6%). We presume that this improvement is chiefly due to knowledge transfer from the KSC and OpenSTT-CS334 datasets. The best average WER result on the test sets for the multilingual models is 21.1%.

Our experiment results show that the multilingual models with the independent grapheme sets (i.e., multi-igs) achieve similar results to the monolingual models for the Kazakh and English languages, and perform slightly worse for Russian. Notably, it achieves further improvement over the monolingual baseline on the test-SF (38.3% versus 41.6%). Overall, the WER performances of the two grapheme set construction methods are comparable, with the independent grapheme set being slightly better. The best average WER result on the test sets for the multi-igs models is 20.5%, which is the lowest of all the E2E ASR models.

6   Discussion and Future Work

Code-Switching. There are two major types of code-switching: inter-sentential and intra-sentential. In the former, the language switch occurs at sentence boundaries, while in the latter, languages switch within sentences, and thus, resulting in a more complex problem. Our multilingual models can deal only with the inter-sentential cases. However, in Kazakhstan, intra-sentential code-switching is commonly practiced, especially switching between Kazakh and Russian languages. Therefore, our future work will focus on recognizing intra-sentential code-switching utterances by collecting code-switching data or by employing special techniques dedicated to utilizing monolingual data [20,36].

Kazakh-Accented English. Since the developed multilingual E2E ASR is intended to be deployed in Kazakhstan, it is important to ensure that it is suited to recognizing Kazakh-accented English utterances. Our experiment results show that using training datasets uttered by native English speakers leads to suboptimal performance. Therefore, future work will focus on improving the recognition of Kazakh-accented English utterances, for example, by applying domain adaptation techniques or collecting in-domain training data. Although most Kazakhs are fluent in Russian, it would be still interesting to explore the performance of multilingual ASR models on Kazakh-accented Russian utterances.

Dataset. In our experiments, for each language we employed different data-sets with varying acoustic and linguistic characteristics (i.e., collected in different ways, and covering different topics and speaking styles). As a result, the Russian and English languages turned out to be more challenging than the Kazakh. Therefore, future work should minimize the impact of domain mismatch between different datasets. This can be achieved by collecting a multilingual dataset under similar conditions or increasing the dataset domain overlap between languages. In addition, future work should also study the data efficiency–that is, an increase in performance due to the addition of new data, to infer additional data required to achieve further WER improvements.

7   Conclusion

In this paper, we explored multilingual E2E ASR applied to simultaneously recognize three languages used in Kazakhstan: Kazakh, Russian, and English. Specifically, we developed both monolingual and multilingual E2E ASR models based on the Transformer networks and compared their performances in terms of WER. To the best of our knowledge, this is the first multilingual E2E ASR work dedicated to these languages. In addition, we compared the use of two different grapheme set construction methods (i.e., combined and independent). We also evaluated the impact of language models and data augmentation techniques on the WER performances of the monolingual and multilingual models and found them extremely effective. Additionally, we introduced two manually-transcribed datasets: OpenSTT-CS334 and test-SF. The first one is a manually cleaned 334-h subset extracted from the OpenSTT dataset. The second one is a 7-h set of Kazakh-accented English utterances designed to be used for evaluation purposes. Given that acquiring high-quality speech data is prohibitively expensive, these datasets will be of great use for the speech community both in academia and industry. Our experiment results show that the multilingual models achieve comparable results to the monolingual models, while having a similar number of parameters. The best monolingual and multilingual models achieved average WERs of 20.9% and 20.5% on the test sets, respectively. We strongly believe that the conducted experiments and reported findings will benefit researchers planning to build multilingual E2E ASR systems for similar languages, especially from the post-Soviet space. We also hope our work will encourage future research that leverages the findings and datasets presented in this paper.

References

1. The state program on development and use of languages in the Republic of Kazakhstan for the years 2011–2020. https://online.zakon.kz/document/?doc_id=31024348. Accessed 22 Apr 2021
2. Voxforge. http://www.voxforge.org/. Accessed 11 May 2021
3. Abdrakhmanova, M., Kuzdeuov, A., Jarju, S., Khassanov, Y., Lewis, M., Varol, H.A.: Speakingfaces: a large-scale multimodal dataset of voice commands with visual and thermal video streams. Sensors **21**(10), 3465 (2021)
4. Adams, O., Wiesner, M., Watanabe, S., Yarowsky, D.: Massively multilingual adversarial speech recognition. In: NAACL-HLT, pp. 96–108. ACL (2019)
5. Akynova, D., Aimoldina, A., Agmanova, A.: English in higher education: pragmatic factors of Kazakh-English code-switching. Life Sci. J. **11**(10), 414–420 (2014)
6. Ardila, R., et al.: Common voice: a massively-multilingual speech corpus. In: LREC, pp. 4218–4222. ELRA (2020)
7. Besacier, L., Barnard, E., Karpov, A., Schultz, T.: Automatic speech recognition for under-resourced languages: a survey. Speech Commun. **56**, 85–100 (2014)
8. Cho, J., et al.: Multilingual sequence-to-sequence speech recognition: architecture, transfer learning, and language modeling. In: Proceedings of SLT, pp. 521–527. IEEE (2018)
9. Dalmia, S., Sanabria, R., Metze, F., Black, A.W.: Sequence-based multi-lingual low resource speech recognition. In: Proceedings of ICASSP, pp. 4909–4913. IEEE (2018)
10. Ghoshal, A., Swietojanski, P., Renals, S.: Multilingual training of deep neural networks. In: Proceedings of ICASSP, pp. 7319–7323. IEEE (2013)
11. Graves, A., Fernández, S., Gomez, F.J., Schmidhuber, J.: Connectionist temporal classification: labelling unsegmented sequence data with recurrent neural networks. In: Proceedings of ICML, Pennsylvania, USA, 25–29 June 2006, pp. 369–376 (2006)
12. Graves, A., Jaitly, N.: Towards end-to-end speech recognition with recurrent neural networks. In: Proceedings of ICML, vol. 32, pp. 1764–1772. JMLR.org (2014)
13. Gülçehre, Ç., Firat, O., Xu, K., Cho, K., Barrault, L., et al.: On using monolingual corpora in neural machine translation (2015). http://arxiv.org/abs/1503.03535
14. Hannun, A.Y., et al.: Deep Speech: Scaling up end-to-end speech recognition (2014). http://arxiv.org/abs/1412.5567
15. Hochreiter, S., Schmidhuber, J.: Long short-term memory. Neural Comput. **9**(8), 1735–1780 (1997)
16. Hou, W., Dong, Y., Zhuang, B., Yang, L., Shi, J., Shinozaki, T.: Large-scale end-to-end multilingual speech recognition and language identification with multi-task learning. In: Proceedings of INTERSPEECH, pp. 1037–1041. ISCA (2020)
17. Kannan, A., et al.: Large-scale multilingual speech recognition with a streaming end-to-end model. In: Proceedings of INTERSPEECH, pp. 2130–2134 (2019)
18. Karafiát, M., et al.: 2016 BUT babel system: multilingual BLSTM acoustic model with i-vector based adaptation. In: Proceedings of INTERSPEECH, pp. 719–723. ISCA (2017)
19. Khassanov, Y., Mussakhojayeva, S., Mirzakhmetov, A., Adiyev, A., Nurpeiissov, M., Varol, H.A.: A crowdsourced open-source Kazakh speech corpus and initial speech recognition baseline. In: Proceedings of EACL, pp. 697–706. ACL (2021)
20. Khassanov, Y., et al.: Constrained output embeddings for end-to-end code-switching speech recognition with only monolingual data. In: Proceedings of INTERSPEECH, pp. 2160–2164. ISCA (2019)

21. Khomitsevich, O., Mendelev, V., Tomashenko, N., Rybin, S., Medennikov, I., Kudubayeva, S.: A bilingual Kazakh-Russian system for automatic speech recognition and synthesis. In: Ronzhin, A., Potapova, R., Fakotakis, N. (eds.) SPECOM 2015. LNCS (LNAI), vol. 9319, pp. 25–33. Springer, Cham (2015). https://doi.org/10.1007/978-3-319-23132-7_3

22. Kim, S., Hori, T., Watanabe, S.: Joint CTC-attention based end-to-end speech recognition using multi-task learning. In: Proceedings of IEEE ICASSP, pp. 4835–4839 (2017)

23. Ko, T., Peddinti, V., Povey, D., Khudanpur, S.: Audio augmentation for speech recognition. In: Proceedings of INTERSPEECH, pp. 3586–3589 (2015)

24. Li, B., et al.: Scaling end-to-end models for large-scale multilingual ASR. CoRR abs/2104.14830 (2021). https://arxiv.org/abs/2104.14830

25. Markovnikov, N., Kipyatkova, I., Karpov, A., Filchenkov, A.: Deep neural networks in Russian speech recognition. In: Filchenkov, A., Pivovarova, L., Žižka, J. (eds.) AINL 2017. CCIS, vol. 789, pp. 54–67. Springer, Cham (2018). https://doi.org/10.1007/978-3-319-71746-3_5

26. Mussakhojayeva, S., Janaliyeva, A., Mirzakhmetov, A., Khassanov, Y., Varol, H.A.: KazakhTTS: an open-source Kazakh text-to-speech synthesis dataset. CoRR abs/2104.08459 (2021). https://arxiv.org/abs/2104.08459

27. Park, D.S., et al.: Specaugment: a simple data augmentation method for automatic speech recognition. In: Proceedings of INTERSPEECH, pp. 2613–2617 (2019)

28. Pratap, V., et al.: Massively multilingual ASR: 50 languages, 1 model, 1 billion parameters. In: Proceedings of INTERSPEECH, pp. 4751–4755. ISCA (2020)

29. Simonyan, K., Zisserman, A.: Very deep convolutional networks for large-scale image recognition. In: Proceedings of ICLR (2015)

30. Slizhikova, A., Veysov, A., Nurtdinova, D., Voronin, D.: Russian open speech to text dataset. https://github.com/snakers4/open_stt. Accessed 15 Jan 2021

31. Solak, I.: The M-AILABS speech dataset. https://www.caito.de/2019/01/the-m-ailabs-speech-dataset/. Accessed 11 May 2021

32. Toshniwal, S., et al.: Multilingual speech recognition with a single end-to-end model. In: Proceedings of ICASSP, Calgary, AB, Canada, 15–20 April 2018, pp. 4904–4908. IEEE (2018)

33. Ubskii, D., Matveev, Y., Minker, W.: Impact of using a bilingual model on Kazakh-Russian code-switching speech recognition. In: Proceedings of MICSECS (2019)

34. Vaswani, A., et al.: Attention is all you need. In: Proceedings of NIPS, pp. 5998–6008 (2017)

35. Watanabe, S., et al.: Espnet: end-to-end speech processing toolkit. In: Proceedings of INTERSPEECH, pp. 2207–2211. ISCA (2018)

36. Zeng, Z., Khassanov, Y., Pham, V.T., Xu, H., Chng, E.S., Li, H.: On the end-to-end solution to Mandarin-English code-switching speech recognition. In: Proceedings of INTERSPEECH, pp. 2165–2169. ISCA (2019)

Dialog Speech Sentiment Classification for Imbalanced Datasets

Sergis Nicolaou[1], Lambros Mavrides[1(✉)], Georgina Tryfou[1], Kyriakos Tolias[2], Konstantinos Panousis[2], Sotirios Chatzis[2], and Sergios Theodoridis[3]

[1] AI Team, Impactech LTD, Limassol, Cyprus
{s.nicolaou,l.mavrides,g.tryfou}@impactechs.com
[2] Cyprus University of Technology (CUT), Limassol, Cyprus
{kv.tolias,k.panousis,sotirios.chatzis}@cut.ac.cy
[3] Aalborg University, Aalborg, Denmark
stheodor@di.uoa.gr
http://ai.impactechs.com

Abstract. Speech is the most common way humans express their feelings, and sentiment analysis is the use of tools such as natural language processing and computational algorithms to identify the polarity of these feelings. Even though this field has seen tremendous advancements in the last two decades, the task of effectively detecting under represented sentiments in different kinds of datasets is still a challenging task. In this paper, we use single and bi-modal analysis of short dialog utterances and gain insights on the main factors that aid in sentiment detection, particularly in the underrepresented classes, in datasets with and without inherent sentiment component. Furthermore, we propose an architecture which uses a learning rate scheduler and different monitoring criteria and provides state-of-the-art results for the SWITCHBOARD imbalanced sentiment dataset.

Keywords: Sentiment analysis · Bi-modal processing · Acoustic classification · Text classification

1 Introduction

In human communication, sentiment is liaised via posture and facial expressions as well as via speech. In this context, sentiment analysis is the task of classifying a segment of spoken text, for example a dialog turn, into a class that better describes the speaker's state of mind, such as positive, neutral or negative. A dialog-based sentiment analysis system can be used for marketing purposes, and for monitoring and optimizing the performance of agents in sales calls [1]. In a different use case, people with a hearing disability can immensely benefit from a machine that can understand and convey human communication. In order to develop such machines, it is paramount that they are able to understand sentiment, with a focus on perceiving subtle positive and negative sentiment cues.

© Springer Nature Switzerland AG 2021
A. Karpov and R. Potapova (Eds.): SPECOM 2021, LNAI 12997, pp. 460–471, 2021.
https://doi.org/10.1007/978-3-030-87802-3_42

Despite the significant role that sentiment analysis plays in different intelligent applications, and the extensive use of modern deep learning methods to address it, it is still a challenging task [17]. The first reason for this is the variance in the way that humans may choose to express sentiment when they speak. They can use the tone of their voice, words or other subtle cues in order to express in a very controlled way strong sentiments. Second, there are still not enough annotated and large corpora that can be publicly found and used for the development of speech sentiment analysis systems. Therefore, systems are often prone to generalization problems. On top of this, the quality of sentiment found in some of the most commonly used speech corpora in the field, is highly affected by the type and original purpose of the corpus [8]. Therefore, there is still a need to investigate speech sentiment analysis, with a focus on the factors that can contribute to improving results for any dataset, and with an emphasis in the underrepresented classes which are often more prone to errors.

In this paper, we investigate in detail the effect of using single modality and bi-modal speech sentiment analysis, *i.e.* sentiment analysis performed simultaneously on speech and text. First, we propose our in-house single modal classification approaches for both modalities, and investigate their behaviour in all classes. We perform a detailed study on how we can improve the behaviour of the single modal classifiers in underrepresented classes, which may often be more important for certain applications. Finally, we investigate how the effects that have been identified in the single modal classification are generalized in the bi-modal scenario.

The remainder of this paper is organized as follows. In Sect. 2, we outline the current state-of-the-art in the area of speech sentiment analysis. In Sect. 3, we present the datasets on which we base our research and quickly outline their main characteristics. In Sect. 4, we review the experimental setup, present the corresponding experiments and discuss the results. Finally, conclusions are drawn and future steps are described in Sect. 5.

2   Related Work

The first attempts at sentiment analysis involved the use of textual data, as this kind of data was easier to find and process. Previous work on textual sentiment analysis is outlined in [18], and it is evident that since the latter half of the 2010s, more and more emphasis was put on deep learning approaches, such as convolutional neural networks (CNN) and recurrent neural networks (RNN). Moreover, many attempts have been made to create hybrid models which combine deep learning methods with each other, or with traditional machine learning approaches like SVM and lexicon-based methods. In addition, the use of attention layers, [19], has become increasingly popular for solving sentiment analysis tasks. The current state-of-the-art results in popular datasets such as Amazon have been achieved using architectures that incorporate attention [20].

As other forms of data, such as audio and video, became more readily available in recent years, their use in sentiment analysis tasks has also increased. In particular, acoustic data from audio has the potential of being a very useful tool in sentiment analysis. This is due to the nature of human speech and the ability of human to convey sentiment using their voice. Various studies such as [11,14] have established that language-independent vocalisations are rich in emotional content and information like sentiment can be conveyed across cultures. These results indicate that acoustic features can be an extremely powerful tool for sentiment analysis. Sentiment analysis using acoustic features has not received as much in-depth research as textual sentiment analysis, and much of the related work is focused in speech emotion recognition rather than sentiment analysis.

Lately, a lot of research is performed in multi-modal systems for sentiment analysis, where features from different input types, such as text, audio and video are processed simultaneously to improve performance. [12] experimented with residual networks and attention on the IEMOCAP dataset [2] and achieved an accuracy of 67.4%. On the same dataset, [16] reported an accuracy of 66.2 % using a bidirectional LSTM architecture.

In [9], acoustic features are fused with lexical features at an early stage, and the fused features are fed to a classification DNN for utterance level emotion classification. The authors reported a classification accuracy of 75.5% on IEMO-CAP. In [4], acoustic features are processed with an LSTM network that predicts emotions and word sequences text features are fed to a multi-resolution CNN trained for the same task. The prefinal outputs of the two are combined with an SVM to produce the final classification verdict. The authors report a significant improvement in the IEMOCAP dataset, but the finding is not confirmed in a proprietary telephone speech dataset that they use. In [7], the authors propose a hierarchical bi-modal architecture with attention and word-level fusion to classify utterance-level sentiment and emotion from text and audio data. A different approach to fuse information from various modalities is presented in [13], where the authors propose to use pre-trained ASR features and solve the sentiment analysis as a down-stream task. With the assumption that ASR features encode acoustic as well as linguistic information the authors achieve state-of-the-art results. Specifically, they achieved an accuracy of 71.7% on the IEMOCAP dataset and 70.1% on the SWITCHBOARD dataset.

Although bi-modal sentiment analysis from speech and text is not a new domain there is not enough research on how the different modalities perform in detecting the various sentiments, and to which extend each modality affects the reported results. Also, the use of different datasets, often with very different class weights, does not allow one to clearly attribute the success of a certain system either in detecting the most popular class or a good prediction of all classes. Fully comprehending the reported results becomes even more challenging as the two modalities may result in contradicting numbers.

3   Data

3.1   SWITCHBOARD-Sentiment Dataset

The SWITCHBOARD-1 Telephone Speech Corpus[1] is a large speech dataset very commonly used for training and bench-marking ASR systems. A subset of

---

[1] https://catalog.ldc.upenn.edu/LDC97S62.

the SWITCHBOARD dataset was annotated with sentiment labels, released as SWBDsentiment dataset[2]. It consists of 3 sentiment labels (positive, negative, and neutral) for approximately 49,500 utterances covering 140 h of SWITCH-BOARD audio. For each segment we selected the sentiment which voted by the majority of the annotators, while discarding the remaining. After this process, the final data constist of 25445 neutral, 15308 positive and 8549 negative examples. Hence the negative class is the minority class in this dataset. For our experiments, we perform stratified 10-fold cross validation. Segments from one dialog are kept in a single fold so as not to bias the model [3,13]. Although the original purpose of the dataset creation was not related to the sentiment analysis task, the speakers did receive a direction to speak as natural as possible and converse in a realistic way. This, along with the wide variety of topics covered in the dataset makes the SWITCHBOARD a valuable resource in the study of bi-modal sentiment analysis

3.2 IEMOCAP-3 Dataset

The IEMOCAP dataset [2] consists of dyadic interactions between actors. There are five sessions, each with a male and a female speaker, for 10 unique speakers total. As commonly performed in the literature, we consider only utterances with majority agreement ground-truth labels. To create the version we are using, which we call IEMOCAP-3, we create three sentiment categories, namely the neutral, positive and negative classes. To create the positive class we combine the happy and excited labels, and to create the negative we combine the angry and sad labels. Following the removal of utterances which contained only non-verbal actions such as breathing and laughing, the dataset contains 4156 negative, 1703 neutral and 1709 positive utterances. In this dataset the negative class is the majority class as it is about 3 times bigger than the other two classes. It is noted here that in the context of sentiment analysis, IEMOCAP is commonly split in the literature into four class, however we believe that for the scope of our research creating three classes is a better fit. For training, we perform the same split approach described above (stratified 10 fold cross validation, without dialog overlap among folds).

4 Experiments and Results

4.1 Acoustic Sentiment Analysis

For acoustic sentiment analysis, our data processing starts with the extraction of acoustic features, using the Librosa python toolkit. We experimented with various features such as spectrograms, MFCCs with their first and second order derivatives, pitch and chroma features. We observed similar behaviour for most of these features. In the following experiments we report results from MFCCs as these showed a slight improvement in the classification accuracy for the under

---

[2] https://catalog.ldc.upenn.edu/LDC2020T14.

represented classes. In order to get the same number of MFCC frames per audio, even though they are of various sizes, we use a variable window length and a 25% overlap so we always get 300 MFCC vectors per audio. This processing approach results in the same time resolution between the different audio files, but the time axis is either stretched or compressed, to ensure the same number of MFCC vectors per audio. The idea is similar to other acoustic data augmentation techniques used in the literature, as for example time warping discussed in [15]. Each MFCC vector contains 20 coefficients, and is then augmented with its first and second order derivatives, resulting to a 300 × 60 feature matrix per signal.

We train a CNN using the above features extracted from the audio. Our architecture consists of consecutive convolutional blocks, each containing two 2D-convolutional layers with batch normalization and ReLU activation, followed by a max pooling and a dropout layer, as shown in Fig. 1. Since we address sentiment analysis as an acoustic classification task, we need to assign the whole audio segment into a single class and disregard the various temporal variations. To achieve this we set the pool size of the last max pooling layer so that its output averages all temporal information into a single temporal dimension. We tune the remaining convolutional block parameters, such as the number and size of filters used in each convolutional layer as well as the number of total blocks. The output of the last convolutional block is then flattened, and mapped into the target number of classes with a final classification layer.

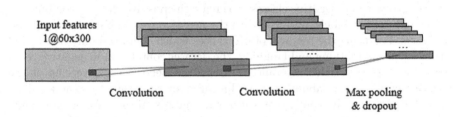

Fig. 1. The convolutional block that we use as a building block for the CNN.

Training Procedure. The acoustic classification model was trained using the Adam optimiser [10] and a *sparse categorical cross entropy* loss function. During training we observed an erratic behavior in most of the validation metrics. This effect is shown in Fig. 2a, where we can also observe that, as training progresses, we get random-like negative class recall values, rapidly changing in the range 0 to 0.4. This indicates that any result is unstable and cannot be generalized.

To overcome this instability issue, we use a learning rate scheduler, which monitors a specific training criterion, and reduces the learning rate by a certain factor once learning stagnates. For our experiments we used 0.5 as a learning rate factor, which results in an controlled reduction in learning rate so that we achieve a good convergence, while we are able to avoid local maxima. Concerning the monitored criterion, we have experimented with the most commonly used metrics in the evaluation of the sentiment analysis task, as for example the

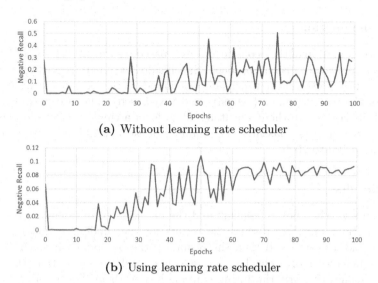

(a) Without learning rate scheduler

(b) Using learning rate scheduler

Fig. 2. The recall in the negative class for the SWITCHBOARD validation set used during training.

weighted accuracy (WA), unweighted accuracy (UA) and the recall values per class. As expected the convergence of the monitored metrics presents the most improvements, although the effects are visible in the remaining metrics as well. For the above example, we can see in Fig. 2b, the effect that the learning rate scheduler has on the monitored metric.

4.2 Text-Based Sentiment Analysis

For the text-based sentiment analysis, we first computed word embeddings for the textual annotations using pre-trained BERT models [5]. The size of each embedding vector was 300 and they were directly used as inputs to the neural network model. The model consisted of consecutive 1D convolutional layers, followed by LSTM layers. The convolutional layers downsampled the input by a factor equal to the stride. Moreover, the kernel size used is always bigger than the stride, meaning the entire inputs are used to compute the output of each layer. The overall effect of this is that model is able to identify useful information while discarding unimportant details, making the output sequences shorter, which in turn can help the LSTM layer in detecting longer patterns [6]. The text-based models were more stable, with regards to metrics like negative class recall, compared to the acoustic classification, therefore we did not introduce a learning rate scheduler for the training.

4.3 Combination

For the combination of the acoustic and text-based results into a bi-modal model, we use a late feature fusion approach. Specifically, we create two feature vectors for each speech utterance, which are calculated in the output of the pre-final layers of the two classifiers (acoustic and text-based). The two output vectors for each utterance are then concatenated to form a single vector and classified using a random forest classifier. The number of estimators hyperparameter was varied from 100 to 1000.

4.4 Results

The results for the above classifiers and the investigated datasets are presented in this section. First, we discuss the results for the single-modality classifiers, *i.e.* text and acoustic, and then the results in the bi-modal approach. We discuss the behaviour of each classifier per class, and the effect that the use of different monitoring criteria during training has on them. We report results for various metrics commonly used in classification tasks: weighted accuracy (WA), unweighted accuracy (UA), negative class recall (Ng. R.), positive class recall (Ps. R) and neutral class recall (Nt. R). WA represents the standard accuracy measure, which is the total number of correct predictions divided by the total number of predictions. UA represents the average accuracy for every class, in other words it is the average of the individual recalls for all classes. Furthermore, we report results for various training stopping criteria in order to understand the way that each classification setup behaves in the different classes, and identify the best approach to optimize the results in the underrepresented classes.

Text Classification. The fine-tuning process for the text-based classification model resulted in three convolutional layers of increasing filter sizes 32, 64, and 128, a kernel size 4 and stride 2, which were followed by an LSTM layer with 128 neurons. These parameters were used for both the SWITCHBOARD and IEMOCAP datasets as the tuning per dataset resulted in very similar setups.

Table 1. The results for the two investigated datasets in the text sentiment classification. For each row we monitor a specific metric.

Monitoring criteria	SWITCHBOARD					IEMOCAP				
	WA	Ng.R	Ps.R	Nt.R	UA	WA	Ng.R	Ps.R	Nt.R	UA
WA	66.0	34.6	60.7	79.5	58.3	64.4	81.7	56.0	31.3	56.3
Ng. R	64.7	45.9	56.0	76.1	59.4	56.0	97.8	13.5	0.0	37.1
Ps. R	63.8	32.4	67.3	72.1	57.3	60.8	76.5	65.2	17.6	53.1
Nt. R	62.9	22.2	39.8	90.2	50.7	62.0	74.7	53.5	40.2	56.2
UA	65.1	38.7	62.2	75.6	58.8	63.8	78.4	59.6	32.8	56.9

In Table 1, we show the results for the text based sentiment classification. For each reported monitoring case, the training runs for a variable number of epochs and stops when the corresponding metric stops improving. First, we observe the difficulty of the classifier in accurately detecting the negative and neutral classes in the SWITCHBOARD and IEMOCAP datasets, which are the smaller classes respectively. In both cases, monitoring the recall value of the smaller class, or directly the UA value, are good methodologies in order to improve the overall UA of the classifier.

Acoustic Classification. After the tuning process, the final acoustic model architecture for SWITCHBOARD consisted of three convolutional blocks with 64, 32 and 30 filters, followed by two fully connected layers of 128 and 64 neurons. The final IEMOCAP acoustic model architecture consisted of one convolutional block with 32 filters, followed by 1 fully connected layers with 32 neurons. The fact that the tuned IEMOCAP model is smaller than the respective SWITCH-BOARD model is expected, since the IEMOCAP dataset is significantly smaller than the SWITCHBOARD dataset.

Table 2. The results for the two investigated datasets in the acoustic sentiment classification. For each row we monitor a specific metric using a learning rate scheduler.

	SWITCHBOARD					IEMOCAP				
Monitoring criteria	WA	Ng.R	Ps.R	Nt.R	UA	WA	Ng.R	Ps.R	Nt.R	UA
WA	57.1	0.0	24.7	95.2	40.0	61.2	90.6	25.5	28.1	48.1
Ng. R	51.5	19.5	34.9	71.9	42.1	56.6	99.0	5.7	8.6	37.8
Ps. R	44.3	11.9	69.7	40.0	40.5	44.7	48.6	71.6	5.5	41.9
Nt. R	56.9	0.0	25.2	94.6	39.9	50.0	53.3	18.4	76.6	49.4
UA	48.4	29.5	53.1	51.8	44.8	59.1	78.1	25.5	49.6	51.1

The results of the acoustic classification on both datasets are shown in Table 2. As before, the monitoring setups concern the use of different stopping criteria. As described before, we also use an learning rate scheduler in matched conditions, meaning that the scheduler and the early stopping callbacks monitor the same value. First, we observe that the acoustic classification results are greatly affected by the selection of the monitoring criterion. For example, in the SWITCHBOARD dataset the negative class recall has increased from 0% to 19% by changing the monitoring from WA to Ng.R. As observed for text classification, selecting the UA offers a good trade-off among the classes. However, in a real application one should consider the expected behaviour of the system. In many cases, improving the prediction in the negative and positive classes is more critical than improving the UA.

Bi-modal Classification. The tuning of the random forest hyperparameters produced similar results, therefore we report the results of the simple classifier with 100 estimators. In Table 3, we report the results from the bi-modal classification. For the combination we use the output of the prefinal layers of the acoustic and text classification. The shapes of the acoustic vector are 64 and 32 for SWITCHBOARD and IEMOCAP respectively, and 128 for each text output. The different monitoring setups here concern the corresponding single modalities used. For instance, a negative class recall monitoring means that both the text and the acoustic classifiers are trained using this stopping criterion. Although the bi-modal classification does help in improving the overall classification metrics, WA and UA, it does not offer overall significant improvements. This may be attributed to the selection of the simple classifier, *i.e* a random forest, as opposed to a more sophisticated neural architecture.

Table 3. The results for the two investigated datasets in bi-modal sentiment classification. For each row we monitor a specific metric.

Monitoring criteria	SWITCHBOARD					IEMOCAP				
	WA	Ng.R	Ps.R	Nt.R	UA	WA	Ng.R	Ps.R	Nt.R	UA
WA	67.0	39.0	61.0	79.0	60.0	67.5	79.0	62.0	44.0	62.0
Ng. R	61.0	30.0	52.0	76.0	53.0	64.0	79.0	50.0	43.0	58.0
Ps. R	65.0	38.0	57.0	79.0	58.0	68.0	82.0	56.0	48.0	62.0
Nt. R	66.0	34.0	59.0	81.0	58.0	63.0	76.0	57.0	41.0	58.0
UA.	67.0	39.0	61.0	79.0	60.0	68.0	79.0	63.0	46.0	63.0

It is interesting though to point out that in the IEMOCAP case, the bi-modal classifier is good at combining complementary information from the two modalities. Notice the improvement that is reported in the underrepresented classes (positive and neutral) while maintaining a good recall in the negative class, when compared with the corresponding results coming from the text modality. The same however is not evident in SWITCHBOARD, something that can be explained by the nature of the dataset. SWITCHBOARD is a dataset built for automatic speech recognition and the conversations regard topics given as a prompt to the speakers. The speakers were not instructed to include any emotional state in their speech and the contents do not cause strong emotions, therefore we expect less sentimental acoustic cues for utterances that are deemed negative or positive. In the positive class, phonations such as laughs may help the model make more accurate predictions.

Nevertheless, the SWITCHBOARD results compare favourably to the results reported in [3], as shown in Table 4. There are no comparable results for 3-class IEMOCAP experiments since most experiments involving this dataset concern emotion recognition and use more classes from the IEMOCAP label set.

Table 4. Comparative results for the SWITCHBOARD dataset.

Modality	Metric	Chen et al. [3]	Proposed solution
5*Acoustic	WA	54.2	48.4
	UA	39.6	44.8
	Ng. R	0.0	29.5
	Ps. R	40.0	53.1
	Nt. R	78.0	51.8
5*Bi-modal	WA	65.6	67.0
	UA	54.6	60.0
	Ng. R	–	39.0
	Ps. R	–	61.0
	Nt. R	–	79.0

5   Conclusion

In this work, we demonstrated that bi-modal analysis perform better when the data have an inherent sentiment component to them, as opposed to an everyday conversational nature. Therefore, according to the nature of each dataset, different configurations may lead to optimal results. For example, in the SWITCHBOARD dataset where sentiment is not expected to be emphasized in oral speech we observed that text is a good source for sentiment analysis. In IEMOCAP where we generally expect strong acted sentiment we observe that the acoustic information becomes much more relevant. In such datasets, bi-modal models are successful in detecting sentiment, also in underrepresented classes using fusion techniques. This conclusion however, indicates the general need for more realistic sentiment analysis corpora for building bi-modal solutions.

In general, we have observed that, as expected, classification accuracy suffers in the smaller classes, which for sentiment analysis are often the non-neutral classes. To address this we introduced a monitoring criterion which focuses on the problematic classes, reduces learning rate in the audio classification, and also selects the best stopping point during training. In any case, the combination strategy that we implement is able to benefit from both information sources, acoustic and text, and significantly improve the results for all sentiment classes.

Finally, to the best of our knowledge, the bi-modal results reported for the SWITCHBOARD dataset are the best achieved from comparable approaches in the literature. In [3], the use of pretrained ASR features is reported to further improve the results, however not in the negative class. Also one needs to take into account the increase in the resources that is required for the training and subsequent use of a sufficiently large pretrained ASR system.

Acknowledgments. This work has received funding from the European Union's Horizon 2020 research and innovation program under grant agreement No 872139, project aiD. We would like to thank our colleagues Steve Barrett, Zacharias Georgiou and Andrey Filyanin for their valuable help and feedback in the preparation of this work.

References

1. Algaba, A., Ardia, D., Bluteau, K., Borms, S., Boudt, K.: Econometrics meets sentiment: an overview of methodology and applications, May 2019. https://doi.org/10.2139/ssrn.2652876
2. Busso, C., Bulut, M., Lee, C.C., Kazemzadeh, A., Mower, E., Kim, S., Chang, J.N., Lee, S., Narayanan, S.S.: IEMOCAP: interactive emotional dyadic motion capture database. Language Resour. Eval. **42**(4), 335–359 (2008)
3. Chen, E., Lu, Z., Xu, H., Cao, L., Zhang, Y., Fan, J.: A large scale speech sentiment corpus. In: Proceedings of the 12th Language Resources and Evaluation Conference, pp. 6549–6555 (2020)
4. Cho, J., Pappagari, R., Kulkarni, P., Villalba, J., Carmiel, Y., Dehak, N.: Deep neural networks for emotion recognition combining audio and transcripts. arXiv preprint arXiv:1911.00432 (2019)
5. Devlin, J., Chang, M.W., Lee, K., Toutanova, K.: BERT: pre-training of deep bidirectional transformers for language understanding. arXiv preprint arXiv:1810.04805 (2018)
6. Géron, A.: Hands-On Machine Learning with Scikit-Learn, Keras, and TensorFlow: Concepts, Tools, and Techniques to Build Intelligent Systems. O'Reilly Media, New York (2019)
7. Gu, Y., Yang, K., Fu, S., Chen, S., Li, X., Marsic, I.: Multimodal affective analysis using hierarchical attention strategy with word-level alignment. In: Proceedings of the Conference. Association for Computational Linguistics, Meeting, vol. 2018, p. 2225. NIH Public Access (2018)
8. Hussein, D.M.E.D.M.: A survey on sentiment analysis challenges. J. King Saud Univ. Eng. Sci. **30**(4), 330–338 (2018)
9. Kim, E., Shin, J.W.: DNN-based emotion recognition based on bottleneck acoustic features and lexical features. In: ICASSP 2019–2019 IEEE International Conference on Acoustics, Speech and Signal Processing (ICASSP), pp. 6720–6724. IEEE (2019)
10. Kingma, D.P., Ba, J.: Adam: a method for stochastic optimization. arXiv preprint arXiv:1412.6980 (2014)
11. Laukka, P., Elfenbein, H.A., Söder, N., Nordström, H., Althoff, J., Iraki, F.K., Rockstuhl, T., Thingujam, N.S.: Cross-cultural decoding of positive and negative non-linguistic emotion vocalizations. Front. Psychol. **4**, 353 (2013)
12. Li, R., Wu, Z., Jia, J., Zhao, S., Meng, H.: Dilated residual network with multi-head self-attention for speech emotion recognition. In: ICASSP 2019–2019 IEEE International Conference on Acoustics, Speech and Signal Processing (ICASSP), pp. 6675–6679. IEEE (2019)
13. Lu, Z., Cao, L., Zhang, Y., Chiu, C.C., Fan, J.: Speech sentiment analysis via pre-trained features from end-to-end ASR models. In: ICASSP 2020–2020 IEEE International Conference on Acoustics, Speech and Signal Processing (ICASSP), pp. 7149–7153. IEEE (2020)
14. Nordström, H., Laukka, P., Thingujam, N.S., Schubert, E., Elfenbein, H.A.: Emotion appraisal dimensions inferred from vocal expressions are consistent across cultures: a comparison between Australia and India. R. Soc. Open Sci. **4**(11), 170912 (2017)
15. Park, D.S., et al.: SpecAugment: a simple data augmentation method for automatic speech recognition. arXiv preprint arXiv:1904.08779 (2019)
16. Poria, S., Majumder, N., Hazarika, D., Cambria, E., Gelbukh, A., Hussain, A.: Multimodal sentiment analysis: addressing key issues and setting up the baselines. IEEE Intell. Syst. **33**(6), 17–25 (2018)

17. Shayaa, S., Jaafar, N.I., Bahri, S., Sulaiman, A., Wai, P.S., Chung, Y.W., Piprani, A.Z., Al-Garadi, M.A.: Sentiment analysis of big data: methods, applications, and open challenges. IEEE Access **6**, 37807–37827 (2018)
18. Shi, Y., Zhu, L., Li, W., Guo, K., Zheng, Y.: Survey on classic and latest textual sentiment analysis articles and techniques. Int. J. Inf. Technol. Decis. Making **18**(04), 1243–1287 (2019)
19. Vaswani, A., et al.: Attention is all you need. arXiv preprint arXiv:1706.03762 (2017)
20. Xie, Q., Dai, Z., Hovy, E., Luong, M.T., Le, Q.V.: Unsupervised data augmentation for consistency training. arXiv preprint arXiv:1904.12848 (2019)

Explicit Control of the Level of Expressiveness in DNN-Based Speech Synthesis by Embedding Interpolation

Tijana Nosek[1](✉), Siniša Suzić[1], Mia Vujović[1], Darko Pekar[2], Milan Sečujski[1], and Vlado Delić[1]

[1] Faculty of Technical Sciences, University of Novi Sad, Novi Sad, Serbia
tijana.nosek@uns.ac.rs
[2] AlfaNum Company, Novi Sad, Serbia

Abstract. The paper proposes a method for controlling the level of expressiveness of speech synthesis by linear interpolation between neural network embeddings corresponding to neutral and fully emotional speech. The deep neural network based speech synthesis model learns the properties of a speech style from a multi-speaker, multi-style speech database. The input features related to speaker and style ID are presented to the model through appropriate embeddings, which allows the model not only to learn the acoustic distance between styles, but also to synthesize speech with an arbitrary level of expressiveness of a particular style. The feasibility of the method has been confirmed by listening tests aimed at establishing the perceived level of style expressiveness, and ensuring that general quality of synthesis from interpolated embeddings is unaffected. The model was trained on approximately 26 h of American English speech by 23 speakers, and the listening tests used speech data of one male and one female speaker. Speech styles considered included happy, angry and apologetic. The results fully confirm that the method is quite successful in controlling the level of style expressiveness, which is one of the key elements of highly natural speech synthesis.

Keywords: Control of expressiveness · Embedding · Neural networks · Speech synthesis

1 Introduction

Applications of speech synthesis are numerous, and the expressiveness of synthesized speech is extremely important for many of them. The main goal of an expressive text-to-speech system (TTS) is to generate a voice as human-like as possible, since such a voice is more pleasant for a human listener [1]. Accordingly, the control over voice characteristics expressing emotions and other information outside the textual content is of great importance.

The support for varying speaking styles and degrees of expressiveness of synthetic speech is becoming a standard for competitive TTS systems, as it has been shown that emotion, mood and sentiment affect attention, memory, performance, judgment and

© Springer Nature Switzerland AG 2021
A. Karpov and R. Potapova (Eds.): SPECOM 2021, LNAI 12997, pp. 472–482, 2021.
https://doi.org/10.1007/978-3-030-87802-3_43

decision making in humans [2]. Furthermore, it has been shown that perceived emotional cues in an interlocutor can affect a person's emotions [3]. For instance, a humorous voice and positive mood can affect the listener's mood, which may have therapeutic implications. Similarly, excitement for a product introduced by an artificial speaker can excite the human listener as well. The importance of expressing emotions and attitudes in human-machine communication has also been shown in [4], where expressive robots have been found to be preferable over efficient ones. However, perceiving an artificial agent as a real person requires not only the presence or absence of a particular emotion in the synthesized speech but also a varying level of expressiveness. At the moment there is not many scientific papers that address this issue.

The simplest approach to achieving a varying level of expressiveness of a speech style is to use a speech database with sections that explicitly correspond to different degrees to which the style is expressed. Then, by using any of the approaches for multi-style speech synthesis [5] and by treating different levels of expressiveness as different styles, TTS with different levels of expressiveness can be created. However, there are several drawbacks of this approach. The first problem is the general complexity related to the control of the level of expressiveness in voice talents whose voices are recorded. Furthermore, only the levels of expressiveness that have been recorded can be reproduced, which implies a rather coarse control of expressiveness. Finally, a more flexible solution may open up more possibilities such as interpolation between different speech styles. One such solution is presented in [6], where an observation vector of an intermediate speaking style in HMM-based speech synthesis is obtained by linearly interpolating observation vectors of the representative speaking styles. Subjective evaluation results showed that speech generated from the interpolated model truly reflects the style between the two representatives. This approach would also allow a finer control over the level of expressiveness of a speech style. The research presented in [7] discusses an approach based on hidden Markov models (HMM) in which, from a simple representation of several basic speech styles as points in a 2-D space, any desired style can be formed by specifying the control vector as a point in that space. Additionally, the level of expressiveness of a particular style can be controlled by choosing the point between two representative styles. The authors report that satisfactory results can be obtained using about 45 min of data for each basic emotion/attitude. However, it is unclear how a new style would fit into the proposed arrangement. In [8], the previously proposed method has been extended by adding information about the subjective perception of the level of expressiveness in the recordings in HMM training. Although this approach resulted in a more precise and intuitive control of expressiveness, it still requires a speech database containing recordings with different levels of expressiveness as well as extensive listening tests.

In the field of speech synthesis based on deep neural networks (DNN), principal approaches for controlling the level of expressiveness have been introduced in [9] and [10]. In [9] a number of approaches making use of perceptual information in the training phase are presented, but they all require extensive evaluation of the training database by human listeners. Although they result in a clearer expression of target emotions, as confirmed by listening tests, attempts at explicit control of the level of expressiveness have not shown to be effective. The idea in [10] identifies different levels of expressiveness in the speech database automatically by using the k-means algorithm on acoustic features extracted from original data. The identified clusters were subsequently associated with different levels of expressiveness through listening tests. Dimensionality reduction over the acoustic features for each sample was performed by using the t-SNE [11] algorithm, and the points in the new space were used as style ID vectors for training. A positive correlation between the level of expressiveness and the values of t-SNE components, allowed explicit control of the expressiveness level by using arbitrary values for the style ID vector in the synthesis stage. However, we failed to confirm these findings on any of our emotional databases, which may imply that the results in [10] appear to be dependent on the speech dataset, e.g. datasets recorded with express intention that different levels of expressiveness should be clearly recognizable.

The method for controlling the expressiveness level proposed in this paper represents an extension of the model based on speaker/style embedding presented in [12]. This model maps different speaker/style combinations into different points in a low-dimensional space, thus efficiently capturing similarities and differences between speakers and speaking styles, even in cases where the quantity of target speech data is quite small. In this paper we explore whether the level of expressiveness can be controlled by choosing a particular point in the embedding space, located between neutral speech and some other speech style of a particular speaker.

The model introduced in [12] will be briefly explained in Sect. 2. The method for controlling the level of expressiveness in speech synthesized by this model will be presented in Sect. 3. Section 4 will describe the database and the details related to the implementation of the model. Results are presented and discussed in Sect. 5, while Sect. 6 concludes the paper and gives an outline of future work.

2 TTS Model from Prior Work

The multi-speaker multi-style TTS model that represents the basis for the idea proposed in this paper [12] is based on speaker/style embedding. Linguistic and prosodic content, i.e., features which describe them, are explicitly separated from the information regarding the speaker and speech style. Although speaker-style combination is presented to the model as a one hot vector, it is embedded before being concatenated with linguistic and prosodic features, and sent as input to the neural network. Allowing the network to establish a speaker-style embedding space on its own from data is beneficial. It enables the network to identify similar speakers, assigning them closer points in the embedding space, while keeping different speakers more distant.

The speaker/style-dependent TTS based on embedding consists of two neural networks: the duration network predicts phone durations and the acoustic network predicts acoustic features. The architecture of both networks is presented in Fig. 1, where it can be seen that the proposed model can handle not only speakers and styles, but also individual clusters within speech data corresponding to particular speaker-style combinations. The clusters within speech data have been identified manually, and have often been found to correspond to single recording sessions of a particular speaker in a particular speech style.

Output features (durations or acoustic parameters)

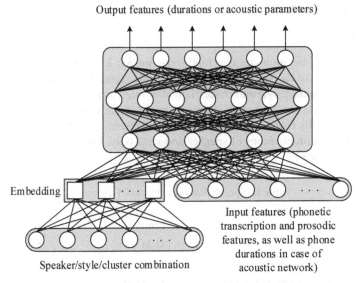

Fig. 1. Architecture of either of the two neural networks that predict phone durations or acoustic features in speaker/style-dependent TTS based on embedding [12].

3 Proposed Idea

We hypothesize that a point in the speaker-style embedding space obtained by linear interpolation between the speaker's neutral and non-neutral (e.g. happy) style representations should correspond to a less expressive non-neutral style. The speaker-style embedding used for synthesis of speech with a specific level of expressiveness of a particular speech style (as opposed to the neutral style) is thus obtained as a linear combination of points from the multidimensional embedding space, i.e.:

$$z = (1 - \alpha)x + \alpha y, \tag{1}$$

where x and y represent the embeddings for the neutral and the desired style of a single speaker, respectively. The coefficient $0 \leq \alpha \leq 1$ corresponds to the contribution of the target style in the final combination, and consequently the greater α should result in a more expressive style. Values of α outside the indicated interval were not included in the listening tests since informal evaluation of results has confirmed a significant decrease in quality in that case.

The feasibility of the proposed method has been verified by listening tests, which have shown that not only there is a strong correlation between the value of α and the perceived expressiveness of a speech style, but also that style interpolation does not impair general quality of synthetic speech. The latter needed verification, having in mind that the embeddings used in synthesizing speech in a style expressive only to a certain extent were not obtained by training on speech data.

4 Data and Implementation Details

4.1 Database

For the creation of the multi-speaker multi-style model, 23 speakers are used. Speech material for many of the speakers contains multiple styles and clusters. Each unique combination of speaker, style and cluster, hereafter referred to as SSC, is represented by a unique one-hot vector. Thus, it should be pointed out that in this research linear interpolation was actually carried out between points representing embeddings of particular SSCs rather than combinations of speaker and style only. More details about the data can be seen in Table 1.

Table 1. Speech data used for model training.

Number of speakers	Female	10
	Male	13
	Total	23
Speaker/style/cluster combinations (SSC)	Total number	82
	Min. duration	0:01:10
	Max. duration	0:59:59
	Mean duration	0:18:58
	Median duration	0:13:48
	Total (hh:mm:ss)	25:54:43

To test the ability to control the level of expressiveness of a speech style, studio quality recordings by two speakers with multiple styles were used, one male with 7 different styles (~5 h of speech, silences excluded), and one female with 8 different styles (~1 h of speech). For the listening tests, only neutral, happy, apologetic and angry styles are used, since other styles, such as promotional or stern, were not present in both speakers. The amounts of speech material for each style used in the listening tests are given in Table 2.

Table 2. Part of the database used for listening tests.

Speaker		Male	Female
Style-cluster combination	Angry-1	0:16:55	0:02:26
	Apologetic-1	0:33:37	0:04:00
	Happy-1	0:26:13	0:01:24
	Neutral-1	0:06:08	0:32:00
	Neutral-2	0:08:45	0:00:00

4.2 Implemented TTS Model

The implementation of the TTS model used in the experiments is based on the Merlin toolkit [13] and the Tensorflow framework [14].The network predicting phone durations (or rather the durations of HMM states) has an input layer of size 577, 3 feedforward layers of size 1024 with rectified linear unit (relu) activation functions, one LSTM layer of size 1024, and a linear output layer of size 5, for the prediction of the durations of each HMM state of a phone. The size of the input layer is determined by the number of questions related to linguistic and prosodic context, while the size of the SSC embedding was heuristically set to 10.

The architecture of the acoustic network is basically the same, with the input layer increased by 9 to accommodate for new frame related features [13]. As in the case of the duration network, hidden layers contain 1024 neurons, while the output layer contains 100 neurons, whose outputs correspond to the values of 30 mel-generalized cepstral coefficients (MGC), 2 band aperiodicity coefficients (BAP), the value of f0, the first and second derivatives of all features previously mentioned, as well as one feature related to the degree of voicing (VUV). Static features represent the data required for the WORLD vocoder [15] used in the final stage of the TTS system.

Both networks also contain dropout layers, with 7% rate, after each hidden feedforward layer. Batch normalization is also included. After a number of experiments, we have concluded that best results are obtained by using batch size of 8 × 50, where 8 represents the number of streams and 50 is the number of phonemes per stream. In the case of the acoustic network, batch size is represented as the product of the number of streams and the number of frames of length 5 ms per stream. By testing different combinations of values, it has been found that best results are achieved with a batch size of 4 × 400.

The duration network was trained for 100 epochs, while the acoustic network was trained for 150 epochs. Stochastic gradient descent is used as an optimizer. Finally, it should be noted that the imbalance between the representation of particular SSCs in the training corpora has been mitigated by using SSC-specific weight coefficients in cost function, as explained in [12].

5 Results

5.1 Subjective Evaluation

For the purpose of subjective evaluation, two listening tests were conducted. No sentence used in any of the listening tests was seen during the training. The goal of the first one was to establish whether embedding interpolation leads to any loss of general quality of synthesized speech. The seen embedding was used for producing utterances which are either purely neutral or express a speech style to its full degree. All levels between neutral and fully expressive were produced using unseen embeddings. A total of 30 utterances were presented to 28 listeners fluent in English, and they were asked to rate the quality of the synthesized voice in terms of intelligibility and naturalness. For each utterance the listeners graded the quality on a MOS scale from 1 to 5, where 1 represents the lowest and 5 represents the highest quality. There were 15 utterances per speaker, 5 utterances for each style. Among these 5 utterances 2 were synthesized with a seen embedding, i.e. one neutral and one happy/apologetic/angry, while the remaining 3 were synthesized with unseen embeddings obtained by setting α to 0.25, 0.50 and 0.75. Values of α outside the interval [0,1] were not included in the listening tests, since an informal evaluation showed that they lead to a significant decrease in quality.

As can be seen from Fig. 2, the use of an unseen embedding in synthesis (α equal to 0.25, 0.50 or 0.75) does not lead to any perceptible loss in general quality. In all cases synthesized speech was given an average grade above 3.0, with no significant differences with respect to speaker gender (both male and female voices were given the same average grade of 3.64) or speech style (average grades of 3.63, 3.62, and 3.53 were given to apologetic, angry and happy style respectively). The perceived quality decreases with an increase of α, i.e. as synthesized speech gets more expressive, which may be due to the fact that a mismatch between the content of the utterance and the speech style used presents a greater problem if a speech style is expressed to its full degree.

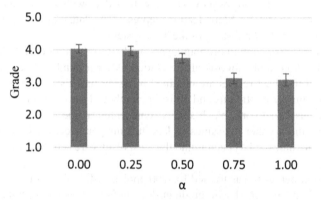

Fig. 2. Average grades for utterances synthesized with different values of α with indicated 95% confidence interval.

The aim of the second experiment was to establish to what extent the value of α is correlated with subjective perception of the level of expressiveness. A total of 18 sets of utterances were presented to 20 listeners fluent in English. Among these 18 sets there were 9 sets per speaker and 3 sets per style (happy, apologetic and angry). Each set contained 5 utterances with the same content, one in the neutral style, while the other 4 represented different levels of a non neutral style, i.e. with the values of α set to 0.25, 0.50, 0.75 and 1.00. The listeners were asked to arrange the utterances in order of increasing expressiveness, i.e. to assign indices from 1 to 5 according to the perceived level of expressiveness of a style.

As can be seen from the confusion matrix shown in Fig. 3, there is a strong positive correlation between the perceived level of expressiveness and the intended one (corresponding to α). In 60% of the cases listeners correctly identified the intended level of expressiveness, and they predominantly confused adjacent levels. Since each sequence of assigned indices represents a permutation of the sequence of intended levels expressed on the same scale, the average of squared distances between the corresponding indices was used as a convenient measure of similarity between two permutations. If this measure is rescaled to the interval $[-1,1]$ to indicate correlation, the average score obtained on all utterances is 0.66 (0.68, 0.86 and 0.43 for angry, happy and apologetic, respectively).

		Intended level				
		1	2	3	4	5
Perceived level	1	**216**	68	27	24	25
	2	74	**195**	55	16	20
	3	28	56	**227**	34	15
	4	20	21	35	**229**	55
	5	22	20	16	57	**245**

Fig. 3. Intended vs. perceived level of expressiveness.

5.2 Objective Evaluation

To further confirm that the intended level of expressiveness, represented by α, is correlated with the actual level of expressiveness of synthesized speech, the influence of α on f0 and energy, acoustic features that are known to be highly dependent on the emotion expressed in speech [16], is also analyzed.

An example of the influence of a gradual increase of α to the mean of the f0 contour is shown in Fig. 4 ($\alpha = 1$ corresponds to happy speech), where it can be seen that a change of α directly influences the values of f0 produced by the network. Furthermore, when α is outside the interval $[0, 1]$, the f0 contour drifts outside its typical boundaries. In this specific example, for $\alpha > 1$ the produced values of f0 are too high, while for $\alpha < 0$ the f0 contour tends to be too flat, and in both cases the correlation between the values of α and the acoustic features is not as strong, as illustrated by Fig. 5, indicating the change of average f0 with respect to α for the happy target style. The degrees of correlation of average f0 and energy with α within the interval $[0,1]$ for each speaker and style are shown in Table 3. It can be seen that there is a strong correlation between α and both acoustic parameters in all cases except when the target style is apologetic and the voice is female. The lack of strong correlation between the level of expressiveness and objective measures of speech in the apologetic style may have been one of the reasons for the lower ability of listeners to identify the degree of expressiveness of this style in synthetic speech.

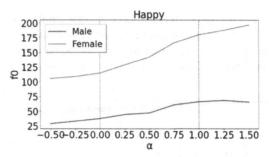

Fig. 4. Dependence between normalized f0 and α.

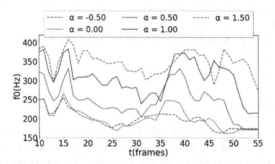

Fig. 5. Influence of α on the shape of the f0 contour (synthesis in female voice, happy target speech style).

Table 3. Correlation between α and energy/f0.

	Happy	Angry	Apologetic
Male	0.93/0.95	0.87/−0.96	−0.93/−0.91
Female	0.99/0.99	0.99/−0.92	0.39/−0.65

6 Conclusions

As confirmed by the results of subjective and objective evaluation, the novel method for the control of the level of expressiveness of synthetic speech presented in the paper is able to produce an arbitrary level of expressiveness of a particular speech style without loss of general speech quality even when just several minutes of target emotional speech data are available. The level of expressiveness of styles more strongly correlated with objective acoustic features of speech (average f0 and energy) has been shown to be more easily identified by the listeners.

The future research will include the investigation of other interpolation methods, since the relationships between points in multidimensional spaces are not as straightforward as they may seem. Furthermore, since the rationale behind the method is equally applicable to the interpolation between voices of different speakers, the future work will also include experiments investigating the perception of naturalness of voices generated by using thus obtained embeddings, as well as the loss of general quality of synthesis that may occur when voices of non-existing speakers are created. The application of the proposed method to voice interpolation is also less straight-forward since it opens up issues related to normalization of acoustic parameters among speakers.

Acknowledgements. This research was supported by Speech Morphing Systems Inc., Campbell, CA, United States of America, as well as the Science Fund of the Republic of Serbia (grant #6524560, AI – S ADAPT). Speech corpora used in the research were provided by Speech Morphing Systems Inc, and the authors note that, to their knowledge, at this moment there is no publicly available corpus suited to the needs of this research.

References

1. Gong, L., Nass, C., Simard, C., Takhteyev, Y.: Usability Evaluation and Interface Design: Cognitive Engineering, Intelligent Agents, and Virtual Reality, When non-human is better than semi-human: Consistency in speech interfaces, vol. 3, pp. 390–394 (2001)
2. Delić, V., et al.: Toward more expressive speech communication in human-robot interaction. In: Ronzhin, A., Rigoll, G., Meshcheryakov, R. (eds.) ICR 2018. LNCS (LNAI), vol. 11097, pp. 44–51. Springer, Cham (2018). https://doi.org/10.1007/978-3-319-99582-3_5
3. Brave, S., Clifford, N.: Emotion in Human-Computer Interaction, the Human-Computer Interaction Handbook: Fundamentals, Evolving Technologies and Emerging Applications. CRC Press, Boca Raton (2002)
4. Hamacher, A., Bianchi-Berthouze, N., Pipe, A.G., Eder, K.: Believing in BERT: Using expressive communication to enhance trust and counteract operational error in physical Human-Robot Interaction. In: Robot and Human Interactive Communication (2016)
5. Suzić, S., Delić, T., Jovanović, V., Sečujski, M., Pekar, D., Delić, V.: A comparison of multi-style DNN-based TTS approaches using small datasets. In: MATEC Web of Conferences, vol. 161, P. 03005, EDP Sciences (2018)
6. Tachibana, M., Yamagishi, J., Onishi, K., Masuko, T., Kobayashi, T.: HMM-based speech synthesis with various speaking styles using model interpolation. In: Speech Prosody 2004, International Conference (2004)
7. Masuko, T., Kobayashi, T., Miyanaga, K.: A style control technique for HMM-based speech synthesis. In: Eighth International Conference on Spoken Language Processing (2004)
8. Nose, T., Kobayashi, T.: An intuitive style control technique in HMM-based expressive speech synthesis using subjective style intensity and multiple-regression global variance model. Speech Commun. **55**(2), 347–357 (2013)
9. Lorenzo-Trueba, J., Henter, G.E., Takaki, S., Yamagishi, J., Morino, Y., Ochiai, Y.: Investigating different representations for modeling and controlling multiple emotions in DNN-based speech synthesis. Speech Commun. **99**, 135–143 (2018)
10. Zhu, X., Xue, L.: Building a controllable expressive speech synthesis system with multiple emotion strengths. Cogn. Syst. Res. **59**, 151–159 (2020)
11. van der Maaten, L., Hinton, G.: Visualizing data using t-SNE. J. Mach. Learn. Res. **9**, 2579–2605 (2008)
12. Sečujski, M., Pekar, D., Suzić, S., Smirnov, A., Nosek, T.: Speaker/style-dependent neural network speech synthesis based on speaker/style embedding. J. Univers. Comput. Sci. **26**(4), 434–453 (2020)

13. Wu, Z., Watts, O., King, S.: Merlin: An Open Source Neural Network Speech Synthesis System. In: Proc. 9th ISCA Speech Synthesis Workshop (2016)
14. Abadi, M., et al.: A System for Large-scale Machine Learning. In: 12th USENIX symposium on operating systems design and implementation (OSDI 16), pp. 265–283 (2016)
15. Morise, W.M., Yokomori, F., Ozawa, K.: WORLD: a vocoder-based high-quality speech synthesis system for real-time applications. IEICE Trans. Inf. Syst. **99**(7), 1877–1884 (2016)
16. Ververidis, D., Kotropoulos, C.: Emotional speech recognition: resources, features and methods. Speech Commun. **48**, 1162–1181 (2006)

Experimental Analysis of Expert and Quantitative Estimates of Syllable Recordings in the Process of Speech Rehabilitation

Dariya Novokhrestova[1](✉) [iD], Evgeny Kostuchenko[1] [iD], Ilya Hodashinsky[1] [iD], and Lidiya Balatskaya[1,2] [iD]

[1] Tomsk State University of Control, Systems and Radioelectronics, Lenina Street 40, 634050 Tomsk, Russia
ndi@fb.tusur.ru, nii@oncology.tomsk.ru
[2] Tomsk Cancer Research Institute, Kooperativniy Av. 5, 634050 Tomsk, Russia
https://www.tusur.ru, https://www.oncology.tomsk.ru/

Abstract. The article proposes analysis and comparison of the estimates of sylla-ble intelligibility obtained from speech therapist (expert) and using an automatic speech quality assessment algorithm. The relevance of the development of algo-rithms for automatic assessment of speech quality and syllabic intelligibility is shown. The estimates were obtained based on the analysis of voice recordings of real patients after surgical treatment of oncological diseases of the oral cav-ity and oropharynx. For comparison with expert opinion, estimates are proposed that were obtained using dynamic time warping (DTW) for time normalization and three metrics: DTW distance, correlation coefficient and Minkowski distance. The obtained quantitative estimates were converted to a binary form using opti-mization methods for comparison with expert estimates, which are initially binary. Errors between expert estimates and converted quantitative estimates are calcu-lated for each patient individually and in general. Of the listed metrics, the DTW distance was chosen for further use, this metric allows to get estimates that are most consistent with the expert opinion. The task of selecting a combination of metrics for further research is proposed, its limitations are indicated.

Keywords: Speech rehabilitation · Syllable intelligibility · Speech quality criteria · Cancer of the oral cavity and oropharynx

1 Introduction

Improving the quality of diagnostics and treatment has led to an increase in the number of timely diagnosed cases of oncological diseases of organs involved in the production of speech [1]. The methods of treatment are improving, their effectiveness is increasing [2, 3], but in most cases (80%) surgical intervention is required. Surgical treatment for cancer of the oral cavity and oropharynx inevitably leads to disruption of such vital functions as speech, voice, breathing, chewing and swallowing. According to the concept of health

© Springer Nature Switzerland AG 2021
A. Karpov and R. Potapova (Eds.): SPECOM 2021, LNAI 12997, pp. 483–491, 2021.
https://doi.org/10.1007/978-3-030-87802-3_44

care development in Russia, oral cavity and oropharynx cancer belongs to the group of the most socially significant diseases, since the violation of sonorous speech leads to disability, reducing the labor potential and quality of life of patients [4, 5]. Thus, after surgical treatment, speech rehabilitation is a mandatory step. Due to the increase in the number of patients, it takes too much time to carry out such rehabilitation by the "manual method" [6], namely when the speech therapist (expert) listens to the recordings several times and gives estimates. This justifies the need for the development of algorithms and software systems that make it possible to evaluate speech quality in an automatic mode. Such algorithms reduce the time spent on estimation, and, accordingly, reduce the processing time of data in the framework of speech rehabilitation.

Previously, various approaches have been investigated for calculating estimates, both at the stage of pre-processing of audio signals [7], and at the stage of direct calculation of estimates [8, 9]. Recently, a large number of works have been published on the analysis of speech through its recognition: analysis of the emotional state of the speaker, age and gender, developmental characteristics [10–12]. This approach can also be applied in speech rehabilitation, but only when calculating phrase intelligibility [13]. For syllable intelligibility, this approach is not suitable. Syllable intelligibility is understood as an assessment of the quality of pronunciation of a syllable and the phonemes in it. Therefore, other algorithms are required for the assessment.

This paper describes an attempt to compare estimates obtained through expert work and estimates according to the developed algorithm using several metrics for calculation. Among the selected metrics, based on the comparison and analysis of the obtained estimates, the best metric for use is chosen.

2 Experiment

2.1 Data Description

For the experiments, we took sound files recorded during the speech quality assessment session. These sessions were carried out as part of the process of speech rehabilitation after the surgical treatment of oncological diseases of the organs of the speech-forming apparatus, carried out on the basis of the Research Institute of Oncology in Tomsk. Recordings of 15 patients were collected. 4 patients had 4 sessions, 11 patients had 3 sessions. The first and the second sessions for each patient were recorded before the surgical treatment and contained the patient's speech close to normal (slight deviations from normal speech may be due to the presence of neoplasms in the oral cavity). The third session was recorded after the surgical treatment and before speech rehabilitation. The fourth session, if available, was recorded during speech rehabilitation. The first session for each patient is a reference, that is, it is with the recordings of this session that the corresponding recordings from the remaining sessions was compared. Thus, 34 sessions were used for calculating estimates and comparison.

In each session, the first 30 recordings were selected. These are notation of syllables with the one of the most problematic phonemes: phoneme [k] and with its soft variant. The most problematic phonemes mean the phonemes that are most often subject to changes after surgical treatment of oncology. The list of the most problematic phonemes was formed after analyzing the database of patient recordings provided by the Research Institute of Oncology in Tomsk. The set of syllables with the problematic phoneme is composed in such a way that there are 5 different syllables for each location of the problematic phoneme in the syllable (at the beginning, in the middle and at the end).

Spectrograms of four recordings of the syllable "кастъ" [kust'] ([kʲasʲtʲ] - according to the international phonetic alphabet [14]) of patient #1 are shown in Figs. 1–4. In Fig. 1 and Fig. 2 spectrograms of preoperative syllable recordings are presented. In Fig. 3 spectrogram recording of a syllable made after surgery and before the speech rehabilitation is presented. In Fig. 4 spectrogram recording of a syllable made during the speech rehabilitation is presented. In all figures, time (s) is displayed along the abscissa, frequency (Hz) is along the ordinate.

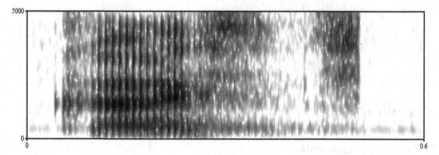

Fig. 1. Spectrogram of the syllable recorded in the first session before the operation. Reference syllable.

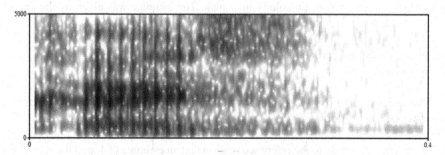

Fig. 2. Spectrogram of the syllable recorded in the second session before the operation.

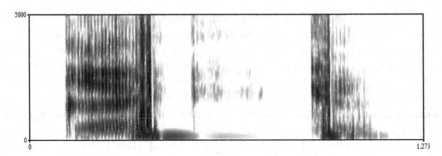

Fig. 3. Spectrogram of the syllable recorded after the operation and before the speech rehabilitation.

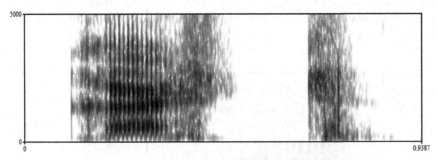

Fig. 4. Spectrogram of the syllable recorded during the speech rehabilitation.

2.2 Evaluation Algorithms

All selected recordings were evaluated using two methods.

The first method. This method is used to assess the quality of speech at the present time at the Research Institute of Oncology in Tomsk. The estimate was given by the expert after listening to the recording:

- 1 if the syllable was pronounced completely correctly;
- 0 - otherwise.

The final estimates of the recording (except for the recordings from the reference sessions) were set as follows:

- 1 if both the recording in the reference session had an estimate of 1, and the recording in the evaluated session had an estimate of 1;
- 0 - otherwise.

The second method. This method includes an algorithm for automatically assessing speech quality. The algorithm receives two sound files as input: a reference recording and an estimated recording (recording from the second, the third or the fourth session).

The output is a quantitative assessment. For time normalization, a dynamic time warping algorithm (DTW) is used. The distance metric for the knot costs in the DTW grid is the Euclidean distance.

In general, the algorithm for calculating the estimate can be described by the following sequence of steps:

1. Converting a reference recording into a sequence of signal amplitude values (sequence #1).
2. Converting an estimated recording into a sequence of signal amplitude values (sequence #2).
3. Converting to one length (time normalization) of sequences #1 and #2 using DTW.
4. Calculating of a quantitative assessment of distance between transformed sequences using a metric.

As part of the experiment three estimates using three different metrics were considered. Selected metrics:

- DTW distance – the total path costs between two sequences. It is the value of the last element of the transformation matrix obtained as a result of DTW.
- Correlation coefficient – Pearson's correlation coefficient:

$$R_{p,q} = \frac{\text{cov}(p, q)}{\sqrt{s_p^2 s_q^2}},$$ (1)

where $R_{p,q}$ is correlation coefficient between sequences p and q,
$cov(p,q)$ is covariance of p and q,
$s^2{}_p$, $s^2{}_q$ are standard deviations.
- Minkowski distance:

$$d_{Mink}(p, q) = \sqrt[\alpha]{\sum_{i=1}^{n} (|p_i - q_i|)^\alpha},$$ (2)

where n is sequence length of p and q,
α is an order of Minkowski distance, in this experiment $\alpha = 3$. This value was selected from the range of the most appropriate values for this parameter [9].

Thus, 1020 recordings were selected for analysis and their estimates were obtained. The purpose of the experiment - to choose the metrics that must be the best way consistent with expert opinion.

Expert estimates are binary (either 0 or 1). The estimates of the algorithm are presented as real numbers. For the DTW distance and the Minkowski distance, the estimate is a positive real number. For the correlation coefficient, the estimate is in the range from −1 to 1. To compare the estimates with each other, decisions were made to convert all estimates to a binary form.

Denote expert estimates as a set of values $X = \{X_1, X_2, ..., X_{1020}\}$, estimates obtained using the DTW distance metric as $Y = \{Y_1, Y_2, ..., Y_{1020}\}$, estimates obtained using the correlation coefficient as $Z = \{Z_1, Z_2, ..., Z_{1020}\}$ and estimates obtained using the Minkowski distance metric as $W = \{W_1, W_2, ..., W_{1020}\}$.

For DTW distance and Minkowski distance, the smaller the estimate, the better. At the same time, for the estimates obtained using the correlation coefficient, the larger the value, the closer to the reference, which means better quality. Therefore, the binary conversion functions are different for these two groups. The functions of converting estimates into binary form for W and W (metrics DTW distance and Minkowski distance) are as follows:

$$F1(Y_i) = \begin{cases} 1, & \text{if } Y_i \leq Y_t, \\ 0, & \text{otherwise} \end{cases}, \tag{3}$$

where Y_t is threshold value.

$$F2(W_i) = \begin{cases} 1, & \text{if } W_i \leq W_t, \\ 0, & \text{otherwise} \end{cases}, \tag{4}$$

where W_t is threshold value.

The converting function for a set of Z values (correlation coefficient metric) is as follows:

$$F3(Z_i) = \begin{cases} 1, & \text{if } Z_i \geq Z_t, \\ 0, & \text{otherwise} \end{cases}, \tag{5}$$

where Z_t is threshold value.

Threshold values were adjusted for each patient's recording set separately. The selection was carried out using optimization methods. The function of the following form was optimized:

$$F(Z_i) = \sum_{i=1}^{n} (X_i - F1(Y_i))^2 \rightarrow 0, \tag{6}$$

where n is number of recordings for the selected patient.

The optimization for the functions F2 and F3 was carried out in a similar way. The value of the function was minimized, the optimization method is evolutionary search. 45 threshold values were selected (3 threshold values for each of the metrics in 15 patients). Thus, all quantitative estimates were converted into binary form.

Threshold values and errors for each patient are presented in Table 1. An error is understood as the ratio of the number of discrepancies between the sets of values X and Y, Z, W, respectively (that is, between expert estimates and converted quantitative estimates) to the total number of recordings for a particular patient. For each metric, a range of possible values is indicated (in the first row of the table). Also, Table 1 shows the common errors for each of the metrics for the full amount of data.

Table 1. Threshold values and errors.

Patient	Yt (0 to inf)	Error for Y	Zt (−1 to 1)	Error for Z	Wt (0 to inf)	Error for W
1	198.89	7/90	0.025	25/90	0.69	19/90
2	149.63	19/90	0.087	31/90	1.42	25/90
3	61.41	5/90	0.07	38/90	0.65	31/90
4	70.44	19/90	−0.19	31/90	0.33	28/90
5	155.27	11/60	−0.11	24/60	1.12	16/60
6	94.5	9/60	0.013	20/60	1.36	19/60
7	42.67	19/60	−0.69	12/60	0.64	11/60
8	53.3	9/60	−0.11	14/60	0.62	9/60
9	26.33	11/60	0.023	17/60	0.5	15/60
10	60.18	8/60	0.01	15/60	0.5	11/60
11	39.22	8/60	0.392	24/60	0.61	10/60
12	31.5	12/60	0.41	19/60	0.34	19/60
13	36.32	11/60	0.15	20/60	0.71	18/60
14	23.73	13/60	0.059	23/60	0.46	17/60
15	29.96	10/60	0.101	21/60	0.3986	22/60
Total error		161/1020		334/1020		270/1020

3   Results

After receiving expert and quantitative estimates, converting them into a binary form, and counting the partial and total number of errors, the data obtained were analyzed. An example of the data obtained for the recordings, the spectrograms of which are presented in Sect. 2.1, is shown in Table 2. Since the first recording was taken as a reference, there is only 1 assessment for it - an expert one, and it is equal to 1. For displaying in the table, the recordings were marked in the following way: recording represented in Fig. 2 was named recording # 2, recording represented in Fig. 3 was named recording # 3, recording represented in Fig. 4 was named recording # 4. Table 2 presents both the initial quantitative estimate and converted to a binary form estimate. The threshold values for conversion are in Table 1 (patient #1).

   The Friedman test was applied to the sequences of transformed estimates. The resulting average ranks are presented in Table 3. The chi-square value is 126.115. The lowest average rank for estimates obtained using the DTW distance metric, the highest rank for estimates using the correlation coefficient. From the given values, it can be concluded the DTW distance can be considered the best metric for application in the framework of the task of assessing syllable intelligibility.

Table 2. Expert, quantitative and converted estimates.

	Recording # 2		Recording # 3		Recording # 4	
	Estimate	Converted estimate	Estimate	Converted estimate	Estimate	Converted estimate
Expert	1		0		1	
DTW distance	2.542	1	450.442	0	96.354	1
Correlation coefficient	0.047	1	0.117	0	0.023	0
Minkowski distance	0.067	1	0.053	1	0.054	1

Table 3. Average ranks obtained using the Friedman test.

	Average rank
DTW distance	1.86
Correlation coefficient	2.12
Minkowski distance	2.02

4 Conclusion

As a result of the analysis of the obtained data, it can be concluded that the optimal metric for application is the DTW distance. With the help of this metric, the estimates obtained are in the best agreement with expert estimates. Accordingly, this metric is used in the automated speech quality assessment algorithm. The algorithm is included in the software package used in the process of speech rehabilitation at the Research Institute of Oncology in Tomsk.

A direct comparison of the values of expert and quantitative assessments is not possible. This is due to the fact that there is a significant difference in the expert estimating method and methods of calculating quantitative estimates. When an expert estimate is given, and if the entire syllable is mispronounced, and if only one phoneme in the syllable is mispronounced, the estimate is 0. When using methods of obtaining quantitative evaluation for these situations, the estimates are different - in the second situation, the estimate will be better (more or less, depending on the metric used) than in the first. This can also explain the relatively large value of the total error calculated in Table 2.

One of the possible directions for further research is the task of selecting combinations of metrics that can give a result better than the DTW distance in the framework of this experiment. However, when assessing syllable intelligibility and speech quality, it is necessary to take into account the need to conduct the assessment in real time or close to it. This is justified by the need to implement the principle of biofeedback in the process of assessing speech in speech rehabilitation. The implementation of this principle allows the patient to immediately, upon pronouncing, find out the assessment of the quality of his speech, which stimulates the patient to further exercise and progress in restoring speech function.

Acknowledgments. The reported study was funded by RFBR, project number 20-37-90082.

References

1. Kaprin, A.D., Starinskiy, V.V., Shahzadova, A.O.: Malignancies in Russia in 2019 (Morbidity and Mortality), p. 252. MNIOI name of P.A. Herzen, Moscow (2020)
2. Method for squamous cell cancer of oral cavity and throat treatment. Boyko, A.V., Gevorkov, A.R., Plavnik, R.N., Bagova, S.Z., Khmelevsky, E.V., Kaprin, A.D.: Patent for invention RU 2715550 C2, 28.02.2020.
3. Oral cavity cancer treatment method. Kaprin, A.D., Ivanov, A.A., Sevryukov, F.E., Panaseikin, Yu.A., and others.: Patent for invention RU 2713530 C2, 05.02.2020.
4. Kulakov, A.A., et al.: Phonation and speech recovery in cancer patients with maxillary defects. Head and neck tumors **1**(2012), 55–60 (2012)
5. Choynzonov, E.L., Balatskaya, L.N., Dubskiy, S.V.: The Quality of Life of Cancer Patients. Printing manufactory, Tomsk (2011)
6. Standard GOST R 50840-95 Voice over paths of communication. Methods for assessing the quality, legibility and recognition, p. 234. Publishing Standards, Moscow (1995)
7. Novokhrestova, D., Kostyuchenko, E., Meshcheryakov, R.: Choice of signal short-term energy parameter for assessing speech intelligibility in the process of speech rehabilitation. In: Karpov, A., Jokisch, O., Potapova, R. (eds.) SPECOM 2018. LNCS (LNAI), vol. 11096, pp. 461–469. Springer, Cham (2018). https://doi.org/10.1007/978-3-319-99579-3_48
8. Kostyuchenko, E., Meshcheryakov, R., Ignatieva, D., Pyatkov, A., Choynzonov, E., Balatskaya, L.: Correlation normalization of syllables and comparative evaluation of pronunciation quality in speech rehabilitation. In: Karpov, A., Potapova, R., Mporas, I. (eds.) SPECOM 2017. LNCS (LNAI), vol. 10458, pp. 262–271. Springer, Cham (2017). https://doi.org/10.1007/978-3-319-66429-3_25
9. Kostyuchenko, E., Roman, M., Ignatieva, D., Pyatkov, A., Choynzonov, E., Balatskaya, L.: Evaluation of the speech quality during rehabilitation after surgical treatment of the cancer of oral cavity and oropharynx based on a comparison of the fourier spectra. In: Ronzhin, A., Potapova, R., Németh, G. (eds.) SPECOM 2016. LNCS (LNAI), vol. 9811, pp. 287–295. Springer, Cham (2016). https://doi.org/10.1007/978-3-319-43958-7_34
10. Alimuradov, A.K., Tychkov, A.Y.: Application of the method empirical mode decomposition for the study of voiced speech in the problem of detecting human stress emotions. PNRPU Bulletin. Electrotechnics, Informational Technologies, Control Systems **35**, 7–29 (2020)
11. Markitantov, M., Verkholyak, O.: Automatic recognition of speaker age and gender based on deep neural networks. In: Salah, A.A., Karpov, A., Potapova, R. (eds.) SPECOM 2019. LNCS (LNAI), vol. 11658, pp. 327–336. Springer, Cham (2019). https://doi.org/10.1007/978-3-030-26061-3_34
12. Lyakso, E.E., et al.: Voice portrait of a child with typical and atypical development. Publishing and Printing Association of Higher Educational Institutions, Saint Petersburg (2020)
13. Kostuchenko, E., et al.: The evaluation process automation of phrase and word intelligibility using speech recognition systems. In: Salah, A.A., Karpov, A., Potapova, R. (eds.) SPECOM 2019. LNCS (LNAI), vol. 11658, pp. 237–246. Springer, Cham (2019). https://doi.org/10.1007/978-3-030-26061-3_25
14. Translator of Russian words in phonetic transcription. https://easypronunciation.com/ru/russian-phonetic-transcription-converter#phonetic_transcription. Accessed 14 June 2021

Methods for Using Class Based N-gram Language Models in the Kaldi Toolkit

Edvin Pakoci[1]([⊠]) [iD] and Branislav Popović[2,3,4] [iD]

[1] AlfaNum Speech Technologies, Bulevar vojvode Stepe 40, 21000 Novi Sad, Serbia
edvin.pakoci@alfanum.co.rs
[2] Faculty of Technical Sciences, Department of Power, Electronic and Telecommunication Engineering, University of Novi Sad, Trg Dositeja Obradovića 6, 21000 Novi Sad, Serbia
[3] Department of Music Production and Sound Design, Academy of Arts, Alfa BK University, Nemanjina 28, 11000 Belgrade, Serbia
[4] Computer Programming Agency Code85 Odžaci, Železnička 51, 25250 Odžaci, Serbia

Abstract. This paper explains in detail several methods for utilization of class based *n*-gram language models for automatic speech recognition, within the Kaldi speech recognition framework. It reexamines an existing implementation for word-level grammars, and then presents two methods of converting ARPA-format language models into a corresponding weighted finite state transducer which is then used for decoding in Kaldi in a usual way. One of the methods relies on implicit expansion of class *n*-grams within the language model during the conversion into the transducer, and the other one on explicit expansion of the ARPA file by changing class *n*-gram entries into an array of regular class instance *n*-grams, while the conversion procedure remains unchanged. Some limitations and optional restrictions for the procedures are discussed as well. The proposed methods are tested on a model trained on a Serbian judicial corpus which includes classes for all types of personal nouns (first names, last names, place names, street names and organization names).

Keywords: Language modeling · Kaldi · ARPA · Class based · Serbian

1 Introduction

Data sparsity is a well-known issue in language modeling [1], especially when it comes to more general models, i.e., models with large vocabularies that are not bound to a specific domain, or models for domains where there is a large number of words that are rare in any training corpus, such as personal names. The problem gets even more pronounced in the case of highly inflective languages, such as Serbian, where each word has many different forms – cases, grammatical numbers, and grammatical genders [2].

A class-based *n*-gram language model can be employed to represent a large number of out-of-vocabulary (OOV) words, or words that are otherwise badly modeled due to missing contexts in the training corpus. It has already been shown that such models can help with reducing perplexities as well as word error rates on different test sets [3, 4].

© Springer Nature Switzerland AG 2021
A. Karpov and R. Potapova (Eds.): SPECOM 2021, LNAI 12997, pp. 492–503, 2021.
https://doi.org/10.1007/978-3-030-87802-3_45

This paper examines various ways to include such language models for Serbian, using the Kaldi language toolkit.

In the rest of this section, word classes in general, along with their usage in language modeling, as well as the Kaldi speech recognition toolkit, are discussed. In Sect. 2, previously completed relevant work related to a method for using word classes in Kaldi is described. The proposed methods are given in Sect. 3. Finally, the results and conclusions are all summarized in Sect. 4.

1.1 Word Classes

Word classes can be defined depending on the desired use of the automatic speech recognition (ASR) system. One way to reduce sparsity is to combine words based on their Part-of-Speech (POS) tags or to perform an automatic clustering of words to better model the contextual information [5]. Another way is to create word classes based on semantics and to combine them with more generalized word-based models [6]. Several experiments have already been conducted for Serbian, where POS-based or automatically extracted word classes have been used both in n-gram models in order to improve calculations of back-off probabilities [7], as well as in neural network based models with output layer factorization [8].

A much more favorable situation occurs when there are already redacted parts of textual corpora related to personal names, locations and organizations, e.g. in anonymized texts from courts and other similar institutions for the dictation of judicial and other legal documents. In cases like these, the classes are basically pre-determined: first names, last names, settlements (cities, towns, villages), streets and organizations, in all the possible cases – for Serbian, these are nominative, genitive, dative/locative (dative and locative have the same form in Serbian), accusative and instrumental. Of course, additional classes are allowed as well. Such a corpus will be discussed in Sect. 4 of this paper.

For the training purposes, the corpus has to include class sequences instead of word sequences (if all words are clustered into classes), or a mixture of class and word sequences (e.g. in the third case mentioned above). Classes should also be non-overlapping (reason for that will be given later in the paper). In this case, the standard word sequence probability for language modeling has to be adjusted. For the sake of simplicity, the original bigram formula for a word sequence $w = \{w_1, w_2, \cdots, w_m\}$ of length m is examined:

$$P(w) = P(w_1) \prod_{i=2}^{m} P(w_i|w_{i-1}). \tag{1}$$

If any given word w_i is part of a class c_i, where c_i can be equivalent to w_i (if it is not part of any class), the formula above needs to be rewritten as:

$$P(w) = P(w_1|c_1)P(c_1) \prod_{i=2}^{m} P(w_i|c_i)P(c_i|c_{i-1}). \tag{2}$$

The within-class probabilities $P(w_i|c_i)$ can be estimated by dividing the number of occurrences of the word w_i in a given corpus with the total number of occurrences of all words within the class c_i in the same corpus.

1.2   The Kaldi Speech Recognition Toolkit

The work described in this paper is implemented within the Kaldi speech recognition framework [9], which is widely used in the ASR community, as it is open-source and provides users with contemporary algorithms and model training recipes which often lead to state-of-the-art results. In the decoding stage, Kaldi uses a graph based on weighted finite state transducers (WFSTs) [10], which combines separate graphs for language model or grammar (this graph models probabilities of word sequences), pronunciation dictionary (i.e., the lexicon, which provides possible phoneme sequences, i.e., pronunciations of words), context (it provides mapping of context-independent to context-dependent phonemes) and acoustic model (more specifically its topology; it provides mapping of context-dependent phonemes to specific transitions between the states of the underlying acoustic model) [9]. All of these graphs are implemented using the OpenFst library [11]. In the rest of this paper, various methods used to modify the language model, i.e., the grammar (G) transducer will be explained.

2   Relevant Work

In [12], the authors have found a way to add word classes into Kaldi by modifying the initial G transducer, which contains class labels. For each of the word classes, a simple sub-language model WFST is created, which contains a path through any of the words within the given class, as well as a couple of class-specific disambiguation symbols at the beginning and at the end in order to keep the decoding graph determinizable. Transitions containing class labels in the original G transducer are then replaced with the appropriate sub-language model WFST using the OpenFst *fstreplace* operation. Finally, the output G transducer is minimized to reduce its size and complexity, while the class-specific disambiguation symbols are added to the lexicon (L) transducer as self-loops, just so that the word classes don't get cut during the following composition of L and G transducers. At the end of this procedure, there are no class labels left in the output G transducer.

The above mentioned procedure was evaluated using small language models with vocabularies of up to 6000 words, for systems such as an automatic spoken dialog telephone system or a more open-domain question-answering system. The number of word classes ranged from 1 to 14 (e.g. city names, celebrities), usually containing not more than 100 words. Although the proposed method slightly improved the word error rate in comparison to the original system which doesn't use class labels, it was not proven that the method can work for larger vocabularies. In our experiments, this approach proved to be useful for more restrictive grammar-like language models, but not in the case of large vocabulary ASR (LVASR) systems based on 3-gram class models, and especially not for larger classes such as personal names and settlements (containing thousands of possibilities to choose from). In these cases, the procedure of building the modified G transducer and the following composition with L was usually very memory-demanding and slow, and the complex nature of LVASR 3-gram language models with back-off probabilities lead to enormous decoding graphs (several gigabytes in size) and also some unexpected behavior (e.g. the recognizer tended to get stuck in a loop recognizing only different personal names or other classes' instances, likely since all of them were equally probable in this approach, while also being extremely slow, i.e., not even close to real time, and memory consuming).

3   Proposed Methods for Modifying the Kaldi Transducer

Both of the approaches proposed in this paper rely on modifying the procedure for the creation of the initial G transducer (*arpa2fst*), instead of modifying it later. They are similar in nature, since they both target the ARPA file format in which *n*-gram models are usually stored in, and process the ARPA lines which include class *n*-grams (i.e., where at least one word in the *n*-gram is a class name). For the first procedure, class *n*-grams are implicitly expanded into class instance *n*-grams while adding new states and transitions to the G transducer (the ones related to the current ARPA line). For the second procedure, class *n*-grams are explicitly expanded by replacing the current line in the ARPA file with new lines for each class instance *n*-gram, and in the end, the new expanded ARPA language model, which includes no class *n*-grams any more, is put through the usual process of conversion into a WFST.

The approach given in Sect. 2 as well as the above proposed approaches are briefly summarized in Fig. 1, where method differences are made apparent.

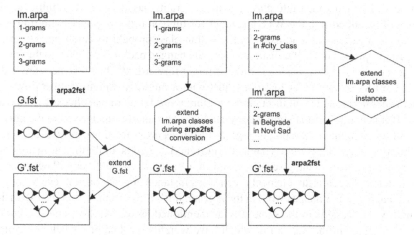

Fig. 1. Diagram of methods of inclusion of class instances into the G transducer: the baseline method (left), the new implicit method (center), and the new explicit method (right).

In relation to the standard G transducer creation procedure in Kaldi, the class definitions in a specific format are used as an additional input. For each class name, an array of possible class instances has to be defined (not required to be unique to a single class by the procedure itself), which are also paired with weights. The weights can be probabilities or counts, previously calculated on the desired corpus. In any case, the weights are transformed into probabilities (if necessary) and then normalized (all between 0–1, and adding up to 1), and then the instances are sorted by weight (larger weights first).

3.1 Implicit Expansion of Class N-Grams

The usual procedure in Kaldi involves conversion of words into integer identifiers, and simply adding a few new transitions into the output WFST. For each but the highest order n-grams, this means adding a new WFST state for the current n-gram and a transition from the parent state (the parent $\{n - 1\}$-gram, or the special empty-string state if $n = 1$) to the new state with the desired weight (probability) and the identifier of the last word in the n-gram as label, as well as a back-off transition from the new state to an existing $\{n - 1\}$-gram state (not the parent, but the "tail" $\{n - 1\}$-gram, i.e., if the first word in the n-gram is dropped out, or again the empty-string state if $n = 1$) with the specified back-off weight. On the other hand, each of the highest order n-grams only create new transitions from the parent $\{n - 1\}$-gram state to the "tail" $\{n - 1\}$-gram state with the specified weight (probability) and the last word identifier as label. For example, in a trigram model, a transition from the "A B" state with the label "C" to the "B C" state with a certain weight represents the trigram "A B C" (that "C" comes after "A B" has been seen) with the probability defined by its weight, after which any of the possible transitions from "B C" represents the next possible trigram. During the procedure, if the current n-gram ends with the end-of-sentence (EOS) marker, the parent $\{n - 1\}$-gram state is simply made final (terminal).

The changes in the new procedure come when a line with a class n-gram is read. Each of these will be expanded into class instance n-grams based on class definitions, new states will be added into the WFST (except for highest order n-grams) with transition weights from parent states adjusted by the within-class probability (multiplied by it), as well as appropriate back-off transitions using unchanged back-off weights. In the case of unigrams ($n = 1$), the expansion is rather straight forward: all class instances are added into the WFST as any other unigrams, just with a modified weight (probability). For higher order n-grams, we go through the n-gram word by word and check if it's a class name. If it is not, a word is simply converted into an identifier and saved to the current index of all elements in the output n-gram instances array for this class n-gram – let's call this array A_{out}. If it is a class name, the current A_{out} will be multiplied as many times as there are instances in the given class, and an instance word identifier will be put at the current index of each array element (each class instance appears once in every copy of the original A_{out}). For the last word in the n-gram, if it's a class name, after the expansion we modify the weights in the same way as mentioned above. At this point, we cut off instance n-grams in the A_{out} array which have weights (probabilities) below a certain threshold. This cutoff weight is usually equal to the pruning cutoff probability used while creating the class n-gram ARPA model, but it can be different (lower, or even higher – in that case, even some regular n-grams can be additionally cut off), and therefore used to control the size of the output WFST. If all instance n-grams of a class n-gram are cut due to low probability, an appropriate warning is displayed, and future child $\{n + 1\}$-grams will also automatically be excluded. In the end, all surviving elements of A_{out} are processed one by one as any regular n-grams.

Another important part of the procedure which saves a lot of time is the fact that the resulting A_{out} array for each input n-gram is being saved after it's formed, for all but the highest order n-grams (because those would not be used) and unigrams (there is really no need to do that since the instance array for class unigrams basically already exists in the input class definition). This saved set of instance n-gram combinations is then simply taken from the save location to be used when we get a parent class $\{n-1\}$-gram (i.e., if we take out the last word) in the future reading of higher order n-grams in the ARPA file, instead of recreating all the combinations again from scratch (with this, we can jump straight to the last word).

Two more optional parameters exist in the procedure, limiting the total number of created instance n-grams from one class n-gram, as well as the size of the saved set of instance n-gram combinations. One is the limiting count of highest order n-grams N_{max}, which limits the number of class instances used for the class n-gram expansion from parent $\{n-1\}$-gram to n-gram (N_{ce}). For each order $n > 1$, these class expansion limits are calculated as:

$$N_{ce}(n) = \sqrt[n]{N_{max}}. \tag{3}$$

The number of unigrams is not limited, as we don't want to out-right exclude any of the instances from the language model. These limits have an effect if there would be more than N_{max} expanded n-gram instances in total if all class entries are taken, and in that case the top N_{ce} class instances by weight are taken. If it is not the case, the limit is ignored. It is generally useful to control the expansion (not let A_{out} to explode too much), and to shorten the procedure to a manageable duration, because when dealing with large classes with thousands of word instances, the amount of possible higher class n-gram combinations can easily get into millions, or even billions in some cases. The number of saved instance combinations for later expansion (N_{sc}) is also limited, for similar reasons. For each $n > 1 \,\&\&\, n < max\_order$, these limits are defined as:

$$N_{sc}(n) = \sqrt[n+1]{N_{max}}. \tag{4}$$

The other optional parameter is a modifier to the previously explained limit, for class n-grams which include more than one class name. This parameter can be used in order to raise the limit for such class n-grams, to include more instances of all classes (since the limit is much more easily reached if there are more classes in the given n-gram), therefore allowing better modeling of more contexts. Using this c_m value, as well as the number of classes N_{cl} in the given n-gram, we calculate a coefficient k for any order $n > 1$:

$$k = \begin{cases} (N_{cl} - 1) \cdot c_m, N_{cl} > 1 \\ 1, N_{cl} \leq 1 \end{cases}. \tag{5}$$

This coefficient transforms the Eqs. (3) and (4) into:

$$N_{ce}(n) = \sqrt[n]{k \cdot N_{max}}, \tag{6}$$

$$N_{sc}(n) = \sqrt[n+1]{k \cdot N_{max}}. \tag{7}$$

As mentioned before, all the limiting is performed by weight, and that is why it's important to sort all class instances by weight beforehand.

The possible issues with this procedure include the inability to normalize the probabilities on the level of the whole model, because we do the expansion and cutting on-the-go. Because of the same reason, it cannot properly handle the situation if different class n-grams can form the same instance n-grams, so it benefits from having unique instances in each class, as well as instances which do not exist elsewhere in the vocabulary. Also, it is impossible to easily predict the total output number of n-grams by order, or to deduce what exactly to do to reach a certain desired n-gram count. Furthermore, the procedure can still get quite long and memory-consuming for larger classes, so very often relatively strict limiting parameters are required. Therefore, a second similar procedure was implemented, which works on the level of the ARPA file instead, and leaves the original generation of G transducer untouched.

3.2   Explicit Expansion of Class N-Grams

The second procedure is more straight-forward, as it inputs an ARPA file, and outputs another one – the first one has class names, while the other one has class instances. It also has the optional parameter N_{max} and the n-gram cutoff probability (or log-probability) like the first procedure, as well as one additional limiting factor, explained in the following paragraphs.

Firstly, for each ARPA file line, it is determined how many class names does the n-gram contain. If it is zero, the n-gram will generally remain the same – it is saved as-is to the output n-grams array A_{all}, except in the case when it has already been seen, i.e., it's already in A_{all} (a class n-gram may in theory create an instance n-gram which already exists elsewhere in the ARPA file), in which case the previously seen n-gram from A_{all} is updated – the log-probabilities are added to each other, and the lower of the two back-off weights remain (the larger possible cost of backing off). If the n-gram is new (generally, that should be the case), it is saved to A_{all}, as well as to the existing n-grams mapping structure M_{ex} (here, it maps itself into a set containing only one element – just itself).

If it was a class n-gram, we first check if it's a unigram, because that's the straight-forward case – we expand it to all class instances, add up the class log-probability and the within-class log-probability for each concrete class instance, and save all of them to A_{all}. The class-to-instance mapping is also saved to M_{ex}. For higher class n-grams, the count of last word instances N_l is obtained first: this can be 1, if it's not a class name, or a larger number than 1 if it is. This count is also limited by the cutoff n-gram log-probability – most of the time, not all class instances are eligible due to their combined class log-probability + instance log-probability being below cutoff. Then, the parent $\{n - 1\}$-gram is searched for in M_{ex}. If it's not there, that means it has been cut due to low probability, and the current ARPA line is skipped completely. If it is there, we obtain the set of instance $\{n-1\}$-grams to which it maps to (if there are class names in the $\{n - 1\}$-gram as well, the set can contain more than one element). Let's label the set size as N_p. If all the last word instances are to be used in the expansion, N_p must be less or equal to N_{max}/N_l. If that is not the case, the procedure lowers N_p. The new value is calculated using the formula:

$$N_p' = \sqrt[n+1]{N_{max}^n}. \tag{8}$$

If the new value N_p' is smaller than N_{max}/N_l, it is set to exactly N_{max}/N_l. In this case, all N_l last word instances are going to be used in the class n-gram expansion. If

N_p' is larger than N_{max}/N_l, during the expansion the procedure will take as many last word instances as possible by going through them from the most to the least probable one, adding N_p' new class n-gram instances for each, while keeping the total number of n-gram instances at most N_{max}. After reaching N_{max}, or going through all N_l instances of the last word, the expansion halts. It also halts if it reaches an instance which lowers the class n-gram log-probability below the cutoff value.

Before saving the expanded class n-gram instances to A_{all} and to M_{ex}, there is an additional check which all instances need to pass. It's the absolute class n-gram instance probability cutoff parameter P_{min}. It relates to the product of within-class probabilities of each word in the n-gram, and helps to limit the expansion of n-grams containing several large classes in particular (e.g. a last name following a first name). Words that are not part of classes have a probability of 1. If the mentioned product is less than P_{min}, the n-gram instance is not saved. During testing, this parameter had the most effect on the procedure speed, memory consumption and the output model size (if it was high enough, the N_{max} parameter could practically be turned off).

Finally, the expanded instance n-grams that pass all the checks are saved to both A_{all} and M_{ex}. If any of the instance n-grams have been seen previously, the matching n-gram from A_{all} is updated instead of putting a new entry into the array, in the same way as described for regular n-grams.

In the end, all the entries from A_{all} are dumped into the output ARPA file, and the regular conversion into a WFST follows.

This procedure allows easier control over the size of the output language model, while even giving an opportunity to normalize the model probabilities, but that did not seem to be an immediate necessity. It also properly takes care of copies of instance n-grams coming from different class n-grams (if such cases exist). It is faster, even including the conversion into a WFST, and if the right parameters are chosen (especially P_{min}), it is also a lot less memory consuming.

One might consider an expansion of the language model training corpus (e.g. by changing classes to certain instances in some of the sentences) instead of this ARPA expansion method, but that may lead to multiple artificial copies of parts of the corpus, especially if working with large classes, which is not recommended for n-gram model training. Furthermore, the problem of multiple classes in the same sentence would have to be solved.

4   Testing and Conclusion

The new methods for utilization of class n-grams in Kaldi were tested on a new Serbian judicial corpus. As hinted in Sect. 1, these are anonymized texts from courts, which means that there are redacted parts of texts related to people, locations and organizations. Each redacted word or phrase was replaced with a marker-word, describing if the original word was one of the following: male first name, female first name, last name, large settlement (city or larger town), small settlement (smaller town, village or part of a larger settlement), street or organization. Also, separate markers were used for all 5 different word cases. The corpus includes around 200,000 generally long sentences and 6.8 million words in total, as well as around 61,000 different words (excluding classes and their instances).

As mentioned before, there are 7 categories, 5 cases each, meaning 35 classes in total. Additionally, since most settlement names (especially in the masculine grammatical gender) have the same nominative and accusative form, the final number of classes ended up being 33 (nominative and accusative classes for both large and small settlements got merged together).

The lists of nominative class instances were obtained from different sources (previously gathered data, existing corpora, Wikipedia, etc.). Taking into account the intended use of the language model (dictation of judicial documents in Serbian courts), we limited the lists to Serbian names, settlements and streets (for organizations, some well-known international ones were allowed too). Using the Serbian morphologic dictionary [13], as well as some rule-based procedures, the other case lists were generated. The instance counts for creating class definitions were obtained by counting them in the largest publicly available Serbian corpus, *srWaC* [14]. Some counts were manually adjusted due to errors in the nominative lists or other unfortunate circumstances (e.g. the last name "Tesla" has a rather high count because of Nikola Tesla and the company of the same name, but as a last name it is very rare).

We also made sure there is no overlap between classes, and also that no class instance exists elsewhere in the vocabulary. This was done by adding distinguishing suffixes to all class members (e.g. '_1', '_2', etc.). This step was important because of the desire to use a reccurent neural network (RNN) based language model for rescoring the lattice after the initial decoding procedure [15]. The RNN had to be trained on the class corpus (it only takes classes as input, not instances), therefore during rescoring it needs to know the correct class of each instance that is found in the lattice – there must be no ambiguity.

The total number of instances for each category (nominative) is given in the following Table 1. The obvious outlier are last names, with more than 50,000 instances. Far behind are streets (more than 9000) and small settlements (more than 5000). By far the smallest category is large settlements (about 100 instances). To combat excessive number of combinations of e.g. last names, it was decided that for all cases except nominative, if the instance word form does not appear at least once in the whole *srWaC* corpus, it is excluded from the class. This rule was used for the three largest categories.

Table 1. Number of nominative instances for each test category.

Category	Examples	#Instances
Male first names	Aleksandar, Milan, Nikola, Dragan	1656
Female first names	Jovana, Marija, Jelena, Ana, Ivana	1104
Last names	Jovanović, Nikolić, Petrović, Ilić	54582
Large settlements	Beograd, Novi Sad, Niš, Zrenjanin	102
Small settlements	Lazarevac, Palić, Vračar, Kostolac	5168
Streets	Matice srpske, Kosovska, Ive Andrića	9644
Organizations	RTS, MUP, Telekom, Samsung, JAT	1386

Of the two desribed methods from Sect. 3, the second one seemed more useful in practice, as it allows more control of the result, and can actually produce a model including exclusively most probable n-grams in the corpus, i.e., all n-grams above the cutoff (if N_{max} is not used), without running into time or memory issues, by limiting the absolute n-gram probability for class n-grams (so too rare combinations are not used). The following Table 2 presents some results regarding the size of the output models. The input is the root model trained on the judicial corpus with class names, with the pruning cutoff probability of 10^{-7}. This was also the n-gram cutoff probability during the procedure. All the models were generated on a machine with 32 GB of RAM. All the procedures (without conversion to WFST) lasted between 1 and 17 min.

Table 2. Sizes of different output models in relation to the input root model.

P_{min}	N_{max}	#Unigrams	#Bigrams	#Trigrams	#n-grams
(root)		61 k	989 k	358 k	1.4 M
$5 \cdot 10^{-3}$	10 k	208 k	1.8 M	5.5 M	7.5 M
$5 \cdot 10^{-3}$	100 k	208 k	2 M	9.8 M	12 M
$5 \cdot 10^{-3}$	5 M	208 k	2 M	17 M	19 M
$1 \cdot 10^{-3}$	1 k	208 k	2.7 M	3.8 M	6.7 M
$1 \cdot 10^{-3}$	10 k	208 k	4.2 M	25 M	29 M
$1 \cdot 10^{-3}$	30 k	208 k	7.2 M	68 M	75 M
$5 \cdot 10^{-4}$	1 k	208 k	3.6 M	4.5 M	8.3 M
$5 \cdot 10^{-4}$	10 k	208 k	5.1 M	25 M	31 M
$5 \cdot 10^{-4}$	30 k	208 k	8.4 M	71 M	79 M
$1 \cdot 10^{-4}$	1 k	208 k	6.4 M	6.6 M	13 M
$1 \cdot 10^{-4}$	10 k	208 k	8.5 M	28 M	37 M
$1 \cdot 10^{-4}$	30 k	208 k	12 M	73 M	85 M
$5 \cdot 10^{-5}$	1 k	208 k	6.7 M	6.8 M	14 M
$5 \cdot 10^{-5}$	10 k	208 k	10 M	30 M	40 M
$5 \cdot 10^{-5}$	30 k	208 k	14 M	75 M	89 M

Table 3 provides some additional information about the created models – the ARPA file size in megabytes, the number of states and arcs in the resulting WFST as well as the calculated perplexity (PPL) on a small test corpus. The test corpus for perplexity calculation is a random subset of 10,000 sentences from the judicial corpus, which includes about 345,000 words in total, 21,000 of which are unique. The class identifiers from the original corpus were changed into random class instances (but taking instance weights into account when choosing). The original 61,000-word model gave a PPL value of 28.61 – all the tested expanded models had 208,000 words, which needs to be taken into account when comparing. Naturally, the more complex models gave better (smaller) PPL values, but the improvement became a lot less significant after moving from P_{min} of

$5 \cdot 10^{-3}$ to P_{min} of $1 \cdot 10^{-3}$. The optimal N_{max} value should be weighed against the output model size (and speed in practice).

Table 3. Output model complexity and calculated perplexity.

P_{min}	N_{max}	Size (MB)	#States	#Arcs	PPL
(root)		39	1.1 M	2.5 M	28.61
$5 \cdot 10^{-3}$	10 k	244	2.2 M	10 M	35.26
$5 \cdot 10^{-3}$	100 k	411	2.5 M	15 M	35.19
$5 \cdot 10^{-3}$	5 M	686	3.3 M	23 M	35.17
$1 \cdot 10^{-3}$	1 k	208	3 M	10 M	33.68
$1 \cdot 10^{-3}$	10 k	987	5 M	34 M	33.01
$1 \cdot 10^{-3}$	30 k	2600	9 M	84 M	32.56
$5 \cdot 10^{-4}$	1 k	256	4 M	12 M	33.35
$5 \cdot 10^{-4}$	10 k	1034	5.9 M	36 M	32.76
$5 \cdot 10^{-4}$	30 k	2724	10 M	89 M	32.27
$1 \cdot 10^{-4}$	1 k	405	7 M	20 M	33.02
$1 \cdot 10^{-4}$	10 k	1219	9.7 M	46 M	32.48
$1 \cdot 10^{-4}$	30 k	2918	14 M	99 M	32.1
$5 \cdot 10^{-5}$	1 k	422	7.4 M	21 M	33.01
$5 \cdot 10^{-5}$	10 k	1331	12 M	52 M	32.41
$5 \cdot 10^{-5}$	30 k	3031	17 M	106 M	32.05

In conclusion, the paper presented two new methods for using class n-gram language models within the Kaldi framework. The new methods are more suited for large, complex models, e.g. for LVASR, than the previous approach. They can be used in combination with RNN language model rescoring too. The second method – explicit expansion of the ARPA file, allows easier control over the output n-gram counts and language model size, and properly solves situations where different class n-grams have identical instances, or they overlap with regular n-grams. The procedures are relatively fast, and work even with very large classes, allowing the inclusion of many words that would otherwise be OOV. The immediate future work should include word error rate testing to find the optimal combination of parameters, as well as testing in practice.

Acknowledgments. This research was supported by the Science Fund of the Republic of Serbia, #6524560, AI-S-ADAPT, and by the Serbian Ministry of Education, Science and Technological Development through the project no. 451 03-68/2020-14/200156: "Innovative Scientific and Artistic Research from the Faculty of Technical Sciences Activity Domain".

References

1. Allison, B., Guthrie, D., Guthrie, L.: Another look at the data sparsity problem. In: Sojka, P., Kopeček, I., Pala, K. (eds.) TSD 2006. LNCS (LNAI), vol. 4188, pp. 327–334. Springer, Heidelberg (2006). https://doi.org/10.1007/11846406_41
2. Pakoci, E., Popović, B., Pekar, D.: Using morphological data in language modeling for Serbian large vocabulary speech recognition. Comput. Intell. Neurosci. (Spec. Iss. Adv. Sig. Process. Adapt. Learn. Methods) **2019**, 1–8 (2019)
3. Brown, P.F., Dellapietra, V.J., de Souza, P.V., Lai, J., Mercer, R.: Class-based N-gram models of natural language. Comput. Linguist. **18**, 467–479 (1992)
4. Kneser, R., Ney, H.: Improved clustering techniques for class-based statistical language modelling. In: Proceedings of the 3rd European Conference on Speech Communication and Technology EUROSPEECH 1993, Berlin, Germany, pp. 973–976. ISCA (1993)
5. Bazzi, I., Glass, J.R.: A multi-class approach for modelling out-of-vocabulary words. In: Hansen, J.H.L., Pellom, B. (eds.) Proceedings of the 7th International Conference on Spoken Language Processing ICSLP 2002 – INTERSPEECH 2002, Denver, Colorado, USA, pp. 1613–1616. ISCA (2002)
6. Schaaf, T.: Detection of OOV words using generalized word models and a semantic class language model. In: Dalsgaard, P., Lindberg, B., Benner, H., Tan, Z. (eds.) Proceedings of the 7th European Conference on Speech Communication and Technology EUROSPEECH 2001 – INTERSPEECH 2001, Aalborg, Denmark, pp. 2581–2584. ISCA (2001)
7. Ostrogonac, S.: Modeli srpskog jezika i njihova primena u govornim i jezičkim tehnologijama (Models of the Serbian language and their application in speech and language technologies). Ph.D. thesis, University of Novi Sad, Serbia (2018)
8. Ostrogonac, S., Pakoci, E., Sečujski, M., Mišković, D.: Morphology-based vs unsupervised word clustering for training language models for Serbian. Acta Polytech. Hungar. (Spec. Iss. Cognit. Infocommun.) **16**(2), 183–197 (2019)
9. Povey, D., et al.: The Kaldi speech recognition toolkit. In: Proceedings of the IEEE Workshop on Automatic Speech Recognition and Understanding ASRU 2011, Waikoloa, Hawaii, USA, pp. 1–4. IEEE (2011)
10. Mohri, M., Pereira, F., Riley, M.: Speech recognition with weighted finite-state transducers. Comput. Speech Lang. **16**(1), 69–88 (2002)
11. Allauzen, C., Riley, M., Schalkwyk, J., Skut, W., Mohri, M.: OpenFst: a general and efficient weighted finite-state transducer library. In: Holub, J., Žďárek, J. (eds.) CIAA 2007. LNCS, vol. 4783, pp. 11–23. Springer, Heidelberg (2007). https://doi.org/10.1007/978-3-540-763 36-9_3
12. Horndasch, A., Kaufhold, C., Nöth, E.: How to add word classes to the kaldi speech recognition toolkit. In: Sojka, P., Horák, A., Kopeček, I., Pala, K. (eds.) TSD 2016. LNCS (LNAI), vol. 9924, pp. 486–494. Springer, Cham (2016). https://doi.org/10.1007/978-3-319-45510-5_56
13. Sečujski, M.: Automatic part-of-speech tagging in Serbian. Ph.D. thesis, University of Novi Sad, Serbia (2009)
14. Ljubešić, N., Klubička, F.: Serbian web corpus srWaC 1.1, Slovenian language resource repository CLARIN.SI (2016). http://hdl.handle.net/11356/1063. Accessed 11 June 2021.
15. Liu, X., Chen, X., Wang, Y., Gales, M.J.F., Woodland, P.C.: Two efficient lattice rescoring methods using recurrent neural network language models. IEEE/ACM Trans. Audio Speech Lang. Process. **24**(8), 1438–1449 (2016)

Spectral Root Features for Replay Spoof Detection in Voice Assistants

Ankur T. Patil[⊠], Harsh Kotta, Rajul Acharya, and Hemant A. Patil

Speech Research Lab, Dhirubhai Ambani Institute of Information
and Communication Technology (DA-IICT), Gandhinagar 382007, India
{ankur_patil,harsh_kotta,rajul_acharya,hemant_patil}@daiict.ac.in

Abstract. In this paper, authors propose spectral root cepstral coefficients (SRCC) feature set to develop the effective countermeasure system for replay attacks on voice assistants (VAs). Experiments are performed on ReMASC dataset, which is specifically designed for the replay attack detection task. Logarithm operation in MFCC extraction is replaced by power-law nonlinearity (i.e. $(\cdot)^\gamma$) to derive SRCC feature set. The proper choice of the γ helps to capture the system information of the speech signal, with a minimum number of cepstral coefficients. We investigated two approaches for proper choice of γ-value, in particular, by estimating the energy concentration in cepstral coefficients and by visualizing the spectrogram w.r.t. γ-value. This system representation of the speech signal, is the discriminative cue for the replay spoof speech detection (SSD) task as replay speech signal consists of additional transmission channel effects convolved with the genuine signal. The performance of the proposed feature set is validated using Gaussian Mixture Model (GMM), and Light Convolutional Neural Network (LCNN). Our primary system shows relative improvement of 47.49% over the baseline system (Constant-Q Cepstral Coefficients (CQCC)-GMM) on the evaluation set. The EER is further reduced to 11.84% on evaluation set by classifier-level fusion.

Keywords: Spectral root cepstrum · SRCC · Replay spoof detection · Power-law · Nonlinearity

1 Introduction

The development in the speech technologies, especially in Distant Speech Recognition (DSR) led to the development of the voice assistants (VAs). VAs use voice commands from an authentic user to control the operation of the many household and personal applications. However, VAs are susceptible to the various spoofing attacks [3,4,6,7,31]. If design of a VA is not ingenious, then these attacks by fraudulent imposter can access personal information, transmit sensitive data, and gain remote access to the system that follows. Considering these threats to VAs, a countermeasure system should be implemented in VAs against the spoofing attacks [17].

© Springer Nature Switzerland AG 2021
A. Karpov and R. Potapova (Eds.): SPECOM 2021, LNAI 12997, pp. 504–515, 2021.
https://doi.org/10.1007/978-3-030-87802-3_46

Earlier, standard databases, and evaluation plans have been released for ASVspoof-2015, -2017, and -2019 challenge campaigns for the Automatic Speaker Verification (ASV) systems [5,29,34]. Few state-of-the-art countermeasure architectures designs for ASV can be found in [2,13,23,28,30]. However, these corpora can be utilized to develop countermeasures for the ASV systems and not for VAs. To design the countermeasures against the replay spoofing attack for VAs, *Realistic Replay Attack Microphone Array Speech Corpus* (ReMASC) dataset is developed [8]. In replay attack, fraudulent imposter attacks the VA using pre-recorded speech sample collected from the authentic user. It can cause severe threat to the voice controlled applications, such as android device and smarthome system. In this paper, we propose a countermeasure for replay attack detection in VAs using this ReMASC dataset. There are important differences in designing the countermeasures for ASV and VAs. In ASV, the microphone is generally placed very close, which enable to capture the close-distance features [26,32]. Whereas, VAs are developed for DSR [8]. Also, strict speaker verification model is utilized for ASV system, whereas VAs use a less strict verification model [35]. Furthermore, VAs use microphone array for speech enhancement purpose, whereas ASV systems primarily use a single microphone to record the speech samples. However, in near future, authors believe that ASV could be an integral part of personalized VA systems and thus, far-field speech becomes more relevant and necessary to analyze.

In this paper, we exploited homomorphic filtering-based approach for feature extraction. For homomorphic filtering-based approaches, the speech signal can be expressed as convolution of the glottal airflow (i.e. speech excitation source) with the impulse response of vocal tract system [21]. A replayed speech signal can be considered as the convolution of natural speech with the impulse responses of recording, and playback devices as well as the acoustic environments [1]. Hence, for replay detection, the challenge is to estimate the characteristics of the extra convolved elements with genuine speech signal. Blind deconvolution approach could be used that requires apriori knowledge of signal components. If one of the convolved components of the signal is known then the other could be easily estimated using linear inverse filtering. Linear Prediction (LP) analysis can be used to estimate the system function, with assumption that the all-pole linear and time-invariant (LTI) system convolves with train of pulses or random noise [16,18]. If the general characteristics of one of the signal component is known, then homomorphic deconvolution system models can be used. In this case, either of logarithmic homomorphic deconvolution system (LHDS) or using spectral root homomorphic deconvolution system (SRHDS) could be used to perform deconvolution operation [20,22,25]. In LHDS, convolutionally-combined signals are mapped to additively combined signals on which time-gating is applied for signal separation [19]. The time-gating in cepstral domain is known as liftering. In SRHDS, convolutional vector space is mapped to another convolutional vector space, where signal components are more easily separable by liftering operation [15]. For replay detection on VAs, we employ SRHDS along with Mel filterbank to derive Spectral Root Cepstral Coefficients (SRCC) [27]. The key novelty in proposed SRCC feature set is the use of power-law nonlinearity that does not depend critically on the input amplitude and thus, suitable for VAs that predominantly use far-field speech. Furthermore, we investigated the two approaches to systematically choose the optimum value of γ-parameter which are explained in detail along with supporting results in Sect. 4.

2   Spectral Root Cepstrum

2.1   Speech Signal Modeling

Speech signal, $x(n)$ can be expressed as the convolution of glottal airflow (i.e., excitation source signal), $g(n)$, with the impulse response of vocal tract system, $v(n)$ [24], i.e.,

$$x(n) = g(n) * v(n), \tag{1}$$

where symbol '*' refers to the convolution operation. For our application, we refer $x(n)$ in Eq. (1) as genuine speech signal. As discussed in Sect. 1, glottal airflow is quasi-periodic (or impulse-like) in nature for voiced speech. It can be approximated as pulse-train for speech signal modeling. The replayed version of the genuine speech signal includes additional components which are impulse responses of playback device $pd(n)$, playback environment $pe(n)$, recording device $rd(n)$, and recording environment $re(n)$ [1]. These components in the replay speech signal, $y(n)$ are convolutionally-combined with the genuine speech signal, $x(n)$, i.e.,

$$y(n) = x(n) * pd(n) * pe(n) * rd(n) * re(n). \tag{2}$$

Equation (2) can be written as,

$$y(n) = x(n) * N(n) = g(n) * v(n) * N(n), \tag{3}$$

where $N(n) = pd(n) * pe(n) * rd(n) * re(n)$, and it is overall impulse response that represents distortion in genuine speech signal due to replay attack. One of the component in $x(n)$ and hence, in $y(n)$, is the glottal airflow $g(n)$, which is quasi-periodic in nature. As the characteristics of one signal, $g(n)$, is known, homomorphic signal processing techniques can be used to estimate the cepstrum for rest of the signal. To that effect, $v(n)$ in genuine and $v(n) * N(n)$ in spoof speech signal can be estimated. These estimated components can serve as discriminative cues for the SSD task.

2.2   Cepstrum Analysis: Logarithmic vs Spectral Root

In evaluation of the logarithmic cepstrum, convolutionally-combined vector space, $x(n) = g(n) * v(n)$, is mapped to the additively combined vector space, $\hat{x}(n) = \hat{g}(n) + \hat{v}(n)$, such that the contribution of glottal airflow $g(n)$, and impulse response of vocal tract system, $v(n)$ can be distinctly observed [22,24]. This transformation takes place in such a way that the duration of the pulse-train, $\hat{g}(n)$ remains the same as that of $g(n)$, however, $\hat{v}(n)$ should get compressed (in quefrency-domain) than the $v(n)$ [22]. Here, $\hat{x}(n)$, $\hat{g}(n)$, and $\hat{v}(n)$ are referred to as logarithmic cepstrum of their corresponding time-domain signals, $x(n)$, $g(n)$, and $v(n)$, respectively. With similar analogy, cepstrum of the replay speech signal is given by,

$$\hat{y}(n) = \hat{x}(n) + \hat{N}(n) = \hat{g}(n) + \hat{v}(n) + \hat{N}(n). \tag{4}$$

Algorithm 1. Computing the Spectral Root Cepstrum

---

1. $x(n) = g(n) * v(n)$
2. On applying Z-transform, $X(e^{j\omega}) = G(e^{j\omega}).V(e^{j\omega})$
3. $X(e^{j\omega})$ raised to γ power, $[X(e^{j\omega})]^{\gamma} = [G(e^{j\omega})]^{\gamma}.[V(e^{j\omega})]^{\gamma}$, i.e., $(\check{X}(e^{j\omega}) = \check{G}(e^{j\omega}).\check{V}(e^{j\omega}))$
4. Applying inverse Z-transform, $\check{x}(n) = \check{g}(n) * \check{v}(n)$.
5. Perform the same operations on $y(n)$ to get $\check{y}(n)$.

Spectral root cepstrum is obtained by transforming the convolutional vector space, $x(n) = g(n) * v(n)$, to another convolutionally-combined vector space, $\check{x}(n) = \check{g}(n) * \check{v}(n)$, such that the elements are more easily separable in transformed vector space than the earlier one. Here, $\check{x}(n)$, $\check{g}(n)$, and $\check{v}(n)$ represents spectral root cepstrum of the signals $x(n)$, $g(n)$, and $v(n)$, respectively. The transformation steps to obtain spectral root cepstrum are shown in Algorithm 1. Here, logarithmic non-linearity in LHDS is replaced by *power-law nonlinearity*, $(\cdot)^{\gamma}$.

Spectral root cepstra for signals, $x(n)$ and $y(n)$ are expressed as follows:

$$\check{x}(n) = \check{g}(n) * \check{v}(n), \tag{5}$$

$$\check{y}(n) = \check{x}(n) * \check{N}(n) = \check{g}(n) * \check{v}(n) * \check{N}(n). \tag{6}$$

In general, pole-zero sequence, $v(n)$ is infinitely long sequence [15]. Hence, $\check{v}(n)$ will also be infinitely long. In this situation, we select 'γ' to maximally compress $\check{v}(n)$ such that it has smallest energy concentration in the low-time region, where $-1 \leq \gamma \leq 1$.

The energy concentration of the first n points of $\check{v}(n)$ relative to its total energy is given by:

$$d(n) = \frac{\sum_{k=1}^{n} |\check{v}(k)|^2}{\sum_{k=1}^{C} |\check{v}(k)|^2}, \tag{7}$$

where n is number of samples in time-gating [15], and C corresponds to total number of cepstral coefficients. For our application, we select γ, and number of samples (n in Eq. (7)) for time-gating such that it can discriminate between $\check{v}(n)$ (Eq. (5)) in genuine speech samples, and $\check{v}(n) * \check{N}(n)$ (Eq. (6)) in spoof speech samples. The application of Eq. (7) to select the appropriate value of γ, is discussed in Sect. 4.1.

Fig. 1. Block diagram of SRCC feature set extraction scheme. After [27].

2.3   Proposed SRCC Feature Set

In this paper, we proposed to use the SRCC feature set, which uses the triangular Mel filterbank along with power-law nonlinearity as shown in Fig. 1. Windowing is performed on the input speech signal with optimum window and hopping length as reported in speech signal processing literature. The qth cepstral coefficient of SRCC is extracted using magnitude spectrum as:

$$SRCC(q) = \sum_{m=1}^{M} (MFM(m))^{\gamma} cos \left[\frac{q(m - \frac{1}{2})\pi}{M} \right],$$ (8)

where the Mel Frequency Magnitude (MFM) spectrum is defined as:

$$MFM(m) = \sum_{k=1}^{K} |X(k)| H_m(k),$$ (9)

where $X(k)$ represents k-point Discrete Fourier Transform (DFT) of the signal, $x(n)$, $H_m(k)$ is the mth Mel-scaled bandpass filter. Root Spectrum in Mel Scale (RSMS) is given by:

$$RSMS(m) = (MFM(m))^{\gamma}.$$ (10)

The value of γ is chosen so as to have maximum distinction between genuine and spoof utterances of the ReMASC dataset.

3   Experimental Setup

3.1   Dataset

We utilized the ReMASC dataset to build the countermeasures against the replay attack for VAs [8]. From the available dataset, ~ 25500 utterances are used. We partitioned the dataset into 3 subsets, i.e., training, development, and evaluation set. Data distribution is shown in Table 1. This publicly available dataset consists of recordings from the 44 subjects. The data partition in Table 1 consists of 22, 17, and 20 speakers in training, development, and evaluation subset, respectively. Most of the speakers in training and development subsets are overlapping. However, speakers selected in evaluation set are disjoint to that of training and development subset. The recordings have been performed in four different environments. The same proportion of all recording environments is maintained in all the subsets.

Table 1. Design of ReMASC database. After [8].

	Training	Development	Evaluation
Genuine	2820	924	3308
Spoof	7392	1884	9203
Total	10212	2808	12511

3.2 Feature Set, Classifier and Evaluation Metric

We have employed two classifiers to validate the efficacy of the proposed feature set, namely, Gaussian Mixture Models (GMM) using 512 mixtures, and Light Convolutional Neural Network (LCNN). To train the GMM, de-correlated features are required and hence, cepstral features are used for this purpose. LCNN architecture on the other hand, uses spectral features as deep learning architectures work well on the correlated features. In this study, Constant-Q Transform-gram (CQT-gram), and RSMS are used as spectral features with LCNN architecture. ReMASC dataset consists of multi-channel speech and hence, only the first channel is considered for feature extraction.

In this paper, Mel Frequency Cepstral Coefficients (MFCC), Linear Frequency Cepstral Coefficients (LFCC), and Constant-Q Cepstral Coefficients (CQCC) are used with GMM classifier, and results obtained are compared with SRCC. The baseline is implemented using CQCC feature set. It includes static, Δ, and $\Delta\Delta$ coefficients which constitutes 90-Dimensional (90-D) feature set. The MFCC (42-D), and LFCC (60-D) features also consists of static, Δ, and $\Delta\Delta$ coefficients. SRCC feature set is extracted with 40 Mel subband filters, and $\gamma = 1/11$. The value of γ is chosen with analysis given in Subsect. 4.1. Initial 13-static coefficients are selected and appended with Δ and $\Delta\Delta$ coefficients. The LFCC, MFCC, and SRCC are derived using 40 number of subband filters in the filterbank. Since SRCC consists of *power-law non-linearity*, experiments are also performed with the other feature sets, namely, Power-Normalized Cepstral Coefficients (PNCC) and Relative Spectral Transform - Perceptual Linear Prediction (RASTA-PLP), which consist of the power-law non-linearity [10–12]. PNCC and RASTA-PLP are of 39-D and 27-D, respectively. Except CQCC, for each of the feature set, framing is performed with 25 ms window length and 10 ms hopping size with Hamming windowing. Performance is evaluated on testing dataset using Equal Error Rate (EER) metric.

LCNN is deep neural network (DNN) architecture which uses Max-Feature-Map activation (MFM) [9,33]. We have designed the architecture as specified in [14]. To train this model, we used RSMS feature representation as per Eq. (10) with 100 subband filters in Mel filterbank.

Score-level fusion of two individual systems, S_1 and S_2, is performed as, $S_f = \alpha \cdot S_1 + (1 - \alpha) \cdot S_2$, where $0 \leq \alpha \leq 1$, and S_f represents the scores after fusion. It helps to capture the possible complementary information of the two individual systems. The fusion parameter α is tuned using development set, and same value of α is used for the fusion on evaluation set.

4   Experimental Results

4.1   Choice of γ

For the given dataset, we have approximated the value of the γ with the help of Eq. (7). Initially, we have chosen three different values of γ, i.e., -0.9, 0.1, and 0.9. The SRCC features are extracted as explained in Subsect. 2.3. We computed the energy concentration over 4000 genuine and spoof samples for $n = 13$ in Eq. (7) and averaged over all utterances. For $\gamma = 0.9$ and -0.9, we obtained 81% energy concentration for $n = 13$ coefficients. Whereas, 87% energy is preserved for the same value of n when γ value is set to 0.1.

Furthermore, we observed the spectrogram obtained using Eq. (10). Figure 2 shows the spectrogram of the genuine and spoof speech signal in Panel-I and Panel-II, respectively. Figure 2(a), (b), (c), and (d) are obtained for the values of γ as 0.9, -0.9, 0.1, and -0.1, respectively. It can be observed that maximal information of the input speech signals is captured in the spectrogram with $\gamma = 0.1$, as seen in Fig. 2(c), where the spectral contents of the speech signal are seems to be well enhanced as compared to Figs. 2(a), 2(b), and 2(d). In [15], the performance of the SRHDS is also evaluated w.r.t. the varying the number of poles and zeros in the system function. The value of γ varies between -1 to 1. If system function consists of only poles then $d(n)$ in Eq. (7) is maximized for $\gamma = -1$. However, for all-zero system, $\gamma = 1$ is the appropriate choice [15,24]. For our case, $d(n)$ is maximized for $\gamma = 1/11$ (obtained after further fine tuning), which suggests that the system function has more zeros than poles. With this analysis, we have chosen the value of γ to be $1/11$ for our SSD system design.

4.2   Spectrographic Analysis

Panel I shows the RSMS for genuine and spoof speech signal in Fig. 3(a) and 3(c), respectively. Figure 3(b) and 3(d) in Panel II shows CQT-gram for genuine and spoof speech signal, respectively. It can be observed that the highlighted region in RSMS is highly *discriminative* than the CQT-gram. It may be due to the fact that the choice of appropriate γ helps by preserving the maximum concentration of signal energy and hence, its behaviour is more profoundly observed. It can be observed from the Fig. 3 that a spoof signal has lesser spectral energy in high frequency region as compared to its genuine counterpart which may be due to energy decay because of replay configuration. Thus, being able to capture the behaviour of the signal in the high frequency region allows RSMS to distinguish genuine and spoof utterances effectively.

4.3   Results

Experiments are performed by varying the value of γ for SRCC feature set along with GMM classifier, and results in %EER are shown in Table 2. It is observed that the $\gamma > 0$ gives better results than $\gamma < 0$, which is exactly opposite to what has been reported for speech synthesis application [24] (pp. 272). In particular,

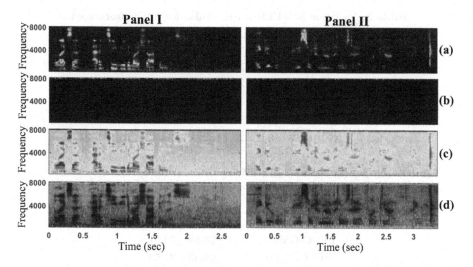

Fig. 2. Panel-I and Panel-II consists of spectrogram of genuine and spoof speech signal, respectively. Figure 2(a) shows spectrogram of the speech signal as given in Eq. (10) for $\gamma = 0.9$. Whereas, Fig. 2(b), 2(c), 2(d) shows the spectrogram for $\gamma = -0.9, 0.1,$ and -0.1, respectively.

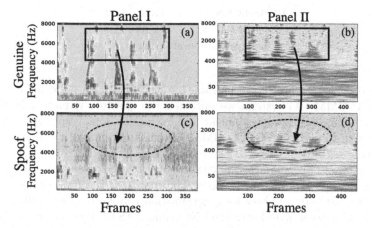

Fig. 3. Plot of RSMS (Panel I) *vs.* CQT-gram (Panel II) feature sets: (a), (b) for genuine speech signal, and (c), (d) for spoofed speech signal.

$\gamma = -1/3$ gave better results in listening test than $\gamma = 1/3$. This is because $\gamma < 0$ emphasize the pole structure (formants) whereas $\gamma > 0$ emphasize the zeros (valleys) in the spectrum. For replay speech, due to bandpass characteristics of the replay mechanism, the spectrum is expected to decay faster, which is essentially encoded in the valleys in the spectrum. Thus, $\gamma > 0$ is able to emphasize this information better than $\gamma < 0$ and hence, gives the relatively better results.

Table 2. Variation in %EER w.r.t. γ value for SRCC feature set.

γ	-1	$-1/2$	$-1/3$	$-1/5$	$-1/7$	$-1/9$	$-1/11$	$-1/13$	$-1/15$
dev	38.78	30.64	27.92	23.04	22.69	21.59	20.94	20.46	20.25
eval	33.33	26.17	23.74	21.59	21.38	21.12	20.74	20.40	20.85
γ	1/15	1/13	1/11	1/9	1/7	1/5	1/3	1/2	1
dev	21.56	20.19	**19.27**	20.28	21.13	21.28	23.78	24.67	32.36
eval	19.23	18.20	**16.16**	19.90	20.79	22.01	24.65	25.75	31.30

Table 3. Results (in % EER) on ReMASC Dataset using various feature sets.

System	Dev	Eval
CQCC-GMM	20.57	23.31
LFCC-GMM	28.89	26.31
MFCC-GMM	36.43	31.53
PNCC-GMM	22.29	25.23
RASTA-PLP - GMM	26.25	29.20
SRCC-GMM (A)	19.27	16.26
CQT-gram-LCNN	13.20	15.14
RSMS-LCNN (B)	13.75	12.24
A + B	**11.39**	**11.84**

'+' denotes score-level fusion.

Results obtained are shown in Table 3 with %EER as a performance metric. For SRCC-GMM (A) system, we obtained the absolute reduction in EER of 1.3% and 7.05% on the development and evaluation sets, respectively, in comparison with the baseline CQCC-GMM system. In addition, it can be observed from Table 3, RSMS-LCNN (B) system performs superior to the CQT-gram-LCNN system. This validates the efficacy of proposed spectral root-based feature sets, irrespective of the classifier. The improved results on evaluation set using SRCC feature set show its generalization capability. The performance of the SRCC is also compared with the PNCC and RASTA-PLP feature sets, which are also power-law nonlinearity-based features. These feature sets are developed to design noise-robust speech recognition system [11]. Because of their noise-robustness property, they may fail to detect the distortions in replayed spoof speech signals. We found that PNCC also works better for the positive values of γ near zero and results in Table 3 are obtained with power-law nonlinearity exponent set to 1/11. Whereas RASTA-PLP shows quite consistent performance with variation of exponent, however, we obtained somewhat better results when it is set to 1/10. We also used LFCC and MFCC feature sets in our experiments. Both MFCC and LFCC feature sets perform poor than CQCC feature set. Our primary system shows the absolute reduction in EER of 6.82% and 11.07% on development and evaluation sets, respectively, compared to the baseline system.

The fusion of the two systems A and B, with fusion parameter $\alpha = 0.33$, gives much better performance suggesting both of these systems capture complementary information. Experiments performed on environment-independent case produces relatively better results than the CQCC-GMM system reported in [8] (i.e., 31.60%, 29.78%, 26.40%, and 36.23% EER in four successive environments).

5   Summary and Conclusion

This study investigated physics of replay attack and spectral root cepstrum, where logarithmic nonlinearity in MFCCs is replaced by power-law nonlinearity for replay SSD in the context of VAs. For power-law nonlinearity, dynamic behavior of the output does not depend critically on the input amplitude. A proper choice of γ in SRCC feature extraction plays a vital role in deconvolving the input signal. The selected γ value also pointed out that this system possess more zeros than the poles. Results suggest that the performance of SRCC is much better as compared to the MFCC, which uses logarithmic nonlinearity. However, this study only captures the magnitude component of the signal and hence, similar study can also be performed in future to capture phase information as well to make front-end more efficient.

References

1. Alegre, F., Janicki, A., Evans, N.: Re-assessing the threat of replay spoofing attacks against automatic speaker verification. In: 2014 International Conference of the Biometrics Special Interest Group (BIOSIG), pp. 1–6. IEEE (2014)
2. Cai, W., Wu, H., Cai, D., Li, M.: The DKU replay detection system for the ASVspoof 2019 challenge: on data augmentation, feature representation, classification, and fusion. In: INTERSPEECH, pp. 1023–1027, Graz, Austria, September 2019
3. Carlini, N., et al.: Hidden voice commands. In: 25th USENIX Security Symposium, pp. 513–530, Austin, USA, August 2016
4. Carlini, N., Wagner, D.: Audio adversarial examples: targeted attacks on speech-to-text. In: IEEE Security and Privacy Workshops (SPW), pp. 1–7, San Francisco, USA, May 2018
5. Delgado, H., et al.: ASVspoof 2017 version 2.0: meta-data analysis and baseline enhancements. In: Odyssey 2018: The Speaker and Language Recognition Workshop, pp. 296–303, Les Sables d'Olonne, France, June 2018
6. Diao, W., Liu, X., Zhou, Z., Zhang, K.: Your voice assistant is mine: how to abuse speakers to steal information and control your phone. In: 4th ACM Workshop on SPSM, pp. 63–74, Scottsdale, USA, November 2014
7. Gong, Y., Poellabauer, C.: An overview of vulnerabilities of voice controlled systems. In: 1st International Workshop on Security and Privacy for Internet-of-Things, Orlando, United States, April 2018
8. Gong, Y., Yang, J., Huber, J., MacKnight, M., Poellabauer, C.: ReMASC: realistic replay attack corpus for voice controlled systems. In: INTERSPEECH, pp. 2355–2359, Graz, Austria, September 2019

9. Goodfellow, I.J., Warde-Farley, D., Mirza, M., Courville, A., Bengio, Y.: Maxout networks. In: International Conference on Machine Learning, pp. 1319–1327, Atlanta, USA, June 2013

10. Hermansky, H.: Perceptual linear predictive (PLP) analysis of speech. J. Acoust. Soc. Am. **87**(4), 1738–1752 (1990)

11. Hermansky, H., Morgan, N.: RASTA processing of speech. IEEE Trans. Speech Audio Process. **2**(4), 578–589 (1994)

12. Kim, C., Stern, R.M.: Power-normalized cepstral coefficients (PNCC) for robust speech recognition. IEEE/ACM Trans. Audio Speech Lang. Process. **24**(7), 1315–1329 (2016)

13. Lai, C.I., Chen, N., Villalba, J., Dehak, N.: ASSERT: anti-spoofing with squeeze-excitation and residual networks. In: INTERSPEECH, pp. 1013–1017, Graz, Austria, September 2019

14. Lavrentyeva, G., Novoselov, S., Malykh, E., Kozlov, A., Kudashev, O., Shchemelinin, V.: Audio replay attack detection with deep learning frameworks. In: INTERSPEECH, pp. 82–86. Stockholm, Sweden, August 2017

15. Lim, J.: Spectral root homomorphic deconvolution system. IEEE Trans. Acoust. Speech Signal Process. **27**(3), 223–233 (1979)

16. Makhoul, J.: Linear prediction: a tutorial review. Proc. IEEE **63**(4), 561–580 (1975)

17. Marcel, S., Nixon, M.S., Li, S.Z. (eds.): Handbook of Biometric Anti-Spoofing. ACVPR, Springer, London (2014). https://doi.org/10.1007/978-1-4471-6524-8

18. Markel, J.D., Gray, A.J.: Linear Prediction of Speech, vol. 12. Springer, Heidelberg (2013)

19. Oppenheim, A., Schafer, R.: Homomorphic analysis of speech. IEEE Trans. Audio Electroacoust. **16**(2), 221–226 (1968). https://doi.org/10.1109/TAU.1968.1161965

20. Oppenheim, A.V.: Superposition in a class of nonlinear systems. MIT Research Laboratory of Electronics (1965)

21. Oppenheim, A.V.: Speech analysis-synthesis system based on homomorphic filtering. J. Acoust. Soc. Am. (JASA) **45**(2), 458–465 (1969)

22. Oppenheim, A.V., Schafer, R.W., Stockham, T.: Nonlinear filtering of multiplied and convolved signals. IEEE Trans. Audio Electroacoust. **16**(3), 437–466 (1968)

23. Patel, T.B., Patil, H.A.: Combining evidences from Mel cepstral, cochlear filter cepstral and instantaneous frequency features for detection of natural vs. spoofed speech. In: INTERSPEECH, pp. 2062–2066, Dresden, Germany (Sept 2015)

24. Quatieri, T.F.: Discrete-Time Speech Signal Processing: Principles and Practice. 1st edition, Pearson Education India, New Delhi (2015)

25. Schafer, R.W.: Echo Removal by Discrete Generalized Linear Filtering. MIT Research Laboratory of Electronics, Cambridge (1969)

26. Shiota, S., Villavicencio, F., Yamagishi, J., Ono, N., Echizen, I., Matsui, T.: Voice liveness detection for speaker verification based on a tandem single/double-channel pop noise detector. In: Odyssey, vol. 2016, pp. 259–263, Bilbao, Spain, June 2016

27. Tapkir, P.A., Patil, A.T., Shah, N., Patil, H.A.: Novel spectral root cepstral features for replay spoof detection. In: APSIPA-ASC, pp. 1945–1950, Honolulu, Hawaii, USA, November 2018

28. Todisco, M., Delgado, H., Evans, N.: Constant Q cepstral coefficients: a spoofing countermeasure for automatic speaker verification. Comput. Speech Lang. **45**, 516–535 (2017)

29. Todisco, M., et al.: ASVspoof 2019: future horizons in spoofed and fake audio detection. In: INTERSPEECH, pp. 1008–1012, Graz, Austria, September 2019

30. Tom, F., Jain, M., Dey, P.: End-to-end audio replay attack detection using deep convolutional networks with attention. In: INTERSPEECH, pp. 681–685, Hyderabad, India, September 2018
31. Vaidya, T., Zhang, Y., Sherr, M., Shields, C.: Cocaine noodles: exploiting the gap between human and machine speech recognition. In: 9th USENIX Workshop on Offensive Technologies (WOOT-2015), Washington, DC, USA, August 2015
32. Wickramasinghe, B., Irtza, S., Ambikairajah, E., Epps, J.: Frequency domain linear prediction features for replay spoofing attack detection. In: INTERSPEECH, pp. 661–665, Hyderabad, India, September 2018
33. Wu, X., He, R., Sun, Z., Tan, T.: A light CNN for deep face representation with noisy labels. IEEE Trans. Inf. Forensics Secur. **13**(11), 2884–2896 (2018)
34. Wu, Z., et al.: ASVspoof 2015: the first automatic speaker verification spoofing and countermeasures challenge. In: INTERSPEECH, pp. 2037–2041, Dresden, Germany, September 2015
35. Zhang, G., Yan, C., Ji, X., Zhang, T., Zhang, T., Xu, W.: Dolphinattack: inaudible voice commands. In: Proceedings of the 2017 ACM SIGSAC Conference on Computer and Communications Security, pp. 103–117. ACM, Dallas, TX, USA, October 2017

Influence of the Aggressive Internet Environment on Cognitive Personality Disorders (in Relation to the Russian Young Generation of Users)

Rodmonga Potapova[1]([envelope]) [iD], Tatyana Agibalova[2] [iD], Vsevolod Potapov[3] [iD], and Olga Tuchina[2] [iD]

[1] Institute of Applied and Mathematical Linguistics, Moscow State Linguistic University, 38 Ostozhenka Street, Moscow 119034, Russia
r.potapova@linguanet.ru
[2] Moscow Research and Practical Centre for Narcology of the Department of Public Health, Lyublinskaya ul., 37/1, 109390 Moscow, Russia
[3] Centre of New Technologies for Humanities, Lomonosov Moscow State University, Leninskije Gory 1, 119991 Moscow, Russia
kedr@philol.msu.ru

Abstract. The study of the clinical and dynamic patterns of auto-aggressive behavior of Internet-addicted users seems very interesting and promising in terms of the appropriate development of effective recommendations for prevention and treatment. All patients had some dissociation, i.e. an addictive dissociation of personality according to the chemical type. Patients are aware of the presence of negative subpersonalities, recognize their identification with them at the moments of actualization of their desire to play or to commit illegal actions. They also emphasize that the activation of the addictive subpersonality leads to the failure of the fulfillment of intentions and intended goals, impulsive behavior and actions. As our research has shown, patients with Internet addiction disorders are characterized by a high suicidal risk, which necessitates specialized psychotherapy aimed at correcting suicidal tendencies in the psyche. The format of the developed and tested no-suicidal psychotherapy for patients with Internet addiction disorders proves its effectiveness and adequacy. Thus, it is necessary to develop an individualized strategy for the primary prevention of emotional disorders and addictive behavior in the future, taking into account the respective age groups.

Keywords: Cognitive personality disorders · Young generation · Internet addiction · No-suicidal psychotherapy

1 Introduction

Over the past decades, there has been not only an increase in addictive behavior, but also an avalanche-like mania for computer games, the Internet and social networks, which in turn leads to the formation of new types of addictive behavior, i.e. non-chemical

© Springer Nature Switzerland AG 2021
A. Karpov and R. Potapova (Eds.): SPECOM 2021, LNAI 12997, pp. 516–527, 2021.
https://doi.org/10.1007/978-3-030-87802-3_47

addictions. In the International classification of diseases-11 (ICD-11 classification) [41], pathological gambling was classified as a substance use disorder and an addictive disorder. ICD-11 introduces separate nosological units for "gambling disorder" and "gaming disorder", combining them under the category "disorders due to substance use or addictive behaviors" ("disorders caused by the use of psychoactive substances or addictive behavior"). Addictive behavior disorders (in their online and offline forms) are defined as "recognizable and clinically significant syndromes associated with distress or impairment in functioning in the individual, resulting from repetitive reinforcing behavior rather than the use of addictive chemicals" [41]. Thus, we are increasingly dealing with individuals who have developed a dependence on various forms of interaction with the Internet. Currently, the presence of addictive "dissociation of personality" has been proven in persons with addictive behavior. For example, in people with alcohol or drug addiction, this dissociation divides into "Alcoholic Self", or "Addictive Self", and "Normative Self" [40]; the addictive process progression [24] results in primary dissociation, and post-traumatic dissociation [23] in secondary dissociation. Accordingly, in individuals with Internet addiction disorders, we also observe addictive dissociation (see, e.g., [12]). This is significantly consistent with the presence of transformation of neurophysiological and cognitive characteristics of the brain, taking into account the reaction of the "electronic personality", i.e. the digital communication user (according to R.K. Potapova ([27, 30]) to the external world, in particular, the polycode Internet. In our opinion, in the formation of addiction, it is the "electronic personality" that is used by the "Addictive Self". A causal relationship arises and develops between the "electronic personality" in social network communication and the product of their communicative activity, which manifests itself on the basis of four sign systems: verbal, non-verbal, paraverbal and extraverbal [29]. All of the above code means are used by the recipient (electronic personality) on the Internet, while the user can be engaged in two types of communication activities: as agents and as patients. Currently, there is no established prophylactic treatment of computer addiction, which requires studying the reasons for its formation. Therefore, it is important to study the factors that contribute to the development of addiction to computer games. Currently, auto-aggressive behavior is one of the urgent problems not only in psychiatry, narcology (e.g., [1, 2, 9, 28], etc.), but also in the entire modern society. A high level of suicides, attempted suicides and other types of auto-aggression is recorded in all types of addictions [14, 22, 25, 32, 34]. According to various researchers, from 13% to 20% of persons with non-chemical addictions commit attempted suicides [16, 26, 39]. At the same time, there are scientific studies confirming the unity of the pathogenetic mechanisms of non-chemical dependence and dependence on psychoactive substances [4, 5, 33, 38].

2 Method

Based on the aforesaid, the study of the clinical and dynamic patterns of auto-aggressive behavior of Internet-addicted users seems to us very interesting and promising in terms of the appropriate development of effective recommendations for prevention and treatment.

Below we will consider Internet users who developed such an addiction (patients) compared to patients with gambling addiction (see also: [3]). To solve this problem, 32 male patients with Internet addiction disorders were examined. It is important to note that addictive behavior has always been implemented using the Internet, social networks and computer network games. The control group included 42 male patients with addiction to gambling, whose non-chemical addiction was realized through gambling behavior, i.e. sports betting through bookmakers' shops. All subjects were without comorbid syndrome of dependence on psychoactive substances and endogenous mental disorders. The age limits of the presented sample are from 18 to 28 years old (average age M = 19.8 (SD = 1.9)). Since patients whose addictive behavior was realized using the Internet without comorbid pathology and without the presence of other dependence on psychoactive substances are quite rare, the sample presented is unique.

1. The anamnestic data and information about auto-aggressive behavior was collected within a provital therapeutic interview [26, 27] modified for the purpose of examining patients with gambling addiction by the authors of the study. A semi-structured therapeutic interview to identify patterns of auto-aggressive behavior in the past and present [26] was originally developed to clarify the suicidological history of patients with alcohol dependence syndrome and was successfully used to solve tasks of a number of thesis researches not only on the material of alcohol dependent subjects [28, 29]. In this study, an abridged version of this interview was used, consisting of 17 questions that had the maximum factor load in relation to the presence of parasuicides in history [30]. The interview is not of only informative, but also therapeutic value, since it increases the level of awareness of maladaptive patterns of thinking and behavior in addicted patients and promotes motivation to continue treatment [35].
2. The following scales and questionnaires were used: Montgomery-Asberg Depression Rating Scale (MADRS), the Yale-Brown Obsessive-Compulsive Scale modified for gambling (PG-YBOCS). For statistical analysis, Microsoft Excel 2007 and STATISTICA 10.0 programs were used. The relative and average values were calculated; the statistical significance of the differences was assessed using the Mann-Whitney and Kolmogorov-Smirnov tests. Differences were considered statistically significant with $p < 0.05$.

The distribution of the subjects' age is presented in Table 1.

Table 1. Age distribution of the study subjects.

Age	Treatment group (N = 32)		Control group (N = 42)	
	Abs. number	%	Abs. Number	%
18–21	6	18.75	6	14.3
22–25	24	75	27	66.1
25–28	2	6.25	9	21.4
Total	32	100.0	42	100.0

In patients of the treatment and control groups, a hereditary burden of drug addiction diseases was often observed (Table 2). In most cases, this is an alcohol dependence on the father's side, less often on the mother's side. There were no significant differences between the treatment and control groups. Data on hereditary burden are presented in Table 2.

Table 2. Hereditary addiction and disorder burden*.

	Father		Mother		Other relatives	
	Number	%	Number	%	Number	%
Treatment group (№ = 32)						
Alcohol dependence	18	56.25	2	6.25	5	16
Drug dependence	1	3	0	0	4	12.5
Gambling addiction	5	16	0	0	9	28
Personality disorders	5	16	0	0	0	0
Neuroses	0	0	5	16	3	9.375
Schizophrenia	0	0	0	0	4	12.5
MDP, cyclothymic disorder	0	0	0	0	2	6.25
Control group (№ = 42)						
Alcohol dependence	18	42.9	2	4.8	5	11.9
Drug dependence	0	0	0	0	2	4.8
Gambling addiction	5	11.9	0	0	4	9.5
Personality disorders	0	0	0	0	2	4.8
Neuroses	0	0	4	9.5	5	11.9
Schizophrenia	0	0	0	0	3	7.1
MDP, cyclothymic disorder	0	0	0	0	1	2.4

The total amount exceeds 100%, since one person could have a hereditary burden related to more than 1 relative.

Patients of the treatment group were characterized by excessive use of computers and the Internet, computer games and social networks with signs of addiction. Patients who mainly played computer games stopped other activities (missed school, work), which led to serious consequences, such as expulsion from universities or job loss.

Currently, ICD-10 is valid. In ICD-10, pathological addiction to computer games, the Internet and social media is classified under Impulse Control Disorder, in (F 63.8) under Habit and Impulse Disorders. All patients of the treatment group demonstrated the following: constantly repeated maladaptive behavior and an inability to resist the attraction to the Internet; there is a prodromal period of tension with a feeling of relief when playing games at the computer, using the Internet and social networks. When making a diagnosis of non-chemical dependence, the ICD-10 criteria for determining the addiction syndrome were used, such as: a combination of physiological, behavioral and cognitive phenomena, in which the use of the Internet takes the lead in the value system; the diagnosis can be made when three or more symptoms have been present for some time in the previous year. Symptoms such as: a strong (sometimes irresistible) need to spend time with a personal computer or smartphone; impairment in ability to control the time spent with the PC or smartphone; discontinuation syndrome with the manifestation of mental, vegetative, somatic disorders; use of other electronic devices that replace games on a computer or smartphone; signs of tolerance with an increase in the time interval spent with a PC or smartphone; progressive forgetting of other interests and pleasures besides the use of the Internet; continued passion for the Internet, despite the negative consequences of this activity. We also used diagnostic criteria, which consist of six components that are universal for all types of addictions: overvalue, mood changes, increased tolerance, discontinuation symptoms, conflict with others and oneself and relapse [15, 17] confirmed in studies by [18].

For patients of the control group the duration of episodic participation in gambling ranged from 5 to 9 months. The discontinuation syndrome after the start of systematic play was formed within one to one and a half years. The patients demonstrated both the constant and periodic form of play behavior, but the periodic form was more common. The duration of the gambling "binges" was from 3 to 14 days. The lucid space was from 14 to 40 days. The maximum number of hours spent in a row in a game was that of sports betting – from 12 to 25. The maximum single loss at the time of the examination was 1.5 million rubles. The maximum single winning was 1.2 million rubles. The maximum debt at the time of the examination was about 15 million rubles. The beginning of the gambling "binge" in most cases was associated with external provoking factors, when the patients experienced negative emotions; as well as with the presence of a sufficient amount of their own money or access to funds. There was a loss of quantitative control, which manifested itself in the fact that patients could not stop playing either when they lost or won. Initially, the patients planned to spend a certain amount of time for sports betting, relying on a sum of money specially allocated for this, but they could not control the time and, as a rule, gambled until the money was played out. Random wins were encouraging, and recurring losses were not taken into account and could not stop them. All patients sought specialized medical treatment for non-chemical dependence. More than 40% (13 people) previously had consulted privately with psychologists and occasionally came to the meetings of Gamblers Anonymous.

The patients in both groups were examined using the Montgomery-Asberg Depression Rating Scale (MADRS) and the Yale-Brown Obsessive Compulsive Scale modified for gambling (PG-YBOCS). The Montgomery-Asberg scale provides a reliable assessment of the depressive state and is sensitive in relation to the assessment of the dynamics of the state [20]. This scale has been used by many researchers to assess depressive disorders.

3   Results

In the Fig. 1, one can see high indicators on the Montgomery-Asberg scale in both the treatment and control groups, reaching a level of significantly pronounced depression; at the same time, in the treatment group, these indicators are statistically significantly higher. Indicators of the Yale-Brown Obsessive Compulsive Scale modified for gambling (PG-YBOCS) are also high in both groups and correspond to mild to moderate disorders, but do not have significant differences across the groups.

These high indicators on the depression scale condition further examination of auto-aggression. When examining our sample, it was found that various suicidal ideas arose in the treatment and control groups (Table 3).

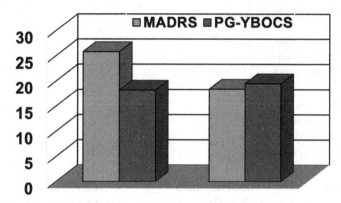

Fig. 1. Indicators of the Montgomery-Asberg Depression Rating Scale and the Yale-Brown Obsessive-Compulsive Scale in the treatment (left) and control (right) groups. (Color figure online)

The patients of the treatment group said that thoughts of dying appeared in connection with a conflict with relatives, who "did not understand them and forced them to work, scolded them for sitting at the computer". The patients in the control group said that suicidal thoughts were more likely to arise in connection with financial debt, after another significant loss. Of special importance were debts to microfinance organizations, where they grew fast beyond measure, and the patients did not have time to track the debt amount, but each time they hoped to "recover their losses and pay off the debts". The patients described their thoughts in the following way: "if I don't win, I will run away from everyone", "I always have a way out – that is, to die", "I am so exhausted, so I'll die and this is a way out". During the period of the discontinuation syndrome, suicidal thoughts were persistent and lasted from 2 to 5–7 days.

Of the entire sample, 3 patients attempted suicides (Table 3). These were demonstratively blackmailing in nature. More often, patients attempted suicides after speaking with their parents, wives or creditors, in response to demands to start schooling or studying, not to play the computer, to stop playing for money, and to pay back debts.

When analyzing the motives of suicidal thoughts and actions of the studied sample of patients, the both groups showed the same results, and two dominant motives were identified. The first one is thoughts of suicide in an attempt to put an end to their suffering, the "eternal" flight from creditors and persecuting relatives, the feeling of hopelessness and seeing suicide as the only possible way to get rid of all this. These patients usually spoke of "intolerance" and "weariness from such a life". The second motive was for cases when patients thought about suicide and attempted suicides trying to manipulate those around them.

Table 3. Suicidal ideas and suicidal actions in the treatment and control groups[1].

Suicidal ideas	Treatment group (N = 32)		Control group (N = 42)	
	Abs. number	%	Abs. number	%
Death wish	9	28.1	11	26.2
Active non-specific thoughts of suicide	4	12.5	4	9.5
Actual suicidal ideas with reflections on the method of suicide, lack of intention to act	1	3.1	1	2.4
Actual suicidal ideas, including intentions to act in the absence of a specific plan	1	3.1	1	2.4
Actual suicidal ideas with a specific plan and intentions	0	0	0	0
Suicidal actions	Treatment group (N = 32)		Control group (N = 42)	
	Abs. number	%	Abs. number	%
Actual suicide attempt	0	0	0	0
Interrupted suicide attempt	1	3.1	1	2.4
Stopped suicide attempt	0	0	2	4.8

[1] *There were no significant differences between the treatment and control groups*

In the studied sample of patients, there is a high suicidal risk, which necessitates maintenance of records on these disorders, including the conclusion of a no-suicide contract.

To prevent and treat anti-vital tendencies in the psyche, we conducted studies of prospective thinking and auto-aggressive behavior of patients with non-chemical dependence and analyzed protocols of examinations and test methods.

The object of the study is prospective thinking and auto-aggressive behavior of patients with non-chemical dependence. The subject of the study in a series of clinical cases is the relationship between the course of non-chemical dependence, prospective thinking and patterns of auto-aggressive behavior.

Purpose of the Clinical Case Study:

- identification of the features of prospective thinking in patients with non-chemical dependence and their potential connection with auto-aggressive behavior and the nature of the course of the disease [8, 13, 19];
- modification of the semi-structured therapeutic interview method to diagnose auto-aggression [36, 37] for using in the gambling addiction clinic;

- development of a protocol for an empirical study of the influence of impairments in prospective thinking caused by gambling addiction on auto-aggressive behavior and the severity of gambling addiction.

Research Objectives: Conduct a series of 3 to 6 counseling sessions with non-chemical addicted patients using semi-structured interviews designed to deal with alcohol dependence syndrome. Based on the data obtained, modify these methods for work with patients with non-chemical addictions; also assess the level of suicidal and non-suicidal auto-aggression in patients with non-chemical dependence. By comparing individual indicators and content analysis of interview texts, identify the features of the explicit and implicit plans of prospective thinking in patients with non-chemical dependence. Analyze the life scenario of patients with non-chemical dependence as a structure of an autobiographical knowledge base of a higher order, implicitly involved in the formation of images of the future. Postulate the possible existence of relationships between the life scenario, auto-aggressive behavior, the severity of the course of non-chemical dependence and impairments of prospective thinking in the examined patients.

The general hypothesis of the study is as follows: patients with non-chemical dependence have specific impairments of prospective thinking that are associated with the influence of an implicit maladaptive life scenario and interfere with the realization of conscious intentions and plans, as well as reinforce auto-aggressive behavior.

3.1   Clinical Case Studies. Conclusions on the Analysis of the Interview Content

Table 4. Family and individual scenarios.

Patient	P4	P5	P1	P2	P3
Name priming	+	+	NA	-	+
Story priming	-	+	NA	-	+
Date/number priming	-	+	NA	-	-
Family secret	+	-	NA	-	-
Favorite story	+	+	NA	-	-
Addictive dissociation metaphors (ME, non-ME parts)	+	+	NA	+	+

1. Patients with non-chemical dependence of the treatment and control groups generally do not have formal disorders of the explicit prospective thought process: they are capable of formal thinking about the future, planning, and goal-setting. At the same time, all patients report that conscious planning, as a rule, turns out to be unrealistic and "fails" (with the exception of planning antisocial actions to accumulate funds for the game or to play directly). Patients emphasize a high proportion of impulsive actions in their behavior.

2. All patients showed a shortened time perspective in relation to the future – long-term planning is formal and usually not visualized. More than 70% of patients report having certain ideas about the "final scene" (the image of death) or a special attitude towards death. They report anxiety about untimely and/or tragic death. Almost 30% of the subjects could not describe either the five-year plan or their final representation, which indicates impairments of long-term projection in these patients. In a similar study of patients with alcohol dependence, patients unable to provide long-term projection (even at the level of fantasies about themselves) showed a greater severity of dependence on a number of indicators.

3. In the majority of patients, indirect indicators of auto-aggression were revealed (the presence of tragic and untimely deaths in the family, hereditary burden of psychopathology and drug addiction, cases of self-injuries, depressive feelings, sense of shame, frustration and futility at certain stages of life). Most patients come from dysfunctional family systems. All patients reported the presence of suicidal ideation – a direct marker of suicidality – as well as the presence of job-related problems, senses of isolation and guilt. Interestingly, the patients' long-term planning had an interpersonal orientation: that is, ideas about the future contained projections about the presence of functional relationships. This observation of a high interpersonal rather than intrapersonal orientation of images of the future correlates with the data of prospective thinking studies in parasuicides, as well as in patients with alcohol dependence. It is assumed that auto-aggressive and dependent patients are guided in the future by the search for supportive (codependent) relationships, and not by intrapersonal growth and development.

4. All patients had some dissociation, i.e. an addictive dissociation of personality according to the chemical type. Patients are aware of the presence of negative subpersonalities, recognize their identification with them at the moments of actualization of their desire to play or to commit illegal actions. They also emphasize that the activation of the addictive subpersonality leads to the failure of the fulfillment of intentions and intended goals, impulsive behavior and actions.

3.2 Algorithm for Conclusion of No-Suicide Contract in Treatment of Patients with Internet Addiction Disorders

The no-suicide contract as a psychotherapeutic method was proposed by R. Goulding and M. Goulding [11] in writing as an agreement, where the patient is considered a potential suicide and undertakes not to commit suicide for a certain time. In the research and recommendations on psychotherapy of patients with suicidal ideas, it is recommended to phrase a no-suicide contract as follows: "I will be (future or indefinite time) here, so that in the meantime I do not feel or think" [10, 21]. The text of the agreement of the founder of psychosynthesis Roberto Assagioli with parasuicide is known all over the world [6]. R. Assagioli [7] noted a positive result in all cases of using this method.

In our study, a no-suicide contract was concluded with 32 patients of the treatment group. The conclusion of such a contract was necessitated either by suicidal thoughts revealed during the inteview, or by the presence of suicidal ideas or parasuicides in their past medical history. With some patients (4 people), no-suicide contracts were concluded in the absence of the above symptoms, since the study of their history showed the need for this procedure, which could significantly reduce conflict tension in the intrapersonal sphere. Patients were sympathetic to the conclusion of the contract; after this procedure they experienced feelings of relief and relaxation or joy. Some patients (7 people) demonstrated reactions of protest and negativism, asserting that "they should not be deprived of the right to die". In these cases, a no-self-injury contract was concluded, a less stricter version of a no-suicide contract, necessary to avoid activating reactions of protest and negativism. To treat these reactions, additional psychotherapeutic sessions were given [40], and distant forms of psychotherapy were provided for support between sessions.

4 Conclusion

The most important criterion of the effectiveness of a no-suicide contract and a no-self-injury contract is the absence of suicidal thoughts and actions in the future. Another criterion is the absence of breakdowns and relapses of non-chemical dependence. Also, one of the effectiveness criteria is a more careful attitude to one's physical health and body. Thus, the study showed that patients with Internet addiction disorders are characterized by a high suicidal risk, which necessitates specialized psychotherapy aimed at correcting suicidal tendencies in the psyche. The format of the developed and tested anti-suicidal psychotherapy for patients with Internet addiction disorders proves its effectiveness and adequacy. Our research has shown once again that excessive use of the Internet [31] negatively affects emotional processes and emotional regulation up to the formation of addictive behavior and suicidal tendencies. In accordance with this, it is necessary to carry out an individualized strategy for the primary prevention of emotional disorders and addictive behavior, taking into account the respective age groups.

Acknowledgments. The research is supported by the Russian Science Foundation, grant #18-18-00477. The method was approved by the Local ethical committee at the Moscow Research and Practical Centre for Narcology of the Department of Public Health, opinions #03-1/20 from August 5, 2020, and #01/19 from February 14, 2019. Conflict of interest: The authors declare no conflict of interest.

References

1. Agibalova, T.V., Rychkova, O.V., Gurevich, G.L., Potapova, R.K.: The relationship of emotional and cognitive impairments in the structure of drug addiction diseases. Narcology **1**, 84–90 (2014). (in Russian)
2. Agibalova, T.V., Rychkova, O.V., Kuznetsov, A.G., Gurevich, G.L., Potapova, R.K.: Dynamics of cognitive functions in patients with alcohol dependence. Bull. East Siberian Scientific Center of the Siberian Branch of the Russian Academy of Medical Sciences **6**(94), 9–15 (2013). (in Russian)
3. Agibalova, T.V., Tuchina, O.D., Buzik, O.Z., Potapova, R.K., Potapov, V.V.: Cognitive deficits in patients with gambling disorder. Counsel. Psychol. Psychother.**4**(28), 167–185 (2020), (in Russian)
4. Anokhina, I.P.: Biological mechanisms of addiction to psychoactive substances. Addiction Issues **2**, 27–32 (1995). (in Russian)

5. Arzumanov, Y.L.: On the medical aspects of gambling addiction. Methods of detection, rehabilitation and prevention: Materials of the conference. Gambling addiction. Myths and reality. May 28, 2003, Moscow. J. Addict. Med.**4**, 15 (2004). (in Russian)

6. Assagioli, R.: Psychosynthesis. A Manual of Principles and Techniques. Dormann & Company, New York, Hobbs (1965)

7. Assagioli, R.: Psychosynthesis: A Collection of Basic Writings. The Synthesis Center, Amherst (2000)

8. Bisaliev, R.V.: Suicidal and non-suicidal forms of self-destructive behavior in opium addiction. Dissertation, University of Astrakhan (2005). (in Russian)

9. Buzik, O.Zh., Rychkova, O.V., Agibalova, T.V., Gurevich, G.L., Shalaeva, E.V., Potapova, R.K.: Emotional and cognitive impairments in the structure of drug addiction diseases: mutual influence and interrelation. J. Neurol. Psychiat. S.S. Korsakov **5**, 79–83 (2014). http://www.mediasphera.ru/journals/korsakov/1174/eng/19112/

10. Clarkson, P.: Transactional Analysis Psychotherapy: An Integrated Approach. Routledge, London (1992)

11. Drye, R., Goulding, R., Goulding, M.: No-suicide decisions: patient monitoring of suicidal risk. Am. J. Psychiatry **130**(2), 171–174 (1973). https://doi.org/10.1176/ajp.130.2.171

12. Egorov, A.Y., Charnaya, D.I., Khutorianskaya, Y.V., Pavlov, A.V., Grechanyi, S.V.: Internet-dependent behavior in adolescents with mental disorders. VM Bechterev Rev. Psychiatry Med. Psychol. **4**, 35–45 (2018). https://doi.org/10.31363/2313-7053-2018-4-35-45

13. Fedotov, I.A.: Clinical and auto-aggressive characteristics of alcohol dependence in patients with various types of parental fixations. Dissertation, University of Moscow (2015). (in Russian)

14. Fedotov, I.A., Shustov, D.I.: Investigation of environmental factors in the transmission of propensity to alcohol dependence by the method of analysis of autobiographical narrative. Problems of Narcology **2**, 69–81 (2015). (in Russian)

15. Frances, A., Clarkin, J.F., Gilmore, M., Hurt, S.W., Brown, R.: Reliability criteria of borderline personality disorder: a comparison of DSM-III and the diagnostic interview for borderline patients. Am. J. Psychiatry **141**, 1080–1084 (1984). https://doi.org/10.1176/ajp.141.9.1080

16. Frank, M.L., Lester, D., Wexler, A.: Suicidal behavior among members of Gamblers Anonymous. J. Gambling Studies **7**, 249–254 (1991). https://doi.org/10.1007/BF01019876

17. Griffiths, M.D.: Internet addiction: an issue for clinical psychology? Clin. Psychol. Forum **97**, 32–36 (1996). http://irep.ntu.ac.uk/id/eprint/25089

18. Malygin, V.L., Khomeriki, N.S., Smirnova, E.A., Antonenko, A.A.: Internet addicted behavior, clinic and diagnostics. J. Neurol. Psychiatry SS Korsakov **4**, 86–92 (2011). (in Russian)

19. Merinov, A.V.: Auto-aggressive behavior and assessment of suicidal risk in patients with alcohol dependence and members of their families. Dissertation, University of Moscow (2012). (in Russian)

20. Montgomery, S.A., Asberg, M.: A new depression scale designed to be sensitive to change. Br. J. Psychiatry **134**, 382–389 (1979). https://doi.org/10.1192/bjp.134.4.382

21. Mothersole, G.: Existential realities and no-suicide contracts. Transact. Anal. J. **26**, 151–159 (1996). https://doi.org/10.1177/036215379602600206

22. Muehlenkamp, J.J., Claes, L., Havertape, L., Plener, P.L.: International prevalence of adolescent non-suicidal self-injury and deliberate self-harm. Child Adoles. Psychiatry Mental Health **6**(10) (2012). https://doi.org/10.1186/1753-2000-6-10

23. Najavits, L.M.: Seeking Safety: A Treatment Manual for PTSD and Substance Abuse. Guilford Press, New York (2002)

24. Nakken, C.: The Addictive Personality: Understanding the Addictive Process and Compulsive Behavior. Hazelden Publishing, Minnesota (1996)

25. Palmer, B.A., Pankratz, V.S., Bostwick, J.M.: The lifetime risk of suicide in schizophrenia: a reexamination. Arch. Gen. Psychiatry **62**, 247–253 (2005). https://doi.org/10.1001/archpsyc. 62.3.247
26. Petry, N.M.: Contingency Management for Substance Abuse Treatment: A Guide to Implementing This Evidenced-Based Practice. Routledge, New York (2011)
27. Potapova, R.K.: New information Technologies and Linguistics. Librokom, Moscow (2017). (in Russian)
28. Potapova, R., Agibalova, T., Bobrov, N., Zabello, N., Yurashko, A., Migunova, E.: Phonetic cues relevant to drug intoxication state identification (experimental research). Linguist. Lit. Stud. **6**(6), 278–284 (2018). https://doi.org/10.13189/lls.2018.060603
29. Potapova, R., Potapov, V.: Kommunikative Sprechtätigkeit. Russland und Deutschland im Vergleich. Böhlau Verlag, Köln (2011)
30. Potapova, R.K., Potapov, V.V.: Fundamentals of a multidimensional study of "electronic personality" on voice and speech in the information and communication environment of the Internet. Man: Image essence **1–2**, 87–111 (2017). (in Russian)
31. Potapova, R.K., Potapov, V.V., Lebedeva, N.N., Agibalova, T.V.: The Polycode Environment of the Internet and the Problems of Valeology. Languages of Slavic Cultures, Moscow (2020). (in Russian)
32. Reutfors, J., et al.: Medication and suicide risk in schizophrenia: a nested case-control study. Schizophr. Res. **150**(2–3), 416–420 (2013). https://doi.org/10.1016/j.schres.2013.09.001
33. Shemchuk, N.V., Oshevsky, D.S.: On a complex clinical and psychological approach to game addiction. In: Materials of the XIV Congress of Russian Psychiatrists. Moscow, 378 (2005). (in Russian)
34. Shustov, D.I.: Auto-aggression and Suicide in Alcohol Addiction: Clinical Aspects and Psychotherapy. Special literature, Saint-Petersburg (2016). (in Russian)
35. Shustov, A.D., Klimenko, T.V.: Study of the effectiveness of provital therapeutic interviews using the SOCRATES method. Issues of Addiction Medicine **11**(182), 65–71 (2019). (in Russian)
36. Shustov, D.I., Merinov, A.V., Valentik, Y.V.: Diagnostics of auto-aggressive behavior with alcoholism by the method of therapeutic interview. Manual for psychiatrists-narcologists and psychotherapists. Section of Narcology of the Ministry of Health of the Russian Federation, Moscow (2000). (in Russian)
37. Shustov, D.I., et al.: Study of addictive disassociation during a provital interview in alcohol-dependent patients with comorbid personality disorders. Issues of Addiction Medicine **11**(182), 38–49 (2019). (in Russian)
38. Skobelin, V.V.: Deficiency of social and emotional intelligence in persons suffering from addiction to gambling, comorbid with alcoholism. Modern achievements of narcology. In: Materials of the International Conference on November 21–22, 2005. Moscow, pp. 98–99 (2005). (in Russian)
39. Thompson, W.N., Gazel, R., Rickman, D.: The social costs of gambling in Wisconsin. Wisconsin Policy Res. Inst. Rept. **9**(6), 1–44 (1996). https://doi.org/10.11575/PRISM/9826
40. Valentik, Y.V.: Continuous psychotherapy of patients with addiction to psychoactive substances. In: Ivanets NN (ed) Lectures on Addiction Medicine. Knowledge, Moscow, pp. 341–364 (2000). (in Russian)
41. World Health Organization. The ICD-11. International Classification of Diseases for Mortality and Morbidity Statistics. Eleventh Revision. (2020) (accessed August 28)

Media Content vs Nature Stimuli Influence on Human Brain Activity

Rodmonga Potapova[1](✉) ⓘ, Vsevolod Potapov[2] ⓘ, Nataliya Lebedeva[3],
Ekaterina Karimova[3] ⓘ, and Nikolay Bobrov[1] ⓘ

[1] Institute of Applied and Mathematical Linguistics, Moscow State Linguistic University,
38 Ostozhenka Street, Moscow 119034, Russia
`{r.potapova,n.bobrov}@linguanet.ru`
[2] Centre of New Technologies for Humanities, Lomonosov Moscow State University,
Leninskije Gory 1, 119991 Moscow, Russia
`kedr@philol.msu.ru`
[3] Institute of Higher Nervous Activity and Neurophysiology of RAS, (IHNA&NPh RAS),
5A Butlerova Street, Moscow 117485, Russia
`lebedeva@ihna.ru`

Abstract. The aim of this study was to identify what neurophysiological and psychophysiological changes in the indicators of the functional state occur during the active perception of media content in comparison with the background contemplative activity when the rest state networks are engaged. Psychophysiological methods showed a more significant decrease in the stress index of cardiovascular activity and an increase in heart rate variability after the passive perception session. The indicators of complex visual-motor response did not differ in the active and passive experiments. However, it was after the passive perception session that the proof test evaluating attention and performance efficiency showed a higher speed of work and a higher volume of the reviewed material. The study showed that the background video sequence, which does not contain information and speech content, contributes to the activation of resting state networks. At the same time, the stress index of the cardiovascular system decreases and the heart rate variability increases; while after a 30-min session of calm wakefulness and contemplation of video sequences of nature, the speed of operator performance increases, as a practical advice, it is suggested not to "surf" the Internet during work breaks, browsing information and entertainment resources, but to look out the window, listen to the sounds of nature, and, contemplating the world around, let one's thoughts flow freely (mind flow). It is at these moments that the default mode networks begin to work, the functioning of which is no less important for the optimal state of the brain and nervous system.

Keywords: Functional state of a person · Perception of media content of different modality · Polycode multimodal signal · Psychophysiological techniques · EEG rhythms · Default mode network

A. Karpov and R. Potapova (Eds.): SPECOM 2021, LNAI 12997, pp. 528–539, 2021.
https://doi.org/10.1007/978-3-030-87802-3_48

1 Introduction

Within the context of the everyday world, one is used to living surrounded by media space. The rapid digitalization of life leads to the situation when it is almost impossible to see a young man in transport or a queue without a gadget in their hands. Young people spend most of their free time watching or listening to blogs, podcasts, news, programs, photographs, during breaks, or often in parallel with their main activities. However, of course, this trend is not observed in the older generation [7].

The high efficiency and low cost of information and communication technologies that have appeared in the last decade have become the substrate for immersion into the media space and digital reality necessary for young people [6]. The rapid development of technological progress also contributes to the entrenchment of the habit of receiving momentary pleasure and postponing the achievement of long-term goals, i.e. procrastination [11].

A distinctive feature of immersion into the Internet environment of the modern generation is the unfocused absorption of information to fill the "pauses" in a person's life (waiting in the queue, traveling by public transport, breaks at work or school). At the same time, this kind of leisure is perceived as a simple and easy way to shift one's attention to something else and relax. In this case, it is not a targeted search for the content of interest, but "surfing" in the network, that is, watching and listening to the content proposed by the site algorithm [2].

As a result of such involvement in the digital environment, a person and a human brain get used to the state of constant consumption of information – visual and auditory stimulation, without which they feel uncomfortable. Continuous processing of vivid visual and emotional auditory stimuli cannot but affect the functional state of the brain, since perception is one of the most complex and resource-intensive processes of cognitive activity affecting all levels from the senses to the association areas of the cerebral cortex [1, 12].

If we consider the functional state as a result of the interaction of the modulating systems of the brain and the higher parts of the cerebral cortex, which determines the current mode of human activity [10], then long-term afferent visual or auditory stimulation before the main labor activity of a person or during pauses can, on the one hand, help maintain a sufficiently high level of the cortex activation, but also leads to stress and overload of analyzers and exhaustion of the nervous system, on the other hand.

For a long time, it was believed that at rest, when a person is not engaged in active motor or cognitive activity, but is in a relaxed state of "quite wake", their brain is resting. Moreover, such rest was considered as something unproductive, useless and shameful. Hardworking members of society have always made fun of those who "sit idle". However, some time ago it turned out that in a state of calmness and "rest" the human brain is extremely active and consumes much more energy than when solving problems – in 1995, resting state networks (RSNs) were discovered [8, 9].

The concept of a resting state network refers to the activity of neural networks in the human (animal) brain that is awake, but not involved in activities requiring direct attention [5]. The concept of resting state networks arose from the work of B. Biswal and his colleagues (1995) [3], in which the authors determined the source of coherent oscillations of the BOLD (blood-oxygen-level-dependent) response of the fMRI signal when performing a simple motor task. Interestingly, it has long been known in EEG studies that at rest, the brain generates the highest-amplitude and rhythmic oscillations, the alpha rhythm, which decreases with concentration and vigorous activity. The activity of these networks can be recorded using fMRIs/EEGs/MEGs [4]. Over the past decade, they have been intensively studied, and it is assumed that the default mode network (DMN), which was one of the first discovered, is closely related to the function of consciousness [15]. All the functions of resting state networks have not yet been discovered, but it has already become clear that in a state of rest, when a person is not busy performing any specific task, the brain remains no less active and performs its equally important tasks.

In this experiment, we modeled two variants for "waiting" behavior: calm contemplation of the background video sequence (for example, when a person taking public transport looks out the window or watches people around him/her, immersed in his/her thoughts) or watching entertainment media material with the option of choosing the most interesting video materials. The aim of this study was to identify what neurophysiological and psychophysiological changes in the indicators of the functional state occur during the active perception of media content in comparison with the background contemplative activity when the rest state networks are engaged.

2 Method

The study involved 16 people: 9 women and 7 men, aged 21–25. Each participant was subjected to two experiments on two different days (active and passive perception); in total, the study included data from 32 experiments. In the "active perception" experiment, the subjects were offered a selection of entertaining videos from YouTube hosting on various topics (interesting facts, travel, countries, popular science, secrets of the planet, etc.) with duration of 10–20 min. The instruction for the subjects was as follows: for 30 min to watch those videos that are most interesting to them, and in this session it was possible to switch from one video to another at any time in order to constantly maintain a high level of interest and attention, as well as bring the situation to the real one as close as possible. In the "passive perception" experiment, the subjects were invited to watch only one video without information content, containing frames and sounds of a summer forest, without the option to switch the video. The session lasted 30 min also. The sequence of sessions was randomized for different subjects.

Before and after each session, the subjects underwent psychophysiological testing and a background EEG recording with eyes closed and open. The EEGs were also recorded while watching the video sequence in both experiments. To assess the functional state of the subjects, the following tests were proposed: complex visual-motor response (CVMR); ECG recording with analysis of heart rate variability (HRV). After the session, the "proof test" (test visual perception) was offered to control the level of attention and quality of activity.

Proof test (Bourdon-Wiersma test) is designed to assess the volume, concentration and stability of attention. As a material, a form is offered for completing the task with rows of randomly arranged letters. The subject should, looking through the form, row by row, circle and cross out the letters indicated in the instructions. For example, "In the form with letters, cross out all the letters I and circle all the letters A, looking through row by row. Every 60 s, at the stop command, mark with a vertical line the place in the form where this command caught you". Time for working on the form was 5 min.

The CVMR test was performed before the session (in a simple version) and after the session (in a three-level version). The recording was made using UPFT-1/30 "Psychophysiologist" (Medikom-MTD, Taganrog). In the two-choice CVMR test, the subject was presented with a series of 75 light stimuli with a random distribution of green and red. The task was to press the right button as quickly as possible in response to the green stimulus, and the left button in response to the red stimulus. The three-level test assumed that after the first variant the instruction was reversed (to press the left button in response to the green stimulus, and the right button in response to the red stimulus); in the third variant it was necessary to press the button only in response to the red stimulus, skipping the green one. The three-level test was performed to assess the flexibility of reactions and the mobility of the nervous system. We analyzed the mean time Tavg, the standard deviation (RMS) of correct responses and the level of sensorimotor reactions (an integral indicator of speed and quality).

The five-minute ECG recording (minimum 300 R-R intervals) was performed in a sitting position in the second standard lead using UPFT-1/30 "Psychophysiologist" (Medikom-MTD, Taganrog); this was processed by the method of variation cardiometry. In addition to the average duration of R-R intervals, its standard deviation (SD) and the Baevsky stress index (SI) were analyzed. The study of HRV is an effective method for assessing the interaction of the cardiovascular and other systems of the body and the use of spectral analysis makes it possible to assess the balance of parasympathetic and sympathetic regulation.

The dynamics of the power of EEG rhythms was analyzed to assess changes in the functional state of the brain, the level of activity and attention. The EEG was recorded in a calm state with eyes open and closed before and after the session (background tests), as well as during the perception of the stimulus material using the "Neurovisor" encephalograph-analyzer with 17 electrodes (F3, F4, F7, F8, Fz, C3, C4, Cz, P3, P4, Pz, T3, T4, T5, T6, O1, O2) located according to the "10–20" system, monopolar with respect to the combined A1 and A2 ear electrodes. For all leads, the sampling rate was 256 Hz, the bandwidth was 0.5–70 Hz, and the impedance was less than 30 kΩ. At the first stage, the EEG was recorded in the "Typology" program, and then, for further processing, the frequency spectra were calculated for epochs equal to 4.75 s in the same program. As a result of the spectral analysis, the values of the amplitudes of the spectral power and the peak values of frequencies in the frequency bands of the theta (4–8 Hz), alpha (8–13 Hz), beta-1 (13–24 Hz), and beta-2 (24–35 Hz) rhythms in each of 17 leads were obtained.

To analyze the power of the rhythm dynamics during the perception of the stimulus material, the entire session time (30 min) was divided into 3 periods (10 min each), i.e. the beginning of the session, the middle of the session and the end of the session (the first, second and third fragments). Further, the average spectral power values recorded in the middle and at the end of the session were normalized to the values obtained at the beginning. Also, the relative changes were recorded in the power of rhythms after the session in tests with closed and open eyes.

To analyze the dynamics of spectral indicators, the relative power values were calculated in the background tests (the "after" values were normalized to the values before the session), as well as during the session – the middle as compared to the beginning (the second fragment to the first), and the end as compared to the beginning (the third fragment to the first). Thus, the relative values of the rhythm power in the background tests with eyes closed and open (normalized to the values before the session) and the dynamics of the power of the EEG rhythms during the session – the middle normalized to the beginning, and the end normalized to the beginning – were considered.

Statistical analysis was performed using Statistica 64 software (StatSoft Inc.). The following methods of analysis were used: Wilcoxon test for matched pairs; repeated measures analysis of variance (ANOVA), ANOVA factor analysis.

All studies were conducted in accordance with the principles of biomedical ethics formulated in the 1964 Declaration of Helsinki and its subsequent updates and approved by the local bioethical committee of the Institute of Higher Nervous Activity and Neurophysiology of the Russian Academy of Sciences (Moscow).

The results obtained in these experiments will help to further establish the prospects for development of an ecological model of health, in particular for student-age population (see also: [13, 14]).

3 Results

Complex Visual-Motor Response Test. Analysis of variance ANOVA with the "session" factor did not show a significant influence of the factor on the dynamics of the complex visual-motor response indicators. Neither the average response speed, nor the standard deviation (SD) of the average response time, nor the level of sensorimotor reactions (where errors in pressing are also taken into account) showed significant differences between the active and passive sessions (Table 1).

Table 1. Average values and standard deviations of the CVMR indicators after the active and passive sessions.

Test level		Estimates of sensorimotor reaction level, rel. units		Average response time (ART), ms		Response time SD, ms	
	Session	Average	RMS	Average	RMS	Average	RMS
TEST 1	Active	0.83	0.20	382	52	87.69	53.16
	Passive		0.32	385	65	75.13	29.44
TEST 2	Active	0.34 0.72	0.31	479	89	479	89
	Passive	0.38	0.33	491	120	491	120
TEST 3	Active	0.09	0.03	385	44	102.31	49.58
	Passive	0.08	0.03	393	71	124.88	101.79

Heart Rate Variability. Analysis of HRV indicators before and after the experiment using the Wilcoxon test for matched pairs revealed significant differences ($p < 0.05$) for all indicators except the scatter of R-R intervals in the active session (Table 2). After the experiment, the duration of R-R-intervals in the subjects increased significantly, and the stress index decreased (Tables 3, 4 and 5). This is ample evidence of relaxation and strengthening of parasympathetic regulation after the sessions.

Table 2. Average values and RMSs of the relative HRV indicators after the active and passive sessions.

	Average duration of R-R intervals, rel. units		RMS of R-R intervals, rel. units		Stress index, rel. units	
Session	Average	RMS	Average	RMS	Average	RMS
Active	0.107	0.095	0.162	0.383	−0.391	0.606
Passive	0.126	0.089	0.271	0.479	−0.564	0.912

Table 3. Distribution of duration values for R-R intervals before and after the active and passive sessions.

Session	25%–75%	Median	Min	Max
Active (before)	670–925	790	550	1210
Active (after)	740–990	950	700	1125
Passive (before)	650–910	800	600	1250
Passive (after)	805–1020	880	680	1315

Even so, the scatter of the duration of the R-R intervals after the video-watching sessions increased significantly (Wilcoxon's paired test, $p < 0.05$) only in the experiment with passive perception. Also, the Baevsky stress index indicator decreased to a greater extent precisely after the passive perception session, which indicates that the relaxing effect of this session was more pronounced.

Proof Test. The Wilcoxon's paired test showed that the total number of reviewed symbols in the "Proof test" was significantly higher after the passive session, and the type of experiment did not affect the quality of the test (see Table 6). Thus, the speed of work was higher after the passive perception session, while the number of errors did not differ significantly.

Table 4. Distribution of RMS values for R-R intervals before and after the active and passive sessions.

Session	25%–75%	Median	Min	Max
Active (before)	32–72	52	8	92
Active (after)	43–67	58	20	121
Passive (before)	27–62	46	17	87
Passive (after)	43–68	59	35	78

Table 5. Distribution of values for stress index before and after the active and passive sessions.

Session	25%–75%	Median	Min	Max
Active (before)	50–290	90	22	825
Active (after)	52–105	65	8	490
Passive (before)	54–335	94	45	1202
Passive (after)	52–110	65	40	208

Table 6. Results of the "proof test": the average number of characters reviewed per minute and the number of errors in the active and passive sessions.

Session	25%–75%	Median	Min	Max
Active (characters reviewed)	147–180	159	112	202
Active (errors)	2–5	3	0	18
Passive (characters reviewed)	142–208	171	92	219
Passive (errors)	1–6	4	0	13

EEG Spectral Analysis.

Comparison of Background Tests with Open and Closed Eyes

Comparison of spectral EEG parameters before and after the session with the analysis of variance showed a significant difference, taking into account the influence of the factors "repeated measurements" (active and passive sessions) and "rhythms" both for the state with closed eyes (p = 0.05) and for the state with open eyes (p < 0.01). The analysis compared the normalized values (the logarithmic ratio of the values after the session to the values before it) of the spectral power of the rhythms. The "localization" factor did not reveal a significant influence of this indicator on the comparison result.

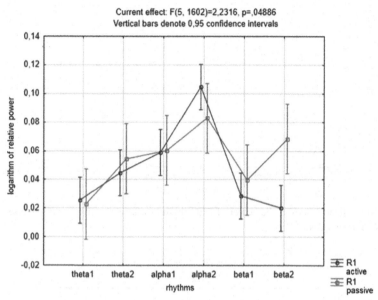

Fig. 1. Normalized values of the power of EEG rhythms after the active and passive sessions in the test with closed eyes.

Figure 1 shows the relative powers of rhythms in the active and passive session "after/before" in the test with closed eyes. After the active session, the power of the alpha2 rhythm increases significantly, and after the passive session, the power of the beta2 rhythm.

Figure 2 demonstrates the relative power of the rhythms in the active and passive session "after/before" in the test with open eyes. This test demonstrates more significant differences in the dynamics of the indicators of the spectral power of rhythms: after the active session, the power of the theta2, alpha1, alpha2 and beta1 rhythms increases significantly, and after the passive session, the power of the beta2 rhythm.

The state after the active session is characterized by the development of inhibition of cortical activity (a significant increase in the power of the theta2 and alpha1 rhythms), which can be attributed to fatigue that is greater than that after the passive session.

The following figures (Fig. 3 and 4) show relative values of the dynamics of the EEG rhythm power while watching videos. Figure 3 shows the spectral power values in the middle of the session relative to the beginning, and in Fig. 4 – at the end of the watching session relative to the beginning (see the methodology).

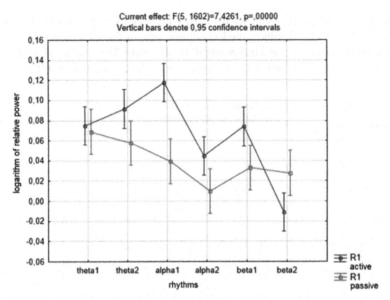

Fig. 2. Normalized values of the power of EEG rhythms after the active and passive sessions in the test with open eyes.

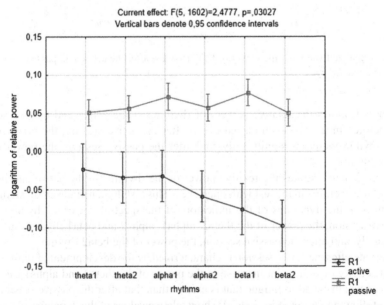

Fig. 3. Changes in the normalized values of the power of EEG rhythms in the middle of the session relative to its beginning while watching the video.

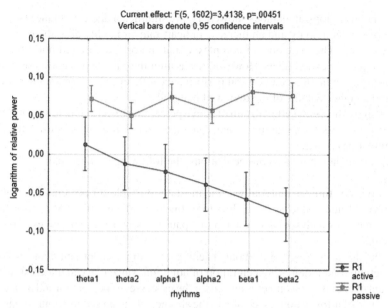

Fig. 4. Changes in the normalized values of the power of EEG rhythms at the end of the session relative to its beginning while watching the video.

In both figures, the dynamics of the spectral power of the rhythms is similar to each other, which means that the main changes occurred in the first 10 min of watching videos. It can be seen that with passive perception of a video with no informative content, an increase in the power of all rhythms occurred, which reflects the synchronous work of subcortical structures and the inclusion of resting state networks. During the active session with various entertainment videos full of polymodal content, all rhythms were desynchronized and the power of the beta frequency range decreased. Desynchronization of the rhythms reflects the process of active perception and an increase in the level of attention, while the work of the cortical and subcortical structures is divided into separate neural ensembles, each of which has to perform its own task of perception, processing, classification and memorization of information.

4   Conclusion

The active process of perceiving a polycode multimodal signal (short entertaining videos from YouTube) differed from passive watching of video material that does not contain any informative part (video and sounds of nature and forest) by desynchronization of all EEG rhythms, which was associated with the processes of perception and increased concentration of attention. In contrast, the passive contemplative process of watching was accompanied by the synchronization of all rhythms and the involvement of resting state networks. Tests with closed and open eyes after the session revealed more significant manifestations of inhibition of cortical processes after the active session.

Psychophysiological methods showed a more significant decrease in the stress index of cardiovascular activity and an increase in heart rate variability after the passive perception session. The indicators of complex visual-motor response did not differ in the active and passive experiments. However, it was after the passive perception session that the proof test evaluating attention and performance efficiency showed a higher speed of work and a higher volume of the reviewed material.

This study shows that after 30 min of active perception of various entertaining videos, a person is in a less favorable functional state than after 30 min of unfocused perception (contemplation) of nature.

Recommendations. As recommendations, the following is suggested:

- the polycode stimulus material was the most comfortable for perception, combining both visual and sound stimuli; therefore, one should give preference to watching video materials with sound to rest and fill "pauses" between various types of business activity;
- one should be more careful about listening to audio content simultaneously with any activity that requires concentration of attention, since one can underestimate the amount of cognitive resources required for the processes of perception and understanding of verbal information, especially in the absence of visual support. Our research has shown a significant activation of cortical processes associated with memory, maintaining attention and emotional responses while listening to audio content without video accompaniment;
- as for watching only video sequences, it can be concluded that the main information channel for human is language (spoken or written), in the absence of which a state of inhibition of cortical activity develops. Therefore, in moments of relaxation and rest, it is necessary to exclude the sources of spoken or written language from the external environment, while the background video will not interfere with the work of the resting state networks;
- the second part of the study showed that the background video sequence, which does not contain information and speech content, contributes to the activation of resting state networks. At the same time, the stress index of the cardiovascular system decreases and the heart rate variability increases; while after a 30-min session of calm wakefulness and contemplation of video sequences of nature, the speed of operator performance increases;
- as a practical advice, it is suggested not to "surf" the Internet during work breaks, browsing information and entertainment resources, but to look out the window, listen to the sounds of nature, and, contemplating the world around, let one's thoughts flow freely (mind flow). It is at these moments that the default mode networks begin to work, the functioning of which is no less important for the optimal state of the brain and nervous system.

References

1. Batuev, A.S.: Chapter 2. Sensory function of the brain. § 1. General principles of sensor systems. Physiology of higher nervous activity and sensory systems. 3. Piter, Sankt-Peterburg (2010). (in Russian)
2. Belozerova, Y.M.: Experience in the use of media technologies, virtual and augmented reality in the formation of professional competencies of employees of service organizations. Digital society as a cultural and historical context of human development: collection of scientific papers/under general editorship of R.V. Ershova. State Social and Humanities University, pp. 41–43. Kolomna (2020). (in Russian)
3. Biswal, B., Yetkin, F.Z., Haughton, V.M., Hyde, J.S.: Functional connectivity in the motor cortex of resting human brain using. Magn. Reson. Med. **34**(4), 537–541 (1995)
4. Fox, M.D., Snyder, A.Z., Vincent, J.L., Corbetta, M., Van Essen, D.C., Reichle, M.E.: The human brain is intrinsically organized into dynamic, anticorrelated functional networks. Proc. Natl. Acad. Sci. **102**(27), 9673–9678 (2005). https://doi.org/10.1073/pnas.0504136102
5. Guo, W., et al.: Iterations of the amplitude of low-frequency fluctuations in treatment-resistant and treatment-response depression: a resting-state fMRI study. Prog. Neuropsychopharmacol. Biol. Psychiatry **37**(1), 153–160 (2012). https://doi.org/10.1016/j.pnpbp.2012.01.011
6. Introduction to the "Digital" economy. In: Budanov, V.G., Dmitrov, I.D., Keshelava, V.B., Rumyantsev, V.Yu., Sorokin, K.S., Khaet, I.L., Shcherbakov, A.V.; under general ed. of Keshelava, A.V. ; chapter "Digit." cons. Zimnenko, I.A. VNIIGeosystem (2017). (in Russian)
7. Kandybovich, S.L.: Peculiarities of students' perception of digital means and communication processes. Digital society as a cultural and historical context of human development: collection of scientific papers/under general editorship of Ershova, V. State Social and Humanities University, pp. 153–158. Kolomna (2020). (in Russian)
8. Lebedeva, N.N., Karimova, E.D.: Neurophysiological manifestations of the state of monotonia in operators with different interhemispheric asymmetries of alpha activity. J. Higher Nerv. Act. **64**(4), 428–438 (2014). (in Russian)
9. Lebedeva, N.N., Mayorova, L.A., Samotaeva, I.S.: Functional connectome: resting state networks in certain neurological and psychiatric conditions. Adv. Physiol. Sci. **48**(3), 29–44 (2017). (in Russian)
10. Maryutina, T.M., Ermolaev, O.Y.: Introduction to psychophysiology: textbook for the course: "General and developmental psychophysiology". In: Moscow Psychological and Social Institute. Flinta, Moscow (1997). (in Russian)
11. Mokhova, S.B., Nevryuev, A.N.: Psychological correlates of general and academic procrastination in students. Psychology **1**, 25–33 (2013). (in Russian)
12. Ostrovsky, M.A., Shevelev, I.A.: Chapter 14. Sensory systems. In: Pokrovsky, V.M., Korotko, G.F. (eds.) Human Physiology. Textbook, vol. 2. Moscow (2003). (in Russian)
13. Potapova, R., Potapov, V., Lebedeva, N., Karimova, E., Bobrov, N.: EEG investigation of brain bioelectrical activity (regarding perception of multimodal polycode internet discourse). In: Salah, A.A., Karpov, A., Potapova, R. (eds.) SPECOM 2019. LNCS (LNAI), vol. 11658, pp. 381–391. Springer, Cham (2019). https://doi.org/10.1007/978-3-030-26061-3_39
14. Potapova, R., Potapov, V., Lebedeva, N., Karimova, E., Bobrov, N.: The influence of multimodal polycode internet content on human brain activity. In: Karpov, A., Potapova, R. (eds.) SPECOM 2020. LNCS (LNAI), vol. 12335, pp. 412–423. Springer, Cham (2020). https://doi.org/10.1007/978-3-030-60276-5_40
15. Verkhlyutov, V.M., Sokolov, P.A., Ushakov, V.L., Velichkovsky, B.M.: Overlapping of large-scale human brain networks recorded by fmri at rest and during mental tasks. In: Cognitive Science in Moscow: New Research. Conference Materials (2015). (in Russian)

Can Your Eyes Tell Us Why You Hesitate? Comparing Reading Aloud in Russian as L1 and Japanese as L2

Valeriya Prokaeva, Elena Riekhakaynen(✉), and Vladislav Zubov

Saint-Petersburg State University, 7/9 Universitetskaya Emb. St, Petersburg 199034, Russia
e.riehakajnen@spbu.ru

Abstract. In the paper, we claim that analyzing eye movement patterns while reading aloud can provide new evidence on multichannel processing. The current study focuses on the unfilled (silent) hesitation pauses that occur during unprepared reading in Russian as a first and Japanese as a second languages. We analyzed the pauses in the oral texts produced by 10 native Russian speakers while reading two text fragments in Japanese and their Russian translations. The eye movements were recorded while the participants were reading the texts. According to the results, the pause duration in L1 can be related to the time spent on the text processing both before and during the hesitation, whereas in L2 the hesitation duration is associated only with the processing time of the following segment. Moreover, when reading aloud in L2, where the number of pauses within the sentences exceeded the number of hesitations at the sentence boundary, the participants spent more time processing the text that followed the hesitation within a sentence, compared to sentence boundaries. In L1, however, we did not find any difference in text processing considering the location of the hesitation, although there were more pauses at sentence boundaries than within one sentence in Russian. The results suggest that in Russian as L1, the readers spend the same time after encountering a difficulty within a sentence and when preparing the next one, whereas in a second language the mid-sentence planning requires more time.

Keywords: Hesitations · Reading aloud · Second language

1 Introduction

1.1 Silent Pauses in Unprepared Reading as a Hesitation Phenomenon

Any natural speech contains speech disfluencies including filled (voiced) and unfilled (silent) hesitation pauses. The earliest classifications of hesitations were proposed in [9, 22]. Such phenomena were then explained exclusively by the difficulties a speaker undergoes while generating an utterance [22]. The majority of studies in the field do use spontaneous (casual, unprepared) speech as the data. However, hesitations frequently occur during reading as well [8, 19]. Using reading as a material makes it possible to obtain more or less homogeneous data from different participants, as all of them

© Springer Nature Switzerland AG 2021
A. Karpov and R. Potapova (Eds.): SPECOM 2021, LNAI 12997, pp. 540–552, 2021.
https://doi.org/10.1007/978-3-030-87802-3_49

can read the same text. Therefore, we suppose reading aloud to be a convenient tool for a comparative study of the hesitation phenomena in the second language acquisition because the content, the format, and the size of the collected data are easy to control, and it is possible to observe the effects of language (the first and the second) on different speech disfluency phenomena. Another methodological advantage of reading over spontaneous speech is that the eye movement technique can be applied to discover what exactly causes hesitations, i.e., how a reader processes the information at the moment of hesitation. The simultaneous registration of eye movements and the recording of speech material in the disfluency research seems to provide a noteworthy alternative to traditional methods that use speech recordings exclusively. For instance, combining eye tracking with a network task paradigm was recently used to demonstrate the effects of speech difficulties on both disfluencies and eye movements in [27]. Thus, we can receive new evidence on multichannel speech processing because reading aloud combines visual word recognition with spoken word production including perceptual control of what is pronounced (i.e., spoken word recognition).

The results obtained in such a study can be potentially used in text-to-speech systems. If we understand not only how frequent hesitations while reading aloud are and where they normally occur, but also what exactly provokes such disfluencies, this information can be applied to automatic text-to-speech systems. We argue that the eye movement patterns can help us find out the factors causing hesitations (e.g., the words before or after the hesitation, the position in the text, etc.).

The current study focuses on unfilled (silent) pauses. The main purpose was to find out the possible connections between eye movement patterns and the occurrence of silent hesitation pauses during reading aloud, and to shed some light on the functions of hesitation phenomena in L1 and L2. The comparison between reading in L1 and L2 is especially interesting from a psycholinguistic point of view, but in the long term can be applied to evaluating language proficiency in L2: if the hesitations in L1 and L2 are caused by different reasons, eye movement patterns analysis can be used to estimate the level of L2 acquisition.

According to some data, the pauses during reading in the first language mostly occur at the ends of sentences [13]. The results of some studies suggest that hesitation pauses may be related to the sentence structure planning, i.e., pursue a stalling strategy [12]. The duration of pauses (along with other hesitation phenomena occurrence) increases with the increase of lexical and syntactic complexity of a clause [3], as well as the sentence length [35], suggesting that hesitation phenomena during reading is mostly associated with the amount of the cognitive load experienced by a speaker [20]. The analysis, however, has mostly been carried out on separate sentences, although reading a text is a more common situation for a speaker. Furthermore, it remains unclear whether the role of silent hesitations is the same during reading in the first and the second languages, which is why we chose reading aloud in Russian as L1 and Japanese as L2 along with the participants' eye movements as our data.

1.2 Eye Tracking Studies of Reading in First and Second Languages

The first paper to describe the eye movements during reading aloud was [4]. Using one of the first eye tracker models, Buswell showed that eye movements during oral reading also include saccades, regressions, word skipping, and other patterns naturally observed during silent reading. Current studies mainly confirm the qualitative similarity of reading aloud to silent reading, but there are significant quantitative differences between the two modalities: the average duration of fixations when reading aloud is about 50 ms longer, the length of saccades is shorter, and regressions are more common [14, 28].

When reading aloud, the gaze is ahead of the articulatory movements. The articulation begins after the identification of several words in the text, and the reader constantly adjusts the time spent processing the subsequent words to keep the eye-voice distance steady. Because of this eye-voice cooperation, the information, which the reader is able to process parafoveally, decreases. A saccade size reduction is also among the reasons for a decrease in the functional visual field during oral reading [14]. According to some data, the parafoveal effects associated with previewing a fragment of the text during reading are stronger in silent reading. However, the change in modality does not lead to significant differences in oculomotor activity [1, 2].

One of the most frequently considered parameters in studies of eye movements while reading aloud is the number of characters at which the gaze is ahead of the voice – the "eye-voice span" (EVS). In the first papers where this parameter was taken into account, EVS was about 15 characters or 2–3 words [7]. According to the data from more recent studies, the duration of this parameter is about 500–600 ms [2, 15] or 13.8 characters [5] for the alphabetic languages. In Japanese reading, EVS seldom exceeds 6 characters (2–3 characters on average, which is considerably fewer than for most European languages), according to [18]. Since the gaze is ahead of the voice, we can expect that when there is a hesitation pause while reading aloud, there will be longer fixations on the characters following the spot where the hesitation takes place.

The comparative studies of written text perception strategies and disfluencies related to them in the first and second languages are quite rare, see [29] for a review. However, since it is possible to examine different (earlier and later) stages of visual processing and to consider different phenomena that are impossible to detect otherwise, applying eye tracking contributes to the research of speech disfluency while reading aloud in a non-native language. Differences in the features of hesitation pauses in L1 and L2 have been demonstrated for different languages [30, 34]. The data indicate that the qualitative differences between speech disfluencies in the first and the second language speech production are few, and the differences are mainly observed in the number of hesitations. Quite predictably, the process of speech production in a second language, being a more cognitively laborious task, entails more pauses, errors, and self-corrections among speakers, which may be explained by the lower level of speech planning skills control [32].

1.3 The Goals of the Study

We are going to analyze and compare the eye movement activity during reading aloud that accompanies silent hesitation pauses in the first (Russian) and second (Japanese) languages in order to find out how the visual information processing differs depending on the hesitation pause length, its location, and the language.

Our hypotheses are as follows:

1) there will be more hesitation pauses in Japanese text reading than in reading in Russian since our participants are native Russian speakers learning Japanese as a second language;
2) in the Russian (first language) data, there will be more pauses at sentence boundaries than within a sentence, similar to the previous studies;
3) there will be differences in eye movement patterns associated with the hesitations within a sentence and on sentence boundaries as well as for long and short hesitations;
4) we will find more differences in the eye movement patterns on the interest areas following the place of hesitation than on the preceding ones, as we assume that thanks to the EVS, during an unfilled hesitation pause a reader is already processing the information following the place of hesitation;
5) there will be differences in eye movement patterns related to the hesitation pauses in L1 and L2.

The first two assumptions seem to be quite evident, but we should check them in order to be sure that our data on hesitations are relevant for further analysis. The third hypothesis considers the role of the hesitation location and length. By checking the latter, we hope to answer the question formulated in the title of the paper. The last two hypotheses may seem quite vague since there are only a few studies concerning both hesitation phenomena and visual information processing. The studies that highlight differences in L1 and L2 text processing are still rare as well. Thus, we would like to shed some light on these issues in our study in order to use the results obtained in our further research.

2 Experiment

2.1 Material

The stimuli were two text fragments (one narrative and one description) from the Japanese novel *Natsu no niwa* by Yumoto Kazumi, and their Russian translations (four texts overall). The text type was defined by the type of predicate prevailing in each text – dynamic (active) for a narration and static (stative) for a description [26, 31].

The dynamic (narrative) and the static (descriptive) Russian texts were similar in difficulty (5.64 and 5.15 respectively), word count (176 and 173 words), sentence count (15 sentences each) and average word count in a sentence (11.73 and 11.53 words). The parameters for texts in Russian were measured automatically using the readability.io resource (last accessed: 29.01.2021). The Japanese Text Readability Measurement System (JReadability PORTAL) resource (https://jreadability.net/sys; last accessed: 02.02.2021) was used to measure the readability of the Japanese texts. Both texts were given the Upper-intermediate level of difficulty. The texts in Japanese were not adapted for reading by Japanese language learners with the only exception. The kanji characters corresponding to the levels of JLPT (Japanese Language Proficiency Exam) N2–N1, as well as characters that are not included in the 常用漢字 (Jōyō kanji) list, were provided with furigana (a reading aid) to facilitate unprepared oral reading. The texts were presented to participants in black Georgia font (16-point size) on a white background, line spacing 1.5.

2.2 Participants

10 Native speakers of Russian (19–28 years old) with some experience of studying Japanese (N3–N1 Japanese Language Proficiency Level JLPT), with normal or corrected to normal vision and no speech or reading impairments took part in the experiment.

2.3 Procedure

The experiment was conducted in accordance with the Declaration of Helsinki and the existing Russian and international regulations concerning ethics in research. All participants provided written consent to take part in the experiment.

The experimental design combined the registration of eye movements and the recording of reading aloud. The recording started as soon as the participants began reading the first text. The participants' oculomotor activity was recorded using an eye tracker Eye-Link 1000+ by SR Research Ltd with a camera-to-screen distance of 190 mm, display resolution 1600:1024. The position of the head was fixated with the upper bar. Reading aloud was recorded using an Olympus DM-720 speech recorder in the Meeting mode, Waveform Audio File Format (WAV), 44100 Hz.

Providing that the participants were asked to read the Japanese texts and their Russian translations, the procedure consisted of two stages with an interval of 1.5–2 weeks in order to distract the participants' attention from the similarity of the Russian and Japanese texts contents. The original text and its translation were presented on different days in randomized order. At each stage of the experiment, the participants read aloud one text in Russian and one in the Japanese language at their own reading pace. Directly after they had read the text, the participants were expected to retell the text and evaluate it on a scale from 1 (easy) to 5 (difficult). The design of the experiment, consisting of two identical sessions, required that we informed all participants about the upcoming task in advance to prevent the effect of the anticipation of the need to retell the text during the second session. We must admit, however, that such a task might have provoked slower processing of a text while reading which resulted in longer pauses. The average duration of speech material from one participant for the reading in Russian was 79 s for the dynamic text and 86 s – for the static one; in Japanese – 150 s for the dynamic text, 186 s – for the static one.

The retelling task was used in the experimental design in order to compare the hesitations in two different types of speech – more and less prepared ones (spontaneous reading aloud and retelling respectively). At this point of the study, we did not use the results of the retelling task as a way to estimate the text comprehension, although it can be considered in our further research. In this paper, we will focus only on spontaneous reading as it allows us to measure eye movements.

2.4 The Principles of Silent Hesitation Pauses Detection

The silent hesitation pauses in the voice recording files transcribed via PRAAT (https://www.fon.hum.uva.nl/praat/) were selected for the analysis manually with the lower boundary of 700 ms. This threshold was chosen in accordance with the data provided in [10]. In a recent study on read speech in Russian [16], mean silent pauses from 433 ms to 645 ms were observed, which is coherent with the previously obtained findings. Goldman-Eisler [10] reported that the mean duration of grammatical reading pauses is mainly less than 500 ms and elaborated that the first 500 ms of a pause located at the end of a clause may represent a standard juncture pause for the clause preceding the addressed one, whereas the remaining 200 ms or longer account for a hesitation pause for the following clause. Along with this data, we will also consider pauses consisting of 700 ms and more to contain both grammatical encoding element of a juncture pause and a hesitation component.

In this study, we differentiated between two types of silent hesitation pauses depending on their length: shorter pauses (700–999 ms) and longer ones (1000 + ms), following the classification presented in [17: 69]. Silent pauses described in our study sometimes included respiratory activity and some minor paralinguistic hesitation phenomena as tongue clicking and suchlike, see [11] for the evidence that the presence of inhalation does not affect the pause structure.

2.5   The Principles of Eye Movements Analysis

In eye movements analysis, we selected the fragments of different length for the texts in Russian and in Japanese. For Russian, we considered three interest areas (IA) before and three interest areas after the place where the hesitation pause occurred (average 16.2 characters). For Japanese – only one interest area before and after (2.3 characters on average each). The thresholds were chosen according to the mentioned in earlier papers EVS value for the alphabetic languages (13.8 characters, up to three words) and for Japanese (2–3 characters). For the mean number of characters in one interest area in all texts, see Table 1.

Table 1. Mean number of characters in one IA in Russian and Japanese texts.

Text type	Dynamic	Static
Russian	5.3	5.5
Japanese	2.2	2.4

The eye movement measure under consideration included the summed duration of fixations in the above-stated interest areas (Dwell Time, DT).

First, we considered the two following conditions depending on the duration of the pause:

1) a short silent hesitation pause (700–999 ms);
2) a long hesitation pause (1000 ms +).

Then, we considered the three following conditions depending on the location and presence of the pause:

1) a silent hesitation pause (700 ms +) within one sentence;

2) a silent hesitation pause (700 ms +) at the sentence boundary;

3) no hesitation pause at the sentence boundary or only a short, syntagmatic pause present.

We excluded from the analysis the hesitation pauses where due to a poor recording quality there were no fixations in the IA under consideration.

2.6 Results

Russian Texts Reading: General Overview. The overall number of silent hesitation pauses of 700 ms and more that corresponded to the registered eye movements was 136, with 48 pauses exceeding 1000 ms. We found 25 pauses to appear inside the sentences and 111 between two sentences (4.4 times more). Therefore, we can assume that hesitation pauses occur more frequently at sentence boundaries than within sentences while reading in L1. Pauses lasting less than 1000 ms appeared to be more frequent than longer ones both within (18/7) and between (70/41) sentences. The overall number of pauses in the static text reading was slightly higher, though the difference in pause distribution between the text types did not reach significance ($t = -0.636$, $df = 9$, $p = 0.540$).

Russian Texts Reading: Eye Tracking Measures Analysis. Using the nonparametric Mann–Whitney U-test, we found that when a long hesitation pause occurred, the readers spent significantly more time processing both three words before hesitation (SFD Before) and three words after (SFD After) than when there was a short hesitation (Table 2).

Table 2. The sum of the fixation durations before and after short or long hesitations when reading in Russian. Here and further on, significant differences are marked with an asterisk (*).

	Long hesitation pauses, N = 48	Short hesitation pauses, N = 88	p-value
SFD Before, the average value (ms)	1648.65	1410.80	$p = 0.018$*
SFD After, the average value (ms)	1556.38	1273.80	$p = 0.013$*

Then, we analyzed how the eye movements differ upon the place of the hesitation pause occurrence. We compared 1) hesitations within a sentence ($N = 25$); 2) hesitations on a sentence boundary ($N = 111$); and 3) cases where there was no pause at sentence boundaries (see Table 3).

The sum of fixations before and after a hesitation did not differ either within a sentence ($W = 150.00$, $p = 1.000$) nor at the end of a sentence ($W = 3682.00$ $p = 0.092$) (Wilcoxon signed-rank test was used for the comparison). When there were no hesitations at sentence boundaries, the sum of the fixations on the three words before was significantly greater than the sum of the fixations on the three words after a sentence boundary ($W = 9068.50$, $p < .001$, see Fig. 1–A).

Table 3. The sum of the fixation durations depending on the location and presence of a hesitation pause while reading in Russian.

	Hesitation within a sentence, N = 25	Hesitation at the end of a sentence, N = 111	No hesitation at the end of a sentence, N = 166
SFD Before, the average value (ms)	1505.52	1492.32	1285.99
SFD After, the average value (ms)	1485.04	1348.41	1107.63

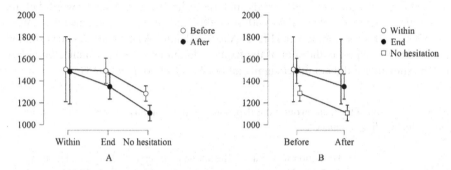

Fig. 1. The sum of the fixation durations (ms) when reading in Russian.

No difference was found between the duration of fixations within one sentence and at sentence boundaries both before hesitation (p = 0.164) and after hesitation (p = 0.200). On sentence boundaries, we found significant differences in eye movements between the cases when hesitations occurred and when they did not: both in the sum of the duration of fixations on the three words before a sentence boundary (p = 0.004) and after (p < .001). The post hoc Dunn test was used for the analysis (see Fig. 1–B).

Japanese Texts Reading: General Overview. In total, we analyzed 548 unfilled hesitation pauses of 700+ ms duration, 307 of hesitations exceeded 1000 ms. 133 pauses appeared at the sentence boundaries, and 415 were found within sentences. Apparently, reading in a second language induces more unfilled pauses within one sentence than at a sentence boundary (3:1). The total number of 1000+ ms pauses within the sentences was 222, at the sentence boundaries – 85. Shorter pauses at sentence boundaries appeared 48 times, within one sentence – 193 times. There were significantly more pauses in the static text reading: t = −2.393, df = 9, p = 0.040.

Japanese Texts Reading: Eye Tracking Measures Analysis. Table 4 shows the average sum of the durations of all fixations within one interest area before and after hesitation when reading in Japanese. We found that the readers spent significantly more time processing words after long hesitations (SFD After). However, the pause length did not affect the time spent processing a word before the hesitation pause.

Table 4. The sum of the duration of fixations before and after short and long hesitations when reading in Japanese.

	Long hesitation, N = 307	Short hesitation, N = 241	p-value
SFD Before, the average value (ms)	881.45	838.17	p = 0.834
SFD After, the average value (ms)	1992.21	1258.18	p < .001*

When hesitation occurred while reading in L2, the participants spent significantly more time visually processing the words after the hesitation pause than the words before, both within a sentence (W = 17316.50; p < .001) and at the end of a sentence (W = 2037.50; p < .001), see Table 5 and Fig. 2–A for the details. When there was no hesitation at the end of a sentence, the sum of the fixation durations before a sentence boundary and the sum after it did not differ significantly (W = 694.50; p = 0.418).

Table 5. The sum of the fixation durations depending on the location and presence of a hesitation pause while reading in Japanese.

	Hesitation within a sentence, N = 415	Hesitation at the end of a sentence, N = 133	No hesitation at the end of a sentence, N = 49
SFD Before, the average value (ms)	912.93	705.04	720.63
SFD After, the average value (ms)	1789.74	1292.37	718.69

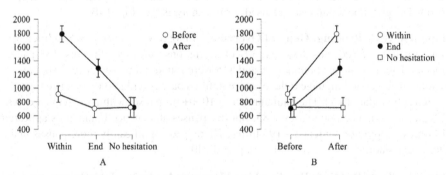

Fig. 2. The sum of the fixation durations (ms) when reading in Japanese.

Dunn's post hoc test showed that before hesitation the readers spent equal time processing words regardless of whether there was hesitation at a sentence boundary or within one sentence (p = 0.360). On sentence boundaries, they spent equal time processing information with the hesitation pause or without it (p = 0.208). At the same time, after the hesitation pause, the readers spent significantly more time if the hesitation appeared within a sentence than at the end of it (p < .001). Processing the following words at a sentence boundary took longer if the hesitation pause occurred, compared to the cases where there was no hesitation at a sentence boundary (p < .001, Fig. 2–B).

3   Discussion and Conclusions

The paper presents the study of eye movement patterns when hesitations occur while reading aloud in Russian as L1 and Japanese as L2. Despite a relatively small number of participants, preliminary results suggest that hesitations when reading in the first and second languages are not always due to the same reasons. The most interesting results are as follows.

As we expected, our data supported the hypotheses that the hesitations are more common for reading aloud in L2 than in L1 and that while reading in L1 silent hesitation pauses occur more often between the sentences than within one sentence. Similar findings were obtained earlier in [13]. Our results show that in L2 (Japanese), however, the within-sentence pauses are more common than those at sentence boundaries. One could suggest that contrary to reading in L1, hesitations while reading in L2 are not simply associated with preparation for the articulation of the next fragment of an utterance, but are caused by the complexity of a particular word or a combination of words.

The pause duration in L1 influenced the time spent processing the text. Presumably, silent hesitation pauses in L1 reading are associated both with the consequent text preparation for the articulation (i.e., speech planning) along with some other factors forcing the speaker to process the text before the hesitation occurs. This suggests that silent pauses in L1 production may not necessarily be associated with speech planning only, as proposed in [30], although the differences in results might be explained by the data from reading and not spontaneous speech. In L2 (Japanese), however, the main role of silent hesitations seems to be the preparation for the articulation of the next segment that is visually processed during the hesitation.

For Russian, the time spent on visual processing did not differ significantly whether the pause appeared within one sentence or at a sentence boundary. Considering that the hesitations in Russian were more frequent at sentence boundaries, we expected that the readers would spend more time processing the beginning of the next sentence than the next words within one sentence in Russian. This, however, was not the case. Thus, we can assume that the eye movement patterns during hesitations in L1 do not depend on the location of hesitation (within a sentence or not). For Japanese, the readers spent significantly more time processing the text after the hesitation if it appeared within a sentence than at a sentence boundary. We suggest several possible explanations of this finding. First, the next word or grammatical structure complexity might serve as a reason for both hesitations occurrence and an increase in the time of processing the fragment that caused the difficulty [33]. Another factor that might have influenced the results is the difference between the Russian and Japanese orthographic systems. Previously obtained data argue in favor of a smaller functional visual field in Japanese text reading (3–4 symbols to the right of a fixation, according to [23, 346]) compared to most languages using alphabetic writing systems. Quite interestingly, some researchers provide similar evidence concerning mean fixation duration (191 ms for Japanese [24], 228 ms for Russian [21]) and saccade size (7.8 symbols for Japanese [25], 8 symbols for Russian [21]). Kana-based (syllabary) text segments, however, are associated with the decrease in the saccade size and the raise of fixation durations among natives; faster kanji processing can be explained by the direct lexical access to such characters without having to render the words into phonetic sequences first [25]. Russian-speaking readers, contrary to Japanese natives, might be less used to the processing of ideographic symbols such as kanji, which can result in the increase of their reading time, e.g., mean fixation durations, as shown in [6], and thus enhance the time spend on the words containing kanji after the hesitation.

To sum up, we found some evidence from eye movements supporting the hypothesis about the differences in the nature of hesitations in L1 and L2. The hypotheses about the different eye movement patterns for hesitation pauses of different length and location and about the difference in processing the words before and after the hesitation were partially supported.

In this paper, we considered only unfilled hesitation pauses. However, hesitation phenomena also usually include filled pauses, as well as, for example, self-corrections or repetitions. The analysis of eye movements during these types of hesitations and their comparison to the data for the unfilled hesitation pauses can be considered as further steps in our research. We also plan to consider the syntactic and semantic structure of the target sentences to find out which factors exactly might serve as the hesitation pause durations determiners. This challenge, indisputably, calls for the changes in the experimental design, for these parameters are difficult to control in a natural text material. We believe that the results will provide new insights into multichannel signal processing.

Our findings can be applied so far only to a specific pair of languages – Russian as a first and Japanese as a second language. However, we hope that the methodology we used in the study, which combines the recording and the analysis of oral speech along with the registration of eye movements, can be further used to study various disfluencies in oral speech using the material of different languages and comparing different writing systems. This will allow us to find out the cases of communication difficulties in processing a written text, and can also be used in the practice of teaching foreign languages, since it will show what exactly causes the greatest difficulties for L2 learners.

We believe that the preliminary results on silent hesitation pauses in L1 that can be potentially used in text-to-speech systems are as follows: 1) such pauses are more common on sentence boundaries than within sentences; 2) they are associated with visual processing of the words both before and after the hesitation and this is the case both within a sentence and on sentence boundaries. Thus, both previous and subsequent information should be regarded in more detail in further research in order to find out which linguistic features of words in a text provoke hesitations and whether these features are the same for the following and preceding hesitations.

Acknowledgements. The study is supported by the research grant #21-18-00429 from the Russian Science Foundation.

References

1. Anderson, I.H., Swanson, D.E.: Common factors in eye-movements in silent and oral reading. Psychol. Monogr. **48**(3), 61–77 (1937). https://doi.org/10.1037/h0093393
2. Ashby, N.J., Dickert, S., Glöckner, A.: Focusing on what you own: biased information uptake due to ownership. Judgm. Decis. Mak. **7**(3), 254–267 (2012)
3. Brown, E., Miron, M.S.: Lexical and syntactic predictors of the distribution of pause time in reading. J. Verbal Learn. Verbal Behav. **10**(6), 658–667 (1971). https://doi.org/10.1016/S0022-5371(71)80072-5
4. Buswell, G.T.: An experimental study of the eye-voice span in reading. Chicago University Press, Chicago (1920)
5. De Luca, M., Pontillo, M., Primativo, S., Spinelli, D., Zoccolotti, P.: The eye-voice lead during oral reading in developmental dyslexia. Front. Human Neurosci. **7** (2013). https://doi.org/10.3389/fnhum.2013.00696
6. Everson, M.E.: The effect of word-unit spacing upon the reading strategies of native and non-native readers of Chinese: an eye-tracking study. Ohio State University, Columbus (1986)
7. Fairbanks, G.: The relation between eye-movements and voice in the oral reading of good and poor silent readers. Psychol. Monogr. **48**(3), 78–107 (1937). https://doi.org/10.1037/h0093394
8. Fant, G., Kruckenberg, A., Ferreira, J. B.: Individual variations in pausing. A study of read speech. Proceedings of Fonetik: Reports in Phonetics. PHONUM 2003, Umeå University, 193–196 (2003)
9. Goldman-Eisler, F.: Psycholinguistics: Experiments in Spontaneous Speech. Academic Press, New York (1968). https://doi.org/10.1016/0024-3841(70)90028-8
10. Goldman-Eisler, F.: Speech production and the predictability of words in context. Q. J. Exp. Psychol. **10**, 96–106 (1958). https://doi.org/10.1080/17470215808416261
11. Grosjean, F., Grosjean, L., Lane, H.: The patterns of silence: Performance structures in sentence production. Cogn. Psychol. **11**(1), 58–81 (1979). https://doi.org/10.1016/0010-0285(79)90004-5
12. Grosjean, F., Collins, M.: Breathing, pausing and reading. Phonetica **36**(2), 98–114 (1979). https://doi.org/10.1159/000259950
13. Grosman, I., Simon, A.C., Degand, L.: Variation de la durée des pauses silencieuses: impact de la syntaxe, du style de parole et des disfluences. Langages **211**(3), 13–40 (2018)
14. Inhoff, A.W., Radach, R.: Parafoveal preview benefits during silent and oral reading: testing the parafoveal information extraction hypothesis. Vis. Cogn. **22**(3–4), 354–376 (2014). https://doi.org/10.1080/13506285.2013.879630
15. Inhoff, A.W., Solomon, M., Radach, R., Seymour, B.A.: Temporal dynamics of the eye-voice span and eye movement control during oral reading. J. Cogn. Psychol. **23**(5), 543–558 (2011). https://doi.org/10.1080/20445911.2011.546782
16. Kachkovskaia, T., Skrelin, P.: Prosodic phrasing in Russian spontaneous and read speech: evidence from large speech corpora. In: Proceedings of the 10th International Conference on Speech Prosody, pp. 166–170. Tokyo, Japan (2020). https://doi.org/10.21437/SpeechProsody.2020-34
17. Kibrik, A.A., Podlesskaya, I.I.: Stories about dreams: a corpus study of Russian oral discourse. Languages of Slavic Cultures, Moscow (2009).(in Russian)
18. Kondo, T., Mazuka, R.: Prosodic planning while reading aloud: on-line examination of Japanese sentences. J. Psycholinguist. Res. **25**(2), 357–381 (1996). https://doi.org/10.1007/BF01708578
19. Krivokapic, J.: Prosodic planning: effects of phrasal length and complexity on pause duration. J. Phon. **35**(2), 162–179 (2007). https://doi.org/10.1016/j.wocn.2006.04.001

20. Lalain, M., Espesser, R., Ghio, A., De Looze, C., Reis, C., Mendonca-Alves, L.: Prosodie et lecture: particularités temporelles et mélodiques de l'enfant dyslexique en lecture et en narration. Rev. Laryngol. Otol. Rhinol. **135**(2), 71–82 (1991)

21. Laurinavichyute, A.K., Sekerina, I.A., Alexeeva, S., Bagdasaryan, K., Kliegl, R.: Russian Sentence Corpus: Benchmark measures of eye movements in reading in Russian. Behav. Res. Methods **51**(3), 1161–1178 (2018). https://doi.org/10.3758/s13428-018-1051-6

22. Maclay, H., Osgood, C.E.: Hesitation phenomena in spontaneous English speech. Word **15**(1), 19–44 (1959). https://doi.org/10.1080/00437956.1959.11659682

23. Osaka, N., Oda, K.: Effective visual field size necessary for vertical reading during Japanese text processing. Bull. Psychon. Soc. **29**(4), 345–347 (1991). https://doi.org/10.3758/BF0333 3939

24. Osaka, N.: Eye fixation and saccade during kana and kanji text reading: comparison of English and Japanese text processing. Bull. Psychon. Soc. **27**(6), 548–550 (1989). https://doi.org/10. 3758/BF03334665

25. Osaka, N.: Size of saccade and fixation duration of eye movements during reading: psychophysics of Japanese text processing. J. Opt. Soc. Am. **9**(1), 5–13 (1992). https://doi.org/ 10.1364/JOSAA.9.000005

26. Papina, A.F.: Text: Is Units and Global Categories. Editorial URSS, Moscow (2020).(in Russian)

27. Pistono A., Hartsuiker R.J.: Eye-movements can help disentangle mechanisms underlying disfluency. Lang. Cog. Neurosci. 1–18 (2021). https://doi.org/10.1080/23273798.2021.190 5166

28. Rayner, K., Pollatsek, A., Ashby, J., Clifton, C. Jr.: Psychology of reading. 2nd ed. Psychology Press, New York (2012). https://doi.org/10.4324/9780203155158

29. Roberts, L., Siyanova-Chanturia, A.: Using eye-tracking to investigate topics in L2 acquisition and L2 processing. Stud. Second. Lang. Acquis. **35**(2), 213–235 (2013). https://doi.org/10. 1017/S0272263112000861

30. Rose, R.L.: A comparison of form and temporal characteristics of filled pauses in L1 Japanese and L2 English. J Phonetic Soc. Japan **21**(3), 33–40 (2017). https://doi.org/10.24467/onseik enkyu.21.3_33

31. Soga, M.: Tense and aspect in modern colloquial Japanese. British Columbia, Vancouver (1983). https://doi.org/10.1080/08351818409389203

32. Temple, L.: Disfluencies in learner speech. Australian Rev. Appl. Linguistics **15**(2), 29–44 (1992). https://doi.org/10.1075/aral.15.2.03tem

33. Watanabe, M., Hirose, K., Den, Y., Miwa, S., Minematsu, N.: Factors influencing ratios of filled pauses at clause boundaries in Japanese. In: Proceedings of ISCA Tutorial and Research Workshop on Experimental Linguistics, Athens, Greece (2006). https://doi.org/10.36505/ExL ing-2006/01/0057/000057

34. Watanabe, M., Rose, R.: Pausology and hesitation phenomena in second language acquisition. In: The Routledge Encyclopedia of Second Language Acquisition, pp. 480–483 (2012)

35. Zvonik, E., Cummins, F.: The effect of surrounding phrase lengths on pause duration. In: Proceedings of Eurospeech 2003, pp. 777–780, Geneva, Switzerland. (2003)

Recognition of Heavily Accented and Emotional Speech of English and Czech Holocaust Survivors Using Various DNN Architectures

Josef V. Psutka[1,2]([⊠])[ID], Aleš Pražák[2][ID], and Jan Vaněk[2][ID]

[1] Department of Cybernetics, University of West Bohemia,
Pilsen, Czech Republic
psutka_j@kky.zcu.cz
[2] NTIS - New Technologies for the Information Society, UWB,
Pilsen, Czech Republic
{aprazak,venekyj}@ntis.zcu.cz

Abstract. The Malach Project [6] verified the possibility of using automatic speech recognition (ASR) methods to search for information in large multilingual archives of Holocaust testimonies. After the end of the MALACH project, in which we participated, we continued to work on the completion and implementation of the project's objectives with priority for two languages - Czech and English. We have developed and implemented a full-text search system that can be used by experts and by the general public in the MALACH Centre for Visual History and Jewish Museum in Prague. ASR is a key technology that ensures the functioning of the whole information retrieval process. To ensure the highest quality searches, we are constantly striving to develop this technology using the state-of-the-art methods. The article presents the latest results obtained in extensive experiments using various DNN architectures in the ASR of the English and Czech MALACH archives. The paper is therefore one of the first responses to M. Picheny's call [10] to the speech community to reconsider this very difficult task of recognizing strongly emotional and heavily accented speech of Holocaust survivors.

Keywords: Speech recognition · Acoustic modeling

1 Introduction

The original MALACH project [6] (Multilingual Access to Large Spoken Archives) was solved between 2001 and 2006 in cooperation with the Shoah Visual History Foundation (VHF), IBM, JHU Baltimore, University of Maryland, Charles University (CU) in Prague and University of West Bohemia (UWB) in Pilsen. The main goal of the project was to develop methods for better access to the large multilingual spoken archives gathered by the VHF. The objective of the MALACH project was to develop and verify techniques of automatic speech

© Springer Nature Switzerland AG 2021
A. Karpov and R. Potapova (Eds.): SPECOM 2021, LNAI 12997, pp. 553–564, 2021.
https://doi.org/10.1007/978-3-030-87802-3_50

recognition (ASR) for spontaneous, accented and highly emotional speech of holocaust survivors and to use an output of the ASR system for automatic indexing and searching for keywords and topics. The researchers focused on the development of ASRs for English, Czech, Russian, Slovak, Polish and Hungarian [2,7,15,20]. Although a great deal of work was done, not all objectives were fully met. After completing the MALACH project in 2006, we decided to continue to work towards achieving its noble goals. Initially, we focused on improving ASR parameters for Czech, including the development of a searching and indexing system [17,18]. Since 2012, we received national funding for this activity (UWB in Pilsen and CU in Prague) with the aim of implementing the system for use by the general public and extending access (in addition to the Czech part) also for English part of archives deposited in Prague [22,23]. This goal has been achieved - there are 2 access points to the MALACH archives in Prague (Charles University and Jewish Museum). The dramatic development of machine learning methods and the use of DNNs in recent years has had a major impact on the rapid increase in ASR accuracy. This article presents the latest recognition results of Holocaust testimonies spoken in English and Czech. Data sources for performed experiments and ASR system setups come from the Linguistic Data Consortium (LDC) MALACH corpora - for English (released in 2012 [21] and for Czech (released in 2014) [19]. To select the optimal acoustic model, we tested various architectures and training criteria of deep neural networks (DNN, TDNN, TDNNF, CNN-TDNNF resp. CE, LF-MMI etc.) [4,9,11,13,25,29] and at very perspective ones we intensively tuned the optimal settings (number of layers, number of neurons in a layer, length of context, etc.).

We also tried the end-to-end architecture [27]. However, neither in English nor in Czech did we surpass the current state of conventional DNN systems in the initial experiments. Although this task seems to be ideal for their use in some aspects.

Due to off-line processing of the archive, we have allowed to work with models with high latency. Structure and parameters of the large-vocabulary continuous speech recognition system (LVCSR) were tuned using KALDI toolkit [12], final recognition was performed using in-house ASR system.

2   Data Sources

2.1   English and Czech Parts of MALACH Archive

This audio-visual archive was originally collected in the 1990s to preserve the memories of the Holocaust survivors. Nowadays are these video-interviews located in the Shoah Foundation Institute at the University of Southern California (USC-SFI) along with another 54,000 video-interviews with witnesses of the history of the entire 20th century. The Shoah part of the archive contains testimonies in 32 languages of personal memories of survivors of the World War II Holocaust, in total it is 116,000 h of video. Approximately 25,000 interviews (average length of each is 2.5 h) are in English, more than 550 are in Czech (almost 1,000 h of video). Testimonies spoken in English thus account for about half of the entire archive, but it should be noted that most of these testimonies were provided by witnesses whose native language was not English. Interviews (in all languages) collected in the corpus contain natural, unrestricted speech, full of disfluencies, emotional excitements, heavy accents, and often influenced by the high age of speakers (problems with keeping ideas).

2.2 English and Czech LDC MALACH Data Used for Experimental Work

English. In 2012, the LDC published approximately 375 English testimonies (audio parts) along with manual transcripts of some of these testimonials - approximately 200 h [21]. Unfortunately, some important metadata of this data source was not made available, e.g. missing phonetic vocabulary, interviewer gender, training development and test parts were not defined. For our further work, we had to define some of these missing meta-data. Since most English testimonies have been pronounced by non-native English speakers, the selection of test speakers from different nations was particularly taken into account (exactly according to the national ratio in the training set). The result is a selection of 10 (5 men, 5 women) testimonies from the entire corpus [21], i.e. 3 Polish, 2 Czech, 2 German, 1 Russian, 1 Hungarian and 1 marginal (Austria)[1]. The rest of the transcribed data formed the training and development part.

Czech. In 2014, the LDC released the Czech part of the MALACH project [19]. There were published 420 testimonies along with their transcripts. The release contains 400 randomly selected testimonies for the purpose of acoustic model training. As only 15-minute segments were transcribed for each testimony, the acoustic training part therefore consists of 100 h of Czech speech from theoretically up to 800 speakers (interviewer and interviewee). The rest of the Czech MALACH corpus consists of 20 testimonies, which have been transcribed in their entirety and are intended for development (10) and testing (10) purposes. This 20 testimonies (10 men and 10 women) have a total length of more than 40 h of speech.

2.3 Annotation and Phonetic Transcription

English. Unfortunately, the analysis of the English transcripts revealed that a small subset was segmented too roughly in [21] (into paragraphs rather than sentences). This caused the problematic parts of the transcripts to be manually re-segmented. Very challenging issue in the Malach project is the pronunciation lexicon due to a large number of non-native named entities. While common

---

[1] Speakers were selected according to several parameters, not only according to nationality. Place of birth (better than nationality), length of transcribed speech and gender formed the basis for the selection of a representative test set. It is well known that the place where the speaker spent his childhood fundamentally influences the way he speaks. This process resulted in these 10 testimonies: 00026, 00055 (only 3th tape), 01032, 19894 (only 3th and 10th tapes), 20806, 22984, 28430, 32907, 33414 and 34024 (MALACH IntCode) [21].

English words exist in any readily available pronunciation dictionary (e.g., CMU-DICT or BEEP), foreign proper names, geographical names, villages, holidays, etc. are not present. Therefore a grapheme to phoneme system [8] was used for those words. Special consideration was given to the German words, which were quite common throughout the Malach corpus. This was achieved by adding the German pronunciation lexicon in G2P training (for more details see [23]).

Czech. The audio files were originally divided into segments (roughly into sentences) and annotated. Special attention was paid to the transcription of colloquial words. These words represent 8.9% of words in the dictionary and 6.8% of tokens in the corpus. Such a high percentage of colloquial words is probably the Czech language specificity. This phenomenon associated with colloquial speech did not appear in any other language that we processed in the MALACH projects (English, Russian, Polish, Slovak and Hungarian). All non-Czech words were marked in the transcript with "[...]" (e.g. [lagerführer]) thus it was easy to find them and rewrite them to the Czech pronounced variant (e.g. lágrfírer). Such modified foreign words along with other Czech words were then rewritten according to Czech phonetic rules into their phonetic form.

2.4 Training and Test Subsets Preparation

LDC provides English [21] speech data as dual channel MP2 files with a sampling rate of 44.1 kHz and Czech [19] data as two-channel files of FLAC type with a sampling rate of 16 kHz. The English part was downsampled to 16 kHz. Although two microphones were used during the recording (one for the interviewer and one for the interviewee) and the interviewer was required to be in the right channel and interviewee in the left channel respectively, these guidelines were not always followed. For all train, dev and test data, the best channels were selected manually (for both the interviewee and interviewer). All important statistics are shown in the Table 1. Unfortunately, the English test is almost half the length of the Czech one, because very few English testimonies have been completely transcribed (and therefore suitable for testing).

Table 1. Statistics of training and test data-sets.

	English		Czech	
	Train	Test	Train	Test
# of speakers	1776	20	776	20
# of words	30.9k	3k	49k	10.3k
# of tokens	1774k	36k	715k	63k
dataset length [hours]	212.5	4.3	87.5	8.9
# of phonemes	38		41	

3 Building LVCSR

3.1 Acoustic Feature Extraction

Mel-frequency cepstral coefficients (MFCCs) were used as input not only to the GMM-HMM but also to the DNN-HMM. The window size was 32 ms. 40 MFCC bandpass filters were applied. This 40-dimensional MFCC feature vectors were computed every 10 ms (100 frames per second). For GMM-HMM training only, the original 40 cepstral coefficients have been extended with both delta and delta-delta sub-features and also the cepstral and variance normalizations were applied.

3.2 Acoustic Modeling

GMM-HMM. The first step is building a monophone acoustic model (AM). A monophone AM is trained from the flat start using the MFCCs features (static + delta + delta delta). Secondly, we trained the triphone AM. As the number of triphones is typically too large, decision trees were used to tie their states. We also applied linear discriminant analysis (LDA) and Maximum Likelihood Linear Transform (MLLT) over a central frame spliced across ±3 frames. LDA+MLLT project the concatenated frames into 40 dimensions space. We used the feature-space Maximum Likelihood Linear Regression (fMLLR) and Speaker-adaptive training procedure (SAT) to adapt GMM-HMM models.

A common approach is to train the GMM-HMM model from scratch. Frame-aligned data for training of all deep-neural nets was generated by forced alignment using the GMM-HMM system.

DNN. We modified a typical Kaldi [12] training recipe S5 for a deep neural network (DNN) acoustic model training. This recipe uses layer-wise RBM pre-training, stochastic gradient descent training, per-frame cross-entropy criterion and multiple iterations of sequence-discriminative training optimizing sMBR criterion. The raw MFCC 40-dimensional features are spliced across ±5 frames of context and used as input to the DNN. The resulting dimension of the input feature vector to the DNN is therefore 440 (11 * 40). In this framework, we used the standard 6 layers topology (5 hidden each with 2048 neurons). The output layer was a softmax layer with dimension equals the number of GMM-HMM clustered context-dependent states.

TDNN_CE. Time Delay Neural Networks (TDNN) have shown to be effective in modeling long-range temporal dependencies [26]. This TDNNs feature is used by AM training that can learn long-term dependencies based on short-term representations (see [9] for more details). The TDNNs used for Cross-Entropy (CE) training were slightly modified to those presented in [9]. The first splicing was moved before the Linear Discriminant Analysis (LDA) transforms layer (−2, −1, 0, 1, 2). The splicing indexes used were (−1, 0, 1) (−1, 0, 1) (−3, 0, 3) (−6, −3, 0). The (−3, 0, 3) means that the hidden layer sees 3 frames of the previous layer, separated by 3 frames. In total we have five hidden layers of

ReLu activation function with 650 nodes. The softmax output layer computes posteriors for clustered GMM-HMM based triphone states. It means that the left context of our DNN was 13 and the right context was 7 frames.

TDNN_LF-MMI. Maximum Mutual Information (MMI) applied during DNN-HMM training uses a full denominator graph (hence the name Lattice-Free) by using a phoneme language model (instead of a word language model) [13]. In place of a frame-level objective, they used the log-probability of the correct phoneme sequence as the objective function to train it. This training procedure (LF-MMI) uses a sequence discriminative training criterion without the need for frame-level cross-entropy pre-training. In regular LF-MMI, all utterances are split into fixed-size chunks (usually 150 frames) to make GPU computations efficient. To obtain the best recognition results, the tuning of hyper parameters was performed. The optimal setting is for the **Czech** LVCSR 14 TDNNF (factorized TDNN [11]) layers, dimension in the hidden layer 1024, bottleneck dimension 512, context ±52 i.e. context per layer (1 1 1 0 3 3 3 5 5 5 5 7 7) and for the **English** LVCRS 15 layers, dimension in the hidden layer 1024, bottleneck dimension 512, context ±57 i.e. context per layer (1 1 1 0 3 3 3 3 5 5 5 5 7 7 7).

The conventional HMM 3*state* topology was replaced in a typical LF-MMI training procedure with a special 1-stage HMM. This 1*state* left-to-right topology has different pdfs on the forward transitions (see *pdf-a* in Fig. 1) and on the self-loop (*pdf-b* in Fig. 1). The observations are associated in this topology with arcs rather than states as in standard HMMs [28]. This HMM can be traversed in a minimum of 1 frame (unlike the typical 3*state* HMM, where 3 frames were needed). This topology allows the use of subsampling, where the output rate at the end of the network is 33.33 Hz (subsampling factor 3) compared to typical setups where it 100 Hz. This subsampling factor (3) speeds up training by a factor of 2. A pruned context-dependent (CD) left-biphone tree is used for regular LF-MMI training instead of commonly used triphones.

CNN-TDNN_LF-MMI. It has been shown [1] that the locality, weight sharing and pooling properties of the convolutional layers have potential to improve the recognition accuracy of ASR. The typical Kaldi CNN-TDNN models consists of 6 CNN layers followed by 10 TDNNF (factorized TDNN [11]) layers and two output layers: chain based (LF-MMI criterion) and cross-entropy criterion (xent). The first convolutional layer receives at input three matrices of speech features (the current, previous and next acoustic frames). It uses 64 filters of size 3×3 to perform time and feature space convolutions and outputs a $64 \times 40 \times 1$ volume. The following convolutional layers apply more filters (128 and finally 256), but preserve the size of the feature volume by decreasing the height from 40 to 20 and finally to 10.

iVector. It has been shown that iVectors capture both speaker and environment specific information that is useful for the instantaneous and discriminative adaptation of the neural network. Along with 40-dimensional MFCCs, 100-dimensional iVectors were optionally appended at each time step (details can be found in [3]).

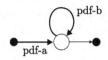

Fig. 1. One state *arc*-based HMM topology.

3.3 Language Modeling

English. The English language model was primarily based on 9.2 MB (1.8M tokens) of training set transcriptions. To deal with very messy transcriptions full of phonetically written names and places, foreign words and word fragments, we made manual vocab-based corrections. All words except common English words were manually checked and either replaced with the correct word spelling (for example word "Czestochowa" which had 14 different transcriptions) or mapped to an unknown word. To expand quite a small vocabulary (22.5k unique words after corrections), we employed the Google "Web 1T 5-gram Version 1" corpus issued by LDC. Only common English words and their bigrams with a frequency of 15 or more and trigrams with a frequency of 7 500 or more were used for language modeling. Resulting trigram language model (with interpolation weight 0.84 for language model from training set transcriptions) with modified Kneser-Ney smoothing contains 243k words (272k phonetical variants). All characteristics are summarized in Table 2.

Table 2. LVCSR setup.

	English	Czech
#vocabulary	243k	237k
#phonetical variants	272k	280k
OOV rate	1.2%	2.6%
#OOV terms	446	1624

Czech. Spontaneous spoken Czech is often colloquial in nature, and colloquial Czech differs significantly from the standard Czech language used in writing or in broadcasting. Coupled with the usual stylistic differences between spontaneous speech and written text, the presence of colloquial language poses major problems in obtaining relevant data for language modeling. As an example, let us mention the Czech word *OBÝVANÝ* (Engl. "inhabited"), which has, in addition to one formal form, another 7 possible colloquial forms. Although each colloquial variant can be written orthographically (in our case: *VOBÝVANÝ, OBÝVANEJ, VOBÝVANEJ, OBEJVANÝ, VOBEJVANÝ, OBEJVANEJ, VOBEJVANEJ*), it must be stated that such orthographic forms of colloquial words appear very rarely in written documents (newspapers, books, etc.), perhaps only when transcribing spontaneous speech. In order to be able to use suitable text sources (books, newspapers, etc.) for language modeling together with transcripts of MALACH testimonies, we approached colloquial words as pronunciation (phonetic) variants [15]. Note that for acoustic modeling, we used the original non-normalized transcriptions with pronounced colloquial words (more details can be found in [14]).

Two basic language models were trained. The first language model was trained on 2.8 MB (715k tokens) of training set transcriptions. The second one was trained from the selection of the Czech National Corpus (CNC). This corpus is relatively large (approximately 400M tokens) and is extremely diverse. Therefore we investigated the possibility of using automatic methods to select sentences from the CNC that are similar in language usage, lexicon, and style to the sentences in the training set transcriptions. This in-domain selection from CNC contains 82 MB of text (16M tokens). An interpolated language model has been created with the ratio 2:1 (transcriptions to the CNC). The resulting tri-gram language model with modified Kneser-Ney smoothing contains 237k words (280k phonetical variants). Details can be found in [16].

3.4 Decoding

All recognition experiments were performed using our in-house real-time ASR system. This LVCSR system is based on left-to-right HMM with "HTK-style" topology [28]. Unfortunately, this brings the need to transform *arc*-based to *state*-based HMM, if necessary. To speed up decoding a parallel approach was used (Viterbi search on CPU and DNN segments scores on GPU [24]).

4 Results

The most interesting results are shown in Table 3. As mentioned in the Sect. 3.2, we started with the **GMM-HMM** model. Frame level alignment (based on GMM-HMM model) is crucial for training many deep neural networks (as stated in Sect. 3.2), unlike e.g. [5] where this alignment is not necessary. Several experiments were performed to determine the optimal number of clustered states concerning the recognition results on the development subset. The result of this optimization process was 4288 states for English and 4496 states for the Czech.

All DNNs topologies were optimized (e.g., number of layers, bottleneck dimensions, dimensions in hidden layers, overall contexts, etc.) on the development parts of the corpora. In the case of training with sequence-discriminative criterion sMBR (**DNN** and **TDNN_CE**), the best result was achieved after several iterations, usually after the first one.

In the Table 3 can be seen the advantages of using biphones together with subsampling (**TDNN_LF-MMI** 1*state* biph.) over the use of the triphones without subsampling (**TDNN_LF-MMI** 3*state* triph. no sub.). Using the left biphones, we reduced the number of clustered states for English to 1784 and for Czech to 1576 (note that the 1*state* *arc*-based HMM has 2 nodes in the DNN output layer).

It is also very interesting to compare the results **TDNN_CE** with sMBR and **TDNN_LF-MMI** for a 3*state* triphone model (without subsampling). Both methods use a sequence criterion over the same HMM topology. Their recognition accuracy is comparable in contrast to the time required to train them, where training of **TDNN_LF-MMI** is much more faster.

The best recognition results were obtained for the optimized **CNN-TDNN_LF-MMI** 1*state* biphones with iVector. The CNN-TDNN employed 8 layers of 2-dimensional convolutional layers (3 × 3). The input-output sizes of these convolutional layers (in the form of filter × height) were 64 × 40, 64 × 40, 128 × 20, 128 × 20, 256 × 10, 256 × 10, 512 × 5, 512 × 5. The optimal settings for sequential TDNNs are for **English** 15 TDNNFs, dimension in the hidden layer 2048, bottleneck dimension 512 in the first layer 256 elsewhere, context per layer (0 1 1 1 3 3 3 3 5 5 5 7 7 7 9) i.e. overall context is ±68 and for the **Czech** 14 TDNNFs dimension in the hidden layer 2048, bottleneck dimension 512 in the first layer 256 elsewhere, context per layer (0 1 1 1 3 3 3 5 5 5 7 7 7 9) i.e. overall context is ±65.

Table 3. The results of recognition experiments.

	WER [%]	
	English	Czech
GMM-HMM	34.27	26.00
DNN	30.91	23.18
DNN sMBR	27.43	20.57
TDNN_CE	29.80	23.27
TDNN_CE sMBR	27.49	20.91
TDNN_LF-MMI 3*state* triph. no sub.	27.72	20.70
TDNN_LF-MMI 1*state* biph.	20.79	17.44
CNN-TDNN_LF-MMI 1*state* biph.	19.72	16.49
CNN-TDNN_LF-MMI iVect 1*state* biph.	17.85	14.65

5   Conclusions

The recognition of testimonies of Holocaust survivors is a very difficult task that we have been working on since the beginning of the MALACH project (y. 2001). The objectives of this project were to show whether it is possible to use automatic speech recognition technology to search for relevant information in large audio-visual archives. Our research group dealt with the development of ASR of some Slavic languages (Czech, Russian, Slovak and Polish) and Hungarian. At the end of the MALACH project in 2006, reached the WER of the Czech ASR system 38.57% [15]. After the end of the MALACH project, we continuously improved the functionality of the Czech ASR system, using new approaches, so that in 2011 we reported a WER of 27.11% [18]. In 2012, our group received national funding, the aim of which was to implement ASR for Czech and English testimonies so that experts and the general public could have access to a quick search in the Czech and English parts of the archive deposited in the Czech Republic. We applied new training methods based on deep neural networks, which brought further improvements in the functionality of the system, see Table 3, where the best result for recognizing Czech testimonies is WER 14.65% and newly for English 15.26%. We analyzed the reasons for the difference between WER for Czech and English for comparable structures of acoustic models (structures of DNN) and we are convinced that the reason for the worse results of the English part is the worse "speech quality" of English-speaking survivors. While Czech utterances were spoken by native Czechs (speaking without a clear accent), the majority of English utterances were spoken by non-native English-speaking survivors who showed less or much accented speech. The results of recognizing their testimonies were then largely dependent on the choice of the test set. This can probably be confirmed by the authors of the article [10], who reported the recognition results of the English part of MALACH testimonies, but worked with other training and test data. However, the latest result in Table 3 shows that the application of CNN-TDNN_LF-MMI with iVectors, which insert important information about a particular speaker, significantly reduces WER, especially in English testimonies burdened by heavily accented speech of non-native English survivors.

In future work, we would like to try the end-to-end architecture in more detail. Such an architecture may be more resistant to speaker characteristics than conventional DNN systems. In addition, pronunciation lexicon issues make this task an ideal candidate for deeper end-to-end system testing. We would also like to perform similar experiments with other Slavic languages (such as Slovak, Polish or Russian).

Acknowledgements. This paper was supported by the Technology Agency of the Czech Republic, project no. TN01000024.

References

1. Abdel-Hamid, O., Mohamed, A., Jiang, H., Deng, L., Penn, G., Yu, D.: Convolutional neural networks for speech recognition. IEEE/ACM Trans. Audio Speech Lang. Process. **22**(10), 1533–1545 (2014). https://doi.org/10.1109/TASLP.2014.2339736

2. Byrne, W., et al.: Automatic recognition of spontaneous speech for access to multilingual oral history archives. IEEE Trans. Speech Audio Process. **12**(4), 420–435 (2004). https://doi.org/10.1109/TSA.2004.828702

3. Dehak, N., Kenny, P.J., Dehak, R., Dumouchel, P., Ouellet, P.: Front-end factor analysis for speaker verification. IEEE Trans. Audio Speech Lang. Process. **19**(4), 788–798 (2011). https://doi.org/10.1109/TASL.2010.2064307

4. Ghahremani, P., Manohar, V., Povey, D., Khudanpur, S.: Acoustic modelling from the signal domain using CNNs. In: Interspeech 2016, pp. 3434–3438 (2016). https://doi.org/10.21437/Interspeech.2016-1495

5. Hadian, H., Sameti, H., Povey, D., Khudanpur, S.: Flat-start single-stage discriminatively trained HMM-based models for ASR. IEEE ACM Trans. Audio Speech Lang. Process. **26**(11), 1949–1961 (2018). https://doi.org/10.1109/TASLP.2018.2848701

6. MALACH project (2006). https://malach.umiacs.umd.edu/

7. Mihajlik, P., Fegyó, T., Németh, B., Tüske, Z., Trón, V.: Towards automatic transcription of large spoken archives in agglutinating languages – Hungarian ASR for the MALACH project. In: Matoušek, V., Mautner, P. (eds.) TSD 2007. LNCS (LNAI), vol. 4629, pp. 342–349. Springer, Heidelberg (2007). https://doi.org/10.1007/978-3-540-74628-7_45

8. Novak, J.R., Nobuaki, M., Keikichi, H.: Phonetisaurus: Exploring grapheme-to-phoneme conversion with joint n-gram models in the WFST framework. Nat. Lang. Eng. **22**(6), 907–938 (2016). https://doi.org/10.1017/S1351324915000315

9. Peddinti, V., Povey, D., Khudanpur, S.: A time delay neural network architecture for efficient modeling of long temporal contexts. In: Interspeech 2015, pp. 3214–3218 (2015)

10. Picheny, M., Tüske, Z., Kingsbury, B., Audhkhasi, K., Cui, X., Saon, G.: Challenging the boundaries of speech recognition: the MALACH corpus. In: Interspeech 2019, pp. 326–330 (2019). https://doi.org/10.21437/Interspeech.2019-1907

11. Povey, D., et al.: Semi-orthogonal low-rank matrix factorization for deep neural networks. In: Interspeech 2018, pp. 3743–3747 (2018). https://doi.org/10.21437/Interspeech.2018-1417

12. Povey, D., et al.: The Kaldi speech recognition toolkit. In: IEEE 2011 Workshop on Automatic Speech Recognition and Understanding 01 (2011)

13. Povey, D., et al.: Purely sequence-trained neural networks for ASR based on lattice-free MMI. In: Interspeech 2016, pp. 2751–2755 (2016). https://doi.org/10.21437/Interspeech.2016-595

14. Psutka, J., Hoidekr, J., Ircing, P., Psutka, J.V.: Recognition of spontaneous speech - some problems and their solutions. In: CITSA 2006, pp. 169–172. IIIS (2006)

15. Psutka, J., Ircing, P., Psutka, J.V., Hajič, J., Byrne, W., Mírovský, J.: Automatic transcription of Czech, Russian and Slovak spontaneous speech in the MALACH project. In: Eurospeech 2005, pp. 1349–1352. ISCA (2005)

16. Psutka, J., et al.: Large vocabulary ASR for spontaneous Czech in the MALACH project. In: Eurospeech 2003, pp. 1821–1824. ISCA (2003)

17. Psutka, J., Švec, J., Psutka, J.V., Vaněk, J., Pražák, A., Šmídl, L.: Fast Phonetic/Lexical searching in the archives of the Czech holocaust testimonies: advancing towards the MALACH project visions. In: Sojka, P., Horák, A., Kopeček, I., Pala, K. (eds.) TSD 2010. LNCS (LNAI), vol. 6231, pp. 385–391. Springer, Heidelberg (2010). https://doi.org/10.1007/978-3-642-15760-8_49

18. Psutka, J., et al.: System for fast lexical and phonetic spoken term detection in a Czech cultural heritage archive. EURASIP J. Audio Speech Music Process. **2011**(1), 1–10 (2011). https://doi.org/10.1186/1687-4722-2011-10

19. Psutka, J.V., et al.: USC-SFI MALACH interviews and transcripts Czech (2014). https://catalog.ldc.upenn.edu/LDC2014S04

20. Ramabhadran, B., Huang, J., Picheny, M.: Towards automatic transcription of large spoken archives - English ASR for the MALACH project. In: ICASSP 2003, p. I (2003). https://doi.org/10.1109/ICASSP.2003.1198756

21. Ramabhadran, B., et al.: USC-SFI MALACH interviews and transcripts English (2012). https://catalog.ldc.upenn.edu/LDC2012S05

22. Stanislav, P., Švec, J., Ircing, P.: An engine for online video search in large archives of the holocaust testimonies. In: Interspeech 2016, pp. 2352–2353 (2016)

23. Švec, J., Psutka, J., Trmal, J., Šmídl, L., Ircing, P., Sedmidubský, J.: On the use of grapheme models for searching in large spoken archives. In: ICASSP 2018, pp. 6259–6263 (2018). https://doi.org/10.1109/ICASSP.2018.8461774

24. Vaněk, J., Trmal, J., Psutka, J.V., Psutka, J.: Optimized acoustic likelihoods computation for NVIDIA and ATI/AMD graphics processors. IEEE Trans. Audio Speech Lang. Process. **20**(6), 1818–1828 (2012). https://doi.org/10.1109/TASL.2012.2190928

25. Veselý, K., Ghoshal, A., Burget, L., Povey, D.: Sequence-discriminative training of deep neural networks. In: Interspeech 2013, pp. 2345–2349 (2013)

26. Waibel, A., Hanazawa, T., Hinton, G., Shikano, K., Lang, K.J.: Phoneme recognition using time-delay neural networks. IEEE Trans. Acoust. Speech Signal Process. **37**(3), 328–339 (1989). https://doi.org/10.1109/29.21701

27. Wang, D., Wang, X., LV, S.: An overview of end-to-end automatic speech recognition. Symmetry **11**(8) (2019). https://doi.org/10.3390/sym11081018

28. Young, S.: The HTK hidden Markov model toolkit: design and philosophy, vol. 2, pp. 2–44. Entropic Cambridge Research Laboratory, Ltd. (1994)

29. Zhang, X., Trmal, J., Povey, D., Khudanpur, S.: Improving deep neural network acoustic models using generalized maxout networks. In: ICASSP 2014, pp. 215–219 (2014). https://doi.org/10.1109/ICASSP.2014.6853589

Assessing Speaker-Independent Character Information for Acted Voices

Mathias Quillot$^{(\boxtimes)}$ ⓘ, Richard Dufour ⓘ, and Jean-François Bonastre ⓘ

Université d'Avignon, 84140 Avignon, France
{mathias.quillot,richard.dufour,jean-francois.bonastre}@univ-avignon.fr

Abstract. While the natural voice is spontaneously generated by people, the acted voice is a controlled vocal interpretation, produced by professional actors and aimed at creating a desired effect on the listener. In this work, we pay attention to the aspects of the voice related to the character played. We particularly focus on actors playing the same video game role in different languages. This article is based on a recent work which proposes to build a neural-network-based voice representation dedicated to the character aspects, namely p-vector. This representation is learnt from recordings only labeled with the acted character. It showed its ability to associate two vocal examples related to the same character, even if the character is unknown during the training phase. However, there is still a possible confusion between speaker and character dimension. To tackle this problem, We propose a protocol to highlight the speaker-independent part of the character information (SICI). We compare the original voice representation with an alternative where the information relating to the characters is neutralised. This experiment shows that performance is not a sufficient metric to assess the quality of a character representation. It also offers the first evidence of the SICI in the voice.

Keywords: Voice casting · Speaker recognition · Character information · Speaker-independent character information · Speaker information

1 Introduction

For decades, the voice has attracted considerable attention from researchers. In speech processing, several areas emerge, such as spoken language recognition [13], automatic speech recognition [14], speaker verification [3], emotion recognition [22], speech understanding [11], voice transformation [21] or conversion [5]. Research efforts in this quite diverse list of areas share one common trait, in terms of the raw material being worked on: most focus on natural voice recordings—spontaneous or read speech, telephone recordings, or speech resulting from human-machine dialogues (through, for example, voice assistants). In comparison, acted voice is poorly represented in speech processing, except in the

© Springer Nature Switzerland AG 2021
A. Karpov and R. Potapova (Eds.): SPECOM 2021, LNAI 12997, pp. 565–576, 2021.
https://doi.org/10.1007/978-3-030-87802-3_51

paralinguistics [6,20] or speech synthesis [10,19] fields, where recordings pronounced by professional actors, playing a specific emotion for instance, are frequently encountered.

Unlike natural speech, acted voice is a controlled vocal interpretation often encountered in audiovisual production. Directed by professional actors, it aims to create a desired effect for the viewer by making manifest the behavior of a fictional character or by facilitating their immersion. The voice is often distorted, sometimes overplayed, in order to make the desired expressive effect more audible. Aspects of the actor's interpretation not related to linguistic contents fall on the listener's side of a complex perception (cultural aspects and stereotypes are obviously there). This interpretation depends on the listeners themselves and their personal history but also on the specific context of each listening. This double complexity, in terms of production and perception, perhaps explains why the acted voice has such little presence in the literature on speech processing. The articles [7–9,15–17] cited in this paper are the only ones dealing with the speech-processing-based automation of Voice Casting in the literature to our knowledge.

In this article, we wish to address some of this complexity and we start with the voices of professional actors playing characters for the gaming industry. We rely on [7], a recent work which defines the p-vector, a neural-network-based representation of the voice dedicated to the character aspects in acted voices. The application context in [7] (like in related previous works [8,9]) is voice casting for audio dubbing. The final objective of this work is to assess how close an actor acting in a target language is to the voice of a given character, speaking in a source language. This can be referred to as character-based voice similarity. In contrast to [16,17], which proposed a voice similarity system for the acted voice based on data labeled with speech classes (age, gender, emotions ...) by an expert, the p-vector approach does not use any expert labels. This representation is learnt from audio associated with the played character label, without any additional information.

Although these approaches deal with final works (video games), another one consists in working directly on the decision data from Artistic Directors. Recently, researchers from Warner Bros. evaluated their models on this kind of data. Unfortunately, these data are sensitive and their acquisition is not trivial since it requires to work on the critical voice casting process. This is why we decided to position ourselves in a task quite different from [15], since we do not use Artistic Director decisions.

In order to evaluate the efficiency of the character representation in the voice dubbing context, [8] proposes to detect whether a pair of speech extracts in the source and the target language belongs, or not, to the same character, knowing that the extracts within a pair are always spoken by different speakers. For that purpose, a Siamese-network-based binary classifier like in [1,12] is trained on the top of p-vectors. Experimental results have shown the ability of the p-vector representation to associate two voice excerpts related to the same character, even when a particularly difficult scenario is employed, where the character and the two speakers of a given pair of recordings are completely unknown during the training phase. However, there are several potential biases in this experiment, like the fact that a given character is represented by a unique pair of actors, the length of the speech extracts, their linguistic content or the influence of speaker-specific information [8]. Even if the proposed protocol allows us to overcome these biases as much as possible, the latter remains debatable because there is still a possible entanglement between the speaker dimension and the character aspects.

Hence, in order to tackle the bias issue of previous evaluation methods, this article proposes a totally new approach to assess the presence of speaker-independent character information (SICI) encoded by a character voice representation like p-vectors. This evaluation can help verifying if systems do not only learn to associate speaker identity but also if they base their decision on character-specific aspects. The main idea is to start with a solution close to the one proposed in [7,8]. Then, we build an alternative model where information about characters is neutralized during the training by swapping the character labels of the voice recordings. This swapping is done at the actor level: all the recordings pronounced by an actor are now wrongly associated to a character label, chosen randomly. It is worth remembering that, because of the voice dubbing context of this work, this is tantamount to breaking the link between an original actor and the dubber associated to him. When comparing the performance of the original system against the second one, we expect to observe a loss proportional to the part of the neutralized (speaker-independent) character information.

The article is organized as follows. In Sect. 2, we give a brief overview of the p-vector representation and the solution to evaluate it. In Sect. 3, we detail the central part of this work, our protocol to estimate the relative quantity of character information. We also present results obtained by applying our modified data. For reproducibility purposes, scripts and models are available on GitHub[1]. Results are then discussed in Sect. 4. We finally conclude in Sect. 5.

2   Character Representation Extraction and Evaluation

In this section, we present an overview of our character similarity system. The p-vector character-based voice representation, close to that proposed in [7,8], is then described, as well as the voice-similarity based approach used to evaluate it. We also propose to evaluate these systems on a closed protocol where the test speakers (and therefore characters) are known to the training phase.

2.1   Character Similarity System Overview

Figure 1 gives an overview of the complete character voice similarity production chain used in this work. A p-vector (*character-oriented representation*) is

---

[1] https://github.com/LIAvignon/specom2021-assessing-speaker-independent-character-information-for-acted-voices.

obtained from a representation of the speech signal (*sequence extractor*). Then, the decision module (*decision*) takes as input a pair of *p*-vectors and generates a *score* about the character similarity between them. Finally, this score is compared to a decision threshold in order to obtain a binary decision.

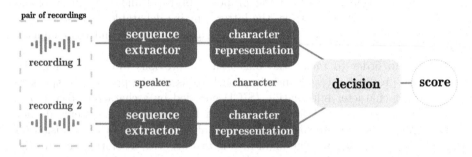

Fig. 1. Production chain of scoring character voice similarity system from the signal to similarity score.

2.2 Character-Oriented Representation

This section describes the character-oriented voice representation, named *p*-vector, introduced in [7]. These *p*-vectors are built from a representation of speech signal and are intended to highlight character information of a given voice recording.

Each recording $r \in train$ is associated with the acted character. We train a Multi-Layer Perceptron (MLP) as classification system in order to recognize the character in a closed space according to the given recording, whatever the language in which it is acted. We give as input to the character extraction system an *i*-vector representation [4] of 400 dimensions obtained from the recording's signal (i.e., indicated as 'sequence extractor' in Fig. 1; details of the extraction are explained in article [8]). The system calculates us back, for each class, the probability that the recording belongs to the class (i.e., the character label). Once the network is trained, [7] propose to use the last layer as embedding, before softmax, as the *p*-vectors.

The neural network is composed of four *Dense* layers, all with 256 neurons, accompanied by a tangent hyberbolic activation function and a dropout of 0.25, except the fourth which is used as embedding, and has only 64 neurons and a dropout of 0.5. A last layer of softmax at the end of the neural network is added. The algorithm we use to train the network is *adadelta* with the cost function *categorical crossentropy*. To avoid overfitting, we apply an early stopping with a minimum delta to 0.1 and a patience of 10 epochs to training algorithm.

2.3 Voice Similarity Model

As said before, in order to evaluate our character representation, we build a character-based voice similarity on top of it. The task consists in deciding if a pair of recordings, one in English and the other in French, belongs to the same character or not. We compute, for each pair of voices X, the score $H_f(X)$ and compare it to a threshold set at the *a posteriori* EER (Equal Error Rate). The voice similarity module is based on the Siamese Neural Network presented in [8].

Performance Evaluation and Confidence Intervals. The voice similarity system (i.e., indicated as 'decision' in Fig. 1) is used in this work to verify the effectiveness of the character-oriented voice representation module (i.e., indicated as 'character representation' in Fig. 1). The performance is computed as the binary accuracy of the voice similarity system, which is the ratio between the number of correctly classified pairs over the total number of classified ones.

We also use a *test of proportion* to assess the statistical significance of accuracy differences. This method takes two proportions p_1 and p_2 and evaluates the hypothesis H_1 saying that the proportions are equivalents. A confidence interval is computed using p_2 and the hypothesis is confirmed if $\hat{p}$ is in this interval. Otherwise, the hypothesis is rejected. We compare accuracy a_1 and a_2 of two given systems by applying this test with a significance level of 5% and with $p_1 = a_1$ and $p_2 = a_2$.

2.4 Corpus Description

The main corpus is composed of voice recordings coming from the *Mass-Effect 3* role-playing game. Originally released in English, the game has been translated and revoiced in several other languages. In our experiments, we use the English and French versions of the audio sequences, representing about 7.5 h of speech in each language. Segments (or recordings) are 3.5 s long on average. A character is then defined by a unique French-English couple of two distinct speakers. To avoid any bias in terms of speaker identity, we consider only a small subset, where we are certain that none of the actors play more than one character. A single audio segment corresponds to a unique speaking slot from an actor in a particular language. We have then applied a filter that keeps only recordings for which the duration is greater than 1 s. Finally, we only keep 16 characters for which we have the largest number of recordings.

Contrary to the article [8] that proposes to apply a 4-fold protocol, we decided in this paper to keep the 16 characters, and their 32 corresponding speakers, for both training and testing phases. We split the corpora in three subsets: training (*train*), validation (*val*), and test (*test*) using a 80/10/10 rule. All these subsets are composed of different recordings but arising from the same 16 characters and 32 speakers. To build respectively the *train*, *val* and *test* subsets, we randomly select for each character 144, 18, and 18 recordings, while balancing the number of French and English recordings. We have then respectively a total of 2, 304, 288 and 288 recordings.

For each subset, we build pairs of recordings where the first element is a voice segment belonging to an actor in the source language (English), and the second is a recording pronounced by another actor, the dubber, in the target language (French). We associate the class *target* to pairs of voices coming from the same character, and *non-target* otherwise. Pairs are made with randomly selected segments while balancing *targets* and *non-targets*. This pairing process is denoted *original data*. We have, for pairs respectively built from *train*, *val* and *test*, $165,888$, $2,592$ and $2,592$ pairs.

2.5   Performance of the *P*-vector Representation

Table 1 shows the performance of the character-oriented voice similarity system (*prot 2*) built upon the *p*-vectors. Performance of a voice comparison system (*prot 1*) based only on the *i*-vectors (in this representation, no specific information about the characters played is used) and of a random system are provided for comparison purposes. A large difference of 7 points in accuracy (87% for *p*-vectors versus 80% for *i*-vectors) is noticed. Looking at the confidence intervals, this difference is strongly significant. It confirms the results observed in [7] (using a different protocol) where it was found that the *p*-vector representation seems to embed specific information about the played characters.

Table 1. Performance of *i*-vectors (*i*-v) and *p*-vectors (*p*-v) on original data. Random is the theoretical performance of random system. 95% confidence interval limits indicated in brackets.

	Sequence extraction	Character layer (*p*-v)	Performance
random	×	×	0.50 [0.48, 0.52]
prot 1	*i*-v	×	0.80 [0.78, 0.82]
prot 2	*i*-v	original	0.87 [0.86, 0.88]

3   Estimation of the Amount of Character Information in the *P*-vector Representation

Previous section empirically proves that the *p*-vector representation improves the performance on a character-based similarity task. Nonetheless, this does not ensure completely that the model captures character information, as the *p*-vector representation is initially based on a speaker representation that may still embody speaker-related information. In order to verify that the improvement observed while using *p*-vector does not come from the ability to associate voices, we propose as a main contribution in this article to train our acted voice similarity systems with misled data where the character information is supposed being neutralized.

3.1 Random Association Protocol

The random association protocol we propose consists in training a neural network on intentionally misled data. As shown by Fig. 2, for each English actor A_i, we associate a new French actor D_j different from the initial dubber one D_i, while keeping the constraint that a French actor is only paired with an English one. To avoid gender bias, we still choose a pair of actors sharing the same gender (*male* or *female*). As a character is represented by a unique pair of speakers, it corresponds to a random labeling of the files in terms of characters. So, the speakers are still associated by pair (one English and one French) but they no longer belong to the same character inside a given pair.

The performance using this new association compared with the system without p-vectors should show the "speaker" power of the p-vector. A performance difference versus the character-based file pairing should indicate the part of character information embed into the p-vectors.

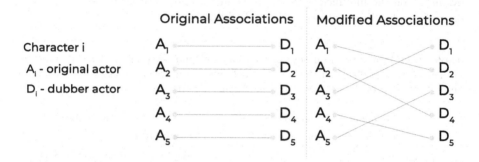

Fig. 2. Random association protocol where each actor A_i is originally associated to the dubber D_i.

3.2 Random Associations Subsets

As explained in Sect. 3.1, the random association protocol consists in intentionally switching the dubber associated with each original actor and then generating new subsets of voice pairs with the modified actor associations using the same steps as presented in Sect. 2.4. This random association dataset is noted *modified*.

Using this new modified protocol, two modules may be impacted, since they can be trained from the original or modified character labels: the p-vector representation (*character representation*) and the Siamese voice similarity system (*decision*). We then train a p-vector extractor, denoted as *modified*, with the new randomly switched character labels for dubbing voices. In the same way, we also train a version of our voice-similarity Siamese system using the *modified* labels. Of course, when the voice similarity system is trained using the *modified* labels, the same *modified* speaker pairing is used to assess the performance (in the test dataset).

3.3   Experiments and Results

Modifying Protocol in Order to Highlight the Speaker-Independent Character Information (SICI). Our first experiment consists in assessing the presence, or not, of SICI on voice representation. The modified protocol is a means of removing character information. Therefore, the absolute difference between the score of systems trained on original or modified data is a clue to assess the presence of SICI. With this in mind, we train an i-vector sequence extractor and then build a p-vector embedding on top of it by using original or modified data. The character representation is then evaluated with a Siamese neural network trained on character voice similarity as explained before. Table 2 summarizes the system performance. To validate that the accuracies of two systems are significantly different, the confidence intervals are written below the performance scores. In this table, *prot 3* and *4* respectively correspond to the modified version of *prot 1* and *2*. We also propose a mixed version named *prot 5* where p-vectors (character module) are trained using original data and are then evaluated on the modified dataset (decision module) in order to assess the presence of speaker information on the embedding.

Table 2. Performance (accuracy) of i-vector (i-v) and p-vector (p-v) representations on modified data. 95% confidence interval limits are given in brackets. The rows for "prot 1" and "prot 2" are repeated from Table 1 for the reader's convenience.

	Sequence extractor	Tying pairs		Performance
		Character layer (p-v)	Decision layer	
prot 1	i-v	×	original	0.80 [0.78, 0.82]
prot 2	i-v	original	original	0.87 [0.86, 0.88]
prot 3	i-v	×	modified	0.80 [0.78, 0.82]
prot 4	i-v	modified	modified	0.84 [0.83, 0.85]
prot 5	i-v	original	modified	0.75 [0.73, 0.77]

Comparison with a Neural Network Sequence Extractor. As we based our systems on i-vector speaker embedding, we also want to compare these results with a neural network sequence extractor. For this purpose, we build an x-vector extractor with the Kaldi [18] toolkit using the Voxceleb corpus [2]. We use it as a sequence extractor in place of i-vectors. Then, we train p-vectors and evaluate them with a Siamese neural network by following exactly the same original and modified protocols used for i-vectors. Table 3 presents the results: protocols from *prot 6* to *prot 10* respectively correspond to protocols from *prot 1* to *prot 5* where the only difference is the replacement of i-vectors by x-vectors approach as sequence extractor.

Table 3. Performance (accuracy) of x-vector (x-v) and p-vector (p-v) representations on modified data. 95% confidence interval limits are given in brackets.

	Sequence extractor	Tying pairs		Performance
		Character layer (p-v)	Decision layer	
prot 6	x-v	×	original	0.85 [0.83, 0.87]
prot 7	x-v	original	original	0.90 [0.89, 0.91]
prot 8	x-v	×	modified	0.76 [0.74, 0.78]
prot 9	x-v	modified	modified	0.90 [0.89, 0.91]
prot 10	x-v	original	modified	0.77 [0.75, 0.79]

4 Discussion

The first part of our analysis will focus on the systems based on i-vectors, listed in Table 2. Since *prot 3* yields the same result as *prot 1* (0.80), we can conclude that neutralizing the character information has no effect on the accuracy of the systems. It confirms that the information encoded by i-vectors is mainly presented from a speaker angle, skewing the Siamese network. These latter consequently has difficulties finding speaker-independent character information (SICI).

We then analyze the contribution of the p-vectors on the information encoding. As we know, building p-vectors on top of i-vectors highlights the character information. This was demonstrated by the fact that p-vector system trained on original data both for the character and decision layers did outperform the one trained on i-vectors, respectively *prot 2* (0.87) and *prot 1* (0.80). We can also notice in the Table 2 that p-vectors bring SICI.

Table 2 also shows the accuracy obtained on *prot 5* (0.75). Even if p-vectors learn to associate speakers with the original associations, the Siamese neural networks trained with modified data manage to find information that allows it to associate speakers. As a consequence, we assume that speaker information is present in p-vectors and that it is legitimate to wonder if this information does not skew the decision module.

Since neural network approaches are state of the art in literature about speaker representation, we have compared the use of i-vectors with a neural-based sequence extractor, the x-vectors. In Table 3, we can observe that all the scores are better than those obtained using i-vectors. While p-vectors built on top of the x-vectors, and the x-vectors themselves, seem to encode more speaker and character information, we can observe an inversion of behaviour when comparing with i-vector performance. Indeed, the absolute difference between *prot 6* (0.85) and *prot 8* (0.76) is about 9%, where similar systems for i-vectors did not display any differences. In addition, we observe no difference between *prot 7* and *prot 9* (0.90) while i-vectors performances show a significant absolute difference of about 3%.

As we observe that no systems trained on modified data perform better than those trained on original data, we assume that we are achieving the objective of neutralizing character information as expected. This consequently allows us to highlight the SICI to prevent speaker skewing.

These experiments also show that while systems based on x-vectors outperform those based on i-vectors (as shown in [7] and Tables 2 and 3), it does not necessarily mean that this encodes a better quality representation. Indeed, the peculiarities of our corpus facilitate the use of speaker information since each actor from each language only plays one character. The system can learn to associate together speaker identities and to disregard character information not related to the speaker dimension. This consequently makes character and speaker dimension really intertwined and difficult to disentangle. Thanks to our approach, new works will be able to assess more precisely their character-based model trained by speaker association and ensure that their system are not too much speaker-oriented.

5   Conclusion and Future Work

In this article, we proposed to highlight the speaker-independent part related to the character played in acted voices. We built up on p-vectors, a representation learning approach dedicated to character's information in acted voices. We used for evaluation purposes a Siamese network binary recognizer capable of deciding whether two voices are linked to the same character or not. We first went through previous paper experiments showing that p-vectors help to achieve this task. Next, we moved on to the first objective of this work, which was to assess whether p-vectors really capture information about the characters and do not just memorize the voices of the speakers. For this, we have designed a specific configuration capable of neutralizing information on the character in the p-vector while retaining intact its capacities for memorizing the speaker-related information.

Our experiment has shown that this configuration neutralizes the character and provides a good framework to analyze speaker bias from character-based systems. Thanks to this method, we have also shown that p-vectors can highlight part of character information related or not to speaker identity. However, we have also highlighted that performance is not a good indicator of representation quality. Indeed, the system achieving the best performances did not encode SICI, leading us to conclude that the system only learns to associate speaker identities.

In future works, we first want to extend our work to other audiovisual productions, such as movies, maybe less stereotypical than video-games. Second, the p-vector character-based representation may suffer from the representation of the speech sequence used in this work, the i-vectors. To overcome this limitation, we will work on end-to-end representations directly trained with the objective of focussing on character dimension.

Acknowledgments. This project is supported by the French National Research Agency (ANR) TheVoice grant (ANR-17-CE23-0025).

References

1. Chopra, S., Hadsell, R., LeCun, Y.: Learning a similarity metric discriminatively, with application to face verification. In: 2005 IEEE Computer Society Conference on Computer Vision and Pattern Recognition (CVPR 2005), vol. 1, pp. 539–546. IEEE (2005)
2. Chung, J.S., Nagrani, A., Zisserman, A.: Voxceleb2: deep speaker recognition. In: Interspeech (2018)
3. Das, R.K., Prasanna, S.R.: Speaker verification from short utterance perspective: a review. IETE Tech. Rev. **35**(6), 599–617 (2018)
4. Dehak, N., Kenny, P.J., Dehak, R., Dumouchel, P., Ouellet, P.: Front-end factor analysis for speaker verification. IEEE Trans. Audio Speech Lang. Process. **19**(4), 788–798 (2011)
5. Ezzine, K., Frikha, M.: A comparative study of voice conversion techniques: a review. In: International Conference on Advanced Technologies for Signal and Image Processing (ATSIP), pp. 1–6 (2017)
6. Gideon, J., Khorram, S., Aldeneh, Z., Dimitriadis, D., Provost, E.M.: Progressive neural networks for transfer learning in emotion recognition. In: Annual Conference of the International Speech Communication Association (INTERSPEECH), pp. 1098–1102 (2017)
7. Gresse, A., Quillot, M., Dufour, R., Bonastre, J.F.: Learning voice representation using knowledge distillation for automatic voice casting. In: Annual Conference of the International Speech Communication Association (INTERSPEECH) (2020)
8. Gresse, A., Quillot, M., Dufour, R., Labatut, V., Bonastre, J.F.: Similarity metric based on siamese neural networks for voice casting. In: IEEE International Conference on Acoustics, Speech and Signal Processing (ICASSP) (2019)
9. Gresse, A., Rouvier, M., Dufour, R., Labatut, V., Bonastre, J.F.: Acoustic pairing of original and dubbed voices in the context of video game localization. In: Annual Conference of the International Speech Communication Association (INTERSPEECH) (2017)
10. Iida, A., Campbell, N., Higuchi, F., Yasumura, M.: A corpus-based speech synthesis system with emotion. Speech Commun. **40**(1–2), 161–187 (2003)
11. Iosif, E., et al.: Speech understanding for spoken dialogue systems: From corpus harvesting to grammar rule induction. Comput. Speech Lang. **47**, 272–297 (2018)
12. Koch, G., Koch, G.: Siamese Neural Networks for One-Shot Image Recognition, vol. 2 (2015)
13. Li, H., Ma, B., Lee, K.A.: Spoken language recognition: from fundamentals to practice. Proc. IEEE **101**(5), 1136–1159 (2013)
14. Lu, X., Li, S., Fujimoto, M.: Automatic speech recognition. In: Kidawara, Y., Sumita, E., Kawai, H. (eds.) Speech-to-Speech Translation. SCS, pp. 21–38. Springer, Singapore (2020). https://doi.org/10.1007/978-981-15-0595-9_2
15. Malik, A., Nguyen, H.: Exploring automated voice casting for content localization using deep learning. SMPTE Motion Imaging J. **130**(3), 12–18 (2021)
16. Obin, N., Roebel, A.: Similarity search of acted voices for automatic voice casting. IEEE/ACM Trans. Audio Speech Lang. Process. **24**, 1642–1651 (2016)
17. Obin, N., Roebel, A., Bachman, G.: On automatic voice casting for expressive speech: Speaker recognition vs. speech classification. In: IEEE International Conference on Acoustics, Speech and Signal Processing (ICASSP) (2014)
18. Povey, D., Ghoshal, A., Boulianne, G., Burget, L., Glembek, O., et al.: The kaldi speech recognition toolkit. In: IEEE 2011 workshop on automatic speech recognition and understanding (2011)

19. Schröder, M.: Emotional speech synthesis: a review. In: European Conference on Speech Communication and Technology (EUROSPEECH), pp. 561–564 (2001)
20. Schuller, B., et al.: The interspeech 2013 computational paralinguistics challenge: social signals, conflict, emotion, autism. In: Annual Conference of the International Speech Communication Association (INTERSPEECH) (2013)
21. Stylianou, Y.: Voice transformation: a survey. In: IEEE International Conference on Acoustics, Speech and Signal Processing (ICASSP), pp. 3585–3588 (2009)
22. Swain, M., Routray, A., Kabisatpathy, P.: Databases, features and classifiers for speech emotion recognition: a review. Int. J. Speech Technol. 21(1), 93–120 (2018). https://doi.org/10.1007/s10772-018-9491-z

Influence of Speaker Pre-training
on Character Voice Representation

Mathias Quillot$^{(\boxtimes)}$ ⓘ, Jarod Duret ⓘ, Richard Dufour ⓘ, Mickael Rouvier ⓘ,
and Jean-François Bonastre ⓘ

Université d'Avignon, Avignon 84140, France
{mathias.quillot,jarod.duret,richard.dufour,mickael.rouvier,
jean-francois.bonastre}@univ-avignon.fr

Abstract. Finding professional voice-actors for cultural productions is
performed by a human operator and suffers from several difficulties.
Researchers have therefore been interested for several years in mimicking the process of vocal casting to help human operators find new voices.
However, voice casting appears to be an underdefined task with many
difficulties. The main issue is that no label is available to accurately
assess the performance of voice casting systems. To tackle these problems, recent works have focused on building a speech representation of
acted voices able to highlight the character dimension. The proposed approach relies on an initial sequence extractor issued from a speaker recognition system which is able to represent a time variable speech sequence
by a unique fixed-size vector, followed by a dedicated neural network
where the character-based embedding, called p-vector, is extracted. It is
legitimate to wonder if the sequence extractor is not guiding p-vectors
too much towards speaker information. We then propose to study the
impact of the speaker pre-training on the character representation learning. In comparison to a directly trained character representation, the
results show that the use of a speaker pre-training provides more character information while retaining the speaker-independent part.

Keywords: Voice casting · Speaker recognition · Character
information · Speaker-independent character information · Speaker
information

1 Introduction

Voice Casting consists in finding professional voice-actors for cultural productions. It is carried out by a human operator and suffers from several difficulties.
Indeed, the cinema market is evolving rapidly with the appearance of streaming
platforms such as Netflix, Amazon Prime Video or Disney+. More and more
audiovisual productions are emerging and it is becoming difficult to find the
actors to dub them, and this, within increasingly tight deadlines (due in particular to the rise of series). Moreover, industrialized productions have a strong
appetite for discovering new vocal talents. Nonetheless, experienced operators

© Springer Nature Switzerland AG 2021
A. Karpov and R. Potapova (Eds.): SPECOM 2021, LNAI 12997, pp. 577–588, 2021.
https://doi.org/10.1007/978-3-030-87802-3_52

usually do not have the time to perform a large number of auditions, and they do not have the memory to keep them all in mind. Of great interest is to come up with an automatic system capable of assisting them by selecting a small number of the best candidates from a large database for dubbing a specific voice. Some researchers have been investigating this question in recent years [6,7,15,16] with the objective of proposing a system to measure vocal similarity, mimicking the decision of a professional operator.

But voice casting is a high level intellectual task difficult to automatize, due to its *underdefined* nature [1]: professional operators themselves find it difficult to precisely define the goals and fundamentals of voice casting, even though they do the job on a day-to-day basis. Working on this type of problem is also complicated because the only sure available knowledge on the vocal casting process concerns the choices previously made by the operators, that is to say the productions already dubbed. We would like to inform the reader that the articles [5–7,14–16] cited in this paper are the only ones dealing with the speech-based automation of Vocal Casting in the literature to our knowledge.

In a recent experiment, authors from WarnerBros. proposed to evaluate a recommendation system by using decision data from Artistic Directors. These data are sensitive and their acquisition is not trivial since it requires working on the critical voice casting process. We therefore position ourselves in a task quite different from [14] since we do not use the Director Decisions – neither for training nor for evaluating our systems. We use the final works (video games) where we have the English and French voices from which we can deduce part of the decision criteria of the Artistic Directors in the form of what we call *character information*.

The work presented in this article follows [5–7] and shares with them the same strong hypothesis: if we do not know the precise criteria that go into the decisions of the operators, we assume that this process involves implicit, high level and commonly shared factors conveyed through the voice. These factors can be linked to the actors (physiology, voice, mode of play, etc.), to national culture and habits (perception of a given trait by a given audience at a given moment), to art (sensitivity and wishes of the original director) and the character played (type of character, state of mind, appearance, etc.). The second shared hypothesis is the fact that it is possible, even if the explicit analysis of these factors is (at least still) impracticable, to highlight their combined effects on the acoustic representation of speech. These combined effects are called *"character information"*.

[5] proposes to build a learning-based voice representation based on the work in [25] dedicated to the "character information", denoted as p-vector. First, a *sequence extractor* transforms a time-variable speech sequence into a fixed length vector representing the general aspects of the vocal excerpt. Second, a specific neural network is trained using these vectors and is optimized for character-related tasks. The p-vectors are extracted from this second neural network [4,8,12,18]. Finally, a Siamese neural network is used in the p-vector space in order to measure the character-oriented distance between two recordings. [5] has shown

that it is possible, thanks to this approach, to link two audio files corresponding to the same character, even if the vocal extracts are spoken by two different actors in two different languages (French and English here). They also showed that the training of the Siamese vocal similarity system at the level of the p-vector improves performance compared to its direct application on the outputs of the sequence extractor.

The *sequence extractor* used in the described approach comes from the speaker recognition domain. It requires a very large amount of training data coming from thousands of speakers, and it is optimized according to a speaker identification task. Its use in a character-based voice representation process seems compulsory because the annotated corpora available in the field are small in size. This sequence extractor process could be considered as "pre-training" [9, 19, 23] within the meaning of the transfer learning approach [9, 10, 13, 17, 24].

Although the use of a pre-trained *sequence extractor* clearly helps in building a character-oriented voice representation, it could also create biases in the system. If certain works [21, 22, 26] have already been interested in the information encoded by the embeddings, it seems however legitimate to wonder if this pre-training does not guide the p-vectors too strongly towards speaker information. This article is dedicated to this question and aims to verify the two following hypotheses:

(A) The more a sequence extractor is dedicated to speaker recognition, the more it integrates specific high-level information about the speaker and risks losing information about the character himself. Thus, taking the embedding at a lower level in the sequence extractor neural network could help capture speaker less-specific information capable of better characterizing the character dimension.

(B) Adapting parts of the sequence extraction model when learning the character-based representation itself could improve that representation and, in particular, its generalization capabilities.

Section 2 presents the character voice representation framework. The corpus and the details of the neural networks are presented in Sect. 3. Results of our experiments are presented for the first and the second hypothesis in Sects. 4 and 5 respectively. For reproducibility reasons, scripts and models are available on GitHub[1]. Finally, we conclude by presenting some takeaways and possible directions for future work in Sect. 6.

2   Neural-Network-Based Character Voice Representation

Figure 1 gives an overview of the character voice similarity framework used in this work. First, a *sequence extractor* outputs a fixed-length vector from a time variable speech excerpt. This output is consumed by the character representation module

---

[1] https://github.com/LIAvignon/specom2021-influence-of-speaker-pre-training-on-character-voice-representation.

to generate *p*-vector. Then, the *decision* module takes as input a pair of *p*-vectors and generates a *score* about the character similarity between them. Finally, this score is compared to a decision threshold in order to obtain a binary decision.

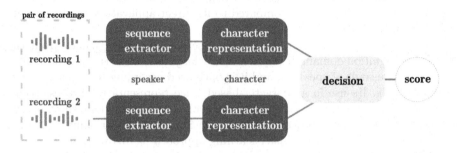

Fig. 1. Character voice similarity framework.

The *character representation* and the *decision* modules are presented in Sects. 2.1 and 2.2 respectively. Finally, Sect. 2.3 focuses on the *sequence extractor* module and its links with the character voice representation system.

2.1   Character-Oriented Representation

The *p*-vectors were first introduced in [5]. They are built from a representation of speech signal and are intended to highlight character-related information in a given recording. To build *p*-vectors, a Multi-Layer-Perceptron (MLP) is trained to classify the character played by the given recording. Once the MLP is trained, the authors propose to use the last layer (before softmax) as an embedding, forming the *p*-vector of a voice extract. In this article, recordings are classified by the MLP among 16 or 12 characters for the protocols described in Sects. 3.2 and 3.3.

2.2   Decision

In order to assess our character representation, we use the character similarity task and *decision* module defined in [6]. The task consists in deciding if two recordings spoken by two speakers belong to the same character or not (in this work, as voice dubbing is targeted, the two recordings are in different languages).

The *decision* module is based on the Siamese Neural Network [2,8,11]. It is composed of two layers (linear, fully-connected, with the hyperbolic tangent activation function) followed by a last neuron which calculates a score between 0 (the two inputs do not belong to the same class) and 1 (the two inputs belong to the same class). Siamese networks are known for their performance on this kind of tasks but also for their instability. To compensate the variation from one training to another, we train 10 systems and select the system with the highest accuracy on the validation set, during the training phase. At each training, only the initialization matrix changes.

2.3 Sequence Extractor

The sequence extractor is based on the speaker recognition x-vector approach [19, 23], described in Fig. 2. It can be decomposed into two parts: 1) the *extraction* part, where acoustic features are extracted from the signal, 2) the *classification* part, dedicated to the targeted task (here, speaker recognition). In this figure, *TDNN* stands for Time Delay Neural Network, as referred to in [23]. *SP* corresponds to a Statistical Pooling. The *XV* is based on a linear from which we classically extract x-vectors in the literature. This layer is followed by a Leaky RELU, a batchnorm, and a dropout. LIN is a linear (fully-connected) layer which precedes a softmax.

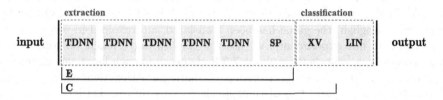

Fig. 2. x-vector extractor architecture.

[22] shown that the layers of such a network encode information with different levels of abstraction depending on the layer. Following hypothesis (A) from Sect. 1, we assume that the closer we get to the objective function (the output), the closer we are to the information dedicated to the speaker and to the risk of having a speaker bias in the character representation system.

In order to verify our hypothesis, we compare p-vectors issued from two different sequence extractors. One, denoted C, is a classical x-vector architecture when the other, denoted E, stops at an earlier layer, the statistical pooling layer. As synthesized in Fig. 3, we use the C or E followed by a dense layer ($DENSE$) and an embedding layer from which we extract the p-vectors (PV). E and C represent the parts pre-trained using a speaker recognition objective and a large dedicated corpus (*VoxCeleb2* [3]). $DENSE$ and PV layers are always trained using a character-oriented objective and a dedicated corpus (*Mass-Effect 3*, see 3.1).

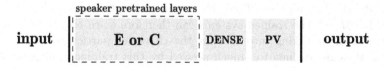

Fig. 3. p-vector extractor architecture. The left part (E or C) corresponds to the sequence extractor while the right part (DENSE and PV) corresponds to the character representation of Fig. 1.

3   Experimental Protocol

We present the data in Sect. 3.1 and how we split them in Sects. 3.2 and 3.3. We then detail the x-vector pre-training and the p-vector training in Sects. 3.4 and 3.5 respectively. Finally, we describe the evaluation in Sect. 3.6.

3.1   Corpora

The main corpus is composed of voice recordings coming from the *Mass-Effect 3* role-playing game. Contrary to movies, voices of video games present some particularities explained in [6] (radio effects are present in the original voices of our corpus). They are also easier to collect since they are separated from the ambient sounds even in their final form, contrary to the dubbed film archives. Originally released in English, the game has been translated and revoiced in several other languages. In our experiments, we use the English and French versions of the audio sequences, representing about 7.5 h of speech in each language. Segments (or recordings) are 3.5 s long on average. A character is then defined by a unique French-English couple of two distinct speakers. To avoid speaker identity biases, we consider only a small subset where we are certain that none of the actors play more than one character. A single audio segment corresponds to a unique speaking slot from an actor in a particular language. We then apply a filter that keeps only recordings longer than 1 s. Finally, we only keep the 16 characters for which we have the largest number of recordings, as [6] did.

3.2   Highlighting the Speaker-Independent Character Information

The *original* protocol is based on a closed space protocol where we keep the 16 characters, and their 32 corresponding speakers (French and English), for both training and testing phases. We split the corpora into three subsets: training (*train*), validation (*val*), and test (*test*) using a 80/10/10 *rule*. All these subsets are composed of different recordings, but coming from the same 16 characters (and so 32 speakers, including both languages). To build the *train, val* and *test* subsets, we randomly select for each character 144, 18, and 18 recordings respectively, while balancing the number of French and English recordings. We then have a total of 2, 304 (*train*), 288 (*val*) and 288 (*test*) recordings. We name S_o the *train, val* and *test* sets deriving from this protocol.

The dataset is composed of only characters played by strictly different actors in each language. The trained systems can therefore learn to associate speaker identities without taking into account the character particularities. To verify that the systems are not too much skewed by this training configuration, we propose a *modified* protocol. This protocol aims at neutralizing the character information by modifying associations between actors, while respecting some constraints to avoid bias (like gender). In other words, the actors (original or dubber) are no longer assigned to the same character and are associated with a new actor (dubber or original). By comparing the absolute difference between scores obtained on the *original* and *modified* protocols, we can then highlight the Speaker-Independent Character Information (SICI) captured by the representation. The presence or absence of such information is a clue to identifying a potential bias in the system. We name S_m the *train*, *val* and *test* sets deriving from this protocol.

3.3 Checking the Generalization Abilities of the Character Representation

In order to measure the ability of our systems to generalize, we propose a protocol that breaks down data differently. This time, we only keep 12 characters, and their 24 corresponding speakers, for the training phase and we use the remaining 4 characters for the testing phase. We still break the corpus down into training, validation and test sets. The *train* and *val* sets are composed of different recordings, but coming from the same 12 characters. To build the *train*, *val* and *test* subsets, we randomly select for each character 144, 36 and 180 recordings respectively, while balancing the number of French and English recordings. We then have a total of $1,728$ (*train*), 432 (*val*) and 720 (*test*) recordings. We name the three sets S_n.

3.4 Pre-training of X-vector Model

The x-vector model is trained on the VoxCeleb 2 corpus. The layer XV from which we extract the x-vectors is accompanied by a LEAKY RELU activation function and a batch normalisation. The last linear layer (*i.e.* LIN in Fig. 2) is attached to a logarithmic softmax at the output. The cost function is the cross-entropy loss.

MFCCs are used as input, extracted using Kaldi tools [20] with the following parameters: 30 cepstral coefficients, 25 ms frame length, $20-7,600$ Hz bandwidth.

3.5 Training of P-vector Neural Network

As in [5], the *DENSE* (see Fig. 3) is composed of a linear layer with hyperbolic tangent activation function and a dropout of 0.25. The p-vector layer (*i.e.* PV in Fig. 3) is composed of the same elements except for the dropout whose value is 0.5. We finally compute a logarithmic softmax at the output of the network. The cost function we have used to train the network is the cross-entropy loss.

3.6 Evaluation

As shown in Sect. 2.2, we evaluate p-vectors on a character voice similarity task using a character-similarity measure based on a Siamese network. We generate *Target* trials composed of pairs of recordings belonging to the same character and *Non-target* trials made up of recordings belonging to two different characters. To avoid any bias, the number of *targets* and *non-targets* is balanced, as well as the number of pairs between two actors. For sets S_o and S_m, we generate $165,888$ (*train*), $2,592$ (*val*) and $2,592$ (*test*) trials. For set S_n, we generate $124,416$ (*train*), $7,776$ (*val*) and $64,800$ (*test*) trials. The threshold is set *a posteriori* at the Equal Error Rate (EER) point. System performance is then expressed in terms of accuracy on the test.

4   Reduce the Speaker Discriminative Information

In order to verify hypothesis Ⓐ from Sect. 1, we propose to reduce the speaker discriminating power of the sequence extractor by using configuration E (extract the sequence vector at the statistical pooling level) instead of configuration C (full classical x-vector extractor).

First, we evaluate the loss in terms of speaker discrimination when using E versus C (see Fig. 2). We measure an EER of 22% (computed on VoxCeleb1) using E, to be compared with an EER of 6% for the configuration C. This result validates the first part of our hypothesis: taking the embedding at a lower level decreases its speaker discriminating power.

We then verify the impact of this decrease on the character representation. For that purpose, we build two p-vector representations, using the outputs of the networks C (*config 1*) and E (*config 2*) respectively. In both cases, we freeze speaker pre-trained layers (C or E) during p-vector training. We then train our two network configurations using the closed space protocol.

We perform a comparative experiment using three data configurations (*original, modified* and *mixed*) and the two sequence extractors already presented (*config 1* and *config 2*). In *original*, p-vectors (character) and the voice similarity system (decision) are trained on the original data S_o (true character-speaker tying). In *modified*, both modules are trained on modified data S_m (artificial tying, but consistent between character and decision levels). In *mixed*, p-vectors are trained on original data S_o while the decision system is using the S_m tying.

We assume that the difference in terms of accuracy between *original* and *modified* is a direct evidence of the amount of character information independent to the speaker embedded in the p-vector representation. We also assume that the accuracy obtained using the *mixed* configuration is a way of measuring the amount of speaker specific information in the p-vector.

Table 1 presents the results of this set of experiments. We observe an absolute difference in accuracy of 3.2 points between *original* and *modified* configurations in the case of *config 1* and 1.7 points in the case of *config 2*. It shows that p-vectors embed speaker-independent character information. Also, the amount of this character information is lower when a sequence extractor with less speaker discriminant power (*config 2*) is used.

The *mixed* protocol shows a high general level and a stronger presence of speaker information for *config 2* than for *config 1*.

Table 1. Accuracy of *config 1* (using C) and *2* (using E) on the test with original, modified and mixed protocol.

	Character module	Decision module	Performance config 1	Performance config 2
Original	S_o	S_o	92.3	95.7
Modified	S_m	S_m	89.1	94.0
Mixed	S_o	S_m	79.7	81.8

5   Give More Power to the Character Classification

This section sets out to test hypothesis Ⓑ from Sect. 1. We propose to give more power to the character classification system during the construction of p-vectors by reducing the influence of pre-training from the sequence extractor. For this purpose, we train p-vectors following two types of configurations presented in Table 2. In configuration 3, we do not freeze the E layers to give more power to the p-vector classification network. In configuration 4, we give all the power to the p-vectors by completely removing pre-training.

Table 2. Training configuration for config 3 and 4 systems.

Config	Layers	Pre-training	Freezing
3	E	VoxCeleb 2	×
4	E	×	×

Table 3 presents the results of the character similarity task obtained on the *config 3* and *4*. Although the results are also high ($\geq 90\%$), we observe less difference in terms of accuracy between the *original* and the *modified* training configurations. We have 0.5 point and -0.8 point difference for *config 3* and *4* respectively. From these results, and compared to those obtained with *config 1*, we observe an evaporation of character information independent to the speaker when we give more power to the character classification.

Table 3. Results obtained in accuracy computed on the test with original, modified and mixed protocol using the *config 3* and *4*.

	Character module	Decision module	Performance config 3	Performance config 4
Original	S_o	S_o	95.6	93.6
Modified	S_m	S_m	95.1	94.4
Mixed	S_o	S_m	81.5	82.1

Table 4 shows the number of modified parameters during training step (*learnable parameters*). It also shows the total number of systems parameters where frozen parameters are taken into account. Since *config 3* and *4* have a higher number of parameters to learn than *config 1* and *2*, we propose to evaluate a smaller system without pre-training having then 664, 144 parameters. We name this system *small*. We obtain accuracies of 92.5 and 89.5 on the *original* and *modified* protocols respectively. This difference of 3 points suggests that reducing the number of parameters brings to light more character information in the *p*-vector representation.

Table 4. Number of parameters and learnable parameters for each studied system configuration.

System	Learnable params	Total params
Config 1	296 528	4 523 492
Config 2	1 570 384	4 260 836
Config 3	4 260 836	4 260 836
Config 4	4 260 836	4 260 836
Small	664 144	664 144

Finally, we seek to verify the generalization abilities of our different system configurations on characters unseen in our training data (S_n protocol). The results of this protocol are shown in Table 5. The systems configured with the *config 1* and *2* respectively obtained a 68.5% and 68.6% accuracy in terms of character similarity. This result strongly suggests that decreasing the amount of speaker discriminant information in the sequence extractor module (*config 2*) does not degrade the generalization abilities of the character representation (*config 1*). As expected, these experiments also tend to demonstrate that the use of a speaker pre-training helps the character representation (*p*-vectors) to generalize to unseen characters, as the *config 3*, *config 4* and *small* (where speaker pre-training is partially or completely removed) obtained lower accuracies than *config 1* and *2* (with speaker pre-training).

Table 5. Speaker-Independant Character Information (SICI), Speaker Information (SI) and Generalization Power (GP) per system. SICI is the accuracy difference between original and modified protocols, SI is the accuracy obtained using the mixed protocol and GP is the accuracy computed using the generalization protocol (S_n).

	GP	SI	SICI
Config 1	68.5	79.7	3.2
Config 2	68.6	81.8	1.7
Config 3	61.2	81.5	0.5
Config 4	61.1	82.1	−0.8
Small	66.9	80.8	3.0

6   Conclusion

This article investigated the influence of speaker pre-training on character voice representation. A first experiment showed that choosing a less speaker discriminative representation for the sequence extractor weakens the presence of speaker-independent character information. A second experiment showed that partially or completely removing speaker pre-training does not make it possible to encode more character information or even to better preserve its part independent to the speaker. We can conclude that the pre-training of the sequence extractor does not guide the p-vectors too strongly towards speaker information and brings useful knowledge to the construction of a character representation. Based on our experimental results, the representation of the characters appear as essentially inseparable from the notion of speaker. We now wish to direct our future work towards the discovery of an "alphabet" of character attributes clustering short voice segments into the p-vector space.

Acknowledgments. This project is supported by the French National Research Agency (ANR) "TheVoice" grant (ANR-17-CE23-0025).

References

1. Bonastre, J.-F.: Representation learning for underdefined tasks. In: Nyström, I., Hernández Heredia, Y., Milián Núñez, V. (eds.) CIARP 2019. LNCS, vol. 11896, pp. 42–47. Springer, Cham (2019). https://doi.org/10.1007/978-3-030-33904-3_4
2. Chopra, S., Hadsell, R., LeCun, Y.: Learning a similarity metric discriminatively, with application to face verification. In: 2005 IEEE Computer Society Conference on Computer Vision and Pattern Recognition (CVPR'05), vol. 1, pp. 539–546 (2005)
3. Chung, J.S., Nagrani, A., Zisserman, A.: Voxceleb2: deep speaker recognition. In: Interspeech (2018)
4. Chung, Y.A., Glass, J.: Speech2vec: A sequence-to-sequence framework for learning word embeddings from speech (2018)
5. Gresse, A., Quillot, M., Dufour, R., Bonastre, J.F.: Learning voice representation using knowledge distillation for automatic voice casting. In: Interspeech (2020)
6. Gresse, A., Quillot, M., Dufour, R., Labatut, V., Bonastre, J.F.: Similarity metric based on siamese neural networks for voice casting. In: IEEE International Conference on Acoustics, Speech and Signal Processing (ICASSP) (2019)
7. Gresse, A., Rouvier, M., Dufour, R., Labatut, V., Bonastre, J.F.: Acoustic pairing of original and dubbed voices in the context of video game localization. In: Interspeech (2017)
8. Hadsell, R., Chopra, S., LeCun, Y.: Dimensionality reduction by learning an invariant mapping. In: 2006 IEEE Computer Society Conference on Computer Vision and Pattern Recognition (CVPR'06), vol. 2, pp. 1735–1742 (2006)
9. Hendrycks, D., Lee, K., Mazeika, M.: Using pre-training can improve model robustness and uncertainty. In: Chaudhuri, K., Salakhutdinov, R. (eds.) Proceedings of the 36th International Conference on Machine Learning, vol. 97, pp. 2712–2721. PMLR (2019)

10. Hinton, G., Vinyals, O., Dean, J.: Distilling the knowledge in a neural network (2015)
11. Koch, G., Zemel, R., Salakhutdinov, R.: Siamese neural networks for one-shot image recognition. In: ICML Deep Learning Workshop, vol. 2. Lille (2015)
12. Levy, O., Goldberg, Y.: Neural word embedding as implicit matrix factorization. Adv. Neural Inform. Process. Syst. **27**, 2177–2185 (2014)
13. Lopez-Paz, D., Bottou, L., Schölkopf, B., Vapnik, V.: Unifying distillation and privileged information (2016)
14. Malik, A., Nguyen, H.: Exploring automated voice casting for content localization using deep learning. SMPTE Motion Imaging J. **130**(3), 12–18 (2021)
15. Obin, N., Roebel, A.: Similarity search of acted voices for automatic voice casting. IEEE/ACM Trans. Audio Speech Lang. Process. **24**, 1642–1651 (2016)
16. Obin, N., Roebel, A., Bachman, G.: On automatic voice casting for expressive speech: Speaker recognition vs. speech classification. In: IEEE International Conference on Acoustics, Speech and Signal Processing (ICASSP) (2014)
17. Pan, S.J., Yang, Q.: A survey on transfer learning. IEEE Trans. Knowl. Data Eng. **22**(10), 1345–1359 (2010)
18. Pascual, S., Ravanelli, M., Serrà, J., Bonafonte, A., Bengio, Y.: Learning problem-agnostic speech representations from multiple self-supervised tasks (2019)
19. Peddinti, V., Povey, D., Khudanpur, S.: A time delay neural network architecture for efficient modeling of long temporal contexts. In: Interspeech (2015)
20. Povey, D., et al.: The kaldi speech recognition toolkit. In: IEEE 2011 Workshop on Automatic Speech Recognition and Understanding. IEEE Signal Processing Society, IEEE Catalog No.: CFP11SRW-USB (2011)
21. Raj, D., Snyder, D., Povey, D., Khudanpur, S.: Probing the information encoded in x-vectors. In: 2019 IEEE Automatic Speech Recognition and Understanding Workshop (ASRU), pp. 726–733. IEEE (2019)
22. Rouvier, M., Favre, B.: Investigation of speaker embeddings for cross-show speaker diarization. In: 2016 IEEE International Conference on Acoustics, Speech and Signal Processing (ICASSP), pp. 5585–5589. IEEE (2016)
23. Snyder, D., Garcia-Romero, D., Sell, G., Povey, D., Khudanpur, S.: X-vectors: Robust dnn embeddings for speaker recognition. In: 2018 IEEE International Conference on Acoustics, Speech and Signal Processing (ICASSP), pp. 5329–5333 (2018)
24. Vapnik, V., Izmailov, R.: Learning using privileged information: similarity control and knowledge transfer. J. Mach. Learn. Res. **16**(1), 2023–2049 (2015)
25. Variani, E., Lei, X., McDermott, E., Moreno, I.L., Gonzalez-Dominguez, J.: Deep neural networks for small footprint text-dependent speaker verification. In: ICASSP, pp. 4052–4056 (2014)
26. Wang, S., Qian, Y., Yu, K.: What does the speaker embedding encode? In: Interspeech, pp. 1497–1501 (2017)

Opinion Classification via Word and Emoji Embedding Models with LSTM

Ilyos Rabbimov[1]([⊠]), Sami Kobilov[1], and Iosif Mporas[2]

[1] Faculty of Digital Technologies, Samarkand State University, Samarkand, Uzbekistan
`ilyos.rabbimov91@gmail.com`, `kobsam@yandex.ru`
[2] School of Physics, Engineering and Computer Science, University of Hertfordshire, Hatfield, UK
`i.mporas@herts.ac.uk`

Abstract. As social networks are rapidly growing, the content created in them is also growing. Mining the emotional tendency of comments on this content through opinion classification technologies is very useful for the timely understanding of public opinion on social media, monitoring of brands, and customer support. Deep learning methods have shown good results in opinion classification. In this paper, we analyze the opinion classification in Uzbek movie reviews taken from YouTube using various pre-trained word embedding models and a classification model based on long short-term memory. Users often use emojis along with text to express their opinions and feelings. Therefore, we also investigated the importance of emojis in opinion classification of Uzbek texts.

Keywords: Opinion classification · Sentiment analysis · Uzbek language · Emoji · Long short-term memory · Word embeddings

1 Introduction

In recent years, online activities such as social networks, blogs, and e-commerce platforms have become very popular. Users freely express their opinions and feedback on products, services, events, various topics in such systems. Opinions classification from comments received from social networking platforms such as Facebook, Twitter, YouTube, and Reddit mainly focuses on the opinion-oriented analysis of the comment corpus, that is, it indicates (expresses) whether users' opinions about products or events are positive, negative, or neutral [1]. The topics of discussion here are also varied, including film reviews analysis [2], product reviews [3], political debates [4], news comments [5], book reviews [6], etc.

Users can express their opinions and feelings on social media with pictures, videos, texts, emojis, emoticons, and more. Among them, emojis can become one of the universal tools of expressing the feelings of people around the world in all languages [7]. Users also often use emojis to express themselves, and they serve to increase or decrease sentimentally separating power (ability) of the text [8]. In most cases, emojis serve as a reliable representative (element) for the emotional content of the text [9]. The importance of emojis in opinion classification and sentiment analysis has been studied in a wide

© Springer Nature Switzerland AG 2021
A. Karpov and R. Potapova (Eds.): SPECOM 2021, LNAI 12997, pp. 589–601, 2021.
https://doi.org/10.1007/978-3-030-87802-3_53

range of studies. Emoji sentiment ranking lexicon presented in [7]. It consists of 751 most common emojis and quantities representing the corresponding sentimental features. Such lexicons are widely used in rule-based, machine learning-based emotion analysis systems. In the sentiment analysis of Arabic tweets, the effect of combining emoji-based features with text features is studied in [10]. Support vector machines (SVMs) are used as the classification algorithm, and the best results are obtained when using emoji-based and skip-gram features.

In recent years, deep learning methods have been addressed in many studies due to their ability to outperform traditional methods in opinion classification [11]. In deep learning approaches, complex models of expressing words in texts in the form of numeric vectors use Word2Vec [12], GloVe [13], and fastText [14]. Just like words, emojis are used in opinion classification [15–17] using distributed representations [18, 19] and deep learning models. An emoji embedding consisting of about 700 emojis was presented in [18] which was trained using the word2vec skip-gram model [12] on a Twitter dataset with over 100 million English tweets. emoji2vec pre-trained emoji embedding demonstrated in [19], which consists of 1,661 Unicode emojis and their corresponding numerical vectors when it is used in opinion classification of Twitter posts, leading to an increase in classification accuracy of 2%. The effectiveness of different pre-trained embedding model combinations in the task of sentiment analysis in tweets was studied in [15]. The classification was performed using Long Short-Term Memory (LSTM), Convolutional neural network, and various pre-trained embedding models. The classification algorithm achieved a high result when Word2Vec, fastText, and emoji2vec pre-trained embedding applied together. The problem of emoji ambiguity was studied in [16], taking into account the location and semantic features of the emoji along with the emotional information of the emoji. This emoji representation method and the Bi-directional gated recurrent unit (BiGRU) neural network has also been used in sentiment analysis in Chinese microblogs. The role of emojis in sarcasm detection was investigated in [17]. Pre-trained GloVe and emoji2vec embedding were used to form the feature vector from the tweets, and sarcasm detection was performed with BiGRU using the attention layer.

Sentiment analysis on emoji for positive, negative, and neural tweets in Turkish was studied at [20]. Bag-of-words and fastText were used to represent the tweets. Sentiment analysis of news articles in Russian and Kazakh using LSTM and Word2Vec, GloVe word embedding were presented in [21]. Replacing emojis with their natural language descriptions and classifying them using pre-trained word embedding models such as simple words was done in [22]. The effectiveness of this approach was evaluated in irony detection and sentiment analysis. Words, emojis, and abbreviations were presented in a concept called Token2Vec [23], which combines into a single vector space. Sentiment analysis was performed using LSTM and Token2Vec. A bi-sense emoji embedding based on positive and negative tweets was explored in [24]. Sentiment analysis was performed in [24] via attention-based LSTM with fastText and bi-sense emoji embedding.

Works on the classification of texts in the Uzbek language were presented in [25, 26]. Approaches to the classification of literary texts on topics were studied in [27]. The thematic classification of a work of medieval scholars was studied in [28]. The classification of news texts using the decision tree algorithm was performed in [29]. A comparative analysis of Naïve Bayes models in text classification was given in [30]. Cluster analysis of text documents by their relevance was presented in [31].

Not many publications in opinion classification in the Uzbek language can be found in the bibliography. An opinion mining dataset collected from the Google Play App Store and manually annotated was presented in [32, 33], with all comments labeled as positive or negative by two native Uzbek speakers. Opinion classification on this dataset using traditional machine learning algorithms like support vector machines, logistic regression and deep learning algorithms recurrent neural network, convolution neural network was performed. The issue of opinion classification of Uzbek movie reviews based on emoji was presented in [8], with opinion classification being performed using statistical features of the text, part-of-speech based features, emoji-based features, and k-nearest neighbors algorithm, Neural network, Support vector machines, Decision tree, Random forest, Naive Bayes classifier algorithms. The discriminative ability of 42 properties evaluated using the ReliefF feature rating algorithm.

An analysis of the available literature shows that there is no research on the application of the LSTM model in opinion classification in Uzbek texts, and the usage of emoji embeddings on Uzbek opinion mining has not yet been studied. In this paper, we use the word embedding and LSTM model for opinion classification of Uzbek movie reviews and investigate the effect of various pre-trained Uzbek word and emoji embedding models in opinion classification taking into account the emojis in the comments.

The rest of the paper is organized as follows. Section 2 describes the architecture being evaluated on opinion classification. Section 3 describes the experimental settings. Section 4 presents the experimental results. Section 5 concludes the paper.

2   Opinion Classification of Uzbek Movie Reviews

The architecture we used for the opinion classification of YouTube movie reviews follows a standard approach, which has been adopted in most studies on opinion classification and sentiment analysis. The block diagram of the evaluated architecture is shown in Fig. 1.

Both training and testing phases involve the pre-processing of data, feature extraction, and the opinion classification stage.

In the training phase, a set of movie review comments in Uzbek collected from YouTube and a set of corresponding comment labels are used to train the opinion classification model. Comments are labeled manually by the native Uzbek speakers. In the test phase unknown (unlabelled) movie review comments are processed by the pre-trained opinion classification models and the corresponding opinion (positive or negative) is automatically identified.

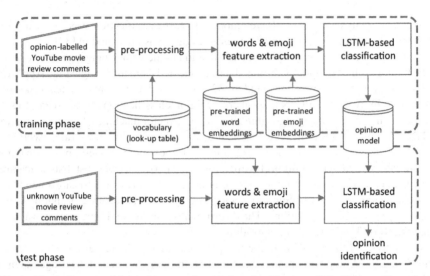

Fig. 1. Block diagram of the architecture for opinion classification of YouTube movie reviews.

2.1 Pre-processing

Initially, each comment is pre-processed, converting all letters in the comments to low-ercase, replacing some letters with the Uzbek Latin alphabet, for example, "õ" → "o'", "ğ" → "g'", "ķ" → "q", deleting special characters, numbers and excess spaces. The sequence of tokens $S = [t_1, t_2, \ldots, t_N]$ is formed from the text of the comment. Here, S is a comment, t_i is a token (word or emoji). When using a word embedding to opinion classification, it is important to define the vocabulary used in the classification. The larger the number of words in the dictionary, the larger the vector representation of the comments. Therefore, when creating a dictionary, we need to choose from the words that are useful for classification. We created a V dictionary using a set of words and emojis from the training set. The 30,000 most used words and emojis were selected to define the V dictionary.

2.2 Feature Extraction

After the pre-processing, the sequence of tokens in the comment is converted to a numer-ical sequence in which the number of elements is fixed L based on the V dictionary. The elements of a numerical sequence are represented by the indexes of the tokens in the V dictionary. A token can be a word or an emoji. If the number of elements of the comment S is less than L, zero paddings are used. If the number of elements of the comment S is greater than L, the most used L token is selected from the content of the comment S on the basis of the dictionary V. In general, we can express the sequence of token indices corresponding to the comment S as $S' = \{i_{t_1}, i_{t_2}, \ldots, i_{t_L}\}$.

Pre-trained word embedding models are used to convert each word into a numeric vector.

$$w_i \rightarrow word\ embedding(w_i) \rightarrow \tilde{w}_i \qquad (1)$$

where w_i is the word in the comment with index i and $\tilde{w}_i$ is the corresponding word embedding for w_i word. Pre-trained Word2Vec and fastText word embedding models are used in this evaluation.

Pre-trained emoji2vec embedding is also used to represent each emoji in the comment as a numeric vector.

$$e_i \rightarrow emoji2vec(e_i) \rightarrow \tilde{e}_i \tag{2}$$

where e_i is the emoji in the comment with index i and $\tilde{e}_i$ is the emoji embedding for e_i emoji. If the w_i word or e_i emoji is not present in pre-trained embedding models, a zero vector is assigned to the corresponding $\tilde{w}_i$, $\tilde{e}_i$. The word and emoji embedding matrix is generated using expressions (1), (2), and the V dictionary. If there is a token word in the V dictionary, then the expression (1) is used, and if there is a token emoji, then the expression (2) is used to create the embedding matrix. This matrix is used in the embedding layer of the LSTM-based classification architecture.

2.3   Opinion Classification

We designed an opinion classification model based on LSTM using word and emoji embeddings, as illustrated in Fig. 2.

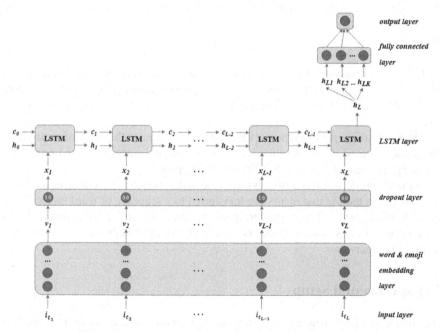

Fig. 2. Block diagram of the proposed classification model.

The input layer contains the vector $S' = \{i_{t_1}, i_{t_2}, \ldots, i_{t_L}\}$ corresponding to the comment S described in the previous section.

The word and emoji embedding layer generate a numeric vector corresponding to the S' vector elements included in it using the word and emoji embedding matrix. That is, $i_{t_j} \rightarrow v_j, j = \overline{1, L}$ transformation is performed.

The Spatial Dropout layer ignores randomly selected neurons during model training. Ignored neurons are not addressed in either the forward pass or the backward pass. Spatial Dropout improves the artificial neural network by reducing overfitting. This method has also been shown to improve neural network performance in document classification [34].

The vectors output from the Spatial Dropout layer are inserted into the sequential LSTM [35] layer. The following calculations are performed at the time step t of the vector x_t entering the LSTM.

$$f_t = \sigma\left(W_f x_t + U_f h_{t-1} + b_f\right) \tag{3}$$

$$i_t = \sigma(W_i x_t + U_i h_{t-1} + b_i) \tag{4}$$

$$\tilde{c}_t = \tanh(W_c x_t + U_c h_{t-1} + b_c) \tag{5}$$

$$c_t = f_t * c_{t-1} + i_t * \tilde{c}_t \tag{6}$$

$$o_t = \sigma(W_o x_t + U_o h_{t-1} + b_o) \tag{7}$$

$$h_t = o_t * \tanh(c_t) \tag{8}$$

Here, h_{t-1} - output of previous hidden layer, c_{t-1} - memory from previous hidden layer, σ - sigmoid function, c_t - new update memory, h_t - current output, $W_f, W_i, W_c, W_o, U_f, U_i, U_c, U_o$ - weights of LSTM, b_f, b_i, b_c, b_o - bias parameters of LSTM.

The h_L vector output from the last LSTM unit is the input to the fully connected layer. The sigmoid is used as the activation function. The output layer consists of 1 neuron and represents a positive (1) or negative (0) identified opinion.

In the test phase, a new comment is pre-processed, in which the words in the processed comment, as in the training phase, are transferred to a sequence of word indices based on the V dictionary, and applying zero padding, and a feature vector is obtained. The trained opinion classification model is used to determine whether a new comment is positive or negative.

3 Experimental Setup

The architecture presented in the previous section for opinion classification of YouTube movie reviews was evaluated using the following dataset, word and emoji embedding-based features, and an LSTM-based classification algorithm.

3.1 Dataset

The Uzbek movie reviews corpus is a set of reviews of Uzbek movies collected using the YouTube Data API. This corpus was manually annotated by six native Uzbek speakers. Of the comments in the corpus, 5,351 are in the Latin alphabet, 7,903 are in the Cyrillic alphabet, 58 are in mixed Latin and Cyrillic alphabets, and 817 are in the form of emojis and other characters. The number of positive comments is 9,732, the number of negative comments is 4,397 and the total number of comments in the corpus is 14,129. Statistical information about the dataset used in this evaluation is presented in Table 1.

Table 1. Statistical information of the evaluated dataset.

Characteristic	Statistical information
# posts in Latin	5,351
# posts in Cyrillic	7,903
# posts in mixed Latin - Cyrillic	58
# posts in non-textual	817
total # posts	14,129
# positive posts	9,732
# negative posts	4,397
minimum # emoji per post	0
maximum # emoji per post	224
average # emoji per post	1.44

All the comments mixed with Cyrillic or Latin with Cyrillic were manually transferred to the Latin scripts corresponding to them. 10-fold cross-validation was applied to the dataset during training and testing of the algorithm evaluation.

3.2 Feature Extraction

In this study, different pre-trained word and emoji embeddings are used, which are trained using fastText and Word2Vec models using various corpora. Information about the word embedding models used in our experiments is presented in Table 2. It tabulates the word embedding technology, the trained dataset, the vocabulary size, and other features.

The UzbekFastText1 word vector is the fastText model trained with crawled texts published on Wikipedia using Common Crawl [36]. UzbekFastText2 was presented in [37] and it is a 300-dimensional Uzbek fastText skip-gram word vector of 119,641 words. UzbekWord2VecCBOW and UzbekWord2VecSkip-Gram pre-trained embeddings contain 797,653 word vectors, which are obtained using the Word2Vec model trained with 45 M tokens collected from news sites in Uzbekistan. The emoji2vec pre-trained embedding model was developed for all Unicode emojis and is presented in [19]. In the evaluation each word embedding model was used separately and each word embedding model along with an emoji embedding model.

Table 2. Pre-trained embedding models used in this evaluation.

Name	Model	Corpus	Corpus size	Vocabulary size	Dimension
UzbekFastText1	fastText	Wikipedia		829,846	300
UzbekFastText2	fastText	Large corpora of Turkic languages	24 M tokens	199,641	300
UzbekWord2VecSkip-Gram	Word2Vec	Uzbek news sites	45 M tokens	797,653	300
UzbekWord2VecCBOW	Word2Vec	Uzbek news sites	45 M tokens	797,653	300
emoji2vec	Word2Vec	Twitter		1,661	300

3.3 Classification Algorithm

The LSTM based opinion classification model was implemented according to the architecture presented in Sect. 2 and the structure described in Fig. 2. The hyperparameters of the proposed model are described in Table 3. The hyperparameters were selected empirically. For the parameters not given in the table, the default values were kept.

Table 3. Hyperparameters of evaluated LSTM based model.

Hyperparameters	Value
Epochs	10
Optimization function	adam
Loss function	binary_crossentropy
MaxLen (L)	50
SpatialDropout1D	0.4
Dropout of LTSM	0.2
Recurrent dropout of LTSM	0.2
Bach size	256
Number of nodes at fully connected layer (K)	10
Word embedding deminsion	300

In all experiments, the values of hyperparameters of the model were kept the same. The proposed LSTM based model was implemented in python using the TensorFlow [38] library.

4 Experimental Results

The proposed model and algorithm for opinion classification of text were evaluated according to the experimental setups in Sect. 3. The performance of the algorithm was measured by metrics such as classification accuracy, F1, Precision, Recall.

$$Accuracy = \frac{TP + TN}{TP + FP + TN + FN} \tag{9}$$

$$Precision = \frac{TP}{TP + FP} \tag{10}$$

$$Recall = \frac{TP}{TP + FN} \tag{11}$$

$$F1 = 2 \cdot \frac{precision \cdot recall}{precision + recall} = \frac{TP}{TP + \frac{1}{2}(FP + FN)} \tag{12}$$

where TP is true positives, TN is true negatives, FP is false positives, FN is false negatives. The LSTM based model was trained with different word embedding models in setups 1–4 without emojis and in setups 5–8 with emojis. The experimental results are presented in Table 4. The best results are given in bold.

As can be seen in Table 4, the best accuracy (91.17%), F1 (93.19%), precision (93.12%) is obtained when UzbekWord2VecSkip-Gram word embedding and emoji2vec emoji embedding are used together. The results of setup 7, which gave the best results, were close to the results of setup 6, and in both cases, emoji was taken into account. Comparing the results of setup 6 and setup 2, it can be seen that the performance of the setup that took emoji into account was higher. There was no increase of performance when using emoji2vec with UzbekFastText1, UzbekWord2VecCBOW pre-trained embedding models. However, the highest classification results were observed when emoji were taken into account.

Table 4. Opinion classification results.

#	Embedding models	Accuracy (%)	F1 (%)	Precision (%)	Recall (%)	Confusion matrix	
1	UzbekFastText1	90.68	92.89	91.77	94.20	3,642	755
						562	9,170
2	UzbekFastText2	90.76	92.86	92.48	93.43	3,728	669
						637	9,095
3	UzbekWor2VecSkip-Gram	90.80	92.90	92.40	93.58	3,719	677
						623	9,110
4	UzbekWor2VecCBOW	90.49	92.69	91.63	94.00	3,636	761
						583	9,149
5	UzbekFastText1 + emoji2vec	90.53	92.75	91.15	**94.66**	3,579	818
						520	9,212
6	UzbekFastText2 + emoji2vec	91.13	93.16	92.70	93.79	3,746	651
						602	9,130
7	UzbekWor2VecSkip-Gram + emoji2vec	**91.17**	**93.19**	**93.12**	93.37	3,789	607
						641	9,092
8	UzbekWor2VecCBOW + emoji2vec	90.32	92.56	91.43	94.03	3,614	783
						585	9,147

5   Conclusion

With the significant growth of content created by users on social networks, it is becoming increasingly important to support them with valuable insights for decision-making by opinion classification. Users often use emojis along with text to express their feelings and opinions. We evaluated various pre-trained embeddings and LSTM based classification models in opinion classification of movie reviews in Uzbek extracted from YouTube. We also investigated the importance of emojis in opinion classification. Experimental results showed that the best results were observed when pre-trained UzbekWord2VecSkip-Gram and emoji2vec embedding models were used together, with the classification accuracy being 91.17%, F1 equal to 93.19%, and precision equal to 93.12%. When using pre-trained UzbekFastText1 and emoji2vec embedding models, the best recall score was 94.66%. Taking emoji into account increased the performance of opinion classification. This is the first study to present a variety of vector representations, such as emoji and word embeddings in opinion classification for the Uzbek language.

References

1. Xu, G., Meng, Y., Qiu, X., Yu, Z., Wu, X.: Sentiment analysis of comment texts based on BiLSTM. IEEE Access **7**, 51522–51532 (2019)

2. Koumpouri, A., Mporas, I., Megalooikonomou, V.: Evaluation of four approaches for "Sentiment analysis on movie reviews": the Kaggle competition. In: Proceedings of the 16th International Conference on Engineering Applications of Neural Networks (INNS), pp. 1–5. ACM, New York (2015)
3. Yang, L., Li, Y., Wang, J., Sherratt, R.: Sentiment analysis for E-commerce product reviews in Chinese based on sentiment lexicon and deep learning. IEEE Access **8**, 23522–23530 (2020)
4. Simaki, V., Paradis, C., Skeppstedt, M., Sahlgren, M., Kucher, K., Kerren, A.: Annotating speaker stance in discourse: the Brexit blog corpus. Corpus Linguist. Linguist. Theory **1** (2017)
5. Ranathunga, S., Liyanage, I.: Sentiment analysis of Sinhala news comments. ACM Trans. Asian Low-Resour. Lang. Inf. Process. **20**, 1–23 (2021)
6. Pecore S., Villaneau J.: Complex and precise movie and book annotations in french language for aspect based sentiment analysis. In: Proceedings of the Eleventh International Conference on Language Resources and Evaluation (LREC 2018), Japan, pp. 2647–2652. ELRA (2018)
7. Novak, P.K., Smailović, J., Sluban, B., Mozetič, I.: Sentiment of emojis. PLOS ONE **10**(12), e0144296 (2015)
8. Rabbimov, I., Mporas, I., Simaki, V., Kobilov, S.: Investigating the effect of emoji in opinion classification of Uzbek movie review comments. In: Karpov, A., Potapova, R. (eds.) SPECOM 2020. LNCS (LNAI), vol. 12335, pp. 435–445. Springer, Cham (2020). https://doi.org/10.1007/978-3-030-60276-5_42
9. Felbo, B., Mislove, A., Søgaard, A., Rahwan, I., Lehmann, S.: Using millions of emoji occurrences to learn any-domain representations for detecting sentiment, emotion and sarcasm. In: Proceedings of the 2017 Conference on Empirical Methods in Natural Language Processing, Denmark, pp. 1615–1625. Association for Computational Linguistics (2017)
10. Al-Azani, S., El-Alfy, E.: Combining emojis with Arabic textual features for sentiment classification. In 2018 9th International Conference on Information and Communication Systems (ICICS), Jordan, pp. 139–144. IEEE (2018)
11. Tang, D., Qin, B., Liu, T.: Deep learning for sentiment analysis: successful approaches and future challenges. WIREs Data Min. Knowl. Discov. **5**, 292–303 (2015)
12. Mikolov T., Sutskever I., Chen K., Corrado G.S., Dean, J.: Distributed representations of words and phrases and their compositionality. Adv. Neural Inf. Process. Syst. 3111–3119 (2013)
13. Pennington, J., Socher, R., Manning, C.: Glove: global vectors for word representation. In: Proceedings of the 2014 Conference on Empirical Methods in Natural Language Processing (EMNLP), Qatar, pp. 1532–1543. Association for Computational Linguistics (2014)
14. Bojanowski, P., Grave, E., Joulin, A., Mikolov, T.: Enriching word vectors with subword information. Trans. Assoc. Computat. Linguist. **5**, 135–146 (2017)
15. Senarath, Y., Thayasivam, U.: DataSEARCH at IEST 2018: multiple word embedding based models for implicit emotion classification of tweets with deep learning. In: Proceedings of the 9th Workshop on Computational Approaches to Subjectivity, Sentiment and Social Media Analysis, Belgium, pp. 211–216. Association for Computational Linguistics (2018)
16. Huang, S., Zhao, Q., Xu, X., Zhang, B., Wang, D.: Emojis-based recurrent neural network for Chinese microblogs sentiment analysis. In: 2019 IEEE International Conference on Service Operations and Logistics, and Informatics (SOLI), China, pp. 59–64. IEEE (2019)
17. Subramanian, J., Sridharan, V., Shu, K., Liu, H.: Exploiting Emojis for sarcasm detection. In: Thomson, R., Bisgin, H., Dancy, C., Hyder, A. (eds.) SBP-BRiMS 2019. LNCS, vol. 11549, pp. 70–80. Springer, Cham (2019). https://doi.org/10.1007/978-3-030-21741-9_8
18. Barbieri, F., Ronzano, F., Saggion, H.: What does this emoji mean? a vector space skip-gram model for twitter emojis. In: Proceedings of the Tenth International Conference on Language Resources and Evaluation (LREC 2016), Slovenia, pp. 3967–3972. ELRA (2016)

19. Eisner, B., Rocktäschel, T., Augenstein, I., Bosnjak, M., Riedel, S.: emoji2vec: learning emoji representations from their description. In: Proceedings of The Fourth International Workshop on Natural Language Processing for Social Media, USA, pp. 48–54. Association for Computational Linguistics (2016)

20. Velioğlu, R., Yıldız, T., Yıldırım, S.: Sentiment analysis using learning approaches over emojis for Turkish tweets. In: 2018 3rd International Conference on Computer Science and Engineering (UBMK), Bosnia and Herzegovina, pp. 303–307. IEEE (2018)

21. Sakenovich, N.S., Zharmagambetov, A.S.: On one approach of solving sentiment analysis task for Kazakh and Russian languages using deep learning. In: Nguyen, N.-T., Manolopoulos, Y., Iliadis, L., Trawiński, B. (eds.) ICCCI 2016. LNCS (LNAI), vol. 9876, pp. 537–545. Springer, Cham (2016). https://doi.org/10.1007/978-3-319-45246-3_51

22. Singh, A., Blanco, E., Jin, W.: Incorporating emoji descriptions improves tweet classification. In: Proceedings of the 2019 Conference of the North American Chapter of the Association for Computational Linguistics: Human Language Technologies, Volume 1 (Long and Short Papers), Minnesota, pp. 2096–2101. Association for Computational Linguistics (2019)

23. Shamal, A.J., Pemathilake, R.G.H., Karunathilake, S.P., Ganegoda, G.U.: Sentiment analysis using Token2Vec and LSTMs: user review analyzing module. In: 2018 18th International Conference on Advances in ICT for Emerging Regions (ICTer), Sri Lanka, pp. 48–53. IEEE (2019).

24. Zhu, P., Yang, Y., Liu, Y.: Sentiment analysis based on hybrid bi-attention mechanism in mobile application. In: Aiello, M., Yang, Y., Zou, Y., Zhang, L.-J. (eds.) AIMS 2018. LNCS, vol. 10970, pp. 157–171. Springer, Cham (2018). https://doi.org/10.1007/978-3-319-94361-9_12

25. Rabbimov, I., Kobilov, S.: Multi-class text classification of Uzbek News articles using machine learning. J. Phys. Conf. Ser. **1546**, 012097 (2020)

26. Rabbimov, I., Kobilov, S., Mporas, I.: Uzbek news categorization using word embeddings and convolutional neural networks. In: 2020 IEEE 14th International Conference on Application of Information and Communication Technologies (AICT), Uzbekistan, pp. 1–5. IEEE (2020)

27. Mukhamedieva, D.T., Zhuraev, Z., Bakaev, I.I.: Approaches to the thematic classification of literary works. Probl. Comput. Appl. Math. **4**(22), 111–117 (2019)

28. Mukhamedieva, D.K., Jurayev, Z.: Classification of content of works. Probl. Comput. Appl. Math. **2**(26), 108–117 (2020)

29. Babomuradov, O.J., Mamatov, N.S., Boboyev, L.B., Otaxonova, B.I.: Classification of texts using decision trees algorithms. Descendants of Muhammad al-Khwarizmi **4**(10) (2019)

30. Babomuradov, O.J., Boboev, L.B., Otaxonova, B.I.: A comparison of naïve bayes models for text classification. Probl. Comput. Appl. Math. **1**(19), 39–43 (2019)

31. Tuliev, U.: Cluster analyse of text documents according to their relation of connectedness. Probl. Comput. Appl. Math. **6**(24), 102–109 (2019)

32. Kuriyozov, E., Matlatipov, S.: Building a new sentiment analysis dataset for Uzbek language and creating baseline models. Multidiscip. Dig. Publ. Inst. Proc. **21**(1), 37 (2019)

33. Kuriyozov, E., Matlatipov, S., Alonso, M., Gómez-Rodríguez, C.: Deep learning vs. classic models on a new Uzbek sentiment analysis dataset. In: Proceedings of the Human Language Technologies as a Challenge for Computer Science and Linguistics, pp. 258–262 (2019)

34. Srivastava, N., Hinton, G., Krizhevsky, A., Sutskever, I., Salakhutdinov, R.: Dropout: a simple way to prevent neural networks from overfitting. J. Mach. Learn. Res. **15**, 1929–1958 (2014)

35. Hochreiter, S., Schmidhuber, J.: Long short-term memory. Neural Comput. **9**, 1735–1780 (1997)

36. Grave, E., Bojanowski, P., Gupta, P., Joulin, A., Mikolov T.: Learning word vectors for 157 languages. In: Proceedings of the Eleventh International Conference on Language Resources and Evaluation (LREC 2018), Japan. ELRA (2018)

37. Kuriyozov, E., Doval, Y., Gómez-Rodríguez, C.: Cross-lingual word embeddings for turkic languages. In: Proceedings of the 12th Language Resources and Evaluation Conference, France, pp. 4054–4062. ELRA (2020)

38. Abadi, M., et al.: TensorFlow: large-scale machine learning on heterogeneous systems (2015). https://www.tensorflow.org. Accessed 21 May 2021

An Equal Data Setting
for Attention-Based Encoder-Decoder
and HMM/DNN Models: A Case Study
in Finnish ASR

Aku Rouhe[1](✉), Astrid Van Camp[2], Mittul Singh[1], Hugo Van Hamme[2],
and Mikko Kurimo[1]

[1] Department of Signal Processing and Acoustics, Aalto University, Espoo, Finland
{aku.rouhe,mikko.kurimo}@aalto.com
[2] Department of Electrical Engineering, KU Leuven, Leuven, Belgium
hugo.vanhamme@esat.kuleuven.be

Abstract. Standard end-to-end training of attention-based ASR models only uses transcribed speech. If they are compared to HMM/DNN systems, which additionally leverage a large corpus of text-only data and expert-crafted lexica, the differences in modeling cannot be disentangled from differences in data. We propose an experimental setup, where only transcribed speech is used to train both model types. To highlight the difference that text-only data can make, we use Finnish, where an expert-crafted lexicon is not needed. With 1500h equal data, we find that both ASR paradigms perform similarly, but adding text data quickly improves the HMM/DNN system. On a smaller 160h subset we find that HMM/DNN models outperform AED models.

Keywords: HMM/DNN · Attention-based Encoder-Decoder · Equal data

A large part of recent speech recognition (ASR) approaches can be divided into two categories: end-to-end attention-based encoder-decoder models (AED) and hybrid hidden Markov model deep neural network (HMM/DNN) models. There are many reasons to choose one approach or the other: some reasons are theoretical (e.g. emphasising the joint optimization of AED models), some practical (e.g. needing the phone-level alignments provided by HMM/DNN models), some simply empirical (which has lower word error rate). The diverged approaches have naturally been compared in terms of performance. Performance comparisons are inherently empirical and the results depend on the constraints of the task [3,17]. These constraints generally mean the data that is available, as well as any technical limitations such as a maximum latency. Without special techniques [9,10,20,27], end-to-end training only uses transcribed speech, but it is typical for standard ASR tasks to also include expert-crafted pronunciation dictionaries and a large amount of text-only data, which standard HMM/DNN models can leverage.

© Springer Nature Switzerland AG 2021
A. Karpov and R. Potapova (Eds.): SPECOM 2021, LNAI 12997, pp. 602–613, 2021.
https://doi.org/10.1007/978-3-030-87802-3_54

In this work we focus on the text resource constraints. From a practical perspective, it is natural to include extra text in standard tasks: text-only data is usually much more plentiful or cheap to produce and thus available to help. From an academic perspective, we argue that experiments with different data constraints could disentangle the effect of differences in data from differences in modeling.

Firstly, we propose an experimental design where the HMM/DNN approach is constrained to use the same data as an end-to-end trained AED model. The experimental design allows us to disentangle the effect of extra text data from model performance. In this constrained setting, the focus shifts to building a suitable language model for the HMM/DNN despite the lack of extra text data, rather than trying to augment the AED approach with extra text data.

Secondly, we find that under this design, in a 1500h Finnish ASR task, the AED and HMM/DNN approaches perform similarly, but on a smaller 10% data task, the HMM/DNN model outperforms the AED model. We find Finnish especially well suited to this constraint, because Finnish has a very transparent orthography, and thus the effect having an expert-crafted lexicon (or lack thereof) is annulled.

Thirdly, we extend the subword lexicon handling to support SentencePiece models for HMM/DNNs, as we find subword models vital for the constrained HMM/DNN.

1   Related Work

Using an external language model with the AED approach in shallow fusion [9] can also achieve an equal data setting, but the resulting system is no longer trained end-to-end. Using more audio data is shown to reduce dependency on an external language model [28].

There are many special methods which extend end-to-end training of AED models so that text-only data can be used, including tighter integration of a language model [27], and synthesizing audio-side information for text-only data [10,20].

Comparisons between AED and HMM/DNN approaches exist, but to the best of our knowledge the equal data experimental design proposed here has not been explored before. It is generally thought that with large data sets, AED performs as well or even better than HMM/DNN [3], and with less data HMM/DNN starts to fare better [30], and that both approaches can be certainly be competitive [8,17].

2   Data

Our training dataset is derived from a combination of three speech datasets: the large Finnish parliament dataset ($\approx$1560h) containing recordings from the Finnish parliments sessions [18], the Speecon corpus ($\approx$160h) containing read speech in various conditions [12], and the Speechdat database ($\approx$220h) containing read and spontaneous, phonetically rich telephone quality (8 kHz) speech from a large number of speakers [21]. After the Kaldi toolkit [19] standard cleanup, a combined ≈1500h training set remains. From this data, 10% of utterances (randomly sampled) are taken to form a ≈160h smaller scale training set.

The transcripts of the full training set consists of ≈9M words, with ≈400k unique words. The 10% subset transcrips have ≈900k words, with ≈100k unique words. In the equal data setting, only the transcripts are used for language modeling. However, there is an order-of-magnitude larger text-only dataset, the Kielipankki text corpus [5] available, consisting of newspaper articles and books. The Kielipankki corpus has a total of ≈143M words, with ≈4.2M unique words.

The main evaluation data is broadcast news shows from Finland's national public service media company YLE. The test set is ≈6h. There is a separate YLE development set of the same type, of ≈5h. However, no matching training set exists for this data. It can be expected that particularly the news articles in the Kielipankki corpus can be helpful on the YLE data. The Finnish parliament data also has a test set, which is in-domain for the training data. It has two sections: one for speakers seen in the training data, one for unseen speakers. Surprisingly, empirically the unseen speakers test data has been *easier*; probably the members of parliament that speak rarely more often read their speech from notes.

3   Attention-Based System

We train AED models end-to-end using the ESPnet toolkit [29]. In initial experiments, Transformer architectures outperformed RNN-based architectures, thus we opt for a Transformer model. This architecture also generally fares well in AED applications [13]. The ESPnet toolkit supports using the CTC criterion in a multi-task setup (with weight α) to aid the encoder training [14]. The separate CTC decoder is can also be used in decoding (with weight γ). We find that it offers a minor improvement in this task.

The common output units for AED models are characters or larger subword units. We conduct experiments with SentencePiece [15] BPE subword units, as they are well integrated into ESPnet, but interestingly find no improvement in this task. Thus we simply use character output units.

For the full 1500h data we tune the model size on the YLE development set, ending with 16 encoder layers and 8 decoder layers of width 2048 each. We also search for ideal weights for the CTC multitask learning and decoding, setting $\alpha = 0.2$, $\gamma = 0.1$. Besides output units, CTC parameters, and model size, we refer to recipes of similarly sized data for the other hyperparameters, using dropout rate 0.1 and label smoothing 0.1. We train the models with early stopping on the YLE development data. Before decoding, we average the last 10 model checkpoints' weights, and decode with the averaged model.

On the smaller 10% data we simply used the same hyperparameters as with the 1500h model. We experimented with a smaller model size (anticipating that having less data could lead to overfitting), but the same model size performed better.

4 HMM System

For the HMM/DNN approach, we use the Kaldi toolkit. As a baseline for acoustic model development we refer to results from [26]. Like [26], we use context- and word-position dependent grapheme-units. However, their models use i-vectors for speaker-aware training, as is typical in the Kaldi toolkit. The AED approach seems to get similar benefit from speaker-aware training as the HMM/DNN methods [1,6,22], and so we argue that either both or neither of the paradigms should use speaker-aware methods. For simplicity, we opt for neither.

We train a new, large (chain-style) time delay neural network (TDNN) based model, without i-vectors. By using more TDNN-layers than Smit et al. we are able to achieve similar performance on the YLE development set without i-vectors, as shown in Table 1. Thus we choose this acoustic model for the HMM approach. On the smaller 10% data, we simply keep the same hyperparameters.

Table 1. Validating the new acoustic model, without i-vectors, against the best published result with TDNN-BLSTM and i-vectors.

Model	YLE Dev WER
TDNN-BLSTM + i-vectors	17.3
Large TDNN	17.4

The Finnish language is agglutinative, which leads to very large vocabularies. Particularly on small text datasets, such as the speech transcripts used here, the data sparsity problem is evident, if using traditional word-based language models. Instead, we use a subword language model, which dramatically reduces the vocabulary size. With subword language models, long n-gram contexts may be necessary for good performance [11], and therefore we use the variKN toolkit [23] to train Kneser-Ney varigram n-gram models of up to 10-gram order. Additionally, we train standard LSTM-based RNNLMs with TheanoLM [7], optimizing network size on the YLE development data transcript perplexity. This leads to network size 1024 units. The RNNLM is applied in lattice rescoring.

To segment the training transcripts into subwords, we use the same SentencePiece BPE algorithm as in the AED approach. This way, both approaches had the same segmentation style available. We optimize the variKN scale parameter, and the number of BPE units, for perplexity on the YLE development set transcripts. Table 2 shows the resulting numbers of BPE merges for different model types and data sizes. We optimize the language model weight for the YLE development set word error rate.

4.1 Correct Subword Handling in Lexicon FST

Using subword-based language models requires some care in constructing the lexicon FST. Firstly, when using word-position-dependent units [16], the lexicon should take subword concatenation into account when handling word-boundary

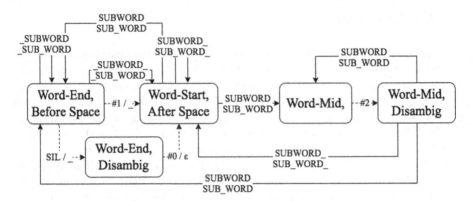

Fig. 1. SentencePiece lexicon FST showing which word positions SentencePiece units can be placed at, depending on where the space character _ appears on example unit SUBWORD (for instance, at the start of the unit: _SUBWORD). Also shows three disambiguation symbols, and two more are needed for spaces inside units.

units [25]. For example, the lexicon should only transduce the word-start and word-end units at true word boundaries, but not at every subword boundary. Secondly, as SentencePiece units may have word boundaries as part of the subword units, the optional silence at word boundaries needs to be handled specially. As part of this work, we extend the tools introduced by [25] to support Sentencepiece segmentation[1].

Figure 1 shows which different word positions SentencePiece units can be placed at, depending on where the space character appears in them. The figure also shows three word-position dependant disambiguation symbols; two more are needed for in-unit spaces.

To validate the proposed SentencePiece lexicon FST, we compare the ASR results to those of Morfessor generated subwords [4, 24] as presented by [25], as shown in Table 3. The SentencePiece models achieve a slightly lower error rate on the larger corpus and slightly higher on the smaller one. The SentencePiece lexicon comes at the cost of larger search graph (HCLG) FSTs compared to Morfessor, for a similar sized language model, because SentencePiece requires a more complex word boundary handling scheme.

5 Results

Table 4 lists the model sizes. Everything combined, the 1500h HMM/DNN system matches the AED model size quite well.

Table 5 shows the performance of the best equal data AED and HMM/DNN systems on the YLE evaluation data. The absolute word error rates are quite similar on the full 1500h data. Note that the percentage in brackets indicates the bootstrap estimate [2] of the probability of improving over the competing

---

[1] https://github.com/aalto-speech/subword-kaldi.

Table 2. Optimal number of BPE merges for different data sizes and model types. In this task the AED systems did not benefit from BPE units, and character-level models were used instead. This was optimized on YLE Development WER (end-to-end). On the HMM side, the number of units was optimized for LM perplexity. With the limited 10% transcripts, a small number of BPE units was marginally better than character units, but with the full transcript and with the ≈17 times larger Kielipankki text data, BPE units clearly improved.

Model	Number of merges
HMM 10% Transcripts	≈100
HMM All Transcripts	≈1700
HMM Kielipankki	≈10000
AED 10% Data	0
AED All Data	0

Table 3. SentencePiece units compared to Morfessor units on the YLE development data, using the same acoustic models. The *small* models used the Parliament transcripts, while the *large* models used the larger Kielipankki corpus.

Model	YLE Dev WER
Morfessor$_{small}$	27.4
SentencePiece$_{small}$	28.4
Morfessor$_{large}$	17.4
SentencePiece$_{large}$	15.8

model (with 10000 repetitions); with strict 95% confidence cutoffs the YLE 1500h WER result would be inconclusive. On the 10% data, the HMM/DNN system outperforms the AED system.

Since Finnish tends to have long words with inflections, character error rate (CER) is a useful metric as well. Table 6 shows the YLE CER evaluation. On the 1500h data this paints a different picture than the WER evaluation: the AED model outperforms the HMM/DNN system. However, on the 10% data the HMM/DNN system has lower CER as well. This CER evaluation did not consider spaces.

The equal data results of Tables 5 and 6 are contrasted by the results in Table 7, which details a set of experiments where a number of random lines was added from the Kielipankki corpus to the HMM/DNN language model training data set (in addition to the speech transcripts). This shows how fast the WER would decrease as slightly better matching text data was added. New language models were trained on the total resulting text data. We optimized the language model and subword segmentation parameters again for each new text corpus obtained this way.

The equal data models from Tables 5 and 6 are also evaluated on the Finnish Parliament test sets. Table 8 shows the WER results and Table 9 shows the CER

Table 4. Comparison of model capacity in terms of number of parameters. N-gram number of parameters measured by number N-grams included in the model; the number of arcs in the resulting finite state transducer is about 50% more.

Model	Number of parameters
AED	35M
HMM Total	35M
Acoustic model	20M
N-gram LM	6M
RNNLM	9M
$AED_{10\%}$	35M
$HMM_{10\%}$ Total	22M
Acoustic model	20M
N-gram LM	2M

Table 5. At the top, the comparison of the best attention (AED) and HMM based models, trained on the 1500h equal data, evaluated on the YLE broadcast data. The percentage in brackets indicates the bootstrap estimate [2] of the probability of improving over the competing model (inside the same horizontal lines). In the middle: the RNNLM (also trained on transcripts only) does not meaningfully improve over the 10-gram Kneser-Ney LM. In the bottom, similar comparison of the best attention and HMM-based models trained on the smaller 10% random subset of the 1500h equal data.

YLE		
Model	Dev WER	Test WER
AED	28.7	**27.8** (78%)
HMM	**28.4** (87%)	28.1
HMM +RNNLM	29.0	28.0
$AED_{10\%}$	36.8	35.8
$HMM_{10\%}$	**35.0** (100%)	**34.0** (100%)

Table 6. Character error rate equivalent of Table 5.

YLE		
Model	Dev CER	Test CER
AED	**5.96** (95%)	**5.57** (99.7%)
HMM	6.13	5.88
HMM +RNNLM	6.29	6.07
$AED_{10\%}$	7.73	7.21
$HMM_{10\%}$	**7.24** (100%)	**6.96** (100%)

Table 7. YLE evaluation WER decreasing as more text data is added to the HMM/DNN approach from the Kielipankki corpus. The number in brackets indicates how large the resulting text dataset is compared to the original.

YLE		
Text data condition	Dev WER	Test WER
Transcripts only	28.4	28.1
+100k KP lines (1.1x)	23.7	23.7
+200k KP lines (1.2x)	22.4	22.1
+500k KP lines (1.7x)	20.3	20.5
+1M KP lines (2.3x)	18.8	19.1
All of KP (16.9x)	15.8	16.2

Table 8. At the top, as a baseline we show Parl-opt HMM, which uses a large (20M token) in-domain text corpus for language modeling, and is optimized for the parliament data. Then, the same models as Table 5, evaluated on the Parliament test set (but models still optimized for YLE). Here the RNNLM improves slightly, indicating it has slightly overfit to the Parliament data compared to YLE data in Table 5.

FINNISH PARLIAMENT		
Model	Test-Seen WER	Test-Unseen WER
Parl-opt HMM [18]	5.9	5.2
AED	**10.2** (95%)	10.2
HMM	10.6	**9.6** (98%)
HMM +RNNLM	**9.7**	**9.0**
AED$_{10\%}$	18.2	18.1
HMM$_{10\%}$	**14.9** (100%)	**13.7** (100%)

Table 9. Character error rate equivalent of Table 8. Character error rates were not available for the Parl-opt HMM.

FINNISH PARLIAMENT		
Model	Test-Seen CER	Test-Unseen CER
AED	**2.91** (81%)	**2.99** (56%)
HMM	2.99	3.01
HMM +RNNLM	**2.80**	**2.85**
AED$_{10\%}$	4.64	4.92
HMM$_{10\%}$	**3.66** (100%)	**3.69** (100%)

results. We emphasize that these models were optimized on the YLE Development data. For constrast, we show a result [18] that was optimized on the Parliament data: this is by far the lowest WER. Based on both WER and CER, the 1500h equal data AED and HMM/DNN models perform similarly. Again, on the 10% data, the HMM/DNN system outperforms the AED system.

6   Discussion

On the whole it can be said that in the full 1500h equal data scenario, the AED and HMM/DNN approaches performed similarly. The CER results on the YLE data favour the AED approach, which may be connected to the observation that character-level units performed better than BPE-subwords for the AED approach, and generally CER evaluation de-emphasizes the role of the language model.

In contrast to the full 1500h data, on the 10% utterances (160h) subset, the HMM/DNN consistently performed better than the AED approach. This is in line with the general understanding that HMM/DNN systems fare better with less data.

Table 7 shows just how much the extra text-only data could help. Text-only data can be naturally leveraged by HMM/DNN models, but improvements could certainly be found with the AED text-data leveraging techniques as well. Which of these techniques works best for AED models is an active research question, but not in the scope of this work. Together these experiments show how the proposed equal data experimental design can provide a new perspective: with the data being equal, the models' inherent strengths and weaknesses are emphasized.

We used our best transformer model to represent the AED approach and the HMM/DNN approach was represented by a strong TDNN acoustic model coupled with our best optimized language model. The models have similar number of parameters. Undoubtedly both approaches could have been optimized further: on competitive datasets such as LibriSpeech, the research community competes for tenths of percentage points of WER. Thus we feel that the differences between AED and HMM/DNN models on the full 1500h data should be seen as inconclusive: both performed similarly. However, some results were clearer: the 10% data favors the HMM/DNN approach and the additional text-only data was obviously the key to better error rates on the YLE data.

Thus the results here suggest there is a medium dataset scale, where the AED and HMM/DNN can perform similarly, as long as techniques for leveraging external text-only data are developed for the AED-models.

7   Conclusion

We have proposed an *equal data* experimental design where HMM/DNN systems and end-to-end trained attention-based systems are compared by artificially limiting the data to transcribed speech only. This sort of task is well suited for Finnish, which has a transparent orthography, ruling out the lexicon's effect. In our equal data experiments, HMM/DNN models and AED models perform similarly at full 1500h data, but HMM/DNN models outperform AED models on a smaller 10% subset. Extra text-only data clearly improves the HMM/DNN models, which emphasizes our argument that when HMM/DNN models and end-to-end trained AED models are compared, unequal data resources can hide differences in modeling.

As part of developing the HMM/DNN models under constraints set by this comparison, we also implement a lexicon FST which handles the SentencePiece subword segmentation correctly.

Acknowledgments. This work was supported by EU's Horizon 2020 research and innovation programme via the project MeMAD (GA 780069). The computational resources were provided by Aalto ScienceIT.

References

1. Bansal, S., Malhotra, K., Ganapathy, S.: Speaker and language aware training for end-to-end asr. In: 2019 IEEE Automatic Speech Recognition and Understanding Workshop (ASRU), pp. 494–501 (2019). https://doi.org/10.1109/ASRU46091.2019.9004000

2. Bisani, M., Ney, H.: Bootstrap estimates for confidence intervals in asr performance evaluation. In: 2004 IEEE International Conference on Acoustics, Speech, and Signal Processing, vol. 1, pp. I–409 (2004). https://doi.org/10.1109/ICASSP.2004.1326009

3. Chiu, C., et al.: State-of-the-art speech recognition with sequence-to-sequence models. In: 2018 IEEE International Conference on Acoustics, Speech and Signal Processing (ICASSP), pp. 4774–4778 (2018)

4. Creutz, M., Lagus, K.: Unsupervised discovery of morphemes. In: Proceedings of the ACL-02 Workshop on Morphological and Phonological Learning, pp. 21–30. Association for Computational Linguistics (Jul 2002). https://doi.org/10.3115/1118647.1118650, https://www.aclweb.org/anthology/W02-0603

5. CSC - IT Center for Science: The helsinki korp version of the Finnish text collection (1998). http://urn.fi/urn:nbn:fi:lb-2016050207

6. Delcroix, M., Watanabe, S., Ogawa, A., Karita, S., Nakatani, T.: Auxiliary feature based adaptation of end-to-end asr systems. In: Proceedings Interspeech 2018, pp. 2444–2448 (2018). http://dx.doi.org/10.21437/Interspeech.2018-1438

7. Enarvi, S., Kurimo, M.: Theanolm - an extensible toolkit for neural network language modeling. In: Interspeech 2016, pp. 3052–3056 (2016). http://dx.doi.org/10.21437/Interspeech.2016-618

8. Gulati, A., et al.: Conformer: convolution-augmented transformer for speech recognition. In: Proceedings of the Interspeech 2020, pp. 5036–5040 (2020). http://dx.doi.org/10.21437/Interspeech.2020-3015

9. Gulcehre, C., Firat, O., Xu, K., Cho, K., Bengio, Y.: On integrating a language model into neural machine translation. Comput. Speech Lang. **45**, 137–148 (2017)

10. Hayashi, T., et al.: Back-translation-style data augmentation for end-to-end asr. In: 2018 IEEE Spoken Language Technology Workshop (SLT), pp. 426–433 (2018). https://doi.org/10.1109/SLT.2018.8639619

11. Hirsimaki, T., Pylkkonen, J., Kurimo, M.: Importance of high-order n-gram models in morph-based speech recognition. IEEE Trans. Audio Speech Lang. Process. **17**(4), 724–732 (2009)

12. Iskra, D., Grosskopf, B., Marasek, K., van den Heuvel, H., Diehl, F., Kiessling, A.: SPEECON - speech databases for consumer devices: database specification and validation. In: Proceedings of the Third International Conference on Language Resources and Evaluation (LREC'02). European Language Resources Association (ELRA), Las Palmas, Canary Islands - Spain, May 2002. http://www.lrec-conf.org/proceedings/lrec2002/pdf/177.pdf

13. Karita, S., et al.: A comparative study on transformer vs rnn in speech applications. In: 2019 IEEE Automatic Speech Recognition and Understanding Workshop (ASRU), pp. 449–456 (2019). https://doi.org/10.1109/ASRU46091.2019.9003750

14. Kim, S., Hori, T., Watanabe, S.: Joint ctc-attention based end-to-end speech recognition using multi-task learning. In: 2017 IEEE International Conference on Acoustics, Speech and Signal Processing (ICASSP), pp. 4835–4839, March 2017. https://doi.org/10.1109/ICASSP.2017.7953075

15. Kudo, T., Richardson, J.: Sentencepiece: A simple and language independent subword tokenizer and detokenizer for neural text processing. arXiv preprint arXiv:1808.06226 (2018)

16. Lee, C.H.: Improved acoustic modeling for speaker independent large vocabulary continuous speech recognition. In: [Proceedings] ICASSP 91: 1991 International Conference on Acoustics, Speech, and Signal Processing, vol. 1, pp. 161–164 (1991). https://doi.org/10.1109/ICASSP.1991.150302

17. Lüscher, C., et al.: RWTH ASR systems for librispeech: hybrid vs attention. In: Proceedings of the Interspeech 2019, pp. 231–235 (2019). http://dx.doi.org/10.21437/Interspeech.2019-1780

18. Mansikkaniemi, A., Smit, P., Kurimo, M.: Automatic construction of the finnish parliament speech corpus. In: Proceedings of the Interspeech 2017, pp. 3762–3766 (2017). http://dx.doi.org/10.21437/Interspeech.2017-1115

19. Povey, D., et al.: The kaldi speech recognition toolkit. In: IEEE 2011 Workshop on Automatic Speech Recognition and Understanding. IEEE Signal Processing Society, December 2011. IEEE Catalog No.: CFP11SRW-USB

20. Rossenbach, N., Zeyer, A., Schlüter, R., Ney, H.: Generating synthetic audio data for attention-based speech recognition systems. In: ICASSP 2020–2020 IEEE International Conference on Acoustics, Speech and Signal Processing (ICASSP), pp. 7069–7073 (2020). https://doi.org/10.1109/ICASSP40776.2020.9053008

21. Rosti, A., Rämö, A., Saarelainen, T., Yli-Hietanen, J.: Speechdat finnish database for the fixed telephone network. Tampere University of Technology, Technical report (1998)

22. Rouhe, A., Kaseva, T., Kurimo, M.: Speaker-aware training of attention-based end-to-end speech recognition using neural speaker embeddings. In: ICASSP 2020–2020 IEEE International Conference on Acoustics, Speech and Signal Processing (ICASSP), pp. 7064–7068 (2020)

23. Siivola, V., Hirsimaki, T., Virpioja, S.: On growing and pruning kneser-ney smoothed n-gram models. IEEE Trans. Audio Speech Lang. Process. **15**(5), 1617–1624 (2007). https://doi.org/10.1109/TASL.2007.896666

24. Smit, P., Virpioja, S., Grönroos, S.A., Kurimo, M.: Morfessor 2.0: toolkit for statistical morphological segmentation. In: Proceedings of the Demonstrations at the 14th Conference of the European Chapter of the Association for Computational Linguistics, pp. 21–24 (2014)

25. Smit, P., Virpioja, S., Kurimo, M.: Improved subword modeling for wfst-based speech recognition. In: Proceedings of the Interspeech 2017, pp. 2551–2555 (2017). http://dx.doi.org/10.21437/Interspeech.2017-103

26. Smit, P., Virpioja, S., Kurimo, M.: Advances in subword-based hmm-dnn speech recognition across languages. Comput. Speech Lang. **66**, 101158 (2021)

27. Sriram, A., Jun, H., Satheesh, S., Coates, A.: Cold fusion: training seq2seq models together with language models. In: Proceedings of the Interspeech 2018, pp. 387–391 (2018). http://dx.doi.org/10.21437/Interspeech.2018-1392

28. Synnaeve, G., et al.: End-to-end asr:from supervised to semi-supervised learning with modern architectures. In: ICML 2020 Workshop on Self-supervision in Audio and Speech (2020)

29. Watanabe, S., et al.: ESPnet: End-to-end speech processing toolkit. In: Proceedings of Interspeech, pp. 2207–2211 (2018). http://dx.doi.org/10.21437/Interspeech.2018-1456

30. Zhou, W., Michel, W., Irie, K., Kitza, M., Schlüter, R., Ney, H.: The rwth asr system for ted-lium release 2: improving hybrid hmm with specaugment. In: ICASSP 2020–2020 IEEE International Conference on Acoustics, Speech and Signal Processing (ICASSP), pp. 7839–7843 (2020). https://doi.org/10.1109/ICASSP40776.2020.9053573

Speaker-Aware Training of Speech Emotion Classifier with Speaker Recognition

Lyudmila Savchenko and Andrey V. Savchenko[✉]

HSE University, Laboratory of Algorithms and Technologies for Network Analysis,
Nizhny Novgorod, Russia
{lsavchenko,avsavchenko}@hse.ru

Abstract. In this paper, we discuss the possibility to improve the accuracy of speech emotion recognition in multi-user systems. We assume that a small corpus of speech emotional data is available for each speaker of interest. It is proposed to train a speaker-independent emotion classifier of arbitrary audio features including deep embeddings and fine-tune it on the utterances of each speaker. As a result, every user is associated with his or her own emotion recognition model. The concrete fine-tuned classifier may be chosen using a speaker recognition algorithm or even fixed if the identity of a user is known. It is experimentally shown that the proposed approach makes it possible to significantly improve the quality of conventional speaker-independent emotion classifier.

Keywords: Speech emotion recognition · Speaker-dependent emotion recognition · Speaker recognition · OpenL3

1 Introduction

Speech emotion recognition (SER) is one of the most challenging tasks in speech processing [1]. In contrast to the recent extreme progress in automatic speech recognition (ASR) [19], the sizes of the datasets available for SER are much smaller and the labeling may be ambiguous. As a result, the performance of even the state-of-the-art SER models is still far from the certain level of maturity. Nevertheless, recent studies [6,7] have reported up to 80–90% accuracy of emotion recognition for several datasets. For example, the pre-trained deep convolutional neural network (DCNN) with a correlation-based feature selection [7] reached 95.1% accuracy for the Emo-DB and 81.3% for the Ryerson Audio-Visual Database of Emotional Speech and Song (RAVDESS) [13]. Leveraging conventional Mel-frequency cepstral coefficient (MFCC) features and bag-of-acoustic-words to feed the neural network was characterized by up to 84.5% accuracy for the latter dataset [6].

It is important to emphasize that these results have been reported for a speaker-dependent mode [4,10], in which the training and testing sets contain audio recordings of the same subjects. Unfortunately, emotion classification performance is 10–30% lower for the speaker-independent mode in which the speakers from the training and testing sets are disjoint [7]. Indeed, it is well known from

© Springer Nature Switzerland AG 2021
A. Karpov and R. Potapova (Eds.): SPECOM 2021, LNAI 12997, pp. 614–625, 2021.
https://doi.org/10.1007/978-3-030-87802-3_55

the studies of ASR that the speaker adaptation may lead to much lower error rate when compared to the speaker-independent mode [20]. However, we would like to highlight the main difference between adaptation of a general speaker-independent model to the voice of a particular speaker or a group of speakers from ASR [17] and experiments for a speaker-dependent SER [6,11] with a single model trained for all speakers. As a result, it is not obvious how to perform adaptation of a SER model for a voice of a particular speaker in, e.g., a federated learning environment [9].

Hence, in this paper we decided to study the ways to use speaker adaptation in SER. We propose an approach using conventional transfer learning and fine-tuning of a neural network-based classifier on audio features including deep embeddings [3]. If the identity of a user in a single-user system, e.g., personal mobile device, is unknown, the speaker verification may be implemented to either choose the speaker-dependent model or general speaker-independent classifier. We may also collect several speaker-specific models for multi-user systems, and choose the particular one using known speaker identification methods [12]. Moreover, face recognition [14] can be applied similarly to the paper [2], in which the concrete acoustic model for ASR was chosen using video modality.

It is necessary to emphasize that data does not come with labels in many real-life examples of SER, e.g., in call centers. Hence, a system should work also for people calling their first time, so that we have to use a speaker-independent model. However, in this paper, it is assumed that the users of emotion recognition system are known and it is possible to gather a speaker-dependent set of utterances with known emotional labels. Potential use cases include emotion recognition for mobile devices, smart houses and smart speakers or analysis of speech from public persons, e.g., politicians in their interviews and debates.

The rest of the paper is organized as follows. In Sect. 2 we introduce the proposed approach. Experimental results for the RAVDESS dataset are presented in Sect. 3. Concluding comments are given in Sect. 4.

2   Methodology

The task of this paper may be formulated as follows. Given an input utterance X from a particular speaker, it is necessary to predict emotional state of this speaker, i.e., the class label $c \in \{1, ..., C\}$, where C is the total number of different emotions. The training set of $N > 1$ speech examples is denoted as $\{X_n\}, n \in \{1, 2, ..., N\}$ from other speakers with known emotion class label c_n. It is assumed that a small set of utterances with corresponding emotions was recorded from expected input speakers in order to improve the overall accuracy by using adaptation of SER model to a voice of particular user.

2.1   Dataset

In this paper, we deal with the English language emotion dataset RAVDESS [13] with 24 actors (12 male and 12 female) and eight emotional classes (angry, calm, disgust, fear, happy, neutral, sad, surprised). All the classes are balanced for each speaker, though there are twice less examples of neutral class when compared to all other categories. The total number of 1440 speech utterances and 1012 songs with a 48,000 Hz sampling rate have been divided into 1932 training and 520 testing examples.

Though this dataset is rather small and simple, it is widely used in recent papers [6,7] which examine both speaker-dependent and speaker-independent scenarios of the SER problem. According to the paper [11], we have implemented two train-test splits, namely:

1. Conventional speaker-dependent random split;
2. Speaker-independent mode, in which the training utterances were taken from actors width id between 1 and 19, while the testing set contains speech signals from other 5 actors.

In order to test the speaker-aware approach for SER, we performed the actor-based split of the testing set from the above-mentioned second item (speaker-independent mode). In particular, five sets of utterances were obtained that correspond to each speaker out of 5 testing actors. Next, each set is randomly split into two disjoint parts, so that the first part with $\delta \cdot N$ speech signals is used as a speaker-specific data to fine-tune the speaker independent classifier, while the second part with the remaining utterances is used to test the accuracy of the proposed speaker-aware approach. Here N is the total size of the set, and $\delta \in (0, 1)$ is the parameter that determines the relative size of the speaker-specific training set.

2.2 Feature Extraction

In order to solve the SER task, it is possible to extract D-dimensional feature vectors $\mathbf{x}$ and $\mathbf{x}_n$ from the input utterance X and training examples X_n, respectively [7,16]. Next, an appropriate classifier may be trained on a set $\{(\mathbf{x}_n, c_n)\}$ to predict the class label of $\mathbf{x}$. We used the following feature extraction methods:

1. Spectrograms obtained by using simple energy-based voice activity detection (VAD) [18], pre-emphasis, framing and mean-normalized filter banks [8]. The resulting images were resized to identical shape (224 × 224), so that the chunks of a different duration were reshaped to the same temporal dimension of the spectrogram image. Next, several pre-trained DCNNs from TensorFlow 2.5 were used as feature extractors. The new fully connected layer is added on top of the penultimate feature extractor layer. In the experimental study the results of MobileNet v1 architecture are reported, because this DCNN has shown the reasonable accuracy and speed.
2. Mel-spectrogram from librosa converted to 224 × 224 images. The ResNet-18 from PyTorch has been fine-tuned to perform classification[1].

---

[1] https://www.kaggle.com/kuntaldas599/emotional-speech-classification2d.

3. Concatenation of traditional acoustic features, namely, 40 MFCC, chroma-gram (normalized energy for 12 chroma bins) and Mel-spectrogram with 128 Mel filters, computed by librosa[2].
4. Scaled acoustic features extracted by OpenSMILE library [5] using two sets, namely, Emobase ($D = 988$ features) and ComParE_2016 ($D = 6373$).
5. The frame-wise average high-dimensional ($D = 6144$) deep audio embeddings extracted by OpenL3 library [3].

The best classifiers for each feature extraction approach by using a small validation (development) set with utterances of one speaker from the given training set. As a result, the frame-wise average $D = 180$-dimensional feature vectors (librosa) are fed into a multi-layered perceptron (MLP) with 1 hidden layer (300 units) as it is done in the above-mentioned example from Kaggle. The OpenSMILE features are better classified by SVM (support vector machine) with RBF (radial basis function) kernel, while the OpenL3 embeddings were classified by using the implementation of SVM with linear kernel from scikit-learn (LinearSVC). However, in the experimental study we report the testing results for the same feature sets with different classifiers.

2.3   Speaker-Aware Fine-Tuning

In this paper, we examine the possibility to improve the quality of SER by using additional speaker-dependent dataset described above. In particular, three identical neural networks with different training procedure have been studied, namely:

1. A pre-trained (hereinafter "speaker-independent") model, for which the average accuracy practically does not depend on δ;
2. A neural network with random initialization of weights that was trained from scratch during 100 epochs on the speaker-specific training set only using Adam optimizer with learning rate 0.0001 (hereinafter "Speaker-data only");
3. The proposed speaker-aware fine-tuned model.

Let us describe the latter model in detail. It is a neural network with the same architectures as in the second item of this list, but the weights of the neural networks for each speaker have been initialized by the weights of the best speaker-independent classifier from the first item, so that the speaker-specific data is used for fine-tuning only. If this speaker-independent model is represented as a neural network, e.g., MLP, this initialization is implemented by simple copying of the pre-trained neural network. However, our experiments demonstrated that several features from Subsect. 2.2 are better classified by using the LinearSVC from scikit-learn. In such case we created a neural network without hidden layers, i.e., multi-class logistic regression, using TensorFlow 2.5 and copied weights and bias of LinearSVC classifier into the weights of this network. In both cases such a neural network was fine-tuned using only utterances from the speaker-specific training set with the relative size δ. The fine-tuning is implemented

---
[2] https://www.kaggle.com/tracyporter/speech-emotion-recognition.

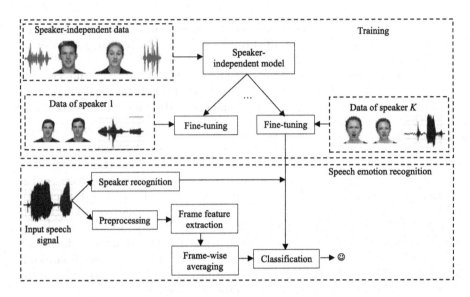

Fig. 1. Proposed pipeline.

using absolutely the same procedure as the training from scratch in item 2 of the above-mentioned list.

2.4   Complete Pipeline

The complete pipeline of the proposed approach is shown in Fig. 1. During training procedure, appropriate speaker-independent SER model is obtained. Next, this model is fine-tuned on the data from specific speaker for all available users. During recognition of an observed speech signal we extract embeddings suitable for speaker recognition/verification with appropriate method, such as Speaker-Net [12]. Second, these embeddings are used in the open-set recognition scenario to look for an appropriate fine-tuned model. If the recognition engine is not confident in the decision, the base speaker-independent model may be used.

The remaining part of Fig. 1 is a general SER pipeline. In particular, we perform conventional preprocessing, such as energy-based VAD, pre-emphasis, etc. Next, the signal is split into short (10–40 ms) partially overlapped frames, and appropriate D-dimensional feature vectors are extracted from each frame using either conventional techniques, such as MFCC and mel-spectrograms, or pretrained DCNN applied for images of a spectrogram. If an input signal is rather short so that only one emotion should be predicted for the whole utterance, it is typical to aggregate frame-wise features into a single descriptor using simple averaging. Finally, this descriptor is classified by the model of a concrete speaker obtained after speaker recognition.

The pipeline may be modified depending on the usage of more complex emotion recognition models or the possibility to gather additional data. For example, if an SER model is an end-to-end neural network, the processing will be slightly changed because the frame feature extraction and decision-making stages are simultaneously implemented using a fine-tuned neural network. If the video data of a speaker's face are available, appropriate video-based face recognition model [14] may be used instead of speaker recognition similarly to [2].

If only one user is available, it will be possible to completely ignore speaker recognition step and always use the fine-tuned model. An example of such a system is the SER for personal devices, which should work only for a specific user. It is important for mobile phones or smart homes with only one owners. However, it is still possible to perform speaker verification to be confident that the input utterance has been produced by this user. If the verification step is not passed, we can use a general speaker-independent model. If the security issues are important, it is even possible to terminate the whole procedure without making a decision about emotional state and raise an alarm about the presence of unknown voice.

3   Experiments

3.1   Speaker-Dependent vs Speaker-Independent Speech Emotion Recognition

In the first experiment we computed the unweighted average recall (UAR) of speaker-dependent and speaker-independent SER for several acoustic features described in Subsect. 2.2. The results for such classifiers as SVM with RBF and linear kernel and random forests (RF) with 1000 trees are shown in Table 1.

Here the spectrogram image recognition techniques are characterized by the worst error rate. It seems that the size of the dataset is too small so that the DCNN-based image classifier overfits rapidly even if the last fully connected layer is trained only. Second, the UAR of traditional emotional features extracted by OpenSMILE is rather high, though it is remarkable that the low-dimensional Emobase features are slightly more accurate than the more widely used ComParE_2016 feature set. Indeed, the classifier for such a small dataset is better trained for the low number of features. Third, simple acoustic features extracted by librosa are recognized surprisingly well: they lead to 4–6% lower error rate when compared to conventional OpenSMILE features in the speaker-dependent mode. However, their accuracy becomes 23% lower for the speaker-independent SER. It is important to emphasize that, in contrast to our experiments with all other features, conventional classifiers (SVM with linear and RBF kernel, random forests, etc.) for these acoustic features are 5–15% worse when compared to the MLP with at least one hidden layer.

Finally, the best results are achieved by the features extracted by OpenL3 library. The latter worked only in very specific environment (TensorFlow 1.x, $x \leq 13$) and sometimes crashed for the large number of input utterances. Despite the usage complexity, our results prove that it is still worth implementing it in

Table 1. Unweighted average recall of speech emotion recognition.

Feature extraction	Classifier	Speaker-dependent UAR	Speaker-independent UAR
Mean-normalized filter banks	MobileNet v1	0.50	0.44
Mel-spectrogram	ResNet-18	0.55	0.49
Frame-wise average acoustic Features (librosa)	linear SVM	0.58	0.43
	MLP	0.78	0.55
	SVM RBF	0.61	0.52
	RF	0.66	0.54
OpenSMILE (Emobase)	linear SVM	0.63	0.50
	SVM RBF	0.74	0.63
	RF	0.69	0.60
OpenSMILE (ComParE_2016)	linear SVM	0.69	0.59
	SVM RBF	0.72	0.57
	RF	0.66	0.55
Frame-wise Average embeddings (OpenL3)	linear SVM	0.83	0.64
	MLP	0.73	0.57
	SVM RBF	0.54	0.52
	RF	0.64	0.54

both modes of SER. It is much better that the capsule networks [11] with 56.2% UAR for speaker-independent scenario with 19 speakers in the training set and 69.4% for speaker-dependent mode with 75% of data (randomly chosen) training examples. The DCNN [7] is also slightly worse than classification of OpenL3 features: 81.3% in a speaker-dependent mode, though a correlation-based feature selection is characterized by up to 73.5% UAR for a leave-one-speaker out scheme of speaker-independent SER. Only the recent approach with the bag-of-acoustic-words [6] has slightly higher UAR (84.5%) for 80%/20% train/test split.

3.2   Speaker-Aware Emotion Recognition

In the second experiment we studied the efficiency of the proposed speaker-aware SER (Subsect. 2.4) depending on the size of the speaker-specific training set. We used the following values of parameter δ: 0.1, 0.3, 0.5, 0.7 and 0.9, which corresponds to 10, 30, 50, 70 and 90 training instances, respectively. Two best feature extraction techniques were used, namely, OpenL3 library and simple frame-wise acoustic features (MFCC, chromagram and mel-spectorgram) extracted by librosa. The dependences of UAR on the remaining testing part are presented in Fig. 2 and Fig. 3 for OpenL3 and librosa features, respectively.

As it was expected, the UAR of the speaker-independent model is approximately identical to its results reported in Table 1. The UAR of other two models is increased with the growth of the size of the speaker-specific training set. If this

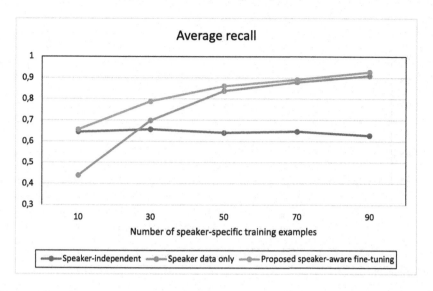

Fig. 2. Dependence of unweighted average recall on the size of the speaker-specific training set in the case of OpenL3 features

size is rather large, then there will be possible to train the classifier from scratch to reach an excellent error rate. Indeed, the proposed fine-tuning has absolutely the same accuracy as the model trained on a speaker data only if 90 training examples for each speaker are available and acoustic features from librosa are used. However, if the size of the speaker-specific training set is relatively small, then the training on the speaker data only will be inefficient. In fact, our approach is 2–21% more accurate for features extracted by OpenL3 for at most 70 speaker-specific training examples (Fig. 2). The gain in accuracy is even more noticeable (not less than 4%) for the frame-wise average simple acoustic features (Fig. 3).

If the amount of the speaker-specific training data is very small ($\delta = 0.1$, i.e., 10 training examples), then our method will have only 1–5% lower error rate when compared to the base speaker-independent model. Hence, we claim that the usage of the speaker-specific data in the proposed fine-tuning pipeline (Fig. 1) is preferable in all cases over speaker-independent model. Figure 4 highlights this difference by demonstrating the confusion matrices for a speaker-independent mode and our technique with 20–40 examples ($\delta = 0.5$) for each emotional class in the speaker-specific training set.

Finally, the most important conclusion is the better performance of our method over conventional speaker-dependent SER, in which a single model is trained using 75% of speech data from all users (Table 1). We should notice that the latter classifier is approximately 6% less accurate when compared to the model fine-tuned only on a voice of a concrete speaker even if we use slightly lower number of his or her utterances ($\delta = 0.7$, i.e., 70%). Comparison with existing methods (Table 2) clearly demonstrates the advantages of the preposed

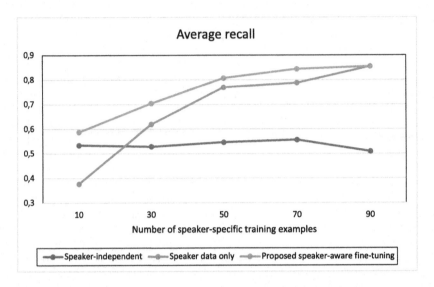

Fig. 3. Dependence of unweighted average recall on the size of the speaker-specific training set in the case of frame-wise average acoustic features (librosa).

Table 2. Average recall for 75%/25% train/test split.

Method	UAR
Capsule routing [11]	0.694
DCNN with feature selection and data resampling [7]	0.813
Hybrid architecture of bag of audio words and DCNN [6]	0.845
Proposed approach for acoustic features (librosa)	0.846
Proposed approach for OpenL3 features	0.901

procedure. In contrast to existing implementations of speaker-dependent SER, in which a training set contain utterances of many speakers, only speaker data are used to fine-tune the model in our method.

In addition, we carried out the preliminarily experiments with speaker recognition using the same training and testing sets of 5 actors. The pre-trained SpeakerNet model [12] extracted $D = 512$ embeddings from each utterance. These embeddings were used to train several classifiers from scikit-learn to recognize speakers based on their voice. As a result, LinearSVC was characterized by 98.08% speaker recognition accuracy only if $\delta = 0.1$ (10 training examples). If the size of the training set becomes greater ($\delta \geq 0.2$), the speakers will be recognized perfectly with 0% error rate. Moreover, SVM with RBF kernel is perfect even when $\delta = 0.1$. Hence, we believe it is better to train several speaker-aware models instead of a single speaker-dependent classifier even for a multi-user system. It is obvious that the speaker identification accuracy will be decreased with an increase of the number of different users, but we believe that our approach will be mainly used if the number of different speakers is rather small.

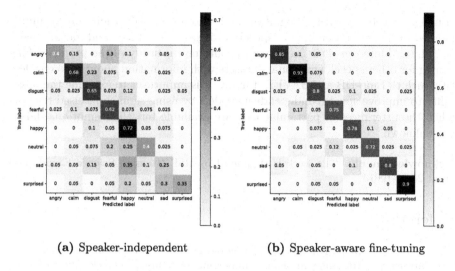

(a) Speaker-independent   (b) Speaker-aware fine-tuning

Fig. 4. Confusion matrix for frame-wise average acoustic features (librosa) with 30 training examples ($\delta = 0.5$): (a) speaker-independent SER; (b) speaker-aware SER.

4   Conclusion

In this paper we proposed an efficient approach for SER (Fig. 1) when the sample speech data from a particular speaker of interest are available. It was demonstrated that our fine-tuning is more accurate when compared to either usage of speaker-independent model (Fig. 4) or training the neural network classifier using speaker data only (Fig. 2, Fig. 3). Our approach becomes a kind of speaker-dependent techniques due to the fact that the system was trained on recordings of the same speakers both in train and test sets. However, our method has 6% higher UAR when compared to conventional speaker-dependent SER [6,7,11] with a single model trained for all users. As a result, we achieved excellent UAR (84–92%) for RAVDESS if the speaker-specific training set contains 70–90% of all data (Table 2).

As the contemporary speaker recognition techniques [12] have rather high quality, it is preferable to use the speaker-specific models even in the multi-user systems. Moreover, speaker verification can be used prior to SER even in a settings with only one expected user to additionally verify his or her identity. It will be possible to implement the proposed user-specific SER for speech processing in personal laptops, mobile devices, smart homes with limited number of users if it is necessary not only understand the user's speech but also predict his or her emotional state. Our method can be applied to predict emotions in dynamics, for example, to analyze the particular answers in political debates or other dialogues of public persons when it is possible to gather the user-specific dataset.

The main direction for future research is the application of our approach to audiovisual emotion recognition. In this case both main parts of our pipeline

(Fig. 1), namely, speaker recognition and emotion classification can be implemented using an ensemble of speech processing methods and facial analysis [14,15]. Moreover, it is necessary to continue the study of the proposed fine-tuning for other speech emotional datasets with information about speaker identity, such as Emo-DB and SAVEE. Finally, it is important to examine the possibility to improve speaker-independent models by using semi-supervised training when the utterances of particular user are available but their emotional labels are unknown.

Acknowledgments. The work is supported by RSF (Russian Science Foundation) grant 20-71-10010.

References

1. Akçay, M.B., Oğuz, K.: Speech emotion recognition: emotional models, databases, features, preprocessing methods, supporting modalities, and classifiers. Speech Commun. **116**, 56–76 (2020)
2. Campr, P., Pražák, A., Psutka, J.V., Psutka, J.: Online speaker adaptation of an acoustic model using face recognition. In: Habernal, I., Matoušek, V. (eds.) TSD 2013. LNCS (LNAI), vol. 8082, pp. 378–385. Springer, Heidelberg (2013). https://doi.org/10.1007/978-3-642-40585-3_48
3. Cramer, J., Wu, H.H., Salamon, J., Bello, J.P.: Look, listen, and learn more: Design choices for deep audio embeddings. In: Proceedings of International Conference on Acoustics, Speech and Signal Processing (ICASSP), pp. 3852–3856. IEEE (2019)
4. Dahake, P.P., Shaw, K., Malathi, P.: Speaker dependent speech emotion recognition using MFCC and support vector machine. In: Proceedings of International Conference on Automatic Control and Dynamic Optimization Techniques (ICACDOT), pp. 1080–1084. IEEE (2016)
5. Eyben, F., Wöllmer, M., Schuller, B.: OpenSmile: the munich versatile and fast open-source audio feature extractor. In: Proceedings of the 18th ACM International Conference on Multimedia, pp. 1459–1462 (2010)
6. Ezz-Eldin, M., Khalaf, A.A., Hamed, H.F., Hussein, A.I.: Efficient feature-aware hybrid model of deep learning architectures for speech emotion recognition. IEEE Access **9**, 19999–20011 (2021)
7. Farooq, M., Hussain, F., Baloch, N.K., Raja, F.R., Yu, H., Zikria, Y.B.: Impact of feature selection algorithm on speech emotion recognition using deep convolutional neural network. Sensors **20**(21), 6008 (2020)
8. Fayek, H.M.: Speech processing for machine learning: Filter banks, Mel-frequency cepstral coefficients (MFCCs) and what's in-between (2016). https://haythamfayek.com/2016/04/21/speech-processing-for-machine-learning.html
9. Guliani, D., Beaufays, F., Motta, G.: Training speech recognition models with federated learning: a quality/cost framework. In: Proceedings of International Conference on Acoustics, Speech and Signal Processing (ICASSP), pp. 3080–3084. IEEE (2021)
10. Haq, S., Jackson, P.J., Edge, J.: Speaker-dependent audio-visual emotion recognition. In: Proceedings of International Conference on Audio-Visual Speech Processing (AVSP), pp. 53–58 (2009)

11. Jalal, M.A., Loweimi, E., Moore, R.K., Hain, T.: Learning temporal clusters using capsule routing for speech emotion recognition. In: Proceedings of Interspeech, pp. 1701–1705. ISCA (2019)
12. Koluguri, N.R., Li, J., Lavrukhin, V., Ginsburg, B.: SpeakerNet: 1D depth-wise separable convolutional network for text-independent speaker recognition and verification. arXiv preprint arXiv:2010.12653 (2020)
13. Livingstone, S.R., Russo, F.A.: The Ryerson audio-visual database of emotional speech and song (RAVDESS): a dynamic, multimodal set of facial and vocal expressions in North American English. PloS One **13**(5), e0196391 (2018)
14. Savchenko, A.V.: Efficient facial representations for age, gender and identity recognition in organizing photo albums using multi-output convnet. Peer J. Comput. Sci. **5**, e197 (2019)
15. Savchenko, A.V.: Facial expression and attributes recognition based on multi-task learning of lightweight neural networks. arXiv preprint arXiv:2103.17107 (2021)
16. Savchenko, A.V., Savchenko, V.V.: A method for measuring the pitch frequency of speech signals for the systems of acoustic speech analysis. Measurement Tech. **62**(3), 282–288 (2019)
17. Sokolov, A., Savchenko, A.V.: Gender domain adaptation for automatic speech recognition. In: Proceedings of 19th World Symposium on Applied Machine Intelligence and Informatics (SAMI), pp. 000413–000418. IEEE (2021)
18. dos SP Soares, A., et al.: Energy-based voice activity detection algorithm using gaussian and cauchy kernels. In: Proceedings of the 9th Latin American Symposium on Circuits & Systems (LASCAS), pp. 1–4. IEEE (2018)
19. Zhang, Y., et al.: Pushing the limits of semi-supervised learning for automatic speech recognition. arXiv preprint arXiv:2010.10504 (2020)
20. Zhao, Y., Li, J., Zhang, S., Chen, L., Gong, Y.: Domain and speaker adaptation for Cortana speech recognition. In: Proceedings of International Conference on Acoustics, Speech and Signal Processing (ICASSP), pp. 5984–5988. IEEE (2018)

Neural Network Recognition of Russian Noun and Adjective Cases in the Google Books Ngram Corpus

Andrey V. Savinkov⬤, Vladimir V. Bochkarev[⊠]⬤, Anna V. Shevlyakova⬤,
and Stanislav V. Khristoforov⬤

Kazan Federal University, Kremlyovskaya 18, Kazan 420008, Russia

Abstract. The article proposes a solution to the problem of automatic recognition of Russian noun and adjective cases in the Google Books Ngram corpus. The recognition was performed by using information on word co-occurrence statistics extracted from the corpus. Explicit Word Vectors composed of frequencies of ordinary and syntactic bigrams that include a given word were fed to the input of the recognizer. Comparative testing of several types of vector representation and preliminary data normalization were carried out. The trained model was a multi-layer perceptron with a softmax output layer. To train and test the model, we selected 50000 adjectives and 50000 nouns that were most frequently used in the Google Books Ngram Russian subcorpus between 1920 and 2009. Parts of speech and cases were determined using the OpenCorpora electronic morphological dictionary. The recognition accuracy of the cases obtained using the trained neural network model was 96.45% for the nouns and 99.63% for the adjectives.

Keywords: Disambiguation · Neural networks · Google books Ngram · Russian cases

1 Introduction

The impact of corpora on linguistics and computer science cannot be underestimated. Corpus linguistics deals with machine-readable texts and offers a fruitful opportunity to study a specific set of research questions. Corpora may encode language produced in any mode. One of the most well-known corpora representing the written form of a language is Google Books Ngram (GBN) [1]. Recently, it has been widely used to study various scientific problems such as linguistic variation and language evolution, culture development and change etc. The GBN corpus includes data on 8 languages.

In particular, the Russian subcorpus of Google Books Ngram contains data on frequencies of words and n-grams based on texts of 1,091 thousand books (published in 1486–2019) with a total number of more than 89 billion words. The Russian subcorpus of GBN includes 4.9 million of unique tokens (case insensitive). This number significantly exceeds the number of words presented in the most complete dictionaries. Currently, it is the largest corpus of the Russian language. By comparison, the amount of linguistic

© Springer Nature Switzerland AG 2021
A. Karpov and R. Potapova (Eds.): SPECOM 2021, LNAI 12997, pp. 626–637, 2021.
https://doi.org/10.1007/978-3-030-87802-3_56

data in the well-known Russian National Corpus is 278 times less than that in GBN. The GBN corpus provides part-of-speech tagging [2]. However, studies of language evolution and solution of other applied linguistics problems may require more detailed description of grammatical characteristics of the lexical units included in the corpus. This paper proposes a solution to the problem of automatic recognition of Russian noun and adjective cases in the GBN corpus.

One of the challenging problems of automatic language processing is disambiguation which is performed for solving a number of practical problems such as increasing the accuracy of methods of text classification and clustering, improving the quality of machine translation, reducing the amount of information in search engines and information retrieval. There are different types of ambiguity and specific methods for recognizing each of the types which are traditionally divided into contextual and statistical-probabilistic [3]. The priority use of one or another method depends on the characteristics of a language. For example, English is a language with poor morphology and a fixed word order. Thus, ambiguity in English is resolved by POS-tagging using statistical model algorithms. Russian is a language with rich morphology and free word order. Therefore, ambiguity is not limited to a part-of-speech ambiguity; free word order increases the number of word contexts resulting in the use of new research methods [4]. One of the important tasks in the disambiguation process is correct recognition of grammatical categories.

As a rule, the problem of grammatical ambiguity in the Russian language is solved using the context analysis. For example, [4] analyzed the use of POS-tagging algorithms based on the Markov model and the Markov model of maximum entropy as applied to the problem of disambiguation in the Russian language. A probabilistic model for resolving morphological ambiguity based on normalizing substitutions and positions of adjacent words was proposed in [5]. The issue of credibility of morphological annotation for the corpora with automatically resolved morphological ambiguity with respect to various metrics was studied in [6] based on the General Internet Corpus of Russian (GICR). This work provides data on accuracy of case recognition in Russian texts using modern taggers.

The problem studied in our work is fundamentally different. GBN does not provide access to the source texts. Therefore, the decision about the case a word is used in should be taken based on the statistics of word co-occurrence. The context analysis aims at determining the case of a word in each specific context; however, our objective is to determine in which cases a given word is used in the corpus.

We use a vector representation of a word meaning, which is being actively developed within the framework of the distributive semantics approach [7–10]. Such approaches have recently been used for solving a wide range of natural language processing tasks, analyzing changes in word semantics and detecting new meanings of words based on the data of diachronic corpora [11–14]. The above-mentioned works discuss various ways of constructing vectors that represent words using their frequencies in different contexts, pairwise mutual information, and other characteristics.

The GBN corpus includes data on frequencies of 1-, 2-, 3-, 4- and 5-grams. There is a certain difficulty explained by the fact that the corpus does not include n-grams with the total frequency of use less than 40 within the target period. Therefore, the database may not include 5-, 4- and even 3-grams for many rare words. Since our goal is to work with the widest possible range of words, the vector representation of words based on 2-gram frequencies will be used in the study. This choice is also supported by the fact that, to determine the case a Russian word is used in, one needs to know direct word distribution and its co-occurrence with other words in the context. The applied method is most similar to the approaches used in [15–17].

One of the features of GBN is that it provides information on frequencies of ordinary and syntactic bigrams. By ordinary bigrams, we understand pairs of words located contiguously in the text. Syntactic bigrams are units of syntactic structures denoting a binary relation between a pair of words in a sentence. In each syntactic bigram, one word is called the head, and the other is its dependent [18]. Approaches based on extraction of syntactic bigrams and analysis of their frequency find application in solving various problems related to natural language processing [18]. Data on frequency of both ordinary and syntactic bigrams are used in the present article the same way as in [16, 17].

To avoid the difficulties associated with the 1918 spelling reform, we considered the period 1920–2019.

2 Data and Method

To train the model, 50,000 nouns and adjectives, that occurred in the corpus most frequently between 1920 and 2009, were extracted from the Google Books Ngram. These nouns and adjectives were selected based on the OpenCorpora morphological dictionary data [19, 20]. According to the dictionary, the words were disambiguated and did not have homonyms referring to other parts of speech. Similar to [15–17], to construct a vector representation of a word, we used information on its co-occurrence with the most frequent words. We selected 20,000 words (context words) that were most frequently used in the Russian subcorpus of GBN between 1920 – 2019. We selected the same number of words as in [16, 17] to be able to compare our results with ones obtained in those studies. A vector of frequencies of bigrams with a dimension of 40,000 was assigned to each of the selected words (hereinafter, the target words). The first 20,000 components of this vector corresponded to the bigram frequencies of the Wx type, where W is the target word, and x is the neighbouring word that directly follows it (hereinafter, the context word). The other 20,000 components corresponded to the bigram frequencies of the xW type, i.e., they described cases when the context word occurred before the target word. Thus, each of the selected 50,000 nouns and adjectives were represented by two vectors of frequencies of the bigrams (of the Wx and xW types) combined into one vector.

Comparative testing of the four ways of representing the input data was carried out. The use of the absolute frequencies of the bigrams as the input data of the model will result in the dependence of the trained model output on the corpus size by which the frequencies are estimated. This problem can be naturally solved by using normalized values instead of absolute frequencies. Various ways of normalizing the input data have been proposed in works using Explicit Word Vectors. The input data matrix (each column of which was composed of the bigram frequencies including some word) was first normalized by rows so that the sum of the elements of the row equaled 1, and then it was normalized by the columns the same way as in [15].

The second way of the input data representation is a simple normalization of the vectors of bigram frequencies per 1. It was proposed in [17] to use neural networks that implement homogeneous input functions to recognize the characteristics of a word. It was also noted in [17] that to do this, it is enough to use the activation function RELU for the hidden layers and impose the condition that the bias of the neurons of these layers is equal to zero. The decision made by such recognizer does not depend on the normalization of the input vector, while, as shown in [17], it trains more efficiently.

One more way of the input data representation is to determine the vector components for each target word by calculating the Pointwise Mutual Information for each bigram [9]:

$$I_{PMI}(c, t) = \log \frac{p(c|t)}{p(c)} = \log \frac{p(c, t)}{p(c)p(t)}, \tag{1}$$

where p(c) and p(t) are individual probabilities (relative frequencies) of the target and context words, respectively, p(c,t) is probability (relative frequency) of a bigram in the Google Books Ngram texts.

Negative values $I_{PMI}(c,t)$ indicate that this bigram occurs less frequently in the texts than it would occur in a random text, where the next word is randomly selected from the dictionary independently of other words. Obviously, the frequencies of such bigrams are not very informative. Large negative values of low-frequency bigrams could have a large impact on the training results of the model; therefore, it is recommended to zero them [9]. To reduce the influence of such low-frequency bigrams, we used another modification of expression (1) by adding one to the expression under the logarithm:

$$\tilde{I}_{PMI}(c, t) = \log\left(\frac{p(c|t)}{p(c)} + 1\right) = \log\left(\frac{p(c, t)}{p(c)p(t)} + 1\right). \tag{2}$$

Following expression (2), the initial vectors of the bigram frequencies were transformed into vectors of the PMI values; and the probabilities of the bigrams $p(c,t)$ and the individual probabilities of the target and context words $p(t)$ and $p(c)$ were determined by normalizing corresponding frequencies to the corpus size.

The last considered way of the input data representation consists in taking the logarithm of the bigram frequencies in accordance with the expression: $log_2(p(c,t) + 1)$. The fact is that frequencies of the bigrams that include the same target word can differ by orders of magnitude, and rarer bigrams have less influence on the decision made by the model. Taking the logarithm raises the significance of the very fact that this bigram is used in the language, which can increase the recognition efficiency. In contrast to the representation methods described above, in this case, the dependence on the corpus size is not excluded, however, it becomes insignificant.

As already mentioned, each word for training and testing the model was selected in accordance with the OpenCorpora dictionary. In OpenCorpora, Russian words are described as belonging to one of 12 case classes. However, all of them are either incomplete (do not apply to all nouns) or degenerate and occur rarely (such cases as vocative, locative, partitive). Therefore, only word forms marked in OpenCorpora as referring to the six main cases (Nominative, Genitive, Dative, Accusative, Instrumental, Prepositional) were selected. However, the homonymy of case forms is widely spread in the

Russian language. For example, the form 'okno' (*window*) is used in both Nominative and Accusative cases. In such cases, morphological analyzers resolve ambiguity based on the context in which the word is used in the text. Google Books Ngram does not provide access to the source texts, but only to the frequencies of n-gram use in different years. Therefore, the task is to determine what case a given word from the corpus is used in. A trained recognizer must indicate one or more cases in which a given word form is used. Therefore, at the first stage, we distinguished 6 classes of words corresponding to the six cases; the words from each class should be used in the corpus only in one of the cases. Then, we introduced classes of words in which a word is used in two cases. For example, the word 'okno' (window) is a frequent word and was used in the GBN corpus in both Nominative and Accusative cases many times. Therefore, we mark this word as belonging to "Nominative + Accusative" class. The following classes were proposed for the nouns: "Nominative + Genitive", "Nominative + Accusative", "Genitive + Accusative", and "Dative + Prepositional". In total, ten classes were introduced. Other cases of ambiguity were found for the selected 50,000 nouns. However, it was inappropriate to create separate classes for them because they were too rare to make a sample with a sufficient number of such cases for training a neural network (words were allocated to a separate case class if their number exceeded 500). As a result, the set of 50,000 words was reduced to 49,400: 40,000 vectors were used to train the model and the remaining 9,400 were used to check the accuracy of the case classification. Each of the selected words was marked as belonging only to one of the indicated ten classes.

The classification of adjectives was carried out based on eight cases. The following additional classes were introduced: "Nominative + Accusative" case and "Dative + Instrumental". The class "Genitive case" was replaced by "Genitive + Accusative" because Russian adjectives are spelled the same in these two cases. After excluding rare classes, the set of examples for adjectives was reduced to 49,980, of which 40,000 were used to train the model, and the remaining 9,980 were used to check the accuracy of the case classification.

Having conducted a number of experiments, a feedforward neural network (a multilayer perceptron) was chosen to solve the problem of case recognition of the selected nouns and adjectives. The neural network consisted of 1) an input layer containing 40,000 neurons, 2) three hidden layers of 64, 128, and 128 neurons, respectively, and 3) an output layer. The number of neurons in the output layer was determined by the number of case classes by which the neural network performed the classification of the input data.

The rectifier activation function (RELU) [21] was used as the activation function for the input layer and all hidden layers. The output layer was activated by softmax [22]. Since a characteristic feature of the application of the softmax function to the layer of artificial neurons is the equality to one of the sums of the output values, this allows one to consider the values of the output layer of the network as a probability distribution over the given case classes.

As the size of the input vector is large, the number of weights between the input layer and the first hidden layer is also large ($40,000 \times 64$), which can result in overfitting of the model. To avoid overfitting, a dropout layer was added in front of the first hidden layer, which randomly "breaks" the connections between a given fraction of neurons in the first hidden layer. In addition, the use of batch normalization applied to the input data of the second and third hidden layers had a positive effect on the speed and quality of training the model.

The model was trained using the backpropagation method applying the Adaptive Moment Estimation ("Adam") [23] algorithm; the Multi-Class Cross Entropy Loss [24] function was used as the loss function.

The neural network was created and trained in the PyTorch framework for machine learning.

3 Result

The described model was trained separately to recognize the cases of nouns and adjectives. At that, two sets of the input data were considered for nouns and adjectives using frequencies of ordinary and syntactic bigrams. Therefore, the model was trained on four datasets (two for nouns and two for adjectives). As mentioned above, the trained recognizer was tested in each case on a sample of examples that were not used in the training process (9400 nouns and 9980 adjectives). Finally, a comparative testing of the four ways of the vector representation mentioned above was performed for each of the four datasets.

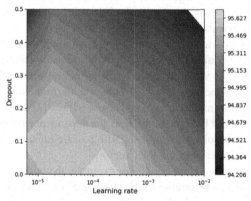

Fig. 1. Dependence of the accuracy of case recognition of nouns using a model trained on ordinary bigrams (depending on the dropout parameter and the learning rate).

The model was trained at various values of the training parameters such as the learning rate and the dropout parameter. As a result, diagrams of the dependency of the recognition accuracy of the noun and adjective cases on the values of the dropout parameter and the initial value of the learning rate were obtained (see Fig. 1). These diagrams were used to determine the optimal values of the training parameters that provide the best recognition accuracy. It was found in the training process that the value $p = 0.1$ for the dropout parameter is usually sufficient to prevent overfitting. The results on the achieved recognition accuracy of the cases of the nouns and adjectives by the trained model are presented in Table 1.

Table 1. The accuracy of case recognition of nouns and adjectives in ordinary and syntactic bigrams using different types of normalization of the model input data (the dropout parameter is 0.1). Four ways of representing the input data are compared: double normalization of the frequencies of bigrams (in accordance with [15]), simple normalization (in accordance with [17]), use of the PMI vectors and simple logarithm of frequencies.

Normalization type	Nouns		Adjectives	
	Ordinary bigrams	Syntactic bigrams	Ordinary bigrams	Syntactic bigrams
[15]	87.66	89.28	93.77	95.46
[17]	93.94	94.46	96.92	98.38
PMI	96.05	96.03	98.14	99.52
$\text{Log}_2(1 + x)$	96.45	96.39	98.37	99.63

As one can see from Table 1, the case recognition accuracy of adjectives is higher than that of nouns. This may result from the fact that adjectives have less case classes. Besides, homonymy is more common among nouns in Russian than among adjectives. It should also be noted that, in case of adjectives, the recognizer using the frequencies of syntactic bigrams provides significantly better results than using the frequencies of ordinary bigrams. As for nouns, the results obtained using syntactic and ordinary bigrams differ to a far smaller extent.

Considering the four ways of input data representation, the worst accuracy results were obtained using the double normalization of the frequency matrix proposed in [15]. Significantly better results were provided by using neural networks that implement a homogeneous function of the input data [17]. However, the highest accuracy was obtained by using vectors of logarithmic frequencies. The use of the PMI vectors provided slightly lower accuracy than the last but one method. As the dependence of the recognition result on the corpus size remains using a simple logarithm of frequencies, one should take into account the results obtained from the PMI vectors.

The recognizer's errors are not equal. For example, the word 'okno' (window) may be mistakenly classified as belonging to the "Genitive" or "Accusative" classes instead of the "Genitive + Accusative" class. Such errors will be considered minor. If, for example, the recognizer mistakenly refers the word 'okno' to any other case, such errors will be considered major. Analysis of the testing results of the trained recognizers shows that a large proportion of errors are minor. Table 2 shows the results of calculating the probabilities of major errors (minor errors are not considered).

Let us consider further how the percentage of the recognizer's errors depends on the word frequency in the corpus. For some selected frequency value, we select all words whose frequency in the corpus differs from this value by no more than $\sqrt{e}$ times and find the total percentage of errors and percentage of major errors for the selected sample. In accordance with the above considerations, the vector representation using the PMI of syntactic bigrams including the given word was chosen for the analysis. The results obtained for nouns and adjectives are shown in Figs. 2,A and 2,B, respectively. As one can see, the error probability for nouns increases significantly when the frequency falls

Table 2. Case recognition of nouns and adjectives in ordinary and syntactic bigrams using different types of normalization of the model input data. Percentage of major errors.

Normalization type	Nouns		Adjectives	
	Ordinary bigrams	Syntactic bigrams	Ordinary bigrams	Syntactic bigrams
[15]	5.98	4.64	3.12	2.39
[17]	2.07	2.27	1.15	0.981
PMI	1.09	1.04	0.662	0.302
$Log_2(1 + x)$	0.839	1.07	0.505	0.205

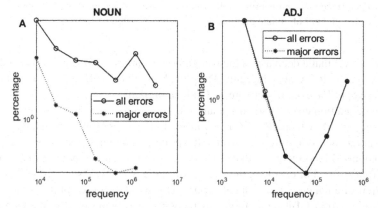

Fig. 2. Dependence of the probability of the classification error on word frequency in the corpus. A - nouns; B – adjectives.

below 10^3 and weakly depends on the frequency at high frequencies. If one considers the probability of major errors, it naturally decreases with frequency increase, and becomes extremely small at frequencies above 10^5. The error probability for adjectives also increases with frequency decrease, however, in this case, the threshold of 1% of errors is exceeded only when the word frequency falls below 8 thousand. The graph also shows unexpected results for adjectives; it is an increase in the error probability with an increase in the word frequency above 10^5. However, it should be taken into account that there are not many adjectives with such frequencies in the sample, and two outlier points of the graph in the frequency range 10^5–10^6 are due to only 7 recognizer's errors. Thus, there is no certainty about the reliability of these points on the graph.

Also, the recognition accuracy may depend on how many different bigrams, including a given word, are found in the corpus. Using the technique described above, we obtained the dependence of the probability of recognition error on the number of unique bigrams including the word (see Fig. 3).

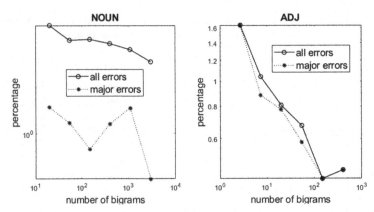

Fig. 3. Dependence of the probability of the classification error (according to the syntactic bigram frequencies) on number of unique bigrams in the corpus. A – nouns; B – adjectives.

One can see that a decrease in the recognition accuracy for nouns is observed in the presence of 20 or less unique bigrams. The probability of recognition error for adjectives is no more than 1% even if there are 7–8 unique bigrams.

The recognition errors were also analysed. The words from the testing sample with a frequency of 10^5 which cases were erroneously recognized were manually selected. There were 94 nouns among such words. It was determined that cases of only 25 nouns were recognized incorrectly. At that, 10 of the 25 words are homonymous that can cause recognition errors. For example, the word form 'pere' (*feather*) is tagged as being used in the Prepositional case in the OpenCorpora. This word denotes a prefix or incorrectly recognized word in GBN; therefore, it is recognized as being used in the Genitive or Accusative cases. Another example is the word 'ukha' which denotes a *fish soup* in the Nominative case or the Genitive form of the word *ear*. In this case, homonymy also results in the incorrect recognition.

In fact, the cases of the latter 69 nouns were recognized correctly. However, the OpenCorpora tags not only the frequently used variants but also the rarest ones which are hardly used in speech and lack in the GBN corpus. Let us consider some examples. According to the OpenCorpora, the word 'Gomera' is tagged as being used in the Nominative case; it is the name of an island in the Atlantic Ocean. In the GBN corpus, this word is used in the Genitive and Accusative cases and means the name of an ancient poet Homer. The word 'masha' is a frequently used Russian name (*Mary*) and is recognized in the OpenCorpora and GBN as being used in the Nominative case. However, it has a rarely used homonymous form 'masha' which denotes a plant (*mung bean*) and is used in the OpenCorpora in the Genitive case.

The cases of 8 frequently used adjectives were incorrectly recognized. This results from morphological homonymy. The considered words can represent two parts of speech. For example, the word 'peremennaya' (*changeable, variable*) can represent adjective and noun, the word 'drugogo' (*another, different*) can be an adjective or a pronoun.

Thus, the performed analysis of the errors showed that, in fact, the percentage of errors is lower than described above. Therefore, the recognizer can also be used to test the dictionaries.

4 Conclusion

The proposed recognizer allows solving the problem of automatic case recognition of Russian nouns and adjectives based on the large corpus data. The recognition is performed by using information on word co-occurrence statistic extracted from the corpus. The recognizer was tested on the data of the Russian subcorpus of Google Books Ngram.

It should be noted that the results obtained using frequencies of syntactic bigrams for adjectives are significantly better than that obtained using ordinary bigrams. In case of Russian nouns, using ordinary and syntactic bigrams showed almost the same result.

Comparative testing of the four ways of representing the input data was carried out. As one can see from Tables 1 and 2, the best results are obtained using the vector representations that utilize the logarithm of the bigram frequencies. The recognition accuracy of the case forms obtained using the vectors consisted of PMI was 96.05% for the nouns and 99.52% for the adjectives. Even higher values of 96.45% and 99.63% can be obtained using a simple logarithm of the frequencies. However, the method using PMI has the advantage of using standardized values that are independent of corpus size. An important issue for a recognizer using a simple logarithm is reproducibility of the results obtained on a corpus of a different size. It should be noted that, in fact, the achieved recognition accuracy is significantly higher since the above-described analysis showed that most of the errors result from the imperfect tagging in the test sample.

The performed analysis showed that it is sufficient to have 20 unique bigrams in the corpus to effectively determine the case of nouns; and it is sufficient to have 7–8 unique bigrams to determine the case of adjectives. This allows one to tag most of the words presented in the Russian subcorpus of Google Books Ngram.

For practical purposes, it is advisable to use the proposed recognizer together with an algorithm based on the analysis of word inflexional endings. The combination of the two approaches can significantly improve the recognition accuracy. It is also of interest not only to perform a qualitative analysis to determine the case a word is used in but also to conduct a quantitative survey to estimate the percentage of use of a word in the given cases. This could be a direction for further research.

Acknowledgements. This research was financially supported by RFBR, grant № 17–29-09163.

References

1. Michel, J.-B., Shen, Y.K., Aiden, A.P., Veres, A., Gray, M.K., et al.: Quantitative analysis of culture using millions of digitized books. Science **331**(6014), 176–182 (2011)
2. Lin, Y., et al.: Syntactic annotations for the Google Books Ngram Corpus. In: Li, H., Lin, C.-Y., Osborne, M., Lee, G.G., Park, J.C. (eds.) 50th Annual Meeting of the Association for Computational Linguistics 2012, Proceedings of the Conference, vol. 2, pp. 238–242. Association for Computational Linguistics, Jeju Island (2012)

3. Gataullin, R.R.: Review of morphological disambiguation methods. Russ. Digit. Libr. J. **19**(2), 98–114 (2016)
4. Lakomkin, E., Puzyrevskij, I., Ryzhova D.: Analiz statisticheskih algoritmov snjatija morfologicheskoj omonimii v russkom jazyke. In: Vserossijskaja nauchnaja konferencija AIST'13 "Analiz izobrazhenij, setej i tekstov". Sbornik dokladov, vol. 2, pp. 184–195. Ekaterinburg, Russia (2013)
5. Zelenkov, Yu.G., Segalovich, I.V., Titov, V.A.: Veroyatnostnaya model snyatiya morfologicheskoy omonimii na osnove normalizuyushchikh podstanovok i pozitsiy sosednikh slov. In: Computational Linguistics and Intellectual Technologies. Papers from the Annual International Conference "Dialogue", pp. 1–22. RGGU, Moscow (2005)
6. Sharoff, S.A., Belikov, V.I., Kopylov, N.Y., Sorokin, A.A., Shavrina, T.O.: Corpus with automatically resolved morphological ambiguity: to the methodology of linguistic research. In: Papers from the Annual International Conference "Dialogue", pp. 109–115. RGGU, Moscow (2015)
7. Weeds, J., Weir, D., McCarthy, D.: Characterising measures of lexical distributional similarity. In: Proceedings of the 20th International Conference on Computational Linguistics, pp. 1015–1021. COLING, Geneva (2004)
8. Pantel, P.: Inducing ontological co-occurrence vectors. In: Proceedings of the 43rd Conference of the Association for Computational Linguistics, pp. 125–132. Association for Computational Linguistics (2005)
9. Bullinaria, J., Levy, J.: Extracting semantic representations from word co-occurrence statistics: a computational study. Behav. Res. Methods **39**, 510–526 (2007). https://doi.org/10.3758/BF03193020
10. Sahlgren, M.: The distributional hypothesis. Italian J. Disabil. Stud. **20**, 33–53 (2008)
11. Gulordava, K., Baroni, M.: A distributional similarity approach to the detection of semantic change in the Google Books Ngram corpus. In: Proceedings of the GEMS 2011 Workshop on Geometrical Models of Natural Language Semantics, pp. 67–71. Association for Computational Linguistics, Edinburgh (2011)
12. Kulkarni, V., Al-Rfou, R., Perozzi, B., Skiena, S.: Statistically significant detection of linguistic change. In: Proceedings of the 24th International Conference on World Wide Web, pp. 625–635. Florence, Italy (2015)
13. Tang, X., Qu, W., Chen, X.: Semantic change computation: a successive approach. World Wide Web **19**(3), 375–415 (2015). https://doi.org/10.1007/s11280-014-0316-y
14. Tang, X.: A state-of-the-art of semantic change computation. arXiv preprint arXiv:1801.09872 (2018). https://doi.org/10.1017/S1351324918000220
15. Xu, Y., Kemp, C.: A computational evaluation of two laws of semantic change. In: Proceedings of the 37th Annual Meeting of the Cognitive Science Society, CogSci 2015. Pasadena, California (2015)
16. Khristoforov, S., Bochkarev, V., Shevlyakova, A.: Recognition of parts of speech using the vector of bigram frequencies. In: van der Aalst, W.M.P., et al. (eds.) AIST 2019. CCIS, vol. 1086, pp. 132–142. Springer, Cham (2020). https://doi.org/10.1007/978-3-030-39575-9_13
17. Bochkarev, V.V., Khristoforov, S.V., Shevlyakova, A.V.: Recognition of named entities in the Russian subcorpus Google Books Ngram. In: Martínez-Villaseñor, L., Herrera-Alcántara, O., Ponce, H., Castro-Espinoza, F.A. (eds.) MICAI 2020. LNCS (LNAI), vol. 12469, pp. 17–28. Springer, Cham (2020). https://doi.org/10.1007/978-3-030-60887-3_2
18. Sidorov, G., Velasquez, F., Stamatatos, E., Gelbukh, A., Chanona-Hernández, L.: Syntactic dependency-based N-grams as classification features. In: Batyrshin, I., Mendoza, M.G. (eds.) MICAI 2012. LNCS (LNAI), vol. 7630, pp. 1–11. Springer, Heidelberg (2013). https://doi.org/10.1007/978-3-642-37798-3_1
19. OpenCorpora dictionary. http://opencorpora.org/dict.php. Accessed 24 July 2021

20. Bocharov, V.V., Alexeeva, S.V., Granovsky, D.V., Protopopova, E.V., Stepanova, M.E., Surikov, A.V.: Crowdsourcing morphological annotation. In: Computational Linguistics and Intellectual Technologies. Papers from the Annual International Conference "Dialogue", 12 (1), pp. 109–115. RGGU, Moscow (2013)
21. Glorot, X., Bordes, A., Bengio, Y.: Deep sparse rectifier neural networks. In: Gordon, G., Dunson, D., Dudik, M. (eds.) Proceedings of the Fourteenth International Conference on Artificial Intelligence and Statistics, vol. 15, pp. 315–323. PMLR, Fort Lauderdale, FL (2011)
22. Goodfellow, I., Bengio, Y., Courville, A.: Deep learning. Adaptive computation and machine learning. MIT Press (2016)
23. Kingma, D., Ba, J.: Adam: a method for stochastic optimization. arXiv preprint arXiv:141 26980 (2014)
24. Bishop, C.: Pattern Recognition and Machine Learning. Springer, NY (2006)

Is It a Filler or a Pause? A Quantitative Analysis of Filled Pauses in Hebrew

Vered Silber-Varod[1]([⊠]) (iD), Mária Gósy[2] (iD), and Anat Lerner[3] (iD)

[1] Open Media and Information Lab (OMILab),
The Open University of Israel, Ra'anana, Israel
`vereds@openu.ac.il`
[2] Linguistics Institute, ELKH and ELTE University, Budapest, Hungary
`gosy.maria@nytud.mta.hu`
[3] Mathematics and Computer Science Department,
The Open University of Israel, Ra'anana, Israel
`anat@cs.openu.ac.il`

Abstract. In this study, we investigate quantitatively the use of Filled Pauses in Hebrew and compare them to the use of silence-based attributes and fluency-based attributes in task-oriented dialogues. Our aim is to explore whether the use of Filled Pauses in Hebrew supports either the filler-as-word hypothesis or the filler-as-pause hypothesis. We computed seven measures as independent variables, among them: Normalized rate of words, Filled Pauses rate, silent pauses rate, and articulation rate. Findings show that Filled Pauses occur twice as many as the most frequent words and on the other hand, Filled Pauses are far less frequent than the overall number of silent pauses. We did find that Filled Pauses are correlated with a sub-category of silent pauses. Our analysis supports that Filled Pauses used by Hebrew speakers are closer to the filler-as-pause hypothesis. Further, speakers would use FPs differently depending on their role in the Map Task dialogues.

Keywords: Filled pauses · Silent pauses · Fillers · Speaker's role · Hebrew · Dialogues · Map task corpus

1 Introduction

The literature suggests several categorization options for Filled Pauses (FPs). The filler-as-pause hypothesis is the most straight-forward approach, as the term itself suggests, but unlike the default silent pause, the filled pause is the marked case. On the other hand, Clark and Fox Tree (2002) argue that uh and um are conventional English words, interjections, therefore they use the term 'fillers' for this phenomenon. They further argue that fillers are indicators of planning difficulties or cognitive load, and that speakers produce them similarly to any kind of word. Their approach is the filler-as-word hypothesis. This approach was adopted for Hebrew by Maschler (1997; 2009), who includes FPs under the category of cognitive discourse markers, hence linking them to wider linguistic categories that characterize spoken language.

© Springer Nature Switzerland AG 2021
A. Karpov and R. Potapova (Eds.): SPECOM 2021, LNAI 12997, pp. 638–648, 2021.
https://doi.org/10.1007/978-3-030-87802-3_57

FPs are phenomena that are connected to speakers irrespective of the language they speak but they are realized language-specifically in several ways (e.g., vocalic forms, occurrences, functions). Other studies also suggested that due to their discriminative prosody, FPs may function as prosodic events (Podlesskaya 2010; Silber-Varod 2013a), a trait that was also used for automatic detection purposes (Vetter et al. 2019), for discourse prosody framework (Tseng et al. 2006), and for studies on prosodic sound fillers (Nenova et al. 2001).

In this paper, we will analyze FPs in Hebrew to highlight the usage of FPs in this language in order to get closer to the answer whether they are fillers or pauses. In the era of data science, we add a quantitative methodology to understand the nature and usage of FPs in Hebrew. Our findings may add useful information on the common debate of the role of FPs in speech by quantitative data of a less analyzed language.

1.1 The Realization of FPs in Hebrew

In Hebrew, like in many other languages, FPs are produced either in a vocalized form or in a nasalized form and are pronounced e and em, respectively. These are signals, though not true words, considered as disfluencies by others (Juste and Andrade, 2006; Oliveira et al. 2010), or else can be identified as nonlinguistic signal used for holding the floor. Studies also showed that FPs are sometimes parasitic to word-level segments (inter alia, Clark and Fox Tree, 2002), as shown also for Hebrew by Silber-Varod (2010; 2013a). Those studies showed how filled pauses in spontaneous Hebrew speech are connecting syntactic clauses. For example, when using conjunctions such as az e … "so uh" and aval e "but uh …". Those studies show that native Hebrew speakers seem to use FPs as predicted fillers: They seek for a word, and they vocally process their demand on specific syntactic locations.

Behavioral differences on FPs use were studied in other languages (e.g., Horváth 2010; Gósy et al. 2017; Pardo et al. 2019). Speakers' age, for example, is one of those factors that influence the occurrences of filled pauses (Gósy et al. 2014). The effect on FP usage in a Map Task dialogues is reported in (Silber-Varod et al. 2020b), where they showed that speakers converge to each other along the course of the tasks.

Phonetically, the vowel e is perceived in Hebrew as /e/, which is one of the vowels in the five-vowel system in the language. Silber-Varod (2013b) reports ten times more e type compared to em in spontaneous spoken Hebrew speech. One of the hypotheses concerning the division between the vocalic FPs and the nasalized version is that choice of a filler is explained by the lengthening hypothesis. For example, in American English, um and u:m is simply lengthened uh and u:h (Clark and Fox tree, 2002, p. 80). In the current paper, we do not discriminate short and long e (or em) since vowel length in Modern Hebrew is environmentally determined by the phonological context and the variants are not phonemic. Therefore, we consider all lengths of e and em as representations of FPs. It is worth mention that although there are Hebrew words that consist of a single vowel, such as /i/ 'island' and /o/ 'or', no word exists in Hebrew pronounced as /e/. Thus, the monosyllabic e is interpreted by Hebrew listeners only as a FP.

1.2 Goal and Hypothesis

The goal of our study is to decide whether FPs in Hebrew support the filler-as-word hypothesis or the filler-as-pause hypothesis.

1. We hypothesize that FPs used by Hebrew speakers are closer to the filler-as-word hypothesis than to the filler-as-pause hypothesis, following Clark and Fox Tree (2002) for American English and Maschler (2009) for Hebrew discourse markers typology.
2. Our second hypothesis is that quantitative patterns of FPs and word metrics would support the filler-as-word hypothesis.
3. Our third hypothesis is that speakers would use FPs differently depending on their role in the task-oriented dialogues (either a leader or a follower).

2   Data and Methods

Our analysis is based on 32 spoken dialogues from MaTaCOp – the Map Task Corpus in Hebrew (Azogui et al. 2015). Map Task dialogue type of discourse is considered task-oriented, unplanned spontaneous speech, in which participants have no a-priori knowledge about the recordings' setting or material (mainly, maps). The setup was the same for all recordings and was based on the original HCRC standard (Anderson et al. 1991; Carletta et al. 1996). Participants sat face to face so they could see each other but could not see each other's map. Each participant was given a map with labeled landmarks, some of them shared with the partner's map, some unique. The map of one participant in a pair, the leader, contained a path among the landmarks. It was the leader's task to describe the path so her partner, the follower, could reproduce it. In MaTaCOp, each speaker participated twice (First task and Second task) with the same interlocutor, each time with a different map but in a different role – once as the information receiver, i.e., a follower, and once as the information giver, i.e., a leader. All speaker pairs discussed the same two pairs of corresponding maps, not necessarily in the same order. The recording device was H4n Handy Recorder (ZOOM) (recording setup is detailed in Lerner et al. (2018)).

This pairwise setting allows comparison of the speaker's behavior in two roles – leader or follower – controlled for the interlocutor. As it was shown in Lerner et al. (2018), Weise et al. (2020), and Silber-Varod et al. (2020a), there are significant differences in various linguistic and acoustic aspects between the roles the speaker played.

Of the 16 pairs of speakers, ten were of same-gender (six of which with two women; four with two men) and six of a mixed gender pair. Note that most paired speakers knew each other prior to the experiment. The average age of the speakers was 41.3 years (ages ranged from 25 to 65 years). More about the demographic background can be found in Weise et al. (2020). The 32 dialogues were first transcribed using PRAAT textgrid tool (Boersma and Weenink, 2018), using the Inter-pausal unit (IPU) as the time-aligned speech unit (Koiso et al. 1998). The minimal silent pause threshold of within-turn (i.e., between adjacent IPUs) was set to 100 ms in duration, following previous studies on Hebrew (Silber-Varod 2013a; Silber-Varod and Lerner 2017) and other languages (e.g., Pardo 2019). The FPs were categorized into two types in the transcription: one without nasalization (transcribed as e) and one with nasalization (transcribed as em). Duration of FPs was not measured in the current study, but previous study showed that the minimum duration of FPs in spontaneous Hebrew is 70 ms and maximum duration is 1.184 s, with an average duration of 0.419 s (standard deviation (SD) = 0.293 s) (Silber-Varod 2013a, p. 72; Silber-Varod et al. 2016). In Silber-Varod (2013a) it was found that telephone conversation yields longer FPs (Mean: 0.502 s; SD: 0.230 s; minimum length: 0.129 s) in yet another study on monologues, it was found that the average duration of FPs is similar (approximately 0.500 s). All FPs were checked by a second phonetician. The inter-rater agreement was 100% due to the ease of detecting FPs in Hebrew (similarly to the detection of uh and uhm in Germanic languages (Wieling et al. 2016) and American English (Pardo et al. 2019)).

In total, our dataset consists of 2,287 FPs, of which 2,046 (89.5%) are e and 241 (10.5%) are em; 12,131 silent pauses, and 47,788 words (all speakers produced more than 400 words each). The total duration of the 32 dialogues is 379.708 min (more than six hours).

2.1 Measurements

In the following, we will describe the quantitative metrics such as relative frequencies, rates, and correlations that are used to compare FPs to fluency-based attributes and to silence-based attributes.

For each map-task task and for each of the two speakers in each task, we computed the rates (occurrences per second) of the selected seven speech attributes, by dividing the attribute's number of occurrences by the speaking time. Attributes 1–2 are fluency-based; attribute 3 is the FPs rate; and attributes 4–7 are silence-based:

1. Fluent Words rate: For each task, the number of words of a given speaker divided by the total speaking duration of that speaker;
2. Articulation rate (syllables per second): we first define articulation rate per IPU as the number of fluent syllables per IPU normalized by the IPU duration. The articulation rate is the average of the articulation rates per IPU over all IPUs of a given speaker in a given task;
3. FPs rate: For each task, the number of filled pauses of a given speaker divided by the total speaking duration of that speaker;
4. Global silent pauses rate: For each task, the number of silent pauses of a given speaker divided by the total speaking duration of that speaker;
5. We further grouped silent pauses into three categories based on their durations (Campione and Véronis 2002): brief (100–200 ms), medium (200–1000 ms), and long (>1000 ms) pauses.
6. Brief silent pauses rate: the number of brief silent pauses of a given speaker normalized by the total speaking duration of that speaker;
7. Medium silent pauses rate: the number of medium silent pauses of a given speaker normalized by the total speaking duration of that speaker;
8. Long silent pauses rate: the number of long silent pauses of a given speaker normalized by the total speaking duration of that speaker.

These attributes were computed twice for each speaker – for the first role in the first task and for the second role in the second task.

We used Pearson's correlation coefficient (ρ) function to measure the strength and direction of the relationship between each two variables.

3   Results

3.1   Use of FPs, Words, and Silent Pauses

We found that speakers differ in the amount of time they spent producing FPs. In terms of FPs rate, attribute #3 above, Fig. 1 presents the usage ratios per speaker, in the first and the second tasks. The slowest rate is 0.02 and the highest rate is 0.38. The average rates in the 1st and the 2nd tasks are 0.12 (SD = 0.08) and 0.11 (SD = 0.07), respectively.

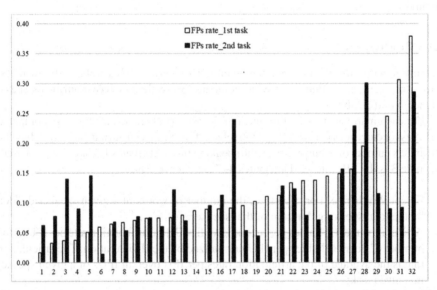

Fig. 1. FPs rate (FPs per second) of the 32 speakers in the first task (white bars; ordered according to rate-size from left to right) and the second task (black bars).

The speakers also varied in the distribution of FP type they used. In general, the nasal FP em is scarcely used in Hebrew compared to e (see Fig. 2). In terms of FPs per 100 words, the average e per 100 words is 3.78 (SD = 2.56); the average em per 100 words is 0.41 (SD = 0.62), ranged from 1.7 to 12.5 FPs per 100 words (median 3.64). In our corpus, four speakers used only e (Speakers' ID 10, 19, 21, and 31 represented in the dark parts of the bars in Fig. 2). No one used only em (represented in the white parts of the bars). Notice that one male participant (speaker's ID 9) did not use any FPs at the second task.

To break-down the fluency-based attributes, we compared the frequency of the most common words in the corpus to the FP frequency and found that compared to 2,287 FPs,

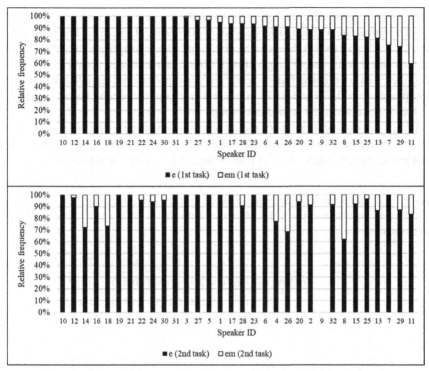

Fig. 2. Relative occurrences of *e* (black part) and *em* (white part) per speaker (32 speakers). The top Figure shows the data from the first task while the bottom figure shows data of the second task.

the three most common words in the corpus are discourse markers, known also as fillers: ken "yes" with 1,399 instances; okey "ok" (1,380 instances); and az "so" with 874 instances.

As to the silence-based attributes, the most frequent are Medium and Long (4,895 and 6,128 instances, respectively), while only 1,108 instances are Brief. Note that the relatively small proportion of Brief is due also to the fact that it ranges between 100 and 200 ms.

3.2 Correlations Between Attributes per Task

Following the descriptive statistics (in Sect. 3.1), we calculated correlations between the 7 attributes, to learn if FPs are more correlated with the fluency-based attributes or with the silence-based one. We calculated separately for all speakers in both tasks so that each participant is included once in each correlation calculation. Findings are presented in Table 1. FP attribute (#3) was not found significantly correlated ($p = 0.039$; the result is not significant at $p < 0.01$ condition) with Words (#1), with Articulation rates (#2), nor with global Silent pauses (#4). Altogether, three correlations were found positively significant ($p < 0.01$) in both tasks: Words rate with Articulation rate ($r = 0.559$ and 0.460 in the first tasks and the second tasks, respectively). The correlation is medium strong, and it indicates that the higher the speaking rate, the more words are articulated. The silent pause rate with long silence type ($r = 0.919$ and 0.952 in the first tasks and the second tasks, respectively) shows high correlation. This is in agreement with the finding that most silent pauses were longer than 1000 ms, as mentioned above. Third, in both tasks, the FPs attribute was found significantly and positively correlated with the brief silent pauses ($r = 0.579$ and 0.678 in the first tasks and the second tasks, respectively; $p < 0.01$). The correlation is medium strong.

Table 1 presents all the data of the correlations according to the seven variables: 1. Fluent Words rate; 2. Articulation rate; 3. FPs rate; 4. Global silent pauses rate; 5. Brief silent pauses rate; 6. Medium silent pauses rate; and 7. Long silent pauses rate.

Table 1. Correlation matrices concerning the seven attributes in the first (top) and second (bottom) tasks (* marks significance; p < 0.01). Values are between −1 (full negative correlation) and 1 (full positive correlation).

First task	2	3	4	5	6	7
1	0.559*	−0.366	0.417	−0.317	0.030	0.387
2		0.316	−0.208	0.135	0.390	−0.328
3			−0.191	0.579*	0.366	−0.363
4				−0.021	−0.180	0.919*
5					0.290	−0.246
6						0.533*
Second task	2	3	4	5	6	7
1	0.460*	−0.205	0.446	−0.126	0.134	0.422
2		0.362	−0.331	−0.014	0.412	−0.431
3			−0.034	0.678*	0.434	−0.220
4				0.380	−0.016	0.952*
5					0.312	0.184
6						−0.305

3.3 Correlations Between Attributes per Role

We wanted to check whether the role of the speaker (a leader or a follower) has an effect on the correlations, as studies showed different FP use according to the role in Map Task corpus (Pardo et al. 2019; Silber-Varod et al. 2020b). We thus divided the data per role and calculated the correlations for each group separately.

For both roles, FP rate is not significantly correlated at $p < 0.01$ condition) either with the two fluency attributes (with word rate $p = 0.018$ and with articulation rate $p = 0.298$) or with global Silent pauses ($p = 0.255$). Altogether, three correlations were found positively significant at $p < 0.01$ for both roles: Fluent words ratio with Articulation rate

($r = 0.736$ for followers and 0.737 for leaders). Second, global silent pause ratio with Long silence type ($r = 0.941$ for followers and 0.710 for leaders). Third, in both roles, the FPs attribute was found significantly and positively correlated with the Brief silent pauses ($r = 0.753$ for followers and 0.582 for leaders; $p < 0.01$). Furthermore, in the leaders' speech, the Brief and Medium silence types were found positively correlated with the global silences ($r = 0.575$ for Brief and Global and 0.688 for Medium and Global). These findings show similar correlation patterns to the tasks (see Sect. 3.2), which implies that the significant correlations are not affected by the role of the speaker.

3.4 Correlations Between Speakers in the Same Task

Finally, we wanted to see if there are correlations between speakers in the same task for the same attribute. Correlation of this kind can show whether the participants of the conversation influence each other. Findings show that the FP attribute is significantly correlated among the pairs in all 32 dialogues (r $= 0.766$ for the first task and 0.673 for the second task; $p < 0.05$). Articulation rate is significantly correlated only in the first task and Brief silences are correlated in the second task (see Table 2 for detailed results).

Table 2. Pearson's correlation coefficient (r) of attributes between speakers in the same task (* marks significance at $p < 0.05$).

Attribute	First tasks r	Second tasks R
1. Word rate	0.456	0.341
2. Articulation rate	0.535*	0.298
3. FP rate	0.766*	0.673*
4. Silent pauses (global) ratio	−0.013	0.016
5. Brief Silence category ratio	0.280	0.527*
6. Medium Silence category ratio	0.055	0.109
7. Long Silence category ratio	−0.337	−0.230

4 Discussion

This study highlights the issue of FPs conception as either filler-as-word hypothesis or filler-as-pause hypothesis. We tried to shed light on this debate using a quantitative approach.

First, we found that speakers differ in the rate they use the language-specific FP-types, e and em. According to Clark and Fox Tree (2002), this fact is an indication that "speakers have characteristic preferences in fillers, just as they do for other words in their vocabulary" (p. 97). The weak point of this statement is that in many languages (e.g.,

Hungarian: Horváth 2010; Gósy et al. 2014), the vocalic versions of FPs are significantly more frequent as opposed to the nasalized versions. This difference may be explained by common articulatory reasons and not necessarily by lexical access the vocabulary. In addition, our analysis showed that FPs occur twice as many as the most common words in the corpus: ok, yes, so, which are considered in the literature as fillers or discourse markers.

Should we therefore define FPs as the most frequent fillers in Hebrew? We might do so since compared to silent pauses, FPs are far less frequent than the overall frequency of silent pauses. However, Brief silent pauses are less frequent than FPs, while Medium and Long silent pauses are relatively more frequent than FPs. FPs seem to have a marked place in the durational series of (silent) pauses. Moreover, FP rate was found to be correlated with the Brief silence rate, in all four tests (two tasks and two roles). The correlation of the FPs with the Brief pauses suggests that the Brief silent pause has a linkage to the FP phenomenon, and that the division of silent pauses into three types (according to their duration) was justifiable. When looking at the durational findings of previous studies on FPs in Hebrew (Silber-Varod 2013a; Silber-Varod et al. 2016; both were mentioned in Sect. 2), we can see even a tighter linkage, since the range of FP duration found in those studies (70 ms to 500 ms) lies between Brief and Medium silent pauses (range 100–200 ms and 200–1000 ms, respectively). Therefore, it is not farfetched to suggest that those brief breaks, either filled or unfilled, are used for the same cognitive purposes during the production of speech.

We can conclude that our first hypothesis that FPs used by Hebrew speakers are closer to the fillers-as-word hypothesis rather than to the filler-as-pause hypothesis was not confirmed. Our second hypothesis that quantitative patterns of FPs would support fillers-as-word hypothesis was not confirmed as well, since our quantitative measures showed a conclusive pattern, but one that strengthens the filler-as-pause hypothesis. Not only that, the filler-as-pause hypothesis is even more robust if we lean on durational measurements that were carried out in previous research and on a different corpus.

Our third hypothesis was that speakers would use FPs differently depending on their role in task-oriented dialogues (either a leader or a follower). This hypothesis was confirmed and is an additional strengthening to studies in other languages that showed the effects of extra-linguistic and sociolinguistic variables on the rate of FPs (e.g., Yuan et al. 2016; Bortfeld et al. 2001; Gósy et al. 2014). Correlations between FP rates of speakers in the same task were positively significant and strong, which may indicate traces of coordination between speakers in their FP use, as suggested in Pardo et al. (2013). This is also in congruence with the findings on the same corpus by Silber-Varod et al. (2020b), albeit using different measures. We suggest that this finding supports that FP patterns are strongly connected to speakers.

We applied a quantitative analysis to seek answer to a typological question: Does the use of Filled Pauses in Hebrew supports either the filler-as-word hypothesis or the fillers-as-pauses hypothesis? The findings support that filler-as-pause hypothesis seems to be characteristic of Hebrew speakers' FP use in the analyzed tasks. We suggest that in Hebrew, FPs are parts of the break, the disfluent unit, within the fluent speech, although FPs show some obvious similarity with interjections in general. Replication of this analysis in other languages would contribute to get closer to the problem solving of this typological question.

Acknowledgements. This work was supported by the Open Media and Information Lab at The Open University of Israel [Grant Number 20184]. The authors wish to thank Mr. Eyal Rabin for his valuable assistance with the statistical tests.

References

Anderson, H., et al.: The HCRC map task corpus. Lang. Speech **34**(4), 351–366 (1991). https://doi.org/10.1177/002383099103400404

Azogui, J., Lerner, A., Silber-Varod, V.: The Open University of Israel Map Task Corpus (MaTaCOp) (2015). http://www.openu.ac.il/en/academicstudies/matacop/

Boersma, P. Weenink, D.: Praat: doing phonetics by computer [Computer program]. ver. 6.0.37 (14 March 2018). http://www.praat.org/

Bortfeld, H., Leon, S.D., Bloom, J.E., Schober, M.F., Brennan, S.E.: Disfluency rates in conversation: effects of age, relationship, topic, role, and gender. Lang. Speech **44**, 123–147 (2001). https://doi.org/10.1177/00238309010440020101

Campione, E., Véronis, J.: A large-scale multilingual study of silent pause duration. Speech Prosody **2002**, 199–202 (2002)

Carletta, J., Isard, A., Kowtko, J., Doherty-Sneddon, G.: HCRC dialogue structure coding manual. Human Communication Research Centre (1996)

Clark, H.H., Fox Tree, J.E.: Using uh and um in spontaneous speaking. Cognition **84**(1), 73–111 (2002). https://doi.org/10.1016/S0010-0277%2802%2900017-3

Gósy, M., Bóna, J., Beke, A., Horváth, V.: Phonetic characteristics of filled pauses: the effects of speakers' age. In: Fuchs, S., Grice, M., Hermes, A., Lancia, L., Mücke, D. (eds.), Proceedings of the 10th International Seminar on Speech Production (ISSP). Köln, 150–153 (2014). http://real.mtak.hu/15491/

Gósy, M., Gyarmathy, D., Beke, A.: Phonetic analysis of filled pauses based on a Hungarian-English learner corpus. Int. J. Learner Corpus Res. **3**(2), 151–176 (2017). https://doi.org/10.1075/ijlcr.3.2.03gos

Horváth, V.: Filled pauses in Hungarian: their phonetic form and function. Acta Linguistica Hungarica **57**(2–3), 288–306 (2010). https://doi.org/10.1556/aling.57.2010.2-3.6

Juste, F., Andrade, C.R.F.D.: Typology of speech disruptions and grammatical classes in stuttering and fluent children. PróFono Revista de Atualização Científica **18**(2), 129–140 (2006)

Koiso, H., Horiuchi, Y., Tutiya, S., Ichikawa, A., Den, Y.: An analysis of turn-taking and backchannels based on prosodic and syntactic features in Japanese map task dialogs. Lang. Speech **41**(3), 295–321 (1998). https://doi.org/10.1177/002383099804100404

Lerner, A., Miara, O., Malayev, S., Silber-Varod, V.: The influence of the interlocutor's gender on the speaker's role identification. In: Karpov, A., Jokisch, O., Potapova, R. (eds.) SPECOM 2018. LNCS (LNAI), vol. 11096, pp. 321–330. Springer, Cham (2018). https://doi.org/10.1007/978-3-319-99579-3_34

Maschler, Y.: Discourse markers at frame shifts in Israeli Hebrew talk-in-interaction. Pragmatics **7**(2), 183–211 (1997). https://doi.org/10.1075/prag.7.2.04mas

Maschler, Y.: Metalanguage in interaction: Hebrew discourse markers, vol. 181. John Benjamins Publishing (2009)

Nenova, N., Joue, G., Reilly, R., Carson-Berndsen, J.: Sound and function regularities in interjections. In: ISCA Tutorial and Research Workshop (ITRW) on Disfluency in Spontaneous Speech (2001)

Oliveira, C.M.C.D., Bernardes, A.P.L., Broglio, G.A.F., Capellini, S.A.: Speech fluency profile in cluttering individuals. Pró-Fono Revista de Atualização Científica **4**(22), 445–450 (2010)

Pardo, J.S., Jay, I.C., Hoshino, R., Hasbun, S.M., Sowemimo-Coker, C., Krauss, R.M.: Influence of role-switching on phonetic convergence in conversation. Discourse Process. **50**(4), 276–300 (2013). https://doi.org/10.1080/0163853X.2013.778168

Pardo, J.S., et al.: The montclair map task: balance, efficacy, and efficiency in conversational interaction. Lang. Speech **62**(2), 378–398 (2019). https://doi.org/10.1177/0023830918775435

Podlesskaya, V.I.: Parameters for typological variation of placeholders. Fillers, pauses and placeholders. In: Typological Studies in Language, pp. 11–32. John Benjamins, Amsterdam (2010). https://doi.org/10.1075/tsl.93.02pod

Silber-Varod, V.: Phonological aspects of hesitation disfluencies. In: Speech Prosody 2010-Fifth International Conference (2010)

Silber-Varod, V.: The SpeeCHain Perspective: Form and Function of Prosodic Boundary Tones in Spontaneous Spoken Hebrew. LAP Lambert Academic Publishing (2013a)

Silber-Varod, V.: Structural analysis of prosodic pattern: The case of excessive prolongations in Israeli Hebrew. Revista Leitura, Special Issue on Speech Prosody **52**, 271–291 (2013b)

Silber-Varod, V., Kreiner, H., Lovett, R., Levi-Belz, Y., Amir, N.: Do social anxiety individuals hesitate more? The prosodic profile of hesitation disfluencies in social anxiety disorder individuals. In: Proceedings of Speech Prosody 2016 (SP 2016), Boston, USA, (2016). https://doi.org/10.21437/SpeechProsody.2016-249

Silber-Varod, V., Lerner, A.: Analysis of silences in unbalanced dialogues: the effect of genre and role. In: Eklund, R., Rose, R. (eds.) Proceedings of DiSS 2017, the 8th Workshop on Disfluency in Spontaneous Speech, TMH-QPSR, 58(1), pp. 53–56 (2017)

Silber-Varod, V., Malayev, S., Lerner, A.: Positioning oneself in different roles: structural and lexical measures of power relations between speakers in map task corpus. Speech Communication **117**, 1–12 (2020a). https://doi.org/10.1016/j.specom.2020.01.002

Silber-Varod, V., Amit, D., Lerner, A.: Tracing changes over the course of the conversation: a case study on filled pauses rates. In: Proceedings of the 10th International Conference on Speech Prosody 2020, pp. 754–758 (2020b). https://doi.org/10.21437/SpeechProsody.2020-154

Tseng, C., Su, Z.Y., Chang, C.H., Tai, C.H.C.: Prosodic fillers and discourse markers–discourse prosody and text prediction. Tonal Aspects of Languages (2006)

Vetter, M., Sakriani, S., Satoshi, N.: Cross-lingual speech-based Tobi label generation using bidirectional LSTM. In: ICASSP 2019–2019 IEEE International Conference on Acoustics, Speech and Signal Processing (ICASSP), IEEE (2019). https://doi.org/10.1109/ICASSP.2019.8682764

Weise, A., Silber-Varod, V., Lerner, A., Hirschberg, J., Levitan, R.: Entrainment in spoken Hebrew dialogues. In: Pardo, J., Pellegrino, E., Dellwo, V., Möbius, B. (eds.), Special Issue on Vocal Accommodation in Speech Communication, Journal of Phonetics, 83 (2020). https://doi.org/10.1016/j.wocn.2020.101005

Wieling, M., Grieve, J., Bouma, G., Fruehwald, J., Coleman, J., Liberman, M.: Variation and change in the use of hesitation markers in Germanic languages. Lang. Dyn. Change **6**(2), 199–234 (2016). https://doi.org/10.1163/22105832-00602001

Yuan, J., Xu, X., Lai, W., Liberman, M.: Pauses and pause fillers in Mandarin monologue speech: the effects of sex and proficiency. Proc. Speech Prosody **2016**, 1167–1170 (2016). https://doi.org/10.21437/SpeechProsody.2016-240

Modified Group Delay Function Using Different Spectral Smoothing Techniques for Voice Liveness Detection

Shrishti Singh[✉], Kuldeep Khoria, and Hemant A. Patil

Dhirubhai Ambani Institute of Information and Communication Technology,
Gandhinagar, Gujarat, India
{shrishti_singh,kuldeep_khoria,hemant_patil}@daiict.ac.in

Abstract. Voice Liveness Detection (VLD) has emerged as a successful technique to detect spoofing attacks in Automatic Speaker Verification (ASV) system. Presence of pop noise in the speech signal of live speaker provides the basic cue to distinguish between genuine and spoofed speech. Pop noise is produced due to the spontaneous breathing while uttering a certain class of phonemes which has low frequency characteristics. Pop noise comes out as a burst at the lips which is captured by the ASV system (as the speaker and microphone are close enough), indicates the liveness of the speaker and provides the basis of VLD. Pop noise characteristics is absent in spoofed speech as generally the original speaker and attacker's recording device are far apart. In this context, we explore relative significance of the phase information present to detect pop noise by utilizing phase-based feature, i.e., modified group delay function. Further, various spectral smoothing techniques have been analyzed, such as cepstral smoothing, spectral root, and linear prediction spectrum in order to enhance the spectral representation of the speech signals through modified group delay functions (MGDF). Better accuracy of 80.13% on development set and 69.79% on evaluation set is obtained when spectral root smoothing is employed in MGDF.

Keywords: Modified group delay function · Voice liveness detection · Pop noise · Spectrum smoothing techniques

1 Introduction

One of the most essential pieces of security is consent and validation of individuals which has motivated to use the biometric system on various platforms. Biometric security systems are becoming a key element to multi-factor authentication as there are various ways of conducting biometric verification, such as voice recognition, facial, and iris recognition, vascular pattern recognition, and fingerprints. Among these, voice biometrics have gained significant importance with the advancements in speech technology and user-machine interface. With these advancements, various spoofing techniques has also been developed to misguide ASV systems. Fraudsters can use advanced speech synthesis, voice conversion or

© Springer Nature Switzerland AG 2021
A. Karpov and R. Potapova (Eds.): SPECOM 2021, LNAI 12997, pp. 649–659, 2021.
https://doi.org/10.1007/978-3-030-87802-3_58

imitation, and recorded replay to try to spoof ASV systems [1,5,6,8,10,22]. The intensity of these attacks has made the spoofing detection as one of the important research issue in the field of ASV. To that effect, several challenges have been organized earlier, such as ASVSpoof challenges during INTERSPEECH conferences with the aim to improve performance of anti-spoofing for attack-resistant design of ASV systems [4,23,26].

The challenge outcomes have provided many countermeasures at the frontend and backend to detect spoofing attacks which has been developed and evaluated on the standard datasets provided by the ASVSpoof challenge organizers. These challenge campaigns focussed on performance of the countermeasure systems for the anti-spoofing. In this paper, the focus is centered to prevent ASV system from spoofing attacks through Voice Liveness Detection (VLD). Recently, POCO (POp noise COrpus) dataset [2] is build to develop various countermeasures against spoofing attacks to detect the human liveness evidence in the speech signal via pop noise detection. Identification of the genuine speaker characteristics (i.e., VLD task) through pop noise detection can be potentially effective when the distance between the testing microphone and the speaker is very less, which consequently leads to detect the spoofing attacks.

In [18], human liveness detection for detecting spoof attacks was proposed for the first time where two approaches for VLD were presented: (a) low-frequency-based single channel detection, and (b) subtraction-based pop noise detection with two channels. In the former approach, entire Short-Time Fourier Transform (STFT) around lower-frequency region is utilized as the pop noise exists in the lower frequency regions. Whereas in the later approach, entire frequency range of the spectrum is utilized. In [12], phoneme-based pop noise detection is performed for VLD along with ASV system, where pop noise duration is detected in the utterance and estimated phonemes in this duration are analyzed for VLD. The similar approach of phoneme-based pop noise detection was utilized in [25] with extended study on Gammatone Frequency Cepstral Coefficients (GFCC) feature set for pop noise detection.

In this paper, the focus is on extracting spectral features from the phase spectrum of the speech signal using group delay function. Phase-based features are not explored much in speech applications, however, the phase contains useful information of speech signal and has been used for the replay spoof detection [19,20,27]. The phase-based features are less investigated for VLD. Moreover, various spectral smoothing techniques based on cepstral, spectral root, and Linear Prediction (LP) spectrum are also investigated, to enhance the group delay spectrum with minimum distortions in the original formant locations [13].

2   Features Used

The speech signal characteristics is usually visualized by using short-time magnitude spectra instead of short-time phase spectra. In the context of speech signal, resonances are formant the peaks formed by the spectral envelope of the short-time magnitude spectra. In short-time phase spectrum, these resonances are observed as transitions. The group delay function is defined as the negative derivative of the unwrapped short-time phase spectrum [15, 16]. Due to wrapping of the phase spectrum at multiples of 2π, it becomes difficult to identify these transitions. Hence, to get any meaningful information from the phase spectrum, the complex process of phase unwrapping has to be performed [24]. The group delay function has the property to resolve resonant peaks of the signal better than the magnitude spectrum, i.e., due to high resolution property of group delay function [14]. Also for minimum phase signal, group delay function effectively extract various source and system parameters [14].

The speech signal $x(n)$ is analyzed with the help of Short-Time Fourier Transform (STFT) to extract the group delay features. The magnitude and phase representation of $x(n)$ is given by Eq. (1):

$$X(\omega) = |X(\omega)| \, e^{j\phi(\omega)}, \tag{1}$$

where $|X(\omega)|$ and $\phi(\omega)$ are the magnitude and phase spectrum at frequency, ω. The group delay function of the signal is given by:

$$\tau(\omega) = -\frac{d}{d\omega}\phi(\omega) = -imag[\frac{d}{d\omega}log(X(\omega))]. \tag{2}$$

The group delay function is also directly computed from the signal by invoking the Fourier Transform (FT) property of differentiation in frequency-domain as shown in Eq. (3):

$$\tau(\omega) = \frac{X_r(\omega)Y_r(\omega) + X_i(\omega)Y_i(\omega)}{|X(\omega)|^2}, \tag{3}$$

where $X(\omega)$ and $Y(\omega)$ are the STFT of the $x(n)$ and $nx(n)$, r and i are the real and imaginary parts, respectively. This method which has the advantage that it can be computed directly from the speech signal without involving complex process of phase unwrapping [24].

2.1   Motivation for Modifying Group Delay Function

The group delay function gives signal information accurately on the condition that the z-transform roots of the signal are not much close to the unit circle in the z-plane [7, 14, 24]. The vocal tract system and excitation contribute to the envelope and fine structure of the speech signal, respectively. When extracting features from the magnitude spectrum, the intention is to obtain the spectral envelope of the spectrum. Similarly, in group delay function, the fine structure has to be suppressed while extracting the vocal tract system characteristics.

The zeros close to the unit circle appears as spikes in the group delay function which distort the original formant locations. The intensity of these spikes is proportional to the distance of these zeroes to the unit circle. These spikes form a significant part of the fine structure and cannot be removed by normal smoothing techniques [7,13]. Therefore, there is a need to modify the group delay function to suppress the effects of these spikes.

In this context, authors have proposed the analysis of the various smoothing techniques applied on the group delay function. The Modified Group Delay Function (MGDF) where historically cepstrally smoothed spectrum is used along with parameters α and γ to reduce the intensity of the spikes present at formant locations and to restore the dynamic range of the speech spectrum [14]. The MGDF is defined in Eq. (4):

$$\tau(\omega) = \frac{X_r(\omega)Y_r(\omega) + X_i(\omega)Y_i(\omega)}{|X_c(\omega)|^{2\gamma}}, \tau_m(\omega) = \frac{\tau(\omega)}{|\tau(\omega)|}|\tau(\omega)|^\alpha, \qquad (4)$$

where $|X_c(\omega)|$ is the cepstrally smoothed version of $|X(\omega)|$. $\tau_m(\omega)$ is the final MGDF. The algorithm for computing MGDF is given in Algorithm 1.

Algorithm 1. Computing the MGDF

1: Compute the STFT of the signal $x(n)$ and $nx(n)$, i.e., $X(\omega)$ and $Y(\omega)$.
2: Perform the cepstral smoothing on $|X(\omega)|$ in order to obtain $|X_c(\omega)|$.
3: Compute the MGDF as given in Eq.(4).
4: Compute the MGDF for different values of the parameter α and γ to get the better results.

The two other approaches introduced for the smoothing of the group delay spectrum are based on Linear Prediction (LP) and Spectral Root (SR). All these smoothing techniques are evaluated for their ability for effective VLD task.

2.2   LP Spectrum-Based Smoothing

LP models the speech signal by approximating in form of all-pole model [3,11]. The basic idea behind LP analysis is that each speech sample is approximated as a linear combination of past speech samples. The LP model is given by

$$\tilde{s}[n] = a_1 s[n-1] + a_2 s[n-2] + ... + a_p s[n-p], \qquad (5)$$

where $a_1, a_2, ..., a_p$ are called as LP coefficients. The system function for p^{th} order predictor is given as

$$P(z) = \sum_{k=1}^{p} \alpha_k z^{-k}. \qquad (6)$$

One of the properties of the LP is formant estimation. It has a tendency to model the peaks of the spectral envelope which corresponds to resonances in the vocal tract system. The formant estimation by linear predictor is based on the fact that the pair of complex poles has peak in the amplitude frequency at angular frequency, θ. The shape of the vocal tract system can be specified with resonant frequencies [17]. Hence, LP effectively extracts vocal tract information. LP spectrum being estimated from all-pole model could help in reducing the effect of zeroes which occurs as spikes in the group delay spectrum. The LP spectrum is incorporated in the modified group delay function (MGDF) as given in Eq. (7):

$$\tau(\omega) = \frac{X_r(\omega)Y_r(\omega) + X_i(\omega)Y_i(\omega)}{|X(\omega)_{LP}|}, \tag{7}$$

where, $|X(\omega)_{LP}|$ is the LP spectrum of the signal $x(n)$. The algorithm to obtain LP-based modified group delay function is given in Algorithm 2.

Algorithm 2. Computing the LP Based MGDF

1: For the given speech segment, compute the LP coefficients for the optimal selected value of p, i.e., order of the linear predictor.
2: Estimate the LP polynomial $A(z) = 1 - \sum_{k=1}^{p} a_k z^{-k}$.
3: Estimate the LP spectrum by calculating the magnitude of the transfer function of the all-pole speech production model $H(z) = 1/A(z)$.
4: Apply this LP spectrum of the signal instead of cepstrally smoothed spectrum in MGDF.

2.3   Spectral Root-Based Smoothing

The spectral root homomorphic filtering helps in separating the contribution of glottal excitation and vocal tract system impulse response by performing the transformation from one convolutional vector space to another convolutionally-combined vector space [9,21]. This means that homomorphic filtering is also considered as a *spectral smoother*. The smoothing of the spectrum can be controlled by a parameter, γ. The criteria for selecting optimum value of γ is discussed in Sect. 4. The process for computing group delay function using spectral root smoothing is given Algorithm 3. The Fig. 1 shows the group delay plots based on different smoothing techniques. It can be observed from Fig. 1 that the cepstral smoothing-based group delay spectrum has reduced the spikes present in original group delay spectrum. The extent of smoothing can be seen with greater intensity in LP spectrum and spectral root-based smoothing methods.

Algorithm 3. Computing the Spectral Root Based MGDF

1: For the given speech segment, apply Z-transform to get $X(e^{j\omega})$
2: Raise $|X(e^{j\omega})|$ to the power γ.
3: Again, apply the Z-transform to the spectral root spectrum obtained in above step.
4: Calculate the absolute value .
5: Apply the obtained value in place of cepstrally smoothed spectrum in MGDF.

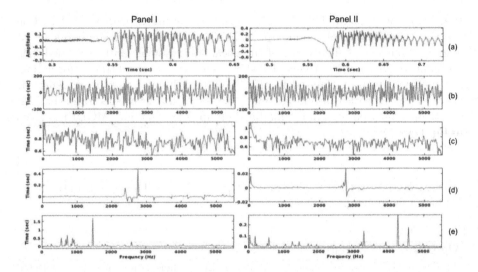

Fig. 1. Panel I (a), (b), (c), (d), and (e) shows the speech segment without pop noise (spoof), group delay, MGDF using cepstral smoothing, LP spectrum smoothing, and spectral root smoothing respectively, and corresponding plots for speech containing pop noise (genuine) utterance is shown in Panel II.

The peaks have been suppressed effectively in both the plots, however, it may be possible that there may have been some information loss of the vocal tract system characteristics occurring in the LP spectrum-based group delay function. This depends on the selection of the optimum value of the, p. Further discussion about selection of the order value is done in Sect. 4.

3   Experimental Setup

3.1   Database Used

In practical scenarios, if an attacker tries to attempt a spoofing attack, he/she must somehow obtain the voice samples of the target (genuine) speaker. The simplest way to do this is by recording (eavesdropping) the voice of target speaker and then using it to mount a replay attack onto the ASV system. Since these recordings will be done from long distances, pop noise will not be recorded by the attacker's microphone and this absence of pop noise in the replayed sample will be able to *flag* the spoofed speech from the genuine speech. In this work, we have used recently released *POCO* dataset [2]. There are total of 66 speakers out of which 34 are male and 32 are female. The words were selected from the English language such that all the 44 phonemes are covered in the recording. The dataset is sampled at 22050 Hz sampling frequency with a bit-depth of *24*-bits. The dataset has three subsets, namely, RC-A (Recording with Microphone),

RP-A (Eavesdropping), and RC-B (Recording with Microphone Array). We have excluded the RC-B subset for our experiments as it consists of microphone array, and it's corresponding spoof speech utterances are not provided. In addition, the experiments in [2] are performed using RC-A and RP-A subsets. The details of RC-A and RC-B are as follows:

Recording with Microphone (RC-A). This subset represents genuine speaker as it was recorded directly with the live speaker and hence, contains pop noise. The recording was done with Audio-Technica AT4040 microphone. The distance between speaker and microphone was fixed to be 10 cm.

Eavesdropping (RP-A). Eavesdropping is done to imitate a scenario where replay attack is done by an attacker from a long distance, i.e., without pop noise. This condition is simulated by using Audio-Technica AT4040 microphone with a suitable pop filter inserted between speaker and microphone. The distance between speaker and microphone was fixed as 10 cm. The dataset is partitioned into training and evaluation subsets as 80% and 20% utterances, respectively. Each of these subsets consists of half of the genuine and half of the spoof speech utterances. We also ensured that the speakers are exclusive in each subset and the ratio between male and female speaker is maintained. The statistics of the data distribution in training and evaluation subset is shown in Table 1.

Table 1. Statistics of the POCO Dataset for Our Experiments.

Subset	# Utterances	# Male	# Female
Training	6952	13	14
Development	3432	6	7
Evaluation	6600	13	13

3.2 Baseline

In our work, detection of pop noise is considered as two-class classification task, where utterances with pop noise are labelled as genuine while utterances with absence of pop noise is labelled as imposter (i.e., spoof). The baseline is implemented with the methodology given in [2]. Spectrograms are used as input features. S_{eng} is obtained by considering spectral energy densities corresponding to $[0, f_{max}]$. Since the pop noise is observed in the lower frequency region of the spectrogram features, f_{max} is considered as $40Hz$. After that f_{avg} is estimated as the average of the spectral energy densities for each frame. Then, the mean and standard deviation are taken for $favg$ across all the frames and is estimated for averaged spectral energies f_{avg} in order to normalize it. Then, 10 frames with largest spectral energies were chosen. This is done by taking 10 frames from normalized f_{avg} having largest value and then taking frames corresponding to that indices from *Seng*. This feature set with appropriate labels, is given as input to Support Vector Machine (SVM) for proposed/VLD task. The more details of this baseline algorithm is given in [18].

3.3   Feature Set, Classifier, and Performance Metric

In this paper, MGDF-based features extracted using three spectral smoothing methods are given as input to Gaussian Mixture Model (GMM) classifier. GMM is used as a two-class classifier, where the two classes correspond to the speech samples containing pop noise (genuine) without pop noise (spoofed). The individual GMM is trained on genuine and spoofed speech using the three different group delay-based feature sets. Total 128 mixtures are used in GMM. The experiments are performed using speaker-independent and customized disjoint partition of the dataset as shown in Table 1. For the classification task, all the variants of group delay feature discussed has been extracted and analyzed for the low-frequency region in order to observe the effect of pop noise only in the different feature sets. The signal is windowed with the help of Hamming window of 25 ms duration and 10 ms shift. The experiments are performed by varying the parameters in the respective features in order to obtain the optimum value of the different parameters. The results are reported in terms of % accuracy. Experimental results are discussed for different values of tuning parameters are discussed in Sect. 4.

4   Experimental Results

For spectral root-based smoothing group delay function, experiments are performed for different values of γ where range of γ varies in $-1 \leq \gamma \leq 1$. From the results, it can be observed that for $\gamma > 0$ accuracy on development and evaluation set is better as compared to $\gamma < 0$. Table 2 represents the classification accuracy for different value of γ. The selection of γ depends on the pole-zero arrangement of the sequence. It has been observed that as the number of poles increases relative to the number of zeros, γ should be made closer to -1, and vice-versa. [9,17]. The negative value of γ results in better pole estimates, whereas $\gamma > 0$ results in a better zero estimates. For the group delay function, the spectral root of the signal is used in the denominator for smoothing. Taking $\gamma < 0$ can lead to enhancing the effect of zeros in the group delay spectrum. Therefore, $\gamma > 0$ has performed better in classification (which can be observed in Table 2).

In estimating LP spectrum for the all-pole model of the vocal tract system, p acts as a controlling degree of smoothing of the measured spectrum [17]. As the order p increases, the harmonic structure is revealed in the all-pole spectrum, indicating the overestimated order of the model. Also, with the decreasing value of p or underestimating the model order may result in loss of the fine resonant structure of the underlying all-pole system and only the largest resonances are represented. For using LP spectrum to smooth with modified group delay function, experiments are performed for various values of p. We got better results on fixing value of p = 24 for VLD task whereas results obtained considering values of p less than 24 are inferior to the baseline. Similarly, for cepstral smoothing-based group delay function, experiments are performed by varying the tuning parameter α and γ. The best results for this experiment were obtained for the value of α and γ to be 0.1 and 0.4, respectively.

Table 3 represents the classification accuracy (in %) for different types of smoothing method and is compared with the baseline. Here, it can be observed that all the three types of smoothing methods, i.e., cepstral smoothing, spectral root smoothing and, LP spectrum smoothing outperforms the baseline. Furthermore, spectral root smoothing method gives us the best classification accuracy as 80.13 % for development set and 69.79 % for evaluation set when compared to the other smoothing techniques.

Table 2. % for Different Values of γ.

γ	Dev	Eval
1/3	**80.13**	**69.79**
1/4	78.29	68.91
1/12	79.05	68.20
−1/3	75.70	66.77
−1/4	76.78	68.68
−1/12	75.17	65.44

Table 3. % Accuracy of Different Smoothing Techniques.

Approach	Parameters	Dev	Eval
Baseline	-	61.52	62.21
Cepstral Smoothing	$\alpha = 0.1, \gamma = 0.4$	71.01	67.73
Spectral Root Smoothing	$\gamma = 1/3$	**80.13**	**69.79**
LP Spectrum Smoothing	p = 24	67.74	64.35

5   Summary and Conclusions

In this paper, we analyzed the effect of different smoothing techniques to counter the problem of emerging spikes due to the zeroes present near the unit circle in the z-plane of the signal. These methods were tested for VLD task to understand the characteristics of pop noise for phase-based features derived from various smoothing methods on MGDF. The purpose of this analysis was to understand the effectiveness of group delay function and how it can be further improved for pop noise detection. From the results, we can conclude that there is potential in spectral-root based smoothing technique which needs to be explored further.

Spectral root method have performed better than other mentioned approaches by giving better classification % accuracy. For future work, estimation of tuning parameters can be explored in detail to get best result depending on the classification task. Also, some improvements can be done in the algorithms of the discussed features for improved performance.

Acknowledgments. The authors would like to thank the authorities at DA-IICT, Gandhinagar for providing resources and kind support towards the completion of this research work.

References

1. Ai, Y., Ling, Z.H.: Knowledge-and-data-driven amplitude spectrum prediction for hierarchical neural vocoders. In: INTERSPEECH, pp. 190–194. Shanghai, China (2020)
2. Akimoto, K., Liew, S.P., Mishima, S., Mizushima, R., Lee, K.A.: Poco: a voice spoofing and liveness detection corpus based on pop noise. In: INTERSPEECH, Shanghai, China, pp. 1081–1085 (2020)
3. Atal, B.S., Hanauer, S.L.: Speech analysis and synthesis by linear prediction of the speech wave. J. Acoustical Soc. Am. (JASA) **50**(2B), 637–655 (1971)
4. Delgado, H., et al.: ASVspoof 2017 version 2.0: meta-data analysis and baseline enhancements. In: Odyssey 2018 The Speaker and Language Recognition Workshop. Les Sables d'Olonne, France, pp. 26–29, June 2018
5. Ding, S., Zhao, G., Gutierrez-Osuna, R.: Improving the speaker identity of nonparallel many-to-many voice conversion with adversarial speaker recognition. In: INTERSPEECH, pp. 776–780. Shanghai, China (2020)
6. Hautamäki, R.G., Kinnunen, T., Hautamäki, V., Laukkanen, A.M.: Comparison of human listeners and speaker verification systems using voice mimicry data. TARGET **4000**, 5000 (2014)
7. Hegde, R.M., Murthy, H.A., Gadde, V.R.R.: Significance of the modified group delay feature in speech recognition. IEEE Trans. Audio Speech Lang. Process. **15**(1), 190–202 (2007)
8. chun Hsu, P., yi Lee, H.: WG-WaveNet: real-time high-fidelity speech synthesis without GPU. In: INTERSPEECH. Shanghai, China, pp. 210–214 (2020)
9. Lim, J.: Spectral root homomorphic deconvolution system. IEEE Trans. Acoustics Speech Signal Process. **27**(3), 223–233 (1979)
10. Lorenzo-Trueba, J., et al.: The voice conversion challenge 2018: promoting development of parallel and nonparallel methods. In: Proceedings of the Odyssey 2018 The Speaker and Language Recognition Workshop, pp. 195–202 (2018). http://dx.doi.org/10.21437/Odyssey.2018-28
11. Makhoul, J.: Spectral analysis of speech by linear prediction. IEEE Trans. Audio Electroacoust. **21**(3), 140–148 (1973)
12. Mochizuki, S., Shiota, S., Kiya, H.: Voice liveness detection using phoneme-based pop-noise detector for speaker verifcation. In: Odyssey 2018 The Speaker and Language Recognition Workshop. ISCA, Les Sables d'Olonne, pp. 233–239 (2018)
13. Murthy, H.A., Gadde, V.: The modified group delay function and its application to phoneme recognition. In: 2003 IEEE International Conference on Acoustics, Speech, and Signal Processing, (ICASSP'03), vol. 1, p. I-68. Hong Kong, China (2003)

14. Murthy, H.A., Yegnanarayana, B.: Group delay functions and its applications in speech technology. Sadhana **36**(5), 745–782 (2011)
15. Oppenheim, A.V., Schafer, R.W.: Digital signal processing(book). Research supported by the Massachusetts Institute of Technology, Bell Telephone Laboratories, and Guggenheim Foundation. Englewood Cliffs, N. J., Prentice-Hall Inc, 1975, p. 598 (1975)
16. Oppenheim, A.V., Willsky, A.S., Hamid, S.: Signals and systems, processing series, 2nd edition (1997)
17. Quatieri, T.F.: Discrete-time Speech Signal Processing: Principles and Practice. 2nd Edition, Pearson Education India, Chennai (2006)
18. Shiota, S., Villavicencio, F., Yamagishi, J., Ono, N., Echizen, I., Matsui, T.: Voice liveness detection algorithms based on pop noise caused by human breath for automatic speaker verification. In: INTERSPEECH, Dresden, Germany, pp. 239–243 (2015)
19. Srinivas, K., Das, R.K., Patil, H.A.: Combining phase-based features for replay spoof detection system. In: 2018 11th International Symposium on Chinese Spoken Language Processing (ISCSLP), pp. 151–155. Taiwan, China (2018)
20. Srinivas, K., Patil, H.A.: Relative phase shift features for replay spoof detection system. In: Proceddings of the Workshop on Spoken Language Technologies for Under-Resourced Languages (SLTU), pp. 1–5. New Delhi, India (2018)
21. Tapkir, P., Patil, H.A.: Novel empirical mode decomposition cepstral features for replay spoof detection. In: INTERSPEECH. Hyderabad, India, pp. 721–725 (2018)
22. Tian, Q., Zhang, Z., Lu, H., Chen, L.H., Liu, S.: FeatherWave: an efficient high-fidelity neural vocoder with multi-band linear prediction. In: INTERSPEECH, pp. 195–199. Shanghai, China (2020)
23. Todisco, M., et al.: Asvspoof 2019: Future horizons in spoofed and fake audio detection. arXivreprint arXiv:1904.05441, pp. 1008–1012 (2019)
24. Tribolet, J.: A new phase unwrapping algorithm. IEEE Trans. Acoustics Speech Sign. Process. **25**(2), 170–177 (1977)
25. Wang, Q., et al.: Voicepop: a pop noise based anti-spoofing system for voice authentication on smartphones. In: IEEE INFOCOM 2019-IEEE Conference on Computer Communications, Paris, France, pp. 2062–2070 (2019)
26. Wu, Z., et al.: ASVSpoof 2015: the first automatic speaker verification spoofing and countermeasures challenge. In: INTERSPEECH, pp. 2037–2041. Dresden, Germany (2015)
27. Yang, J., Wang, H., Das, R.K., Qian, Y.: Modified magnitude-phase spectrum information for spoofing detection. IEEE/ACM Transactions on Audio, Speech, and Language Processing, p. 1 (2021). https://doi.org/10.1109/TASLP.2021.3060810

Complex Rhythm Adjustments in Multilingual Code-Switching Across Mandarin, English and Russian

Tatiana Sokoreva[⊠] [iD], Tatiana Shevchenko[iD], and Mariya Chyrvonaya

Moscow State Linguistic University, 38 Ostozhenka Street, Moscow 119034, Russian Federation

Abstract. The study is concerned with problems facing a multilingual learner in code-switching across three languages: Mandarin, English, Russian. We looked at syllable-based vs. accent-based rhythm dichotomy as accompanied by major rhythm features shared by the three languages, integrating them in the framework of complex rhythm analysis. Segmentation of discourse into larger units (IPs - intonation phrases which could be technically defined as between-pause units) proves to be revealing the way L2 and L3 texts are processed in reading. Advanced learners of Mandarin, English and Russian produced the corpus of 60 texts, code-switching from L1 to L2, then to L3 in one session. Global pitch reset to higher pitch levels could be correlated with rhythm typology of tone language (Mandarin) transition to intonation languages (English, Russian). Global temporal slow-down involved segmentation into shorter IPs by longer pauses, which suggested word-for-word processing of L2 and L3 texts. Similarity of major rhythm adjustments in code-switching by Chinese and Russian learners does not allow to interpret them by transfer of linguistic habits only; they suggest cognitively challenging task of code-switching and the deficiency of teaching practice, namely memorizing Mandarin words separately in lists. Tone cohesion practice and methods of developing fluency employed in teaching English might be suggested.

Keywords: Multilingualism · Code-switching · Mandarin · English · Russian · Rhythm · Segmentation

1 Introduction: An Overview of Rhythm Typology

Rhythm of speech is one of the first characteristics we perceive and identify as similar to our own way of speaking or strange to it [21]. Rhythm facilitates intelligibility and comprehensibility: it provides for predictability of relevant information to turn up at the right place in discourse structure [19, 24].

How do we cope with the task of learning foreign rhythm, especially challenging when we have to codeswitch in between languages whose typology in rhythm is categorically contrastive? We know from psycholinguistics that processing Mandarin prosody is a complex cognitive task even for native speakers [8], and our pilot study supported the idea [20]. The current study is borne of the necessity of teaching two typologically different languages, Mandarin and English, to Russian speakers.

© Springer Nature Switzerland AG 2021
A. Karpov and R. Potapova (Eds.): SPECOM 2021, LNAI 12997, pp. 660–669, 2021.
https://doi.org/10.1007/978-3-030-87802-3_59

Rhythm is "a periodicity of similar and commensurable prosodic events," such as syllable, foot, intonation phrase or larger units, like speech paragraph in prose or stanza in verse [1, 14]. Rhythm units form a hierarchy of events, from which we will consider the three basic ones: the syllable, the foot and the intonation phrase as they are represented in three typologically different languages. Russian, a Slavic language and English, a Germanic one, both belong to the category of intonation languages with an accent-based rhythm. Mandarin is a tone language with a syllable-based rhythm.

At the turn of the century the dichotomy "stress-timed" (accent-based) vs. "syllable-timed" (syllable-based), also known as "Abercrombie-Pike hypothesis," was reconsidered and replaced by a scalar theory of rhythm, which was called "a new paradigm of rhythm" (See review in [7, 11]). The new way of looking at rhythm categories was based on the phonological composition of syllables and phonotactic rules in a particular language, as a result of which English as a prototypical accent-based language was placed at the top of the rhythm continuum together with Dutch and German, while Mandarin occupied the opposite end as the most syllable-based (or the least accent-based) among the 18 languages [9]. The relevant features, according to Dauer [6], were consonant clusters, long and short vowel oppositions and reduction of unstressed syllables in English, which provide for greater variability in adjacent syllables' durations measured by pairwise variability index (PVI) [13]. There was only one research paper known to us in which Russian was measured by similar metrics and assessed as an intermediate case between the prototypical accent-based (Germanic) and the prototypical syllable-based (Romance) languages, in close vicinity to Turkish [23]. In fact, Russian does possess consonant clusters and reduction of unstressed syllables, like English, but has no phonological contrast of long and short vowels. We believe that the present study will find evidence of more specific rhythm features in Russian compared to English and Mandarin due to the introduction of major rhythm dimensions: categorization based on syllable structure (minor rhythm) will be supplemented by foot and intonation phrase (major rhythm) characteristics.

Alongside with specific syllable structures, the three languages have different phonetic prominence-lending means, relevant for creating major rhythm. In English and in Russian there are four prosodic cues of accent which may be in trading relations depending on the dialect: pitch change, duration, intensity and vowel quality [15, 16]. In Mandarin pitch change (tone) dominates both at the lexical level and at the sentence level in rhythm structures. In Mandarin word stress [17] and Mandarin speech rhythm [25] prominence is created either by fully-fledged tone realized on the initial (strong) syllable of a disyllabic word and thus contrasted with the so-called "neutral" tone [4, 10, 22]; or, in discourse, the fully-fledged tone is on the strong syllable in a rhythmic unit constituted by monosyllabic words [25]. Duration and intensity, as M. Kh. Rumyantsev pointed out, are mainly employed as intonation means at sentence level [17, 26]. Mandarin, it is argued, shows similar kinds of duration patterns to English: pragmatically focused words are lengthened [2, 7]. In corpus data tone patterns of prominent words were modified for pitch, amplitude and time [12].

Summing up previous research data we suggest that syllable-centered studies have been fundamental and documented well enough to shift the focus to the other, less researched and more debatable aspect of rhythm typology, i.e. to rhythm units of foot and intonation phrase, marked by prominence and pause placement.

2 Methodology

The goal of the study is to explore the rhythmic effect of code-switching in three languages, Mandarin, English and Russian, for a trilingual speaker, as evidenced by temporal and pitch characteristics in reading authentic texts. In the current study code-switching is synonymous to language or dialect shift by a bilingual or bidialectal speaker caused by the communicative situation (as different from code-mixing which involves the transfer of linguistic elements from one language into another) [5].

The corpus consists of 60 texts read by Chinese (n = 10) and Russian (n = 10) advanced female learners of two foreign languages (BA degree in linguistics) in one session for each individual in the following order: the Mandarin tale (302 words), the English tale (337 words), the Russian tale (320 words). Each reading session lasted around 10 min. The total time of the sound material is 3 h 18 min.

The methods are the perceptual auditory and the acoustic electronic analyses followed by statistical and comparative analyses methods.

Language-specific features are most vivid in L1 performances, while the code-switching effect is found by comparing them with L2 and L3 modifications.

In perceptual analysis the texts were annotated for pauses and accents; thus, the number of major rhythm units, i. e. intonation phrases (IPs) and feet, was established.

Acoustic analysis followed along the following lines:

- in pitch characteristics we searched for a) the global pitch levels in each reading measured by pitch values in the opening and the closing phrases of the texts to check the presence of downdrift in each reading and to compare pitch levels in three languages b) to estimate the local reset of pitch levels at the boundary of adjacent readings.
- in temporal characteristics we had to look for a) the global dynamics of individual reading in three languages b) the amount of IPs determined by pauses c) the number of accented syllables in an IP to determine the amount of feet in an IP;
- in pause characteristics we studied the assumed elongation of pause duration and increased number of pauses in reading in foreign languages as compared to the native language.

The prosodic measurements were taken with PRAAT software [3].

Comparative analysis was made across three readings in the same succession: Mandarin-English-Russian. For rhythmic adjustments evidence we compared reading the text in L1, L2 and L3.

The statistical analysis was carried out in PAWS Statistics applying ANOVA and Kruskal-Wallis test with some figures made in Microsoft Excel.

3 Results

3.1 Auditory Analysis of Pauses and Accents Delimiting IPs and Feet

- By correlating the results of the auditory analysis in pause and accents with the total amount of syllables in the texts (see Table 1) we can describe the structure of major rhythm units in native speakers' performances:
- in Mandarin one foot consists of 3.7 syllables, one IP has 1.73 feet, or 6.5 syllables,
- in English one foot consists of 2 syllables, one IP has 2 feet, or 4.12 syllables,
- in Russian one foot consists of 2.5 syllables, one IP has 2 feet, or 5 syllables.

Thus, we found that Mandarin has the longest rhythmic units of feet and intonation phrases, as was described by previous research data in terms of 'longer between-pause chunks and longer between-words silent pauses' in speaking English [4]. In the model of English text performed by an educated Londoner [18] the rhythm groups are more compact and shorter, while the Russian language tends to occupy an intermediate position between the two languages, closer to English in rhythm structures.

Table 1. Syllables, feet and intonation phrases in the text (Mandarin, English, Russian).

	Syllables	Feet	Intonation Phrases
Mandarin	504	141	78
English	367	186	89
Russian	660	262	133

3.2 Acoustic Analysis of Pitch and Tempo

Pitch Characteristics

Global pitch characteristics reveal the following tendencies:

– within each reading there is a downdrift of pitch levels from the initial to the final IP (see Fig. 1);
– between the end of one reading and the beginning of the adjacent one there is a reset of pitch levels from a lower level to a higher one;
– in reset of pitch levels between Mandarin and English the Chinese subjects make a more considerable shift in pitch levels reaching a higher pitch level than at the beginning of reading the Mandarin text;
– the beginning and end of the Russian text reading have the highest values in Mandarin performances;
– similar tendencies of gradual increase in pitch levels in reset from Mandarin to English, and from English to Russian are found in the Russian subjects' performances.

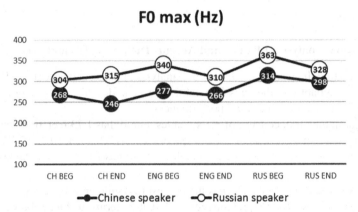

Fig. 1. Maximum fundamental frequency values across the first/last IP in reading the three tales by Chinese and Russian speakers.

Thus, we could observe that transition from a tone language with its focus on minute pitch changes in every lexical unit calls for a global increase in pitch levels for intonation languages. The Russian language turned out to be even more demanding than English in that respect. The emotional-expressive potential of Russian rests mainly on intonation, i.e. pitch variation, employed by the speaker [16], and the subjects in the present experiment proved to be sensitive to that.

Temporal Characteristics

Global temporal characteristics are based on the time spent in reading the three tales. It is found that the Chinese and the Russian subjects tend to demonstrate two opposite tendencies: the Chinese speakers slow down as they proceed from Mandarin to English and then to Russian, whereas the Russians accelerate as they proceed in the course of the session while reading the same sequence.

The analysis revealed that the duration of tales read by Chinese speakers in different languages (see Fig. 2) differs significantly ($F = 92.023$; $p < .000$). Further multiple comparison of each pair of languages used for reading also proved to be significantly various (Mandarin vs English, $p < .05$; Mandarin vs Russian, $p < .000$; English vs Russian, $p < .000$).

As for Russian speakers, the duration of tales read in three languages varies significantly as well ($F = 60.829$; $p < .000$), but the difference is achieved by a distinctive contrast of Mandarin and English and Mandarin and Russian, the difference between English and Russian appeared to be insignificant (Mandarin vs English, $p < .000$; Mandarin vs Russian, $p < .000$).

The assumed pause duration change as a consequence of language shift in reading was confirmed only in Russian speakers ($p < .000$). The significant reduction in pause duration when reading first in Mandarin, then in English and finally in native Russian was verified with mean values being 574 ms–536 ms–469 ms respectively. The corresponding values of mean pause duration of Chinese speakers (535 ms in Mandarin – 572 ms in English – 584 ms in Russian), though showing a tendency to elongation, turned out to be insignificant ($p = .331$).

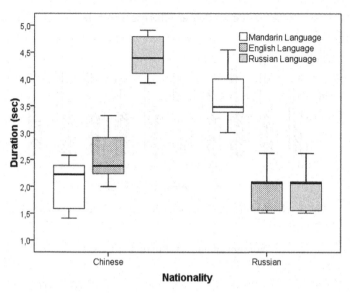

Fig. 2. Time spent for reading the three tales by Chinese and Russian speakers.

The significant change in pause quantity (see Fig. 3, Fig. 4) was revealed both in Chinese and Russian speakers' reading (F = 57.795; p < .000 and F = 49.281; p < .000 respectively). The multiple comparisons between various pairs of languages in each nationality group demonstrated the following difference/absence of difference in pause numbers:

Chinese speakers (see Fig. 3): the number of pauses is significantly larger when reading in Russian compared to reading in native Mandarin (p < .000); significantly larger when reading in Russian compared to reading in English (p. < 000). However, the quantity of pauses in reading in Mandarin and English was not proved to be distinctive (p = .451).

Russian speakers (see Fig. 4): the number of pauses is significantly larger when reading in Mandarin compared to reading in native Russian (p < .000); significantly larger when reading in Mandarin compared to reading in English (p. < 000). However, the quantity of pauses in reading in Russian and English was not proved to be distinctive (p = .216).

Thus, reading in typologically different language causes difficulty in terms of pause quantity for both Chinese speakers (when they read in Russian) and Russian speakers (when they read in Mandarin). In the meantime, reading in English by speakers from Russia and China in terms of pause quantity per tale resembles their native languages.

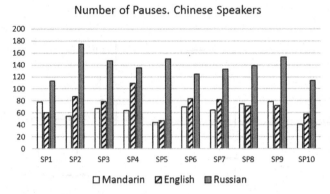

Fig. 3. Number of pauses in each tale read by Chinese speakers.

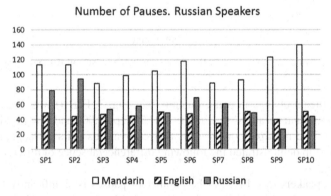

Fig. 4. Number of pauses in each tale read by Russian speakers.

Eventually, when we integrate the features found both in temporal and pitch changes registered in code switching from the tone language to the intonation ones, we can state with confidence that the transition is demanding and strenuous in both respects, calling for a greater articulation effort and time control, just as accurate lexically relevant pitch configurations proved to be challenging in reading the Mandarin text for the Russian learners. The latter also tend to adapt the Mandarin foot and IP structures to bring them closer to the Russian ones. That accounts for a greater number of feet with a smaller number of syllables in the Mandarin text read by the Russian learners.

4   Conclusion and Discussion

Mandarin prosody is known to be processed in the two hemispheres of the brain: the left one is specialized for lexical tones, while the right one caters for the overall prosodic sentence shape according to the syntactic, pragmatic and emotional-expressive connotations of discourse. It is in the latter domain that prominence-lending accents create major rhythm units of feet and IPs, common with intonation languages. Natural speech corpus analysis, Kratochvil argued, evidenced the connection between lexical tones and their realization in running speech due to prominence. Kratochvil called the phenomenon "secondary modifications": lexical tones acquire higher peaks or lower troughs on account of their intonation prominence, which is also associated with amplitude and time changes [12].

However, although there are common major rhythm categories which Mandarin shares with intonation languages, structurally they may be different in length measured by the number of syllables: the feet and especially IPs are longer in Mandarin. Previous research evidenced slower tempo of the Chinese speaking and reading in English [4, 20]. The relevant features were the length of 'between-pause chunks', longer pauses and longer syllable durations.

Alongside with typological differences determined by syllable-based and accent-based nature of Mandarin vs. English comparison, our preliminary study revealed the fact that in their first language reading Mandarin speakers' tempo, as measured by syllable duration, is normal [20]. We could, therefore, suggest that the Mandarin slow-down could be interpreted as a code-switching effect between Mandarin and English. In the current study we made the code-switching task still more complicated by recording multilinguals in three languages within one session with an aim of looking for the prosodic mechanism of transitions across the three languages, based on the performances of Chinese and Russian subjects. Here we could compare their first, second and third languages' temporal and pitch characteristics.

Both the Mandarin and the Russian learners found the code-switching task challenging, which they indicated by slowing down the tempo through the increase of the global time spent on second and third languages' readings. Besides, the Mandarin subjects increased pitch values at the onset of the English text higher than in their first language; still higher are the pitch values for the Russian text, both at the beginning and at the end.

Segmentation of discourse into shorter IPs delimited by longer pauses proved to be the code-switching effect common for both language groups. The results suggest slowing down word-for-word processing of L2 and L3 texts in reading. The most dramatic effect was evidenced by language shift from Russian to Mandarin for the Russian learners and from Mandarin to Russian for the Chinese. The Russian-English shift was not categorical, it could be called gradient.

Thus, by comparing first, second and third language data we could assess the nature of code-shifting effect expressed in duration and pitch values of successive readings. Of particular contrast is the transition between the tone language and intonation language values in the reset area. The difference between the English and the Russian languages is more gradient than categorical: in overall time, for instance, there is no distinction between English and Russian for the Russian learners.

The results of the present study:

- are relevant for integrating approaches based on different dimensions into prosodic typology,
- may help us to achieve a better understanding of brain-related mechanism in code-switching,
- may have applications in multilingual teaching of the Russian and Chinese languages.

Concerning the necessity of developing fluency in both Mandarin and Russian one could find the common practice of learning lists of separate Mandarin words detrimental to connected speech rules, such as tone cohesion in Mandarin and reduction in Russian. Methods of teaching fluent English evidenced by the present study proved to be more successful, and could be recommended for application in teaching the other two languages. That might also facilitate understanding the connection of major rhythm structures with semantic-syntactical composition of discourse.

Further research perspective: more detailed response to the necessity of code-switching (language or dialect shift) in natural conversation, specified for Chinese speakers' regional affiliation, gender, age, proficiency in L2 and L3 and the interlocutor's language.

References

1. Antipova, A.M.: Rhythmic-intonational system of the English language. Higher school, Moscow (1982). (in Russian)
2. Beckman, M.E., Venditti, J.J.: Tone and intonation. In: Hardcastle, W.J., Laver, J., Gibbon, F.E. (eds.) The Handbook of Phonetic Sciences, 2nd edn., pp. 603–652. Wiley-Blackwell, Chichester (2013)
3. Boersma, P., Weenink, D.: Praat: doing phonetics by computer [Computer program]. Version 5.3.80 (2015). http://www.praat.org/. Retrieved 05 April 2015
4. Chen, H.C., Wang, Q.: The effects of Chinese learners' english acoustic-prosodic patterns on listeners' attitudinal judgements. The Southeast Asian J. Eng. Lang. Stud. **22**(2), 91–108 (2018)
5. Crystal, D.: A Dictionary of Linguistics and Phonetics, 6th edn., pp. 82–83. Blackwell Publishing, Oxford (2008)
6. Dauer, R.M.: Phonetic and phonological components of language rhythm. In: Proceedings of the 11th International Congress of Phonetic Sciences, pp. 447–450. Tallinn: Academy of Sciences of the Estonian S.S.R. (1987)
7. Fletcher, J.: The prosody of speech: timing and rhythm. In: Hardcastle W.J., Laver, J., Gibbon, F.E. (eds.) The Handbook of Phonetic Sciences, Second edition, pp. 523–602. Wiley-Blackwell, Chichester (2013)
8. Gandour, J.T.: Neural substrates underlying the perception of linguistic prosody. Tones and Tunes, vol. 2: Experimental Studies in Word and Sentence Prosody, pp. 3–25. Mouton de Gruyter, Berlin (2007)
9. Grabe, E., Low, E.L.: Durational variability in Speech and the Rhythm Class Hypothesis. Papers in Laboratory Phonology 7. C. Gussenhoven, N. Waner (eds). pp. 515–546. Mouton de Gruyter, Berlin (2002)
10. Gussenhoven, C.: The phonology of tone and intonation. Cambridge University Press, Cambridge (2005)
11. Kohler, K.: Rhythm in speech and language. A new research paradigm. Phonetica **1–2**(66), 29–45 (2009)
12. Kratochvil, P.: Intonation in Beijing Chinese. In: Hirst, D., Cristo, A.D. (eds.) Intonation Systems: A Survey of Twenty Languages, pp. 417–431. Cambridge University Press, Cambridge (1998)
13. Low, E.-L.: The rhythmic patterning of English(es): Implications for pronunciation teaching. In: Reed, M., Levis, J.M. (eds.) The Handbook of English Pronunciation, pp. 125–138. Wiley Blackwell, Chichester (2015)

14. Nolan, F., Asu, E.L.: The pairwise variability index and coexisting rhythms in language. Phonetika **66**, 64–77 (2009)
15. Potapova, R.K., Potapov, V.V.: Speech Communication: from sound to utterance. Languages of Slavic Culture, Moscow (2012). (in Russian)
16. Potapova, R.K., Potapov, V.V.: Language, Speech. Personality. Languages of Slavic Culture, Moscow (2006). (in Russian)
17. Rumyantsev, M.K.: Phonetics and phonology of modern Chinese. East-West, AST (2007). (in Russian)
18. Shevchenko, T.I.: Social differentiation of English pronunciation. Higher school, Moscow (1990). (in Russian)
19. Shevchenko, T.I., Sadovnikova, N.A., Sibileva, L.N.: Rhythm and sense of discourse prosody: Cognitive approach and statistics. Bull. Moscow State Linguistic Univer. **1**(634), 175–187 (2012). (in Russian)
20. Shevchenko, T., Sokoreva, T.: Cognitively challenging: language shift and speech rate of academic bilinguals. In: Karpov, A., Potapova, R. (eds.) SPECOM 2020. LNCS (LNAI), vol. 12335, pp. 500–508. Springer, Cham (2020). https://doi.org/10.1007/978-3-030-60276-5_48
21. Sokoreva, T.V., Shevchenko, T.I.: Interaction of regional and age factors in rhythmical and temporal characteristics in American speech. Bull. Moscow State Linguistic Univ. **1**(740), 155–164 (2016). (in Russian)
22. Shu-hui, P., Chan, M.K.M., Tseng, C.-Y., Huang, T., Lee, O.J., Beckman, M.E.: Towards a Pan-Mandarin system for prosodic transcription. In: Jun, S.-A. (ed.) Prosodic Typology: The Phonology of Intonation and Phrasing, pp. 230–270. Oxford University Press, Oxford (2005)
23. Tepperman, J., Nava, E.: Long-distance rhythmic dependencies and their application to automatic language identification. In: Proc. Interspeech 2011, pp. 1061–1064. Communication Association, Florence, Italy (2011)
24. Wichmann, A.: Functions of intonation in discourse. In: Reed, M., Levis, J.M. (eds.) The Handbook of English Pronunciation, pp. 175–189. Wiley Blackwell, Chichester (2015)
25. Zadoenko, T.P.: Rhythmic organization of the Chinese flow of speech. Science, Moscow (1980). (in Russian)
26. Zav'yalova, V.L.: Sound system of English in Eastern Asia: Conception of regional phonetic variation. PhD. Vladivostok (2018). (in Russian)

Increasing the Precision of Dysarthric Speech Intelligibility and Severity Level Estimate

Mohammad Soleymanpour[1]([✉]), Michael T. Johnson[1], and Jeffrey Berry[2]

[1] University of Kentucky, Lexington, KY 40506, USA
{m.soleymanpour,mike.johnson}@uky.edu
[2] Marquette University, Milwaukee, WI 53201, USA
jeffrey.berry@marquette.edu

Abstract. Dysarthria is a speech disorder often characterized by slow speech with reduced intelligibility. Automated assessment of the severity-level and intelligibility of dysarthric speech can improve the efficiency and reliability of clinical assessment as well as benefit automatic speech recognition systems (ASR). However, in order to evaluate them, there are not sentence-level severity and intelligibility label. We only have access to speaker-per-level severity and intelligibility labels. This is a problem as dysarthric talkers might be able to produce some intelligible utterances due to frequent use and short utterances. Therefore, label based analysis might not be very accurate. To address this problem, we explore methods to estimate the severity-level and speech intelligibility in dysarthria given discrete speaker-level labeling in the training set. To accomplish this, we propose a machine learning based method using one-dimensional Convolutional Neural Networks (1-D CNN). The TORGO dataset is used to test the performance of the proposed method, with the UASpeech dataset used for Transfer learning (TL). To evaluate, an Averaged Ranking Score (ARS) and intelligibility probability distribution are used. Our findings demonstrate that the proposed method can assess speakers based on severity-level and intelligibility to provide a more granular analysis of factors underlying speech intelligibility deficits associated with dysarthria.

Keywords: Dysarthria · Intelligibility assessment · Dysarthric speech severity · Convolutional Neural Network · Transfer learning

1 Introduction

Dysarthria is motor speech disorder, often caused by traumatic injury or neurological disfunction, that decreases speech intelligibility through slow or uncoordinated control of speech production muscles [1]. People with moderate and severe levels of dysarthria may be less able to communicate with others through speech due to poor intelligibility [2].

Dysarthria severity-level is conventionally assessed clinically using subjective assessments of neuromuscular function during both speech and non-speech tasks. Standardized testing procedures, such as the Frenchay Dysarthria Assessment (FDA) [3] and

© Springer Nature Switzerland AG 2021
A. Karpov and R. Potapova (Eds.): SPECOM 2021, LNAI 12997, pp. 670–679, 2021.
https://doi.org/10.1007/978-3-030-87802-3_60

the Speech Intelligibility Test (SIT) [4], find common clinical use and prescribe methods for the auditory-perceptual assessment of speech intelligibility [5, 6]. These tests are often time-consuming to implement clinically and some approaches suffer from a lack of intra-rater reliability, due to the subjective nature of these tools [7]. Automated assessment of dysarthria severity-level and speech intelligibility could improve both the efficiency and reliability of clinical assessment. This has led researchers to investigate systems to automatically evaluate these dimensions in dysarthria.

Prior research has investigated automatic assessment of dysarthria severity level and speech intelligibility [8–10]. Automatic Speech Recognition based models have been applied to evaluate dysarthric speech intelligibility [10–12]. K. Gurugubelli et al. have proposed perceptually enhanced single frequency cepstral coefficients (PE-SFCC) as a new perceptually feature representation to assess dysarthric speech [13]. A non-linguistic method of dysarthria severity level has also been presented using audio descriptor, traditional musical-related features [14].

Since the suprasegmental characteristics such as pause occurrence, pause and phonemes duration, speaking rate and f0 decline and overall energy degradation vary across the dysarthric talkers with different degrees of severity and typical talkers, we aim to assess sentence-level dysarthria severity [15–21]. Sentence-level dysarthria severity has been done using Bidirectional Long Short-term Memory BLSTM (BLSTM), in which each sentence is classified into intelligible and non-intelligible groups [22]. Another research [23] has investigated using different DNN frameworks such as CNN and long short-term memory network (LSTM) with MFCC feature to classify dysarthria. In [24], sentence-level features are proposed to capture abnormal variation in the prosodic, voice quality and pronunciation aspects of pathological speech. A final intelligibility decision is made using feature-level fusions and subsystem fusion.

One of the problems in building automatic assessment models is the lack of severity-level and intelligibility labels for individual spoken utterances. Existing dysarthria datasets typically contain only severity-level and intelligibility labels per each speaker. This assumes that all sentences spoken by a speaker have the same degree of dysarthria. However, there is often a varying level of intelligibility in reality. This problem motivated us to use a regression approach to estimate a continuously-valued level of intelligibility.

In this work, we propose using a CNN-based model to automatically analyze dysarthria severity-level and speech intelligibility. Studies shows that one dimensional CNN would perform better over 2-D CNN with limited one-dimensional data [25]. The main dataset used here is TORGO, described in more detail in Sect. 3.1. The features used to represent speech are Mel Frequency Cepstral Coefficients (MFCCs) due to its potential to capture the global spectral envelope characteristics of speech and results of previous studies [23, 24]. Initially, we train the model with four groups of dysarthria severity levels. After this, the model is trained based on speech intelligibility labels. Unlike most of previous works, we use a regression approach to estimate a continuously-valued level of intelligibility rather than applying a simple classification structure. We believe that this approach will enable a more granular assessment of speech, which may be more informative to clinicians.

2 Methodology

We propose a new approach to automatically estimate dysarthria severity and speech intelligibility at a finer-grained level than that given by the dataset labels.

2.1 Model and Experiments

A one-dimensional CNN-based model is used in the proposed approach. Figure 1 shows the model applied for both tasks, containing three 1D-CNN layers, each followed by dropout and maxpooling layers. After the last convolutional layer, two fully connected layers are added for dysarthric severity-level analysis. However, only one fully connected layer is used in the intelligibility detection task. The convolutional layers attempt to capture the local characteristics, while the maxpooling layers reduce the dimensionality. Dropout is also used to avoid overfitting.

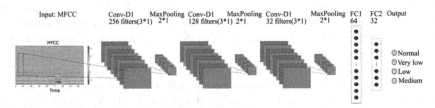

Fig. 1. Block diagram of the proposed architecture.

CNN-based models generally need a large amount of data to capture the varieties between groups. Transfer Learning (TL) is applied to reduce the effect of speaker variability and better learn the spectral features. In addition, since we are using a leave-one-speaker-out classification procedure, training is likely sensitive to the groups with a small number of individuals, in particular the group with only two people (one male and one female). To apply TL, the model is first trained on the UASpeech dataset and then the first three convolutional layers are saved when the model approaches optimal performance. These saved layers are used as initial layers to train the model on the TORGO dataset.

To evaluate, we used the Averaged Ranking Score (ARS) metric as an estimate of dysarthria severity for an individual utterance. For each sentence in the test set, four probabilities were generated to show the probability of the given sentence for each severity level. The final severity level was estimated as the weighted mean from these probabilities, using numeric values 1, 2, 3, and 4 for Normal, Very Low, Low, and Medium dysarthria levels. For example, if the model for a sentence generates the probability of 0.19, 0.15, 0.20, 0.46 for the four classes, respectively, the ranking score would be calculated as follows:

$$ARS = 1 \times 0.19 + 2 \times 0.15 + 3 \times 0.20 + 4 \times 0.46 = 2.93. \tag{1}$$

With this approach, an overall dysarthria severity-level can be obtained for each sentence in the range between 1 to 4. This can be interpreted on a continuous scale with 1 indicating normal and 4 indicating medium severity dysarthria. The average ranking score for each unseen speaker can then be computed across all utterances, allowing us to estimate both the average severity-level of that speaker and variance across utterances.

To estimate overall intelligibility on a per-speaker basis, the posterior probabilities from the intelligibility classifier for each of a speaker's utterances can be used to create a probability distribution for that speaker. The mean of the distribution can be used as an indicator the speaker's overall intelligibility, while the variance can provide information about the consistency of intelligibility.

3   Experimental Setup

We implemented three experiments to evaluate the effectiveness of the proposed method. In the first experiment, the dysarthria estimation model is trained based on four categories of dysarthric speech severity, including Normal, Very Low, Low, and Medium. Before training the model on TORGO, the model was trained on UASpeech.

In the second experiment, we excluded the normal category of speech and only used the dysarthric speech contained in TORGO. Because the categories of normal speech and very low dysarthric speech are quite similar, this allowed us to better distinguish the severity level of dysarthric speech in mild cases. The experimental setup and evaluation were the same as the previous method except for the number of classes. The categories of Very Low, Low, and Medium speech were used with the same ranking factors of 2, 3 and 4, respectively, as used in the first experiment.

The third experiment focused on estimating overall speaker intelligibility from the results of a binary intelligibility classification task. All speech was divided into two groups, intelligible and non-intelligible, which were used to train the model for binary speech intelligibility detection. This model was then used to generate the posterior intelligibility probabilities for individual utterances in the dataset, and the distribution of intelligibility probabilities across utterances from each speaker were used to assess the speaker's overall intelligibility profile.

For both dysarthria severity detection and speech intelligibility, the leave-one-speaker-out cross-validation procedure is applied. Before training, one speaker was kept out for test as unseen speaker and the remaining were used to train the model. 39 MFCC features were extracted for a window of 25 ms with 10 ms overlap. Utterances are zero-padded to the maximum length of training data. For training the model, all words and sentences were exploited whereas only sentences were used for testing. In addition, both words and sentences in UASpeech were used to train the initial TL model.

As described previously, three convolutional layers along with fully connected layers construct the main part of the model. The convolutional layers contain 256, 128 and 32 filters respectively with a kernel length of 3. Each of the convolutional layers is followed by a maxpooling of size 2×1. The coefficient of the dropout layer is 20 percent. The number of neurons in the fully connected layers are 64 and 32, respectively, for the severity detection task and 32 for the one connected layer in the intelligibility task. The optimizer algorithm is Adam with a small learning rate of 0.0001. The number of outputs is four for the dysarthria severity detection and two for intelligibility detection.

3.1 Dataset

The main dataset used in this work is TORGO [26], containing 8 dysarthric speakers and 7 normal speakers. This dataset consists of non-word, short words, restricted and non-restricted sentences. Two types of microphones were used in this dataset, a head-mounted microphone as well as an array of 8 microphones placed approximately 61cm from each speaker. Dysarthric speakers are categorized into three dysarthria severity levels, Very Low, Low, and Medium and into two groups for intelligibility, intelligible and non-intelligible. The standardized Frenchay Dysarthria Assessment by a speech-language pathologist was applied to investigate the motor functions of each subject [26].

The UA-Speech dataset is used for Transfer Learning. This dataset includes speech recordings of 15 dysarthric speakers and control speakers. Each speaker was asked to read utterances containing 10 digits, 26 radio alphabet letters, computer commands, common words from the Brown corpus of written English, and uncommon words from children's novels selected to maximize phone-sequence diversity. All participants produced the same 765 words in citation form, 455 of them unique. Speech was recorded with an eight-channel microphone array at a sampling rate of 48 kHz, but in this experiment only one channel is used. Speakers are categorized in four groups of very low, low, middle and high by five native English listeners for each speaker [27].

4 Results and Discussion

The ARS results for each unseen speaker for the first and second experiments are shown in Table 1. For the first experiment each speaker ranged between 1 (normal) and 4 (medium severity).

Results for the dysarthria severity estimation indicate ARS severity rankings which were ordered in severity and mostly in the expected range. Although the ARS among the normal speakers was lower than those of the very low severity dysarthria group, this was by a small margin with most speakers in the normal category having an ARS close to 2 rather than 1, as might be anticipated. To see the difference between these two groups, Fig. 2 depicts a box plot of dysarthria severity levels. It can be observed that although the mean values of the ARS are similar between the normal and very low category speakers, there is a significant greater variance for the talkers with dysarthria across individual utterances, indicating that talkers with very low severity-level produced some utterances ranking as high as medium severity talkers.

Table 1. Averaged ranking score for the first experiment.

Severity Level	Intelligibility Category	Speaker ID	ARS	
			Exp. 1 4-levels	Exp. 2 3-levels
Normal	Intelligible	FC01	1.98	
		FC02	1.95	
		FC03	1.89	
		MC01	1.98	-
		MC02	1.97	
		MC03	1.77	
		MC04	2.12	
Very low		F03	2.26	2.63
		F04	2.52	2.46
		M03	2.21	2.60
Low		F01	2.97	3.20
		M05	3.85	3.91
Medium	Unintelligible	M01	3.81	3.91
		M02	3.72	3.70
		M04	3.5	3.72

The last column in Table 1 shows the scores for the second experiment which estimated severity for only the dysarthric speech. The results for most speakers align with their labeled severity level; however, the M05 speaker is labeled as having a "low" severity level but the severity estimation for both of the experiments suggests a more severe level, on par with the "medium" speakers.

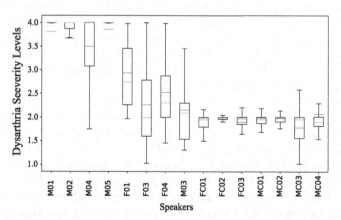

Fig. 2. Box plot of dysarthric severity level for the first experiment. The red line shows the median of the ranking scores, the dashed green line shows the mean (or averaged ranking score), and the box indicates the 25th to 75th percentile range. (Color figure online)

Figure 3 shows the results of the second experiment. This allows visualization of the relative severities as well as the variance within individual utterances. Comparing this to Fig. 2, excluding normal speech from training gives more precise severity estimates and less variation.

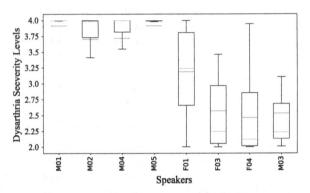

Fig. 3. Box plot of dysarthric severity level, with normal speech excluded. The red line shows the median of the ranking scores, the dashed green line shows the mean (or averaged ranking score), and the box indicates the 25th to 75th percentile range. (Color figure online)

In the third experiment, we analyzed the intelligibility probability distribution across individual utterances. Figure 4 shows the histogram of intelligibility probabilities calculated on individual utterances for select speakers with a bin-size of 0.05. The difference in the mean values of intelligibility is clear between the intelligible and unintelligible groups.

Moreover, with the "intelligible" speakers, "normal" talkers have almost no low-intelligibility utterances but "very low" severity speakers have numerous occurrences of such utterances. There are also notable differences in the distribution patterns across speakers. The extent of this variation suggests the possibility that an utterance-by-utterance assessment of intelligibility variance could be clinically useful, insofar as it could be used as a basis for a phonetic level characterization of the sound contrasts contributing to the intelligibility deficits [28].

To the best of our knowledge, this is the first work to continuously assess dysuria severity level and intelligibility, so there is not a direct way to compare these results with the findings of other works reported in classification metrics. For instance, Bhat et al. [22] have reported an average accuracy of 98.2 percent using BLSTM with transfer learning and balance data. Joshy et al. [23] reported the classification accuracy of 96.1 for TORGO dataset. As we mentioned in introduction section, existing dysarthria datasets like TORGO and UA-Speech contain only severity-level and intelligibility labels per each speaker, lacking severity-level and intelligibility labels for individual spoken utterances. This assumes that all sentences spoken by a speaker have the same degree of dysarthria which is not always correct in reality. Therefore, the classification metrics reported in these papers are based on this assumption.

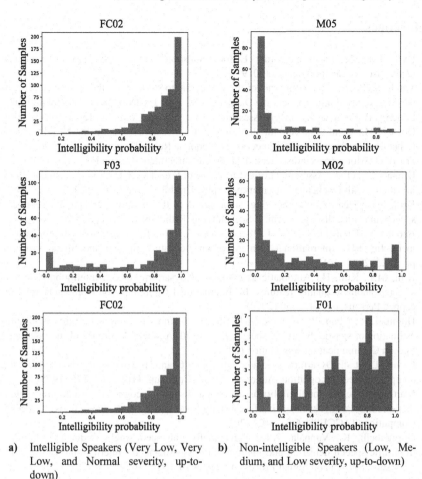

a) Intelligible Speakers (Very Low, Very Low, and Normal severity, up-to-down)

b) Non-intelligible Speakers (Low, Medium, and Low severity, up-to-down)

Fig. 4. The intelligibility probability histogram for each unseen speaker with a bin-size of 0.05.

5   Conclusion

This paper describes an automatic assessment of per-utterance dysarthria severity-level and speech intelligibility of individual speakers using a 1D-CNN-based model with Transfer learning. The models were trained with discrete dysarthria severity-level and speech intelligibility labels per speaker but used weighted probabilities of the discrete categories across individual utterances and speakers to estimate continuously-valued severity and intelligibility assessment metrics. Our findings demonstrate substantial variations across utterances and speakers for multiple dysarthria severity-levels and support the idea that this type of approach could be an effective tool to support objective clinical assessment of dysarthria.

Acknowledgments. This work was supported by National Institutes of Health under NIDCD R15 DC017296-01.

References

1. Duffy, J.R.: Motor speech disorders E-Book: Substrates, differential diagnosis, and management. Elsevier Health Sciences (2019)
2. Mitchell, C., et al.: Interventions for dysarthria due to stroke and other adult-acquired, non-progressive brain injury. Cochrane Database Syst. Rev. 1, CD002088–CD002088 (2007)
3. Enderby, P.: Frenchay dysarthria assessment. Br. J. Disord. Commun. 15(3), 165–173 (1980)
4. Dorsey, M., et al.: Speech intelligibility test for windows. Lincoln, NE: Institute for Rehabilitation Science and Engineering at Madonna Rehabilitation Hospital (2007)
5. Freed, D.: Motor speech disorders: diagnosis and treatment. Nelson Education (2011)
6. Hijikata, N., et al.: Assessment of dysarthria with Frenchay dysarthria assessment (FDA-2) in patients with Duchenne muscular dystrophy. Disabil. Rehabil., 1–8 (2020)
7. Kent, R.D.: Hearing and believing: some limits to the auditory-perceptual assessment of speech and voice disorders. Am. J. Speech Lang. Pathol. 5(3), 7–23 (1996)
8. Berisha, V., Utianski, R., Liss, J.: Towards a clinical tool for automatic intelligibility assessment. In: IEEE International Conference on Acoustics, Speech and Signal Processing, pp. 2825–2828 (2013)
9. Kim, M.J., Kim, H.: Automatic assessment of dysarthric speech intelligibility based on selected phonetic quality features. In: International Conference on Computers for Handicapped Persons, pp. 447–450 (2012)
10. Hummel, R., Chan, W.-Y., Falk, T.H.: Spectral features for automatic blind intelligibility estimation of spastic dysarthric speech. In: Twelfth Annual Conference of the International Speech Communication Association (2011)
11. Ferrier, L., et al.: Dysarthric speakers' intelligibility and speech characteristics in relation to computer speech recognition. Augment. Altern. Commun. 11(3), 165–175 (1995)
12. Martínez, D., et al.: Intelligibility assessment and speech recognizer word accuracy rate prediction for dysarthric speakers in a factor analysis subspace. ACM Transactions on Accessible Computing (TACCESS) 6(3), 1–21 (2015)
13. Gurugubelli, K., Vuppala, A.K.: Perceptually enhanced single frequency filtering for dysarthric speech detection and intelligibility assessment. In: International Conference on Acoustics, Speech and Signal Processing, pp. 6410–6414 (2019)
14. Bhat, C., Vachhani, B., Kopparapu, S.K.: Automatic assessment of dysarthria severity level using audio descriptors. In: International Conference on Acoustics, Speech and Signal Processing, pp. 5070–5074 (2017)
15. Looze, C.D., et al.: Pitch declination and reset as a function of utterance duration in conversational speech data. In: Sixteenth Annual Conference of the International Speech Communication Association (2015)
16. Teodorescu, H.-N.: Pitch analysis of dysarthria helps differentiating between dysarthria mechanisms. Bull. Integr. Psychiatry 84(1), 89–95 (2019)
17. Feenaughty, L., et al.: Speech and pause characteristics in multiple sclerosis: a preliminary study of speakers with high and low neuropsychological test performance. Clin. Linguist. Phon. 27(2), 134–151 (2013)
18. Allison, K.M., Yunusova, Y., Green, J.R.: Shorter sentence length maximizes intelligibility and speech motor performance in persons with dysarthria due to amyotrophic lateral sclerosis. Am. J. Speech Lang. Pathol. 28(1), 96–107 (2019)
19. Patel, R.: Prosodic control in severe dysarthria. J. Speech Lang. Hear. Res. 45, 858–878 (2002)
20. Bunton, K., et al.: Perceptuo-acoustic assessment of prosodic impairment in dysarthria. Clin. Linguist. Phon. 14(1), 13–24 (2000)

21. Bigi, B., et al.: A syllable-based analysis of speech temporal organization: a comparison between speaking styles in dysarthric and healthy populations. In: Sixteenth Annual Conference of the International Speech Communication Association, vol. 1, pp. 2977–2981 (2015)
22. Bhat, C., Strik, H.: Automatic assessment of sentence-level dysarthria intelligibility using BLSTM. J. Sel. Top. Sign. Process. **14**(2), 322–330 (2020)
23. Joshy, A.A., Rajan, R.: Automated dysarthria severity classification using deep learning frameworks. In: European Signal Processing Conference, pp. 116–120 (2021)
24. Kim, J., et al.: Automatic intelligibility classification of sentence-level pathological speech. Comput. Speech Lang. **29**(1), 132–144 (2015)
25. Kiranyaz, S., et al.: 1D convolutional neural networks and applications: a survey. In: Mechanical Systems and Signal Processing, vol. 151, p. 107398 (2021)
26. Rudzicz, F., Namasivayam, A.K., Wolff, T.: The TORGO database of acoustic and articulatory speech from speakers with dysarthria. Lang. Resour. Eval. **46**(4), 523–541 (2012)
27. Kim, H., et al.: Dysarthric speech database for universal access research. In: Ninth Annual Conference of the International Speech Communication Association (2008)
28. Kent, R.D., et al.: Toward phonetic intelligibility testing in dysarthria. J. Speech Hear. Disord. **54**(4), 482–499 (1989)

Articulation During Voice Disguise: A Pilot Study

Lauri Tavi[1,2(✉)], Tomi Kinnunen[2], Einar Meister[3],
Rosa González-Hautamäki[2,5], and Anton Malmi[4]

[1] School of Humanities, University of Eastern Finland, Joensuu, Finland
lauri.tavi@uef.fi
[2] School of Computing, University of Eastern Finland, Joensuu, Finland
tomi.kinnunen@uef.fi
[3] School of Information Technologies, Tallinn University of Technology,
Tallinn, Estonia
einar@ioc.ee
[4] Institute of Estonian and General Linguistics, University of Tartu, Tartu, Estonia
anton.malmi@ut.ee
[5] Electrical and Computer Engineering, National University of Singapore,
Singapore, Singapore
rgonza@cs.uef.fi

Abstract. Speakers can conceal their identity by deliberately changing their speech characteristics, or disguising their voices. During voice disguise, speakers alter their normal movements of the articulators, such as tongue positions, according to a predetermined strategy. Even though technology for accurate articulatory measurements has existed for years, few studies have investigated articulation during voice disguise. In this pilot study, we recorded articulation of four speakers during regular and disguised speech using electromagnetic articulography. We analyzed imitation of foreign accents as a voice disguise strategy and utilized functional t-tests as a novel method for revealing articulatory differences between regular and disguised speech. In addition, we evaluated discovered articulatory differences in the light of the performance of an x-vector-based automatic speaker verification system.

Keywords: Electromagnetic articulography · Functional data analysis · Foreign accent · Voice disguise · Automatic speaker verification

1 Introduction

The human voice is extremely variable and flexible. Besides *inter-speaker* variation due to organic differences in vocal production systems, speakers can modify the content and the style of speaking flexibly, leading to *intra-speaker* speech variation of a given individual. Some of this variation is intentional and controllable by the speaker (*e.g.* whispering to enable private communication) while others are either automatic (*e.g.* Lombard reflex) or only weakly controllable

© Springer Nature Switzerland AG 2021
A. Karpov and R. Potapova (Eds.): SPECOM 2021, LNAI 12997, pp. 680–691, 2021.
https://doi.org/10.1007/978-3-030-87802-3_61

by the speaker (*e.g.* accent of one's mother tongue) [7]. Depending on whether the focus is on speech *science* or speech *technology*, these variations are either the main object of interest or an unwanted nuisance. For automatic speaker verification (ASV), speech variation cause problems as it lowers even the state-of-the-art ASV system's accuracy [6]. Consequently, some speakers might try to exploit this deficiency by deliberately varying their speech features, or disguising their voices.

One highly common form of variation is caused by *foreign accent*, which yields various phonetic changes in speech. Second language (L2) learners also tend to use phonemic substitution rules of their first language (L1), leading to *foreign-accented* speech that shares properties of both L1 and L2 [5]. Consequently, characteristics of L2 speech can be imitated as a form of voice disguise [13].

Human speech is essentially multimodal – it can be analyzed and represented in terms of articulatory, acoustic and perceptual attributes. While research in speech technology and acoustic phonetics has benefited from large acoustic datasets available in many languages, acoustic–articulatory speech data is much scarcer [4]. The study of speech production involves tracking the displacement, timing, and coordination of *articulators* (such as the tongue, the jaw and the lips) inside and outside of the vocal tract. Traditional *imaging* techniques such as x-ray, ultrasound and magnetic resonance imagining have been used to visualize articulators. These methods can be restrictive since speech is characterized by fast, complex and small 3-dimensional movements of the articulators. Our focus, *electromagnetic articulography* (EMA), is a 3D measurement technique designed to track and record articulatory movements during speech production. EMA is an invasive method but it allows precise tracking of the position and orientation of miniaturized sensor coils attached to various places on the articulators. An articulograph records articulator trajectories directly without the need for additional image processing techniques. However, disadvantages of EMA are rather heavy post-processing of raw data and time-consuming data collection.

In this study, we recorded L1 and imitated L2 speech from Finnish and Russian speakers using EMA and explored 1) articulatory differences between L1 and imitated L2 speech and 2) the effect of imitated L2 accent on a modern deep speaker embedding ASV. The latter was tested using an x-vector-based ASV system. In former, we utilized *functional data analysis* (FDA), particularly *functional t-tests*. Although there are existing EMA corpora in English (e.g. MOCHA-TIMIT [24], mngu0 [19], USC-TIMIT [12]), Mandarin-accented English [8], German [2] and Italian [4], the authors are unaware of previous EMA corpora available for the combination of Finnish and Russian. To our knowledge, this study is also the first data collection that addresses voice disguise through EMA measurements.

2   Phonology of Finnish and Russian

Finnish and Russian have numerous differences in their phonological systems [21], which can affect production and imitation of Russian and Finnish accents.

For instance, Finnish has eight vowels, which can occur short or long, while Russian has six. Finnish has also 18 diphthongs that are absent in Russian.

Russian sibilants and affricates can be particularly problematic for Finns. Additionally, in Russian most of the consonants can be *palatalized* in various positions. In palatalization, the place of articulation is higher and more anterior [10]. Palatalized consonants acquire a secondary place of articulation on the *palatal region* of the mouth while preserving the primary constriction. Unlike Finnish, Russian has phonological oppositions in palatalized and non-palatalized consonants, where the usage of palatalization changes the meaning (e.g. мать,, 'mother' and мат, 'check mate'). However, most Finnish consonants can occur either short or long. Furthermore, typical structure of a Finnish syllable is CV(C/V), but Russian syllables can contain one vowel and up to five consonants, e.g. a word взгляд, 'a look'.

Another essential difference between Finnish and Russian phonology is the position of word stress. In Russian, word stress can occur in any syllable resulting in stress-based minimal pairs, e.g. му'ка, 'flour' and мука, 'torment'. In Finnish, the first syllable of a word is always stressed.

3   EMA Data Collection

3.1   Corpus Design

We collected simultaneous recordings of read-aloud speech and articulatory movements tracked by EMA (EMA Wave by Northern Digital) for Finnish and Russian. The collected speech included three different speaking styles from each speaker: speech in native (L1) and non-native (L2) Finnish or Russian, and while imitating Finnish or Russian foreign accent (IL2) in the L1. In the IL2, participants were asked to imitate the foreign accent without further instructions or practise. In this study, we focused on the differences between the L1 and the IL2.

Overall, we collected data from six speakers including one Finnish female, one Finnish male, one Russian female, and three Russian male speakers. To have a balanced set of native languages and sexes for this pilot study, we focused on four speakers summarized in Table 1. Even though four participants can be considered as a limited number of speakers, EMA studies commonly have few participants: for example, [4,12,19] and [24] collected articulatory data from four or less speakers. Yet, we do *not* claim generality of the presented findings beyond the collected material – rather, the point is to demonstrate specific elicited speech variations in terms of articulatory changes, and to address the potential ramification of such changes on ASV performance.

To this end, read-aloud speech is elicited by Finnish and Russian versions of Aesop's Fable 'The north wind and the sun'. Additionally, we collected prompt sentences (ca 70 sentences in both languages) involving most frequent vowels, diphthongs, and consonants in different segmental and prosodic contexts, and text material contained spontaneous speech, elicited by a story telling task based

Table 1. Speaker information. L2 and IL2 (i.e. "imitated L2") levels are self-evaluated by each speaker using categories of low–middle–high and 1–5 scale, respectively. For the IL2 level, the higher the number, the better the imitation.

Speaker	Sex	Age	L1	L2	L2 level	IL2 level
FIN_M_001	Male	28	Finnish	Russian	High	5
FIN_F_001	Female	22	Finnish	Russian	High	2
RUS_M_003	Male	30	Russian	Finnish	Middle	3
RUS_F_001	Female	18	Russian	Finnish	Middle	3

on a cartoon. The prompted sentences and spontaneous speech based on a cartoon were excluded from analyses, but the prompted sentences were included in ASV evaluation (see 4.2).

3.2   Recording Procedure

Recording setup included AKG C444 close-talking microphone (headset), the EMA system and a Windows desktop computer running the EMA recording software. Sensor positions are presented in Table 2.

Table 2. Sensor positions. Left and right are in relation to the experimenter.

Sensor number	Position
10–12	Biteplate (in a triangular shape)
9	Nose
7 and 8	Left and right mastoid
6	Jaw (behind the lower lip, on the gum)
3 and 5	Left and right lateral
4	Laminal
1 and 2	Tongue dorsum and anteo-dorsum

Articulatory movements and the audio signal were recorded simultaneously at sampling frequencies 200 Hz and 22.05 kHz, respectively. The recording procedure included the following steps: 1) gluing reference sensors 9,8 and 7, 2) a *bite-plate* recording, 3) gluing sensors 1–6, 4) doing a palate trace recording, where participant produced syllables *ta*, *ti*, *tu*, *ka*, *ki* and *ku*, and 5) performing a rehearsal run and 6) finally recording itself. The prompt items were displayed on sheets of paper. Figure 1 shows the EMA system and sensors 1–5 glued on the tongue.

Since EMA recordings involve physically attaching sensors on participants, our study underwent detailed ethical and safety evaluation by the Ethics Committee of the University of Eastern Finland. In January 2020, the Committee gave a supporting statement for the proposed research.

Fig. 1. Example of attached sensors on the tongue.

4   Methods

4.1   Functional Data Analysis

FDA involves a set of statistical methods, which are extended from their traditional counterparts to function of time [18]. First step in FDA is to transform discrete data points, such as EMA sensor movements, to continuous curves using basis functions. We used B-splines, a common choice with non-periodic signals. This step also smooths data trajectories, which helps to avoid overfitting [20].

The occurrence of palatalization, which requires tongue dorsum raising and fronting, is one of the major differences between Finnish and Russian accents (see Sect. 2). Therefore, we focused on *sagittal plane* of *tongue dorsum* (TD) sensor which tracks down–up and front–back movement of TD. TD sensor curves were constructed from each word of Finnish and Russian versions of 'The north wind and the sun'. However, words that contained less than 40 measured samples were excluded. This resulted in a total of 531 curves for both the sensor directions.

The second step in FDA is to perform statistical analysis on continuous curves. For comparing the mean TD sensor curves between the L1 and the IL2, we used *functional* t-tests, extensions of classical t-tests, where the t-statistic is defined as

$$T(t) = \frac{|\bar{x}_1(t) - \bar{x}_2(t)|}{\sqrt{\frac{1}{n_1}\text{Var}[x_1(t)] + \frac{1}{n_2}\text{Var}[x_2(t)]}}. \tag{1}$$

In Eq. 1, $\bar{x}$s are the curve means and $\text{Var}(x$s$)$ are the curve variances for the L1 and the IL2. In functional t-tests, the maximum value of $T(t)$ is used as a test statistic, which critical value is found using permutation test. The labels of the curves are randomly shuffled and the maximum value of $T(t)$ is recalculated with new labels. As a result, a null distribution is constructed. In this study, FDAs were carried out using R [16] package fda [17]. WebMAUS [9] and Praat [3] were used to time-align the word segments. Following list will summarize the FDA procedure used in this study:

1. First, TD sensor trajectories were recorded from four participants, who read 'The north wind and the sun' once with their native language and once while imitating a foreign accent.
2. Then, the sensor trajectories were segmented into individual word trajectories using word-level annotations and converted to smoothed functions (i.e. curves) using B-splines.
3. Finally, the means of the word curves of the two speaking styles were compared using functional t-tests; four functional t-tests were performed separately on each participants' speaking styles.

4.2 Automatic Speaker Verification

We considered the effects of accent imitation in an ASV experiment. The L1 read speech from the "The north wind and the sun" was used to train the speaker model (enrollment). In the evaluation phase, we considered gender-dependent trials, same speaker's (*target*) trials correspond to the speaker's audio samples from the prompted sentences, and for different speaker's (*nontarget*) trials the prompted sentences read by the other speaker. The test audio samples average duration is 3.5 s. The trials with L1 are considered as the baseline case, and the effect of including IL2 trials as the disguise case. The number of trials is shown in Table 3.

Table 3. The number of ASV trials per speaking style.

Speaking style	Sex	Target	Non-target
L1	Male	294	294
IL2	Male	302	302
L1	Female	296	296
IL2	Female	296	296

In the experiments, we used an x-vector based ASV system [23]. The system is based on a speaker-discriminative training using deep neural network architecture [22]. The ASV system correspond to the implementation in Kaldi-toolkit [14] with the pre-trained model recipe [1] from augmented VoxCeleb 1 and 2 data [11]. The speech samples were turned from stereo to mono samples by selecting the left channel, and then downsampled to 16 kHz. The feature extraction configuration consists of 23-dimensional Mel-frequency cepstral coefficients (MFCCs) extracted from 25 ms long frames every 10 ms. A cepstral mean subtraction was applied over a 3-second sliding window and energy-based speech activity detection was used to filter out the non-speech frames. A probabilistic linear discriminant analysis (PLDA) [15] was used for scoring the extracted 512-dimensional x-vectors representation of the trial's samples. The x-vectors were centred, whitened, and unit length normalized.

5 Results

5.1 Functional T-Tests

Functional t-tests were applied to check for significant differences between the mean values of the TD sensor curves in the L1 and the IL2. Although the curves contained variation caused by producing different words, the same speech material (i.e. 'The north wind and the sun') was used in comparison of the L1 and the IL2. Consequently, the mean word curves of each speaker's speaking styles show average TD movements revealing plausible articulatory changes related to the IL2.

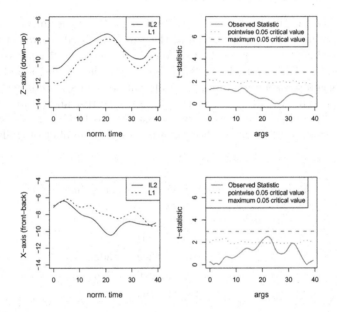

Fig. 2. FIN_F_001's mean TD movements in the IL2 and the L1 (left panels) and functional t-tests (right panels). The panels on the left show the down–up (above) and the front–back (below) movements.

Figures 2–5 show the mean curves in the L1 and the IL2 and the results of the functional t-tests for all four speakers. Comparing T-statistic to conservative reference line, *maximum critical value*, no statistically significant differences between the TD positions in the L1 and the IL2 were found for female speakers (see Figs. 2 and 4). However, male speakers' front–back TD curves differed statistically significantly between the speaking styles. These differences are at strongest approximately on the left and on the right side of the curve, while in the middle they are at weakest. This indicates that especially the beginning and the ending of the words are pronounced differently, i.e. the position of TD in the IL2 is more anterior compared to the TD position in the L1. The down–up sensor

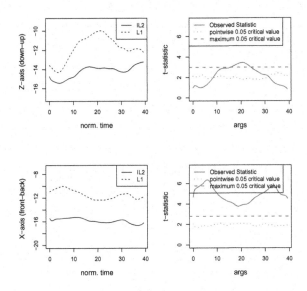

Fig. 3. FIN_M_001's mean TD movements in the IL2 and the L1 (left panels) and functional t-tests (right panels). The panels on the left show the down–up (above) and the front–back (below) movements.

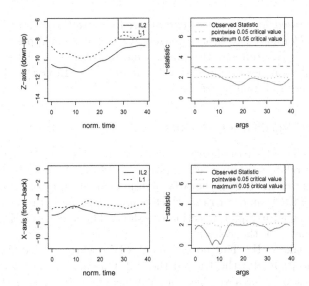

Fig. 4. RUS_F_001's mean TD movements in the IL2 and the L1 (left panels) and functional t-tests (right panels). The panels on the left show the down–up (above) and the front–back (below) movements.

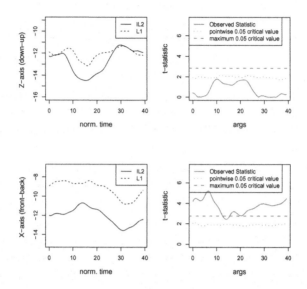

Fig. 5. RUS_M_003's mean TD movements in the IL2 and the L1 (left panels) and functional t-tests (right panels). The panels on the left show the down–up (above) and the front–back (below) movements.

movements showed no differences expect briefly at the middle of FIN_M_001's mean curves. Compared to other speakers, FIN_M_001's TD positions between the L1 and the IL2 differed the most, which most likely related to his self-evaluated imitation performance (i.e. 5 out of 5; see Table 1), which was the highest number of all four speakers.

5.2 Speaker Verification Results

We tested whether the articulatory differences found between the L1 and the IL2 (see Sect. 5.1) relate to the x-vector system (see Sect. 4.2) performance. Table 4 shows the effect of the IL2 on the ASV system as percentage of *equal error rates* (EERs). The EER is an error rate, which equates false acceptance rate and false rejection rate by adjusting a detection threshold. The higher the EER value, the lower the accuracy of the system.

Female speakers' IL2 had no effect on ASV accuracy since the EERs (%) were the same (0.34) for the L1 and the IL2. On the contrary, male speakers' IL2 caused a strong negative effect on ASV accuracy, increasing the EER (%) from 3.06 to 11.59. The same conclusions can be drawn from Fig. 6, where density distributions of genuine trials ASV scores for each speaker are presented. Because male speakers' IL2 yields lower scores compared to their L1 especially for FIN_M_001, the results from the ASV tests support the articulatory data indicating that tongue fronting was used as an effective voice disguise technique.

Table 4. Gender-dependent equal error rates for the L1 and the IL2.

Sex	Speakers	L1–EER(%))	IL2–EER(%)
Male	FIN_M_001 & RUS_M_03	3.06	11.59
Female	FIN_F_001 & RUS_F_01	0.34	0.34

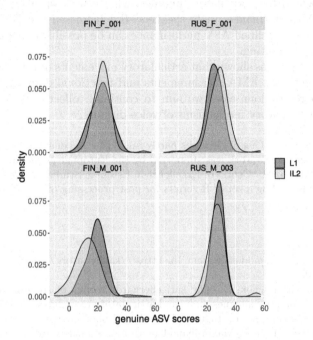

Fig. 6. Density distributions of ASV target scores for each speaker. The lower the ASV scores, the less confident the system is that the speakers are the same.

6   Conclusion

In this study, we investigated articulation of Finnish and Russian speakers during imitation of a foreign accent. The imitation of a foreign accent served as a method of voice disguise. We recorded tongue movements during regular and disguised speech using EMA and performed functional t-tests on the trajectories of TD movements. Additionally, we recorded the audio signal and tested the effect of voice disguise on an x-vector based ASV system. Using these two approaches, it was possible to investigate actual articulatory changes during different speaking styles and the effectiveness of the changes against an x-vector-based ASV system.

Functional t-tests revealed significant differences in the front–back TD movements between male speakers' L1 and IL2; for female speakers, there were no significant differences in the TD positions. Although male speakers had different L2 and IL2, they both fronted their tongues during voice disguise. Fronting the tongue can occur during palatalization, which can be an expected when imitating (palatalized) Russian accent as a Finnish L1 speaker. However, also the Russian speaker's average TD position was more at front while imitating Finnish accent. In this case, the type of imitated Finnish feature was less clear.

The articulatory differences were also evaluated in the respect of ASV performance. The EERs(%), which were calculated using the x-vector-based ASV-system, supported the articulatory findings: while female speakers' IL2 had no effect on ASV performance, male speakers' IL2 increased the EERs(%) from 3.06 to 11.59. The declined ASV performance can be possibly explained by male speakers' tongue fronting.

This pilot study has shown that articulatory movements during voice disguise can be revealed using EMA measurements and functional data analysis. When the Covid-19 restrictions ease, we aim to continue collecting EMA data and reveal more articulatory mechanisms of voice disguise.

Acknowledgments. This project was partly funded by Academy of Finland (project 309629). Einar Meister's work was supported by the European Regional Development Foundation (the project "Centre of Excellence in Estonian Studies"). We thank Fabian Tomaschek for providing a set of R scripts for post processing of raw EMA data.

References

1. VoxCeleb Xvector models system 1a. https://kaldi-asr.org/models/m7. Accessed 10 April 2021
2. Arnold, D., Tomaschek, F.: The karl eberhards corpus of spontaneously spoken southern german in dialogues-audio and articulatory recordings. In: Kleber, C.D.F. (ed.) Tagungsband der 12. tagung phonetik und phonologie im deutschsprachigen raum, pp. 9–11. Ludwig-Maximilians-Universitat Munchen. Retriev (2016)
3. Boersma, P., Weenink, D.: Praat: doing phonetics by computer [computer program] (2020). https://praat.org
4. Canevari, C., Badino, L., Fadiga, L.: A new italian dataset of parallel acoustic and articulatory data. In: Sixteenth Annual Conference of the International Speech Communication Association (2015)
5. Fan, J., Yongbing, L.: The impact of l1 negative phonological transfer on l2 word identification and production. Int. J. Linguist. **6**(5), 37–50 (2014)
6. González Hautamäki, R., Hautamäki, V., Kinnunen, T.: On the limits of automatic speaker verification: explaining degraded recognizer scores through acoustic changes resulting from voice disguise. J. Acoust. Soc. Am. **146**(1), 693–704 (2019)
7. Hansen, J.H., Bořil, H.: On the issues of intra-speaker variability and realism in speech, speaker, and language recognition tasks. Speech Commun. **101**, 94–108 (2018)
8. Ji, A., Berry, J.J., Johnson, M.T.: The electromagnetic articulography mandarin accented english (ema-mae) corpus of acoustic and 3d articulatory kinematic data. In: 2014 IEEE International Conference on Acoustics, Speech and Signal Processing (ICASSP), pp. 7719–7723. IEEE (2014)
9. Kisler, T., Reichel, U., Schiel, F.: Multilingual processing of speech via web services. Comput. Speech Lang. **45**, 326–347 (2017)
10. Malmi, A., Lippus, P.: Keele asend eesti palatalisatsioonis. J. Est. Finno-Ugric Linguist. **10**(1), 105–128 (2019)

11. Nagrani, A., Chung, J.S., Xie, W., Zisserman, A.: Voxceleb: large-scale speaker verification in the wild. Computer Science and Language, p. 101027 (2019)
12. Narayanan, S., et al.: Real-time magnetic resonance imaging and electromagnetic articulography database for speech production research (tc). J. Acoust. Soc. Am. **136**(3), 1307–1311 (2014)
13. Neuhauser, S.: Voice disguise using a foreign accent: phonetic and linguistic variation. Int. J. Speech Lang. Law **15**(2), 131–159 (2008)
14. Povey, D., et al.: The kaldi speech recognition toolkit. In: IEEE 2011 Workshop on Automatic Speech Recognition And Understanding (ASRU). IEEE Signal Processing Society, Hawaii, US (2011)
15. Prince, S.J.D., Elder, J.H.: Probabilistic linear discriminant analysis for inferences about identity. In: Proceedings of ICCV, pp. 1–8. Rio de Janeiro, Brazil (2007). https://doi.org/10.1109/ICCV.2007.4409052
16. R Core Team: R: A language and environment for statistical computing (2020). https://www.R-project.org/
17. Ramsay, J., Graves, S., Hooker, G.: fda: Functional data analysis. R package version 5.1.5.1. (2020). https://CRAN.R-project.org/package=fda
18. Ramsay, J.O., Silverman, B.W.: Functional data analysis (2nd edition). Springer Verlag, NY (2005)
19. Richmond, K., Hoole, P., King, S.: Announcing the electromagnetic articulography (day 1) subset of the mngu0 articulatory corpus. In: Twelfth Annual Conference of the International Speech Communication Association (2011)
20. Schötz, S., Frid, J., Gustafsson, L., Löfqvist, A.: Functional data analysis of tongue articulation in palatal vowels: Gothenburg and malmöhus swedish/i: y: 0ff. In: Proceedings of Interspeech, vol. 2013 (2013)
21. de Silva, V., Ullakonoja, R.: Introduction: russian and finnish in contact. In: de Silva, V., Ullakonoja, R. (eds.) Phonetic of Russian and Finnish: General Description of Phonetic Systems: Experimental Studies on Spontaneous and Read-aloud Speech, pp. 15–20. Peter Lang, Frankfurt a. M. (2009)
22. Snyder, D., Garcia-Romero, D., Povey, D., Khudanpur, S.: Deep neural network embeddings for text-independent speaker verification. In: Proceedings of INTERSPEECH, pp. 999–1003. Stockholm, Sweden (2017)
23. Snyder, D., Garcia-Romero, D., Sell, G., Povey, D., Khudanpur, S.: X-vectors: robust DNN embeddings for speaker recognition. In: IEEE International Conference on Acoustics, Speech and Signal Processing (ICASSP), pp. 5329–5333. IEEE, Calgary, AB, Canada (2018)
24. Wrench, A.: The mocha-timit articulatory database (1999). www.cstr.ed.ac.uk/research/projects/artic/mocha.html

Improvement of Speaker Number Estimation by Applying an Overlapped Speech Detector

Elena Timofeeva[1], Elena Evseeva[1], Valeriia Zaluskaia[1,2(✉)],
Vlada Kapranova[1,2], Sergei Astapov[1], and Vladimir Kabarov[1]

[1] ITMO University, Kronverksky prospekt 49A, St. Petersburg 197101, Russia
`eptimofeeva@itmo.ru`
[2] Speech Technology Center, Vyborgskaya Embankment 45,
St. Petersburg 194044, Russia
`zaluskaya@speechpro.com`

Abstract. The efficiency of modern automatic meeting transcription suffers from the problem of speaker diarization during overlapping speech segments. The problem can be tackled if each segment of a recording could be marked with the number of active speakers. However, overlapped speech recordings with more than two simultaneous speakers serve as a weak point for speaker number estimation. The problem becomes even more complicated if the speaker number estimation system tends to far-field recordings of multiple speakers acquired by a distant microphone. In this paper we propose an improvement for speaker number estimation by combining it with an overlapped speech detector. In our approach we apply different configurations of speaker number estimation and overlapped speech detector models trained and evaluated on the AMI and LibriSpeech datasets with several types of signal representation. Experimental evaluation based on fusion of models yields an improvement of speaker number estimation performance of up to 10% based on the F1-score metric compared with base speaker number estimation model.

Keywords: Speaker number estimation · Overlapped speech detection · Convolutional neural networks · Recurrent neural networks · Fusion

1 Introduction

Speaker diarization [3,4,7,20] to this day forward challenges speech processing, specifically automatic speech recognition and speaker diarization. The destructive effect is greatest in scenarios, where several speakers are simultaneously active [2,9,10]. The main problem is posed by overlapped speech, which naturally occurs during the majority of natural conversations. Such overlaps in speech segments negatively affect the quality of speaker diarization. One of the solutions lies in estimating the number of simultaneous speakers, which serves as a label for overlapped speech and a marker for further speech processing. By marking

A. Karpov and R. Potapova (Eds.): SPECOM 2021, LNAI 12997, pp. 692–703, 2021.
https://doi.org/10.1007/978-3-030-87802-3_62

each input frame with the number of active speakers, the performance of speech processing can be improved by emphasizing recording segments produced by only one active speaker. This allows to model speakers' voice profiles and, thus, improve speaker diarization.

An overlapped speech detector (OSD) is often applied to detect segments of a recording containing overlapped speech. OSD can be used to improve speaker diarization [5,6,13,21,22]; also this method is promising in terms of integration as an intermediate step after performing Voice Activity Detection (VAD) [15]. To determine overlapped speech in a specific short segment of an audio recording, certain models are proposed in the latest research [2,8,12].

In this paper we study several approaches to improving speaker number estimation quality. One of the approaches proposed in the literature involves directly estimating the number of active speakers using the 7th component of the Mel-frequency cepstral coefficients (MFCC) [16]. Several deep learning architectures are also studied [18,19]. Speech segments longer than one second (five seconds being our main focus) are analyzed. This puts a limit to some potential practical applications with the processed segment length of less than one second. If the speaker counting engine operates on long segments, the probability of having overlapped speech in each segment increases, and this can affect the quality of the created voice profiles [2]. On the other hand, processing short speech segments (shorter than one second) does not yield adequate voice profile generation by the state-of-the-art approaches. Therefore, a lower limit of speech segment length equal to one second is justified in this case.

The studied solution targets at most 10 simultaneous speakers, which is far beyond the number of regular human detectability. The speaker number estimation model is trained on segments divided into short signal frames from 100 ms to 1000 ms [2], which makes the models more attractive for improving speaker diarization. The optimal parameters for the convolutional layers of the Convolutional Recurrent Neural Network are investigated and specified [11].

Previously referenced works in the field mainly consider the synthetic mixtures of different speaker recordings acquired by a close-talk microphone and thus obtain permissible results for active speaker number estimation systems. However, estimation quality decreases with the attempts to adapt the system to recordings acquired by a far-field microphone. Segments of overlapped speech, where more than two speakers are active, are an obstacle for systems that estimate active speaker quantities. The performance of such systems in far-field acquired speech was investigated in [10], where the AMI and CHiME-6 corpora were applied for training and evaluation. The results for detecting 2, 3, 4+ simultaneous speakers are shown to be low compared to detecting 0 and 1 speakers. We focus specifically on real life recordings of natural conversations acquired in the far-field.

From this point forward in this paper, we define the operation of speaker number estimation as Speaker counting (SC). The study proposes that combining SC and OSD models can improve the SC performance at the weak points of overlapping speech, which is the determination between 2, 3, and 4+ speakers. This is achieved through fusion of model outputs and yields an increase in quality of up to 10% based on the F1-score metric compared with the baseline SC model.

2   Proposed Approach

This section considers the architectures of SC and OSD models. The principles of fusing the models and the motivation behind the process are addressed.

2.1   Motivation

The proposed method aims at estimating the number of simultaneous speakers by combining two separate systems. The first system is a model that solves the classification problem directly for the number of speakers in a given segment. The architecture of this model is based on existing propositions in this field [19]. The second model is similar in architecture (see Fig. 1), but employs a different type of markup as input and is designed to solve a related problem—overlapped speech detection. Thus, the approach of reusing the architecture for several related tasks with subsequent fusion is being investigated.

We apply the following logic in fusing SC and OSD. Suppose that the SC model does not perform well for speaker number classes of 2, 3 and 4+ simultaneous speakers, but the binary problem of overlap/non-overlap detection yields sufficient estimation quality. If SC is inclined to underestimate the number of speakers, marking most samples as 1 speaker activity, then, fusing SC with OSD one can exclude samples with 1 speaker and, accordingly, eliminate the classification error for samples with more than 2 speakers estimated as 1 speaker. On the other hand, SC may overestimate the number of speakers. Then, by fusing the models and excluding examples containing 2–4+ speakers, the estimation of 0 and 1 speakers can be improved.

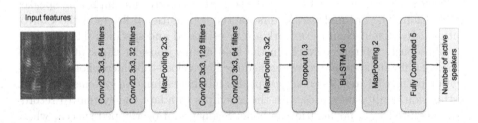

Fig. 1. Speaker Counter and Overlapped Speech Detector model architecture.

2.2   Speaker Counter

From a theoretical perspective, estimation of the number of concurrent speakers is closely related to a more difficult problem of speaker identification, which is one of the speaker diarization tasks. Intuitively, if a system is able to determine "who speaks when", then it is also able to count the number of active speakers. This is a "counting by detection" strategy. In this paper, we estimate the number of audio sources instead of counting these sources after identification, and implementing the "direct count estimation" strategy [19].

We define the speaker number estimation task as a classification task with 5 classes, from 0 to 4 concurrent speakers, while the same architecture as in [18] is applied. The solution is based on the application of several Deep Neural Network (DNN) models, the schematic of which is presented in Fig. 1. These models consist of several Convolutional layers, MaxPooling layers, and a Bi-LSTM layer with 40 hidden units for processing input features, and a fully connected layer for classification by the number of active speakers. The Softmax function is used for the output layer and, as a result, the prediction is specified by the highest probability of the output distribution.

2.3   Overlapped Speech Detector

The Overlapped Speech Detector (OSD) aims to detect the overlapped speech segments in a multi-speaker conversation. This system serves as a binary classifier for overlapped speech. The markup for this task is produced based on the speaker number markup from the SC task:

$$l_{OSD} = \begin{cases} 0, & l_{SC} \in \{0,1\}, \\ 1, & l_{SC} \in \{2,3,4+\}, \end{cases} \tag{1}$$

where l_{OSD} is an OSD segment class label and l_{SC} is a SC segment class label entry. The model presented in Fig. 1 is then trained with OSD labels. The features of short audio segments serve as inputs to this model, while the output is the layer with the probabilities of overlapped speech for the corresponding segment for each class: overlap/non-overlap. The winning label is specified by highest probability.

2.4   Fusion

In this subsection the fusion between the SC and OSD models is described. The diagram of SC and OSD fusion is presented in Fig. 2. The basic principle of the proposed fusion method lies in manipulating the SC class probabilities based on the decision of OSD. If the decisions of the two models are logically in concurrence with one another, the SC probabilities are increased by applying a weight coefficient α. On the other hand, if the decisions are not in concurrence, the SC probabilities are reduced. Namely, if OSD defines a speech segment as non-overlap, then this estimate is used to increase SC probabilities for labels 0 and 1 (no active speaker, one active speaker), and reduce the probabilities for labels 2, 3, and 4+ (2, 3, 4+ speakers active). For estimated overlapped speech segments, the SC probabilities for labels 2, 3, 4+ are increased, and reduced for labels 0 and 1. Thus, the fusion process is defined by the following equation:

$$P_{fusion} = \begin{cases} P_{SC}(l_{SC}) + \alpha \cdot (1 - P_{SC}(l_{SC})), & \hat{l}_{OSD} = 0, \hat{l}_{SC} \in \{0,1\}, \\ P_{SC}(l_{SC}) - \alpha \cdot P_{SC}(l_{SC}), & \hat{l}_{OSD} = 1, \hat{l}_{SC} \in \{0,1\}, \\ P_{SC}(l_{SC}) - \alpha \cdot P_{SC}(l_{SC}) & \hat{l}_{OSD} = 0, \hat{l}_{SC} \in \{2,3,4+\}, \\ P_{SC}(l_{SC}) + \alpha \cdot (1 - P_{SC}(l_{SC})), & \hat{l}_{OSD} = 1, \hat{l}_{SC} \in \{2,3,4+\}, \end{cases} \tag{2}$$

where $P_{SC}(l_{SC})$ are the probabilities of l_{SC} labels for a given signal segment, $\hat{l}_{OSD}$ and $\hat{l}_{SC}$ are the OSD and SC estimates, and α is the weight coefficient. The value for α is chosen equal to 0.5 as it yields the best results of fusion. The presented approach is shown to improve SC on overlapped speech segments in the following section.

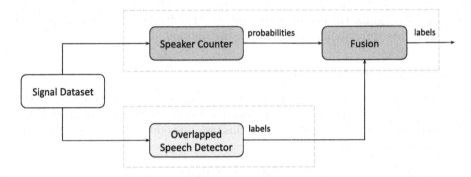

Fig. 2. Diagram of Speaker Counter and Overlapped Speech Detector fusion.

3   Experimental Evaluation

This section considers the datasets and signal representations applied to model training and evaluation. The process of label generation from the original annotation is described, and dataset augmentation required for statistical significance is addressed. In the second part of this section the SC experiments are described and the obtained results are presented and discussed.

3.1   Dataset Description

For experimental evaluation we choose two SC models trained on different datasets to estimate the model performance on both a synthetic dataset (the LibriSpeech corpus) and a real-life dataset (the AMI Corpus). The SC model that demonstrates the best performance with the OSD model (the one trained on the AMI dataset) is applied for fusion. We use two different acoustic features for the SC and OSD models to identify the features most suitable for the corresponding tasks. All these experiments are evaluated on segments of length of 1 s extracted from the AMI test set. For training and evaluation of SC and OSD models we use the AMI corpus and LibriSpeech free access databases.

The LibriSpeech corpus [14] is based on audiobooks; it contains several data sets of a total of 1000 h of read English speech recordings. Combining recordings of various speakers from this database allows to create a huge number of samples for training the models. The AMI Meeting Corpus consists of over 100 h of group meeting recordings, mostly consisting of four people in a group. The meetings were recorded in several instrument halls using various microphone arrays, lapel microphones and headsets. Along with real-life meetings, the corpus contains a significant portion of scenario-driven simulated meetings designed to evoke a wide range of realistic behaviors. The speakers' activity in the recordings was annotated using data from close-talk microphones.

The data for the AMI Meeting Corpus [1] was collected in instrumented meeting rooms constructed at the University of Edinburgh (U.K.), Idiap (Switzerland), and the TNO Human Factors Research Institute (The Netherlands). While the three meeting rooms feature the same types of equipment, there are some minor differences in the ways they were configured, i.e., the distribution of sensors and other equipment and furniture, different room impulse responses, etc. The names of the recordings are formed from the first letter of the facility, the second letter corresponds to the scenario/non-scenario of the recording, so the following names were obtained: ES, EN, IS, IN, TS, TN.

To divide the AMI corpus into train and test sets, we use the division offered by the authors of the corpus (Table 1). The authors of the corpus attempted to create such sets, that they would preserve a variety of speakers and acoustic conditions, while including recordings with different speakers in the training and test sets. In this work, we apply the set distribution that contains scenario and non-scenario meeting recordings.

Table 1. Distribution of recordings in the AMI corpus.

Set	Duration, h	Speakers	Recordings	Rooms					
				ES	EN	IS	IN	IB	TS
Train	70	136	118	44	12	28	10	0	24
Development	15	29	26	8	0	4	0	6	8
Test	15	24	24	8	4	4	0	0	8
Total	100	189	168	60	16	36	10	6	40

To create the markup for the SC model, we use the manual annotations of the AMI corpus, which consist of specified speech segments for each speaker. In order to get the markup by the number of active speakers, the beginnings and ends of all speech segments are combined into one set and then sorted; this sorted set is divided into subsegments, and for each subsegment the number of simultaneous speakers is calculated using the original annotation. Thus, we achieve the subsegments situated between every speaker overlap, with a number of simultaneous speakers specified per each subsegment, including silence.

To train the models we generate a synthetic dataset based on the LibriSpeech corpus and apply data augmentation to the AMI corpus. The LibriSpeech clean-360 dataset is selected, applying the same strategy as proposed in [16]. For the AMI corpus, we apply data augmentation to undermine the poor distribution among class instances. The problem is that the AMI corpus has a poor class balance in the recordings: only 1 speaker is active 70% of the time, about 13% of the time 0 and 2 speakers are active, and only 3% of the time 3 and 4 speakers are active. To prepare data for training we apply augmentation to the AMI Array1-01 signal, i.e., the first channel of Array1. To augment one recording, we use other recordings from the same room only. A segment is randomly selected, where 1 or 2 speakers are active. This segment is added to a segment with a lack of class balance (a segment with 1 or 2 active speakers). Then, the file markup is updated and the procedure is repeated. Thus, we improve the balance of classes for 2, 3 and 4 active speakers by 14%, 9% and 3%, respectively.

3.2   Signal Representations

The input representations, such as the Short-Time Fourier Transform (STFT) and Mel Frequency Cepstral Coefficients (MFCC), are typically chosen for speech applications [2,19]. The STFT spectrogram is popular amongst other features applied in machine learning based speech analysis algorithms. In some solutions, the STFT spectrogram is used in a frame-by-frame manner, while in others the signal spectrogram is used as a 2D matrix, whether the complex or real spectra are used. Mel-frequency cepstral coefficients (MFCCs) have also become the norm in speech processing systems. MFCCs can be applied to larger signal analysis segments with less detail on the frequency side compared to STFT frames, thus reducing the dimensionality of a model.

In our experiments we compute the input features with the following signal representations. For STFT a frame length of 25 ms with a hop size of 10 ms is applied. The magnitude STFT spectrum is computed using the Hann windowing function and has the dimensions of $201 \times N$, where N is the number of frames equal to 100 for the length of the processed segment equal to 1 s. MFCC is computed for 40 coefficients based on STFT with the same parameters and has the dimensions of $40 \times N$. Before feature extraction all the input files are implicitly re-sampled to 16 kHz sampling rate. During the experiments, the models are trained separately on each of the considered signal representations, i.e., magnitude spectra and MFCC are not applied in conjunction.

3.3   Experimental Results

In the first experiment, we compare SC models trained on two different datasets: AMI and LibriSpeech (Table 2). The F1-score metric is chosen to determine the quality of models as it is applicable in conditions when the data is poorly balanced by classes, and allows to get an objective assessment of the quality of the models. The experiment regards the quality of the SC model tested on the far-field AMI testset. For this experiment we apply two SC models trained on the synthetic LibriSpeech train set and on the augmented AMI Array1-01 train set, respectively. SC trained on the augmented AMI Array1-01 set demonstrates better results for all classes. According to class 0 precision results, the model trained on LibriSpeech tends to greatly underestimate the number of speakers, marking the segments with active speakers as silence. The AMI-trained model does not have this problem. Improvements in metrics are visible across most classes. Compared to the Librispeech-trained model, the model trained on the AMI corpus performs better for classes 0–3 according to the f1-score.

Table 2. Results for the SC model trained on two separate training sets.

Class	LibriSpeech			AMI		
	Precision	Recall	F1-score	Precision	Recall	F1-score
0	0.19	0.96	0.31	0.62	0.76	0.68
1	0.68	0.42	0.52	0.74	0.59	0.66
2	0.33	0.03	0.06	0.27	0.39	0.32
3	0.36	0.04	0.07	0.20	0.24	0.22
4+	0.44	0.17	0.25	0.14	0.10	0.11
Weighted	0.53	0.38	0.37	0.59	0.55	0.56

For the second experiment we apply fusion to the SC and OSD model outputs. The SC and OSD models are trained on the AMI dataset, with the segment length being equal to 1 s. Table 3 presents the results for each class as well as their weighted average in the metrics of: accuracy, completeness, and F-measure. The SC model fused with OSD demonstrates a better performance compared with the non-fused SC model. These results show that the classification quality for all classes is increased, in particular for labels 1 and 2 (Fig. 3). The recall metric shows no increase, probably due to the fact that SC is initially efficient in classifying segments with the number of speakers 2+. The recall increases only for the number of speakers equal to 1. This means that SC often overestimates the number of speakers. A noticeable increase occurs in the precision metric, which means that SC has become less deficient on the number of speakers 1, since previously it was inclined to overestimate. The precision confusion matrices before and after fusion are presented in Fig. 4. The matrices show that audio segments with 2, 3 and 4 speakers are classified better by the fused SC model than by the non-fused SC model.

In the third experiment (Table 4), the fusion results for the SC and OSD models trained on different features of the input signal are compared. The experiment results show that the application of STFT features is better suited for speaker counting and overlapped speech detection tasks in our case, since it gives an increase in the quality of both models. The reason behind these results could probably be explained by the fact that the MFCCs are known to perform poorly when used in CNN architectures [17].

General conclusions based on the experimental results are the following. Firstly, the SC model trained on real-life data acquired in the far field yields better results during testing on data acquired in similar conditions than a model trained on synthetic data. Thus, training a synthetic dataset is not representative for applications dealing with real-life data. Secondly, the fusion between the SC and OSD models is proven to benefit speaker number estimation. Thirdly,

Table 3. Speaker Counter and Overlapped Speech Detector fusion results.

Method	Class	Precision	Recall	F1-score
SC	0	0.62	0.76	0.68
	1	0.74	0.59	0.66
	2	0.27	0.39	0.32
	3	0.20	0.24	0.22
	4+	0.14	0.10	0.11
	Weighted	0.59	0.55	0.56
SC+OSD	0	0.62	0.74	0.68
	1	0.78	0.77	0.78
	2	0.40	0.41	0.41
	3	0.30	0.22	0.25
	4+	0.16	0.09	0.12
	Weighted	0.65	0.66	0.66

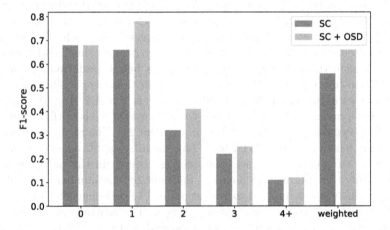

Fig. 3. F1-score fusion result bar for the SC and fused SC+OSD models.

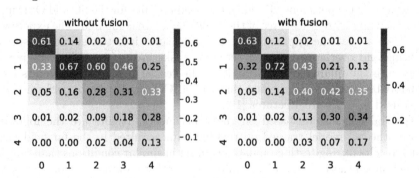

Fig. 4. Confusion matrices for the non-fused and fused SC models.

the question of applying STFT or MFCC features for the tasks of SC and OSD is still debatable due to the specifics of applied datasets and model architectures. Nevertheless, the results obtained are statistically significant since the models are trained and tested on a variety of data recorded by employing different speakers in rooms of different configurations and room impulse responses (see Table 1).

Table 4. SC and OSD results for different signal features.

Method	Precision	Recall	F1-score
SC (mfcc)	0.54	0.53	0.53
SC (stft)	0.59	0.50	0.56
SC (mfcc) + OSD (mfcc)	0.52	0.53	0.52
SC (stft) + OSD (mfcc)	0.55	0.55	0.55
SC (mfcc) + OSD (stft)	0.62	0.63	0.62
SC (stft) + OSD (stft)	0.65	0.66	0.66

4 Conclusion

In this paper we have presented and applied the method to fuse the SC and OSD systems to improve SC performance. A series of experiments employing the SC and OSD models were conducted, which included training on different datasets and applying different signal representation features. It is established that using the augmented AMI data from microphone arrays for training is more efficient in configuring the SC system to estimate the number of simultaneous speakers in a far-field signal than using synthetic mixtures of close-talk microphone recordings. The results of the experiments with different signal representations also show that after using MFCC some information is lost, which affects classification quality. Therefore, STFT features are thought to be more effective than MFCC for the presented system. The results for Speaker Counter appear to be promising, particularly those obtained on real data: scores for each class increase with the F1-score rising by 10%. Future research in this direction includes improving the fused SC and OSD system by training it on more balanced datasets.

Acknowledgments. This research was financially supported by the ITMO University.

References

1. AMI Corpus. https://groups.inf.ed.ac.uk/ami/corpus/. Accessed 10 May 2021
2. Andrei, V., Cucu, H., Burileanu, C.: Overlapped speech detection and competing speaker counting - humans versus deep learning. J. Sel. Topics Signal Process. **13**(4), 850–862 (2019)

3. Astapov, S., Lavrentyev, A., Shuranov, E.: Far field speech enhancement at low SNR in presence of nonstationary noise based on spectral masking and MVDR beamforming. In: Karpov, A., Jokisch, O., Potapova, R. (eds.) SPECOM 2018. LNCS (LNAI), vol. 11096, pp. 21–31. Springer, Cham (2018). https://doi.org/10.1007/978-3-319-99579-3_3

4. Astapov, S., Popov, D., Kabarov, V.: Directional clustering with polyharmonic phase estimation for enhanced speaker localization. In: Karpov, A., Potapova, R. (eds.) SPECOM 2020. LNCS (LNAI), vol. 12335, pp. 45–56. Springer, Cham (2020). https://doi.org/10.1007/978-3-030-60276-5_5

5. Boakye, K., Trueba-Hornero, B., Vinyals, O., Friedland, G.: Overlapped speech detection for improved speaker diarization in multiparty meetings. In: International Conference on Acoustics, Speech and Signal Processing, pp. 4353–4356 (2008)

6. Boakye, K., Vinyals, O., Friedland, G.: Two's a crowd: improving speaker diarization by automatically identifying and excluding overlapped speech. In: INTER-SPEECH, pp. 32–35 (2008)

7. Bredin, H., Yin, R., Coria, J.C., Gelly, G., Korshunov, P.: Pyannote.audio: neural building blocks for speaker diarization. In: International Conference on Acoustics, Speech, and Signal Processing, pp. 7124–7128 (2020)

8. Bullock, L., Bredin, H., Garcia, P.: Overlap-aware diarization: resegmentation using neural end-to-end overlapped speech detection. In: International Conference on Acoustics, Speech and Signal Processing, pp. 7114–7118 (2020)

9. Charlet, D., Barras, C., Liénard, J.-S.: Impact of overlapping speech detection on speaker diarization for broadcast news and debates. In: International Conference on Acoustics, Speech and Signal Processing, pp. 7707–7711 (2013)

10. Cornell, S., Omologo, M., Squartini, S., Vincent, E.: Detecting and counting overlapping speakers in distant speech scenarios. In: INTERSPEECH (2020)

11. Grumiaux, P.A., Kitic, S., Girin, L., Guérin, A.: Multichannel CRNN for speaker counting: an analysis of performance. arXiv preprint arXiv:2101.01977 (2021)

12. Kunešová, M., Hrúz, M., Zajíc, Z., Radová, V.: Detection of overlapping speech for the purposes of speaker diarization. In: Salah, A.A., Karpov, A., Potapova, R. (eds.) SPECOM 2019. LNCS (LNAI), vol. 11658, pp. 247–257. Springer, Cham (2019). https://doi.org/10.1007/978-3-030-26061-3_26

13. Otterson, S., Ostendorf, M.: Efficient use of overlap information in speaker diarization. In: Workshop on Automatic Speech Recognition & Understanding (ASRU), pp. 683–686 (2007)

14. Panayotov, V., Chen, G., Povey, D., Khudanpur, S.: Librispeech: an ASR corpus based on public domain audio books. In: International Conference on Acoustics, Speech and Signal Processing, pp. 5206–5210 (2015)

15. Sajjan, N., Ganesh, S., Sharma, N., Ganapathy, S., Ryant, N.: Leveraging LSTM models for overlap detection in multi-party meetings. In: International Conference on Acoustics, Speech, and Signal Processing, pp. 5249–5253 (2018)

16. Sayoud, H., Ouamour, S.: Proposal of a new confidence parameter estimating the number of speakers-an experimental investigation. J. Inf. Hiding Multimed. Signal Process. 1(2), 101–109 (2010)

17. Seltzer, M.L., Yu, D., Wang Y.: An investigation of deep neural networks for noise robust speech recognition. In: International Conference on Acoustics, Speech and Signal Processing, pp. 7398–7402 (2013)

18. Stöter, R.-F., Chakrabarty, S., Edler, B., Emanuël, H.: Classification vs. regression in supervised learning for single channel speaker count estimation. In: International Conference on Acoustics, Speech and Signal Processing, pp. 436–440 (2018)

19. Stöter, R.-F., Chakrabarty, S., Edler, B., Emanuël, H.: CountNet: estimating the number of concurrent speakers using supervised learning. Trans. Audio Speech Lang. Process. **27**(2), 268–282 (2019)
20. Tranter, S.E., Reynolds, D.A.: An overview of automatic speaker diarization systems. IEEE Trans. Audio Speech Lang. Process. **14**(5), 1557–1565 (2006)
21. Yoshioka, T., Erdogan, H., Chen, Z., Xiao, X., Alleva, F.: Recognizing overlapped speech in meetings: a multichannel separation approach using neural networks. In: INTERSPEECH, pp. 3038–3042 (2018)
22. Zelenak, M., Hernando, J.: On the improvement of speaker diarization by detecting overlapped speech. VI Jornadas en Tecnología del Habla and II Iberian SLTech Workshop (2010)

Mind Your Tweet: Abusive Tweet Detection

Paras Tiwari[1](✉) and Sawan Rai[2]

[1] Department of Computer Science and Engineering, Indian Institute of Technology
(BHU) Varanasi, Varanasi 221005, India
parastiwari.rs.cse19@iitbhu.ac.in
[2] Department of Computer Science and Engineering, Indian Institute of Information
Technology, Design and Manufacturing, Jabalpur 482005, India
sawanrai@iiitdmj.ac.in

Abstract. The abusive posts detection problem is more complicated
than it seems due to its unseemly, unstructured noisy data and unpredictable context. The learning performance of the neural networks
attracts researchers to get the highest performing output. Still, there
are some limitations for noisy data while training for a neural network.
In our work, we have proposed an approach that considers the assets of
both the machine learning and neural network to get the most optimum
result. Our approach performs with the F1 score of 92.79.

Keywords: Abusive · Lexicon · CNN · LSTM · NB

1 Introduction

Language is a loaded weapon that could harm a person to an unmeasurable
depth. Excessive use of online social platforms led people to be more expressive
as well as aggressive. As per a report published by "ScanSafe" [8], 80% of blogs
contained unethical contents, and 74% included obscene content, abusive languages or images. The impact of these contents on youth has been reported as
more critical than we generally assume. There has been a significant increase in
the number of suicide attempts in adolescences due to the cyberbullying [13].
The percentages of individuals who have experienced cyberbullying at some point
during their lifetime have increased, from 18% in 2007 to 36% in 2016 [22]. Also,
it is expected to continue rising with the extreme popularity and dependency on
social networks and mobile devices by children and teenagers [14].

Online social network (OSN) is a very dense community. Creating a graph
of the OSN, assuming each user as a node and connection between them as an
edge, [3] analysed proximity between the nodes (users) by calculating the average
distance between nodes of OSN as 4.74, proceeding the work [11] from Facebook
research team showed the reduction of maximum distance between nodes to 3.57
in 2016. Among various OSN platforms, we opted for "Twitter", as it is the most
popular online social networking platform for text content sharing [16].

© Springer Nature Switzerland AG 2021
A. Karpov and R. Potapova (Eds.): SPECOM 2021, LNAI 12997, pp. 704–715, 2021.
https://doi.org/10.1007/978-3-030-87802-3_63

The abusive tweets are generally considered as tweets containing any highly offensive words. The structure of abusive tweets is so complicated that labelling them perfectly as abusive or normal, even as a challenge for human interpreters. In this paper we have also discussed various challenges and dimensions for labelling the tweet as abusive or normal.

The remainder of the paper is as follows: Sect. 2 defines the problem, challenges in the problem and contribution of people trying to define the problem; Sect. 3 discusses major contributions made so far in the domain, with the limitations and recognition of implemented technique; Sect. 4 discusses the flow of implemented approach; Sect. 5 describes the dataset used as a sample for abusive tweet; Sect. 6 illustrates the pre-processing steps; Sect. 7 illustrates experiment parameters and compared the performance; Sect. 8 discusses the conclusion and future work of the problem.

2   Abusive Content

In the Oxford dictionary[1], "abusive" is defined as an adjective that is extremely offensive and insulting. However, no precise formal definition has yet given to the "abuse". Even the official law firms do not have any entirely acceptable viable definition of abusive content. As per the domestic violence law of California[2], "abuse" is:

- Physically hurting or trying to hurt someone intentionally or recklessly;
- Making someone reasonably afraid that he or she or someone else is about to be seriously hurt (like threats or promises to harm someone); OR
- Behaviour like harassing, stalking, threatening, or hitting someone, disturbing someone's peace, or destroying someone's personal property.

The abusive tweet detection problem is more complex than it seems due to its inept, unstructured noisy data and unpredictable context. There was a general assumption that a tweet is abusive only if it contains abusive lexicons (either text or emoticons). This assumption is correct, but not always. There are tweets that do not have any direct abusive lexicon but still label as abusive. There are abusive tweets, which instead of using exact abusive lexicons, or special characters or a combination of alphabets and characters, still are contextually abusive.

The complexity increases when we honestly consider the relationship between an offensive tweet and abusive tweet. There are tweets unintended to offend with their text, although some readers might find them abusive, and others may not [27]. For example, "you look like a pathetic idiot tonight, how could you @username"; this statement is offensive but not abusive. We should not ignore the point that even the openness for the content varies from person to person. Some people have thin skin for sarcasm, while some have thick. It led to another open debate to label a statement as offensive; the same statement

---

[1] https://en.oxforddictionaries.com/definition/abusive.
[2] https://www.courts.ca.gov/1258.html.

could be offensive to person A, sarcastic to person B, and normal to person C. Figure 1 demonstrates some original screenshots of the Twitter platform, which validates our assumptions. Even the human interpreter face problem in labelling the statements confidently.

Fig. 1. Sample tweets that might offensive, sarcastic or normal.

In [5], authors proposed a set of 30 features from 3 types of attributes to label any tweet as an aggressor, bully, or spammer. In [4], authors deeply reviewed the linguistic challenges faced in natural language processing for identifying abusive statements due to its time-variant creative and highly ambiguous structure. Very similar in [1], authors studied the high variations in linguistic patterns due to factors like socioeconomic status, geo-location, time and peer network. In proceedings, [12] created a low biased dataset with labels "abusive", "hatespeech", "spam", and "normal". This dataset plays the game changer role in abusive tweet detection. It is a well-known fact that, for appropriate neural network training, a large dataset requires. Any minimal quantity dataset usually suffers from low variance, high bias.

3   Related Work

Lexicon meaning, lexical dependency and contextual dependency are three principal techniques used in abusive tweet detection. Each technique individually is not self-sufficient due to the complicated structure of tweets. Tweets are not only unstructured; they are also unordered. Lexicon meaning based models need a rich dataset of abusive words. Authors in [18] manually created a set of abusive lexicons to generate the set of highly offensive words in Hinglish. Creating a dictionary for all the highly offensive words is not feasible. However, [26] created a dictionary that contained 3000 multi-lingual words, among them 2400 belongs to English, 400 in Japanese, and slightly over 100 words each in Bulgarian, Polish, and Swedish. Still, there could not be a claim that any dictionary includes all the abusive words, and no new abusive word will be in the future. Also, there is no pre-defined state of the art for all the terms to be abusive; it solely depends upon the creativity of users, which evolves with time.

There are also cases when an individual lexicon meaning is not sufficient to detect whether the lexicon used for abusive context or other. For example, if multiple abusive label tweets in the dataset contain the lexicon "sex". It will increase the probability of the tweet being abusive whenever the word "sex" come. However, there could be a tweet when any user tweets to draw awareness towards "sex education". As per the dependency on the individual lexicon's meaning, the probability of a tweet about sex education will be miss-label as abusive. So we should also need to take care of multi-unit lexicons and their interdependency. Considering such cases authors in [24] modelled three-level hierarchical classifications, as the top two levels use Naïve Bayes (NB) machine learning model for lexicon dependency followed by the last level consists of a hybrid of NB and decision tree technique. In [30], authors considered the grammatical relationship among lexicons considering lexicon dependency feature. N-gram model is one of the most popular machine learning lexical dependency approaches for abuse detection [19]. As [21], used N-gram technique, including linguistic features like the number of punctuations, the average length of words, etc., as crucial syntactic lexicon dependent features. In [7], authors used the syntactic dependent features to overcome the challenge of unstructured and informal statements in detecting offensive content.

Since lexicons used in tweets are not limited to the standard English words, they include emoticon, symbols and abbreviations. It is a well-known fact that Twitter allows a limited number of characters in a tweet, so popularly users use symbols and abbreviations to express more in the limited number of characters. These abbreviations raise the difficulty level as they do not have any pre-described structure; they also evolve with the trending topics. Symbols used in a tweet have immense contribution in giving meaning to the tweet [19]. Authors in [29] used assumption in their approach that, minimised any set of characters in a tweet repeating thrice consecutively to one only character.

In other text applications like sentiment analysis, sentence classification, etc., Convolution Neural Networks (CNN) is preferred for short length lexicon dependency [10]. CNN outperforms various machine learning techniques in applications on short texts, as CNN's filter size covers the dependence of short length texts appropriately. Considering its outperforming ability to capture lexicon dependency, we have included CNN in our approach. Our work is been inspired by [31].

However, CNN works exceptionally well for the known contents in abusive tokens, but its performance declines for deep contextual dependent abusive tweets. For tweets like "I will broaden the hole between your legs" or "take my banana in your mouth and enjoy the white sauce at last", lexicon dependency model trained with abusive tokens will be inefficient. As there is no limit on user's creativity and the number of highly offensive words, so we must consider the contextual meanings. In [18], authors have proposed Multi-Input Multi-Channel Transfer Learning (MIMCT) based model with parallel channels of CNN and

Long Short Term Memory (LSTM) network to predict abusive tweets in the Hinglish language.

Recurrent Neural Network (RNN) is preferred for long lexicon dependency in the sentence instead of CNN. The RNN overcomes the cons of CNN in terms of contextual dependence. Keeping the confidence in neural networks [15] uses transformer with LSTM in their architecture.

The performance of the neural network lacks for noisy data. Authors in [6] compared the performance of neural network techniques and machine learning techniques over the social media sites dataset and estimated performance of Support Vector Machine (SVM) better in noisy data than neural networks. A neural network works exceptionally well in training weights, but it suffers from unknown lexicons in the hash table for noisy data. As in neural network training, the text is transformed into vectors using an embedding matrix. If the embedding matrix encounters any unknown lexicon that is not in the hash of the embedding matrix, it is marked as ⟨UNK⟩. Since the Twitter dataset has a surplus amount of noises, it leds to an abundance of unknown entries for the neural network. The word embedding for noisy data is a stand-alone problem in the community [15] but out of the scope for this article. Study performed by [9] claims that NB performs slightly better than SVM. Considering these facts and the importance of lexicons, in our approach, we have implemented NB parallel to the neural network.

4   Methodology

In our architecture, we have optimised the strengths of techniques respective all pillars discussed in Sect. 3 to have an optimum performance. As noises in Twitter-data affect architectures' performance, we use pre-processing steps that could generalise these noises. The pre-processing steps are discussed in Sect. 6. The cleaned data is fed parallel into the machine learning model and neural network, as shown in Fig. 2.

In P1, CNN extracts the lexicon dependency features by sliding 1-D filter vectors over the input tweet array. Convolution of filters in one-dimension learns dependency without interruption of any other tweet vector. There are studies that recommended using embedding matrix for a better learning of a neural network, as [20] used syntactic relationships by dependency graph technique for contextualizing word embedding. We are using 300-dimensional GloVe [23] embedding matrix in our experiment.

Let $t_i \in R^d$ be the d-dimensional lexicon vectors for the ith lexicon in a tweet. Let $t \in R^{(L \times d)}$ denotes the input tweet where L is the length of the tweet. Let l be the length of the filter, and the vector $m \in R^{(l \times d)}$ is a filter for the convolution operation. For each position j in the tweet, we have a window vector w_j with l consecutive lexicon vectors, denoted as:

$$w_j = [t_j, t_{j+1}, \cdots, t_{(j+l-1)}] \tag{1}$$

Here, the commas represent row vector concatenation. A filter m generates a feature map $fm \in R^{(L-l+1)}$ where each element fm_j of the feature map for the window vector w_j is produced as follows:

$$fm_j = f(w_j \circ m + b) \tag{2}$$

Where, f is a nonlinear transformation function, $\circ$ is an element-wise multiplication and $b \in R$ is a bias term. With the same length n filters, the generated n feature maps can be rearranged as feature representations for each window w_j.

$$W = [fm_1; fm_2; \cdots ; fm_n] \tag{3}$$

Here, semicolons represent column vector concatenation and fm_i is the feature map generated with the ith filter. Each row W_j of $W \in R^{((L-l+1) \times n)}$, is a new feature representation generated from n filters for the window vector at position j. In our experiment we have used 128 filters of size 4. These window representations are fed into LSTM for learning the contextual dependency.

The LSTM networks are efficient for learning the information in long sequences, hence tends to learn the contextual meaning of lexicon. The action at each time step x_t is evaluated based on three gates, the forget gate f_t, the input gate i_t, and the output gate o_t. These gates collectively decide when to update the current memory cell c_t and the current hidden state h_t. We use t to denote time instance, d to denote the memory dimension in the LSTM and all vectors in this architecture share the same dimension. The LSTM transition functions are defined as follows:

$$i_t = \sigma(W_i \cdot [h_{t-1}, x_t] + b_i) \tag{4}$$

$$f_t = \sigma(W_f \cdot [h_{t-1}, x_t] + b_f) \tag{5}$$

$$q_t = tanh(W_q \cdot [h_{t-1}, x_t] + b_q) \tag{6}$$

$$o_t = \sigma(W_o \cdot [h_{t-1}, x_t] + b_o) \tag{7}$$

$$c_t = f_t \odot c_{t-1} + i_t \odot q_t \tag{8}$$

$$h_t = o_t \odot tanh(c_t) \tag{9}$$

σ is the logistic sigmoid function that has an output in $[0, 1]$, tanh denotes the hyperbolic tangent function that has an output in $[-1, 1]$, and $\odot$ denotes the element wise multiplication. The memory cells c_t carries information that makes it capable of learning the context of a lexicon.

In P2 our architecture learns the probability for meaning of lexicons to be abusive using the NB statistical method. This method calculates the probability of a tweet as:

$$P(\frac{abusive}{l_1 l_2 \cdots l_n}) = \frac{P(\frac{l_1}{abusive})P(\frac{l_2}{abusive})P(\frac{l_3}{abusive}) \cdots P(\frac{l_n}{abusive})P(abusive)}{P(l_1)P(l_2)P(l_3) \cdots P(l_n)} \tag{10}$$

With a naïve assumption that all the lexicons l_i are independent.

The output of both the channels carries the probability of a tweet being abusive and normal. Since we have given equal weightage to each feature, we calculate the average of probabilities being abusive and normal $\bar{X}$. If the average probability score of a tweet being abusive is higher than or equal to the average probability score of a tweet being normal, the tweet is labelled as abusive else normal.

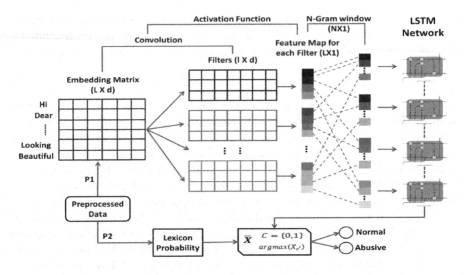

Fig. 2. Complete architecture of proposed model.

5   Dataset

Including the community structure, as per official Twitter blog[3] in 2013, there were an average 5700 tweets per second posted on Twitter. This ample amount of text has no restriction over generation and propagation. To analyze these contents the research community needs appropriate sample data. A small dataset would be also against the sampling strategy for the research work. Authors in [28] analysed and illustrated the issue of biased sampling in dataset creation for abusive language detection. Similarly, [25] discussed various challenges and methods for creating dataset for such task. In [15], authors used cross-domain dataset to promote generalization and avoid any biasness.

For our model training, we use the dataset [12] of 99,996 tweets. Due to its remarkable quantity, this dataset is most suitable for any neural networks. The original dataset consists of four labels as "normal", "abusive", "hatespeech", and "spam". We extracted useful labels, i.e., "normal" and "abusive" each contains 53851 and 27150 tweets, respectively. We ignored the other two classes, as their representation is deficient compared to other classes and the primary scope of this paper is to detect abusive tweets.

---

[3] https://blog.twitter.com/engineering/en_us/a/2013/new-tweets-per-second-record-and-how.htm.

6 Pre-processing

Pre-processing of tweets plays a significant role in model training [2]. It acts as a catalyst for the architectures implemented in abuse detection tweets. It is well-known that the tweet is an unstructured collection of lexicons, which may include any special symbols, numbers, etc. Putting unprocessed tweets directly in the model would lead the model to deal with a lot of unnecessary noises that will affect the performance of the model. We have considerably emphasized on proper pre-processing of the dataset. We have tried our best to generalize noisy content for model training without missing the original context. Following steps are taken in pre-processing of data:

- We have substitute any hyperlink as ⟨url⟩ in any tweet. We are well aware that if any tweet contains spam links in context to abuse any user. These types of tweets should also be label as abusive tweets. However, the spam ⟨url⟩ detection problem is out of the scope of this paper. It is a stand-alone problem to extract tweets containing obscene content's ⟨url⟩.
- We have also understood the importance of smileys in the context of the statement. We have substituted these lexicon into meaningful tags as ⟨face⟩, ⟨smiley⟩, ⟨eye⟩. It helps our model to learn the exceptions between abusive and sarcastic tweets.
- We also assume that if any lexicon consists of any combination of alphabets and special characters. They will be any abusive words as this is very trendy when user type abusive words like, "motherf%%%" or "f##k" for offending. These lexicons are symbolically considered as abusive.
- It is rare that numbers used in tweets (comparatively to alphabets) to express feelings like "143" for "I love you", or "153" for "I adore you". We have generalized any set of numbers as ⟨number⟩.
- There are several tweets consist of user tagging as @user_handel. We need not worry about "who" is tagged in a tweet, so we replaced any user tagging as ⟨user⟩.
- If any lexicon started with an hashtag (#) followed by an alphabet, we have removed the hashtag and kept alphabets.

However, there are no standard benchmark pre-processing steps that have been discussed in this domain.

7 Experiments and Results

We have divided the dataset into 9:1 for training and testing, respectively. We have input the same training data (after processing) individually to our machine learning channel (P2) and neural network channel (P1). We have avoided to shuffle the dataset as we want to avoid any scenario where data trained from one channel is used for testing. In our experiment, we have tried several filter sizes to capture sufficient dependency. However, the change in filter's size did not contributed any significantly, so we have used 128 filters with each filter size of 4. Over-fitting is another issue that needs to be taken care of in neural network training. To avoid over-fitting, we have used L2 weight regularization in our architecture.

Table 1. Noise removal by pre-processing steps.

Original Tweets	After Pre-processing
RT @bicnvcnue:—Huh? Reply ? Sorry my brain is fucked up... https://t.co/UjJKNi0sIo	rt ⟨user⟩:—huh? reply ? sorry my brain is fucked up... ⟨url⟩
@TelaB712 u know my feelings... 143	⟨user⟩ u know my feelings... ⟨number⟩
@_kassmom 😂 😂 seriously yo I got my meal plans together for the whole month of April plus my legs weak as shit I need too get stronger &#128514	⟨user⟩ &⟨number⟩; &⟨number⟩; &⟨number⟩; seriously yo i got my meal plans together for the whole month of april plus my legs weak as shit i need too get stronger & ⟨number⟩

Our approach performs better than all the benchmark models and the latest established technique in terms of F1 measure, as accuracy would not be a comprehensive benchmark for detecting an abusive tweet detection. Since there are several challenges in the dataset like biasness, insufficiency etc., as discussed in Sect. 5. Accuracy will mislead performance evaluation of models. In our experiment, we have considered abusive tweets as positive and normal tweets as negative. As we know, F1 uses two parameters, i.e., precision and recall. The precision measures, accurate detection of abusive tweets among all the abusive labelled tweets that covers the biasness of model performance. And recall measures the performance among actual abusive tweets, so it resolves the dataset biasness issue.

Table 2. Model performance.

Tweet	Actual label	Predicted label
RT @heartlle: Dude looking at his shorty like "Man I'm bout to say fuck this stupid ass prom" https://t.co/caYtV7dKgM	Abusive	Abusive
@GUHoyaFan @ManvilleHoya anyone else feel like we are getting played? Leak Amaker so then we are satisfied with Ewing?	Normal	Normal
@MxVanityFaux I don't fucking know how! I don't even know how to cook Joel. Or what goes with what. I give up. Imma... https://t.co/TfL47kvEfv	Normal	Abusive
Can you please stop shitposting about me or somehow I will lock you up in the tower Sorryyyyyy https://t.co/0B1YuSHuE2	Abusive	Normal

Table 3. Abusive language detection F1 score on the dataset [12].

Technique	F-1 score
NB [17]	0.784
CNN [17]	0.879
RNN [17]	0.887
Hurt-BERT [15]	0.913
Our Approach	**0.927**

8 Conclusion and Future Work

In this paper, we have contributed an approach to detect abusive textual tweets. Specifically, we showed the dependency of abusive tweet detection on the lexicon meaning, the sequence of lexicons, and a lexicon's position for contextual meaning. We have mentioned various merits and demerits of techniques involved to date concerning the task. In our work, features are properly coupled with the efficient technique for better performance. The major challenge of this problem is to deal with the noises and unpredictable contextual features.

For future scope, we can come up with a better techniques that consider features more precisely, including other multi-media content. We also recommend enriching the dataset to motivate the community to work for multi-lingual input and propose a universal technique. There is also a need for standard preprocessing steps that could remove noises without loss of information. We also recommend better tokenization and embedding method for such unstructured data.

References

1. Abitbol, J.L., Karsai, M., Magué, J.P., Chevrot, J.P., Fleury, E.: Socioeconomic dependencies of linguistic patterns in Twitter: a multivariate analysis. In: Proceedings of the 2018 World Wide Web Conference, pp. 1125–1134 (2018). https://doi.org/10.1145/3178876.3186011
2. Alam, S., Yao, N.: The impact of preprocessing steps on the accuracy of machine learning algorithms in sentiment analysis. Comput. Math. Organ. Theory **25**(3), 319–335 (2018). https://doi.org/10.1007/s10588-018-9266-8
3. Backstrom, L., Boldi, P., Rosa, M., Ugander, J., Vigna, S.: Four degrees of separation. In: Proceedings of the 4th Annual ACM Web Science Conference, pp. 33–42 (2012)
4. Castelle, M.: The linguistic ideologies of deep abusive language classification. In: Proceedings of the 2nd Workshop on Abusive Language Online (ALW2), pp. 160–170 (2018). https://doi.org/10.18653/v1/w18-5120
5. Chatzakou, D., Kourtellis, N., Blackburn, J., De Cristofaro, E., Stringhini, G., Vakali, A.: Mean birds: detecting aggression and bullying on Twitter. In: Proceedings of the 2017 ACM on Web Science Conference, pp. 13–22 (2017)

6. Chen, H., McKeever, S., Delany, S.J.: A comparison of classical versus deep learning techniques for abusive content detection on social media sites. In: Staab, S., Koltsova, O., Ignatov, D.I. (eds.) SocInfo 2018. LNCS, vol. 11185, pp. 117–133. Springer, Cham (2018). https://doi.org/10.1007/978-3-030-01129-1_8

7. Chen, Y., Zhou, Y., Zhu, S., Xu, H.: Detecting offensive language in social media to protect adolescent online safety. In: 2012 International Conference on Privacy, Security, Risk and Trust and 2012 International Conference on Social Computing, pp. 71–80. IEEE (2012). https://doi.org/10.1109/socialcom-passat.2012.55

8. Cheng, J.: Report: 80 percent of blogs contain offensive content. ARS Technica. 2011 (2007)

9. Dadvar, M., Trieschnigg, D., de Jong, F.: Experts and machines against bullies: a hybrid approach to detect cyberbullies. In: Sokolova, M., van Beek, P. (eds.) AI 2014. LNCS (LNAI), vol. 8436, pp. 275–281. Springer, Cham (2014). https://doi.org/10.1007/978-3-319-06483-3_25

10. Dos Santos, C., Gatti, M.: Deep convolutional neural networks for sentiment analysis of short texts. In: Proceedings of COLING 2014, the 25th International Conference on Computational Linguistics: Technical Papers, pp. 69–78 (2014). https://www.aclweb.org/anthology/C14-1008.pdf

11. Edunov, S., Diuk, C., Filiz, I.O., Bhagat, S., Burke, M.: Three and a half degrees of separation. Res. Facebook **694** (2016)

12. Founta, A.M., et al.: Large scale crowdsourcing and characterization of Twitter abusive behavior. In: Twelfth International AAAI Conference on Web and Social Media (2018)

13. Hinduja, S., Patchin, J.W.: Cyberbullying fact sheet: identification, prevention, and response. Cyberbullying Research Center (2010). Accessed 30 Jan 2011

14. Hinduja, S., Patchin, J.W.: Cyberbullying fact sheet: identification, prevention, and response. Cyberbullying Research Center (2021)

15. Koufakou, A., Pamungkas, E.W., Basile, V., Patti, V.: HurtBERT: incorporating lexical features with BERT for the detection of abusive language. In: Proceedings of the Fourth Workshop on Online Abuse and Harms, pp. 34–43 (2020). https://doi.org/10.18653/v1/2020.alw-1.5

16. Kwak, H., Lee, C., Park, H., Moon, S.: What is Twitter, a social network or a news media? In: Proceedings of the 19th International Conference on World Wide Web, pp. 591–600 (2010). https://doi.org/10.1145/1772690.1772751

17. Lee, Y., Yoon, S., Jung, K.: Comparative studies of detecting abusive language on Twitter, pp. 101–106 (2018). https://doi.org/10.18653/v1/w18-5113

18. Mathur, P., Sawhney, R., Ayyar, M., Shah, R.: Did you offend me? Classification of offensive Tweets in Hinglish language. In: Proceedings of the 2nd Workshop on Abusive Language Online (ALW2), pp. 138–148 (2018). https://doi.org/10.18653/v1/w18-5118

19. Mehdad, Y., Tetreault, J.: Do characters abuse more than words? In: Proceedings of the 17th Annual Meeting of the Special Interest Group on Discourse and Dialogue, pp. 299–303 (2016). https://doi.org/10.18653/v1/w16-3638

20. Narang, K., Brew, C.: Abusive language detection using syntactic dependency graphs. In: Proceedings of the Fourth Workshop on Online Abuse and Harms, pp. 44–53 (2020). https://doi.org/10.18653/v1/2020.alw-1.6

21. Nobata, C., Tetreault, J., Thomas, A., Mehdad, Y., Chang, Y.: Abusive language detection in online user content. In: Proceedings of the 25th International Conference on World Wide Web, pp. 145–153 (2016). https://doi.org/10.1145/2872427.2883062

22. Patchin, J.W., Hinduja, S.: Summary of our cyberbullying research (2004–2016). Cyberbullying Research Center, pp. 1–2 (2016)

23. Pennington, J., Socher, R., Manning, C.D.: Glove: global vectors for word representation. In: Proceedings of the 2014 Conference on Empirical Methods in Natural Language Processing (EMNLP), pp. 1532–1543 (2014). https://doi.org/10.3115/v1/d14-1162

24. Razavi, A.H., Inkpen, D., Uritsky, S., Matwin, S.: Offensive language detection using multi-level classification. In: Farzindar, A., Kešelj, V. (eds.) AI 2010. LNCS (LNAI), vol. 6085, pp. 16–27. Springer, Heidelberg (2010). https://doi.org/10.1007/978-3-642-13059-5_5

25. van Rosendaal, J., Caselli, T., Nissim, M.: Lower bias, higher density abusive language datasets: a recipe. In: Proceedings of the Workshop on Resources and Techniques for User and Author Profiling in Abusive Language, pp. 14–19 (2020). https://www.aclweb.org/anthology/2020.restup-1.4.pdf

26. Sjöbergh, J., Araki, K.: A multi-lingual dictionary of dirty words. In: LREC. Citeseer (2008)

27. Vidgen, B., Harris, A., Nguyen, D., Tromble, R., Hale, S., Margetts, H.: Challenges and frontiers in abusive content detection. Association for Computational Linguistics (2019). https://doi.org/10.18653/v1/w19-3509

28. Wiegand, M., Ruppenhofer, J., Kleinbauer, T.: Detection of abusive language: the problem of biased datasets. In: Proceedings of the 2019 Conference of the North American Chapter of the Association for Computational Linguistics: Human Language Technologies, (Long And Short Papers), vol. 1, pp. 602–608 (2019). https://www.aclweb.org/anthology/N19-1060.pdf

29. Xiang, G., Fan, B., Wang, L., Hong, J., Rose, C.: Detecting offensive tweets via topical feature discovery over a large scale Twitter corpus. In: Proceedings of the 21st ACM International Conference on Information and Knowledge Management, pp. 1980–1984 (2012). https://doi.org/10.1145/2396761.2398556

30. Xu, Z., Zhu, S.: Filtering offensive language in online communities using grammatical relations. In: Proceedings of the Seventh Annual Collaboration, Electronic Messaging, Anti-Abuse and Spam Conference, pp. 1–10 (2010)

31. Zhou, C., Sun, C., Liu, Z., Lau, F.: A C-LSTM neural network for text classification. arXiv preprint arXiv:1511.08630 (2015)

Speaker Authorization for Air Traffic Control Security

Marian Trnka[1], Sakhia Darjaa[1], Milan Rusko[1(✉)], Meilin Schaper[2],
and Tim H. Stelkens-Kobsch[2]

[1] Institute of Informatics of the Slovak Academy of Sciences (Ústav Informatiky Slovenskej
Akadémie Vied, UI SAV), Bratislava, Slovakia
milan.rusko@savba.sk

[2] Institute of Flight Guidance, German Aerospace Center (Deutsches Zentrum für Luft- und
Raumfahrt e.V., DLR), Braunschweig, Germany

Abstract. The number of incidents in which unauthorized persons break into
frequencies used by Air Traffic Controllers (ATCOs) and give false instructions
to pilots, or transmit fake emergency calls, is a permanent and apparently growing threat. One of the measures against such attacks could be to use automatic
speaker recognition on the voice radio channel to disclose the potential unauthorized speaker. This work describes the solution for a speaker authorization
system in the Security of Air Transport Infrastructures of Europe (SATIE) project,
presents the architecture of the system, gives details on training and testing procedures, analyses the influence of the number of authorized persons on the system's
performance and describes how the system was adapted to work on the radio
channel.

Keywords: ATC security · Radio channel speaker verification · Speaker
authorization

1 Introduction

An unauthorized station can make malicious transmissions on an aeronautical frequency
with the intention of misleading pilots. Such transmissions made at critical stages, e.g.
during the take-off run or landing, can have potentially very dangerous consequences
[1]. For example, in 2005, the pilot of an USAir flight approaching Washington's Reagan
National Airport was instructed to divert his landing by a voice breaking into his frequency, which caused confusion for himself and for two other planes in position to land
[2]. Or, in October 2016 a Virgin Australia flight was about 80 m away from the runway
at Melbourne's Tullamarine Airport when it received instruction from an anonymous
unauthorized person transmitting from an unknown location causing the pilot to pull up
and change course [3]. Advanced automatic speaker verification technologies provide
the ability to detect such attacks. It is possible to a) continuously monitor voice radio
communication and b) verify the authorization of each speaker online. We discuss both
points in 1.1 and 1.2 respectively.

© Springer Nature Switzerland AG 2021
A. Karpov and R. Potapova (Eds.): SPECOM 2021, LNAI 12997, pp. 716–725, 2021.
https://doi.org/10.1007/978-3-030-87802-3_64

1.1 Voice Radio Communication in Air Traffic Control

The analogue radio is still in use in the Air Traffic Control (ATC) voice communication. The radio-voice communication takes place between 118 and 137 MHz. The Very High Frequency (VHF) radio channel spacing is 25 kHz (or the reduced channel spacing 8.33 kHz) and double-sideband amplitude modulation (AM) is utilized. These frequencies are used for the voice communication of Tower (ground movements), Center (air movements) Automatic Terminal Information Service (ATIS). Audio frequency bandwidth for the voice-radio is limited to 300–2700 Hz. For the 8.33-kHz channel spacing, the speech frequency bandwidth was reduced to the 350 Hz to 2.5 kHz range [4].

In contrast to the advantage of relative robustness, this simple system has several disadvantages. One of them is the vulnerability to signals sent by attackers, such as the transmission of deceptive voice commands or interference by audio signals. In the past there were several attempts to increase the security of radio-voice communication using various approaches, such as watermarking [5] or voice biometrics [6] which are being implemented in one of the tools focusing on the security of airports [7].

1.2 Speaker Authorization

Language Dependence. English is used by default in civil international air traffic. Of course, pilots and ATCOs, whose mother tongue is not English, may speak with a strong foreign accent. This can affect automatic speaker verification and, for example, treat voices with the same foreign accent as to be more similar. In the current state of research, this aspect is not addressed. We took advantage of the fact that speaker verification can be considered a language independent task in the first approximation.

Speaker Verification. In the Speaker Verification a Binary Decision is Made and the Claimed Identity of a Speaker is Confirmed or Refused. There Are Two Types of Speaker Verification: Text-Independent Speaker Verification Verifies the Identity Without Constraints on Speech Content, and Text-Dependent Speaker Verification that Requires the Speaker Uttering Exactly the Given Password. The Approach Used in This Work is Text Independent.

Speaker Authorization/Speaker-Group Verification. Speaker authorization (SA) is the ability of a system to identify whether a speaker belongs to those having the permission to access the voice communication channel. The speakers trying to take part in the communication without the permission are designated as intruders. There are dozens of speakers who are authorized to communicate in a certain flight sector in any particular time and the number of potential intruders is practically unlimited.

To address this, a model of the incoming voice is created and compared to the group of models belonging to the authorized persons. The list of authorized persons is called the "whitelist" and the group of persons actually listed is called the "whitelist cohort".

A speaker recognition can generally be done on a closed set of speakers, in which all the possible speakers are known, or on an open set, where the test sample may belong to a speaker that is unknown to the system. The speaker authorization is an open-set task that can be considered as a group-verification problem, as the specific identity of the speaker in the group is not important and only the affiliation to the group is verified.

Consequently, a binary decision is done in the speaker-group verification, by which the affiliation of a speaker to the "authorized" group is confirmed or refused. However, to achieve this goal multiple binary comparisons (speaker verifications) have to be done between the incoming sample and all the enrolled voices from the actual whitelist cohort. If the maximum score of all these comparisons is lower than a pre-defined threshold, the tested speaker is considered an unauthorized person. From a theoretical point of view, this is a special case of the multi-target cohort detection task [8] or open-set text-independent speaker identification [9].

Approach and Challenges. In this paper we present the solution of a speaker authorization module applied in the SATIE project's tool TraMICS (Traffic Management Intrusion and Compliance System), as well as the method and the results of the tests showing its feasibility in the context of the Air Traffic Management (ATM) security. Our approach uses automatic speaker verification to check whether the current speaker in the radio voice communication between the ATCOs and pilots belongs to the group of persons authorized to communicate in the particular time, channel, or sector. Additional challenges arise from the real-world implementation of such a speaker authorization system. First, the nature of a real-time application dictates constraints on robustness or speed. Second, the utterances submitted to the system are typically very short, usually ranging from 2 to 5 s. This is of course challenging since the reliability of the system increases with the amount of speech data under consideration. Additionally, we are facing communication on various channels. For the simulation environment VoIP speech in ATC is used, but the VHF radio channel is used in real operation.

2 Proposed Approach

2.1 Architecture of the Speaker Authorization (SA) Module

The illustrative schematic diagram of the architecture of the SA module is presented in Fig. 1. Technically, the SA module is based on the X-vector approach [10]. The Deep Neural Network (DNN), which was trained to discriminate between speakers, maps variable-length utterances to fixed-dimensional embeddings that are called X-vectors. Simply put, the X vectors serve as speaker models. Reverberation and noising were used for data augmentation. The module was created in the Kaldi environment [11]. In the verification phase an X-vector is extracted from the tested utterance and the Probabilistic Linear Discriminant Analysis (PLDA) is used to calculate a similarity score against the X-vectors of the whitelist cohort [12]. Decision on the affiliation of the speaker to the whitelist cohort is made by comparing the maximum similarity score with a threshold.

2.2 Training Data

The training data must represent a sufficient number of speakers, equipment, transmission channels, acoustic environments and background noises; we chose two large freely available databases VoxCeleb [13] and VoxCeleb2 [14].

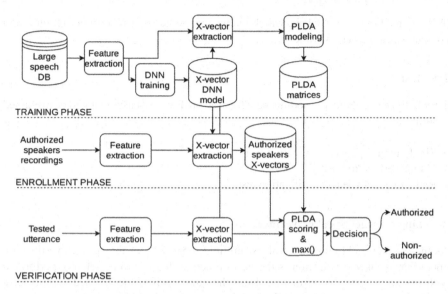

Fig. 1. Schematic diagram of the SA module.

In VoxCeleb the number of speakers in the training set is 1.211 and 40 in the test set. The number of utterances in the training set is 148.642 and 4.874 in the test-set.

VoxCeleb2 contains over 1 million utterances from over 6.000 speakers. The datasets are fairly balanced in terms of gender. The speakers span a wide range of different ethnicities, accents, professions and ages. Records are shot in a large number of challenging auditory environments. They are degraded with real-world noise, consisting of background chatter, laughter, overlapping speech, room acoustics, and there is a broad range in the quality of recording equipment and channel noise [14].

2.3 Test Data

The results of speaker verification tests are highly dependent on the choice of speakers and test utterances. Experiments with users in real operation are not statistically representative, because any time-constrained testing in real operation can provide only a limited number of speakers and acoustic conditions while the variability of speakers and conditions the system has to deal with is enormous. They do not give enough information on the overall reliability of the system. Rather they can confirm usability of SA as an add-on tool in the system of ATC security.

Relevant reliability tests must therefore be performed on speech databases representing a wide variety of speakers and acoustic conditions. It was decided to use the following publicly available speech databases for testing: LibriSpeech, SpeechDatE Sk, and VoxForge.

LibriSpeech [15] offers 2.444 speakers and is large enough for testing the SA module. SpeechDat-E Sk [16] contains telephone speech (1.000 Slovak speakers), and is therefore suitable for some experiments evaluating the channel mismatch. VoxForge

[17] is a medium-size database which allows to conduct tests that do not require high computational power and time.

2.4 Tests

The off-line tests of the SA module were focused on three test cases that will be discussed in turn:

- Single-target speaker verification test;
- Group-verification test;
- Radio channel speaker verification test.

2.5 Single Target Speaker Verification

As the speaker authorization involves multiple repetitions of the speaker verification operation, speaker verification is the basic function that has to be reliably performed with the lowest possible error rate. Here the question is if the claimed identity of a speaker is confirmed or refused. To test this function, each particular utterance from the test database is fed into the speaker verification module and the true and false decisions are counted. The specific threshold value at which False Rejection Rate (FRR) is equal to False Acceptance Rate (FAR) is found and the Equal Error Rate (EER) is determined [18]. The EER gives information on the quality of the verification system when tested on the test-set of the VoxForge database.

Detailed results of the off-line tests on the three databases are presented in Table 1.

Table 1. Detailed results of the off-line single-target speaker verification tests.

Database name	No. of target speakers	No. of test files	EER [%]
LibriSpeech	2.444	24.440	0.86
SpeechDat-E Sk	888	888	0.90
VoxForge	579	7.215	1.63

2.6 Speaker Authorization/Speaker-Group Verification

The VoxForge database contains approximately 500 speakers. All possible groups that can be assembled from speakers in the test database should be considered, but as it will be shown, even when choosing a medium-size DB, the computational and time requirements for such a complete test can quickly exceed the capabilities of the available computational resources.

From a mathematical point of view, creating groups is making combinations without repetition. The number of k-element combinations of n objects, without repetition can be calculated as in (1):

$$C_{n,k} = \binom{n}{k} = \frac{n!}{k!(n-k)!} \tag{1}$$

As it can be seen in Table 2, the number of possible groups of speakers that can be created from the whole test database heavily depends on the number of persons in the group (i.e. currently authorized persons, or the whitelist cohort). It was decided to limit the number of the test-groups to 500.000 for each group size. Although such random selection does not cover all the possibilities of dividing speakers into groups, for the purposes of this paper this is considered a reasonable trade-off between time and computational requirements on the one hand and statistical representativeness of the test on the other hand. All speakers in the database are used for the random selection. All test samples are used in the test.

After this consideration, we are in position to formulate the question for group-verification tests as follows: "Does the test sample belong to some of the authorized speakers?". To answer the question, the test sample has to be compared to each of the members of the whitelist cohort. Naturally, a single comparison may be erroneous with a certain probability. As the size of the whitelist cohort increases, the number of needed comparisons increases, and the overall probability of error is rising.

The overlapping between the distributions of the non-target and the target scores in an open-set identification is greater than the overlapping of impostor scores and target scores in speaker verification. The bigger the target-set size, the greater is this overlapping [19].

For each size of the whitelist cohort the EER (i.e. equality of FRR and FAR) is reached at a different threshold. Therefore, an adaptive-threshold test needs to be performed, in which the threshold is changed so that a respective EER can be computed for each particular size of the authorized group.

Discussions with ATC practitioners have indicated that the number of people authorized to communicate over the voice channel on the given frequency, in the given moment, and in the given sector is typically up to 20. It was therefore decided to choose 30 as the maximum size for the group during the group verification tests. The VoxForge database was used as the test database for this evaluation. The results of speaker authorization tests are presented in Fig. 2.

Table 2. Number of groups that can be created from a test database of 500 speakers in relation to the number of members in the white list cohort.

Whitelist cohort	1	10	20	30
No. of possible groups	5×10^2	2.5×10^{20}	2.7×10^{35}	1.5×10^{48}

Histograms of score distributions of the target speaker and non-target speakers at various whitelist cohort sizes S (S = 1, 10, 20 and 30) are shown. The histogram of target score hardly changes depending on the whitelist cohort size, so only TAR_1 is shown.

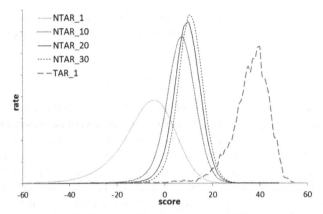

Fig. 2. Histograms of score distributions of the target speaker (TAR_1 - rightmost) and non-target speakers at various whitelist cohort sizes S (S = 1, 10, 20 and 30 – NTAR_1, 10, 20 and 30).

The score distribution of the target speakers' group is reasonably well separated from that of non-target groups even for the size of the whitelist cohort S = 30, indicating that the speaker authorization system is relatively reliable also for larger numbers of the whitelist cohort for the VoxForge database. Detailed results of the tests are presented in Table 3.

Table 3. Detailed results of the off-line multitarget group speaker verification tests - dependence of the EER on the number of currently authorized speakers.

Group size	1	5	10	15	20	25	30
EER [%]	1.6	2.5	2.9	3.2	3.5	3.7	3.8

2.7 Radio Channel Speaker Verification

For the purposes of the project SATIE the SA module was first designed for broadband clean speech signals, and was meant for the DLR's Tower-simulator in Braunschweig that uses VoIP channels for simulating ATC voice communication [20]. (DLR stands for German Aerospace Center, Deutsches Zentrum für Luft- und Raumfahrt e. V., literally German Center for Air- and Space-flight) However, in the real-life operation the system will be monitoring the voice-radio traffic with narrow frequency range, noises, distortions and other effects caused by the transmission via the radio channel.

To ensure that single speaker verification will work well on the radio channel, which is an inevitable condition for speaker authorization to work well, the speaker verification had to be tested on radio speech. There is a difference in the signal quality between the clean training data the original system was trained on and radio-quality test data, which is called channel mismatch. Hence, our task was to determine the influence of channel mismatch on the reliability of speaker verification and eliminate this influence.

No real-life radio communication database was available to the authors that was large enough and appropriately annotated for speaker verification testing. Therefore, it was decided to obtain radio recordings by transmitting an existing VoxCeleb [13] recording via a radio channel. Baofeng UV5R hand-held radios were used as transmitter and receiver. Due to local limitations, the transmission was performed on private mobile radio frequency 446.0 MHz. These frequencies belong to the UHF band, but the distortion and noise caused by the channel are similar to those on the VHF frequencies used in ATC.

Both, the original VoxCeleb database and the newly created radio channel "RadioVoxCeleb" database were split in corresponding non-overlapping training (VoxCeleb_train, RadioVoxCeleb_train) and test sets (VoxCeleb_test, RadioVoxCeleb_test). Detailed results of the off-line tests with various combinations of training and testing data are presented in Table 4.

Table 4. Detailed results of the channel mismatch.

Training data	Test data	EER
VoxCeleb_train	VoxCeleb_test	1.50%
RadioVoxCeleb_train	RadioVoxCeleb_test	2.80%
VoxCeleb_train	RadioVoxCeleb_test	5.90%
RadioVoxCeleb_train	VoxCeleb_test	3.00%
VoxCeleb_train + RadioVoxCeleb_train	VoxCeleb_test	1.20%
VoxCeleb_train + RadioVoxCeleb_train	RadioVoxCeleb_test	**2.60%**

The baseline system reached EER = 1.5% on the "clean" (i.e. original) signal and 5.9% on the radio signal. The best results were achieved by a system with multi-condition-trained models, which achieved an EER of 2.6% on the radio signal. Interestingly, the error in recognizing the clean signal has also been reduced (EER = 1.2%), which is likely a consequence of data augmentation with radio-channel signal.

The influence of the whitelist cohort size on the speaker authorization was tested using a system trained on VoxCeleb_train + RadioVoxCeleb_train set, and tested on RadioVoxCeleb_test set. The results are presented in Table 5.

Table 5. Results of the SA on radio channel with whitelist cohort size from S = 1 to S = 30.

Group size	1	5	10	15	20	25	30
EER [%]	2.6	4.9	6.5	7.2	7.6	8.2	8.6

The EER is relatively high, because the volume of the training data is small. The authors plan to create the radio version of the VoxCeleb2 database and use it for training. It can be assumed that the results will be significantly better.

3   Discussion and Conclusion

We proposed an architecture for a speaker verification system and tested its feasibility for the radio channel that corresponds to real-world use of such a system. In the VoIP mode we showed that the system reaches an EER below 4% even for the whitelist cohort size that exceeds normal application conditions. In the radio-channel mode, a sizeable decrease of the error (2.6% EER) compared to the original channel mismatched data (5.9% EER) was shown when the system was trained on the combination of augmented radio and original training data. The achieved performance meets the current expectations for a real-world air-traffic management application.

One such deployment of the speaker-authorization module is in the Traffic Management Intrusion and Compliance System (TraMICS) that serves as a detector for potential security incidents [21]. TraMICS analyses different indicators of the traffic situation combined with analyzing voices participating in radio-communication. This multimodal system can generate different kinds of alerts that TraMICS aggregates to a security situation indicator.

Due to the COVID 19 pandemic physical access to airports, air traffic control simulator facilities, and other areas where system validation would normally also take place, was drastically limited. Therefore, an on-site validation will be carried out in the near future, which will provide a scientifically based evaluation of personal opinions of future users of the system.

Acknowledgments. This project has received funding from the European Union's Horizon 2020 research and innovation programme under grant agreement No 832969. This output reflects the views only of the author(s), and the European Union cannot be held responsible for any use which may be made of the information contained therein. For more information on the project see: http://satie-h2020.eu/. The results presented in this work were reported in the deliverable D4.2 of the above mentioned project SATIE. The work was also partly funded from the Slovak Scientific Grant Agency VEGA project No 2/0161/18.

References

1. EUROCONTROL: Radio interference (2020). https://www.skybrary.aero/index.php/Radio_Interference
2. Morgan, D.: Hackers attack air traffic control (2006). https://abcnews.go.com/US/story?id=95993&page=1
3. Morris, H.: Hoax caller impersonating air traffic control forces pilot to abandon landing (2016). https://www.telegraph.co.uk/travel/destinations/oceania/australia/articles/hoax-caller-impersonating-air-traffic-control-forces-pilot-to-abort-landing/
4. Eurocontrol: "Implications of end-to-end communication for air traffic control", EUROCONTROL (2009)
5. Hagmüller, M., Kubin, G.: "Speech watermarking for air traffic control", EUROCONTROL (2005)
6. Rusko, M., Trnka, M., Darjaa, S., Rajčáni, J., Finke, M., Stelkens-Kobsch, T.: Enhancing air traffic management security by means of conformance monitoring and speech analysis. In: Klempous, R., Nikodem, J., Baranyi, P. (eds.) Cognitive Infocommunications, Theory and Applications. Topics in Intelligent Engineering and Informatics, vol. 13. Springer, Cham (2019). https://doi.org/10.1007/978-3-319-95996-2_9

7. SATIE project: Security of air transport infrastructure of Europe (2020). http://satie-h2020.eu/
8. Shon, S., et al.: The 1st multi-target speaker detection and identification challenge evaluation. In: Proceedings Interspeech, Graz (2019)
9. Reynolds, D., Singer, E., Douglas, A.: Analysis of multitarget detection for speaker and language recognition. In: ODYSSEY The Speaker and Language Recognition Workshop, number 4 (2004)
10. Snyder, D., Garcia-Romero, G., Sell, D., Povey D., Khudanpur, S.: X-Vectors: Robust DNN embeddings for speaker recognition. In: Proceedings of the International Conference on Acoustics, Speech and Signal Processing (ICASSP), Calgary (2018)
11. Povey, D., et.al: The Kaldi speech recognition toolkit. In: Proceedings of the IEEE 2011 Workshop on Automatic Speech Recognition and Understanding (2011)
12. Kenny, P., et al.: PLDA for speaker verification with utterances of arbitrary duration. In: Proceedings of the IEEE International Conference on Acoustics, Speech and Signal Processing, Vancouver, BC, Canada (2013)
13. Nagrani, A., Chung, J.S., Zisserman, A.: Voxceleb: a large-scale speaker identification dataset. In: Proceedings of INTERSPEECH (2017)
14. Chung, J.S., Nagrani, A., Zisserman, A.: VoxCeleb2: Deep speaker recognition. In: Proceedings INTERSPEECH (2018)
15. Panayotov, V., Chen, G., Povey, D.K.S.: Librispeech: An ASR corpus based on public domain audio books. In: Proceedings of the IEEE International Conference on Acoustics, Speech and Signal Processing (ICASSP), Brisbane (2015)
16. Pollak, P., et al.: SpeechDat(E) – Eastern European telephone speech databases. In: Proceedings of XLDB Workshop on Very Large Telephone Speech Databases, Athens (2000)
17. VoxForge: VoxForge (2006). www.voxforge.org
18. CISSP: The CISSP open study guide web site. https://web.archive.org/web/20081017165633/http://www.ccert.edu.cn/education/cissp/hism/039-041.html. Accessed 2021
19. Zigel, Y., Wasserblat, M.: How to deal with multiple-targets in speaker identification systems? In: Proceedings of IEEE Odyssey - The Speaker and Language Recognition Workshop, San Juan (2006)
20. Institute of Flight Guidance, German Aerospace Center: Apron and Tower Simulator (ATS). https://www.dlr.de/fl/en/desktopdefault.aspx/tabid-1964/1601_read-3011/ Accessed 2021
21. SATIE project D4.2 - Traffic Management Intrusion and Compliance System. SATIE project, 2021

Prosodic Changes with Age: A Longitudinal Study on a Famous European Portuguese Native Speaker

Ana Rita Valente[1,2(✉)] ⓘ, Catarina Oliveira[1,3] ⓘ, Luciana Albuquerque[1,2,4,5] ⓘ, António Teixeira[1,2] ⓘ, and Plínio A. Barbosa[6] ⓘ

[1] Institute of Electronics and Informatics Engineering of Aveiro,
University of Aveiro, Aveiro, Portugal
{rita.valente,coliveira,lucianapereira,ajst}@ua.pt
[2] Department of Electronics, Telecommunications and Informatics,
University of Aveiro, Aveiro, Portugal
[3] School of Health Sciences,
University of Aveiro, Aveiro, Portugal
[4] Center for Health Technology and Services Research,
University of Aveiro, Aveiro, Portugal
[5] Department of Education and Psychology, University of Aveiro, Aveiro, Portugal
[6] Speech Prosody Studies Group, Department of Linguistics,
State University of Campinas, Campinas, Brazil

Abstract. The understanding of human communication development throughout the lifetime involves the characterization of both segmental and suprasegmental parameters. This pilot study intends to analyse suprasegmental (i.e., prosodic) features in conversational longitudinal speech samples in uncontrolled environments. The ProsodyDescriptor Extractor was used to extract 17 prosodic features (intonation, intensity and rhythm measures) in a set of 90 speech intervals of 3 s to 6 s selected from three interviews collected in different ages of the same male public figure. Group mean comparison tests revealed that 14 prosodic features presented statistically significant differences between the three ages. In general, in comparison with his younger age, the speaker got a higher F0 mean level, more F0 variability, higher F0 peaks, more variable F0 peak values, less variable F0 falls, higher F0 min, less steeper F0 rises, less steeper F0 falls, less variable F0 rises, more energy in high frequencies, slower speech and articulation rate, less vocal effort and less variable global intensity. The longitudinal study of age-related changes in speech rhythm and intonation could contribute to the normal ageing process' characterization, being a reference for clinical assessment and intervention.

Keywords: Prosody · Vocal ageing · Longitudinal analysis

© Springer Nature Switzerland AG 2021
A. Karpov and R. Potapova (Eds.): SPECOM 2021, LNAI 12997, pp. 726–736, 2021.
https://doi.org/10.1007/978-3-030-87802-3_65

1   Introduction

The process of ageing is generally associated with a number of changes in physiological, cognitive, psychological and social domains [1,2]. Speech modifications across lifetime reflect the anatomical and physiological changes in the respiratory, laryngeal and supralaryngeal systems, as well as in the speech motor control [1,2].

The comprehension of the human communication process involves the analysis of speech in a fully extension, comprising both segmental and suprasegmental acoustic features. Segmental features concern individual phonemes' characteristics; suprasegmental or prosodic features are spread in syllables, utterances, or sentences and consist in, e.g., acoustic emphasis, rhythm, stress or intonation [3]. Speech prosody encoding is predominantly achieved through the physical correlates of fundamental frequency (F0) modulation, intensity, duration and voice quality [4,5].

Even though it is known that communication changes with age, prosody as a speech component has been scarcely examined, leading to gaps in knowledge about the longitudinal evolution of prosody [6]. For European Portuguese (EP), acoustic studies about age-related prosodic changes are scarce, and, to the best of our knowledge, there are no longitudinal studies of speech changes with age. Preliminary evidence of age-related prosodic variations in EP have emerged in cross-sectional studies with other purposes and using different speech corpora (e.g., reading or conversation) [7–9]. Most of the parameters reported at suprasegmental level are related with mean speaking F0 and rhythm [7–9]. Previous EP studies using connected speech showed a non-consensual trend of F0 for males and a decrease for female speakers [8,9], and a reduce in speech rate [7] with age.

The present study is the first longitudinal investigation of speech prosody production across lifetime in EP and aims to analyse within-speaker trends in intonation, intensity and rhythm through the comparison of prosody features automatically extracted from interviews of a male public figure between 1988 and 2020.

2   Related Work

Although speech can be affected by other factors than chronological age (such as diachronic changes, education, social environment, lifestyle, and health) [10,11], the literature has suggested a set of features typically related to older speech, mainly at segmental level (e.g., increase of segment duration) [1,2,12]. Despite suprasegmental characteristics of speech having been investigated in far less detail, cross-sectional acoustic studies have also revealed age-induced effects on speech prosodic features (i.e., intonation, intensity and rhythm). The reduced speech (or articulation) rate has been the most robust and reported age-related effect, regardless of the speaker's language [1,2,7,13–16]. Most studies have reported that F0 in males decreases from young adulthood into middle age and then rises again into older ages (35 Hz) [1,9,17,18]. Speech intensity appears to remain stable or decrease slightly with ageing, but has also been reported to increase after age 70 in males [1,2,19]. Concerning F0 and intensity range, Volin et al. [16] reported that both F0 variation and the variation in intensity contours increase with age. Other studies have also reported a tendency to F0 range [20] and intensity range [2] increase with age, but contrary findings can be found as well, mainly for speaking F0 range [2,17,21]. Less reported in the literature, but not least, spectral emphasis (emph) displayed a general rise to middle age, followed by a decrease to age 70–80, and a strong rise after age 80 in males [2].

Even though cross-sectional studies provided important findings on the effect of ageing on speech production, this type of methodology presents limitations [22]. The measurements are based on a single-occasion observation, making its generalisation questionable to other time periods [23]. An alternative methodology is the study of age-related variations longitudinally [23]. This methodological approach has been mostly implemented to document age-related changes on vowel-based studies. In general, the segmental analyses revealed gender-related differences, with a decrease in F0 and F1 with ageing for females and a falling-rising pattern in F0 and F1 for male speakers [10,24].

Considering that prosody characteristics in older ages are eminently individual [25], through the assessment of longitudinal prosodic changes using a single speaker, the researchers can measure the impact of healthy ageing on intonation, intensity and rhythm, excluding the influence of inter-speaker variations on within-language prosodic variability [23]. A few studies have been developed using a longitudinal approach for the analysis of prosodic changes with age. A study over a period of 5 years on 11 healthy male speakers only revealed slightly (non significant) variations, i.e., an increase in F0 and a decrease in F0 range and intensity range [26]. A longitudinal study of Queen Beatrix's formal speeches between ages 42 and 74 revealed, in the first decades, a decrease in articulation rate and an increase in the last decade, with a general longitudinally rise. The authors attribute this trend to an accommodation of Queen Beatrix to a generally faster tempo in the Dutch language community and/or effect of learning and practice [27]. A corpus of reading speech collected in 1968 and 2008 of an Italian journalist, Piero Angela, was studied longitudinally concerning rhythmic and intonation parameters. In general, with advancing age, a decrease in speech and articulation rate, an F0 increase and a broaden tonal range was observed [28]. To explore speech production as a biomarker for hypokinetic dysarthria, several Muhammad Ali conversational speech samples, collected before his diagnosis of Parkinson, were analysed [29]. Speech rate presents a statistically significant reduction as age increase and intonational (F0 and intensity) variation also decreases, although not significantly [29]. In this case it is important to note the possible influence of non-healthy ageing in speech prosody. A study on the articulation rate of five German and five French speakers, analysed in two moments with ten years of difference, reported specific language effects: a decrease in the articulation rate for German participants and an increase for French speakers [25]. More recently, 5 public talks produced by Noam Chomsky from the age of 40 to the age of 89 were studied, measuring rhythmic features. A statistically significant decrease in speech rate measures was detected [23]. Globally, longitudinal studies of age-related modifications in prosody revealed a broaden F0 range and a slow rate in speech production as people get older.

3   Method

In order to analyse the age effects in intonation, intensity and rhythm, several prosodic parameters were extracted from three speech interviews of a male speaker.

3.1   Speech Material and Data Annotation

This pilot study analyses longitudinally the speech production of one male public figure, without known voice or age problems, in three different ages: 51 years old (Age51), 74 years old (Age74) and 82 years old (Age 82). The corpus includes three samples of comparable speaking style (i.e., semi-structured interviews conducted by EP interviewers), with a 31 years lag between the age of the first interview and the age of the last interview. The interviews consist in speech data from uncontrolled environments that have been licensed for research purposes from the archive of the public service broadcasting organisation of Portugal (Radio e Televisão de Portugal, RTP). As regards content, the fist speech sample includes an interview about a specific suspicious professional event in which the speaker took part and then talking in unemotional speaking style. The second and third semi-structured interviews are similar and cover the same topic (biographic interview about personal and professional issues).

The duration of the interviews is the following, rounded by excess: Age51, 14 min; Age74, 42 min; Age82, 1 h and 11 min. An experienced rater carefully listened to each interview and marked 30 intervals of 3–6 s (chunks) per interview (a total corpus of 90 chunks), considering research findings of accent groups duration that revealed a mean duration of less than 3 s for the majority of data [30]. The mean number of syllables per chunk was 25.8. (automatically detected as explained in Sect. 3.2). Additional criteria were also applied for chunk determination: 1) subject speech exclusively; 2) complete speech act; 3) absence of non-vocal (e.g., applause), vocal non-lexical (e.g., cough) or verbal non-lexical (e.f., filled pauses) phenomena, and 4) comparable speaking style (i.e., avoiding large prosodic variations).

3.2   Feature Extraction

Two Praat scripts were used in the present study, developed by Barbosa [31]. The `SalienceDetector` was used for a semi-automatic detection of acoustic salience via duration. It was used to segment syllables phonetically by tracking two consecutive vowel onsets (V-V units). The thresholds used were 0.1 and 0.06, the filter was defined as Butterworth and the technique was Amplitude. A second script, `ProsodyDescriptor Extractor` [32], was used to extract several prosodic parameters per manually delimited chunk, described briefly in Table 1. The latter script allows the calculation of duration measures (i.e., speech and articulation rate) from V-V units. The default values of the script were used. The scripts described above were tested for several languages, including EP [31], yielding 17 prosodic parameters per chunk.

Table 1. Systematic overview of the parameters.

Parameter	Description	Unit
Intonation (F0)		
F0med	Median of F0	ST re 1 Hz
F0sd	Standard deviation of F0	ST/Hz
fSAQ	Semi-amplitude of F0 between quartiles	ST/Hz
F0min	Minimum of F0	ST re 1 Hz
F0max	Maximum of F0	ST re 1 Hz
sdF0peak	Standard deviation of F0 maxima	ST/Hz
F0peakwidth	Mean peakness of F0 maximum	ST re 1 Hz
F0peak_rate	Peak rate of F0	peaks/s
sdtF0peak	Standard deviation of the F0 maxima positions	s
dF0posmean	Mean of positive F0 first derivative	Hz/frame
dF0negmean	Mean of the negative F0 first derivatives	Hz/frame
dF0sdpos	Standard deviation of positive F0 first derivative	Hz/frame
dF0sdneg	Standard deviation of negative F0 first derivative	Hz/frame
Intensity		
emph	Spectral emphasis	dB
cvint	Intensity variation coefficient	dB
Rythm		
Speech rate	V-V units per unit of time, including pause intervals	V-V units/s
Articulation rate	V-V units per unit of time, excluding pause intervals	V-V units/s

Figure 1 illustrates some of the parameters related to F0 (in semitones, ST), namely F0min, F0max, sdF0peak, dF0posmean, dF0sdpos, dF0negmean and dF0sdneg.

For computing F0 peak rate a smoothing function (with a cut-off frequency of 1.5 Hz) followed by a quadratic interpolation function was applied before the F0 peak rate computation. Regarding intensity, while the intensity variation coefficient (cvint) allows a measure of how global intensity varies across each chunk (standard deviation of global intensity divided by mean global intensity), spectral emphasis (emph) is an indirect measure of vocal effort, according to Traunmüller and Heldener [33,34]. The rhythm measures were based on automatic vowel onsets detection.

3.3   Statistical Analysis

All acoustic measures extracted by chunk were compiled in a SPSS file (IBM SPSS software package version 25.0; SPSS Inc., Chicago, IL, USA) [35]. The normality of

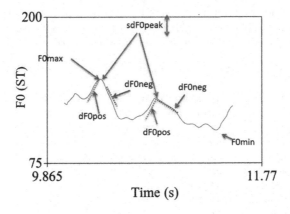

Fig. 1. Description of F0 parameters.

ANOVA residuals was implemented and for the following parameters the normality assumption was insured: F0min, dF0posmean, dF0negmean, sF0sdpos, emph, cvint, speech rate and articulation rate. ANOVAs, followed by the Tuckey HSD post hoc tests, were calculated for inter-group comparison. Concerning F0med, F0sd, fSAQ, F0max, sdF0peak and dF0sdneg, the analysis revealed that normality assumption for ANOVA was violated. For those parameters, Kruskal-Wallis models followed by non-parametric U Mann Whitney post hoc test were employed. All analysis used a significant level of 0.05.

4   Result and Discussion

Data analysis revealed statistically significant differences in 14 prosodic features (see Table 2). Data point to a speech/articulation rate decrease and a reduction in the global intensity range with increasing age. Intonational features revealed, in general, an increase in speaking F0 and a wider range of F0 as age rise.

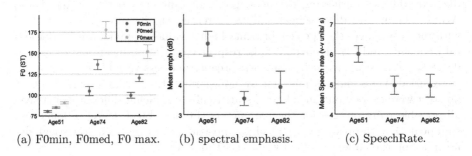

(a) F0min, F0med, F0 max.   (b) spectral emphasis.   (c) SpeechRate.

Fig. 2. Variation of prosodic parameters by age. The Error bars represent 95% Confidence Interval.

Table 2. Mean and standard deviation (SD) of several prosodic parameters by age, with the significant differences highlighted. Results of ANOVA and Kruskal-Wallis models estimate the effect of age on prosodic parameters (right columns).

	Parameter	Age51			Age74			Age82			Age Effect	
		Mean	SD		Mean	SD		Mean	SD		F or H (2,87)	P value
	F0med	85.0	2.3	1;2	136.3	16.1	1;3	120.2	11.5	2;3	67.028*	<0.001
	F0sd	2.3	0.7	1;2	16.9	5.7	1;3	12.1	4.1	2;3	63.923*	<0.001
	fSAQ	1.5	0.6	1;2	10.4	4.5	1;3	8.1	4.1	2;3	60.664*	<0.001
	F0min	80.2	2.6	1;2	104.6	14.7	1	99.6	9.1	2	48.716	<0.001
Intonation	F0max	90.7	3.5	1;2	177.7	26.4	1;3	151.5	22.1	2;3	66.075*	<0.001
(F0)	sdF0peak	2.2	1.0	1;2	18.2	10.3	1;3	13.2	8.1	2;3	56.370*	<0.001
	dF0posMean	3.5	1.4	1;2	2.7	1.1	1	2.2	0.9	2	9.652	<0.001
	dF0neg mean	−3.0	1.1	1;2	−2.4	0.8	1	−1.9	0.6	2	12.711	<0.001
	dF0sdpos	3.0	1.4	1;2	2.3	1.0	1	1.9	1.0	2	7.100	0.001
	dF0sdneg	2.4	1.1	2	2.0	0.7		1.7	0.8	2	9.525*	0.009
Intensity	emph	5.4	1.1	1;2	3.5	0.6	1	3.9	1.4	2	23.133	<0.001
	cvint	14.4	1.4	1;2	10.3	1.6	1;3	12.5	2.1	2;3	41.882	<0.001
Rhythm	Speech rate	6.0	0.7	1;2	5.0	0.8	1	4.9	1.0	2	14.916	<0.001
	Articulation rate	6.2	0.8	1;2	5.2	0.9	1	5.2	1.2	2	9.731	<0.001

1 Significant difference between Age51 and Age74;
2 Significant difference between Age51 and Age82;
3 Significant difference between Age74 and Age82;

* Kruskal-Wallis models followed by non-parametric
U Mann Whitney post hoc tests;

4.1   Intonation

Three intonational prosodic features did not reveal statistical significant differences: F0peakwidth ($H = 3.376$; $df = 2$; $p = 0.185$), sdtF0peak ($H = 3.895$; $df = 2$; $p = 0.143$) and F0peak_rate ($F(2,87) = 0.670$, $p = 0.514$).

Parametric ANOVA with Tukey HDS post-hoc tests revealed significant differences between Age51 and Age74 and among Age51 and Age82 on the following features (as seen in Table 2): F0min, dF0posmean, dF0negmean and dF0sdpos. It can be argued, for the parameters above, that the intonational features extracted from the interview recorded at a younger age (i.e., Age51) presented the most different values, considering the non-significant difference between Age74 and Age82. F0min and dF0negmean values increased significantly, meaning that, with increasing age, the speaker presents higher values of minimum fundamental frequency and less steeper F0 falls, respectively. dF0posmean and dF0sdpos decreased across ages, which means less steeper and less variable F0 rises.

Kruskal-Wallis models followed by non-parametric U Mann Whitney post hoc test were carried out and showed statistically significant differences between all possible pairs of ages for the parameters: F0med, F0sd, fSAQ, F0max and sdF0peak. For the parameter dF0sdneg, post-hoc tests revealed statistical significance on the comparison between Age51 and Age82.

The parameters F0med, F0sd, fSAQ, F0max and sdF0peak presented an inverted v-shape trend, with a significant increase between Age51 and Age74 and a significant decrease between Age74 and Age82. Longitudinally (i.e., comparing feature values for the younger age and values for the older age), those features present a tendency for a significant increase, meaning a higher F0 mean, more F0 variability and higher F0 peaks. dF0sdneg demonstrated a tendency to decrease, which is consistent with less variable F0 falls.

Similar results have been reported in other segmental and suprasegmental longitudinal age-related studies, revealing that F0 in male speakers denotes a non-linear variation with age (see Fig. 2a), with a global tendency to rise, due to changes on the physical properties of the vocal folds [1, 2, 9, 10, 36].

The standard deviation of F0, as well as the variability of F0 maximum or fSAQ, also indicated a longitudinal trend to increase with age, meaning more variability in speaking F0. These results are in line with previous studies on voice ageing that found a significant increase in pitch range in samples of connected speech [16, 20, 37]. This wider range of F0 can be explained both by age changes in speech style and by the decline of phonatory control and the necessary adjustments employed by older speakers [1]. Considering Volin et al. [16], the lower F0 range that is observed in younger adults can be an expression of the fast articulation rate used in these ages, as faster speakers tend to smooth prosodic variations (e.g., fewer prosodic boundaries and prominences). Additionally, and considering that F0 range is associated and it is proportional to the speakers' involvement conveyed by different emotions [38], it is possible that the use of a wider F0 range in this longitudinal data may also be related with emotions of more involvement (e.g., happiness/pleasantness) transmitted by the speaker in the interview recorded with 82 years old.

Less studied, but with a significant decrease with age, were the intonational parameters that analysed the mean and standard deviation of positive and negative F0 derivatives (i.e., dF0pos mean, dF0negmean, dF0sdpos and dF0sdneg). A decrease in those features means less steeper and variable F0 rises and falls. The decline in derivative measures can lead (although not necessarily a direct consequence) to a tendency for less intonational variation with age. Additional studies should be developed using those intonational parameters to acknowledge and discuss the changes' meaning for age-related voice modifications. However, the authors considered that the statistically significant results between ages found in the present study might indicate the potential importance of these parameters in prosodic changes across the lifetime.

4.2 Intensity

Parametric ANOVA models were run for the intensity parameters (i.e., cvint and emph) and the results are presented in Table 2. The speaker showed significant differences in the cvint between all pairs of ages. The global speech intensity tended to be less variable with age, since at Age51 the speaker presented higher global intensity variation than in the last ages, albeit the cvint also increased significantly at the Age82. Most of the previous studies have found an increase in intensity contours variation with age [2, 16]. However, the longitudinal speech study of Muhammad Ali [29] did not reveal significant difference in the intensity range with age. The authors associate the decreases of intensity variation to a "less animated" speech [29]. A decrease of intensity range was found in a longitudinal study with a 5-years time lag, indicating a possible vocal function deterioration with ageing [26].

The spectral emphasis (emph) is displayed in Fig. 2b. Significant differences on emph only occured between the middle age (Age51) and the last ages (Age74 and Age82). Despite the differences in the speech sample used, as in Schötz [2], a general decrease of emph between middle age (Age51) and Age74 was observed in this speaker, followed by a slightly rise to Age82, meaning a lesser vocal effort in the older ages [33,34].

4.3 Rhythm

Parametric ANOVA models were run for the speech rate and articulation rate. Results for both parameters are presented in Table 2. The speaker presented a decrease in speech and articulation rate with age, with significant differences between Age51 and Age74 and Age51 and Age82. As observed in Fig. 2c, speech rate showed a sharp decrease between Age51 and Age74. In the last ages (between Age74 and Age82) the speech rate did not reveal remarkable age changes. As in the current study, most of the literature reported a lower speech rate with age, both in longitudinal [23,25,28] and cross-sectional studies [1,2,7,13–16]. It has been suggested that the age-related decrease in speech (and articulation) rate results from neuromuscular slowing, altered nerve supply and respiratory changes with ageing [1,2,14].

5 Conclusion

The present research study is an ongoing project that implements a longitudinal methodological approach to analyse age-related prosodic changes in EP native speakers (i.e., intonation, intensity, rhythm and vocal quality features). This study adds to the growing body of data on the effects of age on speech prosody for a language other than English.

It can be concluded from the data analysis of this male speaker that, as age increases, significant differences can be observed in both intonation, intensity and rhythm. The subject presents a significant tendency for a higher and more variable F0 range, less intensity variation and slower speech across lifetime. Despite the type of corpus selected (i.e., interviews), in which prosodic parameters may be seemingly more sensitive to paralinguistic effects and variations due to speaker emotion, the results obtained are in accordance with the trends reported in cross-sectional [1,2,7] and longitudinal studies [23,24,27,29,36].

Future research should include longitudinal data for more speakers of both genders, to allow generalisations of patterns in age-related prosodic modifications. It should also address the influence of the speaker emotion in speech prosody [39] and the potential of the less studied intonational parameters (i.e., dF0posmean, dF0negmean, dF0sdpos and dF0sdneg) to explain the age-related prosodic changes.

Acknowledgments. This research was financially supported by the project Vox Senes POCI-01-0145-FEDER-03082 (funded by FEDER, through COMPETE2020 - Programa Operacional Competitividade e Internacionalização (PO-CI), and by national funds (OE), through FCT/MCTES), by the grant SFRH/BD/115381/2016 (funded by FCT, through FSE and by CENTRO2020), and by IEETA (**UIDB/00127/2020**). The last author thanks grant 302194/2019-3 from the CNPq agency, Brazil.

References

1. Linville, S.E.: Vocal Aging. Singular Thomson Learning, San Diego (2001)
2. Schötz, S.: Perception, Analysis and Synthesis of Speaker Age, vol. 47. Linguistics and Phonetics. Lund University (2006)
3. Wang, X.: Segmental versus suprasegmental: which one is more important to teach? RELC J. 1–9 (2020). https://doi.org/10.1177/0033688220925926
4. Crystal, D.: Prosodic Systems and Intonation in English, vol. 1. CUP Archive (1969)
5. Barbosa, P.A.: Prosódia (Prosody), vol. 2. Parábola, São Paulo (2019)
6. Keller, B.Z.: Ageing and Speech Prosody. In: Speech Prosody, Germany (2006)
7. Pellegrini, T., et al.: A corpus-based study of elderly and young speakers of European Portuguese: acoustic correlates and their impact on speech recognition performance. In: INTERSPEECH, Lyon, pp. 852–856. ISCA (2013)
8. Guimarães, I., Abberton, E.: Fundamental frequency in speakers of Portuguese for different voice samples. J. Voice **19**(4), 592–606 (2005)
9. Albuquerque, L., Valente, A.R.S., Teixeira, A., Oliveira, C., Figueiredo, D.: Acoustic changes in spontaneous speech with age. In: VIII Congreso Internacional de Fonética Experimental, Girona (2021, in press)
10. Reubold, U., Harrington, J.: Disassociating the effects of age from phonetic change. In: Language Development: The Life Span Perspective, pp. 9–37 (2015)
11. Pellegrino, E., He, L., Dellwo, V.: The effect of ageing on speech rhythm: a study on Zurich German. In: Speech Prosody, pp. 133–137 (2018)
12. Albuquerque, L., Oliveira, C., Teixeira, A., Sa-Couto, P., Figueiredo, D.: A comprehensive analysis of age and gender effects in European Portuguese oral vowels. J. Voice (2020, in press). https://doi.org/10.1016/J.JVOICE.2020.10.021
13. Hazan, V., Tuomainen, O., Kim, J., Davis, C., Sheffield, B., Brungart, D.: Clear speech adaptations in spontaneous speech produced by young and older adults. J. Acoust. Soc. Am. **144**(3), 1331–1346 (2018)
14. Bourbon, A., Hermes, A.: Have a break: aging effects on sentence production and structuring in French. In: 12th International Seminar on Speech Production (2020)
15. Hermes, A., Bourbon, A., Cecile, F.: Aging effects on prosodic structuring in French. In: SPPL2020: 2nd Workshop on Speech Perception and Production across the Lifespan, p. 119 (2020)
16. Volín, J., Tykalová, T., Bořil, T.: Stability of prosodic characteristics across age and gender groups. In: INTERSPEECH, Stockholm, pp. 3902–3906. ISCA (2017). https://doi.org/10.21437/Interspeech.2017-1503
17. Pegoraro Krook, M.I.: Speaking fundamental frequency characteristics of normal Swedish subjects obtained by glottal frequency analysis. Folia Phoniatr Logop **40**(2), 82–90 (1988). https://doi.org/10.1159/000265888
18. Rojas, S., Kefalianos, E., Vogel, A.: How does our voice change as we age? A systematic review and meta-analysis of acoustic and perceptual voice data from healthy adults over 50 years of age. J. Speech Lang. Hear. Res. **63**(2), 533–551 (2020). https://doi.org/10.1044/2019_JSLHR-19-00099
19. Ryan, W.J.: Acoustic aspects of the aging voice. J. Gerontol. **27**(2), 265–268 (1972). https://doi.org/10.1093/geronj/27.2.265

20. Dimitrova, S., Andreeva, B., Gabriel, C., Grünke, J.: Speaker age effects on prosodic patterns in Bulgarian. In: Speech Prosody, Poznań, Poland, pp. 709–713. ISCA (2018). https://doi.org/10.21437/SpeechProsody.2018-144
21. Nishio, M., Niimi, S.: Changes in speaking fundamental frequency characteristics with aging. Folia Phoniatr Logop **60**(3), 120–127 (2008)
22. Mann, C.J.: Observational research methods. Research design II: cohort, cross sectional, and case-control studies. Emerg. Med. J. **20**(1), 54–60 (2003)
23. Pellegrino, E.: The effect of healthy aging on within-speaker rhythmic variability: a case study on Noam Chomsky. Loquens **6**(1), e060 (2019). https://doi.org/10. 3989/loquens.2019.060
24. Reubold, U., Harrington, J., Kleber, F.: Vocal aging effects on F0 and the first formant: a longitudinal analysis in adult speakers. Speech Commun. **52**, 638–651 (2010)
25. Gerstenberg, A., Fuchs, S., Kairet, J.M., Frankenberg, C., Schröder, J.: A cross-linguistic, longitudinal case study of pauses and interpausal units in spontaneous speech corpora of older speakers of German and French. In: Speech Prosody, Poznan, Poland, pp. 211–215 (2018). https://doi.org/10.21437/SpeechProsody.2018-43
26. Verdonck-de Leeuw, I.M., Mahieu, H.F.: Vocal aging and the impact on daily life: a longitudinal study. J. Voice **18**(2), 193–202 (2004)
27. Quené, H.: Longitudinal trends in speech tempo: the case of Queen Beatrix. J. Acoust. Soc. Am. **133**(6), EL452–EL457 (2013). https://doi.org/10.1121/1. 4802892
28. Massimo, P., Elisa, P.: Age and rhtymic variations: a study on Italian. In: INTER-SPEECH 2014, Singapore, pp. 1234–1237. ISCA (2014)
29. Berisha, V., Liss, J., Huston, T., Wisler, A., Jiao, Y., Eig, J.: Float Like a butterfly sting like a bee: changes in speech preceded parkinsonism diagnosis for Muhammad Ali. In: INTERSPEECH, Stockholm, Sweden, pp. 1809–1813 (2017). https://doi. org/10.21437/Interspeech.2017-25
30. Barbosa, P.A.: Incursões em torno do ritmo da fala (Incursions around the rhythm of speech). FAPESP/Pontes Editores, Campinas (2006)
31. Barbosa, P.A.: Semi-automatic and automatic tools for generating prosodic descriptors for prosody research. In: TRASP, pp. 86–89. Aix-en-Provence (2013)
32. Barbosa, P.A.: ProsodyDescriptorExtractor (2020). https://github.com/ pabarbosa/prosody-scripts/tree/master/ProsodyDescriptorExt-ractor
33. Traunmüller, H., Eriksson, A.: Acoustic effects of variation in vocal effort by men, women, and children. J. Acoust. Soc. Am. **107**(6), 3438–3451 (2000). https://doi. org/10.1121/1.429414
34. Heldner, M.: On the reliability of overall intensity and spectral emphasis as acoustic correlates of focal accents in Swedish. J. Phonetics **31**, 39–62 (2003)
35. IBM Corp: SPSS Statistics for Windows (2017)
36. Pettorino, M., Pellegrino, E., Maffia, M.: "Young" and "Old" voice: the prosodic auto-transplantation technique for speaker's age recognition. In: 7th Speech Prosody, Dublin, Ireland, pp. 135–139. ISCA (2014). https://doi.org/10.21437/ SpeechProsody.2014-15
37. Fougeron, C., Bourbon, A., Delvaux, V.: Age effects on voice and rate in French according to sex. In: 1st International Seminar on the Foundations of Speech (SEFOS): Breathing, Pausing, and the Voice, Denmark, pp. 30–32 (2019)
38. Madureira, S.: Intonation and variation: the multiplicity of forms and senses. Dialectologia. Special Issue **VI**, 57–74 (2016)
39. Cole, J.: Prosody in context: a review. Lang. Cogn. Neurosci. **30**(1–2), 1–31 (2015). https://doi.org/10.1080/23273798.2014.963130

Automatic Selection of the Most Characterizing Features for Detecting COPD in Speech

Loes van Bemmel[1,2(✉)], Wieke Harmsen[1], Catia Cucchiarini[3], and Helmer Strik[3,4]

[1] Department of Artificial Intelligence,
Radboud University Nijmegen, Nijmegen, The Netherlands
{l.vanbemmel,w.harmsen}@student.ru.nl
[2] Institute for Computing and Information Sciences,
Radboud University Nijmegen, Nijmegen, The Netherlands
[3] Centre for Language Studies, Radboud University Nijmegen,
Nijmegen, The Netherlands
{c.cucchiarini,w.strik}@let.ru.nl
[4] Donders Institute for Brain, Cognition and Behaviour, Radboud University
Nijmegen, Nijmegen, The Netherlands

Abstract. Speech can reveal important characteristics of a person such as accent, gender, age, and health. Identifying specific pathologies in a person's speech can be extremely useful for diagnosis, especially if this can be done automatically. In the present research, we investigate which automatically computed speech features are characteristic for distinguishing Dutch COPD patients in exacerbated or stable condition. Read speech of a phonetically balanced story was recorded for COPD patients in exacerbation (n=11), stable condition (n=9), and for healthy controls (n = 29). Several acoustic features automatically computed with Praat and eGeMAPS were ranked by a Recursive Feature Elimination (RFE) method and were used as input for three binary classifications by both Support Vector Machine (SVM) and Linear Discriminant Analysis (LDA) classifiers: I exacerbation vs. healthy, II stable vs. healthy, and III exacerbation vs. stable. Besides the features for the full story, we also computed features on word and phoneme level. For all 9 combinations (3 binary comparisons × 3 feature levels) we used RFE to select the top ten ranked features. The classification results showed: better performance for SVM (vs. LDA), better performance for story level (vs. word and phoneme level), and worse performance for comparison III exacerbation vs. stable (vs. I and II i.e. COPD vs. reference speech). A 100% correct classification could always be obtained at story level, but not for word and phoneme level; and only for a subset of features, not for all features. We discuss these results and consider their implications for future research and applications.

Keywords: Chronic obstructive pulmonary disease (COPD) · Feature selection · Acoustic speech features · Speech classification.

© Springer Nature Switzerland AG 2021
A. Karpov and R. Potapova (Eds.): SPECOM 2021, LNAI 12997, pp. 737–748, 2021.
https://doi.org/10.1007/978-3-030-87802-3_66

1   Introduction

In recent years we have seen an increasing amount of research in which speech analysis is being used for early detection and diagnosis of various diseases. Some diseases would not seem to be related to speech at first sight, but do manifest themselves in speech because they somehow affect one of the many mechanisms involved in speech production. Examples are Alzheimer's [2], Amytrophic Lateral Sclerosis [6], depression level [15], and dysarthria [19].

This type of research has been facilitated by the development of useful research instruments such as the Geneva Minimalistic Acoustic Parameter Set (GeMAPS) [3]. GeMAPS, or the extended version eGeMAPS, is a set of standardized acoustic features with demonstrated theoretical relevance and potential to identify relevant aspects of speech production and ease in automatic computation. GeMAPS features can be extracted from speech using the openSMILE toolkit [4], an open-source implementation kit developed to ensure standardized calculation of all parameters.

One of the diseases that would not necessarily seem to be related to speech, but that does in fact affect speech production is Chronic Obstructive Pulmonary Disease (COPD) [17]. This disease is caused by progressive lung failures associated with airflow limitation. COPD is characterized by so-called exacerbations, which are episodes of extreme worsening of the respiratory symptoms that can lead to hospitalization [20]. Early detection of upcoming exacerbations is crucial to provide timely treatment and prevent hospitalization [21], but so far this has proven to be difficult because the early symptoms are often too subtle to be recognized by the patients [18]. Spirometry is an accurate and established method that is currently used in hospitals to perform pulmonary assessment and detect upcoming exacerbations. Unfortunately, this method is not accessible outside hospital settings since it requires a specialized device and training to operate this device. Therefore, exacerbations are usually identified at a late stage [9]. To overcome this problem, mobile spirometers have been developed, like SpiroCall [5] and SpiroSmart [10], which compute the air flow exiting a patient's mouth using the microphone of a smartphone. These mobile spirometers show promising results in assessing pulmonary function, but a disadvantage is that they do still need high-effort active input (e.g. forcefull blowing) from the user.

Medical professionals maintain that they can hear differences between the speech of COPD patients in stable periods as opposed to their speech during exacerbations [11]. This implies that a passive continuous method to monitor a patient's pulmonary condition can be achieved by extracting and analysing acoustic features from speech of COPD patients. For English COPD speech, this has recently been done in two studies. Both studies extracted features from speech of both healthy individuals and COPD patients and used these features to train a classifier to distinguish between these two types of speech. The studies differ on the type and amount of features that they extract. Nathan et al. [12] computed eight features from continuous running speech. These features are: pause time, pause frequency, relative shimmer, shimmer apq3, shimmer apq5, shimmer apq11, absolute jitter and relative jitter. San Chun et al. [17] initially extracted 15 features from each speech recording and used Recursive Feature Elimination with Cross Validation (RFECV) to select the seven most important features that yield the best classification performance. They used feature selection to avoid overfitting and improve the generalizability. Three of the seven selected features are: the vocalization to inhalation ratio, average phonation time, and relative jitter. Both studies used a Voice Activity Detector (VAD) to identify spoken from unspoken sections in the speech data.

For Dutch speech, only one study tried to identify appropriate acoustic parameters for early detection of exacerbations [11]. In this study, the measures Harmonic to Noise Ratio (HNR), shimmer, duration, the number of syllables per breath group and the number of inhalations per syllable were marked as characterizing COPD speech. Unfortunately, one important limitation of this study is that the inhalation measures were computed manually, by annotating audio files, and therefore cannot be used in applications for early automatic detection of exacerbations. Additionally, the significant automatically computed measures were extracted from sustained vowels and not from spontaneous or read speech.

Therefore, in the current paper we analyze Dutch speech to pursue two distinct, but related research goals: to what extent it is possible to automatically extract and select the most characterizing features to a) distinguish COPD speech from healthy speech and b) to detect exacerbations within COPD speech. In addition, we will extract acoustic features from the read speech on three different levels: for each phoneme, for each word and for the whole story. These features will be computed using the segmentations obtained by a forced aligner. This is a novel approach with respect to the earlier discussed COPD studies by Nathan et al. [12] and San Chun et al. [17].

We will use feature selection, classification and statistical tests to validate the importance of the chosen features for different types of speech. We present and discuss our results in relation to those of previous research and consider future perspectives for fundamental research and application development.

2   Methods

2.1   Acoustic Data

The data used in this study are speech recordings of adult native Dutch speakers reading a story. These recordings can be divided into three groups: speech of COPD patients in exacerbation (n = 11), speech of stable COPD patients (n = 9) and speech of healthy reference speakers, not suffering from COPD (n = 29). The COPD patients' speech was recorded at Radboud University Medical Centre between August 2016 and April 2017. The same COPD speech data was used in Merkus et al. [11], although no sustained vowels are used in the current experiment. Unfortunately, no demographic information of the speakers is available. The speech recordings of the healthy reference speakers were recorded at the Radboud University Medical Center in 2019.

In each speech recording, part of the phonetically balanced Dutch story "De Koning" [8] was read aloud. The COPD patients in exacerbation read the beginning of the story, and later when they had recovered (stable condition), they read the middle of the story in order to avoid a possible learning effect. Two of the patients did not participate in the latter stable recordings.

The reference speakers read the entire story, but these recordings were also split up in beginning and middle parts to match the COPD patients' recordings.

2.2 Data Pre-processing

Pre-processing of the speech recordings consists of three steps.

First, the orthographic transcriptions were checked and corrected if necessary. Some COPD patients were unable to finish the entire selected paragraph during exacerbation, resulting in slightly shorter recordings for this condition. No manual corrections were made for the healthy speakers.

Secondly, the resulting orthographic transcriptions were automatically aligned with their corresponding speech recordings on both word and phoneme level using a Kaldi-based forced aligner developed in-house at the Centre for Language and Speech Technology (https://webservices.cls.ru.nl/forcedalignment). An overview of the segmentations can be seen in Table 1.

Lastly, the COPD speech segmentations at word level were manually checked and corrected if necessary.

Table 1. This table describes the data. For each type of speech, the table contains information about which part of the text "De Koning" was read. For recordings: the number of recordings, and mean duration and mean number of read words per recording. And finally, the total number of segments at the three levels: Story, Words, and Phonemes.

Type of speech	Part of text "De Koning"	Recordings			Total number of segments		
		Number	Mean duration (seconds)	Mean number of read words	Story	Words	Phonemes
COPD exacerbation	Begin	11	38.172	115	11	1266	2775
COPD stable	Middle	9	46.405	160	9	1446	2723
Reference	Begin	29	38.778	125	29	3649	7888
	middle	29	45.068	164	29	4769	8722

2.3 Acoustic Features

For each of the three segmentation levels (full story, word, and phoneme), the same 103 features were automatically calculated using the speech analysis software Praat [1] and the audio feature extraction toolkit openSMILE [4]. For the full story segmentations, two extra features were calculated: the number of words read aloud and the total duration of the audio file.

A Praat script was used to compute a number of features for each word and phoneme segment: duration, the four formants, mean gravity center, and some measures of pitch and intensity (i.e., mean, minimum, maximum and standard deviation). To obtain a value of these features on story level, we summarized the values of these features on word level by taking the mean value per speaker.

The eGeMAPS features [3] were extracted using openSMILE. For the story segmentation, the default configuration for eGeMAPS was used. A custom configuration using the segmentations from the forced alignments was used to compute the eGeMAPS features per word and phoneme.

For a more detailed description of these features including time steps and window sizes, please refer back to the Praat manual and documentation [1] and the eGeMAPS paper [3].

2.4   Classification and Validation

There are many machine learning models available for classification of speech. Two earlier studies that classified English COPD speech reported the best results using a Random Forest model [12,17]. Unfortunately, we do not have enough data to use such a complex model, since it increases the risk of the model overfitting. Therefore, we decided to use relatively simple linear models to classify our data: a Support Vector Machine (SVM) with a linear kernel and Linear Discriminant Analysis (LDA). SVM has also been used quite often for speech classification or analysis in earlier studies. [6,16,22]. Other than the linear SVM kernel, the default parameters from Scikit-learn [14] were used for both classifiers. To prevent the model from overfitting, we also decided to use binary classification. Another reason to study binary classification is that the most interesting comparisons for practical applications are: (1) for presumably healthy persons: are there indications for COPD?; and (2) for presumably stable patients: are there indications for an upcoming lung attack (exacerbation)? Therefore, we studied the following three comparisons: COPD exacerbation vs. reference, COPD stable vs. reference, or COPD exacerbation vs. COPD stable. These three comparisons were carried out for the three segmentation types, resulting in nine combinations.

Because of the differences in story length for the exacerbation and the stable condition, seen in Table 1, three duration-specific features have been removed for the COPD exacerbation vs. COPD stable classification specifically. Since the reference recordings are matched to the COPD recordings in terms of duration, no preemptive feature removal had to be done for those classifications.

To validate the trained models we used Leave-One-Subject-Out (LOSO) cross validation, which means that all samples except the ones belonging to one single speaker are used for training the model and the remaining samples from the one left out speaker are used for validation of the model. We chose to use LOSO cross validation because it maximizes the amount of training data, which is useful since the total amount of data is limited. In addition, it also reduces the impact of subject-based characteristics on the classification [16], and is used by an earlier study in which English COPD speech is classified as well [17].

For training and validation Z-scores were used, which were calculated by means of the StandardScaler function of Python's Scikit-learn package [14]. For every fold in the cross validation, the mean and standard deviation used to calculate the Z-scores were based on the training data only. In this study, we did not evaluate our final model using a test set. We decided to do this because of the limited amount of data that our data set consists of.

For word and phoneme segmentations, classification is initially done at the segment level, and the majority vote of the classification of the segments determines the final classification of the story (speaker) as a whole. A similar strategy was used by Sakar et al. [16].

2.5   Feature Selection

Feature selection is one of the key components for successfully training a model with a limited amount of data. In most cases, the performance improves when only a subset of all available features is used [17,22]. We employed Recursive Feature Elimination (RFE) to select the most relevant acoustic features for each of the nine different binary classifications.

RFE is a wrapper feature selection method that employs greedy search to make a backwards feature elimination [7]. The RFE model also uses an SVM with a linear kernel, but instead of classifying the data it is now used to determine which feature is least informative. This feature is deleted from the complete feature set. We continue deleting features with RFE until only one feature is left. The deletion order of features can also be seen as a list of features ranked on importance, with the last remaining feature being the most important. The RFECV method used by San Chun et al. [17] automatically selects the optimal number of features, but a feature ranking was more useful for this experiment. For each of the nine combinations, we computed this ranking and used it to select the top ten most important features.

2.6   Evaluation of the Models

To evaluate these models, we computed the Matthews Correlation Coefficient (MCC). We chose this metric rather than accuracy because MCC is better suited for unbalanced data [16]. Since our data is severely unbalanced (n = 9, n = 11, and n = 29), MCC is more robust than the standard accuracy measure. The MCC is a score between −1 and 1, in which −1 indicates a very poor classification and 1 indicates a 100% correct classification. The MCC score can be calculated using True Positives (TP), False Positives (FP), True Negatives (TN) and False Negatives (FN) from the binary classification. The confusion matrices from each LOSO fold are combined to compute the final MCC score. The equation for MCC can be seen in Eq. 1.

$$MCC = \frac{TP \times TN - FP \times FN}{\sqrt{(TP + FP) \times (TP + FN) \times (TN + FP) \times (TN + FN)}}. \tag{1}$$

Table 2. The scores of the MANOVA analysis for the top ten features for story segmentation per comparison.

Comparison	Rank	Feature	p	M(SD)		F	η^2
Exacerbation vs. Reference				Exacerbation	Reference		
	1	VoicedSegmentsPerSec	**	1.911(.372)	2.604(.294)	38.180	.501
	2	alphaRatioV_sma3nz_amean	**	−21.626(4.749)	−15.243(2.570)	30.066	.442
	3	pitch_std_mean	**	20.830(10.796)	35.551(13.683)	10.249	.212
	4	F2amplitudeLogRelF0_sma3nz_stddevNorm	**	−0.586(.099)	−.722(.073)	22.852	.376
	5	pitch_var_mean	**	612.438(255.655)	916.693(261.578)	10.918	.223
	6	F1frequency_sma3nz_stddevNorm	*	.281(.0355)	.314(.041)	5.384	.124
	7	intensity_min_mean	**	46.566(6.483)	54.384(3.213)	26.115	.407
	8	MeanUnvoicedSegmentLength	**	.346(.096)	.211(.038)	40.953	.519
	9	pitch_max_mean	**	189.506(48.485)	245.127(57.803)	8.009	.174
	10	F3frequency_sma3nz_amean		2539.975(128.518)	2512.972(74.400)	.690	.018
Stable vs. Reference				Stable	Reference		
	1	intensity_min_mean	**	45.047(5.609)	54.818(3.179)	44.13	.551
	2	StddevUnvoicedSegmentLength	**	.431(.134)	.298(.068)	15.903	.306
	3	mfcc2_sma3_amean	**	12.957(6.692)	2.041(4.660)	30.479	.458
	4	F0semitoneFrom27.5Hz_sma3nz_stddevRisingSlope		246.800(130.1562)	356.301(203.816)	2.283	.06
	5	hammarbergIndexUV_sma3nz_amean		19.925(6.691)	21.780(3.930)	1.076	.029
	6	F2amplitudeLogRelF0_sma3nz_stddevNorm	**	−.621(.091)	−.730(.074)	12.973	.265
	7	F1frequency_sma3nz_stddevNorm	**	.261(.030)	.302(.038)	8.600	.193
	8	spectralFlux_sma3_amean	**	.155(.130)	.435(.176)	19.379	.350
	9	F3bandwidth_sma3nz_stddevNorm		.338(.049)	.326(.037)	.616	.017
	10	pitch_var_mean	*	608.443(213.275)	819.919(238.486)	5.652	.136
Exacerbation vs. Stable				Exacerbation	Stable		
	1	F3bandwidth_sma3nz_amean		908.455(71.025)	857.133(70.351)	2.606	.126
	2	F2frequency_sma3nz_stddevNorm		.159(.024)	.146(.019)	1.680	.085
	3	intensity_std_mean		7.199(.592)	7.448(.840)	.585	.031
	4	logRelF0-H1-A3_sma3nz_stddevNorm		.314(.076)	.363(.098)	.012	.080
	5	mfcc4V_sma3nz_stddevNorm		−.927(6.502)	.391(6.004)	.218	.012
	6	mfcc3V_sma3nz_stddevNorm		4.074(10.823)	−1.359(7.100)	1.670	.085
	7	StddevUnvoicedSegmentLength		.641(.285)	.431(.134)	4.065	.184
	8	F3bandwidth_sma3nz_stddevNorm		.347(.050)	.338(.049)	.187	.010
	9	mfcc2_sma3_amean		13.031(6.490)	12.957(6.692)	.001	.000
	10	StddevVoicedSegmentLengthSec		.142(.028)	.188(.120)	1.312	.068

Note: $^{**}p < 0.01$, $^{*}p < 0.05$

3   Results

Classification performance for both SVM and LDA classifiers is shown in Fig. 1. Different colors are used for the three comparisons, and different line types for the three segmentations. As mentioned above, we start with the full feature set (i.e. at the right), and use RFE to gradually remove features. For each of these feature sets, MCC is calculated and plotted in Fig. 1. The general trend seems to be: better results for the full story (than for word and phoneme level), better results for SVM (than for LDA), scores of COPD exacerbation vs. COPD stable are lower (than for the other 2 comparisons), and the optimal MCC value obtained for a selection of the features is larger than for all features. Using a subset of the features at story level, it is possible to obtain an MCC value of 1, i.e. 100% correct classification, for all three comparisons.

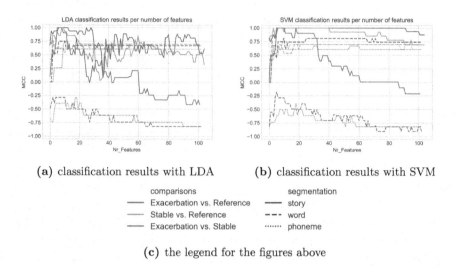

(a) classification results with LDA   (b) classification results with SVM

comparisons   segmentation
—— Exacerbation vs. Reference   —— story
—— Stable vs. Reference   --- word
—— Exacerbation vs. Stable   ······ phoneme

(c) the legend for the figures above

Fig. 1. The MCC classification scores per number of features for the ranked RFE feature set using both LDA and SVM classification.

The top ten features from the story segmentation per comparison were also tested in a MANOVA analysis. The results of this test can be seen in Table 2. All three multivariate tests were significant with $p < 0.01$. The majority of the top ten features separately were significantly affected by speech type as well. However, in the COPD exacerbation vs. COPD stable features this was not the case. None of these features showed a significant univariate effect by speech type, but the multivariate test was significant with $F(10, 9) = 7.103$ and $p = .003$. So, the top ten features combined were affected significantly by speech type.

4   Discussion

We automatically computed speech features for reference, stable COPD and exacerbated COPD speech. Using SVM and LDA, we were able to classify a) COPD speech from healthy speech and b) exacerbated COPD speech from stable COPD speech. For each type of speech, we found a different set of features that are most characteristic and important for classification. In addition, we found that a limited set of features yields better classification than using all possible features.

We see that for a selection of the features, all story segmentation lines reach a classification score of 1, while the word and phoneme level lines do not. A possible explanation is that the story segmentation features contain more information than the word and phoneme segmentations. This is plausible, since shorter segmentations contain more errors and more 'noise', such that classification results are more likely to vary. Furthermore, short segments could be problematic during feature extraction due to the length of time steps in feature computations.

Although we tried to prevent overfitting, these 100% correct classification scores could be (at least partially) due to overfitting, since the number of recordings is small.

Secondly, we found that SVM performs better than LDA in classification, but when comparing the scores of SVM with those of LDA we saw the same trends. For example, the full feature set consistently performs worse than most subsets of the features, proving once again that feature selection is useful for speech classification. However, we need to be careful in drawing conclusions about the SVM performance, since the selected features were ranked using SVM as well.

We observe that COPD exacerbation vs. COPD stable seems to result in lower classification scores than the COPD vs. reference comparisons. This indicates that the classification for COPD exacerbation vs. COPD stable is more complex, probably because the data are more similar. Note that the COPD exacerbation and COPD stable recordings are from the same speakers (i.e. the COPD patients), while the reference recordings are from different speakers. This most likely has impacted the classification scores as well. However, it is also not unlikely that in general the binary classification stable COPD vs. exacerbation is more complex than healthy vs. COPD. Ideally, also the reference recordings should be of the same speakers, but obviously that is not possible.

For each comparison between two types of speech, we found a different set of features that are most important for classification. The top ten story-level features were chosen to be examined more closely since the classification using these features resulted in an MCC score of 1. These features differ from the significant features found by Merkus [11], but have the advantage that they are computed automatically instead of manually, and from read speech rather than sustained vowels. When comparing the top ten ranked features with the features found in English COPD speech by San Chun et al. [17] and Nathan et al. [12], we need to note that they both performed a binary COPD vs. reference speech classification. Additionally, they computed other features than we did in this paper. The only shimmer and jitter features we computed are the ones included in the eGeMAPS featureset, i.e. local shimmer and local jitter. Neither of these were selected in the top ten by the RFE. Other features selected in the literature such as pause frequency, pause time and average phonation time are all related to duration and (un)voiced segments per second measures. For all three of our comparisons, some (un)voiced segment measures were selected in the top ten, illustrating the importance of these kinds of features.

4.1 Limitations

One prominent limitation in this type of research is that there is not a lot of data available in general, and therefore the data set used in this study is limited. This is a problem for most pathological speech research and applications, especially for languages other than English. A risk of using a small amount of data is that overfitting may occur. We tried to prevent this by using simple linear models, LOSO cross validation and the MCC measure. At story level, the RFE method succeeded in selecting a set of features for which MCC is 1, but again, this could be partially due to overfitting. In future research, hopefully more data will be available, which would allow us to use more sophisticated methods, such that we can draw stronger conclusions.

Another limitation is that no demographic information about the speakers was available in our data set, such as accents, place of origin and other relevant metadata. Because of this uncertainty, an unrecognized bias could be present in our research. We stress the importance of this type of information collected in future speech data acquisition studies.

4.2   Future Research

There are multiple routes to explore to possibly improve the methods in future studies. In the first place, other classifiers and feature selection models could be examined as well. There are other binary or multiclass classification methods available that are also suited for the types of classifications we are studying. Similarly, there are other methods that are able to select features.

Secondly, we could also extend the number of features extracted per recording. Currently, we used a rather limited number of Praat and eGeMAPS features, such that the results could be closely examined. However, using the RFE, any number of features could be reduced down to any arbitrary number. There are more features that can be extracted automatically from speech data.

A small variation on our current method could be to calculate Z-scores for each speaker, instead of basing them on the training data of each fold in the cross validation procedure. This will reduce the effects of identity confounding in speech [13]. In addition, the majority of the segmentation classifications per speaker is taken to classify the speaker's type of speech as a whole. In other words, we use a threshold of 50%, which might not be the optimal threshold. We can explore other thresholds and try to find the most optimal one.

In a future study, we can also explore variations of speech data segmentation. Currently, we have studied three different levels of speech segmentations: story, word, and phoneme; other possible options are sentence and syllable. Furthermore, besides read speech, we could also study other speech tasks: vowels sustained as long as possible, vowel glides, diadochokinetic speech, spontaneous speech, etc.

Since we are able to distinguish between COPD exacerbated speech and COPD stable speech, we can imagine that this is extremely useful in remote monitoring of COPD patients and non-invasive early detection of lung attacks using smart applications that continuously analyse speech (in the background). In addition, similar applications for detecting COPD in presumably healthy speakers can realistically be developed since it is possible to distinguish between healthy speech and COPD speech. The current approach is almost completely automatic and could easily be amended to be fully automatic. Instead of checking the orthographic transcription manually, we could simply take the prompt as the transcription. While this will result in a less reliable transcription, this could be handled using an outlier detection method. Another option is to use an Automatic Speech Recognition system to estimate the spoken words.

It is entirely possible that other combinations of features exist that result in a good classification score as well. While we have achieved our goal of finding a subset of characterizing features, it would be interesting to search for other subsets that also result in high classification results. This could be achieved using variations of different feature selection and classification methods.

5   Conclusions

We obtained very promising results in distinguishing Dutch COPD speech from healthy reference speech. However, distinguishing COPD speech from healthy speech seems to be easier than detecting exacerbations within COPD speech. Detecting exacerbations was achieved by using a subset of seven to eleven story segmentation level features from Praat [1] and eGeMAPS [3] selected by an RFE. The features and techniques used in this paper can all be automated. For this reason, our methods are suited for automatic remote analysis of speech and prove to be a first step towards early diagnosis or remote monitoring of Dutch COPD patients. Unfortunately, limited data sets are the norm rather than the exception in pathological speech research. We do fully realize to what extent these kinds of applications are powered by data, and therefore we aim at extending our data set through cooperation with other research and clinical groups. An important aspect in this respect is to make clinicians aware of the importance of data collection and safe data storage.

Acknowledgements. We would like to thank dr. Hanneke van Helvoort and dr. Simone Knuijt from Radboud University Medical Centre for making available the recordings of the COPD and healthy speakers, respectively. We would also like to thank Joop Kerkhoff for providing the Praat scripts.

References

1. Boersma, P., Weenik, D.: Praat: doing phonetics by computer (version 6.1.16) (2020). http://www.praat.org
2. Chen, J., Zhu, J., Ye, J.: An attention-based hybrid network for automatic detection of alzheimer's disease from narrative speech. In: Proceedings Interspeech, vol. 2019, pp. 4085–4089 (2019)
3. Eyben, F., et al.: The Geneva minimalistic acoustic parameter set (gemaps) for voice research and affective computing. IEEE Trans. Affect. Comput. **7**(2), 190–202 (2016)
4. Eyben, F., Wöllmer, M., Schuller, B.: Opensmile: the Munich versatile and fast open-source audio feature extractor. In: Proceedings of the 18th ACM International Conference on Multimedia, pp. 1459–1462 (2010)
5. Goel, M., et al.: SpiroCall: measuring lung function over a phone call. In: Proceedings of the 2016 CHI Conference on Human Factors in Computing Systems, pp. 5675–5685 (2016)
6. Gutz, S.E., Wang, J., Yunusova, Y., Green, J.R.: Early identification of speech changes due to amyotrophic lateral sclerosis using machine classification. In: INTERSPEECH, pp. 604–608 (2019)

7. Guyon, I., Elisseeff, A.: An introduction to variable and feature selection. J. Mach. Learn. Res. **3**(Mar), 1157–1182 (2003)
8. Haasnoot, R.: De ontwikkeling van de fonetisch uitgebalanceerde standaardtekst "de koning" (2012)
9. Hurst, J.R., et al.: Susceptibility to exacerbation in chronic obstructive pulmonary disease. N. Engl. J. Med. **363**(12), 1128–1138 (2010)
10. Larson, E.C., Goel, M., Boriello, G., Heltshe, S., Rosenfeld, M., Patel, S.N.: SpiroSmart: using a microphone to measure lung function on a mobile phone. In: Proceedings of the 2012 ACM Conference on Ubiquitous Computing, pp. 280–289 (2012)
11. Merkus, J., Hubers, F., Cucchiarini, C., Strik, H.: Digital eavesdropper-acoustic speech characteristics as markers of exacerbations in COPD patients. In: LREC 2020 Language Resources and Evaluation Conference, 11–16 May 2020, p. 78 (2020)
12. Nathan, V., Rahman, M.M., Vatanparvar, K., Nemati, E., Blackstock, E., Kuang, J.: Extraction of voice parameters from continuous running speech for pulmonary disease monitoring. In: 2019 IEEE International Conference on Bioinformatics and Biomedicine (BIBM), pp. 859–864 (2019)
13. Neto, E.C., et al.: Detecting the impact of subject characteristics on machine learning-based diagnostic applications. NPJ Digital Med. **2**(1), 1–6 (2019)
14. Pedregosa, F., et al.: Scikit-learn: machine learning in Python. J. Mach. Learn. Res. **12**, 2825–2830 (2011)
15. Rutowski, T., Harati, A., Lu, Y., Shriberg, E.: Optimizing speech-input length for speaker-independent depression classification. In: INTERSPEECH, pp. 3023–3027 (2019)
16. Sakar, B.E., et al.: Collection and analysis of a Parkinson speech dataset with multiple types of sound recordings. IEEE J. Biomed. Health Inform. **17**(4), 828–834 (2013)
17. San Chun, K., et al.: Towards passive assessment of pulmonary function from natural speech recorded using a mobile phone. In: 2020 IEEE International Conference on Pervasive Computing and Communications (PerCom), pp. 1–10. IEEE (2020)
18. van Schayck, O., D'Urzo, A., Invernizzi, G., Román, M., Ställberg, B., Urbina, C.: Early detection of chronic obstructive pulmonary disease (COPD): the role of spirometry as a diagnostic tool in primary care. Primary Care Respir. J. **12**, 90–93 (2003)
19. Shor, J., et al.: Personalizing ASR for dysarthric and accented speech with limited data. arXiv preprint arXiv:1907.13511 (2019)
20. Singh, D., et al.: Global strategy for the diagnosis, management, and prevention of chronic obstructive lung disease: the gold science committee report 2019. Eur. Respir. J. **53**(5), 1900164 (2019)
21. Trappenburg, J.C., et al.: Effect of an action plan with ongoing support by a case manager on exacerbation-related outcome in patients with COPD: a multicentre randomised controlled trial. Thorax **66**(11), 977–984 (2011)
22. Yarra, C., Rao, A., Ghosh, P.K.: Automatic native language identification using novel acoustic and prosodic feature selection strategies. In: 2018 15th IEEE India Council International Conference (INDICON), pp. 1–6. IEEE (2018)

Multilingual Training Set Selection for ASR in Under-Resourced Malian Languages

Ewald van der Westhuizen(✉) [iD], Trideba Padhi[iD], and Thomas Niesler[iD]

Department of Electrical and Electronic Engineering,
Stellenbosch University, Stellenbosch, South Africa
{ewaldvdw,tpadhi,trn}@sun.ac.za

Abstract. We present first speech recognition systems for the two severely under-resourced Malian languages Bambara and Maasina Fulfulde. These systems will be used by the United Nations as part of a monitoring system to inform and support humanitarian programmes in rural Africa. We have compiled datasets in Bambara and Maasina Fulfulde, but since these are very small, we take advantage of six similarly under-resourced datasets in other languages for multilingual training. We focus specifically on the best composition of the multilingual pool of speech data for multilingual training. We find that, although maximising the training pool by including all six additional languages provides improved speech recognition in both target languages, substantially better performance can be achieved by a more judicious choice. Our experiments show that the addition of just one language provides best performance. For Bambara, this additional language is Maasina Fulfulde, and its introduction leads to a relative word error rate reduction of 6.7%, as opposed to a 2.4% relative reduction achieved when pooling all six additional languages. For the case of Maasina Fulfulde, best performance was achieved when adding only Luganda, leading to a relative word error rate improvement of 9.4% as opposed to a 3.9% relative improvement when pooling all six languages. We conclude that careful selection of the out-of-language data is worthwhile for multilingual training even in highly under-resourced settings, and that the general assumption that more data is better does not always hold.

Keywords: Speech recognition · Humanitarian monitoring ·
Multilingual acoustic modelling · Malian languages · Bambara ·
Maasina Fulfulde

1 Introduction

Radio phone-in talk shows have been found to be a popular platform for voicing concerns and views regarding social issues in societies who do not have ready access to the internet. The United Nations (UN) frequently heads humanitarian

© Springer Nature Switzerland AG 2021
A. Karpov and R. Potapova (Eds.): SPECOM 2021, LNAI 12997, pp. 749–760, 2021.
https://doi.org/10.1007/978-3-030-87802-3_67

programmes in regions on the African continent where this is the case[1]. In order to inform and support these efforts, a radio browsing system has been developed with the UN. These ASR-based systems have successfully been piloted in Uganda in three local languages: Luganda, Acholi and English [13,19]. Recently, a focus of UN humanitarian relief efforts has arisen in the West African country of Mali. In this paper we describe our first ASR systems for the severely under-resourced Malian languages Bambara and Maasina Fulfulde. This includes the compilation of annotated radio speech corpora in both languages. Since these new resources are very limited and are time-consuming, expensive and difficult to produce, we incorporate resources from other languages that were at our disposal in various combinations for multilingual acoustic model training [11,20,21].

Multilingual training of deep neural network (DNN) acoustic models includes multiple languages in the training pool and exploits common phonetic structures among the languages. Employing the hidden layers of a DNN as a multilingually-trained universal feature extractor has been shown to achieve good ASR performance [9,10,24]. Model adaptation and transfer learning approaches from other well resourced languages are also popular approaches to acoustic model training in low-resource settings. Here, the initial layers of a DNN trained on a well resourced language are retained, while the output layer is retrained using the smaller dataset in the target language [8]. Finally, multilingually-trained bottleneck features have also been shown to benefit ASR performance for severely under-resourced languages [15,24].

When embarking on multilingual training, an important decision is which languages to include in the training pool. The addition of a language can sometimes lead to an increased mismatch among the datasets that leads to a deterioration in ASR performance. Hence, the specific choice of languages in the training pool becomes a key factor in achieving the best performing ASR system.

In the next section we give an overview of the target languages. In Sect. 3, the speech and text resources are introduced. The description of the pronunciation, language and acoustic modelling follows in Sects. 4, 5 and 6. The experimental results and the discussion thereof are presented in Sect. 7 and we conclude in Sect. 8.

2   Languages

Mali has a multilingual and multiethnic population with 14 officially recognised national languages. We will focus on two of these: Bambara and Maasina Fulfulde. Figure 1 presents a map indicating where these languages are predominantly spoken.

---

[1] https://www.unglobalpulse.org/project/making-ugandan-community-radio-machine-readable-using-speech-recognition-technology/.
https://www.unglobalpulse.org/document/using-machine-learning-to-analyse-radio-content-in-uganda/.

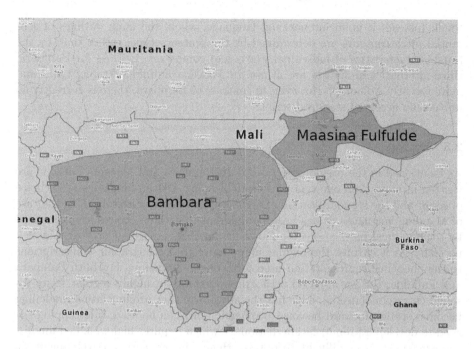

Fig. 1. A map showing the regions of Mali where Bambara and Maasina Fulfulde are predominantly spoken. Adapted from Google Maps.

2.1 The Bambara Language

Bambara is part of the Manding language group which belongs to the greater Mande and Niger-Congo language families [25]. The Manding group is considered to comprise a continuum of languages and dialects that are mutually intelligible. Bambara is used as a *lingua franca* by approximately 14 million Malians.

Bambara is an agglutinative language with seven vowels, 21 consonants and a syllabic nasal [5]. Three distinct alphabets are used to write Bambara: Arabic, Latin and N'Ko [5,6,25]. The Latin-based alphabet is officially recognised in Mali. Bambara is a tonal language and diacritics can be used to indicate the low and high vowel tones.

2.2 The Maasina Fulfulde Language

Maasina Fulfulde is part of the Fulfulde language group which in turn forms part of the Niger-Congo language family. The Fulfulde language group is a continuous chain of dialects that are mutually intelligible and are spoken predominantly in West Africa and a few parts of the Central African region. Maasina Fulfulde is spoken in the central part of Mali in the region of Macina. It is one of Mali's official languages and has an estimated one million speakers [7].

Maasina Fulfulde has 23 consonants, four prenasalised consonants and five vowels [14]. Unlike most of its neighbouring African languages, Fulfulde is not tonal. Instead, it is an intonational language, where the main outlines of sentential pitch contours are determined by the sentence type, rather than by the tonal characteristics of individual words and complexes [1,2]. As for Bambara, three alternative alphabets are in use for Maasina Fulfulde: Arabic, Latin and more recently Adlam [3]. However, in contrast to Bambara, there is currently no universally accepted standard script.

2.3   Scripts

As mentioned in the previous section, both Bambara and Maasina Fulfulde are written in more than one type of script. In many African languages, the choice of script and the standardisation of orthography remains unresolved. In the case of Manding languages, it has been pointed out that these choices are influenced by sociopolitical motivations [6]. However, in ASR, consistent orthography is a necessity, as it ensures the regular mapping of the orthographic transcriptions to the phonemic representation used for acoustic modelling. For both Bambara and Fulfulde, the Latin-based orthography exhibits a highly regular letter-to-sound correspondence [5]. This has the advantage that pronunciation modelling becomes straightforward because graphemic units can be used, sidestepping the need to develop a pronunciation dictionary which requires highly-skilled linguistic expertise that is difficult to obtain. Hence, in our corpus development we have chosen to use the Latin script for both languages.

3   Speech and Text Corpora

No speech or text resources were available for Bambara or Maasina Fulfulde. In this section we describe the corpora that were compiled as part of this work in order to develop acoustic and language models for use in the radio browsing systems.

3.1   Monolingual Speech Corpora

Our Bambara and Maasina Fulfulde speech corpora are under active development. Transmissions from public broadcast radio are recorded and stored as 5-min segments. The speech in these recordings is manually segmented and transcribed by first-language speakers using Praat [4]. We chose to use the Latin script for both languages, as shown in Table 1. Although Bambara and Fulfulde are tonal and intonational languages, respectively, tone markers were not included in order to simplify and expedite the transcription process. At the time of writing, 180 Bambara and 190 Fulfulde recordings have been transcribed, yielding approximately 10 h of speech in each language. Table 2 summarises the extent of the training, development and test sets into which the two corpora have been partitioned.

Table 1. Alphabets used to transcribe Bambara and Fulfulde.

Bambara	
Consonants	b, c, d, f, g, h, j, k, l, m, n, ɲ, ŋ, p, r, s, t, u, w, y, z
Vowels	a, e, ɛ, i, o, ɔ, u
Maasina Fulfulde	
Consonants	', b, ɓ, c, d, ɗ, f, g, h, j, k, l, m, mb, n, nd, ng, nj,
	ŋ, ɲ, p, r, s, t, w, y, yˀ
Vowels	a, e, i, o, u

Table 2. Training, development and test sets for the Bambara and Maasina Fulfulde radio speech corpora. (m: minutes; h: hours).

Bambara	Utterances	Duration
Training	14 037	8.7 h
Development	1 177	49.5 m
Test	933	43.5 m
Total	16 147	10.3 h
Maasina Fulfulde	Utterances	Duration
Training	14 433	10.0 h
Development	322	7.7 m
Test	1 479	31.4 m
Total	16 234	10.6 h

3.2   Multilingual Speech Corpora

Besides the transcribed Bambara and Maasina Fulfulde corpora described above, we had at our disposal speech corpora in a number of other languages. These include radio speech datasets collected for the previously-developed radio browsing systems in Luganda, Acholi and Ugandan English [13]. The data collection procedure for these three languages was similar to that employed for Bambara and Maasina Fulfulde, thus providing a degree of uniformity. In addition, we included Arabic[2], since it is a national language of Mali. Finally, we have collected a small corpus of radio speech in Malian French, which is also a national language of Mali. However, inclusion of this data led to consistent deterioration in preliminary experiments and hence it will not be reported on. The statistics for the four corpora used for multilingual training are summarised in Table 3.

3.3   Text Corpora

Digital text resources in Bambara and Maasina Fulfulde have been compiled from the internet, and this process of identification and collection of additional

---

[2] OpenSLR Tunisian Modern Standard Arabic corpus, accessed 2021-02-21 at http://www.openslr.org/46/.

Table 3. Additional speech corpora used for multilingual acoustic modelling. Duration in hours.

Corpus	Utterances	Duration
Luganda	9 001	9.8
Acholi	4 860	9.2
Ugandan English	4 402	5.7
Tunisian Modern Standard Arabic	11 688	11.2
Total	29 951	35.9

Table 4. Text corpora collected for Bambara and Maasina Fulfulde.

Corpus	Types	Tokens
Bambara	19 992	553 640
Maasina Fulfulde	25 637	665 775

text is ongoing. To the best of our knowledge, no freely or commercially available resources exist in these severely under-resourced languages. The corpora in Table 4 represent the full extent of text available for language modelling in addition to the training transcriptions described in Table 2. Sources include Wikipedia, newspaper articles, blog posts and comments and religious texts.

4   Pronunciation Modelling

As discussed in Sect. 2.3, Bambara and Fulfulde have highly regular letter-to-sound correspondence. We have therefore constructed the pronunciation dictionary using graphemes. This is a simple, fast and automated process that does not rely on skilled linguistic expertise. For example, the dictionary entry for the Bambara word, *angɛrɛ*, is:

    angɛrɛ a_bam n_bam g_bam ɛ_bam r_bam ɛ_bam

A language tag is appended to each grapheme-based phoneme label to disambiguate the labels from similar symbols that may exist in other languages in the multilingual training pool. The same process is applied to create the grapheme-based pronunciation dictionary for Fulfulde. The pronunciation dictionaries for the other languages in the multilingual training pool (Table 3) have been manually compiled by language experts and use true phoneme labels. A multilingual pronunciation dictionary is constructed by concatenating all the dictionaries of the languages in the mulitlingual training pool.

5   Language Modelling

The vocabularies of the language models were closed to include the word types in the training, development and test sets. The vocabularies of the Bambara and Fulfulde language models contain 15 526 and 12 368 word types respectively.

Table 5. Perplexity (PP) of the baseline (transcriptions only) and interpolated (transcriptions and additional text) language models.

Bambara	Word tokens	PP
Baseline language model	137 250	202.46
Interpolated language model	690 890	193.33
Maasina Fulfulde	Word tokens	**PP**
Baseline language model	135 054	522.59
Interpolated language model	800 809	504.56

The SRILM toolkit [22] was used to train trigram language models. Preliminary experiments indicated that higher order models did not provide any further benefit. The same training procedure was used to obtain the language models in each of our two target languages. First, a baseline language model is trained using the training transcriptions (Table 2). Thereafter, language models trained on the additional text resources (Table 4) are interpolated with the baseline to obtain the final language model that is used in the ASR experiments. The interpolation weights were chosen to optimise the development set perplexity. The test set perplexities for the baseline and interpolated language models are given in Table 5. The fairly small perplexity improvements (<5%) indicate a mismatch between the language style in the speech transcripts and the additional text resources.

6   Acoustic Modelling

The acoustic models were trained and evaluated using Kaldi [17]. We followed the standard practice of training a hidden Markov model/Gaussian mixture model (HMM/GMM) system to obtain alignments for DNN training. The DNN architecture used for the multilingual acoustic modelling follows the Librispeech recipe and consists of six convolutional neural network (CNN) layers followed by twelve factorised time-delay deep neural network (TDNN-F) layers, as shown in Fig. 2. The hidden layers and the output layer are shared between languages and the LF-MMI criterion is used as training objective [18]. A *SpecAugment* layer precedes the CNN layers as it has proved beneficial in all experiments [16]. Each ASR system is trained from scratch for six epochs from a randomly initialised network. Three-fold speed perturbation is used during training [12].

In our experiments, we investigate how the composition of the multilingual training pool affects ASR performance. With no prior knowledge about the relatedness of the corpora and languages, a reasonable approach might be to pool all the data that we have at our disposal. This training set composition of six pooled languages is indicated by ALL. We also considered several possible subsets of the six languages for multilingual training, with the constraint that the target language was always included. In each case, a multilingual model is trained on the selected pool of languages, after which it is evaluated on the target language. Adaptation subsequent to multilingual training was attempted in several ways,

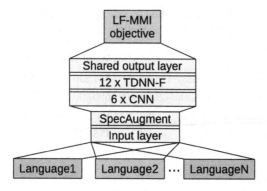

Fig. 2. Multilingual training DNN architecture.

but in all cases led to deteriorated performance. Similar observations have for example been made for Ethiopian languages [23]. For computational reasons, we did not explore all the language combinations exhaustively. We compare the speech recognition performance of these multilingually-trained systems with each other and with the baseline monolingual systems (denoted Bmono and Fmono) trained on only the target language corpora.

7   Results and Discussion

The plots in Fig. 3 depict the test set word error rates (WER) of the monolingual and multilingual systems for Bambara and Maasina Fulfulde. The datasets used in these experiments have been described in Sect. 3. In these plots, the wide blue bars indicate the test set word error rate (left vertical axis). The narrow stacked bars indicate the sizes of the constituent corpora making up the training pool (right vertical axis). Each colour represents a language, as indicated in the legend.

Firstly, we observe that the inclusion of any additional dataset, however small it is, leads to an improvement over the baseline monolingual system. This indicates that, in our under-resourced setting, multilingual training is always beneficial. Secondly, we observed that although the ALL set is able to outperform the monolingual baseline, it is by no means the best performing combination. Hence a decision to simply pool all available out-of-language data is not the best strategy. For Bambara, the best performing ASR system was trained in combination with Fulfulde and for the Fulfulde system the best result was obtained in combination with Luganda. An interesting observation is that the inclusion of the Ugandan English dataset, which is the smallest among the six corpora (5.7 h), results in a notable improvement in ASR performance (Bmono vs B+U and Fmono vs F+U). In comparison, the inclusion of the Tunisian Arabic dataset, which is the largest among the six corpora (11.2 h), resulted in a smaller improvement in ASR performance (WER for B+T>B+U and F+T>F+U). This further affirms that the size of additional datasets cannot be considered a reliable indicator of the expected performance improvement.

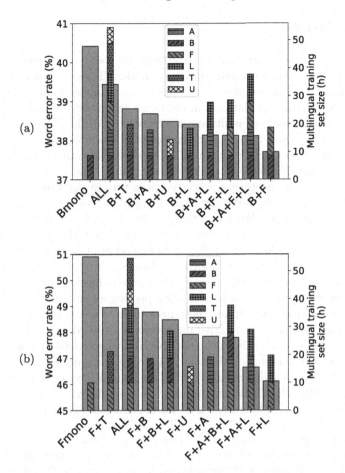

Fig. 3. Word error rate results for the (a) Bambara and (b) Fulfulde ASR for the different multilingual training set combinations. (Bmono: Monolingual Bambara; Fmono: Monolingual Fulfulde; A: Acholi; B: Bambara; F: Fulfulde; L: Luganda; T: Tunisian Modern Standard Arabic; U: Ugandan English).

The reasons for why one language combination results in better ASR performance than another are still not clear. We have performed an analysis of the phonetic overlap between the languages, but this did not provide conclusive insight. In particular, the phonetic overlap between the four Niger-Congo languages is fairly even, with Bambara sharing approximately 80% of its phonetic inventory with the other three, while for Fulfulde it is approximately 68%. We suspect that there may be other factors at play, such as language characteristics besides common phonology, or similarities in recording and channel conditions. This warrants further investigation.

8   Conclusions

We present first speech recognition systems for the two severely under-resourced Malian languages Bambara and Maasina Fulfulde. These systems will be used by the United Nations to inform and support its humanitarian programmes in that country. Because the datasets in the target languages are very small, extensive use has been made of multilingual acoustic modelling. Since a number of datasets in other under-resourced languages were available for experimentation, some from related projects, a key question has been what the composition of the pool of data should be for best multilingual training. We consider various combinations of up to six languages, whose corpora vary in size from 5.7 to 11.2 h of speech, and compare the performance of the resulting acoustic models in speech recognition experiments. We found that, while including all six languages leads to improved speech recognition for both Bambara and Maasina Fulfulde, best performance is achieved when placing only one additional language in the pool. For the case for Bambara, this additional language was Maasina Fulfulde, and its introduction leads to a relative word error rate reduction of 6.7%, as opposed to a 2.4% relative reduction achieved when pooling all six additional languages. For the case of Maasina Fulfulde, best performance was achieved when adding only Luganda, leading to a relative improvement in word error rate of 9.4% as opposed to a 3.9% relative improvement observed when pooling all six languages. We conclude that maximising the pool of multilingual data does not necessarily lead to the best-performing acoustic model for an under-resourced language, and that substantially better performance may be possible by a more judicious configuration of the pool of languages used for multilingual neural network training.

Acknowledgments. We would like to thank United Nations Global Pulse for collaboration and supporting this research. We also gratefully acknowledge the support of NVIDIA corporation with the donation GPU equipment used during the course of this research, as well as the support of Council for Scientific and Industrial Research (CSIR), Department of Science and Technology, South Africa for provisioning us the Lengau CHPC cluster for seamlessly conducting our experiments. We also gratefully acknowledge the support of Telkom South Africa.

References

1. Arnott, D.W.: The Nominal and Verbal Systems of Fula. Clarendon Press, Oxford (1970)
2. Arnott, D.W.: Some aspects of the study of Fula dialects. Bull. Sch. Oriental Afr. Stud. Univ. Lond. **37**(1), 8–18 (1974)
3. Barry, A., Barry, I., Constable, P., Glass, A.: Proposal to encode ADLAM nasalization mark for ADLaM script (2018)
4. Boersma, P., Weenink, D.: Praat: doing phonetics by computer [Computer program]. Version 6.1.39. http://www.praat.org/. Accessed 26 Mar 2021
5. Donaldson, C.: Clear Language: Script, Register and the N'ko Movement of Manding-speaking West Africa. Ph.D. thesis, University of Pennsylvania (2017)

6. Donaldson, C.: Orthography, standardization, and register: the case of Manding. In: Lane, P., Costa, J., Korne, H.D. (eds.) Standardizing Minority Languages: Competing Ideologies of Authority and Authenticity in the Global Periphery, 1st edn., pp. 175–199. Routledge (2017). https://doi.org/10.4324/9781315647722

7. Fagerberg-Diallo, S.: A Practical Guide and Reference Grammar to the Fulfulde of Maasina 1 & 2. Joint Christian Ministry in West Africa, Jos (1984)

8. Grézl, F., Karafiét, M., Veselý, K.: Adaptation of multilingual stacked bottle-neck neural network structure for new language. In: Proceedings of 2014 IEEE International Conference on Acoustics, Speech and Signal Processing (ICASSP), Florence, Italy (2014)

9. Heigold, G., et al.: Multilingual acoustic models using distributed deep neural networks. In: Proceedings of 2013 IEEE International Conference on Acoustics, Speech and Signal Processing (ICASSP), Vancouver, Canada (2013)

10. Huang, J.T., Li, J., Yu, D., Deng, L., Gong, Y.: Cross-language knowledge transfer using multilingual deep neural network with shared hidden layers. In: Proceedings of 2013 IEEE International Conference on Acoustics, Speech and Signal Processing (ICASSP), Vancouver, Canada (2013)

11. Katzner, K., Miller, K.: The Languages of the World. Routledge (2002)

12. Ko, T., Peddinti, V., Povey, D., Khudanpur, S.: Audio augmentation for speech recognition. In: Proceedings of Interspeech 2015, Dresden, Germany (2015)

13. Menon, R., Saeb, A., Cameron, H., Kibira, W., Quinn, J., Niesler, T.: Radio-browsing for developmental monitoring in Uganda. In: Proceedings of 2017 IEEE International Conference on Acoustics, Speech and Signal Processing (ICASSP), New Orleans, USA (2017)

14. Osborn, D.W., Dwyer, D.J., Donohoe, J.I.J.: A Fulfulde (Maasina) - English - French Lexicon: A Root-Based Compilation Drawn from Extant Sources. Michigan State University Press (1993)

15. Padhi, T., Biswas, A., de Wet, F., van der Westhuizen, E., Niesler, T.: Multilingual bottleneck features for improving ASR performance of code-switched speech in under-resourced languages. In: Proceedings of the First Workshop on Speech Technologies for Code-switching in Multilingual Communities (WSTCSMC), Shanghai, China (2020)

16. Park, D.S., et al.: SpecAugment: a simple data augmentation method for automatic speech recognition. In: Proceedings of Interspeech 2019, Graz, Austria (2019)

17. Povey, D., et al.: The Kaldi speech recognition toolkit. In: Proceedings of 2011 IEEE Workshop on Automatic Speech Recognition and Understanding (ASRU), Hawaii, USA (2011)

18. Povey, D., et al.: Purely sequence-trained neural networks for ASR based on lattice-free MMI. In: Proceedings of Interspeech (2016)

19. Saeb, A., Menon, R., Cameron, H., Kibira, W., Quinn, J., Niesler, T.: Very low resource radio browsing for agile developmental and humanitarian monitoring. In: Proceedings of Interspeech 2017, Stockholm, Sweden (2017)

20. Schultz, T., Kirchhoff, K.: Multilingual Speech Processing. Elsevier (2006)

21. Schultz, T., Waibel, A.: Language-independent and language-adaptive acoustic modeling for speech recognition. Speech Commun. 35(1–2), 31–51 (2001)

22. Stolcke, A.: SRILM - an extensible language modeling toolkit. In: Proceedings of Interspeech 2002, Denver, Colorado (2002)

23. Tachbelie, M.Y., Abate, S.T., Schultz, T.: Development of multilingual ASR using globalphone for less-resourced languages: the case of Ethiopian languages. In: Proceedings of Interspeech 2020, Shanghai, China (2020)

24. Veselý, K., Karafiát, M., Grézl, F., Janda, M., Egorova, E.: The language-independent bottleneck features. In: Proceedings of 2012 IEEE Spoken Language Technology Workshop (SLT), Miami, USA (2012)
25. Vydrine, V.: Manding-English Dictionary: Maninka, Bamana, vol. 1. MeaBooks Inc. (2015)

Human and Transformer-Based Prosodic Phrasing in Two Speech Genres

Jan Volín[1]([✉])(iD), Markéta Řezáčková[2](iD), and Jindřich Matoušek[2,3](iD)

[1] Institute of Phonetics, Charles University, Prague, Czech Republic
jan.volin@ff.cuni.cz
[2] New Technologies for the Information Society, Pilsen, Czech Republic
juzova@ntis.zcu.cz, jmatouse@kky.zcu.cz
[3] Department of Cybernetics, Faculty of Applied Sciences,
University of West Bohemia, Pilsen, Czech Republic

Abstract. The chief objective of the study was to observe phrasing behaviour of transformer-based neural networks from the linguistic point of view. The transformer-based architecture mapped prosodic phrasing in isolated sentences read out on request, but was commanded to predict prosodic phrases in continuous texts of journalistic style taken from radio news bulletins. The transfer was quite successful in that most of the prosodic phrase boundaries in the actual newsreading (established by expert auditory analysis) were correctly suggested by the machine. This result is not unexpected as both genres belong to clearly enunciated informative speaking style. The outcome partially rehabilitates the so-called laboratory speech, which is sometimes branded as ecologically invalid. The follow-up analyses revealed that the differences between human phrasing in news bulletins and the partition suggested by the machine can be classified into meaningful linguistic categories based on the syntactic structure or semantic contents, and as such, they can inform further research design.

Keywords: Phrasing · Prosodic boundaries · Prediction · Syntactic constituents · Transformers · T5

1 Introduction

1.1 The Importance of the Topic

Utterances as logical wholes can range in length from one syllable to a large number of words. The longer ones (which is for the speaker to judge) are divided into smaller units that receive various names in different scholarly traditions (e.g., tone-units, tone-groups, phonological phrases, phonological clauses, sense-groups). Currently, the most widely used terms are *prosodic* or *intonation phrases*. We will use the former term throughout this paper, together with the methodology of their identification after [1]. Prosodic phrases are defined by their perceived coherence, i.e., the decisive criterion for their identification is

A. Karpov and R. Potapova (Eds.): SPECOM 2021, LNAI 12997, pp. 761–772, 2021.
https://doi.org/10.1007/978-3-030-87802-3_68

the perceptual one. In other words, to be functional in speech communication, the prosodic phrases have to be perceptually identifiable, even if the current descriptions struggle with the complex interplay of acoustic cues that mark both the prosodic boundaries (PBs) between phrases, and prosodic coherence within phrases. (Intermediate phrases described in [1] will be ignored in the present study.)

The studies that investigated ambiguity of referential meanings (e.g., relative clause ambiguity in the case of complex noun phrases [5] and sources listed there) highlighted the role of phrasing in comprehension. However, prosodic phrasing seems to facilitate cerebral speech processing even when there is no clash of two competing meanings, only a 'contrast' between getting the meaning of the messages effortlessly or laboriously [6, 22]. Adequate prosodic phrasing influences the implicit processing costs. The consequences of high costs are known to be, e.g., irritation, unwillingness to comply, and decreased level of veracity of statements. Acknowledging the importance of this phenomenon we wish to contribute to its research in our domain, which is automatic prediction of prosodic phrasing by artificial neural networks trained on annotated written texts.

Adequate prosodic phrasing is also crucial for speech technologies to be widely accepted in real-life applications; specifically, it has a large impact on naturalness of synthetic speech [20, 24].

1.2   Current Objectives

A key questions asked in prosodic research is often the one of 'grammar', which translates as: What are the rules for the correct prosodic boundary placement? We are not aware of any language where such grammar has already been completed. This is not only due to problems with the definition of *correctness*, but also due to the dependence of prosodic phrasing on the context, which can be extremely varied and perhaps impossible to capture in its entirety. Thus, the *reference state* in our present study will be limited to the speech of professional presenters.

We are aware of the major caveat in is approach: there is no guarantee that a highly skilled speaker produces only correct forms. First, more options of prosodic form are often acceptable in a given communicative situation. Second, news readers (such as those in our present study) are typically under pressure, since they have to perform rapidly on-line with no editing. Therefore, speech errors in their performance happen. However, our goal is not to design prescriptive rules. Various speech styles or even speech genres may require diverse phrasing strategies and, actually, testing the genre differences is one of our current goals. It follows that our chief motivation is merely to observe how humans and machines produce prosodic phrases.

The last important aspect of the present study that has to be explained concerns the training domain. Our deep transformer neural network was trained solely on the structure of written transcripts of speech performances. One might wonder how a phonetic experiment can be done without any reference to acoustics. The explanation is straightforward. The last decades have seen a merger of phonetics with other disciplines into modern speech science [10], and it is widely accepted that expanded scope of inquiry is desirable. Therefore, broader considerations of the linguistic structure of spoken texts are imperative.

Specifically here, the questions asked are the following:

- To what extent is the transformer-based phrasing comparable to human performance?
- Are the differences between human and machine phrase boundary placement linguistically interpretable/classifiable?
- Is the training in one speaking genre (isolated sentences) transferrable to another genre (news reading)?
- Does small-scale adaptation of the transformer in the new speaking genre make any difference?

2   Method

The core of our approach lies in using transformer-based architecture for training a phrasing model, i.e., a model that is capable of predicting phrase boundaries in an input automatically. The machine predictions will be subsequently contrasted with the performance of human speakers.

In *sequence-to-sequence* (seq2seq) learning, a model transforms a given sequence of elements, such as words in a sentence, into another sequence: the output sentence with predicted phrase boundaries (e.g. [17,19,21,23]). In general, the seq2seq models consist of two parts: an *encoder* which maps the input into n-dimensional vectors, and a *decoder* which turns the numeric vectors back into an output sequence. *Transformer* is a novel architecture of a seq2seq neural network model introduced in [25]. Apart from the encoder and decoder part, it also uses the *attention-mechanism* [12] which, at each step, focuses only on crucial parts of the input sequence and provides this information to the decoder together with the encoded input sentence. We worked with the pre-trained Text-to-Text TransferTransformer (T5) model [18] and used the ability of weights pre-training from a huge amount of unlabeled text in the language [4,18] – for this task we used Czech CommonCrawl corpus, collected at the end of August 2020 [30]. For training the model we used the Tensorflow implementation of HuggingFace Transformers [28] together with the T5s library [29].

2.1   Data Description

The *Laboratory Speech* (LS) data consist of text sentences extracted from 6 large-scale Czech speech corpora (3 female + 3 male speakers) created for the purposes of speech synthesis in the TTS system *ARTIC* [14,24]. The sentences in the corpora were selected at random from a large collection of texts (more than 500,000 sentences from various domains – news, culture, economy, sport, etc.) using the greedy algorithm described in [13,16] to ensure maximal coverage of all phonetic units (phones, diphones) in all prosodic and phonetic contexts.

The corpora consist of 10,000–12,000 sentences each. The recording procedure required a detached informative style in a sentence-by-sentence manner, i.e., the sentences were isolated and did not influence one another. After the recording, they were automatically segmented and prosodic boundaries (PBs) were automatically labeled [8,15]. The labels of PBs were then sent back to the original texts and considered correct PBs in the written text. (All the speakers were professionals and their appropriate phrasing was closely monitored.) The mean length of a prosodic phrase was 4.8 words. For evaluating the accuracy of our trained model, we split the available sentences into two groups – the training and the testing data. The testing set contained 40 sentences per speaker (380 words on average).

The texts representing the *News-Reading Speech* (NRS) were extracted from authentic recordings of news-bulletins from a national broadcaster (Channels 1 and 2 of the Czech Radio). The current Czech Radio readers are considered guarantors of the model Czech speech production without any colloquialisms, salient idiosyncrasies or fashionable mannerisms. Our sample consisted of 12 such experienced professionals (6 female + 6 male). The news bulletins are typically 3 to 4 min long (with voices of correspondents between paragraphs excluded). An average composition of a news bulletin in our sample was 40.5 sentences, which is 517 words or 1223 syllables. The mean length of a prosodic phrase in the sample was 4.56 words [26]. As above, the phrases in NRS were established by expert auditory analysis guided by [1].

2.2   Evaluation Measures

Since phrase boundary prediction can be viewed as a two-class classification task, standard metrics as *recall* (R, also known as *sensitivity*, Eq. (1)), interpreted as the ability of a predictor to find all phrase boundaries, *precision* (P, Eq. (2)), the ability of a predictor not to predict false phrase boundaries, *F1-score* ($F1$, Eq. (3)), a combined measure that results in a high value if, and only if, both precision and recall are high, and *accuracy* (Acc, Eq. (4)), a proportion of correct predictions in all predictions, were used to evaluate the performance of PB prediction. The higher the value of all scores, the more successful the prediction is. The symbols stand for: tp, the number of the correctly predicted phrase boundaries (*'true positives'*), tn, the number of correctly predicted no-breaks (*'true negatives'*), fp, the number of falsely predicted phrase boundaries (*'false positives'*) and fn, the number of missed phrase boundaries (*'false negatives'*).

$$R = \frac{tp}{tp + fn} \tag{1}$$

$$P = \frac{tp}{tp + fp} \tag{2}$$

$$F1 = 2 \cdot \frac{P \cdot R}{P + R} \tag{3}$$

$$Acc = \frac{tp + tn}{tp + tn + fp + fn} \tag{4}$$

Note that due to the unbalanced distribution of PB/no-PB, $F1$ score will be used as the main indicator of success during the evaluation in Sect. 3.

2.3 Experiment 1

First of all, we trained a *general* phrasing model using the T5 model and the LS data described in Sect. 2.1, excluding the testing set of sentences (40 per speaker). 10 % of the training data were also excluded for validating the model during the training process after each of 50 epochs (with 1000 steps per epoch). This way, we prepared a speaker-independent phrasing model since the mixed input data originated from more speakers. The core idea was to train a model that would be sufficiently general and easily transferable to unknown speakers. Nevertheless, if we wanted to decrease the errors in model's predictions, we would rather train a speaker-dependent one for each speaker, as e.g., in [9,11].

2.4 Experiment 2

As described in Sect. 2.1, NRS data consisted of continuous texts in journalistic style from Czech radio news, as opposed to the isolated sentences that originated from speech corpora for TTS, so the prosodic partition of these NRS sentences potentially differed from that of the LS material. Thus, our second experiment consisted in testing the *general* phrasing model on sentences of target NRS speakers, which should reveal whether the model was also able to correctly predict phrase boundaries for new unseen speakers and a different genre.

2.5 Experiment 3

Finally, we focused on building a phrasing model for the target genre, the news-reading speech. In general, the deep transformer-based models need a large amount of data to be able to learn a specific issue. The NRS data, however, consisted of only 486 sentences in total, which was not enough to train a new phrasing model from scratch. Therefore, we decided to use the trained T5 *general* phrasing model and to adapt it to the new NRS data. To obtain results for all 12 speakers, we applied a *leave-one-out* approach: We trained 12 different phrasing models, always using 11 speakers for adaptation and the remaining speaker for testing. The training process was significantly shorter – the models stabilized after a few epochs. Due to that, we obtained predictions of phrase boundaries (for all 12 speakers in NRS) suggested by the transferred phrasing model (using a small amount of training data for adaptation) and compared them to the boundaries predicted by the general model from Sect. 2.4 and to those established by phonetic experts in the human performance.

Table 1. Overall results (Acc, P, R, F1 in %).

	speaker	No. of sents	Acc	P	R	F1	tp	fp	fn	tn
(a) General model, LS	LS01	40	99.20	100.00	95.24	97.56	60	0	3	312
	LS02	40	97.38	87.50	96.55	91.80	56	8	2	316
	LS03	40	96.63	89.39	90.77	90.08	59	7	6	314
	LS04	40	96.86	94.12	85.71	89.72	48	3	8	291
	LS05	40	96.63	85.71	93.75	89.55	60	10	4	342
	LS06	40	95.42	94.23	77.78	85.22	49	3	14	305
	all	240	97.02	91.46	89.97	90.71	332	31	37	1880
(b) General model, NRS	NSR01	36	90.61	97.37	45.68	62.18	37	1	44	397
	NRS02	60	93.19	90.74	52.69	66.67	49	5	44	622
	NRS03	38	93.12	86.00	60.56	71.07	43	7	28	431
	NRS04	31	92.81	93.02	57.14	70.80	48	11	22	386
	NRS05	48	90.60	86.54	47.87	61.64	45	7	49	495
	NRS06	45	89.58	96.36	47.75	63.86	53	2	58	463
	NRS07	33	94.13	97.62	63.08	76.64	41	1	24	360
	NRS08	37	91.37	95.12	48.75	64.46	39	2	41	416
	NRS09	50	93.99	84.85	60.87	70.89	56	10	36	664
	NRS10	34	93.35	94.59	57.38	71.43	35	2	26	358
	NRS11	35	94.01	91.67	58.93	71.74	33	3	23	375
	NRS12	39	92.59	91.67	57.89	70.97	44	4	32	406
	all	486	92.44	90.48	55.05	68.46	523	55	427	5373
(c) Adapted model, NRS	NSR01	36	91.65	88.68	58.02	70.15	47	6	34	392
	NRS02	60	94.86	84.15	74.19	78.86	69	13	24	614
	NRS03	38	95.09	83.82	80.28	82.01	57	11	14	427
	NRS04	31	92.81	81.36	68.57	74.42	40	3	30	378
	NRS05	48	92.28	85.29	61.70	71.60	58	10	36	492
	NRS06	45	89.76	87.14	54.95	67.40	61	9	50	456
	NRS07	33	94.84	92.16	72.31	81.03	47	4	18	357
	NRS08	37	92.97	89.47	63.75	74.45	51	6	29	412
	NRS09	50	94.82	77.78	76.09	76.92	70	20	22	654
	NRS10	34	95.49	90.38	77.05	83.19	47	5	14	355
	NRS11	35	94.49	82.00	73.21	77.36	41	9	15	369
	NRS12	39	93.83	85.94	72.37	78.57	55	9	21	401
	all	486	93.52	85.96	67.68	75.74	643	105	307	5307

3   Results

3.1   Experiment 1 – The General Model on LS

The predictions given by the model are evaluated in Table 1(a) and indicate the ability of the transformer-based architecture to learn the specifics of PB placement. The success is substantiated especially by the high values of *F1-score* (around 90 %) and low numbers of false positives and false negatives. In fact, some of these "errors" (or more precisely mismatches) may have been just different representations of prosodic phrasing as explained in the follow-up analyses in Sect. 3.4.

3.2   Experiment 2 – The General Model on NRS

The results of the general phrasing model applied on NRS data are shown in Table 1(b). The values of all the evaluation measures are lower compared to the Table 1(a) which reflects the difference between the two genres. The largest drop can be seen in *recall*, which determines the probability of a positive instance to be predicted as positive. Thus, the general model used on NRS makes more errors of type *false negatives*, i.e., more phrase boundaries are unseen, (also noticeable in the *fn* columns). However, the precision values in Table 1(b) are almost the same (just slightly lower on average) so the numbers of false alarms (*fp*) do not increase significantly, compared to the results in Sect. 3.1. Since the *F1-score* measure combines both precision and recall, the values of *F1* also decreased.

3.3   Experiment 3 – Adaptation to a New Genre

As described in Sect. 2.5, 12 new transferred phrasing models were built from the general model tested before. The results for each speaker (excluded from the training data for building a particular phrasing model) are presented in Table 1(c) and they document increase of *F1-score*, mostly caused by significantly higher *recall* values (fewer false negatives, i.e., missed PBs). Although the incidence of false alarms is slightly higher and the corresponding *precisions* lower, we can see that the model transfer was successful even with the considerably small amount of data.

3.4   Follow-Up Analyses

Due to their immense complexity, neural networks do not produce any explicit rules describing their predictive work. In this section, therefore, we are taking a closer look at the differences between human and machine phrasing in news reading (NRS) in order to establish some linguistically interpretable regularities. As pointed out above, however, that we do not consider the human readers correct without reservations (see Sect. 1.2).

The sentences that were predicted under both G (General) and A (Adapted) conditions exactly as they were pronounced by the news readers made 33.1 %

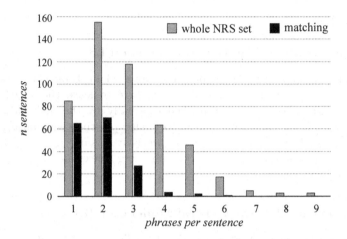

Fig. 1. Occurrences of sentences with various numbers of prosodic phrases in them. Grey – all sentences in the sample; black – sentences with matching solution by humans and T5.

of the whole sample. If we add the cases where at least one machine condition was matching, we get 54.2 %. (Adding the G condition leads to 40.5 %, while the A condition produces 47.8 %). These numbers differ from the measures in Table 1 because here we consider the whole sentence a unit of analysis, and there are unequal counts of prosodic boundaries per sentence (PB/sent). The mean "prosodic complexity" of our NRS sentences was 2.87 PB/sent, ranging from 0 to 8 PB/sent (i.e., from 1 sent. = 1 phrase to 1 sent. = 9 phrases). The sentence length in phrases affects the match between humans and machine in an anticipated way. Figure 1 shows that the ratio of matching solutions is better for the prosodically simpler sentences, and worsens with the increasing complexity.

Non-matching cases were usually caused by missing boundaries, i.e., false negatives. The composition of mismatches within a sentence as a unit of analysis is displayed in Fig. 2. Apart from already known higher matching rate, the A condition produced lower number of missed boundaries than G condition (specifically 32.5 % against 50.4 %).

Syntactic-semantic analysis produced 23 categories, of which 8 occurred more than ten times in the set of mismatched cases. They are listed in Table 2. The table also informs about the number of acceptable cases and the ratio among the missed, extra, and different boundaries. Acceptability was assessed only categorically: a binary decision was based on (a) the danger of ambiguities, (b) the length of the phrases (fewer than 2 or more than 10 words were considered less acceptable), and (c) reputation (i.e., consensus in literature, e.g., [2, 3, 7, 27]).

There are several observations to be made. To begin with, the split of sentences into a subject and predicate part was by far the most frequent problem (line 1 of the table). The orthographic rules of Czech do not allow for subject-predicate partitioning by any punctuation, yet both syntactic constituents can

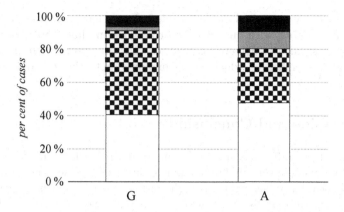

Fig. 2. Four types of the 'whole-sentence solutions' by general (G) and adapted (A) models: white – humanlike, checkered – missing PBs, grey – extra PBs, black – other placement.

Table 2. The main syntactic/semantic categories in mismatched boundaries with the number of cases.

Category	Total	Acceptable	Miss	Extra	Else
1 Subject-predicate division	146	115	109	23	14
2 Post-positioned attribute	85	64	70	4	11
3 Sentence-initial adverbiale	71	51	55	4	12
4 Grammatical object	45	33	35	4	6
5 Numerals	36	22	25	2	9
6 Conjunction 'a' or 'i'	35	29	19	9	7
7 Apposition	32	21	21	7	4
8 Verb/Copula Elipsis	19	14	16	1	2

be complex. When they are, speakers use the opportunity for PB insertion, which makes them prosodically independent (i.e., stand-alone). Our T5 often missed this opportunity, even if mostly with acceptable results. An interesting detail is that all 23 extra PBs in this category were acceptable. Another well-represented category involved an attribute in post-position (line 2 of Table 2). The unmarked position of an attribute in Czech is before the noun, but post-position is legal if the attribute is not an adjective. Again, no punctuation is allowed, although PBs are quite natural to avoid long strings of words. Compared with the previous category, there is a slightly higher rate of missed PBs, but much lower rate of extra PBs. Third, Czech with its relatively free word order (especially compared to English) allows for beginning a sentence with an adverbial constituent. Although the orthography bans punctuation, a PB after an adverbial structure is quite common, even though it is not used in newsreading if the adverbial is expressed by one word only. Line 3 of Table 2 shows that most of the mismatches here were acceptable, with missed PBs forming again almost 80 % of the cases.

To conclude, all the detected categories that are displayed in Table 2 have their linguistic specificities, which will be exploited in further research (see below, Sect. 4).

4   Discussion and Conclusion

Predictions of prosodic phrasing by T5 models (which reflect the deep structure of texts) are comparable to human performances. The accuracy in terms of individual boundary placement was high, and even when the whole sentence was taken as a unit of analysis, most of the mismatches were in line with literature and a simple quantity rule.

What has to be done in the future are perceptual experiments that would test individual alternatives suggested by the machine. A tentative hypothesis based on informal observations is that some of the sentences would actually 'sound better' as planned by our T5 models. Another task for future research concerns the 'emphatic boundaries'. A PB is sometimes used to emphasise the consequent lexical item. Often, they are linked with conative or affective components of the meaning (adding implicit messages like, e.g., "I care about the things I am talking about" or "You must agree that this is unusual"). There were 52 such cases in our NRS material (4.34 per speaker) and all of those led to mismatch between human and T5 performance.

Our findings should not be generalized beyond what we have done. Both LS and NRS genres share certain features like, e.g., very clear sentence-final boundaries. It is known that conversational speech differs considerably in this respect – people do not necessarily 'chat' in sentences. Nevertheless, our findings are already useful in that we can experiment with NRS data and retrain/adapt only selected layers, contrary to the whole model as it was done presently. It is also obvious that the small NRS corpus could be expanded if higher accuracy is required.

Acknowledgments. This work was funded by Czech Science Foundation (GA–CR), project GA21-14758S, and by the grant of the University of West Bohemia, project No. SGS-2019-027. Computational resources were supplied by project "e-Infrastruktura CZ" (e-INFRA LM2018140) within Projects of Large Research, Development and Innovations Infrastructures.

References

1. Beckman, M.E., Ayers Elam, G.: Guidelines for ToBI Labelling, version 3. The Ohio State University Research Foundation, Ohio State University (1997)
2. Cruttenden, A.: Intonation. In: Cambridge Textbooks in Linguistics, 2nd edn. Cambridge University Press, Cambridge (1997)
3. Daneš, F.: Intonace a věta ve spisovné češtině. ČSAV, Praha (1957)

4. Devlin, J., Chang, M.W., Lee, K., Toutanova, K.: BERT: pre-training of deep bidirectional transformers for language understanding (2019). http://arxiv.org/abs/1810.04805arXiv:1810.04805
5. Foltz, A., Maday, K., Ito, K.: Order effects in production and comprehension of prosodic boundaries. In: Frota, S., Elordiet, G., Prieto, P. (eds.) Prosodic Categories: Production. Perception and Comprehension. Studies in Natural Language and Linguistic Theory. Springer, Dordrecht (2011). https://doi.org/10.1007/978-94-007-0137-3_3
6. Friederici, A., Alter, K.: Lateralization of auditory language functions: a dynamic dual pathway model. Brain Lang. **89**(2), 267–276 (2004)
7. Halliday, M.A.K.: Intonation and Grammar in British English. The Hague, Paris (1967)
8. Hanzlíček, Z., Vít, J., Tihelka, D.: LSTM-based speech segmentation for TTS synthesis. In: Ekštein, K. (ed.) TSD 2019. LNCS (LNAI), vol. 11697, pp. 361–372. Springer, Cham (2019). https://doi.org/10.1007/978-3-030-27947-9_31
9. Jůzová, M., Tihelka, D.: Speaker-dependent BiLSTM-based phrasing. In: Sojka, P., Kopeček, I., Pala, K., Horák, A. (eds.) TSD 2020. LNCS (LNAI), vol. 12284, pp. 340–347. Springer, Cham (2020). https://doi.org/10.1007/978-3-030-58323-1_37
10. Kohler, K.: Editorial. Phonetika **65**, 189–193 (2008)
11. Louw, J.A., Moodley, A.: Speaker specific phrase break modeling with conditional random fields for text-to-speech. In: 2016 Pattern Recognition Association of South Africa and Robotics and Mechatronics International Conference (PRASA-RobMech), pp. 1–6 (2016)
12. Luong, T., Pham, H., Manning, C.D.: Effective approaches to attention-based neural machine translation. In: Proceedings of the 2015 Conference on Empirical Methods in Natural Language Processing, Lisbon, Portugal, pp. 1412–1421. Association for Computational Linguistics, September 2015
13. Matoušek, J., Romportl, J.: On building phonetically and prosodically rich speech corpus for text-to-speech synthesis. In: Proceedings of the 2nd IASTED International Conference on Computational Intelligence, San Francisco, USA, pp. 442–447. ACTA Press (2006)
14. Matoušek, J., Tihelka, D.: Annotation errors detection in TTS corpora. In: Proceedings of INTERSPEECH 2013, Lyon, France, pp. 1511–1515 (2013). http://www.kky.zcu.cz/en/publications/MatousekJ_2013_AnnotationErrors
15. Matoušek, J., Tihelka, D., Psutka, J.: Experiments with automatic segmentation for Czech speech synthesis. In: Matoušek, V., Mautner, P. (eds.) TSD 2003. LNCS (LNAI), vol. 2807, pp. 287–294. Springer, Heidelberg (2003). https://doi.org/10.1007/978-3-540-39398-6_41
16. Matoušek, J., Tihelka, D., Romportl, J.: Building of a speech corpus optimised for unit selection TTS synthesis. In: LREC 2008. Proceedings of 6th International Conference on Language Resources and Evaluation, Marrakech, Morocco, pp. 1296–1299. ELRA (2008)
17. Prahallad, K., Raghavendra, E.V., Black, A.W.: Learning speaker-specific phrase breaks for text-to-speech systems. In: SSW (2010)
18. Raffel, C., et al.: Exploring the limits of transfer learning with a unified text-to-text transformer (2020). arXiv:1910.10683
19. Read, I., Cox, S.: Stochastic and syntactic techniques for predicting phrase breaks. Comput. Speech Lang. **21**(3), 519–542 (2007). https://doi.org/10.1016/j.csl.2006.09.004

20. Romportl, J., Matoušek, J.: Formal prosodic structures and their application in NLP. In: Matoušek, V., Mautner, P., Pavelka, T. (eds.) TSD 2005. LNCS (LNAI), vol. 3658, pp. 371–378. Springer, Heidelberg (2005). https://doi.org/10.1007/11551874_48

21. Rosenberg, A., Fernandez, R., Ramabhadran, B.: Modeling phrasing and prominence using deep recurrent learning. In: Interspeech 2015, pp. 3066–3070. ISCA (2015)

22. Steinhauer, K., Alter, K., Friederici, A.D.: Brain potentials indicate immediate use of prosodic cues in natural speech processing. Nature Neurosci. 2, 191–196 (1999)

23. Taylor, P., Black, A.: Assigning phrase breaks from part-of-speech sequences. Comput. Speech Lang. 12, 99–117 (1998)

24. Tihelka, D., Hanzlíček, Z., Jůzová, M., Vít, J., Matoušek, J., Grůber, M.: Current state of text-to-speech system ARTIC: a decade of research on the field of speech technologies. In: Sojka, P., Horák, A., Kopeček, I., Pala, K. (eds.) TSD 2018. LNCS (LNAI), vol. 11107, pp. 369–378. Springer, Cham (2018). https://doi.org/10.1007/978-3-030-00794-2_40

25. Vaswani, A., et al.: Attention is all you need (2017). arXiv:1706.03762

26. Volín, J.: The size of prosodic phrases in native and foreign-accented read-out monologues. Acta Universitatis Carolinae - Philologica 2, 145–158 (2019)

27. Wells, J.C.: English Intonation. An Introduction. Cambridge University Press, Cambridge (2006)

28. Wolf, T., et al.: Transformers: state-of-the-art natural language processing. In: Proceedings of the 2020 Conference on Empirical Methods in Natural Language Processing: System Demonstrations, pp. 38–45. Association for Computational Linguistics, Online, October 2020

29. Švec, J.: t5s–T5 made simple (2020). http://github.com/honzas83/t5s. Accessed 02 Apr 2020

30. Švec, J., et al.: General framework for mining, processing and storing large amounts of electronic texts for language modeling purposes. Lang. Res. Eval. 48(2), 227–248 (2013). https://doi.org/10.1007/s10579-013-9246-z

Learning Efficient Representations for Keyword Spotting with Triplet Loss

Roman Vygon[1,2] and Nikolay Mikhaylovskiy[1,2(✉)]

[1] Higher IT School, Tomsk State University, 634050 Tomsk, Russia
[2] NTR Labs, 129594 Moscow, Russia
{rvygon,nickm}@ntr.ai

Abstract. In the past few years, triplet loss-based metric embeddings have become a de-facto standard for several important computer vision problems, most notably, person reidentification. On the other hand, in the area of speech recognition the metric embeddings generated by the triplet loss are rarely used even for classification problems. We fill this gap showing that a combination of two representation learning techniques: a triplet loss-based embedding and a variant of kNN for classification instead of cross-entropy loss significantly (by 26% to 38%) improves the classification accuracy for convolutional networks on a LibriSpeech-derived LibriWords datasets. To do so, we propose a novel phonetic similarity based triplet mining approach. We also improve the current best published SOTA for Google Speech Commands dataset V1 10 + 2 -class classification by about 34%, achieving 98.55% accuracy, V2 10 + 2-class classification by about 20%, achieving 98.37% accuracy, and V2 35-class classification by over 50%, achieving 97.0% accuracy. (Code is available at https://github.com/roman-vygon/triplet_loss_kws).

Keywords: Potting · Spoken term detection · Triplet loss · kNN · Representation learning · Audio classification

1 Introduction

The goal of keyword spotting is to detect a relatively small set of predefined keywords in a stream of user utterances, usually in the context of small-footprint device [1]. Keyword spotting (KWS for short) is a critical component for enabling speech-based user interactions for such devices [2]. It is also important from an engineering perspective for a wide range of applications [3]. In this article, we show how the use of the triplet loss-based embeddings allows us to improve the classification accuracy of the existing small-footprint neural network architectures.

© Springer Nature Switzerland AG 2021
A. Karpov and R. Potapova (Eds.): SPECOM 2021, LNAI 12997, pp. 773–785, 2021.
https://doi.org/10.1007/978-3-030-87802-3_69

1.1 Previous Work on KWS

The first work on KWS was most likely published in 1967 [4]. Over years, a number of machine learning architectures for small-footprint KWS have been proposed (see, for example [5–9]). With the renaissance of neural networks, they become the architecture class of choice for KWS systems (see, for example, [1, 2, 10–14]). Probably, the only – but notable – exception from this trend is the very recent work of Lei et al. [15] that uses Tsetlin machines for keyword spotting for their extremely low power consumption.

Publication of the Google Speech Command dataset [16] have provided a common ground for KWS system evaluation and allowed for accelerating research. Further, we denote V1 and V2 versions 1 and 2 of this dataset, respectively. When publishing the dataset, Warden [16] have also provided a baseline model based on the convolutional architecture of Sainath and Parada [11], achieving the accuracy of 85.4% and 88.2% on V1 and V2, respectively. The related Kaggle competition winner has achieved 91% accuracy on V1.

Since the publication of the Google Speech Command dataset led to a vast corpus of work appearing in the past three years, we will only briefly discuss the most relevant recent work. Jansson [17] suggested an interesting fully-convolutional model working out of raw waveforms, but, probably, a bit ahead of time and did not improve on previous results. de Andrade et al. [3] have proposed an attention-based recurrent network architecture and achieved the SOTA on 2, 10, 20-word and full-scale versions of the dataset. Majumdar and Ginsburg [18] have published a lightweight separable convolution residual network architecture MatchboxNet, achieving the new SOTA of 97.48% on V1 and 97.63% on V2. Mordido et al. [19] have suggested an interesting improvement to MatchboxNet model, replacing 1x1-convolutions in 1D time-channel separable convolutions by constant, sparse random ternary matrices with weights in $\{-1; 0; +1\}$.

Rybakov, Kononenko et al. [20] tested many of the existing models and proposed a multihead attention-based recurrent neural network architecture, achieving a new SOTA of 98% on V2. Wei et al. [20] proposed a new architecture, EdgeCRNN, which is based on depthwise separable convolution and residual structure, apparently drawing inspiration from MatchboxNet [18] and Attention RNN [3], to achieve a slight improvement in accuracy and a SOTA of 98.05%. Tang et al. [22] have released Howl - a productionalized, open-source wakeword detection toolkit, explored a number of models and achieved nearly-SOTA accuracy.

1.2 Previous Work on the Use of Triplet Loss for the Metric Embedding Learning

The goal of metric embedding learning is to learn a function $f : R^F \rightarrow R^D$, which maps semantically similar points from the data manifold in R^F onto metrically close points in R^D, and semantically different points in R^F onto metrically distant points in R^D [23].

The triplet loss (TL for short) for this problem was most likely first introduced in [24] in the framework of image ranking:

$$l\left(p_i, p_i^+, p_i^-\right) = \left\{0, g + D\left(f(p_i), f\left(p_i^+\right)\right) - D\left(f(p_i), f\left(p_i^-\right)\right)\right\} \tag{1}$$

where p_i, p_i^+, p_i^- are the anchor image, positive image, and negative image, respectively, g is a gap parameter that regularizes the gap between the distance of the two image pairs: (p_i, p_i^+) and (p_i, p_i^-), and D is a distance function that can be, for example, Euclidean distance in the image embedding space:

$$D(f(P), f(Q)) = \|f(P) - f(Q)\|_2^2 \tag{2}$$

A similar loss function was earlier proposed by Chechik et al. in [25], but the real traction came to the triplet loss in the area of face re-identification after the works of Schroff et al. on FaceNet [26] and Hermans et al. [23].

In the speech domain, the use of triplet loss is more limited, but there still are several important works to mention. In particular, Huang J. et al. [27], Ren et al. [28], Kumar et al. [29], and Harvill et al. [30] use triplet loss with varied neural network architectures for the task of the speech emotion recognition. Bredin [31] and Song et al. [32] use triplet-loss based learning approaches for the speaker diarization, and Zhang and Koshida [33] and Li et al. [34] – for the related task of speaker verification. Turpault et al. [35] propose a strategy for augmenting data with transformed samples, in line with more recent works in varied machine learning areas.

The most similar works to ours are probably [36–39], and [40], but there are important differences with each of these works:

- Sacchi et al. [36] operate in the open-vocabulary setting, which required the authors to design a system with a common embedding for text and speech, while we concentrate on improving the quality of existing low-footprint architectures for closed-vocabulary keyword spotting.
- Shor et al. [37] concentrate on building an unified embedding that works well for non-semantic tasks, while we concentrate on the semantic task of keyword spotting
- Yuan et al. [38] operate in a two-stage detection / classification framework and use a BLSTM network with a mix of triplet, reverse triplet and hinge loss.
- Huh et al. [39] start from the same res15 model as we do, but primarily focus on detection metrics and use SVM for classification, so our classification metrics are significantly better.
- Huang et al. [40] concentrate on Query-by-Example KWS application and adopt the softtriple loss - a combination of triplet loss and softmax loss.

1.3 Our Contributions

Our contributions in this work are the following:

- We show that combining two representation learning methods: triplet-loss based metric embeddings and a kNN classifier allows us to significantly improve the accuracy of CNN-based models that use cross-entropy to classify audio information and achieve the SOTA for the Google Speech Commands dataset.
- We propose a novel batch sampling approach based on phonetic similarity that allows to improve F1 metric when classifying highly imbalanced datasets.

2 Model Architectures

Most of the current state-of-the-art keyword spotting architectures are present in the work of Rybakov et al. [20], with the best model to date being the Bidirectional GRU-based Multihead Attention RNN. It takes a mel-scale spectrogram and convolves it with a set of 2D convolutions. Then two bidirectional GRU layers are used to capture two-way long term dependencies. The feature in the center of the bidirectional LSTM's output sequence is projected using a dense layer and is used as a query vector for the multi-head attention (4 heads) mechanism. Finally, the weighted (by attention score) average of the bidirectional GRU output is processed by a set of fully connected layers for classification.

We have mostly experimented with ResNet-based models res8 [1, 22] and res15 [1, 41]. The initial experiments have shown that RNN-based architectures show significantly worse results when trained for the triplet loss, so they were discarded in our later work. We used the encoder part of each of the models above to generate triplet-loss based embeddings that are later classified using the K-Nearest Neighbor (kNN) algorithm.

2.1 Input Preprocessing

64-dimensional (for LibriWords) or 80-dimensional (for Google Speech Commands dataset) mel-spectrograms are constructed and stacked using a 25-ms window size and a 10-ms frame shift. Our implementation stacks all such windows within the one-second sample of Google Speech Commands. LibriWords samples are constrained to have a duration of 0.1–3 s.

2.2 Resnet Architecture

Our resnet implementation is taken directly from [41] with very minor code changes and is depicted in Fig. 1. When working with triplet loss, the softmax layer is removed.

Table 1. Encoder model sizes for the key models studied.

	Embedding dimension	Model encoder size, [K]
Mh-Att-RNN	256	743
res8	128	885
res15	45	237
Att-RNN	128	202

Table 1 above compares the model sizes for the main models studied.

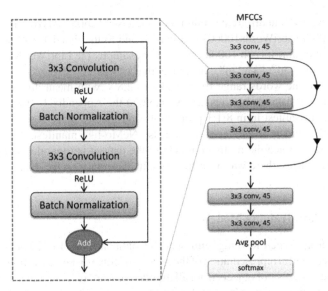

Fig. 1. res* architecture (from [1]).

3   Experiments

3.1   Datasets and Tasks

Speech Commands.   Google Speech Commands dataset Version 1 has 65K utterances from various speakers, each utterance 1 second long. Each of these utterances belongs to one of 30 classes corresponding to common words like "Go", "Stop", "Left", "Down", etc. Version 2 has 105K utterances, each 1 second long, belonging to one of 35 classes. The sampling rate of both datasets is 16kHz. In our experiments we have considered the following tasks based on these datasets [3, 16]:

- Recognition of all 35 words using Google Speech Dataset V2
- Recognition of 10 words ("Yes", "No", "Up", "Down", "Left", "Right", "On", "Off", "Stop", and "Go") and additional labels for "Unknown" and "Silence" using either V1 or V2 datasets.

For these tasks and each architecture studied, we have measured top-1 classification accuracy.

LibriWords Datasets.   To further explore the possibilities of triplet loss models we needed a dataset that consists of a large number of different words to classify. Thus, we have used LibriSpeech [42] - a a collection of 1,000 h of read English speech. The dataset was split on the word level by Lugosch et al. [43]. Since LibriSpeech is aligned on sentence level only, the Montreal Forced Aligner [44] was used to obtain intervals for individual words. The alignments are available online [43]. Further we call this derived dataset LibriWords.

We have created four different versions of the dataset (LibriWords10, LibriWords100, LibriWords1000, LibriWords10000) that correspond to the first 10, 100 etc. words by popularity in the LibriSpeech 1000h corpus. For example, the LibriWords10 words are: "the", "and", "of", "to", "a", "in", "he", "I", "that", "was".

Durations of the words range from 0.03 s to 2.8 s, with mean duration of 0.28 s. The details on the datasets metrics are available in the Appendix 1. We have split the dataset into train\val\test in in 8:1:1 proportion, and tried to make sure this proportion holds for each word in the dataset. We release NeMo-like manifests for ease of use and reproduction. Since the motivation behind the dataset is to model real-life speech recognition scenarios, there was no further quality assurance on the data.

3.2   Approach to Training Models

Batch Sampling. When working with Speech Commands and LibriWords10 datasets, to ensure a meaningful representation of the anchor-positive distances, following [26], we sample an equal number of objects from all the classes available. For unbalanced datasets with a large number of words, we also needed an efficient class-sampling method; otherwise, the network will often train on irrelevant batches where embeddings of the words are already far from each other. To achieve better class selection we have used three sampling approaches:

- Uniform: sample *batch_size* classes randomly from a uniform distribution.
- Proportional: sample *batch_size* classes randomly from a distribution proportional to the word distribution in the dataset. Motivation behind this approach is twofold. First, the popular words are short (the, a, I)) so they are not easy to distinguish from the rest. Second, if you equally train on them, there will be the same amount of errors, and that's a lot in terms of the absolute value. (If we classify 2% of a popular word incorrectly, this would significantly spoil the metric for the entire dataset).
- Phonetic: Calculate a matrix of phonetic similarity for all the words in the dataset, sample batch_size/2 classes, then, for each sampled class add a random phonetically similar word from the closest three to the batch. Similarity score is calculated using SoundEx, Caverphone, Metaphone and NYSIIS algorithms [46].

Comparing Phonetic Distance Methods. To compare the phonetic similarity algorithms, a model was trained using phonetic sampling only, while the similarity matrix was calculated with each of the methods separately. For each phonetic similarity algorithm, we have trained a model for two epochs on LibriWords10000 dataset. The results are listed in the Table 4. While the difference between the algorithms is not large, Metaphone leads in both the accuracy and F1.

Table 2. Phonetic similarity metric comparison

Method	Accuracy	F1
CaverPhone	64.0	41.0
NYSIIS	63.8	40.5
Soundex	64.8	43.2
Metaphone	65.3	43.8

Phonetic Distance. On LibriWords dataset, we used a weighted average of distances calculated using all 4 algorithms weighted as follows:

$$D_{Phonetic} = D_{Soundex} \times 0.2 + D_{caverphone} \times 0.2 + D_{metaphone} \times 0.5 + D_{nysiis} \times 0.1$$
(3)

The weights reasonably reflect the efficiency of each method as per Table 2. The optimal use of these algorithms is a matter of future research, for example, we had to adjust manually the distances of a handful of pairs of words: e.g. the pair "know-no" had a large distance while being similar. The problem was found while analyzing the confusion matrix.

We have evaluated these three triplet mining approaches alone and in combinations, mixing them with equal probabilities. Thus, for example, Uniform + Phonetic in the Table 3 below means 50% probability to sample with the Uniform approach, and 50% with the Phonetic approach, and Uniform + Proportional + Phonetic means 1/3 probability to sample with the Uniform approach, 1/3 with the Phonetic approach, and 1/3 with the Proportional approach.

The results in the Table 3 show that the proportional sampling method improves the accuracy by increasing the score of more popular words while the phonetic sampling method improves the F1 metric due to better classification of difficult pairs like "at"-"ate", "an"-"anne". Uniform sampling usage is essential as one of the sampling strategies, as it provides the proper class coverage.

Table 3. The effects of the different sampling strategies for triplet loss of res15 model on LibriWords10000.

Method(s)	Accuracy	F1
Uniform	79.4	0.72
Proportional	77.1	0.61
Phonetic	76.9	0.73
Uniform + Phonetic	78.9	0.76
Uniform + Proportional	81.2	0.74
Proportional + Phonetic	80.0	0.72
Uniform + Proportional + Phonetic	80.8	0.75

Triplet Selection. An important part of TL models is the selection of triplets used to calculate the loss, since taking all possible triplets from a batch is computationally expensive. We have used a randomized approach to the online batch triplet mining based on [23], where the negative sample to a hard pair of the anchor and a positive sample is selected randomly from the set of negative samples resulting in non-zero loss. Our initial experiments have shown that this modification of the online batch triplet mining performs better than hard or semi-hard batch loss options.

Optimization and Training Process. Baseline models were trained until they reached a plateau on a validation set. We monitored the validation accuracy of triplet loss models each 1k batches and stopped the training process if the accuracy didn't increase for more than .1% for 3 consecutive times. The number of epochs is listed in the Table 4 below.

Table 4. The number of epochs models were trained for.

	TL, epochs	Baseline, epochs
Speech Commands	30	30
Libri10	10	30
Libri100	5	10
Libri1000	5	7
Libri10000	3	5

Three augmentation techniques were used:

1. Shifting samples in range $(-100$ ms; $+100$ ms$)$.
2. SpecAugment.
3. Adding background noise from audio files in Google Speech Commands Dataset.

The decrease in epochs for larger datasets is due to class-imbalance – triplet models sample classes directly, so instead of seeing all objects in the dataset it sees the same number of objects, but distributed more evenly between classes. The baseline, cross-validation based models converge to predict the most popular words well, while ignoring the rest. One can see this from the low F1 metric on LibriWords10000 dataset. The batch size was 35*10 for TL-res8, 35*4 for TL-res15 and 128 for the baseline models. Training was done using the Novograd [47] algorithm with initial learning rate of 0.001 and cosine annealing decay to 1e-4.

Influence of kNN. We have tested kNN for several values of k, and have found that for LibriWords the best performing value varies depending on the dataset size, while for Speech Commands the best performing value was $k = 5$ (see Table 5).

As the model size is of a great concern for the keyword spotting application, and for the larger datasets kNN part of the model can take a lot of memory, we have also studied the effect of kNN quantization available from [13] on the size, speed and accuracy of the resulting model, varying the number of segments for the Product Quantizer.

Table 5. Classification accuracy for res15 model triplet loss embeddings with kNN classification for various k.

k	1	5	10	30
Speech Commands V2/12	98.18	98.37	98.27	98.29
LW10	89.91	91.48	91.74	91.72
LW100	83.93	86.53	86.9	86.98
LW1000	80.43	83.82	84.29	84.37
LW10000	77.57	80.82	81.17	80.62

For each dataset/task there is an optimal number of segments that reduces accuracy by 1.6%–13.6%, and reduces the memory consumption by a factor of 7 to 13.

We should note that the use of kNN is essential for the accuracy we achieve. We have tried to replace kNN with a two-layer fully-connected network with ReLU between the layers, but the results were drastically worse. Specifically, we experimented with intermediary dimensions of 64, 128 and 256 between the two fully connected layers (see Table 6). We have frozen the same triplet loss based encoder as used with kNN and optimized each fully-connected decoder with a cross-entropy loss using Novograd optimizer for 30 epochs with cosine annealing from 1e-3 to 8e-5. The resulting accuracy was around 90% and F1 around 82% independently of the intermediary dimension. This means that the embeddings generated by the triplet loss are not linearly separable and using kNN is really critical for high-quality decoding the triplet loss embeddings.

Table 6. Classification accuracy and F1 for res15 model triplet loss embeddings with kNN and fully-connected network classifiers.

Metric	kNN	FC64	FC128	FC256
Accuracy	98.37	90.04	89.88	90.16
F1	0.98	0.822	0.821	0.825

4 Results and Discussion

The results below were obtained by training a model for 3 different runs in each scenario and averaging the results to avoid the "lucky seed" effect. We can see that triplet loss + kNN based models provide better accuracy than baseline ones, achieve state of the art results on Speech Commands dataset, while being more lightweight and faster in convergence than the mh-att-rnn [20] model.

In particular, triplet loss + kNN based models improve the accuracy on the datasets studied by 25% to 38% and F1 measure by 16% to 57% compared to extremely strong crossentropy based baselines (see Table 7). The bigger the number of classes in the dataset, the bigger the difference between crossentropy and triplet loss based classifiers. Our res15 network trained with triplet loss and kNN classifier achieves state of the art on Google Speech Commands datasets V2/35, V2/12 and V1/12, improving the best previously published results [3, 20, 22] by 50%, 16% and 34% respectively (the best results are bold and the previous best results are italic in Table 8).

Table 7. Comparison of accuracy and F1 measure of triplet loss and crossentropy loss based res15 models.

Task	Triplet Loss		Crossentropy		Relative improvement	
	Accuracy, %	F1	Accuracy, %	F1	Accuracy, %	F1, %
Speech Commands V2 35	97.0	0.965	95.96	0.955	25.74	22.22
Speech Commands V2 12	98.37	0.980	97.8	0.963	25.91	45.95
Speech Commands V1 12	98.56	0.978	97.7	0.967	37.39	33.33
LibriWords10	91.7	0.90	88.8	0.88	26.25	16.67
LibriWords100	86.9	0.87	82.3	0.81	25.99	31.58
LibriWords 1000	84.3	0.86	78.2	0.78	27.94	36.36
LibriWords 10000	81.2	0.75	69.3	0.41	38.66	57.63

Table 8. Model accuracy comparison on Google Speech Commands dataset tasks.

Model	Loss	Model Size, KB	V2 35 accuracy	V2 12 accuracy	V1 12 accuracy
res8 (ours)	Triplet	901	95.33	97.48	
	Crossentropy	885	95.25	97.39	96.03
res15 (ours)	Triplet	252	97.0	98.37	98.56
	Crossentropy	237	95.96	97.8	97.7
EdgeCRNN 20	Crossentropy			98.05	
Mh-Att-RNN 20	Crossentropy	743		98.0	
Attention RNN 3	Crossentropy	202	93.9		
res8 (Howl) 22	Crossentropy				97.8

Acknowledgments. The authors are grateful to:
- colleagues at NTR Labs Machine Learning Research group for the discussions and support;
- Prof. Sergey Orlov and Prof. Oleg Zmeev for the computing facilities provided;
- Nikolay Shmyrev for pointing out to the works [38, 39].

References

1. Tang, R., Lin, J.: Deep residual learning for small-footprint keyword spotting. In: International Conference on Acoustics, Speech and Signal Processing, pp. 5484–5488 (2018)
2. Zhang, Y., Suda, N., Lai, L., Chandra, V.: Hello Edge: Keyword Spotting on Microcontrollers
3. de Andrade, D., Sabato, L., Viana, M., Bernkopf, C.: A neural attention model for speech command recognition
4. Teacher, C., Kellett, Y., Focht, L.: Experimental, limited vocabulary, speech recognizer. IEEE Trans. Audio Electroacoust. **15**(3), 127–130 (1967)
5. Rohlicek, J.R., Russell, W., Roukos, S., Gish, H.: Continuous hidden Markov modeling for speaker-independent word spotting. In: Acoustics, Speech, and Signal Processing, pp. 627–630 (1989)
6. Szöke, I., Schwarz, P., Matějka, P., Burget, L., Karafiát, M., Černocký, J.: Phoneme based acoustics keyword spotting in informal continuous speech. In: Matoušek, V., Mautner, P., Pavelka, T. (eds.) TSD 2005. LNCS (LNAI), vol. 3658, pp. 302–309. Springer, Heidelberg (2005). https://doi.org/10.1007/11551874_39
7. Zhang, S., Shuang, Z., Shi, Q., Qin, Y.: Improved mandarin keyword spotting using confusion garbage model. In: 2010 20th International Conference on Pattern Recognition (ICPR), pp. 3700–3703
8. Greibus, M., Telksnys, L.: Speech keyword spotting with rule based segmentation. In: Skersys, T., Butleris, R., Butkiene, R. (eds.) ICIST 2013. CCIS, vol. 403, pp. 186–197. Springer, Heidelberg (2013). https://doi.org/10.1007/978-3-642-41947-8_17
9. Principi, S.S., Bonfigli, R., Ferroni, G., Piazza, F.: An integrated system for voice command recognition and emergency detection based on audio signals. Expert Syst. Appl. **42**(13), 5668–5683 (2015). https://doi.org/10.1016/j.eswa.2015.02.036
10. Chen, G., Parada, C., Heigold, G.: Small-footprint keyword spotting using deep neural networks. In: Acoustics, Speech and Signal Processing, International Conference on, p. 4087–4091 (2014)
11. Sainath, T.N., Parada C.: Convolutional neural networks for small-footprint keyword spotting. In: Sixteenth Annual Conference of the International Speech Communication Association (2015)
12. Arik, S.O., et al.: Convolutional recurrent neural networks for small-footprint keyword spotting (2017)
13. Sun, M., et al.: Max-pooling loss training of long short-term memory networks for small-footprint keyword spotting. In: Spoken Language Technology Workshop, pp. 474–480 (2016)
14. He, Y., Prabhavalkar, R., Rao, K., Li, W., Bakhtin, A., McGraw, I.: Streaming small-footprint keyword spotting using sequence-to-sequence models. In: Automatic Speech Recognition and Understanding Workshop (ASRU), pp. 474–481 (2017)
15. Lei, J., et al.: Low-power audio keyword spotting using Tsetlin machines. J. Low Power Electron. Appl. **11**(2): 18
16. Warden, P.: Speech commands: a public dataset for single-word speech recognition
17. Jansson, P.: Single-word speech recognition with convolutional neural networks on raw waveforms. Degree Thesis, Information technology, ARCADA University, Finland

18. Majumdar, S., Ginsburg, B.: MatchboxNet: 1D time-channel separable convolutional neural network architecture for speech commands recognition. In: Proceedings of Interspeech, pp. 3356–3360. https://doi.org/10.21437/Interspeech.2020-1058 (2020)
19. Mordido, G., Van Keirsbilck, M., Keller, A.: Compressing 1D time-channel separable convolutions using sparse random ternary matrices (2021)
20. Rybakov O., Kononenko N., Subrahmanya N., Visontai M., Laurenzo S.: Streaming keyword spotting on mobile devices. In: Proceedings of Interspeech, pp. 2277–2281 (2020)
21. Wei, Y., Gong, Z., Yang, S., Ye, K., Wen, Y.: EdgeCRNN: an edge-computing oriented model of acoustic feature enhancement for keyword spotting. J. Ambient. Intell. Humaniz. Comput. 1–11 (2021). https://doi.org/10.1007/s12652-021-03022-1
22. Tang, R., et al.: Howl: a deployed, open-source wake word detection system. In: Proceedings of Second Workshop for NLP Open-Source Software (NLP-OSS), pp. 61–65 (2020)
23. Hermans, A., Beyer, L., Leibe, B.: In defense of the triplet loss for person re-identification
24. Wang, J., et al.: Learning fine-grained image similarity with deep ranking. In: 2014 IEEE Conference on Computer Vision and Pattern Recognition, pp. 1386–1393 (2014)
25. Chechik, G., Sharma, V., Shalit, U., Bengio, S.: Large scale online learning of image similarity through ranking. J. Mach. Learn. Res. 11, 1109–1135 (2010)
26. Schroff, F., Kalenichenko, D., Philbin, J.: FaceNet: a unified embedding for face recognition and clustering. In: 2015 IEEE Conference on Computer Vision and Pattern Recognition (CVPR), pp. 815–823 (2015)
27. Huang, J., Li, Y., Tao, J., Lian, Z.: Speech emotion recognition from variable-length inputs with triplet loss function. In: Proceedings of INTERSPEECH, pp. 3673–3677 (2018)
28. Ren, M., Nie, W., Liu, A., Su, Y.: Multi-modal correlated network for emotion recognition in speech. Vis. Informat. 3(3), 150–155 (2019)
29. Kumar, P., Jain, S., Raman, B, Roy, P.P., Iwamura, M.: End-to-end triplet loss based emotion embedding system for speech emotion recognition. In: 2020 25th International Conference on Pattern Recognition (ICPR), pp. 8766–8773 (2021)
30. Harvill, J., AbdelWahab, M., Lotfian, R., Busso, C.: Retrieving speech samples with similar emotional content using a triplet loss function. In: International Conference on Acoustics, Speech and Signal Processing, Brighton, United Kingdom, pp. 7400–7404 (2019)
31. Bredin, H.: Tristounet: triplet loss for speaker turns embedding. In: 2017 IEEE International Conference on Acoustics, speech and Signal Processing (ICASSP), pp. 5430–5434 (2017)
32. Song H., Willi, M., Thiagarajan, J.J., Berisha, V., Spanias, A.: Triplet network with attention for speaker diarization. In: Proceedings of Interspeech, pp. 3608–3612 (2018)
33. Zhang, C., Koishida, K.: End-to-end text-independent speaker verification with triplet loss on short utterances. In: Proceedings of Interspeech, pp. 1487–1491 (2017)
34. Li, C., et al.: Deep speaker: an end-to-end neural speaker embedding system
35. Turpault, N., Serizel, R., Vincent, E.: Semi-supervised triplet loss-based learning of ambient audio embeddings. ICASSP 2019. Brighton, United Kingdom (2019)
36. Sacchi, N., Nanchen, A., Jaggi, M., Cerňak, M.: Open-vocabulary keyword spotting with audio and text embeddings, pp. 3362–3366
37. Shor, J., et al.: Towards learning a universal non-semantic representation of speech. In: Proceedings of Interspeech, pp. 140–144 (2020)
38. Yuan, Y., Lv, Z., Huang, S., Xie, L.: Verifying deep keyword spotting detection with acoustic word embeddings. In: 2019 IEEE Automatic Speech Recognition and Understanding Workshop, ASRU 2019 Proceedings, no. 61571363, pp. 613–620 (2019)
39. Huh, J., Lee, M., Heo, H., Mun, S., Chung, J.S.: Metric learning for keyword spotting, 2021 IEEE Spoken Language Technology Workshop (SLT). In: IEEE, pp. 133–140 (2021)
40. Huang, J., Gharbieh, W., Shim, H.S., Kim, E.: Query-by-example keyword spotting system using multi-head attention and softtriple loss. In: ICASSP 2021–2021 IEEE International Conference on Acoustics, Speech and Signal Processing, pp. 6858–6862 (2021)

41. Tang, R. and Lin, J.: Honk: A PyTorch reimplementation of convolutional neural networks for keyword spotting 2017. http://arxiv.org/abs/1710.06554 (2021)

42. Panayotov, V., Chen, G., Povey, D., Khudanpur, S.: Librispeech: An ASR corpus based on public domain audio books. In: ICASSP, IEEE International Conference on Acoustics, Speech and Signal Processing, pp. 5206–5210 (2015)

43. Lugosch, L., Ravanelli, M., Ignoto, P., Tomar, V.S., Bengio, Y.: Speech model pre-training for end-to-end spoken language understanding. In: Proceedings of the Annual Conference of the International Speech Communication Association, INTERSPEECH, pp. 814–818 (2019)

44. McAuliffe, M., Socolof, M., Mihuc, S., Wagner, M., Sonderegger, M.: Montreal forced aligner: Trainable text-speech alignment using kaldi. In: Proceedings of the Annual Conference of the International Speech Communication Association INTERSPEECH, pp. 498–502 (2017)

45. https://zenodo.org/record/2619474. Accessed 2 Jan 2021

46. Ahmed, A.F., Sherif, M.A., Ngomo, A.C.N.: Do your resources sound similar?: On the impact of using phonetic similarity in link discovery, in K-CAP 2019. In: 10th International Conference on Knowledge Capture 8(19), 53–60 (2019)

47. Ginsburg, B., et al.: Stochastic gradient methods with layer-wise adaptive moments for training of deep networks

48. Johnson, J., Douze, M., Jégou, H.: Billion-scale similarity search with GPUs. IEEE Trans. Big Data 7(3), 535–547 (2021)

Regularized Forward-Backward Decoder for Attention Models

Tobias Watzel$^{(\boxtimes)}$ ⓘ, Ludwig Kürzinger ⓘ, Lujun Li ⓘ, and Gerhard Rigoll ⓘ

Chair of Human-Machine Communication, Technical University of Munich,
Munich, Germany
{tobias.watzel,ludwig.kuerzinger,lujun.li,rigoll}@tum.de

Abstract. Nowadays, attention models are one of the popular candidates for speech recognition. So far, many studies mainly focus on the encoder structure or the attention module to enhance the performance of these models. However, mostly ignore the decoder. In this paper, we propose a novel regularization technique incorporating a second decoder during the training phase. This decoder is optimized on time-reversed target labels beforehand and supports the standard decoder during training by adding knowledge from future context. Since it is only added during training, we are not changing the basic structure of the network or adding complexity during decoding. We evaluate our approach on the smaller TEDLIUMv2 and the larger LibriSpeech dataset, achieving consistent improvements on both of them.

Keywords: Speech recognition · Attention models · Forward-backward decoder · Regularization

1 Introduction

Automatic speech recognition (ASR) systems have increased their performance steadily over the years. The introduction of neural networks (NNs) into the area of speech recognition led to various improvements. Hybrid approaches replaced traditional Gaussian mixture models by learning a function between the input speech features and hidden markov model states in a discriminative fashion. However, these approaches are composed of several independently optimized modules, i.e., an acoustic model, a pronunciation model, and a language model. As they are not optimized jointly, useful information cannot be shared between them. Furthermore, specific knowledge is necessary for each module to retrieve the optimal result.

Recently, sequence-to-sequence (Seq2Seq) models are gaining popularity in the community [1–5,8–11,15–17,19] since they fuse all aforementioned modules into a single end-to-end model, which directly outputs characters (chars). Works like [4,17] have already shown that Seq2Seq models can be superior to hybrid systems [4] if enough data is available. Seq2Seq models can be categorized into approaches based on connectionist temporal classification (CTC) [9,10], on transducer [8,11,15] and on attention [1–5,16,17,19].

© Springer Nature Switzerland AG 2021
A. Karpov and R. Potapova (Eds.): SPECOM 2021, LNAI 12997, pp. 786–794, 2021.
https://doi.org/10.1007/978-3-030-87802-3_70

In CTC, a recurrent neural network (RNN) learns alignments between unlabeled input speech features and a transcript. The basic idea is to assume the conditional independence of the outputs and marginalize over all possible alignments [9]. For ASR, this assumption is not valid, as consecutive outputs are highly correlated. Transducer models relax the conditional independence and add another RNN to learn the dependencies between all previous input speech features and the output [11]. Attention models also combine two RNNs with an additional attention network. One RNN acts as an encoder to transform the input data into a robust feature space. The attention model creates a glimpse given the last hidden layer of the encoder, the previous time-step attention vector and the previous time-step decoder output. The decoder RNN then utilizes the glimpse and the previous decoder output to generate chars [1].

In our work, we propose a novel regularization technique by utilizing an additional decoder to improve attention models. This newly added decoder is optimized on time-reversed labels. Since we primarily focus on improving the training process, we utilize the decoder only during the optimization phase and discard it later in the inference. Thus, the network architecture of a basic attention model is not changed during decoding. A recent study demonstrated that it is beneficial to add a right-to-left (R2L) decoder to a conventional left-to-right (L2R) decoder [12]. The R2L decoder is trained on time-reversed target labels and acts as a regularizer during optimization. Their work focused mainly on the advantage of using the additional information to improve the beam search in decoding. They applied a constant scalar value, which attached a more significant weight on the loss function of the standard L2R decoder. Furthermore, they trained their models on Japanese words whereby label and time-reversed label sequences were equal. Another comparable work has been published in the domain of speech synthesis. In [20], they also utilized a second R2L decoder, combined both losses and added another regularizing function for the L2R and R2L decoder outputs. Similar to [12], they trained only on equal sequence lengths. In the English language, however, byte pair encodings (BPEs) for encoding the target transcripts seem superior [4,17]. As encoding a time-reversed transcript produces unequal sequence lengths between L2R and R2L decoders, regularization of these sequences is challenging. To the best of our knowledge, an in-depth study on how to solve this problem and leveraging the newly added decoder during the optimization process has not been done for attention models. Our contributions are to introduce an optimization scheme inspired by [20] for attention models in ASR and utilize the added decoder during the training. Furthermore, we propose two novel regularization terms for equal and unequal output sequence lengths and demonstrate their superiority over conventional attention models.

2   Proposed Method

2.1   Attention Model

The standard attentional Seq2Seq model contains three major components: the encoder, the attention module and the decoder. Let $\boldsymbol{X} = (\boldsymbol{x}_1, \cdots, \boldsymbol{x}_t, \cdots, \boldsymbol{x}_T)$

be a given input sequence of T speech features and let $\boldsymbol{y} = (y_1, \cdots, y_k, \cdots, y_K)$ be the target output sequence of length K. The encoder transforms the input sequence into a latent space:

$$\begin{aligned}\boldsymbol{H}^{\text{enc}} &= (\boldsymbol{h}_1^{\text{enc}}, \cdots, \boldsymbol{h}_t^{\text{enc}}, \cdots, \boldsymbol{h}_T^{\text{enc}}) \\ &= \text{Encoder}(\boldsymbol{x}_1, \cdots, \boldsymbol{x}_t, \cdots, \boldsymbol{x}_T),\end{aligned} \tag{1}$$

where $\boldsymbol{H}^{\text{enc}}$ encodes essential aspects of the input sequence, i.e., characteristics of the speech signal. The resulting hidden encoder states $\boldsymbol{H}^{\text{enc}}$ and the hidden decoder state $\boldsymbol{h}_{k-1}^{\text{dec}}$ are fed into the attention module to predict proper alignments between the t-th input and k-th output sequences:

$$\begin{aligned}\alpha_{k,t} &= \text{Attention}(\boldsymbol{h}_{k-1}^{\text{dec}}, \boldsymbol{H}^{\text{enc}}) \\ &= \exp(e_{k,t}) / \sum_{t'=1}^{T} \exp(e_{k,t'}),\end{aligned} \tag{2}$$

where $\boldsymbol{\alpha}_k = (\alpha_{k,1}, \cdots, \alpha_{k,t})$ are the attention weights and $e_{k,t}$ is the output of a scoring function:

$$e_{k,t} = \text{Scoring}(\boldsymbol{h}_{k-1}^{\text{dec}}, \boldsymbol{h}_t^{\text{enc}}, \boldsymbol{\alpha}_{k-1}). \tag{3}$$

Depending on the task, there are several ways to implement scoring functions. We choose the content-based and location-aware attention from [6] for scoring. Based on the attention weights $\boldsymbol{\alpha}_k$, a context vector $\boldsymbol{c}_k$ is created to summarize all information in the hidden states of the encoder for the current prediction:

$$\boldsymbol{c}_k = \sum_t \alpha_{k,t} \boldsymbol{h}_t^{\text{enc}}. \tag{4}$$

The decoder generates the output distribution using the context vector $\boldsymbol{c}_k$ and the decoder hidden state $\boldsymbol{h}_{k-1}^{\text{dec}}$:

$$p(y_k | p_{1:k-1}, \boldsymbol{X}) \sim \text{Generate}(\boldsymbol{h}_{k-1}^{\text{dec}}, \boldsymbol{c}_k), \tag{5}$$

where $\boldsymbol{h}_{k-1}^{\text{dec}}$ is a recurrency, usually a long short-term memory (LSTM):

$$\boldsymbol{h}_k^{\text{dec}} = \text{LSTM}(\boldsymbol{h}_{k-1}^{\text{dec}}, \boldsymbol{c}_k, y_{k-1}), \tag{6}$$

with y_{k-1} being the predicted target label of the previous prediction step. The resulting model is optimized by cross-entropy loss $\mathcal{L}_{\text{CE}}$.

2.2   Adding a Backward Decoder

For a traditional attention model, the char distribution $p(\overrightarrow{y}_k | p_{1:k-1}, \boldsymbol{X})$ is generated by a single L2R decoder. This distribution is dependent on the past and thus, has no information about the future context. For this reason, we extend the model by adding a second R2L decoder, which is trained on time-reversed output labels to generate $p(\overleftarrow{\boldsymbol{y}}_l | p_{L:l+1}, \boldsymbol{X})$. The reverse distribution contains beneficial information for the L2R decoder since the decoder has no access to future labels. The R2L decoder contains an individual attention network, which includes a likewise scoring mechanism as the L2R decoder. The decoders learn to create the posterior $p(\overrightarrow{\boldsymbol{y}} | \boldsymbol{X}, \overrightarrow{\theta})$ for the L2R and $p(\overleftarrow{\boldsymbol{y}} | \boldsymbol{X}, \overleftarrow{\theta})$ for the R2L case, respectively. Thus, $\overrightarrow{\theta}$ represents the attention and decoder parameters for target labels, which are typically time encoded (e.g., *cat*) and $\overleftarrow{\theta}$ are the attention and decoder parameter of the time-reversed target labels (e.g., *tac*).

In an ideal case, the posteriors of both decoders should satisfy the following condition:

$$p(\overrightarrow{\boldsymbol{y}} | \boldsymbol{X}, \overrightarrow{\theta}) = p(\overleftarrow{\boldsymbol{y}} | \boldsymbol{X}, \overleftarrow{\theta}), \tag{7}$$

as both networks receive the same amount of information. However, the decoders depend on a different context, i.e., the L2R on past context and the R2L on future context, which results in a similar but not equal training criterion.

2.3 Regularization for Equal Sequence Lengths

If we apply chars as target values for training the attention model, we are dealing with equal output sequence lengths since there is no difference between the forward and reverse encoding of a word. Therefore, we extend the loss $\mathcal{L}_{\mathrm{CE}}$ similar to [20] with a regularization term to retrieve the global loss $\tilde{\mathcal{L}}$:

$$\tilde{\mathcal{L}} = \alpha \mathcal{L}_{\mathrm{CE}}(\overrightarrow{\theta}) + (1 - \alpha)\mathcal{L}_{\mathrm{CE}}(\overleftarrow{\theta}) + \lambda \Omega(\overrightarrow{\theta}, \overleftarrow{\theta}), \tag{8}$$

where α defines a weighting factor for the losses, and $\Omega(\overrightarrow{\theta}, \overleftarrow{\theta})$ is a regularizer term weighted by λ. We apply the L_2 distance between the decoder outputs $\overrightarrow{\boldsymbol{y}} \in \mathbb{R}^K$ and $\overleftarrow{\boldsymbol{y}} \in \mathbb{R}^L$ with $K = L$ as regularization. Thus, $\Omega(\overrightarrow{\theta}, \overleftarrow{\theta})$ is defined it as:

$$\Omega(\overrightarrow{\theta}, \overleftarrow{\theta}) = \frac{1}{K} \sum_{k=1}^{K} ||\overrightarrow{\boldsymbol{y}}_k - \overleftarrow{\boldsymbol{y}}_k||_2. \tag{9}$$

The regularization term forces the network to minimize the distance between outputs of the L2R and R2L decoders. Therefore, the L2R network gets access to outputs that are based on future context information to utilize its knowledge and increase the overall performance. Note that this kind of regularization is only feasible as we are dealing with equal sequence lengths, which makes it simple to create $\Omega(\overrightarrow{\theta}, \overleftarrow{\theta})$.

2.4 Regularization for Unequal Sequence Lengths

We can extend the approach above by applying BPE units instead of chars. However, in contrast to chars, we face the problem of obtaining unequal sequence lengths $\overrightarrow{\boldsymbol{y}} \in \mathbb{R}^K$ for L2R and $\overleftarrow{\boldsymbol{y}} \in \mathbb{R}^L$ for R2L decoders with $K \neq L$. In fact, we create the same number of BPE units, however, they differ between the L2R and

R2L decoders, which results in a difference encoding (e.g., c a t_ for L2R and ta c_ for the R2L). Thus, the proposed regularization in Eq. 9 is not feasible. We resolve this issue utilizing a differentiable version of the dynamic time warping (DTW) algorithm [7] as a distance measurement between temporal sequences of arbitrary lengths the so-called soft-DTW algorithm. By defining a soft version of the *min* operator with a softening parameter γ:

$$\min{}^\gamma\{a_1, \cdots, a_n\} := \begin{cases} \min_{i \leq n} a_i & \gamma = 0 \\ -\gamma \log \sum_{i=1}^{n} e^{-a_i/\gamma} & \gamma > 0, \end{cases} \tag{10}$$

we can rewrite the soft-DTW loss as a regularization term $\Omega(\overrightarrow{\theta}, \overleftarrow{\theta})$ similar as above:

$$\Omega(\overrightarrow{\theta}, \overleftarrow{\theta}) = \min{}^\gamma\{\langle A, \Delta(\overrightarrow{y}, \overleftarrow{y})\rangle, A \in \mathcal{A}_{k,l}\}. \tag{11}$$

Here, $\langle \cdot, \cdot \rangle$ is the inner product of two matrices, A is an alignment matrix of a set $\mathcal{A}_{k,l} \subset \{0,1\}^{k,l}$ which are binary matrices that contain paths from $(1,1)$ to (k,l) by only applying $\downarrow$, $\rightarrow$ and $\searrow$ moves through this matrix and $\Delta(\overrightarrow{y}, \overleftarrow{y}) := [\delta(\overrightarrow{y}_k, \overleftarrow{y}_l)]$ is defined by a distance function $\delta(\overrightarrow{y}_k, \overleftarrow{y}_l)$ (e.g., Euclidean distance). Based on the inner product, we retrieve an alignment cost for all possible alignments between $\overrightarrow{y}$ and $\overleftarrow{y}$. Since we force the network to also minimize $\Omega(\overrightarrow{\theta}, \overleftarrow{\theta})$, it has to learn a good match between the different sequence lengths of the L2R and R2L decoders.

3   Experiments

3.1   Training Details

All our experiments are evaluated on the smaller dataset TEDLIUMv2 [14] and the larger dataset LibriSpeech [13]. TEDLIUMv2 has approximate 200 h of training data, whereas LibriSpeech contains of 960 h of training data.

We preprocess both datasets by extracting 80-dimensional log Mel features and adding the corresponding pitch features, which results in an 83-dimensional feature vector. Furthermore, we apply chars and BPE units as target labels. The chars are directly extracted from the datasets, whereas the BPE units are created by a language-independent sub-word tokenizer. For all experiments, we select 100 BPE units, which seem sufficient for our approach.

The proposed architecture is created in the ESPnet toolkit [18] and trained by the standard training script for attention models. The encoder is built up by four bidirectional long short-term memory projected (BLSTMP) layers of dimension 1024. Each decoder contains a single LSTM network with 1024 cells and a linear output layer.

We perform a three-stage training scheme inspired by [20]. In the first stage, we train a standard attentional network with a L2R decoder. Then, we apply the pretrained encoder, freeze its weights and train the R2L model. Finally, we combine both networks into one model to receive the final architecture. In all stages, we optimize the network with Adadelta initialized with an $\epsilon = 10^{-8}$. If we do not observe any improvement of the accuracy on the validation set, we decay ϵ by a factor of 0.01 and increment a patience counter by one. We apply an early stopping of the training if the patient counter exceeds three. The batch-size is set to 30 for all training steps.

Depending on the target labels in the third training stage, i.e., chars or BPE units, we deploy two different techniques to regularize the L2R decoder. For chars, forward sequences $\overrightarrow{y}$ and backward sequences $\overleftarrow{y}$ have equal lengths. Thus, we add a L_2 regularizer identical to Eq. 8 and scale it with $\lambda = 1$ for the smaller and $\lambda = 0.1$ for the bigger dataset, which we determined heuristically. On the other hand, for BPE units, we utilize the soft-DTW from Eq. 11 as a regularizer since it represents a distance measurement between the unequal sequence lengths $\overrightarrow{y}$ and $\overleftarrow{y}$, which we want to minimize. Here, we set $\gamma = 1$ and scale the regularization with $\lambda = 10^{-4}$ for both datasets. Besides the added regularizations for chars and BPE units, we regularize the L2R network further by applying $\alpha = 0.9$ in all the experiments. Thereby, we ensure that the overall training is focused on the L2R decoder network. During decoding, we remove the R2L network since it is only necessary in the training stages. As a result, we are not changing or adding complexity to the final model during decoding.

3.2 Benchmark Details

We evaluate our approach on five different setups. In the *Forward* setup, a model is trained with a standard L2R decoder, which is the baseline for all experiments. The second setup is the *Backward* setup, where a model is trained on time-reversed target labels, which results in a R2L decoder. We perform a similar approach in *Backward Fixed*, however, we apply the pretrained encoder from the L2R model and freeze its weights during training. To solely investigate the effect of the R2L decoder as regularization, we define the *Dual Decoder* setup. The model consists of a shared encoder from *Forward* and the pretrained L2R and R2L decoder from the *Forward* and *Backward Fixed* setups. The combined model is trained with $\alpha = 0.9$ and $\lambda = 0.0$. In the last *Dual Decoder Reg* setup, which is similar to the *Dual Decoder* setup, we include the L_2 distance [20] for chars and the soft-DTW loss [7] for BPE units as target labels. Instead of performing the forward and backward beam search as in [12], we only apply a forward beam search deploying the L2R decoder with a beam size of 20.

3.3 Results

In Table 1 and Table 2, we present the results of our approach applying chars and BPE units for the TEDLIUMv2 [14] and LibriSpeech [13] datasets.

For the smaller dataset TEDLIUMv2, we observe a clear difference in WERs between the *Forward* and the *Backward* setup. Ideally, the performance of these setups should be equal, as both networks receive the same amount of information. However, we observe an absolute difference of 1% WER for all evaluation sets, except for the test BPE set. One explanation for this variation may be that the

Table 1. Evaluation of our approach on TEDLIUMv2 with the resulting WERs (%) for all five setups.

TEDLIUMv2 [14]				
Methods	char		BPE	
	dev	test	dev	test
Forward	16.77	17.32	17.83	18.00
Backward	18.12	18.47	18.57	17.99
Backward fixed	23.34	23.77	25.55	25.01
Dual decoder	16.47	17.12	17.70	18.08
Dual decoder reg	**15.68**	**15.94**	**16.75**	**17.42**

Table 2. Evaluation of our approach on LibriSpeech with the resulting WERs (%) for all five setups.

LibriSpeech [13]								
Methods	char				BPE			
	dev-clean	dev-other	test-clean	test-other	dev-clean	dev-other	test-clean	test-other
Forward	7.69	20.67	7.72	21.63	7.59	20.98	7.67	21.92
Backward	7.60	20.78	7.54	21.83	7.53	20.94	7.60	21.71
Backward fixed	11.39	28.36	11.75	28.53	12.07	28.63	12.39	29.06
Dual decoder	7.29	20.99	7.60	22.00	7.46	21.29	7.70	22.01
Dual decoder Reg	**7.24**	**19.96**	**7.02**	**20.95**	**7.17**	**20.01**	**7.33**	**20.63**

Backward setup is more complex. Since the dataset contains only around 220 h of training data, the number of reverse training samples could not be sufficient. In the bigger dataset LibriSpeech, the first two setups obtain nearly the same WER with only a minor difference. This dataset contains nearly five times the data of the smaller dataset and therefore, the network in the *Backward* setup receives enough reverse training examples. It seems, that the amount of data seems crucial for the R2L decoder to satisfy Eq. 7.

In the *Backward Fixed* setup, we can verify the strong dependency of the decoder, relying on the high-level representation of features created by the encoder. Although we do not change the information of the target labels by reversing them, the fixed encoder from the *Forward* setup learned distinct, high-level features, which are based on past context. We observe this by a decline of the WERs in both datasets. Even though, the utilized BLSTMPs in the encoder network receive the complete feature sequence in the input space, they generate high-level features based on past label context, since they do not have access to future labels. As a result, the R2L model applying a fixed encoder from the *Forward* setup is worse compared to the trainable encoder in the R2L model.

In the *Dual Decoder* setup, we follow the idea of [12] to apply the R2L model as a regularizer of the L2R network. Interestingly, the R2L decoder is not able to effectively support the L2R decoder. We recognize only a slight improvement of the WER, which is not consistent in both datasets. Therefore, a simple weighting of the loss during training is not sufficient to enhance the L2R decoder. One reason might be that the L2R decoder receives only implicit information from the R2L decoder by weighting the losses, which is considered not valuable for the optimization of the L2R decoder.

To induce valuable information, we add our proposed regularization terms in the last *Dual Decoder Reg* setup. The overall network is forced to minimize the added regularization terms explicitly. The L2R decoder can directly utilize information of the R2L decoder to improve its predictions. We receive the overall best WER for the last setup. For the TEDLIUMv2 dataset, we recognize an average relative improvement of 7.2% for the char and 4.4% for the BPE units. For the LibriSpeech dataset, we are able to receive an average relative improvement of 4.9% for the char and 5.1% for the BPE units.

Compared to other state-of-the-art approaches, we decided not to include CTC and a language model since their integration into our approach raises several issues as we deal with a shared encoder and unequal sequence lengths among the two decoders.

4   Conclusion

Our work presents a novel way to integrate a second decoder for attention models during the training phase. The proposed regularization terms support the standard L2R model to utilize future context information from the R2L decoder, which is usually not available during optimization. We solved the issue of regularizing unequal sequence lengths, which arise applying BPE units as target values, by adding a soft version of the algorithm. We outperform conventional attention models independent of the dataset size. Our regularization technique is simple to integrate into a conventional training scheme, does not change the overall complexity of the standard model, and only adds optimization time.

References

1. Bahdanau, D., Cho, K., Bengio, Y.: Neural machine translation by jointly learning to align and translate. arXiv preprint arXiv:1409.0473 (2014)
2. Bahdanau, D., Chorowski, J., Serdyuk, D., Brakel, P., Bengio, Y.: End-to-end attention-based large vocabulary speech recognition. In: 2016 IEEE International Conference on Acoustics, Speech and Signal Processing (ICASSP), pp. 4945–4949. IEEE (2016)
3. Chan, W., Jaitly, N., Le, Q., Vinyals, O.: Listen, attend and spell: a neural network for large vocabulary conversational speech recognition. In: 2016 IEEE International Conference on Acoustics, Speech and Signal Processing (ICASSP), pp. 4960–4964. IEEE (2016)
4. Chiu, C.C., et al.: State-of-the-art speech recognition with sequence-to-sequence models. In: 2018 IEEE International Conference on Acoustics, Speech and Signal Processing (ICASSP), pp. 4774–4778. IEEE (2018)

5. Chorowski, J., Bahdanau, D., Cho, K., Bengio, Y.: End-to-end continuous speech recognition using attention-based recurrent NN: first results. arXiv preprint arXiv:1412.1602 (2014)
6. Chorowski, J.K., Bahdanau, D., Serdyuk, D., Cho, K., Bengio, Y.: Attention-based models for speech recognition. In: Advances in Neural Information Processing Systems, pp. 577–585 (2015)
7. Cuturi, M., Blondel, M.: Soft-DTW: a differentiable loss function for time-series. In: Proceedings of the 34th International Conference on Machine Learning, vol. 70, pp. 894–903. JMLR.org (2017)
8. Graves, A.: Sequence transduction with recurrent neural networks. arXiv preprint arXiv:1211.3711 (2012)
9. Graves, A., Fernández, S., Gomez, F., Schmidhuber, J.: Connectionist temporal classification: labelling unsegmented sequence data with recurrent neural networks. In: Proceedings of the 23rd International Conference on Machine Learning, pp. 369–376. ACM (2006)
10. Graves, A., Jaitly, N.: Towards end-to-end speech recognition with recurrent neural networks. In: International Conference on Machine Learning, pp. 1764–1772 (2014)
11. Graves, A., Mohamed, A.R., Hinton, G.: Speech recognition with deep recurrent neural networks. In: 2013 IEEE International Conference on Acoustics, Speech and Signal Processing, pp. 6645–6649. IEEE (2013)
12. Mimura, M., Sakai, S., Kawahara, T.: Forward-backward attention decoder. In: Interspeech, pp. 2232–2236 (2018)
13. Panayotov, V., Chen, G., Povey, D., Khudanpur, S.: LibriSpeech: an ASR corpus based on public domain audio books. In: 2015 IEEE International Conference on Acoustics, Speech and Signal Processing (ICASSP), pp. 5206–5210. IEEE (2015)
14. Rousseau, A., Deléglise, P., Esteve, Y.: Enhancing the TED-LIUM corpus with selected data for language modeling and more TED talks. In: LREC, pp. 3935–3939 (2014)
15. Sak, H., Shannon, M., Rao, K., Beaufays, F.: Recurrent neural aligner: an encoder-decoder neural network model for sequence to sequence mapping. In: Interspeech, pp. 1298–1302 (2017)
16. Sutskever, I., Vinyals, O., Le, Q.: Sequence to sequence learning with neural networks. In: Advances in NIPS (2014)
17. Tüske, Z., Audhkhasi, K., Saon, G.: Advancing sequence-to-sequence based speech recognition. In: Proceedings of the Interspeech, vol. 2019, pp. 3780–3784 (2019)
18. Watanabe, S., et al.: ESPnet: end-to-end speech processing toolkit. arXiv preprint arXiv:1804.00015 (2018)
19. Weng, C., Cui, J., Wang, G., Wang, J., Yu, C., Su, D., Yu, D.: Improving attention based sequence-to-sequence models for end-to-end English conversational speech recognition. In: Interspeech, pp. 761–765 (2018)
20. Zheng, Y., et al.: Forward-backward decoding for regularizing end-to-end TTS. arXiv preprint arXiv:1907.09006 (2019)

Induced Local Attention for Transformer Models in Speech Recognition

Tobias Watzel$^{(\boxtimes)}$ (ID), Ludwig Kürzinger (ID), Lujun Li (ID), and Gerhard Rigoll (ID)

Chair of Human-Machine Communication, Technical University of Munich,
Munich, Germany
{tobias.watzel,ludwig.kuerzinger,lujun.li,rigoll}@tum.de

Abstract. The transformer models and their variations currently are considered the prime model architectures in speech recognition since they yield state-of-the-art results on several datasets. Their main strength lies in the self-attention mechanism, where the models receive the ability to calculate a score over the whole input sequence and focus on essential aspects of the sequence. However, the attention score has some flaws. It is heavily global-dependent since it takes the whole sequence into account and normalizes along the sequence length. Our work presents a novel approach for a dynamic fusion between the global and a local attention score based on a Gaussian mask. The small networks for learning the fusion process and the Gaussian masks require only few additional parameters and are simple to add to current transformer architectures. With our exhaustive evaluation, we determine the effect of localness in the encoder layers and examine the most effective fusion approach. The results on the dataset TEDLIUMv2 demonstrate a steady improvement on the dev and the test set for the base transformer model equipped with our proposed fusion procedure for local attention.

Keywords: Speech recognition · Transformer · Local attention · Attention fusion

1 Introduction

Over the last years, sequence-to-sequence (Seq2Seq) models gain popularity as they are simple to train and require only little expert knowledge. The introduction of the transformer [18] proposed a novel way to eliminate the computational demanding long short-term memory (LSTM) layers by heavily relying on the self-attention (SA) mechanism. Despite the ordinary architecture, which mostly depends on feed-forward networks (FFNs), end-to-end speech recognition models based on the transformer were able to further reduce their word error rate (WER) on several different datasets. Nowadays, most state-of-the-art (SOTA) approaches rely on transformer model structure or its variations [2,10,13,17].

The SA is one of the critical elements in the transformer. This mechanism is based on an operation that predicts attention scores for the complete input

© Springer Nature Switzerland AG 2021
A. Karpov and R. Potapova (Eds.): SPECOM 2021, LNAI 12997, pp. 795–806, 2021.
https://doi.org/10.1007/978-3-030-87802-3_71

sequence. These attention scores are gathered in global attention maps containing the relevance of each input element in the overall sequence and are normalized across the complete sequence. As a result, these attention maps describe a strong global dependency of the overall sequence. Therefore, the model is able to attend to all information in the input sequence and it can focus the importance of every element in the sequence by itself. However, this can be problematic. The SA mechanism performs the normalization by applying the softmax operation, whereby small values are getting smaller and large values are getting even larger. The valuable and important local context in the sequence is suppressed as only dominant values remain after the softmax operation.

A simple approach to support local context information is to restrict the global context. Diminishing the impact of the global context, i.e., create a local window, is already known. Luong et al. [5] proposed one of the first approaches in machine translation based on attention models [15]. The model predicts an aligned position token for each target word. Then, they utilized the predicted position as the mean of a Gaussian distribution to limit the computation context of the following context vector.

Later, the approach of adding a Gaussian window to focus more on the local context was transferred to the transformer [18] model in several works [12,13,20]. Shaw et al. [12] proposed to add a trainable parameter to the key vector. These parameters are the edges of a fully connected, directed graph, representing the relative positions in a predefined clipping range. Sperger et al. [13] utilized a Gaussian mask and added it to the attention maps. This mask acts as a bias onto the SA mechanism and does not work for the cross-attention between encoder and decoder. Instead of applying a single fixed window size (i.e., a fixed standard derivation parameter σ), they proposed a trainable σ for every head. This approach ensures that each head of the SA can determine its specific parameters to achieve local attention where it is necessary. In [20], the approach of adding a Gaussian mask was further extended. They proposed a flexible way to adjust the window size (the standard derivation σ) and the position (the mean μ) of the mask. Therefore, the limitation for only utilizing the mask in the SA was eliminated, and they demonstrated a solution for masking the cross-attention in the transformer. However, similar to [13], their main focus relied on determining the window size. Multiple approaches for predicting this window size were compared, from fixed window sizes to layer-dependent window sizes. Even though this solution was capable of inserting the mask to the cross-attention, most of the improvement was still achieved when a Gaussian mask was added to the encoder's SA.

Recently, Nguyen et al. [6] closed this gap by proposing a fully differentiable window, which is also applicable to the SA in the encoder, and the decoder, and in the cross-attention between encoder and decoder. They investigated different ways of adding the local window to the SA mechanism and where the local mask had the most significant impact on the performance of the overall transformer model. Their study demonstrated that in the case of machine translation, the best model is returned by utilizing an additive window in the encoder's SA, an additive segment-based window in the cross-attention, and a multiplicative window in the decoder's SA.

Nearly all these approaches are proposed in the domain of machine translation, where they return consistent improvements in their translation score. Even though [13] shows a way to utilize localness in automatic speech recognition (ASR), their best model applies an LSTM for modeling the positional encoding. To the best of our knowledge, direct integration of localness into the global score of a transformer model for ASR has not be done. Our contributions are the following:

- We transfer the idea of local attention to the domain of ASR.
- We demonstrate that solely the encoder's SA can already benefit from localness.
- We propose a novel approach to fuse the local and global attention scores.

2 Proposed Method

2.1 Transformer Network

The transformer network relies on the SA mechanism to calculate a score of importance for each input element. As this SA takes into account the complete sequence, it can be considered as an attention with strong global context. The network itself is built up by stacked encoder and stacked decoder networks, connected by a cross-attention mechanism. In this work, we only examine the influence of localness on the stacked encoder. The standard SA is defined as a scoring between the query sequence $Q = (q_1, \cdots, q_i, \cdots, q_I)$ and the key sequence $K = (k_1, \cdots, k_i, \cdots, k_I)$ of length I:

$$\text{Score}(Q, K) = \frac{(QW^Q)(KW^K)^T}{\sqrt{d}}. \tag{1}$$

Since the scoring values are not normalized, a softmax operation is applied, followed by the value sequence $V = (v_1, \cdots, v_i, \cdots, v_I)$ to return the final SA:

$$\text{SelfAttention}(Q, K, V) = \text{Softmax}(\text{Score}(Q, K))VW^V. \tag{2}$$

Here, $q_i, k_i, v_i \in \mathbb{R}^d$ with the vector dimension d are combined into the matrices $Q, K, V \in \mathbb{R}^{I \times d}$, respectively and connected to the corresponding trainable weight matrices $W^Q, W^K, W^V \in \mathbb{R}^{d \times d}$. Note that in case of the SA, $Q = K = V$ and correspond to the output of the previous layer.

For a single attention head, the model would be restricted to certain positions learned during training. We obtain a more flexible model by splitting the single SA to a multi-head attention (MHA) approach [18]:

$$\text{MultiHeadAttention}(Q, K, V) = \text{Concat}(h_1, \cdots, h_n, \cdots, h_N)W^O, \tag{3}$$

where we concatenate the output of each head h_n and transform the concatenation into the output space by $W^O \in \mathbb{R}^{d \times d}$. Each head h_n corresponds to a SA:

$$h_n = \text{SelfAttention}(\boldsymbol{Q}_n, \boldsymbol{K}_n, \boldsymbol{V}_n)$$

$$= \text{Softmax}\left(\frac{(\boldsymbol{Q}_n\boldsymbol{W}_n^Q)(\boldsymbol{K}_n\boldsymbol{W}_n^K)^T}{\sqrt{d_{\text{mha}}}}\right)(\boldsymbol{V}_n\boldsymbol{W}_n^V), \tag{4}$$

where $d_{\text{mha}} = \frac{d}{N}$, $\boldsymbol{Q}_n, \boldsymbol{K}_n, \boldsymbol{V}_n \in \mathbb{R}^{I \times d_{\text{mha}}}$ and $\boldsymbol{W}_n^Q, \boldsymbol{W}_n^K, \boldsymbol{W}_n^V \in \mathbb{R}^{d_{\text{mha}} \times d_{\text{mha}}}$ are trainable parameters. The number N of total heads h_n can be chosen freely.

2.2   Local Attention via Flexible Gaussian Window

In the following, we demonstrate the local attention only for the SA since the formulas would be heavily cluttered with indices in the case of MHA. The approach can seamlessly be transferred to the MHA with its parameters.

Local attention can be achieved by defining a Gaussian mask $\boldsymbol{G}$:

$$G_{i,j} = -\frac{(j - P_i)^2}{2\sigma_i^2}, \tag{5}$$

where $\boldsymbol{G} \in \mathbb{R}^{I \times I}$ with $\boldsymbol{G}_{i,j} \in [0, -\infty)$. The mask is adjustable in its position P_i and its window size $\sigma_i = \frac{D_i}{2}$. The parameter P_i and D_i are learned by a FFNs and restricted to the current input length I, which is defined below. The mask provides the model with the ability to determine localness by itself if necessary. For example, if the model is lowering the standard deviation σ_i via D_i, it is able to focus on relevant parts of the sequence and ignore the irrelevant ones. On the other hand, if it is crucial to have global sequence information, the model can widen its focus by increasing σ_i.

2.3   Trainable Parameters of the Gaussian Mask

In order to predict the central position p_i and the window size z_i, we follow the approach in [20]:

$$\begin{pmatrix} P_i \\ D_i \end{pmatrix} = I \cdot \text{Sigmoid}\begin{pmatrix} p_i \\ z_i \end{pmatrix}. \tag{6}$$

The values p_i and z_i are learned by FFNs and are integrated into the SA procedure. The predict values define a well-fitting Gaussian mask, which induces local attention in the SA.

Central Position Prediction. The score in Eq. 1 is calculated between the key sequence $\boldsymbol{K}$ and the query sequence $\boldsymbol{Q}$. In our case, we add the local attention to the encoder's SA. Therefore, we make our prediction for the central position p_i dependent on $\boldsymbol{K}$ or $\boldsymbol{Q}$. Similar to [20], we also utilize the query sequence $\boldsymbol{Q}$ to transform it into a hidden positional state p_i:

$$p_i = \boldsymbol{u}_{\text{p}}^T \tanh(\boldsymbol{W}_{\text{p}}\boldsymbol{q}_i), \tag{7}$$

where $\boldsymbol{u}_{\text{p}} \in \mathbb{R}^d$ and $\boldsymbol{W}_{\text{p}} \in \mathbb{R}^{d \times d}$ are trainable linear transformations.

Window Size Prediction. There are several ways to set or learn a specific window size z_i [20]. Besides setting a fixed window size, it is possible to make the prediction dependent on the mean of the key sequence K. In this way, we condense all the information of K into a layer-dependent value z. However, we want to give the model as much flexibility as possible. Thus, we select the approach where we depend on all the predictions of the query sequence Q:

$$z_i = u_d^T \tanh(W_p q_i), \tag{8}$$

where $u_d \in \mathbb{R}^d$ denotes a trainable linear transformation. The advantage of reusing the transformation $W_p q_i$ is that we receive enough flexibility to learn the corresponding parameters p_i and z_i with only a few additional parameters [20].

2.4 Global and Local Attention Score Fusion

There are multiple ways, how to integrate the Gaussian mask G into the SA mechanism. First, we revisit the fusion approach from [20]. We propose two refinements for the fusion process to enhance the integration of the local attention.

Bias Attention Fusion. The simplest method is to add the local score G to the global scoring in Eq. 1, where the mask acts like a bias [20]:

$$\text{Score}(Q, K) = \frac{(QW^Q)(KW^K)^T}{\sqrt{d}} + G. \tag{9}$$

We believe that it is challenging for the model to create a local mask utilizing the standard weight matrices $W^Q, W^K, W^V \in \mathbb{R}^{d \times d}$, transforming the queries, keys, and values into their own space containing global information.

Improved Attention Fusion. Inspired by [6], we add weight matrices W_{local}^Q, $W_{\text{local}}^K, W_{\text{local}}^V \in \mathbb{R}^{I \times d}$ for the local attention. However, in [6], they utilize a differential window instead of a Gaussian mask. For that reason, we transfer the idea of their fusion process to our approach:

$$S_{\text{global}} = (QW^Q)(KW^K)^T \tag{10}$$

$$S_{\text{local}} = (QW_{\text{local}}^Q)(KW_{\text{local}}^K)^T \odot G = S_{\text{local}}' \odot G, \tag{11}$$

where $\odot$ denotes an element-wise multiplication and set the final scoring in Eq. 9 with the attention score:

$$\text{Score}(Q, K) = \frac{S_{\text{global}} + S_{\text{local}}}{\sqrt{d}}. \tag{12}$$

The local weight matrices share the same dimensionality as the global weight matrices. Now, the model is more flexible in generating local attention masks since the dependency of the global weight matrices is removed.

Adjustable Attention Fusion. Although the SA is now split into two independent attention branches, the additional term in Eq. 12 still weights the global score S_{global} and the local score S_{local} equally, which could not be optimal, e.g., if S_{global} is more relevant for a precise prediction. To cope with this issue, we insert a weighting parameter α to Eq. 12:

$$\text{Score}(\boldsymbol{Q}, \boldsymbol{K}) = \frac{\alpha\, S_{\text{global}} + (1 - \alpha)\, S_{\text{local}}}{\sqrt{d}}, \tag{13}$$

The parameter α is learned by FFNs:

$$\alpha = \text{Sigmoid}(\boldsymbol{u}_\alpha^T \tanh(\boldsymbol{W}_\alpha \overline{\boldsymbol{k}})), \tag{14}$$

where $\boldsymbol{u}_\alpha \in \mathbb{R}^d$, $\boldsymbol{W}_\alpha \in \mathbb{R}^{d \times d}$ and $\overline{\boldsymbol{k}} \in \mathbb{R}^d$ is the mean key over the key sequence $\boldsymbol{K}$.

3   Experiments

3.1   Training Setup

In order to test our approach for local attention, we evaluate our model on the dataset TEDLIUMv2 [9]. The dataset combines more than 200 h of training data which is already transcribed. The overall data is divided into train, test, and dev set with a lexicon of 150 k words. Furthermore, we perform different augmentation techniques. Before the actual training, we enhance the training data by applying speed perturbation [4], where the original signal is resampled with three different speed factors: 0.9, 1.0, and 1.1. Then, we extract 80-dimensional log Mel filterbanks as feature vectors, followed by 3-dimensional pitch features vectors with Kaldi [8], and concatenated the resulting vectors to the final 83-dimensional feature vector. Moreover, we generate byte pair encoding (BPE) units [11] of size 500 by utilizing the transcript and set these units as our target values. During training, we apply another augmentation technique SpecAugment [7], which warps the created features and blocks certain frequency channels or time steps via masking.

The transformer model is implemented in the ESPnet toolkit [19], where the pre-processed dataset is fed to the front-end of the transformer model. This front-end network sub-samples the input feature sequence utilizing two conv2D layers with ReLU activation functions. Each convolutional layer has $d_{\text{att}} = 256$ channels and employs a 3×3 kernel with a stride of length two. A linear layer with $d_{\text{att}} = 256$ dimensions serves as the output of the front-end, to which the position encoding from [18] is added.

The transformer contains an encoder and a decoder branch. The stacked encoder branch is built up by 12 layers with 2048 units, respectively. The decoder branch has only six layers and shares an equal amount of units as the encoder branch. We set the dimension of the SA mechanism to $d_{\text{att}} = 256$, which is applied to all encoder and decoder layers. We also utilize the benefit of the MHA and set the number of heads $N = 4$.

All our experiments are based on the identical training setup, whereas we vary between the different fusion approaches for adding localness. The local attention is only applied in the SA of the encoder layers. We train all our models for 50 epochs and set the batch size to 128. The transformer models are optimized by the Adam optimizer [3]. To avoid an early local minimum, we perform a warm-up phase [18], in which the learning rate is slowly increased until it is steadily decreased in the regular training setup. The warm-up phase includes 25 000 steps. For regularization purposes, we follow the approach in [18], where we apply the standard and residual dropout [14] with a rate of 0.1 in each encoder and decoder layer and smooth the target labels by 0.1 [16].

The resulting transformer model is trained by the Kullback-Leibler (KL) loss, which is guided by the auxiliary loss of the connectionist temporal classification (CTC) [1] network on top of the encoder branch. The CTC loss is weighted by 0.3.

During decoding, we combine the transformer and the corresponding CTC outputs. The predictions of the CTC network are weighted with 0.3. We apply a standard beam search with a beam size of 20 and omit the language model.

3.2 Ablation Study

Since the improvement mentioned in [6,20] is located in the domain of machine translation and language modeling, it is not clear if the same application holds for the local attention in ASR. Therefore, we perform a short ablation study where to apply localness and to identify the most effective way to fuse the global score from Eq. 10 and local score from Eq. 11.

Table 1. Ablation study of how to fuse the local attention. The results are in WER and evaluated on TEDLIUMv2 [9].

TEDLIUMv2		
Model	dev	test
Baseline w/o localness	10.0	9.2
+ Bias Attention Fusion [20]	10.1	9.0
+ Improved Attention Fusion	10.3	8.8
+ Adjustable Attention Fusion	9.8	9.1

Table 2. Ablation study of the layer location for integrating the local attention from Eq. 13. The results are in WER and evaluated on TEDLIUMv2 [9].

TEDLIUMv2		
Model	dev	test
Baseline w/o localness	10.0	9.2
Layer 1–3	10.1	8.8
Layer 1–6	10.2	8.9
Layer 1–9	10.0	8.8
Layer 1–12	9.8	9.1

Effective Fusion. We examine different approaches to effectively fuse the local and global attention score in the encoder. The standard transformer model without local attention acts as the baseline for our study. The comparison of the different fusion setups share the procedure described in Sect. 3.1 and results are exhibited in Table 1.

Our baseline model achieves a WER of 10.0% on the dev and 9.2% on the test set, which is close to the SOTA results reported in the ESPnet repository[1]. The only difference is that we trained our model for only 50 epochs and decoded it with a beam size of 20.

In the first *Bias Attention Fusion* setup, we integrate the Gaussian mask to the transformer model, similar as proposed in [20]. During our experiments, we faced the problem that the proposed mask returned only minor WER reductions compared to the baseline model. Although we reduce the WER on the test set from 9.2% to 9.0%, we do not observe a similar performance gain on the dev set, where the WER increases from 10.0% to 10.1%. Since the improvements are not consistent, we think it is challenging to learn a favorable Gaussian mask if there is no local branch available which is entirely focusing on inducing localness.

For this reason, we extend the latter approach to the *Improved Attention Fusion* setup, where we separate the local and global attention scores. The extension further reduces the WER on the test set from 9.2% to 8.8%, though we notice an increase of the WER in the dev set from 10.0% to 10.3%. It seems that the model benefits from a separate local attention branch, however, without consistent WER reductions. A reason for these divergent results could be the final fusion between both scores, which is still equally weighted.

In the *Adjustable Attention Fusion* setup, we equip the model with the ability to weigh the global and local scores by itself. Therefore, we utilize the mean key $\bar{k}$ of the key sequence K to predict an α value, which defines a fusion weight between the local and global attention score. We obtain a highly flexible model which returns consistent WER reductions. The final model reduces the WER for the dev set from 10.0% to 9.8% and for the test set from 9.2% to 9.1%.

Location of Localness. Recent approaches as [6,20] already demonstrated that the location of the local attention in the encoder's SA of the model is relevant and improves the transformer performance. They argue that the improvement results in the fact that the lower layers of the model process more low-level features, which contain more local information. As we do not know if it also holds for ASR, we define four setups, where we integrate localness in the encoder with our *Improved Attention Fusion* approach continuously. We begin with the *Layer 1-3* setup, where we apply the local attention from Eq. 13 in the first three SA encoder layers. In the following three setups, we always add our local attention approach for the next three SA encoder layers until the complete encoder is equipped with it.

Our results in Table 2 reveal only a minor impact to the layer location of the local attention. For the *Layer 1-3* setup, we observe an improvement on the test set from 9.2% to 8.8% and a minor increase on the dev set from 10.0% to 10.1%. We obtain a similar result for localness in the first six layers, where the model

---

[1] https://github.com/espnet/espnet/blob/master/egs/tedlium2/asr1/RESULTS.md (commit c881192).

Table 3. Final results in WER trained for 100 epochs between the current SOTA result and our best approach. Evaluation was done on TEDLIUMv2 [9] and was decoded with a beam size of 40.

TEDLIUMv2 [9]			
Model	#Param	dev	test
Baseline ESPnet	28 M	10.1	8.9
+ Adjustable Attention Fusion	29 M	10.0	8.7

achieves a decline in the WER on the test to 8.9%, however, a slight increase to 10.2% on the dev set. In the *Layer 1-9* setup, we are able to equalize with the baseline setup, where the model returns a WER of 10.0% on the dev set and reduces the WER on the test set from 9.2% to 8.8%.

The most consistent improvements are returned for the local attention employed in all SA layers of the encoder. For this setup, we are able to reduce the WER on the dev set from 10.0% to 9.8% and gain a slight decline on the test set from 9.2% to 9.1%. All in all, we do not observe similar findings as in [6, 20]. One reason might be the length of the input feature sequence. Although the input sequence is sub-sampled to reduce its length, it is still several times longer than the output sequence. For machine translation, this is not the case since the input sentence and the output sentence share a high length overlap.

3.3   Final Results

For the final results, we trained our approach with a similar training setup as the current SOTA results reported in the ESPnet repository (c.f. footnote above). The baseline model and the extension *Adjustable Attention Fusion* are optimized for 100 epochs and decoded with a beam size of 40. The extension requires a minor increase from 28 M to 29 M total model parameters.

Our results in Table 3 demonstrate that our approach is competitive with current SOTA transformer model, hence, localness is also beneficial for transformer models in the domain of ASR. We are able to slightly reduce the WER on the dev set from 10.1% to 10.0% and on the dev set from 8.9% to 8.7%.

Furthermore, we depict in Fig. 1 the qualitative results of our approach. In the upper row, we can observe the process of generating the local score S_{local}. First, in Fig. 1a the model branch for the local attention determines the local score S'_{local} without the Gaussian mask G. Then, in Fig. 1b two FFNs predict the position p_i and window size z_i for each entry in G. As the input sequence length increases, the position p_i of the Gaussian mask slowly transits to the end of the output sequence where the more relevant information of the score is. After the multiplication of S'_{local} and G, we observe in Fig. 1c that certain values of the local score are raised since the color shading is brighter, whereas other parts are lowered noticeable by the darker shading.

The fusion process of the S_{local} and S_{global} is shown in the lower row of Fig. 1. In Fig. 1d, the standard score S_{global} is plotted without applying any

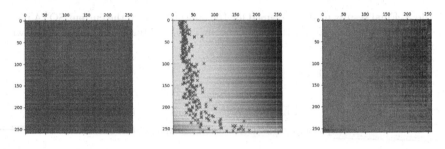

(a) S'_{local} without the Gaussian mask G.

(b) The learned Gaussian mask G with the marked positions p_i.

(c) The final score S_{local}, where S'_{local} is multiplied by G.

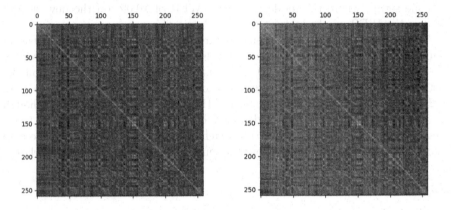

(d) The global score S_{global} without inducing local attention.

(e) The final attention score out of S_{global} and S_{local}, where $\alpha = 0.423$.

Fig. 1. The procedure of the *Adjustable Attention Fusion* with the final attention score. The global score S_{global} and the local S_{local} are determined and weighted by the parameter α. Certain parts of the final attention score in Fig. 1e are getting boosted by S_{local}.

local attention. If the fusion from Eq. 13 is applied, we obtain the final score in Fig. 1e. There, it is observable that some values of the final score are assigned with higher importance since at the positions that plot is much brighter. As a result, we are able to demonstrate that our approach is visible in the quantitative as well as the qualitative results.

4   Conclusion

Our work presented a novel approach to induce localness into the global score of the transformer network's attention mechanism. Thereby, the local attention score is achieved by employing a Gaussian mask, where it is essential to fuse the global and local scores efficiently. Our novel fusion approach provides an excellent way to do so, with only a minor increase of the total model parameters. In our future work, we plan to integrate the local attention mechanism to the SA of the decoder network and the cross-attention between the encoder and decoder network.

References

1. Graves, A., Fernández, S., Gomez, F., Schmidhuber, J.: Connectionist temporal classification: labelling unsegmented sequence data with recurrent neural networks. In: Proceedings of the 23rd International Conference on Machine Learning, pp. 369–376. ACM (2006)
2. Gulati, A., et al.: Conformer: convolution-augmented transformer for speech recognition. arXiv preprint arXiv:2005.08100 (2020)
3. Kingma, D.P., Ba, J.: Adam: a method for stochastic optimization. arXiv preprint arXiv:1412.6980 (2014)
4. Ko, T., Peddinti, V., Povey, D., Khudanpur, S.: Audio augmentation for speech recognition. In: Sixteenth Annual Conference of the International Speech Communication Association (2015)
5. Luong, M.T., Pham, H., Manning, C.D.: Effective Approaches to Attention-Based Neural Machine Translation. arXiv preprint arXiv:1508.04025 (2015)
6. Nguyen, T.T., Nguyen, X.P., Joty, S., Li, X.: Differentiable window for dynamic local attention. arXiv preprint arXiv:2006.13561 (2020)
7. Park, D.S., et al.: Specaugment: a simple data augmentation method for automatic speech recognition. arXiv preprint arXiv:1904.08779 (2019)
8. Povey, D., et al.: The Kaldi speech recognition toolkit. In: IEEE 2011 Workshop on Automatic Speech Recognition and Understanding. No. CONF, IEEE Signal Processing Society (2011)
9. Rousseau, A., Deléglise, P., Esteve, Y.: Enhancing the TED-LIUM corpus with selected data for language modeling and more TED talks. In: LREC, pp. 3935–3939 (2014)
10. Salazar, J., Kirchhoff, K., Huang, Z.: Self-attention networks for connectionist temporal classification in speech recognition. In: ICASSP 2019-2019 IEEE International Conference on Acoustics, Speech and Signal Processing (ICASSP), pp. 7115–7119. IEEE (2019)
11. Sennrich, R., Haddow, B., Birch, A.: Neural machine translation of rare words with subword units. arXiv preprint arXiv:1508.07909 (2015)
12. Shaw, P., Uszkoreit, J., Vaswani, A.: Self-attention with relative position representations. arXiv preprint arXiv:1803.02155 (2018)
13. Sperber, M., Niehues, J., Neubig, G., Stüker, S., Waibel, A.: Self-attentional acoustic models. arXiv preprint arXiv:1803.09519 (2018)
14. Srivastava, N., Hinton, G., Krizhevsky, A., Sutskever, I., Salakhutdinov, R.: Dropout: a simple way to prevent neural networks from overfitting. J. Mach. Learn. Res. **15**(1), 1929–1958 (2014)
15. Sutskever, I., Vinyals, O., Le, Q.: Sequence to sequence learning with neural networks. In: Advances in NIPS (2014)
16. Szegedy, C., Vanhoucke, V., Ioffe, S., Shlens, J., Wojna, Z.: Rethinking the inception architecture for computer vision. In: Proceedings of the IEEE Conference on Computer Vision and Pattern Recognition, pp. 2818–2826 (2016)

17. Tian, Z., Yi, J., Tao, J., Bai, Y., Wen, Z.: Self-attention transducers for end-to-end speech recognition. In: Proceedings of Interspeech 2019, pp. 4395–4399 (2019)
18. Vaswani, A., et al.: Attention is all you need. In: Advances in Neural Information Processing Systems, pp. 5998–6008 (2017)
19. Watanabe, S., et al.: Espnet: end-to-end speech processing toolkit. arXiv preprint arXiv:1804.00015 (2018)
20. Yang, B., Tu, Z., Wong, D.F., Meng, F., Chao, L.S., Zhang, T.: Modeling localness for self-attention networks. arXiv preprint arXiv:1810.10182 (2018)

Applying EEND Diarization to Telephone Recordings from a Call Center

Zbyněk Zajíc(✉) , Marie Kunešová , and Luděk Müller

Faculty of Applied Sciences, NTIS - New Technologies for the Information Society
and Department of Cybernetics, University of West Bohemia,
Univerzitní 8, 301 00 Plzeň, Czech Republic
{zzajic,mkunes,muller}@ntis.zcu.cz

Abstract. In this paper, we focus on the issue of speaker diarization of data from a real call center. We have previously proposed a specialized solution to the problem, which employed additional knowledge about the identities of the phone operators (in our case, the language counselors from the Language Consulting Center), thus improving performance over the baseline. But a recent end-to-end diarization method, EEND, has since proven very successful on other data and was shown to surpass the previous state of the art in the field. Thus, we chose to compare this new method with our own previous approach. Using an existing implementation of the EEND method (adapted using a small amount of the target data from the Language Consulting Center), we successfully surpass the performance of our previous approach (17.42% vs. 19.39% DER), without the need for any additional information about speaker identities. The majority of the remaining diarization error of the EEND system is due to incorrect decisions between speech and silence, rather than speaker confusion. For comparison, we also show the results of a more standard diarization approach, represented by the method used in the Kaldi toolkit.

Keywords: Diarization · End-to-end · X-vector · EEND

1 Introduction

The central question of diarization, "Who spoke when?", is of great importance for commercial and forensic applications, but also as a stand-alone task to provide speaker-specific meta information for audio retrieval. Speaker diarization (SD) has drawn a great amount of attention in recent years, in part due to several organized challenges which focused on this topic – such as the DIHARD challenge [14,15] or the VoxCeleb Speaker Recognition Challenge 2020 [10]. These competitions involved data from a broad variety of acoustics conditions, encouraging more generic approaches to the problem. But in this paper, we focus on a more specific application, and discuss some of the challenges, as well as opportunities, that were encountered when applying diarization techniques to data from a real call center.

© Springer Nature Switzerland AG 2021
A. Karpov and R. Potapova (Eds.): SPECOM 2021, LNAI 12997, pp. 807–817, 2021.
https://doi.org/10.1007/978-3-030-87802-3_72

The standard diarization approach, which has been commonly used in past years, consists of the splitting of an input signal into short speech segments, which are then represented via speaker embedding such as x-vectors [20] and merged into clusters corresponding to individual speakers [13,16,19]. This is optionally followed by resegmentation [17].

More recently, with the rise of deep learning technology, there has been intense development towards end-to-end approaches which are completely driven by a neural network [6,23]. Examples also include [22], an end-to-end system which performs diarization via source separation, or [8], a hybrid diarization framework combining end-to-end and clustering approach. A more detailed review of deep learning in speaker diarization can also be found in [11].

In this paper, we are comparing three systems on a set of data from the Language Consulting Call Center. The baseline diarization approach is based on Kaldi [12]. The second is our previous system [25], which was specifically proposed for the data in question by exploiting the known information about the identity of one speaker in each conversation - the language counselor employed in the call center. The third option is the end-to-end (EEND) system based on the work in [6], trained for conversations with two speakers[1].

2   Call Center Data Description

The Language Consulting Center (LCC) of the Czech Language Institute of the Academy of Sciences of the Czech Republic provides a unique language consultancy service in the matters of the Czech language (e.g. grammar and spelling advice). This is conducted mostly via a telephone line open to public calls.

The recordings of these calls became the subject of the project "Access to a Linguistically Structured Database of Enquiries from the Language Consulting Center"[2]. The main goal of the project was to analyze these data and provide access via a structured database, searchable by topic. This requires the use of an Automatic Speech Recognizer (ASR) and other language processing methods like topic detection and keyword spotting. More about the development can be found in [27,28].

Unfortunately, a large number of the telephone calls from the LCC, nearly eight thousand recordings from the 2013–2016 time period, were recorded on an analog telephone line (8 kHz, μ-law resolution) and stored only in mono channel - the language counselor and client are mixed in one channel.

The diarization of these data can improve the results of the ASR, by allowing us to adapt the acoustic and language model to specific speakers. The topic identification method, which we use for categorizing the topic of each conversation, has also proven more accurate when used only on the answer from the language counselor, rather than the entire recording [28]. Therefore, our goal is to apply

---

[1] https://github.com/hitachi-speech/EEND.
[2] https://starfos.tacr.cz/en/project/DG16P02B009.

speaker diarization to separate the question of the LCC's client from the answer of the language counselor.

The dataset consists of only speech, without music or other noise. There are always only two speakers in each conversation, the client and the operator (the language counselor), and while the sound quality of the clients' side varies, the operators always have relatively clean speech. On the other hand, there are often very short utterances (e.g. agreement) and overlapping speech, and the timings of the overlaps are not included in the available transcripts.

In the course of the project, approximately 10% of the single-channel data were manually transcribed. As this was done primarily for the purpose of ASR and topic detection, the annotators were instructed to focus on accurate transcription of the spoken words, but were not required to precisely indicate the timing or position of words in overlapped speech. Additionally, the role of each speaker (client vs. operator) was noted, and the gender of each client was added to the transcription.

The manually transcribed data were then force-aligned to find the precise time where each word or phone is spoken and also which part of the data belongs to each speaker. These data were used to train the individual models of the operators and to test our diarization system.

3   Speaker Diarization Based on X-Vectors

As the baseline system, we have chosen to employ the standard Kaldi recipe for diarization[3] [18], which is based on x-vectors.

The baseline system uses Mel Frequency Cepstral Coefficients (MFCCs) features and the input recording is segmented into intervals of uniform length (1.5 s, 0.75 s overlap). Individual segments are then represented by x-vectors, extracted from the MFCCs using a Time Delay Neural Network (TDNN).

The x-vectors are also whitened by subtracting the mean and transforming by the Linear Discriminant Analysis (LDA) matrix.

The whitened x-vectors are then clustered using Agglomerative Hierarchical Clustering (AHC), with the similarity between the individual segments calculated using a Probabilistic Linear Discriminant Analysis (PLDA) model [7]. As there are only two speakers in each recording, we set the stopping threshold for two clusters.

The initial rough segmentation can optionally also be refined by feature-wise resegmentation using Variational Bayes (VB) inference [2]. We evaluated the output of the system both with and without this resegmentation.

4   Diarization System Based on Identification

The second diarization system, proposed in our previous paper [25], was specifically designed for the LCC's dataset. Like the baseline, this system is also based

---

[3] https://github.com/kaldi-asr/kaldi/tree/master/egs/callhome_diarization/v2.

on comparing speech segments represented by x-vectors. However, instead of clustering the x-vectors [18, 26], we have decided to incorporate known information about the identity of one participant of the conversation, the language counselor. The list of the language counselors answering the language queries is limited and known. The actual identity of the counselor in each recording is also known: they introduce themselves by name at the start of each call, and so the identification of the counselor is reduced to finding one name from the list appearing at the beginning of the ASR transcription.

For each counselor, we have obtained an identity x-vector, extracted from some of the speaker's oldest transcribed recordings. We have also obtained a pair of universal x-vectors to represent unknown male and female clients. The specific details will be listed in Sect. 7.1.

The pipeline of the system (see Fig. 1) is similar to the previous one described in Sect. 3 until the clustering step. Instead of using AHC, each x-vector is compared with the limited set of identities in the recordings. This set consists of the detected counselor's x-vector and unknown client's identity represented by the universal male and female x-vectors. The segment is assigned to the identity (counselor or client) with the highest PLDA similarity.

The universal client models are more generic than the counselors' identity vectors and this can lead to some incorrect decisions about the identity of the segments. For this reason, the next step is resegmentation where only the representative segments are used. The representative segments are those with sufficient similarity between the segment and the identity models. Instead of the universal models, we obtain a new specific client model by averaging the x-vectors of the representative segments which were initially assigned to the client. Then, the entire recording is resegmented according to two x-vectors – the known counselor's model and the new client model.

5   End-to-End Diarization System

In this work, we apply the recently introduced EEND diarization approach [6] to our data, using the available opensource implementation[4]. The approach in question is a follow-up on the previous systems proposed by the same team in [4,5], extended by the encoder-decoder based attractor calculation (EDA) and allowing the diarization for an unknown number of speakers. But because our target data contains a limited number of speakers in the recording (counselor and client), we do not use the second of these features. Following is a brief description of the system, summarizing the original authors' work.

The EEND-EDA (see the Fig. 2) takes a T-length sequence of the log-scaled Mel-filterbank based features and processes it using Transformer encoders to obtain an D-dimensional embedding $e_t \in \mathbb{R}^D$. This approach is based on the self-attention mechanism (SA) [9] proposed for embeddings in text processing task. For the end-to-end diarization approach, SA was applied in [5] where the

---

[4] https://github.com/hitachi-speech/EEND.

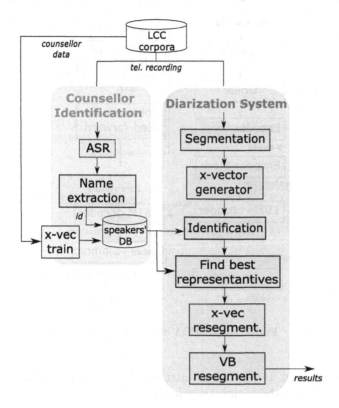

Fig. 1. Diagram of the diarization based on identification.

output of the encoder part was considered as an embedding of the speaker. Authors replaced the original bidirectional long short-term memory (BLSTM) architecture (used in work [4]) by SA embedding.

Furthermore, whereas in [4,5] the embeddings are mapped into the posteriors via a linear transformation (represented by an element-wise sigmoid function), in the EEND-EDA version the authors calculate the attractors from an embedding sequence and obtain the diarization results using embedings along with these attractors.

5.1 EDA Calculation

Long short-term memory (LSTM) [21] encoder is used to obtain the final hidden state embedding $h_0 \in \mathbb{R}^D$ and the cell state $c_0 \in \mathbb{R}^D$ from the sequence of embeddings $(e_t)_{t=1}^T$:

$$h_0, c_0 = Encoder(e_1, \cdots, e_T). \tag{1}$$

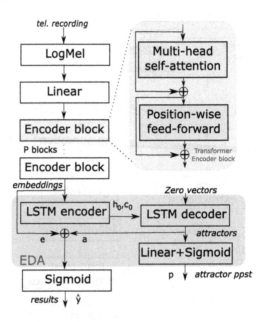

Fig. 2. EEND-EDA diarization system.

Next, time-invariant D-dimensional attractors $(\boldsymbol{a}_s)_{s=1}^{S}$ are calculated using a LSTM decoder with the initial states $\boldsymbol{h}_0$ and cell state $\boldsymbol{c}_0$:

$$\boldsymbol{h}_s, \boldsymbol{c}_s, \boldsymbol{a}_s = Decoder(\boldsymbol{h}_{s-1}, \boldsymbol{c}_{s-1}, \boldsymbol{0}). \tag{2}$$

Theoretically, infinite numbers of attractors can be calculated using this strategy. The probability p_s of whether or not the attractor a_s exists and to stop the calculation is computed using a fully-connected layer with a sigmoid function. In the inference phase, only the first S attractors are used (the number of speakers S is given in our case).

The posterior probabilities $\hat{\boldsymbol{y}}_t$ can be calculated using the inner product of every embedding-attractor pair. The output size is determined using the number of attractors (allowing the detection of the speaker overlaps). The final loss is calculated as linear combination of the permutation invariant training (PIT) [24] and the attractor existence loss [6].

6   Voice Activity Detector

The EEND system does not have a separate step for voice activity detection (VAD). Rather, this functionality is achieved as a side-product of the main diarization process itself.

On the other hand, the Kaldi system uses external VAD to distinguish between speech and silence in the recordings. The default option is a relatively standard energy-based VAD. The same is also used for our own identification-based system.

However, to better compare the results of the three systems, we have also tried replacing Kaldi's VAD with the speech/silence information from the EEND system. This will be included in the results section.

7 Experiments

This section describes our experiments on 715 recordings, a small part of the mono channel data from the LCC which contains a manual transcription. This amounts to approximately 21.5 h of speech total, of which 19 h were used for the actual evaluation (adaptation/training data was only 2.5 h).

7.1 Training Data

The following LDC corpora were used as training data for VB, TDNN and PLDA: *NIST 2004, 05 and 06* (LDC2006S44, LDC2011S01, LDC2011S04, LDC2011S09, LDC2011S10, LDC2012S01, LDC2011S05, LDC2011S08), *SWBD Cellular1 and 2* (LDC2001S13, LDC2004S07) and *SWBD2 Phse2 and 3* (LDC99S79, LDC2002S06). Additionally, data augmentation (additive noise, music, babble and reverberation) was applied to this data.

The list of language counselors in the LCC data consisted of 9 speakers (3 males and 6 females). We selected the 10 oldest recordings from each counselor as training and development data (9 files and 1 file, respectively), while the remaining 625 files were used for evaluation.

For the identification-based system, each counselor's x-vector is generated from the corresponding 9 recordings from the training set, using only the counselor's part of the recording – which is 500 s on average for each counselor. To represent the client's model, general male and female x-vector models were generated from the client side of *all 715* recordings (210 males and 505 females).

The hyper-parameters for the Kaldi diarization process (length of the segmentation window, whitening transformation, etc.) were tuned on a related task with CallHome corpus [1], so a development set was not needed for the two x-vector based systems.

For training the EEND-EDA, we also used the corpora which were listed in the first paragraph, but without augmentation. After 100 epochs, the parameters of the last 10 models (from the models of 91 up to 100 epochs) were averaged and this averaged model was further adapted on the telephone recordings from the target LCC set. Only the 81 training recordings (9 recordings for each counselor) were used for adaptation, as with the identity models mentioned above, but with the difference that the full recordings were used – both the client and the counselor sides. The total amount of adaptation data was only 2.5 h. One additional recording for each counselor was used for development data to set the final epoch of the EEND model training (averaging the models from epochs 91–100), and the threshold for evaluating the EEND result (speaker's posteriors) was set experimentally to 0.5.

7.2 Results

Table 1 shows the results of the three compared systems: the baseline Kaldi diarization system, the diarization system based on identification against the counselors' models and the end-to-end system with EEND neural network model. The results are included with and without VB resegmentation. Compared to our previous paper [25], where the results were presented with oracle speech activity detection, these results are computed with real VAD, without this oracle information. When computing overall speaker diarization error (DER) [3], we did not use any tolerance collar at the start and the end of each speaker segment, and overlapping regions were included in the evaluation.

As the systems use different VAD, we list not only the final DER, but also the individual components: the miss rate, false alarm and speaker confusion error. For a better comparison of these systems, we also include results where the output from the EEND system was used in place of the Kaldi VAD.

Table 1. Missed speaker time (Miss), False alarm speaker time (FA), Speaker confusion error (Err), DER [%] of the three diarization systems: a baseline Kaldi system, our identification-based system and the EEND system.

System	Miss	FA	Err	DER
VAD from Kaldi				
Kaldi SD system	0.9	10.1	10.0	21.05
+ VB resegment.	0.9	10.1	8.9	19.95
SD based on ident.	0.9	10.1	9.2	20.19
+ VB resegmentat.	0.9	10.1	8.4	19.39
VAD from EEND				
Kaldi SD system	6.7	5.5	7.9	20.17
+ VB resegment.	6.8	5.5	6.5	18.80
SD based on ident.	6.7	5.5	6.9	19.16
+ VB resegment.	6.8	5.5	5.6	17.95
EEND system	6.4	7.0	4.0	**17.42**
+ VB resegmentat.	7.6	5.6	4.9	18.07
EEND system without adaptation	4.1	23.6	3.1	30.82

8   Discussion

As seen in Table 1, the EEND system achieves the lowest DER of the three options.

We can notice that the EEND system's integrated VAD has a substantially greater *miss* rate (i.e., speech incorrectly labeled as silence) than the other two systems using Kaldi VAD. It is quite possible that this higher miss rate excludes some of the more problematic parts of the recording, thus making the clustering of the remaining speech easier.

However, even after eliminating the influence of the VAD by using the same voice activity information for all compared systems ("VAD from EEND"), the EEND system remains the best. It surpasses even our previous specialized solution, which utilized information about the identity of one of the speakers in each recording.

The EEND system achieves this without having any of this information beyond the small amount of initial adaptation data. And while the adaptation data did include recordings from all 9 counselors, this was mixed with a broad set of clients, and so we consider it unlikely that the system could have learned to specifically recognize these particular speakers.

The recordings contain some amount of overlapping speech, but due to the annotation process, overlaps are not included in the references. As currently implemented, the Kaldi system, our identification-based system and the VB resegmentation are also unable to find more than one simultaneous speaker at any specific point in the recordings. On the other hand, the EEND system does automatically detect overlaps, which in this case will be evaluated as false alarm. Analyzing the results from EEND, approximately 1.2% of the test data is labelled as overlapping speech.

9   Conclusion

In this paper, we explored the issue of speaker diarization on real data from the archives of the Language Consulting Center. We have compared three different approaches: the classic diarization method, represented by the Kaldi implementation, our previously proposed solution which employs identity models of the phone operators, obtained in advance, and finally a state-of-the art end-to-end diarization method represented by the EEND approach. By adapting the EEND model on a limited amount target data, we can achieve the superior result, overcoming even the results of the system with extra information about the identity of the counselor.

Acknowledgments. The work described herein has been supported by the Ministry of Education, Youth and Sports of the Czech Republic, Project No. LM2018101 LINDAT/CLARIAH-CZ. Access to computing and storage facilities owned by parties and projects contributing to the National Grid Infrastructure MetaCentrum, provided under the program "Projects of Large Research, Development, and Innovations Infrastructures" (CESNET LM2015042), is greatly appreciated.

References

1. Canavan, A., Graff, D., Zipperlen, G.: CALLHOME American English speech, LDC97S42. In: LDC Catalog. Linguistic Data Consortium, Philadelphia (1997)

2. Diez, M., Burget, L., Matejka, P.: Speaker Diarization based on Bayesian HMM with Eigenvoice priors. In: Odyssey - Speaker and Language Recognition Workshop, pp. 147–154 (2018)

3. Fiscus, J.G., Ajot, J., Michel, M., Garofolo, J.S.: The rich transcription 2006 spring meeting recognition evaluation. In: Renals, S., Bengio, S., Fiscus, J.G. (eds.) MLMI 2006. LNCS, vol. 4299, pp. 309–322. Springer, Heidelberg (2006). https://doi.org/10.1007/11965152_28

4. Fujita, Y., Kanda, N., Horiguchi, S., Nagamatsu, K., Watanabe, S.: End-to-end neural speaker diarization with permutation-free objectives. In: Interspeech, pp. 4300–4304 (2019)

5. Fujita, Y., Kanda, N., Horiguchi, S., Xue, Y., Nagamatsu, K., Watanabe, S.: End-to-end neural speaker diarization with self-attention. In: IEEE Automatic Speech Recognition and Understanding Workshop, pp. 296–303. Institute of Electrical and Electronics Engineers Inc., December 2019

6. Horiguchi, S., Fujita, Y., Watanabe, S., Xue, Y., Nagamatsu, K.: End-to-end speaker diarization for an unknown number of speakers with encoder-decoder based attractors. In: Interspeech, pp. 269–273 (2020)

7. Ioffe, S.: Probabilistic linear discriminant analysis. In: Leonardis, A., Bischof, H., Pinz, A. (eds.) ECCV 2006. LNCS, vol. 3954, pp. 531–542. Springer, Heidelberg (2006). https://doi.org/10.1007/11744085_41

8. Kinoshita, K., Delcroix, M., Tawara, N.: Integrating end-to-end neural and clustering-based diarization: getting the best of both worlds. Arxiv (2020)

9. Lin, Z., et al.: A structured self-attentive sentence embedding. In: ICLR (2017)

10. Nagrani, A., et al.: VOXSRC 2020: The Second Voxceleb Speaker Recognition Challenge. Arxiv (2020)

11. Park, T.J., Kanda, N., Dimitriadis, D., Han, K.J., Watanabe, S., Narayanan, S.: A Review of Speaker Diarization: Recent Advances with Deep Learning. arXiv, January 2021

12. Povey, D., et al.: The Kaldi speech recognition toolkit. In: Workshop on Automatic Speech Recognition and Understanding. IEEE Catalog No.: CFP11SRW-USB, Hawaii (2011)

13. Rouvier, M., Dupuy, G., Gay, P., Khoury, E., Merlin, T., Meignier, S.: An open-source state-of-the-art toolbox for broadcast news diarization. In: Interspeech, Lyon, pp. 1477–1481 (2013)

14. Ryant, N., et al.: The second DIHARD diarization challenge: dataset, task, and baselines. In: INTERSPEECH, Gratz (2019)

15. Ryant, N., et al.: The Third DIHARD Diarization Challenge. arXiv, p. 5 (2020)

16. Sell, G., Garcia-Romero, D.: Speaker diarization with PLDA I-vector scoring and unsupervised calibration. In: IEEE Spoken Language Technology Workshop, South Lake Tahoe, pp. 413–417 (2014)

17. Sell, G., Garcia-Romero, D.: Diarization resegmentation in the factor analysis subspace. In: ICASSP, pp. 4794–4798. IEEE, April 2015

18. Sell, G., et al.: Diarization is hard: some experiences and lessons learned for the JHU team in the inaugural DIHARD challenge. In: Interspeech, Hyderabad, pp. 2808–2812 (2018)

19. Senoussaoui, M., Kenny, P., Stafylakis, T., Dumouchel, P.: A study of the cosine distance-based mean shift for telephone speech diarization. IEEE/ACM Trans. Audio Speech Lang. Process. **22**(1), 217–227 (2014)

20. Snyder, D., Garcia-Romero, D., Sell, G., Povey, D., Khudanpur, S.: X-vectors: robust DNN embeddings for speaker recognition. In: ICASSP, pp. 5329–5333 (2018)

21. Sutskever, I., Vinyals, O., Le, Q.V.: Sequence to sequence learning with neural networks. Adv. Neural. Inf. Process. Syst. **4**, 3104–3112 (2014)
22. Von Neumann, T., Kinoshita, K., Delcroix, M., Araki, S., Nakatani, T., Haeb-Umbach, R.: All-neural online source separation, counting, and diarization for meeting analysis. In: ICASSP, pp. 91–95 (2019)
23. Yin, R., Bredin, H., Barras, C.: Neural speech turn segmentation and affinity propagation for speaker diarization. In: INTERSPEECH, pp. 1393–1397. ISCA, Hyderabad (2018)
24. Yu, D., Kolbæk, M., Tan, Z.H., Jensen, J.: Permutation invariant training of deep models for speaker-independent multi-talker speech separation. In: ICASSP, pp. 241–245, July 2017
25. Zajíc, Z., Psutka, J.V., Müller, L.: Diarization based on identification with x-vectors. In: Karpov, A., Potapova, R. (eds.) SPECOM 2020. LNCS (LNAI), vol. 12335, pp. 667–678. Springer, Cham (2020). https://doi.org/10.1007/978-3-030-60276-5_64
26. Zajíc, Z., Kunešová, M., Radová, V.: Investigation of segmentation in i-vector based speaker diarization of telephone speech. In: Ronzhin, A., Potapova, R., Németh, G. (eds.) SPECOM 2016. LNCS (LNAI), vol. 9811, pp. 411–418. Springer, Cham (2016). https://doi.org/10.1007/978-3-319-43958-7_49
27. Zajíc, Z., Psutka, J.V., Zajícová, L., Müller, L., Salajka, P.: Diarization of the language consulting center telephone calls. In: Salah, A.A., Karpov, A., Potapova, R. (eds.) SPECOM 2019. LNCS (LNAI), vol. 11658, pp. 549–558. Springer, Cham (2019). https://doi.org/10.1007/978-3-030-26061-3_56
28. Zajíc, Z., et al.: First insight into the processing of the language consulting center data. In: Karpov, A., Jokisch, O., Potapova, R. (eds.) SPECOM 2018. LNCS (LNAI), vol. 11096, pp. 778–787. Springer, Cham (2018). https://doi.org/10.1007/978-3-319-99579-3_79

Acoustic Characteristics of Speech Entrainment in Dialogues in Similar Phonetic Sequences

Svetlana Zimina and Vera Evdokimova(✉)

Saint Petersburg State University, Universitetskaya emb., 7-9, St. Petersburg 199034, Russia
svetlanazimina6306@gmail.com, v.evdokimova@spbu.ru

Abstract. The paper presents the study of the speech entrainment in dialogues of two interlocutors playing games. The calculations of the degree of speech entrainment are based on the acoustic characteristics of similar phonetic sequences. Formant values of stressed vowels in these words are considered. The recordings from the new SibLing corpus developed at the Department of Phonetics of St. Petersburg State University, were used as the material for the study. The results of the study confirmed the presence of speech entrainment in the values of the formants of stressed vowels. Based on the calculation of the Euclidean distance and the analysis of the vowel formant patterns, the following conclusions can be drawn: 1) In most cases, there is a mutual shift in the formant characteristics of vowels in the process of dialogue. 2) According to preliminary data, the degree of familiarity of the interlocutors quite strongly affects the speed of speech entrainment. The one case of divergence was observed. The degree of entrainment can be affected by the difference in age and social status. 3) The degree of adjustment of the acoustic characteristics depends on the quality of the vowel. To a greater extent, speakers adapt to each other by the rounded vowels of the back row (/o/, /u/), and also actively change the location of the vowels /a/ and /i/, adapting to each other. Moreover, the speakers often shift the focus of pronunciation of all cardinal vowels at once.

Keywords: Phonetics · Acoustics · Speech adaptation · Formants

1 Introduction

Several approaches to the interpretation of the term communicative entrainment exist. The fundamental work in the field of studying this speech phenomenon can be considered the accommodation theory by Giles [1]. It is assumed that the interlocutors try to achieve successful communication by adapting to each other's speech behavior. In this theory, there are 2 basic terms: convergence and divergence. Convergence refers to the fact that people are more likely to approach the peculiarities of their interlocutor's speech behavior when they want to get social approval from him, as well as when the expected result of this adjustment does not require much effort. Conversely, divergence or the preservation of the manner of speech is manifested when the interlocutors identify themselves as people belonging to different social groups and want to maintain the distance between each other by demonstrating of their peculiarities and differences in interpersonal communication.

© Springer Nature Switzerland AG 2021
A. Karpov and R. Potapova (Eds.): SPECOM 2021, LNAI 12997, pp. 818–825, 2021.
https://doi.org/10.1007/978-3-030-87802-3_73

Also, depending on the approach of Levitan and Hirschberg, the direction of the adaptation can differ [2]. The authors distinguish 3 gradations: proximity, convergence, and synchrony.

Communicative adaptation emerges at all levels of the language, from the highest to the lowest [3]. Moreover, it is important to note that there is a balance between the processes of speech production and its perception. Receptivity to the communicative situation in a general sense affects the process of adjusting the speech of the interlocutors, which, moreover, occurs regardless of their desire and awareness of this fact.

This is the increased interest in the topic of tuning acoustic characteristics in the process of communication in recent years that should be marked. The number of works conducted on the material of various languages is quite large. The most popular among them are the studies that were carried out using the material of the English language [4, 5], including its dialects [6].

The studies conducted in Germany [7], France [8], Italy [9], Spain [10], Japan [11] are worth noting. In these works, different methods of conducting an experiment and calculating the degree of communicative adaptation are considered. Moreover, scientists make attempts to explore this issue in terms of sociolinguistics.

Nevertheless, in the Russian academic literature one cannot find much information concerning research in this area. The studies that have been carried out are of a general nature [12]. Also they can refer to related areas – for example, forensic phonetics [13]. In the latter work the emphasis is placed on the psychological side of the issue of adaptation rather than on acoustic characteristics.

Research in the field of communicative adaptation nowadays is gaining popularity. However, there are quite a few works in Russian devoted to the topic of acoustic charac-teristics of communicative entrainment. Due to these facts a need to create a new speech corpus seems to be quite relevant. The new SibLing corpus was recorded in 2019–2020 at the Department of Phonetics Saint Peterburg State University for the task of speech adaptation [14]. Some work was performed on this material and the significant results were obtained [15–18].

The SibLing corpus was used for the presented work. The Structure of the corpus allows studying the influence of various factors on the conversation.

Formant frequencies of stressed vowels were chosen as a measure for estimation of the presence or absence of communicative adaptation. Based on the acoustic theory of speech production [19] and the theory of communicative adaptation [20], we allow that the adjustment of interlocutors to each other's speech behavior can have an impact on the change in formant values. This may happen because the speakers will begin shifting the articulation of vowels from those familiar to their speech to those that are acoustically close to the places of articulation of the interlocutor.

There are quite a few methods of spectral analysis of the acoustic characteristics of a speech signal, both automated and not. Among them is the wavelet transform [21], the Kalman filter, LPC-transform, SWLP-transform, MDVR, building formant trajectories in the program PRAAT, HLP, Liljencrantz-Fant model [22], neural networks [23], method of zeros of the signal [24], cepstral analysis [25] and spectral analysis of signals produced under and above the vocal cords [26].

The method used in this study which is called the construction of formant patterns can be called a partially automated method [22].

2 Material

The SibLing corpus which was developed and recorded at the Department of Phonetics of St. Petersburg State University has been chosen as the material for the study [14]. This corpus was designed purposely for conducting researches on the communicative adaptation of interlocutors in a dialogue. The dialogues are divided into 5 degrees of familiarity of the speakers-from close relatives (brothers/sisters, twins) to strangers with different social status. The speakers are also balanced for the gender and age.

In total, 7 dialogues from the SibLing corpus were processed as part of this work. The list of the dialogues with the main information about the interlocutors is presented in the Table 1.

Table 1. Data on the processed dialogues The first column contains the number of the dialogue according to the encoding assigned to it, the second and fifth columns contain the speakers whose names were also encoded, the third and sixth columns contain the gender of the speakers, the fourth and seventh columns contain the age, the eighth column contains information about the degree of familiarity of the informants.

Number of a dialogue	Interlocutor № 1	Sex	Age	Interlocutor № 2	Sex	Age	Degree of familiarity
D11	S03	F	36	S04	F	38	Sisters
D12				Z11	F	36	Friends
D13				Z12	F	35–40	Strangers
D14				Z13	M	38	Strangers of different genders
D15				Z14 (boss)	F	66	Strangers of different social status
D51	S11	M	24	S12	M	24	Twins
D81	S17	F	23	S18	F	25	Sisters

The construction of the recordings was determined by the structure of the corpus. Thus, similar words were repeated in different parts of the task. In theory the acoustic characteristics of these words can change during the dialogue. These words are key or similar phonetic sequences. During the recording the interlocutors performed 2 types of tasks, which in total lasted from 25 to 60 min. In the first part of the dialogue, the speakers were asked to choose cards with similar elements on them and repeat them. The cards used for the task were taken from a game called "Imaginarium", which is very similar to the game "Dixit" developed by Jean-Louis Rubira. The second part of the dialogue involved mapping. One of the interlocutors had a card with objects and a route and one with objects only. The task was to explain the route. The objects on the card were not identical. Each speaker had a set of 4 cards: 2 complete and 2 incomplete. Each pair of cards contained 5 keywords that were the same in all the recordings. Thus, we managed to get several samples of keywords that were repeated by both participants of the dialogue.

3 Method

The words that were present in the speech of both speakers in the first minutes of each dialogue and at the end the dialogue were selected. Then similar contexts were compared, the keywords were selected in which the target sounds (stressed vowels) were in similar phonetic positions.

Similar phonetic sequences are those words in which the right and left vowel contexts are similar, but which are not necessarily the same. Consider the words "пуговица" /púgavjica/ (a button) and "буковку" /búkafku/ (a letter). The left context of the stressed vowel /u/, the sounds /b/ and /p/, do not match on the basis of sonority, but they have the same place of articulation: they are bilabial occlusives. The right context, the sounds /g/ and /k/, also have the same place of articulation, both are velar occlusives but one of them is also voiceless. The shift of formant values in the transitional parts of a vowel is determined by the environment. That is why the accordance of sounds considering the place of articulation is more important than the difference in such characteristic as sonority.

Once the key words and similar phonetic sequences were picked out, the speech signal was manually segmented at 2 levels. The labels for words and for sounds were set. These labels were used for further processing by a program which used the Python programming language and allowed to cut out the sounds.

The formant frequencies of stressed vowels were chosen as acoustic characteristics. On the basis of the analysis of these sounds it was possible to observe the communicative adaptation. Formant analysis was performed for the selected keywords. Specific software was used to help to calculate the spectral characteristics of sounds [27].

The next step was to get averaged formant values of the stressed vowels of individual words. The obtained values were compared for the interviewees in the dialogues. The averaged values of the formants for each speaker were used for the construction of 2 formant figures corresponding to the location of the vowels at the beginning and at the end of the dialogue.

To confirm the conclusions made on the basis of formant pictures the Euclidean distance was used. This metric allowed determining the distance between the vowels at the beginning and at the end of each dialogue.

4 Results

Considering the Euclidean distance and the analysis of the vowel formant patterns, the following results can be presented:

1) In most cases, there is a mutual shift in the formant characteristics of vowels, which results in the rearrangement of vowel triangles of both speakers. Thus, there is a mutual adjustment of the interlocutors in the process of dialogue.

   For example, in the case of a dialogue between one of the sisters and a stranger it could be observed that the sister moved the focus of the articulation of the vowel /a/ to the range of values which is closer to the second speaker. At the same time the stranger keeping the quality of the vowel /a/ unchanged, began to implement the vowel /i/ as a more forward one (Fig. 1).

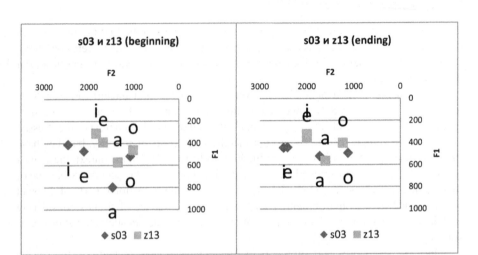

Fig. 1. Changing of formant figures during the dialogue between a sister (s03) and a stranger (z13).

2) According to obtained data the degree of familiarity can affect the speed of communicative adaptation (this can be observed in the dialogue between a sister and a friend);

   Moreover, there is a connection between the degree of familiarity and the degree of adaptation. In the dialogues of close relatives (siblings) there is either an initial similarity of formant characteristics or their convergence in the process of communication. When dealing with strangers, you can talk about convergence rather than divergence.

   The one case of divergence was observed. The degree of entrainment can be affected by the difference in age and social status (Fig. 2).

   According to the data on the Euclidean distance, we can say that the least negative values (the distance of the foci of vowel articulation in the process of communication) is observed in the vowel /i/, in second place is the vowel /o/, /a/ and /e/ occupy the third and fourth places. A similar rating can be formed after the analysis of the maximum values of the Euclidean distance: the convergence of the vowels /i/ is the strongest, the convergence of the vowel /a/ is less strong, for /e/ - is even less, and the vowel /o/is in the last place.

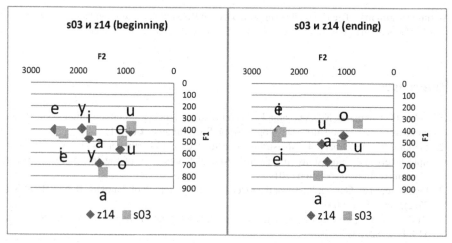

Fig. 2. Changing of formant figures during the dialogue between a sister (s03) and a stranger of the same sex and different social status (z14).

3) At this stage of the study, there is not enough data to judge correctly about the connection between the communicative adaptation and the sex of the interlocutor. According to preliminary data, the communicative entrainment is stronger when interlocutors are of the same sex. However, it should be taken into account the effect of a whole set of factors (sex, age, social status).

5   Conclusion

In most cases, there is a mutual shift in the formant characteristics of vowels, which results in the rearrangement of vowel triangles of both speakers.

The degree of adjustment of the acoustic characteristics depends on the quality of the vowel to some extent. Based on the analysis of formant patterns we can consider that the speakers better adapt to each other by the rounded vowels of the back row (/o/, /u/). Moreover, the location of the vowels /a/ and /i/ is actively changed. It is also worth noting that speakers often shift the pronunciation of all cardinal vowels at once. The cases of vowel shift in the range of height can be found. For example, the vowel /u/ shifts with the vowel /i/ because these are close vowels. Along with the vowel /e/, the vowel /o/ changed its characteristics because these are mid vowels. The same can be said about the shift in the focus of vowel articulation within a row: the change in the quality of /i/ is often accompanied by the dynamics in the quality of /e/.

The data should be widened to judge correctly about the connection between the communicative adaptation and the sex of the interlocutor. According to our experiment the communicative entrainment is stronger when interlocutors are of the same sex. We are planning to take more material and take into account the effect of a whole set of factors (sex, age, social status).

Acknowledgments. The research is supported by the Russian Science Foundation (grant 19-78-10046 "Phonetic manifestations of communication accommodation in dialogues").

References

1. Giles, H., Coupland, N., Coupland, I.: Accommodation theory: communication, context, and contexts of accommodation: Developm. Appl. Sociolinguist. **1** (1991)
2. Levitan, R., Hirschberg, J.: Measuring acoustic-prosodic entrainment with respect to multiple levels and dimensions. In: Twelfth Annual Conference of the International Speech Communication Association (2011)
3. Pickering, M.J., Garrod, S.: Toward a mechanistic psychology of dialogue. Behav. Brain Sci. **27**(2), 169–190 (2004)
4. Pardo, J.S.: On phonetic convergence during conversational interaction. J. Acoust. Soc. Am. **119**(4), 2382–2393 (2006)
5. Namy, L.L., Nygaard, L.C., Sauerteig, D.: Gender differences in vocal accommodation: the role of perception. J. Lang. Soc. Psychol. **21**(4), 422–432 (2002)
6. Krivokapić, J.: Rhythm and convergence between speakers of American and Indian English. Lab. Phonol. **4**(1), 39–65 (2013)
7. Schweitzer, A., Lewandowski, N., Duran, D.: Social attractiveness in dialogs. In: Interspeech, pp. 2243–2247 (2017)
8. Bailly, G., Lelong, A.: Speech dominoes and phonetic convergence. In: 11th Annual Conference of the International Speech Communication Association 2010 (Interspeech 2010), pp. 1153–1156 (2010)
9. Savino, M. et al.: Prosodic convergence in Italian game dialogues. ExLing, pp. 151–154 (2016)
10. San, S.E., Yang, J.: Formant dynamics of Spanish vocalic sequences in related speakers: a forensic-voice-comparison investigation. J. Phonet. **75**, 1–26 (2019)
11. Kawahara, T. et al.: Synchrony in prosodic and linguistic features between backchannels and preceding utterances in attentive listening. In: Asia-Pacific Signal and Information Processing Association Annual Summit and Conference (APSIPA), pp. 392–395. IEEE (2015)
12. Schevchenko, T., Galochkina, I.: Towads the agreement: phonetic adaptation of interlocutors in a dialogue. Bull. Moscow State Linguist. Univ. Human Stud. **1**(740), 185–203 (2016)
13. Zotina, E.: Communicative adaptation as a factor of building of the successful communication (on the material of speech and voice recordings). Stud. Kazan Law Inst. **2**(4), 115–121 (2017)
14. Kachkovskaia, T. et al.: SibLing corpus of Russian dialogue speech designed for research on speech entrainment. In: Proceedings of the 12th Language Resources and Evaluation Conference, pp. 6556–6561 (2020)
15. Menshikova, A., Kocharov, D., Kachkovskaia, T.: Phonetic entrainment in cooperative dialogues: a case of Russian. Proc. Interspeech **2020**, 4148–4152 (2020)
16. Kachkovskaya, T., Mamushina, A.: Phonetic markers of communicative adaptation in a dialogue. Quest. Linguist. **2**, 123–141 (2021)
17. Kholiavin, P., Mamushina, A., Kocharov, D., Kachkovskaia, T.: Automatic detection of backchannels in Russian dialogue speech. In: Karpov, A., Potapova, R. (eds.) SPECOM 2020. LNCS (LNAI), vol. 12335, pp. 204–213. Springer, Cham (2020). https://doi.org/10.1007/978-3-030-60276-5_21
18. Kachkovskaya, T., Menshikova, A., Kholyavin, P.: Do we use different "voices" with a friend and with a stranger? In: The Fifth St. Petersburg Winter Workshop on Experimental Studies of Speech and Language (Night Whites 2019)

19. Fant, G.: Acoustic Theory of Speech Production. Nauka, Moscow (1964)
20. Giles, H., et al.: Speech accommodation theory: the first decade and beyond. Ann. Int. Commun. Assoc. **10**(1), 13–48 (1987)
21. Evdokimova, V.: Acoustic Analysis of the Speech Signal: A Handbook for Seminars and Practical Exercises. University Press of SPbU, Saint Petersburg (2014)
22. Evdokimova, V., Kocharov, D., Skrelin, P.: A method of construction formant figures for research into the phonetic characteristics of vowels. Comput. Sci. Automat. **19**(2), 302–329 (2020)
23. Gurakov, I., Kostuchenko, E., Novokhrestova, D., Silitch, M.: Algorithm of selecting formants and searching for aligned fragments in preparation for conduction of forensic phonetical examination. Pap. Tomsk State Univ. Control Syst. Radioelectr. **21**(2), 48–53 (2018)
24. Sorokin, V., Leonov, A., Makarov, I.: Sustainability of formant frequency estimations. In: Speech Technologies, pp. 3–21 (2009)
25. Ivanov, A., Trushin, V., Markelova, G., Reva, I.: A study of the spectrum of formants in forced speech. Sci. Bull. NSTU **61**(4), 63–73 (2015)
26. Fant, G., Liljencrants, J., Lin, Q.: A four-parameter model of glottal flow. STL-QPSR **4**, 1–13 (1985)
27. Evdokimova, V.: Variability of formant figure of vowels in different types of speech. In: Proceedings of the Second Interdisciplinary Seminar "Analiz razgovornoy russkoy rechi" (AR^3–2008), pp. 49–54. Saint-Petersburg State University of Aerospace Instrumentation (2008)

Predicting Biometric Error Behaviour from Speaker Embeddings and a Fast Score Normalization Scheme

İsmail Rasim Ülgen[1,2]([✉]), Mustafa Erden[1], and Levent M. Arslan[1,2]

[1] Sestek, Istanbul, Turkey
{rasim.ulgen,mustafa.erden,levent.arslan}@sestek.com
[2] Electrical and Electronics Engineering Department,
Bogazici University, Istanbul, Turkey

Abstract. For the task of speaker recognition from audio, it is known that speakers experience different levels of error rates. In this work, predicting the proneness to false alarm and false reject of a given speaker embedding is investigated. Although exact prediction of biometric error behaviour appears to be a difficult problem, it is seen that the tendency to false alarm and false reject errors can be predicted directly from embeddings by training a neural network in a supervised manner. This prediction might be useful for several applications such as normalization of verification scores, incorporating those characteristics in embedding training or using it as an adversarial objective. We have utilized this predicted behaviour for a fast score normalization method. Our approach is compared to the frequently employed biometric normalization method that is s-norm which is a cohort-based technique and accounts only for imposter calibration. The proposed normalization is not only faster than s-norm, but also it outperforms s-norm by 8% and 3% for male and female speakers, respectively.

Keywords: Biometric menagerie · Speaker embeddings · Score normalization

1 Introduction

Research showed that each individual in a biometric system differs in terms of verification performance and individuals can be characterised by menagerie analysis [1]. Menagerie analysis showed that there is a group of individuals that are prone to produce high false alarm (FA) rates, named as wolves, if the individual is on authentication side, lambs if otherwise. In symmetric comparison schemes wolves and lambs are interchangeable. And also, there is a group of individuals that are prone to high false reject (FR) rates named as goats.

Menagerie analysis gives important insights about the performance of a biometric system and their vulnerabilities. Stoll et al. has found that 50% of the FA and FR errors are related to only 15–25% of the speakers [2]. Therefore,

© Springer Nature Switzerland AG 2021
A. Karpov and R. Potapova (Eds.): SPECOM 2021, LNAI 12997, pp. 826–836, 2021.
https://doi.org/10.1007/978-3-030-87802-3_74

to reduce the speaker verification system error rates, it is beneficial to detect these difficult speakers. Focusing on FA errors [3] investigated speaker similarities based on distances or similarities of acoustic features including pitch, jitter, shimmer, formant frequencies and energy.

Once the speakers contributing to increased error rates are detected there are several areas where this information can be utilised. In [4] the wolves/lambs are used to impersonate other speakers. It also can be used to improve the verification performance. In [5] a user-specific threshold is applied during verification. In [6] a score-normalization technique is proposed based on assessing the biometric characteristics by using distributions derived from scores against imposter and genuine cohorts and it became one of the most popular score normalization methods.

In this paper, biometric error behaviour is predicted directly from x-vector speaker embeddings by a feed-forward regression network. That prediction opens up new possibilities to use that information. For example, it might be used as an additional objective for training speaker embeddings network to make it more robust. Also, those characteristics can be incorporated in score normalization. A fast and efficient score normalization scheme is proposed as a use case of prediction of biometric characteristics. The implemented normalization differs from the baseline s-norm method since it is not based on cohort set scoring.

In Sect. 4 we propose the prediction of error proneness and score normalization method. In Sect. 5 we define the dataset and evaluation protocol for assessing the performance of the proposed normalization technique. In Sect. 6, prediction results and comparative results of proposed scheme along with no-normalization and s-norm is presented.

2   Speaker Embeddings

For speaker recognition one of the most popular methods is x-vector embeddings which are extracted from one of the last layers of a deep neural network that is trained to classify among large number of speakers [8]. Extracted embeddings from utterances are compared via PLDA and a similarity score is obtained. In this work an E-TDNN network, defined in [9], is trained and embeddings from that network is used. The topology of the network is given in Table 1.

3   Biometric Menagerie

It is shown that in a biometric system, speakers can be split into groups in terms of their behaviour of two main error types: false alarm and false reject. Although the definitions are extended in recent works, there are four types of basic behaviour in biometric menagerie: goats, wolves, lambs, and sheep. These main groups may not appear or may not be clear in some other biometric systems. However, in voice biometrics such a phenomenon exists [7] and it is illustrated in Fig. 1 where geuine and imposter scores are calculated in voxceleb1 [11]. The figure tells us that there is a continuity in those behavioural patterns.

Table 1. The E-TDNN network which extracts speaker embeddings.

Layer	Layer type	Context	Size
1	TDNN-ReLU	$t-2; t+2$	512
2	Dense-ReLU	t	512
3	TDNN-ReLU	$t-2, t, t+2$	512
4	Dense-ReLU	t	512
5	TDNN-ReLU	$t-3, t, t+3$	512
6	Dense-ReLU	t	512
7	TDNN-ReLU	$t-4, t, t+4$	512
8	Dense-ReLU	t	512
9	Dense-ReLU	t	512
10	Dense-ReLU	t	1500
11	Pooling	Full seq	2×1500
12	Dense(Embedding)-ReLU		512
13	Dense-ReLU		512
14	Dense-Softmax		Num. spks.

The experiment also shows that given speaker can have different imposter mean scores across his/her single utterances. This suggests that the phonetic content and environmental effects for an utterance are also significant for showing different behaviour types along with speaker characteristics.

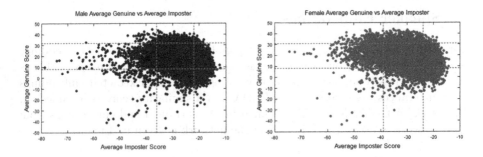

Fig. 1. Exploratory menagerie analysis.

3.1 Goats

Individuals that are prone to have low genuine scores against their own biometric models are defined as goats in a biometric system. They have higher FR rates compared with other speakers. They represent left hand side of the genuine mean scale.

3.2 Wolves and Lambs

Individuals, whose biometric models can be easily matched by other speakers, are defined as lambs. On the other hand, speakers that can easily match other speaker models are defined as wolves in a biometric system. Both wolves and lambs are prone to have high imposter scores thus they have higher FA rates compared with the rest of the population. Normally, they are defined as separate groups based on different characteristics of enrollment and authentication scenario and scoring scheme. However, in this work, scoring is symmetric and enrollment/authentication is sampled from the same dataset having the same characteristics, and wolves/lambs are treated as one group.

3.3 Sheep

Individuals, that are not distinctly prone to FA or FR rate, are defined as sheep in a biometric system. Most of the population fall into this group and it corresponds to middle region in Fig. 1, although the graphs suggest that there is a continuity of characteristics and it is somewhat hard to define exact borders.

The aim of this work is to predict FA proneness (wolf-lamb behaviour) and FR proneness (goat behaviour) of a given speaker embedding.

4 Prediction of Biometric Error Behaviour

In the literature, Stoll et al. [2] focused on classifying the extreme individuals of the scale, with basic features and a support vector machine classifier. But the analysis in Fig. 1, suggests that there is rather a continuous scale and it is hard to find a classification boundary unless we ignore the middle portion like Stoll et al. [2]. It is also shown that x-vectors contain valuable information [10] and the proneness for FA and FR might also be contained in x-vectors. Thus, we propose two feed-forward regression modules that predict the FA and FR proneness of a given speaker embedding separately.

4.1 Annotation of Data

The expression of proneness for FA and FR is not a fixed concept, there might be many things that can express the biometric characteristics. The most straightforward one is the FA and FR counts for a given utterance in a predefined, closed set. Another one is using the mean of scores against some group of utterances from imposter speakers when assessing FA behaviour. Similarly, utterances from same speaker are utilized for assessing the FR behaviour. Using FA and FR counts depends on a specific threshold, and with systems having low EER's some speakers cannot be involved in the assessment process correctly. Also, the characteristics show continuous behaviour, thus using mean imposter and mean genuine scores as expression of error proneness seemed more suitable for this task.

Annotations can be defined for different levels: speaker-level or utterance level. For the speaker level annotation, a single value for each speaker can be obtained by averaging corresponding statistics over that speaker's utterances. Most of the previous work focused on single utterances, and different error proneness values of a single speaker's utterances suggests utterance level annotation. Speaker embeddings extracted from a single speaker's utterances, despite being close to each other they are scattered in the embedding space. Trying to predict a single value for all those embeddings seems infeasible and utterance level prediction suits to analysis results of error characteristics, as analysis shows an overall continuity and variation between utterances of a given single speaker.

After annotation, the Pearson correlation between actual FA count and mean imposter score; correlation between actual FR count and mean genuine score are calculated. The correlations can be found in Table 2.

Table 2. Correlations between error types and mean score statistics.

Correlation type	Gender	Pearson
FA count vs Mean Imposter	Male	0.814
FA count vs Mean Imposter	Female	0.745
FR count vs Mean Genuine	Male	−0.642
FR count vs Mean Genuine	Female	−0.627

There are strong correlations between FA counts and mean imposter score as expected, less in the female case, in which mean imposter score variation between a single speaker's utterances has been found higher than the male case. The correlation between FR count and mean genuine score is also strong; but less than FA-mean imposter case that goes parallel to the more ambiguous definition of goats, and probably goat behaviour is more dependent to external factors such as it is more likely to have a false reject, when the utterance is extremely noisy, than to have a false alarm.

Table 3. Correlations between imposter and genuine score statistics.

Correlation type	Gender	Pearson
Mean Genuine vs Mean Imposter	Male	0.277
Mean Genuine vs Mean Imposter	Female	0.263

Correlation values in the Table 3 shows that there is a small correlation between the mean imposter and the mean genuine score; suggesting that a score normalization technique that is fusion of two methods compensating FA and FR can be applicable in a speech based biometric system.

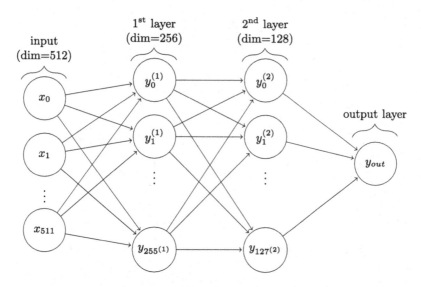

Fig. 2. The structure of the Regression Network where input is the x-vector embedding output is the proneness to error value.

4.2   Regression Module

Since embeddings that are extracted from utterances are single vectors of fixed dimension, which is 512 in our experiments, and are already organized in classification space, a simple feed-forward regression network is suitable for this problem. Input layer takes an x-vector of a given utterance as input; then fed to 2 hidden layers of the network with dimensions 256 and 128, respectively. ReLU activation function is used at hidden units and output unit. Then value at the output layer is taken as the regression of proneness to corresponding error type (FA or FR) which is mapped mean imposter or mapped mean genuine score described in Sect. 5.2. The topology of this network is depicted in Fig. 2. This structure is used for both FA and FR proneness predictor, and it is also seen that the gender of speakers creates two modalities. Thus, we also separated networks for genders. In total, 4 networks having the described structure is trained and tested.

4.3   Score Normalization Module

Although the beforehand prediction of biometric error behaviour can be used differently, a simple yet fast and efficient score normalization method using that information is proposed. Most score normalization methods use score statistics against fixed cohorts whereas our method uses error proneness value obtained from the regression module directly. For FA compensation, the average of FA proneness values is scaled and subtracted from the standard PLDA verification score. For FR compensation, the average of FR proneness values for enrollment

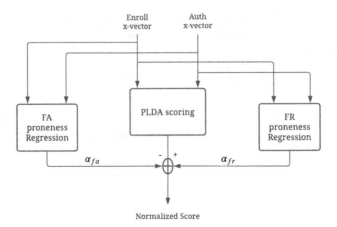

Fig. 3. Block diagram of the score normalization method.

and authentication utterance is scaled and added to the standard PLDA verification score. In equations, s(e,a) is the verification score between enrollment(e) and authenticate(a) utterances, S_e and S_a are sets of imposter scores between given utterance and its imposter cohorts.

$$s(e,a)_{s-norm} = \frac{1}{2}\left(\frac{s(e,a) - \mu(S_e)}{\sigma(S_e)} + \frac{s(e,a) - \mu(S_a)}{\sigma(S_a)}\right). \qquad (1)$$

In proposed normalization that compensates FA errors; $r_{wolf-lamb}$ is the regression value of FA proneness for a given utterance; and α_{fa} is the scale used when subtracting the average regression values for enroll and authenticate.

$$s(e,a)_{proposed(fa)} = s(e,a) - \alpha_{fa}\left(\frac{r_{wolf-lamb}(e) + r_{wolf-lamb}(a)}{2}\right). \qquad (2)$$

Similarly in normalization that compensates false reject errors; r_{goat} is the regression value of FR proneness for a given utterance; and α_{fr} is the scale used when subtracting the average regression values for enroll and authenticate.

$$s(e,a)_{proposed(fr)} = s(e,a) + \alpha_{fr}\left(\frac{r_{goat}(e) + r_{goat}(a)}{2}\right). \qquad (3)$$

The scales α_{fa} and α_{fr} are set to 2.4 and 2.6 by experimental results.

$$s(e,a)_{proposed(fused)} = s(e,a) - \alpha_{fa}\left(\frac{r_{wolf-lamb}(e) + r_{wolf-lamb}(a)}{2}\right)$$
$$+ \alpha_{fr}\left(\frac{r_{goat}(e) + r_{goat}(a)}{2}\right). \qquad (4)$$

For the fusion of FA and FR compensations, basically addition and subtraction by scale done at the same time. Figure 3 shows the overall score normalization scheme.

5   Experimental Setup

5.1   X-Vector Embedding Training

For x-vector training, E-TDNN structure described in Sect. 2 is trained on all voxceleb2 (6112 speakers, 1128336 utterances) [12] for 6 epochs with default parameters in [9]. Trained x-vector model has 2.27% verification EER on voxceleb1-e test set.

5.2   Regressor Annotation and Training

For biometric error characteristics analysis and prediction, voxceleb1 dataset[11] is used. Mean imposter and mean genuine score statistics are calculated per utterance with cross-scores between a sampled subset of voxceleb1 for the sake of computational burden. For FA proneness mean imposter scores of utterances are mapped linearly to 0–10 range as 0 corresponds to global minimum mean imposter score, 10 corresponds global maximum mean imposter score.

Similarly for FR proneness mean genuine scores of utterances are mapped linearly to 0–10 range as 0 corresponds to global maximum mean genuine score, 10 corresponds global minimum mean genuine score. Mean-squared-error(MSE) loss is used in training with respect to described annotation values.

After creating annotations, sampled voxceleb1 dataset is split into train and test sets with no speaker overlap. Training split has 497 speakers and 17413 utterances, test split consists of 168 speakers 5777 utterances for the male gender. For the female part training split has 408 speakers and 13338 utterances; test split consists of 138 speakers 4379 utterances.

5.3   Score Normalization

In order to see the effect of score normalization, test utterances in the regression split are cross-scored against each other and the verification EER is measured. For s-norm trials, gender-dependent cohorts are selected randomly from train set split of the regression module. Each cohort set consists approximately of 1000 utterances from 200 speakers. For the s-norm and proposed normalization, speakers are split in terms of gender by using gender annotations of voxceleb1, in order to eliminate the effect of gender detection accuracy.

6   Results

6.1   Regression Results

Mean squared error (MSE) on the train and test set is calculated to evaluate the regression performance. Table 4 shows MSE between annotations and regression results on train and test set.

Table 4. Regression results for FA proneness and FR proneness.

Predicted parameter	Gender	Train MSE	Test MSE
FA proneness	Male	0.29	0.36
FA proneness	Female	0.31	0.43
FR proneness	Male	0.38	0.57
FR proneness	Female	0.42	0.62

For the true values between 0–10 range, MSE is around the 0.3–0.6 range. The error is not very small for the value range, but it seems good enough, meaning that exact prediction is hard but regressor predicts values roughly. Since the definitions of behaviour do not have a clear boundary, even rough predictions would be sufficient for applications, such as score normalization and extra objective function for embedding training.

6.2   Score Normalization Results

For score normalization results in Table 5, s-norm accounts for imposter score adjustment and in fact improves performance in a limited way. One reason for the limitation is that when s-norm tries to decrease a verification score of imposter trials having high scores, it also decreases genuine trials' scores. This is harmful since the correlation between high imposter scores and high genuine scores is very small. The proposed normalization for FA compensation suffers from the same problem but this problem is eliminated to some extent by fusion with FR compensation. Proposed FR compensation method; improves performance more than FA adjustment, might be caused by a smaller number of genuine trials in the evaluation. FR errors might also be more compensable, it comes from the same speaker essentially. The fusion of FR compensation and FA compensation also works, and improves normalization by focusing on both types of errors for both genders.

The improvement for female speakers is less for all normalizations; but the verification performance is also worse in female speakers; mostly caused from similar genuine scores with males but higher imposter scores. Female gender having higher imposter scores was also experimented in [4]. It degrades FA compensation performance as well as FR compensation performance.

Table 5. Verification score normalization results.

Model	Scoring	Normalization	Male EER (%)	Female EER (%)
E-TDNN	PLDA	no-normalization	2.87	3.75
E-TDNN	PLDA	s-norm	2.77	3.69
E-TDNN	PLDA	proposed(fa)	2.77	3.71
E-TDNN	PLDA	proposed(fr)	2.69	3.69
E-TDNN	PLDA	proposed(fusion)	**2.56**	**3.61**

6.3 Normalization Speed

The process times for s-norm and proposed normalization is measured; for enrollment and authentication embeddings. Embedding extraction and PLDA scoring are excluded from the measurement since they are the same for both methods. Measurements done on single-core of Intel(R) Xeon(R) CPU 3.00 GHz and listed in Table 6.

Table 6. Process times for normalization methods.

Method	Process time (per comparison)
s-norm	14.59 ms
proposed(fusion)	**1.08 ms**

S-norm is slower mainly because it has to perform PLDA scoring between a given embedding and a large number of cohort embeddings. The speed can be increased by decreasing the cohort set size, but a small cohort set results in less reliable statistics. In this work a cohort size of 1000 is used, usually larger cohort sets are employed, thus the results seem optimistic for s-norm. S-norm has also a memory burden to store those cohort embeddings but it is ignored since modern hardware is capable of this kind of memory.

7 Conclusion and Future Work

Biometric system users are split into categories according to their compliance with the system. Most of them have expected behaviour in terms of FA and FR errors. Some deviate from the majority by one or both of the error types. Predicting these divergent behaviors is critical for improving the system performance and building new robust techniques.

State-of-the-art audio speaker recognition systems are mostly based on speaker embeddings extracted from utterances. In this work, we have shown that information about error behaviours is contained in speaker embeddings. A new method based on feed-forward regression neural networks is applied in order to predict the speaker error behaviours. Separate models are trained to for FA and FR error proneness regression.

Additionally, we have proposed a score normalization method based on the speaker error behaviour predictions. This approach improves the system performance by a substantial amount. Also, it is faster and more efficient than the standard normalization methods. Another advantage of the proposed method over existing ones is that the false reject compensation can be applied without presence of different utterances of a given speaker.

The next step of this work would be to explore the different use cases of predicted error behaviour information such as a speaker embedding training scheme incorporating that prediction.

References

1. Doddington, G., Liggett, W., Martin, A., Przybocki, M., Reynolds, D.: Sheep, goats, lambs and wolves: a statistical analysis of speaker performance in the NIST 1998 speaker recognition evaluation. National Inst of Standards and Technology Gaithersburg Md (1998)
2. Stoll, L.L.: Finding difficult speakers in automatic speaker recognition. Doctoral dissertation, UC Berkeley (2011)
3. Stoll, L., Doddington, G.R.: Hunting for wolves in speaker recognition. In: Odyssey, p. 29 (2010)
4. Marras, M., Korus, P., Memon, N.D., Fenu, G.: Adversarial optimization for dictionary attacks on speaker verification. In: Interspeech, pp. 2913–2917 (2019)
5. Chen, K.: Towards better making a decision in speaker verification. Pattern Recogn. **36**(2), 329–346 (2003)
6. Kenny, P.: Bayesian speaker verification with heavy-tailed priors. In: Odyssey, vol. 14, June 2010
7. Yager, N., Dunstone, T.: The biometric menagerie. IEEE Trans. Pattern Anal. Mach. Intell. **32**(2), 220–230 (2008)
8. Snyder, D., Garcia-Romero, D., Sell, G., Povey, D., Khudanpur, S.: X-vectors: robust DNN embeddings for speaker recognition. In: 2018 IEEE International Conference on Acoustics, Speech and Signal Processing (ICASSP), pp. 5329–5333. IEEE, April 2018
9. Snyder, D., et al.: The JHU speaker recognition system for the VOiCES 2019 challenge. In: Proceedings of Interspeech 2019, pp. 2468–2472 (2019). https://doi.org/10.21437/Interspeech.2019-2979
10. Raj, D., Snyder, D., Povey, D., Khudanpur, S.: Probing the information encoded in x-vectors. In: 2019 IEEE Automatic Speech Recognition and Understanding Workshop (ASRU), pp. 726–733. IEEE, December 2019
11. Nagrani, A., Chung, J.S., Zisserman, A.: VoxCeleb: a large-scale speaker identification dataset. In: INTERSPEECH (2017)
12. Chung, J.S., Nagrani, A., Zisserman, A.: VoxCeleb2: deep speaker recognition. In: INTERSPEECH (2018)

Author Index

Printed in the United States
by Baker & Taylor Publisher Services

Printed in the United States
by Baker & Taylor Publisher Services